# INFORMATION TECHNOLOGY
# FOR MANAGEMENT

# INFORMATION TECHNOLOGY FOR MANAGEMENT

## Making Connections for Strategic Advantage

**Second Edition**
UPDATE

**EFRAIM TURBAN**
City University of Hong Kong

**EPHRAIM MCLEAN**
Georgia State University

**JAMES WETHERBE**
Texas Tech University

*With Contributions by*
**RALPH WESTFALL,** California Polytechnic University, Pomona

**KELLY RAINER,** Auburn University
*and*

**LINDA LAI,** City University of Hong Kong

## JOHN WILEY & SONS, INC.
**New York   Chichester   Weinheim   Brisbane   Singapore   Toronto**

ACQUISITIONS EDITOR   Beth Lang Golub

ASSOCIATE DIRECTOR OF DEVELOPMENT   Johnna Barto

MARKETING MANAGER   Jessica Garcia

PRODUCTION EDITOR   Patricia McFadden

COVER & TEXT DESIGNER   Dawn L. Stanley

COVER PHOTO © 1997 Chlaus Lotscher/Alaska Stock Images

FREELANCE PRODUCTION MANAGEMENT   Suzanne Ingrao/Ingrao Associates

PHOTO EDITOR   Jill Tatara

ILLUSTRATION EDITOR   Anna Melhorn

This book was set in 10/12 Meridien by York Graphic Services and printed and bound by Von Hoffmann Press. The cover was printed by Phoenix Color Corp.

This book is printed on acid-free paper. ∞

The paper in this book was manufactured by a mill whose forest management programs include sustained yield harvesting of its timberlands. Sustained yield harvesting principles ensure that the number of trees cut each year does not exceed the amount of new growth.

ISBN: 0-471-38919-6

Printed in the United States of America

10 9 8 7 6 5 4 3

As we begin a new millennium, we witness the tremendous importance of computerized information systems and their applications in business, education, government, the military, medicine, and at home. Computerized systems can be found today in even the smallest businesses. It is impossible to run a competitive business without a computerized information system. Indeed, global competitive pressures and continuous innovations are forcing many organizations to *rethink* how they do business. To do so requires the ability to successfully incorporate *electronic commerce, enterprise resource planning,* and *supply chain management* into an organization.

Much has changed since the Second Edition of this text was published in 1999. To help keep students up-to-date in this fast-moving field, we felt it necessary to update key sections of the text including electronic commerce, supply chain management, and enterprise resource planning. Consequently we have updated and revised the following: Chapter 4 on business process reengineering now includes extensive coverage of supply chain management and more on enterprise resource planning. Chapter 6 on electronic commerce is completely rewritten and updated to reflect the great expansion of e-commerce over the past couple of years; we've included up-to-the-minute coverage of the Internet, intranets, and extranets to conduct business. Chapter 8 has more coverage on integration of innovative functional systems to keep pace with what is happening in business today. (A special appendix presenting the basic concepts of BPR is also available on our Web site.) Finally the Technology Guides are fully updated with technological advances of the last two years.

## ▶ MAKING CONNECTIONS FOR STRATEGIC ADVANTAGE

This book is based on the fundamental premise that the major role of information technology is to provide organizations with *strategic advantage by facilitating problem solving, increasing productivity and quality, improving customer service, and enabling business process reengineering.* By taking a practical, managerial-oriented approach, the book demonstrates that IT can be provided not only by information systems departments, but by end users and vendors as well. Managing information resources, new technologies, and communications networks is becoming a—or even *the*—critical success factor in the operations of many companies, and will be essential to the survival of businesses as we reach the year 2000.

Many introductory texts on information systems are geared toward yesterday's environment, where the important issues were the technology, the construction of information systems, and the support of traditional business functional applications. This book's approach is different. While recognizing the importance of the technology, system development, and functional transaction processing systems, we emphasize the *innovative* uses of information technology. The rapidly increased use of the Web, the Internet, intranets, extranets, and electronic commerce change the manner in which business is done in almost all organizations. This fact is reflected in our book where every chapter and major topic points to the role of the Web in facilitating competitiveness, effectiveness, and profitability. Of special importance is the emergence of the Enterprise Resource Planning (ERP) concept and the integrated information systems (such as those provided by SAP AG) that support it.

## ▶ FEATURES OF THIS TEXT

In developing the second edition of *Information Technology for Management,* we have tried to craft a book that will serve the needs of tomorrow's managers. During the process of revising and reorganizing this edition, we have been guided by certain recurring themes that are important to succeed in business as we move into the twenty-first century.

This book reflects our vision of where information systems are going and the direction of IS education in business programs. This vision is represented by the following features that we have integrated throughout the book.

▶ *Managerial Orientation.* Most IS textbooks identify themselves as either technology or sociobehavioral oriented. While we recognize the importance of both, our emphasis is on managerial orientation. To do so *we assembled all the major technological topics in the four technology guides at the end of the book.* Furthermore, we attempted not to duplicate detailed presentations of behavioral sciences topics, such as dealing with resistance to change, or motivating employees. Instead, we concentrate on managerial decision making, cost-benefit justification, supply chain management, and business process reengineering as they relate to information technology.

▶ *Functional Relevance.* Frequently, non–IS major students wonder why they must learn technical details. In this text the relevance of information technology to the major functional areas is an important theme. Also, we show, through the use of icons, the relevance of topics to accounting, finance, marketing, production/operations management, and human resource education. Furthermore, we show the relevance to public services and health care management, using additional icons. Finally, our examples cover small businesses as well.

▶ *Real-World Orientation.* Extensive, vivid examples from large corporations, small businesses, and government and not-for-profit agencies will make concepts come alive by showing students the capabilities of information technology, its cost and justification, and some of the innovative ways real corporations are using IT in their operations.

▶ *Solid Theoretical Backing.* Throughout the book we present the theoretical foundation necessary for understanding information technology, ranging from Moore's Law to Porter's competitiveness models. Furthermore, we provide extensive references and many exercises to supplement the theoretical presentations.

▶ *Most Current.* The book presents the most current topics of information technology as evidenced by the many 1998 and 1999 citations. Topics such as electronic commerce, extranets, chief knowledge officers and knowledge bases, Web-based supply chain systems, data warehousing, knowledge discovery, and information economics are presented both from the theoretical point of view and from the application side.

▶ *Electronic Commerce and the Use of the Web.* We strongly believe that electronic commerce and the use of the Internet, intranets, and extranets are changing the world of business. Not only is an entire extended chapter (6) dedicated to electronic commerce, but we demonstrate our belief in every chapter and major topic. The world of commerce is changing and it is important that students understand these changes and their implications. For example, world-class companies such as FedEx, Dell computers, and Wal-Mart are introducing extremely innovative logistics systems supported by information technologies. This text tells you about all these innovations.

▶ *Economic Justification.* Information technology is mature enough to stand the difficult test of economic justification, a topic which is ignored by most textbooks. It is our position that investment in information technology must be scrutinized like any other investment, despite the difficulties of measuring technology benefits. In addition to discussion throughout the text, we are unique in devoting a complete Chapter (13, "Information Technology Economics") to this subject.

▶ *Integrated Systems.* In contrast with many books that highlight isolated functional information systems, we emphasize those systems that support Enterprise Resources Planning (ERP) and supply chain management. Interorganizational systems are particularly highlighted, including the latest innovations in global commerce.

▶ *Global Perspective.* The importance of global competition, partnerships, and trading is rapidly increasing. IT facilitates export and import, managing multinational companies, and trading electronically around the globe. International examples are highlighted in a Special Global Index in the back of the book, and the book's Web site includes several international cases.

▶ *Comprehensiveness and Ease of Reading.* All major topics of information technology are covered, many with more details than you will find elsewhere. Furthermore, the book is very user friendly, easy to understand and follow, and it is full of interesting real-world examples and "war stories" that keep the reader's interest at a very high level.

## ▶ ORGANIZATION OF THE BOOK

The book is divided into four major parts composed of 15 regular chapters with four technology guides supplementing them.

**Part I** introduces the drivers of the use of information technology in the new world of business.

It also introduces the foundations of information systems and their strategic use. Special attention is given to the role information systems play in facilitating business process reengineering.

**Part II** introduces network computing, the various applications of telecommunication networks and the role of the Internet, intranets, and extranets in contributing to communication, collaboration, and information discovery. Electronic commerce is presented in a most comprehensive way, followed by an analysis of information technology impacts on individuals, groups, organizations, and society.

**Part III** discusses the many ways information systems can be used to support the day-to-day operations of a company, with a strong emphasis on the use of IT in managerial decision making. The four chapters in this part address some of the ways businesses are using information technology to solve specific problems and build strategic, innovative systems that enhance quality and productivity. Special attention is given to innovative applications of intelligent systems and to integrated systems, not only within organizations but also between and among business partners and customers. Also highlighted are the new approaches to marketing databases and knowledge management.

**Part IV** explores many topics, related to the planning, evaluation, construction, operation, security, and maintenance of information systems. We consider several issues ranging from the economics of information to outsourcing.

The four **technology guides** cover hardware, software, databases, and telecommunications, including the essentials of the Internet. They contain condensed up-to-date presentations of all the material necessary for the understanding of these technologies. They can be used as a self-study refresher or as a basis for a class presentation. The technology guides are supplemented by a glossary, questions for review and discussion, and case studies, all of which are available on our Web site.

# ▶ PEDAGOGICAL STRUCTURE

We developed a number of pedagogical features to aid student learning and tie together the themes of the book.

▶ *Chapter outline.* The outlines provide a quick indication of the major topics covered. Detailed outlines are provided at the beginning of the book.

▶ *Learning objectives.* Learning objectives are provided at the beginning of each chapter to help students focus their efforts and alert them to the important concepts discussed.

▶ *Opening cases (Connections).* Each chapter opens with a *real-world* example that illustrates the importance of information technology to modern corporations. These cases were carefully chosen to demonstrate the relevance, for business students, of the topics introduced in the chapter.

▶ *"A Closer Look" boxes.* These contain detailed, in-depth discussions of specific concepts or procedures, often using real-world examples. Some boxes enhance the in-text discussion by offering an alternative approach to information technology.

▶ *"IT at Work" boxes.* These spotlight some real-world innovations and new technologies that companies are relying on to solve organizational dilemmas or create new business opportunities. Each box concludes with "for further exploration" issues.

▶ *Highlighted icons.* Icons appear throughout the text to relate the topics covered within each chapter back to some major themes of the book. The icons alert students to the related functional areas, and to human resource management and health care applications.

▶ *Student Annotations.* To help business students understand the relevance of the topics in this book, we asked students who also hold jobs to add their comments about how the concepts are applied in the business world. Their remarks appear in the margins throughout the book.

▶ *Managerial Issues.* The final section of every chapter explores some of the special concerns managers face as they adapt to an increasingly technological environment. Thought-provoking questions can serve as a springboard for class discussion and challenge business students to consider some of the actions they might take if placed in similar circumstances.

▶ *Key Terms.* All boldfaced, new terms introduced within the chapter appear in a list at the end of the chapter and are defined in the end-of-book glossary.

▶ *Chapter Highlights.* A list of all the important concepts covered, the chapter highlights are linked to the learning objectives introduced at the beginning of each chapter to reinforce the important ideas discussed.

▶ *End-of-Chapter Exercises.* Different types of questions measure student comprehension and their ability to apply knowledge. Questions for

Review ask students to summarize the concepts introduced. Discussion Questions are intended to promote class discussion and develop critical thinking skills. Exercises are challenging assignments that require students to apply what they have learned. The Group Assignments are class projects designed to foster teamwork.

▶ ***Internet Exercises.*** Over 100 hands-on exercises send the students to the most interesting Web sites to conduct research, investigate an application, or learn about the state of the art of a topic.

▶ ***Minicases.*** Real-world cases highlight some of the problems encountered by corporations as they develop and implement information systems. Discussion questions and group assignments are included.

▶ ***Part Ending Cases.*** Longer real-world cases were chosen specifically for their ability to bring together many of the overriding concepts from each part of the text. These can be found on our Web site.

▶ ***International cases.*** Several cases from countries around the globe (including multinational corporations) are available on our Web site.

# ▶ SUPPLEMENTARY MATERIALS

An extensive package of instructional materials is available to support this edition:

▶ ***Instructor's Manual*** (0471-28333-9). Written by Tushar Hazra (University of Baltimore), this manual presents objectives from the text with additional information to make them more appropriate and useful for the instructor. Chapter overviews provide an explanation of how each chapter fits in with previous chapters and the entire course. The manual also includes practical applications of concepts, case study elaboration, answers to end-of-chapter questions, questions for review, questions for discussion, and Internet exercises.

▶ ***Test Bank*** (0471-29933-2). Written by Lisa Friedrichsen (instructor at the Keller Graduate School of Management), the test bank contains approximately 1,000 questions and problems (about 50 per chapter) consisting of multiple-choice, short answer, fill-ins, and critical thinking/essay questions.

▶ ***Computerized Test Bank*** (0471-29927-8). This electronic version of the Test Bank allows instructors to customize tests and quizzes for their students.

▶ ***PowerPoint Presentation*** (0471-29928-6). A series of slides designed around the content of the text incorporates key points from the text and illustrations where appropriate. These were prepared by Wade Jackson of University of Memphis.

▶ ***Video Series*** (0471-29929-4). A collection of videos which provide the students and instructors with dynamic and interesting business examples directly related to the concepts introduced in the text. The video clips illustrate the ways in which computer information systems are utilized in various companies and industries.

▶ ***Business Extra Website: Wall Street Journal Interactive and the On-Line Business Survival Guide.*** Wiley has teamed up with the Wall Street Journal to bring you instant access to a wealth of current articles dealing with all aspects of today's volatile business world. Use this resource to get up-to-date articles dealing with issues in information systems. The *On-Line Business Survival Guide* (0-471-25503-3) covers everything your students need to know to become master sleuths at finding critical information on the Internet. Each copy of the Survival Guide includes a special password for Wiley's *Business Extra Website* that allows students access to a series of relevant clippings from news wires and Dow Jones publications. For more information, go to www.wiley.com/college/businessextra

▶ ***The Turban Web Site*** (www.wiley.com/college/turban2e). The Web site extends the content and theme of the text to provide extensive support for instructors and students. Organized by chapter, it includes cases, questions and exercises for the technology guides, and downloadable PowerPoint slides, self-testing material for students, working student's experiences with using IT, links to many of the companies discussed in the text, and a link to a unique supplement called "The Virtual Company" described below.

▶ ***The Virtual Company.*** A Web-based case, The Virtual Company features Internet and intranet sites for a simulated company that produces snowboards. Students are "hired" by the company as consultants and given assignments which require the students to use the information in the Internet and intranet sites to develop the solutions and produce deliverables to present to the company. These exercises get the student into active, hands-on learning to complement the conceptual coverage of the text.

# ACKNOWLEDGMENTS

Special recognition goes to Ralph Westfall (California State University Long Beach) and Kelly Rainer (Auburn University). Ralph wrote the chapter on information economics (Chapter 13) and contributed major portions to Chapters 12 and 14. Kelly created the technology guides to this book and updated the relevant technological topics. Also, we recognize the contribution of Kent Sandoe (formerly of Fordham University and now California State University at Chico), who reviewed the entire manuscript for completeness, accuracy, and consistency. And we thank Christine Bullen who helped to set up a student focus group at Fordham University.

Many other individuals provided assistance in the creation of the second edition. First, dozens of students participated in the class testing of the material and helped develop exercises and find illustrative applications, and contributed valuable suggestions and annotations for the text. It is not possible to name all of them, but they certainly deserve recognition and thanks.

Faculty feedback was essential to the development of the book. Many individuals participated in focus groups and/or acted as reviewers. Several others created portions of chapters or cases, especially international cases, some of which are in the text and others are on the Web site. We are grateful to the following faculty for their contributions to the second edition:

Christine P. Andrews, *SUNY at Fredonia;* Marzi Astanti, *Winona State University;* V. Bose, *Texas A&M University;* Marek Ejsmont, *Keyano College (Alberta, Canada);* George Fettes, *Camosun College;* David R. Fordham, *James Madison University;* Lisa Friedrichsen, *Keller Graduate School;* David Hale, *University of Alabama;* Fred G. Harold, *Florida Atlantic University;* Jeff Harper, *Athens State College;* Myron Hatcher, *California State University, Fresno;* Chin-Yuan Ho, *National Central University (Taiwan);* Change T. Hsieh, *University of Southern Mississippi;* Grace Johnson, *Marietta College;* Dorothy Leidner, *Baylor University;* James Linderman, *Bentley College;* Munir Mandviwalla, *Temple University;* Ji-Ye Mao, *University of Waterloo;* Vicki McKinney, *University of Texas, Arlington;* Derrick Neufeld, *University of Manitoba;* E. F. Peter Newson, *University of Western Ontario;* Floyd D. Ploeger, *Southwest Texas State University;* Larisa Preiser-Houy, *California State University, Pomona;* Mary Ann Robbert, *Bentley College;* Dolly

Samson, *Weber State University;* Vijay Sethi, *Nanyang Technological University (Singapore);* Kathy Stewart, *Georgia State University;* Ted Strickland, *University of Louisville;* Edward Tsang, *University of Essex (United Kingdom);* and Liang Chee Wee, *Luther College.*

The following individuals participated in focus groups and/or acted as reviewers of the first edition: Mary Anne Atkinson, *University of Delaware,* Benedict Arogyaswamy, *University of South Dakota,* James Carroll, *Georgian Court College,* Paul Cheney, *University of South Florida,* Candace Deans, *Thunderbird School, AGIM,* Bill DeLone, *American University,* Phillip Ein-Dor, *Tel Aviv University (Israel),* Michael Eirman, *University of Wisconsin-Oshkosh,* Paul Evans, *George Mason University,* Deb Ghosh, *Louisiana State University,* Oscar Gutierrez, *University of Massachusetts-Boston,* Rassule Hadidi, *Sangamon State University,* Fred Harold, *Florida Atlantic University,* Jaak Jurison, *Fordham University,* Eugene Kaluzniacky, *University of Winnipeg,* Astrid Lipp, *Clemson University,* Jo Mae Maris, *Northern Arizona University,* E. F. Peter Newson, *University of Western Ontario,* Michael Palley, *CUNY-Baruch College,* Keri Pearlson, *University of Texas,* Bill Richmond, *George Mason University,* Larry Sanders, *University of Buffalo,* A. B. Schwarzkopf, *University of Oklahoma,* Henk Sol, *Delft Institute of Technology (The Netherlands),* Timothy Smith, *DePaul University,* Timothy Staley, *DeVry Institute of Technology,* Shannon Taylor, *Montana State University,* Robert Van Cleave, *University of Minnesota,* Kuang-Wei Wen, *University of Connecticut,* Anthony Wensley, *University of Toronto (Canada),* Jennifer Williams, *University of Southern Indiana,* G. W. Willis, *Baylor University,* Gayle Yaverbaum, *Pennsylvania State University*

Also, we recognize those faculty who contributed cases to the first edition of the text.

Kimberly Bechler, *International Institute of Management Development (Switzerland)* Christer Carlsson, *Abo Akademi University (Finland);* Guy Fitzgerald, *University of London (United Kingdom);* Young Moo Kang, *Dong-A University (Korea);* Ossi Kokkonen, *Metsa-Serla Oy (Finland);* Donald Marchand, *International Institute of Management Development (Switzerland);* David McDonald, *Georgia State University;* Boon-Siong Neo, *Nanyang Technological University (Singapore);* Nicolau Reinhard, *University of Sao Paulo (Brazil);* Chris Sauer, *University of New South Wales (Australia);* Scott Schneberger, *Georgia State University;* Pirkko Walden, *Abo Akademi University (Finland);* Leslie Willcocks,*

*Templeton College, Oxford University (United Kingdom);* and Ronaldo Zwicker, *University of Sao Paulo (Brazil).*

We would like to thank Tushar Hazra of the University of Baltimore for creating the Instructor's Manual and Lisa Friedrichsen of the Keller Graduate School of Management for generating the Test Bank that accompanies this edition.

Many individuals helped us with the administrative work; of special mention are Judy Lang, who devoted considerable time to typing and editing. Hugh Watson of the University of Georgia, the Information Systems Advisor to Wiley, guided us through various stages of the project. Finally, we would like to thank the dedicated staff of John Wiley & Sons, Cindy Rhoads, Carlise Paulson, Kim Khatchatourian, Jeanine Furino, and Trisha McFadden. A special thank you to Matthew Van Hattem, Johnna Barto, Beth Lang Golub, Shelley Flannery, and Suzanne Ingrao of Ingrao Associates, who contributed their considerable energy, time, and devotion to the success of this project.

Finally, we recognize the various organizations and corporations that provided us with material and permissions to use it.

Efraim Turban
Ephraim McLean
James Wetherbe

# ABOUT THE AUTHORS

## DR. EFRAIM TURBAN

**Dr. Efraim Turban** obtained his MBA and Ph.D from the University of California, Berkeley. His industry experience includes eight years as an Industrial Engineer, three of which were spent at General Electric Transformers Plant. He also has extensive consulting experience to small and large corporations as well as to foreign governments.

In his thirty years of teaching, Professor Turban has served as Distinguished Professor at Eastern Illinois University, and as Visiting Professor at Nanyang Technological University in Singapore. He has also taught at UCLA, USC, Simon Fraser University, Lehigh University, California State University, Long Beach, and Florida International University.

Dr. Turban was a Co-Recipient of the 1984/85 National Management Science Award (Artificial Intelligence in Management). In 1997 he received the Distinguished Faculty Scholarly and Creative Achievement Award at California State University, Long Beach.

Dr. Turban has published articles in over 100 leading journals, including the following: *Management Science, MIS Quarterly, Expert Systems, Operations Research, Expert Systems With Applications, Journal of MIS, Communications of the ACM, Decision Support Systems, International Journal of Information Management, Heuristics, International Journal of Applied Expert Systems, The Journal of Investing, Accounting, Management and Information Systems, Computers and Operations Research, Computers and Industrial Engineering, IEEE Transactions on Engineering Management, Omega, Human Systems Management and Information Resources Management*. He has also published eighteen books, including bestsellers such as *Electronic Commerce: A Managerial Perspective* (Prentice Hall, 2000); *Neural Networks: Applications in Investment and Financial Services*, 2nd edition (co-editor with R. Trippi) (Richard D. Irwin, 1996); *Decision Support Systems and Expert Systems*, 6th edition (Prentice Hall, 2001); and *Expert Systems and Applied Artificial Intelligence* (MacMillan, 1992). Books in progress include *Essentials of Managing Information Systems* (Wiley, 2001).

Professor Turban is currently on the faculty at City University of Hong Kong, Department of Information Systems, College of Business Administration. Professor Turban's current major interest is electronic commerce.

## DR. EPHRAIM McCLEAN

**Dr. Ephraim McLean** obtained his Bachelor of Mechanical Engineering degree from Cornell University in 1958. After brief service in the U.S. Army Ordnance Corps, he worked for Procter & Gamble Co. for seven years, first in manufacturing management and later as a computer systems analyst. In 1965, he left P&G and entered the Sloan School of Management at the Massachusetts Institute of Technology, obtaining his master's degree in 1967 and his doctorate in 1970.

While at M.I.T., he began an interest in the application of computer technology to medicine, working on his dissertation at the Lahey Clinic in Boston. While there, he was instrumental in developing the Lahey Clinic Automated Medical History System. During the same period, he served as an instructor at M.I.T. and also assisted in the preparation of the books *The Impact of Computers on Management* (MIT Press, 1967); *The Impact of Computers on Collective Bargaining* (MIT Press, 1969); and *Computers in Knowledge-Based Fields* (MIT Press, 1970).

Dr. McLean left M.I.T. and joined the faculty of the Anderson Graduate School of Management at the University of California, Los Angeles (UCLA) in the winter of 1970.

He was the founding Director of the Information Systems Research Program and the first Chairman of the Information Systems area, both within the Anderson Graduate School of Management. In the Fall of 1987, he was named to the George E. Smith Eminent Scholar's Chair at the College of Business Administration at Georgia State University in Atlanta, Georgia.

Dr. McLean has published over 80 articles in such publications as the *Harvard Business Review; Sloan Management Review; California Management Review; Communications of the ACM; MIS Quarterly; Information Systems Research, Information & Management; Journal of MIS; Journal of Risk and Insurance; DATA BASE; InformationWEEK; Datamation; ComputerWorld;* and the *Journal of the American Hospital Association.* He is the co-author of *Strategic Planning for MIS* (Wiley Interscience, 1977) and co-editor of a book of programs entitled *APL Application in Management.* He was a founding Associate Editor for Research of the *MIS Quarterly* and is currently senior co-editor of the *DATA BASE for Advances in Information Systems.* He was twice on the national Executive Council of the Society for Information Management (SIM). In 1980, he helped organize the International Conference on Information Systems (ICIS) and was Conference Co-chairman in 1981 in Cambridge, Massachusetts; Conference Chairman in 1986 in San Diego, California; and Conference Co-chairman in 1997 in Atlanta, Georgia. He is currently Vice President for Affiliated Organizations of the new Association for Information Systems (AIS).

In addition to university work, he has served as a consultant to such firms as the IBM Corporation, General Electric Company, Atlantic Richfield Company, Digital Equipment Corporation, BellSouth Corporation, the National Science Foundation, American Hospital Supply Corporation, McCormick & Company, Security Pacific National Bank, Pennsylvania Financial Corporation (now Primerica), and Citibank, N.A. of New York. He has also made executive presentations and conducted management workshops in Asia, Australia, Europe, South Africa, and throughout North America.

## DR. JAMES WETHERBE

**Dr. James Wetherbe** is FedEx Professor of Excellence and the Executive Director of the FedEx Center for Cycle Time Research at the University of Memphis, as well as Professor of MIS and the Director of the MIS Research Center at the University of Minnesota. He is internationally known as a dynamic and entertaining speaker, author, and leading authority on the use of computers and information systems to improve organizational performance and competitiveness. He is particularly appreciated for his ability to explain complex technology in straightforward, practical terms that can be strategically applied by both executives and general management.

Quoted often in leading business and information system journals, Dr. Wetherbe writes regular columns and serves as a consulting editor for publishing companies. He is the author of 17 highly regarded books and over 200 articles in the field of management and information systems.

# STUDENT PANEL

Written with students in mind, this book tries to present materials as they relate to today's world of commerce. To help business students understand the importance of these concepts and applications, we asked several students to provide annotations for *Information Technology for Management* to show how the information in the text can be applied directly to their careers, whatever function they may serve in their organization. We are grateful to the following students for their thoughtful annotations, which can be found in the margins throughout the text.

Kristin Borhofen
*(Training Coordinator)*
*Fordham University,*
*Marketing and Finance major*

Dave Gehrke
*(Manufacturing Engineer)*
*California State University, Long Beach,*
*Information Technology major,*
*MBA Candidate*

Karen Miller
*(Health Care Manager)*
*California State University, Long Beach*
*Information Technology major,*
*MBA Candidate*

Michael M. Rewald
*(Assistant Controller)*
*California State University, Long Beach*
*B.A. in Finance; Information Technology Major*
*MBA Candidate*

James Rolstead
*(Sales Manager)*
*California State University, Long Beach*
*Information Technology major,*
*MBA Candidate*

Blake Thompson
*(Systems Administrator)*
*University of Memphis,*
*Management Information Systems major*

Brad White
*(Family Nurse Practitioner)*
*University of Texas, Arlington,*
*Nursing major*

# Brief Contents

# CONTENTS

# P A R T I
# IT IN THE ORGANIZATION

## PART I
### IT in the Organization

1. Organizations, Environments, and Information Technology
2. Information Technologies: Concepts and Management
3. Strategic Information Systems
4. Supply Chain, Enterprise Resources Planning, and Business Process Reengineering

## PART II
### Networks and IT

5. Network Computing: Discovery, Communication, and Collaboration
6. Electronic Commerce
7. Impacts of IT on Organizations, Individuals, and Society

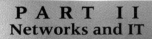

## PART III
### Using IT

8. Transaction Processing, Innovative Functional Systems, and Integration
9. Supporting Management and Decision Making
10. Data and Knowledge Management
11. Intelligent Support Systems

## PART IV
### Managing IT

12. Planning for Information Technology and Systems
13. Information Technology Economics
14. Systems Development
15. Managing Information Resources, Control, and Security

| Hardware | Software | Databases | Telecommunications and Internet |

Today's business environment is undergoing rapid changes due to the globalization of business, technological innovations, social and political changes, and increased awareness and demands from customers. These changes result in a tough competitive environment in which many organizations cannot survive. Organizations, private and public, must take measures to increase their productivity, quality of service, and competitive ability. New management approaches—ranging from mass customization to electronic commerce—are being used to counter increasing pressures on organizations. The major driving force of many of the changes is information technology, which is also at the core of most of the innovations used by organizations to succeed or even survive.

Part I places information technology in the context of organizations, focusing on business pressures and the strategies used to counter them, especially through the use of strategic information systems and supporting business process reengineering.

**Chapter 1** provides an overview of business pressures resulting from environmental, organizational, and technological issues. Information systems are viewed as systems that support the critical response activities of organizations, such as increasing productivity, increasing speed, and improving customer service.

**Chapter 2** is dedicated to the various species of information systems. The major categories of systems are those intended to support the functional areas, business transaction processing, and various groups of people and their tasks. The chapter also outlines the architecture and infrastructure of information technology, and the relationship between the information system department and the end users.

**Chapter 3** deals with strategic information systems. Based on Porter's models of value chain and competitive advantage, the chapter introduces several frameworks which illustrate the role of information technology (IT) in supporting strategic initiatives.

**Chapter 4** concludes Part I. The welfare and survival of many organizations depend on their ability to reengineer their business processes. Chapter 4 provides an introduction to and overview of the concept of the business processes reengineering and the role that IT plays in it. Furthermore, the chapter compares and contrasts this approach with total quality management, a complementary strategy of incremental improvement.

Part I is loaded with real-life examples showing how companies practice what we preach. A Part I end case which is available on our Web site (www.wiley.com/college/turban2e) describes the manner in which Metsä-Serla Corp (of Finland) is using an intelligent decision support system.

# CHAPTER 1

# Organizations, Environments, and Information Technology

## Learning Objectives

*After studying this chapter, you will be able to:*

❶ Recognize the relationships between business pressures, organizational responses, and information systems.

❷ Identify the major pressures in the business environment and describe the major organizational responses to them.

❸ Describe the role of the information technology in organizational activities.

❹ Define computer-based information systems and information technology.

❺ List the essentials of networked computing.

# THE HARPER GROUP COLLABORATES WITH HONDA IN INTERNATIONAL TRADE

## The Problem

THE HARPER GROUP is an international freight moving company that uses information technology to support the services it provides to its clients who export and/or import goods. International trade is complex because it involves exporters and importers, customs services, ports, storage companies, and transportation companies. Harper operates in a highly competitive environment where hundreds of freight moving companies in the United States and abroad serve an international market. In this market, large amounts of information flow among several trading partners and support services. This information includes orders, biddings, billings, status queries, contracts, payments, and so on. Harper manages this information for its customers, the exporters and importers. The problem faced by Harper is how to effectively manage the information at competitive prices.

## The Solution

To improve information flow so that it will move more consistently, freely, and rapidly, and thus to expedite the movement of cargo, the Harper Group is using **electronic data interchange (EDI)** technology (see Chapter 6). EDI links the computers of involved organizations, resulting in a paperless flow of routine information. Harper has an EDI arrangement with 500 of its largest customers, one of which is Honda Motor Company of Japan. Honda ships over 300,000 cars and trucks to the United States each year. Harper takes care of all the necessary arrangements, including those involving the United States Customs. Harper can also tap into Honda's computers to deposit or retrieve information required by Customs.

The EDI transaction begins when Honda exports cars from Japan to the United States. Honda sends its export documents electronically from its headquarters in Japan to the American Honda offices in Los Angeles. The information is then transferred electronically to Harper's mainframe in San Francisco. The complete files (one order may include several hundred pages of data) are then transferred electronically to U.S. Customs several days before the ship carrying the cars docks in a U.S. port. Customs agents calculate the duty fees and send them to Harper via EDI. Honda's duty payment for each shipment is then transferred electronically from a bank to the Customs' bank. Finally, Harper bills Honda electronically for its services and is paid via electronic transfer of funds.

## The Results

This electronic communication system, which includes EDI and e-mail, allows cheaper, faster, and more reliable information to flow and support Harper's global business. IT enables Harper to maintain its position as the second largest importer in the United States (Harper filed over 320,000 customs entries in 1997, which gave it about 6 percent of the total United States market share). In addition, Harper operates in an industry with thin profit margins, yet its profit margins are substantially above the industry's average.

As of the end of 1996, Harper, a subsidiary of Circle International (www.circleintl.com) is using the Internet to enhance its communication and research and development activities. In 1997, the company started to adopt an intranet for improving its internal operations.

SOURCE: Guglielmo (1992) and *Information Week*, June 20, 1994, and private communication with the company, 1998.

 ## 1.1 THE NEW WORLD OF BUSINESS

Harper's case illustrates the realities of doing business as we approach the twenty-first century. Business is now done in many cases globally. The transactions surrounding each shipment of cars are complex, involving several trading partners in Japan and the United States as well as government officials. Therefore, they are difficult to manage. Harper must be effective and efficient, otherwise Honda will select a competing vendor.

*Electronic Commerce and Networked Computing.* Harper's use of information technology to support the business electronically is an example of **electronic commerce (EC)**. In EC computers communicate with computers via telecommunication networks. EC could become a very significant global economic element in the twenty-first century (see Clinton and Gore [1997]). The infrastructure for EC is **networked computing**, which is emerging as the standard computing environment in business, home, and government. Networked computing connects several computers and other electronic devices by telecommunication networks. This allows users to access information stored in many places and to communicate and collaborate with others from their desktop computers. While some people still use a standalone computer exclusively, or a network confined to one organization, the vast majority use computers connected to a global networked environment known as the **Internet**, or its counterpart within organizations, called the **intranet**.

> Computer networks make it a lot easier to share everyone's data.
>
> — *Blake Thompson*

This new breed of computing is helping companies not only to excel but also frequently to survive. Harper Group is not the only company that uses electronic commerce to facilitate its business. As a matter of fact, almost all organizations, private or public, in manufacturing, agriculture, or services, use various types of information technologies, including electronic commerce, to support their operations.

Why is this so? The reason is simple. **Information technology (IT)** has become the major facilitator of business activities in the world today (see for instance, Tapscott and Caston [1993], Mandel et al. [1994], and Gill [1996]). IT is also a catalyst of fundamental changes in the structure, operations, and management of organizations (see Dertouzos [1997]) due to the capabilities shown in Table 1.1. These capabilities, according to Wreden (1997), support the following five business objectives: improving productivity (in 51% of corporations), reducing cost (39%), improving decision making (36%), enhancing customer relationships (33%), and developing new strategic applications (33%).

---

### *Table 1.1* Major Capabilities of Information Systems

- Perform high-speed, high-volume, numerical computations.
- Provide fast, accurate, and inexpensive communication within and between organizations.
- Store huge amounts of information in an easy-to-access yet small space.
- Allow quick and inexpensive access to vast amount of information, worldwide.
- Increase the effectiveness and efficiency of people working in groups in one place or in several locations.
- Vividly present information that challenges the human mind.
- Automate semiautomatic business processes and manually done tasks.
- Speed typing and editing.
- Accomplishs all the above much less expensively than when done manually.

***The New World of Business.*** Environmental, organizational, and technological factors are creating a highly competitive business environment in which customers are the focal point. Furthermore, these factors can change quickly, sometimes in an unpredictable manner (see Knoke [1996]). Therefore, companies need to react frequently and quickly to both the *problems* and the *opportunities* resulting from this new business environment (see Drucker, [1995]). Because the pace of change and the degree of uncertainty in tomorrow's competitive environment are expected to accelerate, organizations are going to operate under increasing pressures to produce more, using fewer resources. We have already seen organizations such as IBM, General Motors, and Digital Equipment Corporation going through major restructuring, eliminating over 100,000 jobs during the early 1990s in an attempt to get "lean and mean" and to be competitive in the marketplace.

Boyett and Boyett (1995) emphasize this dramatic change and describe it with a set of **business pressures** or drivers. They maintain that in order to succeed (or even to survive) in this dynamic world, companies must take not only traditional actions such as lowering cost, but also innovative activities such as empowering employees. We refer to these activities, some of which are interrelated, as **critical response activities**. They can be performed in some or all of the processes of the organization, from the daily routine of preparing payroll and order entry to strategic activities such as the acquisition of a company. A response can be a reaction to a pressure already in existence, or it can be an initiative that will defend an organization against future pressures. It can also be an activity that exploits an opportunity created by changing conditions. Most response activities can be greatly facilitated by IT. In some cases IT is the only solution to these business pressures (see Larson [1996] and Callon [1996]).

The relationship between business pressures, organizational responses, and IT is shown in Figure 1.1. This figure illustrates a model of the new world of business.* The business drivers create pressures on organizations. Organizations

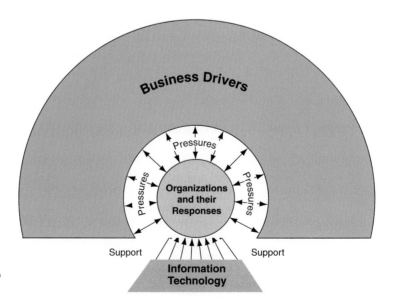

FIGURE 1.1 IT support to organizational responses.

---

*In this book a reference to a "business" means either a private or a public organization. Pubic and not-for-profit organizations should both be managed like a business.

respond with activities supported by IT. And the core of today's IT, as we will see throughout the book, is networked computing. Now, let's examine the components of the model in more detail.

### BUSINESS PRESSURES

To understand the role of information technology in today's organization, it is useful to review the major business environmental factors that create pressures on organizations. The business environment refers to the social, legal, economic, physical, and political factors that affect business activities. Significant changes in any part of this environment are likely to create pressures on organizations. Figure 1.2 presents a schematic view of the major pressures, which may interrelate and affect each other.

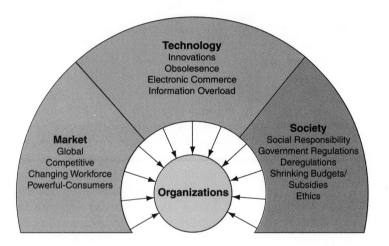

**FIGURE 1.2** The major business pressures.

In this book, the business pressures are divided into the following categories: market, technology, and society. These are described next.

**MARKET PRESSURES.** A global economy and strong competition, unique work force, and powerful consumers can characterize today's market.

*Global Economy and Strong Competition.* The fairly stabilized world political environment that resulted from the collapse of the Soviet Union, and the moves toward market economy by many countries (including China and Russia), have created the foundation necessary for a global economy (see Naisbitt [1994]). This move to globalization is facilitated by advanced telecommunication networks and especially by the Internet (see Clinton and Gore [1997], Negroponte [1995], and Kanter [1995]). Regional agreements such as North American Free Trade Agreement (United States, Canada, and Mexico) contribute to increased world trade. Reduction of trade barriers allows products and services to flow freely around the globe.

Labor costs differ widely from one country to another, as shown in Figure 1.3. While the hourly industrial wage rate (excluding benefits) is over $15 in some Western countries, it is only $1 to $2 in many developing countries, including those in Asia, South America, Eastern Europe, and Africa. The lowest

Hourly Industrial Wages in Different Countries (in US $)

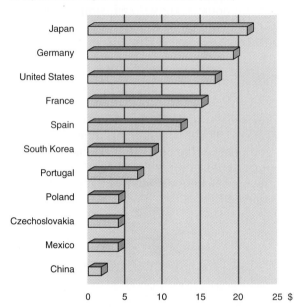

**FIGURE 1.3** Labor costs in different countries. (*Source*: Based on data published by the Institute for the German Economy, 1998.)

labor cost for industrial employees can be found in China, where the hourly wage rate is 50 cents to $1.00. In addition, companies in developed countries usually pay high fringe benefits and environmental protection costs; thus, they have difficulty competing in labor-intensive industries with developing countries. Therefore, companies are moving their manufacturing facilities to countries with low labor cost. Such a global strategy requires extensive communication, frequently in several languages and under several cultural, ethical, and legal conditions. The complexity of the communication system may greatly hinder competition unless it is properly supported by IT.

*Global competition* is especially intensified when governments become involved through the use of subsidies, tax policies, and import/export regulations and incentives. Rapid and inexpensive communication and transportation modes increase the magnitude of international trade even further. Previously confined within an industry or a region, competition is now becoming truly global.

***Changing Nature of the Workforce.*** The workforce, particularly in developed countries, is changing rapidly and becoming more diversified. An increasing number of females, single parents, minorities, and handicapped persons work today in all types of positions. More employees prefer to defer retirement than ever before. Information technology is easing the integration of the above employees into the traditional workforce (see discussion of telecommuting and support for the disabled in Chapter 7).

***Powerful Customers.*** Consumer sophistication and expectations increase as consumers become more knowledgeable about the availability and quality of products and services. Consumers are demanding ever more detailed information about products and services. They want to know what features are available, what warranties they will receive, what financing is available, and so on, and they want to know now. Companies need to be able to deliver information quickly to satisfy these customers. Advances in the use of the Internet and elec-

Consumers are at a great advantage at this time. With the Internet, there is no longer a reason not to be a well informed buyer.
— *Blake Thompson*

tronic commerce bring customers information about thousands of products, including cost and quality comparisons.

Customers want customized products, at high quality and low prices. Vendors must respond. For example, a large department store in Japan offers refrigerators in 24 different colors with a delivery time of less than two weeks (see Stalk and Weber [1993]); and, Dell computers will take the order of the computer of your choice over the Internet, and deliver it to your home within 72 hours.

## TECHNOLOGICAL PRESSURES

*Technological Innovation and Obsolescence.* Technology is playing an increased role in manufacturing and services. New and improved technologies create or support substitutes for products, alternative service options, and superb quality. In addition, some of today's state-of-the-art products may be obsolete tomorrow. Thus, technology accelerates the competitive forces. Many technologies affect business in areas ranging from genetic engineering to food processing. However, probably the technology with the greatest impact is information technology (see Larson [1996] and Dertouzos [1997]).

*Information Overload.* The Internet and other telecommunication networks increase the amount of information available to organizations and individuals. The amount of information available on the Internet more than doubles every year, and most of it is free! The information and knowledge generated and stored inside organizations is also increasing exponentially. It looks as though the world is going to be drowned in a flood of information. Thus, the accessibility, navigation, and management of data, information, and knowledge which is necessary for managerial decision making become critical.

## SOCIETAL PRESSURES

The impact of societal pressures is on the increase, especially in developed countries.

*Social Responsibility.* The interfaces between organizations and society are increasing and changing rapidly. Social issues on which business impinges range from the state of the physical environment to the spread of AIDS. Corporations are becoming more aware of these problems and some are willing to contribute toward improvements. Such activity is known as organizational *social responsibility* (see Table 1.2).

---

### *Table 1.2* Major Areas of Social Responsibility

- Environmental control (pollution, noise, trash removal, and animal welfare)
- Equal opportunity (minorities, women, elderly, and physically handicapped)
- Employment and housing (the aged, poor, teenagers, and unskilled)
- Health, safety, and social benefits to employees (the role of employer vs. that of the government)
- Employee education, training, and retraining
- External relationships (community development, political, and other interfaces)
- Marketing practices (fairness, truth)
- Privacy and ethics

Other societal pressures are:

▶ *Government regulations.* Several social responsibility issues are related to government regulations regarding health, safety, environmental control, and equal opportunity. For example, companies that spray parts with paint must use paper to absorb the overspray. The paper must then be disposed of by a licensed company at a high cost. Such regulations not only cost money and make it more difficult to compete with countries that lack such regulations, but they also create changes in organizational structure and processes.

▶ *Government deregulation.* While government regulations are usually viewed as expensive constraints, deregulation can be a blessing to one company and a curse to another company previously protected by the regulation. In general, deregulation intensifies competition.

▶ *Shrinking budgets and subsidies.* The U.S. budget deficit skyrocketed during the late 1980s and early 1990s. At the same time, the U.S. economy entered an economic recession. As a result, there was less funding for social programs available from federal, state, and municipal sources. Also, government subsidies were reduced. The budget "crunch" and the attempt to balance the budget forced many public organizations to streamline their operations.

Ethical IT issues include email monitoring, data file monitoring, and appropriate Internet access at work.

— *Mike Rewald*

*Ethical Issues.* Organizations must deal with ethical issues of their employees, customers, and suppliers. Also, what is ethical in one country may be unethical in another. Ethical issues are very important since they can damage the image of an organization as well as destroy the morale of the employees.

The use of information technology raises many ethical issues, ranging from the surveillance of electronic mail to the potential invasion of privacy of millions of customers whose data are stored in private and public databases (see Chapter 7). Since IT is new and rapidly changing, there is little experience or agreement on how to deal with related ethical issues.

The environments that surround organizations are increasingly becoming more complex and turbulent. Advancements in communications, transportation, and technology create many changes. Other changes are the result of political or economic activities; thus, the pressures on organizations are mounting and organizations must take responsive actions. In addition, organizations may see opportunities in these pressures. How all this is accomplished is described next.

## ORGANIZATIONAL RESPONSES

In order to understand the impact of the business pressures on organizations we will use a classical management framework which was originally developed by Leavitt and later modified by Scott-Morton (see Scott-Morton and Allen [1994]), and by the authors, to reflect the role of IT. The framework is depicted in Figure 1.4.

Organizations are composed of five major components—one of which is IT—and they are surrounded by an environment. These components are in a stable condition, called equilibrium, as long as no significant change occurs in the environment or in any of the components. However, as soon as a significant change occurs, the system becomes unstable and it is necessary to adjust some or all of the internal components. As you can see in the figure, the inter-

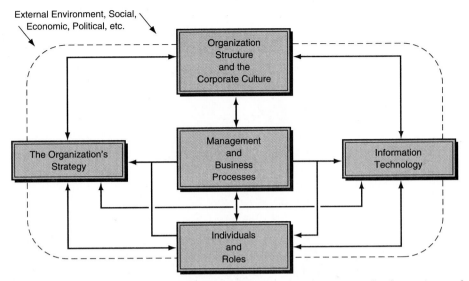

**FIGURE 1.4 Framework for organizational and societal impacts of information technology.** (*Source*: Adapted from M. Scott-Morton, "DSS Revisted for the 1990s," paper presented at *DSS 1986*, Washington, DC, 1986. Used with permission. Also see Scott-Morton and Allen [1994].)

nal components are interrelated. For example, a significant change in an organization's strategy may create a change in the corporate structure. Unstable organizations may be unable to excel or even survive; therefore, organizations need to respond by what we call *critical response activities*. Notice that such activities deal not only with long-term strategies, but also with the basic daily business activities.

Traditional responses may not work with new problems, so many old solutions need to be modified, supplemented, or eliminated. Organizations can also take *proactive* measures to create a change in the market place. Such activities also include *exploiting opportunities* created by the external pressures. The major critical response activities are summarized in Figure 1.5.

Organizations' major responses are divided here into five categories: strategic systems for competitive advantage, continuous improvement efforts, business process reengineering, business alliances, and electronic commerce. (Since many responses can be interrelated, they can be found in more than one category.)

*Strategic Systems.* Strategic systems (see Callon [1996]) provide organizations with strategic advantages, thus enabling them to increase their market share, to better negotiate with their suppliers, or to prevent competitors from entering into their territory. There are a variety of IT-supported strategic systems, as we will show in Chapter 3. An example is Federal Express's overnight delivery system and the company's ability to track the status of every individual package anywhere in the system. Federal Express's system is heavily supported by IT. A major challenge with this kind of strategic system is the difficulty of sustaining competitive advantage. Most of Federal Express's competitors have already duplicated the system. So FedEx moved the system to the Internet. However, the competitors quickly followed, and FedEx is now introducing new activities as described in the following *IT at Work* story.

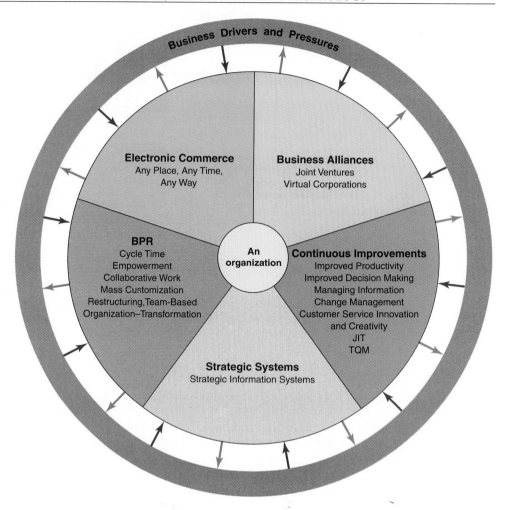

**FIGURE 1.5** Critical response activities.

---

### IT At Work   FEDERAL EXPRESS: AN INFORMATION TECHNOLOGY COMPANY

**USING IT**
→
...in Production &
Operations Management

FedEx executives like to describe themselves as an IT company. Here are some of FedEx's activities conducted on the Web (www.fedex.com):

▶ Customers can calculate the cost of any shipment and order a pickup.
▶ Customers can track the whereabouts of packages they send.
▶ Customers can prepare and verify shipping documents using electronic forms on the Web site.
▶ Customers can print shipping labels and other documents.
▶ Customers can find the closest of the 50,000 drop boxes in the United States.
▶ Businesses can sell products via a special FedEx Web system that presents electronic catalogs on special home pages hosted by FedEx. FedEx handles all the logistics of this electronic commerce (see details of the system in Chapter 6).

The Web services are growing rapidly, saving time for customers and money for FedEx. For example, in 1997, FedEx users placed more than 500,000 electronic tracking inquiries per month. Even at a conservative estimate of a $1.00 saving as compared to a telephone inquiry, this amounts to savings of $6 million per year.

   **For further exploration:** why is FedEx called an IT company? Can a smaller competitor compete without heavy investment in IT? ▲

***Continuous Improvement Efforts.*** Many companies continuously conduct programs in an attempt to improve their productivity and quality. Examples of such programs are:

▶ ***Improved productivity.*** Productivity is the ratio of outputs to inputs. A firm can improve productivity by increasing output, reducing costs, increasing output faster than cost, and so on. IT is used extensively for productivity improvement, as we illustrate throughout the book and especially in Chapter 8.

▶ ***Just-in-time.*** The **just-in-time (JIT)** approach is a comprehensive production scheduling and inventory control system that attempts to reduce costs and improve work flow by scheduling materials and parts to arrive at a workstation exactly when they are needed. JIT minimizes in-process inventories and waste and saves space. While some just-in-time systems can be managed manually, IT makes it easier to implement large and complex JIT systems (see Chapters 4 and 8).

▶ ***Total quality management.*** **Total quality management (TQM)** is a corporatewide organized effort to improve quality wherever and whenever possible. Information technology can enhance TQM by improving data monitoring, collection, summarization, analysis, and reporting. Information technology can also increase the speed of inspection, raise the quality of testing, and reduce the cost of performing various quality control activities. Finally, IT can help avert quality problems before they arise. This topic is further developed in Chapters 4 and 8.

▶ ***Improved decision making.*** The term management implies making decisions. Appropriate decision making attempts to select the best, or at least a good enough, alternative course of action. This task becomes difficult in a frequently changing environment, when the number of alternative choices can be very large and the impacts of the decision can be far reaching as well as difficult to forecast. The complexity of organizations, that is, their diversity, and the large number of constraints (such as government regulations) makes it even more difficult to make decisions. Also, the cost of making wrong decisions can be very high. Decisions require information that is timely and accurate. So it is obvious that IT plays a major role in providing such information, as well as in supporting difficult decision-making processes (see Chapter 9).

▶ ***Managing information and knowledge.*** One of the major pressures described earlier was information overload. To deal with the problem, organizations need to build an appropriate IT infrastructure (Chapter 12) and use effective methods to store, access, navigate, and properly use the vast amount of knowledge and information (see Fried [1995]). For example, an appropriate database marketing approach is considered one of the most critical success factors of organizations today. In addition to effectively managed data and databases (Chapter 10), it is necessary to find and properly interpret information. Intelligent systems are perhaps the most promising approach here (see Chapter 11).

▶ ***Innovation and creativity.*** Frequent environmental and technological changes require innovative approaches to organizational responses. Innovation and creativity can be facilitated by various information technologies as we will see in Chapters 9 and 11.

▶ ***Change management.*** Firms' responses to environmental changes may alter the manner in which organizations are structured and operated. Therefore, appropriate change management methodologies are needed. Several informa-

This text has helped me think creatively about how to manage people better, using IT as an enabler.
— *Karen Miller*

tion technologies can facilitate change management activities such as training and presentations (see Chapter 8).

▶ *Customer service.* The increased power of customers and the stiff competition force organizations to improve customer service. In addition to the traditional activities of customer service, organizations are developing innovative approaches to satisfy customers. As we'll see in Chapters 4, 6, 8, 9, and 11, IT plays a major role in supporting customer service. This important topic is also considered part of electronic commerce and of the business process reengineering approach, described next.

*Business Process Reengineering.* Organizations may discover that continuous improvement efforts have limited effectiveness in an environment full of strong business pressures. Therefore, a new approach called **business process reengineering (BPR)** is needed.

Business process reengineering refers to a major innovation in the organization's structure and the way it conducts its business. Technological, human, and organizational dimensions of a firm may all be changed in BPR (see Hammer and Champy [1993]). Over 70 percent of all large U.S. companies claim to be doing reengineering of some sort. As part of BPR, there are management realignments (see Drucker [1995]), mergers, consolidations, operational integrations, and reoriented distribution practices.

Information technology plays a major role in BPR. It provides automation; it allows business to be conducted in different locations; it provides flexibility in manufacturing; it permits quicker delivery to customers; and it supports rapid and paperless transactions among suppliers, manufacturers, and retailers.

The major areas in which IT supports BPR are:

▶ *Reducing cycle time and time to market.* Reducing the business process time (cycle time) is extremely important for increasing productivity and competitiveness (see Wetherbe [1996]). Similarly, reducing the time from the inception of an idea until its implementation—time to market—is important because those who can be first on the market with a product, or who can provide customers with a service faster than competitors, enjoy a distinct competitive advantage. Information technology can be used to expedite the various steps in the process of product or service development, testing, and implementation. An example of how cycle time is reduced in bringing new drugs to the market is shown in the following.

---

**IT At Work**    THE INTERNET AND THE INTRANET SHORTEN TIME TO MARKET OF NEW DRUGS

**U**SING IT

...in Health Care

**THE PROBLEM.** The Food and Drug Administration (FDA) must be extremely careful in approving new drugs. At the same time, there is public pressure on the FDA to approve new drugs quickly, especially for cancer and AIDS. The problem is that in order to assure quality, the FDA requires companies to conduct extensive research and clinical testing. The development programs of such research and testing cover 300,000 to 500,000 pages of documentation for each drug. The subsequent results and analysis are reported on 100,000 to 200,000 additional pages. These pages are reviewed by the FDA prior to approval of new drugs. Manual processing of this information significantly delays the work of the FDA, so the total process takes 6 to 10 years.

**THE SOLUTION.**  *Computer-Aided Drug Application Systems* (from Research Data Corporation of New Jersey) is a software program that uses a network-distributed document processing system. The pharmaceutical company scans all its related documents into a database. The documents are indexed, and full-text-search-and-retrieval software is attached to the system. Using key words, corporate employees can search the database via the intranet. The database is also accessible, via the Internet, to the FDA employees, who no longer have to spend hours looking for a specific piece of data (it takes only six to eight seconds to access an image in the database; see the screen below). Any viewed information can be processed or printed at the user's desktop computer. The system not only helps the FDA but also the companies' researchers, who have any required information at their fingertips. Remote corporate and business-partner users can also access the system. The overall results: The time to market of a new drug is reduced by up to a year (each week saved can be translated into the saving of many lives and can also yield up to $1,000,000 profit). The system also reduces the time it takes to patent a new drug.

Today the process can be expedited even further. An example is ISIS pharmaceuticals, a company that develops drugs for treating cancer. The company submits its reports to the FDA electronically, on a CD-ROM. This cuts the FDA's review time by several months. Furthermore, by using an intranet the company can expedite the internal preparation of the report. Smithkline Beecham quickens the process further by using an electronic publishing solution. Using automated hypertext links and sophisticated software, navigation through information is much faster (see www.openmarket.com/products/folio/Smitklin.htm.)

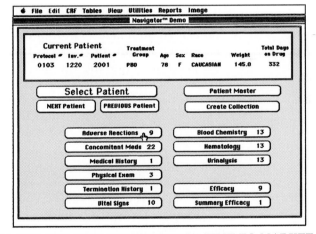

**THE INTERNET AND THE INTRANET SHORTEN TIME TO MARKET OF NEW DRUGS**

**For Further Exploration:**  It is said that this system helps communication, collaboration, and discovery. Explain. ▲

SOURCE: Condensed from *IMC Journal* May/June 1993, pp. 23–25. The ISIS case is based on a story in *Inc. Technology*, No. 3, 1997, p. 48.

▶ *Empowerment of employees and collaborative work.* Giving employees the authority to act and make decisions on their own is a strategy used by many organizations as part of their BPR. Empowerment is related to the concept of self-directed teams (see Mankin et al. [1996] and Lipnack and Stamps [1997]). Management delegates authority to teams who can execute the work faster and with fewer delays. IT allows the *decentralization* of decision making and authority but simultaneously supports a centralized control. For example, the Internet and intranets enable empowered employees to access data, information, and knowledge they need for making quick decisions. Networked expert systems can give experts' advice to team members whenever human experts are not available. In addition, computer networks allow team members to communicate with each other effectively as well as to communicate with other teams in different locations.

▶ *Customer-focused approach.* Companies are increasingly becoming more customer oriented (see Whiteley [1992]). In other words, they must pay more attention to customers and their preferences and reengineer themselves to meet consumer demands. This can be done in part by changing manufacturing processes from mass production to *mass customization* (see Pine [1993]). In mass production, a company produces a large quantity of identical items. In mass customization, items are produced in a large quantity but are customized to fit the desires of each customer. Information technology supports mass customization (see Chapter 4) and other customer-focused approaches.

▶ *Restructuring and team-based structure.* One of the major premises of BPR is that the organizational structure should fit the business processes. One way to attain this goal is to create many teams, each responsible for a complete business process. As we will see in Chapter 4 such a structure, called a **networked organization** and often supported by IT, reduces or eliminates many of the problems created by the business pressures.

▶ *Enterprise Resource Planning and supply chain management.* **Enterprise Resource Planning (ERP)** (Chapters 4 and 8) is a new concept which attempts to integrate the various functional areas in organizations and further extend them to business partners usually using integrated software such as SAP R/3. Such an integration is done through **supply chain management.** Extranets are secured networks that connect the intranets of several business partners. The delivery of ERP is now done via intranets and **extranets.**

*Business Alliances.* Many companies realize that alliances with other companies, even competitors, can be very beneficial. For example, General Motors and Ford created a joint venture to explore electronic commerce applications. There are several types of alliances: sharing resources, establishing permanent supplier-company relationship, and creating joint research efforts. One of the most interesting types is the temporary joint venture, where companies form a special company for a specific, limited-time, mission. This is an example of a **virtual corporation** and, according to Davidow and Malone (1992), it could be a common business organization in the future. More details of virtual corporations are provided in Chapter 4. An example of how IT supports the international virtual corporation follows.

*IT At Work*  **IT ENHANCES AN INTERNATIONAL VIRTUAL CORPORATION**

*U*SING IT
...in Production &
Operations Management

An international virtual corporation was established in 1994 in Southeast Asia to set up a satellite-based mobile (wireless) telephone communication system in the region. The one-billion-dollar project serves one million subscribers in China, India, Japan, Singapore, Thailand, Malaysia, and other neighboring countries. The international consortium includes companies from the various Asian countries as well as Hughes Communications of the United States. The project is the first of its kind in Asia, and was completed 1998.

While it is based on telecommunication via satellites, the project is supported by other information technologies. Due to the different locations of the participating members and vendors, for example, communication is improved by using the Internet, computerized fax, e-mail, and computer conferencing.

**For Further Exploration:** Why is the idea of a virtual corporation appealing? What role does IT play in supporting the concept? ▲

SOURCE: Based on a story in *The Straits Times,* August 6, 1994.

A more permanent type of business alliance that links manufacturers, suppliers, and finance corporations is known as *keiretsu* (a Japanese term). This and other types of alliances can be heavily supported by information technologies ranging from electronic data interchange to electronic transmission of maps and drawings.

***Electronic Commerce.***  Doing business electronically is the newest and perhaps most promising strategy that many companies can pursue (see Turban et al. [1999]). While it may be viewed as a part of BPR, it certainly deserves special attention (see Chapter 6).

## INFORMATION SYSTEMS AND INFORMATION TECHNOLOGY

While some critical response activities can be executed manually, the vast majority require the use of information systems. Before we provide more examples on the role of information systems and IT, let us briefly explore the terms *information system* and *information technology.*

**WHAT IS AN INFORMATION SYSTEM?**  An **information system (IS)** collects, processes, stores, analyzes, and disseminates information for a specific purpose. Like any other system (see the appendix at the end of the chapter), an information system includes *inputs* (data, instructions) and *outputs* (reports, calculations). It *processes* the inputs and produces outputs that are sent to the user or to other systems. A *feedback* mechanism that controls the operation may be included (see Figure 1.6). Like any other system, an information system operates within an *environment.*

***Formal and Informal Information Systems.***  An information system can be formal or informal. Formal systems include agreed-upon procedures, standard inputs and outputs, and fixed definitions. Informal systems take many shapes, ranging from an office gossip network to a group of friends exchanging letters electronically. It is important to understand the existence of informal systems. They may consume information resources and sometimes interface with the formal systems. They may also play an important role in resisting and/or encouraging change.

**WHAT IS A COMPUTER-BASED INFORMATION SYSTEM?** A **computer-based information system (CBIS)** is an information system that uses computer technology to perform some or all of its intended tasks. Such systems can

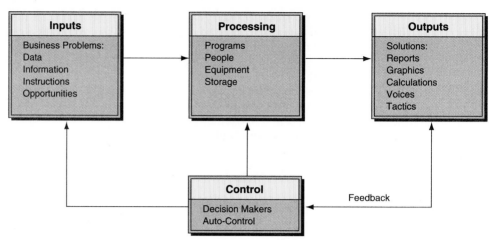

**FIGURE 1.6** A schematic view of an information system.

include a personal computer and software, or it may include several thousand computers of various sizes with hundreds of printers, plotters, and other devices, as well as communication networks and databases. In most cases an information system also includes people. The basic components of information systems are listed below. Note that not every system includes all these components.

▶ *Hardware* is a set of devices such as processor, monitor, keyboard and a printer (see Figure 1.7) that accepts data and information, processes them, and displays them.

▶ *Software* is a set of programs that enable the hardware to process data.

▶ A *database* is a collection of related files, tables, relations, and so on, that stores data and the associations among them.

▶ A *network* is a connecting system that permits the sharing of resources by different computers.

▶ *Procedures* are the set of instructions about how to combine the above components in order to process information and generate the desired output.

▶ *People* are those individuals who work with the system or use its output.

In addition, all systems have a purpose and a social context. A common *purpose* is to provide a solution to a business problem. In the Harper-Honda case, the system helped in reducing cost, improving communication, and expediting administrative processes. The *social context* of the system consists of the values and beliefs that determine what is admissible and possible within the culture of the people and groups involved.

To really unlock the potential of a computer, you need to have your software and hardware attuned to your business, whether you're selling golf balls or mortgages. Your Information System will only do for you what you tell it to.

— *Blake Thompson*

**THE DIFFERENCE BETWEEN COMPUTERS AND INFORMATION SYSTEMS.** Computers provide effective and efficient ways of processing data, and they are a necessary part of an information system (IS). An IS, however, involves much more than just computers. The successful application of an IS requires an understanding of the business and its environment that is supported by the IS. For example, to build an IS that supports transactions executed on the New York Stock Exchange, it is necessary to understand all the procedures related to buying and selling stocks, bonds, options, and so on, including irregular demands made on the system.

**FIGURE 1.7** Some components of a computer-based information system.

In learning about IS, it is therefore not sufficient just to learn about computers. Computers are only one part of a complex system that must be designed, operated, and maintained. A public transportation system in a city provides an analogy. Buses are a necessary ingredient of the system, but more is needed. Designing the bus routes, bus stops, different schedules, and so on requires considerable understanding of customer demand, traffic patterns, city regulations, safety requirements, and the like. Computers, like buses, are only one component in a complex system. The purpose of this book is to acquaint you with all aspects of information systems.

**WHAT IS INFORMATION TECHNOLOGY?** *Information technology*, in its narrow definition, refers to the technological side of an information system. It includes the hardware, databases, software, networks, and other devices. It can be viewed as a subsystem of an information system. Sometimes, the term *IT* is also used interchangeably with *information system*, or it may even be used in a broad way to describe a collection of several information systems, users, and management for an entire organization. In this book, we use the term IT in this broadest sense. Now that the basic terms have been defined, we present some examples of IS applications worldwide.

## ▶ 1.2  EXAMPLES OF INFORMATION SYSTEMS AT WORK WORLDWIDE

Millions of different information systems are in use throughout the world. The following examples are intended to show the diversity of applications and the benefits provided. At the end of each example, we list the critical response activities supported by the system.

## MANAGING ACCOUNTING INFORMATION ACROSS ASIA

*U*SING IT

...in Accounting

Le Saunda Holding Company (Hong Kong) manages 32 subsidiaries in four Asian countries, mostly in the manufacturing, import, and sale of shoes. Managing the financing and cash flow is a complex process. All accounting information flows to headquarters electronically. Sales data are electronically collected at point-of-sale (POS) terminals and, together with inventory data (which are updated automatically when a sale occurs), they are transferred to headquarters. Other relevant data such as advertising and promotions, merchants, and cash flow, are also transmitted electronically and collected in a centralized database for storage and processing.

To cope with the rapid growth of the company, a sophisticated accounting software package, SunAccount, was installed in 1995. The result was radical improvements in accounting procedures. Today, for example, it takes less than 10 minutes rather than a day to produce an ad hoc special report. Many reports are generated, helping functional managers make quicker and better decisions. The system is also much more reliable, and internal and external auditing is easier. Headquarters knows what is going on almost as soon as it occurs. All these improvements have led to a substantial growth in revenue and profits for the firm. (SOURCE: Condensed from *IT Asia,* August 1995.)

**CRITICAL RESPONSE ACTIVITIES SUPPORTED:** Decision making, managing large amounts of information, improving quality, reducing cycle time.

## RUSSIANS LIVE IN MOSCOW AND WORK IN CALIFORNIA

*U*SING IT

...in Production &
Operations Management

Sixty highly computer-skilled Russians (some with Ph.D. degrees) live in Moscow but commute electronically to a small software company called Pick Systems in Irvine, California where they work on advanced software projects. Richard Pick, President of Pick Systems, has been employing Russian scientists since 1990. The company revealed its Russian venture only in 1994, after keeping it secret from its competitors for four years. Communication is done through the Internet. To exercise management control, the company is using mirrored systems; what the Russians are doing in Moscow is mirrored in the systems in California. The Russians are paid relatively low salaries, because there is a huge pool of skilled employees who were laid off from space and military programs after the collapse of the Soviet Union. This case is an example of telecommuting, where employees work at their home or in centers away from the corporate facilities (see Chapter 7). The ability to use employees that live in other countries can result in substantial savings.

**CRITICAL RESPONSE ACTIVITIES SUPPORTED:** Strategic advantage (cost reduction, use of experts).

## TRACKING UPS PACKAGES WITH PEN COMPUTERS

*U*SING IT

...in Production &
Operations Management

More than 65,000 UPS drivers are using hand-held pen computers and telecommunication to improve the accuracy of their package delivery records and increase their record-keeping efficiency by eliminating paperwork. Each computer has a keypad, infrared bar code scanner, small liquid-crystal display screen, and

1. UPS driver enters data on hand-held terminal when package is delivered.

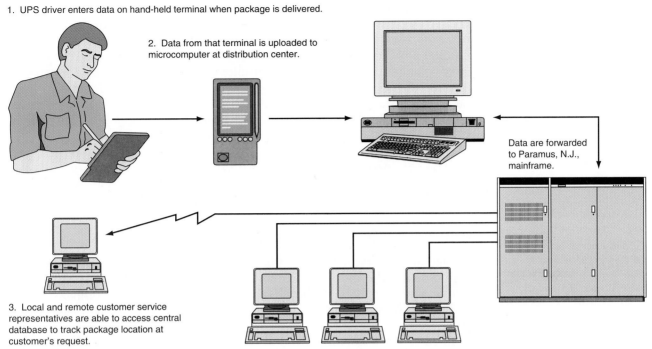

2. Data from that terminal is uploaded to microcomputer at distribution center.

Data are forwarded to Paramus, N.J., mainframe.

3. Local and remote customer service representatives are able to access central database to track package location at customer's request.

**FIGURE 1.8 UPS electronic package tracking system (www.ups.com).** (*Source*: Courtesy of United Parcel Service Inc., Atlanta, GA.)

electronic pad for capturing customer signatures. When delivering a package, the driver inputs delivery information via the keypad to a computer at UPS headquarters using a telecommunication network (see Figure 1.8). Customers are equipped with software that allows them to access UPS's corporate database electronically via the Internet and find out the status of their packages. Alternatively, the customer can call a UPS customer representative, who will access the database and provide a reply within a few seconds.

In 1998, UPS started to use the Internet for secured delivery service of documents. (SOURCE: Condensed from *InternetWeek,* March 9, 1998.)

**CRITICAL RESPONSE ACTIVITIES SUPPORTED:** Customer service, quality.

## MERCY HOSPITAL PROVIDES PATIENT-FOCUSED CARE

**U**SING IT

...in Health Care

Health care costs, as well as health care quality, are ranked as a prime concern of people in the U.S.. As a result, some hospitals are restructuring their operations and renovating facilities to provide patient-focused care while at the same time containing costs. In the patient-focused model, a team of multidisciplinary caregivers provides about 80 percent of what patients need.

San Diego's Mercy Hospital placed computer terminals in all patients' rooms, allowing the nurses to communicate with doctors, specialists, medical records, laboratories, and so on. Orders for tests, special diets, and medications are all entered from the patient's room. Also, information about the patient, such as nearest relative, can be found within seconds directly from the patient's room. There are no more busy telephone lines, unavailable data, or errors in information. Health team members do not have to run to use the computer at the nursing station any more. This system reduced operating costs by 10 percent and increased quality of care. Patients, employees, and doctors have expressed enthusiasm for the system, and surveys indicated a 5 to 13 percent improvement in patients' satisfaction (SOURCE: Condensed from Borzo, G., "Patient-Focused Hospitals Begin Reporting Good Results," *Health Care Strategic Management*, August 1992, pp. 17–22.)

**CRITICAL RESPONSE ACTIVITIES SUPPORTED:** Productivity, BPR, quality, cycle time, customer service.

## BOEING TRAINS ITS EMPLOYEES ELECTRONICALLY

*U*SING IT
→
...in Human Resources
Management

The aviation industry needs to continuously train its employees on the new airplanes. Boeing, the industry's leader in manufacturing of airplanes, used to spend millions of dollars in traditional classroom training. The company had to pay hundreds of instructors worldwide as well as employees while they attended classes.

In early 1995, Boeing moved to computer-based training in order to teach its employees the ins and outs of new planes. The computer-based training program is basically a graphical representation of the new airplane. It documents every part of the plane and closely mimics all the plane's flying characteristics. For example, the training takes the pilots through the whole preflight operations, training them on what instruments need to be looked at and adjusted. The training modules also show pilots how to configure the airplanes' flight-management computer system. The computer-based training also acts as a problem-solving tool. The training program, for instance, simulates a mechanical problem with one of the engines, and it is up to the mechanic to diagnose and suggest how to fix the problem. During this interactive process, the program offers hints to the mechanic.

The training programs were placed on hundreds of CD-ROMs. However, the CD-ROMs needed to be continually updated to comply with federal regulations, and there was a logistics problem and costs with distributing them to Boeing's employees all over the world.

> The Lockheed Martin intranet at my workplace is an integral part of training — all training procedures are on-line.
>
> — *Dave Gehrke*

Boeing solved all of these problems by transferring the entire program to its intranet. Now it is possible to make updates to the training program in real time. Before the advent of its intranet, Boeing's engineers would have to collaborate with the programmers of the computer-based training face-to-face because the engineers had to make sure that the programmers got all of the details right. Now, the engineers and programmers can collaborate through e-mail and video teleconferencing. By moving the training online, assembly line workers can also be educated about parts of a plane which they are working on. Boeing estimates that by using its intranet for computer-based training, it saves approximately 25 percent of the training costs. (SOURCE: Condensed from Mermon, F., "Boeing Flies High with Computer-based Training," *Interactive Week*, October 7, 1996.)

**CRITICAL RESPONSE ACTIVITIES SUPPORTED:** Cost reduction, and training cycle time reduction.

## INTEGRATING FINANCE, MANUFACTURING, AND SALES INCREASES CUSTOMER SATISFACTION AND PRODUCTIVITY

*I*NTEGRATING IT

...for Finance, Marketing, Accounting

Headquartered in Santiago Tianguistenco in the federal state of Mexico, Mercedes-Benz Mexico S.A. de C.V. assembles Mercedes-Benz and Freightliner trucks, C and E class passenger cars, and engines for the Mexican and South American marketplace.

The company was looking for a modern, 90s solution to improve processes and meet customers' objectives, as well as guarantee successful operation in the future.

The solution was found in an integrated software, called R/3, from SAP AG. Three of the software modules—Financial Accounting, Controlling, and Sales and Distribution—were implemented in three months. They allow the company to integrate several resources and functions.

The process-oriented integration between functions within R/3 has led to a reduction in tasks in each of the different areas. And the information between sales and finance is now consistent. Mercedes-Benz customers have noticed the change, especially in how quickly they can get information from the company. R/3 has also speeded up Mercedes-Benz's warranty payment system.

The flip side of that increase in customer responsiveness is enhanced internal productivity. "R/3 has really allowed us to optimize our processes," explains Victor Carrasco, manager for Accounting and Administrative Systems. "As a result of that significant reduction in tasks and time, we are able to do the same amount of work with less people." (SOURCE: Condensed from success story #469KB, at www.sap.com, 1998.)

**CRITICAL RESPONSE ACTIVITIES SUPPORTED:** Customer service, productivity improvement, and distribution of information.

## CRIME FIGHTING INFORMATION TECHNOLOGY

*U*SING IT

...in Public Service

The national Crime Information Center (CIC) in the United States contains a crime-related database operated by the FBI. Law enforcement agencies throughout the country file all their outstanding arrest warrants on this system. A highway patrol officer can use the telecommunication network (or call in) to transmit a name or driver's license number to find out whether a person is wanted, or the officer can use the vehicle ID number to find out whether a car is stolen. Some police cars are equipped with devices that read fingerprints and/or take pictures of suspects, transmit them electronically to CIC, and obtain identifications in a matter of seconds.

In February 1993, the system helped the New York police arrest two suspects in the Valentine's Day murder of six people. The suspects used the nicknames Tato and Ding Ding. The police matched the nicknames with the actual names in the database and quickly arrested the suspects. When crime is considered a critical national issue, information systems are certainly an important crime-fighting technique.

Police departments in California use a database called Law Enforcement Automated Data System (LEADS) to track parolees and match them quickly against suspects. (SOURCE: *California Computer News*, June 1992.)

**CRITICAL RESPONSE ACTIVITIES SUPPORTED:** Cycle time, information management, and productivity.

## MAXIMIZING THE VALUE OF JOHN DEERE'S PENSION FUND

Managing the pension fund of John Deere & Co., a large manufacturer of earth-moving machines, agricultural machines, and other heavy equipment, is not simple. About $1 billion of the over $5 billion fund is managed internally by the corporate finance department. In order to achieve a better return on the invest-ment, the finance department has been using neural computing (see Chapter 11) since 1993.

Here is how the process works. Using historical data, an individual artificial neural network is built for each of the 1,000 largest U.S. corporations. The data include 40 fundamental and technical variables, such as growth rate, financial ratios, price movements, market share, and earning per share. Once a week, the current data of each of these companies is entered into a model that predicts the future performance of each stock (see Figure 1.9). The model then ranks the 1,000 stocks, based on their anticipated performance in the stock market. A port-folio of the top 100 stocks is selected and the funds' money is allocated in pro-portion to the predicted return.

While the internal structure and success rate of the model are trade secrets, it is known that returns are well in excess of industry benchmarks.

**CRITICAL RESPONSE ACTIVITY SUPPORTED:** Decision making.

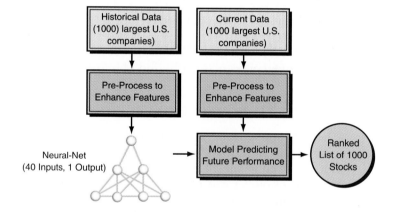

**FIGURE 1.9** Schematic representation of the stock portfolio process. (*Source*: Courtesy of John Deere & Co.)

## WEB-BASED INFORMATION SYSTEMS AT OREGON STATE

Students at Oregon State are using browsers to find their grades, to replace cata-logs, to register, to change their address, to access account information, and to get academic counseling. These are only some of the things that students can do on the network. Students can also use the Web-based system to apply for admis-sion and communicate with faculty. And it's not just the students who are bene-fiting from the system (www.osu.orst.edu). Faculty and administrative work also is simplified, since admissions applications can be processed and instructors can advise students on transcripts over the Internet. The registrar's office reduced its staff considerably. The GartnerGroup estimates that in 1998 over 80 percent of the universities already have some of these capabilities. (SOURCE: Condensed from *PC Week*, Sept. 8, 1997 and www.gartner.com, 1998.)

**CRITICAL RESPONSE ACTIVITIES SUPPORTED:** Improved customer service, reducing cost, reducing cycle time, and improving access to information.

**AMAZON.COM CHANGES THE BOOK SELLING INDUSTRY**

*U*SING IT

...in Marketing

Amazon.com is known as the first Internet-based bookstore, and its revenue increased by more than 800% in 1997. Offering over 2.5 million books on-line, Amazon can get you almost any book in a very short time and at a discount of up to 40%. In addition, Amazon provides comprehensive reviews of books, the possibility of electronic communication with some authors, bibiliographies of any topic you desire with table of contents, and other information on many books. With Amazon's of home shopping, you also get some entertainment and a chance to win $100 in the "customer review contest." You can chat in Internet communities with people of the same interest, join a book club, and more.

If you have an intersest in seeing the list of forthcoming books on your favorite topic or reviews by professionals or customers, there is no problem; all you need to do is ask.

Amazon is changing the manner in which books are marketed, worldwide. The competition in the industry is increasing, traditional bookstores (such as Barnes and Noble) are adding on-line services. Weak competitors, such as Crown Books, are in big trouble. Amazon.com is a vivid example of the impact IT has on both the manner in which business is conducted and on our life. The technology used is known as *electronic commerce.*

**CRITICAL RESPONSE ACTIVITIES SUPPORTED:** Improve cycle time, strategic advantage, customer service, BPR, cost reduction and improved access to information.

## ▶ 1.3 INFORMATION TECHNOLOGY DEVELOPMENTS AND TRENDS

In the previous section, we described the role of IT in supporting business activities. We also pointed out some of the capabilities (Table 1.1) that enable IT to play such a role. Next we will describe some of IT's developments and trends, and especially the move toward networked computing. But first imagine this scenario:

It's a Monday morning in the year 2002. Executive Joanne Smith gets into her car, and her voice activates a remote telecommunications-access workstation. She requests that all voice and mail messages open and pending, as well as her schedule for the day, be transmitted to her. The office workstation consolidates these items from home and office databases. The message-ordering knowbot (knowledge robot), a computer program Joanne developed, delivers the accumulated messages (in the order she prefers) to the voice and data portable computer in her car. By the time Joanne gets to the office, she has read the necessary messages, sent some replies, revised her day's schedule, and completed a "to-do" list for the week, all of which have been filed in her virtual database by her personal organizer knowbot.

The virtual database and the intranet have made Joanne's use of IT much easier. No longer does she have to be concerned about the physical location of data. She is working on a large proposal for the Acme Corporation today; and although segments of the Acme file physically exist on several databases, she can access the data from her *wireless workstation* wherever she happens to be. To help manage this information resource, Joanne uses an *information visualizer* that enables her to create and manage dynamic relationships among data collections. This information visualizer has extended the graphical user interface of the early

1990s to a three-dimensional graphic structure. (SOURCE: Compiled from Benjamin and Blunt [1992], p. 7.)

Joanne could do even more work if her car were able to drive itself. While this kind of a car is still in an experimental stage, it will probably be in commercial use sometime during the twenty-first century. As a matter of fact, a limited use of such a car is expected in California by the year 2002 (see Chapter 11).

This year-2002 scenario is becoming a reality even sooner, owing to important trends in information technology. These trends, which are listed in Table 1.3 and described next, fall into two categories: general and networked computing.

*Table 1.3* **Major Technological Developments and Trends**

*General:*

- The cost-performance advantage of computers over manual labor will increase.
- Graphical and other user-friendly interfaces will dominate PCs.
- Storage capacity will increase dramatically.
- Data warehouse will store terabytes of information.
- Multimedia use will increase significantly.
- Intelligent systems, especially artificial neural computing and expert systems, will increase in importance.
- Object-oriented programming and document management will be widely accepted.
- Computers will be increasingly compact.

*Networked Computing:*

- Client/server architecture will be the predominant architecture.
- Computers will be more portable. Mobile and wireless applications will become a major component of IT.
- Home computing will be integrated with the telephone, television, and other electronic services.
- The use of the Internet will grow, leading to information superhighways.
- Intranets will be the dominating network systems in most organizations.
- Electronic commerce will grow rapidly, changing the manner in which business is conducted.
- Intelligent software agents will roam through databases and networks conducting time-consuming tasks for their masters.

## GENERAL TECHNOLOGICAL TRENDS

General trends are relevant to any computing system. They include:

***Cost-Performance Ratio: Improvement by a Factor of at Least 100.*** In about 10 years, a computer will cost the same as its costs today but will be about 50 times more powerful (in terms of processing speed, memory, and so on). At the same time labor costs could double, so the cost-performance ratio of computers versus manual work will improve by a factor of 100. This means that computers will have increasingly greater comparative advantage over people. As time passes, more and more routine tasks will be economically done by a computer rather than by a human.

The U.S. Department of Labor estimates that 75 percent of all work in U.S. service firms can be technologically automated by the year 2000. (*Note:* Even if a job can be technologically automated, it needs to be *economically justifiable* before a human is replaced.) While the replacement of people by computers will continue, there will be some jobs whose automation cost will be so high that it may take generations before these jobs can be fully automated. Also, there are jobs that may never be automated.

***Graphical and Other User-Friendly Interfaces.***  A graphical user interface (GUI) is a set of software features that provides users with direct control of visible objects and actions on the screen to replace complex command syntax. GUI creates a user-friendly human-machine interface with icons, pull-down menus, windows, and a mouse. GUI is becoming the major interface in PCs.

The trend is to make the interface as simple as possible. One way to do that is to introduce intelligent interfaces that understand the user's wishes even when expressed in everyday language.

***Storage and Memories.***  CD-ROMs and other storage devices will increase secondary storage, thereby allowing a vast amount of information to be stored. Large memories will support the use of multimedia and emerging computer technologies such as artificial intelligence.

***Data Warehouse.***  To store the ever-increasing amount of information, companies are building gigantic "warehouses" that contain terabytes (one trillion bytes) of data, organized for easy access by end users. These warehouses are integrated with the Internet so they can be accessed from any location at any time.

***Multimedia and Virtual Reality.***  Computers will play a major role in integrating various types of media (voice, text, graphics, full motion video, and animation) to improve education, training, advertising, communicating, and decision making. Virtual reality (Chapter 11) is an implementation of interactive 3-D graphics that allows users to enter a virtual world.

***Intelligent Systems.***  Intelligent systems such as expert systems, natural language processors, and neural computing increase productivity and ease the execution of complex tasks. They also provide support when the information flow is incomplete or "fuzzy." Intelligent systems can be used individually, but in many cases they are integrated among themselves and with other information systems. The result is powerful systems that can support many of the critical response activities described earlier. Intelligent systems also play an important role in improving computing security.

***Object-Oriented Environment and Document Management.***  An object-oriented environment is an innovative way of programming and using computers that is expected to significantly reduce the cost of both building and maintaining information systems. The environment includes object-oriented programming, databases, and operating systems that increase the capabilities of IT and its cost effectiveness. The increased use of multimedia and object-oriented systems will make electronic document management one of the most important topics of IT.

***Compactness.***  While the capabilities and the benefit/cost ratio of computers are increasing, their size is decreasing.

### NETWORKED COMPUTING

The technology of networked computing is emerging rapidly. This technology enables users to reach other users and access databases anywhere in the organization and in any other place. The major applications of networked computing are the following.

*Portability.* Compact computers can now be attached to cars and other machines as well as to consumer products. They can be carried to almost any place you go. Their portability allows employees in the field to enter and access data, thus reducing the time between data collection and processing. Portable computer devices that can be used in many places and are supported by wireless technologies are revolutionizing the computing environment by creating a large number of new applications (see Box 1.1).

## A Closer Look BOX 1.1

### MOBILE AND WIRELESS APPLICATIONS

Mobile computing supports existing and entirely new kinds of applications, for example:

▶ Mobile personal communications capabilities, such as the personal digital assistants (PDAs) for networked communications and applications.
▶ On-line transaction processing, for example, where a salesperson in a retail environment can enter an order for goods and also charge a customer's credit card to complete the transaction.
▶ Remote database queries, for example, where a salesperson can use a mobile network connection to check an item's availability or the status of an order, directly from the customer's site.
▶ Dispatching like air traffic control, rental car pick up and return, delivery vehicles, trains, taxis, cars, and trucks.
▶ Front-line IT applications, where instead of the same data being entered multiple times as it goes through the value chain, it is entered only once.

Wireless communications support both mobile computing applications and low cost substitutions for communication cables, for example:

▶ Temporary offices can be set up quickly and inexpensively by using wireless network connections.
▶ Wireless connections to permanent office locations are often practical in difficult or hazardous wiring environments.
▶ Installing a wireless connection can replace leased lines that are used to connect LANs, thus eliminating the costs of monthly line leases.

There are mobile and wireless application opportunities in many industries, such as:

▶ Retail—a very successful application to date, particularly in department stores where there are frequent changes of layout; retail sales personnel conduct inventory inquiries or even sales transactions on the retail floor with wireless access from their PCs.
▶ Wholesale/distribution—wireless networking is used for inventory picking in warehouses with PCs mounted on forklifts, and for delivery and order status updates with PCs inside distribution trucks.
▶ Field service/sales—dispatching, on-line diagnostic support from customer sites, and parts ordering/inventory queries in all types of service and sales functions.
▶ Factories/manufacturing—environments and applications include mobile shop-floor quality control system or wireless applications that give added flexibility for temporary setups.
▶ Healthcare/hospitals—healthcare personnel need to access and send data to patient records, or consult comparative diagnosis databases wherever the patient or the healthcare worker may be located.
▶ Education—pilot applications equip students with PCs in the lecture halls, linked by a wireless network, for interactive quizzes, additional data and graphics lecture support, and on-line handout materials.
▶ Banking/finance—mobile transactional capabilities can assist in purchasing, selling, inquiry, brokerage, an other dealings.

SOURCE: Publicly distributed information of Digital Equipment Corporation.

Client/server architecture is used in most businesses today, and all employees are required to have some knowledge of it.
— *Dave Gehrke*

***Client/Server Architecture.***   Client/server architecture, the subject of Chapter 12, is growing rapidly. PCs, viewed as "clients," are linked to specialized, powerful "servers" (databases, communication devices, mainframes, and very powerful PCs), which they share via local or global networks. Such architecture requires telecommunication standards that will allow interconnection of different types of software and hardware. The client/server architecture is used to support the Internet and the intranets.

***The Network Computer.***   In 1997, the *network computer* was introduced. This computer does not have a hard drive; it is served by a central computing station through a network similar to a dumb terminal in a miniframe. Also called "thin clients," network computers are designed to provide the benefits of desktop computing without the high cost of PCs.

***Integrated Home Computing.***   Home computing, television, telephone, home security systems, and other devices will be integrated and managed in one unit. Assuming such a unit will be easy to operate, the integrated system will facilitate telecommuting and the use of the Internet.

***Intranets and Extranets.***   As the intranet concept spreads and the supporting hardware and software are standardized, it is logical to assume that most organizations will use it for internal communication. Combining an intranet with the Internet (in what is called an extranet) creates a powerful interorganizational communications and collaboration system.

***Electronic Commerce.***   Approaching several billion dollars of business volume in 1997 and growing rapidly, electronic commerce may cover as much as 15 percent of all U.S. trade within 10 years. Electronic commerce, as shown in the Harper-Honda case, may provide a significant competitive edge and it could change organizational structure, processes, procedures, climate and management—a true **organizational transformation.**

***Intelligent Agents.***   The success of the Internet and EC depend on the development of intelligent software agents (see Chapters 5, 6, and 11) that will help in navigating the Internet, accessing databases, and helping users to conduct certain EC activities.

***The Internet and Information Superhighways.***   From about 50 million Internet users in 1997, there could be as many as 750 million in less than 10 years. The integration of television and computers will allow the Internet to reach every networked home, business, school, and other organization. This will lead to an **information superhighway,** which is a national fiber-optic-based network that will change the manner in which we live, learn, and work. Singapore is likely to be the first country to have such a national information superhighway completely installed (see Box 1.2).

***The Networked Enterprise.***   The components and technologies just described can be integrated together into an enterprisewide network which is extended to all business partners. Netscape describes this concept in a white paper titled "The Networked Enterprise" (http://search.netscape.com/comprod/at-work/white-paper/vision/intro.html; 12/21/97) in the following way:

The **networked enterprise** comprises one seamless network, extending

## *A Closer Look*   BOX 1.2

### A NETWORKED INTELLIGENT COUNTRY

In Singapore, information technology is a national priority. This country of 3 million people is preparing itself to be, by 2000, the first country with an advanced nationwide information infrastructure, which will connect virtually every home, office, school, and factory. The computer will evolve into an information appliance, combining the functions of the telephone, TV, computers, and more. A nationwide network will provide a wide range of communication means and access to services. Singaporeans will be able to tap into vast reservoirs of electronically stored information and knowledge to improve their businesses and quality of life. Text, sound, pictures, videos, documents, designs, and other forms of media will be transferred and shared through the high capacity of the national fiber optic telecommunication system working in tandem with a pervasive wireless network. A wide range of new infrastructural services—linking government, businesses, and people—will be created to take advantage of new telecommunications.

The plan, which has been in implementation for several years as a joint government-industry project, is based on five strategic thrusts:

1. Developing Singapore as a global hub for business, services, and transportation.
2. Improving the quality of life for Singaporeans.
3. Boosting the economic engine, increasing the competitiveness of the island's industries, and decreasing unemployment.
4. Linking communities locally and globally.
5. Enhancing the capabilities of individuals.

By 1998 the Singaporean government had launched several projects aiming to boost the use of electronic commerce in the country.

**IT enables monitoring of operations at Singapore's ports, a major hub for business.**

SOURCE: Condensed from "A Vision of an Intelligent Island: The IT 2000 Report," National Computer Board of Singapore, 1992, and from www.ncb.gov.sg, 1998.

---

the corporate contacts to all the entities a company does business with. The networked enterprise provides two primary benefits:

▶ By creating new types of services, businesses can engage customers in a direct interactive relationship that results in customers getting precisely what they want when they want it, resulting in stronger customer relationships. Also, relationships with suppliers and other business partners are improved.

▶ By taking the entire product design process online—drawing partners and customers into the process and removing the traditional communication barriers that prevent rapid product design and creation—companies can bring products and services to market far more quickly.

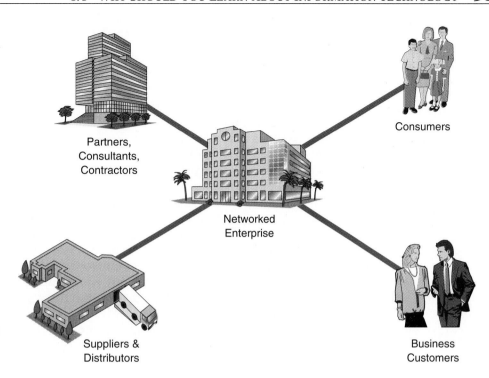

**FIGURE 1.10 The networked enterprise.** (*Source*: Courtesy of Netscape Corporation.)

The networked enterprise is shown schematically in Fig. 1.10. As a result of the technology pressures discussed earlier, companies that implement standards-based intranets can quickly create networked enterprises via extranets, as will be discussed in Chapter 6.

All these developments and prospects will increase the importance of IT both at home and at work. Therefore, it is only logical to learn about IT.

## ▶ 1.4 WHY SHOULD YOU LEARN ABOUT INFORMATION TECHNOLOGY?

We demonstrated in this chapter that we live in the information and knowledge age, and that the way we do business is changing drastically. The field of IT is also growing rapidly, especially with the introduction of the Internet and EC, so the organizational impacts keep increasing. As a result, the manner in which business is managed changes too. In this part of the chapter we describe some specific benefits you can derive from studying IT.

This opening chapter stressed the role of IT as a facilitator of organizational activities and processes. That role will become more important as time passes. Therefore, it is necessary that every manager and professional staff member learn about IT not only in his or her specialized field, but in the entire organization, as well as in interorganizational settings. IT is important not only in its supporting role, but also for its potential impacts on people, organizational structure, organizational strategy, and business and management processes.

Obviously, we need to learn how to build, use, and manage successful systems, but we also need to learn how to avoid unsuccessful systems and failures (see Chapter 13). Finally, we should learn about IT because of the many employment opportunities in this field.

> If you're in a field unrelated to IT (finance, marketing, etc.) you are still affected heavily by IT. If you're in an outside area your tools are put in place by IT for utilization. It has moved beyond a room full of nerds playing Doom.
>
> — *Blake Thomson*

## EMPLOYMENT OPPORTUNITIES IN INFORMATION TECHNOLOGY

Some mention of IS knowledge is a requirement on a resume today. I expect everyone in my organization, from senior accountants to filing clerks to have more than just a basic knowledge of information systems.

*— Mike Rewald*

Addressing the issues listed in the previous sections requires considerable knowledge about IT and its management (see Fried [1995]). However, being knowledgeable about information technology can also increase employment opportunities. Even though computerization eliminates some jobs, it also creates many more.

The demand for traditional information technology staff—such as programmers, systems analysts, and designers—is substantial. In addition, many well-paid opportunities are appearing in emerging areas such as the Internet and electronic commerce, network security, client/server, object-oriented programming, telecommunications, multimedia designers, artificial intelligence, and document management. The U.S. Department of Labor projected that among the 12 fastest growing employment areas, four will be IT related. These four will account for about 50 percent of all additional jobs in the 12 areas by the year 2000. A study of the Information Technology Association of America (www.itaa.org) documented in early 1998 a shortage of employees for about 350,000 IT positions in the United States. Similar conclusions were derived by the U.S. Department of Commerce. (See *Infoworld*, Feb. 23, 1998.) Thus, salaries for IT employees are very high (see Table 1.4).

To exploit the high-paying opportunities in IT, a college degree in computer

### *Table 1.4* Typical Job Openings

| Title | Industry | Compensation | Location |
|---|---|---|---|
| CIO | Medical laboratory | $100,000-$150,000 + bonus + options | Virginia |
| CIO | Banking | $100,000-$110,000 + bonus ($10K-$15K) | Western Massachusetts |
| CIO | National services | $120,000-$150,000 + bonus | West Michigan |
| CTO | Local government | $100,000-$134,000 + bonus (10%) | Seattle |
| Development manager | Online services | $100,000+ | Atlanta |
| Director, IT | Manufacturing | $70,000-$125,000 | Midwest |
| Director, IT | Window manufacturing | $100,000 + bonus | Rocky Mount, Va. |
| Internet/intranet architect | Financial services | $90,000s-$100,000s | Dallas |
| Manager, call center technology | Consulting | $100,000+ | Various locations |
| Network administrator | Fortune 500 | $60,000-$90,000 + bonus (10%-15%) | Fairfield County, Conn. |
| Network control group manager | Financial markets | $80,000-$110,000 | Houston |
| Outsourcing network operations manager | High tech | $65,000-$84,000 | Hong Kong |
| VP/CIO | Financial services | To $150,000 + bonus ($40K-$60K) + stock options + car | Philadelphia |
| VP, IS | Manufacturing | $90,000-$100,000 (CDN) + bonus (20%) | Ontario, Canada |
| VP, technology | Accounting services | $125,000 + bonus | Fort Worth, Texas, area |

The jobs are actual positions listed with Exec-U-Net, a Norwalk, Conn.-based career information service and networking organization for executives (www.execunet.com).

(SOURCE: Compiled from *InternetWeek*, March 16, 1998, p. 43.)

> I've had three job offers already (not bad for a senior), and with the highest starting salaries of a business major. Why not IT? MIS instead of computer science for people who don't like math or science.
> — *Blake Thompson*

science, computer information systems (CIS), management information systems (MIS), or a combination of the above is advisable. Several schools offer graduate degrees with specialization in information technology. Majoring in such programs can be very rewarding. For example, students graduating with Baccalaureate in MIS degrees usually attain the highest starting salaries of all undergraduate business majors (more than $40,000 per year). Many students prefer a double major, one of which is MIS. Similarly, MBAs with an undergraduate degree in computer science or CIS have no difficulty getting well-paying jobs, even during recessionary times. Many MBA students select IS as a major, a second major, or an area of specialization. Finally, nondegree programs are also available on hundreds of topics. For details about careers in IT see *Computerworld*'s special issue (vol. 10, no. 2, Fall 1997).

## 1.5 PLAN OF THE BOOK

A major objective of this book is to demonstrate how IT supports different organizational activities. In addition, we will illustrate the role that networked computing plays in our society today and will play tomorrow. Furthermore, we describe how information systems should be developed, maintained, and managed.

We have divided the book into five parts. Figure 1.11 shows how the chap-

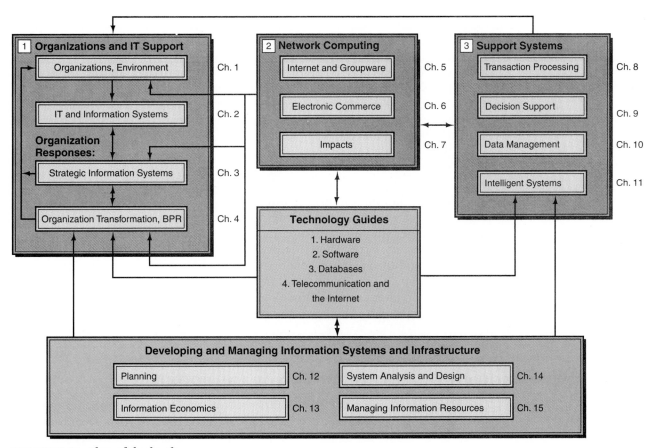

**FIGURE 1.11** Plan of the book.

ters are positioned in each part and how the parts are connected. The contents of the parts follow.

**PART I**  The operation of modern business in a turbulent environment can be so complex that the support of information systems is a critical necessity (see Chapter 1). However, there are many configurations of information systems and several ways in which they can be classified (see Chapter 2). A significant use of IT is to support strategic management (Chapter 3) and BPR (Chapter 4).

**PART II**  The Internet, intranets, and groupware (Chapter 5) provide organizations with the means of communicating among their internal components and with the environment, where their business partners are located. These systems also facilitate groupwork, access to information, and collaboration. Internet, intranets, and other networks provide for electronic commerce (Chapter 6), including business-to-business and business-to-individual transactions. IT in general, and network computing in particular, have a significant impact on the manner in which business is done, on individuals, and on society (Chapter 7).

**PART III**  Information technology support is essential for dealing with many problems and opportunities, especially complex ones. Support is provided by the transaction processing system (Chapter 8) and by management support systems (Chapter 9). Of special interest is data and its management (Chapter 10) and intelligent support systems, which provide access to massive databases, and support and even automate decision making (Chapter 11).

**PART IV**  Specific information systems are built upon an infrastructure, which must be planned for carefully. The planning process and the various architectures for putting together the infrastructure are discussed in Chapter 12. The investment in IT may be very large. Therefore, it should be scrutinized. However, it is very difficult to conduct an IT cost-benefit analysis, and several approaches may be attempted (Chapter 13). Building information systems is a complex process that can be done in alternative methodologies (Chapter 14). Finally, information systems must be properly managed, secured, and controlled (Chapter 15).

### TECHNOLOGY GUIDES (AT THE END OF THE BOOK)

The technology that is used for the infrastructure and the specific applications can be divided into four major categories: hardware (Technology Guide 1), software (Technology Guide 2), databases and their management (Technology Guide 3), and telecommunications and the Internet (Technology Guide 4).

## ▶ MANAGERIAL ISSUES

Here are some managerial issues regarding the topics in this chapter:

1. *How can we recognize the opportunities for using IT?* The answer can be found in most chapters of the book, but especially in Chapters 3, 4, 12, and 13.

2. *Who is going to build, operate, and maintain the information systems?* This is a critical issue because management wants to minimize the cost of IT while maximizing its benefits. Some alternatives are subcontracting (outsourcing) portions, or even all of the IT activities, and dividing work between the IS department and the end users. Details will be provided in Chapters 12 through 15.

3. *How much IT?* This is a critical question related to IT planning. IT does not come free, but not having it may be much costlier. Chapters 12 and 13 deal with this issue.

4. *How important is IT?* In some cases, IT is the only approach that can help organizations. As time passes, the comparative advantage of IT increases.

5. *Is the situation going to change?* Yes, the pressures will be stronger as time passes. Therefore, the IT role will be even more important.

6. *How about globalization?* Global competition will have an impact on many companies. However, globalization opens many opportunities ranging from selling products and services in foreign markets to conducting joint ventures or investing in them. IT supports communications, collaboration, and discovery of information regarding all the above.

7. *What about ethics and social issues?* The implementation of IT involves many ethical and social issues that are constantly changing due to new developments in technologies and environments. These topics should be examined any time an IT project is undertaken. ☆

## KEY TERMS

Business pressures *6*

Business process reengineering (BPR) *14*

Computer-based information system (CBIS) *17*

Critical response activities *6*

Electronic commerce (EC) *5*

Enterprise Resource Planning (ERP) *16*

Electronic data interchange (EDI) *4*

Extranet *16*

Information superhighway *29*

Information system (IS) *17*

Information technology (IT) *5*

Internet *5*

Intranet *5*

Just-in-time (JIT) *13*

Networked computing *5*

Networked enterprise *29*

Organizational transformation *29*

Supply chain management *16*

Total quality management (TQM) *13*

Virtual corporation *16*

## CHAPTER HIGHLIGHTS *(L–x means learning objective number x)*

▶ Many pressures surround the modern organization, which is responding with critical response activities supported by information technology. (L–1)

▶ An accelerated rate of change, complexity, and turbulence and a move toward a global economy today characterize the business environment. The competition faced by businesses is ever increasing. (L–2)

▶ Corporations are increasingly concerned about social responsibility. (L–2)

▶ Business alliances among organizations are spreading, largely due to the support of information technology. (L–2)

▶ Organizations are adapting a customer-focused approach in order to succeed. (L–2)

▶ Organizations are reengineering their business processes in order to cope with rapid environmental changes. IT plays an important role. (L–2)

▶ Organizations are changing their mode of operation by using IT-supported innovative approaches such as just-in-time, total quality management, and empowerment of employees. (L–2)

▶ The cost-performance advantage of information technology is increasing with time, due to increasing processing speed and storage capability. (L–3)

▶ Communication networks will be the core of IT in the next century. (L–3)

▶ Information technology is a major agent of change, supporting critical response activities. (L–3)

▶ Information technology refers to the network of all information systems in an organization. (L–4)

▶ An information system collects, processes, stores, and disseminates information for a specific purpose. (L–4)

▶ Networked computing via the Internet and intranet is becoming the centerpiece of information technology. (L–5)

## QUESTIONS FOR REVIEW

1. Define an information system and list its major components.

2. What are the major pressures in the business environment?

3. List the major critical response activities used by organizations.

4. What is a virtual corporation?

5. What is business process reengineering?

6. What do we mean by empowerment of employees?

7. What is total quality management?

8. What is time-to-market? Why is it so important?

9. Describe the concept of cycle time reduction.

10. List the major capabilities of IT.

11. Define the Internet, intranet, and electronic commerce.

12. Define networked computing and networked organizations.

## QUESTIONS FOR DISCUSSION

1. Describe how information systems can support the just-in-time approach.

2. IBM has been under attack because of its perceived poor leadership. In April 1993, the company replaced its chief executive by hiring the chief executive of RJR Nabisco (a large diversified food and tobacco company). The decision brought immediate debate. Some people felt that a company like IBM needed a technology-oriented chief. Others considered general managerial skills more important than technological experience. Discuss.

3. What are the relationships between increased social responsibility and IT?

4. It is said that IT supports business reengineering. It is also said that IT creates the need for business reengineering. Discuss.

5. Explain the relationship between empowerment of employees and total quality management.

6. Explain why the cost-performance ratio of IT will improve by a factor of 100, while performance is expected to improve only by a factor of 50.

7. What is the difference between programs such as JIT, TQM, and BPR?

8. Is IT a strategic weapon or a survival tool? Discuss.

9. It is said that networked computing changes the way we live, work, and study. Why?

10. Relate cycle-time reduction to improved performance.

11. Distinguish between network computers and networked computing.

## EXERCISES

1. Read the Clinton and Gore framework (www.iitf.nist.gov/eccomm/ecomm.htm).
   a. Summarize the content.
   b. What is the importance of this framework?
   c. What is the most important managerial lesson?
   d. Discuss the major proposed government policies.

2. Review the examples of IT applications (Section 1.2), and identify the business pressures in each example.

3. The market for optical copiers is shrinking rapidly. It is expected that by 2000 as much as 70 percent of all duplicated documents will be done on computer printers. Can a company such as Xerox Corporation survive?
   a. Identify all the business pressures on Xerox.
   b. Find Xerox's response strategies (see *Datamation,* June 1997, p. 42 and www.Xerox.com).

c. Identify the role of IT as a contributor to the business technology pressures.
d. Identify the role of IT as a facilitator of the critical response activities.
e. Review the role of the CIO in the revitalization project.

## GROUP ASSIGNMENT

Review the *Wall Street Journal, Fortune, Business Week,* and local newspapers of the last three months to find stories about the use of IT as an enabler in organizations. Each group will prepare a report describing five applications. The reports should emphasize the role of IT and its benefit to the organizations. Issues such as productivity, quality, cycle time, globalization, and so on, which were discussed in this chapter, should be covered. One of the groups should concentrate on the Internet, intranet, and electronic commerce. Present and discuss your work.

## INTERNET EXERCISES

Note: The URLs included here were current when the book went to press. However, they are subject to change without notice. Please consult the Turban Web site (www.Wiley.com/college/turban2e).

1. Enter the Web site of UPS (www.ups.com).
   a. Find out what information is available to customers before they send a package.
   b. Find out about the "package tracking" system; be specific.
   c. Compute the cost of delivering a 10″ × 20″ × 15″ box, weighing 40 lb, from your hometown to Long Beach, CA. Compare the fastest delivery against the least cost.

2. Surf the Internet and find information about:
   a. International virtual corporations (at least two examples).
   b. Virtual corporations in general.

3. Enter the Web site of Harper group (www.circleintl .com). Find out what services they offer. Do you think they offer quality services?

4. Enter the Web site of National Computer Board (NCB) in Singapore (see Box 1.2). Examine the plans for information superhighways.

5. Visit some Web sites that offer employment opportunities in IT (such as www.execunet.com). Prepare a report on job availability and salaries. Compare to salaries offered to accountants. Check *Computerworld*'s annual salary survey. For 1997 check www.computerworld.com:8080/home/online9687.nsf/all/970901/survey.

6. Prepare a short report on the role of information technology in government. Start with www.ctg .albany,edu.

---

▼ **M**inicase 1

## Computers in Mid-Sized Business: Killington Ski Resort

As baby boomers began to enter their forties and the number of teenagers shrank, business at many U.S. ski resorts declined. By 1990 the problem got worse in New England, where the economy was declining. In addition, nature provided only meager snowfall for several years in a row. Many ski resorts were struggling to survive. One exception was **SKI Ltd.,** (now Killington Ski resort) which operates a resort in Killington, Vermont. This company stays profitable by using information systems. Here is how IT is used at SKI Ltd.

▶ Sensors track temperature and other weather data in many places around the slopes. They also collect information about the condition of all equipment (such as snowmaking machines and ski lifts). This information is interpreted by computers, thereby helping staff to make quicker and better decisions. Only two people control the entire operation.

▶ The ski season has been extended about one month per year due to computerized planning and scheduling, and management has been able to justify the expense of creating artificial snow by attracting enough customers to the additional period.

▶ A computerized program selects seats and prints tickets for the resort's stadium events.

▶ An existing lodging reservation system has been modified to be more flexible and effective. A customer database of 2.5 million (growing by 200,000 names per year) includes information ranging from the level of skiing ability to skiers' preferences (services desired, times when they ski). This information allows effective advertisement and promotion of special discounts and better customer service.

▶ The computer monitors the whereabouts of each of the company's 3,000 employees. When an employee arrives at any location, he or she runs a barcoded ID card through a special device, and the information is transmitted to a minicomputer. In this way, unutilized employees can be quickly located and transferred to areas that need help. This arrangement allows better utilization of personnel and better customer service. The system also tracks employees' hours and jobs for better staffing decisions and improved productivity.

▶ The company developed a customized accounting system in conjunction with a standard off-the-shelf product to create a sophisticated financial control system. The system provides a detailed picture of each resort's revenue and costs on a *daily* basis. Comparisons with historical data are provided, as well as comparisons of actual results to budgets and plans. The information generated by the system is used at the weekly management meeting.

▶ Since competitors are also introducing IT applications, SKI Ltd. created a software division that sells its software products to other ski resorts.

▶ Recent projects include: (1) touch-screen "information booths" (kiosks) installed at various sites (including locations on the slopes), (2) an automated lodging reservation system (no operators), (3) artificial intelligence systems to assist decision making regarding snow making and staffing, (4) issuance of "frequent skier" cards, and (5) an intranet.

### Questions for Minicase 1

1. Enter the Web site of SKI Ltd., www.killington. com. Identify some of its marketing strategies.

2. SKI Ltd.'s CEO insists that SKI Ltd. is in no danger of selling off its competitive edge by selling its software to competitors. Do you agree with this statement? Why or why not?

3. The CEO said, "The customer is like a Rubik's Cube. Figuring out and responding to his [or her] needs is a complex puzzle, and there is always some better way to solve it." How can IT be utilized to find a better way?

4. The CEO said his company "created a culture where people are addicted to information." What does he mean by that, and what are the benefits and drawbacks of such a culture?

5. What kind of trends in the business environment, in management and organizations, and in technology are evidenced in this case?

6. Why is the system considered to be customer focused?

7. Relate the IT applications to the critical response activities discussed in this chapter.

SOURCE: Based on Freedman, D. H., "An Unusual Way to Run a Ski Business," *Forbes ASAP,* December 7, 1992, pp. 27–30 and information provided by the company in 1998.

# Minicase 2

## Can Information Systems and the Internet Help a Small Business in Distress?

**Sports for All**, one of the most successful stores in Middletown, Illinois, is privately owned by Nancy Knowland. It employs 12 people with sales of about $3 million per year. Nancy's family started the sporting goods store over 60 years ago. The store grew slowly over the years, attracting customers from several communities around Middletown. The store's strategy was to provide a large variety of products at low prices. Because of low expenses in Middletown (labor, taxes, rent), the store was able to compete successfully against both K-Mart's and Wal-Mart's sporting goods departments.

Lately, however, the situation changed. Sports for

All was losing customers to Wal-Mart because Wal-Mart was importing extremely inexpensive goods from sources that were not available to Sports for All. Furthermore, several customers opted to travel as much as 150 miles to St. Louis and pay high prices for special products that were customized for them by a new and fashionable sporting goods store there.

Nancy became concerned last summer when total sales showed a clear trend of decline for four consecutive quarters. Yesterday, the monthly sales data were compiled and showed the lowest monthly sales level in 10 years. Nancy called in all the key people of the store for an emergency meeting.

Nancy's son, David, an MBA student at the University of Illinois, has been urging his mother for years to install a modern computerized information system in the store. Last summer, he purchased several computers and an accounting package and transferred most of the manual accounting transactions (billing, purchasing, and inventory) to the computer. The store also handles all its correspondence on word processors. Nancy objected to further investment in computer systems, especially since profits were declining.

During the meeting, David proposed the installation of a sophisticated information system that would improve purchasing, inventory management, and customer service. "Some major manufacturers will not sell products to us because we are not on their electronic data interchange (EDI) system. We need to expedite the receipts of shipments and buy directly from manufacturers so we can be more responsive to customers. We also need to control costs and inventories," he explained. He said it is necessary to create an Internet presence by building a Web site. The existing internal systems should be migrated to an intranet, and electronic commerce applications should be explored. Furthermore, "we should explore the feasibility of constructing an extranet with our business partners."

Jim Park, who helps Nancy with finance and marketing, was not too enthusiastic. "David's proposal will cost more than $160,000, and it will not reduce our labor force by even one employee. We are just too small for these fancy machines. We will be better off applying this money toward advertisement and providing special sales to attract customers," he said.

### Questions for Minicase 2

As a consultant to Sports for All, complete the following:

1. Prepare a report in which you explain to management the changing business environment and why traditional actions such as an increase in advertisement may not be effective.

2. Use the trends described in this chapter and the capabilities of IT to demonstrate to Nancy why she may have to use IT in order to survive.

3. Why was David pushing the use of the Internet?

4. What specific factors need to be considered in order to make a decision on whether or not to accept David's proposal?

## REFERENCES AND BIBLIOGRAPHY

1. Benjamin, R. I., and J. Blunt, "Critical IT Issues: The Next Ten Years," *Sloan Management Review,* Summer 1992.

2. Boyett, J. H., and J. T. Boyett, *Beyond Workplace 2000: Essential Strategies for the New American Corporation,* New York: Dutton, 1995.

3. Bradley, S. P., et al. (eds.), *Globalization, Technology and Competition: The Fusion of Computers and Telecommunciations in the 1990s,* Boston: Harvard Business School Press, 1993.

4. Callon, J. D., *Competitive Advantage Through Information Technology,* New York: McGraw-Hill, 1996.

5. Clinton, W. J., and A. Gore, Jr., "A Framework for Global Electronic Commerce," www.iitf.nist.gov/eleccomm/ecomm July 1997.

6. Davidow, W., and M. S. Malone, *The Virtual Corporation,* New York: HarperCollins, 1992.

7. Dertouzos, M., *What Will Be: How the New World of Information Will Change Our lives,* San Francisco: Harper Edge, 1997.

8. Devenport, T. H., *Information Ecology: Mastering the Information Knowledge Environment,* New York: Oxford University Press, 1997.

9. Drucker, D. F., *Managing in a Time of Great Change,* New York: Truman Tally Books, 1995.

10. Fried, L., *Managing Information Technology in Turbulent Times,* New York: Wiley, 1995.

11. Galbraith, J. R., and E. E. Lawler III, *Organizing for the Future,* San Francisco: Jossey-Bass, 1993.

12. Gill, K. S. (ed.), *Information Society,* London: Springer Publishing, 1996.

13. Hammer, M., and J. Champy, *Reengineering the Corporation,* New York: Harper Business, 1993.

14. Jarvenpaa, S., and B. Ives, "The Global Network Organization of the Future: Information Management Opportunities and Challenges," *Journal of Management Information Systems,* Spring 1994.

15. Kalakota, R., and A. B. Whinston, *Electronic Commerce: A Manager's Guide,* Reading, PA: Addison Wesley, 1997.

16. Kanter, R. M., *World Class: Thriving Locally in the Global Economy,* New York: Simon and Schuster, 1995.

17. Knoke, W., *Bold New World: The Essential Road Map to the 21st Century,* New York: Rodensha America, 1996.

18. Larson, T., "Global Information Technology Utilization Trends," *Journal of Global Information Management,* Spring, 1996.

19. Mandel, M. J., et al., "The Information Revolution: Special Report," *Business Week,* June 13, 1994.

20. Mankin, D., et al., *Teams and Technology,* Boston: Harvard Business School, 1996.

21. Naisbitt, J., *Global Paradox,* London: N. Breadly, 1994.

22. Negroponte, N., *Being Digital,* New York: Knopf, 1995.

23. Perry, L. T., et al., *Real-time Strategy,* New York: John Wiley & Sons, 1993.

24. Pine, J. B. II, *Mass Customization,* Boston: Harvard Business School Press, 1993.

25. Rhinesmith, S. H., *A Managers Guide to Globalization,* Homewood, IL: Business One IRWIN, 1993.

26. Scott-Morton, M., and T. J. Allen (eds.), *Information Technology and the Corporation of the 1990s,* New York: Oxford University Press, 1994.

27. Stalk, B. Jr., and A. M. Weber, "Japan's Dark Side of Time," *Harvard Business Review,* July/August, 1993.

28. Steven, T. A., "Managing in a Wired Company," *Fortune,* July 11, 1994.

29. Tapscott, D., *The Digital Economy,* New York: McGraw-Hill, 1996.

30. Tapscott, D., and A. Caston, *Paradigm Shift: The New Promise of Information Technology,* New York: McGraw-Hill, 1993.

31. Turban, E., et al., *Electronic Commerce,* Upper Saddle River, NJ: Prentice Hall, 1999.

32. Van Gigch, J. P., *Applied General Systems Theory,* 2nd ed., New York: Harper and Row, 1978.

33. Wetherbe, J. C., *The World on Time,* Santa Monica, CA: Knowledge Exchange, 1996.

34. Whiteley, R. C., *The Customer Driven Company,* Reading, MA: Addison-Wesley, 1991.

35. Wigand, R., et al., *Information, Organization, and Management: Expanding Markets and Corporate Boundaries,* New York: John Wiley & Sons, 1997.

36. Wreden, N., "Business Boosting Technologies," *Beyond Computing,* Nov./Dec. 1997.

## APPENDIX: SYSTEMS

A *system* is a collection of elements such as people, resources, concepts, and procedures intended to perform an identifiable function or serve a goal. A clear definition of that function is important to the design of an information system. For instance, the purpose of an air defense system is to protect ground targets, not to just destroy attacking aircraft or missiles.

### Levels and Structures of Systems

The notion of levels (or a hierarchy) of systems reflects that all systems are actually subsystems, since all are contained within some larger system. For example, a bank system includes such subsystems as the commercial loan system, the consumer loan system, and savings system, and so on.

Systems are divided into three distinct parts: inputs, processes, and outputs. They are surrounded by an environment and frequently include a feedback mechanism that controls some aspect of the operation. In addition, a human, the decision maker, is considered a part of the system.

▶ *Inputs* include those elements that enter the system. Examples of inputs are raw materials entering a chemical plant, patients admitted to a hospital, or data inputted into a computer.

▶ All the elements necessary to convert or transform the inputs into outputs are included in the *processes*. For example, in a chemical plant a process may include heating the materials, following operating procedures, operating the materials-handling subsystem, and utilizing employees and machines. In a computer, a process may include activating commands, executing computations, and storing information.

▶ *Outputs* describe the finished products or the consequences of being in the system. For example, fertilizers are one output of a chemical plant, cured people are the output of a hospital, and reports may be the output of a computerized system.

▶ The connections among subsystems are the flow of information and materials among the subsystems. Of a special interest is the flow of information from the output component to a control unit (or a decision maker) concerning the system's performance. Based on this information, which is called *feedback*, the inputs or the processes may be modified.

▶ The *environment* of the system is composed of several elements that lie outside it, in the sense that they are not inputs, outputs, or processes. However, they have a significant impact on the system's performance and consequently on the attainment of its goals. One way to identify the elements of the environment is by answering two questions:

1. Is the element significant to the system's goals?

2. Is it possible for the decision maker to manipulate this element?

If, and only if, the answer to the first question is *yes,* and the answer to the second is *no,* should the element be considered part of the environment. Environmental elements can be social, technological, political, legal, physical, and economic. For example, in a system that deals with capital budgeting, the Dow-Jones database, the manufacturing system, the telecommunications network, and the personnel department may represent some elements of the environment.

> ▶ A system is separated from its environment by a *boundary*. The system is inside the boundary, whereas the environment lies outside. Boundaries may be physical or nonphysical. For example, a system can be bounded by time.

Because every system can be considered a subsystem of another, the application of system analysis may never end. Therefore it is necessary, as a matter of practicality, to confine the system analysis to defined manageable boundaries. Such confinement is termed *closing* the system. A *closed system* represents one extreme along a continuum of independence (the *open system** is at the other extreme). A closed system is totally independent, whereas an open system is very dependent on its environment (and/or other systems). The open system accepts inputs (information, energy, and materials) from the environment and may deliver outputs into the environment.

When determining the impact of changes on an open system, it is important to check the environment, the related systems, and so on. In a closed system, however, it is not necessary to conduct such checks because it is as-

---

*The term *open systems* in IT has a different meaning. It refers to the ability of software to run on any hardware.

sumed that the system is isolated. Traditional computer systems like transaction processing systems (TPSs) are considered to be closed systems while the newer decision support systems (DSSs) are open.

## System Effectiveness and Efficiency

Systems are evaluated and analyzed along two major dimensions: effectiveness and efficiency. *Effectiveness* is the degree to which the right goals are achieved. It is concerned with the results or the outputs of a system. The outputs may be the total sales of a company or of a salesperson, for example. *Efficiency* is a measure of the use of inputs (or resources) to achieve results; an example of efficiency might be how much money is used to generate a certain level of sales. An interesting way to distinguish between the two terms is as follows:

Effectiveness = Doing the "right" thing
Efficiency = Doing the "thing" right.

## General Systems Theory

The term *general systems theory* refers to the discipline that deals with the field of systems and their analysis, design, and improvement. It includes the concepts, methods, and knowledge pertaining to the field of systems and systems thinking. It is an interdisciplinary, holistic approach to the study of systems. For details, see Van Gigch (1978).

# CHAPTER 2

# Information Technologies: Concepts and Management

## Learning Objectives

*After studying this chapter, you will be able to:*

❶ Describe various information systems and their evolution, and categorize specific systems you observe.

❷ Describe transaction processing and functional information systems.

❸ Identify the major support systems, and relate them to managerial functions.

❹ Discuss information architecture and infrastructure.

❺ Compare legacy systems, client/server architecture, and enterprisewide computing and analyze their interrelationship.

❻ Describe how information resources are managed.

❼ Describe the role of the information systems department and its relationship with end users.

**2.1**
Information Systems: Concepts and Definitions

**2.2**
Classification of Information Systems

**2.3**
Transactional and Functional Processing

**2.4**
Operational, Managerial, and Strategic Systems

**2.5**
Information Infrastructure and Architecture

**2.6**
Managing Information Resources

## PAN ENERGY CORPORATION: IMPROVED CUSTOMER SERVICE AND COMPETITIVENESS

PAN ENERGY CORPORATION (PEC), previously Panhandle Eastern Corporation, owns and operates one of the nation's largest natural gas transmission networks. It employs over 5,000 people in 28 states, transporting natural gas in underground pipes from sources in the southern United States to markets in the Northeast. The company competes with other natural gas providers as well as with companies that provide alternative sources of energy.

### The Problem

In order to survive, PEC needed to provide a superb service to its customers at competitive prices. This is a difficult task since the company collects data in more than 13,000 entry locations along its pipelines that cover 28 states. These data need to be shared by em-

ployees in more than 100 facilities and processed on more than 3,000 computers. Information must flow quickly and smoothly and be shared among employees in the production, marketing, and finance departments. All of this must be accomplished at a low cost.

### The IT Solution

The company constructed its own electronic communication network, based on the latest microwave telecommunication technologies. The massive network allows enterprisewide communication over an intranet, as well as enabling the company to communicate with customers, suppliers, and other business partners in the outside world (using private networks and the Internet). It supports information processing on projected and actual gas flows, personnel availability, and much more.

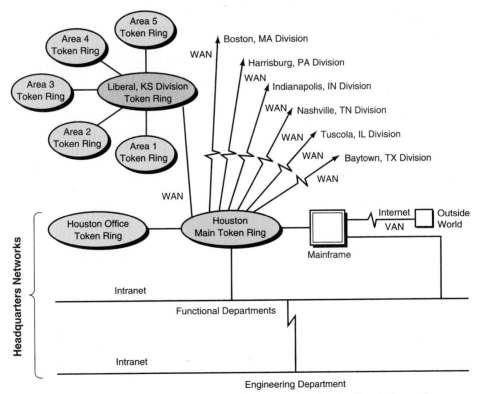

**FIGURE 2.1 Pan Energy Corporation wide area network pipeline information system.** (*Source*: Provided by Mark Robben of PEC at Houston, TX.)

Figure 2.1 provides a high-level schematic view of the system at PEC. The core of the system is the corporate network at the headquarters in Houston, Texas, shown in color. This network is connected to an IBM mainframe application server, which is also connected via a local network (LAN) to many small and large computers. The corporate network is connected to seven divisions by a wide area network (WAN). Only one of the divisions is shown in the figure (Liberal, KS). Each divisional network is connected to several work areas, and all have their own LANs (structured in a token ring arrangement).

The network allows the collected data to be stored in several databases. These data are used in hundreds of software applications that were built by both information system professionals and end users in all functional areas. These applications track information ranging from the incoming and outgoing gas flow to the storage of gas and scheduling of personnel. For example, a comprehensive accounting system has dozens of modules ranging from general ledger to tax-related depreciation schedules. A financial management system handles the corporate lines of credit and sources of financing. Customer files are a part of a marketing system, and a complete inventory control system of all spare parts can be accessed in seconds. There are also many decision support systems constructed by end users that help the company to best utilize resources and cut costs.

**The Results**

Without this kind of information system, PEC would be unable to operate successfully, compete, and meet customer demand in the 1990s and beyond. Of special importance is the collaboration within and among the divisions, headquarters, and the customers. Customer satisfaction, demand, and profit are continuously increasing. Pan Energy is considered one of the best companies in its industry, and therefore it was acquired recently by a larger utility.

SOURCE: Based on a paper written by Mark Robben of PEC at Houston, Texas.

## ▶ 2.1 INFORMATION SYSTEMS: CONCEPTS AND DEFINITIONS

The opening case illustrates a networked corporate information system with the following characteristics that can be found in many other organizations:

▶ Several different information systems can exist in one organization. As a matter of fact, PEC's information system contains hundreds of smaller information systems.

▶ A collection of several information systems is also referred to as an information system.

▶ Some of these systems are completely independent but most are interconnected.

▶ Information systems are connected by means of electronic networks. If the entire company is networked and people can communicate with each other and access information throughout the organization, then the arrangement is known as an *enterprisewide system*.

▶ Information resources are managed both centrally by the information systems department (ISD) and locally by users in functional units.

▶ The system is composed of large and small computers and hardware connected by different types of networks (intranets, the Internet, LANs, and WANs). It also includes software, databases, data, procedures, and of course, people. These are the components of any information system.

These characteristics point to the complexities involved in organizing and managing information systems. Therefore, before one learns about IT and its management, it is necessary to define the major concepts and organize them in some logical manner. This will be accomplished in this chapter.

Information systems are built to attain several goals. One of the primary goals is to economically process **data** into **information** or **knowledge.** Let us define these concepts:

▶ *Data* items refer to an elementary description of things, events, activities, and transactions that are recorded, classified, and stored, but not organized to convey any specific meaning. Data items can be numeric, alphanumeric, figures, sounds, or images. A *database* consists of stored data items organized for retrieval.

▶ *Information* is data that have been organized so that they have meaning and value to the recipient. The recipient interprets the meaning and draws conclusions and implications. Data processed by an *application* program represent a more specific use and a higher value added than simple retrieval from a database. Such an application can be an inventory management system, a university online registration system, or an Internet-based stock buying and selling system.

▶ *Knowledge* consists of data or information that have been organized and processed to convey *understanding, experience, accumulated learning,* and *expertise* as they apply to a current problem or activity. Data that are processed to extract critical implications and to reflect past experience and expertise provide the recipient with *organizational knowledge,* which has a very high potential value.

These three terms, especially data and information, are often used interchangeably. Data, information, and knowledge can be inputs to an information system; they can also be outputs. For example, data about employees, their wages, and time worked are processed to produce payroll information. Payroll information itself can later be used as an input to another system that prepares a budget or advises management on salary scales.

**INFORMATION SYSTEMS CONFIGURATIONS.** Information systems components can be assembled in many different configurations, resulting in a variety of information systems, much as construction materials can be assembled to build different homes. The size and cost of a home depend on the purpose of the building, the availability of money, and constraints such as ecological and environmental factors. Just as there are many different types of housing, so there are many different types of information systems. Therefore, it is useful to classify information systems into groups that share similar characteristics. Such a classification may help in identifying different systems, analyzing them, planning new systems, planning integration of systems, and making decisions such as regarding the possible outsourcing of systems.

## ▶ 2.2  CLASSIFICATION OF INFORMATION SYSTEMS

Information systems can be classified in several ways: by organizational levels, major functional areas, support provided, and the IS architecture. Note that regardless of how they are classified, the structure of these systems is the same, namely each contains hardware, software, data, procedures, and people. Several major classification schemes are described next.

## CLASSIFICATION BY ORGANIZATIONAL STRUCTURE

Organizations are made up of components such as departments, teams, and work units. For example, most organizations have a human resources department, a finance and accounting department, and perhaps a public relations unit. These components form an organization that may report to a higher organizational level, such as a division or a headquarters, in a traditional *hierarchical* structure. Although some organizations are reengineering themselves into innovative structures, such as those based on cross-functional teams, today the vast majority of organizations still have a traditional hierarchical structure.

One way to classify information systems is along organizational structure lines. Thus, we can find information systems built for headquarters, for divisions, for departments, for operating units, and even for individual employees. Such systems can stand alone or they can be interconnected.

Typical information systems that follow the organizational structure are: departmental, enterprisewide, and interorganizational.

▶ *Departmental information systems.* Frequently, an organization uses several **application programs** in one functional area or department. For instance, in managing human resources, it is possible to use one program for screening applicants and another for monitoring employee turnover. Some of the applications might be completely independent of each other, whereas others are interrelated. The collection of application programs in the human resources area is called a *human resources information system.* That is, it is referred to as a single *departmental* information system even though it is made up of several application subsystems. In large organizations, several departments in the same functional area may exist in different corporate locations. For example, a human resources department might exist at the corporate level as well as in each division. The designers of the IS then have two options: they can design a *divisional* information system that includes a human resources subsystem, or they can design a *centralized* human resources system for the entire corporation.

▶ *Enterprise information systems.* While a departmental IS is usually related to a functional area, the collection of all departmental applications comprises the *enterprisewide* information system. The PEC corporate information system is an example of an enterprisewide information system.

▶ *Interorganizational systems.* Some information systems connect several organizations. For example, the worldwide airline reservation system is composed of several systems belonging to different airlines. Of these, American Airlines' SABRE system (see Figure 2.2) is one of the largest. **Interorganizational information systems (IOS)** are systems connecting two or more organizations, and are common among business partners and are extensively used for electronic commerce, frequently via an *extranet.* A special IOS is an international or multinational corporation, whose computing facilities are located in two or more countries. Interorganizational information systems play a major role in *electronic commerce*, as shown in the opening case to Chapter 1 as well as in supply chain management support.

**FIGURE 2.2** American Airlines SABRE reservation system. The system is available for travel agents, corporations, and individuals. It is also accessible through the Internet and online services such as AOL.

## CLASSIFICATION BY FUNCTIONAL AREA

> Not having these systems interface (talk) with each other was one of the biggest mistakes my company ever made. Much of my job is correcting mistakes caused by information being entered into one system but not another.
>
> — *Mike Rewald*

Information systems at the departmental level support the traditional functional areas of the firm. The major functional information systems are:

- ▶ *The accounting information system*
- ▶ *The finance information system*
- ▶ *The manufacturing (operations/production) information system*
- ▶ *The marketing information system*
- ▶ *The human resources management information system*

In each functional area, some routine and repetitive tasks exist that are essential to the operation of the organization. Preparing a payroll and billing a customer are typical examples. The information system that supports these tasks is called the *transaction processing system (TPS)*. TPSs,* which are described in Section 2.4, support tasks performed in all functional areas but especially in the areas of accounting and finance.

## CLASSIFICATION BY SUPPORT PROVIDED

A third way to classify information systems is according to the type of support they provide, regardless of the functional area. For example, an information system can support office workers in almost any functional area, and managers, regardless of where they work, can be supported by a computerized decision-making system. The major types of systems under this classification are:

- ▶ *Transaction processing system (TPS)*—supports repetitive, mission-critical activities and clerical staff
- ▶ *Management information system (MIS)*—supports functional activities and managers

---

*The acronym TPS can be read either as singular or plural, as can many of the other acronyms related to information systems such as MIS and IS.

▶ *Office automation system (OAS)*—supports office workers

▶ *Decision support system (DSS)*—supports decision making by managers and analysts

▶ *Executive information or support system (EIS)*—supports executives

▶ *Group support system (GSS)*—supports people working in groups

▶ *Intelligent support systems*—supports mainly knowledge workers, but can support other groups of employees, *expert systems* being the major technology

Brief descriptions of these systems are provided next; they are also described in Chapters 5, 8, 9, and 11. Doke and Barrier (1994) provide an in-depth assessment of these and some other support systems.

## THE EVOLUTION OF THE SUPPORT SYSTEM

The first computers were designed to compute formulas for scientific and military applications during and immediately after World War II. The first business applications began in the early 1950s, and the computers did repetitive, large-volume transactions computing tasks. The computers "crunched numbers," summarizing and organizing data in the accounting, finance, and personnel areas in what is known as a **transaction processing system (TPS).** These TPSs (see Chapter 8 for details) were easy to justify since they automated manual computations. The reduction in clerical employees was sufficient to cover the cost of the technology.

As the cost of computing decreased and computers' capabilities increased, it became possible to justify IT for less repetitive tasks than TPS. In the 1960s, a new breed of IS started to develop. Systems arrived that accessed, organized, summarized, and displayed information for decision making in the functional areas. Such systems are called functional **management information systems (MISs)** and are geared toward middle managers. MISs are characterized mainly by their ability to produce periodic reports such as a daily list of employees and the hours they work, or a monthly report of expenses as compared to a budget. Initially, MISs had a *historical orientation;* they described events after they occurred. Later, they were also used to forecast trends, to support routine decisions, and to provide answers to queries. Today, MIS reports might include summary reports even for periods that are different from the periods of the scheduled reports.

The main types of support systems described in this book are shown in Table 2.1, together with the employees they support and the chapters in which they are described.

Support systems began to emerge in the late 1960s and early 1970s when networked computing and electronic communication became prevalent. Airline reservation systems are perhaps the best example of this development. Electronic communications is only one aspect of what is now known as an **office automation system (OAS).** Another, word processing systems, spread to many organizations in the 1970s. At about the same time, computers were introduced to manufacturing environments. Applications ranged from robotics to computer-aided design and manufacturing (CAD/CAM).

By the early 1970s, the demand for all types of IT had begun to accelerate. Increased capabilities and reduced costs justified computerized support for a growing number of nonroutine applications and the **decision support system (DSS)**

*Table 2.1* **Main Types of IT Support Systems**

| System | Employees Supported | Detailed Discussion in: |
|---|---|---|
| Office automation | Office workers | Chapters 5, 6, 8 |
| CAD/CAM | Engineers, draftsmen | Chapter 8 |
| Communication | All employees | Chapter 5 |
| Group support system | People working in groups | Chapter 5 |
| Decision support system | Decision makers, managers | Chapter 9 |
| Executive information | Executives, top managers | Chapter 9 |
| Expert system | Knowledge workers, nonexperts | Chapter 11 |
| Neural networks | Knowledge workers, professionals | Chapter 11 |

concept was born. The basic objective of a DSS is to provide computerized support to complex, nonroutine decisions, as illustrated in the following *IT at Work.*

*IT At Work* **GLAXO WELLCOME SAVES LIVES WITH DSS**

**U**SING IT

...in Health Care

**I**NTEGRATING IT

...for Production & Operations Management and Marketing

Glaxo Wellcome of the United Kingdom is one of the largest pharmaceutical companies in the world. In 1996, the company found that a combination of two of its existing drugs, Epirir and Retrovir, was effective in treating some cases of AIDS. Doctors worldwide began writing prescriptions en masse almost overnight. Such a tidal wave of demand depleted the inventories of the two drugs in the pharmacies.

Glaxo needed to produce and ship Epirir and Retrovir quickly, but demand, which is used to determine production, shipping scheduling, and inventory levels was too difficult to forecast.

To solve the problem, Glaxo developed a special corporatewide networked information system based on relational online analytical processing technology (see Chapter 9). The system works with a vast amount of internal and external data stored in a data warehouse (Chapter 10). Using these data and DSS models, market analysts at Glaxo were able to track and size the sources of demand, generating summary reports and projections in minutes. The projected demand was inputted into DSS models to figure appropriate production plans, delivery schedules, and inventory levels along the supply chain.

As a result, Glaxo streamlined its distribution process so wholesalers and retailers around the world never ran out of the drugs. An added benefit was that operational costs were reduced. Finally, the system provided Glaxo's employees with a tool that allows them to quickly and easily access information from different sources that is now stored in one place. Finally, the network allows for efficient internal and external collaboration and communication.

**For Further Exploration:** Why was a DSS needed in this case and why is quick data consolidation so important? ▲

SOURCE: Condensed from Fryer, B., "Fast Data Relief," *Information Week,* December 2, 1996.

At first, the high cost of building DSSs constrained their widespread use. However, the microcomputer revolution, which started around 1980, changed that. The availability of desktop computers, which were easily programmable thanks to high-level programming languages, made it possible for a person who knows little about programming to build DSS applications. This was the beginning of the era of *end-user computing*, in which analysts, managers, many other professionals, and even secretaries build their own systems (see McLean [1979]).

Decision support expanded in two directions. First, **executive information systems (EISs)** were designed to support senior executives. These were expanded later to support managers around the enterprise. The second direction was the support of people working in groups. **Group support systems (GSSs)** that initially supported people working in a special decision-making room expanded, due to network computing, to support people working in different locations. An example of how an intranet is used by Hershey foods to support group work is illustrated in the following *IT at Work*.

## *IT At Work*    HERSHEY FOODS ENHANCES GROUP WORK WITH AN INTRANET

Hershey bars and kisses can be found on the shelves of convenience stores and supermarkets in over 100 countries, competing with both local brands and brands from other countries. The transportation cost and the low labor cost in many foreign countries are factors that reduce the competitiveness of Hershey. But the Internet and intranet more than compensate for the disadvantages. Thus, Hershey runs one of the most efficient food processing businesses in the world. Recognizing the importance of group work, internal communication, and collaboration, the company established a Director of Corporate Communications who initiated an Internet Web site as early as 1994, and who also created a comprehensive intranet in 1996.

By 1998, more than 4,000 key employees were on the intranet. Corporate information such as annual reports, press releases, information on quality, and internal newsletters are published electronically, saving paper and delivery cost. All departments have their own home pages. This enables improved communications and collaboration within and among departments. John Long, Director of Corporate Communications, said that to him the intranet is much more exciting than the Internet since there is a greater opportunity to defray costs and measure the system's worth. Here are some of the intranet applications: Most corporate internal communications are now paperless, training is delivered to the desktop of the employees, and the intranet includes e-mail and software to support the work of groups (such as video teleconferencing). The intranet also empowers employees by allowing them access to information in a clear and unadulteratable form. This motivates people to be creative. All in all, Hershey can produce high-quality products at a low cost.

**For Further Exploration:** Why is group work important for Hershey? Who is communicating with whom? How does IT help? ▲

SOURCE: http://www.itaa.org/13.htm, May 1997 (intranets).

*I*NTEGRATING IT

...for Production & Operations Management and Human Resources Management

By the mid-1980s the commercialization of managerial applications of artificial intelligence (AI) began. Of special interest were **expert systems (ES).** These advisory systems differ from TPS, which centered on data, and from MIS and DSS, which concentrated on processing information. ES provide the stored knowledge of experts to nonexperts, so the latter can solve difficult problems.

All the above systems are very beneficial, but their support is fairly passive and limited. Even expert systems are unable to learn from experience. By the beginning of the 1990s, a new breed of systems emerged, with learning capabilities. Systems such as **artificial neural networks (ANNs),** *case-based reasoning,* and *genetic algorithms* can learn from historical cases. This capability enables machines to process vague or incomplete information, as shown in the following *IT at Work.*

## *IT At Work*  DETECTING BOMBS IN AIRLINE PASSENGERS' LUGGAGE

The Federal Aviation Administration (FAA) in the United States is making continuous efforts to improve safety and prevent terrorists from sneaking bombs aboard airplanes. Since it is practically impossible to open and search every piece of luggage, the FAA uses computer technologies in an attempt to find different types of explosives. One approach is to bombard each piece of luggage with gamma rays that are collected by a sensor and then interpreted. The FAA is using statistical analysis and expert systems to conduct the interpretation. However, these technologies cannot detect all types of explosives. Since 1993, artificial neural networks have been added to improve detection effectiveness. The ANN is exposed to a set of historical cases (a training set), that is, it is shown pictures obtained by gamma rays. It is also told whether each specific piece of luggage contains an explosive or not. Once trained, the system is used to predict the existence of explosives in new cases. It can detect an explosive even if the explosive device is somewhat different from those used for training. The objective is not only to detect explosives successfully, but also to minimize false alarms caused by the fact that many things (including clothing) contain nitrogen, a major component of bombs.

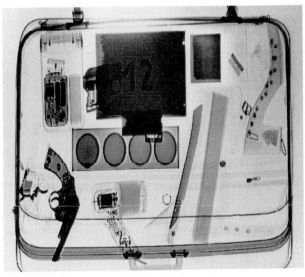

Color x-ray system used for airport security.

**For Further Exploration:** It is said that two heads are better than one. Can the addition of ANN be considered an extra head? Why? ▲

SOURCE: Informal information provided by Scan-Tech Security, Northvale, NJ, a developer of one of these systems, 1998.

The relationship among the different types of support systems can be summarized as follows:

▶ Each support system has sufficiently unique characteristics so it can be classified as a special entity.

▶ The interrelationships and coordination among the different types of systems are still evolving.

▶ In many cases, two or more systems are integrated to form a hybrid information system.

▶ There is information flow among the systems. For example, MIS extracts information from TPS and EIS receives information from both TPS and MIS (see Figure 2.3).

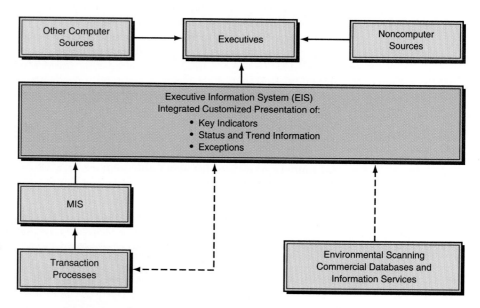

FIGURE 2.3 Interrelated support systems. The TPS collects information that is used to build the MIS and EIS. The information in the MIS as well as information that flows from other systems can be used as an input to the EIS. (*Sources*: Millet et al. [1991]; see also Millet [1992].)

**INTEGRATION.** Providing a computerized solution to a business problem may require integrating two or more of the systems mentioned above. For example, a decision support system combined with an expert system can be built to support a marketing promotion program. Therefore, it is more appropriate to view IS applications as a matrix where the major functional areas are shown on the left side and the entities receiving support are at the top. The cells of the matrix are the areas in which specific applications are defined. Such a matrix is introduced in Section 2.5, where the concept of system architecture is presented.

## CLASSIFICATION BY SYSTEM ARCHITECTURE

The manner in which an information system is organized depends on what it is intended to support. Therefore, before designing an information system, a key task is to conceptualize the information requirements of the core business of the organization, including the way these requirements are to be met. This conceptualization is called the **information architecture.**

A related concept is the **information infrastructure,** which tells us how *specific* computers, networks, databases, and other facilities are arranged and how they are connected, operated, and managed. Architecture and infrastructure are interrelated aspects of IS design. Analogous is the *conceptual planning* of a house (the architecture) and the specific components such as the foundation, walls, and roof (the infrastructure).

Information systems can be classified according to three types of architecture:

- ▶ A mainframe-based system
- ▶ A standalone personal computer (PC)
- ▶ A distributed or a networked computing system (several variations exist)

A brief description of these types is provided in Section 2.5

Now that we have introduced the different types of systems involved in the evolution of IT, let us look at some of the key systems in more detail.

 ## 2.3 TRANSACTIONAL AND FUNCTIONAL PROCESSING

### TRANSACTION PROCESSING

Any organization that performs financial, accounting, and other daily business activities faces routine, repetitive tasks. For example, employees are paid at regular intervals, customers place purchase orders and are billed, and expenses are monitored and compared to the budget. Table 2.2 presents a partial list of business transactions in a manufacturing organization.

The information system that supports such a process is the *transaction processing system (TPS)*. A TPS (frequently several TPSs exist in one company) supports the monitoring, collection, storage, processing and dissemination of the organization's basic business transactions. It also provides the input data for many applications involving other support systems such as DSS. The transaction processing systems are considered critical to the success of any organization since they support core operations, such as purchasing of materials, billing customers, preparing a payroll, or shipping goods to customers.

> Even though mainframe systems are being replaced by client/server architecture, the student will learn that TPS is still used frequently in business.
> — *Dave Gehrke*

---

*Table 2.2*  **Business Transactions in a Factory**

---

| **Payroll** | **Manufacturing** |
|---|---|
| Employee time cards | Production reports |
| Employee pay and deductions | Quality-control reports |
| Payroll checks | |
| | |
| **Purchasing** | **Finance and accounting** |
| Purchase orders | Financial statements |
| Deliveries | Tax records |
| Payments (accounts payable) | Expense accounts |
| | |
| **Sales** | **Inventory management** |
| Sales records | Material usage |
| Invoices and billings | Inventory levels |
| Accounts receivable | |
| Sales returns | |
| Shipping | |

The TPS collects data continuously, frequently on a daily basis, or even in real time (as soon as they are generated, as in the PEC case). Most of these data are stored in the corporate databases and are available for processing. Further details on TPS are provided in Chapter 8.

## FUNCTIONAL MANAGEMENT INFORMATION SYSTEMS

The transaction processing system covers the core activities of the organization. The functional areas, however, perform many other activities; some of them are repetitive while others are only occasional. For example, the human resources department hires, advises, and trains people. Each of these tasks can be divided into subtasks. Training may involve selecting topics to teach, selecting people to participate, scheduling classes, finding teachers, and preparing class materials. These tasks and subtasks are frequently supported by information systems specifically designed to support functional activities, and they are referred to as functional MIS, or just MIS.*

**WHAT IS AN MIS?** Functional information systems are put in place to ensure that business strategies come to fruition in an efficient manner as shown in Chapter 8. Typically a functional MIS provides periodic information about such topics as operational efficiency, effectiveness, and productivity by extracting information from the corporate database and processing it according to the needs of the user. MISs can be constructed in whole or in part by end users.

MISs are also used for planning, monitoring, and control. For example, a sales forecast by region is shown in Figure 2.4.

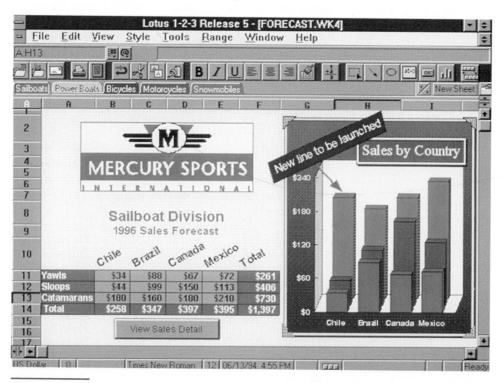

**FIGURE 2.4** Sales forecast by region generated by marketing MIS.

---

*The term MIS here refers to a specific application in a functional area. MIS is also used to describe the management of information systems.

This report can help the marketing manager make better decisions regarding advertisements and pricing of products. Another example is that of a human resources information system (HRIS), which provides a manager with a daily report of the percentage of people who were on vacation or called in sick as compared to forecasted figures.

## ▶ 2.4 OPERATIONAL, MANAGERIAL, AND STRATEGIC SYSTEMS

### CLASSIFICATION BY THE ACTIVITY SUPPORTED

Another important way to classify information systems is by the nature of the activity they support, which can be either operational, managerial, or strategic.

**OPERATIONAL SYSTEMS.** *Operational systems* deal with the day-to-day operations of an organization, such as assigning employees to tasks and recording the number of hours they work, or placing a purchase order. Operational activities are short-term in nature. The information systems that support them are mainly transaction processing, MIS, and simple decision support systems. Operational systems are used by supervisors (first-line managers), operators, and clerical employees.

**MANAGERIAL SYSTEMS.** *Managerial systems,* also called *tactical* systems, deal with middle management activities such as short-term planning, organizing, and control. Computerized managerial systems are frequently equated with MISs, because MISs are designed to summarize data and prepare reports. Middle managers also like to get quick answers to queries that an MIS can provide.

Managerial information systems are broader in scope than operational systems, but like operational systems, they use mainly internal sources of data. They provide the following types of support:

> *Statistical summaries.* Statistical reports include summaries of raw data such as daily production, weekly absenteeism rate, and monthly usage of electricity.

> *Exception reports.* To relieve managers of the information-overload syndrome, an information system can extract (or highlight) exceptions.

> *Periodic and ad hoc reports.* Users can get on a periodic basis or on demand both statistical summaries and exception reports. Users request **ad hoc reports** because they need information not available in the routine reports, or because they cannot wait for the scheduled **periodic report.** Managers now can view current, or even real-time information, any time they wish to do so.

> *Comparative analysis.* Managers like to see performance values and other information compared to their competitors, to past performance, or to industry standards.

> *Projections.* In contrast to an operational system, which has only a historical orientation, managerial information systems also provide projections, such as trend analysis, projection of future sales, projection of cash flows, or forecast of market share.

> *Early detection of problems.* By comparing and analyzing data, managerial information systems can detect problems in their early stages. For example,

These are crucial, as management is always in need of "what if" reports or comparison reports. A flexible database and good report writers save a lot of time and effort.

— *Mike Rewald*

statistical quality-control reports can reveal that a trend for reduced quality is developing.

▶ *Routine decisions.* Middle managers are involved in many routine decisions. They schedule employees, order materials and parts, and decide what to produce and when. Standard computerized mathematical, statistical, and financial models are available for the support of these activities.

▶ *Connection.* Functional managers need to interact frequently with each other and with specialists. The functional MISs provide email and messaging systems which are not part of the operational systems. Such systems were developed since the mid-1960's when MISs were initiated. While other managerial systems are confined to one company, email can be extended to business partners as in strategic systems.

**STRATEGIC SYSTEMS.** **Strategic systems** deal with decisions that significantly change the manner in which business is being done. Traditionally, strategic systems involved only **long-range planning.** Introducing a new product line, expanding the business by acquiring supporting businesses, and moving operations to foreign countries are prime examples of long-range activities. A long-range planning document outlines strategies and plans for five or even ten years. From this plan, companies derive their shorter range planning, budgeting, and resource allocation. Today, however, strategic systems help organizations in two other ways.

First, *strategic response systems* can respond to a major competitor's action or to any other significant change in the environment of the enterprise. Although they can sometimes be planned for as a set of contingencies, strategic responses are usually not included in the long-range plan because they are unpredictable. IT is often used to support the response or to provide the response itself. When Kodak Corp. learned that the Japanese were developing a disposable camera, for instance, the company decided to develop one too. However, the Japanese were already in the middle of the development process. By using computer-aided design and other information technologies, Kodak was able to cut its design time and beat the Japanese in the race to be the first to have cameras in retail outlets.

Second, instead of waiting for a competitor to introduce a major change or innovation, an organization can be the initiator of change. Such *innovative strategic systems* are frequently supported by IT, as is shown in Chapter 3. Federal Express's package tracing system is an example of such an innovative strategic system supported by IT.

## THE RELATIONSHIP BETWEEN PEOPLE AND INFORMATION SYSTEMS

Top management usually makes strategic decisions. Managerial decisions are made by middle managers and line managers and operators make operational decisions. The relationships between the people supported and the decision type are shown in Figure 2.5. The figure is organized as a triangle to illustrate the number of employees involved. Top managers are few, and they sit at the top of the triangle.

As you can see, an additional level of staff support is introduced between top and middle management. These are professional people (such as financial and marketing analysts). They act as advisors to both top and middle management. Many of these professional workers can be thought of as knowledge workers.

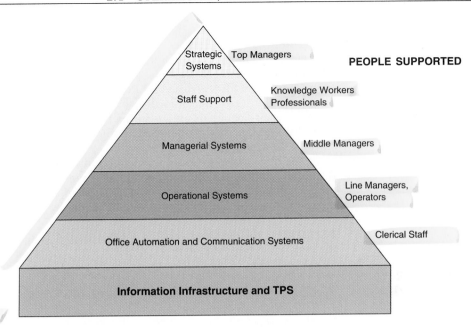

**FIGURE 2.5** The information systems support of people in organizations.

**Knowledge workers** are people who create information and knowledge as part of their work and integrate it into the business. Knowledge workers are engineers, financial and marketing analysts, production planners, lawyers, and accountants, to mention just a few. They are responsible for finding or developing new knowledge for the organization and integrating it with existing knowledge. Therefore they just keep abreast of all developments and events related to their profession. They also act as advisors and consultants to the members of the organization. Finally, they act as change agents by introducing new procedures, technologies, or processes. In many developed countries, 60 to 80 percent of all workers are knowledge workers.

Knowledge workers can be supported by a large variety of information systems ranging from Internet search engines that help them find information and expert systems that support information interpretation, to computer-aided design and hypertext that help them increase their productivity and quality of work. Knowledge workers are the major users of the Internet. They need to learn what is new, to communicate with corporate managers and colleagues, and frequently to collaborate with knowledge workers in other organizations. Knowledge workers need to learn and relearn. One way to assist them in improving their performance is through the use of expert systems. Expert systems can provide the knowledge of super experts and can facilitate training. The manner in which expert systems can be used is shown in the *IT at Work* story that follows.

> In MIS, good communication skills are essential. Often you are called upon to put the tools in someone else's hands. You must understand the requirements to build the correct tool.
>
> — *Blake Thompson*

---

*IT At Work*     AN EXPERT SYSTEM INCREASES PRODUCTIVITY AT FORD MOTORS, INC.

On Ford production lines, manufacturing processes are achieving major productivity increases through the adoption of a computer integrated manufacturing (CIM) strategy. CIM provides access to the information flowing from robots and other machines and allows federation of all the resources of the plant into a unified network.

Cadiz Electronica of Spain, a subsidiary of Ford Motors, Inc., employs about 480 people on two production lines. The first one produces electronic engine control modules, at a rate of 330 modules per hour. The second builds the anti-lock brake system modules at a rate greater than 170 per hour.

The System for Diagnosis and Repair (SEDYR) is an expert system that detects and diagnoses printed circuit malfunctions by analyzing the CIM system information flow and assisting repair operations online during the production process through a sophisticated graphical interface. Each component is automatically diagnosed, in real time, while it is still on a manufacturing line.

The system also provides access to the manufacturing process history located on a relational database. It maintains a real-time connection with the main CIM computer, informing it about failures in processing. The failed boards are eventually separated from the boards that pass the functional tests and enter the repair zone.

**BENEFITS.** The ability to visualize the boards and highlight failed components, linking the graphical representation of the problem with appropriate comments or providing tips for the treatment of the failures, drastically lowered the time needed to repair a board.

Another benefit provided by this approach of manufacturing supervision is the ability to use the system as a realistic and cost effective simulation-training tool.

**For Further Exploration:** How is productivity increased? Why is a real-time connection necessary? ▲

SOURCE: ILOG Corporation Web site: www.ilog.com/html/customer_success_ford.html, 1998.

---

Another class of employees is clerical workers who support managers at all levels. Among clerical workers, those who use, manipulate, or disseminate information are referred to as *data workers*. These include bookkeepers, secretaries who work with word processors, electronic file clerks, and insurance claim processors. Clerical employees are supported by office automation and communication systems including document management, workflow, e-mail, and coordination software.

All the systems in the triangle are built on the information infrastructure. Consequently, all of the people supported work with infrastructure technologies such as the Internet, intranets, and corporate databases. The infrastructure that is shown as the foundation of the triangle in Figure 2.5 is described in the next section.

##  2.5 INFORMATION INFRASTRUCTURE AND ARCHITECTURE

### INFRASTRUCTURE

An *information infrastructure* consists of the physical facilities, services, and management that support all computing resources in an organization. There are five major components of the infrastructure: computer hardware, general-purpose software, networks and communication facilities (including the Internet and intranets), databases, and information management personnel. Infrastructures include these resources as well as their integration, operation, documentation, maintenance, and management. Infrastuctures are further discussed in Chapter 12, and in Broadbent and Weill (1997). If you will examine Figure 2.1, which describes the architecture of PEC, and substitute specific names instead of general ones, you will get a picture of the infrastructure. For example, instead of a mainframe there will be an IBM/3010, and instead of a WAN there will be a T 1 line.

## ARCHITECTURE*

Recall that an *information architecture* is a high-level map or plan of the information requirements in an organization. It is a guide for current operations and a blueprint for future directions. It assures us that the organization's IT meets the strategic business needs of the corporation. Therefore, it must tie together the information requirements, the infrastructure, and the support technologies as shown in Figure 2.6.

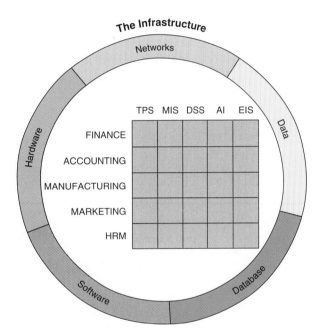

**FIGURE 2.6** Schematic view of the information architecture, which combines the functional areas, the general support systems, and the infrastructure, The inside matrix includes specific applications in an organization. The outside ring includes the computing resources of the infrastructure.

Remember the analogy of the architecture for a house. When preparing a conceptual high-level drawing of a house, the architect needs to know the purpose of the house, the requirements of the dwellers, and the building constraints (time, money, materials, etc.). In preparing information architecture, the designer needs similar information, which can be divided into two parts:

1. The business needs for information, that is, the organizational objectives and problems and the contribution that IT can make. The potential users of IT must play a critical role in this part of the design process. An architect cannot plan without knowing the purpose of the house and the requirements of the owners.
2. The information systems that already exist in an organization and how they can be combined among themselves or with future systems to support the organization's information needs.

---

*Information architecture needs to be distinguished from computer architecture (see Technology Guide 1). For example, the architecture for a computer may involve several processors, or special features to increase speed such as reduced instruction set computing (RISC). Our interest here is in information architecture only.

A system's architecture cannot be completed until the planning for the business is complete. However, IT architecture and business planning, for either a new business or the restructuring of an existing organization, are interrelated. This important topic will be revisited in Chapter 12.

**AN INFORMATION ARCHITECTURE MODEL.** The information architecture, according to Synnott (1987), is a conceptual framework for the organizational IT infrastructure. It is a plan for the structure and integration of the information resources in the organization. Synnott proposes a model for information architecture, shown in Figure 2.7, which divides the information architecture into two major parts. The centralized portion serves the entire organization and it includes the business architecture (information needs of the organization), the data architecture, and the communications architecture. The decentralized (upper) portion focuses on an organizational function or on some service or activity (e.g., human resources, computers, end-user computing, and systems). Each entity in the upper part includes operational, managerial and strategic applications.

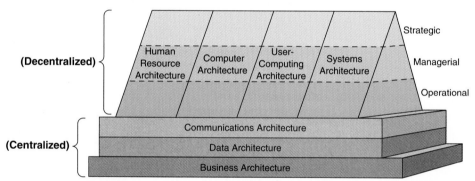

**FIGURE 2.7** The information architecture model. (*Source*: W. R. Synnott, *The Information Weapon: Winning Customers and Markets with Technology*, p. 199. Copyright 1987 John Wiley & Sons. Reprinted by permission of John Wiley & Sons, Inc.)

**GENERAL TYPES OF INFORMATION ARCHITECTURE.** One way to classify information architecture is by the role the hardware plays. It is possible to distinguish two extreme cases: a mainframe environment and a PC environment. The combination of these two creates a third type of architecture, the distributed or networked environment.

1. *Mainframe environment.* In the mainframe environment, processing is done by a mainframe computer. The users work with passive (or "dumb") terminals, which are used to enter or change data and access information from the mainframe. This was the dominant architecture until the mid-1980s. Very few organizations use this type of architecture exclusively today. An extension of it is an architecture where PCs are used as smart terminals. Yet, the core of the system is the mainframe with its powerful storage and computational capabilities. The network computers (NCs) that were introduced in 1997 are redefining the role of the centralized computing environment.

2. *PC environment.* In the PC configuration, only PCs form the hardware information architecture. They can be independent of each other, but nor-

mally the PCs are connected via electronic networks. This architecture is common for many small- to medium-size organizations.

3. *Networked (distributed) environment.* **Distributed processing** divides the processing work between two or more computers. The participating computers can be all mainframe, all midrange, all micros, or, as in most cases, a combination. They can be in one location or in several. **Cooperative processing** is a type of distributed processing in which two or more *geographically dispersed* computers are teamed together to execute a specific task. Another important configuration of distributed processing is the *client/server* arrangement, where several computers share resources and are able to communicate with many other computers via LANs. When a distributed system covers the entire organization, it is referred to as an **enterprisewide system** and its parts are frequently connected by an intranet.

A distributed environment with both mainframe and PCs is very flexible and is commonly used by most medium- and large-size organizations. This basic classification is analogous to a transportation system. You can travel three ways. First, you can use public transportation, such as a train or a plane. In this case, several riders share the vehicle and use it at specified times, and must obey several rules. This is like using a mainframe. Second, you can use your own car, which is like using a PC. Third, you can use both; for example, you can drive to the train station and take the train to work, or you can drive to the airport and take a plane to your vacation destination. This last arrangement, which is analogous to a distributed system, is flexible, providing the benefits of the other two options.

Thanks to communication networks and especially the Internet and intranets, *networked computing* is becoming the dominant architecture of most organizations. This architecture permits intra- and interorganizational cooperation in computing; accessibility to vast amounts of data, information, and knowledge; and high efficiency in the use of computing resources. The concept of networked computing drives today's new architecture. An example is provided in the *IT at Work* box that follows.

---

## IT At Work     FLEXIBLE IT ARCHITECTURE AT CHASE MANHATTAN BANK

Chase and Chemical Bank merged in 1996, creating the largest bank in the United States. The unified bank had to process 16 million checks daily across 700 locations in 58 countries. It also had to serve 25 million retail and thousands of institutional customers. (These figures are growing by 6 to 10% a year.) The problem was how to merge the different information systems of the bank and create IT architecture that will support the bank's activities including its future growth (more acquisitions are planned). Previous mergers and acquisitions involving both Chase and Chemical resulted in many problems in developing the IT architecture. "We needed to blueprint an architectural platform that provided operational excellence and customer privacy," says Dennis O'Leary, CEO and executive vice president of the new bank. "The platform also had to be functional and have the ability to integrate business at the retail, national, and global enterprise levels."

One problem was the worldwide connectivity among more than 60,000 desktop computers, 14 large mainframes, 300 minicomputers, 1100 T 1-telecommunication lines, and more than 1,500 core applications.

The new architecture was constructed around the TCP/IP model (see Chapter 5 and Technology Guide 4). An innovative three-layer system was designed. First, there is a global infrastructure, then there are distribution networks that route traffic among business units, and third, numerous access networks were provided. This is a flexible structure that will allow the addition of more networks in the future. The global infrastructure is a network built on WANs, satellites, and so on. The architecture plan includes several firewalls, mainly in the distribution network layer. The accessed networks are the internal networks (now intranets) of the different business units. They also have many client/server applications as well as mainframes. All the desktops are managed on Windows NT.

All this massive networking has one goal: giving customers extensive real-time access to accounts and a view of their assets.

**For Further Exploration:** Why are banks so dependent on networks? Why is a three-layer system preferable? ▲

SOURCE: Condensed from Girishankar, S., "Modular Net Eases Merger," www.techweb.com/se/directlink.cgi CWK19970421S0005, April 1997.

## New Architectures: Client/Server, Enterprisewide Computing, Intranets, the Internet, and Extranets

The Internet, intranet, and extranets are based on **Client/server architecture** and **enterprisewide computing,** the newest architectural concepts. The principles of these concepts are briefly explained in this section, while the details are provided throughout the book.

**CLIENT/SERVER ARCHITECTURE.** A client/server arrangement divides networked computing units into two major categories: clients and servers, all of which are connected by LANs and possibly VANs. A *client* is a computer such as a PC or a workstation attached to a network, which is used to access shared network resources. A *server* is a machine that provides clients with these services. Examples of servers are a database server that provides a large storage capacity and a communication server that provides connection to another network, to commercial databases, or to a powerful processor. In some client/server systems there are additional computing units, referred to as middleware (see Chapter 12 and Technology Guides 2 and 4).

The purpose of client/server architecture, is to maximize the use of computer resources. Client/server architecture provides a way for different computing devices to work together, each doing the job for which it is best suited. The role of each machine need not be fixed; a workstation, for example, can be a client in one task and a server in another. Another important element is *sharing*. The clients, which are usually inexpensive PCs, share more expensive devices, the servers.

There are several modules of client/server architecture. In the most traditional model, the mainframe acts as a database server providing data for analysis, done by spreadsheets, database management systems, and other 4GLs, for the PC clients. For other models and more details see Technology Guide 2.

Client/server architecture gives a company as many access points to data as there are PCs on the network. It also lets a company use more tools to process data and information. Client/server architecture has changed the way people work in organizations; for example, people are empowered to access databases at will.

**ENTERPRISEWIDE COMPUTING.** Client/server computing can be implemented in a small work area or in one department on a LAN. Its main benefit is the sharing of resources within that department. However, many users frequently need access to data, applications, services, electronic mail, and real-time flows of data which are in different LANs or databases, so that they can improve their productivity and competitiveness. The solution is to deploy an *enterprisewide* client/server architecture, that is, to combine the two concepts to form a cohesive, flexible, and powerful computing environment. An example of such an architecture is provided in the PEC opening case and in the *IT at Work* illustration about Burlington, which follows.

*IT At Work* A CLIENT/SERVER SYSTEM AT BURLINGTON, INC.

**U**SING IT
...in Finance

**U**SING IT
...in Accounting

Burlington, Inc. operates about 200 textile retail stores and two distribution centers in various parts of the United States. Its headquarters are in New Jersey. The company runs its entire business from an enterprisewide client/server system. The figure below shows how the system works.

The cash registers and other PCs are networked to a main processor (a Sun workstation) in each store, which acts as a file server for the registers. It also acts as a communication gateway to the corporate mainframe computers for processing. Such communication is done via a WAN using satellite technology. At headquarters, data can be processed or moved to several destinations such as the VISA/MasterCard system for credit card transactions. Routine transactions are executed on the corporate Sequent computers, which process the transactions in parallel. Users can feed information from the corporate databases into spreadsheets or word processors on their desktop computers for end-user computing. The system handles everything from conveyor-belt scanners that generate database transactions to PCs with a graphical user interface, where users can enter queries. The terminal servers shown in the figure allow data entry and queries from workstations.

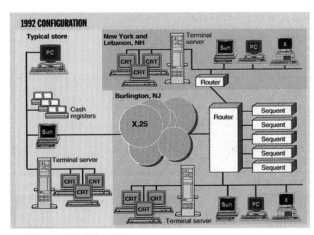

Burlington's client/server system.

**For Further Exploration:** How would Burlington be conducting its business today if it had not adopted a client/server enterprisewide architecture? ▲

SOURCE: Condensed from Ullman, E., "Client/Server Frees Data," *Byte*, June 1993, p. 99.

An enterprisewide client/server architecture provides total integration of departmental and corporate IS resources, thereby allowing for a new class of applications that span the enterprise and benefit both corporate central management (providing controls) and end-user systems (providing empowerment). It also provides better control and security over data in a distributed environment. By implementing client/server computing as the architecture for enterprisewide information systems, organizations maximize the value of information by increasing its availability. Enterprisewide client/server computing enables organizations to reengineer business processes, to distribute transactions, to streamline operations, and to provide better and newer services to customers. In short, by using an enterprisewide client/server architecture, a corporation can gain a significant competitive advantage.

The client/server architecture can be implemented in different ways, depending on what hardware and software one is using, and what role the servers and the clients play (see Technology Guide 4). Many new IT developments are based on the client/server concept. These include enterprise group support technologies such as Lotus Notes/Domino and Netscape Communicator (see Chapter 5) as well as the Internet and the intranets

**THE INTERNET AND INTRANETS.** While the concept of client/server architecture dominates IT architecture, specially structured client/server applications that were considered revolutionary in the mid-1990s may become obsolete due to the rapid development of the Internet and especially intranets and extranets. Even though these technologies are based on the concept of client/server, their implementation is considerably less expensive than that of many specially structured client/server systems. Furthermore, the conversion of existing systems to an intranet can be much easier and faster, while the capabilities of an intranet can be more powerful. Therefore, as is shown throughout the book and especially in Chapters 5 and 6, the Internet, intranets, and sometimes extranets are becoming an indispensable portion of most IT architectures in today's organizations. New architectures may replace old architectures, or may integrate them into their structure. These old architectures are referred to as legacy systems.

**LEGACY SYSTEMS.** **Legacy systems** are older, usually mature, information systems. Few of them have been around for 30 or 40 years; mostly they are 15 to 25 years old and some are less than 10 years old. They are usually pure mainframe or distributed systems in which the mainframe plays the major role and the PCs act as smart terminals. Newer legacy systems may include one or more LANs and even early client/server implementations.

Legacy systems were developed from the late 1950s through the 1980s for general-purpose business use in medium- to large-size companies where they were the primary mechanism for high-volume processing applications. Legacy systems are housed in a secured and costly data (or computer) center. They occupy one or several rooms and are operated by IS professional staff rather than by end users. Much of their work is routine, mainly in transaction processing. Some legacy systems are very large, including hundreds or even thousands of remote terminals networked to the mainframe processor. The role of legacy systems and the mainframe is changing rapidly (see Chapter 12).

Regardless of its type, an architecture is the basis for infrastructures that are major information resources. These and other information resources are ex-

> Given compatability and connectivity to older systems, intranets are becoming more vital every day. They've gone beyond optional. It's hard to see how a business does business without one.
>
> — *Blake Thompson*

> The understanding of the concept of legacy systems gained in this course has been very useful to me in communication with our MIS department. They are dealing with a legacy system that they did not create.
>
> — *Karen Miller*

tremely important organizational assets that need to be managed. This topic is presented next.

## ▶ 2.6 MANAGING INFORMATION RESOURCES

A modern organization possesses several information resources. In addition to the infrastructures, many software applications exist and new ones are continuously being developed. These systems have enormous strategic value and firms rely on them so heavily that, in some cases, when information systems are not working, even for a short time, an organization cannot function. Furthermore, the acquisition, operation, and maintenance of these systems may cost a considerable amount of money. Therefore, it is essential to manage information systems properly; the planning, organizing, implementing, operating, and controlling of the infrastructures and the organizations' portfolio of applications must be done with great skill.

The responsibility for the management of information resources is divided between two organizational entities: the information systems department (ISD), which is a corporate entity, and the end users, who are scattered throughout the organization. This division raises important questions such as:

▶ Which resources are managed by whom?

▶ What is the role of the ISD, its structure, and its place in the organization?

▶ What are the relationships between the ISD and the end users?

Brief answers to these questions are provided next.

### WHICH RESOURCES ARE MANAGED BY WHOM?

There are many types of information resources and their components may be from multiple vendors and of different brands. The major categories are hardware (all types of computers, servers, and other devices), software (development tools, languages, and applications), databases, networks (local, wide, Internet and intranets, and supporting devices), procedures, security facilities, and physical buildings. The resources are scattered throughout the organization and some of them are changing frequently. Therefore, it may be rather difficult to manage IS resources.

There is no standard menu for the division of responsibility for the development and maintenance of IS resources between the ISD and end users. In some organizations, the ISD manages most of these resources, regardless of where they are located and how they are used. In others, the ISD manages only a few. The division depends on the size and nature of the organization, the amount and type of IT resources, the organization's attitudes toward computing, the philosophy of top management, the maturity level of the technology, the amount and nature of outsourced IT work, and even the country in which the company operates.

Generally speaking, the ISD is responsible for corporate-level and shared resources, while the end users are responsible for departmental resources. Regardless of who is doing what, there are several activities involved in managing each resource. Thus, responsibilities range from planning and purchasing to application development and maintenance. Sometimes the division between the

ISD and the end users is based on such activities. For example, the ISD may acquire or build systems and the end users operate and maintain them.

Because of interdependencies of information resources, it is important that the ISD and the end users work closely together and cooperate regardless of who is doing what. We discuss this below and in Chapter 15.

## WHAT IS THE ROLE OF THE INFORMATION SYSTEMS DEPARTMENT?

The role, structure, and place of the ISD in the organization hierarchy and the department's leadership vary considerably, depending upon the amount and importance of information resources to be managed, the extent of outsourcing, and the role that end users play. These issues will be described in Chapter 15. Here, we provide only some major observations.

> The director of ISD in my company is no longer viewed as an electronic geek, but as a vital player in strategic management.
> — *Mike Rewald*

1. The role of the ISD is changing from purely technical to more managerial and strategic (see Table 2.3).
2. As a result, the position of the ISD within the organization tends to be elevated from a unit reporting to a functional department, to a unit reporting to a senior vice president of administration or to the CEO (see Minicase 2).
3. The role of the director of the ISD is changing from a technical manager to a senior executive, sometimes referred to as the chief information officer (CIO).
4. The internal structure of the ISD is changing to reflect its new role (see Minicase 2).

*Table 2.3* **The Changing Role of the Information Systems Department**

*Traditional major IS functions:*
- Managing systems development and systems project management
- Managing computer operations, including the computer center
- Staffing, training, and developing IS skills
- Providing technical services

*New (additional) major IS functions:*
- Initiating and designing specific strategic information systems
- Infrastructure planning, development, and control
- Incorporating the Internet and electronic commerce into the business
- Managing system integration including the Internet, intranets, and extranets
- Educating the non-IS managers about IT
- Educating the IS staffs about the business
- Supporting end-user computing
- Partnering with the executive level that runs the business
- Actively participating in business processes reengineering
- Proactively using business and technical knowledge to "seed" the line with innovative ideas about IT
- Creating business alliances with vendors and IS departments in other organizations

**5.** The ISD can be centralized or decentralized or a combination of the two.

**6.** The ISD must work closely with external organizations such as vendors, business partners, research institutions, universities, and consultants.

**7.** The key issues in information systems management change with time. The most important issues for 1994/1995 were researched by Brancheau et al. (1996), and their relative importance was traced over time. The 12 most important issues are listed in Table 2.4, together with a reference to the chapter in this book where they are discussed.

*Table 2.4*  **Key MIS Issues for 1994/95**

| Rank | Key Issue | Mean Rating | Chapter in Book |
|------|-----------|-------------|-----------------|
| 1 | Building a Responsive IT Infrastructure | 9.10 | 12 |
| 2 | Facilitating and Managing Business Process Redesign | 7.79 | 4 |
| 3 | Developing and Managing Distributed Systems | 7.73 | 5, 14 |
| 4 | Developing and Implementing an Information Architecture | 7.62 | 12 |
| 5 | Planning and Managing Communication Networks | 7.58 | 5 |
| 6 | Improving the Effectiveness of Software Development | 7.50 | 14 |
| 7 | Making Effective Use of the Data Resource | 7.46 | 10 |
| 8 | Recruiting and Developing IS Human Resources | 7.31 | 8, 15 |
| 9 | Aligning the IS Organization Within the Enterprise | 7.11 | 12, 15 |
| 10 | Improving IS Strategic Planning | 6.82 | 3, 12 |
| 11A | Implementing and Managing Collaborative Support Systems | 6.59 | 5 |
| 11B | Measuring IS Effectiveness and Productivity | 6.59 | 13, 15 |

SOURCE: Compiled from Brancheau et al. (1996).

Highest rating = 10

Note that in a study conducted in late 1997 (Wreden [1997]), the five most important issues were (in descending order): (1) improving productivity, (2) reducing cost, (3) improving decision making, (4) enhancing customer relationships, and (5) developing new strategic applications. All of these issues are covered in many places throughout this book.

## MANAGING RELATIONSHIPS WITH END USERS

The ISD and the end-user units must be close partners. Some mechanisms that build the required cooperation are:

▶ A *steering committee* that represents all end users and the ISD. This committee sets IT policies, provides for priorities, and coordinates IS projects.

▶ *Joint ISD/end-users project teams* for planning, budgeting, application developments, and maintenance.

▶ ISD representation on the *top corporate executive committee.*

▶ *Service agreements* that define computing responsibilities and provide a framework for services rendered by the ISD to end users.

▶ *Technical and administrative support* (including training) for end users.

▶  A *conflict resolution unit* established by the ISD to handle end-user complaints quickly and resolve conflicts as soon as possible.

Details on these are provided in Chapter 15.

# ▶ MANAGERIAL ISSUES

1. *The transition to networked computing.* Converting the IT in organizations to networked computing may be a complicated process. It requires a client/server infrastructure, an Internet, and electronic commerce policy and strategy, all in the face of many unknowns and risks. However, such a potentially painful conversion may be, in many organizations, the only way to succeed or even to survive. When to do it, how to do it, and what the impacts will be of such a conversion are major issues for organizations to consider.

2. *From legacy systems to client/server.* A related major issue is whether and when to move from the legacy systems to a client/server enterprisewide architecture. While the general trend is toward client/server, there have been several unsuccessful transformations. Client/server and enterprise computing are relatively new, and so there are many unresolved issues regarding the implementation of these systems. The introduction of intranets seems to be much easier than that of other client/server applications. Yet, moving to any new architecture requires new infrastructure, and it may have a considerable impact on people, quality of work, and budget. These important issues are discussed in detail in Chapters 12 through 14.

    It should be noted that many companies need high-speed computing of high-volume data. Here the client/server concept may not be effective. Management should consider transformation of the legacy systems to new types of mainframes that use innovations that make the systems smaller and cheaper.

3. *How much infrastructure?* Justifying information system applications is not an easy job due to the intangible benefits and the rapid changes in technologies that often make systems obsolete. Justifying infrastructure is even more difficult since many users and applications share the infrastructure. This makes it almost impossible to quantify the benefits. Basic architecture is a necessity, but there are some options. Various justification methodologies are discussed in Chapter 13.

4. *The role of the ISD.* The role of the ISD can be extremely important, yet top management frequently mistreats it. By constraining the ISD to technical duties and considering it a second-class area, an organization may jeopardize its entire future. For appropriate roles see Chapter 15.

5. *The role of end users.* End users play an important role in IT development and management. The end users know best what their information needs are and to what degree they are fulfilled. Also, it is not economically feasible for the ISD to develop and manage all IT applications. Properly managed end-user computing is essential for the betterment of all organizations (see Chapter 12).

6. *Ethical issues.* Systems developed by the ISD and used and maintained by end users may introduce some ethical issues. The ISD's major objective is to

build efficient and effective systems. But, such systems may invade the privacy of the users or create advantages to certain individuals at the expense of others. See Chapter 15 for details.

## KEY TERMS

Ad hoc reports  *55*

Application programs  *46*

Artificial neural network (ANN)  *50*

Client/server architecture  *62*

Cooperative processing  *61*

Data  *45*

Decision support system (DSS)  *48*

Distributed processing  *61*

Enterprisewide computing  *61*

Enterprisewide system  *61*

Executive information system (EIS)  *50*

Expert system (ES)  *50*

Group support system (GSS)  *50*

Information  *45*

Information architecture  *52*

Information infrastructure  *52*

Interorganizational information system (IOS)  *46*

Knowledge  *45*

Knowledge workers  *57*

Legacy system  *64*

Long-range planning  *56*

Management information system (MIS)  *48*

Office automation system (OAS)  *48*

Periodic reports  *55*

Strategic system  *56*

Transaction processing system (TPS)  *48*

## CHAPTER HIGHLIGHTS  *(L–x means learning objective number x)*

▶ Information systems can be organized according to business functions, the people they support, or both. (L–1)

▶ The transaction processing system (TPS) covers the core repetitive organizational transactions such as purchasing, billing, or payroll. (L–2)

▶ The data collected in a TPS are used to build other systems. (L–2)

▶ The major functional information systems in an organization are accounting, finance, manufacturing (operations), human resources, and marketing. (L–2)

▶ Management information systems refers to functional information systems. But MIS is also used to describe the field of IT. (L–2)

▶ The main general support systems are office automation systems, decision support systems, group support systems, executive support systems, expert systems, and artificial neural networks. (L–3)

▶ Managerial activities and decisions can be classified as operational, managerial, and strategic. (L–3)

▶ An information architecture provides the conceptual foundation for building the information infrastructure and specific applications. It maps the information requirements as they relate to information resources. (L–4)

▶ There are three major configurations of an information architecture: the mainframe environment, the PC environment, and the distributed environment. (L–4)

▶ The information infrastructure refers to the shared information resources (such as corporate database) and their linkages, operation, maintenance, and management. (L–4)

▶ Legacy systems are older systems in which the mainframe is at the core of the system. (L–5)

▶ In a client/server architecture, several PCs (the clients) are networked among themselves and are connected to databases, telecommunications, and other providers of services (the servers). (L–5)

▶ An enterprisewide information system is a system that provides communication among all the organization employees. It also provides accessibility to any data or information needed by any employee at any location. (L–5)

▶ Information resources are extremely important and they must be managed properly by both the ISD and end users. (L–6)

▶ In general, the ISD manages shared enterprise information resources such as networks, while end users are responsible for departmental information resources, such as PCs. (L–6)

▶ The role of the ISD is becoming more managerial and its importance is rapidly increasing. (L–7)

▶ Steering committees, service agreements, and conflict-resolution units are some of the mechanisms used to facilitate the cooperation between the ISD and end users. (L–7)

## QUESTIONS FOR REVIEW

1. Describe a TPS.
2. What is an MIS?
3. Explain the role of the DSS.
4. What is the purpose of an EIS?
5. Describe operational, managerial, and strategic activities.
6. Define data, information, and knowledge.
7. What information systems support the work of groups?
8. What is an enterprisewide system?
9. What is an information architecture?
10. Describe information infrastructure.
11. Discuss the evolution of support systems over time.
12. Distinguish among periodic, ad hoc, and exception reports.
13. Define business transactions and give some examples.
14. List the information resources that are usually managed by end users.
15. Distinguish between a mainframe and a distributed environment.
16. Describe a legacy system.
17. What is a client/server system?
18. What mechanisms can be used to assure ISD and end-user cooperation?

## QUESTIONS FOR DISCUSSION

1. Review the analogy between means of transportation and an information architecture. Show the equivalence and indicate the major advantages and disadvantages of each of the three subsystems.
2. Discuss the logic of building information systems in accordance with the organizational hierarchical structure.
3. Distinguish between information architecture and information infrastructure.
4. Information systems evolved over time starting with TPS. What is the logic of such evolution?
5. Explain how operational, managerial, and strategic activities are related to general support systems.
6. Relate the following concepts: client/server, distributed processing, and enterprisewide computing.
7. Some believe that client/server architecture, when organized in an enterprisewide setting, is the most desirable option for many companies. Explain why.
8. The allocation of information resources between two entities may create some conflicts. Provide examples of potential conflicts.
9. Discuss the relationship between infrastructure and architecture.
10. Is the Internet an infrastructure, an architecture, or an application program? Why? If none of the above, then what is it?
11. What is the advantage of classifying information systems according to the support provided to different groups of employees?

## EXERCISES

1. Classify each of the following systems as one (or more) of the general support systems:
   a. A student registration system in a university
   b. A system that advises farmers about which fertilizers to use
   c. A hospital patient admission system
   d. A system that provides a marketing manager with demand reports regarding the sales volume of specific products
   e. A robotic system that paints cars in a factory
2. Review the list of key MIS issues in Table 2.4.
   a. Present these issues to IT managers in a company you can access (you may want to develop a questionnaire).
   b. Have the managers vote on the importance of these items. Also ask them to add items. Report the results. Try to explain the differences between this and the original study.
3. Review the following systems in Chapter 1 and classify each of them according to the inside cells in the matrix in Figure 2.6. Try to match each system with at least one cell. Note that one system can be classified in several ways. The systems in Chapter 1 are:

   Harper Group

   UPS

   Oregon State

   La Saunda Holding

   Mercy Hospital

   John Deere and Company

Boeing Inc.

FDA (Box 1.1)

Killington Ski Resort (Minicase 1)

Hershey Food

Ford Motors, Inc.

Detecting bombs

Burlington Inc.

Atlantic Electric Co. (Minicase 1)

Chase/Chemical Bank

**4.** Review the following systems in this chapter and classify each of them according to the triangle of Figure 2.7.

Pan Energy Corporation

Glaxo Wellcome

## GROUP ASSIGNMENT

**1.** Observe a checkout counter in a supermarket that uses a scanner. Find some material that describes how the scanned code is translated into the price that the customers pay.
   **a.** Identify the following components of the system: inputs, processes, outputs, feedback.
   **b.** What kind of a system is this (TPS, DSS, EIS, MIS, etc.)? Why?

   **c.** Having the information electronically in the system may provide opportunities for additional managerial uses. Identify such uses.
   **d.** Research and report on how such systems will be operating in the future. Describe them.

## INTERNET EXERCISES

Note: The URLs included here were current when the book went to press. However, they are subject to change without notice. Please consult the Turban Web site (www.Wiley.com/college/turban2e).

**1.** Enter the site of Pan Energy Corporation and find the amount of profit the company made during each of the last five years. Also, check into their customers and products.

**2.** Surf the Internet for information about airport security via bomb detecting devices (*IT at Work:* Detecting Bombs

in Airline Passengers' Luggage). Examine the available products and comment on the IT techniques used.

**3.** Visit the site of American Airlines. Find out how the Internet is being used for advertisement, auctions, etc.

**4.** Enter the Web site of Hershey (www.hersheyfoods .com). Examine the information about the company and its products and markets. Explain how an intranet helps such a company compete in the global market.

## Minicase 1

### Information Technology Helps Atlantic Electric Co. Survive

**Atlantic Electric Co. of New Jersey** is losing the monopoly it once held. Some of its clients are already buying electricity from a new, unregulated brand of competitor—an independent cogenerator that generates its own electricity and sells its additional capacity to easy-to-serve commercial accounts at low prices. Atlantic Electric Co. may even lose some of its residential customer base if the local regulatory commission rules that the customers would be better served by another utility.

In order to survive, the company must become the least expensive provider in its territory. One way to do that is to provide the company's employees with the information they need to make more up-to-date and accurate business decisions. The current IT system in-

cludes a mainframe and a corporate network providing mainframe access. The users have both dumb and smart terminals. However, this system is unable to meet the new challenge. It is necessary to develop new user applications, in a familiar format, and to do it rapidly with minimum cost. This can be done on PCs but not on the mainframe.

Some of the needed applications include the following:

**1.** A database and decision support system for fuel purchasing.

**2.** A database for customers and their electricity usage pattern, and a DSS for customizing rates.

3. A DSS for substations' design and transmission.

4. A cash management DSS for the treasury department.

The company decided to explore an enterprisewide option, with departmental LANs connected to the corporate network. The estimated cost of the proposed system is $1.5 million.

### Questions for Minicase 1

1. Is an enterprisewide system the best option in this case, or will departmental client/server systems be sufficient? Why?

2. The existing legacy system is using the networks as a traditional distributed system, in which people can download and upload information with their PCs. Why not just modify this system?

3. The concern of Atlantic Electric Co. is survival. What kind of information technologies can be used to help survival in this case?

4. What business pressures described in Chapter 1 are affecting Atlantic Electric?

5. If this incident had occurred today, what IT arrangement would you recommend?

SOURCE: Based on Goff, L., "Old Game, New Rules," *Info-World Direct*, May 1993, p. 30.

# Minicase 2

## Centralized Information System at Mead Corporation

Mead Corporation in Dayton, Ohio is a large U.S. paper and forest products company. Mead is also in the information business as the owner of LEXIS (a legal online research service) and NEXIS (a news information retrieval service). Due to its large size, the company has been decentralized. Its divisions have the option of maintaining their own IS departments or using the centralized ISD for corporatewide applications.

In 1980, management realized that it was necessary to reorganize the ISD. In the old structure, ISD reported to a VP of operations and included six units in the information service organization: operations, telecommunications, technical services, system development, operational systems, and operations research (for system analysis). The company needed a corporatewide network, as well as information resources, planning and control, and decision support applications. The function was relocated, and its CIO now reports directly to the CEO. After two additional reorganizations, IS has shifted its emphasis from end-user computing and small systems to building a networked computing infrastructure and integrating application development. A major task has been to permit end-user applications and large-scale business systems to cross-fertilize each other using an intranet.

In 1994, IT started to support the corporate business process reengineering efforts at Mead. Mead is also changing its relationships with its customers, so that it will be easier for them to do business with Mead. EDI and terminals at customers' sites are some examples of its electronic commerce activities.

A basic tactic of Mead is to retain central control of the IT infrastructure and distribute responsibility for building and maintaining small and medium-size applications to the business units. Yet, as the use of information technology has changed, Mead's centralized ISD has reorganized to focus on those new uses, especially those involving the Internet and intranets. The name of the centralized department has been changed (in 1994)

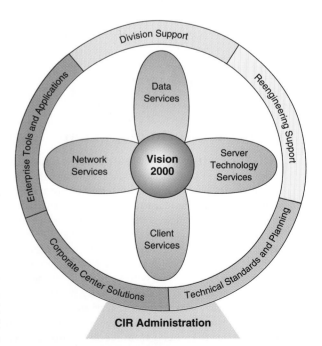

The 1997 organization structure.

to the *information resources department*. The latest reorganization (1997) is aimed at supporting Mead's Vision 2000. This vision foresees computing to be in the form of a three-tiered mainframe, midrange, and desktops. Applications will be of three types: enterprisewide, divisional, and local; they will use a global network that reaches out beyond Mead. The structure of the ISD is shown in the figure on p. 72. This structure was designed to match the corporate client/server architecture. For details see McNurlin and Sprague (1998).

### Questions for Minicase 2

1. Trace the changes in the centralized IS department, and relate them to the material discussed in this chapter.

2. Discuss the relationships between the centralized IS departments and end users as described in this case.

3. Analyze the tactic of centralized control over the infrastructure, and decentralized authority over building and maintaining applications.

4. Review Mead's organizational structure as shown in the figure. What unique feature exists in this structure?

SOURCE: This minicase was condensed from McNurlin and Sprague (1998). The figure was reproduced with permission from Barbara McNurlin.

## REFERENCES AND BIBLIOGRAPHY

1. Aituv, N., et al., "Factors Affecting the Policy of Distributed Computing Resources," *MIS Quarterly,* December 1989.

2. Brancheau, J. C., et al., "Key Issues in Information Systems Management: 1994–95, SIM Delphi Results," *MIS Quarterly,* June 1996.

3. Broadbent, M., and P. Weill, "Management by Maxim: How Business IT Managers Can Create IT Infrastructures," *Sloan Management Review,* Spring 1997.

4. *Datamation,* special supplement on client/server computing, June 15, 1993.

5. Doke, R. E., and T. Barrier, "An Assessment of Information Systems Taxonomies: Time to Re-evaluate," *Journal of Information Technology,* Vol. 3, 1994.

6. Fried, L., *Managing Information Technology in Turbulent Times,* New York: John Wiley & Sons, 1995.

7. Khama, R. *Distributed Computing Implementation and Management Strategy,* Englewood Cliffs, NJ: Prentice Hall, 1994.

8. McLean, E., "End-Users as Application Developers," *MIS Quarterly,* December 1979.

9. McLeod, R., Jr., "Systems Theory and Information Resource Management: Integrating Key Concepts," *Information Resource Management Journal,* Spring 1995.

10. McNurlin, B., and R., Sprague, *Information Systems Management in Practice,* 4th ed., Upper Saddle River, NJ: Prentice Hall, 1998.

11. Millet, I., and C. H. Mawhinney, "Executive Information Systems," *Information & Management,* Vol. 23, 1992.

12. Millet, I., et al., "Executive Information Systems," *DSS 91 Transactions,* Zigurs I., ed., Providence, RI: Institute of Management Sciences, 1991.

13. Palvia, P. C., et al., "The Prism System: A Key to Organizational Effectiveness at Federal Express Corporation," *MIS Quarterly,* September 1992.

14. Sinha, A., "Client-Server Computing," *Communications of the ACM,* July 1992.

15. Synnott, W. R., *The Information Weapon,* New York: John Wiley & Sons, 1987.

16. Turban, E., and J. Aronson, *Decision Support Systems and Intelligent Systems,* 5th ed., Upper Saddle River, NJ: Prentice Hall, 1988.

17. Wreden, N., "Business Boosting Technologies," *Beyond Computing,* Nov./Dec. 1997.

# CHAPTER 3
# Strategic Information Systems

## *Learning Objectives*

*After studying this chapter, you will be able to:*

❶ Describe strategic information systems and explain their advantages.

❷ Describe Porter's competitive forces model and how information technology helps companies improve their competitive positions.

❸ Describe Porter's value chain model and its relationship to information technology.

❹ Describe several frameworks that show how IT supports the attainment of competitive advantage.

❺ Describe global competition and its SIS framework.

❻ Describe representative strategic information systems and the advantage they provide with the support of IT.

# CONNECTIONS

## CATERPILLAR INC. FENDS OFF COMPETITION

### The Problem

CATERPILLAR INC. (CAT) of Peoria, Illinois, is a world leader in manufacturing heavy machinery. In 1982, the company entered a difficult period. Komatsu of Japan, a major competitor, was offering bulldozers in the United States at prices 40 percent lower than CAT's. Caterpillar was forced to cut prices. A poor economy and a lengthy labor strike worsened the situation. By 1985, the accumulated losses amounted to $953 million. Caterpillar, which sells its products all over the world, responded to the downturn in all the usual ways: it closed plants, laid off workers, and slashed expenses. But the usual ways did not work: market share declined and losses increased.

### The IT Solution

Management decided that the only solution lay in a state-of-the-art information technology. CAT would not be globally competitive without it. The first phase of the information technology project lasted eight years and cost $2 billion. What did it accomplish?

Computer-integrated manufacturing (CIM) (see Chapter 8), a dream at many companies, is a reality at CAT. Robots, computer-aided design, and computer-aided manufacturing are functioning throughout the various plants. These and other computerized systems resulted in in-process inventory reductions of 60 percent and savings of several million dollars. Nonessential labor was eliminated, production processes were simplified, costly plants and warehouses were closed, lead time to build a product was reduced from 45 days to 10, and on-time deliveries to customers increased by 70 percent. Modern management techniques, such as a computerized Materials Requirement Planning II (see Chapter 8), were installed, and computerized purchasing and logistics systems were put into operation. A sophisticated system for managing repairs and providing replacement parts to dealers and customers was installed. This system enabled dealers to provide parts to their clients quickly yet maintain low inventories.

Some other important IT applications at CAT are these:

▶ A global network with 7,000 terminals connects 50,000 employees and 180 dealers in 1,000 locations (Caterpillar uses both its fiber optic network and a leased satellite service). This network is used for an EDI, for the Internet, for other telecommunications applications, and intranet activities.

▶ An executive information system enables business units to analyze data, identify trends, and evaluate each dealer's performance.

▶ CAT's dealers and suppliers are on an EDI system.

▶ The telecommunication system includes a "CAT TV" link to dealers, as well as audio and video teleconferencing capabilities.

▶ Ninety-five percent of the company's employees can access data on the company's enterprisewide system (an intranet).

▶ A world-class repair and part inventory system was developed (see *IT at Work* in Section 3.6).

The IT project supported a massive reengineering of the company.

### The Results

By 1993, Caterpillar had become stronger than its competitors, controlling more than 30 percent of the U.S. construction equipment market. The firm was able to export more than half its sales to foreign buyers yet keep its manufacturing plants and the jobs in the United States. For its efforts, CAT was a winner of *Information Week's* 1991 "Excellence in IS" award. And what about CAT's chief rival, Komatsu of Japan? Komatsu shifted its construction-equipment strategy away from bulldozers in order to avoid head-to-head competition with CAT.

SOURCE: Condensed from Bartolomew, D., "Caterpillar Digs In," *InformationWeek,* June 7, 1993, pp. 36–41, 59, and from *Harvard Business Review,* March/April 1996, p. 89.

## 3.1 STRATEGIC ADVANTAGE AND INFORMATION TECHNOLOGY

The opening case is a vivid example of a company that has achieved competitive advantage by using IT. Caterpillar's experience illustrates the following points:

1. Global competition is not just about price and quality; it is about service and time as well.
2. Competitive situations can involve several parties such as buyers, sellers, dealers, suppliers, financial institutions, and labor unions.
3. IT is a major tool for gaining competitive advantage.
4. IT may require a large investment over a long period of time.
5. A reengineered system provides benefits to the company, its customers, dealers, and suppliers.
6. Extensive networked computing infrastructure is necessary to support a large global system.
7. Successful strategic information systems can force even fierce competitors to quit.

### STRATEGIC INFORMATION SYSTEMS

**Strategic information systems (SISs),** like the one developed at Caterpillar, are systems that *support* or *shape* a business unit's competitive strategy (Callon [1996] and Neumann [1994]). An SIS is characterized by its ability to change *significantly* the manner in which business is done. This can give the company a *competitive advantage.* The system does this through its contribution to the strategic goals of an organization and/or its ability to increase performance and productivity significantly. For example, Caterpillar's provides superb dealer services, quick shipments, on-time deliveries, an effective parts replacement program, and an electronic transaction processing system. Its competitors have been unable to match the services that IT allows Caterpillar to provide.

Neumann (1994) maintains that conventional information systems, when used in innovative ways, can become strategic. Originally, strategic systems were considered to be *outwardly* aiming at direct competition in their industry, for example, by providing new services to customers and/or suppliers with the specific objective of beating their competitors. But starting in the late 1980s, strategic systems are also being viewed *inwardly*: they are focused on enhancing the competitive position of the firm by increasing employees' productivity, improving teamwork, and enhancing communication. Caterpillar has combined both outward (the use of EDI and CAT TV) and inward (computer-integrated manufacturing) orientations to its advantage.

In addition to the inward and outward approaches, there is another dimension to SIS—**strategic alliances**—wherein two or more companies share a strategic information system. For example, many banks share the same ATM network. Strategic alliances were introduced in Chapter 1 and will be revisited throughout this book, especially in Chapter 4.

As you may recall from Chapter 1, *corporate strategy* is one of the five major internal organization components. Strategic systems are also one of the organiza-

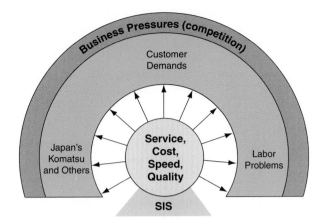

**FIGURE 3.1** Strategic information systems at Caterpillar—defending against business pressures and competition.

tion's critical responses to business pressures. In its successful IT-supported strategic management effort, Caterpillar used IT to facilitate the reengineering of its business processes; to increase service, speed, and quality; and to reduce cost, in order to fend off competition (see Figure 3.1).

In order to understand better how SIS works, let us first review some generic aspects of strategic management.

## ELEMENTS OF STRATEGIC MANAGEMENT

*Strategic management* is the way an organization maps the strategy of its future operations. It has long been associated with long-range planning. Today, strategic management includes three complementary activities: **long-range planning, response management,** and **innovation** (see Figure 3.2). The topic of long-range planning is outside the boundaries of this book (see Huffman [1996]). Response management includes many of the critical response activities presented in Chapter 1.

**FIGURE 3.2** Strategic management has three complementary elements.

*Innovation.* Strategic information systems support some response systems, but mostly reactive systems in an attempt to provide competitive advantage. *Innovation* is one of the most important business concepts for the 1990s (see Davenport [1993]). As a matter of fact, when one company introduces a major successful innovation, other companies in the industry need to respond to the threat. Innovation is strongly related to information technologies, which can facilitate cre-

*Table 3.1* **Areas of IT Related to Technological Innovations**

| Innovation | Advantage |
|---|---|
| New products | Constantly innovating with new competitive products and services. Electronic Art Inc. was first to introduce CD ROM-based video games. |
| Extended products | Leveraging old products with new competitive extensions. A Korean company was the first to introduce "fuzzy logic" in its washing machines; sales went up 50% in a few months. |
| Differentiated products | Gaining advantage through unique products or added value. Compaq Computers became the leading PC seller after providing self-diagnostic disks with its computers. |
| Super systems | Erecting competitive barriers through major system developments that cannot be easily duplicated. American Airlines' reservation system, SABRE, became so comprehensive that it took years to duplicate; a super system always stays ahead of the competition. |
| Customer terminals | Putting computer terminals in customer's offices to lock out the competition. American Hospital Supply did this during the 1980s, to great effect. |
| Electronic delivery | Using EDI as a substitute for paper transactions and as a means of global expansion. |
| Computer-aided sales | Offering systems that provide computer support to marketing and sales; for example, equipping salespeople with wireless hand-held computers that allow them to provide quotations at the customer's location. |
| Internet Web sites for wholesalers | Putting electronic catalogs and ordering systems on the Internet sites of your wholesalers. Fruit of the Loom has installed a Web site for each of 50 independent wholesalers with whom they do business. |

SOURCE: Based on Synnott (1987) and on www.fruit.com, 1998.

ativity and the generating of ideas, as shown in Table 3.1 and as we will see in Chapters 9 and 11.

**THE ROLE OF IT.** Information technology contributes to strategic management in many ways (see Ross [1996] and Callon [1996]). Consider these three:

1. Information technology creates *applications* that provide direct strategic advantage to organizations. For example, Federal Express was the first company in its industry to use information technology for tracking the location of every package in its system.

2. IT supports strategic changes such as *reengineering*. For example, IT allows efficient decentralization by providing speed communication lines, and it streamlines and shortens product design time with computer-aided engineering tools.

3. IT provides *business intelligence* by collecting and analyzing information about innovations, markets, competitors, and environmental changes. Such information provides strategic advantage because, if a company knows something important before its competitors, or if it can make the correct interpretation of the information before its competitors, then it can introduce changes first and benefit from them.

**COMPETITIVE INTELLIGENCE.** Information about the competition can mean the difference between winning and losing a business battle. Many companies continuously monitor the activities of their competitors (see Wreden [1994]). For example, Frito Lay distributors, when they deliver to a store, will count what their competitors have on the shelves, enter the information into hand-held computers, and transmit it to the corporate database daily. An executive information system at Hertz monitors car rental prices of their competitors on a daily basis. An EIS at Kraft, the giant food maker, closely monitors the performance of Kraft's competitors. Such activities are part of **competitive intelligence,** which drives business performance by increasing market knowledge, improving internal relationships, and raising the quality of strategic planning.

Information about markets, technologies, and government's actions is also collected by competitive intelligence. Several information technologies can be used for collecting such information, ranging from text retrieval to optical character recognition.

Analyzing and interpreting the information is as important as collecting it. Here, one can use anything from spreadsheets to expert systems. For example, Chase Manhattan Bank (New York) uses expert systems to track several sources of information to determine their possible impacts on the bank, the customers, and the industry.

Competitive intelligence means looking at internal sources as well. Much informal information and knowledge can be collected and stored in what some companies call "institutional memory" or a "corporate knowledge base" (see Chapter 10). Competitive intelligence can be enhanced by several information technologies, including intelligent agents (see Chapter 11). Research has indicated that the percentage of companies using IT to support competitive intelligence has increased from 31 percent in 1993 to about 50 percent in 1997. This increase is due primarily to the use of the Internet.

***The Internet and Competitive Intelligence.*** The Internet plays an increasingly important role in supporting competitive intelligence. Power and Sharda (1997) proposed a framework in which the Internet capabilities are shown to provide information for strategic decisions. According to the framework (see Figure 3.3) the external information required (upper left) and the methods of acquiring information (upper right) can be supported by Internet tools via processes such as organizational experience with the Internet and the strategic planning process.

Power and Sharda emphasize the search capability of the various tools of the Internet. Using these tools one can implement specific search strategies as illustrated in Box 3.1, on page 81.

There is another aspect to competitive intelligence: *industrial espionage.* Corporate spies are looking for marketing plans, cost analyses, new products/services, and strategic plans. Such espionage can be unethical and illegal. Another problem is the theft of portable computers at conferences, which is spreading all over the world. Many of the thieves are interested in the information stored in the computers, not in the computers themselves. Protecting against such activities is important and is discussed in Chapter 15.

Before discussing how organizations apply IT to facilitate their competitiveness, it is necessary to introduce the concepts of competitive strategy, competitive advantage, and sustainable strategic advantage. The distinction among these concepts is important.

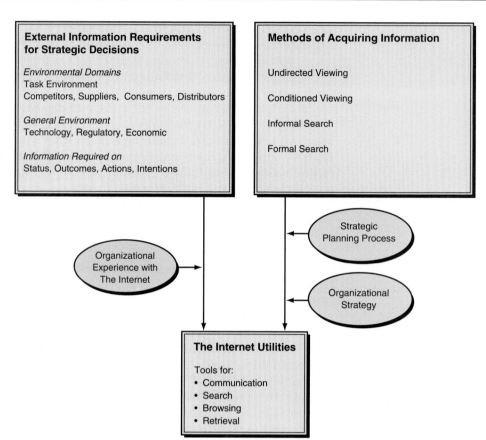

**FIGURE 3.3** A framework for the Internet as a source of information for strategic decision making. (*Source:* Power and Sharda [1997], p. 111.)

Large hospitals are striving to achieve the competitive edge in the marketplace. They are creating large networks to provide a wide range of services and keep cost in control.
— *Brad White*

***Competitive Strategy and Sustainable Advantage.*** *Competition,* according to Porter (1985 and 1996), is at the core of a firm's success or failure. *Competitive strategy* is the search for a **competitive advantage** in an industry, leading to control of the market and to larger-than-average profits. Such a strategy aims to establish a profitable and *sustainable* position against the forces that determine industry competition. SISs are designed to provide for competitive advantage, or to support competitive strategy. Indeed, during the 1970s and 1980s, there were a number of successful implementations of SIS applications. Now, entering the twenty-first century, as a result of the widespread adoption of information technology, it has become increasingly difficult to *sustain* an advantage for an extended period. Competitors can imitate systems in months rather than in years. New technological innovations today make yesterday's innovations obsolete. Furthermore, experience indicates that information systems, by themselves, can rarely provide a sustainable competitive advantage. Therefore, a modified approach is used.

When SISs are combined with structural changes in the organization, they can provide a sustainable *strategic advantage.* (The term "strategic" points to the long-term nature and to the large magnitude of the advantage an organization has over its competitors.) For example, PRISM is a comprehensive strategic information system used by Federal Express to manage its human resources and increase the effectiveness and efficiency of its operation (see Palvia et al. [1992]).

## *A Closer Look* BOX 3.1

### COMPETITIVE INTELLIGENCE ON THE INTERNET

The Internet can be used to help a company conduct competitive intelligence easily, quickly, and relatively inexpensively in the following ways:

1. *Review competitor's Web sites.* Such visits can reveal information about new products or projects, potential alliances, trends in budgeting, advertising strategies used, financial strength, and much more.
2. *Analyze related newsgroups.* Internet newsgroups help you find out what people think about a company and its products. For example, newsgroup participants state what they like or dislike about products provided by you and your competitors. You can also examine people's reactions to a new idea by posting a question.
3. *Examining publicly available financial documents.* This can be accomplished by entering a number of databases. While some databases charge nominal fees, others are free. The most notable is the Securi-

ties and Exchange Commission EDGAR database (see Chapter 6 and www.sec.gov/edgarhp.htm).

4. *You can give prizes* to those visitors of your Web site who best describe the strengths and weaknesses of your competitor's products.
5. *Use an information delivery service* (such as Info Wizard, My Yahoo, or PointCast) to find out what is published in the Internet, including newsgroup correspondence about your competitors and their products. Known as *push technologies* (see Chapter 6), these services provide any desired information including news, some in real-time, for free or a nominal fee.
6. *Corporate research companies* such as Dun & Bradstreet and Standard and Poor, provide information ranging from risk analysis to stock market analysts' reports about your competitors, for a fee. These are available electronically.

The system does not compete directly with any company, but it does provide a strategic advantage by building and maintaining a first-class personnel system. The shift of corporate operations from a *competitive* to a *strategic* orientation (of which competition is only one aspect) is significant as illustrated in the McKesson example that follows.

### *IT At Work* McKESSON DRUG COMPANY'S ECONOMOST

*I*NTEGRATING IT

...for Marketing and Production & Operations Management

McKesson Drug Company is a wholesale drug distributor, operating in a very competitive market and known for its extensive use of IT. One example is Economost, its electronic order-entry system for drug distribution.

McKesson had an important motivation to install Economost as early as 1975. Its primary customers were small, independent pharmacies at risk of going out of business because they were unable to compete with the large pharmacy chains. Economost was aimed at giving these pharmacies many of the advantages enjoyed by the large chains, thereby preserving their business.

Here is how the system works. The customer's order is phoned in, faxed, or transmitted electronically to McKesson's data center. The order is then entered into a computer and acknowledged. Next, the orders are transferred to an IBM mainframe for storage. Regional distribution centers pull their shipment orders from the mainframe at regular intervals and deliver the drugs quickly to the pharmacy that placed the order.

The IT has been combined with *structural changes.* The distribution centers are designed for maximum efficiency. For example, "pickers" walk through McKesson's warehouses, pushing carts on rollers and filling the orders. Warehouse shelves are arranged to correspond to pharmacy departments and are laid out to minimize the pickers' effort. Each distribution center has a minicomputer that runs the entire operation from bar-code order-identification labels that are used to sort and route the products. Distant customers that are not tied directly to a warehouse are served from "mother trucks," which are sent to switching points where their content is transferred into smaller trucks for local deliveries.

Benefits accrue to both customers and to McKesson. The benefits to customers include:

▶ More reliable order filling   ▶ Reduced inventory holding costs
▶ Reduced transaction costs     ▶ Faster delivery service

And the benefits to McKesson include:

▶ Rapid, reliable, and cost-effective customer order processing (the number of order-entry clerks has been reduced from 700 to 15).
▶ Sales personnel are no longer primarily order takers (their number has been cut in half)
▶ Productivity of the warehouse staff has increased by 17 percent and the volume has increased substantially.
▶ Purchasing from suppliers has been reorganized to tightly match actual sales.
▶ Customers are loyal to McKesson because of the benefits they enjoy.

The impact of Economost for McKesson has been significant. Although the company's total market share has not increased significantly, Economost changed the manner in which business is done so that both McKesson and its customer pharmacies have been able to survive and McKesson's revenues have escalated.

Economost has been expanded and modernized and is now incorporated using the Internet.

**For Further Exploration:** Does Economost provide McKesson with a sustainable strategic advantage? Why or why not? ▲

SOURCE: Based on Clemons and Row (1988) and corporate information (www.mckesson.com), 1998.

---

Some studies (see McNurlin [1991]) show that in the 1990s fewer top executives feel that IT holds the major key to competitive advantage. However, more than 90 percent of these same executives strongly agree that IT has a significant impact on profitability and even survival by facilitating a strategic advantage.

In order to understand the role of IT in strategic advantage, we now examine two of Michael Porter's classical models.

## ▶ 3.2 PORTER'S COMPETITIVE FORCES MODEL AND STRATEGIES

### THE MODEL

One of the most well-known frameworks for analyzing competitiveness is Porter's **competitive forces model** (1985). This model has been used to develop strategies for companies to increase their competitive edge. It also demonstrates how IT can enhance the competitiveness of corporations. The model recognizes five major forces that could endanger a company's position in a given industry. (Other forces, such as those cited in Chapter 1 and including the impact of government, affect all companies in the industry and therefore may have less impact on the relative success of a company within the industry.) Although the

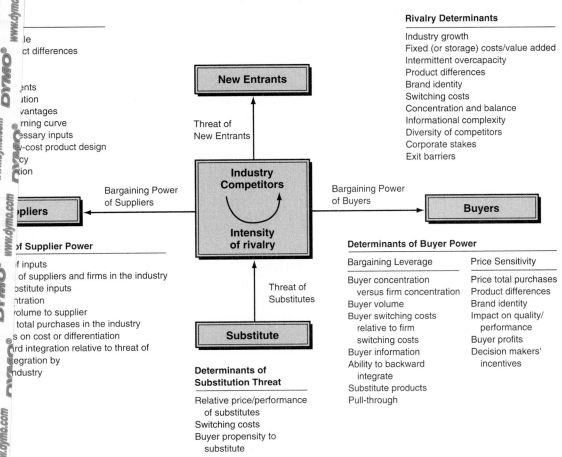

**Rivalry Determinants**

Industry growth
Fixed (or storage) costs/value added
Intermittent overcapacity
Product differences
Brand identity
Switching costs
Concentration and balance
Informational complexity
Diversity of competitors
Corporate stakes
Exit barriers

**New Entrants**

Threat of
New Entrants

**Industry
Competitors**

Bargaining Power
of Suppliers

Bargaining Power
of Buyers

**Buyers**

**Intensity
of rivalry**

le
ct differences

ents
ution
vantages
rning curve
essary inputs
v-cost product design
cy
tion

ppliers

f Supplier Power

f inputs
of suppliers and firms in the industry
stitute inputs
ntration
olume to supplier
total purchases in the industry
s on cost or differentiation
rd integration relative to threat of
egration by
ndustry

Threat of
Substitutes

**Substitute**

**Determinants of
Substitution Threat**

Relative price/performance
 of substitutes
Switching costs
Buyer propensity to
 substitute

**Determinants of Buyer Power**

| Bargaining Leverage | Price Sensitivity |
|---|---|
| Buyer concentration  versus firm concentration | Price total purchases |
| Buyer volume | Product differences |
| Buyer switching costs  relative to firm  switching costs | Brand identity |
| Buyer information | Impact on quality/ performance |
| Ability to backward  integrate | Buyer profits |
| Substitute products | Decision makers'  incentives |
| Pull-through | |

**Figure 3.4** Porter's five forces model (including the major determinant of each force). (*Source:* Porter [1985], p. 6.)

details of the model differ from one industry to another, its general structure is universal (see Figure 3.4). The five major forces can be generalized as follows:

1. The threat of entry of new competitors.
2. The bargaining power of suppliers.
3. The bargaining power of customers (buyers).
4. The threat of substitute products or services.
5. The rivalry among existing firms in the industry.

The strength of each force is determined by several factors of the industry structure, which are also shown in Figure 3.4. Most of the forces and determining factors Porter identified in the early 1980s are still valid and are related to the pressures identified in Chapter 1.

## RESPONSE STRATEGIES

Porter (1985 and 1996) suggests how to develop a *strategy* aimed at establishing a profitable and sustainable position against these five forces. To do so, a company needs to develop a strategy of performing activities differently than a competitor. Porter (1985) proposed the following generic strategies:

▶ *Cost leadership:* Producing products and/or services at the lowest cost in the industry. An example is Wal-Mart, which through business alliances supported by computers and by computerized purchasing and inventory management is able to provide low-cost products at its stores.

▶ *Differentiation:* Being unique in the industry, for example, providing high-quality products at a competitive price. Caterpillar provides its customers with a product maintenance service that no other competitor can match (see the opening case).

▶ *Focus:* Selecting a narrow-scope segment (niche market) and achieving either a **cost leadership** or a **differentiation** strategy in this segment. For example, several chip manufacturers make customized chips for specific industries or companies. Such customization is supported by computers. Another example is frequent flyer programs that allow airlines to identify frequent travelers and offer them special incentives. Some airlines have several million customers registered in the programs, which can be managed efficiently only with the help of computers.

▶ *Additional strategies:* In 1996, Porter expanded the generic strategies to include strategies that emphasize the sustainability of competitive advantage. These include "strategic positioning," improved operational effectiveness (internal efficiency), and customer service. Several of these were pointed out earlier by Wiseman and MacMillan (1984) and others.

Examples of the various strategies can be found in Section 3.6. Other examples can be found throughout the entire book. In certain industries there may be a greater emphasis on one strategy rather than another. For example, in the trucking industry, cost leadership is critical and companies are using innovative techniques to achieve it as illustrated below.

*I learned that differentiation in my job as an engineer is important in order to build better missiles than those of competitors.*

— *Dave Gehrke*

---

**IT At Work**    TRUCKING COMPANIES USE IT FOR GAINING COST LEADERSHIP

USING IT

...in Production & Operations Management

The trucking business is very competitive. Here are some examples of how IT helps in significant cost savings.

**J. B. Hunt** of Lowell, Arkansas, is a large truckload carrier. Its corporate PCs are connected to the fuel commodity market for minute-by-minute monitoring of the greatly fluctuating fuel prices and can trigger the purchase of fuel at the lowest possible prices (fuel costs represent 18–35 percent of the company's total operating cost). In addition, the system allows J. B. Hunt to pass on a very accurate fuel surcharge to its customers; the company tailors surcharges to individual customers on a percent-per-mile basis every week.

**Roadway Express,** another trucking company, owns several hundred gas pumps nationwide. Using computers, the company continuously compares six vendors' prices and related expenses to purchase the least expensive gas available at any given time.

**Leaseway Trucking** does not own pumps, but it centrally controls the purchasing of gas by over 10,000 drivers. Using geographical position systems (GPS), the company knows where its trucks are at any given time. Knowing where the nearest, least expensive gas station is located, corporate headquarters instructs drivers in real time, where to buy gas. This strategy has reduced fuel costs by 10 percent.

Computers are also used by large companies to monitor drivers' and trucks' productivity. Using telecommunication and GPS, companies can monitor the exact location of trucks at any given time, study their performance, and thereby improve it. In addition, large trucking companies use DSS and EIS to optimize their operations. IT provides large companies with a competitive edge against the small companies and allows truckers to survive in an extremely competitive business.

**For Further Exploration:** How can trucking companies achieve cost leadership? Can smaller truckers defend themselves against the giants? How? ▲

SOURCE: Based on *Computerworld,* April 7, 1991, p. 59, and on material available on the Internet, 1998.

Before we discuss how IT supports Porter's strategies, let us see how the generic model works.

## HOW THE MODEL IS USED

Porter's model is an industry-related model that shows the position of a company in its industry. Companies can use the model for non-IT analysis to suggest specific actions. However, in most cases, such actions involve the use of IT, as will be shown in the Wal-Mart example (see Figure 3.5).

Using the model one follows these four steps:

In Step 1, the players in each force are listed. An illustration of a competitive threat is electronic shopping, which may be a substitution for going shopping at a Wal-Mart store—the buyers can be anywhere.

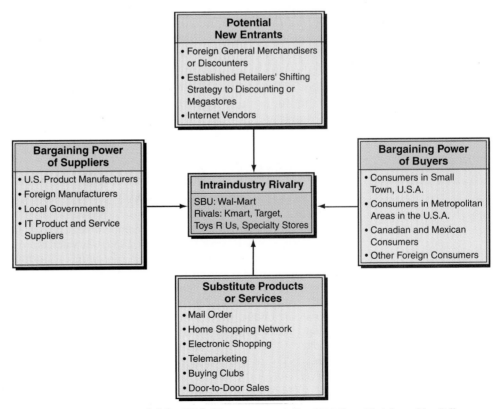

**FIGURE 3.5** **Porter's model for Wal-Mart.** (*Source:* Callon [1996], p. 40. Adapted by Callon from Porter, in *Harvard Business Review,* March/April, 1979, p. 141.)

In Step 2, an analysis is made to relate the determinants shown in Figure 3.4 (and similar determinants) to each player listed in Figure 3.5. For example, with respect to electronic shopping, we can check the switching cost of the buyers, the buyers' propensity to substitute, the price advantage of the electronic shopping, and so forth.

In Step 3, we can devise a strategy for Wal-Mart to defend itself against these forces, based on the specific players and the determinants. For example, to counter electronic shopping, Wal-Mart can provide a playground for children, hand out free samples of products, and recognize frequent shoppers personally. Wal-Mart can also respond by imitating the competition (the company actually did just that by introducing Wal-Mart Online).

In Step 4, we can look for supportive information technologies. An illustration of this step is managing frequent shoppers. It will be necessary to use a gigantic database and an online processing system with a good database management system and analytical capability to assess shoppers' activities accurately.

A similar process can be employed when the model is used by a Wal-Mart competitor. A competitor can use a similar process to portray all the determinants and then look for information technology to increase the competitive pressure on Wal-Mart.

Here are some additional examples of businesses defending themselves against the five competitive forces proposed by Porter.

▶ Extranets and EDI can shrink order times and costs and thus increase the profitability of the supplier and their desire to do business with your company. By being involved in the design phase, the supplier may help you design a higher quality part, or a less expensive one, and will be able to supply the part in a shorter time frame. This approach helped Chrysler to cut billions of dollars from the cost of their parts and helped the company both in competing in their industry as well as in reducing the bargaining power of their suppliers, as shown in the *IT at Work* case.

## *IT At Work*   CHRYSLER LINKS ELECTRONICALLY WITH SUPPLIERS—SAVES BILLIONS

The automotive industry is very competitive. Chrysler has been using the Internet and Lotus Notes to save billions. In 1989, Chrysler offered its parts' suppliers a plan in which they get an opportunity to share savings resulting from cost-cutting suggestions they made. The program was not very successful when it was conducted manually. In 1993, Chrysler lost $2.6 billion. Then the program went online! Using Lotus Notes (Chapter 5) and the Internet, the suppliers submit proposals to Chrysler's buyers. Since the proposals are online, they can be transferred quickly to evaluators, via the intranet. Furthermore, all communication among all participants is paperless and fast. Using special forms makes the filing of the suggestions easy. It then becomes easy to evaluate it. To expedite the process, the proposers must first discuss the idea, usually electronically with the part's buyer. Only if the buyer is impressed is the proposal submitted. Using the workflow capabilities of Notes, the proposals are routed to the appropriate evaluators. In 1998 Chrysler started to use the Web-based Lotus Domino to publish measurement reports to static HTML Web pages. Suppliers are able to view the reports using an Internet browser. Also, in the fall of 1997, Chrysler moved the system onto the Automotive Network eXchange (ANX) extranet. This is a private automotive industry extranet developed by the Automotive Industry Action Group, which is a collaborative effort between the Big Three and several thousand industry suppliers. The new ANX system functions like a giant intranet. It provides secured communication between Chrysler and its business partners. ▲

SOURCE: http://www.techweb.com/se/directlink.cgi?CWK19970428S0002, April 28, 1997, and *Internet Week*, March 9, 1998.

▶ Via the Internet or other telecommunication networks, Federal Express offers self-tracking of packages, thereby reducing the chance of new companies entering the overnight delivery business.

▶ Automobile manufacturers use computerized quality-control systems to make steel producers (the suppliers) more conscious of quality and reduce their bargaining power.

▶ Allowing the suppliers of funds to financial institutions (depositors, investors) to electronically transfer funds rapidly and easily is an example of influencing the bargaining power of suppliers through the use of IT.

▶ Many companies provide their customers with free software and other computer services, thus reducing the customers' bargaining power.

▶ Frequent flyer programs in the airline industry and discount brokering in the securities industry have significantly changed rivalries among existing firms.

▶ Domino's Pizza lost market shares to competitors. Using a sophisticated ordering system, the company is trying to lure customers, as illustrated in the example that follows.

## IT At Work   DOMINO'S PIZZA MATCHES CUSTOMERS' CALLS TO THE CLOSEST OUTLET

Domino's Pizza and AT&T teamed up to create a service that speeds up the ordering and delivery of pizzas to customers' homes and reduces transportation costs to the customers. To begin the process, the customer dials a special number (see Step 1 in the figure attached). The calls are received at the AT&T Store Locator Service Node (Step 2). Using an automotive number identification system, the Store Locator finds the address of the caller. The computer then matches the caller's address with the nearest open Domino's Pizza restaurant (Step 3) and dials that restaurant (Step 4). The entire process takes 7 to 11 seconds. An employee at the restaurant picks up the phone, talks with the customer, and arranges the delivery. The system is especially useful in large cities. For example, in Los Angeles there are over 300 Domino's restaurants, and many customers do not know which restaurant is nearest to them or which one is open for business at certain hours.

**INTEGRATING IT**

...for Marketing and Production & Operations Management

Domino's is facing competitive pressures, especially from Pizza Hut. Domino's share of the pizza delivery market has declined from close to 100 percent to less than 50 percent in less than ten years. The new service fundamentally changes the manner in which pizzas are being ordered. It is also used to generate bills immediately and to store market information about customers (for such purposes as issuing sales coupons). Using this technology, the company hopes to increase customers' loyalty and ultimately its market share. (Pizza Hut's reply to this innovation has been to set up an ordering system on the Internet.)

Domino's Pizza and AT&T have joined forces to test Store Finder, which matches customers' calls to the closest Domino's outlet.

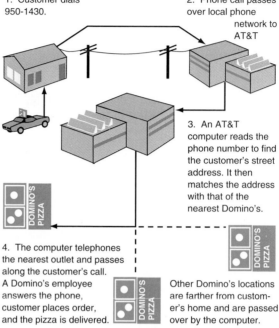

1. Customer dials 950-1430.

2. Phone call passes over local phone network to AT&T

3. An AT&T computer reads the phone number to find the customer's street address. It then matches the address with that of the nearest Domino's.

4. The computer telephones the nearest outlet and passes along the customer's call. A Domino's employee answers the phone, customer places order, and the pizza is delivered.

Other Domino's locations are farther from customer's home and are passed over by the computer.

AT&T plans to create similar alliances with other national businesses that depend on a network of outlets. Rental car agencies, florists, clothing stores, repair shops, insurance companies, and auto dealerships would be the most likely participants.

**For Further Exploration:** How can the new service improve the delivery of pizza? How can the information collected be used to improve marketing and customer service? ▲

SOURCE: Condensed from the *New York Times,* September 9, 1991 and Domino's Web site (www.dominos.com), 1998.

Ward and Griffiths (1997) provide a summary of the role of IT in each competitive force (see Table 3.2 on p. 89). Additional IT strategies have been proposed by others; some are described in Sections 3.4 and 3.5. Examples of IT facilitating additional strategies can be found in Section 3.6. A different way to analyze competition and the role of IT is provided in Porter's value chain model, which is the subject of the next section.

## ▶ 3.3 PORTER'S VALUE CHAIN ANALYSIS MODEL

According to the **value chain model** (Porter [1985]), the activities conducted in any manufacturing organization can be divided into two parts: *primary activities* and *support activities*. The five **primary activities,** are: (1) inbound logistics (inputs), (2) operations (manufacturing and testing), (3) outbound logistics (storage and distribution), (4) marketing and sales, and (5) service.

**Table 3.2** Impact of Competitive Forces and Role of IT

| Key Force Impacting the Industry | Business Implications | Potential IT Effects |
|---|---|---|
| Threat of new entrants | Additional capacity | Provide entry barriers/reduce access by: |
| | Reduced prices | exploiting existing economies of scale |
| | New basis for competition | differentiate products/services control distribution channels segment markets |
| Buyer power high | Forces prices down Demand higher quality Require service flexibility Encourage competition | Differentiate products/services and improve price/performance Increase switching costs of buyers Facilitate buyer product selection |
| Supplier power high | Raises prices/costs Reduced quality of supply Reduced availability | Supplier sourcing systems Extended quality control into suppliers Forward planning with supplier |
| Substitute products threatened | Limits potential market and profit Price ceilings | Improve price/performance Redefine products and services to increase value Redefine market segments |
| Intense competition from rivals | Price competition Product development Distribution and service critical Customer loyalty required | Improve price/performance Differentiate products and services in distribution channel and to consumer Get closer to the end consumer— understand the requirements |

SOURCE: Ward and Griffiths (1997), p. 86.

These activities together with the support activities are shown in Fig. 3.6.

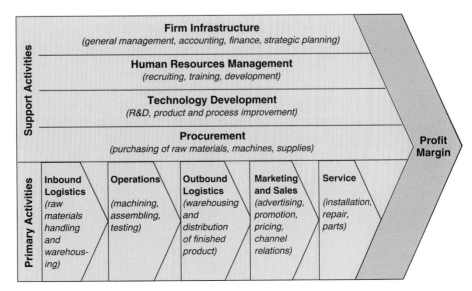

**FIGURE 3.6** Porter's value chain model for a manufacturing firm. (*Source:* Reprinted with permission of the Free Press, a Division of Simon & Schuster Inc. from *Competitive Advantage: Creating and Sustaining Superior Performance.* Copyright © 1985 by Michael Porter.)

In industry one hears the term "value added" frequently, and it is a part of every function in the value chain.

— *Dave Gehrke*

These primary activities are sequenced, and work progresses according to the following manner while value is added in each activity.

The incoming materials are processed (in receiving, storage, etc.) and so value is added to them in what is called inbound logistics. Then, the materials are used in operations, where more value is added in making products. The products need to be prepared for delivery (packaging, storing, and shipping), and so more value is added. Then marketing and sales deliver the products to customers. Finally, after-sales service is performed for the customer. All these value-adding activities result (it is hoped) in profit. They are supported by the following **support activities:** (1) the firm infrastructure (accounting, finance, management), (2) human resources management, (3) technology development (R&D), and (4) procurement. Each support activity can support any or all of the primary activities; they may also support each other.

A firm's value chain is part of a larger stream of activities, which Porter calls a **value system.** A value system includes both the suppliers that provide the inputs necessary to the firm and their value chains. Once the firm creates products, they pass through the value chains of distributors (who also have their own value chains), all the way to the buyers (customers), who also have their own value chains. Gaining and sustaining a competitive advantage, and supporting that advantage by means of IT, requires an understanding of this entire value system.

The value chain and value system concepts can be drawn for both products and services and for any organization, private or public. Although the initial purpose of the value chain model was to analyze the internal operation of a corporation to increase its efficiency, effectiveness, and competitiveness, the model was later used as a basis for explaining the support IT can provide. It is also the basis for the *supply chain* concept, which we present in Chapters 4 and 8.

## HOW THE MODEL IS USED

The value chain model can be used in different ways. First, we can use it for company analysis by systematically evaluating a company's key processes and core competencies. Attention is given to strengths and weaknesses of all activities and the values added by each activity. The activities that add more values are those that might provide strategic advantage.

Then we investigate whether or not by adding IT we can get even greater added value and where in the chain its use is most appropriate. For example, Caterpillar uses EDI to add value to its inbound and outbound activities; and it uses its intranet to boost customer service. In Chapters 8 through 11, we show through dozens of examples how IT supports the various activities of the value chain. The manner in which Frito Lay uses IT to support the value chain is shown in this *IT at Work* example.

*IT At Work*   FRITO LAY USES IT
AND THE VALUE CHAIN

Frito Lay, the world's largest snack food producer and distributor, is known for its extensive use of IT. Its strategic information system gives managers the ability to visualize nearly every element of the company's value chain as part of an integrated whole. The SIS is a central nervous system within the business that integrates marketing, sales, man-

*U*SING IT

...in Marketing

ufacturing, logistics, and finance, and it provides managers with information about suppliers, customers, and competitors.

Frito's employees in the field collect sales information daily, store by store, across the United States and in some other countries. They feed this information electronically to the company. The employees also collect information about the sales and promotions of competing products or about new products launched by competitors at select locations. By combining this field data with information from each stage of the value chain, Frito's managers can better determine levels of inbound supplies of raw materials, allocate the company's manufacturing activity across available production capacity, and plan truck routing for the most efficient coverage of market areas. The company's ability to target local demand patterns with just the right sales promotion means that it can continuously optimize profit margins and reduce inventory costs. Frito can also use this information to identify and react to environmental pressures and competitive forces.

**For Further Exploration:** Why does Frito Lay pay such attention to the value chain? Who are the customers? Can smaller competitors use such a system? ▲

SOURCE: Condensed from Rayport and Sviokla (1996), p. 78, and www.fritolay.com, 1998.

Second, the value chain can be used for an industry analysis, as shown for the airline industry in Figure 3.7. Once the various activities have been identified, then it is possible to search for specific information systems to facilitate these activities. For example, in "marketing and sales," advertising can be done on the Internet, and "agent training" can be enhanced by multimedia.

Finally, the model can be used either for an individual company or for an industry by superimposing different types of information systems that may help special activities. For example, EDI can help inbound and outbound logistics while virtual reality can help both advertising and product development.

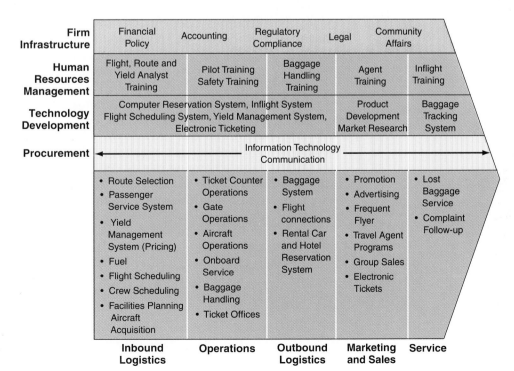

**FIGURE 3.7** The airline industry value chain superimposed on Porter's value chain. (*Source:* Callon [1996], p. 74.)

## 3.4 STRATEGIC INFORMATION SYSTEMS FRAMEWORKS

A framework for SIS is a descriptive structure that helps us understand and classify the relationships among strategic management, competitive strategy, and information technology. A framework is basically a classification language, a subjective conceptual model that helps us understand how IT can support the business. One reason for the abundance of frameworks is that there are many different types of information systems, as we saw in Chapter 2. Neumann (1994) advocates the use of SIS frameworks and provides a detailed description of (and references for) the most important ones. For additional frameworks and models see Elliot and Melhuish (1995). In this book, we will present only a few of the more important frameworks, basically to illustrate their role in the study of SIS.

We introduce the following:

▶ Three frameworks that are directly related to Porter's models.

▶ A customer resource life cycle framework.

▶ A global business drivers' framework for multinational corporations.

For other approaches see Buchanan and Gibb (1998) and Lederer and Salmela (1996).

### PORTER AND MILLAR'S FRAMEWORK

Porter and Millar (1985) concluded that competition has been affected by IT in three vital ways. First, industry structure and the rules of competition have changed. Second, organizations have outperformed their competitors by using IT. Finally, organizations have created new businesses by using IT. Based on this conclusion, they developed a five-step framework that organizations can take to exploit the strategic opportunities IT creates (see Box 3.2).

Porter and Millar have developed a m°atrix that indicates the high and low values of the interrelated information. They then use this matrix to identify the role that information plays in product offerings, as well as the process used to deliver the product to customers. The framework enables managers to assess the *information intensity* and role of IT in their businesses, thus setting priorities for using IT to achieve a strategic advantage. The basic idea is to determine how specific information technologies can enhance various links in the value chain, whether in internal operations or in the external marketplace. The framework relates the information intensity of a product's chain to the information content of the product.

One should distinguish between **information intensity** which measures the actual, or planned, usage of information (high intensity means high level of information usage), and **information content** which refers to the amount of information included in the creation of a product or a service. Information intensity, which is measured separately for each link in the chain, may be low for a high level of information content of a product, and may vary from one link to another. However, in many cases both concepts are difficult to measure, and in most cases companies use estimates that vary from expert to expert.

## *A Closer Look* BOX 3.2

### PORTER AND MILLAR'S FIVE-STEP PROCESS

**STEP 1.** *Assess information intensity.* Organizations need to assess the information intensity of each link in each of their value chains. Higher intensity implies greater opportunity. If the customers or suppliers are highly dependent on information, then intensity is high and strategic opportunities are likely to exist.

**STEP 2.** *Determine the role of IT in the industry structure.* An organization needs to know how buyers, suppliers, and competitors might be affected by and react to IT.

**STEP 3.** *Identify and rank the ways in which IT can create competitive advantage.* An organization must analyze how particular links of the value chain might be affected by IT.

**STEP 4.** *Investigate how IT might spawn new businesses.* Excess computer capacity or large corporate databases can provide opportunities for spinoff of new businesses. Organizations should answer the following three questions:

▶ What information generated (or potentially generated) by the business should be sold?
▶ What IT capacities exist to start a new business?
▶ Does IT make it feasible to produce new items related to the organization's current products?

**STEP 5.** *Develop a plan for taking advantage of IT.* Taking advantage of strategic opportunities that IT presents requires a plan. The process of developing such a plan should be business driven rather than technology driven.

SOURCE: Compiled from Porter and Millar (1985).

Several companies have used Porter and Millar's model successfully as shown in the *IT at Work* example that follows.

### *IT At Work* BENETTON SPA—A SUCCESS STORY

Benetton SPA, the highly successful Italian fashion retailer, has effectively exploited the information-intensive nature of the retail fashion industry to its own benefit. Though its products have very low information content, its cloth design production and marketing processes, which are part of its value chain, are highly information intensive (Step 1 in Porter and Millar's model).

As much as 20 percent of new fashion ideas depend on previous fashion ideas. Benetton has been able to leverage its expertise in information systems by recording its previous fashions on a laser-disc-based computer database, which can easily be accessed by personal computers via the intranet. Benetton can now reduce the time spent in designing new clothes, improving response time to customer requests (Step 2 in the model).

**I**NTEGRATING IT

...for Marketing and Production & Operations Management

By virtue of its innovative investments in information technology for production and marketing processes, Benetton has been able to respond to changes in fashion trends faster than anyone else in the industry. Its ability to provide overnight adjustments of production, via its highly computerized manufacturing environment, allows its worldwide licensees to receive items two to three weeks after ordering (Step 3 in the model). This is about three times faster than the major competitors.

Benetton developed a plan (Step 5 in the model) that enabled it to take advantage of IT. The company can delay production of garments until an order is placed by a franchisee, thereby eliminating inventory costs. The flexibility offered by the computerized manufacturing system allows Benetton to respond quickly to changes in fashion trends. It can delete slow-selling items from its product lines and expand the production of fast-selling clothes. For example, Benetton receives information from each of their stores immediately after each sale. This allows the company to dye their sweaters to match demand.

By utilizing the information-intensive nature of the fashion industry, Benetton has achieved tremendous success. From a meager $2,000 investment in 1955, Benetton has become a company with sales of $2.5 billion in 1987 and sales of over $5.0 billion in 1997.

**For Further Exploration:** What makes Benetton's business amenable to IT? What is the advantage to Benetton of using Porter and Millar's model? ▲

SOURCE: Condensed from Martin, J., "Benetton's IS Instinct," *Datamation,* July 1, 1989, pp. 15–16 and updated with information provided by the company, April 1998.

## WISEMAN AND MACMILLAN FRAMEWORK

Wiseman and MacMillan (1984) and Wiseman (1988) added the four defense strategies, *innovation, growth, alliance,* and *time,* to Porter's three strategies. Then, they created a matrix in which they use the defense strategies as rows and "suppliers," "customers," and "competitors" as columns. The cells in the matrix can direct IT applications. For example, in the row differentiation and column customer, one can utilize IT-supported mass customization. Thus, each cell in the matrix identifies the available strategies for an external industry force.

An important implementation question is how to find applications for the cells in this matrix. An example of a company that used this framework to find applications is GTE Corporation. The company employed a brainstorming procedure and identified more than 300 ideas for strategic applications of IT. (For other suggestions about how to find IT-based ideas see Bergerson [1991], Boynton et al. [1993], and Callon [1996].)

## BAKOS AND TREACY FRAMEWORK

According to Bakos' and Treacy's framework (1986), the two major sources of Porter's competitive advantage are bargaining power and comparative efficiency

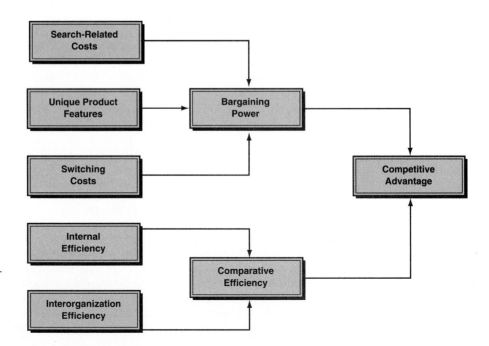

**FIGURE 3.8** Bakos and Treacy's causal model of competitive advantage. (*Source:* "Information Technology and Corporate Strategy: A Research Perspective," reprinted with permission from the *MIS Quarterly,* June 1986.)

(see Figure 3.8). These sources are determined by five specific items: search-related costs, unique product features, switching costs, internal efficiency, and interorganizational efficiency. Initially, IT efforts were aimed at increasing comparative efficiency. Lately, however, IT is also dealing with enhancing bargaining power activities.

Let us consider some ways in which IT can support the five activities (shown on the left side of Figure 3.8) that drive bargaining power and comparative efficiency from the point of view of a company planning a defensive strategy.

1. IT can increase the cost to a company's suppliers and customers of searching for other clients.
2. IT can create unique product features.
3. IT is known for its effectiveness in reducing costs and increasing productivity.
4. IT can increase interorganizational efficiency through *synergy*, enhancing business partnerships, joint ventures, and other alliances.

### CUSTOMER RESOURCE LIFE CYCLE FRAMEWORK

The customer resource life cycle (CRLC) framework (Ives and Learmouth [1984]) focuses on the relationship with the customer. The idea behind CRLC is that an organization differentiates itself from its competition in the eyes of the customer. Therefore, concentrating on the relationship to the customer is the key to achieving a strategic advantage. CRLC postulates that the customer goes through 13 fundamental stages in its relationship with a supplier and that each stage should be examined to determine whether IT can be used to achieve a strategic advantage. This approach is used, for example, in developing electronic commerce systems, as will be shown in Chapter 6. The 13 stages are listed in Table 3.3.

*Table 3.3* **Stages in the Customer Resources Life Cycle**

| Stage | Description |
|-------|-------------|
| 1 | Establish customer requirements |
| 2 | Specify customer requirements |
| 3 | Select a source, match customer with a supplier |
| 4 | Place an order |
| 5 | Authorize and pay for goods and services |
| 6 | Acquire goods or services |
| 7 | Test and accept goods or services |
| 8 | Integrate into and manage inventory |
| 9 | Monitor use and behavior |
| 10 | Upgrade if needed |
| 11 | Provide maintenance |
| 12 | Transfer or dispose of product or service |
| 13 | Accounting for purchases |

## 3.5   A FRAMEWORK FOR GLOBAL COMPETITION

Many companies are operating in a global environment. First, there are the truly global or multinational corporations. Second are the companies engaged in export or import. Third, a large number of companies face competition from products created in countries where labor and other costs are low, or where there is an abundance of natural resources. Finally, other companies have low-cost production facilities in these same countries. Thus, globalization is increasing rapidly. However, doing business in a global environment is becoming more and more challenging as the political environment improves and telecommunications and the Internet open the door to a large number of buyers, sellers, and competitors worldwide. The increased competition forces companies to look for better ways to do business and IT is frequently evaluated as a potential solution. Porter and Youngman (1995), for example, propose an approach that focuses on employment policies and government regulations.

### THE GLOBAL BUSINESS DRIVERS FRAMEWORK

Ives et al. (1993) have proposed a comprehensive framework that connects IT and global business. According to this framework, the success of companies doing business in a competitive global environment depends on the alignment of the information system and the global business strategy. This connection was demonstrated in the Caterpillar case, where a business strategy of strong support to dealers and customers worldwide was accomplished by developing an effective global information system.

The success of multinational firms and companies engaged in export and import, in a highly competitive global market, is thus strongly dependent on the link between their information systems and their business strategy. Information managers must be innovative in identifying the IT systems that a firm needs in order to be competitive worldwide and must tie them to the strategic business imperatives.

The global business driver framework provides a tool for identifying the business entities such as customers, suppliers, projects, and orders that will benefit most from an integrated global IT management system. The basic idea is to apply IT through a firm's **global business drivers.** Business drivers are quality, risk reduction, and suppliers, for example. They are considered to be drivers if they can benefit from global economies of scale and scope, and thus add value to the global business strategy. They are the means for assessing high-level global information requirements. The drivers look at the current and future information needs and focus on worldwide implementation.

The global drivers are determined by the global vision and strategy. To identify them, we can use the critical success factors (CSF) methodology described in Chapter 12. The CSF method can be applied across country units, functional areas, and levels of management. Once the drivers have been identified, they form the basis for the IT strategy as well as for the specific data, applications, and infrastructure needed. In addition, they determine the necessary organization structure and communication networks for sharing data across the entire corporation. The model can address both the firm's internal value chain and its external value system (like suppliers and customers). The model is shown in

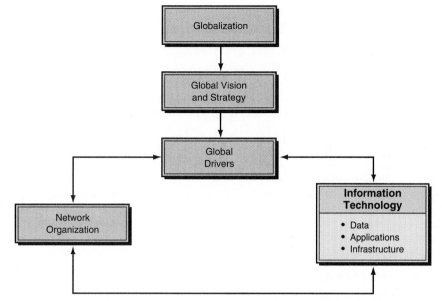

**FIGURE 3.9** Alignment of global vision with information technology using global drivers. (*Source:* Ives, et al. [1993]. Copyright © 1993 International Business Machines Corporation. Reprinted with permission from *IBM Systems Journal.*

Fig. 3.9. To build it one needs to pose a series of questions to uncover the global drivers and their importance. Representative questions are shown, together with business drivers and example entities in Table 3.4. These business entities are places where global coordination can provide a competitive advantage and where an integrated global IT application portfolio and infrastructure can realize that advantage.

Advances in Internet and electronic commerce are of special interest to global traders. First, many of the business drivers can be facilitated by the Internet, which is much cheaper and more accessible than private communication networks. Second, the Internet and EC are answers to several of the analysis questions shown in Table 3.4.

## ▶ 3.6 STRATEGIC INFORMATION SYSTEMS APPLICATIONS

The frameworks presented in the previous two sections suggest strategies that companies can use to gain strategic advantage. In this section, we provide examples of how companies use, and how IT supports, the following strategies:

▶ *Cost leadership.* By reducing the cost of products or services (e.g., by increasing productivity or decreasing inventories), a company can gain a competitive advantage with its customers. This strategy can also lead to reduced costs for customers and suppliers.

▶ *Differentiation.* By offering products or services that are significantly different from competitors', companies can sell more. Differentiation is achieved by offering unique features, high quality, and/or special services.

▶ *Growth.* Increasing market share, acquiring more customers, or selling more products strengthens a company and increases profitability in the long run.

### *Table 3.4* Analysis of Some Global Business Drivers

| Global Business Drivers | Analysis Questions | Examples of Entities |
|---|---|---|
| Joint resources | Can you electronically move work to countries with a highly skilled workforce and favorable wage levels?<br>Can you compose and manage work teams with globally dispersed members?<br>Do you manage human resources skills on a global level? | Employee location, employee skill, employee position, work assignments, employee compensation, standard work tools, relationship history between customers and employees |
| Rationalized and flexible operations | Can you move production around the world?<br>Can you rapidly move knowledge work around the world?<br>Can you share production resources across country boundaries?<br>Are you optimizing plant locations and production planning on a global scale? | Production plan, production schedule, product demand, plant capacity, vehicles, storage facilities |
| Risk reduction | Do you manage your monetary flows and the associated risks on a daily and hourly basis at the global level?<br>Are you vulnerable to political and economic conditions in particular countries? | Investments, pending investments, foreign exchange, assets, safety of assets |
| Global products | Are there opportunities for global product and brands?<br>Do you need to launch synchronized product introductions on a global basis? | Product standards, process, standards, legal requirements, repair records, marketing plans |
| Quality | Can you identify the source of a defective component on a global basis?<br>Are you conducting competitive benchmarking on a worldwide basis? | Competitive benchmarks, internal performance standards |
| Suppliers | Can volume discounts be negotiated on a global scale?<br>Do you know your global position with a major supplier? | Supplier information, parts and material, procurement standards, innovations |
| Corporate customers | Are your leading-edge customers becoming global?<br>Can you ensure consistent product and service regardless of the location?<br>Can you provide seamless worldwide ordering, order tracking, and billing?<br>Do the needs of global customers provide new business opportunities? | Customer information, customer quality standards, customer product specification, local preferences, preorder history, order status |

SOURCE: Ives et al., 1993. Copyright 1993 International Business Machines Corporation. Reprinted with permission from *IBM Systems Journal*, Vol. 32, No. 1.

▶ ***Alliances.*** Working with business partners creates synergy, allows companies to concentrate on their core business, and provides opportunities for growth.

▶ ***Innovation.*** Developing new products and services, new features in existing products and services, and new ways to produce them provides companies with a competitive advantage. Also included are innovative information systems applications.

> Internal efficiency is not only increased by layoffs and restructuring. We're always asking "why are we doing this?" and "how can we improve this process?" to make our department more efficient.
> — *Mike Rewald*

▶ *Improve internal efficiency.* The manner in which business programs are executed can be improved in many ways. Such improvements increase employee and customer satisfaction, quality, and productivity, while decreasing time to market. Improved decision making and management activities also contribute to improved efficiency.

▶ *Customer-oriented approaches.* Strong competition and the realization that the customer is king leads to a strategy that concentrates on making customers happy.

These strategies are interrelated. For example, innovation is achieved through alliances that reduce cost and increase growth. Cost leadership improves customer satisfaction and may lead to growth.

In this section we present several examples of how IT has successfully supported these strategies. Several of the cases illustrate support for more than one strategy, as you will see in the summary table at the end.

***Computerized Total Quality Management at Florida Power and Light.*** Florida Power and Light (FPL) is the fourth largest U.S. utility and has one of the best information systems in the industry. It is also a leader in implementing *total quality management,* and was awarded the prestigious Deming Prize, Japan's highest reward for quality.

*U*SING IT

...in Production & Operations Management

FPL's IT includes many interesting applications. One is the Generation Equipment Management System (GEMS), which tracks electrical generators at 13 oil-fired power plants. When a generator goes down, GEMS diagnoses the problem and recommends a remedy. Once the remedy has been approved, GEMS automatically budgets the repair, orders the parts, and issues work orders. GEMS also predicts mechanical breakdowns, allowing preventive maintenance work to be scheduled. This has cut downtime from 14 to 8 percent, saving about $5 million per year while also increasing customer satisfaction.

FPL has implemented over 20 different quality-control applications. These programs have reduced customer complaints by over 50 percent and have assisted the company in improving its financial position. Another application that has led to increased customer satisfaction is the Trouble Call Management System. It collects complaints from blacked-out customers and analyzes the causes of the malfunction. This analysis helped reduce the average black-out time from 70 to 48 minutes. Recognized all over the world for its computerized quality control programs, FPL created a subsidiary, Qualtec Inc., that sells quality control software to other companies including non-utilities. (SOURCE: Based on information provided by FPL, Miami, FL.)

*U*SING IT

...in Health Care

***Intranet Gives Geisinger a Shot in the Arm.*** Health Maintenance Organizations (HMOs) are growing very rapidly in the United States as an approach to containing health care costs. However, HMOs face strong competition among themselves and from physicians' groups. The rapid growth of some HMOs creates problems of inefficient operation and poor customer services, as in the case of Geisinger, a rural HMO in Danville, Pennsylvania.

The company, which grew through mergers and acquisitions, had 40 different IT legacy systems that needed to be upgraded and integrated. In 1993, Geisinger started to modernize its systems. An innovative approach required use of an intranet to deal with the complexity of this integration. Not only does its intranet allow Geisinger to integrate its systems, but it also allows the HMO to offer innovative services such as "Tel-a-Nurse," which provides ways for patients to communicate with their nurses. Patients can easily ask medical questions through the intranet. Moreover, Geisinger installed a clinical management system to work with its intranet. Doctors use digital cameras to take pictures of patients' injuries and the pictures are then accessible through the intranet. Having information about the patients on the intranet reduces unnecessary reordering of tests and X-rays.

The intranet is also used for patient education, human resources management, routine paper work, and library systems. Geisinger's radiology department, which performs diagnostic procedures such as X-rays, mammograms, and MRIs, has placed an electronic information kiosk in its waiting rooms. Patients can click on the homepage to find a list of 20 procedures, described in nontechnical terms, which are performed in the department.

Geisinger, which was named the premier network health care organization of 1996, uses its intranet to improve its quality, creativity, and innovation. Moreover, utilization of its intranet helps the company reduce costs and unnecessary work. (SOURCE: Condensed from *PC Week*, Feb. 3, 1997, pp. 27, 39.)

**I**NTEGRATING IT

...for Marketing and Production & Operations Management

*J.C. Penney Provides Custom-Made Suits.* In mass customization, J.C. Penney has responded to the trends in men's clothing by using information systems to take orders for customized men's suits. Systems linking J.C. Penney and its distributors, garment makers, and textile mills allow customers to select fabric, cut, and size at a J.C. Penney store and obtain a custom-made suit in a week. This is an interorganizational system that reduces cycle time and provides customization. The garment manufacturer makes the suits using CAD/CAM systems. This allows the manufacturer to run off an economical order quantity of an hour's worth of suits rather than a month's worth. The distributor can monitor orders regionally and adjust stock to reflect local tastes (a fabric that sells in the North may not sell well in the South). Rather than have one purchasing agent make blanket decisions a year in advance, the process is highly customized. A similar system is used by Levi Strauss to make custom jeans.

**I**NTEGRATING IT

...for Marketing and Accounting

*EDI Helps MacGregor Compete.* Makers of golf clubs and other golf equipment and accessories face tough competition. MacGregor Golf Company, a surviving pioneer in the industry, is no exception. MacGregor sells its products to large retailers such as K-mart and Service Merchandise. The company has a competitive advantage in terms of quality and customer service. But it has become much more difficult to sustain this competitive advantage. MacGregor recently decided to improve relationships with its retailers by retooling its information systems with state-of-the-art software and by using electronic data interchange (EDI) to enhance transaction processing. MacGregor receives and acknowledges purchase orders on the EDI, and transfers them for appropriate processing through an intranet. Customers are billed nightly. The system has increased order volume by 25 percent in the first year. It also saves the company $3 million each year on inventory costs. (SOURCE: Condensed from McLain, K., "Surviving into the Future," *EDI Work*, September 1996.)

*Otis Is Using IT to Block Competitors.* Otis Elevator's toll-free maintenance service number and self-diagnosing elevators blocked competing maintenance providers from the lucrative elevator maintenance business. With its online cus-

**U**SING IT
...in Production &
Operations Management

tomer service system, Otis can quickly troubleshoot calls because it has access to an elevator's maintenance history. It can locate and dispatch the appropriate mechanic from virtually anywhere in the country, and it records the mechanic's work for future troubleshooting purposes. Otis has subsequently installed telephones on elevators for direct maintenance communications, which further discouraged competitors' efforts. (SOURCE: Neumann ([1994]) and Jelassi, T., "Gaining Business From Information Technology," *European Management Journal,* March 1993.)

**U**SING IT
...in Production &
Operations Management

***The Port of Singapore Competes by Using Intelligent Systems.***  The Port of Singapore, the second largest container port in the world, is facing strong competition from neighboring ports in Malaysia, Indonesia, and the Philippines. In all the neighboring countries labor, space, utilities, and services are significantly cheaper. The Port of Singapore automates many of its port services to reduce costs. But its most innovative applications are the intelligent systems designed to reduce the cycle time of unloading and loading vessels. This cycle time is most important to ships whose fixed cost is very high. (Consequently, the stay in the port is very expensive.)

For example, an intelligent system is used to expedite trucks' entry into and exit from the port (using neural computing, it is down to 30 seconds per truck). Expert systems plan vessel loading, unloading, and container configuration, so cycle time can be as little as four hours (versus 16 to 20 hours in a neighboring port). Expert systems also are used for improved resource allocation that makes customers happy while reducing costs. (SOURCE: Condensed from Tung, L.L. and E. Turban, "Expert Systems Support Container Operations in the Port of Singapore," *New Review of Applied Expert Systems,* March 1996.)

**I**NTEGRATING IT
...for Marketing and
Production & Operations
Management

***Volvo Speeds Cars to Buyers via a Global Network.***  Selling new cars is becoming more difficult as global competition intensifies and trade agreements expand. Volvo of North America is known for its quality cars, but they are relatively expensive. Also, delivery times are slow, so customers have been going to competitors. A new strategy has been undertaken involving a complex network for both internal operations and external dealer applications.

The creation of a global ISDN-based network between the dealers in the United States and Canada and the headquarters in Sweden allows orders to be placed in real time; thus, inventories of cars and parts are reduced. In addition, Volvo believes that the new system helps the company understand who its customers are and what they really need. Overall, delivery time has been reduced from 12 to 16 weeks to 4 to 6 weeks for customized cars. The cost of doing business has also significantly been reduced along with the price of the car. Volvo's $35 million IT investment is expected to pay for itself in less than five years. (SOURCE: Condensed from *PC Week,* Feb. 3, 1997, pp. 71, 78.)

**U**SING IT
...in Health Care

***Computer Terminals at Customers' Locations: Baxter International.***  Baxter International Corporation acquired American Hospital Supply (AHS), in the 1980s. AHS had previously installed computer terminals in its clients' hospitals so that hospitals could order their supplies electronically. Quick deliveries allowed customers to maintain low inventories. This arrangement had a powerful effect on the hospital supply business. It significantly reduced the time between order placement and order delivery, essentially eliminating one person in the vendor-customer relationship in each hospital and giving the customer more control over its sources of supply.

Even more significantly, it controlled a channel of distribution and placed AHS in a position of considerable strategic advantage. Customers found it inconvenient to do business with other suppliers. Switching suppliers meant learning a new system, which was time consuming and error prone. Furthermore, competitors were thwarted from offering price advantages. American Hospital Supply had struck deals with suppliers two years earlier, and thus the company had price advantages and product-line breadth that was unmatched by any of its competitors. This system was one of the main reasons that the company was purchased by Baxter International. Others have emulated AHS's system, but the company still maintains a significant market advantage over its competitors. It took competitors years to duplicate the system. (See Chapter 1 of Neumann [1994] for more details.)

**I**NTEGRATING IT

...for Accounting and Finance

*Merrill Lynch's Cash Management Accounts System Creates a New Idea.* Merrill Lynch bundled together a number of financial services (brokerage, deposit accounts, credit cards, money market funds, and so on), resulting in a single combined monthly statement for each customer. The company achieved a differentiation strategy by delivering a service not provided by any competitor. The individual services were not new, but bundling them together was.

It took competitors several years to imitate the system, since they did not have the necessary integrated technology infrastructure. (Today, such a system could have been duplicated in only a few months.)

**I**NTEGRATING IT

...for Marketing and Production & Operations Management

*American Airlines Computerizes Reservation System.* The SABRE system was developed by American Airlines in the early 1960s. By the mid-1970s, the company began installing SABRE in travel agencies across the country. Despite the fact that there have been several attempts to copy it, SABRE continues to dominate the market. In fact, rather than developing their own reservation systems, many airline carriers now subscribe to SABRE.

The system did not show a profit until the early 1980s, but it has sustained its competitive advantage by continually adding new capabilities. For example, the airline has created an office automation software package for travel agencies, called Agency Data Systems, that enables travel agents to manage their offices and communicate with airlines and clients. SABRE now encompasses hotel reservations, car rentals, train schedules, theater tickets, and limousine rental. It even has a feature that lets travelers use the system interactively from their PCs at home.

Despite SABRE's comprehensiveness, several airlines now have similar reservations systems. Therefore, American Airlines must continue to look for further enhancements to SABRE to maintain its role as an industry leader. For example, easy SABRE (www.easysabre.com) is one of the most comprehensive on-line travel services that enables customers to make reservations and buy tickets.

*Odense Shipyard Built the Largest Ships in the World.* Odense shipyard in Denmark faced strong competition from South Korean companies, whose labor costs are about one-third less, and from the former East Germany, where the government subsidizes the shipyards. The company also faced competition from Japan, where high technology and ample financial resources (until 1997) are used ex-

**U**SING IT

...in Production &
Operations Management

tensively. Yet, Odense is able to compete successfully, especially in its area of specialty—building the world's largest ships. Information technology makes the difference between winning and losing.

For example, using IT Odense was able to successfully compete against the Japanese and to win a construction contract for a supertanker. A special department was established to find ways of using IT, plant automation, and robots. One hundred fifty special computer-aided design (CAD) machines help in expediting design by as much as 600 percent. In addition, CAD allows the creation of alternative designs that can be evaluated quickly for durability and efficiency. IT also helps in cutting costs. Additional software assists with labor and logistic decisions (there are more than 400,000 different parts in a large ship). IT also allows for just-in-time construction, a concept that enables operations with very little inventory. Many more things have been done with computers such as costing, scheduling, and project management.

IT is not only a condition for survival for Odense, but it also helped it capture 20 percent of the world market of container ships and 10 percent of the supertanker market. (SOURCE: Based on *Forbes, ASAP,* December 5, 1994.)

**U**SING IT

...in Finance

***Dun and Bradstreet Corporation Evaluates Credit.*** Dun & Bradstreet's (D&B) credit clearinghouse provides risk analysis to manufacturers, wholesalers, jobbers, and marketers in the apparel industry. D&B actually maintains and updates a database of credit ratings on approximately 220,000 businesses, of which the apparel industry is only a portion. Customers who pay D&B for the credit analysis of companies in the apparel business used to complain about long waiting periods and inaccuracies (it is difficult to update the material constantly), inconsistencies (such as different interpretations by different risk analysts), and slow response time. An expert system is now capable of handling more than 95 percent of all requests. As a result, response time has been reduced from about three days to a few seconds, and the credit recommendations are more accurate. As soon as there are changes in a retailer's data, the expert system reevaluates the implications for creditworthiness and informs its clients if needed. Similar systems are in operation in other business units at D&B. Together they help the company maintain its position as a leading information provider. The clients communicate with D&B via the Internet or value added network. Once a report is purchased from D&B it can be placed on the buyer's intranet and accessed by all authorized employees.

**I**NTEGRATING IT

...for Marketing and
Production & Operations
Management

***National Car Rental Makes a Quick and Satisfactory Car Pickup.*** National car rental has been an innovator in using information technology to become competitive in the car rental business. Research into issues that most concerned customers revealed that customers were tired of long delays, waiting in line, and providing the same information again and again (driver's license, car preferences, features in rental cars, and so on). Customers were also frustrated because cars were assigned to them; they could not select the exact model, color, or features. When customers tried to specify car model or color, it resulted in delays and upset other customers waiting in line.

After conducting a strategic planning exercise using the techniques discussed in this chapter—competitive strategy and customer resource life cycle—National Car Rental came up with an innovation called the Emerald Card. The Emerald Card prequalifies customers; they simply make a reservation, skip the line, and select a car of their choice from the rental lot. When they leave the lot, they use the Emerald Card as documentation to show that they rented a car and are leaving with it. When they return the car, they again use the Emerald Card to indicate the return and an invoice is generated automatically. (SOURCE: www.nationalcar.com.)

***Summary.*** The relationships between the suggested corporate strategies and the cases presented here are summarized in Table 3.5.

***Table 3.5*** **Company Cases and Competitiveness Strategies**

| Company | Cost Leadership | Differentiation (Quality, Speed), Customization etc.) | Growth | Alliances | Innovation | Internal Efficiency | Customer Orientation |
|---|---|---|---|---|---|---|---|
| American Airlines | | X | | X | | | |
| American Hospital Supply | | | | X | | | |
| Dun and Bradstreet | | X | | | | | X |
| Florida Power & Light | | | | | | X | X |
| Geisinger | | X | X | | | X | X |
| J.C. Penney | | X | | | | | X |
| MacGregor Golf | | | | X | | | X |
| Merrill Lynch | | X | | | | | |
| National Car Rental | | X | | | X | | X |
| Odense of Denmark | X | | | | | X | |
| Otis | | X | | | X | | |
| Port of Singapore | | X | | X | X | X | |
| Volvo | X | X | | | | | X |

## SUSTAINING A STRATEGIC ADVANTAGE

The strategic information systems of the 1970s and 1980s enabled a number of companies to enjoy a competitive advantage for several years. For example, Federal Express's package tracking system was copied by UPS, DHL, and others after only three to five years. The SISs of the 1970s and 1980s were primarily *outward systems*, which are visible and can now be duplicated quickly. Advances in computerized system development methodologies, such as CASE tools and object-oriented programming, allow companies today to duplicate visible systems in months rather than years. Therefore, the major problem that companies face now is how to sustain their competitive advantage. Ross et al. (1996) suggests the following three IT assets—people, technology, and "shared" risk and responsibility—as a way to develop sustainable competitiveness. Porter (1996) expanded his classical model to include strategies such as growth and internal efficiency to facilitate sustainability. Here are some ways to accomplish sustainability with the help of IT:

One popular approach is *inward systems* that are not visible to competitors. Companies such as General Motors and American Airlines, for example, use intelligent systems in a number of ways, but the details are secret. It is known that several investment companies are using neural computing, but again the details are not known. The use of such inward systems is sustainable as long as they remain a secret, or as long as competitors do not develop similar or better systems.

Another approach is to provide a comprehensive, innovative, and expensive system that is very difficult to duplicate. This is basically what Caterpillar is doing as demonstrated below.

---

## IT At Work  MAKING GLOBAL CONNECTIONS
### AT CATERPILLAR

Consider the following scenario.

A part on a Caterpillar machine operating at a copper mine in Chile begins to deteriorate. A district center that continuously monitors the health of all the Caterpillar machines in its area by remotely reading the sensors on each machine spots the problem in the making and sends an electronic alert to the local dealer's field technician through his portable computer. The message describes all the necessary details that sparked the alert and its diagnosis. Then, with the aid of a DSS and expert system, the technician validates the diagnosis and determines the service or repair required, the cost of labor and parts, and the risks of not performing the work.

The computer also tells the technician exactly which parts and tools are needed to make the repair. Then, the technician determines the best sources of the necessary parts and the times each source can deliver them to the dealer's dropoff point.

Next, the technician sends a proposal to the equipment owner (customer). If approved, a time frame is agreed upon and the technician orders the parts from the factories or warehouses that can supply the parts in time. At the factories and warehouses, the message triggers the printing of an order ticket and automatically sets into motion, if necessary, a robot that retrieves the parts from a storage rack.

**INTEGRATING IT**

...for Production & Operations Management, Marketing, and Accounting

An interactive manual on his computer provides the technician with knowledge about the latest best-practice procedures for carrying out the repair. As soon as the repair is completed, an invoice is printed. The machine's history is updated accordingly. Also, the repair's information is added to Caterpillar's databases, which helps the company spot any common problems that a particular model might have and thereby continually improves the machine designs.

Sound like science fiction? It isn't. Caterpillar has such a system in place around the world. Most of the pieces were completed by 1996—sensors in the machines, computers that diagnose problems and instruct technicians in how to make repairs, and the information system that ties together Caterpillar's factories, distribution center, dealers, and large customers. The system currently links some 1,000 locations across 23 time zones and 160 countries. The last two missing pieces—the remote monitoring system and the worldwide sharing of inventories by Caterpillar and its dealers and suppliers—were implemented in 1998.

The global information system is a critical part of Caterpillar's drive to expand its industry-leading position by minimizing the downtime and cost of operating and servicing its machines. The system promises to help Caterpillar, its dealers, and customers do an even better job of heading off major machine failures.

Another advantage is that by treating their inventories as one, Caterpillar and its suppliers, dealers, and customers are able to reduce their combined inventories significantly. (Caterpillar and its dealers have a total of about $2.5 billion worth of parts in their inventories.) Even bigger savings flow from reductions in the time that technicians require to diagnose and repair machines. The amount of time saved is in the range of 20 to 30 percent. When you consider that field service workers are billed out at $20 to $50 an hour, that's a significant savings.

With Caterpillar's models proliferating and becoming more complex, and with business outside the United States accounting for more than half its sales, the company believes that its ambitious information system is a necessity that support dealers and customers wherever they are.

Caterpillar is spending in excess of $250 million on the system, and that does not include their dealers' investments. That is a lot of money for their competitors to try to match. Will the competitors be able to copy the system eventually? Sure, it's possible, but it will take them considerable time. By that time Caterpillar will continue to move ahead, making it tough for competitors to catch up.

**For Further Exploration:** Why is such a system difficult to duplicate? What are the benefits to CAT? ▲

SOURCE: Condensed from Prokesch, S. E., *Harvard Business Review,* March/April 1996, p. 89.

Finally, another approach is to combine an SIS with structural changes. We alluded to this possibility in differentiating competitive advantage from strategic advantage. This is basically what is attempted in business processes reengineering and organizational transformation, which are the subjects of the next chapter.

## ▶ MANAGERIAL ISSUES

1. *Implementing Strategic Information Systems Can Be Risky.* The investment involved in implementing an SIS is high. Frequently these systems use new concepts. Considering the contending business forces, the potential damage, the probability of success, and the cost of investment, a risk analysis should be done.

2. *Strategic Information Systems Requires Planning.* Planning for an SIS is a major concern of organizations, according to Earl (1993). He surveyed 27 companies and reported on major SIS planning approaches. Exploiting IT for competitive advantage can be viewed as one of four major activities of SIS planning. The other three (which will be discussed later) are aligning investment in IS with business goals (see Chapter 12), directing efficient and effective management of IS resources (see Chapters 13 and 15), and developing technology policies and architecture (see Chapter 12). It is interesting to note that the Porter and Millar framework is one of several methods that can be used to plan and develop a strategy of how to use an SIS.

3. *Sustaining Competitive Advantage Is Challenging.* As companies become larger and more sophisticated, they develop sufficient resources to duplicate the successful systems of their competitors quickly. For example, Alamo Rent-a-Car now offers the Quick Silver card similar to National's Emerald card. Sustaining strategic systems is becoming difficult and is related to the issue of being a risk-taking leader or a follower in developing innovative systems.

4. *Ethical Issues.* Gaining competitive advantage through the use of IT may involve unethical or even illegal actions. Companies use IT to monitor the activities of other companies and may invade the privacy of individuals. In using business intelligence (e.g., spying on competitors), companies may engage in unethical tactics such as pressuring competitor's employees to reveal information or using software that is the intellectual property of other companies (frequently without the knowledge of these other companies).

> It is difficult to predict the IS changes to come, but to predict that there will be no changes is a recipe for disaster.
>
> — *Mike Rewald*

Companies may post unethical questions and place unethical material about their competitors on Internet newsgroups. Many such actions are technically not illegal, due to the fact that IT is new and its legal environment is not well developed as yet.

## KEY TERMS

Competitive advantage *80*

Competitive forces model *82*

Competitive intelligence *79*

Cost leadership *84*

Differentiation *84*

Global business drivers *96*

Innovation *77*

Information content *92*

Information intensity *93*

Long-range planning *77*

Primary activities *88*

Response management *77*

Strategic information system (SIS) *76*

Strategic alliances *76*

Support activities *90*

Value chain model *88*

Value system *90*

## CHAPTER HIGHLIGHTS *(L–x means learning objective number x)*

▶ Strategic information systems (SISs) support or shape competitive strategy. (L–1)

▶ SIS can be outward (customer) oriented or inward (organization) oriented. (L–1)

▶ Strategic management involves long-range planning, response management, and technological innovation. (L–1)

▶ SISs not only help companies perform above average, but they may also help companies survive tough competition. (L–1)

▶ Cost leadership, differentiation, and focus are Porter's major strategies for gaining a competitive advantage. (L–2)

▶ Porter's model of competitive industry forces is frequently used to explain how SIS works. (L–2)

▶ The value chain model can be used to identify areas in which IT provides strategic advantage. (L–3)

▶ Different frameworks can be used to describe the relationship between IT and attainment of competitive advantage. (L–4)

▶ Multinational corporations and international traders need a special approach to support their business strategies. (L–5)

▶ Some SISs are expensive and difficult to justify, and others turn out to be unsuccessful. Therefore, careful planning and implementation are essential. (L–6)

## QUESTIONS FOR REVIEW

1. What is an SIS?

2. Describe the three dimensions of strategic management.

3. List the major benefits of SISs.

4. Describe Porter's value chain model and its view regarding competition.

5. List Porter and Millar's steps of exploiting strategic opportunities.

6. Describe Porter's competitive forces model.

7. Explain the meaning of cost leadership, differentiation, and focus.

8. Describe the global business drivers model.

9. Compare the value chain to the value system.

10. List all the major variables in the Bakos and Treacy model that provide a competitive advantage.

11. Describe the customer resource life cycle framework.

## QUESTIONS FOR DISCUSSION

1. Review the opening case and *IT at Work:* Making Global Connections at Caterpillar and identify all the "outward-looking" and "inward-looking" aspects of Caterpillar's system.

2. Identify the information technologies used in Caterpillar's *IT at Work* story.

3. A prominent IT researcher said, "now that Caterpillar has strengthened its market leadership, cheaper labor is no longer the biggest issue. It is service, quality, mass customization, and lead time that count." Explain this statement.

4. Review the opening case (and read the original article if possible). Explain how the use of IT can help Caterpillar in its mass customization approach.

5. Discuss the relationship between the critical organizational responses of Chapter 1 and a differentiation strategy.

6. Provide three examples of IT being used to build a barrier to entry for new competitors or new products.

7. Discuss the idea that IS by itself can rarely provide a sustainable competitive advantage.

8. Give two examples that show how IT can help a defending company *reduce* the impact of the five forces in Porter's model.

9. Give two examples of how attacking companies can use IT to *increase* the impact of the five forces in Porter's model.

10. Why is it so difficult to justify SIS and why is it that some systems do not work?

11. Explain what unique aspects are provided by the global business drivers model.

12. What is the importance of business intelligence in SIS?

## EXERCISES

1. Review the applications in Section 3.6 and relate them to Porter's five forces.

2. The use of intelligent agents for *business intelligence* is on the increase. Conduct a search on vendors, software agents, and implementing companies.

3. Study the Web sites of Amazon.com and Barnes and Noble (www.barnesandnoble.com). Also, find some information about the competition between the two. Analyze Barnes and Noble's defense strategy using Porter's model and its 1996 extension. Prepare a report.

## GROUP ASSIGNMENTS

1. Assign group members to each of the major car rental companies. Find out their latest strategies regarding customer service. Visit their Web sites, compare the findings, and prepare a report on competitiveness in the car rental industry and the role of IT. Prepare a Porter's forces model to substantiate your findings.

2. Assign group members to each of the major airlines. Read Callon's (1996) chapter on the competition in the airline industry. Visit the Web sites of the major airlines. Explain how they deal with "buyers." What information technologies are used in the airlines' strategy implementation?

3. Each student is assigned to a company to which he or she has an access. The objective is to prepare a value-chain chart and discover how specific IT applications are used to facilitate the various activities. Compare these charts across the companies.

4. Assign members to UPS, FedEx, and the United States Postal service (see *Internet Week*, March 9, 1998). Each group will study the strategies of one company with respect to overnight delivery and the use of the Internet as a transport medium.

## INTERNET EXERCISES

**Note:** The URLs included here were current when the book went to press. However, they are subject to change without notice. Please consult the Turban web site (www. Wiley.com/college/turban2e).

1. McKesson Drugs has become the largest wholesale drug distributor in the world. Visit the company Web site (www.mckesson.com). What can you learn about its strategy toward retailers? What about toward its customers?

2. Enter the Web site of Dell Computers (www.dell.com) and document the various services available to customers. Then enter IBM's site (www.ibm.com) and compare the services provided to PC buyers. Discuss the differences.

3. Fruit of the Loom, Inc. (www.fruit.com) helps its wholesalers create Web sites that are used for advertisement of products to retailers. Compare this approach to what American Hospital Supply did with hospitals. Comment on the similarities in strategies. Use the Internet to collect information about both cases.

4. Enter Caterpillar's Web site. Identify the services and activities intended for the dealers and those for the users of the company's products.

5. Enter SEC's EDGAR database. Prepare a list of the documents that are available and discuss the benefits one can derive in using this database for conducting a competitive intelligence.

6. Locate which company takes orders for delivery of pizzas on the Internet (check the Web sites of Domino's Pizza, Pizza Hut, and local companies). Compare Internet ordering to telephone ordering.

7. Enter the Web site home.dti.net/shadow/sourcebook and review it. Why is it considered the "corporate intelligence sourcebook"?

# Minicase 1

## 7-Eleven Japan: Giving Customers a Voice

Ito-Yokado Company is Japan's most profitable retailer. In 1974, Ito-Yokado bought the franchise rights to 7-Eleven in Japan from Southland Corporation (Houston, TX). The first store opened in May 1974, and by 1998 the Japanese franchise grew to over 5,000 stores. In the meantime, 7-Eleven's parent company—Southland—was also expanding its operations. However, heavy debt forced it to seek court protection from its lenders. In an attempt to raise cash, Southland was forced to sell assets. In 1990, Ito-Yokado Corporation purchased 70 percent of Southland Corporation.

While 7-Eleven in the United States was losing a considerable amount of money, 7-Eleven Japan made over 40 percent profit on its sales ($680 million on sales of $1.44 billion in 1992). Such a high level of profit is extremely unusual, not only in Japan but in other countries. How could a franchiser of 7-Eleven achieve such a high profit margin while its parent company was filing for bankruptcy? The answer is: A *consumer-focused* orientation based on *information technology.*

7-Eleven Japan created in the early 1990s a $200-million information system for its stores in Japan. The purpose of the system was to (1) discover who the customers are and what they want and (2) create a sophisticated product-tracking system. How does such a system work? Every clerk in every store keys in *customer information,* such as gender and approximate age, at the time purchases are made. In this way, the company knows who buys what, where, and at what time of day, so it can track customer preferences. Clerks also key in information about products requested by customers that are not included in the store's inventory. Such information leads to stocking the appropriate products and even to the customization of products, manufactured by specially created companies in Japan.

The information system is also used for other purposes such as monitoring inventories. By implementing the *just-in-time approach,* a minimum inventory is kept on the shelves. However, because stores know customer's preferences, they seldom run out of stock. In addition, most stores have arrangements for quick delivery of products they sell, and so they do not need large inventories. Other uses of the information system are (1) electronically transmitting orders to distribution centers and manufacturers (via satellite), (2) determining which products to keep in each store (70 percent of the products are replaced each year), (3) determining how much shelf space to allocate to each product, and (4) tracking employee performance (for rewarding high performers).

In addition, the company maintains a high level of quality. A team of 200 inspectors visits 7-Eleven stores regularly. Even the company's president occasionally drops into stores incognito to check quality. Quality control data are collected and analyzed continuously by a computerized decision-support system at headquarters. Brands that do not meet strict quality requirements are immediately discontinued. Quality is extremely important in Japan, where fresh hot meals are sold at convenience stores.

As a result of its information system, 7-Eleven Japan has extensive knowledge of its market. It maximizes sales in limited space and optimizes its inventory level. Also, knowing exactly what the customers want helps the company to negotiate good prices and high quality with its vendors, who support the just-in-time approach. (About 20 manufacturers have special factories that make only or mostly 7-Eleven products.)

7-Eleven has also created a time-distribution system that changes the product mix on display in its stores at least twice a day, based on careful and continual tracking of customers' needs. The company knows that customers' needs in the morning are completely different from those in the evening. Space is very expensive in Japan, and the stores are small. So the system allows them to display the most appropriate items at different hours of the day.

The company is in the process of reshaping its U.S. operations. The Japanese are interested in changing the U.S. way of doing business before they improve the U.S. information systems. Thus, they are concentrating on transforming 7-Eleven into a high-quality, profitable, and truly *convenience* store operation.

In late 1997, 7-Eleven was the first convenience store chain to introduce Internet access stations in their Seattle area stores. These stations allow customers that do not have computers to access the Internet by paying a user fee to 7-Eleven. In 1998 it introduced a computerized system to track inventory and forecast sales in the United States.

### Questions for Minicase 1

1. 7-Eleven competes both with other chains of convenience stores and independent stores. What

competitive advantages can you identify in this case?

2. Which of the five forces of Porter are countered by the 7-Eleven systems?

3. Which strategies of those suggested in the various frameworks are noticeable in this case?

4. Which of the business pressures discussed in Chapter 1 are evidenced in this case?

5. Which of the corporate response activities of Chapter 1 are evidenced in this case?

6. Is the system infringing on the customer's privacy? Why or why not?

SOURCE: Based on stories in *Business Week,* January 1992 and Sept. 1, 1997, and on information provided by 7-Eleven, 1998. See also *Forbes,* June 21, 1993, pp. 44–45 and www.businesswire .com, Sept. 15, 1997.

# Minicase 2

## New Entrants to the Dutch Flower Market

The Dutch auction flower market in the Netherlands is the largest in the world, attracting sellers from dozens of countries such as Thailand, Israel, and East African States; 3,500 varieties of flowers are sold in 120 auction groups. The auctions are semiautomated; buyers and sellers must come to one location where the flowers are shown to the buyers. The auctioneer of each variety of flower uses a clock with a large hand which he starts at a high price and drops until a buyer stops the clock by pushing an ordering button. Using an intercom, the quantity is clarified and the clock hand is reset, at the high price, for the next batch of flowers. The process continues until all the flowers are sold.

In September 1994, the Dutch growers who own the auction organization (called the Dutch Flower Auctions, or DFA) decided to ban foreign growers from participating during the summer months in order to protect the Dutch growers from low prices from abroad. By March 1995 some foreign growers, together with several local buyers, created a competing auction called the Tele Flower Auction (TFA). TFA is an *electronic auction* that enables its initiators to penetrate the Dutch flower market. Here is how it works:

In the TFA, buyers can bid on flowers via their PCs from any location connected to the network. The process is similar to the traditional one and the auction clock is shown on the PC screen. The buyers can stop the clock by pushing the space bar. The auctioneer then converses with the buyers by telephone, a sale is concluded, and the clock is reset. The flowers are not physically visible to the buyers; however, a large amount of relevant information is available, for example, the time flowers are picked up, quality, and arrival time to the Netherlands. The buyers are alerted to a specific auction, in real time, when their item of interest is auctioned.

Initial results indicated that buyers and growers are enthusiastic. While prices are about the same as in the regular auctions, the process is much quicker, and the after-sale delivery is much faster than in other markets (less than half an hour). A major issue could be the quality of the flowers, since the buyers cannot see them; but the quality is actually better since there is less handling (no need to bring the flowers to an auction site) and the growers stand behind their products. As a result, there is enough trust so that everyone is happy.

The TFA has gained considerable market share at the expense of existing organizations—a real new-entrant success story. Using IT, the new entrant quickly built a competitive advantage. While some minor competitors decided to install a similar system in order to compete immediately, it took the major Dutch Growers Association more than a year to cancel the import restrictions and implement their own electronic clearinghouse for flowers.

### Questions for Minicase 2

1. Why was the TFA successful?

2. How can the TFA sustain its success while competitors are copying its new concept?

3. The cancellation of the import restrictions is not working too well for the Dutch Growers Association. Advise the CEO of the DFA what to do.

4. Can this concept be extended to the Internet? If so, how can real-time auctions be implemented?

SOURCE: van Heck, E., et al., "New Entrants and the Role of IT—Case Study: The Tele Flower Auction in the Netherlands," *Proceedings of the 30th Hawaiian International Conference on Systems Sciences,* Hawaii, January 1997. For details see http://kam-bik.stern.nyu.edu/teaching/cases/auction/flowerscase/html. Also see *Electronic Markets,* Dec. 1997.

# REFERENCES AND BIBLIOGRAPHY

1. Atkinson, A. A., "A Stakeholder Approach to Strategic Performance Management," *Sloan Management Review,* Spring 1997.

2. Bakos, J. Y., and M. W. Treacy, "Information Technology and Corporate Strategy: A Research Perspective," *MIS Quarterly,* June 1986.

3. Bergerson, F., et al., "Identification of Strategic Information Systems Opportunities: Applying and Comparing Two Methodologies," *MIS Quarterly,* March 1991.

4. Boynton, A. C., et al., "New Competitive Strategies: Challenges to Organizations and Information Technologies," *IBM Systems Journal,* Vol. 32, No. 1, 1993.

5. Buchanan, S., and F. Gibb, "The Information Audit: An Integrated Strategic Approach," *Inter. Jour. of Info. Mgt.,* Feb. 1998.

6. Callon, J. D., *Competitive Advantage Through Information Technology,* New York: McGraw Hill, 1996.

7. Ciborra, C., and T. Jelassi (eds.), *Strategic Information Systems: A European Perspective,* Chichester (UK): John Wiley & Sons, 1994.

8. Clemons, E. K., and M. Row, "A Strategic Information System: McKesson Drug Company's Economost," *Planning Review,* September/October 1988.

9. Davenport, T. H., *Process Innovation: Reengineering Work Through Information Technology,* Boston: Harvard Business School Press, 1993.

10. Elliot, S., and P. Melhuish, "A Methodology for the Evaluation of IT for Strategic Implementation," *Journal of Information Technology,* Vol. 10, 1995.

11. Ives, B., and G. P. Learmouth, "The Information System as a Competitive Weapon," *Communications of the ACM,* December 1984.

12. Ives, B., et al., "Global Business Drivers: Aligning IT to Global Business Strategy," *IBM Systems Jurnal,* Vol. 32, No. 1, 1993.

13. Kim, W. C., and R. Mauborgne, "Value Innovation: The Strategic Logic of High Growth," *Harvard Bus. Review,* Jan./Feb. 1997.

14. Lederer, A. L., and H. Salmela, "Toward a Theory of Strategic Information Systems Planning," *Jour. of Strategic Information Systems,* Vol. 5, 1996.

15. Loebbecke, C., and P. Powell, "Competitive Advantage from IT in Logistics: The Integrated Transport Tracking System," *Inter. Jour. of Info. Mgt.,* Feb. 1998.

16. Luftman, J., *Competing in the Information Age: Strategic Alignment in Practice,* London: Oxford University Press, 1996.

17. McNurlin, B. (ed.), *Trends in Information Technology,* Chicago, IL: Andersen Consulting, Fall 1991.

18. Mata, F. J., et al., "Information Technology and Sustained Competitive Advantage: A Resource-based Analysis," *MIS Quarterly,* December 1995.

19. Neumann, S., *Strategic Information Systems—Competition Through Information Technologies,* New York: Macmillan, 1994.

20. Palvia, P. C., et al., "The Prism System: A Key to Organizational Effectiveness at Federal Express Corporation," *MIS Quarterly,* December 1992.

21. Porter, M. E., *Competitive Advantage: Creating and Sustaining Superior Performance,* New York: Free Press, 1985.

22. Porter, M. E., "What Is a Strategy?," *Harvard Business Review,* November/December 1996.

23. Porter, M. E., and V. E. Millar, "How Information Gives You Competitive Advantage," *Harvard Business Review,* July/August 1985.

24. Porter, M. E., and J. A. Youngman, *Keeping America Competitive: Empoyment Policy for the Twenty-first Century,* Lakewood, CO: Glenbridge Publishing, 1995.

25. Powell, T. C., and A. Dent/Micallef, "IT as Competitive Advantage: The Role of Human, Business, and Technological Resources," *Strategic Management Journal,* May 1997.

26. Power, B. S., and R. Sharda, "Obtaining Business Intelligence on the Internet," *Long Range Planning,* April 1997.

27. Prakash, A., "The Internet as a Global Strategic IS Tool," *Information Systems Management,* Summer 1996.

28. Ramarapu, N. K., and A. A. Lado, "Linking Information Technology to Global Business Strategy to Gain Competitive Advantage: An Integrative Model," *Journal of Information Technology,* Vol. 10, 1995.

29. Rayport, J. F., and J. J. Sviokla, "Exploring the Virtual Value Chain," *Harvard Business Review,* November/December 1996.

30. Ross, J. W. et al., "Develop Long-term Competitiveness Through IT Assets," *Sloan Management Review,* Fall 1996.

31. Synnott, W. R., *The Information Weapon: Winning Customers and Markets with Technology,* New York: John Wiley & Sons, 1987.

32. Ward, J., and P. Griffiths, *Strategic Planning for Information Systems,* 2nd ed., Chichester: John Wiley & Sons, 1997.

33. Wiseman, C., *Strategic Information Systems,* Homewood, IL: Dow Jones-Irwin, 1988.

34. Wiseman, C., and I. MacMillan, "Creating Competitive Weapons from Information Systems," *Journal of Business Strategy,* Fall 1984.

35. Wreden, W., "Get Smart—Competitive Intelligent Networks," *Beyond Computing,* January/February 1994.

# CHAPTER 4

# Supply Chain, Enterprise Resource Planning, and Business Processes Reengineering

## Learning Objectives

*After studying this chapter, you will be able to:*

① Understand the concept of the supply chain, its importance, and management.

② Describe the problems of managing the supply chain and some innovative solutions.

③ Trace the evolution of software that supports activities along the supply chain.

④ Define business processing reengineering (BPR) and understand its relationship with the supply chain.

⑤ Describe the networked organization and identify its benefits.

⑥ Demonstrate the role of IT in supporting BPR.

⑦ Describe mass customization, cycle time reduction, self-directed teams, and empowerment.

⑧ Define business alliances and virtual corporations.

⑨ Understand the relationships among enterprise resources planning (ERP), supply chain management (SCM), and electronic commerce.

Note: Appendix on the basics of BPR can be found on our Web site (www.wiley.com/college/turban2e).

112

# HOW DELL REENGINEERED AND MANAGED ITS SUPPLY CHAIN TO BECOME #1

## The Problem

MICHAEL DELL started his business as a student, from his university dorm, by using a mail-order approach to selling PCs. This changed the manner by which PCs were sold. The customer did not have to come to a store to buy the computer, and Dell was able to customize the computer to the specifications of the customer. The direct mail approach enabled Dell to underprice his rivals, who were using distributors and retailers, by 10 percent. For several years the business grew slowly, but Dell constantly captured market share. In 1993, the PC market leader, Compaq, decided to drastically cut prices to drive Dell out of the market. As a result of the price war, Dell Computers Inc. had a $65 million loss from inventory writedowns in the first 6 months of 1993 alone. The company was on the verge of bankruptcy.

## The Solution

Dell realized that the only way to win the marketing war was to introduce fundamental changes (termed *reengineering*) in its own business and along the supply chain from its suppliers all the way to its customers. In addition to competing on *price* and *quality,* Dell started competing on *speed.* Since 2000, if you order a standard PC on any working day, the computer will be on the delivery truck the next day; a complex custom-made PC will be delivered in 5 days or less.

Among the innovations used to reengineer the business, many of which are IT-supported, were:

▶ Dell builds many computers only after they are ordered. This is done by using just-in-time manufacturing, which also enables quick deliveries, low inventories, little or no obsolescence, and lower marketing and administrative costs.
▶ Dell uses an approach called *mass customization,* meaning that it produces large quantities of customized products, at a low cost.
▶ Component warehouses, which are maintained by Dell's suppliers, are located within 15 minutes of Dell factories. Not only can Dell get parts quickly, but also it can get parts that are up to 60 days newer than those of its major competitors.

▶ Shipments, which are done by UPS and other carriers, are all arranged by electronic mail.
▶ Most orders from customers and to suppliers are done on the Web.
▶ Dell collaborates electronically with its major buyers to pick customers' brains.
▶ Most of Dell's sales are to large corporations. While individual buyers want their units customized, large corporations may prefer standard computers. For example, Eastman Chemical Company needed 10,000 PCs, all with exactly the same parts and software, regardless of *when* and *where* in the world they were needed. The standardization saved operations and training maintenance costs of about $5 million annually for Eastman. Dell was the only vendor that was able to fulfill this need.
▶ Dell's new PC models are tested at the same time as the networks that they are on are tested. This cooperation with another vendor reduced the testing period from 60 or 90 days to 15.
▶ Dell's employees constantly monitor productivity and rate of return on investments, on all products.

## What Role Did Information Technology Play?

Most significant for Dell has been the emergence of *electronic commerce.* In 2000, Dell was selling more than $2.5 million worth of computers each day on its Web site, and this amount was growing by 10 percent per month! In 1999 Dell added electronic auctions as a major marketing channel. Dell is aiming to sell most of its computers on the Web (www.dell.com). Customers can create their own Dell home page and track their orders online, to see if the computers are in production or already on the shipping track. Customers can access detailed diagrams of the computers and get information about troubleshooting. By using viewer-approved configurations and pricing and by eliminating paperwork, Dell has been able to cut administrative process expenses by 15 percent. In addition, Dell created home pages for its biggest buyers, such as Eastman Chemical, Monsanto, and Wells Fargo. These sites enable customers' employees to place orders quickly and easily. These employees can also order PCs for their own homes and receive the corporate price! The electronic ordering makes customers happy, but it also enables Dell to collect payments very quickly. Dell is frequently cited as an example of a top customer relationship management (CRM) provider.

Dell is using several other information technologies, including e-mail, EDI, video teleconferencing, electronic procurement, computerized faxes, an intranet, DSS, Web-based call center and more. Computerized manufacturing systems tightly link the entire demand and supply chains from suppliers to buyers. This system is the foundation on which the "building-to-order" strategy rests.

Dell created customized Web pages to its top 30 suppliers on an extranet. Thus suppliers' employees can log on to view actual demand, request forecasts, and find out who Dell's customers are and how many Dell computers they order. This helps the suppliers to better gauge demand which helps them to improve their production schedules in order to meet Dell's just-in-time delivery requirements in an economical way.

Dell also passes along data about its defect rates, engineering changes, and product enhancements to these suppliers. Since both Dell and its suppliers are in constant communication, the margin for error is reduced. Also, employees are now able to collaborate in real time on product designs and enhancements. In turn, suppliers are required to share sensitive information with Dell, such as their own quality problems. It was easy to get suppliers to follow Dell's lead because they also reap the benefits of faster cycle times, reduced inventory, and improved forecasts.

Dell also uses the Internet to create a community around its supply chain. The Web sites all have links to bulletin boards where partners from around the world can exchange information about their experiences with Dell and its value chain. The Internet provides the capacity to improve the flow of information, eliminate paper-based functions, and link global organizations. Dell is also using the Internet to form tighter links with customers. For many of its business users, the company has created Premier Pages containing approved configurations, prenegotiated prices, and workflow capabilities, so when an employee in a business client organization requests a new computer, the order is automatically routed to the appropriate person within that client organization for approval.

**The Results**

By the year 2000, Dell has become the #1 PC seller. It is considered one of the world's best-managed and profitable companies. Its stock zoomed over 3,000% in the period 1995–2000.

SOURCE: Compiled from several articles in *Business Week* (1997–99), *Information Week* (1998–2000), cio.com (2000), and www.us.dell.com/dell/media.

## 4.1 ESSENTIALS OF THE SUPPLY AND VALUE CHAINS

The Dell case demonstrates the following points:

1. By introducing a new business model one can change the manner in which business is done and may even capture the leadership in its industry.

2. By introducing major customer-related changes, Dell enables customers to order what they like, do it from home, and get it quickly, at a very competitive price and with high quality. Improved communications and customer service are the cornerstones of Dell's success.

3. Another major success factor in Dell's plans was the improvements made in its logistics system along the entire supply chain. Using Web technologies, Dell integrated its own suppliers into its supply chain efficiently and effectively.

4. Dell created flexible and responsive manufacturing systems.

5. The changes introduced by Dell were so fundamental that they are considered to be a complete reengineering.

6. Dell supports all of the above by extensive use of information technologies. Of special interest is its use of *electronic commerce*, the *Internet*, and *intranets*.

Dell implemented successfully the concepts of *supply chain management, enterprise resources planning,* and *business processing reengineering* which are the topics of this chapter, as well as *customer relationship management* which is described in Chapter 8.

## DEFINITIONS AND BENEFITS

Initially the concept of a *supply chain* referred to the flow of materials from their sources (suppliers) to the company, and then inside the company to places where they were needed. There was also recognition of a **demand chain,** which described the process of taking and fulfilling orders. Soon it was realized that these two concepts are interrelated, so they were integrated under the single concept of *extended supply chain,* or just *supply chain.*

**DEFINITION.** A **supply chain** refers to the flow of materials, information, and services from raw material suppliers through factories and warehouses to the end customers. A supply chain also includes the *organizations* and *processes* that create and deliver these products, information, and services to the end customers. It includes many tasks such as purchasing, materials handling, production planning and control, logistics and warehousing inventory control, and distribution and delivery.

The function of the **supply chain management (SCM)** is to plan, organize, and coordinate all the supply chain's activities. Today the concept of SCM refers to a total systems approach to managing the entire supply chain.

**BENEFITS.** The goals of modern SCM are to reduce uncertainty and risks in the supply chain, thereby positively affecting inventory levels, cycle time, business processes, and customer service. All these benefits contribute to increased profitability and competitiveness. The benefits of supply chain management have long been recognized both in business and in the military. Clerchus of Sparta said, as early as 401 B.C., that the survival of the Greek army depended not only upon its discipline, training, and morale, but also upon its supply chain. The same idea was echoed later by famous generals such as Napoleon and Eisenhower.

In today's competitive business environment, the efficiency and effectiveness of supply chains in most organizations are critical for their survival and are greatly dependent upon the supporting information systems.

## THE COMPONENTS OF SUPPLY CHAINS

The term *supply chain* comes from a picture of how the partnering organizations in a specific supply chain are linked together. As shown in Figure 4.1, a simple supply chain links a company that manufactures or assembles a product (the entity in the middle of the chain) with its suppliers (on the left) and its distributors and customers (on the right). The upper part of the figure shows a generic supply chain; the lower part shows a specific example of a cereal manufacturer.

Note that the supply chain involves three parts:

1. ***Upstream supply chain.*** This part includes the organization's *first-tier* suppliers (which themselves can be manufacturers and/or assemblers) and their suppliers. Such relationship can be extended, to the left, in several tiers, all the way to the origin of the material (e.g., mining ores, growing crops).

2. ***Internal supply chain.*** This part includes all the processes used by an organization in transforming the inputs of the suppliers to outputs, from the

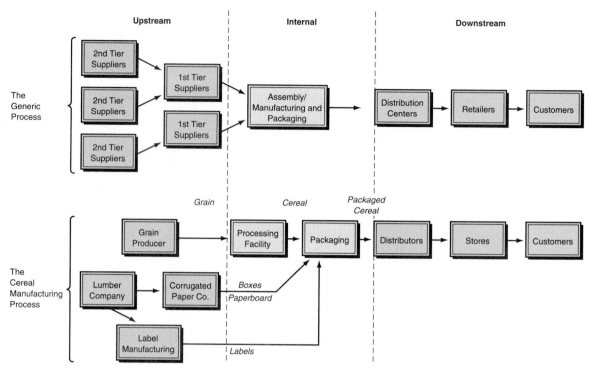

**FIGURE 4.1 Supply chains.** (*Source*: Adapted from Handfield and Nichols, *Introduction to Supply Chain Management* (Prentice Hall, 1999).)

time materials enter the organization to the time that the product goes to distribution outside the organization.

**3. *Downstream supply chain.*** This part includes all the processes involved in delivering the product to final customers. Looked at very broadly, the supply chain actually ends when the product reaches its after-use disposal—presumably back to Mother Earth somewhere.

As you can see, a supply chain involves a **product life cycle** from "dirt to dust." However, supply chain is more than just the movement of tangible inputs, since it also includes the movement of information and money and the procedures that support the movement of a product or a service. Finally, the organizations and individuals involved are part of the chain as well.

Supply chains come in all shapes and sizes and may be fairly complex, as shown in Figure 4.2. As can be seen in the figure, the supply chain for a car manufacturer includes hundreds of suppliers, dozens of manufacturing plants (parts) and assembly plants (cars), dealers, direct business customers (fleets), wholesalers (some of which are virtual, e.g., www.cardirect.com), customers, and support functions such as product engineering and purchasing.

Notice that in this case the chain is not strictly linear as it was in Figure 4.1. Here we see some loops in the process. In addition, sometimes the flow of information and even goods can be bidirectional. For example, not shown in this figure is the *return* of cars (known as **reverse logistics**) to the dealers in cases of defects or recalls by the manufacturer. Also notice that the supply chain is much more than just being physical. It includes both information and financial flows. As a matter of fact the supply chain of a service or a digitizable product may not include any physical materials.

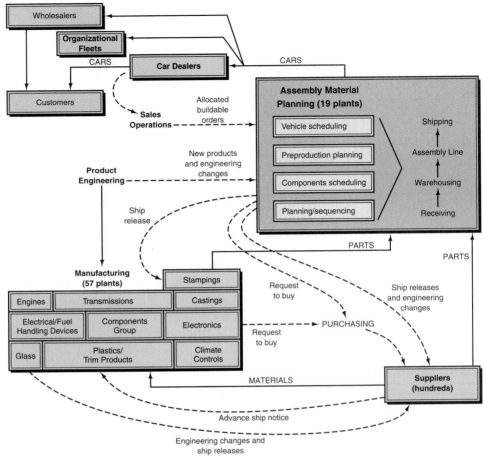

**FIGURE 4.2** An automotive supply chain. (*Source*: Modified from Handfield and Nichols, *Introduction to Supply Chain Management* (Prentice Hall, 1999).)

The flow of goods, services, information, and financial resources is usually designed not only to effectively transform raw items to finished products and services, but also to do so in an efficient manner. Specifically, the flow must be followed with an increase in value, which can be analyzed by the *value chain*.

## THE SUPPLY CHAIN AND THE VALUE CHAIN

In Chapter 3 we introduced the concepts of the value chain and the value system. A close examination of these two concepts shows that they are closely related to the supply chain. The *primary activities* of the value chain correspond to the generic model of Figure 4.1 and were shown as a chain in Figure 3.6 (page 89). Some of the support activities of the value chains can be identified in Figure 4.2. Note also that the *value system* concept corresponds to the concept of an *extended supply chain*, which includes suppliers, warehousing, distribution, and other business partners. Porter's contribution was in concentrating on the values added in moving along the chain. One of the major goals of supply chain management is to maximize this value, and this is where IT in general and electronic commerce in particular enter the picture, as will be shown in sections 4.3 and 4.8. But let us first see why it is difficult to maximize or optimize the value chain.

## 4.2  SUPPLY CHAIN PROBLEMS AND SOLUTIONS

### BACKGROUND

Adding value along the supply chain is essential for competitiveness or even survival. Unfortunately such addition is limited by many potential problems along the chain.

Supply chain problems have been recognized both in the military and in business operations for generations. Some even caused armies to lose wars and companies to get out of business. The problems are most evident in complex or long supply chains and in cases where many business partners are involved. For example, a well-known military case is the difficulties the German army in World War II encountered in the long supply chain to its troops in remote Russian territories, especially during the winter months. These difficulties resulted in a major turning point in the war and the beginning of the Germans' defeat. Note that during the Gulf war, the allied armies had superb supply chains which were managed by the latest computerized technologies including DSS and EIS applications. These chains were a major contributor to the swift victory in this war.

In the business world there are numerous examples of companies that were unable to meet demand, had too large and expensive inventories, and so on. Some of these companies paid substantial penalties; others went out of business. On the other hand some world-class companies such as Wal-Mart, Federal Express, and Dell have superb supply chains with innovative applications.

A recent example of a supply chain problem was the difficulty of fulfilling orders received electronically for toys during the 1999 holiday season. During the last months of the year online toy retailers, including eToys, Amazon.com, and Toys 'R' Us, conducted a massive advertising campaign for Internet ordering. This included a $20–$30 discount voucher for shopping online. Customer response was overwhelming, and the retailers that underestimated it were unable to get the necessary toys from the manufacturing plants and warehouses and deliver them to the customers' door by Christmas Eve. Toys 'R' Us, for example, offered each of its unhappy customers a $100 store coupon as a compensation. Despite its generous gift, over 40 percent of Toys 'R' Us unhappy customers said they will not shop online at Toys 'R' Us again.

These and similar problems create the need for innovative solutions. For example, during the oil crises in the 1970s, Ryder Systems, a large trucking company, purchased a refinery to ensure availability of gasoline for its trucks. Such vertical integration was effective in some cases but very ineffective in others. In the remaining portion of this section we will look closely at some of the major problems in managing the supply chain and some of the proposed solutions, many of which are supported by IT.

### PROBLEMS ALONG THE SUPPLY CHAIN

The problems along the supply chain stem mainly from uncertainties and from the need to coordinate several activities, internal units, and business partners.

The major source of supply chain uncertainties is the demand forecast, which may be influenced by several factors such as competition, prices, weather conditions, technological development, customers' general confidence, and more. Other uncertainties exist in delivery times which depend on many factors ranging from machine failures to road conditions and traffic jams that may interfere with shipments. Quality problems of materials and parts may also create production delays.

A major symptom of poor SCM is poor customer service, which hinders people from getting the product or service when and where needed, or gives them a product of poor quality. Other symptoms are high inventory costs, loss of revenues, extra cost of expediting shipments, and more.

## SOLUTIONS TO THE SUPPLY CHAIN PROBLEMS

Over the years organizations have developed many solutions to the supply chain problems. One of the earliest solutions was vertical integration. For example, Henry Ford purchased rubber plantations in South America in order to control tire production for his cars. Undoubtedly, the most common solution used by companies is *building inventories* as an "insurance" against supply chain uncertainties. This way products and parts flow smoothly through the production process. The main problem with this approach is that it is very difficult to correctly determine inventory levels for each product and part. If inventory levels are set too high, the cost of keeping the inventory will be very large. If the inventory is too low, there is no insurance against high demand or slow delivery (lead) times, and revenues (and customers) may be lost. In either event the total penalty cost, including sales opportunities lost and bad reputation, can be very high. Thus, companies make major attempts to control inventory, as shown in the *IT at Work* example that follows.

### IT At Work    HOW LITTLEWOODS STORES IMPROVED ITS SCM

Littlewoods Stores is one of Britain's largest retailers of high-quality clothing, with 136 stores around the U.K. and Northern Ireland. The retail clothing business is very competitive, so in the late 1990s the company embarked on an IT-supported initiative to improve its supply chain efficiency. A serious SCM problem for the company was *overstocking*.

In order to get better SCM, the company introduced a Web-based performance reporting system. The new system analyzes, on a daily basis, marketing and finance data, and space planning, merchandising, and purchasing data. For example, merchandising personnel can now perform sophisticated sales, stock, and supplier analyses to make key operational decisions on pricing and inventory.

Using the Web, analysts can view sales and stock data in veritably any grouping of levels and categories. Furthermore, users can easily drill down to detailed sales and other data.

The system uses a data warehouse decision support system (DSS), and other end-user oriented software to make better decisions. Here are some of the results:

▶ The ability to strategically price merchandise differently in different stores saved $1.2 million in 1997 alone.
▶ Reducing the need for stock liquidations saved $1.4 million in a single year.
▶ Marketing distribution expenses were cut by $7 million a year.
▶ The company was able to reduce staff from 84 to 49 people, a saving of about $1 million annually.
▶ Back-up inventory expenses were cut by about $4 million a year. For example, due to quick replenishment, stock went down by 80%.

Within a year the number of Web-based users grew to 600, and the size of its data warehouse grew to over 1 gigabytes.

**For further exploration:** Explain how integrated software solved the excess inventory problem. Also, review the role of data warehouse decision support in this case. ▲

SOURCE: Condensed from www.microstrategy.com (Jan. 2000, Customers' Success Stories)

Proper supply chain and inventory management requires coordination of all different activities and "links" of the supply chain. Successful coordination enables goods to move smoothly and on time from suppliers to customers, which enables the firm to keep inventories low and costs down. The coordination is needed since companies depend on each other but do not always work together toward the same goal.

Business partners must trust each other. Both suppliers and buyers must participate together in the design of the supply chain to achieve their shared goals.

To properly control the uncertainties mentioned earlier, it is necessary to identify and understand the causes of the uncertainty, determine how uncertainties will effect other activities up and down the supply chain, and then formulate specific ways to reduce or eliminate the uncertainty. Combined with this is the need for an effective and efficient communication environment among all business partners. A rapid flow of information along the supply chains makes them very efficient. For example, computerized point-of-sale (POS) information can be transmitted once a day, or even in real time, to distribution centers, suppliers, and shippers. This enables firms to achieve optimal inventory levels.

Here are some other solutions used to solve SCM problems:

▶ Use outsourcing rather than do-it-yourself during demand peaks.

▶ Similarly, "buy" rather than "make" production inputs whenever appropriate.

▶ Configure optimal shipping plans.

▶ Create strategic partnerships with suppliers.

▶ Use the *just-in-time approach* to purchasing, in which suppliers deliver small quantities whenever supplies, materials, and parts are needed. (See the Dell opening case.)

▶ Reduce the lead time for buying and selling.

▶ Use fewer suppliers.

▶ Improve supplier-buyer relationships.

▶ Manufacture only after orders are in, as Dell is doing with its custom-made computers.

▶ Achieve accurate demand by working closely with suppliers. (See Minicase 2 in Chapter 8.)

Most of the above solutions are enhanced by IT support.

## ▶ 4.3 COMPUTERIZED SYSTEMS: MRP, ERP, AND SCM

The concept of the supply chain is interrelated with the computerization of its activities, which has evolved over 50 years.

### THE EVOLUTION OF COMPUTERIZED AIDS

Historically, many of the supply chain activities were managed with paper transactions, which can be very inefficient. Therefore, since the early business utilization of computers attention was given to automation of processes along the supply chain. The first software programs appeared in the 1950s and early 1960s. They supported short segments along the supply chain. Typical examples are inventory management systems, scheduling, and billing. The major objective was to reduce cost, expedite processing, and reduce errors. Such applications were developed in the functional areas, independent of each other, and became more and more sophisticated with the passage of time, as will be shown in Chapter 8. Of special interest were transaction processing systems and decision support procedures such as management science optimization and financial decision making formulas (e.g., for loan amortization).

In a short time it became clear that interdependencies exist among some of the supply chain activities. One of the earliest realizations was that production schedule is related to inventory management and purchasing plans. As early as the 1960s, the *material requirements planning* (MRP) model was devised (see Chapter 8). Then it became clear that in order to use this model, which may require daily updating, one needs computer support. This resulted in commercial MRP software packages coming on the market.

While MRP packages were useful in many cases, helping to drive inventory levels down and streamlining portions of the supply chain, they failed in as many (or even more) cases. One of the major reasons for the failure was the realization that schedule-inventory-purchasing operations are closely related to both financial and labor resources. This realization resulted in an enhanced MRP methodology and software called *manufacturing requirements planning*, or MRP II.

During this evolution there was more and more integration of information systems. This evolution continued, leading to the *enterprise resources planning* (ERP) concept which integrates the transaction processing activities of the entire enterprise. ERP was expanded to include internal suppliers and customers and later to incorporate external suppliers and customers in what is known as *extended ERP/SCM software*. This evolution is shown in Figure 4.3. The next step in this evolution, which is just beginning to make its way into business use, is the inclusion of markets and communities. (See mySAP.com for further details.)

Notice that throughout this evolution there have been more and more integrations along several dimensions (more functional areas, combining transaction processing and decision support, inclusion of business partners). Therefore, before we describe the essentials of ERP and SCM software it may be beneficial to analyze the reasons for software integration.

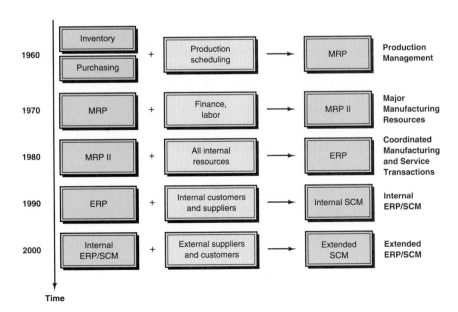

**FIGURE 4.3** The evolution of integrated systems.

## WHY INTEGRATION?

Creating the twenty-first century enterprise cannot be done effectively with twentieth-century computer technology, which is *functionally* oriented. Functional systems may not let different departments communicate with each other in the same language. Worse yet, crucial sales, inventory, and production data often have to be painstakingly entered manually into separate computer systems every time a person who is not a member of a specific department needs ad hoc information related to the specific department. In many cases employees simply do not get the information they need, or they get it too late.

Sandoe and Saharia (2001) list the following major benefits of integration (in order of importance):

*Tangible benefits:* Inventory reduction, personnel reduction, productivity improvement, order management improvement, financial-close cycle improvements, IT cost reduction, procurement cost reduction, cash management improvements, revenue/profit increases, transportation logistics cost reduction, maintenance reduction, and on-time delivery improvement.

*Intangible benefits:* Information visibility, new/improved processes, customer responsiveness, standardization, flexibility, globalization, and business performance.

Notice that in both types of benefits many items are directly related to improved supply chain management. (For further discussion on the improvements that integration provided to SCM, see "Competition's New Battleground: The Integrated Value Chain," at www.cambridgetechnology.com.)

## INTEGRATING THE SUPPLY CHAIN

For generations companies managed the various links of the supply chain independently of each other. However, since the 1950s and thanks to the introduction of computer-based information systems, companies started to integrate the links. The integration was facilitated by the need to streamline operations in order to meet customer demands in the areas of product and service cost, quality, delivery, technology, and cycle time brought by increased global competition. Furthermore, new forms of organizational relationships and the information revolution, especially the Internet and electronic commerce, have brought SCM to the forefront of management attention. This attention created willingness to invest money in hardware and software that are needed for seamless integration, as shown in the example of Warner-Lambert Corp.

*IT At Work*    **HOW WARNER-LAMBERT APPLIES AN INTEGRATED SUPPLY CHAIN**

It all begins in eucalyptus farms in Australia, where these fast-growing trees produce some of the materials used in one of Warner-Lambert's major products: Listerine antiseptic mouthwash. From Australia, the materials collected from eucalyptus trees are shipped to the Warner-Lambert (WL) manufacturing plant in New Jersey, U.S.A. The major problem there is to determine how much Listerine to produce. Listerine is purchased by thousands of retail stores, some of which are giants such as Wal-Mart and many of which are small. The problem that the manufacturing plant faces is to forecast the overall demand. A wrong forecast will result either in high inventories at WL, or in shortages. Inventories are expensive to keep, and shortages may result in loss of business and reputation.

Warner-Lambert forecasts demand with the help of Manugistic Inc.'s Demand Planning information system. (Manugistic is a vendor of IT software for SCM.) Used with other products in Manugistics' Supply Chain Planning suite, the system analyzes manufacturing, distribution, and sales data against expected demand and business climate information to help WL decide how much Listerine (and other products) to make and distribute and how much of each raw ingredient is needed. For example, the model can anticipate the impact of seasonal promotion or of a production line being down. The sales and marketing group of WL also meets monthly with WL employees in finance, procurement, and other departments. The group enters the expected demand for Listerine into a Marcam Corp. Prism Capacity Planning system, which schedules the production of Listerine in the amounts needed and generates electronic purchase orders for WL's suppliers.

WL's supply chain excellence stems from its innovative Collaborative Planning, Forecasting, and Replenishment (CPFR) program. WL launched CPFR a few years ago when it started sharing strategic plans, performance data, and market insight with Wal-Mart, Inc., over private networks. The company realized that it could benefit from Wal-Mart's market knowledge, just as Wal-Mart could benefit from WL's product knowledge. During the CPFR pilot, WL increased its products' shelf-fill rate—the extent to which a store's shelves are fully stocked—from 87 percent to 98 percent, earning the company about $8 million a year in additional sales (the equivalent of a new product launch) for much less investment. WL is now using the Internet to expand the CPFR program to all its suppliers and retail partners.

Warner-Lambert is a major player in two collaborative retail industry projects. One is the Collaborative Forecasting and Replenishment Project (CFAR), described in Chapter 8. In CFAR, trading partners collaborate on demand forecast using electronic commerce technology. The project includes major SCM and ERP vendors such as SAP and Manugistics. The other project is Supply-Chain Operations Reference (SCOR), an initiative of the Supply-Chain Council in the United States. SCOR decomposes supply-chain operations into component parts, giving manufacturers, suppliers, distributors, and retailers a framework with which to evaluate the effectiveness of their processes along the same supply chains.

**For further exploration:** Can you find other industries, besides retailing, for which such collaboration will be beneficial? Why is Listerine a target for the SCM collaboration? ▲

## ENTERPRISE RESOURCES PLANNING (ERP)

With the advance of enterprisewide client-server computing comes a new challenge: how to control all major business processes with a single software architecture in real time. The integrated solution, known as **enterprise resources planning (ERP)**, promises benefits from increased efficiency to improved quality, productivity, and profitability (see Appleton [1997] for details). The name enterprise resources planning is misleading because the software does not concentrate on either *planning* or *resources*. ERP's major objective is to *integrate all departments and functions across a company* onto a single computer system that can serve all of the enterprise's needs. For example, improved order entry allows immediate access to inventory, product data, customer credit history, and prior order information. This availability of information raises productivity and increases customer satisfaction. ERP, for example, helped Master Product Company increase sales by 20 percent and decrease inventory by 30 percent (Caldwell et al. [1997]).

For businesses that want to use ERP, one option is to self-develop an integrated system by using existing functional packages, or by programming one's own systems. The other option is to use commercially available integrated ERP software. The leading software for ERP is **SAP R/3** (see Box 4.1). Oracle, J.D. Edwards, Computer Associates, PeopleSoft, and Baan Company make similar products. These products include Web modules (see *Interactive Week*, Nov. 3, 1997).

## *A Closer Look* BOX 4.1

### SAP—THE COMPLETE SOLUTION

SAP R/3 from Germany-based SAP AG Corporation is the leading integrated enterprise software. It is comprised of four major application categories—accounting, manufacturing, sales, and human resources—containing more than 70 modules. R/3 is a totally integrated system, allowing companies to automate or eliminate many costly and error-prone manual communication procedures. R/3 can work for multinational corporations as well, since it can handle different currencies, different languages, different tax laws and regulations, and different requirements of several countries. SAP can be used to support interorganizational activities of the supply chain management.

Let us assume that a company has several manufacturing facilities, each with several production lines. SAP can help utilize excess capacity quickly or reschedule the production when a malfunction occurs. SAP empowers employees to make complex decisions instantaneously.

SAP forces organizations to operate along business processes. By doing so it not only supports business process reengineering, but also permits organizations to grow globally and operate efficiently.

Implementing SAP is a difficult process, especially for large corporations. Not only is it necessary to modify business procedures to conform to SAP's strict integration requirements, but SAP implementation is very complex and consequently very expensive (up to $200 million for a large company). For example, there are over 8,000 tables in the SAP database containing both user data and system data. These complicated tables direct the users through many menus and screens. Implementing these tables in a multilanguage, multicurrency, multifunction, multiproduct environment can take 2 to 4 years. Interfacing SAP's client/server architecture with legacy systems adds to the complexity. As a result, introducing SAP means significant changes in organizational structure, job descriptions, business processes, and organizational strategy.

SAP has proven to be ideal for medium-sized corporations of about $500 million annual sales. For large companies the problems cited above could be difficult, though successful implementation can be very rewarding. The following steps illustrate a simple example of how R/3 works (*Business Week*, Nov. 3, 1997):

**STEP 1.** Brazilian retailer orders, via the Internet, 1,000 shoes from International Shoe Co. A sales rep takes the order, routes it to R/3's *ordering* module, R/3 checks the retailer credit, price, etc. The order is approved.

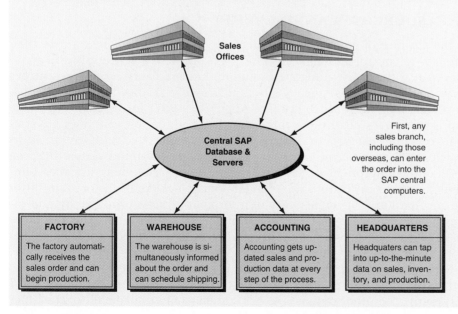

**Sales Offices**

First, any sales branch, including those overseas, can enter the order into the SAP central computers.

**Central SAP Database & Servers**

| FACTORY | WAREHOUSE | ACCOUNTING | HEADQUARTERS |
|---|---|---|---|
| The factory automatically receives the sales order and can begin production. | The warehouse is simultaneously informed about the order and can schedule shipping. | Accounting gets updated sales and production data at every step of the process. | Headquaters can tap into up-to-the-minute data on sales, inventory, and production. |

With **SAP** software, a company can keep different departments updated with crucial product information. For example, once the sales department enters an order, it goes to a central computer system where others can access it. (*Source*: Lieber [1995], p. 122.)

**STEP 2.** Simultaneously R/3's *inventory* module checks the stocks and notifies the rep that half the order can be filled immediately from stock. The other half will be manufactured and delivered in 5 days directly from the factory in Taiwan.

**STEP 3.** R/3's *manufacturing* module schedules the production in Taiwan and instructs the warehouse (in Chinese) to ship the shoes to Brazil and print up an invoice (in Portuguese).

**STEP 4.** R/3's *human resources* module calculates labor requirements. Due to a shortage, the personnel manager in Taiwan is instructed to get temporary workers.

**STEP 5.** R/3's *material planning* module notifies the purchasing manager about a shortage of purple dye. A purchase order is automatically issued.

**STEP 6.** The customer logs on via the extranet to the company's sneakers division. He can see that 500 shoes were shipped from the regional warehouse. This is done with R/3 *tracing* capabilities.

**STEP 7.** Based on data from R/3's *forecasting and financial* modules, the CEO can determine both profitability per product and demand. The financial module also converts all foreign moneys to $U.S., whenever needed.

The ERP software crosses functional departments. An ERP suite provides a single interface for managing all the routine activities performed in manufacturing—from entering sales orders, to coordinating shipping and after-sales customer service. More recently, ERP systems have begun to be extended along the supply chain to suppliers and customers. They can incorporate functionality for customer interaction and for managing relationships with suppliers and vendors, making the system less inward-looking.

Companies have been successful in integrating several hundred applications using ERP software, saving millions of dollars and significantly increasing customer satisfaction. For example, Mobil Oil consolidated 300 different information systems by implementing SAP R/3 in U.S. petrochemical operations alone. ERP forces discipline and organization around business processes, making the alignment of IT and business goals more likely. Such change is related to business process reengineering (BPR) (see sections 4.4 through 4.7). Also, by implementing ERP a company can discover all the "dusty corners" of its business.

However, due to the extreme complexity in implementing SAP, the need to change existing business processes to fit SAP's format, and the fact that some companies require only some of R/3's 70 software modules, SAP may not be attractive to everyone. For example, Caldwell (1999) reports that Inland Steel Industries, Inc., opted to write its own system (containing 7 million lines of code), which supports 27 integrated applications, rather than use SAP.

ERP has played a critical role in getting small- and medium-sized manufacturers to focus on business processes, thus facilitating business process changes across the enterprise. By tying multiple plants and distribution facilities together, ERP solutions have also facilitated a change in thinking that has its ultimate expression in an enterprise that is better able to expand operations and in better supply-chain management. (For a comprehensive treatment of ERP, its cost, implementation problems, and payback, see Koch [1999]).

But ERP was never meant to fully support supply chains. ERP solutions are "transaction-centric," that is, centered around business transactions. As such, they do not provide the computerized models needed to respond rapidly to real-time changes in supply, demand, labor, or capacity. This deficiency has been overcome by the second generation of ERP.

## POST-ERP (SECOND GENERATION ERP)

The first generation ERP aimed at automating key office processes. And indeed ERP projects save companies millions of dollars. A report by Merrill Lynch & Co.

noted that nearly 40 percent of all U.S. companies with more than $1 billion in annual revenues have implemented ERP systems. However, by the late 1990s the major benefits of ERP had been fully exploited. It became clear that with the completion of the Y2K projects that were an integral part of many ERP implementations, the first generation of ERP was nearing the end of its life. But the ERP movement was far from over. A second, more powerful generation of ERP development started. Its objective is to leverage existing systems in order to increase efficiency in handling transactions, improve decision making, and further transform ways of doing business. Let's explain:

The first generation of ERP basically supported routine transactional activities. In other words, ERP has traditionally excelled in transaction management, i.e., the ability to manage administrative activities like payroll, financials inventory, and order processing. For example, an ERP system has the functionality of electronic ordering or the best way to bill the customer—all it does is to automate the transactions.

The reports generated by ERP systems gave planners statistics about what happened in the company, costs, and financial performance. However, the planning systems with ERP were rudimentary. Reports from ERP systems provided a snapshot of the business at a point in time. But they did not support the continuous planning that is central to supply chain planning, one that continues to refine and enhance the plan as changes and events occur, up to the very last minute before executing the plan. Attempting to come up with an optimal plan using first generation ERP-based systems has been compared to steering a car by looking in the rear-view mirror.

This created the need for systems oriented toward decision making, and this is what the SCM software vendors provided. To illustrate, we look at how ERP and SCM approach a planning problem. There is a fundamental difference: The question in SCM becomes "Should I take your order?" instead of the ERP approach of "How can I best take or fulfill your order?"

Thus SCM systems have emerged as a *complement* to ERP systems, to provide intelligent decision support capabilities. An SCM system is designed to overlay existing systems and to pull data from every step of the supply chain. It thus is able to provide a clear, global picture of where the enterprise is heading. Creating a plan from an SCM system allows companies to quickly assess the impact of their actions on the entire supply chain, including customer demand. Therefore, it makes sense to integrate ERP and SCM.

How is such an integration done? One approach is to work with different softwares from different vendors. For example, a business might use SAP as an ERP and add to it Manugistics' manufacturing-oriented software, as shown earlier in the Warner-Lambert case. Such an approach requires fitting different softwares, which may be complex, unless special interfaces exist.

The second approach is for the ERP vendors to add decision support and business intelligence capabilities. This solves the integration problem. But as is the case with integration of database management systems (DBMS) and spreadsheets in Excel or Lotus 1-2-3, the result can be a product with some not-so-strong functionalities. However, most ERP vendors are adding such functionalities for another reason: it is cheaper for the customers. The added functionalities, which create the second generation ERP, include not only decision support, but also CRM (Chapter 8), electronic commerce (section 4.8), and data warehousing and mining (Chapter 10).

Companies are eager to use the post-ERP systems, as shown in the *IT At Work* examples that follow.

**IT At Work**   HOW U.S. COMPANIES ARE USING POST-ERP

Owens Corning, a maker of building materials, changed its business model and corporate thinking in 1999. Instead of separately selling shingles and roofing vents, it now sells complete roofing systems which include parts, installation, delivery, and other services. To do it economically, the company is using business intelligence (data warehousing and mining) to analyze the data generated by the ERP system (from SAP). The data warehouse provides valuable information on customer profitability, product-line profitability, sales performance, and SCM activities. The ERP is also integrated with shop-floor process control that uses SCM software.

General Instruments, a telecommunications equipment maker, uses SCM software to enter parts data into Metaphase's product management tool. From there data are entered to Oracle's ERP system. Previously, product data were entered manually into each system, resulting in high cost and errors. The company is also using a product configuration tool that assists the sales force and manufacturing to ensure that certain product configurations requested by customers are possible before orders are placed on the ERP. More than 3,000 component suppliers have direct access to product data over the Web using Metaphase's technology.

At in-line skate maker Rollerblade, Inc., an ERP (from J.D. Edward) is the platform for the company's forecasting, sales-force automation, and data warehousing systems. The new integrated platform now allows a profitability and sales analysis by product, region, and time period to be done regularly.

Mott's North America installed a first generation ERP and found that it did not address the company's marketing and customer service needs properly. Using SAP's advanced features, the company has now added production planning and shipment scheduling optimization, along with an integration of electronic commerce. For example, distributors can now use the Web to check order status by themselves in the R/3 system. ▲

## APPLICATION SERVICE PROVIDERS AND ERP OUTSOURCING

The first option tried by many businesses that want ERP functions is to lease applications rather than to build systems. In leasing applications, the ERP vendor takes care of the functionalities and the integration problems. This relatively new approach is known as the "ASP alternative." An *application service provider (ASP)* is a software vendor that offers to lease ERP-based applications to other businesses. The basic concept is the same as the old-fashioned time share. The outsourcers set up the systems and run them for you. ASP is considered a product risk-management strategy, and it best fits small- to mid-size companies.

The ASP concept is especially useful in ERP projects, which are expensive to install and take a long time to implement, and for which staffing is a major problem. However, ASP offerings are also evident in ERP-added functions such as electronic commerce, customer relationship management (CRM), datamarts, desktop productivity, human resources information systems (HRIS), and other supply chain-related applications.

The use of ASP has some downsides. First, ERP vendors typically want a 5-year commitment. In 5 years ERP may be bundled with a PC and given away for free. Second, you lose flexibility. Rented systems are fairly standard and may not fit your need. (For further discussion of ASPs, see *Datamation*, July 1999).

### GLOBAL SUPPLY CHAINS

Supply chains that involve suppliers and/or customers in other countries are referred to as *global supply chains*. The introduction of electronic commerce has made it much easier to find suppliers in other countries (e.g., by using electronic bidding; see section 4.8). Also, e-commerce has made it much easier and cheaper to find customers in other countries (see Turban et al., [2000]).

Global supply chains are longer than domestic ones and may be complex. Therefore additional uncertainties are likely. Information technologies are found to be extremely useful in supporting global supply chains. For example, TradeNet in Singapore connects sellers, buyers, and government agencies via electronic data interchange (EDI). TradeNet's case is described in detail on the Web site of this book. A similar network, TradeLink, operates in Hong Kong, using both EDI and EDI/Internet to connect about 70,000 trading partners. The book's opening case (in Chapter 1) introduced the Harper Group, which uses EDI and other information technologies extensively. Some of the issues that may create delays in global flows are legal issues, customs fees and other taxes, language and cultural differences, fast changes in currencies' exchange rates, and political instabilities.

IT facilitates global SCM. It provides not only EDI and other communication options, but also online expertise in sometimes difficult and fast-changing regulations. IT also can be instrumental in helping businesses find trade partners (via electronic directories and search engines). Finally, IT facilitates outsourcing of products and services, especially IT programming, to countries with a plentiful supply of labor, at low cost.

The major reasons why companies go global are: lower prices of material, products, and labor; availability of products that are unavailable domestically; the firm's global attitude; advanced technology available in other countries; high quality of products available; intensification of global competition which drives companies to cut costs; the need to develop a foreign presence; and fulfillment of counter trade.

## ▶ 4.4  THE NEED FOR BUSINESS PROCESS REENGINEERING AND THE ROLE OF IT

The major environmental pressures faced by any business were described in Chapter 1. They are summarized by Hammer and Champy (1993) as the three Cs—customers, competition, and change.

▶ *Customers* today know what they want, what they are willing to pay, and how to get products and services on their own terms.

▶ *Competition* is continuously increasing with respect to price, quality, selection, service, and promptness of delivery. Removal of trade barriers, increased international cooperation, and the creation of technological innovations cause competition to intensify.

▶ *Change* continues to occur. Markets, products, services, technology, the business environment, and people keep changing, frequently in an unpredictable and significant manner.

> Change can also be the result of internal growth, expansion, and mergers. Ideally, preparing for change would eliminate the need of BPR. Unfortunately, too many things aren't considered during the change, and costly BPR is often the result.
> — *Mike Rewald*

Since the old methods are not always working, organizations face situations like the one described in the following example.

| IT At Work | ALMOST EVERY INSURANCE COMPANY |

Nick Simmons had accepted an executive position with Honeywell in Minneapolis, so he contacted his insurance company in his home city, Detroit. He had been a customer for the past 25 years and wanted to transfer his insurance to the Minneapolis office, keeping the same life, health, personal liability, and auto coverage.

**U**SING IT

...in Marketing

Much to Nick's disappointment, he found that he would have to contact an agent when he arrived in Minneapolis and reapply for insurance. Nick asked his agent in Detroit whether she could at least give him the name of a good agent in Minneapolis. He was told the best thing to do would be to look up an agent in the Yellow Pages. Nick had been loyal for over 25 years and was trying to remain a customer. Yet, it was as if the insurance company was deliberately trying to alienate him.

When he arrived in Minneapolis Nick checked competitive rates on the Internet and found several quotes for low rates. After making an evaluation, he ended up selecting a new insurance company.

**For Further Exploration:** Assume that Nick's problem resulted from poor communication and information flow in the Detroit office of his insurance company, and the lack of access to the data stored in Detroit from the Minneapolis office. How could the incident have been avoided? ▲

Assuming an insurance company is concerned about retaining customers, the above *IT At Work* illustrates an organization that is probably not accomplishing its objectives very well. It needs a CRM initiative. Research shows that it is five to six times more difficult and expensive to obtain a new customer than it is to retain an existing one. Figure 4.4 indicates what customers often find as they try to get service from many organizations. What went wrong with these organizations? What needs to be done to correct the problem?

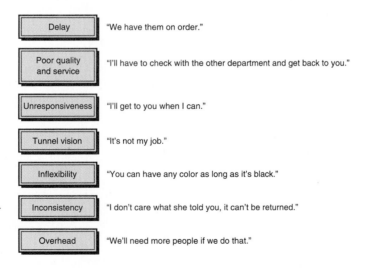

**FIGURE 4.4** Organizations need to be more responsive than ever to customers to succeed in today's environment. But what do we often find?

### PROBLEM OF THE STOVEPIPE

All organizations have both horizontal and vertical dimensions. The organization's layers (usually top, middle, and supervisory management) define the horizontal dimensions; the organization's functional departments define the vertical dimensions.

The *vertical dimension* of the organization, primarily focused on functional specialization, has caused many problems in organizations as they have tried to

This seems humorous, but sadly most of the companies I know of still don't encourage "crossing the stovepipes" to share information with those in other departments who may need it.

— *Mike Rewald*

move into the information-based economy. Such problems are sometimes referred to as "stovepipes" because of the lack of cooperation between functional areas. Interaction among vertical functions (across the stovepipes) turns out to be crucial in order for organizations to operate efficiently and effectively.

Often, the difference between duties of functional units and business processes in an organization is confused. Figure 4.5 illustrates how an organization can have vertical functions but have processes that transcend departmental boundaries. These are sometimes referred to as **cross-functional activities.** Product development, order processing, planning, resourcing, control, and customer service are processes that can transcend the functional boundaries of distribution, purchasing, research and development, manufacturing, and sales.

Here is an example of a stovepipe problem: A customer places an order with Sales. After a few days, she calls Sales to find out the status of the order. Sales calls various departments. Frequently, it is difficult to trace the order. People push the order from place to place and feel only a small sense of responsibility and accountability, so Sales may not be able to give the customer an answer in time, or may even give an incorrect answer. The problem of the stovepipe can intensify if the supporting information systems are structured improperly.

Focusing on vertical functions and their corresponding information systems to support the business has resulted in fragmented, piecemeal information systems that operate in a way in which the "left hand doesn't know what the right hand is doing." Integration of information is required for good decision making. Achieving it is one of the goals of **business process reengineering (BPR),** which undertakes a fundamental change in specific business processes. Dell Computer Inc. was successful in integrating the information received from its customers with that of its just-in-time manufacturing and parts suppliers, along the expanded supply chain. Many companies, however, are not so successful. They face the need for information integration.

## NEED FOR INFORMATION INTEGRATION

In a hospital setting the necessity of protecting confidential patient information is a barrier to information integration.

— *Brad White*

Besides creating inefficient redundancies, information systems developed along departmental or functional boundaries cause difficulties in the *integration* of information that is required for decision making. A loan officer, for instance, may

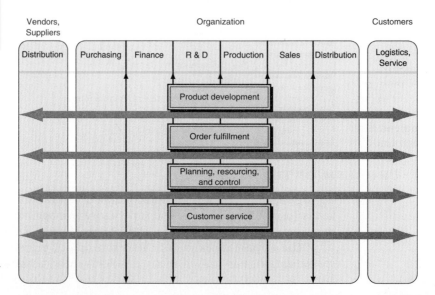

**FIGURE 4.5** Business processes across functional areas and organizational boundaries.

want to check information pertaining to a loan applicant's savings accounts. However, there is no linkage to these data from the loan system. Indeed, the loan officer may have to ask the loan applicant if he or she has a savings account with the bank and what the account number is.

Or, consider a case where the management of the bank wants to offer more mortgage loans to utilize large savings deposits. Management decides to send letters encouraging specific customers to consider buying homes, using convenient financing available through the bank. Management also decides that the best customers to whom to send such letters are the following:

1. Customers who do not currently have mortgage loans or who have loans for a very small percentage of the value of their homes.

2. Customers who have good checking account records (i.e., few or no overdrafts).

3. Customers with sufficient funds in their savings accounts to make a down payment on a home.

4. Customers who have good payment records on any installment loans with the bank.

Because the data necessary to identify such customers may be available in different files of different information systems, there may be no convenient or economic way to integrate them. Using innovations such as data warehouses and special integrated software can be helpful but expensive. Therefore, extensive programming and clerical work are required to satisfy such an information request. Management is understandably disappointed and unable to function effectively. The scenario of the bank can be translated into other organizational settings.

Integration should cross not only departmental boundaries but also organizational ones, reaching suppliers and customers. Namely, it should work along the *extended supply chain*. An example of an internal integration followed by an integration with dealers is provided in the following case.

---

### *IT At Work*  VW OF MEXICO SHIFTED TO HIGH GEAR

**I**NTEGRATING IT

...for Accounting, Marketing, Finance, and Production & Operations Management

Facing strong competition and the North American Free Trade Agreement (NAFTA) environment, Volkswagen of Mexico resorted to IT. In 1996 VW implemented an enterprise resource planning system, using SAP R/3 software. By 1998, the company integrated its enterprise system, which was used to cut inventory and production costs, with an extranet, which streamlined spare-part ordering by its dealers in Mexico. The integrated system allows people at every level of the company, from manufacturing to car servicing at the dealership, to take advantage of the SAP system. The SAP system integrates manufacturing, finance, marketing, and other departments among themselves and, thanks to the extranet, with the dealers and business partners. Flora Lopez, production software manager, said that the R/3 system orchestrates all the different areas of the manufacturing and parts-ordering tasks, such as supplier orders, reception, warehousing, client orders, packing, and billing. By tapping into R/3 modules, the dealers can cut the turnaround time for ordering spare parts from 10 days to fewer than 5—a very important competitive advantage. The dealers can check the status of their orders on the computer.

The major reason for the project is the increased demand that resulted from NAFTA and from VW's decision to market the Beetle (called the "New Beetle") in the United States and Canada. These cars are manufactured in Mexico, where labor and services are cheaper.

One problem is that some of the dealers in Mexico are not ready to buy, install, and use computers. However, the fact that the new system means a low inventory level, which can save the dealers considerable money, is motivating the dealers to join in. The company projects the application will result in $50 million in cost savings over three years for the dealers.

**For Further Exploration:** Can VW's suppliers be added to the system? What competitive advantage can be realized with such an addition? ▲

SOURCE: Condensed from *PC Week*, Jan. 12, 1998, pp. 29, 39.

The integration of an organization's information systems enables BPR innovations such as the introduction of a single point of contact for customers, called a "case manager" or a deal structurer (see the following *IT At Work*).

## IT At Work    IBM CREDIT CORPORATION
## REDUCED CYCLE TIME BY 90 PERCENT

IBM Credit Corporation provides credit to customers who purchase IBM computers. The process of credit approval used to take an average of seven days. Because of the long processing time, salespeople felt that they were losing many potential customers; therefore, reducing processing time became critical.

### THE OLD PROCESS
**STEP 1:** The IBM salesperson telephones in, requesting credit approval for a customer.

**STEP 2:** A clerk logs the call on paper; a messenger takes it to the credit department.

**STEP 3:** A specialist enters the data into the computer, checks creditworthiness of the potential customer, and prepares a report.

**STEP 4:** The report is physically moved to the business practices department.

**STEP 5:** The business practices department modifies a standard loan to fit the customer's needs.

**STEP 6:** Using a spreadsheet, a pricer determines the appropriate interest rate and payment schedule. Another piece of paper is added to the application.

**STEP 7:** An administrator uses the information to develop a quote letter.

**STEP 8:** The quote letter is delivered to the salesperson, who submits it to the customer.

Incremental attempts to increase productivity improved some of the activities, but the overall time reduction was minimal.

**THE REENGINEERED PROCESS.** One person, called a deal structurer, conducts all the above steps. One generalist replaces four specialists. To enable one person to execute the above steps, a simple DSS provides the deal structurer with the guidance needed. The program guides the generalist in finding information in the databases, plugging numbers into an evaluation model, and pulling standardized clauses—"boilerplate"—from a file. For difficult situations, the generalist can get help from a specialist.

**THE RESULTS.** The turnaround time has been slashed from seven days to four hours! Furthermore, IBM credit can handle a volume of business up to 100 times larger now.

**For Further Exploration:** Why is this change considered a BPR? What role did IT play in supporting the BPR? ▲

SOURCE: Compiled from Hammer and Champy (1993).

*I*NTEGRATING IT

...for Finance, Accounting, and Marketing

## THE ENABLING ROLE OF INFORMATION TECHNOLOGY IN BPR

IT has been used for several decades to improve the productivity and quality by automating existing processes. However, when it comes to reengineering, the traditional process of looking at problems first and then seeking technology solutions for them needs to be reversed. Now it is necessary to first recognize powerful solutions that BPR makes possible, and then to seek the process that can be helped by it. Such an approach requires *inductive* rather than *deductive* thinking. It requires innovation, since a company may be looking for problems it does not even know exist.

IT can break old rules that limit the manner in which work is performed. Some typical rules are given in Table 4.1.

## *Table 4.1* Changes Brought by IT

| Old Rule | Intervening Technology | New Rule |
|---|---|---|
| Information appears in only one place at one time. | Shared databases, Internet client/server architecture, intranet | Information appears simultaneously wherever needed. |
| Only an expert can perform complex work. | Expert systems, neural computing | Novices can perform complex work. |
| Business must be either centralized or decentralized. | Telecommunication and networks: client/server intranet | Business can be both centralized and decentralized. |
| Only managers make decisions. | Decision support systems, enterprise support systems, expert systems | Decision making is part of everyone's job. |
| Field personnel need offices to receive, send, store, and process information. | Wireless communication and portable computers, the Web, electronic mail | Field personnel can manage information from any location. |
| The best contact with potential buyers is a personal contact. | Interactive videodisk, desktop teleconferencing, electronic mail | The best contact is the one that is most cost-effective. |
| You have to locate items manually. | Tracking technology, groupware, workflow software, search engines | Items are located automatically. |
| Plans get revised periodically. | High-performance computing systems, intelligent agents | Plans get revised instantaneously whenever needed. |
| People must come to one place to work together. | Groupware and group support systems, telecommunication, electronic mail, client/server | People can work together while at different locations. |
| Customized products and services are expensive and take a long time to develop. | CAD/CAM, CASE tools, online systems for JIT decision making, expert systems | Customized products can be made fast and inexpensively (mass customization). |
| A long period of time is spanned between the inception of an idea and its implementation (time-to-market). | CAD/CAM, electronic data interchange, groupware, imaging (document) processing | Time-to-market can be reduced by 90 percent. |
| Organizations and processes are information-based. | Artificial intelligence, expert systems | Organizations and processes are knowledge-based. |
| Move labor to countries where labor is inexpensive (off-shore production). | Robots, imaging technologies, object-oriented programming, expert systems, geographical information systems (GIS) | Work can be done in countries with high wages and salaries. |

SOURCE: Compiled from Hammer and Champy (1993).

The following *IT at Work* example shows how a water-products company used several IT tools in support of a complex reengineering effort.

---

### *IT At Work* McKESSON WATER PRODUCTS CO. REENGINEERS OPERATION

McKesson, the number one supplier of noncarbonated bottled water in the United States located in Pasadena, California, went through a $5 million reengineering effort of several business processes. New computer systems were installed to integrate sales, service, and customer relations into a new teleservice center. Route management was greatly enhanced through the use of a geographical information system (GIS), and hand-held terminals with wireless communication links to the central database greatly improved inventory control, distribution, and overall efficiency. The January 1994 earthquake in Los Angeles put McKesson's new systems to the test, which it passed with flying colors. This is why:

1. ***IT supports changes in the organization structure.*** The sales organization, service, and customer relations were consolidated in a single location by installing a computerized telephone switch that routed calls from seven regional offices into a teleservice center.

2. ***IT supports changes in the business process.*** The teleservice center staff now combines the functions of sales, service, and customer relations. A GIS was installed to optimize the process of adding new customers to existing routes. Previously 100,000 addresses had to be looked up manually on key maps, so that they could be added to the appropriate delivery routes. With the GIS, route allocation is fully automatic, and the entire route structure can be quickly reconfigured automatically. Hand-held wireless terminals and pagers provide instant information, and allow the central database to be updated at all times from all locations, without depending on public telephones, paper records, redundant data entry, and inevitable human errors.

3. ***IT supports shortening the time-to-market.*** The teleservice center installed a standard software package that automatically identified telephone numbers and displayed a customer's background information on the staff member's screen. This technology made data instantly available to the service representatives, and therefore to the customer. Since all data was available online, immediate follow-up activities could be carried out, resulting in drastically reduced delivery times.

4. ***IT supports customer-centered organizations.*** The integrated customer service center is focusing on improving customer satisfaction; faster order processing at lower cost.

5. ***IT enhances empowerment of employees.*** All sales, service, and customer service information is available to all service center employees. Enhanced team operations resulted in greater productivity, employee morale, and independence.

6. ***IT enhances TQM programs.*** The integrated systems guaranteed consistent, timely, and verifiable data, and resulted in improved quality and efficiency.

**U**SING IT

...in Production & Operations Management

The BPR efforts resulted in an annual cost reduction of $7 million; in addition staffing was reduced by 60 percent.

**For Further Exploration:** Why do we consider this use a BPR? What role did IT play in supporting the change? ▲

SOURCE: Condensed from Bartholomew, D., "Keeping Water Flowing in L.A.," *InformationWeek*, February 14, 1994.

---

IT-supported BPR examples can be found in any industry, private or public. The role of IT can be very critical and is increasing due to the Internet/intranet. Geoffrey (1996) provides several examples of how intranets have *rescued* BPR projects. One of these, the AT&T case, is described next.

## IT At Work   AT&T USED AN INTRANET TO ASSURE BPR IMPLEMENTATION

The telephone industry is one of the most competitive industries, where billions of dollars of business are at stake. The largest player, AT&T, is under constant attack from its competitors.

A substantial business area is the commercial (organizational) customers, some of which pay millions of dollars a year. These customers need special attention since when their telephones do not work their business does not work either. Also, thousands of new customers call daily, billing mistakes need to be corrected, and rates and contracts are frequently negotiated. The traditional solution was to set up specialized units which customers call for help by using 800 numbers. Unfortunately, there were 23 different such units. Customers calling one 800 number were frequently told to call a different number, which again might redirect the frustrated customer to another number. This cost AT&T millions of dollars. A combined 800 number was introduced, as a BPR, to solve the problem. However, this required highly trained operators. To teach these operators about the previous 23 different specialized services required a 40-week intensive class. Such training meant a multimillion-dollar special training budget.

**_U_SING IT**

...in Human Resources
Management

To reduce training costs, AT&T deploys an intranet that the operators can use to access the experience of specialists which is now documented and catalogued in the intranet database. Also the operators can share knowledge and experiences among themselves. Using browsers and search engines operators can find quick answers to customer queries. Also, the operators can train themselves by examining the databases and the answers to frequently asked questions (FAQs). The system eliminated the need of 40-week classes. Thus, the unified 800 system was implemented quickly, making AT&T customers happy and saving the company several million dollars.

**For Further Exploration:** In what other ways can intranets facilitate BPR? ▲

SOURCE: Condensed from Geoffrey (1996).

## RETOOLING OF IT FOR BPR

Information systems designed along hierarchical lines are usually ineffective in supporting the networked organization. Therefore, it is often necessary to reengineer the information systems. This process is referred to as _retooling_. Retooling focuses on making sure the information systems are responsive to the reengineering effort. Many organizations found that once they realized they had a problem and wanted to do something about it, their information systems function could not accommodate it. They were being "held hostage" by their information systems. For example, a government agency in Singapore decided to defer a badly needed BPR project when it discovered that it would cost over $15 million to rewrite the applicable computer programs.

To retool for reengineering, the key issue is getting a good understanding of the current installed base of information systems applications and databases. It is also important to understand the existing infrastructure in terms of computing equipment, networks, and the like, and their relationships to the current available software, procedures, and data. The key is an assessment of what the ideal IT architecture would be for the organization in terms of hardware and software, as well as an appropriate information architecture.

During this stage, it is very important to _benchmark_ the technology being used in the organization against what the best competitors are using. It is also imperative to find out what the latest technologies are and determine in what direction the organization needs to go. For an example of a massive IT retooling in a public agency where the technology enabled the company to reengineer all its major business processes, read on.

---

**IT At Work** THE NATIONAL HOUSING BOARD IN SINGAPORE RETOOLS ITS INFORMATION SYSTEMS

**USING IT**

...in Production & Operations Management

More than 87 percent of the population in Singapore live in housing units provided by the government. A government agency called the Housing Development Board (HDB) manages over a million properties. HDB must be responsive to its customers, business partners, and changing government policies. The organization faces a shortage of manpower as well as several of the business pressures described in Chapter 1.

Due to its rapid growth rate, HDB was unable to meet all of the demands placed on it without reengineering its business processes. To succeed in its reengineering efforts, HDB decided to retool its information services department. Starting in 1991, the IT area became one of the most sophisticated IT-based organizations in the world. HDB is committed to a process of continuously improving its IT tools, which will enable it to become perhaps the best housing authority in the world within a few years. The technology retooling completed by 1995 included:

▶ A sophisticated graphical-based property database.
▶ A large resident database.
▶ 200 CAD workstations that have increased the productivity of the office draftsmen.
▶ More than 2,600 users of Lotus Notes.
▶ An integrated land information system.
▶ A voice-response system that serves about a million residents 24 hours a day.
▶ Electronic hand-held terminals that enable HDB's parking wardens to print parking violation notices on site.
▶ An integrated payment collection system that includes conveniently located payment kiosks for electronic transfer of funds by residents.
▶ Sophisticated local area and wide area networks connecting 3,400 workstations in hundreds of HDB and business partner sites throughout Singapore. These networks are ISDN-based and are part of Singapore's information highway system.
▶ An elevator telemonitoring system that handles 1,400 calls per day. If rescue is needed, it is provided in less than 30 minutes.
▶ A client/server technology that is replacing many of the mainframe applications.
▶ EDI technology to reengineer business processes with partners.
▶ Imaging and workflow applications.

The latest additions to the IT retooling are:

▶ Interacting with residents at their homes (using interactive TV or the Internet).
▶ Customer information smart cards that store all pertinent customer information on one card. By running the card through an input device, all the necessary information appears on a screen. There is no more keying in information or filling out forms.

The retooling paid for itself very quickly. Every dollar spent returned $2.53 in less than four years.

**For Further Exploration:** Why does HDB need all this technology? How can an IT retooling help BPR in this case? ▲

SOURCE: Condensed from Vision 2000, HDB's Strategic IT Plan, HDB Corporate Internal Report Singapore (1994), and Tung and Turban (1996).

---

**THE TOOLS FOR BPR.** A large variety of IT tools can be used to support BPR and organizational transformation. The major categories of support tools are:

1. *Simulation and visual simulation tools.* Simulation is essential to support the modeling activities of BPR. In addition to conventional simulation and visual simulation tools (see Chapter 9), there are simulation tools that are specifically oriented for BPR such as SIMPROCESS (from CACI), ProModel (from ProModel Corp), BPSimulator (from Technology Economics), Witness (from Visual Interactive Systems, Inc.), and BPR Workflow (see El Sawy [1998]).

2. *Flow diagrams.* Flow diagrams can be made with CASE tools or other systems development charting tools. They can also be made by specialized BPR tools that are usually integrated with other tools.

3. *Work analysis.* Analyzing both existing processes and proposed solutions can be accomplished with tools that conduct forecasting, risk analysis, and optimization, such as I-think (from Performance Systems, Inc.) and BizCase and Turbo SPR (from SRA International).

4. *Application development.* BPR applications can be built with some of the tools described earlier.

5. *Other tools.* Several special tools were designed to plan and manage the BPR process and the organization transformation. Information tools and technologies can also be part of the BPR solution itself. For example, CAD/CAM and imaging technologies contribute to cycle time reduction, EDI supports virtual corporations and other interorganizational systems, and expert systems support case managers and mass customization.

6. *Integrated tool kits.* Several integrated tool kits are available to support BPR. The most well known tool is SAP R/3.

7. *Workflow software.* In redesigning business processes, it is usually necessary to analyze the work to be done and the manner in which it flows from one place to another. A workflow system is a powerful business process automation tool that places system controls in the hands of end-user departments. Not only does workflow automate business processes, it also provides a quality interface between business systems. As a result, workflow installations have evolved into enterprisewide computing solutions at major companies. There are three types of workflow software: *administrative*—expense reports, travel requests and messages; *ad hoc*—product brochures, sales proposals, and strategic plans; and *production*—credit card mailings, mortgage loans, and insurance claims.

## ▶ 4.5 RESTRUCTURING PROCESSES AND ORGANIZATIONS

Reengineering efforts involve many activities, four of which are described in this section: redesign of processes, mass customization, cycle time reduction, and restructuring the organization. Several other BPR activities are described in subsequent sections.

### REDESIGN OF PROCESSES

One of the most publicized examples of business process redesign is the accounts payable process at Ford Motor Company.

## IT At Work — REENGINEERING PROCESSES AT FORD MOTOR COMPANY

**U**SING IT

...in Accounting

As part of its productivity improvement efforts, Ford management put its North American Accounts Payable Department under the microscope in search of ways to cut costs. Management thought that by streamlining processes and installing new computer systems, it could reduce the head count by some 20 percent to 400 people.

But after visiting Mazda's payables department (Ford is part owner of Mazda), Ford managers increased their goal: perform accounts payable with only 100 clerks. Analysis of the existing system revealed that when the purchasing department wrote a purchase order, it sent a copy to accounts payable. Later, when material control received the goods, it sent a copy of the receiving document to accounts payable. Meanwhile, the vendor also sent an invoice to accounts payable. If the purchase order, receiving document, and invoice matched, then the accounts payable department issued a payment. Unfortunately, the department spent most of its time on the many mismatches. To prevent them, Ford instituted "invoiceless processing." Now, when the purchasing department initiates an order, it enters the information into an online database. It does not send a copy of the purchase order to anyone. The vendor receives notification through an EDI.

When the goods arrive at the receiving dock, the receiving clerk checks the database to see whether the goods correspond to an outstanding purchase order. If so, he or she accepts them and enters the transaction into the computer system. (If there is no database entry for the received goods, or if there is a mismatch, the clerk returns the goods.)

Under the old procedures, the accounting department had to match 14 data items among the receipt record, the purchase order, and the invoice before it could issue payment to the vendor. The new approach requires matching only four items—part number, amount, unit of measure, and supplier code—between the purchase order and the receipt record. The matching is done automatically, and the computer prepares the check, which accounts payable sends to the vendor (or an electronic transfer is done). There are no invoices to worry about since Ford has asked its vendors not to send them. The reengineered system as compared to the old one is shown in the figure below.

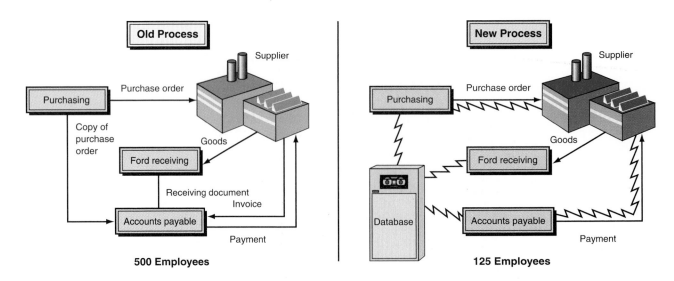

Ford did not settle for the modest increases it first envisioned. It opted for a radical change and it achieved dramatic improvement: a 75 percent reduction in head count, not the 20 percent it would have achieved with a conventional improvement program. And since there are no discrepancies between the financial record and physical record, material control is simpler, receipts are more likely to be correct, and financial information is more accurate.

**For Further Exploration:** How did the EDI help attain the reduction? What other support was provided by IT? ▲

SOURCE: Condensed from Hammer and Champy (1993).

## FROM MASS PRODUCTION TO MASS CUSTOMIZATION

One of the most innovative concepts of the Industrial Revolution was *mass production*. In mass production, a company produces a large quantity of an identical standard product. The product is then stored for future distribution to many customers. Because the concept of mass production results in a low cost, products are relatively inexpensive and sold in department or specialty stores to unknown customers. The concept of mass production was adapted to thousands of products, ranging from simple watches to major appliances, vehicles, and computers.

A major change in marketing started about 30 years ago with the increased competition between automobile manufacturers. Customers were able to select "options," such as an air conditioner or automatic transmission. Manufacturers collected the customized orders. Once they accumulated enough similar orders to justify manufacturing the customized product, they produced the items. The result was a waiting time of several months. A similar strategy was developed in other relatively expensive products. However, today's customers are not willing to wait so long (see the Volvo case in Chapter 3, Section 3.6). The solution was found in mass customization.

The concept **mass customization** may be essential to the survival of many companies as we enter the twenty-first century. The basic idea is to enable a company to produce large volumes, yet to customize the product to the specifications of individual customers (e.g., see Pine [1993]). Mass customization enables a company to provide flexible and quick responsiveness to a customer's needs, at a low cost and with high quality. It is made possible by allowing fast and inexpensive production changes, by reducing the ordering and sales process, by shortening the production time, and by using prefabricated parts and modules as shown in the following *IT at Work* example.

*IT At Work*  **BALLY REENGINEERS TO PROVIDE MASS CUSTOMIZATION**

*I*NTEGRATING IT

...for Marketing and Production & Operations Management

Bally Engineered Structures of Bally, Pennsylvania, was established in 1933 as a producer of custom-made, insulated products for commercial and industrial uses. When the market matured in the 1970s, Bally found itself competing in a price-sensitive market, and the company developed into a mass production operation in order to reduce cost. However, with the beginning of the 1990s, the competition shifted from an emphasis on price alone to price-and-customized products. Bally (which employs 400 people) established new goals. They included: (1) customizing of products to suit the needs of the individual customers, (2) continuously developing new products, (3) delivering products to customers faster than the competition, and (4) reducing the overall manufacturing and administrative costs. These goals required a massive reengineering of the manufacturing process and other company processes.

First Bally introduced a computer-driven intelligent system to reengineer sales and ordering processes, which were composed of 86 sequential tasks which could take five to seven weeks. A redesign of the sales and order entry system allowed salespeople to access information directly from a minicomputer via their own personal computers. Salespeople are able to provide customer requirements, receive price quotations, identify order status and shipment information, receive specification drawings, and communicate with anyone in the company through the electronic mail system. As a result, the sales and ordering process was reduced to less than 20 tasks and took only one to two weeks.

Another improvement of the computerized system was the direct input of customer configurations into a CAD system. From the initial design, bills of materials were generated and copies could be sent via fax machine (now Internet fax) directly to the customer. This also allowed the elimination of a complex system of checking and comparing the components. Every employee has access to all data needed for his or her job, and unnecessary paperwork has been minimized. As a result, the number of customer options has soared from 12 to 10,000, making Bally a true *mass customizer.* Bally also developed a computerized network that links sales representatives, customers, production people, and suppliers into one system which shares information across the entire supply chain. This system evolved by 1998 into an *Internet community* (see Chapter 7).

Without mass customization, Bally would be a struggling company fighting to cut prices with other competitors. Today, however, the company has a leading position, with 12 to 15 percent of the $500 million U.S. market.

**For Further Exploration:** How much more are you willing to pay for a customized rather than a standard product, and why is mass customization better than regular customization? ▲

SOURCE: Condensed from Pine, B. J. II and T. W. Pietrocini, "Standard Modules Allow Mass Customization at Bally Engineered Structures," *Planning Review,* July/August 1993, pp. 20–22.

---

An important point here is that mass customization involves not only the operations function but also marketing and sales, personnel, and finance.

Digital Equipment Corporation (DEC) is another example of a company that has successfully employed mass customization. DEC manufactures minicomputers to order: each unit is customized, and yet millions of systems are sold annually. DEC purchases the necessary subassemblies, which are made in mass production, and then assembles them as needed. A plan for each order used to be compiled manually, which was expensive as well as error prone. Now, the compilation is done by an expert system in about 20 percent of the time and the error rate has decreased drastically.

The role of IT in supporting mass customization is illustrated in the case of flexible manufacturing systems. A *flexible manufacturing system (FMS)* is a group of machines designed to provide the flexibility of individual machines, yet handle a united production process. An FMS saves space, provides high consistency and quality, uses little manual labor, and increases capacity. Virtually unmanned, FMS systems include a series of identical machines, an automated, computer controlled materials handling system, and other equipment, such as coordinate measuring machine, robots, and loading/unloading stations. The FMS is supervised by a work station computer, which interfaces with a central corporate computer when it needs additional data or when it is feeding data back. FMS is flexible enough to all rapid changes in manufacturing, thus enabling mass customization.

> Also crucial is accounting, or billing, or whoever issues the customer the invoice for goods or services.
> — *Mike Rewald*

According to Kalakota and Whinston (1997), electronic commerce transforms the supply chain from a traditional *push model* to a *pull model.* In the push model, the business process starts with manufacturing and ends with consumers buying the products or services. In the pull model (see Figure 4.6), the process starts with the consumer ordering the product (or service) and ends with the

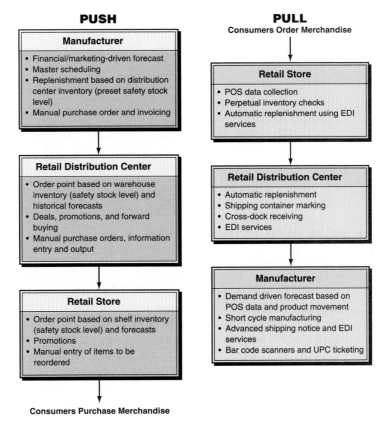

**FIGURE 4.6** Push-based supply chain versus pull-based supply chain. (*Source:* Kalakota and Whinston [1996] p. 289.)

manufacturer making it. The pull model enables customization since orders are taken first. By organizing production to handle a large volume, mass customization is achieved. Dell Computer's success is basically due to reorganizing the supply chain as a pull system.

Mass customization, according to Pine and Gilmore (1997) and Gilmore and Pine (2000), can be facilitated by the Web in four different approaches, for which they give the following examples:

▶ *Collaborative customizers* refers to establishing a dialogue with individual customers to help them figure out what they want to buy. An example is MySki (www.myski.com), which suggests selections of standard skis and then allows each customer to tailor the look of the skis (colors, logos, locations and so forth). Dell uses this approach as do most car manufacturers. The Web is an ideal tool for such customization (Chapter 6).

▶ *Adaptive customizers* refers to offering one standard but customizable product that is designed so users can alter it themselves. A Web example might be a grocery delivery company called Peapod (see Chapter 6) that creates a learning relationship with their customers. With each interaction and service, it becomes more tailored to you. Peapod provides one standard diskette/interface, which each customer then adapts to himself.

▶ *Cosmetic customizers* present a standard product differently to different customers. This approach is ideal when customers use a product the same way and differ only in how they want it presented. The product doesn't change—it's really the packaging or sizes that differ. A Web example is Interactive Custom Clothing (www.ic3d.com), which tailors jeans to your specifications over the Web. Levi's and J. C. Penny are providing a similar service over their private networks.

▶ *Transparent customizers* provide customers with unique goods or services without letting them know that these products have been customized for them. It is adapting a product for you based upon observed behavior. One example is BOC Gases Americas, of Murray Hill, New Jersey, whose parent company, The BOC Group, recently placed No. 1 in the *PC Week Fast-Track 500*, based upon innovations such as tailoring its Web catalog of gas products to clientele, utilizing knowledge of their previous purchases.

Additional examples are provided in Chapter 6.

## CYCLE TIME REDUCTION

Cycle time refers to the time it takes to complete a process from beginning to end. As discussed earlier, competition today focuses not only on cost and quality, but also on time. Time is recognized as a major element that provides competitive advantage, and **cycle time reduction** is a major business objective.

> Cycle time reduction has been a big part of an engineer's job. Using information systems to eliminate/combine production/inspection operations is an example.
>
> — *Dave Gehrke.*

The success of Federal Express, for example, is clearly attributable to its ability to reduce the delivery time of packages with complex computer-supported systems that allow flexible planning, organization, and control (see Wetherbe [1996]). The comeback of Chrysler Corporation and its success in the 1990s can be attributed largely to its "technology center," which has brought about a more than 30 percent reduction in its time to market (the time from beginning the design of a new model to the delivery of the car). Boeing Corporation reengineered its design of airplanes by moving to total computerization. The first airplane designed in this manner was the 777. In a fundamental change to Boeing's processes, a physical prototype was never built. In addition to reducing the cycle time, quality has been improved and costs reduced. Because of this, Boeing was able to compete successfully with Airbus Industries. Notice that both in Boeing's and Chrysler's cases the change was fundamental and dramatic. First, the role of the computer was changed from a tool to a platform for the total design. Second, it was not just a process change, but a cultural change relative to the role of the computer and the design engineers. According to Callon (1996), the engineers are now a part of a computer-based design system. Computing also played a major communications role during the entire design process.

There is an old saying that "time is money," so saving time saves money. But cycle time reduction does more than save money. If you beat your competitors with a new product, a product improvement, or a new service, you can gain a substantial market share. Pharmaceutical companies, for example, are desperately trying to reduce the cycle time of new drugs. If successful, they will be the first on the market, they may receive a patent on the innovation, and revenues will begin flowing sooner to repay their huge investments.

As shown in the Ford and McKesson Water Products cases, IT makes a major contribution in shortening cycle times by allowing the combination or elimination of steps, and the expedition of various activities in the process.

Finally, telecommunications (see Keen [1988]) and especially the Internet and intranets provide a means of economically reducing cycle time by cutting communications time through the use of e-mail and EDI, and by allowing collaboration in design and operations of products and services (see Dietz [1996]).

Cycle time reduction can be very beneficial, but to obtain maximum results from reengineering efforts, it may be necessary to restructure not just one or a few processes, but the entire organization, as we describe next.

## RESTRUCTURING ORGANIZATIONS

We've seen that one problem in many current organizations is vertical structures. How should a contemporary organization be organized? Answers come from two directions. First, management theories advocate a structure that provides leadership and support for critical activities and strategies. For example, cost reduction can be achieved when some layers of middle management are eliminated. Second, we can examine the relationships between organizations and information systems.

**REENGINEERING THE ORGANIZATION.** The fundamental problem with the hierarchical approach is that any time a decision needs to be made, it must climb up and down the hierarchy. All it takes is one person who does not understand the issues to say "no," and everything comes to a screeching halt. Also, if information is required from several "functions," getting all the right information coordinated can be a time-consuming and frustrating process for employees and customers alike.

So, how is reengineering done? It all depends. For example, providing each customer with a single point of contact can solve the fundamental problem just described. Figure 4.7 illustrates the traditional bank, where each department views the same customer as a separate customer. Figure 4.8 depicts a reengineered bank. The customer deals with a single point of contact, the account manager. The account manager is responsible for all bank services, and provides all services to the customer, who receives a single statement for all his accounts. Notice the role of IT is to back up the account manager by providing her with expert advice on specialized topics, such as loans. Also, by allowing easy access to the different databases, the account manager can answer queries, plan, and organize the work with customers.

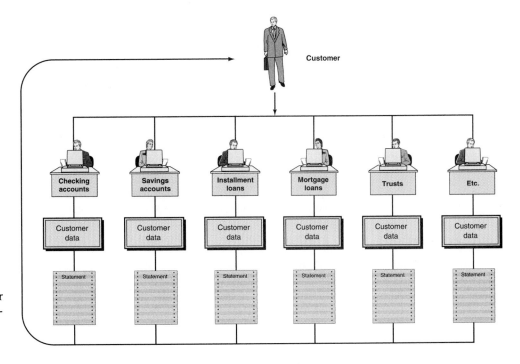

**FIGURE 4.7** Bank before reengineering—customer has to go to every department and he gets different statements.

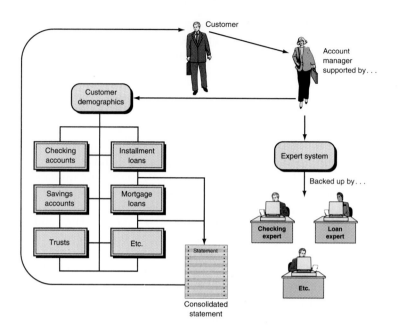

**FIGURE 4.8**
Reengineered bank
with integrated system.

The bank example illustrated how a single point contact provides a high level of customer service. A variation is where several people working in a networked structure can provide excellent service, as demonstrated in the case of the insurance company. A networked structure would have allowed the firm to give Nick Simmons the service he needed, because all agents would have access to all customer data. Another model, used by companies such as USAA, Otis Elevator, and others, is to have all agents located in one city and give customers an 800, toll-free number or an e-mail address. In this model, the company can install a computer-based call-center technology, which brings up complete customer information (or a customer's elevator in the case of Otis) on the computer screen, whenever a customer calls. This means that anyone who picks up the telephone would know all the information necessary to make a quick decision. There is no need to ask questions of the customer, and any agent can give personalized and customized service. This is especially important in reservation systems such as for hotels and airlines, as illustrated in the following *IT at Work*.

## IT At Work    THE TRAVEL COMPANY

**I**NTEGRATING IT

...for Marketing and
Production & Operations
Management

James Williams made extensive use of The Travel Company to coordinate his various speaking and consulting engagements. Because of his specific travel requirements, he always liked to deal with Kathy, a senior travel agent who was familiar with his travel requirements.

The problem was that when Jim called The Travel Company, Kathy was frequently on the line with another customer. Jim would leave a message for her to call him back, but then he would be tied up. So telephone tag inevitably developed, which is a typical frustration of dealing with any travel company.

One day Jim called in to book a flight; as usual, Kathy was busy, so he left a message for her to return his call. The person taking the message said, "Mr. Williams, how was your flight to London last week?"

"Fine."

"Did you receive an aisle seat and a low-cal, low-fat meal as requested?"

"Yes."

"Was the limo service there to pick you up as arranged?"

"Yes," said Jim. "Who is this?"

"This is Mary."

Jim replied, "Well, perhaps *you* could help me."

Jim was now willing to talk to any agent who picked up the phone at the company. Why? Because the travel company installed call-center technology. Now, customer service has improved while costs have declined due to better utilization of the agents.

**For Further Exploration:** Why is IT important in this case? Also, some people suggest that you really do not need a travel agency; you can use the Internet to make reservations on your own. Can Jim get the customer service he gets now from the travel agency from a do-it-yourself system? (*Note:* You can explore this issue further after reading Chapter 6.) ▲

Reengineering is not limited to a specific type of organization. As a matter of fact, studies indicate that 70 percent of all large U.S. corporations are reengineering or considering reengineering. In addition, the public sector, including the U.S. federal government, is implementing reengineering (see the following *IT at Work*).

## *IT At Work*   REENGINEERING THE FEDERAL GOVERNMENT WITH INFORMATION TECHNOLOGY

*USING IT*

...in Public Service

The U.S. Federal Government is using IT to streamline its bureaucracy and improve public services. The program has strong backing, with Vice President Albert Gore acting as leader of the National Performance Review (NPR) team. The team's plan is to create an "electronic government," moving from the Industrial Age into the Information Age.

Information technology is playing a key role in this reengineering of government operations and services. As in any project, top management support is vital. In this case, the President has issued directions that those agencies should coordinate new programs for distributing information to the public through the IT team.

The IT team describes the new electronic government systems as a "virtual agency" in which information is shared throughout the government. The U.S. Department of Agriculture already distributes food stamps electronically. Medicare and social security payments may also be integrated. Other services being proposed by the NPR team include a national network serving law enforcement and public safety agencies; electronic linkage of tax files at federal, state, and local agencies; an international trade data system; a national environmental data index; governmentwide electronic mail; and an integrated information infrastructure, including consolidated data centers. The IT team is also looking at client/server networks and intranets to eliminate the need for large mainframe data centers. Tens of millions of Americans receive Social Security and other payments periodically. The distribution of these services is moving to the Internet for greater savings and shorter cycle times. The NPR made many recommendations about how to use IT for improving the operations of the federal government.

**For Further Exploration:** Why is this system referred to as an electronic agency? Is so much computerization of the government beneficial? Why or why not? ▲

SOURCE: Condensed from Anthes, G. H., "Feds to Downside with IT," *Computerworld*, September 13, 1993, and www.npa.gov, 1998.

The examples in this section demonstrate some approaches that can be helpful in solving the stovepipe and other problems created by the new business environment. Such approaches can be part of an enterprisewide networked structure, which we discuss next.

 ## 4.6 THE NETWORKED ORGANIZATION

### THE STRUCTURE OF NETWORKED ORGANIZATIONS

Many writers have advocated the concept of networked organizations (see Cash et al. [1994], Majcharzak and Wang [1996], Nohria and Eccles [1994], Byrne [1993], and Garvin [1993]). The major characteristics of the **networked organization** are shown in Figure 4.9 (right side) and compared to the characteristics of the hierarchical organization (left side).

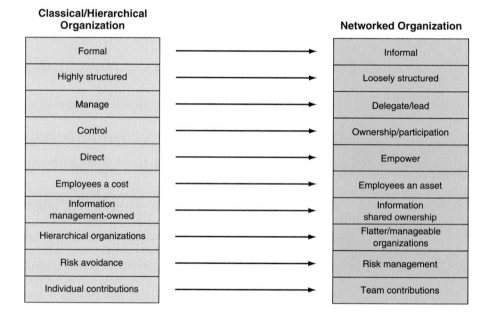

**Classical/Hierarchical Organization** → **Networked Organization**

| Classical/Hierarchical Organization | Networked Organization |
|---|---|
| Formal | Informal |
| Highly structured | Loosely structured |
| Manage | Delegate/lead |
| Control | Ownership/participation |
| Direct | Empower |
| Employees a cost | Employees an asset |
| Information management-owned | Information shared ownership |
| Hierarchical organizations | Flatter/manageable organizations |
| Risk avoidance | Risk management |
| Individual contributions | Team contributions |

FIGURE 4.9 Networked versus hierarchical organization.

The hierarchical and network approaches to management obviously present significant contrast, and each has its successes and failures. There is, in fact, no single, best way to manage all organizations. Rather, the best management approach is *contingent* on characteristics of the organization being managed.

However, today some organizations are turning away from the hierarchical organization toward the networked organization. This trend is being brought about by the evolution from an industrial-based economy to an information-based economy. Today, most people do **knowledge work,** in which the intellectual context of the work increases to the point where the subordinate often has more expertise than the "hierarchical" supervisor. If managers knew "everything," they could use hierarchical methods to tell employees what to do, how to do it, and when to do it. But physicians, scientists, engineers, and similar employees in an organizational network are not just "cogs" in a hierarchical "machine." Each employee has special expertise and information. Therefore, it is better to view the information-based organization as a client/server network. The best "node" should be used to solve the problem.

This is seriously true. When my employees come to me with a problem, my first question is, "How do you think we should solve it?" This will make them ready for my job one day.

— *Mike Rewald*

Figure 4.10 portrays the continuum from the hierarchical approach to the network approach. The nodes in the network can be individuals or teams, as will be described later. Note that in the middle is the **flattened organization,** which has fewer layers of management and a broader span of control than the hierarchical organization, and can be considered to be an improved structure.

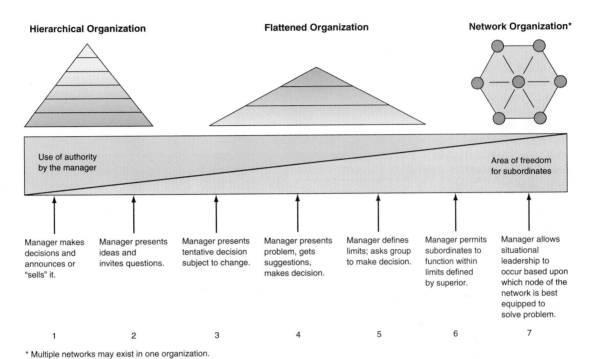

* Multiple networks may exist in one organization.

**FIGURE 4.10** The roles of managers and subordinates in the different types of organizations.

As a straightforward example of a network approach to problem solving, let us say a student in class begins to have cardiac arrest. What should happen? If one student in the class knows CPR, she should become a situational leader and configure a team to solve the problem. That person is the best-equipped "node" in the network. Note that she might be temporarily hierarchical in behavior. For example, she might tell one person to call 911, another to get some blankets, and another to keep the hallways clear for the ambulance personnel. The professor should relinquish authority, and those people assigned tasks by the CPR expert should not argue about who should call 911! The goal is to recognize the most important task. In this case, saving a life preempts teaching, and the situational leader needs to emerge from the network.

Traditional, multilevel hierarchies can become too bureaucratic and slow to be as responsive to dynamic problem solving as in our hypothetical class. In the flattened networked organization, there are fewer layers of management and a broader span of control. In the networked organization, management plays a different role (see Cash et al. [1994]). As a result, in the United States alone, over two million middle management positions have been eliminated in the last 15 years. Why are these jobs not needed? A nationwide recession and competition forced companies to make these staffing reductions in order to survive. The result has gone beyond mere survival to improvements in information management and more empowered and knowledgeable employees working with less supervision.

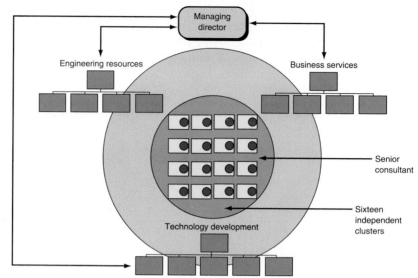

**FIGURE 4.11 British Petroleum Engineering networked with self-directed teams.** (*Source:* Mills, Quinn D., *Rebirth of the Corporation.* Copyright © 1991 John Wiley & Sons, Inc. Reprinted by permission of John Wiley & Sons, Inc.)

Figure 4.11 provides a graphic portrait of the network organization for a division of British Petroleum. Note the *standing teams* (green) of Engineering Resources, Technology Development, and Business Services. The 16 independent clusters represent *pickup teams* (yellow) assigned to solve problems that develop.

## EMPOWERMENT

Self-directed or autonomous teams make their own decisions. In order to do this, they must be empowered.

*Empowerment* is the vesting of decision-making or approval authority in employees where, traditionally, such authority was a managerial prerogative. As a philosophy and set of behavioral practices, empowerment means allowing self-managing teams and individuals to be in charge of their own career destinies, as they meet and exceed company and personal goals through a shared company vision. As an organizational program, empowerment means giving permission to the workforce to unleash, develop, and utilize their skills and knowledge to their fullest potential for the good of the organization as well as for themselves, and it means providing the framework in which this can be done.

For example, the empowerment program of Trane Air Conditioner (Macon, GA), according to Garwood (1991), is designed to achieve the following goals, which are good models for other firms to consider:

1. Increase motivation to reduce mistakes and have individuals take more responsibility for their own actions.

2. Increase the opportunity for creativity and innovation.

3. Support the continuous improvement of processes, products, and services.

4. Improve customer satisfaction by having the employee closest to the customer make rapid, relevant decisions.

5. Increase employee loyalty, while at the same time reducing turnover, absenteeism, and illness.

6. Increase productivity by increasing employee pride, self-respect, and self-worth.

7. Use peer pressure and self-managing team methods for employee control and productivity.

8. Relieve middle and upper management from being "control dogs" and from doing lower level tasks, thereby allowing them more time to do strategic planning, focusing on increasing market share and customer satisfaction.

9. Increase the bottom line by such methods as reducing waste and building quality, while meeting customer requirements.

10. Increase upper management time for development of strategy plans.

11. Reduce the excessive need for quality assurance personnel, lawyers, and historian accountants.

12. Maintain and increase competitiveness.

**EMPOWERMENT'S RELATIONSHIP TO INFORMATION TECHNOLOGY.** Empowerment can be enhanced through IT. Perhaps IT's most important contribution is the provision of the right information, at the right time, at the right quality, and at the right cost. Information is necessary, but it may not be sufficient. To be fully empowered means to be *able to make decisions,* and these require *knowledge.* Knowledge is scarce in organizations, and specialists usually hold it. Accessibility to knowledge may not be easy or cheap. To empower employees means to increase the availability of such knowledge. Expert systems and other intelligent systems can play a major role in providing knowledge, as can the Internet and intranets.

Empowered employees are expected to perform better. To do so, they need new tools. Information technology can provide tools that will enhance the creativity and productivity of employees, as well as the quality of their work. These tools can be special applications for increasing creativity, spreadsheets for increasing productivity, and hand-held computers to improve communication.

Finally, empowerment may require training. People may need more skills and higher levels of skills. Self-directed teams, for example, are supposed to have all the necessary skills to achieve their goal. Once organized, teams will require training, which can be enhanced by IT. For example, many companies provide online training, use multimedia, and even apply intelligent computer-aided instruction. Many companies are using intranets to provide training as in the cases of AT&T and Boeing, cited earlier. Levi Strauss & Company uses a program called Training for Technology, which aims at training people to use the skills and tools they need in order to be able to find information and use it properly.

**EMPOWERMENT OF CUSTOMERS, SUPPLIERS, AND BUSINESS PARTNERS.** In addition to empowering employees, companies are empowering their customers, suppliers, and other business partners. For example, Levi Strauss allows its textile suppliers to access its database, so they know exactly what Levi Strauss is producing and selling and can ship supplies just-in-time. The company is using a similar approach with all its suppliers. Federal Express is using the Internet to empower its customers to check prices, prepare shipping labels, find the location of the nearest drop box, and trace the status of packages. Finally, Dell empowers their customers to track orders and troubleshoot problems. Of special interest is the concept of **extranets,** a combination of Internet and intranet which allows companies to empower their business partners, as will be described in Chapter 6.

### TEAMS

A survey conducted by the Center for Effective Organizations at the University of Southern California in 1994 showed that 68 percent of the largest U.S. corporations are using self-managed teams. However, the survey also showed that only 10 percent of the employees are in such teams. These figures, which were not changed much by 1998, suggest that while most companies use teams, they are not replacing the hierarchical organizational structure with the flat team-based structure. This is because: (1) not all organizations can be structured as team-based organizations, (2) not all processes should be converted to team-based processes, and (3) transforming organizations takes a long time.

Whether teams are all over the organization or only in some parts of it, they can be extremely valuable. Types of teams include (1) *permanent or work group teams*, usually multiskilled, which are **self-directed (managed) teams** that conduct the routine work of the organization; (2) *problem-solving teams*, usually multidisciplinary, multiskilled, established for the purpose of solving a specific problem and then dismantled; (3) *quality circles*, which meet intermittently to find and solve workplace-related problems; (4) *management teams* consisting mainly of managers from different functional areas, whose major objective is to coordinate the work of other teams; and (5) *virtual teams*, whose members are in different places, frequently belong to different organizations, and communicate electronically. In all these cases, IT plays a critical role in empowering team members and providing the necessary communication links among teams (see the following *IT at Work* example).

---

**IT At Work**    HOW GE OF CANADA SUPPORTS TEAMS WITH INFORMATION TECHNOLOGY

One of the most highly publicized examples of a company that transformed itself to a self-directed team structure is GE of Canada. Its being relatively small (360 employees), and in the financial services industry, made it easier to reengineer the entire company, which is now composed of 20 teams (see the figure on page 141) heavily supported by IT.

From the beginning, the steering committee that planned the reengineering recognized IT as a critical factor in the transformation—both for communication and collaboration among teams, and as a tool to support the work of team members. Here are some of the IT applications.

1. Since all secretarial and administrative resources were eliminated, it was necessary to provide productivity software support applications (such as word processing and electronic calendars).
2. Special applications were written to provide user-friendly access to databases. For example, an online access to financial data was created to facilitate data analysis by the payroll and control teams. Downloading data from the mainframe was made simple and easy.
3. Employees were empowered to make their own travel arrangements electronically. (GE has an agreement with a large travel agency that allows these activities.)
4. Robots were installed to deliver mail and supplies.
5. E-mail, voice mail, and fax were made available to all employees.
6. Training in spreadsheet software and in downloading data to the spreadsheet was provided online.
7. Special hardware and software needed for improving productivity, quality, and communication was provided (scanners and imaging technology, for instance). As a matter of fact, employees were encouraged to find ways in which IT could be of help.

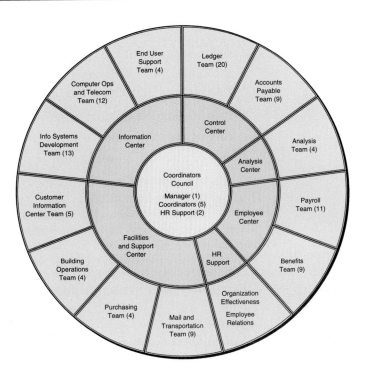

**U**SING IT

...in Production &
Operations Management

The results of the GE reengineering were dramatic indeed. The number of employees was reduced by 50 percent, while the productivity of the company and the quality of its operations (especially in terms of customer service) were drastically improved.

**For Further Exploration:** Who is the boss in this structure? How are employees empowered and how can one control such an organization? ▲

SOURCE: Condensed from Applegate, L.H., and J.J. Cash, "GE Canada: Designing a New Organization," *Harvard Business School Case* 9-189-138, 1989.

The networked organization and self-directed teams are related to another BPR innovation—the virtual corporation, which is presented next.

## ▶ 4.7 VIRTUAL CORPORATIONS

One of the most interesting reengineered organizational structures is the virtual organization, usually referred to as a *virtual corporation (VC)*. The creation, operation, and management of a VC is heavily dependent on IT and is especially facilitated by the Internet and electronic commerce.

### DEFINITIONS AND CHARACTERISTICS

A **virtual corporation** is an organization composed of several business partners sharing costs and resources for the purpose of producing a product or service. The virtual corporation can be temporary, with a onetime mission such as launching a satellite, or it can be permanent. The virtual corporation is usually composed of several components, each in a different location. Each partner contributes complementary resources that reflect its strengths, and determine its role in the virtual corporation. Virtual corporations (VCs) are not necessarily organized along the supply chain. For example, a business partnership may include several partners, each creating a portion of a product or service, in an area in which they have special advantage such as expertise or low cost.

According to Goldman et al. (1995), permanent virtual corporations are designed to do the following:

▶ Create or assemble productive resources rapidly.

▶ Create or assemble productive resources frequently and concurrently.

▶ Create or assemble a broad range of productive resources.

The concept of virtual corporations is not new, but recent developments in IT allow new implementations that exploit its capabilities (see O'Leary, et al. [1997]). The modern virtual corporation can be viewed as a *network* of creative people, resources, and ideas connected via online services and/or the Internet, who band together to produce products or services.

The major attributes of virtual corporations are:

> It's important that we, the next generation of IT managers, understand these concepts, so we can implement these in our businesses. If our business already takes advantage of these techniques, it's beneficial that we understand their concepts so that we won't have to play catch-up when we enter "the working world."
>
> — *Blake Thompson*

▶ **Excellence.** Each partner brings its core competency so an all-star winning team is created. No single company can match what the virtual corporation can achieve.

▶ **Utilization.** Resources of the business partners are frequently underutilized, or utilized in a merely satisfactory manner. In the virtual corporation, resources can be put to use more profitably, thus providing a competitive advantage.

▶ **Opportunism.** The partnership is opportunistic. A virtual corporation is organized to meet a market opportunity.

▶ **Lack of borders.** It is difficult to identify the boundaries of a virtual corporation; it redefines traditional boundaries. For example, more cooperation among competitors, suppliers, and customers makes it difficult to determine where one company ends and another begins in the virtual corporation partnership.

▶ **Trust.** Business partners in a VC must be far more reliant on each other and require more trust than ever before. They share a sense of destiny. For example, Minicase 2 in Chapter 3 (the Dutch Flower Auctions) shows that trust is essential.

▶ **Adaptability to change.** The virtual corporation can adapt quickly to the environmental changes discussed in Chapter 1 because its structure is relatively simple.

▶ **Technology.** Information technology makes the virtual corporation possible. A networked information system is a must.

## THE VIRTUAL CORPORATION AND INTERORGANIZATIONAL INFORMATION SYSTEMS

According to Goldman et al. (1995), in a VC the resources of the business partners remain in their original locations but are integrated. Since the partners are in different locations, they need information systems for supporting communication and collaboration (see Figure 4.12). Such systems are a special case of interorganizational information systems (IOS). An IOS is an information system that crosses organizational lines to one or more business partners (see Chapter 6).

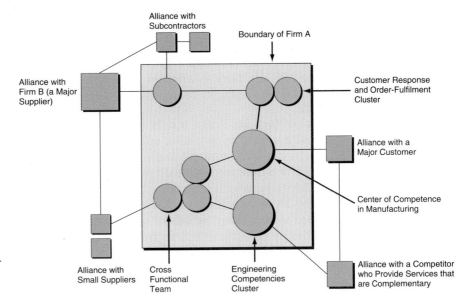

**FIGURE 4.12** A network structure facilitates the creation of virtual companies. (*Source:* Cash, et al. [1994], p. 34.)

## HOW IT SUPPORTS VIRTUAL CORPORATIONS

There are several ways for IT to support virtual corporations. The most obvious are those that allow communication and collaboration among the dispersed business partners. For example, e-mail, desktop videoconferencing, screen sharing, and several other groupware technologies described in Chapter 5 are frequently used to support virtual corporations. Standard transactions in the interorganizational information systems are supported by electronic data interchange (EDI) and EFT (see Chapter 6). The Internet is the infrastructure for these and other technologies. Virtual office systems, for example, can be supported by intelligent agents (see O'Leary et al. [1997] and Chapter 11). Modern database technologies and networking permit business partners to access each other's databases. Lotus Notes and similar integrated groupware tools permit diversified interorganizational collaboration. Kalakota and Whinston (1997) provide numerous examples of intranet/Internet applications. ERP software is extensively used to support standard transactions among business partners. In general, most VCs cannot exist without information technology.

## SOME EXAMPLES OF IT-SUPPORTED VIRTUAL CORPORATIONS

*IBM Ambra.* IBM's Ambra was formed to take advantage of an opportunity to produce and market a PC clone. Ambra's headquarters were in Raleigh, North Carolina. There, 80 employees used global telecommunications networks to coordinate the activities of five companies that were business partners in the virtual company.

Wearnes Technology of Singapore did engineering design and subsystem development services and manufactured or contracted for Ambra PC components. SCI Systems assembled the Ambra microcomputers in its assembly plants on a build-to-order basis from order data received by its computers from AI Incorporated. AI, a subsidiary of Insight Direct, a national telemarketing company based in Tempe, Arizona, received orders for Ambra computers from customers over its 800-number telephone lines. Merisel Enterprises provided the product and delivery database used by AI and handled Ambra order fulfillment and customer delivery. Finally, another IBM subsidiary provided field service and customer support. (SOURCE: Based on Goldman, et al. [1995].)

***Steelcase Inc.*** Steelcase Inc. is a major U.S. maker of office furniture. It has formed a virtual corporation subsidiary called Turnstone that sells its products through catalogs designed and printed by a third-party company. Customers of Turnstone phone in credit card orders to a telemarketing company based in Denver, Colorado, which transmits the order data to computers at warehouses operated by Excel Logistics, Inc. in Westerville, Ohio. From there the products are shipped to customers by subcontracted carriers. Excel's computer systems handle all order processing, shipment tracking, and inventory control applications. Marketing, financial management, and coordinating the virtual company's business partners are the only major functions left to Turnstone's managers. (SOURCE: Based on King [1994].) See www.steelcase.com

*I*NTEGRATING IT

...for Marketing and Production & Operations Management

***The Agile Web, Inc.*** The concept of Agile Web, Inc. emerged at Lehigh University when administrators considered how they could combine the resources of small to medium-size manufacturing companies that had complementary capabilities. The network was designed to address needs of customers who required high value design and manufacturing capabilities involving different technologies and processes, but who did not have the time and/or resources of their own to develop and manage a supplier team for each order.

As business practices became established at the Agile Web, it became clear that information technology was needed to support the network. To leverage the growing body of information on the Agile Web, a communications infrastructure was needed. First, information access and information exchange capabilities were provided by equipping all the member companies with personal computers, EDI software, and connections to a *value added* network. Second, communications capabilities were extended with e-mail and the use of ProShare video software to allow interactive videoconferencing. Most of these services are accessed today through the Internet.

A capabilities database for processes, product customers, and facilities was developed for marketing systems. Finally, long-term goals include implementation of state of the art interfirm project management software. It is expected that the sharing of resources, including actual production facilities, along with the exchange of engineering and design talent, will ultimately lead to fully linked business processes. (SOURCE: Condensed from Sherer [1997].)

## ▶ 4.8 SCM AND ELECTRONIC COMMERCE

Electronic commerce (EC) is emerging as a superb approach for providing solutions to problems along the supply chain. As seen in Dell's example at the beginning of the chapter, many supply chain activities, from taking customers' orders to procurement, can be conducted electronically as part of EC initiatives. The SCM–EC connection can be explained by viewing Figure 4.1 (p. 116) and dividing the EC activities into upstream, internal, and downstream.

### BUYING AND SELLING ALONG THE SUPPLY CHAIN

A major role of EC is to facilitate buying and selling along the supply chain. The major activities are described as follows:

**UPSTREAM ACTIVITIES.** There are many innovative models of EC that improve the upstream activities. These models are described as *e-procurement*, and several are presented in Chapter 6. Here are the highlights of some.

*Bidding.* Companies can place on the Web *requests for quotes* (RFQ) for parts, products, or services. Approved bidders are asked to bid on these jobs during a certain period of time. Many companies, government agencies, and public institutions use the process. There are several variations of bidding:

▶ Large companies conduct the bidding on their own Web site.

▶ Small companies place the RFQ on an intermediary's bidding place. (See www.tpn.geis.com.)

▶ Bids can be made during a certain bidding period until the bids are closed.

▶ Bids can be made in real time.

*Consolidation of Vendors' Catalogues in Buyer's Site.* Large companies and government agencies that have many purchasing departments in various locations and that buy from many vendors use the following process usually for maintenance, repairs, and operations (MRO), parts, products, and jobs. They follow this process:

1. Conduct bids or negotiate prices with approved vendors and agree on prices.
2. Place the vendors' catalogues and price lists on the buyer's central Web site, and add a search engine and electronic ordering forms.
3. Buyers anywhere in the organization can place orders on the corporate central Web site.

*Onsite Specialty Stores.* Fatbrain (www.fatbrain.com), a technical bookseller that establishes onsite electronic bookstores in large companies, initiated this model. Employees buy the books they need (also for personal use) at a discount. Dell is using a similar approach by opening special Web pages for its large companies.

*Other Purchases.* Purchases of services such as bank services, travel, and insurance, can be done electronically at great savings of time and money.

*Buying Knowledge.* Companies also can purchase expertise and consulting services on the Internet at low prices and with fast delivery.

*Internal SCM Activities.* Internal SCM activities include different *intrabusiness EC* activities, which are usually conducted over an intranet, from entering orders of materials, to recording sales, to tracking shipments.

**DOWNSTREAM ACTIVITIES.** Typical models of downstream SCM activities are:

*Selling on Your Own Web Site.* Large companies such as Intel, Cisco, and IBM use this model. Buyers review catalogues from which they buy. Large buyers have their own pages and customized catalogues. (See Dell's opening case.)

*Auctions on Your Web Site.* Large companies such as Dell use this model.

**UPSTREAM AND DOWNSTREAM COMBINED.** It is also possible to combine upstream and downstream EC activities. These are basically electronic markets organized by electronic intermediaries, where many buyers and sellers meet.

Most of these markets are centered on specialized products or services. A typical market is the one organized by Chemdex (www.chemdex.com) for specialty bioscience products. Similar markets exist for flowers, metals, electricity (which is sold among electric-generating companies), certain commodities, and even pigs (in Singapore and Taiwan! See Minicase 2 at the end of the chapter.) Auctions on intermediary sites are also very popular ways to either buy or sell.

## STREAMLINING THE FLOW OF INFORMATION AND EXECUTING PROCEDURES

SCM includes not only flow of goods but also flow of information and the execution of certain procedures (e.g., contracts). Electronic commerce has been contributing to streamlining these flows by providing the EDI infrastructure and protocol since the 1970s. Today EC also uses additional methods such as EDI/internet and extranets for streamlining these flows.

## IMPLEMENTING ELECTRONIC COMMERCE SOLUTIONS ALONG THE SUPPLY CHAIN

Developing EC applications can be done in several ways. Here are some alternatives to consider:

**BUILD IT YOURSELF, IN HOUSE.** This approach may be suitable only for large corporations. It requires a large internal staff and coordination and cooperation from the business partners. This approach is also used in industry-type extranets for certain activities along the supply chain. This approach may be mixed with outsourcing some of the project's tasks.

**OUTSOURCE THE JOB.** Companies that choose to outsource EC solutions usually go to vendors who offer Internet start-up software. Several companies provide EC software for certain segments of the supply chain. Companies such as Ariba (www.ariba.com) and Commerce One (www.commerce.com) provide software for the upstream activities, primarily e-procurement. These companies will install the systems for you, or you can engage major IT outsourcers to do it. The price is not cheap, but the speed is fast and the system will work with less trial-and-error than would exist in option #1. A possible problem with this approach, especially in downstream EC, is that you need to interface with the administrative functions and the logistics system. These systems may already be automated and may be difficult to integrate with ERP software.

**INTEGRATE EC WITH ERP.** Since most middle-sized and large companies already have an ERP system, or are installing one, and since EC needs to *interface* with ERP, it makes sense to interconnect the two. The problem is that ERP vendors started to do this only since 1997 on a small scale and only in 2000 as a major initiative. For example, SAP started building some EC interfaces in 1997, but only in 1999 did it introduce mySAP.com as a major initiative. Its multi-faceted Internet strategy includes EC, online trading sites, an information portal, application hosting, and more user-friendly graphical interfaces. The logic behind the latest move is that by extending the existing ERP system to support e-commerce, organizations not only leverage their investment in the ERP solution, but also speed up the development of EC application. The problem with this approach is that the ERP software is very complex and inflexible (difficult to change), so it is difficult to achieve easy, smooth, and effective integration.

One potential problem is that ERP systems deal more with back-office (administrative) applications, whereas EC deals with front-office applications such as sales and order taking, customer service, and other customer relationship management (CRM) activities. What makes it all even more complex is the need to integrate the company's ERP with business partners. Several vendors are providing software for trading-partner integration, which is a problem that exists in all three options.

**INTEGRATION WITH CRM AND DSS.** The integration of ERP and EC is related to the integration with customer relationship management (CRM). As you will see in Chapters 6 and 8, several CRM activities are part of EC customer service. Furthermore, CRM is considered a value-added function for the ERP vendors. Integration provides a single data model for ERP, CRM, and EC, which enables strong operational efficiencies.

EC activities themselves can be enhanced with analytical tools. For example, Influence Software Inc. has a set of canned enterprise analytical tools for EC analysis. Finally the set of tools of business intelligence, from instantaneous on-line analytical processing of data (OLAP) to data mining, are now integrating with both ERP and electronic commerce.

**COMPONENTIZATION.** *Componentization* refers to breaking large ERP systems into individual components that would work together. By breaking up the large applications into components, vendors would be able to more quickly fix or add functionality. The accounts payable component, for example, could be enhanced without having to touch the other financial components or any of the other components, such as planning or logistics. And once the ERP vendor has established a component architecture, it becomes easier and safer for IT to customize the systems. Componentization also helps the vendors extend the core ERP system with supply chain, CRM, and sales force automation solutions.

Componentization not only would make it easier for ERP vendors to enhance their solutions but also would make it easier for customers to upgrade the software. A customer could selectively upgrade some components without having to upgrade the entire ERP solution, which usually entails a substantial effort and expense. The newest e-commerce capabilities are being delivered as individual components.

# ▶ MANAGERIAL ISSUES

1. *Ethical issues.* Conducting an SCM project or a BPR may result in the need to lay off, retrain, or transfer employees. Should management notify the employees in advance regarding such possibilities? And what about those older employees who are difficult to retrain? Other ethical issues may involve sharing of personal information, which may be part of the new organizational culture. Finally, individuals may have to share computer programs that they designed for their personal use. Such programs may be considered the intellectual property of the individuals.

Implementing organization transformation by the use of IT may involve unethical or even illegal actions. Companies may need to use IT to monitor the activities of their employees and customers and so they may invade the privacy of individuals. When using business intelligence to find out what the competitors are doing, companies may be engaged in unethical tactics such as pressuring competitor's employees to reveal information, or using software that is the intellectual property of other companies (frequently without the knowledge of these other companies).

2. *BPR implementation.* While a large number of companies report that they are reengineering their processes, only a few conduct a true companywide BPR. Remember that SCM, ERP, and BPR are interrelated.

3. While companies should consider extreme integration projects, including ERP, SCM, and electronic commerce, they should recognize that managing long and complex supply chains may result in a failure. Many times companies tightly integrate the upstream, inside company, and downstream activities, and loosely connect these three.

4. *BPR Tools.* BPR utilizes some tools and techniques that have been in existence for years. What is new is the framework that recognizes BPR as a major reorganizational effort, undertaken with clear objectives.

5. *Role of IT.* Almost all major SCM and/or BPR projects use IT. However, it is important to remember that in most cases the technology plays a supportive role, and the primary role is organizational and managerial in nature. On the other hand, without IT, most SCM and BPR efforts do not succeed.

6. *Failures.* A word of caution: One of the lessons from the history of IT is that very big projects have a tendency to fail when expectations exceed real capabilities. For example, many of the early material requirements planning (MRP) systems, artificial intelligence, and complex transaction processing systems never worked. BPR and some ERP are no exception. They too fail for many reasons. One of the reasons for failure is a miscalculation of the required amount of IT. It simply may be too expensive to rebuild and retool the IT infrastructure and adjust applications that are necessary for BPR. The solution may be to defer the BPR and use incremental improvement instead, or to reengineer the most critical processes only.

> One word of wisdom given to me when I left my old job to become a system analyst: "We must focus our attentions to making everyone happy, keeping our promises, and not promising things we can't deliver."
>
> — *Blake Thompson*

## KEY TERMS

Business process reengineering (BPR) *130*

Cross-functional activities *130*

Cycle time reduction *142*

Demand chain *115*

Enterprise resources planning (ERP) *123*

Extranet *149*

Flattened organization *147*

Knowledge work *146*

Mass customization *139*

Networked organization *146*

Product life cycle *116*

Reverse logistics *116*

SAP R/3 *124*

Self-directed teams *150*

Supply chain *115*

Supply chain management (SCM) *115*

Virtual corporation (organization) (VC) *151*

## CHAPTER HIGHLIGHTS *(L–x means learning objective number x)*

▶ It is necessary to properly manage the supply chain to assure superb customer service, low cost, and short cycle time. (L-1)

▶ The supply chain must be completely managed, from the raw material to the end customers. (L-1)

▶ It is difficult to manage the supply chain due to the uncertainties in demand and supply and the need to coordinate several business partners' activities (L-2)

▶ Innovative approaches to SCM require cooperation and coordination of the business partners, which is facilitated by IT innovations such as extranets, that allow suppliers to view company's inventories in real time. (L-2)

▶ During the last 50 years, software integration has increased both in coverage and scope, from MRP to MRP II, to ERP, to enhanced ERP and SCM. (L-3)

▶ Today ERP software, which is designed to improve standard business transactions, is enhanced with decision support capabilities as well as Web interfaces. (L-3)

▶ Implementing SCM projects, or using ERP software, frequently requires changing organizational processes. (L-4)

▶ BPR is the fundamental rethinking and radical redesign of business processes to achieve dramatic improvements. (L-4)

▶ The trend is for organizations that are reengineered to behave like networks and operate in an online, real-time, seamless, empowered mode of operation. (L-5)

▶ Network organizations are flattened and make extensive use of self-directed teams. (L-5)

▶ A major goal of the network organizational paradigm is to allow customers to have straightforward, simple contact with organizations. (L-5)

▶ IT helps not only to automate existing processes, but to introduce innovations which change structure (e.g., create case managers and interdisciplinary teams), reduce the number of processes, combine tasks, enable economical customization, and reduce cycle time. (L-6)

▶ Mass customization which is facilitated by IT, enables production of customized goods by methods of mass production at a low cost. (L-7)

▶ Cycle time reduction is an essential part of many BPR projects and is usually attainable only by IT support (L-7)

▶ One of the most innovative BPR strategies is the creation of business alliances and virtual corporations. (L-8)

▶ Electronic commerce is able to provide new solutions to problems along the supply chain by integrating the company's major business activities with both upstream and downstream entities via an electronic infrastructure. (L-9)

## QUESTIONS FOR REVIEW

1. Define supply chain and supply chain management.

2. Define BPR.

3. How did organizations arrive at the hierarchical structure?

4. What are the limitations of the hierarchical structure in service organizations, such as banks, from a customer's perspective? from an organization perspective?

5. What is meant by mass customization? Give examples.

6. What are the characteristics of a network? How would those characteristics be applied to an organization if it were trying to mirror networks?

7. Explain the role of the self-directed team in the context of a network organization.

8. Contrast the difference between a permanent team and a temporary (pickup) team.

9. Describe the enabling role of IT in BPR.

10. How can IT empower people?

11. Define cycle time reduction.

12. Define a virtual corporation.

13. Describe the major characteristics of empowerment and describe its benefits.

14. Define ERP.

15. List the major components of ERP.

16. Define extended supply chain.

17. Describe a virtual corporation.

## QUESTIONS FOR DISCUSSION

1. Identify the supply chain and the processes that were reengineered by Caterpillar (Chapter 3), and identify the information technologies that supported the reengineered processes.

2. Relate the concepts of supply chain and its management to BPR and IT.

3. Examine the McKesson Water Case. Identify all the BPR activities and describe the information technologies used to support these activities.

4. Identify the supply chain activities in the Dell Computers case.

5. Discuss the Warner-Lambert Listerine case. Was there a need for BPR when the system was implemented?

6. How can an extranet improve the SCM?

7. Explain why IT is such an important BPR enabler.

8. Some people say that BPR is a "capital-labor struggle in disguise." Comment.

9. Some people say that BPR is a special case of SIS, whereas others say that the opposite is true. Comment.

10. Distinguish between ERP and SCM software.

11. What are some quick intermediate steps that could have been taken to solve the problem that Nick Simmons (p. 129) was facing? Consider something that could be implemented in a week or two to provide some value-added services to customers.

12. Relate VC to networked organizations. Why is a VC considered to be a BPR?

13. It is said that SCM software created more change in logistics more than 100 years of continuous improvement did. Discuss.

14. Discuss what it would be like if the registration process and class scheduling process were reengineered to an online, real-time, seamless basis with good connectivity and good empowerment in the university organization. Explain the supply chain.

15. Review the GE Canada *IT at Work*. What are the strengths and weaknesses of the new organizational design at GE Canada?

16. What are some of the reasons for maintaining a functional structure of an organization?

17. Explain how a bank could end up with fragmented information systems so that one customer with several accounts may be perceived as several customers. What would a reengineered bank be like from a customer perspective?

18. It is said that intranets revived the BPR movement. Comment.

19. Explain the role intranets can play in lessening the stovepipe problem.

20. Relate the concept of supply chain management to value system (Chapter 3).

21. How can cooperation between a company and its suppliers reduce inventory cost?

## EXERCISES

1. Find examples of how organizations improve their supply chains in manufacturing, hospitals, retailing, education, construction, and shipping.

2. Contact several banks about opening up multiple accounts (checking, savings, installments, and so on), and ask them to send you the necessary applications for opening the accounts. Assess if the banks are moving toward an integrated network organization.

3. The normal way to collect fees from travelers on expressways is to use tollbooths. Automatic coin collecting baskets can expedite the process, but not eliminate the long waiting lines during rush hours. About 80 percent of the travelers are frequent users of the expressways near their homes, and they complain bitterly. The money collection process in some highways has been reengineered, reducing travelers' waiting time by 90 percent and money processing cost by 80 percent.
   a. Identify the supply chain.
   b. Several new information technologies including smart cards are used in the process. Find information on how this is accomplished.

4. Some say that intranets and extranets will make ERP obsolete. Find information in CIO Magazine, PCWeek, and other periodicals regarding this possibility. Find arguments why this is not possible. Prepare a report.

5. Carlson Travel Network of Minneapolis is the second largest travel agency in the country. It provides an agentless service to corporate clients, the first of which was General Electric Company in April 1993. A computerized system allows GE employees to book trips by filling out a form on their PCs. The system is available 24 hours a day. It is connected with the computer reservation systems of major airlines, car rental companies, and hotel chains. The automated system generates detailed spending reports, enabling GE to negotiate special rates for their employees. Complex travel itineraries are still handled manually, but they account for less than 5 percent of the total trips. The system saves GE several million dollars each year.
   a. Identify the supply chain activities.
   b. Describe the support provided by IT.
   c. Can this be considered a BPR? Why or why not?

## GROUP ASSIGNMENTS

1. Each group in the class will be assigned to a major ERP/SCM vendor such as SAP, PeopleSoft, Oracle, etc. Members of the groups will investigate topics such as:
   a. Web connections.
   b. Use of business intelligence tools.
   c. Relationship to BPR.
   d. Major capabilities.
   e. Use of ASP.
   f. Low cost approaches.

   Each group will prepare a presentation for the class.

2. Mass Customization Review

   Group members should search for cases of mass customization such as those cited in this chapter. Describe the various types of mass customization and the supportive role of IT. Collect more information on what is going on at Levi Strauss and J. C. Penney.

3. Explore the concept of *virtual classrooms* and universities. Start by visiting www.cs.unc.edu/caeti and www.arpa.mil/sisto/Overview/CAETI.html. Each member will explore an actual case. Prepare a summary report.

4. Universities and many other organizations order periodicals for their libraries constantly. New periodicals appear every day, people change their preferences, and the librarians are busy. Typically, the university will contact an agent to place their order. The agent, who is in contact with hundreds (thousands) of publishers, consolidates orders from several universities and then places orders with the publishers. This process is both slow and expensive to the library, which pays 3 percent commission and loses a 5 percent discount that the publisher passes on to the agent.

   The University of California at Berkeley pioneered an electronic ordering system in 1996, which enabled the university to save about $365,000 per year. Furthermore, the cycle time is cut by as much as 80 percent, providing subscribers with the magazine one to three months earlier.

   The electronic ordering is coordinated by Rowe .Com. Inc. The system, called Subscribe (see http://

rowe.com.subscribe/html), enables the university to electronically submit its encrypted orders and a secure payment authorization to a central computer via EDI. The program verifies the order and the authorization, transfers the order via EDI to the publisher and the payment authorization to the automated clearing house, for EFT from the buyers' bank to the payers'.

The cost to the university is $5/order. That is, for an average periodical with annual subscription fee of $400, the cost is more than 80 percent lower ($5 vs. $32).

**a.** Prepare a flowchart of how the new purchasing process works. Show all the business partners (the university, Rowe.Com, publishers) and the flow of information (orders, etc.), journals, and money.

**b.** Prepare a flowchart for the traditional process which involves placing an order to an agent who places the order with the publishers and bills the university. The university pays the agent who pays the publisher. One agent can work with many publishers.

**c.** What are the advantages to the university? What are the disadvantages?

**d.** Identify the various software programs that support the new system. Where are they located and what is the role of each program?

**e.** What other services related to the ordering of journals (not books!) could Rowe.Com offer to the university?

**f.** What will happen to the middleman (the agent)?

**g.** What can Rowe.Com do to stay ahead of potential competitors in this market? What will be the cost of such a strategy?

**h.** Enter the Web site of Rowe (www.Rowe.com). Find more information about their recent Subscribe program.

**i.** What is the EDI and the Internet used for?

## INTERNET EXERCISES

Note: The URLs included here were current when the book went to press. However, they are subject to change without notice. Please consult the Turban Web site (www.Wiley.com/college/turban2e).

**1.** Access the Web site of Bank of America or Wells Fargo. Find some information about their home-banking program. Download the demo they provide. Can home shopping cure the problems cited in this chapter? Why or why not?

**2.** There is an increased use of the Internet/intranet to enable employees to make their own travel arrangements. Several Internet travel companies provide opportunities for companies to reengineer their travel processes. Surf the Internet to find some vendors that provide such services. Also check what the airlines are doing (e.g., electronic ticketing). Prepare a report that summarizes all the various activities. Also discuss the potential impact on the travel agency industry.

**3.** Access the site of Levi Strauss. Find information about how to order their customized jeans. E-mail the company to find out more about their mass customization plan. Also, try to find any information about their electronic communications with their wholesalers and suppliers.

**4.** Surf the Internet to find some recent material on the role IT plays in supporting BPR. Search for products and vendors and download an available demo. Try http://raider/mgmt.purdue.edu/~/shashi/bpr.html.

**5.** Identify some newsgroups that are interested in BPR. Initiate a discussion on the role of IT in BPR.

**6.** Surf the Internet to find information about BPR vendors and tools. Try the following vendors: CACI, SAP/AG, Baan Co NV, Oracle, and PeopleSoft.

**7.** Enter www.supply-chain.org and www.cio.com, and identify recent issues in supply chain management.

**8.** Dell Computer Corporation (www.dell.com) mass customizes its PC production. Find out how they do it.

# Minicase 1

## Case: Green Mountain Coffee Roasters Integrates Electronic Commerce and Supply Chain Management

**Green Mountain Coffee Roasters (GMCR)**, a medium-sized distributor of quality coffee in the U.S., experienced a high growth rate (from $34 million in 1996 to about $70 million in 1999). Sales are done through over 5,000 wholesalers and resellers, including supermarkets, restaurants, and airlines. In addition, mail order shipments are made to over 40,000 loyal individual customers.

The rapid expansion of the business made if necessary to provide all employees access to the latest data so they can make better decisions regarding demand forecast, inventory management, and profitability analysis. To meet this need the company decided to install ERP software.

In 1997 GMCR replaced its custom legacy information system with an ERP from PeopleSoft. The ERP includes functional modules such as production and inventory control, financial management, and human resources management. GMCR decided in 1998 to hook the ERP to the Internet for the following reasons:

▶ The company expects to double its sales to individual customers. This is going to be done by displaying the culture and image of the company, allowing customers to learn more about coffee, and actually creating a "GMCR coffee community."

▶ The existing coffee tours and coffee club will adapt well to the Internet.

▶ It is forecasted that at least 30% of the 5,000 business partners prefer to do business online.

▶ The company needed a better mechanism for customer relationship (both with individuals and businesses). The company wants to get quick feedback, be able to solve customer problems quickly, and provide an efficient and easy order taking facility.

The integration of the Web with the ERP provides the following capabilities:

▶ Many of the business customers are small proprietor-managed shops. They are busy during the day, so they prefer to place orders in the evenings when GMCR's call center is closed.

▶ The customers like to know, immediately, if a product is in stock and when it will be shipped.

▶ Customers want to see their order histories, including summaries such as most-frequently-ordered product list.

All of the above can be done by customers themselves, anytime and from anywhere. In addition the system can support the requests of GMCR's sales force for instant information about customers, inventory levels, prices, competition, overnight delivery services, etc.

PeopleSoft's eStore, an Internet storefront that is tightly integrated with the ERP suite from order fulfillment to the rest of the supply chain management, was implemented in 1999. GMCR benefited not only from improved customer service and efficient online marketing, but also from provision of access to the latest data to all employees. Some of the results so far: Forecasts have improved, inventory is minimized (using the just-in-time concept), and profitability analysis by product and/or customer can be done in minutes.

### Questions for Minicase 1

1. Enter www.gmcr.com and identify the major customer-related activities. How are such activities supported by information technology?

2. Coffee club members make up about 90% of all the company's direct mail business. Why? (Check the Web site.)

3. How can the ERP system improve GMCR inventory system?

4. It is said that "Internet sales data must be taken into account by enterprise planning, forecast demand, and profitability studies." Explain why.

5. It is said that "Because the customer's account and pricing information are linked to the order, accurate invoicing will flow automatically from the Internet transaction." Explain, and relate to the concept of supply chain.

SOURCE: Condensed from customer success stories at www.peoplesoft.com, Jan. 2000.

# Minicase 2

## Electronic Pig Auctioning in Singapore

Pork is the main meat item consumed by about 2.5 million Chinese in Singapore. To meet this demand, there is a need for between 2,000 and 3,000 pigs every day. The pigs are raised on about 120 farms, mostly in Malaysia, although some are in Indonesia. The business used to be controlled by 4 out of 23 importers. Prices were set by the major importers, allowing them to make substantial profits at the expense of the consumers.

In order to protect customers, the government decided to change pig trading by using open electronic auctions. This idea was adapted from Taiwan, where a similar system was working successfully. The pig trad-

ing is done in a system called Hog Auction Market (HAM). As in any auction, bidders are competing against each other by placing bids. Refer to the accompanying figure to see how the bidding is conducted.

On the left side of the figure are the pigs. On the right side are the bidders. Importers bring pigs into the auction area where data (such as the type of pig) are entered into the computer. Using a lottery, the sequence of auctioning is determined. Then, the pigs are washed (guess who is considered to be the cleanest country in the world), marked for identification, and weighed. At that point, everything is ready for the auc-

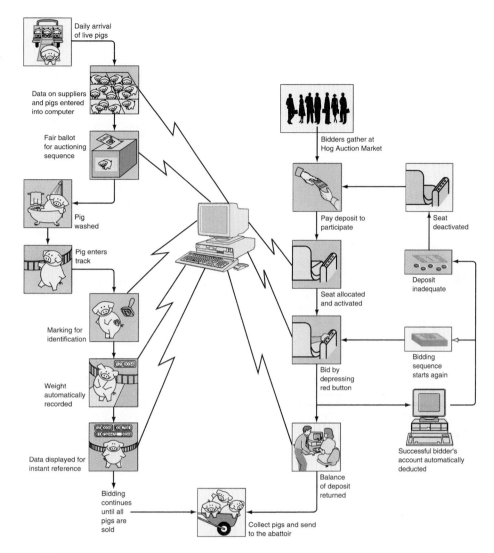

Daily arrival of live pigs

Data on suppliers and pigs entered into computer

Fair ballot for auctioning sequence

Pig washed

Pig enters track

Marking for identification

Weight automatically recorded

Data displayed for instant reference

Bidding continues until all pigs are sold

Bidders gather at Hog Auction Market

Pay deposit to participate

Seat allocated and activated

Bid by depressing red button

Balance of deposit returned

Seat deactivated

Deposit inadequate

Bidding sequence starts again

Successful bidder's account automatically deducted

Collect pigs and send to the abattoir

tion. About 40 bidders, licensed by the government, enter the area and pay the necessary participation fees.

When a pig is ready to be auctioned, its ID number, type, weight, and starting bidding price are displayed on a large screen visible to all bidders. The pig is moved to a track where it can be visually assessed by bidders. The bids are executed by pressing a "bid" button, signifying that the bidder is willing to pay the displayed price. If two or more bidders press buttons, the price is automatically raised by $0.02 per kilogram. The process continues until only one bidder remains. Once a bid is awarded, the computer checks the adequacy of funds, and the successful bidder gets his pig. Using computers makes the process very efficient. A pig is usually shown for five seconds or less before it is sold.

The system helped to increase the quality of meat, since pigs are now being sold individually. Commission was dropped from between 7 and 10 percent to 3 percent. Farmers are being paid in three days instead of

three to four weeks. Most importantly, the consumers are paying about 20 percent less (prices dropped from $2.80 to $2.30 per kilogram in 1992).

### Questions for Minicase 2

1. Why is this considered a BPR?
2. What specific information technologies are involved in the systems?
3. Can the Internet be added to this auctioning process? How?
4. What are the advantages over a manual auction system?
5. Who are the major beneficiaries of the system?
6. Compare this case to the flower auctioning in the Netherlands (Minicase 2 in Chapter 3). What can you learn from either case to improve the other?

SOURCE: Condensed from Neo, B. S., "The Implementation of an Electronic Market for Pig Trading in Singapore," *Journal of Strategic Information System,* December 1992.

# REFERENCES AND BIBLIOGRAPHY

1. Allen, T. J., and M. Scott-Morton, *Information Technology and the Corporation of the 1990s,* Oxford: Oxford University Press, 1993.

2. Alt, R., et al., "Interaction of Electronic Commerce and Supply Chain Management: Insights from 'The Swatch Group,' *Proceedings 33rd HICSS,* Hawaii, Jan. 2000.

3. Appleton, E. L., "How to Survive ERP." *Datamation,* March 1997.

4. Ayers, J., "A Primer on Supply Chain Management," *Information Strategy: The Executive's Journal,* Winter 2000.

5. Blackburn, J. D., ed., *Time-based Competition: The Next Battleground in American Manufacturing,"* Homewood, IL: Business One Irwin, 1991.

6. Byrne, J. A., "The Horizontal Corporation," *Business Week,* December 20, 1993.

7. Caldwell, B., "Taming the Beast," *Information Week,* March 10, 1997.

8. Caldwell, B., and T. Stein, "Beyond ERP: New IT Agenda," *Information Week,* Nov. 30, 1998.

9. Candler, J. W., et al., "The ORION Project: Staged BPR at Fed EX," *Communications of the ACM,* February 1996.

10. Champy, J., *Reengineering Management: The Mandate for New Leadership,* New York: Harper Collins, 1995.

11. Chase, R. B., et al., *Production and Operations Management,* 8th ed., Homewood, IL. Irwin, 1998.

12. cio.com, "Supply Chain Integration: The Name of the Game Is Collaboration," Special Advertising Supplement, *CIO Magazine,* Nov. 1, 1999.

13. Clark, T. H., and D. B. Stoddard, "Interorganizational Business Process Redesign: Merging Technological and Process Innovation," *Journal of MIS,* Fall 1996.

14. Cleland, D. I., *Strategic Management of Teams,* New York: John Wiley & Sons, 1996.

15. Connoly, J., "ERP Corporate Cleanup," *Computerworld,* vol. 33, 1999, pg. 74 – 78.

16. Cross, J., et al., "Transformation of the IT Function at British Petroleum," *SIM 1996 International Paper Award* (www.simnet.org/public/programs/captial/97paper/paper1/1.html).

17. Currid, C., et al., *Computing Strategies for Reengineering Your Organization,* Rocklin, CA: Prima Publishing, 1994.

18. Davenport, T. H., *Process Innovation: Reengineering Work Through Information Technology,* Boston: Harvard Business School Press, 1993.

19. Davenport, T., "Putting the Enterprise in the Enterprise System," *Harvard Business Review,* vol. 76, 1998, pp. 121 – 131.

20. Davenport, T., and N. Nohria, "Case Management and the Integration of Labor," *Sloan Management Review,* Winter 1994.

21. El Sawy, O., *The BPR Workbook,* New York: McGraw Hill, 1998.

22. Fugleseth, A. M., and K. Gronhaug, "IT-enabled Redesign of Complex Dynamic Business Process: The Case of Bank Credit Evaluation," *Omega,* Vol. 25, No. 1, 1997.

23. Garvin, D. A., "Building a Learning Organization," *Harvard Business Review,* Vol. 71, No. 4, 1993, p. 78.

24. Geoffrey, J., "Intranets Rescue Reengineering," *Datamation,* December 1996.

25. Grenier, R., and G. Metes, *Going Virtual: Moving Your Organization into the Twenty-First Century,* Upper Saddle River, NJ: Prentice Hall, 1995.

26. Hammer, M., and J. Champy, *Re-engineering the Corporation,* New York: Harper Business, 1993.

27. Hammer, M., and S. A. Stanton, *The Reengineering Revolution: A Handbook,* New York: Harper Collins, 1995.

28. Handfield, R. B., and E. L. Nichols, Jr., *Introduction to Supply Chain Management,* Upper Saddle River, NJ: Prentice-Hall, 1999.

29. Jacobs, F. R., and D. C. Whybark, *Why ERP,* Boston: McGraw-Hill, 2000.

30. Kalakota, R., and A. B. Whinston, *Electronic Commerce: A Manager's Guide,* Reading, MA: Addison, Wesley, 1997.

31. Keen, P., *Competing in Time: Using Telecommunications for Competitive Advantage,* Cambridge, MA: Ballinger, 1988.

32. Ketting, W. J., et al., "Business Process Change: A Study of Methodologies, Techniques and Tools," *MIS Quarterly,* March 1997.

33. Khalil, O. E. M., "Implications for the Role of Information Systems in BPR Environments," *Information Resources Management Journal,* Winter 1997.

34. Koch, C., et al., "The ABCs of ERP," *CIO Magazine* (www.cio.com), December 22, 1999.

35. Lampel, J., and H. Mintzberg, "Customization Customization," *Sloan Management Review,* Fall 1996.

36. Lieber, R. B., "Here Comes SAP," *Fortune,* Oct. 2, 1995.

37. Lipnack, J., and J. Stamps, *Virtual Teams,* New York: John Wiley & Sons, 1997.

38. Majcharzak, A., and Q. Wang, "Breaking the Functional Mind-set in Process Organizations," *Harvard Business Review,* September/October 1996.

39. Markus, M. L., and R. I. Benjamin, "The Basic Bullet Theory in IT-enabled Transformation," *Sloan Management Review,* Winter 1997.

40. Neumann, S., *Strategic Information Systems,* New York: MacMillan, 1994.

41. Nolan, R. L., and C. C. Crosson, *Creative Destruction,* Boston, MA: Harvard Business School Press, 1995.

42. O'Leary, D., et al., "Artificial Intelligence and Virtual Organizations," *Communications of the ACM,* January 1997.

43. Parr, A. N., and Shanks, G., "A Taxonomy of ERP Implementation Approaches," *Proceedings 33 HICSS,* Hawaii, Jan. 2000.

44. Peppard, J., "Broadening Vision of BPR," *Omega,* June 1996.

45. Pine, B. J. II, *Mass Customizations,* Boston: Harvard Business School Press, 1993.

46. Pine, B. J., and J. Gilmore, "The Four Faces of Mass Customization," *Harvard Business Review,* Jan./Feb. 1997.

47. Poirier, C. C., *Advanced Supply Chain Management: How to Build a Sustained Competition,* Publishers' Group West, 1999.

48. Pollalis, Y. A., "A Systematic Approach to Change Management: Integrating IS Planning, BPR, and TQM," *Information Systems Management,* Spring 1996.

49. Rayport, J. F., and J. J. Sviokla, "Exploiting the Virtual Value Chain," *Harvard Business Review,* November/December 1995.

50. Russell, R. S., and Taylor, B. W., *Operations Management,* 3rd ed., Upper Saddle River, N.J., Prentice-Hall, 2000.

51. Sandoe, K., and A. Saharia, *Enterprise Integration,* New York: John Wiley & Sons, 2001.

52. Sieber, P., and J. Griese, "Virtual Organizing as a Strategy for the 'Big Six' to Stay Competitive in a Global Market," *Proceedings of the 30th Hawaiian International Conference on Systems Sciences,* Hawaii, January 1997.

53. Stein, T., "Orders from Chaos" (supply chain systems), *Information Week,* June 23, 1997.

54. Teng, J. T. C., et al., "Re-designing Business Processes with Information Technology," *Long Range Planning,* February 1994.

55. Tung, L. L., and E. Turban, "The Reengineering of the ISD of the Housing Development Board in Singapore," in Neo, B. S., ed., *Exploring Information Technology for Business Competitiveness,* Addison Wesley, 1996.

56. Turban, E., et al., *Electronic Commerce. A Managerial Perspective,* Upper Saddle River, NJ: Prentice-Hall, 2000.

57. Utterback, J., *Mastering the Dynamic of Innovation,* Boston: Harvard Business School, 1996.

58. Wetherbe, J. C., *The World on Time,* Santa Monica, CA: Knowledge Exchange, 1996.

59. Wigand, R., et al., *Information, Organization and Management: Expanding Markets and Corporate Boundaries,* New York: John Wiley & Sons, 1997.

60. Wysocki, R. K., and R. L. Denrichiell, *Managing Information Across the Enterprise,* New York: Wiley, 1996.

**Note:** An integrated case study for Part I, *Woodstrat: A Support System for Strategic Management,* is available on the Turban Web site (www.wiley.com/college/turban2e).

# PART II
## NETWORKS
## AND IT

### PART I
### IT In the Organization

1. Organizations, Environments, and Information Technology
2. Information Technologies: Concepts and Management
3. Strategic Information Systems
4. Supply Chain, Enterprise Resources Planning, and Business Process Reengineering

### PART II
### Networks and IT

5. Network Computing: Discovery, Communication, and Collaboration
6. Electronic Commerce
7. Impacts of IT on Organizations, Individuals, and Society

### PART III
### Using IT

8. Transaction Processing, Innovative Functional Systems, and Integration
9. Supporting Management and Decision Making
10. Data and Knowledge Management
11. Intelligent Support Systems

### PART IV
### Managing IT

12. Planning for Information Technology and Systems
13. Information Technology Economics
14. Systems Development
15. Managing Information Resources, Control, and Security

| Hardware | Software | Databases | Telecommunications and Internet |

An executive forum organized by *Beyond Computing* magazine in late 1997 discovered that executives today have a lot in common. Most notably it was found that information technologies are helping to reshape organizations in dramatic ways (*Beyond Computing,* July/Aug. 1997). The most frequently mentioned topics were the Internet, intranet, and electronic commerce and their impact on employees, customers, competition, and business operation. These topics are also the subject of Part II (Chapters 5 through 7).

**Chapter 5** deals with the three major capabilities of network computing. First is the *discovery* of information, which is done by using the Web and the Internet and/or intranets. Various tools can be used to facilitate discovery—ranging from search engines to intelligent agents. Some of these tools are described in Technology Guide #4 and in Chapters 6 and 11. Second, it is *communication*, which is also facilitated by a variety of tools, and it is done over the Internet, private networks, and intranets. Several tools are described here as well as in Technology Guide #4. Finally, *collaboration* among people who are in different locations, possibly at different times, is facilitated by several tools over the networks.

Discovery, communication, and collaboration is the basis for *electronic commerce,* which is the topic of Chapter 6. **Chapter 6** is divided into four major parts: essentials of electronic commerce, applications, customer and market research, and infrastructure and support services. The coverage of electronic commerce in Chapter 6 is very comprehensive, making it the longest chapter in the book.

The Internet, electronic commerce, and the conventional information technologies impact on people and organizations and society. **Chapter 7** begins with a look at some negative effects of IT. Then ethical issues are placed into perspective, especially privacy and the protection of intellectual property. The many dimensions of organizational impacts are described next, followed by a discussion of the impacts on individuals, including their health and safety. The chapter and the part end with a discussion of the societal impacts of IT, ranging from unemployment to telecommuting.

The Part II end case demonstrates the implementation of a global EC. Tradenet, a pioneering application of EDI in the Port of Singapore, is enabling the country to successfully compete with its neighboring ports who enjoy low labor cost. It is available on our Web site (www.Wiley.com/college/turban2e).

# CHAPTER 5
# Network Computing: Discovery, Communication, and Collaboration

**5.1**
**The Internet**

**5.2**
**Groupware Technology and Infrastructure**

**5.3**
**Some Internet Implementation Topics**

## *Learning Objectives*

*After studying this chapter, you will be able to:*

❶ Understand the concept of the Internet, its importance, and its capabilities.

❷ Identify the various ways in which communication is executed over the Internet.

❸ Demonstrate how people collaborate over the Internet and use the various supporting tools, including voice technology and teleconferencing.

❹ Describe group support systems and Lotus Notes.

❺ Describe intranets.

❻ Describe and analyze the role of software agents.

❼ Consider ethical issues related to the use of the Internet.

*167*

# NATIONAL SEMICONDUCTOR CORPORATION

## The Problem

The semiconductor (or chip) industry is one of the most competitive global industries. The rivalry among Japan, Korea, Taiwan, and the United States is fierce and prices are continuously being driven down. When the economy is weak, demand for computers weakens, resulting in price cuts and losses to the chip manufacturers.

One way to survive is to customize products. National Semiconductor Corporation (NSC) has over 30,000 products (40,000 in 1998); however, this creates a problem for the customers. When customers need a chip, they provide specifications to several chip manufacturers, collect catalogs and samples from these manufacturers, and then contact them for prices and technical details. This takes a considerable amount of time and effort.

Connectivity problems due to different hardware, software, and communication standards had forced NSC to resort to the telephone, fax, and regular mail to communicate and collaborate with its customers. It was just too expensive and cumbersome to handle these activities electronically with the old system. The communication channels that were available prior to the Internet were either regular telephone lines or private communication lines, all of which were expensive. EDI was in use, but it was limited to transaction processing and was carried on an expensive VAN. Transmission of pictures, charts, and diagrams, a major part of the NSC product catalog, was a very difficult task.

## The Solution

NSC introduced an innovative solution. The company posts detailed descriptions about its 40,000 products on its *Web site** and allows its customers to access this information 24 hours a day. *Browsing* through the information, customers are able to download the documents they need. The Web site is also used by the company's employees to search out information quickly and accurately, and to receive more direct feedback from their customers. This application is part of the corporate *extranet* system.

The *World Wide Web* services of NSC (www.nsc.com) uses innovative technologies such as a *Java search engine*

*The Internet terms used in this case are italicized here and are defined in Technology Guide #4 or in Chapter 6. For an Internet dictionary and tour guide see www.whatis.com.

that can help find a matching product for a customer, based on product specification, and custom software that can extract information from existing databases and automatically format it in the *HTML* programming language. HTML (see Technology Guide #4) helps in preparing documents that appear on the Internet.

NSC has created direct links between its Web site and the Web pages of many of its customers. Thus, customers can access their own Web pages and easily interface with NSC. This arrangement also allows NSC to watch the inventory level of chips at their customers' facilities (they are allowed to enter a portion of their customers' intranets). The Internet links enable Tektronix Inc., for example, to discontinue the need to maintain paper files of past and current parts. Product specifications and availability are automatically updated and linked to Tektronix's system. This has enabled NSC to reengineer its distribution system. NSC can manage their customers' inventory and automatically ship products to them when the inventories are low.

Designing its Web site was a complex job for NSC since the company had to satisfy many different people. Using focus groups, the company's engineers identified the information needs of its customers. Another problem was collecting the data to be used with the Web site. These data resided in several databases protected behind a company *firewall*. A special program was written to collect these data and format them in HTML. Three search engines were used:

▶ Swish (a freeware package), which does a keyword or full-text search.

▶ An in-house program for writing the HTML instructions and providing product lists.

▶ Krakatoa (from Cadis Inc., Boulder, CO), which finds products based on customers' technical requirements.

The search process is supported by an *electronic form* that is easily filled in by customers, and by a menu of *hyperlinks* to related products and services. The system is used both by customers and by NSC engineers. Its benefits are:

▶ Reducing the sample ordering process by days or weeks.

▶ Expediting the design of new products.

▶ Increasing the exposure of NSC products by a factor of ten. (Customers are now downloading ten times as many documents as they did previously using e-mail.)

▶ Providing more information to the customers.

▶ Providing direct and expeditious feedback from customers.

▶ Increasing quality and productivity.

▶ Improving the company's relations with its business partners.

▶ Increasing profitability and competitiveness.

**The Results**

The Internet solution enables NSC to use **electronic catalogs** instead of paper catalogs. In addition, it lets customers view these catalogs from their own sites and download detailed documents in order to analyze products more closely. The Internet's electronic mail capabilities allow rapid communication between NSC engineers and customers. Recently added software and hardware, such as videoconferencing and screen sharing, let NSC engineers collaborate with customers electronically, allowing them to work on the same documents from different locations. All this is done at a relatively low cost. NSC's sales and profitability increased significantly in 1996 and 1997 due to the Internet solution.

Since 1997, the company tracks its visitors' movements in its site trying to predict their buying habits (see *Internetweek,* Oct. 6 and 13, 1997). In 1998, NSC earned the best extranet application award (*Internetweek,* March 9, 1998).

*Source:* Condensed from Corcoran, C., "National Semiconductor Uses Web to Ease Support Services," *Infoworld,* July 22, 1996.

## ▶ 5.1 THE INTERNET

### OVERVIEW AND DEFINITIONS

The NSC opening case demonstrates the increasing role the Internet, intranets, and extranets play in organizations and their potential benefits to an organization.

Because of its capabilities, the Internet is rapidly becoming one of the most important information technologies today. It is clearly the most widely discussed IT topic during the latter part of the 1990s and special terminology has even been developed to support it (see the italicized words in the opening case).

The **Internet** is a *global network of computer networks,* frequently referred to as the "Net." It links the computing resources of businesses, government, and educational institutions using a common computer communication protocol, TCP/IP, which we describe in Technology Guide #4. The Internet supports applications in the following major categories:

> Almost every job I've applied for has had some Internet skills listed in the requirements.
>
> — *Blake Thompson*

1. *Discovery.* Discovery involves browsing and information retrieval. As demonstrated in the opening case, it provides customers the ability to view documents and download whatever they need. This topic is discussed in Section 5.1.

2. *Communication.* The Internet provides fast and inexpensive communication channels that range from messages posted on bulletin boards to complex exchanges among many organizations. It also includes information transfer (among computers) and information processing. E-mail, chat groups, and newsgroups are examples of major communication media presented in Section 5.1 and in Technology Guide #4.

**3. *Collaboration.*** Due to improved communication, electronic collaboration between individuals and/or groups is on the rise. Several facilities can be used, ranging from screen sharing and teleconferencing to group support systems, as we will illustrate in Sections 5.2 and 5.3. Collaboration also includes resource-sharing services, which provide access to printers and specialized servers. Several collaboration tools, called groupware, can be used on the Internet and on other networks.

The Net is also used for education and entertainment. Moreover, its ever-increasing capabilities allow companies to conduct many types of business activities on the Net. Termed **electronic commerce (EC),** these activities range from just advertising to rendering a full range of customer services, as we will see in Chapter 6.

Some of the tools developed for the Internet are listed in Technology Guide #4. These tools can be used not only on the Internet, but also on a conceptually similar system called an **intranet,** which is a network used within an organization (see the description in Section 5.2).

The amount of material available on the Internet doubles every year. To build indices to this information, some companies use automation called software agents (described in Section 5.3). Some important emerging ethical issues relating to the Internet and intranets are also discussed in Section 5.3.

> Allows me to train my salespeople in product knowledge in geographically dispersed areas.
> — *James Rolstead*

## THE INFORMATION SUPERHIGHWAY

Many aspects of the way we work and live in the twenty-first century will be determined by a vast web of electronic networks which has been dubbed the **information superhighway** (see Figure 5.1).

**CD-ROM:** The utmost multimedia combination at your fingertips for education, entertainment, and business.

**VIDEO PHONE:** You will be able to conduct a face-to-face conversation from any video phone to others.

**HDTV:** High-resolution TV will provide much sharper TV pictures for the viewer's enjoyment.

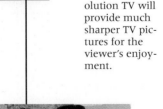

**VIRTUAL REALITY:** You will be able to feel the sensation of being in any place you ever wanted to be. Will simulate just about any human activity.

**LAPTOP:** Powerful and portable. Enables you to work anywhere; with wireless telecommunication it is even more useful.

**EDUCATION:** Children as well as adults will be able to learn at home and explore libraries and museums around the globe.

**FIGURE 5.1** What the information superhighway may bring to your home.

This system is envisioned as being able to deliver large amounts of services to our homes, offices, and factories, including telephone calls, TV programs and other video images, text, and music. The system will enable students at rural schools to use computers to tap the resources of Stanford University or MIT, and researchers in a small college in Lapland, Finland to use the power of the supercomputer located at the University of Illinois. The superhighway will allow a doctor to check patients from their homes, and it will let doctors in different cities collaborate on a patient's care by immediately sharing his medical history, including X-rays and videos from arthroscopic surgery, using multimedia computer screens. Consumers will be able to shop for goods and services from all over the world in the comfort of their home. The information superhighway will connect people like the railroad system of the nineteenth century and the interstate highway system of the twentieth. Fiber-optic cables, satellites, and wireless grids will link millions of computers, telephones, faxes, and other electronic devices around the world. A large portion of the information superhighway in developed countries is already constructed so most of the capabilities described above already exist. Future superhighways will allow larger volume and a more rapid flow of information. Eventually we may see several information superhighways. For example, it is probable that the original concept of a scientific–educational system will be separated from the commercial one. This will make it possible to provide value-added services to the commercial sector, but charge fees for the usage.

The term electronic or information superhighway is a catchall name for several different architectures. Most people envision the information superhighway as a more comprehensive version of the Internet, accessible by all. To rewire the United States completely with fiber-optic lines that will reach every individual and organization may take 50 years and cost $500 billion. Smaller countries will do this much sooner. Singapore, a small island with population of less than three million, will have a national digital network largely based on fiber optics by 2000 (see Box 1.2 in Chapter 1). Japan, France, and Germany plan to complete their national networks by 2015. Korea and China are implementing several national projects (see the following *IT at Work*).

---

**IT At Work**   **BUILDING NATIONAL INFORMATION SUPERHIGHWAY**

Several countries are moving rapidly to utilize the information superhighway infrastructure (even before the highway is complete), in order to provide for innovative applications. Here are two examples.

**U**SING IT
...in Public Service

**KOREA.** By 2000, the government of Korea intends to complete what it calls "informationization," a project meant to improve civil services, boost government productivity, improve living standards, and enhance national competitiveness. For example, in 1997, all citizens were issued electronic ID cards that integrated seven existing ID cards such as driver's license, medical insurance, and pension cards. Medical records will be on the network by 2000. This information will be available via the Internet to public insurance offices and tax authorities. Different governmental departments are establishing Web sites and databases in order to access, exchange, and utilize information more effectively.

One interesting application monitors the country's environmental management. Citizens are now able to check the degree of air and water pollution on a daily basis. This helps them cope with pollution in a more efficient and timely manner.

All corporate information is computerized, including industry trade, energy, and labor, as well as current cultural and sports activities. (SOURCE: Based on *Korea Money,* October 1996.)

**CHINA.** At the end of 1996, the government established four information services programs: major cross-regional networks, regional and sector networks, technological services, and regional information joint groups. These projects promote the wider use of information resources, since the country is weak in these areas. China also plans to establish centers for information collection, processing, and storage to help develop its national information resources.

Central and local governments will assist in these projects, especially the information organizations set up by the government ministries. In addition, China is focusing on the expansion of the current Scientific and Technological Information Networks (STnet) and the construction of a computerized catalog of foreign documents.

The STnet is the largest network of its kind in China, covering more than 20 provinces, municipalities, and autonomous regions. The STnet is expected eventually to spread to all the provinces and regions, including some relatively underdeveloped areas. It will also link networks in research and higher education institutions in order to exchange data among all sectors of the national economy. In addition, China is developing a commerce net which will be used exclusively by businesses and government organizations. (SOURCE: Based on *China Daily,* October 17, 1996.) For further details see Liu (1997). ▲

*U*SING IT
...in Public Service

---

The information superhighway will have two groups of customers. The first group is individuals at home who will shop, bank, work, and entertain themselves without leaving their homes. These customers will pay for the services they get, just as we pay for telephone or cable TV services. The second group of customers is organizations. These customers will use the networks for hundreds of applications, a number of which are described in this book. Companies will conduct important electronic meetings and train employees in many locations simultaneously, using advanced multimedia tools and intelligent computer-aided tutoring.

Using the information superhighway, people will be able to see places before they travel to them and even "feel" scenarios using virtual reality. Students will be able to take classes from home and even pursue a degree program consisting of courses taken at several universities. Shopping will be changed, not only for individuals who will use home shopping, but also for corporations that will buy directly from producers without the need for retailers and wholesalers. Products will be demonstrated to potential buyers in three dimensions. Frequently, customers will be able to see the various colors, designs, and sizes of the product they want before these products are made. Ultimately, customers will be able to interface electronically with designers and order custom-made products. Companies will buy knowledge electronically. Experts and consultants will deliver their services across the world at a small cost. All of the above capabilities are already a reality, but only a small percentage of businesses and individuals participate. However, the rate of participation is increasing rapidly.

Building the information superhighway will not be a simple undertaking. In addition to the high cost, and the question of how it will be financed, there are a number of other issues and factors that could slow or limit its development, such as technological obstacles, privacy, security, ethics, government regulations, or political considerations for information crossing national borders. The project also faces many conflicting interest groups, especially telephone companies, cable TV operators, cable manufacturers, and the manufacturers of telecommunication hardware and software.

## BENEFITS OF THE INTERNET

The Internet is valuable because it can be used to:

▶ Send and receive messages and documents around the world, at low or no cost, almost in real time.

▶ Review many government-published documents and monitor government grant opportunities.

▶ Locate any material cataloged by the U.S. Library of Congress.

▶ Provide a forum for exchanging opinions and information.

▶ Download documents and software.

▶ Conduct many electronic commerce activities (see Chapter 6).

▶ Read newspapers, magazines, and books.

▶ Listen to music, see movies, and view other cultural events.

▶ Play games and entertain.

▶ Conduct collaborative research.

▶ Conduct free telephone calls and videoconferencing.

▶ Visit many major museums and galleries worldwide.

▶ Read material in other languages using Web translators.

Examples of specific Internet applications are provided throughout the book. An example of how NASA is using the Internet is shown in Figure 5.2. The upper part illustrates how the results of data analysis done at NASA are accessible to companies that work with NASA (such as McDonnell Douglas). The lower part shows how NASA researchers collaborate with their research partners (for example, at Boeing).

## SUPPORTING DISCOVERY: USING THE WEB

The Internet permits users to access information located in databases all over the world. Although only a small portion of organizational data may be accessible to Internet users, even that limited amount is enormous. Many fascinating resources are accessible, ranging from the content of most major libraries and museums to the archives of cities and public hospitals. The discovery capability can facilitate education, government services, entertainment, and commerce. Discovery is done by *browsing* and *searching* of the Web. (See Technology Guide #4.)

**BENEFITS OF THE WEB.** The *discovery, communication,* and *collaboration* capabilities available on the Internet at low cost provide for a large number of useful applications. Many of these are presented in Chapter 6. According to Udell (1996), some of the reasons that the Web is becoming so important are:

By using search engines I can identify and qualify potential customers.
— *James Rolstead*

▶ *It's open.* The Web is platform-neutral and global, and Web browsers function as universal clients.

▶ *It's resourceful.* Using the Web, you can update the look and capabilities of legacy and previously programmed applications.

▶ *It's efficient.* Web-server applications are becoming simpler to create and faster to use.

▶ *It's dynamic.* Tools like Java and Active X can help you build information-rich and customizable client applications quickly.

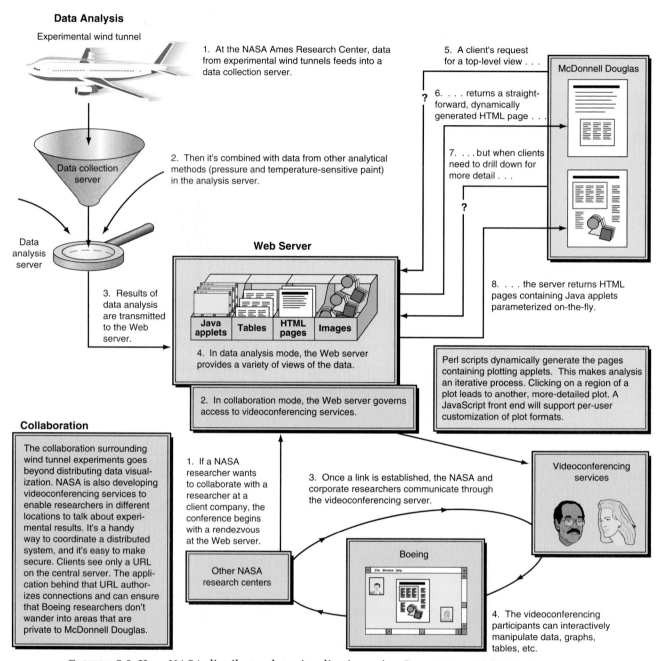

**Data Analysis**

Experimental wind tunnel

1. At the NASA Ames Research Center, data from experimental wind tunnels feeds into a data collection server.

Data collection server

2. Then it's combined with data from other analytical methods (pressure and temperature-sensitive paint) in the analysis server.

Data analysis server

3. Results of data analysis are transmitted to the Web server.

5. A client's request for a top-level view . . .

6. . . . returns a straight-forward, dynamically generated HTML page . . .

McDonnell Douglas

7. . . . but when clients need to drill down for more detail . . .

**Web Server**

Java applets | Tables | HTML pages | Images

4. In data analysis mode, the Web server provides a variety of views of the data.

8. . . . the server returns HTML pages containing Java applets parameterized on-the-fly.

2. In collaboration mode, the Web server governs access to videoconferencing services.

Perl scripts dynamically generate the pages containing plotting applets. This makes analysis an iterative process. Clicking on a region of a plot leads to another, more-detailed plot. A JavaScript front end will support per-user customization of plot formats.

**Collaboration**

The collaboration surrounding wind tunnel experiments goes beyond distributing data visualization. NASA is also developing videoconferencing services to enable researchers in different locations to talk about experimental results. It's a handy way to coordinate a distributed system, and it's easy to make secure. Clients see only a URL on the central server. The application behind that URL authorizes connections and can ensure that Boeing researchers don't wander into areas that are private to McDonnell Douglas.

1. If a NASA researcher wants to collaborate with a researcher at a client company, the conference begins with a rendezvous at the Web server.

Other NASA research centers

3. Once a link is established, the NASA and corporate researchers communicate through the videoconferencing server.

Videoconferencing services

Boeing

File Window Help

4. The videoconferencing participants can interactively manipulate data, graphs, tables, etc.

FIGURE 5.2 How NASA distributes data visualization using Java. (*Source*: Udell [1996], pp. 68–69.)

## SUPPORTING COMMUNICATION

*Communication* is an interpersonal process of sending and receiving symbols with messages attached to them. Through communication, people exchange and share information as well as influence and understand each other.

Most managers spend as much as 90 percent of their time communicating. Managers serve as "nerve centers" in the information-processing networks called organizations, where they collect, distribute, and process information continuously. Since poor communication can mean poor management, managers must communicate effectively among themselves and with others, both inside and outside of organizations. The Internet has become a major supporter of interactive communications. People are using Internet phone, videoconferencing, Internet radio, and more (see Comerford [1996] and the *IT at Work* that follows).

## *IT At Work*    INTERNET HELPS A SMALL MANUFACTURER

$U$SING IT

...in Production & Operations Management

Improving coordination and maintaining simplicity was the challenge facing Ti Cycles, a Seattle-based manufacturer and retailer of high-end, titanium bicycles. With just seven employees, Ti Cycles makes quantity production models for bicycle dealers throughout the United States. It also does a profitable business in custom road, mountain, racing, and tandem bicycles for individual customers.

The company had an information problem. Information about its business, products, and customers was stored on a variety of computers around the company, and every time an employee needed information, the employee first had to determine on which computer it was stored. Ti Cycles wanted to simplify this process and also better coordinate its sales, production, and customer service operations. Finally, Ti Cycles needed a system that was easy to maintain. "We can't justify hiring a separate technical person," says Martin Criminale, retail manager. "Our most technical person also happens to be one of our key bike-frame builders, so anything we do with technology has to be as simple as possible."

The technology approach that Ti Cycles chose was a system that centralizes all information, communication, and collaboration around a single computer server. That server provides all of the technology capabilities and information employees need to work individually or within a team. Employees are able to share files and access fax and Internet services from their desktop. They can also exchange documents and communicate while at home or on the road. More importantly, the system allows the exchange of information with clients and key vendors.

The software the company selected to operate this "command center" approach was the Microsoft BackOffice Small Business Server. Small Business Server lets businesses share files, databases, printers, and computer software on up to 25 workstations. It also provides Internet access and the ability to build a Web site.

"We've improved nearly every one of our competitive factors," explains Criminale. "The communications and collaboration benefits have made this a tauter ship to run. Every employee is better tuned-in to what everyone else is doing and our problem-solving cycle is shorter. We're also responding faster and smarter to queries from dealers and individual customers." ▲

SOURCE: Compiled from www.microsoft.com (small business software), 1998.

## FACTORS DETERMINING THE USES OF INFORMATION TECHNOLOGIES

Several factors determine the IT technologies that could be used to provide communication support to a specific organization or group of users. The major ones are the following:

▶ *Participants.* The number of people sending and receiving information can range from two to many thousands.

▶ *Nature of sources and destinations.* Sources and destinations of information can include people, databases, sensors, and so on.

▶ *Location.* The sender(s) and receiver(s) can be in the same room, in different rooms at the same location, or at different locations.

▶ *Time.* Messages can be sent at a certain time and received almost simultaneously. In such a case, communication is synchronous. Telephones, teleconferencing, and face-to-face meetings are examples of **synchronous (real time) communication. Asynchronous communication,** on the other hand, refers to communication whereby the receiver gets the message at a different time than it was sent.

▶ *Media.* Communication can involve one or several media. Today's IT can handle several types of media such as text, voice, graphics, pictures, and animation. Using different media for communicating can increase the effectiveness of a message, expedite learning, and enhance problem solving. Working with multiple media may, however, reduce the efficiency and effectiveness of the system (its speed, capacity, quality) and may significantly increase its cost.

**A TIME/PLACE FRAMEWORK.**   A framework for classifying IT communication support technologies has been proposed by DeSanctis and Gallupe (1987). According to this framework, communication is divided into four cells (see Figure 5.3 for the cells with a representative technology in each):

1. *Same-time/same-place.* In this setting, participants meet face-to-face in one place and at the same time. An example is communication in a meeting room.

2. *Same-time/different-place.* This setting refers to a meeting whose participants are in different places but communicate at the same time. A conference telephone call and desktop videoconferencing are examples of such situations.

3. *Different-time/same-place.* This setting can materialize when people work in shifts. The first shift leaves electronic or voice messages for the second shift.

4. *Different-time/different-place.* In this setting, participants are in different places, and they send and/or receive messages (for example, via the Internet) at different times.

Businesses require that messages be transmitted as fast as they are needed, that the intended receiver properly interprets them, and that the cost of doing this be reasonable. Communication systems that meet these conditions have several characteristics. They allow two-way communication: messages flow in different directions, sometimes almost simultaneously, and messages reach people regardless of where they are located. Efficient systems also allow people to access

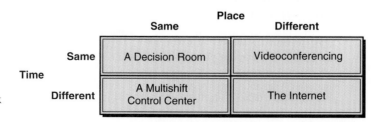

**FIGURE 5.3** A framework for IT communication.

various sources of information (such as databases). IT can meet these requirements through the electronic transfer of information using tools such as e-mail.

Next, we discuss e-mail; other specific communication tools and technologies are described in Technology Guide # 4.

**ELECTRONIC MAIL. Electronic mail (e-mail)** is the most used service of the Internet (see Technology Guide #4). E-mail can be enhanced to provide valuable services as shown in the *IT at Work* case.

---

### IT At Work · E-MAIL AT HUGHES AIRCRAFT CORPORATION AND AT UNITED TECHNOLOGY

**U**SING IT

...in Production &
Operations Management

Hughes Aircraft Corporation is a multinational aerospace and electronic division of General Motors that employs 25,000 people worldwide. A leader in electronics, the company was using more than ten different e-mail systems in order to link all its employees. The company unified its e-mail system in 1992. Not only are the 25,000 employees linked with each other, they also are connected with over 75,000 employees of General Motors and have access to the Internet.

The real value of the system is the infrastructure it provides for companywide applications that streamline business processes and speed up the dissemination of critical information. The e-mail is integrated with a videotext database network that can be accessed for a variety of applications, including electronic routing and approval (ERA).

ERA provides electronic forms and routes them among employees. The user imports standard information from the database to complete the forms. Thus the time needed for data entry and approval has been significantly reduced. For example, documents that used to take weeks to be processed are now processed in minutes, reducing cycle time. Employees are getting individually tailored information extracted from sources such as *Commerce Business Daily*. People get the right information fast, and they are not charged for the service. On the contrary, they are encouraged to use it as much as possible.

By 1997, the e-mail was incorporated with the corporate intranet allowing for browsing and internal database searches.

Another aerospace company, United Technologies Corp., was not so successful in their e-mail consolidation, migration, and integration. Building a common mail backbone for over 50,000 users was found to be difficult. The e-mail integration will be finished only by 2000, save communication costs, and increase efficiency and functionality.

**For Further Exploration:** Why is e-mail so important for such companies? ▲

SOURCE: *CIO*, January 1992, updated November 1997, and *InternetWeek*, January 12, 1998, pp. 33–35.

---

E-mail in the medical field allows consultation about difficult medical problems with experts anywhere in the world in a very short period of time.
— *Brad White*

*E-mail on the Internet and Intranet.* E-mail systems have been used for many years as an internal medium of communication. For example, IBM's PROFS (Professional Office System) enables employees to communicate with each other all over the world. With the Internet, e-mail is able to connect people in different organizations who are working on different LANs using different hardware, operating systems, and communication systems. People can use such e-mail systems from home or while they are on the road, using regular telephone lines. Wireless e-mail connects remote users with corporate e-mail systems via paging technology and the Internet. This capability allows mobile users such as salespeople and repair people to enter the corporate e-mail system quickly, to send and receive messages, and to initiate communication in workgroups.

## SUPPORTING COLLABORATION

One of the abiding features of a modern organization is that people collaborate to perform work. **Collaboration** refers to mutual efforts by two or more individuals who perform activities in order to accomplish certain tasks. Group members work together on tasks ranging from designing products and documents to teaching each other and to executing complementary subtasks. Also, people work with customers, suppliers, and other business partners in an effort to improve productivity and competitiveness. Finally, group members participate in decision making. In all the above cases they need to collaborate, which can be supported electronically by several technologies (see Smith and Rist [1998]). Group work is increasing in importance; it is a cornerstone in some BPR projects and continuous improvement programs. Also, group work is needed in virtual corporations as well as in multinational organizations. The use of group work is also increasing due to the support provided by IT, especially the support provided to groups whose members are in different locations. To understand such support, let us first examine how groups work.

**THE NATURE OF GROUP WORK AND CONVENTIONAL SUPPORT.** The term **work group** refers to two or more individuals who act together in order to perform some task. The group can be permanent or temporary. It can be in one location or several. Members can meet concurrently or at different times. The group can be a committee, a review panel, a task force, an executive board, a team, or a department.

*Conventional Approach.* For years, people have recognized the benefits of collaborative work. Typical benefits that relate to decision making are shown in Table 5.1. But despite the many benefits of group interaction, groups are not always successful. The reason is that the *process* of collaborative work is frequently plagued by dysfunction (see Table 5.2).

---

### Table 5.1  Benefits of Working in a Group

- Groups are better than individuals at understanding problems.
- People are accountable for decisions in which they participate.
- Groups are better than individuals at catching errors.
- A group has more information (knowledge) than any one member and, as a result, more alternatives are generated for problem solving.
- Synergy can be produced, so the effectiveness and/or quality of group work can be larger than the sum of what is produced by independent individuals.
- Working in a group may stimulate the participants and the process.
- Group members have their egos embedded in the decision they make, so they will be committed to its implementation.

### Table 5.2  Dysfunctions of Group Processes

- Social pressures to conform ("groupthink") may eliminate superior ideas.
- Group process can be time-consuming, slow, and costly.
- Work done in a group may lack appropriate coordination.
- Some members may dominate the agenda.
- Some group members ("free riders") may rely on others to do most of their work.
- The group may compromise on solutions of poor quality.
- The group may be unable to complete a task.
- Unproductive time is spent socializing, getting ready, waiting for people, or repeating what has already been said.
- Members may be afraid to speak up.

To reconcile these differences, researchers have worked for many years to improve the work of groups. If we could eliminate or lessen some of the causes of dysfunctional behavior, the benefits of group work would be greatly enhanced. Many approaches have been developed to attempt to solve these problems. Two representative methods are the *nominal group technique* and the *Delphi method.*

The **nominal group technique (NGT)** is a group communication method that includes a sequence of activities: (1) the silent generation of ideas in writing, (2) a round-robin listing of ideas on a flip chart, (3) a serial discussion of ideas, (4) a silent listing and ranking of priorities, (5) a discussion of priorities, and (6) a silent reranking and rating of priorities (see Lindstone and Turroff [1975] for more details).

The **Delphi method** is used with a group of experts who do not meet face-to-face and do not know who the other group members are. The experts provide individually written opinions on an issue along with supporting arguments and assumptions. These opinions are then distributed as anonymous feedback to all participants along with a second round of questions. The questions and feedback continue in writing for several rounds, becoming increasingly more specific, until consensus among the panel members is reached, or until the experts no longer change their positions.

Both methods take time and organizational resources and require a trained facilitator or coordinator, and each eliminates only a few dysfunctions of the group process. So, their success is limited.

## ▶ 5.2 GROUPWARE TECHNOLOGY AND INFRASTRUCTURE

The limited success of methods such as the nominal group technique and the Delphi method has created an opportunity for information technology to support groups electronically. The name for the supporting software products is *groupware.*

**Groupware** refers to software products that support groups of people who share a common task or goal and collaborate on its accomplishment. It provides a way for them to share opinions and resources. Groupware implies the use of networks to connect people, even if they are in the same room. Many groupware products are available on the Internet or an intranet, enhancing the collaboration of a large number of people worldwide. Ozer et al. (1996) has identified 41 different approaches and technologies for the support of groups on the Internet.

Groupware products come either as a standalone product supporting one task (such as an e-mail), or as an integrated kit that includes several tools (e-mail, workflow, etc.). In general, groupware technology products are fairly inexpensive and can be easily incorporated into existing information systems. The Internet, intranets, extranets, and private communication lines provide the infrastructure needed for the hardware and software of groupware.

The software products are either Web-based, which is the trend today (e.g., see Smith and Rist [1998]), or they are not related to the Internet and work with other networks. Representative areas of support and some products are described next. (For a detailed list see Haskin [1997].)

In this section we present the major groupware technologies.

## WORKFLOW AND SCREEN-SHARING SYSTEMS

**WORKFLOW SYSTEMS.** **Workflow systems** are business process automation tools that place system controls in the hands of user departments. They are highly flexible and can be designed to automate almost any information processing task. The primary purpose of workflow systems is to provide users with tracking, routing, document imaging, and other capabilities designed to improve business processes (see the following examples).

---

*IT At Work*    **WORKFLOW SOFTWARE AUTOMATES BUSINESS PROCESSES**

*U*SING IT

...in Finance

**B**ankers Trust Company of New York replaced its manual customer requests system with an automated one. The system is based on Action software (from Action Technologies) and it works together with Lotus Notes. Cases are placed into Notes, where Action routes them to the appropriate employees to work on them. The software tracks the status of every case and whether employees complete each task as scheduled. In case of deviations, a reminder is automatically generated.

**Carold Corporation,** a mortgage-banking firm in New York, services about 13,000 loans and about 12,000 insurance policies a year. Scanning related documents and pictures and integrating them with the workflow system greatly increased the productivity of accessing information, conducting analyses, and answering queries.

**For Further Exploration:** How can workflow software increase productivity? ▲

SOURCE: Condensed from Sullivan, K. B., "Workflow Applications Can Change the Way of Doing Business, Buyers Say," *PC Week,* April 5, 1993.

---

Expense reports are filed via LAN on common drive.

— *James Rolstead*

There are three types of workflow software: *administrative*—focused on the tracking of expense reports, travel requests, and messages; *ad hoc*—dealing with the shaping of product brochures, sales proposals, and strategic plans; and *production*—concerned with tracking credit card mailings, mortgage loans, and insurance claims. There are many workflow software packages on the market. Some are Internet-based and may be combined with e-mail; others use a shared database or a file on a server that people can log into. Notable software in the latter category is Lotus Notes.

**SCREEN SHARING.** Another technique to support group work is **screen sharing.** In collaborative work, members are frequently in different locations. Using special software, it is possible for them to work on the same document, which is shown on the screens of each of the participants. For example, two authors can work on a single manuscript. One may suggest a correction and execute it so the other author can see the change. Collaborators can work together on the same spreadsheet (only one of them needs to have the spreadsheet software), or on the resultant graphics. Changes can be done by using the keyboard or by touching the screen. This capability can expedite the design of products, the preparation of reports and bids, and the resolution of conflicts.

**WHITEBOARDING.** IT allows you to create what is called a *virtual whiteboard*. This means that the two parties can view changes made to a single document "pasted" onto an electronic whiteboard, as in the screen sharing described earlier.

Take, for example, an advertisement that needs to be cleared by a senior manager. Once the proposed ad has been scanned into a PC, both parties can see it on their screens. If the senior manager does not like something, he or she can use a stylus pen and highlight what needs to be changed. This makes communications between the two parties both easier and clearer. The two parties can also share applications. For example, if party A works with Excel, party B can see A's screen and make amendments to it even if party B does not have Excel. Desktop videoconferencing can also be used by advertising agencies to show their clients creative concepts and ideas. A client can make changes online that can be seen immediately by the advertising agency. Marketers can also use it to make remote presentations to customers.

Computerized real-time whiteboarding makes a lot of sense given the way people like to work. It's about sketching out ideas, sharing ideas quickly. And it's a medium with which many people are familiar.

Whiteboarding with a computer works like the real-world version with markers and erasers, with one big difference: Instead of one person standing in front of a meeting room drawing on the whiteboard, all participants can join in. Each user can view and draw on the whiteboard throughout the meeting. You also can save digital whiteboarding sessions for later use. Some products let you insert graphics files that can be annotated by the group (e.g., CoolTalk, from Netscape communication). (See Haskin [1997].)

## VISUAL COMMUNICATIONS

Visualization and voice communications play an increasingly important role in facilitating communication and group work. Of the various supporting technologies, the two most frequently used with networked computing are desktop teleconferencing and voice technologies.

*My company currently links globally via satellite for conferencing.*
*— James Rolstead*

**Teleconferencing** is the use of electronic communication that allows two or more people at different locations to have a simultaneous conference. There are several types of teleconferencing (see Storm [1997]). The oldest and simplest is a telephone conference call, wherein several people talk to each other from three or more locations. The biggest disadvantage is that it does not allow for face-to-face communication. Also, participants in one location cannot see graphs, charts, and pictures at other locations. While the latter disadvantage can be overcome by using a fax, this is a time-consuming, expensive, and frequently poor-quality process. One solution is video teleconferencing, where participants can see each other as well as the documents.

**VIDEO TELECONFERENCING.** In a **video teleconference,** participants in one location can see participants at another location or in several locations. Dynamic pictures of the participants can appear on a large screen or on a desktop computer. Originally, video teleconferencing was the transmission of live, compressed TV sessions between two or more points. Video teleconferencing (or videoconferencing) today, however, is a digital technology capable of linking various types of computers across networks. Once conferences are digitized and transmitted over networks, they become a computer application. (For details see Storm [1997].) Advanced systems utilize virtual reality, as shown in the following application.

*IT At Work* **INFORMATION TECHNOLOGY MAKES TELECONFERENCING ALMOST REAL AT HILTON HOTELS**

**U**SING IT

...in Production & Operations Management

Hilton Hotels, TelePort, and IBM have teamed up to develop TeleSuite systems, which utilize virtual reality–based group videoconferencing techniques that permit users to experience life-size, virtual person contact while in remote locations. The first publicly accessible virtual conferencing TeleSuite systems have been introduced at two Hilton properties: The Waldorf-Astoria in New York City and The Capital Hilton in Washington, DC.

During a TeleSuite conference, all participants appear without any delay simultaneously on screen, life-size, appearing to be across a table from each other. Through the use of a video mirror concept, the suites provide a natural setting that gives users the perception of being together in one location. Participants communicate in fully synchronized audio and video, with each person making "virtual eye contact" with the image of others on screen. In addition to virtual conferencing, the suites can accommodate food service, allowing users to participate in a "teledining" experience. ▲

SOURCE: Condensed from *Expert Systems,* November 1996, p. 317.

With videoconferencing, participants can share data, voice, pictures, graphics, and animation. Data can also be sent along with voice and video (**data conferencing**). So it is possible to work on documents together and to exchange computer files during such conferences. This allows several geographically dispersed groups to work on the same project and to communicate by video simultaneously. The major benefits of video teleconferencing are given in Table 5.3

---

*Table 5.3* **The Benefits of Teleconferencing**

- Provides the opportunity for face-to-face communication for individuals in different locations.
- Supports several types of media during conferencing, including voice and radio.
- The primary reasons for teleconferencing are savings in productivity and travel costs.
- Conserves the time and energy of key employees and increases the speed of business processes (including product development, contract negotiation, and customer service).
- Improves the efficiency and frequency of communications.
- Makes available different types of systems to provide flexibility to meet different needs.
- Saves messages in the computer to reconstruct specific parts of a meeting for future purposes.
- Makes it possible to hold classes at different locations.

---

**Video mail** is an example of videoconferencing as a computer application. It is similar to voice mail; however, the voice and image components of video mail can be created from portions of conferences and stored on a file server.

While the first generation of computerized video teleconferencing was conducted in special rooms with large screens, cameras, and recorders, the second generation has moved to the desktop, using special equipment such as PC

**FIGURE 5.4** ShareVision, a comprehensive desktop teleconferencing system from Creative Technology, Ltd.

Videophone and LANs in conjunction with other desktop facilities (see Figure 5.4).

However, several factors limit the growth of video teleconferencing. These include a lack of standards, the cost of setup and maintenance, lack of connectivity, problems with network security, and network capacity. Technological developments are reducing the seriousness of these factors as time passes.

Computer programs can enable people at different locations to work together on the same screen, exchanging voice files, spreadsheet analysis, and/or keyed-in ideas and comments (see the following illustration).

---

*IT At Work*   VIDEO TELECONFERENCING SAVES MONEY

**U**SING IT
...in Health Care

**U**SING IT
...in Human Resources Management

**B**ull HN Information Systems (Billerica, MA) used to spend several millions of dollars a year on travel between its headquarters in Billerica and its Phoenix office. To save money, Bull installed a PictureTel System video teleconferencing system at the two locations. Bull was then able to increase the number of meetings and yet contain costs, since no travel was required. Many other companies have reported similar savings. For example, **BASF Corporation's** fiber division (Williamsburg, VA) saves over $1 million a year in travel expenses alone. Video teleconferencing can also be used among several companies. For example, **Sun Health Corporation** (Charlotte, NC) purchases supplies for 250 hospitals in 15 states. The member hospitals decided to install video teleconferencing equipment in all their hospitals so that they could conduct face-to-face meetings without the need to travel.

In an attempt to cut trips to their offshore drilling sites and their European office in Aberdeen, Scotland, **Global Marine** (Houston, TX) installed Fujitsu's Desktop Conferencing system. One application was to train the IS employees in Aberdeen in a new client/server system that had replaced the mainframe. Other applications have enabled managers at different locations to review contracts, spreadsheets, and proposals. For example, a manager in one location can change online a cell value in a spreadsheet and discuss the change with colleagues in other locations.

**For Further Exploration:** Is it really necessary to see the person you are conferring with on a screen? Why not use telephone conferencing? ▲

SOURCE: Condensed from *Computerworld*, May 3, 1993.

Companies such as PictureTel, Fujitsu, and Creative Technology market several interesting products. Many products can now work on the Internet. Some of these use analog telephone lines and run either as standalone units or across a LAN. The digitally based products provide better quality, but they are more expensive.

In military and security applications, desktop videoconferencing can be used as a remote surveillance tool because the video camera can capture movements that can then be interpreted by security personnel located elsewhere. A particular benefit here is that a single frame of the video can be captured and enlarged to spot security breaches. An application in transportation is similar. Traffic officers, stationed strategically along highways during peak traffic hours, can transmit maps showing congested areas and decide how to divert traffic.

Businesses can conduct videoconferencing and collaborative work sessions over the Internet or corporate intranets easily and inexpensively, with a quality that approaches that of TV. The latest technological innovations permit both business-to-business and business-to-consumer applications. Banks, insurance agents, and others can conduct videoconferencing sessions over the Internet with a customer at home. Banks in Alaska use *video kiosks* in sparsely populated areas instead of building underutilized branches. The video kiosks operate on the banks' intranet and provide videoconferencing equipment for eye-to-eye interactions.

## ELECTRONIC VOICE COMMUNICATION

The most natural mode of communication is voice. When people need to communicate with each other from a distance, they use the telephone more frequently than any other communication device. Voice communication can now be done on the computer using a microphone and a sound card. You can even talk long distance on the Internet without paying the normal long distance telephone charges.

Voice and data can work together to create useful applications. For example, operators of PBXs are letting callers give simple computer commands using interactive voice response. The number and type of voice technologies applications is growing (see the following example).

**IT At Work**    HOW COMPANIES
USE VOICE TECHNOLOGIES

Here is a sample of voice applications compiled from miscellaneous issues of *Communications News*.

*U*SING IT

...in Human Resources
Management

1. **Duke Power Company** (Charlotte, NC) has a 24-hour interactive voice response system that addresses questions about fringe benefits via the telephone.
2. **Fleet Services Corporation** allows its 30,000 employees to register for their flexible benefit program (once each year) via the telephone, supported by a voice response system.

3. **Dixie Electric Management Corporation** uses voice recognition (and interpretation, using expert systems) of customers who are calling in to report downed lines, power outages, or transformer fires.

**U**SING **IT**

...in Finance

4. **Toronto Dominion Bank** (Canada) customers can use voice commands to transfer funds between accounts and authorize bill payments. They can request, by voice, that the bank fax copies of interim statements. In addition, they can buy savings bonds, roll-over term deposits, and trace checks. Voice orders can be given both in English and in French.

5. **Bidwell and Company** (Portland, OR) enables customers to find stock prices simply by saying the stock symbol.

6. **U.S. West Communications** (Denver, CO) allows customers to say the name of the person they want to call (up to 75 names) rather than dial the number. A voice recognition system matches the name to a phone number and does the dialing.

7. **Voice terminals in a warehouse** can provide the following applications.

▶ *Forklift material movement.* Drivers can send and receive information while operating the forklifts, yielding 20 to 50 percent productivity improvement.

▶ *Receiving inspection.* Employees who receive or inspect materials are generally busy. Results of inspection are communicated by voice while inspection is going on.

**U**SING **IT**

...in Production &
Operations Management

▶ *Inventory taking and location reporting in floor stack warehouses.* When items are set on the inventory floor, they have no fixed location. Therefore, a description of what is available and where it is located can be done rapidly and accurately by voice.

▶ *Inventory taking in a refrigerated or dusty warehouse.* Other methods like reading bar codes may not work in some environments; voice input has no such drawbacks.

While most of these applications are not related to the Internet, similar applications can be combined with the Internet/intranet. ▲

Voice technologies have the following advantages:

1. Hands-free and eyes-free operations increase the productivity, safety, and effectiveness of operators ranging from forklift drivers to military pilots.

2. Disabled employees can enter voice data to command the computer to perform various tasks.

3. Voice terminals are designed for portability. Workers do not have to go to the computer. They can communicate with the computer from their work areas, even when they are on the move, using telephone lines and/or wireless equipment.

4. Voice terminals are more rugged than keyboards, so they can operate better in dirty or moving environments.

5. It is about two-and-a-half times faster to talk than to type.

6. In most circumstances, fewer errors in voice data entry are made compared to keyboard data entry, assuming a reliable voice recognition system is used.

There are many other applications of voice technologies; here is a sampling:

▶ **Interactive voice recognition.** Interactive voice recognition, one of the most popular applications, enables a computer to understand the content of incoming telephone calls.

▶ **Voice annotation.** A combination of recorded voice messages with electronic mail, spreadsheet, and other applications, voice annotation can be used to add comments to documents. Prerecorded voices of experts can add background information, or users can enter a request for advice or explanations on their

PC. A computer program orders the telephone system to dial the user, who can then pick up the phone to receive recorded instructions.

▶ *Automated attendant.* An automated attendant system transfers calls, monitors them for completion, streamlines call flow, and shortens call hold times. Applications are in call routing, call screening, and receptionist backup.

▶ *Voice mail.* **Voice mail** is a computerized system for storing, forwarding, and routing telephone messages. Applications include personal greetings, front-end beepers and pagers, departmental messaging, message broadcasting to groups, and emergency notifications.

▶ *Audiotext.* Audiotext plays and records information in any sequence and/or in response to touch-tone input.

## GROUP DECISION SUPPORT SYSTEMS (GDSS)

Although most business organizations have traditionally been hierarchical, decision making is frequently a shared process. Meetings among groups of managers from different areas are an essential element for reaching consensus. The group may be involved in making a decision or in a decision-related task, like creating a short list of acceptable alternatives or deciding on criteria for accepting an alternative. When a decision-making group is supported electronically, the support is referred to as a group decision support system.

A **group decision support system (GDSS)** is an interactive computer-based system that facilitates the solution of semistructured and unstructured problems by a group of decision makers. Components of a GDSS include hardware, software, people, and procedures. These components are arranged to support the *process* of arriving at a decision. Important characteristics of a GDSS, according to DeSanctis and Gallupe (1987), are those summarized in Table 5.4.

*Table 5.4* **The Characteristics of GDSS**

- Designed with the goal of supporting groups of decision-makers in their work.
- Easy to learn and use. It accommodates users with varying levels of knowledge regarding computing and decision support.
- Can be designed for one type of problem or for a variety of group-level organizational decisions.
- Encourages generation of ideas, resolution of conflicts, and freedom of expression.
- Contains built-in mechanisms that discourage development of negative group behaviors, such as destructive conflict, miscommunication, and "groupthink."
- Is a specially designed information system, not merely a configuration of already existing system components.

SOURCE: Compiled from DeSanctis and Gallupe (1987).

The goal of GDSS is to improve the productivity of decision-making meetings, either by speeding up the decision-making process or by improving the quality of the resulting decisions, or both. This is accomplished by providing support to the exchange of ideas, opinions, and preferences within the group.

GDSS can increase decision-making process gains (see Table 5.5) and reduce process losses listed in Table 5.2.

*Table 5.5*  **Process Gains from Group Decision-Support Systems**

- Supports parallel processing of information and idea generation by participants.
- Enables larger groups with more complete information, knowledge, and skills to participate in the same meeting.
- Permits the group to use structured or unstructured techniques and methods.
- Offers rapid and easy access to external information.
- Allows nonsequential computer discussion (unlike oral discussions, computer discussions do not have to be serial or sequential).
- Produces instant, anonymous voting results.
- Provides structure to the planning process, which keeps the group on track.
- Enables several users to interact simultaneously.
- Automatically records all information that passes through the system for future analysis (develops organization memory).

**SUPPORTING FACE-TO-FACE MEETINGS.**  The first generation of GDSS was designed to support face-to-face meetings in what is called a **decision room.** Such a GDSS is composed of hardware, software, people, and procedures.

*Hardware.*  A group can use two basic types of hardware configurations. The first is a decision room, a GDSS facility designed for electronic meetings. It is equipped with state-of-the-art workstations, a local-area network, a server, and a "facilitator station," which controls a large-screen projection system. An electronic decision room requires a trained facilitator.

The second configuration is basically a collection of PCs, each equipped with keypads for voting and other groupware activities. The machines can be in

**FIGURE 5.5** The Group-Systems 24-station decision center is used for electronic meetings.

one location or in different locations. Simple to operate, such PCs are usually part of a network, and can be connected to the Internet.

***Software.*** Typical GDSS software is a collection of about a dozen tools or packages, which are integrated into a comprehensive system. GDSS software (such as GroupSystems) includes modules such as idea generation, idea organization, prioritizing (by votes), and policy formulation. This software can be used in a decision room or for a group of people who are all at different locations, in some cases using Internet or intranet technology. Lotus Notes and Netscape Communicator offer some of these capabilities.

Advanced software packages support conflict resolution among participants, communication with commercial databases, and execution of quantitative analysis. Advanced software includes artificial intelligence capabilities such as intelligent agents.

***People.*** The people component of the GDSS includes the group members and the facilitator. The facilitator is present in all group meetings at a single site. He or she coordinates dispersed-participation groups and serves as the group's "chauffeur," operating the GDSS hardware and software and displaying requested information to the group as needed. Distributed meetings usually require a coordinator.

***Procedures.*** The final component of the GDSS consists of procedures that allow for ease of operation and effective use of the technology by the group members.

**SOME APPLICATIONS OF GDSS.** An increasing number of companies are using GDSS. One example is the Internal Revenue Service, which used a GDSS to implement its quality improvement programs based on the participation of a number of its quality teams. The GDSS was helpful in identifying problems, generating and evaluating ideas, and developing and implementing solutions. Another example follows.

---

### *IT At Work*　USING GDSS TO EXAMINE THE FUTURE EUROPEAN AUTOMOBILE INDUSTRY

The automotive industry competes in a global market. Some well-established European companies such as Fiat feel strong competition from Japanese and U.S. manufacturers. Several years ago the automotive industry in Europe established groups of experts in Geneva, Switzerland and Frankfurt, Germany and supported these groups with a GDSS named DELWARE. DELWARE incorporates the Delphi forecasting method with cross-impact analysis in an attempt to examine the business environment of the European automobile industry looking toward the year 2000.

The specific task of the experts was to refine their initial estimates about the probability and desirability of 34 business events and trends in Europe. The GDSS enabled the experts to achieve this refinement by arriving at a consensus electronically.

Communication among the experts was done in an asynchronous mode, since the experts were unable to meet together at specific times. In addition to the telephone they used special GDSS software that enhances the implementation of the Delphi procedure. The results showed a great improvement in communication among the experts who were quickly able to acquire an understanding of the project. As a result, they agreed on the major business events. The final list has been used by the automotive industry in Europe

*U*SING IT

...in Production & Operations Management

for the purposes of strategic planning. A similar effort is now being undertaken to forecast for 2010.

**For Further Exploration:** Anonymity is required in a Delphi study and it is provided by a GDSS. Do you support anonymity in this situation? Why or why not? ▲

SOURCE: Condensed from Vickers (1992).

---

San Trans, a Tucson, Arizona bus company, used the University of Arizona GDSS facility to negotiate a labor contract with the Teamsters Union, which represents 300 of its blue-collar employees. Management and union representatives met for nine sessions, concluding with a new contract after only 30 hours of electronic meetings. El Rio Health Care facility, also of Tucson, used the same facility to negotiate a labor contract with its union. The union and management teams had a history of difficult negotiation. The university's GDSS tools, which were customized to handle the negotiations, helped in reaching a satisfactory contract much faster than in the past.

The City of Louisville, Kentucky, used a GDSS to prioritize the ten most important areas of public education. The prioritization was needed for planning and allocation of resources and the views of a number of different constituencies had to be taken into account.

## INTEGRATED TECHNOLOGIES AND LOTUS NOTES/DOMINO

**INTEGRATED TECHNOLOGIES.** Groupware technologies can be used as stand-alone, independent technologies. However, because these technologies are computer based, it makes sense to integrate them with other computer-based or computer-controlled technologies. Integrating several technologies can save time and money for users. Here are some examples:

> *It is not about "off the shelf" solutions any more. In many cases you find yourself pulling together loosely related applications or technologies to meet a need. It takes a creative person to do a job these days, but that person must also be attuned to the technologies.*
>
> *— Blake Thompson*

- ▶ PictureTel Corporation formed an alliance with Lotus and developed an integrated desktop video teleconferencing product that uses Lotus Notes. Using this integrated system, Reader's Digest (Pleasantville, NY) has built several applications combined with videoconferencing capabilities. This product is now available on the Internet.
- ▶ Cardiff Software (Solana Beach, CA) developed a fax machine that is integrated with an optical character recognition device and a database. *PC World* uses this product to analyze results of questionnaires that its readers fax to the editors. When a fax is received, the questionnaire is scanned automatically, and the results are stored in the database.
- ▶ Netscape Communicator (Web-based), LiveLink from Abitech, Inc. (Web-based), Microsoft Exchange, Novell GroupWise, and Lotus Notes/Domino (described in detail below) have developed a set of comprehensive integration tools in an effort to provide tools that support many groupwork needs. (See *InfoWorld,* March 2, 1998 for a comparison.)

**LOTUS NOTES/DOMINO. Lotus Notes** is a Windows-based client/server platform for developing and deploying groupware applications. It improves the business performance of people working together by compressing the time and improving the quality of everyday business processes, such as customer service, sales, account management, and product development.

Lotus Notes is software that acts as a group communications environment to allow users to access and create shared information. It provides workgroup e-mail, distributed databases, bulletin boards, text editing, document management and a forms generator, workflow capabilities, and various applications development tools, all integrated into an environment with a graphical menu-based user interface. Lotus Notes is used for many applications, including fostering virtual corporations and similar intercompany alliances. The software can be integrated with Internet and intranet infrastructure and applications. As such it is known as Lotus Domino. The following discussion concerns both Notes and Domino. Overall, Lotus Notes can provide a considerable competitive advantage for the users, as shown in the following illustration.

---

### *IT At Work*   USING LOTUS NOTES AT PRICE WATERHOUSE

**U**SING IT

...in Accounting

Price Waterhouse (PW) is one of the largest accounting CPA firms in the world. In March 1989, PW named Sheldon Laube as the director of information technology. A few months later, in a bold, unorthodox move, Laube licensed 10,000 copies of Lotus Notes at a cost of $2 million, while it was still in the testing phase. By 1992, Lotus Notes had fundamentally altered PW's business processes and brought an end to the chaos that existed in 1989. Here is how PW operated before Lotus Notes was introduced.

▶ Highly paid associates were shuffling between floors with stacks of paperwork, desperately trying to get signoffs on top priority products.
▶ Partners in regional offices were struggling to decipher complex accounting rules without the aid of centralized databases.
▶ Out-of-town partners were unable to use local offices to print out data from their portable disks.
▶ Partners had to wait weeks to find information about specific tax court rulings.
▶ Local offices adopted their own technology without a strategy for data sharing.

Here is a sample of what Lotus Notes has enabled PW's employees to do.

▶ View, from inside a database, a collection of the firm's analysis of tax rulings and opinions.
▶ Share, within hours, all information describing a court tax ruling and read the ruling itself.
▶ Build upon the labor of others by accessing every business proposal PW has submitted to clients since 1989, thus reducing preparation time and improving the chance of winning contracts.

The initial system included about 125 servers and 11,000 PCs residing on PW's worldwide network. In addition to its information-sharing capabilities, the system is used to create new applications. More than 500 were created by end users and 100 by the IS department during the first three years of the operation. These applications include generation of billing reports and compilation of marketing data by the partners themselves. "The system puts knowledge at the senior managers' fingertips; that is why they use it," commented Laube. Lotus Notes can also quickly put the experience of many experts at the service of clients.

After Notes became operational, PW was invited to bid on a multimillion-dollar consulting job. The proposal was due in four days, and the four executives who were needed to write the proposal were in three different states. With Lotus Notes, not only did they work on the same document, but they also extracted key components of the proposal from various databases. From around the world they pulled resumes of the company's experts who could be consulted when needed. A draft was written, and each executive modified it or made comments and other executives looked at the proposal via Lotus Notes and contributed valuable suggestions. The proposal was ready on time, and the consulting job was awarded to Price Waterhouse. Notes also changed PW's organizational culture. People who never used computers use them extensively now.

**For Further Exploration:** How could Lotus Notes eliminate the chaotic situations that existed before? Is there any other way to prepare a bid as quickly and economically?

▲

SOURCE: Based on Mehler, M., "Notes Fanatic," *Corporate Computing,* August 1992 and on "Groupware Goes Boom," *Fortune,* December 27, 1993.

*Capabilities of Lotus Notes.*  Notes/Domino is designed to handle these four main types of applications:

1. *Tracking.* This helps users follow what is happening in their business. For example, management may want to track all activities related to a specific customer (agreements, volume of purchase, meetings conducted), or track all potential candidates for an open position. Yet another application is to track a specific meeting (prepare agendas, send invitations, prepare minutes).

2. *Team discussion.* Lotus Notes helps in sharing information and conducting discussions among participants who may be in different locations and available at different times.

3. *Broadcasting.* Lotus Notes helps deliver announcements or post information on its bulletin boards. Also, technical notes and tips can be posted so that everyone can benefit from individual expertise.

4. *References.* Lotus Notes helps users sift through the many documents stored in Notes servers.

In addition there are specialized application categories such as the following:

▶ *Things to do.* Lotus Notes reminds individuals or groups about action items that must be completed to keep projects on schedule.

▶ *Contract library.* Lotus Notes can be used as a central repository for all legal contract templates.

▶ *Corporate policy documents.* Lotus Notes maintains all organizational policy documents and communicates them to all employees worldwide.

*Notes' Databases.*  Lotus Notes utilizes distributed document databases that allow users to store, distribute, and organize information so they can retrieve it. The following three basic types of databases are used in Lotus Notes:

1. *Discussion databases* enable users to participate in written meetings. The databases are usually classified by subject.

2. *Document libraries* store written information normally printed on paper. Databases can be created to contain reports, memos, forms, and so on.

3. *Information services* enable users to obtain the latest information about selected topics. Information from any document can be replicated automatically in all authorized servers, both internal and external.

***Lotus Domino and the Internet and Intranets.***  The early releases of Lotus Notes included several capabilities that are now available on the Internet and intranets. These included e-mail, bulletin boards, chat groups, accessibility to databases, and provision of information services. Therefore, some people initially saw intranets as inexpensive competitors to Notes (but less secure and less capable). In late 1995, Lotus Development Corporation redefined the scope of Lotus Notes to include the Internet and intranets so as to reach beyond private LANs. In late 1996, Lotus provided direct Web access as well. Lotus then renamed the product Lotus Domino 4.5 (Domino 5.0 in 1998). Additional functionality provided by Domino Server is its access to Web browsers, accomplished by converting Notes documents into standard HTML format, and there is a Weblicator, a browser add-on that gives Web browsers the Notes replication features (for further discussion see Ouellette [1996]). Several competitors such as Netscape Communicator and Livelink provide many of these same features via the Web. The power of combining Notes and the intranet is demonstrated next.

---

*IT At Work*    NOTES AND THE INTRANET
AT CIRCUIT CITY

**U**SING IT

...in Marketing

Circuit City Stores Inc. is the nation's largest retailer of brand-name consumer electronics and major appliances and a leading retailer of personal computers and music software. The company also pioneered the auto superstore concept with the 1993 opening of CarMax, a used-car retail format.

Circuit City deployed more than 9,500 Notes seats during 1997 and 1998 to provide industry-standard intranet and messaging connectivity between its home office and growing chain of Circuit City Superstores and CarMax Superstores.

With headquarters in Richmond, Virginia, it operates 390 Superstores, five consumer electronics-only stores, 39 mall-based Circuit City Express stores and five CarMax Superstores throughout the United States. Continuing its expansion, the company opened 65 Superstores and two CarMax locations in its 97/98 fiscal year.

"Circuit City is breaking major new ground in its field, largely due to its innovative application of human and technology resources to traditional retailing challenges," said Eileen Rudden, Lotus senior vice president of communications product development. "They have recognized the incredible competitive advantages that can be derived by interactively sharing information in a timely, cost-effective manner among large groups of employees, suppliers and customers through Lotus Notes/Domino."

**For Further Exploration:** How is the Web related to such a project? ▲

SOURCE: Lotus Development Corporation press release, Jan. 4, 1997. See www.lotus.com.

---

**ORGANIZING TEAMS ON THE WEB USING INVOLV.** Based on Domino technology, Involv (from Changepoint Corporation) helps organize Web teams in minutes. The technology is especially useful when the team members are in different locations. Members may belong to different organizations. The software includes several modules such as project collaboration tools, e-mail, document management, and workflow. Task assignments, discussion teams, task by project, work groups, and all project documents are included (for details see www.involv.net). In Figure 5.6 we can see some of the functionalities of Involv.

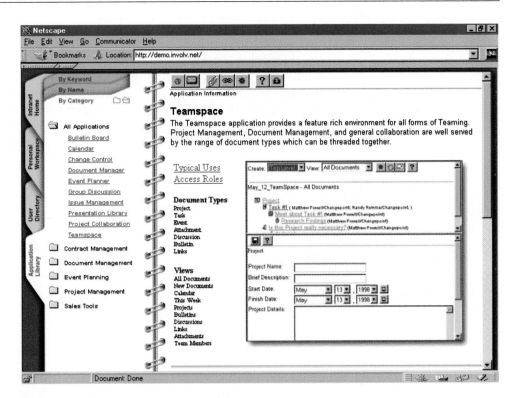

**FIGURE 5.6** Working together remotely using Involv.

## THE INTRANET AND THE EXTRANET

An *intranet*, or an *internal Web*, is a network architecture designed to serve the internal informational needs of a company using Web concepts and tools. It provides Internet capabilities, namely easy and inexpensive browsing, communication, and collaboration. Using a Web browser, a manager can see resumes of employees, business plans, corporate regulations and procedures; retrieve sales data; review any desired document; or call a meeting. Using hyperlinks to expedite searches for material in a database, employees can check availability of software for particular tasks and test the software from their workstations. Intranets are frequently connected to the Internet, enabling the company to conduct electronic commerce activities, such as cooperating with suppliers and customers, checking a customer's inventory level before making shipments, and more. Such activities are facilitated by *extranets*, as described later in this chapter and in Chapter 6. Using screen sharing and other groupware tools, the intranets can be used to facilitate the work of groups. Companies also publish newsletters and deliver news to their employers on their intranet. Detailed applications of intranet commerce are provided in Chapter 6.

The cost of converting an existing network to an internal Web is relatively small, especially when a company is already on the Internet (see Minicase 1 at the end of the chapter). Many computing facilities can be shared by both the Internet and intranets. An example is a client/server-based electronic conferencing software (from Picture Talk, Inc.) that allows users to share documents, graphics, and video in real time. This capability can be combined with an electronic voice arrangement.

Intranets are safe, operating within the company's firewalls. A **firewall** is a method of isolating the company's computers behind a device that acts as a gatekeeper. All outgoing requests for information go to a special computer, which hides the sender's machine address but passes on the request. All incoming information is also checked by the firewall computer. Employees can venture out into the Internet, but unauthorized users cannot come in. This arrangement lets companies speed information and software safely to their own employees and business partners. For a description of firewalls see Chapter 15 and Figure 5.7.

Intranets change organizational structures and procedures and help reengineer corporations. According to a cover story in *Datamation* (December 1996), reengineering fails for three major reasons: (1) it is a top-down process resisted by employees who fear layoffs, (2) massive personnel retraining is necessary, and

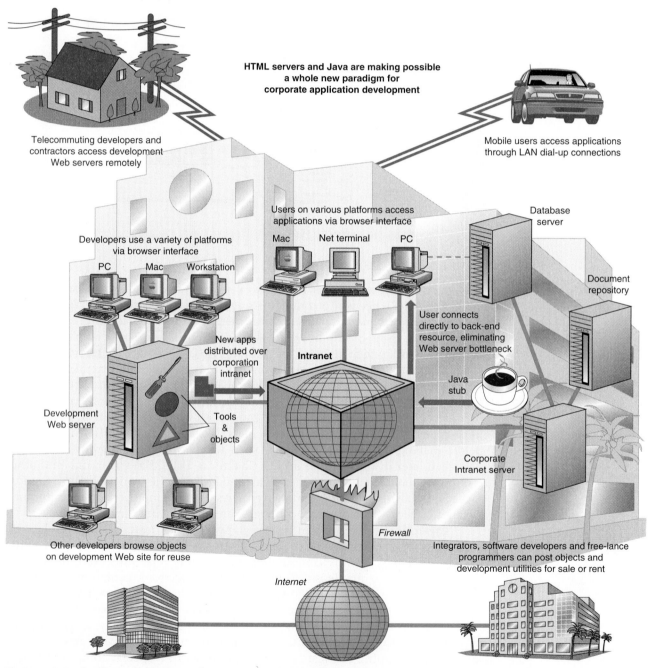

FIGURE 5.7 The firewall between the intranet and its connection to the Internet. (*Source*: *CommunicationsWeek,* April 29, 1996.)

(3) participation of several departments is also needed. Intranets can be useful to rectify the situation, because (1) they support a participative bottom-up process, (2) they are easy to use and facilitate information sharing and cooperation, and (3) they can usually support a diversity of computer platforms in different departments.

At Eli Lilly in Indianapolis, Indiana, 16,000 out of its 26,000 employees were on an intranet by 1996 (*BusinessWeek*, February 26, 1996). But intranets are also affordable for small companies. For example, Geffen Records of Los Angeles supports all its 225 employees with an intranet. Using the existing infrastructure and HTML, an intranet was built at a minimal cost. It enables Geffen's Mac and PC users to work together and share information (*InfoWorld*, February 12, 1996).

All the Hawaiian islands are linked by a state educational, medical, and other public services network (www.htdc.org). This ambitious intranet will help in providing quality services to residents of all islands (*Interactive Week*, January 12, 1998).

A June 1996 fire destroyed much of Utah's Sundance Ski Resort's IT infrastructure. An intranet was built to replace it. Sundance's intranet runs functions including e-mail, reservations, billings, guest requests, catering, food services, and food inventory. In addition, the network allows the resort to improve customer service by distributing customer information like photos and personal preferences to hostesses and managers. The intranet has also improved efficiency in internal operations by facilitating better collaboration and communication among the staff (*Computerworld*, January 27, 1997).

There are many other innovative intranet applications as demonstrated in Box 5.1. Applications related to electronic commerce are provided in Chapter 6.

---

## *A Closer Look*   BOX 5.1

### REASONS COMPANIES USE INTRANETS

According to a special report published in *Information-World* (November 18, 1996), the top ten intranet applications are:

▶ *Extranets.* Linking customers and suppliers to authorized sections of your intranet can create happier customers and more efficient suppliers, and reduce your staff costs (see Chapter 6).

▶ *Interactivity.* Intranets can provide more than fancy e-mail. Online financial planning, creating task forces, and project management are just a few examples.

▶ *Customer service.* FedEx, UPS, and other service-oriented companies have proved that information about product shipments and availability makes customers happier.

▶ *Time-to-market.* Easy online access speeds teamwork in product development.

▶ *Empowerment.* Everything should be available to everyone with the right to know.

▶ *Video.* Face-to-face meetings take on a whole new meaning. But should you do performance reviews online?

▶ *Audio.* The public address system of the twenty-first century.

▶ *Virtual organization.* Incompatible technology is no longer a barrier if you need subcontractors.

▶ *Telephony.* All the hype about consumers avoiding AT&T, Sprint, and MCI misses the bigger opportunity—intranets are the perfect conduit for computer-based telephony.

▶ *Software distribution.* Don't put a copy of each application on each desktop. Use the intranet server as the applications warehouse and avoid many maintenance support problems.

Additional applications such as training, publishing, and providing human resources services are described in Chapter 6.

**EXTRANETS.** An intranet's infrastructure is confined to an organization's boundaries while the Internet is an infrastructure that is used to connect organizations. Another type of infrastructure is called an **extranet.** An extranet is an infrastructure that allows secure communications among business partners. It enables limited accessibility to the intranets of the participating companies as well as the necessary interorganizational communications using Internet technology. The use of extranets is increasing rapidly due to the large savings in communication costs that can materialize. The extranets enable innovative applications of electronic commerce (Chapter 6). Finally, extranets are closely related to improved communications along the supply chain (for details see Chapter 6 and Technology Guide #4).

## ▶ 5.3 SOME INTERNET IMPLEMENTATION TOPICS

Of the many topics involved in implementing the Internet, only two will be discussed here due to space limitations.

### INTERNET-BASED SOFTWARE AGENTS

The amount of information on the Internet is at least doubling every year. This makes navigating through the Internet and gaining access to necessary information more and more difficult. The most effective solution to this problem is the automation of routine activities conducted over the Internet by means of **software agents** or **intelligent agents.** (See the July/Aug. 1997 special issue of *Internet Computing.*) A software agent is a computer program that helps the user with routine computer tasks. The topic of intelligent agents is discussed more fully in Chapter 11. Here we present only some examples of Internet-based agents, which appear under names, such as wizards, softbots, and knowbots. Five major types of Internet agents are e-mail agents, Web-browsing-assisting agents, FAQ agents, Internet softbot, and indexing agents.

**E-MAIL AGENTS.** These agents assist users with the often time-consuming task of managing their e-mail. For example, Maxims (see Maes [1994]) monitors what each user routinely does with his or her e-mail and memorizes the user's situation-action pairs. These pairs are stored in a "memory of examples," described in terms of a set of features including the names of those who send or receive messages to or from the user. When a new situation occurs, the agent analyzes the features of the situation and suggests an action to the user (read, delete, forward, and archive). The agent communicates with Eudora, a Windows-based e-mail software system.

The agent measures the confidence (or fit) of a suggested action to a situation. If the confidence is high, the agent executes the suggestion with the approval of the user; otherwise, the agent waits for instructions. The agent's performance improves with time as the collection of examples increases.

Several other e-mail agents help users handle large numbers of messages. For example, Motiwalla (1995) developed an intelligent agent for prioritizing e-mail messages based on users' preferences or knowledge. American Finance and Investment, Inc. uses intelligent agents to control their e-mail flood. The application reduced the number of employees answering e-mail from four to one.

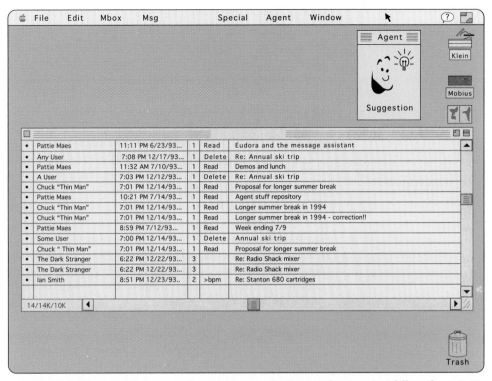

**FIGURE 5.8** The e-mail agent makes recommendations to the user (middle column). It predicts what actions the user will perform on messages, such as which messages will be read and in which order, which messages will be deleted, forwarded, archived, and so on. (*Source*: Maes [1994], p. 34.)

(For details see R., Gotcher in *InfoWorld*, 8, 1997.) An example of an e-mail agent's output is shown in Figure 5.8.

**WEB-BROWSING-ASSISTING AGENTS.**  Some agents can facilitate browsing by offering the user a tour of the Internet. Known as *tour guides*, they work while the user browses. For example, WebWatcher helps find pages related to the current page, adding hyperlinks to meet the user's search goal and giving advice on the basis of user's preference.

Another example is Letizia. This agent monitors the user's activities with a browser. Using various heuristics, the agent tries to anticipate additional items that might be of interest to the user. A similar agent is Netcomber Activist from IBM. The agent monitors you when you surf through the Yahoo catalog. The agent builds your interest profile; then it recommends newspapers for daily reading, and so on (O'Leary [1996] and Etzioni and Weld [1995]).

**FREQUENTLY ASKED QUESTIONS (FAQ) AGENTS.**  These agents guide people to the answers to frequently asked questions. People tend to ask the same or similar questions. In response, newsgroups, support staffs, vendors, and others have developed files of those FAQs and the most appropriate answer to each. But there is a problem in that people use natural language, asking the same questions in several different ways. The agent (such as FAQFinder) addresses this problem by indexing large numbers of FAQ files, and providing an interface by which people can post their questions in natural language. Using the text of a question the agent can locate the appropriate answer. Due to the limited number of FAQs and the semistructured nature of the questions, the reliability of FAQ agents is very high. GTE Laboratories developed an FAQ agent that accepts questions from users of Usenet News Groups in natural language and answers them by matching question–answer pairs (Whitehead [1995]).

**INTELLIGENT INDEXING AGENTS.** Web robots, spiders, wanderers, and similar names describe agents that traverse the Web and perform tasks such as information retrieval and discovery, validating links or HTML, and generating statistics.

Indexing agents can carry out a massive autonomous search of the Web on behalf of a user or, more commonly, a major commercial *search engine* like HotBot or Altavista. First, they scan millions of documents and store an index of words found in document titles, key words, and texts. The user can then query the search engine to find documents containing certain key words (Etzioni and Weld [1995]). Special indexing agents are being developed for knowledge sharing and acquisition in large databases and documents. *Metasearch engines* (such as *Spider, Savvy Search, Metacrawler, All in One,* and *Web Compass*) integrate the findings of the various search engines to answer queries posted by the users.

**INTERNET SOFTBOT.** Search agents suggest locations on the Web to the user. Such suggestions are based on a relatively weak model of what the user wants and what information is available in the suggested location. *Internet softbots,* developed at the University of Washington (Etzioni and Weld [1994]), attempt to determine what the user wants and they also understand the contents of information services. The first generation of softbot agents was only effective with structured information such as stock quotes, weather maps, or Federal Express's package tracking service.

**INTERNET-BASED DATA MINING.** Appropriate data mining tools can give users a necessary edge when sifting through large amounts of information. Data mining permits new patterns and relationships to be revealed through the implementation of software that can do much of the mining process (see Chapter 10). Intelligent agents are most useful in discovering previously unknown relationships especially in complex data structures. Query-and-reporting tools, on the other hand, demand a predefined database structure and are most valuable when asking particular questions to confirm hypotheses.

*Web mining* is an important part of data mining, and, according to Etzioni (1996), it can perform the following functions:

▶ *Resource discovery.* Locating unfamiliar documents and services on the Web.

▶ *Information extraction.* Automatically extracting specific information from newly discovered Web resources.

▶ *Generalization.* Uncovering general patterns at individual Web sites and across multiple sites.

Some of the agents described earlier can assist in these activities. For example, WebCrawler and MetaCrawler can facilitate resource discovery. Internet Learning Agent and Shopbot are Web miners that rely on a combination of test queries and domain-specific knowledge to learn descriptions of Web services automatically. The learned descriptions are then used to extract information.

## ETHICS ON THE NET

Several ethical, legal, and security issues have been raised as a result of the use of electronic networks in general and the Internet in particular. For example:

▶ Is someone's desire to download pornographic images from a newsgroup protected by freedom of speech and privacy laws?

▶ Does an employer have the right to look at your e-mail without your permission?

▶ Can someone post critical comments about a product or service to a newsgroup?

▶ Can a network provider be held liable for the content of the traffic on the network?

Whenever there are no specific answers to such questions and their legal dimensions are vague, ethics become an important factor (see Chapter 7). Here are some representative issues:

1. *Privacy and ethics in e-mail.* The increased use of e-mail raises the question of privacy. While letters are sealed, e-mail material is open (unless encrypted). Many organizations are monitoring e-mail, which raises questions of invasion of privacy (see discussion in Chapter 7). Other issues include the use of e-mail at work for personal purposes and for sending and receiving material that is not related to work, including electronic junk mail. For privacy protection tips see *PC World,* February 1997, pp. 223–229.

2. *Right of free speech.* The dissemination of information such as pornographic and racist material via e-mail, newsgroups, electronic bulletin boards, and public networks may offend some people. But dissemination of such information is believed to be a right prescribed by the U.S. Constitution. At the time of this writing, the degree of freedom in the online world, and who should be liable for transmissions that are illegal, is still very much in debate. Legislation has been proposed that would require providers to create filters allowing adults to keep children from accessing inappropriate material. In fact, the commercial online providers have largely done so. The Internet, however, remains entirely accessible for anyone with a direct connection.

3. *Copyright.* The material you access on the Internet may be marked as being in the public domain; then it can be used by anyone for any purpose. Some material is marked as "copyrighted," which indicates that you need permission from the author for anything other than a "fair use." Fair use refers to educational and not-for-profit activities. If you make a profit from copyrighted material, you should pay the owner of the copyright some royalties.

   Much of the material on the Internet is not marked as either in the public domain or copyrighted. Therefore, at least from an ethical point of view, it should be considered copyrighted. This includes software—you cannot legally copy any licensed software. However, *freeware* on the Internet can be downloaded and distributed, while *shareware* can be downloaded for review but you are expected to buy it if you decide you want to use it.

4. *The privacy of patients' information.* In the United States, several specialized healthcare networks exist such as Telemed, a network that tracks tuberculosis patients in order to prescribe the most suitable drugs. These sys-

tems could be abused. How do patients know they are getting qualified advice? What if personal medical records fall into the wrong hands? The growth of computerized networks makes medical confidentiality harder to preserve. The problem is how to strike a balance between the benefits of health information systems and their potential ethical problems.

5. *Internet manners.* It is very easy to offend people or tread on their toes when you cannot see their faces or you do not know who they are. Two well-known behaviors on the Internet are spamming and flaming. **Spamming** refers to indiscriminate distribution of messages, without consideration for their appropriateness. Some people spam newsgroups repeatedly. Spamming is frequently answered by **flaming,** which refers to sending angry messages. The Internet can become a war zone between spammers and flamers. Both sides may be equally guilty for ruining newsgroups. Flamers are known for their attacks on inexperienced visitors to newsgroups as well as on those that make spelling errors. A *spam shield* can stop spamming (for examples see Ipwa.com.8000/).

There are certain rules, called **netiquette** (network etiquette), governing Internet manners; some are shown in Box 5.2.

Likewise, it is far easier to take offense because online interaction excludes the nuances of body language, rhythm, mood, and context. E-mail

---

## A Closer Look   BOX 5.2

### HOW TO BEHAVE ON THE INTERNET— REPRESENTATIVE NETIQUETTE

▶ Never respond rashly to provocation on the Internet. Although "flame wars" have often broken out on unmoderated mailing lists and Usenet newsgroups, they are generally frowned on. If you must respond, do it offline (that is, in private e-mail, not to the group as a whole).

▶ Criticize ideas, not people. Try to be as constructive in your criticism as possible.

▶ Watch or monitor for a while any mailing list or newsgroup you want to participate in, to get a feel for the tone and to avoid asking "newbie" (newcomer) questions.

▶ Do your homework before asking questions. Look for the relevant Frequently Asked Questions (FAQ) files to avoid asking questions that have already been answered.

▶ Think carefully before sending a message. Remember that you are making your reputation internationally through the messages you send out.

▶ Stay on the topic of the newsgroup or mailing list. No matter how strongly you feel about a subject, it is not appropriate to send information or opinions about it to unrelated groups.

▶ Do not shout. (Typing messages in ALL CAPS is shouting.) A single word in uppercase for emphasis is fine, but no more.

▶ Don't post commercials. Ads have their place in the online world, but make sure you understand just where that place is. The vast majority of usenet groups eschew ads. Indeed, posting an advertisement in the wrong place will surely provoke a flame attack and worse.

▶ Know whereof you speak. Don't pass along unsubstantiated rumors or anything you yourself don't believe to be true.

▶ Don't be the skunk at the picnic. If you don't accept the underlying premise of a discussion group, don't disrupt it; just go away. An atheist, for example, needn't bother joining a conference of nuns who are debating church matters.

▶ Apply the Golden Rule. Do unto others in cyberspace as you would do unto them face to face, which is, of course, how you would want them to do unto you.

## *A Closer Look* BOX 5.3

### THE UNOFFICIAL SMILEY GUIDE

Smileys are simple but creative drawings of expressions. They are used very often in electronic messages in place of facial and tonal expressions. For example, if I say, "Get lost!" you may think that I am really angry at you. But if I say, "Get lost :-)" you know I don't really mean it. The remark becomes something like a secret between us and

I am really giving you a pat on your back. There may be more than one explanation for each Smiley and some are more obvious than others. You can design your own Smileys too. Some typical Smileys are listed below.

(*Note:* If you cannot see the faces, turn this page clockwise 90 degrees.)

| | | | |
|---|---|---|---|
| :-) | Basic smiling smiley | :-X | A big wet kiss |
| :) | Smiley midget | :-x | My lips are sealed |
| :-D | A big smile | #-) | Partied all night |
| ;-) | Winking | %-| | Been working all night |
| <:-O | Eeek! | %+{ | Lost a fight |
| 8-O | Omigod!! | 8-) | Wears glasses |
| :-o | Shocked | (:-{~ | Bearded |
| **-( | Too many shocks | :=~) | Has a cold |
| %-( | Confusion | :^D | "Great! I like it!" |
| &-| | Tearful | |-{ | "Good grief!" |
| :'-( | Crying | >-< | Absolutely livid!! |
| :-( | Frowning | 0:-) | Angel |
| :-* | Kissing | | |

users developed a similar language that can be used to overcome the problem. A sample is shown in Box 5.3.

6. ***Monitoring employees' use of the Internet.*** Some companies use special software that monitors time spent on the Internet, by employee and by site address. The objective is to eliminate abuse of access during working hours and the accessing of "indecent" sites. It seems to be a good idea, but is it ethical? Other companies simply disconnect sites they do not want their employees to visit. It sounds good, but what about freedom of speech?

## ▶ MANAGERIAL ISSUES

Providing timely, relevant, and correct information is a critical factor for the success of almost any organization. In implementing IT to support communication and collaborative work, the following issues may surface.

1. ***Security of communication.*** Communication via networks raises the issue of the integrity, confidentiality, and security of the data being transferred. The protection of data in networks across the globe is not simple. A 1996 survey (*Communications Week*, November 25, 1996) indicated that about 50 percent of the *Fortune* 1000 companies were successfully attacked and penetrated during that year. Most of the invasions were network related.

2. *Data crossing national borders.* Governments cannot or do not wish to control data that crosses their borders via regular mail. However, it is easier to control data crossing national borders electronically. Such control, which is commonly justified as a protection of citizens' privacy, is sometimes done to preserve jobs.

3. *Congestion.* Some people believe the increased use of the Internet will clog it; therefore, companies should develop a plan to limit the use of the Internet (Mann [1995]). Others believe that technological developments will solve the capacity and security problems of the Internet (Gilder [1996]).

4. *Control of employee time and activities.* "Surfing the Internet" is an exciting, yet time-consuming activity. Employees may be tempted to conduct private surfing during work hours. Control can be achieved by limiting the information that employees have access to, and by using special monitoring software. Providing guidelines is simple and fairly effective.

5. *Questionnaires and referenda.* An increasing number of researchers and pollsters are using the Internet for conducting marketing surveys or running national referenda on political issues. Some researchers have questioned the reliability and validity of such surveys because of possible response biases.

6. *Organizational impacts.* Technology-supported communication may have major organizational impacts. For example, intranets and groupware force people to cooperate and share information. Therefore, their use can lead to significant changes in both organizational culture and the execution of business process reengineering. Further impacts may be felt in corporate structure and the redistribution of organizational power.

7. *The use of a decision room.* A GDSS decision room is expensive to build and requires a professional facilitator. Building a decision room with off-the-shelf components is an option that can reduce its cost at the expense of some capabilities. In addition, the room may be little used, since it is mainly suitable for resolving conflicts, and its use requires a great deal of preparation and professional support. Therefore, companies should consider renting one in order to gain experience before constructing their own.

8. *Cost-benefit justification.* The technologies described in this chapter do not come free and many of the benefits are intangible. For example, Price Waterhouse invested $2 million in Lotus Notes. However, with the introduction of intranets and other competing products, the price of Lotus Notes is decreasing. Distributed GDSS and the availability of competing products reduce the cost of the technology even further.

9. *Legal issues.* There are many unresolved legal issues. For example, international groups are struggling over jurisdiction of trademarks and names on the Web. In one instance, when Carl's Jr. Corporation, a fast-food chain, applied for a Web site by this name (for which it has the trademark), it found the name had been granted to a youngster named Carl Junior. Other examples are the use of the Internet for misrepresentation, fraud, and other illegal transactions.

10. *Controlling the access and managing the content of the material on the intranet.* This is becoming a major problem due to the ease of placing material on the intranet and the huge volume of information. Flohr (1997) suggests tools and procedures to manage the situation.

## KEY TERMS

Asynchronous communication  176

Collaboration  178

Data conferencing  182

Decision room  187

Delphi method  179

Electronic catalogs  169

Electronic commerce (EC)  170

Electronic mail (e-mail)  177

Extranet  196

Firewall  193

Flaming  200

Group decision support system (GDSS)  186

Groupware  179

Information superhighway  170

Intelligent agents  196

Internet  169

Intranet  170

Lotus Notes  189

Netiquette  200

Nominal group technique (NGT)  179

Screen sharing  180

Software agents  196

Spamming  200

Synchronous (real time) communication  176

Teleconferencing  181

Video teleconference  181

Video mail  182

Voice mail  186

Workflow systems  180

Work group  178

## CHAPTER HIGHLIGHTS *(L–x means learning objective number x)*

▶ Information superhighways will enable us to integrate voice, text, and other interactive media and bring them into every home, school, and business. (L–1)

▶ The Internet is a network of many networks. It is the predecessor of the information superhighway. (L–1)

▶ There are four ways of supporting communication in meetings: same-time/same-place, same-time/different-place, different-time/same-place, and different-time/different-place. (L–2)

▶ Electronic mail allows quick communication across the globe at minimal cost. (L–2)

▶ Electronic meeting systems, computer-supported cooperative work, groupware, and other names designate various types of computer support to groups. (L–3)

▶ Video teleconferencing utilizes several technologies that allow people to communicate and view each other as well as view and transfer documents. (L–3)

▶ Voice technologies can be used to increase productivity and usability of communication. (L–3)

▶ A corporate group decision support system is usually structured on a LAN and is conducted in a decision-room environment with a facilitator. (L–4)

▶ Lotus Notes is the major integrated software that supports the work of dispersed individuals and groups. (L–4)

▶ Intranets are an implementation and deployment of Web-based network services within a company. (L–5)

▶ Software agents help to carry mundane tasks on the Internet such as searching, browsing, and sorting e-mail. (L–6)

▶ Ethical behavior on the Internet is critical to its success. You need to know what is right and wrong. (L–7)

## QUESTIONS FOR REVIEW

1. List the major advantages of the Internet.

2. Define an intranet.

3. Define browsing.

4. What are some major benefits of working in groups?

5. Are there any major limitations to working in groups?

6. Define a GDSS, and list three of its benefits.

7. Explain the major characteristics of a GDSS.

8. Describe a decision room, and contrast it with other GDSS scenarios.

9. Compare GDSS to noncomputerized group decision making.

10. Define groupware.

11. Describe the major capabilities of Lotus Notes.

12. List the major capabilities of teleconferencing.

13. Define e-mail, and describe its capabilities.

14. Define workflow systems.

15. Describe software agents.

16. List the major Internet-based agents.

17. What are information superhighways?

18. Define voice technology, and list its uses.

19. Define flaming and contrast it with spamming.

20. Define netiquette.

## QUESTIONS FOR DISCUSSION

1. Identify some commercial tools that allow users to conduct browsing, communication, and collaboration simultaneously.

2. Explain why the topic of group work and its support is getting increased attention.

3. Explain the advantages of electronic mail over regular mail.

4. Compare and contrast GDSS to noncomputerized group decision making.

5. How can GDSS support creativity?

6. It is said that Lotus Notes can change organizational culture. Explain how.

7. How can computers support a team whose members work at different times?

8. Based on what you know about Lotus Notes, can it support different-time/different-place work situations?

9. Relate flaming to netiquette.

10. Discuss the need for Internet-based software agents.

11. Describe how agents can help people find specific information quickly.

## EXERCISES

1. From your own experience or from the vendor's information, list all the major capabilities of Lotus Notes and Domino and explain how they can be used to support knowledge workers and managers.

2. The University of Arizona adopted GroupSystems for use in a distributed mode on the Internet. Determine which software modules are especially suitable for a distributed mode. (You may need to contact the Ventana Corporation, makers of GroupSystems.)

3. Sears had some problems with its Prodigy system in 1992 and 1993, regarding dissemination of information that offended people. Find material about this or similar incident. Use the Internet for your search. Summarize and prepare a report.

4. Visit www.picturetel.com and sites of other companies that manufacture conferencing products for the Internet. Prepare a report. Why is it called video commerce?

## GROUP ASSIGNMENTS

1. You are a member of a team working for a multinational finance corporation. Your team's project is to prepare a complex financing proposal for a client within one week. Two of the team members are in Singapore, one is in Seoul, Korea, one is in London, and one is in Los Angeles. You cannot get the team members together in one place. Your team does not have all the required expertise, but other corporate employees may have it. There are 8,000 employees worldwide; many of them travel. You do not know exactly who the experts are in your company. Your company has never prepared such a proposal, but you know that certain parts of the proposal can be adapted from previous proposals. These proposals are filed electronically in various corporate databases, but you are not sure exactly where (there are over 80 databases, worldwide). Finally, you will need a lot of external information, and you will need to communicate with your client in China, with investment groups in Japan and New York, and with your corporate headquarters in London.

   If the client accepts your proposal, your company will make more than $5 million in profit. If the contract goes to a competitor, you may lose your job.

   Your company has all the latest information and communication technologies.

   a. Prepare a list of tasks and activities that your team will need to go through in order to accomplish the mission. (Look at www.knowldgespace.com.)

   b. Describe what information technologies you would use to support the above tasks. Be specific, explaining how each technology can facilitate the execution of each task.

2. The world of the Internet is growing very fast, and it keeps changing. An additional task for the group is to report on the latest developments on the Internet's uses. Members of the group will prepare a report to include the following.

   a. New business applications on the Internet.

   b. New books about the Internet.

   c. Information about new software products related to the Internet.

   d. New managerial and technological issues related to the Internet.

   Also, send an e-mail message about a topic of concern to you to the White House and include the reply in your report.

3. Assign each group member to an integrated group support tool kit (Notes, GroupWise, Communicator, etc.). Have each member visit the Web site and obtain information about this product. The group should prepare a comparative table of the major similarities and differences among the kits.

4. Trace some of National Semiconductor's latest utilization of the Internet-intranet and extranet. Visit www.national.com, and www.natsem.com and NSC

news releases (e.g., wgaultier@hoffman.com). Of special interest is the manner the company tracks the movements of visitors in an attempt to predict their buying habits. (See *Internetweek*, Oct. 13, 1997.)

## INTERNET EXERCISES

Note: The URLs included here were current when the book went to press. However, they are subject to change without notice. Please consult the Turban Web site (www.Wiley.com/college/turban2e).

1. Your friend wishes to pursue graduate studies in accounting in the United States. She is especially interested in two universities: the University of Illinois (U of I) and the University of Southern California (USC). Use the Internet to find information that will help your friend choose between the two universities. Such information should include, *but not be limited to,* the following:
   a. the types of degree programs in accounting offered by the two universities.
   b. the admission procedures and school calendar.
   c. coursework and dissertation requirements of the programs under consideration.
   d. the costs of tuition and other expenses associated with the programs.

2. You plan to take a three-week vacation in Hawaii this December, visiting the Big Island of Hawaii. Using the Internet, find information that will help you plan the trip. Such information includes, *but is not limited to,* the following:
   a. geographical location and weather conditions in December.
   b. major tourist attractions and recreational facilities.
   c. travel arrangements (airlines, approximate fares).
   d. car rental, local tours.
   e. alternatives for accommodation (within a moderate budget) and food.
   f. estimated cost of the vacation (travel + lodging + food + recreation + shopping + . . .).
   g. state regulations regarding the entrance of your dog that you plan to take with you.
   h. shopping (try to find an electronic mall).

3. Your friend manufactures canned food products (vegetables, beef) and wants to export them to Mexico. He has heard about the North American Free Trade Agreement (NAFTA) and wishes to find out how it may affect his business prospects. Surf the Internet to find information that will help your friend address his concerns about NAFTA. Such information includes, *but is not limited to,* the following:
   a. the nations involved in NAFTA.
   b. the scope of NAFTA (with specific reference to food products).

Finally, find how the company is using their Lotus Domino with the extranet (see *Internetweek*, March 9, 1998).

   c. the time-table for the provisions of NAFTA (what went or goes into effect when).
   d. the expected benefits to the participants in NAFTA.
   e. implications of NAFTA for businesses located in your state.
   f. implications of NAFTA for businesses located in a food-exporting country (e.g., Australia).

   Join a discussion group or newsgroup whose major concern is NAFTA. Post a question regarding your friend's issues of concern.

   Based on the information you collect, provide your friend with a report and recommendations on whether to pursue his project or not.

4. Visit Georgia Tech's sites (www.cc.gatech.edu/gvu /user_surveys).
   a. Find the latest studies about Internet users.
   b. Compare with previous studies.

5. Visit www.cdt.org.
   a. Find what technologies are available to track users' activities on the Internet.

6. Visit the ON Technology Corporation Web site (http://www.on.com). Describe the capabilities of the current version of Meeting Maker. Download the Meeting Maker demo software, try it with a group, and report your findings. Visit and download the demo of "The Meeting Room" from Eden Systems Corporation (http://www.iquestnet/edensys/index.html). Compare its functionality to that of Meeting Maker.

7. You are assigned the task of buying desktop teleconferencing equipment for your company. Using the Internet:
   a. Identify three major vendors.
   b. Visit their Web sites and find information about their products and capabilities.
   c. Compare the least expensive products of two vendors.
   d. Find a newsgroup that has an interest in video-teleconferencing. Post new questions regarding the products selected (for example, what are the users' experiences?).
   e. Prepare a report of your findings.

8. Both Microsoft Explorer and Netscape Navigator have the capability for telephony; all you need is a sound card, microphone, and speakers on your PC. (If you

do not have these browsers, access the VocalTech Web site at http://www.vocaltech.com/, and download and install its fully functional Internet long distance telephone software). Get a friend in another city to do the same. Contact each other via the Internet using your computer as a telephone. What are the advantages and disadvantages of using the Internet for telephone service? Compare your experience to that of making a standard telephone call.

# Minicase 1

## Marine Forces Reserve Streamlines Communications

Like organizations in the private sector, the Marine Forces Reserve (MARFORRES) is always seeking ways to make its operations more efficient. MARFORRES trains 14,000 reserve personnel at any given time, for a war or national emergency, in 200 locations around the United States. Reservists are at their training centers only one weekend a month. This created a communication problem.

Until recently even relatively simple administrative requests from reservists, especially those not at bases, could take months to process. The 100,000 reservists are submitting many requests. The delays caused frustration and loss of productivity among the reservists during their training.

The solution was the creation of a Web site and an internal communication system for the 200 training centers based on Lotus Notes/Domino. The system includes both e-mail and groupware, and it contains several Notes applications which both solve the above communication problem and facilitate the reduction of the administrative manpower. One of the first areas addressed was the hierarchical communications bottlenecks. Reservists now submit requests electronically. Using workflow software, the requests are automatically routed to the proper authorities. If more information is needed, a request is instantly routed back to the sender. The reservists can track the status of their requests at any time. The results were staggering: Processes that had been taking six months were now down to three days!

In order to reduce administrative overhead, MARFORRES replaced the manual system with Notes databases in which all directives are stored and changed centrally. Other applications include: e-mail for the internal system, a platform for decisions, and planning and awareness tools (e.g., to plan training exercises and to manage the number of people, where they are to be transported, and other cost and logistics issues).

Notes is also used for internal collaboration. MARFORRES knowledge sharing database (R-NET) allows technical experts to answer users' questions.

The MARFORRES Web site (www.marforres .usmc.mil) is integrated with Lotus Domino server. This Web site provides considerable information to 100,000 reservists in any location in the world.

The entire system was deployed rapidly. User (the permanent staff of the bases) training was facilitated by computer-based, video-based, and self-paced courseware at each of the 200 sites.

### Questions for Minicase 1

1. Communication among the 200 training centers and the MARFORRES headquarters is conducted over dedicated military lines. In each training center there is one Notes server. However, there is only one Domino server at the headquarters. Why?

2. Examine some of the capabilities of Notes. What other applications can you envision at MARFORRES? You may check www.lotus.com for the newest capabilities of Notes and Domino.

3. Training in Lotus Notes takes 2–3 days, but it is automated at MARFORRES. Why?

4. Which of Notes' capabilities do you think is used by the reservists and which by the bases' permanent staff? Why?

5. Log on to the Web site. What information/services available on the Web are related to the Notes system? Why?

6. How can Notes contribute to the reduction of the administrative manpower of MARFORRES?

SOURCE: Condensed from *Lotus Solutions Now,* Winter 1998, pp. 10–11.

# ▼ Minicase 2

## Which Technology to Use?

Marketel is a fast-growing telemarketing company whose headquarters are in Colorado, but the majority of its business is in California. The company has eight divisions, including one in Chicago. (The company has just started penetrating the Midwest market.) Recently the company was approached by two large telephone companies, one in Los Angeles and one in Denver, for discussions regarding a potential merger.

Nancy Miranda, the corporate CEO who was involved in the preliminary discussions, notified all division managers on the progress of the discussions. Both she and John Miner, the chief financial officer, felt that an immediate merger would be extremely beneficial. However, the vice presidents for marketing and operations thought the company should continue to be independent for at least two to three years. "We can get a much better deal if we first increase our market share," commented Sharon Gonzales, the vice president for marketing.

Nancy called each of the division managers and found that five of them were for the merger proposal while three objected to it. Furthermore, she found that the division managers from the West Coast strongly opposed discussions with the Colorado company, while the other managers were strongly against discussions with the Los Angeles company. Memos, telephone calls, and meetings of two or three people at a time resulted in frustration. It became apparent that a meeting of all concerned individuals was a must. Nancy wanted to have the meeting as soon as possible in spite of the busy travel schedules of most division managers. She also wanted the meeting to be as short as possible. Nancy called Bob Kraut, the chief information officer, and asked for suggestions about how to conduct a conference electronically. The options are as follows.

1. Use the corporate intranet. Collect opinions from all division managers and vice presidents, then disseminate them to all parties, get feedback, and repeat the process until a solution is achieved (similar to the Delphi method).

2. Fly all division managers to corporate headquarters and have face-to-face meetings until a solution is achieved.

3. Use the distributed version of GroupSystem software. Conduct a facilitated real-time meeting where the participants stay at their locations.

4. Fly all division managers to corporate headquarters. Rent a decision room and a facilitator from the local university for $2,000 per day and conduct the meetings there.

5. Conduct a videoconference. Unfortunately, appropriate facilities exist only at the headquarters and in two divisions. The other division managers can be flown to the nearest division that has equipment. Alternatively, videoconferencing facilities may be rented in all cities.

6. Use a telephone conference call.

### Questions for Minicase 2

1. Which of these options would you recommend to management and why?

2. Is there a technology not listed that might do a better job?

3. Is it possible to use more than one alternative in this case? If yes, which technologies would you combine and how would you use them?

## REFERENCES AND BIBLIOGRAPHY

1. Berghel, H., "E-mail—The Good, the Bad, and the Ugly," *Communications of the ACM*, April 1997.

2. Bernard, R., *The Corporate Intranet*, New York: John Wiley & Sons, 1997.

3. Coleman, D., *Collaborative Strategies for Corporate LANs and Intranets*, Upper Saddle River, N.J.: Prentice Hall, 1996.

4. Comerford, R., "Interactive Media: An Internet Reality," *IEEE Spectrum*, Apr. 1996.

5. Cortese, A., "Here Comes the Intranet," Special Report, *BusinessWeek*, February 26, 1996.

6. Cox, N., *Building and Managing a Web Services Team*, New York: Van Nostrand Reinhold, 1997.

7. Cronin, M. J., *Global Advantage on the Internet*, New York: Van Nostrand Reinhold, 1996.

8. DeSanctis, G., and B. Gallupe, "A Foundation for the Study of Group Decision Support Systems," *Management Science*, Vol. 33, No. 5, 1987.

9. Editorial, "Free Phone! Free Video! Free E-mail! Free Fax!— on the Web," *PC Computing*, February 1997.

10. Ellsworth, J. H., and M. V. Ellsworth, *The Internet Business,* 2nd edition, New York: John Wiley & Sons, 1996.

11. Etzioni, O., "The WWW: Quagmire or Gold Mine?" *Communications of the ACM,* November 1996.

12. Etzioni, O., and D. S. Weld, "A Softbot-based Interface to the Internet," *Communications of the ACM,* Vol. 37, No. 7, 1994.

13. Etzioni, O., and D. S. Weld, "Intelligent Agents on the Internet: Fact, Fiction, and Forecast," *IEEE Expert,* August 1995.

14. Flohr, U., "Intelligent Intranets," *Byte,* August 1997.

15. Gilder, G., "Will the Internet Collapse? No Way!" *Forbes ASAP,* August 26, 1996.

16. Haskin, D., "Meetings Without Walls," *Internet World,* October 1997.

17. Jessup, L. M., and J. Valacich (eds.), *Group Support Systems: New Perspectives,* New York: Macmillan, 1993.

18. Johnsen, R., *Groupware: Computer Support for Business Teams,* New York: Free Press, 1988.

19. Khoshafian, S., and M. Buckiewicz, *Introduction to Groupware, Workflow, and Workgroup Computing,* New York: Wiley Computer Publishing, August 1996.

20. Krantz, S., *Building Intranets with Lotus Notes and Domino,* Gulf Breeze, FL: Maximum Press, 1998.

21. Lawrence, P. (ed.), *Workflow Handbook,* New York: John Wiley & Sons, 1997.

22. Lindstone, H., and H. Turroff, *The Delphi Method: Technology and Applications,* Reading, MA: Addison-Wesley, 1975.

23. Liu, Z. "China's Information Superhighway: Its Goal, Architecture and Problems," *Electronic Markets,* Vol 7., No. 4, 1997.

24. McKeown, P. G., and R. T. Watson, *Metamorphosis—A guide to the WWW and Electronic Commerce,* New York: John Wiley & Sons, 2nd ed. 1998.

25. McKim, G. W., *Internet Research Companion,* Indianapolis, IN: Que Publishing Company, 1996.

26. Maes, P., "Agents that Reduce Work and Information Overload," *Communications of the ACM,* July 1994.

27. Maitra, A. K., *Building a Corporate Internet Strategy: The IT Manager's Guide,* New York: Van Nostrand Reinhold, 1997.

28. Mann, C. C., "Is the Internet Doomed?" *Inc. Technology,* No. 2, 1995.

29. Motiwalla, L. F., "An Intelligent Agent for Prioritizing E-mail Messages," *Information Resources Management,* Spring 1995.

30. Nelso, S. L., *The WWW for Busy People,* New York: Berkeley Osborne/McGraw Hill, 1996.

31. NII—"National Information Infrastructure—Agenda for Action" (http://sunsite,unc.edu/nii/toc.html), 1993.

32. O'Leary, D., "AI and Navigation on the Internet and Intranet," *IEEE Expert,* April 1996.

33. Ouellette, T., "Notes Changes Name, Shifts Focus to Internet," *Computerworld,* Vol. 30, No. 45, November 4, 1996.

34. Ozer, J., et al., "Collaboration on the Web," cover story, *PC Magazine,* October 6, 1996, pp. 100–230.

35. Pitkow, J. E., and G. M. Kethoe, "Emerging Trends in the WWW User Population," *Communications of the ACM,* June 1996.

36. Rebstock, S., et al., "Group Support Systems, Power and Influence in Organizations: A Field Study," *Decision Sciences Journal,* Fall 1997.

37. Smith, G. S., and O. Rist, "Collaboration (Groupware)," *Internetweek,* January 19, 1998.

38. Sterne, J., *Customer Service on the Internet: Building Relationship, Increasing Loyalty, and Staying Competitive,* New York: John Wiley & Sons, 1997.

39. Storm, D., "Videoconferencing," *Internet World,* Sept. 1997.

40. Stull, A. T., *Surfing for Success in Business: A Student Guide to the Internet,* Upper Saddle River, NJ: Prentice Hall, 1997.

41. Udell, J., "Your Business Needs the Web," *Byte,* August 1996.

42. Vickers, B., "Using GDSS to Examine the Future European Automobile Industry," *Futures,* October 1992.

43. Zieger, A., "IP Telephony Gets Real," *Infoworld,* January 5, 1998.

# CHAPTER 6

# Electronic Commerce

## Learning Objectives

*After studying this chapter, you will be able to:*

❶ Describe electronic commerce, its dimensions, benefits, limitations, and process.

❷ Describe the major applications of electronic commerce, both business-to-customer and business-to-business.

❸ Discuss the importance and activities of market research and customer service.

❹ Describe the electronic commerce infrastructure and EDI.

❺ Compare the various payment systems and describe the role of smart cards.

❻ Describe the relationship between EC, supply chain management, ERP, and EDI.

❼ Discuss legal and ethical issues related to e-commerce.

# CONNECTIONS

## INTEL CORPORATION EMBRACING THE WEB

### The Problem

Intel Corporation, the world's largest producer of microprocessor chips, sells its products to thousands of manufacturers. Much of its business is in the personal computer market, in which companies such as Dell Computers use Intel's chips ("Intel Inside" logo). Competition in the chip market is intense. Intel creates customized catalogs and sends them to its potential customers together with information on product availability. Until 1997 it was all done on paper. Furthermore, orders from Intel's thousands of customers, distributors, and business partners worldwide were received by fax and phone, making the distribution process slow, expensive, and frequently not up to date. During 1997 a number of departments launched their own electronic order handling that resulted in incompatible and inefficient systems.

### The Solution

So, in 1998, Intel established its e-business program extranet, that is focused on procurement and customer support for a range of products, including microprocessors, motherboards, embedded chips, chipsets, and flash memory.

Order placing is only part of what Intel offers. The site also features self-service order tracking and a library of product documentation and road maps that re-place the work of customer service representatives who previously sent information manually to customers.

Intel specifically targeted the small and midsize customers, the majority of which operate outside the U.S. These companies had previously communicated with Intel mostly by phone and fax, whereas larger companies typically were connected to Intel on *electronic data interchange* (EDI) networks. Eleven of Intel's larger customers were connected in fall 1998 to another system called Supply Line Management, which lets Intel link to customers' plants across the Internet to track part consumption. Intel is using the system to deliver personalized information to its customers and employees. New applications include procurement of material and services from suppliers. Intel claims that it is doing e-business more than any other company in the world.

### The Results

The e-business initiative enhances Intel's competitive advantage by giving its customers better tools for managing transactions. At the same time the system brings substantial tangible savings. For example the company has been able to eliminate 45,000 faxes per quarter to Taiwan alone.

*SOURCES:* Compiled from *InternetWeek* (November 23, 1998), pp. 1, 98, and from "Intel Goes E-Business" (*www.intel.com/eBusiness/enabling/ebusiness.htm*) December 28, 1999.

# CONNECTIONS

## TOSHIBA'S EXTRANET KEEPS DEALERS ON TIME

### The Problem

Toshiba America works with 300 dealers. Dealers that needed parts quickly had to place a telephone or fax order by 2 P.M. for next-day delivery. To handle the shipments, Toshiba's Electronic Imaging Division (EID) (fax machines and copiers) spent $1.3 million on communication and charged $25/shipment from the dealers. In addition, dealers had to pay the overnight shipping fee. A cumbersome MS-DOS order-entry system was created in 1993, but no significant improvement was achieved.

**The Solution**

In August 1997, Toshiba created a Web-based order entry system using an extranet (an extended intranet). Dealers can place orders for parts until 5 P.M. for next-day delivery. The company placed the warehouse in Memphis, Tennessee, near Federal Express headquarters. Dealers can also check accounts receivable balances and pricing arrangements, and can read service bulletins, press releases, and so on. Once orders are submitted, a computer checks for the parts' availability. If a part is available, the order is sent to Toshiba's warehouse in Memphis over a dedicated leased line. Once at the warehouse site, the order pops up on a hand-held RF (radio frequency) monitor. Within a few hours the part is packed, verified, and packaged for FedEx.

**The Results**

Using the extranet, the cost per order has been reduced to about $10. The networking cost of EID has been reduced by more than 50 percent (to $600,000/year). The low shipping cost results in 98 percent overnight delivery, which increases customer satisfaction.

SOURCE: Compiled from *InternetWeek,* Feb. 2, 1998, p. 44.

 ## 6.1 FOUNDATIONS OF ELECTRONIC COMMERCE

The opening two examples illustrate a new way of conducting business, called **electronic commerce (EC),** in which business transactions take place via telecommunications networks, primarily the Internet. Electronic commerce may occur between businesses and consumers (such as takes place when a consumer orders a book from Amazon.com) or between businesses (as in both the Toshiba and Intel cases).

The term electronic commerce is viewed by some as referring only to transactions conducted in a *marketspace,* which is an electronic market place. Therefore, the term electronic commerce seems to some people to be fairly narrow; thus, many use the term **e-business** (or e-Biz). It refers to a broader definition of EC, not just buying and selling, but also servicing customers, collaborating with business partners, and conducting electronic transactions within an organization. According to Lou Gerstner, IBM's CEO, "e-business is all about cycle time, speed, globalization, enhanced productivity, reaching new customers, and sharing knowledge across institutions for competitive advantage." In this book we use the term electronic commerce in its broadest scope, which is basically equivalent to e-business.

Electronic commerce is a very diverse and interdisciplinary topic, with issues ranging from technology, addressed by computer experts, to consumer behavior, addressed by behavioral scientists and marketing research experts. In this section we include a brief history, classification of the field, descriptions of electronic commerce benefits, and a description of how a company uses several EC initiatives.

> In my field, a traditional consumer-oriented business has been dramatically impacted by e-commerce. The customers no longer have to go out to our retail shops, and we have to apply our main retail service to the virtual store.
> — *Kristin Borhofen*

### HISTORY AND SCOPE

Electronic commerce applications began in the early 1970s with such innovations as electronic transfer of funds. However, the applications were limited to large corporations and a few daring small businesses. Then came electronic data interchange (EDI), which expanded EC from financial transactions to other kinds of transaction processing and extended the types of participating companies from financial institutions to manufacturers, retailers, services, and other forms of business. Since the commercialization of the Internet and the introduction of the Web in the early 1990s, EC applications have expanded rapidly. Over the last 5 years we have witnessed many innovative applications, from large-scale direct marketing to auctions and procurement. In fact, buying food from a vending machine with a smart card or with a cellular phone (new technology, in experimentation in Israel, Finland, and Japan) is also considered electronic commerce. Today, almost every company in the United States has a Web site. Many are extensive. For example, in 2000 General Motors Corporation (www.gm.com) offered over 18,000 Web pages of information that included over 100,000 links to its products, services, and related topics.

## THE ELECTRONIC COMMERCE FRAMEWORK

Many people associate EC with having a presence on the Web or advertising on Web sites. While advertisement is probably the most popular activity of EC, the EC field is much broader than that. The framework pictured in Figure 6.1 shows the content of the field of EC. The top of the figure shows some major applications of EC. These include direct marketing, home banking, shopping in electronic stores and malls, buying stocks, finding a job, conducting auctions and bids, collaborating electronically with business partners around the globe, and providing customer service.

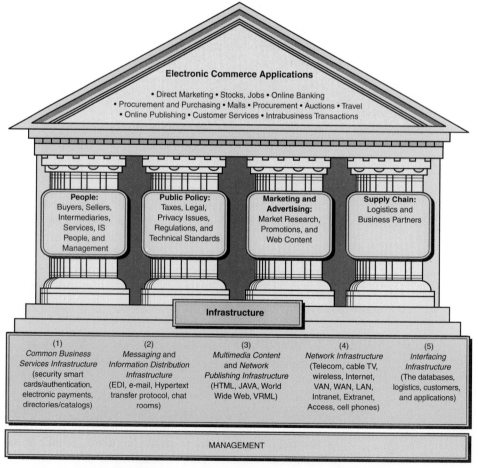

**FIGURE 6.1 A framework for electronic commerce.** (*Source*: Modified from Kalakota and Whinston [1997], p. 12, and from a list provided by Zwass [1996], p. 6.)

These applications are supported by four major support categories (shown as supporting pillars in the figure): (1) people, including business partners; (2) public policy, standards, and regulations, including security, protocols, and government incentives; (3) marketing and advertisement; and (4) logistics and supply chain management, including business partners. As shown at the bottom of the figure, EC management coordinates all of the above and makes decisions on strategy, outsourcing, joint ventures, and the like.

Figure 6.1 can be used as a framework for understanding the relationships among the EC components. It also provides a preview of this chapter.

## ELECTRONIC MARKETS AND INTERORGANIZATIONAL INFORMATION SYSTEMS

> By providing electronic markets, companies can gain customers without spending money and resources.
>
> — *James Rolstead*

**ELECTRONIC MARKETS.** Electronic markets are rapidly emerging alongside interorganizational systems as a vehicle for conducting business. A *market* is a network of interactions and relationships where information, products, services, and payments are exchanged. When the marketplace is electronic, the business center is not a physical building but a network-based location where business interactions occur. The market handles all the necessary transactions, including the transfer of money.

In electronic markets, the principal participants—transaction handlers, buyers, brokers, and sellers—not only are at different locations but seldom even know one another. The means of interconnection vary among parties and can change from event to event, even between the same parties.

**INTERORGANIZATIONAL INFORMATION SYSTEMS.** An **interorganizational information system (IOS)** involves information flow among two or more organizations. Its major objective is efficient transaction processing, such as transmitting orders, bills, and payments using EDI. All relationships are predetermined; there is no negotiation, just execution. Interorganizational systems are used exclusively for business-to-business applications, while electronic markets exist in both the business-to-business and business-to-consumer cases.

*Drivers of Interorganizational Systems.* IOSs are a direct result of the growing desirability of interconnecting business partners to streamline business processes. The reasons to do so are many: They reduce the costs of routine business transactions and eliminate paper, inefficiencies, and costs associated with paper processing. They improve the quality of the information flow by reducing or eliminating errors. They compress cycle time in the fulfillment of business transactions regardless of geographical distance. They make the trading process easy for users, and they facilitate coordination and collaboration along the supply chain.

*Types of Interorganizational Systems.* Interorganizational information systems include a variety of business activities, some of which are used in non-EC-related activities. The five most prominent types of interorganizational systems are:

▶ Electronic data interchange (EDI) (see Section 6.6).

▶ Electronic funds transfer (EFT) (see Section 6.6).

▶ Extranets (see Section 6.4).

▶ Integrated messaging—Delivery of electronic mail and fax documents through a single electronic transmission system that can combine EDI, electronic mail, and electronic forms.

▶ Shared databases—Information stored in repositories that can be shared between trading partners and is accessible to both. Such databases are often used to reduce elapsed time in communicating information between parties as well as arranging cooperative activities.

The last two activities are described in Chapters 5 and 10, as well as in Technology Guides 3 and 4.

## BENEFITS AND LIMITATIONS OF ELECTRONIC COMMERCE

Few innovations in human history encompass as many benefits as electronic commerce. The global nature of the technology, the low cost, the opportunity to reach hundreds of millions of people, the interactive nature, the variety of interaction possibilities, and the resourcefulness and rapid growth of the Internet, result in many benefits to organizations, individuals, and society. These benefits are just starting to materialize, but they will increase significantly as EC expands.

**BENEFITS TO ORGANIZATIONS.** The major benefits of EC to organizations are:

▶ Electronic commerce allows a vendor to *reach a large number of customers, anywhere* around the globe, at a very *low capital outlay and operating cost.*

▶ Companies can procure material and services from other companies *rapidly* and 15 to 30 percent *less expensively* than what they can get otherwise.

▶ Marketing distribution *channels* can be *drastically cut* or even eliminated, simultaneously making products cheaper and vendors' *profits higher.* Ultimately, intermediaries are eliminated, allowing true direct *one-to-one marketing* and sales.

▶ Electronic commerce *decreases the cost* of creating, processing, distributing, storing, and retrieving paper-based information by as much as 90 percent.

▶ Electronic commerce allows *reduced inventories* and overhead by facilitating "pull"-type supply chain management. In a pull-type system the process starts from customer orders and uses just-in-time production and delivery processing. This allows *product customization* and *lower inventory costs.*

> A business where e-commerce will really prove its worth is one where scheduling is critical. If you implement a "just in time" inventory system, you can minimize your warehousing requirements and inventory levels.
>
> — *Blake Thompson*

▶ Customer relationships are facilitated by *interactive, one-to-one* communication.

▶ Electronic commerce *reduces the time* between the outlay of capital and the receipt of products and services.

▶ Electronic commerce *lowers telecommunications cost,* as the Internet is much cheaper than value-added networks (VANs).

▶ Electronic commerce allows for *superb customer service* at relatively low cost.

▶ *Advertisement* can be *media-rich,* be *changed* frequently, reach *large audiences,* and be *customized.*

Electronic commerce can also help small businesses to compete against large companies. For example, Egghead Software closed all of its physical stores in 1998 and moved completely to the Web because of its inability to compete in the conventional marketplace with large software distributors, such as CompUSA. Egghead added items other than software to its product mix, and in 1999 merged with the online auction company Onsale, adding another distribution channel. This example demonstrates a case of a changing *business model.* New and modified business models are greatly facilitated by EC.

**BENEFITS TO CONSUMERS.** EC's major benefits to consumers are:

▶ Electronic commerce frequently provides customers with *less expensive* products and services by allowing them to shop in many places and conduct online quick comparisons.

▶ Electronic commerce provides customers with *more choices;* they can select from many vendors and from more products.

▶ Electronic commerce enables customers to shop or do other transactions *24 hours* a day, year round, from almost any location.

▶ Customers can receive relevant and *detailed information* and *other services* in seconds, rather than in days or weeks.

▶ Electronic commerce enables consumers to get *customized products and services,* from PCs to cars, at competitive prices.

▶ Electronic commerce makes it possible to *participate in virtual auctions.* Thus, customers can obtain unique products and collectors' items that might otherwise require them to travel long distances to a particular auction place at a specific time.

▶ Electronic commerce allows customers to *interact* with other customers and with vendors in *electronic communities* and to exchange ideas as well as compare experiences.

**BENEFITS TO SOCIETY.** EC's major benefits to society are the following:

▶ Electronic commerce enables more individuals to *work at home* and to do *less traveling,* resulting in less traffic on the roads and *lower air pollution.*

▶ Electronic commerce allows some merchandise to be sold at lower prices, so less affluent people can *increase their standard of living.*

▶ Electronic commerce enables people in third-world countries and rural areas to *enjoy products and services that otherwise are not available* to them. This includes opportunities to learn professions and earn college degrees, or to receive better medical care.

▶ Electronic commerce *facilitates delivery of public services,* such as government entitlements, reducing the cost of distribution and fraud, and increases the quality of the social services, police work, health care, and education.

**LIMITATIONS OF ELECTRONIC COMMERCE.** The spread of EC has been slowed somewhat by some limitations, which can be classified as technical and nontechnical and are listed in Table 6.1 on page 216.

As time passes, these limitations, especially the technical ones, will lessen or be overcome; also, appropriate planning can minimize the impact of the limitations. Despite these limitations, very rapid progress is occurring in EC, especially in selected fields such as auctions, buying stocks, buying books, CDs and computers. Also, corporate procurement and direct sale to businesses (B2B) is expanding. As experience accumulates and technology improves, the ratio of EC benefits to cost will increase, resulting in a greater rate of EC adoption.

## ELECTRONIC COMMERCE IN ACTION

Organizations are using EC for three major purposes: (1) facilitating direct sale, online; (2) conducting intrabusiness applications; and (3) enhancing customer service.

*Table 6.1* **Limitations of Electronic Commerce**

| *Technical limitations* | *Non-technical limitations* |
|---|---|
| **1.** Lack of universally accepted standards for quality, security, and reliability. | **1.** Many legal issues are as yet unresolved. |
| **2.** Insufficient telecommunication bandwidth. | **2.** National and international government regulations and standards are not developed for many circumstances. |
| **3.** The software development tools are still evolving. | **3.** Benefits of some EC, such as Web advertisements, are difficult to measure. Mature methodologies for justifying EC are not available. |
| **4.** Difficulties in integrating the Internet and EC software with some existing (especially legacy) applications and databases. | **4.** Many sellers and buyers are looking for EC to stabilize before they engage in EC. |
| **5.** The added cost of special Web servers in addition to the network servers. | **5.** Customers resist the change from a real to a virtual store. People do not yet sufficiently trust paperless, faceless transactions. |
| **6.** Accessibility to the Internet is still expensive and/or inconvenient. | **6.** There is a perception that electronic commerce is expensive and unsecured, so many do not want even to try it. |
| | **7.** There is not yet the sufficiently large number (critical mass) of sellers and buyers in many EC activities that is needed for profitable EC operations. |

For these activities, they use the following major support infrastructures: Internet, intranet, and EDI or extranet. Some companies use only one of the above; others use all of the above. Let's examine how this is done in a hypothetical company, Toys Inc. As shown in Figure 6.2, Toys Inc. has a corporate intranet for conducting all its internal communication, collaboration, dissemination of information, and accessing databases. It uses a corporate extranet (on the left side of the figure) to cooperate with its large business partners (e.g., suppliers, distributors, noncorporate retail stores, salespeople, liquidators) and with large customers. In addition, the company is connected to the toy industry extranet (upper right portion of Figure 6.2) which includes other manufacturers, professional associations, and large suppliers.

The company may also be networked to additional extranets. For example, some major corporations may allow Toys Inc. to connect to their intranets, via their extranets. Toys Inc. is also connected with its banks and other financial institutions (loan providers, stock issuers) over a highly secured EDI that runs on a VAN. The company also uses the VAN-based EDI with some of its largest suppliers and other business partners. An Internet-based EDI is used with smaller business partners that are not on the corporate EDI or extranet. The company communicates with others on the regular Internet.

Many companies are moving toward a similar network configuration. Today, it is almost impossible to do business without being connected through an EDI, extranets, and the Internet to one's business partners.

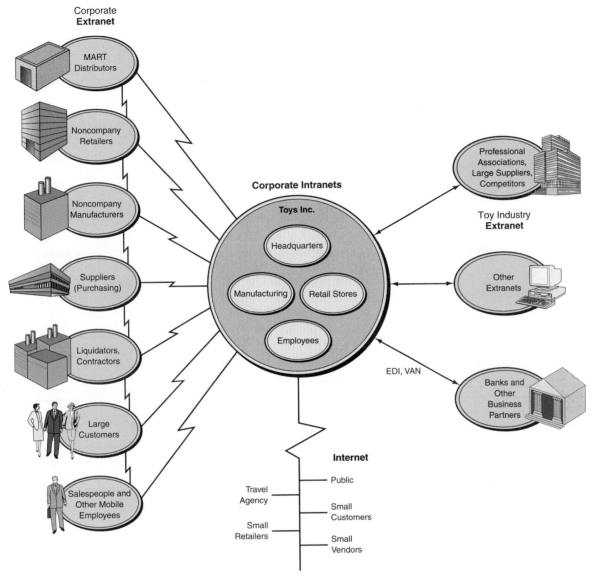

**FIGURE 6.2** How a company uses the Internet, intranet, and extranets.

## ▶ 6.2 DIRECT RETAIL MARKETING AND ADVERTISEMENT

There are many potential applications of EC that will foster trading between businesses and individual customers. The projected 750 million Internet users within 10 years could generate a huge volume of **business-to-consumer (B2C)** transactions. Because of limited space, we can describe here only some of the major categories of such applications.

### INTERACTIVE ONE-TO-ONE MARKETING

The availability of EC provides companies with unprecedented opportunity to conduct one-to-one marketing, which is a type of relationship marketing. **Rela-**

tionship marketing, according to Mowen and Minor (1998), is the "overt attempt of exchange partners to build a long-term association, characterized by purposeful cooperation and mutual dependence on the development of social, as well as structural, bonds" (p. 540). **One-to-one marketing** is basically a simple idea: "Treat different customers differently." It is based on the fact that no two customers are the same.

One-to-one marketing involves much more than just sales and marketing, because a firm must be able to change how its products are configured or its service is delivered, based on the needs of individual customers. Smart companies have always encouraged the active participation of customers in the development of products, services, and solutions. For the most part, however, being customer-oriented has meant being oriented to the needs of the *typical* customer in the market—the average customer. In order to build enduring one-to-one relationships, a company must continuously interact with customers, individually.

The actual, detailed mechanics of building a one-to-one relationship depend on understanding the various ways customers are different and how these differences should affect the firm's behavior toward particular, individual customers. One reason so many firms are beginning to focus on one-to-one marketing is that this kind of marketing can create high customer loyalty.

**How One-to-One Relationships are Practiced.** Doing business over the Web enables companies to better understand their customers' needs and buying habits, which in turn enables them to improve and customize their future marketing efforts. There are several ways to build one-to-one relationships around the Web. The GartnerGroup, an IT consulting company, proposed what it calls "The New Marketing Cycle of Relationship Building." Their proposal, shown in Figure 6.3, views relationships as a two-way street in which customer information is collected and placed in a database. Then a customer's profile is developed and the so-called four marketing P's (product, place, price and promotion) are updated on a one-to-one basis. Based on this, appropriate advertisement is prepared, possibly leading to a purchase by the customer. The detailed transaction is then added to the database and the cycle repeats. EC can facilitate this process, as will be shown later.

Ideally, in **interactive marketing**, marketers and advertisers use customized, one-on-one advertising, followed by a sale. The term "interactive" points to the ability to address an individual, to gather and remember the responses of that individual, and to serve that customer based on his or her previous, unique responses. Alternatively, using the Internet, companies can segment the market into groups (e.g., by age, gender, or location), and then use different ads for different segments. When the Internet is combined with marketing databases, interactive marketing becomes a very effective and affordable competitive strategy. (See Box 6.1, page 220.)

It is obvious that interactive marketing and advertisement are interrelated. However, before describing Internet advertisement let us see how the B2C electronic retail market, for which advertisement is critical, operates.

## Individual Storefronts and Malls

For generations home shopping from catalogs has flourished, and television shopping channels have been attracting millions of shoppers for over a decade. However, television shopping is limited to what is shown on the screen, and

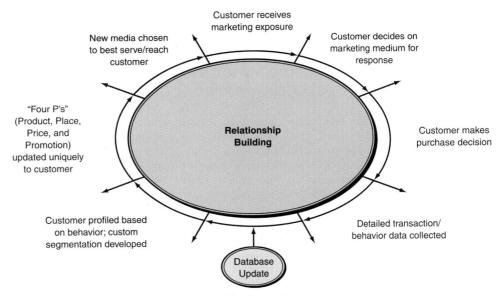

**FIGURE 6.3  The New Marketing Model.** (*Source*: Courtesy of GartnerGroup.)

paper catalogs become quickly outdated. The limitations of conventional home shopping can be overcome by electronic retailing.

> Often you're not just selling a product, you're selling value added services along with it. The Main Street store has moved online and taken all its friendly, helpful advice with it.
>
> — *Blake Thompson*

**ELECTRONIC RETAILING.** With electronic commerce you can buy from home, 24 hours a day, 7 days a week. The difference is that the Web offers you a wide variety of products and services, including the most unique items, usually at lower prices. In addition, you can get very detailed information on products in seconds, and you can easily search items and compare prices. Finally, you can easily interact and communicate with vendors and other shoppers. **Electronic retailing** is the direct sale (B2C) through electronic storefronts or in electronic malls, usually designed around an electronic catalog format. Some companies such as Wal-Mart Online sell to corporations as well (B2B), usually at discounts for large quantities.

Electronic retailing is mushrooming on the Web. There are two types of vendors: solo electronic storefronts and electronic malls. Solo **electronic storefronts** maintain their own Internet name and Web site and may or may not be affiliated with electronic malls. Electronic retail stores may be extensions of physical stores, such as Disney Online, The Sharper Image, and Wal-Mart Online. Others are new businesses started by entrepreneurs who saw a niche on the Web. Examples of pioneering sites are Virtual Vineyards, Peapod, and eToy.

**WHAT DO PEOPLE BUY MOST ONLINE?** Goods that are sold most often online are: computers and computer-related items, books and magazines, CDs, cassettes, movies, videos, clothing and shoes, toys, and food. There are two types of storefronts; *general* and *specialized*. The latter sell one or few products (flowers, wines). The general stores sell many products. Services that are sold most often online include: travel services, stocks and bonds trading, electronic banking, insurance, and job matching. (Online service industries are presented in Section 6.3).

## *A Closer Look* BOX 6.1

### HOW DOES INTERACTIVE MARKETING WORK?: THE DOUBLECLICK APPROACH

Interactive marketing can take many forms. Assume that 3M Corporation wants to sell its $10,000 multimedia projectors. It knows that potential buyers are people who work in advertising agencies or in IS departments of large corporations, or companies that use Unix as their operating system. 3M approaches DoubleClick Inc. and asks the firm to identify such potential customers. How does DoubleClick find them? Clever and simple.

In 1997, DoubleClick (www.doubleclick.net) monitored people browsing the Web sites of about 100 cooperating companies such as Quicken, Travelocity, and Virtual Comics and Books That Work. By inspecting Internet addresses of the visitors to these 100 companies' Web sites and matching them against a database with 70,000 Internet domain names that include a line-of-business code, DoubleClick can find those people working for advertising agencies. By checking the browsers, it can also find out which visitor is using a Unix system. While DoubleClick cannot find out your name, it can build a dossier on you, attached to an ID number that was assigned to you during your first visit to any of the 100 cooperating sites. As you continue to visit the 100 sites, an intelligent software agent builds a relatively complete dossier on you, your spending, and your computing habits. This process is done with a device known as a **cookie,** a file created at the request of a Web server and stored on the user's hard drive. So, the Web site can "remember" your past behavior on the Internet.

DoubleClick then prepares an ad for 3M projectors. The ad is targeted for people whose profile matches what is needed for 3M. So, if you are a Unix user or employed by an advertising agency, on your next browsing trip in any of the 100 participating Web sites, you will be surprised to find exactly what you wanted: information about the multimedia projector.

How is all this financed? 3M pays DoubleClick for the ad. The fee is then split with the Web sites that carry the 3M ads, based on how many times the ad is matched with a visitor.

NOTE: You can avoid the creation of a cookie on your hard drive if you elect to do so, using software such as Cookie Cutter. However, only a few people know this fact. In most cases the cookie is placed on your hard drive without your knowledge.

SOURCE: Condensed from Moukheiber (1996).

**ELECTRONIC MALLS.** An **electronic mall,** also known as a **cybermall,** is a collection of individual shops under one Internet address. The basic idea of an electronic mall is the same as that of a regular shopping mall, namely, to provide a one-stop shopping place that offers many products and services. With a keystroke, browsing people become potential shoppers as they explore cybermalls. As is true of regular shopping malls, a vendor that locates itself in a mall gives up a certain amount of independence: Its success depends on the popularity of the entire collection of stores as well as on its own efforts. On the other hand, malls generate streams of prospective customers who otherwise might never have stopped by the store.

Representative cybermalls are: Downtown Anywhere (www.da.awa.com), HandCrafters Mall, America's Choice Mall (www.choicemall.com), www.shopnow.com, and Shopping 2000 (www.shopping2000.com). Each of these malls may include thousands of vendors. For example, www.shopnow.com listed over 30,000 stores in 1999. Of special interest is the Internet Shopping Network (http://www.internet.net), a futuristic mall. A cybermall may supply the same look and feel to all its tenants, or it may just link its tenants' own electronic home pages. Some malls offer prizes and entertainment; for example, America's Choice Mall offers a "5-minute multimedia tour" contest for success stories about products, services, or leasing associated with the mall. An overview of mall shopping and a list of major malls is available at www.cybermall.com.

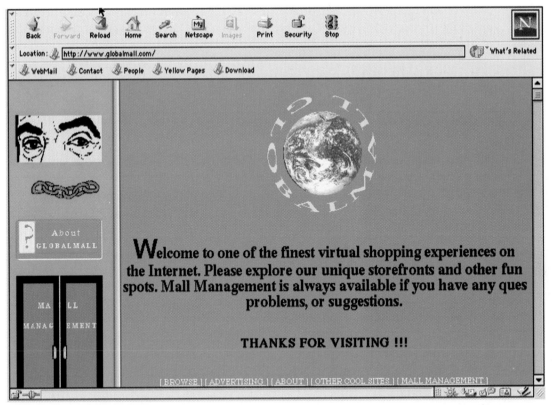

An electronic mall Web site.

**METAMALLS.** In an attempt to make shopping easier, the next logical step is to provide one-stop shopping over multiple malls. This concept is referred to as **metamalls.** Metamalls allow customers to shop in different department stores and many individual stores using one search engine to find items. In addition, customers are able to pay only once in a highly secure system. The metamall can provide other services such as comparative pricing and finding substitute products. An example of a pioneering metamall is Metaland of Korea (www.metaland.com). Major department stores, banks, and manufacturers sponsor Metaland. The services it provides are of the highest quality and include a superb search engine, a secure payment system, and sophisticated customer services.

Hundreds of thousands of solo storefronts can be found on the Internet. Directories and hyperlinks from other Web sites and the use of intelligent agents help buyers find the best products to match their needs. But how to attract buyers to your store? Of course you need to advertise.

## ADVERTISING ONLINE

Opening a storefront is necessary but is seldom sufficient to attract visitors and buyers. Being in a mall may generate some additional traffic. But the best solution to attract visitors is in most cases advertising.

**INTERNET ADVERTISEMENT.** *Advertisement* is an attempt to disseminate information in order to affect a buyer-seller transaction. Traditional advertisement on

TV or newspapers is impersonal, one-way mass communication. Using telemarketing to reach individual customers personalizes advertisement and marketing. But when it is done on the phone, or with direct mail, it is expensive, slow, and ineffective at times. *Internet advertisement* redefines the meaning of advertisement. It is media-rich, dynamic, and interactive, and can reach large numbers of people at relatively low cost.

*Why Internet Advertisement?* The major reasons for advertising on the Internet are as follows:

▶ Ads can be updated any time with a minimal cost, so they can always be timely.

▶ Ads can reach very large numbers of potential buyers all over the world.

▶ Online ads are frequently cheaper in comparison to television, radio, newspaper, or magazine ads. Traditional ads are expensive since they are determined by space occupied (print ads), how many days (times) they are shown, and in how many media they are run.

▶ Web ads can efficiently use text, audio, graphics, and animation.

▶ The use of the Internet itself is growing very rapidly, so the audience for Internet advertising is growing.

▶ Web ads can be interactive and targeted to specific interest groups and/or individuals.

▶ Customers can move easily and quickly from viewing an ad to getting details and to ordering.

To better understand why businesses would choose to advertise on the Internet, see Table 6.2, which compares the benefits and the shortcomings of the major advertisement media.

There are several advertisement methods on the Internet. The most common ones are banners, e-mail, and URL placement.

**BANNER ADVERTISEMENT.** Banner advertisement is the most commonly used form of advertising on the Internet. A banner is like a billboard. As you drive along a highway, you see countless billboards on the sides of the road. The same is true for the Internet. As you surf your way through the Internet, banners are everywhere. Designers of banners pay a lot of attention to the content, media, and size of the image of the banner, because long downloading times may cause a viewer to become impatient and move on even before the banner is fully displayed. Typically, a banner contains a short text or graphical message to promote a product or a vendor and frequently connect to its Web site ("click on the link"). Advertisers go to great length to design a banner that catches consumers' attention. Banners may contain video clips and sound.

There are two types of banners: *keyword banners* and *random banners.* **Keyword banners** are banners that appear when a predetermined word is queried from the search engine. It is effective for companies who want to narrow their target. **Random banners** appear randomly. A main purpose for using random banners could be to introduce new products, or to keep a well-known brand, such as Amazon.com or IBM, in the "public eye."

A 1998 study by AOL showed that 9 out of 10 people responded favorably to banner advertisement, and about 50 percent of the viewers recalled ads immediately after seeing them (www.adage.com, March 15, 1998).

*Table 6.2*  **Benefits and shortcomings of the major advertisement media**

| Medium | Benefits | Shortcomings |
|---|---|---|
| TV | • Intrusive impact—high awareness getter.<br>• Ability to demonstrate product and feature "slice of life" situations.<br>• Very "merchandisable" with media buyers. | • Ratings fragmenting, rising costs, "clutter."<br>• Heavy "downscale" audience skew.<br>• Time is sold in multiprogram packages. Networks often require major upfront commitments. Both limit the advertiser's flexibility. |
| Radio | • Highly selective by station format.<br>• Allows advertisers to employ time-of-day or time-of-week to exploit timing factors.<br>• Copy can rely on the listener's mood or imagination. | • Audience surveys are limited in scope, do not provide socioeconomic demographics.<br>• Difficult to buy with so many stations to consider.<br>• Copy testing is difficult, few statistical guidelines. |
| Magazines | • Offer unique opportunities to segment markets, demographically and psychographically.<br>• Ads can be studied, reviewed at leisure.<br>• High impact can be attained with good graphics and literate, informative copy. | • Reader controls ad exposure, can ignore campaign, especially for new products.<br>• Difficult to exploit "timing" aspects. |
| Newspapers | • High single-day reach opportunity to exploit immediacy, especially on key shopping days.<br>• Reader often shops for specific information when ready to buy.<br>• Portable format. | • Lack of demographic selectivity, despite increased zoning—many markets have only one paper.<br>• High cost for large-size units.<br>• Presumes lack of creative opportunities for "emotional" selling campaigns.<br>• Low-quality reproduction, lack of color. |
| Internet | • Internet advertisements are accessed on demand 24 hours a day, 365 days a year, and costs are the same regardless of audience location.<br>• Accessed primarily because of interest in the content, so market segmentation opportunity is large.<br>• Opportunity to create one-to-one direct marketing relationship with consumer.<br>• Multimedia will increasingly create more attractive and compelling ads.<br>• Distribution costs are low (just technology costs), so the millions of consumers reached cost the same as one.<br>• Advertising and content can be updated, supplemented, or changed at any time, and are therefore always up-to-date. Response (click-through rate) and results (page views) of advertising are immediately measurable.<br>• Ease of logical navigation—you click when and where you want, and spend as much time as desired there. | • No clear standard or language of measurement.<br>• Immature measurement tools and metrics.<br>• Although the variety of ad content format and style that the Internet allows can be considered a positive in some respects, it also makes apples-to-apples comparisons difficult for media buyers.<br>• Difficult to measure size of market, therefore difficult to estimate rating, share, or reach and frequency.<br>• Audience is still relatively small. |

SOURCE: Based on Meeker (1997), pp. 1–10.

A major advantage of using banners is the ability to customize them. At minimum, the advertiser can target a group of market segments. Optimally, banners can be customized to one-to-one targeted advertisement. As will be shown, if the computer knows who you are or what your profile is, advertisers can send a banner that matches your interests. Also, a *forced advertising* marketing strategy is utilized. Customers are forced to see the banners which come into view before the content the customer was searching for. The disadvantage of banner advertising would be high overall cost. Another major drawback of using banners is that limited information is allowed. Hence advertisers need to think of creative but short messages to attract viewers.

**E-MAIL ADVERTISEMENT.** E-mail is emerging as a marketing channel that offers cost-effective implementation and a better and quicker response rate than other advertisement channels. Marketers develop or purchase a list of e-mail addresses, place them in a customer database, and then send advertisement to them via e-mail. A list of e-mail addresses can be a very powerful tool that enables marketers to target a group of people with similar profiles, or even specific individuals. What happens, though, when every marketer starts inundating prospects and customers with e-mail? How will consumers respond? What must marketers focus on to ensure e-mail marketing success? The answers to these and similar questions determine the success of e-mail marketing. Unfortunately the answers to these questions are not always known.

Undoubtedly, the quantity of e-mail that consumers receive is exploding. According to a study by Jupiter Communications, messages per consumer are expected to increase from 1,166 per user per year in 1998 to 1,606 per user per year by 2002. In light of this, marketers employing e-mail must take a long-term view and work toward the goal of motivating consumers to continue to open and read messages they receive. This is especially important as even now nearly one-third of consumers read e-mail only from senders with whom they have a relationship. As the volume of e-mail increases, consumers' tendency to screen messages will rise as well.

When considering who they should send e-mail to, marketers must supplement existing database information with data relevant to e-mail campaigns. When deciding e-mail topics, marketers must integrate inbound customer service e-mail with outbound marketing efforts. Finally, with regard to the "how" or the execution of the message, marketers must develop e-mail–specific editing skills and the ability to deliver multimedia-rich e-mail. A major issue related to e-mail is spamming (sending "junk mail").

*How E-Mails Are Used in EC.* E-mail can be used in different ways. The most common usage is to send advertisement material to potential buyers. The recipient can then be linked to a Web site to receive more information and to place an order. E-mail can also be used for customer service. Customers can e-mail queries to a company and get answers. Also a company can send information about products or services.

**URL ADVERTISEMENT.** The major advantage of using a URL (universal resource locator) as an advertising tool is that it is free. Any company can submit its URL to a search engine and be listed. Also, by using a URL the targeted audience can be locked and uninterested viewers can be filtered because of the key word function. However, the URL method has several drawbacks. First, due to intense competition, even if a company is placed at the top of the list generated by a search engine, its position can easily be downgraded by others. Moreover, different search engines index their listings differently. Therefore, the chance to be placed at the top of the list is low. To overcome this limitation, a company may decide to register with several search engines. However, with close to 1,000 search engines, deciding which ones to register with becomes complex. Professional vendors are ready to help (for a fee) both to register and to optimize the chance to make the top of the list.

**OTHER FORMS OF INTERNET ADVERTISEMENT.** Online advertisement can be done in several other ways including chat rooms, newsgroups, and kiosks. Advertisement on Internet radio is just beginning, and soon advertising on Internet television will commence. Of special interest is advertisement to members of **Internet communities.** Community sites such as www.geocities.com offer a targeted advertisement opportunity, where members can buy the advertised products at a discount. There are also ads that link consumers to other sites that might be of interest to the type of community they are members of. Targeted ads may also go to members' personalized Web pages.

**SOME ADVERTISEMENT ISSUES.** How to design ads for the Internet? Where and when to advertise? How to integrate the online and offline ads? These are only some of the implementation issues. (See O'Keefe [1997], Meeker [1997], and Sterne [1999].) We present here, in brief, several important issues of designing Internet advertising.

*Customizing Ads.* Because there is so much information on the Internet for customers to view, filtering the irrelevant information by providing *customized ads* can be beneficial to customers and advertisers alike. BroadVision's Web site is a example of a customized ad platform (www.broadvision.com). Its software, named One-to-One, allows the rapid creation of secure and robust visitor-centric Web sites. The heart of One-to-One is a customer database, with registration data and information gleaned from site visits. Using this software, a marketing manager can customize display ads based on users' profiles. For an example of how to customize ads see the demos in www.micromass.com.

Another model of customized ads can be found in Webcast (www.webcast.com). Webcast provides free Internet news service that broadcasts personalized news and information. This technology is called **push technology.** When a user establishes his/her system, the user selects the type of desired information, such as sports, news, headlines, stock quotes, etc. The user then gets the information he or she wants, but at the same time also gets banner ads. The initiator of this technology was www.pointcast.com.

*Measuring the Effectiveness of Advertisements.* Justifying advertising expenses, including awarding prizes and delivering entertainment, is a difficult task. Therefore the pricing of ads on Web sites becomes an important issue in EC. The major methods of charging for ads are the following:

1. The most common measure used to determine ad payments is ad view (or impressions). An *ad view* is the number of times users see the banner ad during a specific time period.

2. Another measure by which ads are charged is clicking on a banner and moving to the advertiser's Web home page. This method is used by some large advertisers, such as Procter & Gamble.

**3.** The number of potential customers who seek product leads or fill out questionnaires is a more accurate measure.

**4.** Finally, the number of actual purchases on the Web is a fairly precise measure.

It is difficult to know what the real benefits to advertisers are because:

▶ It is difficult to relate the number of *hits* or ad views. One problem is that 100 ad views can be recorded by one person visiting the site 100 times or by 100 users visiting it once each. Obviously, there is a major difference between the two.

▶ The use of the gross number of visits (occasions on which a user looks up a site) as a possible measure of effectiveness is also inadequate. (Visiting an entertaining site may not result in a purchase.)

▶ The number of *unique users* at a site during a specific time can be calculated by recording some form of user registration or identification. An ad placed in such a site has a greater potential of attracting a viewer, but there is no guarantee that a purchase will be made.

▶ It is not known whether visitors who do not buy online while visiting a site will buy offline later; such purchases may or may not be related to the online advertising.

***Attracting Visitors to a Site.*** A site without visitors has little value. However, visiting a site is no guarantee that a purchase will be made. There are several ways to attract visitors to a Web site and induce them to buy. Here we will discuss some of the issues involved in attracting visitors.

***Online Events and Promotions.*** Contests, quizzes, coupons, and give-away samples are an integral part of Internet commerce as much as, or even more than, in offline commerce. There promotions are designed to attract visitors and their attention. There are dozens of innovative ideas in use. Here are some examples:

**1.** Yoyodyne Inc. conducts give-away games, discounts, contests, and sweepstakes, whose entrants agree to read product information of advertisers ranging from Major League Baseball to Sprint Communication. For example, Yoyodyne organized a contest in 1997 in which H&R Block, the tax-preparer, paid $20,000 toward the winner's federal taxes. Yoyodyne also offers multisponsor games.

**2.** Netzero and others offer free Internet access in exchange for viewing ads.

**3.** Both www.egghead.com and www.lucent.com use real people to talk to you over the phone about your interests and then they "push" ads to your computer.

**4.** Cybergold (www.cybergold.com), Goldmine (www.goldmine.com), and others connect you with advertisers who *pay you* money or give you discounts in exchange for reading ads and exploring the Web.

**5.** Riddler (www.riddler.com) provides an opportunity to play games in real time and win prizes. People also play games for no prizes at all.

**6.** Netstakes runs sweepstakes that, in contrast with contests, require no skills. You register only once and can randomly win prizes (see http://webstakes.com). Prizes are given away in different categories. The site is divided into channels, each with several sponsors. The sponsors pay Netstakes to send them traffic. Netstakes runs online ads, both on the Web and in many e-mail lists that people requested to be on.

**7.** Other ideas include giving free PCs to qualified customers (www.freepc.com), paying a penny a page for viewing ads (www.gotoworld.com and www.tripod.com), and free samples and coupons (www.clickrewards.com).

The marketing principles behind running promotions on the Internet are similar to those used for running offline promotions (Aronson et al. [1999], Chase [1998], O'Keefe [1997], and Sterne [1999]).

*Coupons Online.* You can gather any discount coupons you want by accessing www.hotcoupons.com or www.supermarkets.com, selecting the store where you plan to redeem the coupons, and printing them. In the future, transfer of coupons directly to the virtual supermarket (such as www.peapod.com or www.netgrocer.com) will be available so that you can receive discounts on the items you buy there.

## INTELLIGENT AGENTS IN ELECTRONIC COMMERCE AND RETAILING

Intelligent software agents play an increasingly important role in EC. **Intelligent agents** are computer programs to help users to conduct routing tasks, to search and retrieve information, to support decision making, and to act as consulting experts. (See Chapter 11.)

**OVERVIEW.** Agents sense the environment and act autonomously without human intervention. This results in a significant savings of time (up to 99 percent) for users. There are various types of agents, ranging from those with minimal or no intelligence, which are called **software agents,** to *learning agents* that exhibit some intelligent behavior. One of the primary reasons for using such agents is to overcome the tremendous amount of *information overload.*

In this section we will concentrate on intelligent agents for retailing and advertisement. However, before we do this, it will be beneficial to distinguish between search engines, which are usually software agents, and the more intelligent type of agents. A *search engine* is a computer program that can automatically contact other network resources on the Internet, search for specific information or key words, and report the results. Unlike search engines, an *intelligent agent* can do more than just "search and match." For example, it can monitor movement on a Web site to check whether a customer seems lost or ventures into areas that may not fit his profile; the agent can notify the customers and frequently provides assistance.

**INTELLIGENT AGENTS FOR INFORMATION SEARCH AND FILTERING.** Intelligent agents can help consumers determine what to buy to satisfy a specific need. The agent looks for specific product information, critically evaluates it, and reports the results to the consumer. One of the first intelligent agents available on the market for this task was PersonalLogic (www.personalogic.com), an agent that narrows down product selection through a *filtering process.* Consumers specify requirements and constraints, and the system returns a list of products that best meet the desired product.

Another agent that helps people find what they want is Firefly's Passport (www.firefly.net), which generates a customer's personal profile. It stores information about who you are, what you like, and what you do not like. By using your Passport at different sites that use Firefly software (such as Barnes and Noble, My Yahoo, and Filmfinder), you can have access to personalized content, Internet communities, and services—while maintaining your privacy. To do so, Firefly uses a *collaborative filtering* process that can be described as "word of mouth" to build the profile. The consumer is asked to rate a number of products; the system then matches his or her ratings with the ratings of other consumers, and relying on the ratings of other consumers with similar tastes, recommends products that he or she has not yet rated. In other words, Firefly uses the opinions of like-minded people to make recommendations.

This type of intelligent agent is called a *product broker* (see Maes, 1999). It alerts users to new product releases or recommends products based on past selections or requirements specified by the buyer. Examples of companies using such agents are Amazon.com, Fastparts, and Classified 2000. In addition to Firefly, vendors such as Net Perceptions, Personal Logic, Broadvision, ZineZone and others have built such agent systems. Here is an example how such agent works:

### *IT At Work*   FUJITSU'S INTELLIGENT AGENTS FIND CUSTOMERS

Fujitsu, a major Japanese vendor of consumer products, is using an agent-based technology called Interactive Marketing Interface (iMi) that allows advertisers to interact directly with targeted customers and provides valuable services and information. The system enhances the customers' Internet experience.

iMi allows advertisers to interact directly with specific segments of the consumer market through the use of software agents, while ensuring that consumers remain anonymous to advertisers. Consumers submit a personal profile to iMi, indicating such characteristics as product categories of interest, hobbies, travel habits, and the maximum number of e-mail messages per week they are willing to receive. In turn, via electronic mail, customers receive product announcements, advertisements, and marketing surveys from advertisers based on their personal profile information. By answering the marketing surveys or acknowledging receipt of advertisements, consumers earn iMi points, redeemable for gift certificates and phone cards.

*For Further Exploration:* How is privacy protected in systems such as this one? What is unique about this system? ▲

### ELECTRONIC CATALOGS

Printed catalogs have been a medium of advertisement for a long time. However, electronic catalogs on CD-ROM and on the Web have recently gained popularity. The merchants' objective in using **online catalogs** is to advertise and promote products and services, whereas customers use them as a source of information on products and services. With the help of search engines, customers can quickly search electronic catalogs and can compare products very effectively. Electronic catalogs consists of product database, directory, search capability, and a presentation function.

In the early stage of online catalogs, most were a replication of text and pictures from the vendors' printed catalogs. Today, electronic online catalogs are dynamic, customized, and integrated with selling and buying procedures such as order taking and payment.

**COMPARING ONLINE CATALOGS WITH PAPER CATALOGS.** Table 6.3 contrasts the advantages and disadvantages of online catalogs with those of paper catalogs. Online catalogs have significant advantages, but one big disadvantage: customers need computers and the Internet to access online catalogs. However, since computers and Internet access are spreading rapidly, we can expect many paper catalogs to be replaced by, or at least supplemented by, electronic catalogs. Nevertheless, considering the fact that printed newspapers and magazines have

*Table 6.3* **Comparisons of Online Catalogs with Paper Catalogs**

| Type | Advantages | Disadvantages |
|---|---|---|
| Paper Catalogs | • Easy to create a catalog without high technology<br>• Reader is able to look at the catalog without a computer system<br>• More portable than electronic catalog | • Difficult to update changed product information promptly<br>• Only a limited number of products is displayed<br>• Limited information through photographs and textual description is available<br>• No possibility for advanced multimedia such as animation and voice. |
| Online Catalog | • Easy to update product information<br>• Able to integrate with the purchasing process<br>• Good search and comparison capabilities<br>• Able to provide timely, up-to-date product information<br>• Provision for global range of product information<br>• Possibility of adding voice and motion pictures<br>• Cost savings<br>• Easy to customize<br>• More comparative shopping<br>• Ease of connecting order processing, inventory processing, and payment processing to the system | • Difficult to develop catalogs, large fixed cost<br>• There is a need for customer skill to deal with computers and browsers |

not diminished due to the online ones, we can guess that paper catalogs will not disappear (at least for a decade or two) in spite of the popularity of online catalogs. Both media seem to survive complementarily.

**CUSTOMIZED CATALOGS.** A *customized catalog* is a catalog assembled specifically for a company, usually a customer of the catalog owner. It can be also tailored to individual consumers in certain cases. There are two approaches to customized catalogs. The first approach is to let the customers identify the interesting items out of the total catalogs, as is done by One-to-One (www.broadvision.com). Then, customers do not have to deal with irrelevant topics.

The second approach is to let the system automatically identify the characteristics of customers based on their transaction records and build a catalog accordingly. For collecting data on individuals, *cookie* technology is used to trace the transactions. However, to generalize the relationship between the customer and items of interest, data mining technology support by intelligent systems is necessary. This second approach can be effectively combined with the first one. Customized catalogs are used mainly in B2B, as will be described in section 6.4.

## THE IMPACT OF EC ON TRADITIONAL RETAILING SYSTEMS

What is the impact of EC on traditional retailing systems? Let's look at two representative issues: the elimination of traditional distribution channels and the rise of new ones, and the impact of EC on distribution strategy.

**DISINTERMEDIATION AND REINTERMEDIATION.** In the traditional distribution channel, there are intermediating layers, such as wholesaler, distributor, and retailer, between the manufacturers and the consumers. In Japan, there sometimes exist 10 layers, which add a 500 percent markup. Owing to the presence of the Internet as a marketing and product selection vehicle, customers are beginning to question the value offered by traditional distribution channels. By using the Internet, manufacturers can sell directly to customers and provide customer support online. In this sense, the traditional intermediaries are eliminated. We call this phenomenon **disintermediation.**

In response to this change, traditional intermediaries like retailers and department stores have initiated online stores while still keeping their traditional way of doing business. Some manufacturers, like automakers, still need to cooperate with dealers, though in a different way. These are evolutionary steps. In addition, new electronic intermediaries—e-malls and product selection agents—are emerging. Occurrence of a new breed of electronic intermediaries is called **reintermediation.**

In some cases it is characterized by the shifting or transfer of the intermediary function, rather than the complete elimination of it. The new class of intermediaries includes e-malls, directory and search engine services, market makers, and comparison-shopping agents. Another form of reintermediation can emerge by differentiating the services of traditional intermediaries from online intermediation. This can be realized, for instance, by offering recreation during shopping.

**IMPACT OF EC ON MANUFACTURERS' DISTRIBUTION STRATEGY.** In addition to disintermediation and reintermediation, interesting manufacturers' distribution strategies also are developing. Distribution strategies in the era of EC include the following:

1. **Manufacturer's monopolistic Internet-based distribution.** Levi Strauss did not allow anyone else to sell the Levi's product on the Internet. The company wanted customers to have a single contact point in cyberspace for purchasing this product that has high name value. (The company is changing now its policy, to expand its market.)
2. **Coexistence with the dealers.** This is the case in car distribution. Automakers need to keep the traditional dealers as test-drive servers (and for maintenance support) even though the automakers sell on the Internet. However, direct car selling and even car auctions are becoming popular.
3. **Regionally mixed strategy.** In a certain region a company may sell on the Internet, while in another region it sells through traditional retailers. For instance, Nike sells on the Internet but only in the United States.
4. **Restraint of competition by powerful distributors.** Home Depot tried to pressure its suppliers not to market online. The company reminded its major suppliers, such as Whirlpool.com, that Home Depot has the right not to distribute products of suppliers who are actually competitors (*Fortune,* 1999).

# ▶ 6.3 SERVICE INDUSTRIES ONLINE

Selling books, computers, toys, and most other products on the Internet reduces the cost to the customers by 20 to 40 percent. Further reduction is difficult to achieve since physical products must be manufactured and delivered physically. Only a few products can be digitized to be delivered online for additional savings. On the other hand, delivery of services, such as buying stocks or insurance online, can be done close to 100 percent electronically, with cost reduction of as much as 99 percent. Therefore, online delivery of services is growing very rapidly, with millions of new customers added annually. The major online services to be discussed here are: banking, personal finance, investing, job matching, travel, real estate, and auctions. In addition to these, many other services are becoming available online. Examples are supermarkets and groceries, insurance, and any matching service (try www.match.com).

## CYBERBANKING

**Cyberbanking**, also known as **electronic banking**, virtual banking, home banking, and online banking, includes all major banking activities (from paying bills to securing a loan) conducted from home, a business, or on the road instead of at a physical bank location. Electronic banking saves time and is convenient for customers. For banks, it offers an inexpensive alternative to branch banking (costing about 2 cents per transaction vs. $1.07 at the physical branch) and a chance to enlist remote customers. Many banks are beginning to offer home banking, and some use EC as a major competitive strategy. Electronic banking offers several of the benefits listed for EC in section 6.1, such as expanding the customer base and saving the cost of paper transactions. In addition to regular banks with added online services, we see the emergence of virtual banks, such as www.netbank.com, dedicated solely to Internet transactions. Here is how a major California bank practices cyberbanking.

*IT At Work*    **CYBERBANKING AT WELLS FARGO**

***U*SING IT**
→
...in Finance

Wells Fargo is a large California Bank (over 1,700 branches). The bank has been known for generations for its financial services, dating back to the days of the wild West. Wells Fargo's declared competitive strategy is cyberbanking. It plans to move mil-

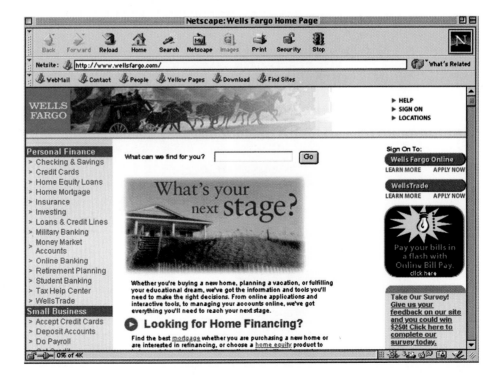

lions of customers to the Internet and close hundreds of branches. A visit to the Wells Fargo Web site (www.wellsfargo.com) indicates the richness of services available.

The services are divided into five major categories: online (personal) banking, personal finance services, small business, commercial banking, and international trade. In addition, there are employment opportunities, and even shopping. The bank offers many services in all categories. Most interesting are the services that cover all the needs of small businesses which are extremely user friendly and can run even on an old 386 computer. The bank also saves money for the customer by offering lower rates.

The bank facilitates shopping by offering a virtual mall in which you can buy from the Wells Fargo Museum Store as well as from many other virtual stores such as Amazon.com.

**For Further Exploration:** Why is a bank getting involved in shopping? ▲

SOURCE: Compiled from *Communications Week,* May 27, 1997, p. 44, and *Datamation;* June 1997, pp. 91–93.

**THE CYBERBANKING PIONEER SFNB.** The Security First Network Bank (SFNB) was the first bank offering secure banking transactions on the Web (www.sfnb.com). The home page (see Figure 6.4) looks like the lobby of a bank. The bank offers savings and checking accounts, certificates of deposit, money market accounts, joint accounts, check imaging, and other services. To attract customers, SFNB offers relatively high interest yields for CDs and money market accounts. You can transfer money between accounts, review past statements and credit card transactions, pay bills, check balances in all your accounts and credit cards, and calculate the interest to be paid on loans and credit cards. If you have an account with your parents and you are away from home, both you and your

**FIGURE 6.4** Security First Network Bank.

parents can view the account and add or withdraw funds. (*Note:* In March 1998 SFNB sold its online banking operations to Royal Bank of Canada, but continues to operate under its original name. The Canadian bank needed the online services to serve its customers while they are vacationing in the United States. The original company is now a software company which is marketing online banking software to many banks.)

This presents great potential for export business.
— *James Rolstead*

**INTERNATIONAL AND MULTIPLE-CURRENCY BANKING.** International banking and the ability to handle trading in multiple currencies is critical for international trade. Although some international retail purchasing can be done by giving your credit card number, other transactions may require international banking support. Two examples of such cross-border support follow:

▶ **Hong Kong Bank** has developed a special system called HEXAGON to provide electronic banking in Asia. Using this system, the bank has leveraged its reputation and infrastructure in the developing economies of Asia to become a major international bank rapidly, without developing an extensive new branch network. For more detail, see the case on our Web site.

▶ **Mark Twain Bank** in the United States is using electronic cash to support trading in about 25 currencies. Teamed with DigiCash, the bank attracts international traders. For details see www.marktwain.com.

**THE FUTURE OF BANKING.** A 1998 study by the Boston Consulting Group (BCG), titled "The Information Superhighway and Retail Banking," painted a challenging picture for today's banking institutions. Rapid obsolescence will be the norm in the immediate future, since the online transaction cost can be as low as 1 percent of an offline one. Therefore, it is necessary to have a successful online banking strategy that will depend on factors such as:

▶ Building alliances quickly with banks, software vendors, and information providers.

▶ Effective outsourcing without neglecting to build in-house skills, particularly with respect to customer information systems.

▶ Focusing on the profitable customer (including business customers) to provide broad channels for services and products.

▶ Keeping a central role in the payment environment.

The study suggests that banks have three core strategies to pursue. They can become one of three types: customers' agents, product manufacturers, or integrated players.

1. *Customers' agents.* There will be a number of banks that will see themselves as unable to achieve economies of scale due to disadvantages in putting together banking products and in transaction processing. In many cases they may choose to leave that part of the business but to focus on acting as agents for the bank's customers. Consistent with this option would be a strategy to offer customers the widest possible choice of banking products from multiple outside sources, and to provide customers with information-integrated services.

2. *Product manufacturers.* Conversely, some banks will see themselves as able to achieve economies of scale in developing new banking products and in transaction processing, and they may choose to position themselves as ei-

ther a branded or unbranded wholesaler of product and processing services to other banks (such as to customers' agents banks).

3. ***Integrated players.*** Remaining as integrated players will be an option only for banks with a strong brand as well as a strong position from "manufacturing" of banking products to delivery. The study states "the banks may determine that if they sold third party products to increase choices for their customers, sales would not increase sufficiently to offset lost margins."

## PERSONAL FINANCE AND PAYING BILLS ONLINE

**PERSONAL FINANCE.** Electronic banking is often combined with personal finance and portfolio management. Also, brokerage firms such as Schwab offer personal finance services such as retirement planning in addition to stock transactions. However, specialized personal finance vendors offer more diversified services. For example, both Quicken (from Intuit) and Money (from Microsoft) offer the following capabilities:

▶ Bill paying and electronic check writing

▶ Tracking bank accounts, expenditures, and credit cards

▶ Budget organization

▶ Record keeping of cash flow and profit and loss computations

▶ Portfolio management, including reports and capital gains (losses) computations

▶ Investment tracking and monitoring of securities

▶ Quotes and tradelines, historical and current prices

▶ Tax computations

▶ Retirement goals, planning, and budgeting

**PAYING BILLS ONLINE.** In August 1998, 90 percent of people surveyed in the Bay Area in California indicated a desire to pay bills on the Internet. Mostly people prefer to pay online monthly payments, such as telephone, utilities, credit cards, and cable TV. The recipients of such payments are even more eager than the payers to receive money online since they can reduce processing cost significantly.

The following are the major existing payments systems:

1. ***Automatic payment of mortgages.*** This method has been in existence since the 1980s. The customer authorizes its bank to pay the mortgage, including tax, every month, and payments are made automatically thereafter.

2. ***Automatic transfer of funds to pay monthly utility bills.*** Since fall 1988 the city of Long Beach, California, has allowed its customers to pay their gas and water bills automatically from their bank accounts. Many other utility companies, worldwide, offer such services.

3. ***Paying bills from online banking account.*** Monthly bill payments can be made from the customer's bank account to creditors' accounts. Many people pay their monthly rent and their credit card and other bills directly to the payees' bank accounts.

4. ***Merchant-to-customer direct billing.*** Under this model, a merchant like American Express posts bills on its Web site, where customers can view and pay them. Several utilities in Los Angeles allow customers to pay bills on the utilities' Web sites, charging customers 20 cents per transaction, which

is less than the price of a postage stamp. However, this means that customers have to go to many Web sites to pay all their bills.

5. *Using an intermediary.* In this model, a third party like Microsoft's Money-Center consolidates all bills related to each customer in one site and in a standard format. Collecting a certain commission, the intermediary makes it convenient both to the payee and payer to complete transactions. The payer pays all bills in one place. Several companies offer bill consolidation services.

## ONLINE INVESTMENT TRADING

It is estimated that in the year 2000, about 30 million people in the United States alone are using computers to trade stocks, bonds, and other financial instruments. Why? An online trade typically costs between $5 and $30 compared to an average fee of $100 from a full-service broker or $35 from a discount broker. There is no waiting on busy telephone lines, and the chance of making mistakes is small since there is no oral communication that traditionally took place in a frequently very noisy physical environment. Orders can be placed from anywhere, any time, and you can find a considerable amount of information regarding investing in a specific company or in a mutual fund.

How does online trading work? Let's say you have an account with Schwab. You access Schwab's Web site (www.schwab.com/schwabonline), enter your account number and password, and click on stock trading. Using a menu, you enter the details of your order (buy, sell, margin or cash, price limit, or market order, etc.). The computer tells you the current "ask" and "bid" prices, much as your broker would do on the telephone, and you can approve or reject the transaction.

Some well-known companies that offer online trading are E\*Trade, Ameritrade (see Figure 6.5), and Suretrade. E\*Trade offers many services and also challenges you to participate in a simulated investment portfolio. (See Internet Exercise #1 in this chapter.) The ability to trade financial securities online may have a major impact on individual investors because they now have tools that enable them to perform as well or even better than financial institutions.

In addition to stocks and bonds, online trading is expanding to include financial derivatives, commodities, mutual funds, and more. Futures exchanges around the world are positioning themselves for a market that many participants now agree will be dominated by electronic trading.

**INVESTMENT INFORMATION.** There is an almost unlimited amount of investment information, mostly available for free, on many Web sites. Here are some examples:

▶ For municipal bond pricing, see www.bondmarkets.org.

▶ For overall market information and many links, see www.cyberinvest.com.

▶ For free Gurus' advice, see www.upside.com.

▶ For stock screening and evaluation, try www.marketguide.com.

▶ Articles from the *Journal of the American Association of Individual Investors* can be read on www.aaii.com.

▶ For chart lovers, try www.bigcharts.com.

▶ For mutual fund evaluation and other interesting investment information, see www.morningstar.net.

► Almost any investment information that you need will be provided to you by www.yahoo.com.

► Earning estimates and much more are found on www.firstcall.com.

► For current news and much more, try www.cnnfn.com.

Most of these services are provided free, together with financial news, global investment, portfolio tracking, investor education, and much more.

**INITIAL PUBLIC OFFERINGS AND THE INTERNET.** An *initial public offering (IPO)* is the first public sale of a company's stock. IPOs are attractive to investors because of the possibility of buying at a low price a stock that will experience significant price increases.

The first successful IPO offered for sale on the Internet was that of a beer-making company called Spring Street Brewing. The owner created a special company, Wit Capital Corporation, to offer initial secondary securities trading over the Internet. Several other successful offerings followed. For example, Internet Venture Inc. raised $5 million in the spring of 1998 (www.perki.net and www.ivn.net). Also, Direct IPO (www.directipo.com) is active in this area. Virtual Wall Street brings together investors and companies interested in raising capital via direct public offering rather than using an underwriting syndicate. Auctions on IPOs are being conducted by www.openipo.com.

## THE JOB MARKET ONLINE

The Internet offers a perfect environment for job seekers and for companies searching for hard-to-find employees. The job market is especially effective for technology-oriented jobs. However, thousands of companies and government

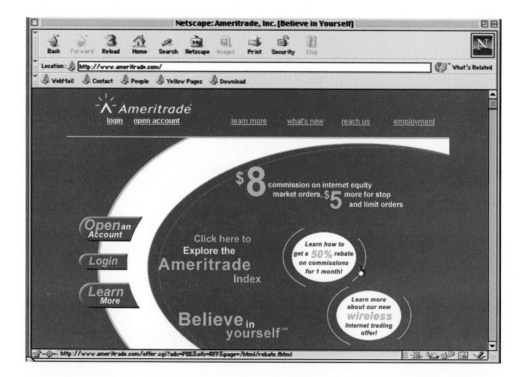

**FIGURE 6.5** Trading stocks electronically.

agencies advertise available positions in all types of jobs, accept resumes, and take applications via the Internet.

**THE PARTICIPANT IN THE JOB MARKET.** The job market is used by the following parties:

1. *Job seekers.* Job seekers can reply to employment ads posted online. Alternatively, they can take the initiative and place resumes on their own home pages or on others' Web sites, send messages to members of newsgroups asking for referrals, and use recruiting firms such Job Center (www.jobcenter.com) and Monster Board (www.monster.com). For entry-level jobs and internships for newly minted graduates, job seekers can use www.jobdirect.com. Need help to write your resume and post it on the Net? Try www.resume-link.com or www.jobweb.com.

2. *Job offerers.* Many organizations advertise openings on their Web sites. Others use other sites ranging from popular general sites (such as Yahoo) to online services, bulletin boards, and recruiting firms.

3. *Recruiting firms.* Thousands of job placement brokers are active on the Web. They use their own Web pages to post available job descriptions and to advertise their services in electronic mail and in others' Web sites. Recruiters use newsgroups, online forums, bulletin boards, and chat rooms. Job-finding brokers help candidates write their resumes and get the most exposure. Matching of candidates and jobs is done by companies such as www.discoverme.com.

4. *Newsgroups.* Job finding is of interest to many newsgroups. Jobs in certain categories or locations are posted, discussions are conducted, and resumes can be sent. (Visit 1a.job for examples.)

Smart Business Supersite (www.smartbiz.com) provides links to many sources for conducting further research, for accessing job listings, and for finding counselors for-fee.

> An easy and cheap way to recruit potential employees.
> — *James Rolstead*

**ADVANTAGES OF THE ELECTRONIC JOB MARKET.** The major advantages are:

### For Job Seekers

- ► Ability to find information on a large number of jobs and employing companies worldwide
- ► Ability to quickly communicate with potential employers
- ► Ability to write and post resumes for large-volume distribution
- ► Ability to customize resumes quickly and at no cost
- ► Ability to search for jobs quickly from any place at any time
- ► Several support services available at no cost
- ► Ability to learn how to use your voice in an interview (www.greatvoice.com)

### For Employers

- ► Ability to advertise to a large number of job seekers
- ► Ability to save on advertisement costs

> ▶ Ability to post job openings quickly

> ▶ Lower cost of processing applications (using electronic application forms)

> ▶ Ability to provide greater "equal opportunity" for job seekers

> ▶ Ability to find highly skilled employees, including those outside the area

**THE LIMITATIONS OF THE ELECTRONIC JOB MARKET** Probably the biggest limitation of the electronic job market is the fact that many people do not use the Internet. This limitation is even more serious with nontechnology-oriented jobs. To overcome the problem, companies may use both traditional approaches and the Internet. However, the trend is clear: over time, more and more of the job market is moving to the Internet.

Security and privacy may be another limitation, but one that is diminishing with security improvements. The electronic job market may also accelerate people's movements to better jobs, creating high and expensive turnover. Finally, there is a problem of information overload. In early 2000, it was estimated that over 5,000,000 resumes are on the Internet as well as 2,000,000 job openings. This problem may be addressed by companies such as resumix (www.resumix.com).

## TRAVEL AND TOURISM

Any experienced traveler knows that good planning and shopping around for the best rates can save a considerable amount of money. The Internet is an ideal place to plan, explore, and arrange almost any trip. Potential savings are available through special sales, auctions, and the elimination of travel agents. Examples of comprehensive travel online services are www.expedia.com, www.travelocity.com, and www.travelweb.com. Services are also provided online by all major airline vacation services, large conventional travel agencies, car rental agencies, hotels, and tour companies. Their online travel services allow you to purchase airline tickets, reserve hotel rooms, and rent cars. Most sites also support an itinerary-based interface, including a fare-tracker feature that periodically sends you e-mail messages about low-cost flights to your favorite destinations.

Travel Dispatch (from Expedia) is a digest of news stories that may affect your travel plans, including links to weather sites, currency converters, adventure magazines, and chat forums where users can share travel tips. Links to city maps, events, and ticket agencies online (such as www.ticketmaster.com) are also available. Some sites also include frequent-flier deals and special discounts. An interesting new travel-related site is www.priceline.com which allows you to set a price you are willing to pay for an airline ticket and hotel accommodations. The company then attempts to fulfill your wish.

## REAL ESTATE

Real estate transactions are an ideal arena for electronic commerce, for the following reasons. First, you can view many properties on the screen, saving time for you and the broker. Second, you can sort and organize properties according to your criteria and preview the exterior and interior design of the properties, shortening the search process. Finally, you can find detailed information about the properties and frequently get even more detail than brokers will provide. In some locations brokers allow the use of such databases only from their offices, but considerable information is now available on the Internet. For example, www.realtor.com allows you to search a database of over 1 million homes all over the United States. The database is composed of local "multiple listings" of all available properties, in hundreds of locations. You also can apply for a mortgage online (www.eloan.com) or bid on a loan (www.priceline.com).

Home builders now use virtual-reality technology on their Web sites to demonstrate three-dimensional floor plans to potential home buyers. They use "virtual models" that enable buyers to "walk" through mockups of homes that can be built.

### AUCTIONS, BIDDING, AND BARTERING

Auctions, bidding, and bartering are growing rapidly on the Internet.

**AUCTIONS.** Electronic auctions started in the 1980s on private networks. But their use was very limited (cars in Japan, pigs in Singapore [see Chapter 4], and flowers in the Netherlands). The Internet opens many new opportunities for electronic auctions, and millions of shoppers participate.

A few examples of auctions on the Internet are described next. B2B auctions are described in section 6.4

1. *Specialized auction sites.* Onsale (www.onsale.com) conducts live online auctions, mostly of computers and electronic consumer products. There are several types of auctions. For example, Figure 6.6 shows Yankee Auction, with eight identical items offered for sale. The seven highest bids are shown. In order to be included, you must enter a bid at least $10 above the lowest bid. The eight highest bidders win the available inventory at their offered price. A detailed list of all the product specifications, war-

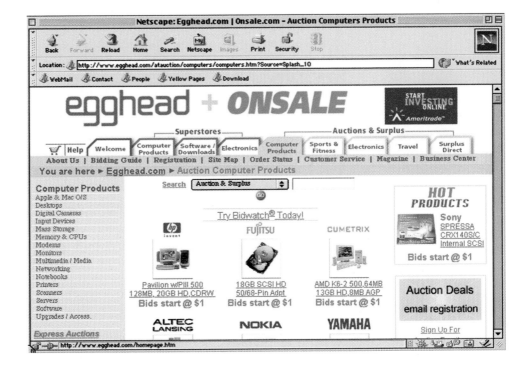

**FIGURE 6.6** A real-time Yankee-type auction.

ranties, and so forth, is included and purchases are made using a credit card. eBay offers hundreds of thousands of different items in several types of auctions. Over 300 other companies, including Amazon.com, offer online auctions as well.

2. *Auctioning cars.* As of Fall 1999, several web sites started to auction new and/or used cars (notably www.autobytel.com and www.autoweb.com). Manheim Online (www.manheim.com) brings the Web to the used car supply chain—auto dealers, banks, leasing companies, rental companies, and users of fleet vehicles—by conducting dealers-only auctions. Dealers visit "cyberlots" where they see pictures of the cars. A buyer in city A can buy a car in city B, with transportation costs also quoted online. Aucnet conducts auctions on the Internet for used cars in Japan.

3. *Art auctions.* Artwork is sold online at various sites, including www.onlineart.com, Auctions On-line (www.auctions-on-line.com), and Internet Liquidators. The large offline art auction houses, such as Christie's, offer limited online auctions.

4. *Airlines.* Several airlines auction tickets on their Web sites. See American Airlines (www.americanair.com) and Cathay Pacific (www.cathay-usa.com).

In the future it is expected that online auctions will allow you to leave instructions for your agent on the price that you are willing to bid and other specifications. Your agent will contact other agents and attempt to conclude a transaction for you. While initially most auctions were open for days until winners were announced, today some auctions last only a few hours.

**BIDDINGS.** A special type of auction is corporate bidding. Details are provided in section 6.4.

**BARTERING.** Related to auctions and bids is **electronic bartering,** the *exchange* of goods and/or services. In addition to the individual-to-individual bartering ads that appear in some newsgroups, bulletin boards, and chat rooms, there are several companies that arrange for corporate bartering (e.g., www.barterbrokers.com). These companies try to find partners to a barter.

## A NON-INTERNET APPLICATION

The applications presented so far have all been Internet-based. Electronic commerce is also being conducted on private lines (usually EDI) and increasingly offline, mainly with the use of smart cards (section 6.6). Here is an example of a smart-card based, B2C non-Internet service.

**THE HIGHWAY 91 PROJECT.** Route 91 is a major eight-lane, east–west highway east of Los Angeles. Traffic is especially heavy during rush hours. California Private Transportation Company (CPT) built six express toll lanes along a 10-mile stretch in the median of the existing Highway 91. The express lanes system has only one entrance and one exit, and it is totally operated with electronic commerce technologies. Here is how the system works:

1. Only prepaid subscribers can drive the road. They receive an automatic vehicle identification (AVI) device that is placed on the rearview mirror of the car. The device, about the size of a thick credit card, includes a microchip, an antenna, and a battery.

2. A large sign over the tollway tells drivers the current fee for cruising the express lanes. In 2000 it varied from $0.50 in slow traffic hours to $3.25 during rush hours.

3. Sensors in the pavement let the tollway computer know that a car has entered; the car does not need to slow or stop.

4. The AVI makes radio contact with a transceiver installed above the lane.

5. The transceiver relays the car's identity through fiber-optic lines to the control center, where a computer deducts the fee from the driver's prepaid account.

6. Surveillance cameras record the license numbers of cars without AVIs. These cars can be stopped by police at the exit or fined by mail.

7. Video cameras along the tollway enable managers to keep tabs on traffic, for example, sending a tow truck to help a stranded car. Also, through knowledge of the traffic volume, pricing decisions can be made. Raising the price ensures the tollway will not be jammed.

8. The system accesses the driver's account which is automatically debited for the fare. A monthly statement is sent to the subscriber's home.

The system saves commuters between 40 and 90 minutes each day, so it is in high demand. An interesting extension of this system is the use of the same AVIs for other purposes. For example, they can be used in paid parking lots. And one day you may be recognized when you enter the drive-through lane of McDonalds and a voice asks you, "Mr. Smart, do you want your usual meal today?"

## 6.4 BUSINESS-TO-BUSINESS APPLICATIONS

In this section we give attention to typical **business-to-business (B2B)** applications, namely, the buyers, sellers, and transactions involving only organizations. B2B composes the majority of EC volume (about 80 to 85 percent). B2B covers a broad spectrum of applications that enable an enterprise or business to form electronic relationships with their distributors, resellers, suppliers, customers, and other partners. This covers all activities along the supply chain (see Handfield and Nichols [1999]), including all internal operations.

B2B applications offer enterprises access to the following types of information:

- Product—specifications, prices, sales history
- Customer—sales history and forecasts
- Supplier—product line (catalogs) and lead times, sales terms and conditions
- Product process—capacities, commitments, product plans
- Transportation—carriers, lead times, costs
- Inventory—inventory levels, carrying costs, locations
- Supply chain alliance—key contacts, partners, roles and responsibilities, schedules
- Competitor—benchmarking, competitive product offerings, market share
- Sales and marketing—point of sale (POS), promotions
- Supply chain process and performance—process descriptions, performance measures, quality, delivery time, customer satisfaction

When using B2B e-commerce, businesses may need to reengineer their business processes along the supply chain as discussed in Chapter 4.

## B2B BUSINESS MODELS

There are several business models for B2B e-commerce. The major ones are: seller-oriented marketspace, buyer-oriented marketspace, intermediary-managed marketspace, buyer internal market place, and auctions.

**SELLER-ORIENTED MARKETSPACE.** In the seller-oriented marketspace model, organizations attempt to sell their products or services to other organizations electronically. This model is similar to the B2C model in which the buyer is expected to come to the seller's site or to a mall, view catalogs, and place an order.

In the B2B case, the buyer is an organization that may be a regular customer of the seller. The key mechanisms in such a model are electronic catalogs that can be customized for each large buyer, the ordering system, the payment system, and due to their large size, the integration of the incoming orders with the vendor's logistics system. Examples of companies using such a model are Cisco, IBM, and Intel. This model is used by thousands of companies and is especially powerful for companies with superb reputations, such as Intel. Large sellers sell directly from their Web sites. Alternatively, catalogs can be placed in industry malls or in distributors' Web sites.

EC is used in the seller-oriented model to increase sales, reduce selling and advertisement expenditures, increase delivery speed, and reduce administrative costs (for example, by using electronic catalogs and providing electronic-based customer service). An example is Cisco Systems.

---

*IT At Work*　　**CISCO SYSTEMS ONLINE—A BILLION-DOLLAR BUSINESS**

*U*SING IT

...in Marketing

Cisco Systems is the major producer of routers, switches, and related network products sold to information systems departments worldwide. Cisco decided to go online since virtually all its customers were regular Web users. The company started to sell its products in 1996, and reached over $1 billion business in 1997. By the end of 1996 more than 8,000 customers had registered for online trading.

Cisco Connection is an extranet enabling customers to communicate and collaborate regarding any issue related to their orders, such as checking current purchasing order status. Customers can configure, price, and submit orders on line with direct access to Cisco's database for pricing and configuration information. By correctly configuring and pricing equipment before submitting orders, customers and resellers eliminate rework, which can delay order processing. Submitted orders are deposited directly into Cisco's procurement database, where they are quickly queued for scheduling.

Built-in security features such as automatic encryption and password protection ensure that orders cannot be changed or deleted without authorization. Customers and credit lines are preapproved, and payments are settled separately, offline.

Customers like Cisco's electronic purchasing for its:

▶ Up-to-the-minute price information (available 24 hours a day)
▶ Quick replies to queries (hours, compared to days)
▶ Ability to configure the needed system and price it very quickly
▶ Easy order status and invoice checking

▶ Easy accessibility to maintenance contracts
▶ Availability of online technical support

The benefits to Cisco are:

▶ Reduced customer service cost and improved service
▶ Reduced marketing costs
▶ Reduced shipping cost

In summary, the site combines three major functions: product configuration, pricing, and order processing.

     **For Further Exploration.** Compare Cisco Connection to Disney Online. What are the similarities and differences? ▲

SOURCE: *Industry Week,* April 21, 1997, pp. 69–70.

**BUYER-ORIENTED MARKETSPACE (PROCUREMENT AND BIDDING).** One variation of the buyer-oriented marketspace model involves placing a request for quotation (RFQ) on the buyer's Web site, or in a bidding marketplace, like the one managed by General Electric (www.geis.com; see TPN Post). Once RFQs are posted on this trading process network (TPN), bids are submitted electronically (usually by approved bidders), and routed via the buyers' intranet to the engineering and finance departments for evaluation. Clarifications are made via e-mail. The winner is notified electronically. Such bids attract larger pools of suppliers because they are cheaper to prepare. GE, the originator of the concept, saves 10 to 15 percent on the cost of the items placed for bid and up to 85 percent on the administrative cost. In addition, cycle time is reduced by about 50 percent.

     GE has also organized a market for small companies that use GE's TPN to post their RFQs. They pay GE a fee for this, as well as for handling processes like payments. In this capacity, GE acts as an intermediary.

**INTERMEDIARIES IN ELECTRONIC COMMERCE: MARKET MAKERS.** Electronic intermediaries provide different services for buyers and sellers. Their main function is *market making.* Take, for example, Boeing PART which manages the market for airplane replacement parts. About 300 parts suppliers and dozens of airlines participate in this market. Another example is ProcureNet, which runs dozens of seller sites (similar to malls) where more then 150,000 products, known as MROs (maintenance, repairs, and operations) are displayed. Another, Industry.net, has about 300,000 members, from 37,000 organizations. Hosting fees charged by electronic intermediaries range from $2,000 to $250,000 per year for hosting the site. Several other business models of intermediaries exist. In all models, the purpose of the intermediation is to make money or (as in the case of Boeing) improve service for customers. Boeing also saves money by reducing the search time of its own staff, who used to spend too much time locating parts. In turn, Boeing customers reduce airplanes' idle time (waiting for parts) that is very costly. Intermediaries use various infrastructures, but lately the extranet became a mode of choice.

**BUYER'S INTERNAL MARKETPLACE.** The buyer's internal marketplace model is fairly new and best suited for large companies. Here is how the model works at MasterCard International: MasterCard buys large numbers of supply items from many vendors. Once prices are agreed upon, the items are approved for purchase and placed on MasterCard's internal procurement system. About 10,000 items are listed in the company's catalog, from dozens of vendors. Over 2,300 purchasers at various MasterCard offices around the world now view the catalog, select the appropriate products, electronically place orders, and pay with a Master-Card procurement card. This model is especially suitable for small items, such as office supplies, cleaning materials, and replacement parts. This model enabled MasterCard to consolidate buying activities from many corporate locations and reduce the administrative processing costs. Also, procurement cycle time has been reduced in many cases from 20 days to just one. Finally, since MasterCard now has a smaller supplier base to buy from, the quantities purchased from each vendor are larger, so MasterCard has been able to negotiate larger purchase discounts.

**BUSINESS-TO-BUSINESS AUCTIONS.** An increasing number of organizations, including Dell Computer, are utilizing auctions as a substantial business model. The U.S. federal government, for example, conducts auctions of houses and apartments to real estate brokers. Two major options exist: to use the organization's own Web site, as in the case of Dell or Ingram Micro, or to use an auction site of an intermediary. In either case companies can reduce commissions by 50 to 80 percent and can also sell, and especially liquidate, products quickly. Corporations use auctions mainly as a B2B tool, but an increasing number use them also as a direct marketing channel to both companies and individuals.

The major benefits of such auctions are:

1. *Generating revenue.* As a new sales channel, auctions support existing online sales. For example, Weirton Steel Corp. doubled its customer base when it started auctions (Fickel [1999]). Auctions also offer a new venue for disposing of excess, obsolete, and returned products quickly and easily.

2. *Increasing page views.* Auctions give sites "stickiness." Auction users spend more time on a site and generate more page views than other users, so companies can sell ad space at auction sites for higher prices.

3. *Acquiring and retaining members.* All bidding transactions result in additional registered members, which increases the value of companies.

*Types of B2B Auctions.* There are four basic types of auctions:

1. *Independent auctions.* In this case companies use a third-party auctioneer to create the site and sell the goods (e.g., www.fairmarket.com, www.imxexchange.com, and www.auctiongate.com). Such as arrangement can be fairly complex as shown in the case of FreeMarkets Online Inc.

---

**IT At Work**    **HOW FREEMARKET OPERATES: A NEW B2B MODEL**

Imagine this scenario: United Technologies Corp. needs suppliers to make $24 million worth of circuit boards. Twenty-five hundred suppliers were identified as possible contractors. These were found in electronic registries and directories. The list was submitted to FreeMarkets On-Line Inc. (www.freemarket.com). FreeMarkets' experts reduced the list to 1,000, based on considerations ranging from plant location to the size of the supplier. After further analysis of plant capacity and customers' feedback, the list was reduced to 100. A detailed evaluation of the potential suppliers resulted in 50 qualified suppliers who were invited to bid.

Three hours of online competitive bidding was conducted. FreeMarkets divided the job into 12 lots, each of which was put up to bid. At 8:00 A.M., the first lot, valued at $2.25 million, was placed on the Net. The first bid was $2.25 million, which was seen by all. Minutes later, another bidder placed a $2.0 million bid. Using the reverse (Dutch) method, the bidders further reduced the bids. Minutes before the bid closed, at 8:45 A.M., the 42nd bidder placed a $1.1 million bid. When it all ended, the bids for all 12 lots totaled $18 million (about 35 percent savings to United Technologies).

To finalize the process, FreeMarkets conducted a very comprehensive analysis on several low bidders of each lot, attempting to look at other criteria in addition to cost. FreeMarkets then recommended the winners and collected its fees.

**For further exploration:** What are the unique aspects of this B2B model? ▲

2. *Commodity auctions.* In this case many buyers and sellers come together to a third-party Web site. For example, energy access, utilities, and telecommunications are sold at www.band-x.com. Typical intermediaries are www.metalsite.net and www.fastparts.com.

3. *Private auctions by invitation only.* Several companies bypass the intermediaries and auction their products by themselves. Ingram Micro has its own site, www.auctionblock.com, for selling obsolete computer equipment to its regular business customers.

4. *Auctions at the company web site.* A growing number of companies build an auction capability on their web site. Dell Computers is an example. Companies like www.opensite.com and www.fairmarket.com provide software, hosting it, and consulting if needed.

## INTRABUSINESS COMMERCE ON INTRANETS

Electronic commerce is growing rapidly within companies in what is called **intrabusiness EC.** Intrabusiness is mainly done on intranets (see Chapter 5). An **intranet** uses Internet-based technology, including browsers and search engines, to provide access to a variety of information within a firm. The use of intranets is increasing rapidly not only for internal communications but also as a facilitator of electronic commerce. Intranets can be used to sell corporate products to employees, or to sell or trade services and products among business units. Intranets can facilitate transaction processing by providing efficient transaction entry, and enabling transactions to be reported in a consistent form, using common procedures. Finally, an intranet can be used to increase productivity and reduce costs along the internal supply chain.

Main intranet applications exist (see Box 6.2). Examples include: publishing, sharing corporate knowledge, group calendaring and scheduling, data and information searches, group document editing and management, distributed project management, distributed applications access, facilitated training, office productivity, and support of mobile workers. Client access to certain parts of a firm's intranet via an extranet is a value-added service at relatively low cost that acts as a powerful marketing and communication tool.

## *A Closer Look* BOX 6.2

### INTRANET EXAMPLES FROM AROUND THE GLOBE

Some examples of how businesses around the world are making use of intranets for the benefit of their employees and customers are as follows.

▶ **Credit Lyonnais,** Paris, publishes reports prepared by its department of financial and economic studies.

▶ **Harris,** Melbourne, FL, offers documentation of company policies and procedures from purchasing to health benefits.

▶ **Industry Canada,** the Canadian Department of Commerce, uses an intranet to distribute corporate information and policies, human resources information, financial manuals, job listings, and access to its library system.

▶ **Intel,** Santa Clara, CA, distributes human resources information, online documentation, and supply ordering.

▶ **Fujitsu,** Tokyo, maintains its company telephone book, corporate information, and internal communications on an intranet.

▶ **Post AG,** Darmstadt, Germany, offers software manuals, software purchasing, and IS department rules and procedures on its intranet.

▶ **Sun Microsystems,** Mountain View, CA, deploys intranet technologies widely inside the company. These include corporate documents, searchable directories, simple groupware applications, software distribution, and e-mail.

▶ **Sparbanken Sverige AB** of Sweden uses an intranet in its 1,300 branches to disseminate news and internal information about banking procedures to all of its employees. The intranet is connected to an electronic storage and retrieval system that includes push technology for customized news and updates to key employees. A newsgroup of employees raises and discusses difficult questions electronically. The system is combined with an extranet for customer service and cooperation with business partners.

▶ **The Social Security Administration** in the United States is using an intranet as a base for an extensive groupware for communication and decision making. A major objective is to increase employees' productivity by enabling them to handle an inquiry electronically from start to finish. Also, the system is used to disseminate information and facilitate training (see *Information Week,* May 5, 1997.)

### THE EXTRANETS AND WHOLE INDUSTRY MARKETS

The use of an extranet (see Chapter 5) as an interorganizational infrastructure is increasing rapidly. In contrast with electronic data interchange (EDI), which mostly supports transaction processing between two business partners, an extranet can be used for collaboration, discovery of information, trading, and other activities. The exact definition of an **extranet** is still evolving, but the most universally accepted one is a network that links business partners to one another over the Internet by tying together their corporate intranets. The term "extranet" comes from "extended intranet." The main goal of extranets is to foster collaboration between organizations. In Figure 6.2 (pg. 217) we showed two extranets. On the right side was the toy industry extranet and on the left side, the company's extranet with its major business partners.

An extranet uses the same basic infrastructure components, including servers, TCP/IP protocols, e-mail, and Web browsers, as the Internet. It basically makes communication over the Internet secure. It links the company's intranet with suppliers, customers, and trading partners. Extranets may be used, for example, to allow inventory databases to be searched by outsiders, or to transmit information on the status of an order. An extranet enables people who are located outside a company to work together with the company's internally located employees.

An extranet, like an intranet, is typically protected by a firewall and is closed to the public. It is open to selected suppliers, customers, and other business partners, who access it on a private wide-area network over the Internet or on a virtual private network (VPN), which increases security and functionality.

Here are few examples of extranets:

▶ By year-end 1996, Chrysler Corporation, General Motors Corporation, and Ford Motor Company had linked their intranets with a limited number of suppliers and business partners. The resulting network is a pilot version of a global project called Automotive Network Exchange (ANX) sponsored by the Automotive Industry Action Group. Participants are linked to the system through multiple Internet service providers, putting ANX on the cutting edge. The network is used as of 1999 for EDI, the exchange of large engineering files, and other forms of business-to-business electronic commerce.

▶ Ho Chi Minh City in Vietnam uses an extranet to help attract foreign investment and develop exports. The extranet is linked with the intranet to introduce Vietnam's export potential and projects calling for outside investment. The extranet also links Vietnam's small- and medium-size export enterprises among themselves and with government agencies, and it also connects Vietnamese import–export businesses with the outside business world. (*Source: Saigon Times*, April 4, 1998.)

**I**NTEGRATING IT

...for Marketing and Production & Operations Management

▶ Marshall Industries of El Monte, CA, is a large electronics distributor. An extranet helps facilitate the flow of information from Marshall Industries to its hundreds of suppliers, systems integrators, and other customers. The system lets the company's suppliers get point-of-sale reports at any time, day or night, and it also enables Marshall Industries to offer real-time inventory access. The customers can track the status of their orders. Says Marshall Industries vice president Bob Edleman,

> **Thirty thousand companies do business with us, and we're trying to figure out a way to reach both ends of that supply chain. In our industry, time is compressed. You go from 2-1/2 years for a design cycle to a few months. We had to make it so people could see status of orders immediately and interact with other parts of our company. A guy in San Diego can get in and find out that type of information. That's something he needs now, not a month from now.**

Along with the increased customer service, which indirectly leads to cost savings, Marshall Industries has discovered that the network has helped increase productivity. Although the company has cut its sales staff from 1,600 to 1,450 employees, Edleman says it has been able to double its sales and profits.

Extranets allow the use of capabilities of both the Internet and intranet. External partners and telecommuting employees can use the Internet to access data, place orders, check status, and send e-mail. The Internet-based extranet is far more economical than the creation and maintenance of proprietary networks. It is a nonproprietary technical tool that can support rapid evolution of electronic commerce, as illustrated in the *IT at Work* case that follows.

*IT At Work*     HOW AN EXTRANET

FACILITATES HOME LOANS

**U**SING IT

...in Finance

Countrywide Home Loans of Pasadena, CA, is the nation's largest independent mortgage lender, with nearly 330 branch offices nationwide. It is using extensive Internet, intranet, and extranet solutions that serve its employees, business partners, and consumers.

Every day, Countrywide processes thousands of transactions that are influenced by continuous fluctuations in lending rates and product offerings. To improve processing, the company has embarked on a long-term project to eliminate paper from its operating environment. The system provides a completely open, networked environment that seamlessly ties into the mountains of legacy data that must be accessed by people using various computer platforms, both inside and outside the corporate firewall.

Countrywide's IS department has developed a corporatewide intranet system servicing more than 5,000 employees at the company's headquarters and branch locations. This far-reaching network provides employees with online access to product guidelines, forms, and corporate information. Countrywide programmers develop intranet applications for such corporate functions as mortgage origination, mortgage servicing, and back-office operations.

The company has also developed a powerful extranet accessible only to Countrywide's lending partners, brokers, and real estate agents. These parties require secure access to valuable information, such as account and transaction status, loan status, company contacts, and company announcements. A total of 500 Countrywide lenders use Netscape Navigator client software to access the extranet, which uses a sophisticated routing program. This program automatically identifies each lender and provides him or her with his or her own customized information on premium rates, discounts, and special arrangements.

The same server deployed for the extranet is also being used to develop a host of customer-oriented applications for use on a publicly accessible Internet site. These applications come online as part of a Web service offered free by Countrywide. For example, consumers can calculate home mortgage rates based on any number of market variables and product offerings. Countrywide integrated its consumer Web services with massive legacy databases that contain pertinent information on loan offerings, loan rates, and mortgage products.

**For Further Exploration.** Identify the collaboration and communication activities that are facilitated by the extranet. Why is this so beneficial? ▲

SOURCE: Compiled from Netscape Corporation news release No. 220 (1996) available at http://home.netscape.com.; also see *Computer World,* August 12, 1996.

A major issue in implementing an extranet is whether it can be accessed via the Internet. If such access is permitted, communication costs are reduced, but security and performance levels are also lower. If an extranet is truly private, then it is more secure but also more expensive.

## ▶ 6.5 CONSUMERS, MARKET RESEARCH, AND CUSTOMER SUPPORT

In this section, we explore several issues related to consumers. First, it is important to know *who* the potential cyber consumers are and *how* they make purchasing decisions. This knowledge can be gained through *market research.* It is also important to understand the role of customer service. Finally, customer-related activities may require considerable effort; therefore automation using intelligent agents may be beneficial. All of these topics are discussed in this section.

## CONSUMERS AND THEIR BEHAVIOR

Two major types of consumers buy EC products and services: individuals and organizations. Most of the discussion in this section concentrates on the individual B2C shopper. The issue of the organizational buyer is briefly presented at the end of this section. We will refer to the buyers as consumers or customers interchangeably.

A key activity in EC implementation is finding out who are the actual and potential customers. Several studies periodically conducted at Georgia Tech University (see www.gtech.edu/gvu.user_surveys) and at Ernst and Young (www.ey.com/industry/consumer/internetshopping) attempt to assess the demographics of Internet users and the activities of EC shoppers. They have found that initially the vast majority of Internet users were mostly 15- to 35-year-old males. Now the situation is changing. The number of female users nearly equals that of males, and both younger and older surfers have joined the party. However, it may take several years before the Internet population matches exactly the general population mix.

The largest group of Internet users are married and highly educated; almost 90 percent are white. Most users are working in educational institutions, the computer industry, professions, and organizations. The surfers have high household incomes. The amount of money spent on the Internet is increasing with users' experience. Men buy more expensive items, usually computers. The two major reasons that people *do not buy* over the Internet are fear of inadequate security and quality uncertainty. (Both are discussed later.)

Online purchasing constitutes a fundamental change for customers. If the customer has previously used mail-order catalogs or television shopping, the change will not be so drastic. But moving away from a physical shopping mall to an electronic mall may not be simple. Furthermore, shopping habits keep changing as a result of innovative marketing strategies. The key to finding out what certain groups of consumers (such as teenagers or residents of certain geographical zones) want is the role of market research. However, even if we know what consumers in general want, each individual consumer is very likely to want something different. Some like classical music, while other like jazz. Some like brand names, others like fancy items, and price is important to many others. A major advantage of EC is its ability to *customize* products, services, advertisements, and customer service at a reasonable cost as compared to traditional retailing.

The importance of understanding consumer behavior can be seen by comparing two electronic vendors, Peapod and Amazon.com. Peapod (www.peapod.com) provides supermarket products online. Customers view electronic catalogs picturing available items. Once in the virtual supermarket, customers can request itemized lists of products by brand name, type of food, and so forth. The items are then ranked by price per ounce or nutritional value. Once the customer decides on all items, he or she arranges payment and delivery time. The cost is slightly higher than in a regular supermarket, but Peapod's customers are repeat customers (75 percent of whom are female) interested in saving time. The major problem faced by Peapod is its small customer base. In 1999, the company was still incurring losses. One reason is that customers like to see and feel items before they buy them. To alleviate this problem, Peapod plans to use virtual-reality technology in the future that lets customers "pick up" items and "place" them in virtual shopping carts.

A different story is that of books sold at Amazon (www.Amazon.com). Like Peapod, Amazon is an intermediary, selling books published by others. Here, cus-

*U*SING IT
...in Marketing

tomers also buy from electronic catalogs. However, in contrast to Peapod, Amazon's business is growing very rapidly. Special customer services such as book reviews, chat rooms, bibliographical lists, and automatic notifications on new books are available online, attracting many customers to the Web site. Amazon.com's CEO said that when he planned to open his business he assessed the potential customers' reaction and correctly projected books to be a desirable item for online sale.

Thus, learning about customers is extremely important for any successful business, especially in cyberspace. Such learning is facilitated by market research.

## MARKET RESEARCH

Market research has been conducted for years in order to find out what motivates consumers to buy.

**MODELS OF MARKET RESEARCH.** Researchers have developed models (frameworks) that explain consumer behavior regarding purchasing decisions. We have developed a similar model for explaining consumer buying decisions on the Internet, as shown in Figure 6.7.

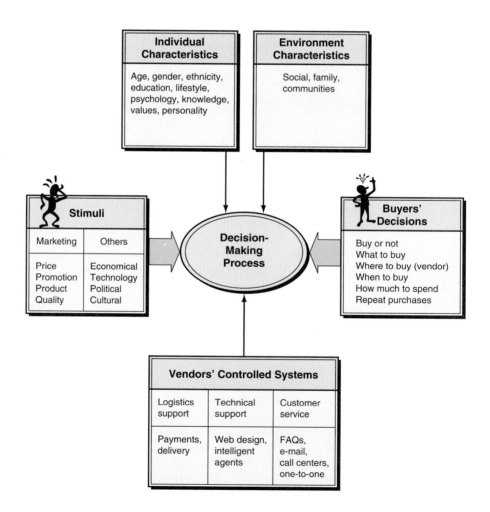

FIGURE 6.7 Electronic commerce consumer behavior model.

The purchasing process starts on the left, where factors that stimulate a consumer to think about buying are shown. As the consumer considers the need to buy, two types of factors influence the decision-making process (center): personal factors (top left), and environmental factors (top right). In EC there are several others factors that influence shoppers' decision making. These are shown at the bottom of the figure. These factors, which are controlled by the seller and/or the intermediary, range from technology to customer service. The model shows us that cybershopping is a complex process. The seller controls all the factors shown at the bottom of the figure, as well as being able to influence some of the stimuli factors (for example, through advertisement). Such knowledge is provided by market research, much of which is done online.

The Internet is a powerful and cost-effective tool for conducting market research regarding consumer behavior, for identifying new markets, for investigating competitors and their products, and for testing consumer interest in new products. The findings of such research are essential for *one-to-one marketing*. This new interactive style of marketing allows one-to-one personal contact with customers, and it provides marketing organizations with greater ability to understand the consumers, market, and competition. For example, it can identify early shifts in consumer tastes and trends, enabling marketers to identify, or if necessary design, products, and marketing opportunities that match these shifts. Market research also tells management when a product or a service is no longer popular. For a suggested process for market research, see Box 6.3.

**HOW TO FIND OUT WHAT CUSTOMERS WANT.** There are basically two ways to find out what customers want. The first is to ask them, and the second is to infer what they want by observing what they do. Such observation is relatively easy in cyberspace.

*Asking Customers What They Want.* The Internet provides easy, fast, and relatively inexpensive ways for vendors to interact directly with consumers to find

---

## A Closer Look  BOX 6.3

### HOW MARKET RESEARCH IS CONDUCTED

**PROCESS OF CONDUCTING THE RESEARCH**
1. Define the target market.
2. Identify newsgroups to study.
3. Identify topics for discussion.
4. Subscribe to the pertinent groups.
5. Search discussion group topic and content lists to find target market.
6. Search e-mail discussion group lists.
7. Subscribe to filtering services that monitor groups (such as www.reference.com).
8. Read FAQs and other instructions.

**CONTENT OF THE RESEARCH INSTRUMENT**
1. Post strategic queries to groups.
2. Post surveys on your Web site.
3. Post strategic queries on your Web site.
4. Post relevant content to groups with a pointer to your Web site survey.
5. Post a detailed survey in special e-mail questionnaires.

**TARGET AUDIENCE OF THE STUDY**
1. Identify the demographics of your Web site visitors. Compare them to the population demographics.
2. Determine your editorial focus.
3. Determine your content.
4. Determine what Web services to create for each type of audience.

SOURCE: Compiled from Vassos (1996), pp. 66–68.

out what they want. The simplest way is to ask potential customers to fill in electronic questionnaires. To do so, vendors need to use some inducements. For example, in order to play a free electronic game, or participate in sweepstakes, you are asked to fill in a form and answer some questions about yourself. Frequently you are asked to "sign" an electronic agreement. Be sure to *read it very carefully.* Marketers not only learn what you want from your direct answers, but also try to infer from your preferences in music, for example, what type of books, clothes, or movies you may be likely to prefer. This is done with the help of *intelligent agents,* as we will describe later.

Asking customers what they want may not be feasible in some cases. Customers may refuse to answer questionnaires, or they may provide false information (in about 40 percent of the cases, per Georgia Tech University Studies). Also, the administration of questionnaires can be lengthy and costly. Therefore, it may be necessary to use a different approach.

***Tracking Customer Activities on the Web.*** Today it is possible to learn about customers by observing what they do on the Internet. Many companies offer site-tracking services, based on cookies or other approaches. For example, Internet Profile Corporation collects data from client/server logs and provides periodic reports that include demographic data such as where customers come from or how many customers have gone straight from the home page to ordering. The company translates Internet domain names into real-company names and includes general and financial corporate information. However, tracking customers' activities without their knowledge or permission may be unethical, even though the tracker does not know the name of the customer. This is an issue we'll discuss in section 6.7.

**ORGANIZATIONAL BUYERS AND THEIR BEHAVIOR.** Although the number of organizational buyers is much smaller than the number of individual buyers, their transaction volumes are far larger and the terms of negotiations and purchase are more complex. In addition, the purchasing process may be more important than advertising activities in making sales to organizational buyers. In general, factors that affect individual consumer behavior and organizational buying behavior are quite different.

***A Behavioral Model of an Organizational Buyer.*** The behavior of an organizational buyer can be described by a model similar to that of the individual buyer we showed in Figure 6.7. However, the specific variables may differ (for example, the family and the Internet communities may have no influence). What is added in this model is an *organizational module* that includes the organization's purchasing guidelines and constraints, the relationship among various buyers, the possibility of group decision making, and the organizational structure. Also important are interpersonal variables of the organizational buyer and the seller, such as authority, status, empathy, and persuasiveness. (For a detailed discussion of organizational buying, see Chapter 6 in Kotler and Armstrong [1999]).

## INTELLIGENT AGENTS FOR PRODUCT/VENDOR FINDING AND FOR NEGOTIATION

One of the most interesting tools for finding products and vendors on the Internet (as well as helping in negotiations) is intelligent agents.

**INTELLIGENT AGENTS FOR PRODUCT AND VENDOR FINDING.** Intelligent agents help consumers decide where to buy by comparing merchants' offers. A pioneering intelligent agent for online price comparison was Bargainfinder from Andersen Consulting. This agent was used only in online shopping for CDs. The agent queried the price of a specific CD from a number of online vendors and returned the list of vendors and prices. However, this system encountered several problems because vendors that did not want to compete on price only managed to block out the agent's requests.

The blocking problem has been solved by Jango (from NetBot/Excite). This agent originates the requests from the customer's site instead of Jango's. This way, vendors have no way of determining whether the request is directly from the customer or from the agent. Jango is also more complete than Bargainfinder as it includes more categories of products like computers, software, appliances, groceries, flowers, and even Beanie Babies! Furthermore, Jango provides product reviews in addition to price comparisons.

Another agent worth mentioning is Kasbah (http://ecommerce.media. mit.edu/kasbah). In Kasbah (from MIT Laboratories), users who want to sell or buy a product assign the task to an agent that is then sent out to proactively seek buyers or sellers. In creating the agent, users must specify constraints, including desired price, highest (or lowest) acceptable price, and a date by which to complete the transaction. The agent's goal is to complete an acceptable transaction based on these parameters. This intelligent agent also can negotiate on the part of the buyers, as will be discussed next.

**NEGOTIATION AGENTS.** Before people buy, they may negotiate the price and other terms of the transactions. Intelligent agents can be particularly useful in this stage, because they can take away some of the real-world problems associated with negotiation such as the frustration some customers experience in the process, and the technical limitations of being physically in different locations. For example, a buyer agent may negotiate with agents of several sellers. One area where such agents are being developed is in supporting auctions.

Auctions are one of the most popular activities on the Web. However, almost all auctions require users to personally execute the bidding. This is not the case with AuctionBot, developed by the University of Michigan (http://auction.eecs.umich.edu), where users can create intelligent agents that will take care of the bidding process. In AuctionBot users create auction agents by specifying a number of parameters that vary depending on the type of auction selected. After that, it is up to the agent to manage the auction until a final price is met or the deadline of the offer is reached.

Kasbah, which was cited earlier, is a multi-agent, classified ad system in which users create agents for the purpose of selling or buying goods. Kasbah agents are capable of negotiating with each other, following specific strategies assigned by their creators. However, the Kasbah agent's usefulness is limited by the fact that price is the only parameter considered.

A more powerful agent, called Tete-@-tete, has been developed by creators of Kasbah. Tete-@-tete is unique compared to other online negotiation systems because its agents negotiate with each other considering a number of different parameters: price, warranty, delivery time, service contacts, return policy, loan options, and other value-added services. Another innovative feature of this system is that unlike the Kasbah, where negotiation is conducted along the lines of simple price increase or decrease functions, negotiation of Tete-@-tete agents is argumentative (see http://ecommerce.media.mit.edu/tete-tete).

**LEARNING AGENTS.** A *learning agent* (also called *remembrance*) is capable of learning an individuals' preferences and making suggestions. An example is Memory Agent, developed by IBM. Memory Agent uses a neural network technique that learns by creating a knowledge database of attributes of cases.

## CUSTOMER SERVICE

**THE PROCESS OF CUSTOMER SERVICE.** In many cases, a competitive edge is gained by providing superb customer service. In electronic commerce, customer service becomes even more critical, since customers and merchants do not meet face to face (see Sterne [1999]). According to McKeown and Watson (1998), customer service should be approached as a life cycle process with the following four phases:

> **Phase 1.** *Requirements.* Assisting the customer to determine needs (providing photographs of a product, video presentations, textual descriptions, articles or reviews, sound bites on a CD, and downloadable demonstration files).

> **Phase 2.** *Acquisition.* Helping the customer to acquire a product or service (online order entry, negotiations, closing of sale, and delivery).

> **Phase 3.** *Ownership.* Supporting the customer on an ongoing basis (interactive online user groups, online technical support, FAQs and answers, resource libraries, newsletters, and online renewal of subscriptions).

> **Phase 4.** *Retirement.* Helping the client to dispose of a service or product (online resale, classified ads).

**EXAMPLES OF CUSTOMER SERVICE.** Many activities are conducted in each of the above phases. A few examples are:

...in Marketing

▸ **American Airlines** (www.americanair.com) offers flight and fare information such as flight schedules, fare quotes, and much more. This is an example of support for phases 1 and 2.

▸ **Dell, Compaq, and other computer vendors** provide an electronic help desk for their customers. This is an example of supporting phase 3.

...in Finance

▸ **Fidelity Investments** (www.fidelity.com) provides investors with "the right tools to make their own best investment decisions." The site has several sections, which include daily updates of financial news, information about Fidelity's mutual funds, material for interactive investment and retirement planning, and brokerage services. This is an example of support given to phase 1.

**FACILITATING CUSTOMER SERVICE.** Several tools are available for facilitating customer service. The major tools, with their functionalities, are:

▸ *Personalized Web pages:* Customers build individualized pages at the vendor's site. Customized information is provided there.

▸ *A chat room:* Customers can interact with each other and with vendor's personnel, who monitor the chat room.

▸ *E-mail:* Send confirmation, product information, and instructions to customers. Take orders, complaints, and other inquiries.

▶ *FAQs:* Provide online answers to questions customers ask most and place them online.

▶ *Tracking capabilities:* Enable customers to track the status of their orders, services (such as FedEx shipments), or applications. Customers can find the status of their banking and stock activities, and more.

▶ *Web-based call centers:* A comprehensive communication center takes customers' inquiries in any form they come (fax, telephone, e-mail, letters) and answers them quickly. Provides for quick problem resolution.

An application of Web-based call centers is becoming very popular as shown in the case of Canada Tire.

---

## *IT At Work*    CANADIAN TIRE PROVIDES SUPERB CUSTOMER SERVICE VIA INTEGRATED CALL CENTER

Canadian Tire Acceptance Ltd. (CTAL), the financial services division of the $4 billion Canadian Tire Corp., Ltd., serves 4 million Canadian Tire credit card holders. In 1998 it became the primary call center of the company. It expects to increase sales and enhance customer retention systematically through a new effort to develop an integrated call center. It intends to eliminate annoying and time-consuming call transfers, ensuring that customers are treated on an individual basis. "The call center is a strategic asset," says Mary Turner, vice president of customer services at CTAL. "This is our main point of contract with the customer. We have to maximize it."

Canadian Tire operates 10 call centers, each dealing with a different subject area (general information and retail, wholesale, service, etc.), or with a geographical zone. The demands are heavy. CTAL's 10 call centers operate 24 hours a day, 7 days a week, and respond to more than 16 million calls each year. Call center representatives are expected to provide personalized service while handling a diverse set of customer needs—responding to more than 200 types of customer requests. CTAL's new system ensures that any representative can resolve any customer need without handing it off to another department or departments.

CTAL has several key business objectives:

▶ Greater customer loyalty to Canadian Tire as a result of enhanced service.
▶ Personalized customer attention and reduced transfers.
▶ Rapid introduction of new products or changes to existing business services.
▶ Reduced training requirements for customer-service representatives.
▶ Integration of all customer touch points via a single system capable of handling Web, e-mail, and call center interactions.

"When we began the project, we took a look at our operations and saw too many independent call centers," Turner continues. "It seemed that every time we introduced a new product or service, we set up a new call center. We decided to streamline operations to make it possible for customers to reach the right representative whenever they called."

The call center integrates telephone, fax, e-mail, and the Web. One of its major capabilities is to build customer profiles and act on them when needed, providing one-to-one relationships. The call center can be viewed as an *interaction center* that immediately recognizes the individual customer and integrates data that reflects on the relationship. The Web-based call center is expected to pay for itself quickly.

**For further exploration:** Why did the company have several call centers? What are the advantages of the Web-based system, and what are the capabilities of the Web-based system? ▲

SOURCE: Peppers et al. (1999).

## 6.6 INFRASTRUCTURE: EDI, PAYMENTS, AND SUPPLY CHAIN MANAGEMENT

For electronic commerce applications to succeed, it is necessary to provide them with all the needed support as shown in Figure 6.1. This is not a simple task because of the large number of issues to be considered and the large number of companies and government agencies involved. Here we present only the major issues.

First, an infrastructure must be in place. Electronic commerce transactions must be executable worldwide without any delays or mistakes. Some transactions involve several trading partners, requiring a more complex infrastructure. An important part of this infrastructure is EDI and EDI/Internet. Second, electronic payment issues must be addressed. Payments need to be secure, convenient, fast, and inexpensive to process. Third, support services along the supply chain must be in place. These topics are the subject of this section.

> EDI allowed one company to offer direct deposit paychecks. Not only is this better for employees, but the time and expense to stuff and distribute paycheck envelopes has significantly decreased.
>
> — *Mike Rewald*

### ELECTRONIC COMMERCE INFRASTRUCTURE

Electronic commerce infrastructure requires a variety of hardware and software. The major components are summarized in Table 6.4.

### ELECTRONIC DATA INTERCHANGE (EDI)

**EDI** can be defined as the electronic movement of specially formatted standard business documents, such as orders, bills, and confirmations sent between busi-

---

**Table 6.4** Electronic Commerce Infrastructure

| Component | Description and Issues |
|---|---|
| Networks | A shift from VANS to the Internet. Increased use of VPNs to enhance security and capabilities over the Internet. |
| Web servers | Specialized servers are usually superior to dual-purpose servers. They are available for rent. Interface to legacy systems may be a problem. |
| Web server support and software | (1) Web site activity tracking. (2) Database connectivity. (3) Software for creating electronic forms. (4) Software for creating chat rooms and discussion groups. |
| Electronic catalogs | Product description, multimedia use, customized catalogs, inclusion in Web site design and construction, templates for construction. |
| Web page design and construction software | Web programming languages (HTML, JAVA, VRML, XML). |
| Transactional software | (1) Search engines for finding and comparing products. (2) Negotiating software. (3) Encryption and payment capabilities. (4) Ordering (front office), inventory, and back office software. |
| Others | Firewalls, e-mail, HTTP (transfer protocols), smart cards. |
| Internet access components | TCP/IP package, Web browsers, remote access server, client dial-in software, Internet connection device, leased-line connection, connection to leased line, Internet kiosks. |

ness partners (Figure. 6.8). Like e-mail, EDI allows sending and receiving of messages between computers connected by a communication link. However, EDI has the following special characteristics:

▶ *Business transactions messages.* EDI is used primarily to electronically transfer *repetitive* business transactions. These include purchase orders, invoices, approvals of credit, shipping notices, confirmations, and so on.

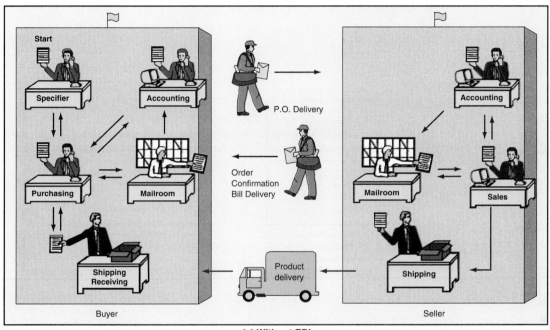

**(a) Without EDI**

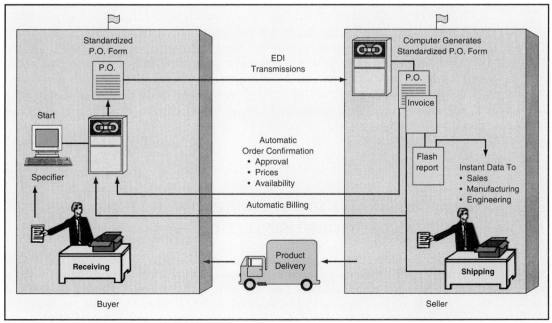

**(b) With EDI**

**FIGURE 6.8** Order-delivery cycle with and without EDI. (*Source*: From Stalling [1990].)

▶ ***Data formatting standards.*** Since EDI messages are repetitive, it is sensible to use some formatting (coding) standards. Standards can shorten the length of the messages and eliminate data entry errors, since data entry occurs only once. In the United States and Canada, data are formatted according to the ANSI X.12 standard. An international standard developed by the United Nations is called EDIFACT.

▶ ***EDI translators.*** An *EDI translator* does the conversion of data into standard format. An example of such formatting for a shipping company is shown in Figure 6.9.

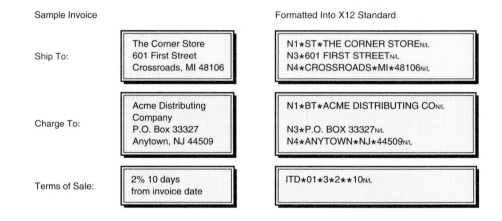

**FIGURE 6.9** Translating data to an EDI code.
(*Source*: From Guglielmo [1992], p. 242.)

▶ ***Private lines versus the Internet.*** In the past, EDI ran on expensive value-added networks. These networks provided sufficient security and capacity; however, their implementation was confined to large trading partners. There were also problems of compatibility. As a result, large companies doing business with thousands of other companies were unable to place most of them on the EDI. For example, according to Varney and McCarthy (1996), Boeing Commercial Airplane Group, which sells aircraft parts, was using EDI with only 30 out of 500 customers. This situation is changing rapidly with the emergence of Internet-based EDI, as shown in the case of Hewlett-Packard.

*IT At Work*   **HP CONDUCTING MILLIONS OF TRANSACTIONS USING EDI**

***I*NTEGRATING IT**

...for Finance, Accounting, and Marketing

Hewlett-Packard (HP), the giant computer manufacturer, performs over a million transactions electronically each month using EDI. Most of them are now Internet-based. HP uses Net-based EDI to do business with small companies that otherwise would never be able to afford the cost and complexities of the traditional EDI. The Net-based EDI is not as integrated as the traditional one, but it provides alternatives where EDI had not been appropriate before. Special tools can be placed on the system to make forms-based entry look like EDI. The user does not see EDI at all, but the application does.

Net-based EDI not only supplements the traditional Web but can replace VAN-based EDI for many applications, especially when Internet security and capacity is improved.

**For Further Exploration.** Is the traditional EDI doomed? Read Tucker's (1997) paper and Varney and McCarthy (1996). ▲

Note that Internet-based EDI does not have the same capabilities as VAN-based EDI. Therefore, at least in the short run, it is viewed as supplementary to the VAN, permitting more companies to use EDI. Also, Internet EDI may be cheaper, but it is still an EDI and requires coordination and integration with the company's back-end processing systems.

**HOW DOES EDI WORK?** Box 6.4 illustrates how EDI works. Information flows from the hospital's information systems into an EDI station which includes a PC and an EDI translator. From there, the information moves, using an modem if necessary, to a VAN. The VAN transfers the formatted information to a vendor(s) where an EDI translator converts it to a desired format.

## A Closer Look   BOX 6.4

### HOW EDI CUTS HOSPITAL COSTS

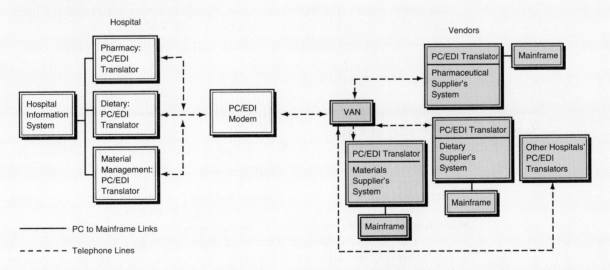

An average hospital generates about 15,000 purchase orders each year at a processing cost of about $70 per order. The Health Industry Business Communication Council estimates that EDI can reduce this cost to $4 per order—potential yearly savings of $840,000 per hospital. The required investment ranges between $8,000 and $15,000, which includes purchase of a PC with an EDI translator, a modem, and a link to the mainframe-based information system. The hospital can have two or three ordering points. These are connected to a value-added network (VAN), which connects the hospital to its suppliers. (See above figure.)

The system also can connect to other hospitals, or to centralized joint purchasing agencies.

SOURCE: Based on Nussbaum (1992).

**ADVANTAGES AND DISADVANTAGES OF EDI.** The use of EDI is rapidly increasing. Many companies use it to foster relationships with their suppliers and/or customers. The major advantages of EDI are summarized in Table 6.5.

Electronic data interchange has its limitations and costs. A company may have to use several EDI translators; the VAN services may be expensive; there could be security problems on the networks; and there could be communication problems with some of the business partners. Internet-based EDI solves these problems, except for security, which is a serious shortcoming. Moreover, network capacity may be insufficient.

*Note:* An Internet-based EDI functions very similar to an extranet, a topic which will be discussed later.

**INTERNET-BASED EDI.** There are several reasons for firms to create EDI ability over the Internet:

▶ The Internet is a publicly accessible network with few geographical constraints.

▶ The Internet global internetwork connections offer the potential to reach the widest possible number of trading partners of any viable alternative currently available.

▶ The Internet's largest attribute—large-scale connectivity (without the need to have any special networking architecture)—is a seedbed for growth of a vast range of business applications.

▶ Using the Internet can cut EDI communication costs by over 50 percent.

▶ Using the Internet to exchange EDI transactions is consistent with the growing interest of businesses in delivering an ever-increasing variety of products and services electronically, particularly through the Web.

▶ Internet-based EDI can complement or replace current EDI applications.

▶ Internet tools such as browsers and search engines are very user-friendly, and most users today know how to use them.

*Table 6.5* **The Benefits of EDI**

- EDI enables companies to send and receive large amounts of routine transaction information quickly around the globe.
- There are very few errors in the transformed data as a result of computer-to-computer data transfer.
- Information can flow among several trading partners consistently and freely.
- Companies can access partners' databases to retrieve and store standard transactions.
- EDI fosters true (and strategic) partnership relationships since it involves a commitment to a long-term investment and the refinement of the system over time.
- EDI creates a complete paperless TPS environment, saving money and increasing efficiency.
- Payment collection can be shortened by several weeks.
- Data may be entered offline, in a batch mode, without tying up ports to the mainframe.
- When an EDI documents is received the data may be used immediately.
- Sales information is delivered to manufacturers, shippers, and warehouses almost in real time.
- EDI can save a considerable amount of money.

## ELECTRONIC PAYMENT SYSTEMS

Payments are an integral part of doing business, regardless of how the business is done. In most cases, traditional payment systems are not effective for EC.

**LIMITATIONS OF TRADITIONAL PAYMENT INSTRUMENTS.** Nonelectronic payments methods such as paying cash, writing a check, sending a money order, or paying by giving your credit card number over the telephone have many limitations in EC. First, cash cannot be used since there is no face-to-face contact. Second, if a payment is sent by mail, it takes time for it to be received. Even if a credit card number is provided by phone or fax, it takes time to process it. It is inconvenient and less secure for the online buyer to stop surfing and use the telephone or "snail mail" to send a payment, especially to another country, than to finish the transaction on a computer. Also, not everyone accepts credit cards or checks. Finally, some buyers do not have credit cars or checking accounts.

Another issue is that many electronic commerce transactions are valued at only a few dollars or cents. The cost of processing such **micropayments** needs to be very low; you would not want to pay $5.00 to process a purchase valued at only a few dollars, and many payments are even less than $1.00. The cost of paying micropayments offline is too high.

For all the above reasons it is clear that a better way is needed to pay in cyberspace. This way is referred to as *electronic payment systems*. As in a marketplace, a diversity of payment methods in cyberspace allows customers to choose how they wish to pay. The following instruments are acceptable means of electronic payment: electronic cash, electronic credit cards, electronic checks, smart cards, and electronic funds transfer (EFT). Before we describe the various methods, we will describe the *security requirements* necessary in EC.

**SECURITY REQUIREMENTS.** There are several security requirements for conducting electronic commerce:

1. *Authentification.* The buyer, seller, intermediary, and paying institutions need to be assured of the *identity* of the party with whom they are dealing.
2. *Privacy.* Many customers want their identity to be secured. They want to make sure others do not know what they buy. Some prefer complete anonymity like they have when they pay with cash.
3. *Integrity.* It is necessary to assure that data and information transmitted in EC, such as orders, reply to queries, payment authorization, and so on, are not accidentally or maliciously altered or destroyed during transmission.
4. *Non-repudiation.* Merchants need protection against the customer's unjustifiable denial of placing an order. On the other hand, customers need protection against the merchants' unjustifiable denial of payments made.
5. *Safety.* Customers want to be sure that it is safe to provide a credit card number on the Internet. They also want protection against fraud by sellers.

Several methods and mechanisms can be used to fulfill the above requirements. One of the primary mechanisms is encryption which is used in some of the most useful security schemes.

**ENCRYPTION. Encryption** is a process of making messages indecipherable except by *those who have an authorized decryption key.* A **key** is a code composed of very large collection of letters, symbols, and numbers. For example, the letter

"A" might be coded as: ABQ8iF + 73 Rjbj / 83 ds + 22 m × 3 SP = Qqm2z. Two basic encryption methods exist: one key and two keys (and their combination).

***Single-key (Symmetric) Encryption.*** In early encryption technologies only one key was used. The sender of the message (or payment) encrypted the information with a key. The receiver used an identical key to **decrypt** the information to a readable form. Therefore, the same code had to be in the possession of both the sender and the receiver. This created problems. For example, if a key were transmitted and intercepted illegally, the key could have been used to read all encrypted messages or to steal money. Since keys are changed frequently, the problem becomes even more difficult in cyberspace. To increase the safety of a single key, we usually encrypt it with a public/private keys system.

***Public/Private Key System.*** **Public Key encryption** uses two different keys. One key is called *public,* the other one, *private.* Several authorized people may know the public key, while only its owner knows the private key. Every person (business) has one private key and one public key. Encryption and decryption can be done with either key. However, if encryption is done with the public key, the decryption can only be done with the private key, and vice versa. There are several public key encryption algorithms; the most well known is RSA (www.rsa.com).

Here are some examples of the use of the two keys:

1. Adam (A) wants to be sure that Barbara (B) will be the only one able to read a message. A encrypts the message with B's public key. B decrypts it with her private key.

2. Adam (A) wants to assure Barbara (B) that A is the author of a message. A encrypts a signature (as a message) in his own private key. B uses A's public key to decrypt the signature. The signature is attached to the original message. This is called a **digital signature** (see Figure 6.10).

The *privacy* of the message is assured by using Barbara's public key for the encryption, and the digital signature assures the identity of the sender. We still face one problem: How do we assure Adam that the public key he uses really be-

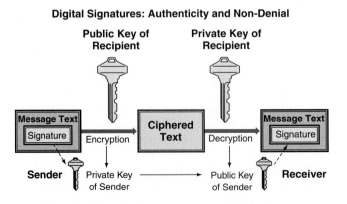

**FIGURE 6.10** Two-key encryptions with digital signature.

longs to Barbara? And how can Barbara be sure that the public key she has used to verify Adam's signature really belongs to Adam? Such assurances are provided by *certificates.*

**ELECTRONIC CERTIFICATES. Electronic certificates** are issued by a trusted third party, called a *certificate authority (CA),* in order to verify that a specific public key belongs to specific individual. In addition to a name, a certificate may verify age, gender, and other attributes of the individual to whom the public key belongs. Also, if the CA is not well known to the user of the certificate, it may be necessary to certify the CA by another, more trustworthy legal body. Thus, there could be several levels of certification. Certificates are valid until an expiration date and are signed by the CA. A major issuer of certificates is VeriSign, Inc. (www.versign.com). A higher certificate authority that guarantees certifiers (in many countries) is the Post Office.

The public/private key security system with digital signature and certification is the backbone of the various payment mechanisms that are described later. However, to assure the acceptance of payments anywhere in the world, it is necessary to have some universal protocol (standards).

**PROTOCOLS.   A protocol** is a set of rules and procedures that govern the transfer of information on the Internet. It is the software that also helps in authentication, security, and privacy. Two major protocols are used in EC: SSL and SET.

*Secure Socket Layer (SSL).*   The secure socket layer (SSL) is the most common protocol used in EC. Its main capability is to encrypt messages. For example, any time you order merchandise from Wal-Mart, Amazon.com, or most other large vendors on the Internet, your order is encrypted automatically by the SSL in your computer browser *before* being sent over the Internet. This includes the encryption of credit card numbers. Credit cards are the major payment method in B2C.

*Secure Electronic Transaction Protocol (SET).*   A new, major, proposed standard for credit card processing is secure electronic transaction protocol (SET). It is designed to allow you to shop anywhere as conveniently and securely as possible by incorporating digital signatures, certification, encryption, and an agreed-upon payment gateway (to banks). In 1999, SET was still under development; only very few large companies were utilizing it. Due to its complexity, SET was temporarily abandoned by VISA in June 1999. The manner in which SET is designed to work is shown in Fig. 6.11.

Now that we have discussed the supporting instruments, we can look at the various payment mechanisms.

**ELECTRONIC CREDIT CARDS.**   The most common method of paying in B2C e-commerce is by means of **electronic credit cards,** which can be used in any of the following methods:

1. *Payments using unencrypted credit card.* In this method the buyer e-mails her or his credit card number to the seller on the Internet. The risk here is that hackers can read the credit card number. Sender authentication is also difficult; however, the method is simple and inexpensive and used with some small vendors as an option.

2. *Encrypted payments.* Using SSL encryption, credit card details are encrypted for security. This is done at the buyer's browser, automatically

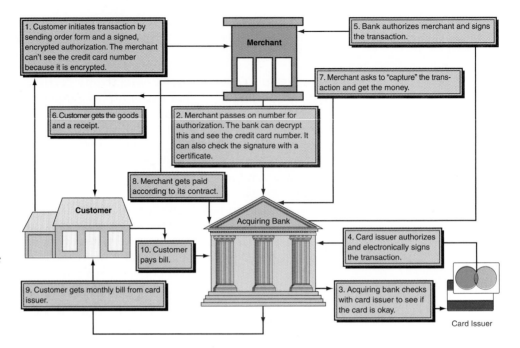

**FIGURE 6.11** How secure Electronic Transactions protocol (SET) works. (*Source:* Modified from P. Wayner, "Who Goes There," *Byte*, June, 1997.)

when an order is placed, and it is used by most major vendors (e.g., Amazon.com). However, this way the vendor knows who you are.

3. *High level of security and privacy.* Using the SET protocol or a third-party intermediation, you will get a very high level of security, integrity and privacy.

The encrypted payment process involves the buyer's and seller's banks and an intermediary. One of the most secure processes works as follows:

**Step 1.** After the consumer enters the payment and shipping information at his or her browser, the information travels to the merchant's Web site. The merchant site reviews (electronically) the purchase request and returns a summary of the order for an approval.

**Step 2.** The consumer verifies the information and then clicks on the "pay" button to send the information back to the merchant.

**Step 3.** The merchant receives the information, retrieves the order information (but cannot see the credit card number), and forwards the encrypted payment information digitally signed to an intermediary server.

**Step 4.** The intermediary server receives the information, moves the transaction behind its firewall and off the Internet, decodes the information, reformats the transaction, and forwards the encrypted information to the merchant's bank.

**Step 5.** The merchant's bank then forwards the consumer's request to the card's issuing bank, and the approval or denial is sent back by the bank to the intermediary.

**Step 6.** The intermediary returns the approval or denial response to the merchant. The merchant, in turn, passes the information to the consumer.

This process is very very secure, but it is slow and expensive. Using SET will be less expensive, but it requires a feature for the certificate and therefore is not in wide use as yet.

**ELECTRONIC CHECKS.  Electronic checks (e-checks)** are similar to regular checks. They are secured by public-key encryption and may be suitable for some micropayments. Here is how the experimental systems (as of 1999) work:

**Step 1.** The customer establishes a checking account with a bank.

**Step 2.** The customer contacts a seller, buys a product or a service, and e-mails an encrypted electronic check signed with a digital signature and two certificates, one for the bank, one for the buyer.

**Step 3.** The merchant deposits the check in his or her account; money is debited in the buyer's account and credited to the seller's account.

Like regular checks, e-checks carry a signature (a digital one) that can be verified. Properly signed and endorsed e-checks are exchanged between financial institutions through electronic clearinghouses. An e-check can also be used as a payment instrument in EDI applications. (For further details see www.fstc.org.)

**ELECTRONIC CASH.** Cash is the most prevalent non-Internet consumer payment instrument. Merchants prefer cash since they do not have to pay commissions to credit card companies, and they can put the money to use as soon as it is received. Also, some buyers pay with cash because they do not have checks or credit cards, or because they want to preserve their anonymity. Banks like cash because it is inexpensive to process, more secure than checks or credit cards, and if used instead of credit cards, costs the bank less. It is logical, therefore, that EC sellers, some buyers, and banks prefer **electronic cash (e-cash).**

Electronic cash appears in two forms: cash on a PC and on a smart card.

*Electronic Cash in Your PC.*  The use of this approach (still experimental in 1999) involves a six-step process:

**Step 1.** A customer opens an account with a bank, and receives special software for PCs, either by downloading it or by working with the bank's software via the Internet.

**Step 2.** The customer "buys" electronic money from the bank by using the software. His or her bank account is debited accordingly.

**Step 3.** The bank sends an electronic money note to the customer, endorsing it with a digital signature (made with the bank's private key). The customer can verify that the money is real by using the bank's public key and also checking the certificate.

**Step 4.** The money is stored on the buyer's PC and can be spent in any electronic store that accepts e-cash.

**Step 5.** The software is also used to transfer the e-cash from the buyer's computer to the seller's computer. The seller uses the bank's and customer's public keys to verify that the money belongs to the specific buyer and is indeed at hand.

**Step 6.** The seller can deposit the e-cash in a bank, crediting his or her regular or electronic account, or use the e-cash to make a purchase elsewhere.

In 1999, the major vendors experimenting with such an e-cash payment system were DigiCash, Inc., CyberCash, and Mondex. To ensure that purchasers do not overpay and that the money is real, e-cash in a PC requires considerable verification, making it uneconomical for micropayments. For these small payments of a few dollars or even cents, smart card-based systems are more appropriate.

*Electronic Payment Cards (Smart Cards) with E-cash.* Electronic payment cards have been in use for several decades. The best known are credit cards, which use magnetic strips that contain limited information, such as the card's ID number. A more advanced form of payment card is the one that you use in your library to pay for photocopies, or to pay for telephone calls. Such cards store a fixed amount of prepaid money; each time you use the card, the amount is reduced. A successful example is used by the New York Metropolitan Transportation Authority (MTA), which operates buses, trains, interstate toll bridges, and tunnels. Nearly 5 million customers use these cards on buses, subways, and road tollbooths each day. Similar cards are in use in many other cities, including Tokyo where one card is used for all types of transportations, including taxis. Some of these cards are reloadable, but most are discarded when the money is depleted.

A Smart Card.

A more enhanced card, also referred to as **smart card,** is a card that contains a microprocessor. This type of card can store a considerable amount of information (100 times more than a regular credit card). Smart cards also allow money to be stored in quantities that can be increased (reloaded) as well as decreased. These cards contain diversified information about the cardholder and can be used for several purposes, as at Takashimaya, in Japan.

*IT At Work*     SMART CARDS MOVE SHOPPERS TO THE TWENTY-FIRST CENTURY

*U*SING IT

...in Marketing

Takashimaya is a giant retailer based in Japan with stores in Asia, Europe, and the United States. The company was the first to introduce in Singapore an international loyalty smart credit card. The card, called Takashimaya VISA Smart Card, can be used as a regular VISA credit card worldwide. It also features a microchip that stores a wealth of information, such as bonus points earned by shopping at Takashimaya stores. Cardholders can redeem these bonus points for such privileges as free car parking, free delivery, lucky draws, gifts, and gift coupons. The card also stores information about the cardholder's shopping habits and target direct mail programs.

The smart card system consists of an electronic data capture terminal, a card reader, and a printer. It is integrated with the point-of-sale (POS) terminal and a hand-held scanner.

The information collected at the POS is used to create a customer information system. The card includes the customer's address, age, and shopping preferences, which are transferred via an intranet to the corporate databases. Mr. Chen Seong Leng, the MIS Manager at Takashimaya Singapore, said, "at today's competitive environment, a retailer has to find a better means of identifying shopping trends and habits." Retailers must know exactly who has bought what merchandise.

The system saves time for cashiers, who now make one entry instead of two (one at the POS, the other one for a credit payment). The Singapore store is located on Orchard Road, one of the most competitive shopping streets in the world. Since the introduction of smart cards, business has been booming as never before. The information collected is also processed by a decision-support system for pricing, designing advertisements, and other promotional decisions.

**For Further Exploration.** Newer smart cards that are issued to students in universities include additional features such as keys to the dormitory and the computer room. What is the logic of such an inclusion, and what other information can be stored on the cards? ▲

SOURCE: Based on a story in *ITAsia*, December 1993, and on communications with VISA International, Spring 1998.

**USING SMART CARDS.** Enhanced cards can combine several credit cards, debit cards, and stored electronic cash. In the future they will have the ability to transfer funds, pay bills, buy from vending machines, or pay for services such as those offered on television or PCs. Money values can be loaded at ATMs, kiosks, or at your PC. For example, VISA Cash Card now allows you to buy at participating gas stations, fast-food outlets, pay phones, discount stores, post offices, convenience stores, coffee shops, and even movie theaters. Smart cards are ideal for micropayments. Used for that purpose, smart cards become an electronic purse. An **electronic purse** is a wallet-sized smart card that stores money for making small payments in any place there is a card reader. This is not a simple task since you need to get the cooperation of banks, retailers, and government regulators (who are concerned about collecting sales taxes). Some banks are still not interested in doing business on the Internet since the banks' mainframes don't talk easily to the Internet, and replacing them with client/server systems would cost a lot of money.

Smart cards can also be used to transfer benefit payments from companies to their employees, as when retirees get their pension payments, and from governments that pay citizens different entitlements. The money is transferred electronically to a smart card at an ATM, kiosk, or PC.

**ELECTRONIC PAYMENT FROM CELLULAR PHONES.** This new technology that is just starting to appear will enable people to make payment from their cell phone. In Japan you can even pay vending machines this way, and in Finland you can pay for gasoline in some areas.

**ELECTRONIC FUNDS TRANSFER. Electronic funds transfer (EFT)** is the electronic transfer of money to and from financial institutions using telecommunication networks. Electronic funds transfer is now widely used—with funds, debits and credits, and charges and payments electronically routed via clearinghouses among banks and between banks and customers. Examples of EFT include:

- ▶ Interbank transactions around the globe
- ▶ Paying university tuition using an ATM
- ▶ Direct deposit of salaries in employees' accounts
- ▶ Paying mortgages, utility bills, or car loans through monthly bank account deductions

EFT is fast; it reduces delays associated with sending hard-copy documents, and it eliminates returned checks. It has become the only practical way to handle the large volume of financial transactions generated daily in the banking industry. EFT-based ATMs are increasingly available in shopping centers and business areas, allowing individuals to make deposits, withdrawals, and money transfers 24 hours a day.

## SUPPLY CHAIN MANAGEMENT AND ELECTRONIC COMMERCE

In order to understand the scope of supply chain management (SCM) in Chapter 4 we looked at a typical food processing company, Kellogg's. We return to this example now.

**ELECTRONIC COMMERCE AND ENTERPRISE RESOURCES PLANNING.** Let us assume that Kellogg's decides to go online to sell its products. To do so the company needs to create electronic catalogs, marketing, and advertisement systems, an ordering system for customers, and a payment system. These activities are called **front-end activities,** and they relate mainly to customers and perhaps to intermediaries. Several vendors provide the software needed for the above (e.g., Yahoo, Netscape, IBM, and Excite).

Once orders are received they enter the company's *internal supply chain.* First the customer's credit line is checked. If the order is approved financially, the inventory is checked for product availability. If the order can be supplied from existing stock, then a shipment is ordered. In a B2B operation, especially on a large scale, rather than asked to pay in advance customers are billed; therefore billing is required. If the inventory is too low, an order to produce is generated. These activities are part of the **back-office activities.** They involve the purchasing of materials from suppliers as well as the use of human and other resources internally. A process for a manufacturing company selling in B2B e-commerce is shown in Figure 6.12. Notice the involvement of all the corporate functional areas. Such an involvement can be made effective and efficient by using enterprise resources planning (ERP) which is facilitated by integrated software such as SAP R/3.

To properly execute the EC process with the support of ERP software it may be necessary to change some, or all, of the business processes, as described in Chapter 4. The point is that the initiation of EC may require the organization to go through a radical structural and procedural change, which may be both painful and expensive. However, by using intrabusiness EC over the intranet and cooperation with business partners over extranets, EC can increase the effectiveness of supply chain management of companies that operate in the conventional physical world.

**INTEGRATION OF EC WITH BACK-END INFORMATION SYSTEMS.** *Back-end information systems* support back-office activities and the preparation of data for business analysis. Back-end information systems may be implemented using intranet-based workflow, database management systems (DBMS), application packages, and ERP. In a supplier-oriented business model, the integration of EC with suppliers' back-end information systems is relatively easy because the suppliers keep the platform for both EC and their back-end systems in their servers.

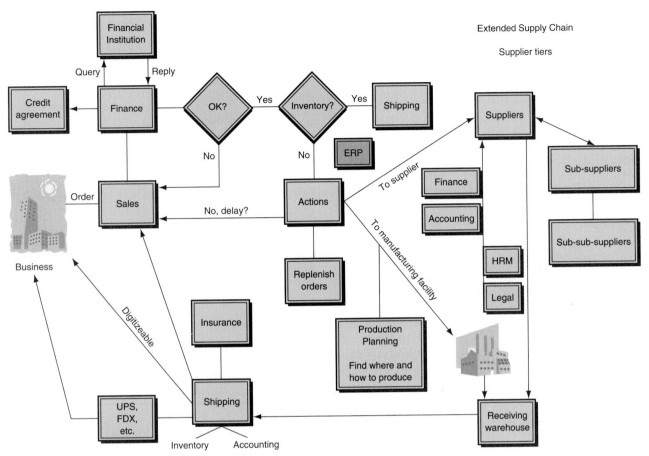

**FIGURE 6.12** B2B Logistics System

However, it is not easy for the buyers to trace their transactions that are scattered in various suppliers' servers. By the same token, in a buyer-oriented business model, business buyers, but not suppliers, can integrate EC with their back-end information systems easily. In the intermediary-oriented business model, neither buyers nor sellers can organize their transactions easily. This difficulty is a challenge to the participating buyers and sellers in B2B e-commerce but is a good opportunity for the intermediary.

## ▶ 6.7   LEGAL AND ETHICAL ISSUES IN ELECTRONIC COMMERCE

Several legal and ethical issues are associated with the implementation of EC. Representative issues are discussed in this section.

### MARKET PRACTICES AND CONSUMER AND SELLER PROTECTION

When buyers and sellers cannot see each other (they may even be in different countries), there is a chance for dishonest people to commit fraud and other crimes over the Internet. During the first few years of EC, we witnessed many of these, ranging from the creation of a virtual bank that disappeared together with the investors' deposits, to manipulating stocks on the Internet.

# *A Closer Look*   BOX 6.5

## HOW FRAUD IS COMMITTED ON THE INTERNET

David Lee, a 41-year-old Hong Kong resident, replied to an advertisement in a respected business magazine that offered him free investment advice. When he replied, he received impressive brochures and a telephone sales speech. Then he was directed to the Web site of Equity Mutual Trust (Equity) where he was able to track the impressive daily performance of a fund that listed offices in London, Switzerland, and Belize. From that Web site he was linked to sister funds and business partners. He monitored what he believed were independent Web sites that provided high ratings on the funds. Finally, he was directed to read about Equity and its funds in the respected *International Herald Tribune*'s Internet edition items which appeared as news but were actually advertisements. Convinced that he would receive good short-term gains, he mailed US$16,000, instructing Equity to invest in the Grand Financial Fund. Soon he grew suspicious when letters from Equity came from different countries, telephone calls and e-mails were not an-

swered on time, and the daily Internet listings dried up.

When David wanted to sell, he was advised to increase his investment and shift to a Canadian company, Mit-Tec, allegedly a Y2K bug troubleshooter. The Web site he was directed to looked fantastic. But David was careful. He contacted the financial authorities in the Turks and Caicos Islands—where Equity was based at that time—and was referred to the British police.

Soon he learned that chances were slim that he would ever see his money again. Furthermore, he learned that several thousand victims paid billions of dollars to Equity. Most of the victims live in Hong Kong, Singapore, and other Asian countries. Several said that the most convincing information came from the Web sites, including the "independent" Web site that rated Equity and its funds.

SOURCE: Based on a story in the *South China Morning Post* (Hong Kong), May 21, 1999.

**FRAUD ON THE INTERNET.** Internet fraud and its sophistication have grown as much and even faster than the Internet itself, as can be seen in the following examples.

*Internet Stocks Fraud.* In fall 1998, the SEC brought charges against 44 companies and individuals who illegally promoted stocks on computer bulletin boards, online newspapers, and investment Web sites. (See details on both settled and pending cases at www.sec.gov.) In many cases, stock promoters falsely spread positive rumors about the prospects of the companies they touted. In other cases the information provided might have been true, but the promoters did not disclose that they were paid to talk up the companies. Stock promoters specifically target small investors who are lured by the promise of fast profits. Such actions trigger frantic buying. When prices go up, the promoters sell the stocks they purchased at a low price. Consequently prices decline significantly, and the investors lose money.

*Other Financial Fraud.* Stocks are only one of the many areas in which swindlers are active. Other areas include selling bogus investments and phantom business opportunities. Financial criminals have access to far more people than ever before, due mainly to the availability of the Web and electronic mail. An example is provided in Box 6.5.

**THE FEDERAL TRADE COMMISSION CONSUMER ALERTS.** The Federal Trade Commission (FTC) provides a list of 12 scams most likely to arrive via e-mail or the Web. They are:

1. **Business opportunities.** Easy-to-start businesses that will earn you a fortune. Also illegal pyramid schemes are being offered.

2. **Bulk mail solicitors.** These offer to sell you lists of e-mail addresses. If you use them, you usually violate the terms of service of your Internet service provider.

3. **Chain letters.** You are asked to send money to some people and your name is placed on a list. This is usually illegal to do.

4. **Work-at-home schemes.** These are usually worthless and cost you money.

5. **Health and diet schemes.** You usually get worthless products that do not work.

6. **Effortless income.** Do not believe these "easy to make money" opportunities. They will take your money.

7. **Free goods.** You pay to join a club and recruit others. It is usually an illegal pyramid scheme.

8. **Investment opportunities.** Do not believe in "investment with no risk" and "high return." There are many scams to watch for.

9. **Cable descrambler kits.** These kits usually do not work, and it is illegal to use them.

10. **Guaranteed loans or credit, on easy terms.** You usually pay application fees and then are turned down.

11. **Credit repair.** Again, you pay a service fee, but get no repair.

12. **Vacation prize promotions.** These electronic certificates are usually scams. You will be asked to upgrade and it will be very expensive.

The FTC shows examples in each of these categories at its Web site (www.ftc.gov/bcp/conline/pubs/alerts/doznalrt.htm, July 1998). Lately, the FTC has been trying to deal with fraud in auctions. About 65 percent of all complaints to the FTC are auction-related.

There are several ways buyers can be protected against EC fraud. The major methods are described below.

**BUYER PROTECTION.** Buyer protection is critical to the success of any commerce, and especially of electronic commerce, where buyers do not see the sellers. Tips for safe electronic shopping include:

1. Look for reliable brand names at sites like Wal-Mart Online, Disney Online, and Amazon.com. (Make sure that the sites are authentic; if you are linked to a site, it may not be what its name shows!)

2. Search any unfamiliar selling site for the company's address and phone and fax numbers. Call up and quiz the employees about the sellers.

3. Check the seller with the local Chamber of Commerce and/or Better Business Bureau (www.bbbonline.org), or look for seals of approval such as TRUSTe.

4. Investigate how secure the seller's site is and how well it is organized.

5. Examine the money-back guarantees, warranties, and service agreements.

6. Compare prices to those in regular stores; too-low prices are too good to be true.

7. Ask friends what they know. Find testimonials and endorsements.

8. Find out what you can do in case of a dispute.

9. Consult the National Fraud Information Center (http://nfic.inter.net/nfic).

10. Check www.consumerworld.org for other useful resources.

11. Be aware that you have shopper's rights (see Box 6.6).

## A Closer Look BOX 6.6

### INTERNET SHOPPING RIGHTS

Although the Web offers new ways to shop, you can still benefit from legal protections developed for shopping by telephone, mail, and other means. The two most important consumer protection laws for online shopping come from the U.S. government: the Mail/Telephone Order Rule and the Fair Credit Billing Act.

**MAIL/TELEPHONE (E-MAIL) ORDER RULE.** Sellers must deliver your goods within certain time periods or they can face penalties from the Federal Trade Commission. If the seller advertises or tells you a delivery date before your purchase, it must deliver by that date.

If the seller does not give you a delivery date, it must deliver within 30 days after receiving your order. If the seller cannot deliver by the required date, it must give you notice before that date, so you can choose either to cancel your order and receive a full and prompt refund or to permit the seller to deliver at a later date.

If delivery problems continue, look at the resources below for additional rights and how to make a complaint.

**FAIR CREDIT BILLING ACT.** Using your credit card on the Web is like using it at a store. The Fair Credit Billing Act gives you certain rights if there is an error or dispute relating to your bill. If there is an error on your statement, you can withhold payment for the disputed amount while you notify the creditor.

You can withhold payment when your bill contains a charge for the wrong-amount, for items you returned or did not accept, or for items not delivered as agreed. Notify the creditor of the error promptly, no later than 60 days after the first bill on which the error appeared. Put it in writing. Describe the error clearly and include your name, address, and credit card number. After you send

the notice, the creditor must give written acknowledgment within 30 days and must resolve the error within 90 days.

**NEW PAYMENT METHODS: A WORD OF CAUTION.** While consumer protections for traditional credit cards are well established, the protections for those who use new forms of "digital payment," "digital case," and the like are unclear. Some resemble credit cards; others resemble ATM cards; still others are brand-new forms of payment. Look at the resources below for the latest information on new regulations that may be developed to protect consumers using these payment methods.

### RESOURCES FOR FURTHER INFORMATION

▶ **Federal Trade Commission:**
   http://www.ftc.gov; Tel: (202) 326-2222
   If you have a complaint, write:
▶ **Division of Enforcement:**
   Federal Trade Commission, Washington, DC 30580
▶ **National Fraud Information Center:**
   http://nfic.inter.net/nfic
▶ **Consumer Information Center:**
   http://www.pueblo.gsa.gov; Tel: (729) 948-4000
▶ **Direct Market Association:** Tel: (202) 347-1222
▶ Remember to look up your local or state consumer protection agency for additional protections.

**DISCLAIMER:** This is general information on certain consumer rights. It is not legal advice on how any particular individual should proceed. If you want legal advice, consult an attorney.

SOURCE: Based on Rose, L., "Internet Shopping Rights," *Internet Shopper,* Spring 1997, p. 104.

**SELLER PROTECTION.** Sellers, too, need safeguards. They must be protected against:

▶ Consumers who refuse to pay, or pay with bad checks.

▶ Use of sellers' names by others.

▶ Buyers' claims that the merchandise did not arrive

▶ Use of sellers' unique words and phrases, names, slogans, and Web address (trademark protection).

▶ Customers downloading copyrighted software and/or knowledge and selling it to others.

## OTHER LEGAL ISSUES SPECIFIC TO E-COMMERCE

Many legal issues relate to e-commerce. We discuss the most important ones here.

**DOMAIN NAME.** Internet addresses are known as **domain names.** Domain names appear in levels. A top-level name is www.wiley.com, or www.stanford.edu. A second level name will be www.wiley.com/turban2e or www.ibm.com.hk (for IBM in Hong Kong). Top-level domain names are assigned by central non-profit organizations that check for conflicts and possible infringement of trademarks. Problems arise when several companies that have similar names compete over a domain name that is not a registered trademark. Several cases are already in court. The problem of domain names was alleviated somewhat in 1999 after several upper level names were added to "com" (such as "firm" and "web").

**TAXES AND OTHER FEES.** Federal, state, and local authorities are scrambling to figure out how to get a piece of revenue created electronically. The problem is particularly complex for interstate and international trades. For example, some claim that even the state where a server is located deserves some tax. Others say that the state where the seller is located deserves the entire tax. In addition to sales tax, there is a question about where to pay business license tax, income tax, franchise fees, gross-receipts tax, excise tax, privilege tax, and utility tax. Furthermore, how should tax collection be controlled? Legislative efforts are opposed by the Internet Freedom Fighters. At the moment there is a ban on taxing business done on the Internet (sales tax) in the United States and many other countries, which will remain valid until fall 2001.

**COPYRIGHT.** The U.S. legal system provides creators of *intellectual property* with protection of that property through copyrights. Nevertheless, protecting software and other intangible creations is difficult over the Web. Copyright issues and protection of intellectual property are discussed in Chapter 7.

**OTHER ISSUES.** Several other legal issues are a challenge to the existing system:

▶ What are the rules of *electronic contracting,* and whose *jurisdiction* prevails when buyers, brokers, and sellers are in different states and/or countries?

▶ When are electronic documents admissible evidence in courts of law? What evidence does one have if they are not?

▶ Time and place can carry different dates for buyers and sellers when they are across the ocean. For example, an electronic document signed in Japan on January 5 may have the date January 4 in Los Angeles; which date is legal?

▶ The use of multiple networks and trading partners makes the documentation of responsibility difficult. How is such a problem overcome?

▶ Liability for errors, malfunction of software, or theft and fraudulent use of data may be difficult to prove. How is such liability determined?

▶ What is considered misrepresentation? Where should one take legal action against misrepresentation?

▶ Much of the law hinges on the physical location of files and data. With distributed databases and replication of databases, it is difficult to say exactly where data are stored at a given time. How is electronic storage related to existing legalities?

> ► Online corporate reports are difficult to audit since they can be changed frequently and auditors may not have sufficient time to perform with due diligence. There are no established auditing standards. How should such auditing be conducted and what legal value does it have?

> ► What *encryption* software can be exported from the United States?

## ETHICAL ISSUES

Many of the ethical and global issues related to IT apply also to EC. Some particular issues are:

1. *Privacy.* Most electronic payment systems know who the buyers are; therefore, it may be necessary to protect the buyers' identities. Other privacy issues may involve tracking of Internet user activities by intelligent agents and cookies, and in-house monitoring of Web activities. Privacy issues are related to both customers and employees.

2. *The human element.* A possible difficulty in implementing EC relates to human nature. The technology is new to many IS directors and employees and so may require new sets of skills. Another human factor is related to the nature of sales. Salespeople who work on commission are accustomed to being in control of the flow of certain information, and the implementation of an EC can lead to personnel dissatisfaction and loss of salespeople's income as customers bypass the salesperson and revenues become more widely distributed within the company.

3. *Web tracking.* By using sophisticated software it is possible to track individual movements on the Internet. Programs such as cookies raise a batch of privacy concerns. The programs can be stored on your PC, organized by Web site, and then accessed every time you go back to that site. Programs such as Cookie Cutter are designed to allow users to have some control over cookies. (For more information, see www.commerceNet.com.)

4. *Disintermediation.* The use of EC may result in the elimination of a company's employees as well as brokers and agents (disintermediation). How these people, especially employees, are treated may raise ethical issues, such as how to handle the displacement.

Chapter 7 further discusses ethical issues as they relate to IT in general.

## THE FUTURE OF ELECTRONIC COMMERCE

Forrester Research Institute predicts that online B2C shopping will be a $15 billion business in the year 2000, up from $518 million in 1996 (www.forrester.com). In 1995, $10 billion worth of B2B transactions were executed in the United States. This amount grew to more than $100 billion in 1999. Predictions on the total size of commerce vary. For 2002, the total B2C and B2B are estimated to be in the range of $500 to $4,000 billion (4 trillion). Electronic commerce is growing at an average rate of 10 percent per month. Some EC applications grew by 25 percent per month in the late 1990s—an astounding phenomenon!

# ► MANAGERIAL ISSUES

The electronic commerce field is growing and changing rapidly, resulting in many managerial issues to consider; such as:

1. *Managing resistance to change.* Electronic commerce can result in a fundamental and radical change in the manner in which business is done. Therefore, resistance to change from employees, vendors, and customers may develop. Education, training, and publicity over an extended time period are some possible solutions to the problem.

2. *Integration of electronic commerce into the business environment.* Electronic commerce needs to be integrated with the rest of the business. Some of the integration issues involve planning, competition for corporate resources with other corporate projects, and interfacing EC with databases, existing IT applications, and infrastructure.

3. *Lack of qualified personnel and outsourcing.* Very few people have expertise in electronic commerce. There are many implementation issues that require expertise, such as when to offer special promotions on the Internet, and what kind of customer incentives are appropriate under what circumstances. For this reason, it may be worthwhile to outsource some electronic commerce activities. As usual, outsourcing decisions are not simple.

4. *Alliances.* It is not a bad idea to join an alliance or consortium of companies to explore electronic commerce and its implementation before making implementation decisions. The problem is which alliance to join, or what kind of alliance to form and with whom.

5. *Implementation plan.* Because of the complexity and multifaceted nature of EC, it makes sense to prepare an implementation plan. Such a plan should include goals, budgets, timetables, and contingency plans and should address the many legal, financial, technological, organizational, and ethical issues that can surface during implementation.

6. *Responding to e-mail.* Some companies are flooded by e-mail queries, requests, or complaints. The problem is that it may be expensive to answer them quickly. Slow response may be damaging to the company. Many companies develop an optimal response time policy (e.g., within 24 or 48 hours).

7. *What is the company's strategy toward electronic commerce?* Generally speaking there are three major options:

   ▶ **To Lead:** Conduct large-scale innovative electronic commerce activities.

   ▶ **To Watch:** Do nothing, but carefully watch what is going on in the field in order to determine when electronic commerce is mature enough to enter it.

   ▶ **To Experiment:** Start some electronic commerce experimental projects (learn by doing).

   Each of these has its advantages and risks (see Exercise 2).

8. *Privacy.* Most electronic payment systems know who the buyers are; therefore, it may be necessary to protect their identity. Other privacy issues may involve tracking of Internet user activities by intelligent agents and cookies and in-house monitoring of Web activities. Privacy issues are related to both customers and employees.

9. *Justifying electronic commerce by conducting a cost-benefit analysis is very difficult.* Many intangible benefits and lack of experience may make costs and benefits estimates grossly inaccurate. Nevertheless, a feasibility analysis and estimates of costs and benefits must be done. For example, a proposal for assessing EDI investment is presented by Hoogewelgen and Wagenaar (1996).

10. *The human element.* A possible difficulty in implementing EC relates to human nature. The technology is new to many IS directors and employees

and so may require new sets of skills. Another human factor relates to the nature of sales. Salespeople who work on commission are accustomed to being in control of the flow of certain information, and the implementation of an EC can lead to personnel dissatisfaction as customers bypass the salesperson and revenues become more widely distributed within the company.

11. *The impacts.* The impacts of electronic commerce on organizational structure, people, marketing procedures, and profitability may be dramatic. Therefore, establishing a committee or organizational unit to develop strategy and to manage electronic commerce is necessary.

## KEY TERMS

Back-office activities *268*

Business-to-business EC (B2B) *241*

Business-to-consumer EC (B2C) *217*

Cookie *220*

Cyberbanking (electronic banking) *231*

Cybermall (electronic mall) *220*

Decryption *262*

Digital signature *262*

Disintermediation *230*

Domain names *273*

E-business *211*

Electronic banking *231*

Electronic bartering *240*

Electronic cash (e-cash) *265*

Electronic certificates *263*

Electronic checks (e-checks) *265*

Electronic commerce (EC) *211*

Electronic credit cards *263*

Electronic data interchange (EDI) *256*

Electronic funds transfer (EFT) *267*

Electronic mall *220*

Electronic purse *267*

Electronic retailing *219*

Electronic storefront *219*

Encryption *262*

Extranet *246*

Front-end activities *268*

Intelligent agents *227*

Internet communities *225*

Interactive marketing *218*

Interorganizational systems (IOS) *213*

Intrabusiness EC *245*

Intranet *245*

Key *261*

Keyword banner *222*

Metamalls *221*

Micropayments *261*

One-to-one marketing *218*

Online (electronic) catalogs *228*

Private key *262*

Protocol *263*

Public key *263*

Public/private key encryption *262*

Push technology *225*

Random banners *222*

Reintermediation *230*

Relationship marketing *217–218*

Smart cards *266*

Software agents *227*

## CHAPTER HIGHLIGHTS *(L–x means learning objective number x)*

▶ Electronic commerce can be conducted on the Web, by e-mail, and on other networks. (L – 1)

▶ Electronic commerce is divided into three major areas: business to consumer, business to business, and intra-business. (L–1)

▶ Electronic commerce offers many benefits to the organization, consumer, and society. (L–1)

▶ Electronic commerce limitations are technical and nontechnical. The current technical limitations are expected to lessen with time. (L–1)

▶ The major applications, which occur for both business-to-business and business-to-consumer operations, are advertisement, manufacturer-to-customer sale of products and services, electronic banking, electronic stock trading, travel, job market, auctions, and real estate. (L–2)

▶ The major pure business-to-consumer applications are retail and personal finance. (L–2)

▶ Electronic data interchange (EDI) deals with predetermined standard transactions (such as placing purchasing orders and billing) among regular trading partners. (L–4)

▶ Customer behavior is critical to electronic commerce; it can be studied by questionnaires or by automatic observation of people's movements on the Internet. (L–3)

▶ There are several ways to conduct market research on the Internet utilizing newsgroups, Web sites, FAQs, and "cookies." (L–3)

▶ Customer service occurs before purchase, while purchasing, after purchasing, and during disposal of products. (L–3)

▶ Electronic commerce (software) agents help customers find products and services, monitor events and notify customers, and negotiate on behalf of the customer. (L–3)

▶ The major electronic commerce infrastructure components are networks, Web servers, Web tools, programming languages, transactional software, and security devices. (L–4)

▶ Nonelectronic payment systems are insufficient or inferior for doing business on the Internet. Therefore, electronic payment systems are used. (L–5)

▶ Electronic payments can be made by e-cash, e-card, e-checks, and smart cards. (L–5)

▶ Execution of EC requires connection to the supply chain that can be facilitated by ERP software and by EDI communication system. (L–6)

▶ Many unresolved legal issues surround electronic commerce implementation. Protection of customers and intellectual property is a major concern, but so is the value of contracts, domain names, and how to handle legal issues in a multicountry environment. (L–7)

▶ Security is a major issue in electronic commerce. Secure transactions and payments receive most attention, but protection of privacy must also be addressed. (L–7)

▶ Implementing electronic commerce is not simple, and multiple financial, organizational, technological, and managerial issues must be addressed. (L–7)

## QUESTIONS FOR REVIEW

1. Define electronic commerce and e-business.

2. Define business-to-consumer, business-to-business commerce, and intrabusiness EC.

3. Define private and public keys.

4. Define electronic funds transfer (EFT).

5. List the organizational benefits of electronic commerce.

6. List consumers' benefits of electronic commerce.

7. List societal benefits of electronic commerce.

8. Define digital signature.

9. Define market research for EC.

10. Define one-to-one marketing.

11. Describe the four phases of the customer service life cycle.

12. List the major electronic commerce infrastructure elements.

13. Define micropayments.

14. Define disintermediation and reintermediation.

15. Describe electronic cash.

16. Define smart cards.

17. List the different Internet advertisement options.

18. Define "cookies."

19. Describe banners and their use.

20. Describe an electronic mall.

21. Define EDI and describe its capabilities.

22. Define extranet.

## QUESTIONS FOR DISCUSSION

1. Compare and contrast electronic markets and interorganizational information systems; describe the major characteristics of each.

2. Discuss the major limitations of electronic commerce. Which of them are likely to disappear? Why?

3. Describe the advantages of electronic home shopping over regular shopping.

4. Describe the benefits of electronic stock trading.

5. Why is the electronic job market so popular, especially among the high-tech professions?

6. Discuss the relationship between digital signature, certification, and the public-key system.

7. Relate the intranet to the extranet.

8. Why is EDI moving from VANs to the Internet? What are some of the limitations of such a move? In what ways can VAN and Internet EDI complement each other?

9. Identify the electronic commerce elements in the Highway 91 project.

10. If you had a chance to select between an electronic auction and a face-to-face auction, which one would you select and why?

11. Compare the following advertisement effectiveness measures: ad view, clickthrough, lead and purchase. What are the advantages and disadvantages of each?

12. Compare consumers' behavior at Peapod and Amazon.

13. Describe the benefits of a smart card.

14. Explain how electronic credit cards work. How can a third-party intervention be useful in electronic card payments?

15. What might be the impact of widely accepted electronic banking on the banking industry (try www.Ramresearch.com/crdflash/cf12_6e.html)?

16. Why might people object to the use of a "cookie" to build their profile? After all, no one knows whose profile is being constructed.

17. Discuss the major issues related to electronic payments.

18. Describe the role of intelligent agents in EC.

19. Compare and contrast EDI and e-mail.

20. The Highway 91 Express system is centered around a transponder. Can a debit smart card be used instead? What are the advantages and disadvantages of each?

21. What is interactive advertisement? What are its major benefits?

22. Why is it so difficult to measure the effectiveness of advertisements on the Internet?

23. Relate push technology to mass customization.

24. Why it is necessary to use different keys for a message and for its attached signature?

## EXERCISES

1. Examine the customer service life cycle model. Find one real-life example for each phase.

2. Compare B2B and B2C auctions. Also, find information about auction brokers (such as auctionwatch.com). Why is eBay at odds with such brokers?

3. Contact U.S. West and find any information on the company's intranet network called Global Village. You may also contact John Deere Corporation, which uses a large intranet system.

4. Contact PictureTalk (www.picturetalk.com) and find information about its products. Discuss their advantages.

5. General Electric saved $240,000 in 1996 in printing costs by using its intranet to publish a simple directory of company information (see "The New Way to Share Workgroup Information," White Paper, Netscape Communications Corporation at: http.netscape.com/comprod/at_work/white_paper/gold_white paper.html, January 1997). How is this possible? Explain.

6. You want to open a baby diaper factory in China. You consider the following alternatives.
   a. Organize a partnership between an existing small diaper manufacturer in another country and a Chinese partner that will provide the facilities in China and do the marketing and sales. You will be the organizer. Your first mission is to find on the Web a suitable diaper manufacturer. How would you go about it?
   b. Buy the necessary machines and knowledge required for such a factory. Then organize a company in China. Locate such machines on the Web. Identify sources of the required knowledge.
   c. Buy an existing factory and transfer it to China. For this option you need venture capital. How would you go about finding it? Try www.investerguide.com/VC.htm. Find all the options regarding venture capital. Communicate electronically with one of the companies to discuss your options and the chances for finding financial support.
   d. You are considering expansion from baby diapers to adult diapers, dog diapers (www.dog-diaper.com) and more. Explore and report.

7. Find information about how to conduct a new business. Go to http://catalog.com/intersoft/commerce/entrepre.html, and to www.Financehub.com.

8. Find information on the Web on:
   a. Getting an MBA degree at a virtual university
   b. Going public on the Internet with stocks
   c. Business credit verification

9. Describe how public and private keys are used in the following instances:
   a. A wants to send a secure message to many, but only authorized people.
   b. A pays B in digital cash via a digital bank's currency server. How can security be assured?
   c. A received an e-check from B. How can he or she be sure it is real?

10. Relate Clinton and Gore's (1997) paper to Figure 6.1.

## GROUP ASSIGNMENTS

1. Wells Fargo Bank is well on its way to a cyberbank. Hundreds of branch offices are being closed. In early 1998 the bank served over 230,000 cyber accounts (see www.wellsfargo.com; also read the October 21, 1996 issue of *Forbes* magazine). Research the bank's strategy and the benefits and limitations.

2. Studying consumer behavior can be done with the consumer's cooperation, such as asking the consumer to answer a questionnaire and then analyzing it. Likewise, it can be done without the consumer's knowledge (using a "cookie" or methods used by DoubleClick). Divide the class into two groups; each

will research one approach. Then the two groups prepare a comparative report.

3. Research the various measures that are available to protect customers shopping on the Internet. Prepare a list of such measures; include at least five not listed in this book. Prepare a report.

4. Surf the Internet to find articles, cases and vendors related to internet-based EDI.
   a. Join a newsgroup whose interest is EDI on the Internet. Identify the major issues of concern.

b. Find the benefits and limitations of EDI/Internet.

5. Amazon is a giant bookstore on the Internet with a list of over 10,000,000 titles; yet it does not have much book inventory.
   a. Enter the company site at www.amazon.com.
   b. Print lists of books on: Electronic commerce and EDI.
   c. Find out what professional advice on buying books you can get at the site.
   d. What other services do you get there that you normally do not get in a leading bookstore?

## INTERNET EXERCISES

Note: The URLs included here were current when the book went to press. However, they are subject to change without notice. Please consult the Turban Web site (www.Wiley.com/college/turban2e).

1. Access www.etrade.com and register for their Internet stock games. You will be bankrolled with $100,000 in a trading account every month. Try to win the game! Alternatively, try the $200,000 game available on http://pawws.secapl.com.

2. Access the Web site of Computer Associates (www.cai.com) and search for information on Kiplinger's Simple Money. Then access Microsoft's site and find information about Money. Compare the capabilities of the two. Finally, find information about Quicken. Why is Quicken's market share the largest? Access www.edify.com and find information about its Electronic Workforce and Electronic Banking System (EBS) software. Compare the capabilities.

3. Take an electronic tour of Wells Fargo bank (www.wellsfargo.com). Examine its services and fees. Assuming it is cheaper to do business there, would you open an account? Why or why not?

4. Select one of the following destinations you want to visit: Australia, Nepal, Israel, Thailand, or Finland. Access the Expedia Web site.
   a. Find the lowest airfare.
   b. Examine a few hotels.
   c. Get suggestions of what to see.
   d. Find out about local currency.
   e. Compile travel tips.

   Prepare a report.

5. Access www.realtor.com. Prepare a list of services available on this site, then prepare a list of advantages derived by the users and the advantages to realtors. Are there any disadvantages? To whom?

6. Access www.zinezone.com. Review all the capabilities of this agent. Write a report on what you find.

7. Access the site of www.hothothot.com. Do you like this site? Why or why not? Examine the ordering and payment mechanisms. Do you think the site is more appealing to a male or to a female? Why? This site cost only $5000 to develop and 10 percent of the sales go to the Web hosting company. Is this a good arrangement for a business that sells about $10,000 of goods per month online? Why?

8. Visit the following sites and prepare a research report on the current status of electronic commerce: www.intet.it/asptit/mccann.com; www.forrester.com; www.nielsenmedia.com; and www.zonaresearch.com.

9. Discuss the status of the proposed Internet Tax Freedom Act by visiting: www.house.gov/republicanpolicy.global.html.

10. Access the Web sites of DigiCash and CyberCash. Find out the latest developments of e-cash and e-credit. What are they offering to the merchants? What other services do they provide?

11. Access www.mondex.com. Discuss the Mondex card and its benefits.

12. Access the Web site of Happy Puppy. Examine the various features offered. Download a demo and play it. What do you like most about visiting this site? What do you not like? Why?

13. Access the site of Firefly (www.firefly.net), and fill in their questionnaire to learn about the services. Do you feel that giving out the information about yourself is justified by what you are getting in return?

14. Try to find a unique gift on the Internet for a friend. Several sites help you do it. Describe your experience with such a site. Try www.shopping.com.

15. Access the sites of Pizza Hut and Domino's to find what they are doing in your area with respect to take-home orders. Also check their distribution of coupons and any other strategic activities.

## Grocery Supermarket Keeps It Fresh

Perishable goods such as fruit, vegetables, meat, and milk are significant in any retail marketplace. Innovative start-up companies like Peapod (U.S.), and Greengrocer.com (Australia) have found new ways to satisfy customers.

How is a well-established major player to respond? With huge investments in bricks-and-mortar stores, Woolworths of Australia found itself dealing with just this question. The grocery market in Australia is dominated by three major players: Coles-Myers, Woolworths, and Franklins. Between them they control some 80 percent of the marketplace. Franklins, which is Hong Kong–owned, takes a low-cost minimum service approach; the others, both Australian-owned, provide a full range of products, including fresh foods and prepared meals.

Woolworths' initial approach was to set up a standard Web site offering a limited range of goods, but excluding perishable items. This was trialed in areas near major supermarkets. The company felt that it had to respond to the newly emerging approaches from entrepreneurs. If those organizations were allowed to take over a sizeable segment of the market, it could be difficult to recover it.

It was not long before management realized that this was not an attractive approach. Woolworths' staff had to walk the aisles, fill the baskets, pack the goods, and deliver them. For an organization that had optimized its supply chain in order to cut costs, here was a sudden explosion in costs. When gross margins are only 10 percent and net margins around 4 percent, it was very easy to become unprofitable.

Furthermore, Woolworths has established its place in public perceptions as "the fresh food people" with fruit and vegetables, freshly-baked bread, meat, and prepared meals being promoted heavily. If home shopping ignores these, Woolworths is avoiding its strengths.

Woolworths' Homeshop, its second-generation home shopping site (www.woolworths.com.au), is designed with freshness in mind, and all the fresh food is available for delivery. Deliveries are arranged from major regional supermarkets, rather than from every local store. There is an A$50 minimum order, 7.5 percent surcharge for home delivery, as well as an A$6 delivery charge. This helps in recovering the additional costs, but an average order around A$200 still returns little profit.

New users can register only if deliveries are possible to their postal address. On first use of the system, customers are guided to find the products that they want with suggestions from the list of best-selling items. Alternatively customers can browse for items by category or search by keyword. Items are accumulated in the "shopping trolley" (cart). The first order can form a master list for future orders, as can subsequent orders.

When customers have selected the required items, they select "checkout," where the total value is computed and the customer confirms that delivery is required. Payment is made only at time of delivery using a mobile (cellular) electronic funds transfer (EFTPOS) terminal, and either a credit card or a debit card. In this way, precise charges can be made based on weight of meat or fish, as well as allowing for out-of-stock items.

The customer has to set the delivery time and day, and will bear an additional charge if not at home to accept the delivery.

Additional services that are available include dietary advice, recipes, and recording of preferred food items. At the present, these do not link directly into the shopping trolley.

### Questions for Minicase

1. Visit the Woolworth's Homeshop site and find new activities not mentioned above.

2. Who would be the target customers for this site?

3. How easy is it to order regularly used items from this site? One-off items? Suggest some improvements to the design.

4. How does this service disrupt the previously highly-tuned supply chain?

5. Compare the advantages and disadvantages of the EFTPOS payment mechanism used with the more usual "credit card at time of order."

6. Should the newer start-ups such as greengrocer.com and Peapod be threatened by this service? How about the traditional local grocery stores, such as Dewsons Wembley (www.dewsons.com.au)?

SOURCE: Written by Prof. Ernie Jordan, Macquarie Graduate School of Management, Sydney, Australia. More details of the case may be found at the text's Web site.

# REFERENCES AND BIBLIOGRAPHY

1. Adam, N., and Y. Yesha, *Electronic Commerce: Current Research Issues and Applications*, New York: Springer, 1996.
2. Aronson, B., et al. *Advertising on the Internet*, New York: John Wiley & Sons, 1999.
3. Asokan, K., et al. "The State of the Art in Electronic Payment Systems," *Computer*, Sept. 1997.
4. Benjamin, R., and R. Wigard, "Electronic Markets and Virtual Value Chains on the Information Superhighway," *Sloan Management Review*, Winter 1995.
5. Bernard, R., *Corporate Intranet*, New York: John Wiley & Sons, 1997.
6. Blanning, R., and D. King, "Electronic Commerce — A Tutorial," presented at *Hawaii International Conference on System Sciences*, Jan. 1997.
7. Chase, R. D., et al., *Production Operations Management*, 8th ed., Richard D. Irwin, 1998.
8. Choi, S. Y., et al., *The Economics of Electronic Commerce*, Macmillan, Technical pub., 1997.
9. Clark, T. H., "Financial Times: Reengineering Logistics Using the Internet," *Proceedings, HICSS 31*, Hawaii, Jan. 1998.
10. Clark, T. H., and H. G. Lee, "Security First Network Bank: A Case Study of an Internet Pioneer," *Proceedings HICSS 31*, Hawaii, Jan. 1998.
11. Clinton, W. J., and A. Gore Jr., "A Framework for Global Electronic Commerce," http://www.iitf.nist.gov/eleccomm/ecomm.htm, July 1997.
12. Deighton, J., et al., "The Future of Interactive Marketing," *Harvard Business Review*, Nov./Dec. 1996.
13. "Electronic Commerce on the Internet," Special issues of *Communications of the ACM*, June 1996.
14. Farrell, P. B., *Investor's Guide to the Net*, New York: John Wiley & Sons, 1996.
15. Guglielmo, C., "Toy 'R' US: Special Report," *Interactive Week*, Nov. 1, 1999.
16. GVU: Graphics, Visualization & Usability Center at Georgia Institute of Technology, www.cc.gatech.edu/gvu/user surveys.
17. Hamilton, S., "E-Commerce for the 21st Century," *Computer*, May 1997.
18. Hampton, T., and S. Hampton, *Creating Commercial Web Sites*, Indianapolis: Semos.net, 1996.
19. Handfield, R, and E. Nichols, *Supply Chain Management*, Upper Saddle River, NJ: Prentice-Hall, 1999.
20. Hills, M., *Intranet Business Strategy*, New York: John Wiley & Sons, 1996.
21. Hutheeing, N., "HP's Giant ATM," *Forbes*, Feb. 9, 1998.
22. Jarvenpaa, S. L., and P. A. Todd, "Consumer Reactions to Electronic Shopping on the WWW," *Inter. Jour. of Electronic Commerce*, Winter 1996/1997.
23. Kalakota, R., and A. B. Whinston, *Frontiers of Electronic Commerce*, Reading, MA: Addison-Wesley, 1996.
24. Kalakota, R., and A. B. Whinston, *Electronic Commerce: A Manager's Guide*, Reading, MA: Addison-Wesley, 1997.
25. Kimbrough, S. O., and R. M. Lee, "Formal Aspects of Electronic Commerce: Research Issues and Challenges," *International Journal of Electronic Commerce*, Summer 1997.
26. Komenar, M., *Electronic Marketing*, New York: John Wiley & Sons, 1997.
27. Kosiur, D., *Understanding Electronic Commerce*, Microsoft Press, Redwood, WA, 1997.
28. Kotler, P., and G. Armstrong, *Principles of Marketing*, 8th ed., Upper Saddle River, NJ: Prentice-Hall, 1999.
29. Maes, P., et al., "Agents that Buy and Sell," *Communications of the ACM*, March 1999.
30. Mahan, J. S., "Electronic Commerce and the Future of Banking," *The Banker's Magazine*, Mar./Apr. 1996.
31. Martin, C., *The Digital Estate: Strategies for Competing, Surviving, and Thriving in an Internetworked World*, New York: McGraw Hill, 1997.
32. Martin, J., *Cybercorp: The New Business Revolution*, New York: Amacom, 1996.
33. McElroy, D., and E. Turban, "Using Smart Cards in Electronic Commerce," *International Journal of Information Systems*, Feb. 1998.
34. McGonagle, J., Jr., and C. Vella, *A New Archetype for Competitive Intelligence*, Greenwood Publishing Group and Quorum Books, 1997.
35. McKeown, P. G., and R. T. Watson (2nd edition), *Metamorphosis — A Guide to the WWW and Electronic Commerce*, New York: John Wiley & Sons, 1998.
36. McLaughlin, T., "Electronic Benefits Transfer: Should Banks Be Interested?" *The Banker's Magazine*, Mar./Apr. 1996.
37. Meeker, N., *The Internet Advertising Report*, New York: Morgan Stanley Corp., 1997.
38. Mowen, J. C., and M. Minor, *Consumer Behavior*, Upper Saddle River, N. J.: Prentice Hall, 1998.
39. Moukheiber, Z., "DoubleClick Is Watching You," *Forbes*, Nov. 4, 1996.
40. Nussbaum, G., "EDI: First Aid for Soaring Hospital Cost," *Corporate Computing*, Aug./Sept. 1992.
41. O'Keefe, S., *Publicity on the Internet*. New York: John Wiley & Sons, 1997.
42. Panurach, P., "Money in Electronic Commerce," *Communications of the ACM*, June 1996.
43. Pawar, B. S., and R. Sharda, "Obtaining Business Intelligence on the Internet," *Long Range Planning*, Vol. 30, No. 1, 1997.
44. Peffers, K., and V. K., Tunnainen, "Expectation and Impacts of a Global Information Systems: The Case of a Global Bank from Hong Kong," *Journal of Global IT Management*, Vol. 1, #4, 1998.
45. Peppers, D., et al., *The One to One Fieldbook*, New York: Currency & Doubleday, 1999.
46. Perry, T. S., "Electronic Money: Toward a Virtual Wallet," Special Issue, *IEEE Spectrum*, Feb. 1997 (13 papers).
47. Pitkow, J. E., and C. M. Kehoe, "Emerging Trends in the WWW User Population," *Communications of the ACM*, June 1996.
48. Powell, T. A., "Don't Get Pushed Around," *Communications Week*, May 26, 1997.
49. Randall, D., "Consumer Strategies for the Internet: Four Scenarios," *Long Range Planning*, Vol. 30, No. 2, 1997.
50. Senn, J. A., "Capitalization on Electronic Commerce," *Information Systems Management*, Summer 1996.
51. Selz, D., and P. Schubert, "Web Assessment — A Model for the Evaluation of Successful Electronic Commerce Applications," *Proceedings HICSS 31*, Hawaii, Jan. 1998.
52. Seybold, P. B., customers.com, New York: Random House, 1998.
53. Siebel, T. M., and M. S. Malone, *Virtual Selling*, New York: Free Press, 1996.
54. Stalling, W., *Business Data Communications*, New York: Macmillan, 1990.
55. Sterne, J., *WWW Marketing*, 2nd ed. New York: John Wiley & Sons, 1999.
56. Tucker, J. M., "EDI and the Net: A Profitable Partnering," *Datamation*, Apr. 1997.
57. Turban, E., et al., *Electronic Commerce: A managerial perspective*. Upper Saddle River, NJ: Prentice-Hall, 2000.
58. Tyson, E., "Best Ways to Manage Your Money," *PC World*, Jan. 1997.
59. Waltner, C., "EDI 'Travels the Web,'" *Communications Week*, June 16, 1997.
60. Wang, S., "Analyzing Agents for Electronic Commerce," *Information Systems Management*, Winter 1999.
61. Wayner, P., *Digital Cash*, Boston: AP Professional, 1997.
62. Wolff, L., "For EFT, the Future Is Now," *Business Credit*, April 1996.
63. Zwass, V., "Electronic Commerce: Structures and Issues," *International Journal of Electronic Commerce*, Fall 1996.

# CHAPTER 7

# Impacts of IT on Organizations, Individuals, and Society

## 7.1
**Does IT Have Only Positive Effects?**

## 7.2
**Ethical Issues**

## 7.3
**Impacts on Organizations**

## 7.4
**Impacts on Individuals at Work**

## 7.5
**Societal Impacts and the Internet Community**

### Learning Objectives

*After studying this chapter, you will be able to:*

❶ Understand the major impacts of information technology on organizations, individuals, and society.

❷ Describe the major ethical issues related to information technology, and identify situations in which they occur.

❸ Explain the various aspects of privacy and its possible invasion by organizations or individuals using information technology.

❹ Consider the potential dehumanization of people by computers and other potential negative impacts of information technology.

❺ Identify the major impacts of information technology on organizational structure, power, jobs, supervision, and decision making.

❻ Identify some of the major societal impacts of information technology, such as electronic communities.

# CONNECTIONS

## SOFTWARE DILEMMA AT AGRICO, INC.

AGRICO INC. (DES MOINES, IA) manages over 350 farms in several midwestern states. Prior to 1987, Agrico outsourced most of its computer services. However, due to the growth of its business and its reliance on information, the company decided to build its own IS department. Unfortunately, Agrico was unable to find an off-the-shelf farm management software package. After advertising its needs, the company received several bids and selected AMR, a small software company in Omaha, Nebraska, to develop its information system. AMR had only 12 customers, 10 employees, and one product: an integrated farm management software package. While the basic software was similar, AMR provided customizations for each customer.

Agrico and AMR signed an agreement that the source code (Technology Guide #2 ) of the new program would be maintained in escrow with a third party, for backup and accessibility. Due to frequent modifications, Agrico needed to have access to the code for "viewing listings necessary to test the system." In addition, since AMR is a very small company, Agrico needed to have access to the code in the event that AMR had problems. Agrico found that there were several variations of the code (because of the other 11 clients).

Agrico requested that the source code be placed in escrow. John Rogers, AMR's president, claimed that Agrico should be satisfied with his backup plan, according to which he occasionally took computer tapes to his bank's vault in Omaha.

However, Agrico had no independent way to verify that the source code in the vault was indeed Agrico's and that it was a current version. Due to the importance of the information for Agrico and its 350 customers, it became critical for Agrico to be assured that the actual source code would be in an independent, accessible escrow location. Rogers, however, refused to do so. AMR was afraid that placing the code with a third party would put its own survival at risk because an unauthorized person could copy the software and then compete with AMR. Since AMR was small and basically has one product, the company's survival was dependent on the security of its product. Agrico was very upset, but it was unable to change vendors because it had already invested time and money in the software. Also, AMR was still the best vendor. Consequently, the two companies were in dispute. Legal experts advised Agrico that the contract was not clear on the location of the escrow.

Because of its big development efforts, AMR assigned Jane Seymour to work full-time at Agrico's premises. She was aware of the dispute and was very uncomfortable because of the situation. Shortly after, Agrico's vice president of information systems entered the computer room. Jane Seymour was on her dinner break. The source code had been left on the computer screen (either deliberately or accidentally). The vice president immediately called the president of Agrico and asked, "Should I copy the source code to disk? We only have one hour to do it." Agrico's president called his lawyer, who advised him that copying the software might be illegal, and if he should be caught, he could be sued by AMR.

While the president did not want to do something illegal, he felt that Agrico was entitled to the code as an assurance for the safety of the client's assets. He called the vice president back and they made a quick decision (see Exercise 2).

SOURCE: Condensed from "Agrico, Inc.—A Software Dilemma," Harvard Business School Case #9-189-085, Boston: Harvard Business School Press, 1989.

## ▶ 7.1 DOES IT HAVE ONLY POSITIVE EFFECTS?

The decision faced by Agrico's president is a major one; it can determine the future of the company and have ethical and possible legal consequences. Yet it is typical of a new type of situations created by the use of IT. IT has had an effect on private and public organizations as well as on employees, customers, clients, and

## A Closer Look BOX 7.1

### SOME GOOD REASONS TO HATE COMPUTERS

▶ They cost too much.

▶ They break down all the time.

▶ You can't fix them by whacking them a few times with a hammer.

▶ The different brands are incompatible.

▶ They take up too much desk space.

▶ They become obsolete five minutes after you leave the store.

▶ They don't understand plain English.

▶ You have to know how to type to use them.

▶ They lose your data every time there is an electrical storm in the Western Hemisphere.

▶ They give off radiation that may cause cancer, but we won't find out until we all have it.

▶ They have three-pronged plugs and it is a two-pronged world.

▶ Our grandparents never had them, and they got along just fine.

▶ They're taking away people's jobs.

▶ They don't do anything the average person needs.

▶ They think the world can be reduced to strings of ones and zeros.

▶ Storing words on disks never made any sense, and it never will.

▶ Five cables sticking out of an appliance is cruel and unusual punishment.

▶ Computer furniture is uncomfortable and looks lousy around the house.

▶ Instruction manuals are written by illiterate sadists.

▶ When they sell you a $1,500 computer, they forget to mention that you have to spend another $1,500 in order to do anything with it.

▶ How can you respect any machine controlled by a mouse?

▶ It hurts your back to sit in front of one for a long time.

▶ They don't make good conversation at parties.

▶ When you make a mistake using one, you can't blame it on anybody.

▶ Worst of all, the guy down the street has a better one than I do.

SOURCE: Compiled from Gutman, D., "43 Good Reasons to Hate Computers," *Miami Herald,* August 18, 1989.

society. Indeed, everyone—from the living room to the boardroom—has been touched in some way by IT. However, not everyone likes computers and IT, and even those who do may not like them at all times (see Box 7.1).

Concern about technology's effect on people, organizations, and society is not new. British intellectuals expressed philosophical arguments about the effects of the Industrial Revolution on society as early as 170 years ago. In Samuel Butler's book, *EREWHON* (anagram for *nowhere*), a man loses his way in a strange land and wanders into a society that has rejected machines. The people have frozen technology at a predetermined level and outlawed all further technological development; they have made a conscious decision to reject new technology.

While there are many philosophical, technological, social, and other differences between that society and our own, there are many people today who believe that humankind is threatened by the evolution of technology. Our society, however, has not rejected technology. In contrast, we recognize that computers and technology are essential to maintaining and supporting our culture as we know it. We are in a symbiotic relationship with technology. We must be aware of its effect on us as individuals and as members of organizations and society.

Throughout this book, we note the manner in which information systems are being justified, constructed, used, and maintained. In all these discussions we assume that members of an organization will reap the fruits of new technology and that computers have no major negative impact on people, organizations and society.

However, information technology *has* also raised a multitude of negative issues, ranging from illegal copying of software programs to planned surveillance of employees' electronic mail files. Health and safety issues are also of major concern, as are the impact of IT on employment levels and the quality of life. In this chapter, some of these issues will be discussed, especially ethics and the impact of IT on organizations, individuals, and society.

##  7.2 ETHICAL ISSUES

### A FRAMEWORK

**Ethics** is a branch of philosophy that deals with what is considered to be right and wrong. In one of the oldest codes of ethics, the Ten Commandments, clear specifications are given about what an individual should and should not do. Over the years, philosophers have proposed many ethical guidelines, yet what is unethical is not necessarily illegal. Thus, in most instances, an individual faced with an ethical decision is *not* considering whether or not to break the law. In today's complex environment, the definitions of "right" and "wrong" are not always clear (see the Agrico case and Table 7.1).

*Table 7.1* **What Is Right and What Is Wrong?—A Self-Assessment***

| Scenario | Unethical | Not unethical | Not an ethics issue |
|---|---|---|---|
| | *The behavior is (choose one for each scenario)* | | |
| 1. A software developer continued to work on a project, even though he knew that using the software would produce incorrect results. It was because part of the input information could not be trusted. | ( ) | ( ) | ( ) |
| 2. A programmer developed profiles of potential customers from publicly available information and sold the list to mail-order firms. Some of the profiles were inaccurate; consequently people received numerous pieces of inappropriate mail and unsolicited telephone calls. | ( ) | ( ) | ( ) |
| 3. Management allowed employees to use computers for approved personal uses, then monitored usage without employees' knowledge. | ( ) | ( ) | ( ) |
| 4. The president of a software development companys marketed a tax advice program, knowing it had bugs. As a result, some users filed incorrect tax returns and were penalized by the IRS. | ( ) | ( ) | ( ) |
| 5. A computer scientist worked on two research projects for developing systems. She diverted funds from one project to another, completing both projects successfully. | ( ) | ( ) | ( ) |

*In this self-assessment you can express your opinion as to the ethics of each situation. Ask your instructor for the national results of this survey.

SOURCE: Adapted from Weiss (1990).

A debate is also occurring about who should teach ethics. Some people believe that families and schools should teach ethics, not companies. Others believe it is the duty of a company to develop a code of ethics to guide its employees.

The spread of IT has created many new ethical situations. For example, the issue of a company monitoring electronic mail is very controversial (47 percent of the readers of *Information Week* believe companies have the right to do so, 53 percent disagree). Obviously, there are major differences among companies and individuals with respect to what is right and wrong.

There are also differences regarding ethics among different countries. What is unethical in one culture may be perfectly acceptable in another. Many Western countries, for example, have a much higher concern for individuals and their rights to privacy than some Asian countries. In Asia, more emphasis is, in general, placed on the benefits to society than on the rights of individuals. Some countries, like Sweden and Canada, have very strict laws; others have none. For example, at this writing, Italy, Belgium, Spain, Portugal, and Greece lack legislation protecting an individual's right to control personal data in governmental or commercial databases. This obstructs the flow of information among countries in the European Community. To overcome this problem, the European Community Commission has issued guidelines to all its member countries regarding the rights of individuals to access information about themselves and to correct errors.

> Ethics gets to be touchy enough when you try to manage a group of people, but what if those people are all from other countries, or better yet still in those countries, but working for your company? The water gets real muddy real quick.
>
> — *Blake Thompson*

Many companies and professional organizations develop their own codes of ethics. A **code of ethics** is a collection of principles intended as a guide for members of a company or an association (see Oz [1994]). For a discussion of the code of the Association for Computing Machinery (ACM), see Anderson, et al. (1993).

The diversity of IT applications and increased use of the technology have created many ethical issues, as illustrated throughout this text. An attempt to organize these issues into a framework was undertaken by Mason (1986) and Mason et al. (1995), who categorized ethical issues into four kinds: privacy, accuracy, property, and accessibility.

▶ *Privacy.* Collection, storage, and dissemination of information about individuals.

▶ *Accuracy.* Authenticity, fidelity, and accuracy of information collected and processed.

▶ *Property.* Ownership and value of information and intellectual property.

▶ *Accessibility.* Right to access information and payment of fees to access it.

Representative questions and issues in each category are listed in Table 7.2. (page 287). Of these, the issues of privacy and intellectual property are discussed in detail in this section.

Mason et al. (1995) also developed a model for ethical reasoning that shows the process that leads to ethical judgment when an individual is faced with an ethical issue.

## PROTECTING PRIVACY

*Privacy* means different things to different people. A former U.S. Supreme Court Justice, Potter Stewart, said the following about pornography, which could be applied to privacy: "I cannot define it, but I know it when I see it." It is common to identify four states of privacy: (1) solitude—the state of being alone, away

*Table 7.2*  **A Framework for Ethical Issues**

| *Privacy* | *Accuracy* |
|---|---|
| ▶ What information about oneself should an individual be required to reveal to others? | ▶ Who is responsible for the authenticity, fidelity, and accuracy of information collected? |
| ▶ What kind of surveillance can an employer use on its employees? | ▶ How can we ensure that information will be processed properly and presented accurately to users? |
| ▶ What things can people keep to themselves and not be forced to reveal to others? | ▶ How can we ensure that errors in databases, data transmissions, and data processing are accidental and not intentional? |
| ▶ What information about individuals should be kept in databases, and how secure is the information there? | ▶ Who is to be held accountable for errors in information, and how is the injured party compensated? |

| *Property* | *Accessibility* |
|---|---|
| ▶ Who owns the information? | ▶ Who is allowed to access information? |
| ▶ What are the just and fair prices for its exchange? | ▶ How much should be charged for permitting accessibility to information? |
| ▶ Who owns the channels of information? | ▶ How can accessibility to computers be provided for employees with disabilities? |
| ▶ How should one handle software piracy (copying copyrighted software)? | ▶ Who will be provided with equipment needed for accessing information? |
| ▶ Under what circumstances can one use proprietary databases? | ▶ What information does a person or an organization have a right or a privilege to obtain—under what conditions and with what safeguards? |
| ▶ Can corporate computers be used for private purposes? | |
| ▶ How should experts who contribute their knowledge to create expert systems be compensated? | |
| ▶ How should access to information channels be allocated? | |

SOURCE: Compiled from Mason (1986) and Mason et al. (1995).

from outside interference; (2) intimacy—the state of privacy one wants to enjoy from the outside world; (3) anonymity—the state of being free of external surveillance; and (4) reserve—the ability to control information about oneself.

In general, privacy is the right to be left alone and the right to be free of unreasonable personal intrusions. A definition of **information privacy,** according to Agranoff (1993), is the "claim of individuals, groups, or institutions to determine for themselves when, and to what extent, information about them is communicated to others."

Privacy has long been a legal and social issue in the United States and many other countries. The right to privacy is recognized today in virtually all U.S. states and by the federal government, either by statute or common law. The definition of privacy can be interpreted quite broadly. However, according to Freedman (1987), the following two rules have been followed fairly closely in past court decisions: (1) The right of privacy is not absolute. Privacy must be balanced against the needs of society. (2) The public's right to know is superior to the individual's right of privacy. These two rules show why it is difficult, in some cases, to determine and enforce privacy regulations. (Federal privacy legislations are listed in Table 7.3.)

*Table 7.3* **Federal Privacy Legislation**

| Legislation | Content |
| --- | --- |
| Fair Credit Reporting Act of 1970 | Allows individuals to access information that credit bureaus (e.g., Equifax) maintain. Individuals can correct inaccuracies. |
| Freedom of Information Act of 1970 | Permits individuals to access any information about themselves stored by the federal government. |
| Privacy Act of 1974 | Prohibits the government from collecting information secretly. Information collected must be used only for a specific purpose. |
| Right to Financial Privacy Act of 1978 | Guards the safety of data in financial institutions. People must be notified if the government wants access to the data. |
| Privacy Protection Act of 1980 | Provides protection of privacy in computerized and other documents. |
| Electronic Communications Privacy Act of 1986 | Prohibits private citizens from intercepting data communication without authorization. |
| Computer Security Act of 1987 | Requires security of information regarding individuals. |
| Computer Matching and Privacy Act of 1988 | Regulates the matching of computer files by state and federal agencies. |
| Video Privacy Protection Act of 1988 | Protects privacy in transmission of pictures. |
| Telephone Consumer Protection Act of 1992 | Limits telemarketers' practices. |
| Fair Health Information Practices Act of 1997 | Provides a code of fair information (pending). |
| Consumer Internet Privacy Protection Act of 1997 | Requires prior written consent before a computer service can disclose subscribers' information (pending). |
| Social Security Online Privacy Protection Act of 1997 (H.R. 1287) | Its purpose is to limit disclosure of Social Security numbers and related information (pending). |
| Federal Internet Privacy Protection Act of 1997 (H.R. 1367) | Its purpose is to prohibit federal agencies from disclosing personal records via the Internet (pending). |
| Communications Privacy and Consumer Empowerment Act of 1997 (H. R. 1964) | Its purpose is to protect privacy rights in online commerce (pending). |
| Data Privacy Act of 1997 (H. R. 2368) | Its purpose is to limit the use of personally identifiable information and to regulate "spamming" (pending). |
| Social Security Information Safeguards Act of 1997 (H. R.1331) | Its purpose is to develop online security mechanisms for Social Security data (pending). |

The complexity of collecting, sorting, filing, and accessing information manually from several different agencies was, in many cases, a built-in protection against misuse of information. It was simply too expensive, cumbersome, and complex to invade privacy. However, personal computers, powerful software, large databases, and the Internet have created an entirely new dimension of accessing and using data. The inherent power in systems that can access vast amounts of data could be used for the good of society. For example, by matching records with the aid of a computer, it is possible to eliminate or reduce fraud, government mismanagement, tax evasion, welfare cheats, family support filchers, employment of illegal aliens, and so on. The question is: what price must every individual pay in terms of loss of privacy so that the government can better apprehend criminals? (See the group assignment at the end of this chapter.)

Unfortunately, the same system that helps the government could be used to blacklist innocent citizens. For example, people who have filed workers' compensation or product-liability lawsuits or have used legitimate benefits extensively (such as health care) could be blacklisted by providers and denied benefits. These decisions can be made without an individual's even knowing the basis for them. With the widespread use of the Internet and electronic commerce, the issue of privacy becomes more critical (see Exercise 1). A special organization called the Electronic Privacy Information Center (www.epic.org) is trying to protect privacy. Also see Cavoukian and Tapscott (1997) and Schneier and Banisar (1997) for a comprehensive coverage. Some issues of privacy are discussed next.

**ELECTRONIC SURVEILLANCE.** According to the American Civil Liberties Union (ACLU), monitoring computer users—**electronic surveillance**—is a widespread problem. The ACLU estimates that tens of millions of computer users are monitored, many without their knowledge. While surveillance is one of the most extensively debated privacy issues, the practice is widely used.

For example, a survey conducted by *MacWorld* magazine in May 1993 indicated that about 22 percent of all U.S. employers engage in surveillance of employee computer files, electronic mail files, and voice mail boxes. Among companies with more than 1,000 employees, the figure rises to 30 percent. Only 18 percent of the companies have written policies on electronic privacy, and 35 percent said that it was "never acceptable" to eavesdrop electronically on employees. Most surprising is that in less than one-third of the cases of such surveillance, employees were warned about such a possibility.

Employees have very limited protection against employers' surveillance. Although several legal challenges are now underway, the law appears to support employers' rights to read electronic mail and other electronic documents. Legislation now before the U.S. Congress attempts at least to require employers to inform employees that their on-the-job activities might be monitored electronically.

**PERSONAL INFORMATION IN DATABASES.** Information about individuals is being kept in many databases. When you apply for a new telephone, for example, you may be asked to fill in a two-page questionnaire. The questionnaire is reviewed and then stored in a database. Perhaps the most visible locations of such records are credit reporting agencies. Other places personal information might be stored are banks and financial institutions; cable TV, telephone, and utilities companies; employers; apartment (renters) and equipment rental companies; hospitals; schools and universities; supermarkets, retail establishments, and mail-order houses; government agencies (Internal Revenue Service, Census Bureau, your municipality); libraries; and insurance companies.

There are several concerns about the information you provide to these record keepers. Under what circumstances will personal data be released? Do

> In the medical field there is a great concern about personal medical information being used inappropriately, i.e., to refuse insurance coverage.
>
> — *Brad White*

you know where the records are? Are these records accurate? Can you change inaccurate data? How long will it take to make a change? How are the data used? To whom are they given or sold? How secure are the data against unauthorized people?

Having information stored in many places increases the chance that the information is inaccurate, not up-to-date, or not secured properly. Here are some examples of potential problems.

▶ An entire city in New England was unable to get financing. An investigation discovered that all the taxpayers were wrongly labeled as people who had failed to pay their property taxes.

▶ Landlords refuse to rent apartments to individuals because of identification errors in databases.

▶ People experience difficulties in financing or refinancing homes because of delayed or even incorrect information in databases.

▶ Individuals may be fired from their jobs when management discovers private information on their e-mail that may not be related to work.

▶ Confidential information such as health status or sexual preference of an individual may have a negative impact on hiring, promotion, or other personnel decisions.

▶ Databases are used to compile different mailing lists. Such lists are sold to various vendors, who then call upon people as potential customers.

To assist individuals in the control of personal records it is possible to use the services of a commercial company. For example, Privacy Guard Corporation advises individuals about how to protect their rights, and it monitors several databases. Many companies do attempt to protect the privacy of their employees and/or customers as shown in the following example.

---

*IT At Work* **AMERICAN EXPRESS USES CUSTOMER INFORMATION FOR MARKETING DECISIONS. IS PRIVACY PROTECTED?**

*I*NTEGRATING IT

...for Finance and Marketing

American Express (AmEx) was one of the first financial service companies to adopt a formal privacy policy regarding information about its customers. These policies restrict disclosure of data to those with a "business need" to see it. AmEx also gives its customers the choice not to receive promotional material. However, AmEx is using its vast database internally to generate lists for mass mailings and specialized promotions.

Stephen Cone, senior vice president for direct marketing, uses sophisticated mathematical models to sift through billions of bits of data to predict what products a person might be interested in. For example, all information—from the original application to each card transaction—is accessed to build individual profiles. These profiles can be used to determine marketing strategies and generate a list of potential customers.

From purchased lists, AmEx compiles a list of almost every potential cardholder in America. The records note every solicitation AmEx has ever sent to each person. The lists also contain demographic data and lifestyle indicators. AmEx produces many specialized models from this data. For example, AmEx has a "who's moving" model that is extremely valuable because people who are relocating tend to make several other changes at the same time. The company also has a "lifestyle" model that decides which solicitation letters to send to a prospect. The effect of this selective, direct marketing tool is that response rates are up 7 to 10 percent over previous years.

Even though AmEx does not rent out its list, it does enter into joint ventures with merchandising companies that conduct several thousand promotions a year. They offer everything from invitations to local pizzerias to solicitations for potential buyers of luxury cars. AmEx can pinpoint the cardholders most likely to respond to each offer.

American Express has realized that information about actual consumer behavior is extremely valuable. How consumers spend their money is a better measure of their needs and desires than any marketing survey could ever be.

**For Further Exploration:** Do you think that what AmEx is doing is ethical? How would you feel as a customer? How well is your privacy protected? What can you do if you are unhappy? ▲

SOURCE: Based on Hansell, S., "Getting to Know You," *Institutional Investor,* June 1991.

An area of major concern is the privacy protection in companies engaged in Web-based personalization products, such as that of Firefly (see discussion in Chapter 6). On the Firefly Network, it is possible to build a user profile, and carry it securely and privately (using the P3P standard) to other Web sites. (For details, see *Internetweek,* Feb. 16, 1998.)

> Negative information that may be untrue is being posted on newsgroups. This spreads misinformation.
>
> — *James Rolstead*

**INFORMATION ON BULLETIN BOARDS AND INTERNET NEWSGROUPS.** Every day there are more and more *electronic bulletin boards, newsgroups,* and *electronic discussion arrangements,* such as chat rooms, both nationally and within corporations. It is estimated that in 1998 there were 30 million users of over 100,000 commercial bulletin boards of all types. How does society keep owners of bulletin boards from disseminating information that may be offensive to readers (see Box 7.2)? The difficulty we have addressing this problem highlights the conflict between freedom of speech, privacy, and ethics.

## *A Closer Look*   BOX 7.2

### PRODIGY BANS BIAS NOTES FROM ITS ELECTRONIC BULLETIN BOARD

Prodigy operates one of the largest electronic bulletin boards in the United States. Two types of messages can be transmitted: public messages, which are posted by individuals and/or organizations, and private messages, which are sent usually by one individual to another (or to several individuals). One day it was discovered that Prodigy had carried two anti-Semitic statements disseminated by one individual to many recipients.

Prodigy has a policy of free expression of ideas on its network. However, at the same time, the company has an explicit policy banning its millions of members from posting public messages that are "obscene, profane, or otherwise offensive references." (The company screens the publicly carried notes, but it does not check the content of each private person-to-person electronic message.) Prodigy's position raised a question regarding the limits of free speech as well as Prodigy's responsibility to prevent transmissions that may offend people.

The company said it would try to reconcile its two policies that seemed to be inconsistent. Prodigy also said that its case is similar to that of any city when it decides what movies and books are acceptable. In January 1993, Prodigy closed down its "frank discussion" channel when the language used by some participants got a little *too* frank for the owners of the company at that time.

Prodigy was sued by Stratton Oakmont Investment firm for libel over a message that appeared in 1994 on the Prodigy Money Talk bulletin board which made derogatory statements about the company. The statement was made through an unused Internet account that Prodigy failed to close.

SOURCE: Condensed from stories in *USA Today, Wall Street Journal, New York Times,* and *Chicago Tribune* during the early part of August 1992, and Charles (1995).

**TRANSFER OF DATA ACROSS INTERNATIONAL BORDERS.** Several countries like Canada and Brazil impose strict laws to control the flow of personal data across their borders. These countries usually justify their acts as protecting the privacy of their citizens. (Other justifications are property protection and keeping jobs within the country by requiring that data processing be done there.) The transfer of information in and out of a nation without knowledge of the authorities or individuals involved raises a number of privacy issues. Whose laws have jurisdiction when records are in a different country for reprocessing or retransmission purposes? For example, if data are transmitted by a Polish company through an American satellite to a British corporation, whose laws control what data and when? Governments must make an effort to develop laws and standards to cope with the rapidly increasing rate of information technology in order to solve some of these privacy issues. The major issues of such transfers are shown in Table 7.4.

**Table 7.4** The Issues of Data Transfer Across International Borders

| Security Issues | Technical Issues |
|---|---|
| ▶ *National security.* Databases may contain classified information relevant to national security. Transfer of such data outside the country may jeopardize the country's security. <br><br> ▶ *Organizational security.* An organization's security may be at risk. France, for example, requires that every database maintained in that country be registered with the government, so classified material can be monitored. <br><br> ▶ *Personal security.* A major issue is privacy. Sweden, Canada, France, and Brazil have strict privacy laws. These countries require that information be processed within their borders as much as possible. The problem is that this may increase the cost of processing. | ▶ *Data vulnerability and accuracy.* This issue is similar to that described in Chapter 15. However, due to global flows, the problems may be more acute. <br><br> ▶ *Technical standards.* There are no global technical standards for transmitting information across borders. Communication infrastructures differ from one country to another. |
| **Sovereignty Issues** | **Developing Issues** |
| ▶ *National sovereignty.* Some countries prefer that hardware, software, and networks used be made in their country. <br><br> ▶ *Economic sovereignty.* Some countries want information to be processed within their boundaries to increase employment and improve the balance of payments. <br><br> ▶ *Cultural sovereignty.* Many countries want to maintain their cultural identities. They are afraid of what is described as "electronic colonialism." They can control what is shown on television, but it is difficult to control what is on the Internet or on a bulletin board. | ▶ *Legal and regulatory issues.* Every country has its own legal system regarding national, organizational, and personal flow and use of data and information. <br><br> ▶ *Intellectual property.* Transfer of data may violate intellectual property laws with regard to copyrights, patents, licenses, and copying of software. There are also different laws in different countries and modes of enforcement differ as well. <br><br> ▶ *Developing countries.* Many so-called Third World nations have fears regarding the use of information flowing to their territories. Also, they lack a robust communication infrastructure. |

**PRIVACY CODES.** One way to protect privacy is to develop **privacy policies** or codes, which can help organizations avoid legal problems. In many corporations, senior management has begun to understand that with the ability to collect vast amounts of personal information on customers, clients, and employees comes an obligation to ensure that the information—and, therefore, the individual—is protected. A sample of privacy policies is given below (condensed from Agranoff [1993]). A privacy code was issued on June 22, 1998 by most major Internet-related companies including IBM and Microsoft.

### PRIVACY POLICY BASICS—A SAMPLE
DATA COLLECTION
- ▶ Data should be collected on individuals only to accomplish a legitimate business objective.
- ▶ Data should be adequate, relevant, and not excessive in relation to the business objective.
- ▶ Individuals must give their consent before data pertaining to them can be gathered. Such consent may be implied from the individual's actions (e.g., applications for credit, insurance, or employment).

DATA ACCURACY
- ▶ Sensitive data gathered on individuals should be verified before it is entered into the database.
- ▶ Data should be accurate and, where and when necessary, kept current.
- ▶ The file should be made available so the individual can ensure that the data are correct.
- ▶ If there is disagreement about the accuracy of the data, the individual's version should be noted and included with any disclosure of the file.

DATA CONFIDENTIALITY
- ▶ Computer security procedures should be implemented to provide reasonable assurance against unauthorized disclosure of data. They should include physical, technical, and administrative security measures.
- ▶ Third parties should not be given access to data without the individual's knowledge or permission, except as required by law.
- ▶ Disclosures of data, other than the most routine, should be noted and maintained for as long as the data are maintained.
- ▶ Data should not be disclosed for reasons incompatible with the business objective for which they are collected.

The organization for Economic Cooperation and Development in Europe has probably provided the best known set of guidelines intended to protect individuals' privacy in the electronic age (for a comprehensive discussion, see O'Leary [1995]).

## PROTECTING INTELLECTUAL PROPERTY

**Intellectual property** is the intangible property created by individuals or corporations, which is protected under copyright, trade secret, and patent laws.

*Copyright* is a statutory grant that provides the creators of intellectual property with ownership of it for 28 years. They are entitled to collect fees from anyone who wants to copy the property. The U.S. Federal Computer Software Copyright Act (1980) provides protection for *source* and *object code,* but one problem is that it is not clear what is eligible to be protected. For example, similar concepts, functions, and general features (such as pull-down menus, colors, or icons) are not protected by copyright law.

A *trade secret* is intellectual work such as a business plan, which is a company secret and is not based on public information. An example is a corporate strategic plan. Laws about trade secrets are legislated at the state level in the United States.

A *patent* is a document that grants the holder exclusive rights on an invention for 17 years. Thousands of patents related to IT have been granted during the years. Examples of IT-related patents are "A method and system for natural language translation" (#5477451), and expert-based systems and methods for managing error events on a local area network (#5483637).

The most common intellectual property related to IT is software. The copying of software without making payment to the owner is a major problem. But there are several other potential violations of intellectual property, as shown in Box 7.3.

---

## *A Closer Look* BOX 7.3

### COPYRIGHT PROTECTION VS. FREE SPEECH ON THE INTERNET

Gil Trevizo is a 25-year-old student who loves the TV science-fiction series *Millennium.* He was able to get a bootlegged video of the first episode and other information and images regarding the show. So he dedicated his Web site at the University of Texas to the show even before its big 1996 network premier. The show belongs to Twentieth Century-Fox, which has its own Web site dedicated to the show. The University switched off Trevizo's Internet account after Fox alerted them to the apparent piracy of its copyrighted material. Gil removed the material from his Web site.

*Millennium*'s Internet fans were unhappy with the situation. The "First Unofficial *Millennium* WWW Site" went up before the second episode. Several dozen other fans activated "protest sites" before the third show aired on November 8, 1996. A university did not control these fans, so their sites remained open. "They [Fox] are shutting us down," the protest sites proclaim, playing on a line instantly recognizable to fans of the *X-Files* series. "Free speech is out there."

Although Gil does not receive any economic benefits, Fox could have been hurt by his site. Fox spent over $100,000 on its *Millennium* Web site and wants the fans to visit this site where promotional material is sold. If fans go to Gil's or similar sites, fewer visitors will come to the official site.

The problem is not unique to Fox. Thousands of Web sites are using unauthorized material and it is unclear whether what is going on in cyberspace is governed by predigital copyright law.

**For Further Exploration:** Who is right—Fox or the fans? Is it possible that some predigital copyright laws may not be logical or practical in the digital world?

SOURCE: Based on Harmon, A., "Web Wars: Companies Get Tough on Rogues," *Los Angeles Times*, November 12, 1996, p. 1.

---

> Some managers who would never steal money from a customer, plan and budget around copying computer programs. They fail to realize this is also stealing.
>
> — *Mike Rewald*

One of the most difficult issues created by IT is *who owns information?* The information in large databases has been compiled by many people at different times. Some information is about consumers. A comprehensive discussion is provided by Wells-Branscomb (1994).

The protection of intellectual property on the Web is an extremely difficult undertaking. Even if the material is protected it is easy to pay for one usage and then distribute it to many without pay. Several federal Acts are pending. For example, "The Electronic Theft (NET) Act," which deals with software piracy, "Digital Copyright Clarification and Technology Act of 1997," which deals with copyright liability in distance learning, and "Online Copyright Liability Limitation Act," which aims to protect from liability certain Internet access providers, are all close to approval (Jan. 1998).

**INTERNATIONAL ASPECTS.** Copyright laws in the digital age are being challenged, and international agreements are needed. In 1996, the World Intellectual Property Organization began to discuss the need for copyright protection of intellectual property delivered on the Internet. More than 60 member countries were trying to bridge cultural and political differences and come up with an international treaty. Part of the agreement is called the "database treaty," and its aim is to protect the investment of firms that collect and arrange information.

## ▶ 7.3 IMPACTS ON ORGANIZATIONS

The use of computers and information technology has brought many changes to business, which are being felt in areas like structure, authority, power, job content, employee career ladders, supervision, and the manager's job—a brief description of each follows.

### STRUCTURE, AUTHORITY, POWER, AND JOB CONTENT

Several issues are related to the changes in these areas. They include:

**FLATTER ORGANIZATIONAL HIERARCHIES.** IT allows for the increased productivity of managers, an increased **span of control** (more employees per supervisor), and a decreased number of experts. It is reasonable to assume, then, that *fewer* managerial levels will exist in many organizations; there will be fewer staff and line managers. This trend is already evidenced by the continuing phenomenon of the "shrinking size of middle management." (See Pinsonneault and Kraemer [1993].)

Flatter organizational hierarchies will also result from reduction in the total number of employees, reengineering of business processes, and the ability of lower-level employees to perform higher-level jobs (e.g., by using expert systems). As one example, consider Bank of America's 1985 reorganization and Citicorp's 1991 reorganization, each of which resulted in a smaller corporation, a larger span of control, and a much flatter structure. The downsizing of many organizations is supported by the use of computers.

**STAFF-TO-LINE RATIO.** The ratio of staff-to-line workers has increased in most organizations as computers replace clerical jobs, and as the need for information systems specialists increases. Expansion of IT, and especially expert systems, may reverse this trend. Specifically, the number of professionals and specialists could *decline* in relation to the total number of employees in the organizations.

**SPECIAL UNITS.** Another change in organizational structure is the possibility of creating a technology center, an Internet/electronic commerce unit, a decision support system department, and/or an intelligent systems department. Such units may have a major impact on organizations especially when they are well supported by top management.

**CENTRALIZATION OF AUTHORITY.** The relationship between computerized systems and the degree of centralization of authority (and power) in the organizations that these systems serve has been debated extensively, especially since the introduction of microcomputers. It is still difficult, however, to establish a clear pattern. For example, the introduction of expert systems in General Electric's maintenance area increased the power of the decentralized units because they became less dependent on the company's headquarters. On the other hand, expert systems can be used as a means of increasing control and enhancing centralization.

Because of the trend toward smaller and flatter organizations, centralization may become more popular. However, this trend could be offset by specialization in more decentralized units. Whether extensive use of IT will result in more centralization or decentralization of business operations and management may depend on top management's philosophy.

**POWER AND STATUS.** Knowledge is power—this fact has been recognized for generations. The latest developments in computerized systems are changing the power structure within organizations. The struggle over who will control the computers and information resources has become one of the most visible conflicts in many organizations, both private and public. Expert systems, for example, may reduce the power of certain professional groups because their knowledge will be in the public domain. On the other hand, individuals who control electronic commerce application may gain considerable prestige, knowledge, power, and status. As a result, there is a *power redistribution* in many organizations. Managers and employees who control information and IT are likely to gain power at the expense of others.

**JOB CONTENT.** One major impact of IT is on the content of many jobs in both private and public organizations. **Job content** is important not only because it is related to organizational structure, but also because it is interrelated with employee satisfaction, compensation, status, and productivity. Changes in job content occur when work is redesigned, for example, when business process reengineering (BPR) is attempted or when electronic commerce changes the marketing system (see Baatz [1996]).

**ROLE AMBIGUITY AND CONFLICT.** Changes in job content may result in opportunities for promotion and employee development. But these changes could create problems of role conflict and **role ambiguity,** especially in the short run. In addition, there may be considerable resistance to changes in roles, primarily from managers who favor noncomputerized information systems.

Many workers feel out of place in their positions when they see computers executing many of the tasks they used to do. Management sometimes fails to discuss such changes with workers, or to revise the affected job descriptions. Consequently, these individuals are left without a clear understanding of what their jobs are supposed to be and what they are supposed to do.

## PERSONNEL ISSUES

The IT revolution may result in many changes in personnel management and human resources management. These include:

**EMPLOYEE CAREER LADDERS.** Increased use of IT in organizations could have a significant and somewhat unexpected impact on career ladders. Today, many highly skilled professionals have developed their abilities through years of experience, holding a series of positions that expose them to progressively more difficult and complex situations. The use of IT, and especially computer-aided instruction over the intranet, may short cut a portion of this learning curve. However, several questions remain unaddressed. How will high-level human expertise be acquired with minimal experience in lower-level tasks? What will be the effect on compensation at all levels of employment? How will human resource development programs be structured? What career paths will be offered to employees?

**CHANGES IN SUPERVISION.** The fact that an employee's work is performed online and stored electronically introduces the possibility for greater electronic supervision. For professional employees whose work is often measured by their completion of projects, "remote supervision" implies greater emphasis on completed work and less on personal contacts. This emphasis is especially true if employees, such as telecommuters, work in geographically dispersed locations away from their supervisors. In general, the supervisory process may become more formalized, with greater reliance on procedures and measurable outputs than on interpersonal processes.

**OTHER CONSIDERATIONS.** Several other personnel-related issues could surface as a result of using IT. For example, what will be the impact of IT on job qualifications, on training requirements, and on worker satisfaction? How can jobs that use IT be designed so that they present an acceptable level of challenge to users? How might IT be used to personalize or enrich jobs? What can be done to make sure that the introduction of IT does not demean jobs or have other negative impacts from the workers' point of view? What principles should be used to allocate functions to people and machines, especially those functions that can be performed equally well by either one? Should cost or efficiency be the sole or major criterion for such allocation? All these and even more issues could be encountered in any system implementation.

## THE MANAGER'S JOB

The most important task of managers is making decisions. IT can change the manner in which many decisions are being made and consequently change the managers' jobs. The most probable areas of change are listed here:

> This allows empowerment of employees and definitely increases productivity.
> — *James Rolstead*

- ▶ Automation of routine decisions.
- ▶ Less expertise required for many decisions.
- ▶ Less reliance on experts to provide support to top executives.
- ▶ Power redistribution among managers.
- ▶ Electronic support of complex decisions (intelligent agents, executive support systems).

According to Huber (1990), the use of computer-assisted communication technologies leads to the following organizational changes:

- ▶ A large number and variety of people participating in decision making.
- ▶ A decrease in the number and variety of people participating in traditional face-to-face communication.

▶ Fewer organizational levels involved in authorizing actions.

▶ More rapid and accurate identification of problems and opportunities, so better decisions are made.

▶ Organizational intelligence (scanning, monitoring) that is more accurate, comprehensive, timely, and available.

▶ Shorter time required to authorize actions and make decisions.

Many managers have reported that the computer has finally given them time to "get out of the office and into the field." They also have found that they can spend more time planning activities instead of "putting out fires." Another aspect of the management challenge lies in the ability of IT to support the process of decision making. IT could change the decision-making process and even decision-making styles. For example, information gathering for decision making will be done much more quickly. Most managers currently work on a large number of problems simultaneously, moving from one to another as they wait for more information on their current problem or until some external event "interrupts" them. IT tends to reduce the time necessary to complete any step in the decision-making process. Therefore, managers will work on fewer tasks during each day but complete more of them. The reduction of startup time associated with moving from task to task could be the most important source of increased managerial productivity.

Another possible impact on the manager's job could be a change in leadership requirements. What are generally considered to be good qualities of leadership may be significantly altered with the use of IT. For example, when face-to-face communication is replaced by electronic mail and computerized conferencing, leadership qualities attributed to physical appearance could be minimal.

 ## 7.4 IMPACTS ON INDIVIDUALS AT WORK

Information systems affect individuals in various ways. What is a benefit to one individual may be a curse to another. Some of the ways that IT may affect individuals, their perceptions, and behaviors will be considered next.

### JOB SATISFACTION

Although many jobs may become substantially more "enriched" with IT, other jobs may become more routine and less satisfying. For example, as early as 1970 Argyris predicted that computer-based information systems would reduce managerial discretion in decision making and thus create dissatisfied managers.

### DEHUMANIZATION AND PSYCHOLOGICAL IMPACTS

**DEHUMANIZATION.** A frequent criticism of traditional data processing systems is their negative effect on people's individuality. Such systems are criticized as being impersonal; they *dehumanize* and depersonalize activities that have been computerized. Many people feel a loss of identity; they feel like "just another number" because computers reduce or eliminate the human element that was present in the noncomputerized systems.

While the major objective of newer IT technologies, such as expert systems, is to increase productivity, they can also create *flexible* systems that allow individuals to include their opinions and knowledge in the system. These technologies attempt to be people oriented and user friendly.

Kaltnekar (1991) has posed the question whether IT exists for the sake of people or whether people exist for the sake of the technology. He addressed the importance of achieving a balance between technology and the significance of the individual in an organization. He also asked whether IT is just an organizational function, or the organization is a function of IT. Technical solutions to organizational problems can easily subvert the need to consider relationships among people in an organization. He stated that the basic requirement for system development is the recognition that all work processes should be designed because of people and for people. Hardware and software accomplish many difficult tasks previously performed by people. This enables people to devote time to more creative tasks. Now, however, expert systems and artificial intelligence are increasingly replacing people in the creative arena. People have become dependent on technology and may become a mere link in the chain. Kaltnekar (1991) says, ". . . one faces a half-serious yet worrying question: will there be any place for man in the future automated world?"

**PSYCHOLOGICAL IMPACTS.**  Home computers threaten to have an even more isolating influence than was created by television. If people are encouraged to work and shop from their living rooms, then some unfortunate psychological effects—such as depression and loneliness—could develop. Another example is distance learning. Children can be schooled at home through IT, but the lack of social contacts could be damaging to their development.

## IMPACTS ON HEALTH AND SAFETY

Computers and information systems are a part of the job environment that may adversely affect our health and safety. To illustrate, we will discuss the effects of three issues: *job stress, video display terminals,* and *long-term use of the keyboard.* For further discussion see the *Wall Street Journal,* April 9, 1996, p. 1.

**JOB STRESS.**  An increase in workload and/or responsibilities can trigger **job stress.** Although computerization has benefited organizations by increasing productivity, it has also created an ever-increasing workload. Some workers feel overwhelmed and start feeling anxious about their jobs and their performance. These feelings of anxiety can adversely affect workers' productivity. Management's responsibility is to help alleviate these feelings by redistributing the workload among workers or hiring more individuals.

> Studying how prolonged computer use can result in carpal tunnel syndrome has resulted in my use of correct posture, monitor breaks, and keyboard/mouse pads.
> — *Dave Gehrke*

**REPETITIVE STRAIN INJURIES.**  Exposure to video display terminals (VDTs) raises the issue of the risk of radiation exposure, which has been linked to cancer and other health-related problems. For example, lengthy exposure to VDTs has been blamed for miscarriages in pregnant women. However, results of the research done to investigate this charge have been inconclusive. It is known that exposure to VDTs for long periods of time can affect an individual's eyesight.

Other potential hazards, though not direct results of the VDT, are backaches and muscle tension in the wrists and fingers. *Carpal tunnel syndrome* is a pernicious and painful form of repetitive strain injury that affects the wrists and hands. It has been associated with the long-term use of keyboards. Repetitive strain injuries can be very costly to corporations. According to Cone (1994), there have been more than 2,000 lawsuits against computer manufacturers and employers. For example,

## ERGONOMIC PRODUCTS PROTECT COMPUTER USERS

Many products are available to improve working conditions for people who spend much of their time with a computer. The following pictures are representative examples.

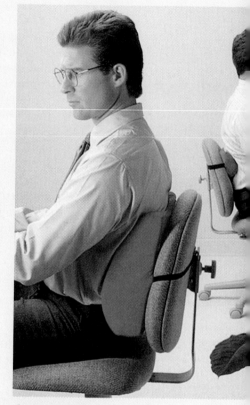

(a) Wrist support.

(b) Back support.

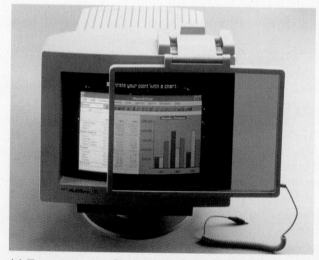

(c) Eye-protection filter (optically coated glass).

(d) Adjustable foot rest.

SOURCE; Based on information taken from vendors' catalogs.

a lawsuit was filed against IBM requesting $11.5 million because of the inappropriate design of a keyboard that supposedly caused carpal tunnel syndrome.

**LESSENING THE NEGATIVE IMPACT ON HEALTH AND SAFETY.** Designers are aware of the potential problems associated with prolonged use of computers. Consequently, they have attempted to design a better computing environment. Research in the area of **ergonomics** (or human factors) provides guidance for these designers. For instance, ergonomic techniques focus on creating an environment for the worker that is well lit and comfortable. Devices such as antiglare screens have helped alleviate problems of fatigued or damaged eyesight, and chairs that contour the human body have helped decrease backaches (see Box 7.4).

**OTHER IMPACTS.** Interactions between individuals and computers are so numerous that entire volumes can be written on the subject. An overview of such interactions is provided by Kanter (1992) and illustrated in Figure 7.1. The figure shows the individual encircled by the electronic transfer of money (as in home shopping and smart cards) that allows purchase of products and services. The intermediate rings identify six areas or systems of human activity affected by computers (consumerism, education, and so on). Finally, the outer ring gives some examples of specific products or services in each system.

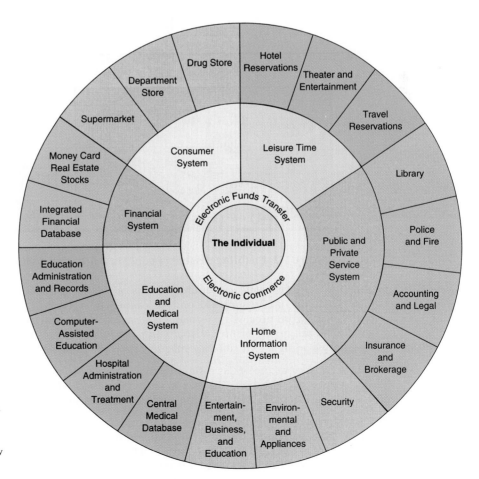

**FIGURE 7.1** Information systems and the individual. (*Source*: Kanter, Jerome, *Managing with Information*, 4th Ed. 1992, p. 350. Reprinted with permission of Prentice-Hall, Upper Saddle River, New Jersey.)

## 7.5 SOCIETAL IMPACTS AND THE INTERNET COMMUNITY

The social implications of IT will be far reaching. This section describes several representative impacts.

### OPPORTUNITIES FOR PEOPLE WITH DISABILITIES

The integration of artificial intelligence technologies, such as speech and vision recognition, into a computer-based information system (CBIS) can create new employment opportunities for people with disabilities. For example, those who cannot type are able to use a voice-operated typewriter, and those who cannot travel can work at home.

(a)

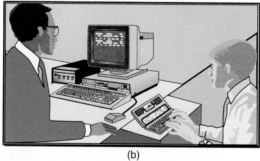

(b)

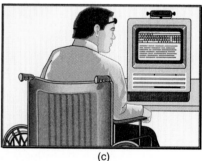

(c)

**FIGURE 7.2** Enabling disabled people to work with computers. (*Source*: Lazzaro [1993].)

(*a*) *A PC for a blind user,* equipped with an Oscar optical scanner and a Braille printer, both by TeleSensory. The optical scanner converts text into ASCII code or into proprietary word processing format. Files saved on disk can then be translated into Braille and sent to the printer. Visually impaired users can also enlarge the text on the screen by loading a TSR software magnification program.

(*b*) *The deaf user's PC* is connected to a telephone via an Ultratec Intele-Modem Baudot/ASCH modem. The user is sending and receiving messages to and from someone at a remote site who is using a telecommunications device for deaf people (right).

(*c*) *This motor-disabled person* is communicating with a PC using a Pointer Systems optical head pointer to access all keyboard functions on a virtual keyboard shown on the PC's display. The user can "strike" a key in one of two ways. He can focus on the desired key for a user-definable time period (which causes the key to be highlighted), or he can click an adapted switch when he chooses the desired key.

Adaptive equipment for computers permits people with disabilities to perform tasks they would not normally be able to do. Figure 7.2 (on p. 302) shows a PC for a deaf user, a PC for a blind user, and a PC for a motor-disabled user. Since the summer of 1994, companies with 15 employees or more have been required to comply with the Americans with Disabilities Act. This act requires companies to take reasonable steps to ensure that employees with disabilities will be able to work with specially adapted computers as well as with other equipment.

## QUALITY OF LIFE IMPROVEMENTS

On a broader scale, IT has implications for the **quality of life.** An increase in organizational efficiency may result in more leisure time for workers. The workplace can be expanded from the traditional nine-to-five job at a central location to twenty-four hours a day at any location. This expansion provides a flexibility that can significantly improve the quality of leisure time, even if the total amount of leisure time is not increased. Our health and safety can also be improved, since robots can work in uncomfortable or dangerous environments, as in the following *It at Work* example.

### IT At Work    NEW TASKS FOR ROBOTS

*U*SING IT

...in Production &
Operations Management

**CALIFORNIA ROBOTS HIT THE ROAD.**  Road signs in California say, "Robots Working." The California Transportation Department and the University of California at Davis have developed robotic road-maintenance systems that save money, reduce congestion, and prevent worker accidents. The robo-repairer, which is operated by only one employee, uses lasers to spot cracks between the pavement and the shoulder. It then dispenses the right amount of patch material (see picture). Incidentally, farmers use a similar machine that dispenses fertilizers and/or pesticides after a robot "sees" the crop and soil and analyzes them.

California Robots on the road.

Caltrans Corporation is using an unmanned machine, based on technology developed for the military, that combines a hovercraft and a video camera to inspect bridges. Other highway robots inspect traffic lanes and identify hazardous materials from a safe distance. Caltrans project manager, Thomas West, says such machines are critical to keeping roads in good shape to handle the ever-increasing traffic.*

**ROBOTS CLEAN TRAIN STATIONS IN JAPAN.** With growing amounts of rubbish to deal with at Japanese train stations and fewer people willing to work as cleaners, officials have started turning the dirty work over to robots. Since May 1993, the Central Japan Railway Company and Sizuko Company, a Japanese machinery maker, have been using robots programmed to vacuum rubbish. A railway official said the robots, which are capable of doing the work of 10 people each, have been operating at the Sizuko station in central Japan. The robots measure about 1.5 meters wide and 1.2 meters long. The railway and Sizuko spent 70 million yen to develop the machines and are planning to program them for other tasks, such as sweeping and scrubbing.

More than any other country, Japan has made extensive use of robots in industry. It also uses them to assist the blind and the elderly as well as to diagnose some illnesses; robots are even being used to clean cemeteries.**

**For Further Exploration:** If robots are so effective, what will be the impact on unemployment when more tasks will be robotized? What will people do if robots take over? ▲

*SOURCE: Based on "California Robots May Soon Hit the Road," *BusinessWeek*, December 7, 1992.

**SOURCE: Based on "Robots Used to Clean Train Station in Japan," *The Sunday Times* (Singapore), June 6, 1993.

**IMPROVEMENTS IN HEALTH CARE.** IT has brought about major improvements in health care delivery, ranging from better and faster diagnoses to expedited research and development of new drugs to more accurate monitoring of critically ill patients. One technology that has made a special contribution is artificial intelligence. Of special interest are expert systems that support diagnosis of diseases and the use of machine vision in enhancing the work of radiologists. Recently, surgeons started to use virtual reality to plan complex surgeries.

The Internet cancer site (http://oncelink.upenn.edu) features more than 8,000 documents (1998) written by experts. It offers information on the latest research studies and cancer pain management. It also helps families cope with emotional and financial burdens. In 1998, the site had more than 1.2 million visitors *each day* from about 80 countries.

Of the thousands of other applications related to health care it is interesting to point out the administrative systems, which range from insurance fraud detection (e.g., by IBM's Fraud and Abuse Management System) to nursing scheduling and financial and marketing management. Also, a sick person who needs help can activate a small transistor that is worn on a necklace. A computer chip automatically activates the telephone to notify an operator who can contact an emergency service or a physician.

On June 26, 1998, the first China-America Internet medical video teleconferencing was initiated. Doctors in Xian Medical University communicated over the Internet with American doctors at Stanford Medical School. Now, doctors can discuss complex medical cases not only on the telephone, but also with the support of pictures and sound.

**CRIME FIGHTING AND OTHER BENEFITS.** Computer applications can benefit society in many ways. Here are some examples:

▶ Electronic sensors and computers reduce traffic congestion in many major cities from Los Angeles to Tokyo.

- ▶ A geographical information system helps the San Bernadino Sheriff's Department to better visualize crime patterns and allocate resources.

- ▶ A computerized voice mail system is used in Rochester, NY so that homeless and other needy people can find jobs, access health care resources, and gain independent living skills.

- ▶ IT provides many devices for disabled people. Examples include a bilingual notebook computer for blind students, a two-way writing telephone, a robotic page-turner, a hair-brusher, and a hospital-bedside video trip to the zoo.

- ▶ In 1997, information about sex offenders was put on the Internet (see related issues of child abuse in "Debate" at the end of the chapter).

- ▶ Los Angeles County has a sophisticated computer program for reporting evaluation and tracking of over 150,000 gang members in the county. The program significantly helps reduce gang crime.

- ▶ Electronic imaging and fax enhance searching for missing children. In addition to its Web site, www.missingkids.com, which attracts more than a million hits each day, the Center for Missing and Exploited Children can send high-quality photos plus text to many fax machines and to portable machines in police cars. Computers improved the quality of fax transmission and increased the number of people exposed to the announcements. Of special interest is the support given by computers in a California kidnapping case shown below.

## *IT At Work*   TRACING KIDNAPPERS VIA THE INTERNET

USING IT

...in Public Service

On October 1, 1993, America was shocked by the abduction of 12-year-old Polly Klaas from a slumber party at her home in Petaluma, California (see picture below). While Polly was only one of 4,500 children missing annually, her case received tremendous pub-

licity due to the unusual nature of the abduction. Normally, the authorities distribute blurry black-and-white snapshots of the victim in the neighborhod of the missing child. The police usually use fax machines that turn out poor reproductions of pictures for dissemination.

Polly's picture and the FBI sketch were scanned into the Internet and several other networks. From there, the information was transmitted to several hundred electronic bulletin boards. In addition, eight computers sent the images via computer fax to grocery stores and transportation hubs around the country at a rate of 1,000 pictures per minute (see picture). Overall, more than seven million high quality copies were distributed.

Since this was the first application of computers for the purpose of distributing high-quality information nationwide, it took about two weeks to complete. The knowledge gained through this experience enabled the National Center for Missing and Exploited Children to solicit the help of millions of searchers for lightning-fast searches.

Based on this case a Web site for helping to find missing children has been created (www.missingkids.com). The site contains pictures and a search engine. Also, the Web is used to distribute photos to local communities (with the help of Kinko's and Sir Speedy).

**For Further Exploration:** How did the Web improve on Klaas's case? A CyberTip line allows people with information about missing kids to send it online. How can this interface with the Web site? ▲

SOURCE: Based on Smolowe, J., "A High-Tech Dragnet," *Time*, November 1, 1993, and *Internet Week*, Nov. 17, 1997.

## THE INTERNET (ELECTRONIC) COMMUNITY

Rheingold (1993) believes that the Web is being transformed into a social Web or community. He thinks that every Web site should incorporate a place for people to chat. His popular Web site, http://www.minds.com, is an interesting place to visit—a kind of virtual community center. It is a place where discussions cover many controversial topics, but mostly the impact of technology on life.

**Electronic communities** are also related to electronic commerce. For example, Champy et al. (1996) describe online, consumer-driven markets where most of the consumers' needs, ranging from finding a mortgage to job hunting, will be arranged from home. Electronic communities will eventually have a massive impact on almost every company that produces consumer goods and services. The electronic communities will change the nature of corporate strategy and the manner in which business is done. For further discussion see *Business-Week*, May 7, 1997.

Electronic communities are spreading quickly over the Internet. Armstrong and Hagel (1996) and Hagel and Armstrong (1997) recognize four types of electronic communities. They are:

▶ *Communities of transaction.* These facilitate buying and selling. Members include buyers, sellers, intermediaries, and so on. In Chapter 6 we provide examples such as virtual vineyards, which in addition to selling wines provide experts' information on wines and a place for wine lovers to chat with each other. GE's TPN network created the infrastructure for many traders to conduct bids or simply buy and sell (TPN-mart). The site www.fishmart.com is another example.

▶ *Communities of interest.* Here people have the chance to interact with each other on a specific topic. For example, if you are interested in gardening try www.gardenweb.com. The Motley Fool (www.motleyfool.com) is a forum for individual investors. City 411 provides comprehensive information about local communities, where many topics such as entertainment, traffic, and weather reports are displayed. Geocities (www.geocities.com) is organized into several dozen communities of interest. More than 1,000,000 members are organized in communities such as Motor City (car lovers), and Nashville (country music). Members have a "marketplace" for buying and selling goods and services. www.agriculture.com is a business-related sharing place for farmers. Thousands of other communities of interest exist on the Web.

▶ *Communities of relations.* These are organized around certain life experiences. For example, the cancer forum on CompuServe contains all information and exchange of opinion regarding cancer. Parent Soup is a favorite gathering spot for parents, seniors like to "SeniorNet," and Women's Wire is a well-known on-line community aimed at women, with regular celebrity chats and discussion.

▶ *Communities of fantasy.* Participants create imaginary environments. For example, AOL subscribers can pretend to be a medieval baron at the Red Dragon Inn. On ESPNet participants can create competing teams.

> Just as our retail stores provide a community meeting place for our customers, Web store offers a virtual community meeting place to shop, learn and interact with others of similar interests.
> — *Kristin Borhofen*

Electronic communities can create value in the following ways: They charge usage fees; they charge users contact fees for downloading an article, music, or picture; they draw revenues from transactions and advertisements; and they may take advantage of synergies by reducing the cost of customer service. For the ways companies can benefit from electronic communities see the book *Net Gain,* by Hagel and Armstrong (1997).

An interesting case is that of N2k corporation which provides multiple Web sites to different communities of interest in music (e.g., see www.classical-insites.com for lovers of classical music). The company sells CDs, T-shirts, and more, and it provides many free services to the members of about 10 communities. Sales have grown by 300% in less than 2 years.

Robert Winer, in his *Cybernetics* (1986), raises some interesting issues, such as: What are the ways in which virtual communities can be arranged effectively, and will virtual communities lead to a fractionalized or integrated society?

An interesting project for the community of design engineers is provided by Analog Devices (www.analog.com). The company allows any design engineer extensive free online access to its technical experts. This is an example of how the concept of communities is utilized to provide commercial benefits. (See *Interactive Week*, Feb. 23, 1998, page 43.)

Finally, a special report of *Business Week* (Hof et al. [1997]) provides an overview of the field with coverage of the most interesting communities and their special terminology. For example, a **Netizen** is a member who surfs the Internet.

## INFORMATION TECHNOLOGY AND EMPLOYMENT LEVEL

The major attribute associated with automation is the replacement of people by machines. From its inception in the eighteenth century, automation has caused people to lose their jobs. Naturally, many people rejected or objected to automation. Butler's work of fiction, described earlier, is an example of the concern people have about automation; so is the classic Charlie Chaplin movie *Modern Times,* which attempted to show how machines displace people and how workers can be dehumanized in a factory.

There is no doubt that many people *have* been displaced by automation, but many more have gained employment due to automation. Machines replaced muscle power in the Industrial Revolution; in the Information Revolution, machines are replacing both muscle and brain power. The increase in productivity provided by computers leads to lower costs and prices for products and services. Computers encourage competition, which leads to further decline in prices. Lower prices mean higher demand, which, in turn, creates more jobs. The computer industry itself has created millions of new jobs.

Unemployment has been one of the major concerns of developing countries. However, during the past decade, this concern has spread to industrialized countries as well (see Ceramalus [1993]). The high unemployment rate in the United States in 1992 was one of the major factors in the 1992 presidential election. In 1994, the United Nations conducted a special investigation to study unemployment, which continues to increase in many countries.

Due to difficult economic times, increased global competition, demands for customization, and increased consumer sophistication, companies have had no choice but to increase their investments in IT. In addition, computers are becoming "smarter" and more capable as time passes. The competitive advantage of replacing people with machines is increasing rapidly. For this reason, some people believe that society is heading toward massive unemployment. The remaining part of this section presents the major arguments of two opposing factions: those who believe that massive unemployment is coming, and those who believe that this is not going to happen.

**ARGUMENTS THAT SUPPORT MASSIVE UNEMPLOYMENT.** Kalman Toth, author of *The Workless Society* (1990), predicted that by 2010 there will be massive unemployment; most of the U.S. workforce will be replaced by machine intelligence. Toth believes that people currently making a living from computers will be replaced by what he refers to as silicon magnetic intelligence (SMI). Eventually, SMI will be able to drive trucks and perform other tasks through development of a stationary body–based intelligence augmented by a visual pattern processed through a video camera. By adding hearing and speech to an artificial intelligence device that can already see, SMI units could take over an unlimited variety of human jobs.

A more plausible argument is provided by Rifkin (1995), who argues that the new wave of IT innovations will result in a sharp decline of administrative and service positions. For example, business process reengineering reduces the number of clerks, the Internet will reduce the sales jobs, and expert systems will reduce analyst jobs. Rifkin does not believe that any economic sector will be able to absorb all those who lose their jobs.

A group of economists (including Nobel Prize winner Wassily Leontief [1986]) presents the following supporting arguments:

1. The need for human labor will be reduced significantly because of computers (productivity increases of 1000 percent or more will be realized in some industries).
2. The skill levels required of people performing many jobs with the help of IT will be low.

3. IT will affect both blue- and white-collar employees (professionals and managers) in all sectors, including service industries and high-technology companies. In the past, service industries and the high-technology sector absorbed employees displaced by computers in other sectors.

4. In the past few years, especially in the early 1990s, several industries—ranging from banking and insurance to computer and automotive industries—have laid off millions of employees.

5. Industry, government, and services already have a substantial amount of **hidden unemployment;** that is, companies retain many employees who are not needed or fully utilized but remain due to humanitarian reasons, union pressures, or government policies.

6. Unemployment levels have grown steadily in the 1980s and early 1990s in spite of increased computerization; the current reduction in the unemployment level (1998) will be followed by an increase sooner or later.

7. The per-capita amount of goods and services that people can consume is limited, and sooner or later it may stop growing. Therefore, the idea that the economy can grow and produce without limit (and create jobs) is highly questionable.

8. Many organizations are reengineering their operations in an effort to remain competitive or to stay within budgets. This will reduce the demand for labor even further.

9. The use of the Internet for electronic commerce will result in a loss of millions of jobs in marketing and brokerage services (see Baatz [1996]).

**ARGUMENTS CONTRADICTING MASSIVE UNEMPLOYMENT.** While the arguments for massive unemployment in the future are rather convincing, there are many people, including another Nobel Prize winner, Herbert Simon (1977), who believe that IT *will not* cause massive unemployment. Instead, IT will continue to create new jobs and even increase the overall employment level. Their primary arguments are the following:

1. Historically, automation has always resulted in increased employment by creating new occupations and markets.

2. Unemployment is higher in nonindustrialized countries than in industrialized ones.

3. Work, especially the professional and managerial kind, can always be expanded, so there will be work for everyone.

4. The task of converting to fully automated factories and offices is complex and may take several generations.

5. Many tasks cannot be fully automated (top management, nursing, marriage counseling, surgery, the performing arts, and the creative arts).

6. Machines and people can be fully employed, each where its comparative advantage is the strongest.

7. Real wages may be reduced; however, people will have income from other sources (assuming that the government will control the distribution of wealth). Therefore, people will have enough money to spend and thus will help create more jobs.

8. The cost of goods and services will be so low that the demand for them will increase significantly. Automation will never catch up with the increased demand.

9. The downsizing and restructuring of the 1990s is almost over. Organizations are much healthier and employment levels in the United States are at an all-time high in 1998. Other countries will follow sooner or later.

This debate about how IT will affect employment raises a few other questions. Is unemployment really socially undesirable? (People could have more leisure time.) Should the government intervene more in the distribution of income and in the determination of the employment level? Can the "invisible hand" in the economy, which has worked so well in the past, continue to be successful in the future? Will IT make most of us idle but wealthy? (Robots will do the work, and people will enjoy life.) Should the issue of income be completely separated from that of employment? The answers to these questions will be provided in part by the developments in future IT.

## TELECOMMUTING

> Telecommuting has enabled a few of my co-workers to move to different areas in the country but still work for our corporate offices in New York City.
>
> — *Kristin Borhofen*

By **telecommuting,** or *teleworking*, employees can work at home, at the customer's premises, or while traveling, using a computer linked to their place of employment. The first telecommuters were typists and bookkeepers, but now a growing number of professionals do a significant portion of their work at home or on the road. Telecommuting, which is used by many corporations in large cities, is also appealing to small entrepreneurs (see Box 7.5).

---

## *A Closer Look*  BOX 7.5

### THE VIRTUAL ENTREPRENEUR

While many telecommuters work for other companies, there are people who run their own businesses from home. A third kind of telecommuters is people who work for others in specially designed telecommuting centers. Henricks (1993) provides the following examples of all three kinds.

▶ Brenda Clamera Brimages develops math textbooks that sell millions of copies and manages an ever-shifting stable of writers and designers spread across the country, all from her home.

▶ An ophthalmologist, Dr. J. Garden, examines prison inmates without traveling the 40 miles to the prison. Instead, she tests eyes using a PC, modem, and video camera, all from her living room.

▶ Frank Cottle has built nine telecommuting centers in Southern California where close to 1,000 tenants rent space, computers, faxes, Internet access, and phones to work with colleagues thousands of miles away.

▶ Michael Kouloaroudis of Brooklyn, New York, gets leads on overseas companies looking for U.S. products. Using one computer and operating from his home, he grossed over $100,000 on one deal alone by selling U.S.-made window air conditioners to Japan.

▶ All 14 employees of Journal Graphics work from home in several states. The company produces transcriptions of broadcast news and talk shows. Employees can locate where they wish.

---

Telecommuting has a number of potential advantages for employees, employers, and society (see Table 7.5 on next page). However, there are also potential disadvantages. The major disadvantages for the employees are increased feelings of isolation, loss of fringe benefits, lower pay (in some cases), no workplace visibility with the potential of slower promotions, and lack of socialization. The major disadvantages to employers are difficulties in supervising work, potential

**Table 7.5** The Benefits of Telecommuting

*Benefits to the Employee*
- ▶ Less stress (no driving, no office pressure).
- ▶ Ability to go to school while working.
- ▶ Improved family life (fewer family conflicts).
- ▶ Opportunity to make more money (if on an incentive plan).
- ▶ Money saved on lunches, clothes, gas, parking, and car maintenance.
- ▶ Commuting time saved.
- ▶ Ability to control schedule and time better.
- ▶ Employment opportunities for housebound people (single parents of children, handicapped).

*Benefits to the Organization*
- ▶ Increased productivity (15 to 50 percent) is claimed.
- ▶ Reduced real estate (or rent) cost.
- ▶ Reduced cost of employees' parking lots.
- ▶ Ability to retain skilled employees who otherwise would leave.
- ▶ Ability to tap remote labor pool. Greater staffing flexibility.
- ▶ Less paperwork.
- ▶ Less absenteeism.
- ▶ Fewer labor costs (some people will take lower wages in order to stay home).
- ▶ Better interaction of employees with clients and suppliers (work can be done at the customers' sites).

*Benefits to Society*
- ▶ Less air pollution.
- ▶ Less use of fossil fuels.
- ▶ Fewer traffic problems and car accidents.
- ▶ More business for suburbs and rural areas.

data security problems, training costs, and the high cost of equipping and maintaining telecommuters' homes. Despite these disadvantages, the use of telecommuting is on the increase. Some experts predict that in 10 to 15 years, 50 percent of all work will be done at home, on the road, or at the customer's site. On the other side are those that believe that the growth of telecommuting will be very slow due to its disadvantages and employers' resistance to change.

Telecommuting helps health care employees and physicians to treat patients from a distance. This is especially important in rural areas and during disasters or military conflicts. (See *Monitor*, Aug. 1997, p. 38.)

Almost all groupware technologies can be used to support telecommuting. Regular and overnight mail, special messengers, and fax are still used to support telecommuting, but they are slow and expensive. The Internet is gradually replacing them.

Telecommuting can be used on a temporary basis. For example, during the 1996 Summer Olympics, Atlanta employers anticipated that 750,000 additional cars would create a traffic nightmare. So, many Atlanta companies set up temporary ISDN lines to save employees from traffic snarls. Vendors cooperated; Symantec and U.S. Robotics offered companies free software to provide remote access to corporate networks. The Olympics provided many employees and companies with their first taste of telecommuting.

The opportunity to work at home helps women or single parents with young children assume more responsible managerial positions in organizations. This could lead to better pay for women who can devote more attention to business while they still carry on duties at home.

**TELECOMMUTING AND PRODUCTIVITY.** Why would productivity go up if people work at home? Strangely enough, reduced absenteeism has been cited by many organizations as a reason for increased productivity. Paul Ruper, Associate Director of New Ways to Work, claims absenteeism can be reduced by telecommuting because it eliminates "sort of" illnesses. He refers to those mornings when an employee wakes up and just feels "sort of blah." The trip to work and a whole day at the office is not going to make him feel any better, so he stays home.

Telecommuting forces managers to manage by results instead of by overseeing. Telecommuting forces both employees and managers to ask some serious questions about the real purpose of a job. This process, although difficult, could make both the manager and the employee reduce misunderstandings about work. The employee will have a clear understanding of his or her responsibilities and thereby be accountable for his or her actions.

Even though many employees are attracted to telecommuting, it is not for everybody and should not be mandatory. Some employees need to work with others, and for those employees telecommuting may not be an option. Also, not all jobs can be done while telecommuting and not all managers can participate.

## OTHER IMPACTS

**CHALLENGE TO FREE SPEECH VERSUS INTERNET INDECENCY.** Federal lawmakers in the United States and other countries are battling to protect children from being exposed to what is described as the "worst, most vile, and most perverse pornography," by Senator James Exon, sponsor of the 1996 Communication Decency Act. The act was ruled unconstitutional immediately after its passage as a violation of the First Amendment to the Constitution.

> When you are on the Internet as a representative of your company, decency laws should prevail.
>
> — *Blake Thompson*

The problem of pornography is very serious (see Elmer-Dewitt [1995]), since it is difficult to decide what is indecent and impossible to control what is delivered on Web sites from other countries.

The U.S. Supreme Court was considering this issue at the time this book was written. In the meantime, it is clearly the responsibility of Internet companies and advertisers to do whatever they can to minimize the problem by issuing guidelines.

**SOCIAL RESPONSIBILITY.** Organizations need to be motivated to utilize IT to improve the quality of life in the workplace. This challenge relates not only to companies that produce IT hardware and software but also to companies that use these technologies. Increased exposure to the concepts and actual use of IT will bring pressure on public agencies and corporations to employ the latest capabilities for solving social problems outside the workplace as well. This is part of the organization's **social responsibility.** At the same time, conflicting public pressures may rise to suppress the use of IT because of concerns about privacy and "big brother" government.

**INTERNATIONAL IMPLICATIONS.** As a result of advancements in information technology, such as the increased speed of communications and information flow, we are living in a shrinking world. In fact, more than 25 years ago, Marshall McLuhan coined the term "global village" to refer to this very concept. The power of the media is growing as a result of cable television, electronic publishing, and networking through computer modems.

Many countries, willingly or unwillingly, are being westernized as a result of information about western ways of life and values flowing freely across borders. This has the potential to fuel the fires of political unrest, especially in nondemocratic countries. As an example, in 1996, China blocked hundreds of western Web sites from being viewed on the Internet in China. Facsimile, computer disks, electronic publishing, tape recorders, and other forms of information technology could assist the masses in planning revolts. How these advancements in technology are viewed, therefore, would depend upon where one's affiliations lie.

# ▶ MANAGERIAL ISSUES

Management attention must be directed to the social, psychological, ethical, and legal issues surrounding IT. Here are some points to consider:

1. Lawsuits against employers that focus on repetitive strain injuries under the Federal Disabilities Act are on the increase. Because this law is new, court cases may be very costly.

2. Multinational corporations face different cultures in the different countries in which they are doing business. What might be ethical in country A may be unethical in country B. Therefore, it is essential to develop a country-specific ethics code in addition to a corporatewide one. Also, managers should realize that in some countries there is no legislation specifically concerned with computers and data.

3. Issues of privacy, ethics, social responsibilities, and so on may seem to be tangential to running a business, but ignoring them may hinder the operation of many organizations. Privacy protection can cut into profits (see Hildebrand [1996]).

4. The impacts of electronic commerce and the Internet can be so strong that the entire manner in which companies do business will be changed, with significant impacts on procedures, people, organizational structure, management, and business processes.

5. The spread of IT may result in massive layoffs in some companies. Management should be aware of this possibility and have a contingency plan regarding appropriate reaction.

6. Telecommuting is a promising approach, but its implementation is not as simple as it may seem. Therefore, it is spreading very slowly. Expertise is essential since it is necessary to address legal, psychological, technical, and financial issues.

7. Electronic communities are not just a social phenomena. Many communities provide an opportunity for a business to generate sales and profits.

## KEY TERMS

Code of ethics *286*

Electronic communities *306*

Electronic surveillance *289*

Ergonomics *301*

Ethics *285*

Hidden unemployment *309*

Information privacy *287*

Intellectual property *293*

Job content *296*

Job stress *299*

Privacy policies *293*

Quality of life *303*

Netizen *307*

Role ambiguity *296*

Social responsibility *312*

Span of control *295*

Telecommuting *310*

## CHAPTER HIGHLIGHTS  *(L–x means learning objective number x)*

▶ The major negative impacts of IT are in the areas of invasion of privacy, unemployment, and dehumanization. (L–1)

▶ The major positive impacts of IT are its contribution to employment of the disabled, improvements in health, delivery of education, crime fighting, increased productivity, and improvement of the environment as well as the quality of life. (L–1)

▶ Ethical issues can be classified into categories of privacy, accuracy, property, and accessibility. (L–2)

▶ Major privacy issues are electronic surveillance, accuracy and accessibility of personal information in a database, dissemination of offensive information, and the right to privacy. (L–3)

▶ Dehumanization is a major concern that needs to be overcome by proper design and planning of information systems. (L–4)

▶ Computers can increase health risks to eyes, back, bones, and muscles. Ergonomically designed computing facilities can greatly reduce the risks associated with computers. (L–4)

▶ Information technology can make organizations become flatter and change authority, job content, and status of employees. As a result, the manager's job and methods of supervision and decision making may drastically change. (L–5)

▶ Many positive social implications can be expected from IT. They range from providing opportunities to the disabled to reducing people's exposure to hazardous situations. (L–6)

▶ In one view, IT will cause massive unemployment because of increased productivity, reduced required skill levels, and the potential reduction of employment in all sectors of the economy. (L–6)

▶ In another view, IT will increase employment levels because automation makes products and services more affordable, thus increasing demand; and the process of disseminating automation is slow enough to allow the economy to adjust to information technologies. (L–6)

▶ Quality of life, both at work and at home, is likely to improve as a result of IT. (L–6)

▶ IT enables people to work from many places, including home. (L–6)

▶ Electronic communities of different types are spreading over the Web, providing opportunities to some companies to increase revenues and profit. (L–6)

## QUESTIONS FOR REVIEW

1. Describe how IT can have negative effects on people.

2. Define ethics.

3. What are the four categories of ethics as they apply to IT?

4. Explain why some people object to computerization.

5. Define the four states of privacy: solitude, intimacy, anonymity, and reserve.

6. Why do the government and corporations use surveillance?

7. Why is there so much information about individuals in databases?

8. Explain the potential ethical issues involved in using electronic bulletin boards.

9. Describe the content of a "code of ethics" (for privacy).

10. What are some of the major impacts of IT on individuals?

11. Describe some of the potential risks to human health caused by extensive use of computers.

12. List the major societal impacts of IT that are described in this chapter, and categorize each of them as either negative or positive.

**13.** Present the major arguments of those who believe that IT will result in massive unemployment.

**14.** Present the major arguments of those who believe that IT will *not* result in massive unemployment.

**15.** Describe the following organizational impacts: flatter

organizations, increased span of control, power redistribution, supervision, and decision making.

**16.** Define intellectual property.

**17.** Define Internet community and list its four types.

**18.** Define telecommuting.

## QUESTIONS FOR DISCUSSION

**1.** There are three ways to alert employees that information in their computers is under observation: (1) notify all employees upon recruitment that they may be observed while working on their computers, (2) notify employees once a year that they may be under surveillance, or (3) alert employees by a light or visible message on the computer screen (each time the computer is turned on) that they may be under observation. Which alternative would you prefer and why?

**2.** The Internal Revenue Service (IRS) buys demographic market research data from private companies. This data contains income statistics that could be compared to tax returns. Many U.S. citizens feel that their rights within the realm of the privacy act are being violated; others say that this is an unethical behavior on the part of the government. Discuss.

**3.** Clerks at 7-Eleven stores enter data regarding customers (sex, approximate age, and so on) into the computer. These data are then processed for improved decision making. Customers are not informed about this nor are they being asked for permission. (Names are *not* keyed in.) Are the clerks' actions ethical?

**4.** Many hospitals, health maintenance organizations (HMOs), and federal agencies are converting, or plan to convert, all patients' medical records from paper to electronic storage (using imaging technology). Once completed, electronic storage enables quick access to most records. However, the availability of these records in a database and on networks may allow people, some of whom are unauthorized, to view one's private data. To protect privacy fully may cost too much money and/or considerably slow accessibility to the records. What policies could health care administrators use in such situations? Discuss.

**5.** Northeast Utilities (Hartford, CT) has its meter readers gather information about services needed on its customers' homes, such as a driveway or fence requiring repairs. It sells the data to companies that would stand to gain from the information. Customers are then solicited via direct mail, telemarketing, and so on for the services that the meter readers record as

being needed. While some customers welcome this approach, others consider it an annoyance because they are not interested in the particular repairs. Assess the value of the company's IT against the potential negative effects of adverse public reaction.

**6.** IT may have both positive and negative effects in the same situation. Give two examples, and explain how to reconcile such a case.

**7.** Explain why there are such diverse opinions regarding specific ethical issues even within the same company.

**8.** It is said that IT has raised many new privacy issues. Why is this so?

**9.** Discuss the various aspects of relationships between IT and surveillance.

**10.** Several examples in this chapter illustrate how information about individuals can help companies improve their businesses. Summarize all the examples provided in this chapter, and explain why they may result in invasion of privacy.

**11.** Robots are used in California and Japan to support transportation. At the same time, they take jobs away from people. Describe all the considerations that management will be faced with when it needs to decide whether or not to use robots.

**12.** Explore the effects of the Americans with Disabilities Act on productivity and cost as it relates to IT.

**13.** Explain why organizations are becoming flatter and what the implications are for management practices.

**14.** Why do many companies and professional organizations develop their own codes of ethics?

**15.** What are the two major rules of privacy? Why do these rules make privacy issues difficult to enforce?

**16.** The Kennedy Center Web site is being visited by millions of people who enjoy different forms of art. The Center had a plan to offer snippets of classical concerts, plays, etc., so that the public could view some of its programs. Artists and their unions objected. They also wanted royalties, which the Center was unable to pay. The unions of the Center's employees are also complaining. They do not like the online ticketing introduced by the Center. Discuss the ethical (and possible legal) issues of the incident (for details see *Webmaster*, May/June, 1996).

17. Cyber Promotions Inc. attempted to use the First Amendment right in their flooding of America Online (AOL) subscribers with junk e-mail. AOL tried to block the junk mail. The federal judge agreed with AOL that unsolicited mail that is annoying, a costly waste of Internet time, and often inappropriate should not be sent. Discuss some of the issues involved, such as freedom of speech, how to distinguish between junk and nonjunk mail, and the analogy with regular mail.

18. Read "Privacy vs. Profit," *CIO*, Feb. 15, 1996, p. 56 (available at www.cio.com) and discuss the issue of information ownership.

## EXERCISES

1. An information security manager had access to corporate e-mail. She routinely monitored the contents of electronic correspondence among employees. She discovered that many employees were using the system for personal purposes. Some messages were love letters, and others related to a football betting pool. The security manager prepared a list of the employees, with samples of their messages, and gave them to management. Some managers punished their employees. The employees objected to the monitoring, claiming that they should have the same right to privacy as they have using the company's interoffice mail system.
   a. Is monitoring of e-mail by managers ethical?
   b. Is the use of e-mail by employees for personal communication ethical?
   c. Is the submission of a list of abusers by the security manager to management ethical?
   d. Is punishing the abusers ethical?
   e. What should the company do in order to rectify the situation?

   **Note:** In January 1996, a U.S. District court in Pennsylvania reaffirmed that employers can read electronic mail sent over their computer system, even if employees don't know about it. The court ruled that Pillsbury Company could fire a manager who used e-mail to lambaste some bosses as "backstabbing bastards." The district court ruled that Pillsbury had the right to read the e-mail, saying "the company's interest in preventing inappropriate and unprofessional comments" outweighed any privacy rights the employee had. The decision is similar to two earlier California cases that allowed company searches of e-mail.

2. Review the opening case regarding Agrico.
   a. Identify all the ethical issues involved in this case.
   b. Advise Agrico's president as to what action to take, and justify your recommendation.
   c. Assume that Jane left the software on the screen deliberately; is her behavior ethical or not?

3. Schafer (1996) pointed out that companies in key industries (such as the fishing industry) must take advantage of IT to become intensely efficient. But as a result, they simply may run out of scarce natural resources. So, the technology that was a savior may wipe many people out of business. Discuss the dilemma and examine the situation in other industries such as oil and coal. What are the possible solutions?

4. Visit the following communities: www.wbs.net, www.geocities.com, www.well.com, www.electricmind.com, and espnet.sportzone. Join one of the communities. Become a member of the community and report on your experiences.

5. Will the Web eat your job? Read Baatz's (1996) paper. What types of jobs are most likely to disappear or be drastically reduced? Why?

## DEBATES

1. The State of California maintains a database of people who allegedly abuse children (the database also includes the alleged victims). The list is made available to dozens of public agencies and it is considered in child adoption and employment decisions. Computers easily access the list. In 1996, an alleged abuser and her child, whose case was dropped but whose names had remained on the list, sued the State of California for invasion of privacy.
   Some of the issues involved are:
   a. Is there a need to include names of people on the list in cases that were dismissed or declared unfounded?
   b. Who should make the decision about what names should be included, and what should the criteria be?
   c. What is the potential damage to the abusers (if any)?
   d. Should the State of California abolish the list? Why or why not?

2. Milberg et al. (1995) and Johnson and Molvey (1995) pointed out some interesting issues relating to IT and decision making. Specifically, Milberg et al. believe that personal information privacy, the ability to personally control information about oneself, is fast becoming one of the most important ethical issues of the information age. Information technology departments—coupled with the increasing value of information to decision makers—are causing a rising tide of concern about personal information privacy management practices. As such concerns grow, businesses' ability to use personal information may be threatened, and decision makers will have to make trade-offs between the efficient, effective operations of businesses and the protection of personal privacy.

Johnson and Molvey claim that computer decision systems have become an integral part of the decision-making apparatus of many public and private organizations. In the United States, decisions made by Congress and the executive branch are increasingly based on computer models that simulate the effects of public policy decisions. Congress has even passed legislation requiring the development of comprehensive plans and management strategies, which, in effect, mandates the use of computer decision systems. Computer decision systems provide a variety of benefits leading to more informed decision-making assistance in coping with complexity, the ability to manage uncertainty in a rational way, and consistency. At the same time, they raise a variety of ethical issues. The ethical issues center on the values and trade-offs made within the system. (For example, how are risks to human life managed? Is it fair to put dollar amounts on human life?) System designers should articulate standards of behavior as part of a process of professionalization that will create accountability in the field of computer decision systems.

Other issues relate directly to the Internet, such as the flooding of the Internet with pornography, hate material, and junk mail versus the right of free speech or the electronic surveillance of potential criminals versus their privacy.

Identify the debatable issues and prepare a list of the major pros and cons for each point of view.

## GROUP ASSIGNMENT

According to Denning (1993 a, b), a leading researcher on data security, personal privacy must be balanced against our collective interest in law and order. Denning supports proposed legislation which would require providers of electronic communications services and PBX operators to do the following: (1) ensure the government that, in real time, the communication signals of individual(s) named in a court order can be monitored and transferred to a remote government monitoring facility, and (2) ensure that this will be done without detection by the subject and without degradation of service. A special clipper chip, a microprocessor that is linked to a telephone or data terminal, will do monitoring, so federal agents can unscramble coded messages (see Figure 7.3 at the top of page 318).

Opponents raise the following concerns.

▶ The proposal would hold back technology and stymie innovation.

## INTERNET EXERCISES

Note: The URLs included here were current when the book went to press. However, they are subject to change without notice. Please consult the Turban Web site (www.Wiley.com/college/turban2e).

1. Your mission is to identify additional ethical issues related to the Internet and intranets. Surf the Internet, join newsgroups, and read articles from the Internet.

▶ It will jeopardize security and privacy: first, because the remote monitoring capability would make the system vulnerable to attack, and second, because the intercept capability itself would introduce a new vulnerability into the systems.

▶ Implementing the intercept could harm the competitiveness of the United States. (Why?)

▶ The cost of implementing the intercept might not justify the benefits.

▶ It is not clear who must comply with the proposed legislation and what compliance means.

### Questions for Group Assignment

a. Find the status of the proposed federal legislation.

b. Divide the group into pro and con subgroups.

c. Prepare presentations to the class by each subgroup.

d. Prepare a summary statement.

2. There is considerable talk about the impact of the Internet on society. Concepts such as a global village, an Internet community, the Internet society and the like are getting much attention (e.g., see *Harvard Business Review*, May/June 1996 and *BusinessWeek*, May 5, 1997). Surf the Internet (e.g., try http://www.mind.com) and prepare a report on the topic. How can companies profit from Internet communities?

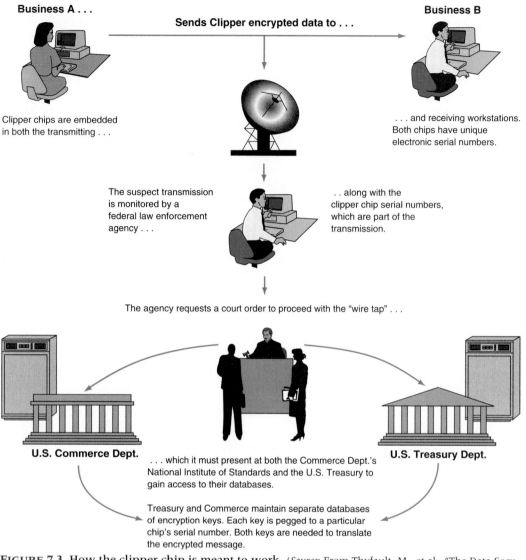

**Business A . . .**

**Sends Clipper encrypted data to . . .**

**Business B**

Clipper chips are embedded in both the transmitting . . .

. . . and receiving workstations. Both chips have unique electronic serial numbers.

The suspect transmission is monitored by a federal law enforcement agency . . .

. . along with the clipper chip serial numbers, which are part of the transmission.

The agency requests a court order to proceed with the "wire tap" . . .

**U.S. Commerce Dept.**

**U.S. Treasury Dept.**

. . . which it must present at both the Commerce Dept.'s National Institute of Standards and the U.S. Treasury to gain access to their databases.

Treasury and Commerce maintain separate databases of encryption keys. Each key is pegged to a particular chip's serial number. Both keys are needed to translate the encrypted message.

**FIGURE 7.3 How the clipper chip is meant to work.** (*Source*: From Thyfault, M., et al., "The Data Security Furor," *Information Week*, February 14, 1994, p. 12.)

3. The Internet and intranets are playing an important role in providing opportunities to disabled people. Find more about the topic by surfing the Internet.

4. Two interesting terms in Internet terminology are *flaming* and *spamming*. Surf the Internet to find more about these terms. How are they related?

5. Many vendors create products to support telecommuting. Find the latest technological support (e.g., http://www.gandalf.ca and www.picturetel.com).

6. Enter www.internetwk.com/links.
   a. Get a listing of industry organizations with privacy initiatives.
   b. Check out the W3C's Privacy Preferences Project.
   c. Find more information about Firefly Network's privacy policies (www.firefly.net).

7. Enter www.nolo.com.
   a. Click on Legal Encyclopedia. Try to find information about the legal issues of IT. Find information about international IT issues.
   b. Click on www.lawstreet.com. Try to find information about international legal aspects of IT.
   c. Support the above with a visit to www.legallink .org and with a search with Yahoo.

# Minicase 1

## Is Neural Computing Appropriate for Personnel Decisions?

Several months ago, the Internal Affairs Division of the Chicago Police started using computer software called neural networks (see Chapter 11), which contains a model that predicts whether each of the 14,000 officers on the force is likely to behave properly or not. The system uses a model that compares certain characteristics of all officers to a profile of about 250 officers who were dismissed or resigned under investigation for actions ranging from insubordination to misconduct. Those that match the profile are classified as "heading for trouble."

This application has been found to be fairly accurate. About half of the 91 individuals identified by the program in its initial use as having a potential problem with misconduct had already been manually identified as such and placed in an improvement program. The neural application created a debate. The Chicago police maintain that it is impossible to manually check so many officers and identify potential misconduct. If early detection of potential offenders is possible, a counseling program can rectify the situation. Only a computer program can screen so many people periodically and there is no way for a supervisor to be biased one way or another. Furthermore, neural networks have already proven to be helpful in similar tasks such as predicting recidivism by criminals on probation.

The labor union was unhappy; they said that the system is unethical. They felt that use of the software was merely a tactic by management to avoid managing the officers. "You got a guy slacking off? Supervise him, correct him." The critics' main objection is that neural networks are a form of black box: they do not indicate how they arrive at a conclusion. So, it is not fair to use a technology that you do not understand.

The software developer said that "Users don't need to know what the software is doing—they only need to know whether it works." The Chicago Police Department believes that the program works very well.

### Questions for Minicase 1

1. Is this another case where the needs of the society are in conflict with the rights of the individual? Why or why not?

2. Is using the program ethical? If you were an officer, would you object to such a program? Why?

3. As a citizen, do you want your police department to use the program? Why or why not?

4. How may a good officer at the police department feel about this issue?

5. Is it necessary to understand a technology in order to use it?

# Minicase 2

## American Stock Exchange Seeks Wireless Trades

For about 120 years, traders at the American Stock Exchange (Amex) have used hand signals to relay information about their trades. But in April 1993 Amex introduced a pilot project to test the use of handheld computers in trading. Previous attempts by the Chicago Board of Trade and by the Chicago Mercantile Exchange were not successful. Amex is using simple, off-the-shelf equipment instead of the highly customized terminals used by the Chicago exchanges. The project was the first in a series designed to make Amex a paperless trading floor.

Omer F. Sykan, director of technical planning at Amex, said that the biggest benefit is to get a real-time

position analysis to the 462 members of the exchange. Experiments are being done with two different devices. One device is used by market specialists to transmit option trades to a PC-based risk-analysis system. The second device is used for equity (stocks) trading.

Wireless technologies are expected to be faster and more cost-effective than hand signals and the paper-and-pencil trading mechanism that has been in use for the past 70 years. In the old system, specialists receive orders by hand signals and scribble their trades on an order slip. Then a clerk manually enters the data into the computer. If the markets are moving rapidly, the information that the clerk gathers from the floor is often

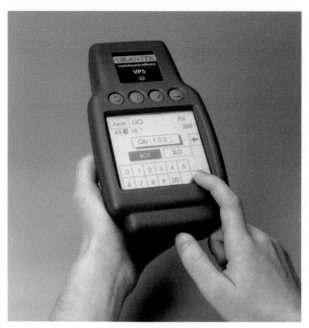

The American Stock Exchange's hand-held computer.

obsolete by the time it is put into the computers. Hand-held devices transmit information instantaneously.

While the devices are extremely easy to use, many traders do not welcome them. "We old guys are faster than most of these computers," says Jack Maxwell, a veteran of 26 years with Amex. "To hell with it; I don't need the handhelds." Attitudes of traders like Maxwell are a big problem facing expanded use of computers.

By 1996, the Amex was in the process of implementing the system, first on a voluntary basis. In summer 1998, Amex agreed to merge with NASDAQ, moving to complete automation.

## Questions for Minicase 2

1. As a consultant to Amex, you need to identify the problems of implementing the handheld computers. How would you approach your case?

2. The President of Amex is considering laying off traders like Maxwell. Would you support this decision or not?

3. Find the status of the computerization that is going on in several stock and commodity exchanges in several countries.

4. How would you convince a trader, who may soon lose his job, to use the new device?

SOURCE: Based on *Computerworld*, May 17, 1993, p. 6, the *Wall Street Journal*, July 19, 1993, p. C1, and *Fortune*, October 28, 1996, p. 52.

## REFERENCES AND BIBLIOGRAPHY

1. Agranoff, M. H., "Controlling the Threat to Personal Privacy," *Jour. of Information Systems Management*, Summer 1993.

2. Anderson, R. E., et al., "Using the New ACM Code of Ethics in Decision Making," *Communications of the ACM*, February 1993.

3. Argyris, C., "Resistance to Rational Management Systems," *Innovation*, November 10, 1970.

4. Armstrong, A., and J. Hagel III, "The Real Value of On-line Communities," *Harvard Business Review*, May–June 1996.

5. Baatz, E. B., "Will the Web Eat Your Job?," *Webmaster*, May/June, 1996.

6. Bellamy, E., *Looking Backward: 1700–1887*, Boston, MA: Houghton, Mifflin, 1989.

7. Butler, S., *EREWHON, or Over the Range* (1923, Reprint), Shrewsbury Edition, New York: AMS Press, 1972.

8. Cavoukian, A., and D. Tapscott, *Who Knows: Safeguarding Your Privacy in a Networked World*, New York: McGraw-Hill, 1997.

9. Ceramalus, N., "The Threat of Workless Future," *Management-Auckland*, November 1993.

10. Champy, J., et al., "Creating the Electronic Community," *Information Week*, June 10, 1996.

11. Charles, R. B., "Online Libel: A 250 Million Bug," *Computerworld*, January 23, 1995.

12. Cone, E., "Keyboard Injuries: Who Should Pay?," *Information Week*, January 27, 1994.

13. Davenport, T. H., "Saving IT's Soul: Human-Centered Information Management," *Harvard Business Review*, March/April, 1994.

14. Dejoie, R., et al., *Ethical Issues in Information Systems*, 2nd edition, Boston, MA: Boyd and Fraser, 1995.

15. Denning, D. E., "To Tap or Not To Tap," *Communications of the ACM*, March 1993a.

16. Denning, D. E., "Forum," *Communications of the ACM*, June 1993b.

17. Diffie, W., and S. Landau, *Privacy on the Line: The Politics of Wiretapping and Encryption*, Boston: MIT Press, 1998.

18. Elmer-Dewitt, P., "On the Screen Near You: Cyberporn," *Time*, July 3, 1995.

19. Garson, G. P., *Computer Technology and Societal Issues*, Harrisburg, PA: The Idea Group, 1995.

20. Hagel, J. III, and A. G. Armstrong, *Net Gain: Expanding Markets through Virtual Communities*, Boston: Harvard Business School Press, 1997.

21. Henricks, M., "The Virtual Entrepreneur," *Success*, June 1993.

22. Hildebrand, C., "Privacy vs. Profit," *CIO*, Feb. 15, 1996.

23. Hof, R. D., et al., "Electronic Communities," Special Report, *Business Week*, May 5, 1997.

24. Huber, G. P., "A Theory of the Effects of Advanced Information Technologies on Organizational Design, Intelligence, and Decision Making," *Academy of Management Review*, Vol. 15, No. 1, 1990.

25. Huxley, A., *Brave New World*, London: Chatto and Williams, 1932.

26. Kalman, E. A., and J. P. Grillo, *Ethical Decision Making and Information Technology*, 2nd edition, New York: McGraw-Hill, 1996.

27. Kaltnekar, Z., "Information Technology and the Humanization of Work," in *Management Impacts of IT: Perspectives on Organizational Change and Growth*, Harrisburg, PA: Idea Group, 1991.

28. Kanter, J., *Managing with Information*, 4th edition, Englewood Cliffs, NJ: Prentice-Hall, 1992.

29. Kugelmass, J., *Telecommuting: A Manager's Guide to Flexible Work*, New York: Lexington Press, 1995.

30. Larsen, T., "Global Information Technology Utilization Trends," *Journal of Global Information Management*, Spring 1996.

31. Lazzaro, J. J., "Computers for the Disabled," *Byte*, June 1993.

32. Leontief, W., *The Future Impact of Automation on Workers*, Oxford: Oxford University Press, 1986.

33. Mason, R. O., "Four Ethical Issues of the Information Age," *MIS Quarterly*, March 1986.

34. Mason, R. O., et al., *Ethics of Information Management*, Thousand Oaks: Sage Publishers, 1995.

35. Mizell, L. R., *Invasion of Privacy*, Berkley: Berkley Pub. Group, 1998.

36. Niles, J. M., *Making Telecommuting Happen: A Guide for Telemanagers and Telecommuters*, New York: John Wiley, 1998.

37. O'Leary, D. E., "Some Privacy Issues in Knowledge Discovery: The OECD Personal Privacy Guidelines," *IEEE Expert*, April 1995.

38. Pinsonneault, A., and K. Kraemer, "The Impact of Information Technology on Middle Managers," *MIS Quarterly*, September 1993.

39. Rheingold, H., *The Virtual Community: Homesteading on the Electronic Frontier*, Reading, MA: Addison Wesley, 1993.

40. Rifkin, J., *The End of Work*, New York: G. P. Putnam and Sons, 1995.

41. Ryker, R., and N. Ravinder, "An Empirical Examination of the Impact of Computer Information Systems on Users," *Information & Management*, Vol. 24, 1995.

42. Schafer, S., "Fished Out," *Inc. Technology*, November 3, 1996.

43. Schneier, B., and D. Banisar, *The Electronic Privacy Paper*, New York: John Wiley, 1997.

44. Schuler, D., "Social Computing—Special Section," *Communications of the ACM*, January 1994.

45. Simon, H., *The New Science of Management Decision*, Englewood Cliffs, N.J., Prentice Hall, 1977.

46. Smith, H. J., et al., "Information Privacy: Measuring Individuals' Concerns about Organizational Practices," *MIS Quarterly*, June 1996.

47. Toth, K., "The Workless Society," *The Futurist*, May/June 1990.

48. Varney, C. A., "Privacy in the Electronic Age," *Credit World*, January/February, 1996.

49. Weiss, E. A., ed., "Self-Assessment Procedure XXII—Ethical Issues," *Communications of the ACM*, November 1990. (Compiled from a report by D. B. Parker et al., SRI International.)

50. Wells-Branscomb, A., *Who Owns Information? From Privacy to Public Access*, New York: Basic Books, 1994.

51. Wilde, W. J., and P. A. Swatman, "Toward Virtual Communities in Rural Australia," *International Journal of Electronic Commerce*, Fall 1997.

52. Winer, R., *Cybernetics, Science and Society* (collected work), Boston: MIT Press, 1986.

Note: An integrated case study for Part II, Tradenet: Singapore's Computerization of International Trade, is available on the Turban Web site ww.wiley.com/college/turban2e).

# PART III
## USING IT

### PART I
#### IT In the Organization
1. Organizations, Environments, and Information Technology
2. Information Technologies: Concepts and Management
3. Strategic Information Systems
4. Supply Chain, Enterprise Resources Planning, and Business Process Reengineering

### PART II
#### Networks and IT
5. Network Computing: Discovery, Communication, and Collaboration
6. Electronic Commerce
7. Impacts of IT on Organizations, Individuals, and Society

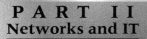

### PART III
#### Using IT
8. Transaction Processing, Innovative Functional Systems, and Integration
9. Supporting Management and Decision Making
10. Data and Knowledge Management
11. Intelligent Support Systems

### PART IV
#### Managing IT
12. Planning for Information Technology and Systems
13. Information Technology Economics
14. Systems Development
15. Managing Information Resources, Control, and Security

| Hardware | Software | Databases | Telecommunications and Internet |

Information systems applications, as described in Chapter 2, can be directed toward the functional areas or built to support certain groups of people or certain processes. Accordingly, this part is divided into four chapters.

**Chapter 8** describes innovative applications mainly within a single organization. This is in contrast with Chapters 5 and 6 where interorganizational systems were described in relationship to the networked world. Here, applications are organized according to the tradition functional areas; in addition, emphasis is placed on their *integration*. We will also show the use of IT to support the core transactions in an organization.

**Chapter 9** focuses on support technologies for executives and managers. Decision making, especially at the managerial and strategic levels, is becoming more and more complex. IT can provide support to all types of decisions, even complex ones. The chapter concentrates on two types of support. First, the support given to unstructured problems is examined under the topic of decision support systems (DSS), which uses a modeling approach to problem solving. Second, the support given to top executives in identifying problems and opportunities, as well as in assessing their importance, is covered under the topic of executive information systems.

**Chapter 10** describes the handling of the increased amount of information in both external and internal databases, which creates both opportunities and problems for organizations. The opportunities allow discovery of information on products, processes, performance, people, competitors, technology, and so on, which is necessary in making decisions, developing strategies, and managing organizations. However, due to the abundance of information it is more and more difficult to find the right information when needed. Help is found in the data warehouse, data mining, and online analytical processing concepts. This chapter also introduces the concept of knowledge bases.

**Chapter 11** directs attention to intelligent and emerging technologies. Intelligent technologies are based on the discipline of artificial intelligence and play a major role in providing innovative applications ranging from SIS and BPR support to enhancing security on the Internet. The major technologies described here are expert systems, artificial neural networks, fuzzy logic, and intelligent agents. As a representative of other emerging technologies, we present virtual reality and some of its business applications.

Part III ends with Nabisco's case describing how a modern organization manages its data for decision support, improved functional operations, and gaining a strategic advantage. The case is available on the Web site. (www.wiley.com/college.turban2e)

# CHAPTER 8

# Transaction Processing, Innovative Functional Systems, and Integration

## Learning Objectives

*After studying this chapter, you will be able to:*

**❶** Relate functional areas and business processes to the value chain model.

**❷** Identify functional management information systems.

**❸** Describe the transaction processing system and demonstrate how it is supported by IT.

**❹** Describe the support provided by IT to each of these: production/operations, marketing and sales, accounting, finance, and human resources management.

**❺** Describe the benefits and issues of integrating functional information systems.

**❻** Describe the role of IT in facilitating customer relationship management (CRM).

## INTEGRATED SOLUTIONS HELP COLONIAL BUILDING SUPPLY STAY COMPETITIVE

### The Problem

Colonial Building Supply (Centerville, UT) is a small company that must compete with chains like Home Depot. Until a few years ago, Colonial and other lumberyards used to run by the "seat of their pants." Managers used to go out into the lumberyard and physically count what was there. In contrast, Home Depot uses sophisticated computers to monitor inventory and support related decisions. Colonial installed a proprietary computer POS/accounting system in 1988, but it quickly reached its capacity. It was impossible to add data collection hand-held units to remotely collect information without a large investment. Also, the store operations were expensive. Furthermore, to remain competitive, Colonial needed a technology to provide it with information about inventory levels and customer buying trends. Lumber is a commodity whose prices fluctuate daily, sometimes hourly. Therefore, lumberyards want to keep large inventories when prices are low to meet customer demand, and they do not want to overstock during high-price periods.

### The Solution

Colonial purchased an *integrated* system from Dimensions Software (Salt Lake City). The system included accounting, POS terminal, inventory control, purchasing/receiving, employee time control and attendance, hand-held automatic identification and data collection, and several other modules, such as truck scheduling. The system runs on an IBM Pentium server with 25 terminals and several peripheral devices to execute the above capabilities. The entire system was installed in five days. The software ties different functions together under one system. Employees have access only to some designated menus, using a password.

When items are purchased they are deducted from the inventory instantly. The software examines past buying patterns and future business conditions and automatically determines amounts for reordering. For example, if building permits are up, the system will increase orders. Purchase orders are sent electronically via the Internet. The system is very user friendly and requires minimal training.

Recent additions are: (1) Document management system that stores all documents electronically. Every piece of paper is scanned, categorized and archived for easy access. (2) RF-based hand-held computers that collect data and transmit it to the computer automatically. (3) Laptops plugged into a cellular phone that allow salespersons in the field to tap into the store's computer and check availability while they meet with contractors at construction sites.

### The Results

Lower costs for data entry labor, reduction in inventory and storage space, fast access to information, better customer service, and higher employee satisfaction all contribute to Colonial's ability to stay competitive and increase its market share and profitability.

SOURCES: Condensed from *Integrated Solutions*, July 1997, pp. 7, 8, and from www.dimensions.com, 1998.

## ▶ 8.1 FUNCTIONAL INFORMATION SYSTEMS

### CROSSING FUNCTIONAL BOUNDARIES

The case of Colonial makes some interesting points about implementing information technology.

▶ IT supported the routine processes of a retailer, enabling it to be *efficient* and *effective* and to satisfy its customers.

▶ The software helped the modernization and reengineering of the company's major business processes.

▶ The software supports several business processes, not just one.

▶ The system's major applications were in logistics. However, the same software vendor provides ready-made accounting, marketing, and operation software modules, which were *integrated* with the inventory module and with each other.

▶ IT can be beneficial to a relatively small company.

▶ The integration includes connection to business partners using the Internet.

This solution was proven useful for a company whose business processes cross the traditional functional departmental lines.

The logistics, accounting operations, marketing, and finance departments are major functional areas at Colonial and at other companies. Traditionally, information systems were designed to support the functional areas by increasing their effectiveness and efficiency. However, as we discussed in Chapter 4, the traditional functional hierarchical structure may not be best for many modern organizations, because certain business processes may involve activities that are performed in several functional areas. Suppose a customer wants to buy a particular product that is stored in the corporate warehouse. An order arrives at the marketing department; then credit is approved by finance. Operations will prepare the product; the shipping department will deliver it. Accounting will bill the customer, and finance may arrange for insurance. In such a case, the customer may not be properly served, and the cost of doing business can be very high. In addition, in the traditional structure, IT is usually organized along fairly independent functional areas rather than business processes. As a result, one may experience problems in both executing the business processes and supporting them with IT.

One possible solution is to reengineer the organization. For example, create cross-functional teams, with each responsible for performing a complete business process. Then it is necessary to create appropriate information systems applications for the reengineered processes. This can be an expensive solution. In other cases, we can use IT to create a change in the business processes and organizational structure. This solution may not be effective or may be too expensive. Therefore, many companies use incremental improvements and ad hoc problem solving as problems occur rather than reengineer.

However, these strategies do not solve problems such as the stovepipe problem or an ineffective supply chain. One remedy may be an *integrated approach,* like the one used at Colonial, which maintains the functional departments. Even if we move to networked organizations, however, the functional areas do not disappear since they contain the expertise needed to run the business. In order to achieve effective and efficient processes, we must redesign or drastically improve operations in the functional areas, increasing productivity, quality, speed, and customer service, as we will see in this chapter. Also, as shown in Chapter 6, an intranet can be used to integrate functional areas and improve their collective operations.

Before we demonstrate how IT facilitates the work of the functional areas, we need to see how they are organized and how they relate to the corporate value chain and the supply chain.

## PORTER'S VALUE CHAIN MODEL AND THE SUPPLY CHAIN

The **value chain model,** introduced in Chapter 3, views activities in organizations as either primary (reflecting the flow of goods and services) or secondary (supporting primary activities). The organizational structure of firms is intended to support these activities. Figure 8.1 maps the typical *functional departments* on the value chain structure.

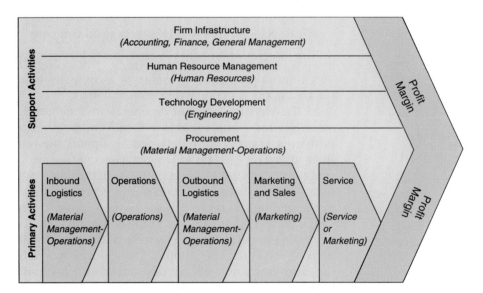

**FIGURE 8.1** Typical functional areas mapped on the value chain of a manufacturing company.

The *supply chain* is a business process that links all the primary procurement activities inside a manufacturing firm and may be extended to include customers, suppliers, wholesalers, retailers, and any other business partners that team up to produce and sell a product or service. Thus, the concept of the supply chain extends the value chain to become a *value system.* In the section that follows we present innovative systems that increase internal functional efficiency, as well as examples of improved communication and collaboration with business partners. But, first, let us examine the characteristics of the functional information systems.

## MAJOR CHARACTERISTICS

The hierarchical organizational structure is built on functional areas that are supported by functional information systems known as *management information systems (MIS).* MIS mainly provides routine middle management support to improve productivity and quality.

Functional information systems share the following characteristics:

1. As shown in the opening case, a functional information system comprises several smaller information systems that support specific activities performed by each functional area. For example, computerized truck scheduling and inventory controls support the logistic system at Colonial.

2. The specific IS applications in any functional area can be integrated to form a coherent departmental functional system, or they can be completely independent. Alternatively, some of the applications within each module can be integrated across departmental lines to match a business process. Several

applications in the logistic information system of Colonial, for example, were integrated with the marketing information system.

**3.** Functional information systems interface with each other to form the organizationwide information system. A specific functional information system may be used as the core of the enterprise information system, such as the inventory information system in the case of Colonial.

**4.** Some organizational information systems interface with the environment. For example, a human resources information system can collect data about the labor market and transmit information to federal agencies about compliance with safety and equal-opportunity regulations and guidelines. Similarly, a manufacturing information system may be connected to the suppliers' logistics information system.

**5.** Information systems applications support the three levels of an organization's activities: *operational, managerial,* and *strategic.*

A model of the information systems applications in the production/operations area is provided in Figure 8.2. Other functional information systems have a similar basic structure. Note that the applications in Figure 8.2 are classified into op-

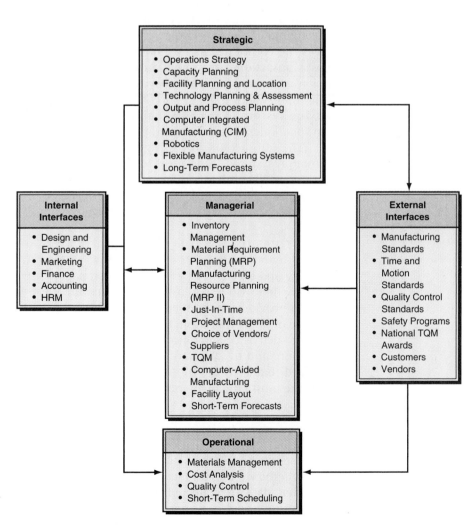

**FIGURE 8.2** A model of information systems in the production/operations functional area.

erational, managerial, and strategic levels. Such classification is useful for understanding the support provided to different levels of managers.

In this chapter we describe IS applications in the major primary and support areas of the value chain. However, since information systems applications receive much of their input from the corporate *transaction processing system (TPS)*, we deal with this subject first.

## ▶ 8.2 TRANSACTION PROCESSING INFORMATION SYSTEMS

### COMPUTERIZATION OF ROUTINE TRANSACTION PROCESSES

In every organization there are major business processes that provide the mission-critical activities. Business transactions occur when a company produces a product or provides a service. For example, to produce toys, a manufacturer needs to buy materials and parts, pay for labor and electricity, build the toys, ship them to customers, bill customers, and collect money. A bank that maintains the company checking account must keep the account balance up-to-date, disperse funds to back up the checks written, accept deposits, and mail a monthly statement.

> This is the most important part of the text. Using BPR, firms can increase their productivity through lower costs, faster service and less personnel.
> — *James Rolstead*

Every transaction may generate additional transactions. For example, purchasing materials will change the inventory level, and paying an employee reduces the corporate cash on hand. Because the mathematical manipulations of most transactions are simple and the volume is large and repetitive, such business transactions are fairly easy to computerize. As defined in Chapter 2, the information system that supports these *transaction processes* is the **transaction processing system (TPS).** TPS mainly includes accounting and finance transactions and some sales, personnel, and production activities as well.

The transaction processing system is the backbone of an organization's information systems. It monitors, collects, stores, processes, and disseminates information for all routine core business transactions. An organization may have one integrated TPS or several, one for each specific business process. In the latter case, the systems should interface with each other.

**OBJECTIVES OF TPS** The primary goal of TPS is to provide all the information needed by law and/or by organizational policies to keep the business running properly and efficiently (see Table 8.1 on page 331). Some specific objectives include the following: to allow for efficient and effective operation of the organization, to provide timely documents and reports, to increase the competitive advantage of the corporation, to provide the necessary data for tactical and strategic systems such as DSS applications, to assure accuracy and integrity of data and information, and to safeguard assets and security of information. It should be emphasized that TPSs are the most likely candidates for reengineering and usually yield the most tangible benefits of IT investments.

### ACTIVITIES AND METHODS OF TPS

Regardless of the specific data processed by a TPS, a fairly standard process occurs, whether in a manufacturer, in a service firm, or in a government organization. First, data are collected by people or sensors and entered into the computer via any input device. Generally speaking, organizations try to automate the TPS

## *Table 8.1* The Major Characteristics of TPS

- *Large amounts of data are processed.*
- *The sources of data are mostly internal, and the output is intended mainly for an internal audience.* This characteristic is changing since trading partners may contribute data and be permitted to use TPS output directly.
- *The TPS processes information on a regular basis:* daily, weekly, biweekly and so on.
- *Large storage (database) capacity is required.*
- *High processing speed is needed due to the high volume.*
- *TPS basically monitors and collects past data.*
- *Input and output data are structured.* Since the processed data are fairly stable, they are formatted in a standard fashion.
- *High level of detail is usually observable,* especially in input data but often in output as well.
- *Low computation complexity* (simple mathematical and statistical operations) is usually evident in TPS.
- *A high level of accuracy, data integrity, and security is needed.* Sensitive issues such as privacy of personal data are strongly related to TPS.
- *High reliability is required.* The TPS can be viewed as the lifeblood of the organization. Interruptions in the flow of TPS data can be fatal to the organization.
- *Inquiry processing is a must.* TPS enables users to query files and databases (even online and in real time).

data entry as much as possible because of the large volume involved (see Figure 8.3). Next, the system processes data in one of two basic ways: *batch* or *online processing.* In **batch processing,** the firm collects transactions as they occur, placing them in groups or batches. The system then prepares and processes the batches periodically (say, every night). In **online processing,** data are processed as soon as a transaction occurs. For example, when an item such as a toy is sold in a store, the POS terminal immediately notifies the inventory system, which triggers a change in the inventory level. The sale of the toy causes other files to be updated in real time (for example, cash on hand or a departmental sales file). Alternatively, a *hybrid system* (a combination of batch and online processing) can collect data as they occur but process them at specified intervals. For example,

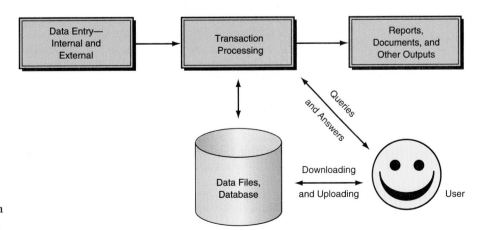

**FIGURE 8.3** The flow of information in transaction processing.

sales at POS terminals are entered into the computer as they occur; however, they are processed only during evenings.

## CLIENT/SERVER AND INTERNET-BASED TPS

> Online transactions processing allows you to capture more data than an order. A customer fills out personal information which can be turned around and stored for customer profiles, instead of implementing a separate form.
>
> — *Blake Thompson*

**CLIENT/SERVER SYSTEMS.** Transaction processing systems may be fairly complex, involving customers, vendors, telecommunications, and different types of hardware and software. Traditional TPSs are centralized and run on a mainframe. However, innovations such as **online transaction processing (OLTP)** created on a client/server architecture can save money by allowing suppliers to enter the TPS and look at the firm's inventory level or production schedule. The suppliers can then assume responsibility for inventory management and ordering. Customers too can enter data into the TPS or query it directly (see the following example).

*IT At Work*  MODERNIZING THE TPS
CUTS DELIVERY TIME AND SAVES MONEY

The **3Es Company** (Des Moines, IA) is a mid-size wholesaler of electrical equipment ($50 million annual sales). Until 1993, its salespeople delivered sales receipts and paper orders by hand to the order entry department, where they were keyed into a mainframe computer. Back orders took about two weeks to fill, and employees had no way of knowing whether an item was in stock or how much time was needed to get it from the producers.

*I*NTEGRATING IT

...for Marketing, Accounting, and Production & Operations Management

The new system is centered around an NCR mainframe. 3Es created a database containing purchasing information and ordering patterns and histories of all its 2,200 customers. Customers now transmit their orders via the Internet and EDI. The customers can query their accounts electronically, 24 hours a day, from any location via the extranet. The savings have been significant. Ninety percent of back orders are now filled in three to five days instead of two weeks. Also, employees are freed from responding to customers' queries and from administrative work.

Several other companies are moving TPS to customers. For example, **Grossman's** (a retailer in Braintree, MA) replaced all its POS terminals with a network of 700 PCs. The network rings up sales, updates inventory, and keeps customers' histories at 125 stores. The PCs automatically record stock from a remote database and trace out-of-stock items available at other stores. This way, customers can get unavailable items within hours. Employees do not have to count inventory or order merchandise any longer. The $3 million investment is expected to pay for itself in less than two years.

Several companies *outsource* their transaction processing. For example, **Citgo Petroleum** must process more than 2.5 million credit card transactions each year. Using a network, these transactions are transferred to **J. C. Penney's Business Services** subsidiary for processing. J. C. Penney has 40,000 other customers for whom they perform transaction processing.

Using an object-oriented approach, **Sprint Inc.** has improved its ordering processing for new telephones. In the past it took a few days to get a new telephone line, now it takes a few hours. The order application is fast (10 minutes) with fewer errors and is executed on electronic forms on the salesperson's laptop computer.

**For Further Exploration:** How do you feel about outsourcing transaction-processing activities? Why is the back-ordering cycle usually reduced with a networked TPS? Why is J. C. Penney in the business of information services? ▲

SOURCE: Condensed from *InformationWeek*, May 24, 1993, and *InfoWorld*, March 25, 1996.

**INTERNET TRANSACTION PROCESSING.** Rather than isolated exchanges of simple text and data over private networks, such as traditional EDI and EFT, transactions are increasingly conducted over the Internet and intranets. As a result, OLTP has broadened to become interactive *Internet transaction processing.* Internet transaction processing software and servers (see Internet Exercise 4) allow multimedia data transfer, fast response time, and storage of large databases of graphics and video—all in real time and at low cost. Here are some of the benefits.

▶ Flexibility to accommodate unpredictable growth in processing demand.

▶ Cost effectiveness for small dollar amounts.

▶ Interactive, automatic billing, enabling companies to offer services to anyone, not just subscribers.

▶ Timely search and analysis of large databases.

▶ Multimedia data such as pictures and sound are handled effectively and efficiently.

▶ High data throughput to support inquiries requiring massive file size.

▶ Fast response time.

▶ Effective storage of huge graphics and video databases.

## TYPICAL TASKS IN TRANSACTION PROCESSING

Transaction processing exists in all functional areas. However, it has a major impact in the accounting and finance areas, as shown in Figure 8.4. The major components of a TPS and its processes are the following:

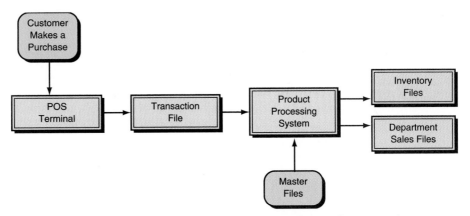

**FIGURE 8.4** Overview of typical transaction processing in the accounting area.

*Order Processing.* Orders for goods and/or services may flow to a company electronically, by phone, or on paper. Salespeople in many companies enter orders from the client's site using portable, even wireless, computers. Orders can also be internal—from one department to another. A computerized system receives, summarizes, and stores the orders. At Otis Elevator Company, repair technicians use wireless hand-held computers to enter maintenance and parts orders [see the *IT at work* case (top of page 334)].

*IT At Work*    HAND-HELD COMPUTERS AND WIRE-
LESS COMMUNICATION AT OTIS ELEVATOR COMPANY

Using hand-held computers, Otis field service technicians and the company's host computer in Farmington, CT communicate instantly about on-site technical assistance, orders, and job dispatching. Previously, field workers were forced to leave the work site, search for a working phone, call the home office, and wait on hold, or call again, wasting large amounts of time. Now, using a wireless network, communications can be initiated from a location as remote as an elevator shaft. Hand-held computers have greatly increased productivity by reducing repair time. Customer satisfaction has also been increased thanks to faster service.

The wireless network is provided by ARDIS, a partnership of IBM and Motorola. ARDIS is part of a new generation of wireless telephones, called "personal communication services," that work in places where cellular telephones are ineffective, such as tunnels. Computers allow documents to be viewed, images examined, and problems diagnosed quickly—even from a distance—using the wireless system.

**For Further Exploration:** If wireless communication is good for elevator repairpersons, can it be useful for *all* repairpersons? ▲

SOURCE: Information provided by Otis Elevator Company, 1998.

Fast and effective order processing is recognized as a key to customer satisfaction. Using object-oriented software, Sprint Telephone Company reduced the waiting time for hookup from days to hours (see *InfoWorld,* March 25, 1996, p. 76). In some cases, orders to warehouses and/or manufacturing are issued automatically. An EDI system would be especially useful in cases involving business partners. A computerized system can track sales by product, by zone, or by salesperson, for example, in an EIS. Some companies spend millions of dollars reengineering their order processing systems. For example, Inland Steel spent $37 million for this purpose (see Caldwell, 1997). Order processing can be reengineered with innovations such as a *GPS,* as shown in the following example.

*IT At Work*    TAXIS IN SINGAPORE
ARE DISPATCHED BY SATELLITES

Taxis in Singapore are tracked by a global positioning system (GPS) of 24 satellites originally set up by the U.S. government for military purposes. The GPS allows its users to get an instant fix on a geographical position. How does the system work?

Customer orders are usually received via telephone or fax. Frequent users enter orders from their office or home by keying in a PIN number in the telephone, which identifies them automatically together with their pickup point. Customers can also dispatch taxis from special kiosks located in shopping centers and hotels. Other booking systems include the Internet and portable taxi order terminals placed in exhibition halls. Infrequent customers use an operator-assisted system. The computerized ordering system is connected to the GPS. Once an order has been received, the GPS finds a vacant cab nearest the caller, and a display panel in the taxi alerts the driver to the pickup address. The driver has five seconds to push a button to accept the order. If he does not, the system automatically searches out the next nearest taxi for the job.

The system completely reengineered customer order processing. First, the transaction time for processing an order for a frequent user is much shorter, even during peak demand, since there is no need for a human operator. Second, taxi drivers are not able to pick and choose which trips they want to take, since the system will not provide the commuter's destination. This reduces the customer's average waiting time significantly, while minimizing the travel distance of empty taxis. Third, the system increases the capacity for taking incoming calls 1,000 percent, providing a competitive edge to the cab companies that use the system. Fourth, frequent commuters get priority, since they are automatically identified. Finally, customers that use terminals do not have to wait a long time just to get an operator (a situation that exists during rush hours, rain, or any other time of high demand for taxis).

**For Further Exploration:** What kinds of priorities can be offered to frequent customers? What tasks do computers execute in this system? ▲

SOURCE: Publicly available information, Singapore, 1998.

---

***The Ledger.*** The entire group of accounts maintained by a company is collectively referred to as the ledger. The ledger keeps all information about changes in specific account balances in one place. Companies may use various kinds of ledgers, but every company has a *general ledger*. A general ledger contains all the assets, liabilities, and owners' equity accounts. Maintaining the general ledger requires a large number of simple transactions and is an ideal application area for computers.

***Accounts Payable and Receivable.*** Accounts payable and accounts receivable list the credit, debit, and balance of each customer or vendor, generated from sales journals or purchase orders, and are updated periodically. The accounts are considered subsidiaries of the general ledger and usually are maintained by the same software. Analysis of accounts receivable can help identify a customer's credit rating and compute the risk of an account not being paid. Accounts receivable information is also important for making decisions about when to send a reminder notice for payments, transfer the account to a collection agency, or declare a debt as a loss. These can be done automatically by tracking software.

***Receiving and Shipping.*** Whenever goods are received or shipped, transactions are created. For example, when items are shipped, customers need to be billed, inventories updated, and the general ledger modified. When items are received, a confirmation is generated to accounts payable so payments can be made and inventories updated. If goods received are deemed substandard, then adjusting transactions are made and the goods are returned to the vendor.

***Inventory on Hand.*** There are several types of inventories in organizations. According to Weygandt et al. (1993), inventory consists of ready-to-sell items in a merchandising enterprise. In a grocery store, canned foods and dairy products are inventory items. In manufacturing companies, there are three categories of inventory: finished goods, work in process, and raw materials. The accounting function must determine the number of units of inventory in each category that are owned by the company on the date that a financial (or tax) statement is prepared.

To determine inventories, companies must count, weigh, or measure each kind of inventory on hand and record the results. Information technology can be used to expedite this process. Computerized voice technology and bar codes on packages are common computerized inventory counting tools.

***Fixed Assets Management.*** Organizations own a large amount of fixed assets such as buildings, cars, and machines. These assets depreciate over time, so it is necessary to keep a record of the original cost of each item, the depreciation rate used for tax purposes, any improvements made, and the book value of each asset. An asset may go through dozens or hundreds of changes during its life. Also, the total of all assets needs to be periodically computed. All these are recorded and are part of fixed assets management.

***Payroll.*** Preparing the periodic payroll was one of the first applications of computers in business. It is a routine job that involves computing gross salary during a given period and determining appropriate deductions and reductions (taxes, insurance, contributions). Most payroll programs will calculate the net pay, and some even print checks or electronically transfer funds to the employee. Many companies outsource the payroll function. Outsourcers use powerful computers to prepare payroll in the most efficient manner (economies of scale). For those that do not, there are dozens of ready-made payroll packages, many of which run on PCs and sell for as little as $100. (You can get some free on the Internet.)

***Personnel Files and Skills Inventory.*** The human resources department in any organization is responsible for keeping a personal file for each employee. All information about a person, beginning with his or her application for employment, is contained in this file. The information includes the skills and experience of the employee, the tests taken and passed by the employee, and performance evaluations over time. In addition, the file includes the employee's preferences for relocation and for changing his or her current jobs. When the personnel files are computerized, it is easy to identify qualified employees within the company for open positions, promotion, transfer, special training programs, and layoffs. Many companies allow employees to update their own personal files (for example, to change an address), saving clerical labor and reducing errors in data entry.

***Government Reports.*** The human resources department is responsible for the completion of several standard state and federal reports that indicate compliance with laws and regulations. Both scheduled and ad hoc reports go to agencies such as the Equal Employment Opportunity Commission (EEOC), Occupational Safety and Health Administration (OSHA), Immigration and Naturalization Service (INS), and Employment Standards Administration (ESA). In the near future, firms will file such reports electronically, just as the SEC receives financial reports from companies and the IRS accepts tax returns.

***Periodic Reports and Statements.*** Many periodic reports and statements are generated from the TPS data. These include external reports to the SEC (such as 10Ks), the IRS, and other state and federal agencies. Many internal periodical reports are also produced daily, weekly, monthly, and annually. Financial statements, payroll summaries, productivity summaries, and sales figures are just a few examples.

## 8.3 INNOVATIVE IT APPLICATIONS IN THE FUNCTIONAL AREAS

Commencing with Chapter 1, we illustrated IT applications as they relate to the functional areas. In this and the following sections we present several innovative applications as they relate to the major business processes which either are completely within the boundaries of a functional area, or are a major responsibility of an area.

Due to space limitations, we cover only the five major functional areas. The topics of managerial decision making and enterprise information systems are deferred to Chapter 9. Our discussion begins with the production/operations and logistics processes.

### MANAGING PRODUCTION/OPERATIONS AND LOGISTICS

The *production and operations management (POM)* function in an organization is responsible for the processes that transform inputs into useful outputs (see Figure 8.5). The POM area is very diversified, in comparison to the other functional areas, and so are its supporting information systems. It also differs considerably among organizations. For example, manufacturing companies use completely different processes than service organizations, and a hospital operates much differently from a university.

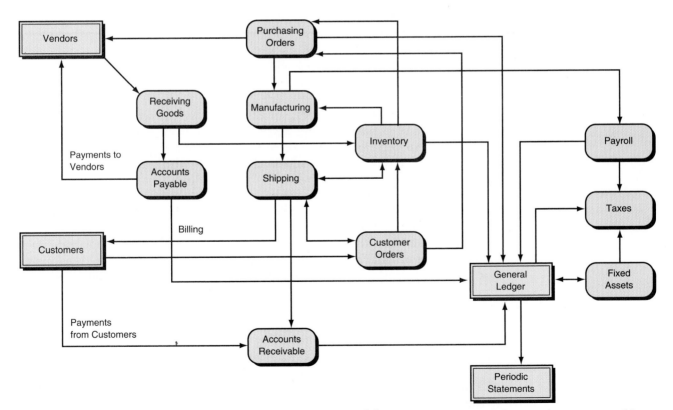

**FIGURE 8.5** The operations process transforms inputs into useful outputs. (*Source*: Meredith, J. R., *The Management of Operations*, 4th Ed., New York: John Wiley & Sons, Inc. Copyright 1992, p. 10. Reprinted by permission of John Wiley and Sons, Inc.)

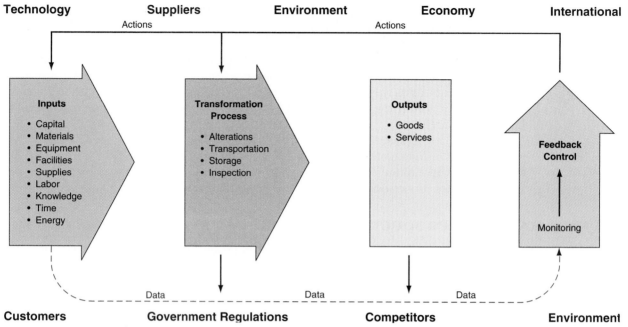

**FIGURE 8.6** The manufacturing process and its interactions with related processes. (*Source*: Narayanan et al., 1993, p. 52.)

An example of the complexity of the field is shown in Figure 8.6. POM here is related to finance and sales (on the left), engineering and design (on the right), and purchasing and logistics (warehousing, on the bottom). Certain processes may involve several or all of these activities.

**SUPPLY-CHAIN MANAGEMENT.** In Chapter 4 we introduced the concept of supply chain and its management. According to Caldwell et al. (1995), U.S. companies spent $670 billion in 1993 on logistics-related activities (about 10 percent of the GNP). The process of the supply chain starts with the suppliers, as shown in Figure 8.7 on page 339.

Figure 8.7a shows a supply chain in which a company delivers products to customers. In Figure 8.7b the supply chain includes wholesalers and retailers. Note the information and cash flows in the process.

The objective of the supply chain is to support the flow of goods and materials from the original supplier through multiple production and logistic operations to the ultimate consumer. **Supply-chain management (SCM)** plans and controls this flow, to speed time to market, reduce inventory levels, lower overall cost, and enhance customer service and satisfaction.

The POM function is responsible for most of these activities. Extensive integrated software is available for managing portions of the supply chain as well as the entire process (see Caldwell et al. [1995]).

Due to the large number of IT-supported topics, both in the supply chain and the entire POM area, here we present only four topics, the first two relating to the supply chain and the last two to production. They are:

1. In-house logistics and material management.
2. Planning production/operations.

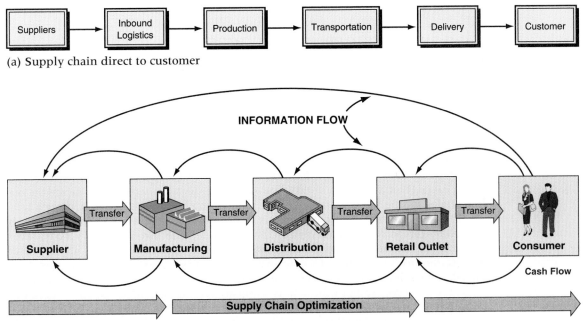

(a) Supply chain direct to customer

(b) Supply chain including wholesalers (distributors) and retailers

FIGURE 8.7 Supply chain management. (*Source*: www.sap.com/products/supchain/sup—exec.html, 1998.)

**3.** Automating design work and manufacturing.

**4.** Computer-integrated manufacturing (CIM).

> In hospitals, patient supplies are counted each morning by scanning a bar code. The central supply area uses this data to restock. The hospital floors order new supplies and generate product use reports.
>
> — *Brad White*

**IN-HOUSE LOGISTICS AND MATERIAL MANAGEMENT.** Logistics management deals with ordering, purchasing, inbound logistics, and outbound logistics activities. Logistics activities are a good example of processes that cross several primary and support activities in the value chain. The purchasing agent decides—with functional area people—what, where, and when to buy. Prices are negotiated with suppliers, and materials (and parts) are ordered and received. The materials received are inspected for quality and then stored. While in storage, they need to be maintained until distributed to those who need them. Some materials are disposed of when they become obsolete or when their quality becomes unacceptable.

All these activities can be supported by information systems. For example, purchasing can place orders with EDI. Scanners and voice technologies can support inspection, and robots can perform distribution and material handling. Large warehouses use robots to bring materials and parts from storage whenever needed. The parts are stored in bins, and the bins are stacked one above the other, similar to the way safe deposit boxes are organized in banks. Whenever a part is needed, the storekeeper keys in the part number. The mobile robot travels to the part's "address," takes the bin out of its location (e.g., using magnetic force), and brings the bin to the storekeeper. Once a part is taken out of the bin, the robot is instructed to return the bin to its permanent location. In intelligent buildings in Japan, robots bring files to employees and return them for storage; and, in some hospitals, robots dispense medicine.

Logistics is related to inventory management as illustrated in the *IT at Work* example that follows.

## IT At Work FEDEX'S WEB SHOPPING/SHIPPING SERVICES

FedEx created a business-to-business service called Virtual Order that integrates the Web catalogs of companies and ordering with fulfillment and delivery using FedEx's own trucks and planes. This move by FedEx marks the first stage in moving its whole logistics and order processing to the Internet. It also marks a new stage for electronic commerce on the Internet because service companies, like FedEx, can offer services to companies that do not want to personally deal with transactions over the Internet—rather they can just subcontract those services.

Virtual Order works like this: FedEx hosts the Web pages for companies that want to put catalogs on the Internet. FedEx provides the software necessary to create the online catalog for the selling company if the selling company does not already have a catalog or Web page set up. These Web pages run on the FedEx servers, but are exclusively the selling company's branded items. Customer orders are taken 24 hours a day, seven days a week. When an order comes through, all of the applicable charges are calculated and are sent to the buyer and to the selling company's server. Also, the information is linked to the selling company's database for real-time inventory management. FedEx offers a secure server so both the selling company and its customers can be assured of a safe, secure transaction. The order then is routed to the selling company's product warehouses where FedEx handles the packaging and shipping of the product. Alternatively, FedEx can manage the inventory of the product on its own premises, usually in Memphis, the hub of its planes. As with any other FedEx shipping, the shipment can be tracked by both the customer and the selling company. FedEx also provides a 24-hour Web-based technical support line for Virtual Order merchants. Finally, FedEx offers other services such as confirmation, invoicing, and after-sales service for returns and repairs. The idea for Virtual Order came to FedEx when it set up a similar process for Insight Direct, a computer equipment and supplies distributor. Insight Direct was shipping more than 1,000 orders per month over the Internet using FedEx technology during the first year of this venture. (See the figure below.)

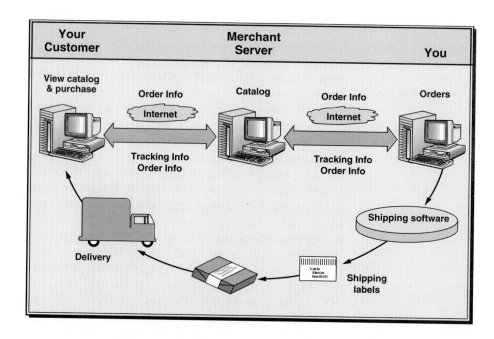

Along with the services offered with Virtual Order, FedEx launched a marketing alliance program. The program is designed to help companies boost their business sales by offering points to the companies using the Virtual Order system. The selling company through the Virtual Order system obtains these points through the direct sale of products. The points can be redeemed for a showcase of rewards that is designed by FedEx.

If you visit the FedEx site you can read success stories and learn more about the service. ▲

SOURCE: www.fedex.com/us/services, 1998.

*Inventory Management.* *Inventory management* determines how much inventory to keep. Overstocking can be expensive; so is keeping insufficient inventory. Three costs play important roles in inventory decisions: the cost of maintaining inventories, the cost of ordering (a fixed cost per order), and the cost of not having inventory when needed (the shortage or opportunity cost).

Two basic decisions are made by operations: when to order and how much. Inventory models such as the economic order quantity (EOQ) model support these decisions. Dozens of models exist, because inventory scenarios can be diverse and complex. For example, discounts can be given for purchasing in large quantities. Demand for parts can fluctuate in a sporadic manner, and delivery times can vary. A large number of commercial inventory software packages are available at low cost.

Once management has made decisions about how much to order and when, an information system can track the level of inventory for each item that management wants to control. When the inventory falls to a certain level, called the *reorder point*, the computer automatically generates a purchase order. The order is transferred electronically either to a vendor, or to the manufacturing department if restocking is done in-house.

*Quality Control.* Quality control systems that are stand alone systems or part of a total quality management (TQM) provide information about the quality of incoming material and parts, as well as the quality of in-process semifinished and finished products. Such systems record the results of all inspections. They also compare actual results to standards. Quality control data may be collected by sensors and stored in a database for analysis. Periodic reports are generated (such as percentage of defects, percentage of rework needed), and comparisons are conducted among departments.

Standard quality control information systems are available from several vendors (like HP and IBM) for executing standard computations such as preparing control charts. After the data have been recorded, it is possible to use expert systems to make interpretations and recommend actions.

**PLANNING PRODUCTION/OPERATIONS.** The extensive POM planning in many firms is supported by IT. Some major areas of planning and their computerized support are these:

*Material Requirements Planning (MRP).* The inventory systems with EOQ are designed for individual items for which the demand is completely independent. However, in manufacturing systems, the demand for some items can be interdependent. For example, a company may make three types of chairs that all use the same legs, screws, bolts, and nuts. Thus, the demand for screws, for example, depends on the shipment schedule of all three types of chairs. The software that facilitates the plan for acquiring (or producing) parts, subassemblies, or materials in such a case is called **material requirements planning (MRP).** MRP is computerized because of the complex interrelationship among many products and their components, and the need to change the plan each time that a delivery date or the quantity ordered is changed. Several MRP packages are available commercially. MRP deals only with production scheduling and inventories. But a more complex process will also involve allocation of related resources. In such a case, more complex, integrated software is available—MRP II.

*Manufacturing Resource Planning (MRP II).* Computerized scheduling systems are frequently tied to other functional areas. **Manufacturing resource planning (MRP II)** is an *integrated* computer system that connects the regular MRP to other functional areas (greater integration can be achieved with enterprise resource planning (ERP), as will be described in Section 8.4). In addition to the output of MRP, MRP II determines the costs of parts and the cash flow needed to pay for parts. It also estimates cost of labor, tools, equipment repair, and energy. Finally, it provides a detailed, computerized budget.

Other company functions can also be tied to this system. Information is needed about when items will be purchased and products will be delivered, so that the finance department can prepare cash flow projections. The human resources department can project hiring and layoff requirements. Finally, the marketing department can determine up-to-date customer delivery times and purchasing lead times. MRP II software is commercially available. The following example shows how MRP II is used at Lipton Company.

---

### IT At Work    LIPTON MAINTAINS QUALITY AND PRODUCTIVITY USING MRP II TO INTEGRATE PRODUCTION, MARKETING, AND ACCOUNTING

*I*NTEGRATING IT

...for Production &
Operations Management,
Marketing, and
Accounting

Thomas J. Lipton Company (Englewood, NJ) is a large international food processor known for its tea products. Food processing is a very competitive global industry in which many government regulations must be observed, and rigorous quality control programs must satisfy not only the government but also consumers. European, Japanese, and U.S. companies are all struggling for market share.

Lipton's prime supplier of packaging materials is Stone Container Corporation, so an electronic data interchange (EDI) system was established between the two companies. Soon, many of Lipton's supermarket customers were added. EDI was part of a major change in Lipton's information system, from a mainframe to client/server architecture based on a minicomputer.

The electronically supported collaboration between Lipton's headquarters staff and operations management at its plants yielded tighter delivery schedules and more consistent levels of production. A key goal at Lipton is to smooth out the peaks and valleys that have whipsawed production levels by using MRP II. For example, orders always skyrocket for holidays and summer vacations, but it's possible to "annualize" those oscillations through the integration of planning, inventory control, sales forecasts, shortened lead times, and faster order processing. A pilot project was done at Lipton's Independence, Missouri plant in which production-line data were uploaded into higher-level MIS functions for integration with plant accounting and business systems. This facilitated the development of an executive information system (EIS) to give top management real-time access and online decision support for plant operations. Today, availability of the latest information makes Lipton more flexible and responsive to shifting consumer preferences. It can more freely pursue a quick response strategy unfettered by outmoded computer architecture. Lipton wants shortened production lead times, decreased changeover times, and improved supply-chain management. It sees its MRP II as essential to these efforts.

**For Further Exploration:** How is MRP II related to EDI? What kind of planning strategy does Lipton use? ▲

SOURCE: Condensed from Sykes, C., "Lipton Maintains Quality Image with Strategic Shift to Unix-based MRP II," *APICS*, May 1993.

---

*Just-in-Time Systems.* MRP systems are conceptually related to (or can even be a part of) the just-in-time concept. **Just-in-time (JIT)** is an attempt to minimize waste of all kinds (space, labor, materials, energy, and so on), continually improve processes and systems, and maintain respect for all workers. For example, if materials and parts arrive at a workstation exactly when needed, there is no need for inventory, there are no delays in production, and there are no idle production facilities.

Just-in-time is achieved by the use of several technologies and management techniques that enable production to move as quickly as possible without interruption. The major elements are low inventories, small lot sizes, fixed production rates, extensive preventive maintenance and quick repairs, few but reliable vendors, high-quality material and work, quick setups, skilled multifunctional workers, cooperative spirit (among departments, employees, and management), a problem-solving environment, continual innovation and improvements, and a *pull system* for moving goods (where control over the work is determined backwards, from the last workstation to previous stations). Other elements are standardized outputs, moderately utilized capacity, and participative management.

JIT systems have resulted in significant benefits. These range at Toyota, for example, from reducing production time from 15 days to 1 day to reducing cost by 30 to 50 percent and at the same time increasing quality.

All elements of JIT can be executed manually. However, the use of IT to support even some of the elements may result in significant enhancement, especially when complex processes are involved. For example, EDI can greatly enhance implementation by reducing cycle time, especially when international business partners are involved. HP Manufacturing Management III (from Hewlett-Packard Company) is a software program that supports multilocation tracking and JIT component ordering; extensive MRP and inventory control execution; and interfaces to financial management, budgeting, and CAD/CAM applications. Control Manufacturing (from Cincom Systems) supports multiple location JIT inventory control, as well as MRP, cost management, and production scheduling. It interfaces with several databases and is fully integrated with accounting and financial planning components. JIT systems are often interrelated with computerized project management systems.

*Project Management.* A *project* is usually a onetime effort composed of many interrelated activities, costing a substantial amount of money, and lasting for weeks to years. The management of a project is complicated by the following characteristics.

▶ Most projects are unique undertakings and participants have little prior experience in the area.

▶ Uncertainty exists due to the long completion times.

▶ There can be significant participation of outsiders, which is difficult to control.

▶ Extensive interaction may occur among participants.

▶ Projects often carry high risk but also high profit potential.

The management of projects is enhanced by project management tools such as the Program Evaluation and Review Technique (PERT) and Critical Path Method (CPM). These tools are easily computerized, and indeed there are dozens of commercial packages on the market.

***Short-Term Schedules.*** Operations managers schedule jobs and employees on a daily or weekly basis, with the support of information systems. For example, paper-based bar or Gantt charts can be computerized. Some complex scheduling situations are supported by expert systems or by intelligent agents (see May and Vargas [1996]). Other complex scheduling can be supported by DSS (see the following *IT at Work* example).

---

*IT At Work*   **DSS ROUTES MILK TANKERS IN INDIA**

**U**SING **IT**

...in Production &
Operations Management

Lipton India Ltd. is an Indian subsidiary of Unilever, and a maker and distributor of Lipton Tiger Tea and dozens of other products including dairy products. About 70 milk collection centers are spread within a radius of 150 kilometers from Etahtown (located 300 km. from New Delhi). Farmers deliver milk every morning to the collection centers, but not all of them are open every day. The collected milk is then delivered from the centers to the dairy by leased tanker. Pickups must be done early in the day due to refrigeration difficulties at the collection centers. The amount of milk at each center varies greatly, so scheduling of the pickups and routing of the tankers, which come in five sizes, is difficult.

The problem is to find the best daily routing plan for the tankers. Lipton wanted to minimize its collection cost, yet it needed to collect all the milk early and if possible with one visit per center per day. To ensure quality, the tankers could not travel more than five hours per trip and also had to meet other constraints.

The company developed an intelligent DSS which includes an expert system that uses a set of rules. For example, one rule might be to go from each center to the nearest one until the tanker is full, or until a constraint is violated. Another rule is that the first pickup must be the farthest from the dairy. The schedule is generated daily on a PC. The company knows which centers are open on what days, and approximately how much milk will be picked up at each station. Since the tankers differ in capacity and cost/ton/mile, it is necessary to best match routes and tankers; thus the computer model included complex cost calculations and "what-if" capability.

In addition to annual savings of $35,000, the company improved the quality of its products due to faster collection.

**For Further Exploration:** What is the role of an expert system here? Why is DSS needed? ▲

SOURCE: Condensed from Shankaran, J. K., and R. R. Ubgade, "Routing Tankers for Daily Milk Pickup," *Interfaces,* September/October 1994.

**AUTOMATIC DESIGN WORK AND MANUFACTURING.**  An important activity in the value chain is the design of products, services, or processes. IT has been successfully used in cutting the time required for design. Following are descriptions of representative information technologies (condensed from Zachary and Richman [1993]) that can be used to facilitate design:

***Computer-Aided Design.***  **Computer-aided design (CAD)** is a system that enables drawings to be constructed on a computer screen and subsequently stored, manipulated, and updated electronically. Most CAD systems allow the designer to draw a model of the design using a set of simple 2-D geometric figures (such as lines and circles) that form a 3-D image. Images can be brought to the screen and resized, reoriented, partially trimmed, or otherwise adjusted to create the desired drawing. Different colors in the display help make drawings even clearer and easier to understand. The ability to rotate or create movement in the design allows testing for clearances and frequently reduces the cost of prototyping.

Having access to a computerized design database makes it easy for a designer to quickly modify an old design to meet new design requirements—an event that occurs quite frequently. This enhances designer productivity; speeds up the design process; reduces design errors resulting from hurried, inaccurate copying; and reduces the number of designers needed to perform the same amount of work. It also means that the designers can focus on doing work that is mostly nonroutine, while the CAD system does most of the routine work (see the following example).

*IT At Work*   **REENGINEERING DESIGN AT KODAK**

**K**odak Corporation was in dire trouble. One of its main competitors, Fuji, announced that it would come out soon with a new product—a cheap, disposable camera that had the potential of garnering huge market share. This camera could be purchased for a nominal retail cost. Once its purchaser had shot the film, the camera would be returned to a developer, who would break down the parts and send them back to the manufacturer. Kodak had no comparable product, and its product development cycle was estimated at 70 weeks to create such a competitive product.

Kodak's business process needed changing to enhance its time-to-market capability. Like many processes, Kodak's development process was primarily sequential. First, the camera body designers had to do their work; then it was forwarded to the shutter designers; then to the film advance mechanism department, and so on. Kodak had tried to use parallel processes. However, quite often the parts wouldn't fit together. Changes in any part of the design affected its overall integration, and if they were not integrated the parts would not fit.

Kodak greatly enhanced its time-to-market cycle and changed its business process by instituting two information technologies: CAD/CAM and integrated product design database. These combined systems resulted in increasing Kodak's designers' productivity. Much of the dramatically improved results came from the integrated database. This system allowed each group of independent designers to view others' changes or improvements and factor those revisions into their own work.

Significant time reductions occurred, since the revisions were identified immediately and could be integrated instantaneously. Employees no longer had to experience the frustrating realization at the very end of the entire process that parts wouldn't fit together. Kodak was able to reduce its time-to-market to 38 weeks, almost half of its previous capability. In addition, Kodak's tooling and manufacturing costs were reduced by 25 percent

**U**SING IT

...in Production &
Operations Management

from former levels. The manufacturing staff could now review the design process while it was still in progress, allowing them to offer valuable cost-effective suggestions. The shorter design time allowed Kodak to offer its products in the U.S. market before Fuji had a chance to do so.

Information technology enabled successful reengineering to take place. In this case, integrated databases allowed a completely new process to materialize, now called *concurrent manufacturing*. This new process has spread to the automotive and aircraft manufacturing industries because it is very effective in reducing time to-market, eliminating costly changes due to last-minute recovery of others' revisions, and integrating cost-saving manufacturing ideas into the design phase.

**VIRTUAL PROTOTYPING ON THE WEB.** Using Web technology, Kodak is able to further reduce cycle time. The developer can design a new product in a virtual environment and both company employees and even customers can test it, even though it only exists in computer memory. Such virtual prototyping is based on advanced modeling, simulation, advanced user interface, and virtual reality (see Chapter 11). Together they simulate the product as realistically as possible. Virtual prototyping also cuts the development cost and improves the quality of the product. Several other companies use it. Virtual prototyping is implemented with VRML and can be reached via intranets or the Internet.

**For Further Exploration:** Find some other applications of IT-supported concurrent engineering. ▲

SOURCE: Compiled form Hammer and Champy (1993) and from Kodak's corporate information (1998).

---

*Computer-Aided Engineering.* Once CAD work has been completed, a designer can use **computer-aided engineering (CAE)** to analyze the design and determine whether it will work the way the designer thought it would. With any kind of CAE, detailed engineering analysis provides data that may be useful when actually manufacturing the product. Such data include not only product specifications but also information about the design of tools or molds and programs used for controlling the motions of numerical control machines or robots. Thus, a database created as a result of CAD/CAE may then be used to support computer-aided manufacturing (CAM).

*Computer-Aided Manufacturing.* **Computer-aided manufacturing (CAM)** encompasses the computer-aided techniques that facilitate planning, operation, and control of a production facility. Such techniques include computer-aided process planning, numerical control part programming, robotics programming, computer-generated work standards, MRP II, capacity requirements planning, and shop-floor control. When CAD feeds information to CAM, the combined system is referred to as *CAD/CAM*.

**COMPUTER-INTEGRATED MANUFACTURING.** **Computer-integrated manufacturing (CIM)** is a concept or philosophy about the implementation of various integrated computer systems in factory automation. CIM has three basic goals.

▶ *Simplification* of all manufacturing technologies and techniques.

▶ *Automation* of as many of the manufacturing processes as possible by the integration of many information technologies. Typical technologies are: flexible-manufacturing systems (FMS), JIT, MRP, CAD, CAE, and Group Technology (GT).

▶ *Integration and coordination* via computer hardware and software of all aspects of design, manufacturing, and related functions.

***The CIM Model.*** All the hardware in the world will not make a computer-integrated manufacturing system work if it does not have the support of the people designing, implementing, and using it. According to Kenneth Van Winkle, manager of manufacturing systems at Kimball International, a furniture manufacturer, "Computer technology is only 20 percent of CIM. The other 80 percent is the *business processes* and *people*." In order to bring people together and formulate a workable business process, CIM must start with a plan. This plan comes from the CIM Model that describes the CIM vision and architecture. (See Fig 8.8.)

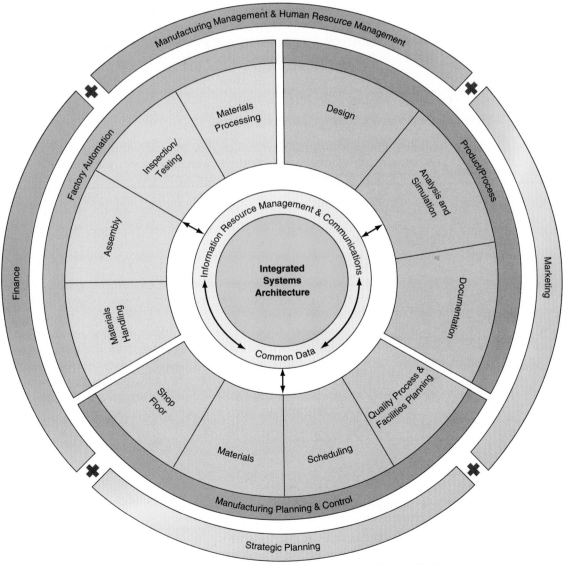

**FIGURE 8.8** The CIM model, integration of all manufacturing activities under unified management.
(*Source*: Society of Manufacturing Engineers, Dearborn, Michigan. Reproduced with permission.)

The CIM model is derived from the CIM Enterprise Wheel developed by the Technical Council of the Society of Manufacturing Engineers. Its outer circle represents general business management. The inner circle represents four major families of processes that make up CIM: *(1) product* and *process definition, (2) manufacturing planning and control, (3) factory automation,* and *(4) information resource management.* Each of these five dimensions is a composite of more specific manufacturing processes, and each dimension is interrelated with the others. Thus, when we plan a CIM system, no dimension can be ignored.

The hub of the wheel represents the IT resources and technologies necessary for the integration of CIM. Without an integrated plan, trying to implement CIM would be next to impossible. There must be communication, data sharing, and cooperation among the different levels of management and functional personnel.

The major advantages of CIM are its comprehensiveness and flexibility. These are especially important in business process reengineering, where processes are completely restructured or eliminated. Without CIM, it may be necessary to invest large amounts of money in changing existing information systems to fit the new processes.

## MANAGING MARKETING AND SALES

In Chapters 1 through 6 we emphasized the increasing importance of customer focus and the trend toward customization and consumer-based organizations. How can IT help? First we need to understand how products reach customers.

## CHANNEL SYSTEMS

**Channel systems** are all the systems involved in the process of getting a product or service to customers and dealing with all customers' needs. The complexity of channel systems can be observed in Figure 8.9 (top of page 349), where six major systems are interrelated.

Channel systems can link and transform marketing, sales, supply, and other activities and systems. Added market power comes from the integration of channel systems with the corporate functional areas. The problem is that a change in any of the channels may affect the other channels. Therefore, the supporting information systems must be coordinated or even integrated. We describe only a few of the many channel systems' activities here, organizing them into four groups:

1. The customer is king (queen).
2. Telemarketing.
3. Distribution channels.
4. Marketing management.

**THE CUSTOMER IS KING (QUEEN).** It is essential for companies today to know more about their customers and to treat them like royalty. New and innovative products and services, successful promotions, and superb customer service are becoming a necessity for many organizations.

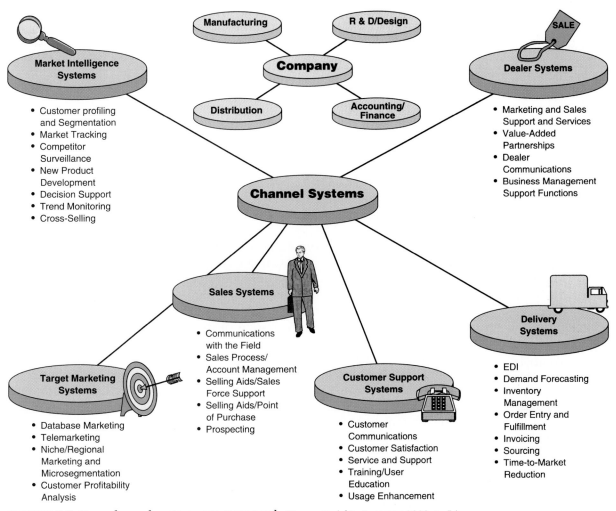

**FIGURE 8.9** How channel systems are composed. (*Source: Insights,* Summer 1989, p. 5.)

***Customer Profiles and Preference Analysis.*** Information about existing and potential customers is critical for success. Sophisticated information systems are
being developed to collect data on customers, demographics (ages, sex, income
level), and preferences (see the following illustration).

---

**IT At Work**     FINNISH NEURAL NETWORKS
HELP IN CUSTOMER ANALYSIS

*U*SING IT
...in Marketing

**I**nfomarket Corporation (Lappeenranta, Finland) developed a neural network-based
application for customer analysis. It enables a retailer, retail chain, or other seller to analyze its customer structure on the basis of purchasing behavior.

Modern supermarkets are visited by tens of thousands of customers every week,
buying thousands of different brands of goods. Therefore, accurate information about customers' purchases is registered in the checkout terminals and it can be analyzed on a daily
basis by Infomarket's neural network. The system provides the retailer's management
with a concrete picture of the structure of customer classes, the retailer's share of sales in

the region, and the demand for different goods in different customer classes. The network also analyzes the impact of various promotions and price variations. Finally, the program makes it possible to compare and analyze the performance of resalers and sales agents. The neural software is often more accurate and faster than traditional statistical methods and is in use in many countries worldwide.

**For Further Exploration:** In what other businesses can similar systems be used? ▲

SOURCE: Condensed from *Finnish Trade Review,* March 1993.

---

Customer data are stored in a corporate database or in special marketing databases for future analysis and use (we discuss database marketing in Chapter 10). Another approach for targeted marketing and/or advertising is intelligent agents in electronic commerce as described in Chapter 6.

***Prospective Customer Lists and Marketing Databases.*** All firms need to know something about customers and their preferences. IT can help create customer databases of both existing and potential customers. It is possible today to purchase computerized lists from several sources and then merge them electronically. Once prospective customer lists have been stored electronically, they can be easily accessed and sorted by any desired classification for direct mailing or for telemarketing.

Several U.S. retailers ask customers to tell them only the zip code in which they live. This way the retailers do not get involved in privacy issues, yet they gather valuable locational information they match with the items purchased. Using geographical information systems (GIS), for example, retailers can make better decisions about where to open new branches and outlets.

***Mass Customization.*** Today's customers want customized products; there can be many different configurations, especially in some products where dozens of options are available. This has led to **mass customization.** The Web can be used to expedite the ordering process of customized products, as demonstrated next.

> We mass customize our monthly invoice billing statements. Each customer has their own template, which prints in the same time it takes to print a regular invoice. Customers think we do each one by hand—they feel special, and we haven't spent any extra time.
>
> — *Mike Rewald*

**IT At Work** CONFIGURE YOUR NEXT
BMW OR CHRYSLER ON THE WEB

Using the Web, new-car shoppers can customize cars as of late 1997. For example, at BMW's www.bmw.com/dialog site you can customize a car with many desirable options and see how much it would cost. (However, the company's policy of 1998 was not to let you consummate the purchase online.) Similar capabilities are offered by other car manufacturers. The shoppers then go to the nearest dealer to arrange financing and pickup. The software for such ordering is made by www.trilogy.com and www.calicoth.com. Trilogy offers a laptop-based product configuration and pricing software for cars and for many other products.

Customers can test virtual cars and conduct comparisons of different manufacturers and models. To negotiate prices customers can go to the dealers or use Auto By Tel (www.autobytel.com), which connects nearby dealers to the customer.

**Chrysler** believes that the Web offers a way to market to customers they might not reach normally. However, delivery may take a few weeks, and it is not yet clear if the Web customers will mind waiting for product delivery.

*U*SING IT
...in Marketing

**For Further Exploration:** Why would manufacturers be interested in the Web if the actual purchase is done at the dealers' site? ▲

SOURCE: *PC Week,* July 28, 1997; also www.zdnet.com/PCweek/news/0728/28auto.html and www.autobytel.com, 1998.

*Targeted Advertisement on the Web.* By checking the demographics of its millions of customers and their locations, America On-Line can match appropriate ads of advertisers with specific customers. The effectiveness of such ads is very high and so are the fees charged by AOL to the advertising companies.

*Customer Inquiry Systems and Automated Help Desk.* Organizations are flooded with inquiries from customers, sometimes thousands per day. The usual way to handle inquiries is to establish a **help desk** that answers the telephone, e-mail, faxes, or face-to-face inquiries. Many help desks are clogged, resulting in considerable waiting time. An automatic voice system is useful in some cases, while in others the customer wastes a lot of time moving from one voice menu to another and not being properly served. Information technology can provide several alternative solutions to the problem. For example, some companies use expert systems to expedite the search for information. This speeds up the work of the help desk employees. A more sophisticated solution is to enable customers to electronically enter the corporate database and find answers by themselves (see Internet Exercise 2). The use of intelligent agents is expected to completely reengineer the manner in which customer inquiry systems operate.

**TELEMARKETING.** *Telemarketing* is a process that uses telecommunications and information systems to execute a marketing program for customers who want to shop from their homes. It can be done by telephone calls generated by computer programs and by computer-generated messages delivered by voice technologies. A telemarketing process can be divided into five major activities: advertisement and reaching customers, order processing, customer service, sales support, and account management, all of which are supported by IT.

Home shopping via television is a fast growing business. Shoppers watch a special TV channel that displays products and, when interested, they call and order, using a credit card to pay. The orders are entered into computers as soon as the telephone operators receive them. Such entry helps to determine whether to continue with the advertisement of an item or to discontinue advertising. (TV time is very expensive; if an item is not selling well the advertising is stopped.) In addition, the computer entry triggers an order to the warehouse, instructions regarding shipment, and a bill to the credit card company.

Through home shopping via computers, described in Chapter 6, shoppers can request information about *any* desired products and buy them. This is in contrast to home shopping via TV, where you can buy only what is displayed on the TV screen. Also, additional information and further product viewing can be accomplished on the computer.

Telemarketing benefits include generating sales leads, gathering information, providing information, improving cash flow, selling, and enhancing customer service.

***Table 8.2*** **Capabilities and Limitations of Telemarketing**

*Capabilities*
- Telemarketing uses a targeted marketing strategy. It uses a personalized contact with the customers.
- Telemarketing's order processing allows customers to buy at their convenience.
- Message-on-hold feature is effective in informing customers about a company's products and services. It is the least expensive form of company advertisement, but it can be the most effective.
- Telemarketing reduces operating costs and cuts the number of salespeople, along with travel expenses, entertainment costs, and travel time.
- Telemarketing is a versatile and cost-effective method to increase sales, manage accounts, and make the outside sales force more productive.
- Sales support improves the effectiveness and efficiency of the sales force.
- Customer service features allow customers to voice their concerns and gain ongoing support after purchasing products. The result is a positive image and a loyal customer.
- Telemarketing can collect information about customer needs and wants quickly, inexpensively, and accurately.
- Telemarketing is done primarily by phone, but computers support it. It is starting to use the computer as a communications tool with customers.

*Limitations*
- Cost of telemarketers, commissions, training, equipment, and telephone can be very high, depending on the scope of the operation and its overall objectives.
- It is difficult to find good telemarketers.
- Telemarketing is seen by many as a nuisance.
- Unlisted telephone numbers, devices that enable people not to accept calls, and telephone answering machines present telemarketing companies with challenges in reaching people.

In addition to its capabilities, telemarketing has limitations (Table 8.2). Despite these limitations, telemarketing is growing very fast, especially when the customer uses the computer interactively. The Internet, for example, is becoming a prime telemarketing vehicle. According to the U.S. Department of Labor, the number of telemarketing employees in the United States is expected to increase from over five million in 1997 to eight million by 2000.

## DISTRIBUTION CHANNELS

***Distribution Channels Management.*** Organizations can distribute their products and services through several available delivery channels. For instance, a company may use its own outlets or distributors. In addition, the company needs to decide on the transportation mode (trains, planes, trucks). Deliveries can be accomplished by the company itself, by a trucker, or by a subcontractor. DSS models are frequently used to support this type of decision.

Once products are in the distribution channels, firms need to monitor and track them, since only fast and accurate delivery times guarantee high customer satisfaction and repeat business. FedEx, UPS, and other large shipping companies use some of the most sophisticated tracking systems.

***Improving Sales at Retail Stores.*** The home-shopping alternative puts pressure on retailers to offer more products in one location and provide better service. The increased number of products, and the customers' desire to get more information while at the store, results in a need to add many salespeople. This increases costs. Also, long lines are in evidence in some stores. Using information technology, it is possible to improve the situation by reengineering the checkout process (as illustrated in the following example).

## *IT At Work*  TANDY CORPORATION REENGINEERS SHOPPING PROCESSES

**INTEGRATING IT**

...for Marketing and Production & Operations Management

In order to keep aisles from getting clogged with shopping carts and checkout lines from becoming too long, Tandy Corporation introduced a wireless portable system in its large Incredible Universe stores. (See Tech America stores, www.tandy.com.)

Each Incredible Universe has 15,000 or more different products, ranging from refrigerators to computers. To manage such a store, Tandy joined forces with IBM to create a unique information support system.

Here is how the system works. When a customer enters the store she receives a smart card. To make a purchase, the shopper presents the card to a sales representative, who runs a bar code reader attached to a PalmPad computer over the card and then scans the bar code reader over the UPC on the desired appliance or other product (see figure). Pricing, inventory status, product options, and service (warranty) options, as well as delivery schedules then appear on the PalmPad screen, visible to the sales representatives and to the customer. When a customer decides to buy an item, the information is transmitted from the wireless PalmPad to a PC, which is connected to a LAN and to the IBM store control information system. When the customer finishes shopping, she presents the card to the cashier; the bill appears in a split second and the customer can pay cash or use a credit or debit card. The payment processing time takes less than one minute compared with five to ten minutes in an ordinary store. (This *includes* time working on warranties and making shipping arrangements for home deliveries of large items.)

The new process enables Tandy to accommodate more than 50,000 customers per store per month, and the customers are happy. Furthermore, the system allows management to run the store at a low cost.

**For Further Exploration:** Small retail stores cannot afford to provide such a service. Will they be able to compete? ▲

SOURCE: Condensed from *ComputerWorld*, July 19, 1993.

An alternative to the hand-held computer is the information kiosk, but kiosks only provide information and do not take orders.

**MARKETING MANAGEMENT.** Many marketing management activities are supported by computerized information systems (see Figure 8.10). Here are some representative examples of how this is being done.

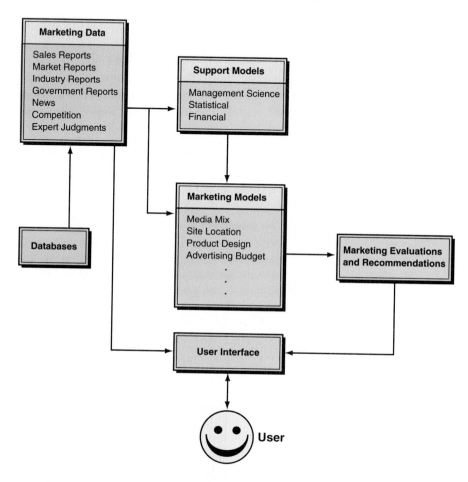

**FIGURE 8.10** Marketing decision support.

***Pricing of Products or Services.*** Sales volumes are largely determined by the prices of products or services. Price is also a major determinant of profit. Pricing is a difficult decision, and prices may need to be changed frequently. For example, in response to price changes made by competitors, a company may need to adjust its prices or take other actions. Many companies are using online analytical processing to support these and other marketing decisions.

***Salesperson Productivity.*** Salespeople differ from each other; some excel in selling certain products, while others excel in selling to a certain type of customer or in a certain geographical zone. This information, which is usually collected in the marketing TPS, can be analyzed, using a comparative performance system, where sales data by salesperson, product, region, and even the time of day can be compiled. Actual current sales can be compared to historical data and to standards. Multidimensional spreadsheet software facilitates this type of analysis.

Alignment of salespeople to regions and/or products and the calculation of bonuses can also be supported by this system.

Salesperson productivity can greatly be increased by what is known as **sales-force automation,** namely, providing salespeople with portable computers, access to databases, and so on. It empowers the sales force in the field to close deals at the customer's office and configure marketing strategies at home (for details see Schafer [1997]). For the use of the Web by the sales force see Varney (1996).

*Productivity Software.* *Nation's Business* of March 1996 reported that **sales automation software** is especially helpful to small businesses, enabling them to rapidly increase sales and growth. This refers to PC software that manages telephones, written contracts, and scheduling; assists with appointments, word processing, taxes, and e-mail; and helps with mailing lists and follow-up letters.

*Product-Customer Profitability Analysis.* In deciding on advertisement and other marketing efforts, managers often need to know the profit contribution of certain products, services, or customers. In Chapter 9, we demonstrate how this is done by Hong Kong Bank. Profitability information can be derived from the cost-accounting system. Identification of profitable customers and the frequency with which they interact with the organization can be derived from special promotional programs, such as the frequent flyer programs used by airlines and hotels. Both the operations and the analysis of such programs are fully computerized. For example, profit performance analysis software is available from Comshare. It is designed to help managers assess and improve the profit performance of their line of business, products, distribution channels, sales regions, and other dimensions critical to managing the enterprise. Northwest Airlines uses expert systems and DSS to check the profitability of more than 40,000 special agreements for calculating commissions to travel agents.

*Sales Analysis and Trends* The marketing TPS collects sales figures that can be segregated by an EIS along several dimensions for early detection of problems and opportunities, usually by searching for trends. For example, if sales of a certain product show a continuous decline in certain regions but not in other regions, management needs to investigate the declining region. Similarly, an increasing sales volume of a new product, if it is found to be statistically significant, calls attention to an opportunity. This application demonstrates the reliance of an EIS on the TPS.

An interesting computerized technology that can support this type of sales analysis is a geographical information system (GIS). Using prestored maps at various levels of detail, a marketing manager can learn a lot about the company's customers and competitors and experiment with potential strategies, as shown in Chapter 10.

*New Product, Service, and Market Planning.* The introduction of new or improved products and services can be expensive and risky. An important question to ask about a new product or service is, "Will it sell?" An appropriate answer calls for careful analysis, planning, and forecasting. These can best be executed with the aid of IT because of the large number of determining factors and uncertainties that may be involved.

Market research can be conducted on the Internet, as described in Chapter 6. In the DSS arena market research, simulation, and detailed analysis are integrated to support critical decisions.

Marketing concludes the primary activities of the value chain. In the next three sections we look at the secondary systems of accounting, finance, and human resources management.

## MANAGING THE ACCOUNTING AND FINANCE SYSTEMS

**INTRODUCTION.**  A primary mission of the accounting/finance functional area is to manage money flow into, within, and out of organizations. This is a very broad mission since money is involved in all functions of an organization. Some repetitive accounting/financing activities such as payroll, billing, and inventory were computerized as early as the 1950s. Today, however, accounting/finance information systems are so diverse and comprehensive that to describe them would require several books.

The general structure of an accounting/finance system is presented in Figure 8.11. It is divided into three levels: operational, tactical, and strategic. Information technology can support all the activities listed as well as the communica-

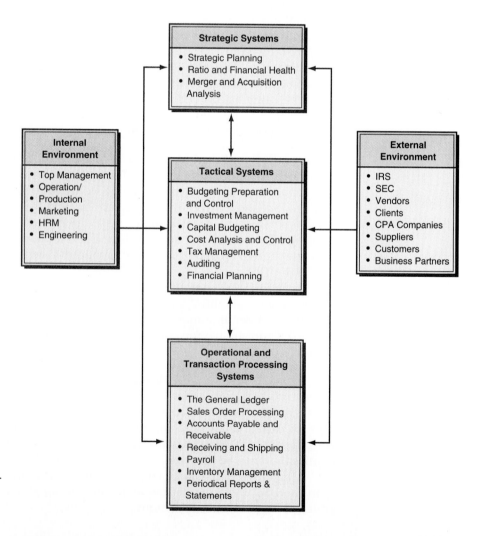

**FIGURE 8.11**  Major activities of the accounting/finance system.

tion and collaboration of accounting/finance with internal and external environments. We describe some selected activities in the remaining section.

**MANAGING FINANCIAL TRANSACTIONS.** An accounting/finance information system is responsible for gathering the raw data necessary for the transaction processing system, transforming the data into information, and making the information available to users, whether aggregate information about payroll or external reports to the Securities and Exchange Commission (SEC).

Many packages exist to execute routine transaction processing activities. Several are available free on the Internet (try http://www.oak.oakland.edu). Many software packages are integrated, such as M.A.S. 90 (from State of the Art, Inc.), a collection of standard accounting modules as shown in Figure 8.12 (the "wheel" in the diagram). Communication and inquiry modules (right side) support the accounting modules. The user can integrate as many of the modules as needed for the business. On the left side, there is a list of other business processes and functional applications that can interface with accounting applications.

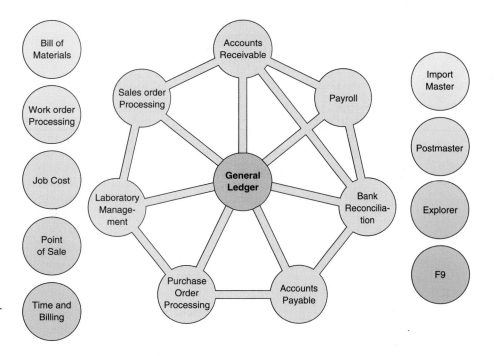

**FIGURE 8.12** Integrated accounting/business software. (*Source*: Courtesy of the State of the Art, Inc.)

The transaction processing system also provides a complete reliable audit trail of all transactions transmitted through the network, which is vital to accountants and auditors. The data collected and managed for the transaction processing system are input for the various functional information systems.

**FINANCIAL PLANNING AND BUDGETING.** Appropriate management of financial assets is a major task in financial planning and budgeting. Managers must plan for both the acquisition of financial resources and their use. Financial planning, like any other functional planning, is tied to the overall organizational planning and to other functional areas. It is divided into short-, medium-, and long-term horizons, much like activities planning. The best-known part is the annual budget that allocates the financial resources of an organization among participants and activities. Prior to discussing the budget, we will discuss IT support for the following related activities: financial and economic forecasting, planning for incoming funds, budgeting, and capital budgeting. Financial analysts using PCs and spreadsheets can accomplish some of the activities listed next.

***Financial and Economic Forecasting.*** Knowledge about the availability and cost of money is a key ingredient for successful financial planning. Especially important is the projection of cash flow (inaccurate cash flow projection is the major reason many small businesses go bankrupt), which tells organizations what they need and how they will acquire it. Availability and cost of money depend on corporate financial health and the willingness of lenders and investors to infuse money into the corporation. Such analysis is facilitated by intelligent systems such as neural computing.

Forecasting is a difficult task since many interrelated financial and economic indicators need to be considered. Background information about the economy, competition, government regulations, labor movements, international exchange rates, and so on are essential to conducting a good forecast. Much of the background information is available on the Internet. Many software packages are available for conducting business, economic (using econometric models), and financial forecasting and planning. Economic and financial forecasts are also available for a fee, frequently over the Internet.

***Planning for Incoming Funds.*** Funds for organizations come from several sources, including shareholders' investments, sale of bonds, loans from banks, and corporate sales and investments. Using the information generated by financial and economic forecasts, the organization can build a decision support model for planning incoming funds. For example, if the forecast indicates that interest rates will be high, the company can defer borrowing until the interest rate drops. Decisions about when and how much to refinance can be supported by expert systems.

***Budgeting.*** The budget is the financial expression of the organization's plans. It allows management to allocate resources in the way that best supports achieving the organization's mission and goals.

Several software packages are available to support budgeting (Budget 2000 from EPS Consultants and Comshare BudgetPlus from Comshare Inc.) and to facilitate communication among all participants in the budget preparation. For example, daily file updates can be sent via the intranet to all those who request funds and submit proposals. Since budget preparation can involve both top-down and bottom-up processes, modeling capabilities in some packages allow the budget coordinator to take the top-down numbers, compare them with the bottom-up data from the users, and reconcile the two.

Software also makes it easier to build complex budgets that involve multiple sites including foreign countries. Budget software also allows various internal and external comparisons. The latest trend is industry-specific packages such as for hospitals, banks, or retailing. Budgeting software is frequently bundled with financial analysis and reporting.

The major benefits of using budgeting software according to Freeman (1997) are that it can:

▶ Reduce the time and effort in the budget process.

▶ Explore and analyze the implications of organizational and environmental changes.

▶ Facilitate the integration of the corporate strategic objectives with operational plans.

▶ Maintain data integrity of budgets and planning.

▶ Make planning an ongoing, continuous process.

▶ Explore and analyze across various planning and reporting dimensions.

▶ Automatically monitor exceptions for patterns and trends.

*Capital Budgeting.* Capital budgeting is the financing of planned acquisitions or the disposal of major organizational assets during the current year. It usually includes a comparison of options, such as keep the asset, replace it with an identical new asset, replace it with a different one, or discard it. The capital budgeting process also evaluates buy versus lease options. Using standard financial models such as net present value (NPV), internal rate of return (IRR), and payback period it is possible to conduct capital budgeting analysis. Most spreadsheet packages include built-in functions of these models so financial analysts can easily build capital budgeting evaluation applications. Consolidation loans, deferring payments, and leasing instead of buying are all related to capital budgeting.

**INVESTMENT MANAGEMENT.** Organizations invest large amounts of money in stocks, bonds, real estate, and other assets. Some of these investments are short term in nature, others are long term. If you examine the financial records of publicly traded corporations, you will see that some of them have billions of dollars of assets. Furthermore, organizations need to pay pensions to their employees, so they need to manage the pension funds as an asset (see the case of John Deere & Co. in Chapter 1). Investment management is a difficult task for the following reasons:

1. There are thousands of investment alternatives. As an example, there are more than 2,000 stocks on the New York Stock Exchange, and millions of possible combinations for creating portfolios.

2. Investment decisions are based on economic and financial forecasts—no one of these is a perfect predictor.

3. The investment environment includes opportunities in other countries, providing both high potential rewards and risks.

4. Investments made by many organizations are subject to complex regulations and tax laws.

5. Investment decisions need to be made quickly and frequently. Decision makers can be in different locations, and they need to cooperate and collaborate.

6. Several multiple and conflicting objectives exist in making investments, including high yield, safety, and liquidity.

For these reasons the results of investment decisions differ greatly, and many organizations outsource some of their investment management to professional investment institutions. (You may recall that John Deere & Company outsourced approximately 80 percent of their multibillion-dollar pension fund management, while they self-managed the rest.) Computerization is especially popular in financial institutions that are involved in investments, as illustrated in the Daiwa Securities scenario.

*IT At Work*   MATLAB MANAGES EQUITY PORTFOLIOS AT DAIWA SECURITIES

**U**SING IT

...in Finance

Daiwa Securities of Japan is one of the world's largest and most profitable multinational securities firms. Many of the company's traders are engineers and mathematicians who use computers to constantly buy and sell securities for the company's own portfolio. Daiwa believes that identifying mispricings in the stock markets holds great profit potential. Toward this end the company uses leading-edge computerized quantitative analysis. Comparisons are conducted on stock price performance of individual companies versus that of other companies in the same market sector. In an attempt to minimize risk, the model then suggests a buy, sell, or sell "short" solution for each investigated security.

The company is using an arbitrage approach. It may own undervalued stocks, but sell short overvalued stocks and futures. The recommendations are generated by a system called MATLAB, which is based on modern portfolio theory (see Markowitz [1991]). MATLAB uses two models: one for the short term (three to ten days) and one for the longer term (3 to 6 weeks). MATLAB follows over 1,200 stocks and includes many variables, some of which are very volatile. Using 4GL tools, changes in MATLAB can be made quickly. Complex statistical tools, such as *symmetric correlation,* are used for the computations. MATLAB attempts to minimize the risk of the portfolio yet maximize its profit. Since these two goals usually contradict each other, trade-offs must be considered.

MATLAB is based on neural networks and fuzzy logic. The advantage of neural networks is that they can closely approximate the underlying processes that may be moving the financial markets in a particular direction.

To motivate the traders to use the system, as well as to quickly build modifications using Excel, the company pays generous bonuses for successful trades. As a matter of fact, some young MBA and Ph.D. traders are commanding bonuses of hundreds of thousands of dollars each year. ▲

SOURCE: Pittaras, A., "Automated Modeling," *PC AI,* Jan./Feb. 1996.

The following are the major areas of support IT can provide to investment management.

***Access to Financial and Economical Reports.*** Investment decisions require managers to evaluate financial and economical reports and news provided by federal and state agencies, universities, research institutions, financial services, and corporations. There are hundreds of online sources (see Farrell [1996]); a sample is listed in Table 8.3 on page 361.

To cope with the large amount of financial online data, investors use three supporting tools:

▶ Internet meta-search engines for finding financial data.

▶ Internet directories and yellow pages.

▶ Software for monitoring, interpreting, analyzing financial data, and alerting management.

### *Table 8.3*  Online Financial Sources: A Sampler

*Government economic and monetary statistics*

 U.S. Census Bureau (http://www.census.gov; www.census.gov)

 University of Michigan economic bulletin board
 (http://www.una.hh.lib.umich.edu)

 U.S. Dept. of Commerce (http://www.stat-usa.gov)

 World bank (http://www.worldbank.org)

*Industry sector and company analysis fundamentals*

 Dun & Bradstreet corporate and industry research (www.dnb.com)

 Value Line's electronic publishing (www.wsdinc.com)

 Dow Jones News/Retrieval (www.dis.dowjones.com)

 CompuServe's Company and Industry Sector Analysis (www.compuserve.com)

*Security filing*

 EDGAR (www.sec.gov/edgar.html)

 The Disclosure Database (www.web.worldinc.com)

*Security exchanges*

 The Chicago Mercantile Exchange (www.cme.com)

 The New York Stock Exchange (www.nyse.com)

 MIT Stock Market Data (www.mit.edu/stocks)

 NETworth (www.networth.galt.com)

 PAWWS: Free Quotes (www.pawws.com)

 International Stock Exchanges (www.ino.com/chart-html)

*Special Internet services*

 Bloomberg (www.nando.net)

 Knight-Ridder (www.kri.com)

 Microsoft Network (www.microsoft.com)

 CNN (www.cnn.com)

 Dow Jones (www.dowjones.com)

 Reuters (www.reuters.com)

*Investment advisory newsletters on the Internet*

 Investor Square (10,000 funds, 3,500 indices, etc.) (www.investment.square.com)

 Investor home (includes financial analysts exams) (www.investorhome.com)

*News services: digest and clipping services*

 CompuServe (Executive News Service) (www.compuserve.com)

 NewsNet (www.newsnet.co.jp)

 InfoManager (www.infomanager.fi)

 Newswire services (many)

*Financial newspapers*

 The Wall Street Journal Online (www.wsj.com)

 London's Financial Times (www.ft.com)

 Investor's Business Daily (www.investors.com)

 New York Times Business Page (www.nytimes.com)

 Los Angeles Times Business Page (www.latimes.com)

 Time Warner (www.pathfinder.com)

*Newsgroups for investors*

 Miscellaneous investments, miscellaneous stocks, miscellaneous funds

*Financial Analysis.* Information analysis can be executed with a spreadsheet program, or with commercially available ready-made decision support software. It can be more sophisticated, involving intelligent systems. Other information technologies can be used as well. For example, Morgan Stanley and Company uses virtual reality on its intranet to display the results of risk analysis in three dimensions. Seeing data in 3-D makes it easier to make comparisons and intuitive connections than a 2-D chart.

To illustrate the diversity of financial analyses we examined the use of an emerging tool, neural computing. Here are typical applications, per Trippi and Turban (1996):

▶ Analyzing the financial health of corporations in which you plan to invest.

▶ Analyzing business failures and bankruptcies of companies, banks, and thrift institutions.

▶ Conducting debt risk analysis of bonds, mortgages, real estate, and other financial instruments.

▶ Ranking companies by creditworthiness.

▶ Predicting economic and financial performance.

▶ Designing stock market investment strategies such as arbitrage.

▶ Pricing initial public offerings.

▶ Developing commodities trading models.

▶ Pricing and hedging financial derivatives.

▶ Recommending appropriate investment mix.

▶ Predicting foreign exchange rates.

Several financial analyses can be supported by custom-made or commercially available software, as seen in the following example.

 *IT At Work* **OBJECT-ORIENTED DSS REDUCES BANKBOSTON RISKS**

**USING IT**

...in Finance

In the banking industry, assessing risk is essential to staying competitive or even solvent. Since banking and economics are constantly changing, banks must be flexible in calculating, assessing, and managing risks. Banks face many different types of risks, including market, credit, liquidity, and operations, that must be assessed and managed constantly. Each type of risk has its own set of characteristics and is calculated using methods distinctly proprietary to each bank.

At BankBoston, limited information was shared through a variety of databases running on a variety of hardware platforms. Traders on the floor and their managers could not instantly analyze their positions and the potential risk of each trade. Instead they had to wait for the back-office systems to process the data they had to input.

Therefore, when BankBoston saw the need to rebuild its entire trading structure and risk management systems early in the 1990s, a decision was made to use an object-oriented client/server computing infrastructure.

The treasury risk management system (TRMS) was the first application. It was developed entirely with C++ object-oriented language that resides on the bank's intranet. The TRMS was first deployed to users in the bank's Boston headquarters in 1995, and then spread to offices across the United States. It enables traders and managers to instantly calculate by DSS models the risk of a trade before it is executed. The trader can enter the pending-trade into the system, and within seconds, up to 10,000 calculations can be carried out against real-time data. This allows traders to assess the risk and simulate the bank's position in the marketplace. The users can "slice and dice" the data many different ways. The bank continually analyzes the project's cost-to-savings ratio.

**For Further Exploration:** Can such sophisticated analyses be done manually? What about a small bank that cannot afford such systems? ▲

SOURCE: Condensed from "Object-oriented Technology Reducing BankBoston Risks," *Application Development Trends*, Vol. 3, No. 11, November 1996, pp. 14, 18.

**CONTROL AND AUDITING.** The major reason organizations go out of business is their inability to secure sufficient cash flow. Underestimating expenses, overspending, fraud, and financial mismanagement can lead to a disaster. Good planning is necessary but not sufficient and must be supplemented by skillful control. Control activities in organizations take many forms, including controls on the information systems themselves (see Chapter 15). Information systems play an extremely important role in supporting controls, as we show throughout the text.

*Budgetary Control.* Once the annual budget has been decided upon, it is divided into monthly allocations. Corporate expenditures are then monitored and compared against the budget and operational progress of the corporate plans. Simple reporting systems summarize the expenditures and provide exception reports by flagging any expenditure that exceeds the budget by a certain percent or that falls significantly below the budget. More sophisticated software attempts to tie expenditure to program accomplishment. Numerous software programs can be used to support budgetary control, most of them combined with budget preparation packages such as Comshare BudgetPlus (from Comshare, Inc.). For further details see Freeman (1997).

*Auditing.* The major purpose of auditing is to ensure the accuracy and condition of the financial health of an organization. Internal auditing is done by the accounting/finance department, which also prepares for external auditing by CPA companies. There are several types of auditing, including financial, operational, concurrent, and internal design systems. In financial auditing the accuracy of the organization's records are verified. The operational audit attempts to validate the effectiveness of the procedures of collecting and processing the information, for example, the adequacy of controls and compliance with company policies. When the operational audit is ongoing all the time it is called concurrent. For new information systems the design is checked before the systems are implemented.

Support software ensures consistency and impartiality as well as increasing the productivity of internal and external auditors. Auditing software is especially suitable when computerized information systems are audited (see Chapter 15). For example, it provides access to the computer files, and allows the auditors to create audit files, extract data, analyze data statistically, summarize samples, and generate reports. Auditing software also provides checklists and other prompts for examining procedures, as well as security.

IT can facilitate auditing when, for example, intelligent systems can uncover fraud by finding financial transactions that deviate significantly from previous payment profiles.

*Financial Health Analysis.* A major task of the accounting/finance department is to watch the financial health of the company by monitoring and assessing a set of financial ratios. While collection of data for ratio analysis is done by the transaction processing system and computation of the ratios is done by simple financial analysis models, the *interpretation* of the ratios, and especially the prediction of their future behavior, requires expertise and is sometimes supported by expert systems (see Trippi and Turban [1990]). Financial ratios are also important in investment analysis. For example, moneylenders conduct a careful ratio analysis prior to the approval of commercial loans. Expert systems can help with the interpretation of ratios. Using neural computing, it is possible to predict the chance of a failure.

Financial health analysis is done not only on the company itself, but also on its partners, potential merger and acquisition candidates, and companies whose stocks are considered for purchase.

*Profitability Analysis and Cost Control.* Many companies are concerned with the profitability of individual products or services as well as the entire organization. Profitability analysis software allows accurate computation of profitability. It also allows allocation of overheads.

A study sponsored by the Bank Administration Institute revealed the existence of generally sophisticated performance measurement software. The study also showed that at times banks struggle to keep pace with emerging needs for tactical and strategic performance information. They spend substantial sums to replace or enhance aging information management platforms aimed at improving the breadth, accuracy, and relevance of performance measures. Performance measurement is closely related to executive information systems, a topic we will present in Chapter 9.

*Product Pricing.* Product pricing is an important corporate decision since it determines competitiveness and profitability. The marketing department may wish to reduce prices in order to increase market share, but the accounting/finance system must check the relevant cost in order to provide guidelines for such price reductions. Decision support models can facilitate product pricing. Accounting, finance, and marketing can team up to jointly prepare appropriate product prices supported by integrated software and intranets.

**CONCLUSION.** Several applications in the financial/accounting area described earlier are demonstrated in the following illustrations.

*IT At Work*    HOW INFORMATION TECHNOLOGY IS USED TO ENHANCE ACCOUNTING/FINANCE TASKS

*U*SING IT

...in Accounting

*U*SING IT

...in Finance

The **U.S. General Accounting Office** uses neural computing to facilitate detection of fraud (estimated to cost the taxpayers about $100 billion per year) and abuse against the health care system. The system detects subtle patterns of collusion associated with fraud. (SOURCE: *National Underwriter,* July 28, 1996, pp. 2, 8.)

**Air Canada Vacations** uses a computer-based fax to send invoices and confirmations to travel agents. A substantial savings was achieved in billing, booking, payment cycle time, and customer service. (SOURCE: *Communication News,* August 1996, p. 29.)

**Toro Company** shelters itself from seasonal and economical fluctuations by tracking and analyzing data from 175 units by division, product line, geographical location, and distribution channels. Using Comshare's executive information system (Chapter 9) and financial software, the company predicted economic shifts and took appropriate action to minimize negative effects and enhance positive trends. (SOURCE: *Management Accounting,* July 1996, pp. 52–53.)

**Plantation Resorts Management Inc.** manages its Gulf Shores Plantation resort in Alabama with a fully integrated accounting system. The system facilitates standard transaction processing and provides information on cost control, resource allocation, and scheduling. (SOURCE: *Hotel and Motel Management,* June 17, 1996, p. 53.)

**Union Bank of California** uses a client/server system to process car loan applications generated at 20 car dealerships in southern California. Using imaging technologies, large databases, and decision support systems, bank loan officers evaluate loan applications so quickly that in some cases a response is provided in a minute. Related to this is the automation of an administrative environment of 100,000 business accounts and 1,000,000 regular banks accounts. (SOURCE: *InfoWorld,* September 25, 1995, pp. 96–97.)

The **City of Philadelphia** was heading toward bankruptcy in the early 1990s. One problematic area was the management of the 1,500 contractors with whom the city was doing business. Using a client/server-based decision support system, the city was able to reduce the contract review to 13 from 44 steps and increase reliability. An intranet that connects the 40 departments and agencies in 21 locations allows information sharing and collaboration. Using imaging systems and query tools, vendor management improved drastically in less than three years and the city's financial health was restored. (SOURCE: *American City and County,* July 1996, p. 12.)

**For Further Exploration:** Does the increasing use of automation imply that fewer accounting and financial analysts will be needed? ▲

## MANAGING HUMAN RESOURCES SYSTEMS

Recent developments in database management systems and client/server architecture suggest that human resources information systems (HRISs) are spreading (for examples see Martinson [1997], James [1997], and Broderick and Boudreau [1992]). Initial HRIS applications were mainly related to TPS. However, in the last decade we have seen considerable computerization activities in the managerial and even strategic areas (see Byun and Suh [1994]).

Managing human resources (HR) is a complex job that starts with the hiring of an employee and ends with his or her retirement or departure. It includes several business processes; a few of them are described next.

> Employee recruitment in my company is a people-driven task. Out in the retailing field where competition for strong candidates is high, a mall-based recruiting kiosk supported by an expert system may be the wave of the future. The kiosk could match people to retailers and save both the job hunter and retail manager a lot of time.
>
> — *Kristin Borhofen*

**RECRUITMENT.** Recruitment is finding employees, testing them, and deciding which ones to hire. While some companies are flooded with applicants, in other cases it is difficult to find the right people. Information systems can be helpful in both cases. Here are some examples.

*Position Inventory.* Large organizations need to fill vacant positions frequently, so they maintain a file that lists all open positions by job title, geographical area, task content, and skills required. Like any other inventory, this position inventory is updated each time a transaction occurs.

An advanced computerized position inventory system keeps the list current, matches openings with available personnel, and allows data to be viewed by an employee over the intranet from any location at any time outsiders can view openings on the Internet. In addition, it is possible to match openings to available personnel. By analyzing the position inventory and its changes over time, human resources personnel can find those jobs with high turnover, for example. This information can support decisions about promotions, salary administration, and training plans.

*Employee Selection.* The human resources department is responsible for screening job applicants, evaluating, testing, and selecting them in compliance with state and federal regulations. To expedite the testing and evaluation process and ensure consistency in selection, companies use information technologies such as expert systems. For an example, see the following *IT at Work* illustration.

---

*IT At Work* **CYDSA USES AN EXPERT SYSTEM TO ASSESS FUTURE PERFORMANCE OF JOB CANDIDATES**

*U*SING IT

...in Human Resources Management

The human resources department of CYDSA, a large company in Mexico, administers a behavioral profile test to measure the capabilities of individuals under consideration for employment. The test results were analyzed manually by experts and divided into three categories: candidate style, candidate values, and candidate thought preferences. Due to the large number of applicants, the many locations of the corporation, and the high level of expertise required for the analysis, it was very difficult to execute a quality analysis in a timely manner. To overcome these problems, an expert system was developed that includes eleven knowledge bases.

The basic objective of the system is to assess the candidates' directional initiative, potential performance problems, and supervision effectiveness. Analysis of an average applicant, which takes an hour when done manually, can be performed in about five minutes when supported by the expert system. The system was available via satellites to all corporate sites. In 1998 it was placed on the corporate intranet.

**For Further Exploration:** What were the benefits to CYDSA of this expert system? How would you feel if your job application were assessed by a machine for a yes-or-no decision? ▲

SOURCE: Condensed from Terashima, H. Sehusi, "An Expert System for Describing Human Behavior in Work Environments," in Cantu-Ortiz, F. J., ed., *Operational Expert Systems in Mexico,* New York: Pergamon Press, 1991; also, communication with CYDSA, 1998.

---

*Using the Internet.* Many companies advertise position openings on the Internet and intranet. In addition, there are several thousand employment agencies on the Internet that attempt to match job seekers and positions (see Exercise 3). Finally, intelligent agents help companies to find relevant resumes on the Internet. (For details and examples, see *Beyond Computing,* July/Aug. 1997, and *InformationWeek,* Aug. 4, 1997.)

**HUMAN RESOURCES MAINTENANCE AND DEVELOPMENT.** Once recruited, employees become part of the corporate human resources pool, which needs to be maintained and developed. Some activities supported by IT are the following:

*Performance Evaluation.* Most employees are evaluated periodically by their immediate supervisors. Peers or subordinates may also evaluate others. Evaluations are usually recorded on forms and can be keyed in or scanned into the information system. Once digitized, evaluations can be used to support many decisions, ranging from rewards to transfers to layoffs. Using such information manually is a tedious and error-prone job. Managers can analyze employees' performances with the help of expert systems, which provide an unbiased and systematic interpretation of performance over time. Several universities evaluate professors online. The evaluation form appears on the screen, and the students fill it in. Results can be tabulated in minutes.

Wage review is related to performance evaluation. For example, Hewlett-Packard's Atlanta-based U.S. Field Services Operations Group (USFO) has developed a paperless wage review (PWR) system, according to Blanchard (1996). The system uses intelligent agents to deal with quarterly reviews of HP's 11,000 employees. The agent software lets USFO managers and personnel access employee data from both the personnel and e-mail databases, drive e-mail communications, and initiate phone and fax transactions through the telecommunications network.

Via software agents, the PWR system tracks employee review dates and automatically initiates the wage review process. It sends wage review forms to first-level managers by e-mail or fax every quarter, reminding them about the appropriate evaluation dates, and speeds up all the administrative tasks, eliminates paper-pushing, and improves the accuracy of the information throughout the entire process.

*Training over the net would enhance my firm's person-to-person commitment to training in sales and customer service. When updated training materials are readily available on a company intranet, our management team will have a valuable resource at their disposal.*
— *Kristin Borhofen*

***Training and Human Resources Development.*** Employee training and retraining is an important activity of the human resources department. Major issues are planning of classes and tailoring specific training programs to meet the needs of the organization and employees. Sophisticated human resources departments build a career development plan for each employee. IT can support the planning, monitoring, and control of these activities by using workflow and project management applications.

IT also plays an important role in training. Some of the most innovative developments are in the areas of intelligent computer-aided instruction (ICAI) and application of multimedia support for instructional activities. Instruction can be provided online at different sites of an organization as shown in the following example.

### IT At Work    TRAINING OVER THE NETS

Training salespeople is an expensive and lengthy proposition ($8,000/person). To save money companies are providing sales skills over the Internet or intranet. Here are a few examples.

*U*SING IT
...in Human Resources Management

▶ **Sun Microsystems** is using intranet. The users log on to a centralized server and call up a browser that steps them through the courses. Sun needs to train 5,000 distributors and 2,000 salespeople each time it comes up with a new product. Regular classes are for 25 people. For 7,000 people you need 250 classes. This is big money. Sun saves money (about 50%) and shortens the training time by 75 percent.

▶ **KN Energy**, a Lakewood, Colorado natural gas company, uses Internet-based courses to train remote employees on an array of Microsoft programs.

▶ At **Hewlett-Packard**, classes are delivered via a broadcast medium and then lab exercises are posted on the intranet so that trainees can review material as needed. Post-class discussions also take place on the intranet.

▶ Employees at **Digital Equipment** can search and browse through 11,000 training courses. Schedules and enrollment are also available on the intranet. Training is provided for business partners as well.

▶ **Ernst & Young** delivers multimedia training over the intranet, replacing CD-ROM-based training.

**For Further Exploration:** Why is the CD-ROM-based training inferior? ▲

SOURCE: Condensed from Kahn, R. H., and M. Sloan, "Twenty-First Century Training," *Sales and Marketing Management,* June 1997; also see *Training and Development,* Feb. 1997 (several papers), and Wreden (1977).

Training can be improved using videotapes produced by using IT. According to *InfoWorld,* Dairy Queen did just that. By using a video-editing system with the addition of a digital video-editing system for Windows NT, the in-house video production department produces a higher-quality training video at 50 percent lower cost, which encourages more Dairy Queen franchisees to participate in the program. Encouraging franchisees to purchase more training videos improves customer service as well as employee skill. Training can be facilitated by CD-ROM and by intelligent systems. Finally, training can be enhanced by virtual reality. Intel, Motorola, Samsung Electronic, and IBM are using VR (see Chapter 11) to simulate different scenarios and configurations. The training is especially effective in complex semiconductor environments where mistakes can be very costly (see Greengard [1998] for details).

***Turnover, Tardiness, and Absenteeism Analyses.*** Replacing a skilled employee may cost as much as $25,000. Therefore, it is important to learn why employees leave. The same is true for tardiness and absenteeism. Data on these topics are collected in the payroll system and personnel files. By using DSS models, for example, it is possible to identify causes and patterns as well as to assess the impact of programs that aim to reduce turnover, tardiness, and absenteeism.

**HUMAN RESOURCES PLANNING AND MANAGEMENT—LABOR NEGOTIATIONS.** Managing human resources in large organizations requires extensive planning. Here are some examples of how IT can help.

***Personnel Planning.*** The human resources department forecasts requirements for people and skills. In some geographical areas and for overseas assignments it may be difficult to find particular types of employees. Then the HRM plans how to find (or develop from within) sufficient human resources.

Large companies develop qualitative and quantitative workforce planning models. Such models can be enhanced if IT is used to collect, update, and process the information.

***Succession Planning.*** Replacement of top managers can be a difficult, lengthy, and expensive process. Therefore, prudent corporations prepare long-range plans for replacing departing managers, especially those who are due to leave soon. In some cases, the succession plan includes a contingency plan for replacing executives whose departure times are unknown. The plan, which includes selection and training, protects against sudden departures. Expert systems have been successfully used to support succession planning.

***Labor–Management Negotiations.*** Labor–management negotiations can take several months, during which time employees may present management with a large number of demands. Both sides need to make concessions and trade-offs.

Large companies (like USX (steel group) in Pittsburgh, PA) have developed computerized DSS models that support such negotiations. The models can simulate financial and other impacts of fulfilling any demand made by employees, and they can provide answers to queries in a matter of seconds.

Another information technology that has been used successfully in labor–management negotiations is group decision support systems, which have helped improve the negotiation climate and considerably reduced the time needed for reaching an agreement.

*Benefits Administration.* Employees' contributions to their organizations depend on the rewards they receive, such as salary, bonuses, and other benefits. Managing the benefits system can be a complex task, due to its many components and the tendency of organizations to allow employees to choose and trade off benefits ("cafeteria style"). In some organizations, employees can learn about benefits and/or register for specific benefits using networks and voice technology. In large companies, using computers for benefits selection can save a tremendous amount of labor and time.

Providing flexibility in selecting benefits is viewed as a competitive advantage in large organizations. It can be successfully implemented when supported by computers. Some companies have automated benefits enrollments. Employees call in or use the intranet and select desired benefits from a menu. The system specifies the value of each benefit and the available benefits balance of each employee. Some companies use intelligent agents to assist the employees and monitor their actions.

**INTRANET APPLICATIONS.** Web applications facilitate the use of IS in the human resources department (see Row [1996]). Many corporations use their Web sites to advertise job openings and conduct online hiring. Here are some other examples:

▶ Edify Corporation's employee service system allows users to access information via PCs, voice-recognition phone, kiosks, or faxes. The package offers intranet-based automation of company procedures, collective bargaining agreements, employees' handbooks, phone directories, pay scales, job banks, benefits, and training.

▶ Oracle Corporation conducts its flexible benefits enrollment program on the intranet. The employees give the program high marks because they feel it is simple and fast. Employees do not have to wait for a starting date and forms do not get lost. Furthermore, employees can see the trade-offs between various benefits, since the cost of each benefit is calculated. Oracle allows new hires to input benefit data online. Finally, Oracle created links from its intranet pages to Fidelity Investments' 401(k) pages, so employees can learn about funds and pension plans online as well as register for the plans.

▶ Aetna Health Plan's directory of primary care physicians, hospitals, medical services, and health information is available to employees online around the clock. The company also offers insurance options online.

▶ Apple Computers Inc. conducts extensive education and development activities on the intranet, including a remote management-training program.

▶ Merck and Company Inc. found that the cost of an HR transaction on the intranet is only $2.32 compared to $16.96 when done by HR employees. Also, when employees enrolled by themselves and conducted other tasks electronically, there were very few errors. Finally, intelligent agents supervise employees' activities, calling their attention to existing or potential errors.

Perhaps the biggest benefit to companies is the release of HR staff from intermediary roles so they can focus on strategic planning and human resources organization and development.

Companies take strict measures to protect the privacy of their employees. Oracle, for example, allows employees to enroll in benefits programs over the Web, but the information is then encrypted and sent to the headquarters over a secure T1 line.

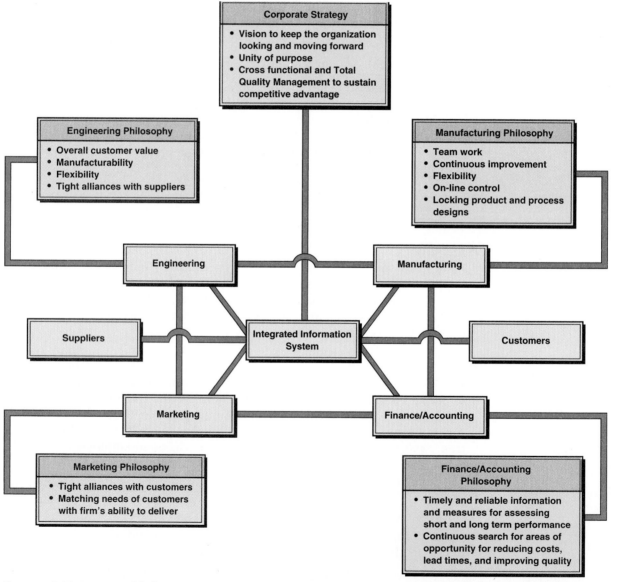

**FIGURE 8.13 Integrated information systems—sharing data and business processes across functional lines.** (*Source*: Yakhou and Rahali, 1992. Reprinted from *APICS—The Performance Advantage*, December 1992, p. 36.)

## ▶ 8.4 INTEGRATING INFORMATION SYSTEMS AND FACILITATING CRM

### REASONS FOR INTEGRATION

> Note that there are no "disadvantages" to integrating functional systems. It's amazing that more companies didn't have the foresight to design integrated systems.
>
> — *Mike Rewald*

For many years most IS applications were developed in the functional areas, independent of each other. Many companies developed their own customized systems that dealt with standard procedures to execute transaction processing/operational activities. These procedures are fairly similar, regardless of where they are being performed. Therefore, the trend today is to buy commercial, off-the-shelf functional applications. The smaller the organization, the more attractive such an option is. Indeed, several hundred commercial products are available to support each of the major functional areas. Development tools are also available to build custom-made applications in a specific functional area. For example, there are software packages for building financial applications, a hospital pharmacy management system, and a university student registration system.

However, to build information systems along business processes, which cross functional lines, requires a different kind of approach. Matching business processes with a combination of several functional off-the-shelf packages may be a solution in some areas, but not in all. For example, we saw in the Colonial case that it is possible to integrate manufacturing, sales, and accounting software. However, combining existing packages may not be practical or effective in other cases. To build applications that will easily cross functional lines and reach separate databases requires new approaches such as client/server architecture and integrated software.

Information systems integration tears down barriers between and among departments and corporate headquarters and reduces duplication of effort. A structure for an integrated information system was developed by Yakhou and Rahali (1992) and is shown in Figure 8.13 (on page 370). There is data sharing as well as joint execution of business processes across functional areas, allowing individuals in one area to quickly and easily provide input to another area. Various functional managers are linked together in an enterprisewide system.

Integrated information systems can be built not only in a small company like Colonial, but also in large organizations, and even in multinational corporations, as shown in the following illustration.

### *IT At Work* INTEGRATED CLIENT/ SERVER SYSTEM AT EUROPCAR

**INTEGRATING IT** ➤

...for Production & Operations Management, Finance, and Accounting

Major reengineering of Europcar Internet, the largest European-based car rental agency, changed the structure of the entire organization, in addition to changing everyday work processes and methods. To support these changes, the company combined 55 different mainframe and minicomputer systems into a single client/server center known as Greenway. Located at corporate headquarters near Paris, the $400 million system combines data from nine different countries within Europe.

The 55 independent systems used various data types, many of which were incompatible and needed to be integrated. Europcar was interested in integrating their business practices, customer preferences, and related data into a single system. To complicate matters, the company had to simultaneously develop a uniform set of business practices, or corporate standards, to support the new single business entity. Furthermore, Europcar had to consider the variety of languages spoken in the nine countries involved, as well as different currencies and cultures.

Key business processes—including reservations, billing, fleet management, cost control, and corporate finance—were all integrated into Greenway. Customer-related benefits include (1) fast service since clerks no longer have to manually verify credit cards or calculate bills, (2) reservation desks linked to airline reservation systems like SABRE or Amadeus, and (3) corporate customers managed from one location.

Three thousand Europcar employees at 800 offices throughout the continent utilize Greenway. Europcar originally grew through the acquisition of geographically and culturally disparate entities. Through reengineering, IT helps support these business alliances to present more of a multicountry team-based organization.

**For Further Exploration:** What are some of the difficulties of integrating 55 systems from nine countries speaking different languages? What functional areas can you identify in the integrated system? ▲

SOURCE: Based on Greenbaum, J., "A Bumpy Road for Europcar," *InformationWeek*, February 7, 1994.

---

In addition to using ERP to achieve integration, companies can choose the "best of bread" systems on the market, or use their own home-grown systems and integrate them. The latter approach may not be simple, but it may be more effective.

Integrating information systems helps to reduce cost, increase employees' productivity, and facilitate information sharing and collaboration which are necessary for improving customer service.

## CUSTOMER RELATIONSHIP MANAGEMENT

One area where all functional departments must work very closely together is in **customer relationship management (CRM).** This approach recognizes that customers are the core of the business and that the company's success depends on effectively managing relationships with them. (See Brown [2000].) Peppers et al. (1999) classify customers along two dimensions. The first is the *diversity* of customers' needs. For example, in a gas station, customers have only a few products to choose from, so their diversity is low. In a bookstore the diversity is high (many books to choose from). The second dimension is *customer valuation*, which is the measure of the customer's value to the organization. In a business such as an airline or a department store, a few customers (those who fly first class, for example) contribute more to profit, so they are more valuable. Peppers et al. (1999) maintain that businesses with relatively undiversified customer needs and relatively uniform customer valuations—e.g., the gas station—will do best with *mass marketing* techniques. Those with diversified customer needs but relatively uniform valuations—such as a bookstore—can benefit from *target marketing* (marketing to segments or groups). Those companies with diversified customer needs and highly valued customers, such as a pharmacy or a computer system company, will benefit most from CRM.

The concept of CRM is usually referred to also as *one-to-one marketing*, and it is considered a type of relationship marketing.

**RELATIONSHIP MARKETING.** According to Mowen and Hinor (1998), **relationship marketing** is the "overt attempt of exchange partners to build a long-term association, characterized by purposeful cooperation and mutual dependence on the development of social, as well as structural, bonds" (p. 540). It includes the concepts of *loyalty* and *trust*. But not everything that could be called relationship marketing is in fact CRM. To be a genuine one-to-one marketer, a company must be able and willing to change its behavior toward an individual customer, based on what it knows about that customer. So, CRM is basically a simple idea: "Treat different customers differently." It is based on the fact that no two customers are the same.

CRM involves much more than just sales and marketing, because a firm must be able to change how its products are configured or its service is delivered, based on the needs of individual customers. Smart companies have always encouraged the active participation of customers in the development of products, services, and solutions. For the most part, however, being customer-oriented has meant being oriented to the needs of the typical customer in the market—the *average* customer. In order to build enduring one-to-one relationships, a company must continuously interact with customers, *individually*. One reason many firms are beginning to focus on CRM is that this individualized kind of marketing can create high customer loyalty, which in turn can help the firm's profitability.

**HOW IS CRM PRACTICED?** There are many strategies for conducting CRM, and they appear under several names: customer asset management, customer service, help-desk management, customer-centric system, sales force automation, and more (e.g., see www.crmassist.com, www.bring.com, and www.cio.com).

To correctly manage customer relationships, a company must first know who its current and potential customers are, not just as groups or segments of customers, but as individual customers. They need to know who is a good customer, and who are the most profitable customers for the business. Furthermore, it is important to know why a certain customer is in the market, why he or she does business with the company, what the customers like and dislike about the business, and so on.

With such knowledge, companies can develop CRM programs, and there are many of them (see www.crmassist.com). Both the knowledge about customers and their behavior, and the CRM programs themselves are greatly facilitated by several information technologies, frequently integrated as enterprise-wide systems.

**THE ENABLING ROLE OF INFORMATION TECHNOLOGY.** IT plays a diversified role in supporting CRM activities. Let's look at some examples:

▶ Using intelligent agent technology, American Airlines generates personalized Web pages for each of about 800,000 registered travel-planning customers.

▶ Manchester Metropolitan University (U.K.) tracks a population of 30,000 students, manages modular courses, and keeps the student management system updated. The system is based on databases and parallel processing.

▶ Charles Schwab's call center handles effectively over 1 million customer calls every day.

▶ State Farm Insurance Co. makes retaining customers its primary objective. Using a computerized incentives system, the company manages several initiatives for retaining customers.

Some generic CRM activities and the IT support required for them are shown in Table 8.4.

*Table 8.4* **CRM Activities and IT Support**

| CRM Activity | IT Support |
|---|---|
| Information about choice of doctors, hospitals, and alternative medicine offered by HMO's. | Internet; online customer surveys; groupware; expert systems for giving advice. |
| Customized information and services in many languages; discounts based on healthy lifestyle; appointment reminders; information on doctors; and medical research. Help center to solve HMO member problems. (Medical centers, hospitals, HMO's). | E-mails (push technology, see Chapter 6); data warehouse for customer information; data mining; intelligent translating systems; search engines on the Web help center. |
| Web-based integrated call centers; quick reply to customers' inquiries. | Facilitates help-desk activities; intelligent agents for answering FAQs. |
| Monitoring of customers' orders inside the company. | Workflow software for planning and monitoring; intranets. |
| Appointment of account managers (BPR activity); creation of specialized teams (BPR). | Expert systems for advice; groupware for collaboration. |
| Seminars and educational activities for customers (Banks, hospitals, universities). | Online training; Internet. |
| Self-tracking of shipments and orders. | Web-based training software; workflow. |
| Segmenting of customers. | Data mining in data warehouses. |
| Matching customers with products and services. | Web-based intelligent agents. |
| Customizing products to suit customers' specific needs. | Intelligent agents to find what customer wants; CAD/CAM to reduce cost of customization. |
| Customer discussion forums. | Chat rooms; sponsored newsgroups. |
| Loyalty programs for repeat customers (frequent fliers and buyers—gas companies, airlines, retailers). | Data warehouses and data mining of customers' activities; smart cards that record purchasers' activities. |
| Customer participation in product (service) development. | Online surveys; newsgroups; chat rooms; e-mail. |
| Proactive approach to customers based on their activity level. | Data warehouses; data mining. |

Many organizations are using the Web to facilitate CRM. Examples range from Web-based call centers, to tracking overnight packages on the Internet, to identifying customers' needs by using data mining tools to analyze e-mails.

# ▶ MANAGERIAL ISSUES

1. *Integration of Information Systems.* Integration of existing standalone information systems is a major problem for many organizations. While client/server and open systems solve some technical difficulties, there are still problems of integrating different types of data and procedures used by functional areas. Also, there is an issue of information sharing, which may contradict existing practices and culture.

2. *Layoffs and Change Management.* The introduction of IT may result in massive layoffs and morale problems. Therefore, managers must anticipate

resistance to IT, especially when combined with BPR. Managing change is an important issue that organizations must deal with, especially when the change is radical (see Kotler [1996]).

3. **Priority of Transaction Processing.** Transaction processing may not be an exotic application, but it deals with the core processes of the organization. It must receive top priority in resource allocation, balanced against innovative applications needed to sustain competitive advantage and profitability, because TPS collects the information needed for most other applications.

4. **The Customer Is King (Queen).** In implementing IT applications, management must remember the importance of the customer, whether external or internal. Some innovative applications intended to increase customers' satisfaction are difficult to justify in a traditional cost-benefit analysis. Corporate culture is important here, too. Empowering customers to enter into a corporate database can make customers happy (since they get quick answers to their queries) and can save money for a company. But it may raise security concerns. Everyone in the organization must be concerned about customers. Management should consider installing a formal CRM program for this purpose.

5. **Finding Innovative Applications.** Tools such as Lotus Notes, intranets, and the Internet enable the construction of many applications that can increase productivity and quality. Finding opportunities for such applications can best be accomplished cooperatively by end users and the IS department.

6. **System Integration.** Although functional systems are necessary, they may not be sufficient if working independently. It is difficult to integrate functional information systems, but there are several approaches to doing so. In addition to ERP and SCM discussed in Chapter 4, one may consider a "best of bread" integration by finding the most suitable functional systems and tying them together.

7. **Modeling and Decision Making.** The application of financial, marketing, and other functional modeling is much more than just using software. Most important is the quality and relevance of the input data and the reliability and validity of the models. And knowledge of the business processes and functional areas is critical. Finally, judgmental elements that are based on expertise, group discussion, and intuition play a very important role in implementing IT.

## KEY TERMS

Batch processing *331*

Channel systems *348*

Computer-aided design (CAD) *345*

Computer-aided engineering (CAE) *346*

Computer-aided manufacturing (CAM) *346*

Computer-integrated manufacturing (CIM) *346*

Customer relationship management (CRM) *372*

Help desk *351*

Just-in-time (JIT) *343*

Manufacturing resource planning (MRP II) *342*

Mass customization *350*

Material requirements planning (MRP) *342*

Online processing *331*

Online transaction processing (OLTP) *332*

Relationship marketing *372*

Sales automation software *355*

Sales-force automation *355*

Supply-chain management *338*

Transaction processing systems (TPS) *330*

Value chain model *328*

## CHAPTER HIGHLIGHTS *(L–x means learning objective number x)*

▶ Information systems applications can support many functional activities. Considerable software is readily available on the market for much of this support. (L–1)

▶ The major business functional areas are accounting, finance, production/operations, marketing, and human resources management. (L–2)

▶ The backbone of most information systems applications is the transaction processing system, the routine, mission-central operations of the organization. (L–3)

▶ The major area of IT support to production/operations management is in logistics and inventory management: MRP, MRP II, JIT, CAD, CAM, mass customization, and CIM. (L–4)

▶ Channel systems deal with all activities related to customer orders, sales, advertisement and promotion, market research, customer service, and product and service pricing. (L–4)

▶ Accounting information systems cover many non-TPS applications in areas such as cost control, tax, and auditing. (L–4)

▶ Financial information systems deal with topics such as investment management, financing operations, raising capital, risk analysis, and credit approval. (L–4)

▶ All tasks related to human resources development can be supported by human resources information systems. These tasks include employee selection, hiring, performance evaluation, salary and benefit administration, training and development, labor negotiations, and work planning. (L–4)

▶ Integrated information systems are necessary to ensure effective and efficient execution of activities that cross functional lines or require functional cooperation. (L–5)

▶ Effective CRM programs require IT support and integrated efforts of all functional areas. (L–6)

## QUESTIONS FOR REVIEW

1. What is a functional information system?
2. List the major characteristics of a functional information system.
3. What are the objectives of a TPS?
4. List the major characteristics of a TPS.
5. Distinguish between batch and online TPS.
6. Define a general ledger and demonstrate how it is supported by IT.
7. Explain how the Web enables mass customization.
8. Describe the managerial applications of finance and accounting.
9. Describe MRP.
10. Describe MRP II.
11. Describe CAD. Explain CAE and CAM.
12. Define CIM, and list its major benefits.
13. Define channel systems.
14. What is telemarketing?
15. Define JIT, and list some of its benefits.
16. Describe tactical and strategic accounting/finance applications.
17. Explain human resources information systems.
18. Define CRM.

## QUESTIONS FOR DISCUSSION

1. Why is it logical to organize IT applications by functional areas?
2. Describe the role of a TPS in a service organization.
3. Why are TPSs a major target for reengineering?
4. Which functional areas are related to payroll, and how does the relevant information flow?
5. Relate CAD to CAE and to CAM.
6. It is said that in order to be used successfully, MRP must be computerized. Why?
7. The Japanese implemented JIT for many years without computers. Discuss some elements of JIT, and comment on the potential benefits of computerization.
8. Conduct some research on MRP and MRP II, and discuss the relationship between these two products.
9. Describe how IT can enhance mass customization.
10. Describe the role of computers in CIM.
11. Describe the benefits of an accounting integrated software such as M.A.S. 90.
12. Discuss how IT facilitates the budgeting process.
13. Why is risk management so important and how can it be enhanced by IT?
14. Explain how IT can make the customer king (queen).
15. Why are information systems so critical to sales order processing?

16. Explain how IT can enhance telemarketing.

17. Geographical information systems are playing an important role in supporting marketing and sales. Provide some examples not discussed in the text.

18. Marketing databases play a major role in channel systems. Why?

19. How can the Internet support investment decisions?

20. Discuss the role IT plays in support of auditing.

21. Discuss the need for software integration.

22. Human resources information systems (HRISs) are a relatively new IT arrival. Many routine applications in this area could have easily been computerized long ago. Speculate on the reasons for the delay in introducing HRIS.

23. Discuss how IT facilitates CRM.

## EXERCISES

1. Compare the way Colonial integrated its software to an integration in a business process reengineering via software such as SAP R/3.

2. The chart shown in Figure 8.6 portrays the flow of routine activities in a typical manufacturing organization. Explain in what areas IT can be most valuable.

3. The introduction of software like SAP/R3 transforms the way business is done and the organizational culture (see Stein [1997]). Review some cases (try www.sap.com and www.peoplesoft.com). Prepare a report on the major impacts.

4. **FUNCTIONAL INFORMATION SYSTEMS AT ARGOT INTERNATIONAL.** Argot International (a fictitious name) is a medium-sized company in Peoria, Illinois with about 2,000 employees. The company manufactures special machines for farms and food processing plants, buying materials and components from about 150 vendors in six different countries. It also buys special machines and tools from Japan. Products are sold either to wholesalers (about 70) or directly to clients (from a mailing list of about 2,000). The business is very competitive.

   The company has the following information systems in place: financial/accounting, marketing (primarily information about sales), engineering, research and development, and manufacturing (CAM). These systems are independent of each other, and only the financial/accounting systems are on a local area network.

   Argot is having profitability problems. Cash is in high demand and short supply, due to strong competition from Germany and Japan. The company wants to investigate the possibility of using information technology to improve the situation. However, the vice president of finance objects to the idea, claiming that most of the tangible benefits of information technology are already being realized.

   **QUESTIONS.** You are hired as a consultant to the president. Respond to the following:
   a. Prepare a list of ten potential applications of information technologies that you think could help the company. Prioritize them.
   b. From the description of the case, would you recommend any telecommunication arrangements? Be very specific. Remember, the company is in financial trouble.
   c. How can the Internet help Argot?

5. Refer to the FedEx *IT at Work* in Section 8.3 and answer the following questions:
   a. What are the major benefits for a seller to use this service?
   b. What companies are most likely to use the service?
   c. What will be the impact on packaging companies, freight-forwarding companies, and transportation companies?
   d. How is the role of wholesalers going to be impacted?
   e. It is said that, "ABC Widget Distribution Corporation will find out soon that cyberspace means their backyard is the world and all of a sudden FedEx is in your backyard." Discuss.
   f. What are the strategic advantages for FedEx?

## GROUP ASSIGNMENTS

1. Visit a large company in your area and identify its channel systems. Prepare a diagram that shows the six components in Figure 8.9. Then find how IT supports each of those components. Finally, suggest improvements in the existing channel system that can be supported by IT technologies that are not in use by the company today.

2. Preparing an advertising program for a client is a long process, involving many individuals and groups. The process starts with a work order generated by an account executive and distributed to a creative services department, which prepares the concepts of the program and layouts. The layouts must be approved, distributed, and filed. The art director, production

manager, and media planner must prepare cost estimates. The client must approve the program and the cost. Then, final art must be prepared and again approved by the client. Finally, purchase orders must be created. All this is done manually, creating a paper nightmare.

Your group acts as a consultant to Young and Rubicam, one of the nation's largest advertising agencies. The company wants to improve quality, productivity, and customer service by using IT. Cost of IT is not a problem.

Prepare a report that includes:

a. Material on the advertisement business and on Young and Rubicam.
b. A diagram that shows how you envision the exe-

cution of an advertising program.
c. A list of information technologies that can be used to improve the advertising program process.
d. Explain how each of the technologies is going to be used, and be specific.
e. For each technology proposed, find a vendor who distributes the technology. Get information about the cost and the possible integration of the various technologies.

3. The class is divided into groups of five. Each member represents a major functional area. Prepare several examples of processes that require the integration of functional information systems in a company of your choice.

## INTERNET EXERCISES

Note: The URLs included here were current when the book went to press. However, they are subject to change without notice. Please consult the Turban Web site (www.Wiley.com/college/turban2e).

1. Surf the Net and find a free accounting software (try shareware and www.oakland.edu). Download the software and try it.

2. Enter the site of Federal Express (www.fedex.com/usa) and learn how to ship a package, track the status of a package, calculate cost, etc.

3. Finding a job on the Internet is challenging; there are almost too many places to look. Visit the following sites: www.careermosaic.com, www.careermag.com, www.jobcenter.com, and www.monster.com.

4. Enter the Web site www.tandem.com and find information about Tandem's iTP solutions. Identify the software that allows Internet transaction processing. Prepare a report about the benefits of iTP.

5. Enter the Web site www.peoplesoft.com and identify products and services in the area of integrated software. E-mail PeopleSoft to find out whether their product can fit the organization where you work or one with which you are familiar.

6. Locate a newsgroup that is interested in CRM. Research the positive experiences and the concerns of the members.

7. Examine the capabilities of the following financial software packages: Comshare BudgetPlus (from Comshare), Financial Analyzer (from Oracle), and CFO Vision (from SAS Institute).

8. Surf the Internet and find information on sales-force automation (try www.sybase.com/products/system11/workplace/sapaper.html). Prepare a report on the state of the art.

9. Enter www.crmassist.com and www.cio.com, and identify the most recent IT products and services that support CRM.

# ▼ Minicase 1

## Extranet for Improved Research Chemicals Procurement

**The Problem.** The 1 billion a year research chemicals industry includes over 1500 suppliers, mostly small companies. The buyers constitute a population of over 300,000 researchers who work in more than 25,000 universities, hospitals, biotech and pharmaceutical companies.

The market is very inefficient. The sellers have difficulties in locating the scattered buyers. The buyers have a problem finding what they want for a reasonable price, since it is difficult to compare many catalogs, some of which are not up to date. Therefore price differentials of up to 40% exist on similar items. Buyers frequently need to pay wholesalers high commissions to help in securing the needed chemicals quickly. A printed catalog of multiple vendors exists, but it covers only 15% of the market.

**The Solution.** Chemdex Corp. is a new company that provides an online catalog Web site (www.chemdex.com). The site includes several dozen suppliers, and many more are expected soon. The online service provides technical details of all products, and customers can find what they want quickly. Previously it took four to six hours on the average to compare about ten catalogs. Now it can be done in minutes. Small vendors are really excited, because now their products are displayed to hundreds of thousands of researchers. The buyers find what they want and place the order on Chemdex's site. Chemdex charges 5% commission, far less than the 40% markup distributors now charge.

**Implementation.** Chemdex started the site with Genetech, a large biotech company and with about 100 suppliers. The system runs on a procurement software called Purchasing Commerce (from www.connect.com) and became operational in April 1998.

**Competition.** Sigma-Aldrich Corp. is a leading manufacturer of chemicals and a distributor of other vendors in a combined paper catalog. It dominated 15% of the market prior to the initiation of Chemdex. Sigma officials declined to comment on Chemdex.

### Questions for Minicase 1

1. What makes this industry a natural target for a Web market?

2. What are the necessary conditions for the success of Chemdex?

3. Which functional areas in both the buyers' and sellers' companies are involved in this process?

4. Enter the www.connect.com Web site and explore the procurement software.

5. The U.S. government is moving its procurement system to the Web, claiming a savings of 80% or more in the administrative expenses. Why is this so?

SOURCE: Condensed from *Interactive Week,* January 26, 1998, p. 42.

# Minicase 2

## Wal-Mart Reengineers Itself Through Extreme Integration

Being the world's largest retailer (over $100 billion sales in 1997) does not guarantee success. Stiff competition drove even very large retailers, such as Montgomery Ward, to file for bankruptcy. Wal-Mart is well aware of the need to innovate, use IT, and quickly respond to market fluctuations. To deal with today's business pressures, organizations recognized the need to integrate their internal systems. By doing so, production, marketing, finance, and other functional areas can coordinate their efforts to provide cost-effective products or services. Moreover, integrated operations are critical for providing outstanding customer service. And, indeed, Wal-Mart embarked on using computers, networks, and specialized software to integrate its internal operations. However, approaching the year 2000, such integration was not sufficient. To excel, Wal-Mart recognized the need to integrate its efforts with that of its suppliers and customers. To remain a player in the twenty-first century, Wal-Mart found it necessary to integrate its internal systems and tie them in with its supply and demand chains. According to Martin (1996), intercorporate networks and computing are changing worldwide patterns of commerce. Wal-Mart, for example, provides each of

its major suppliers with a profit-and-loss statement for the goods received from that supplier.

One of the major reasons for the integration was the difficulty with the demand forecast, which is key for inventory management and delivery scheduling. Usually, the retailer makes its forecast, the supplier makes its forecast, and the difference is systematic inefficiency: excess inventory, out-of-stock products, lost opportunity, and competitive disadvantage. The major retailers, under Wal-Mart leadership, created an initiative called Collaborative Forecasting and Replenishment (CFAR) to help retailers and their suppliers collaborate on a *single,* short-term forecast, and then freeze it, moving it from the realm of wishes to the reality of work orders. Since the retailers and the suppliers are committed to the forecast, it becomes a plan that enables much lower fluctuations and inventories. Also, out-of-stock situations, a major reason why customers leave stores, are reduced drastically. Finally, the retailers can offer a marketing plan since they no longer fear the suppliers' reactions.

A schematic view of a pilot project of CFAR that links Wal-Mart with a major supplier, Warner-Lambert, is shown in the figure on page 380.

**A CFAR Pilot**

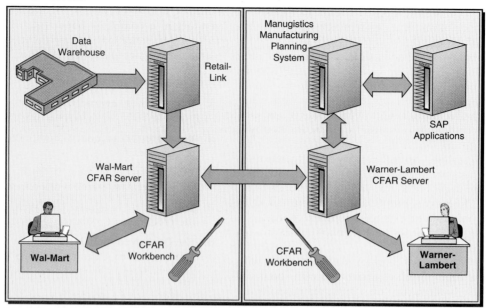

In a pilot project, Wal-Mart has linked up with one of its key suppliers–Warner-Lambert, manufacturer of consumer products like Listerine–by using the Collaborative Forecasting and Replenishing (CFAR) standard. Through CFAR workbenches (spreadsheet-like documents with ample space for collaborative comments), Wal-Mart buyers and Warner-Lambert planners are able to jointly develop product forecasts.

The process starts from the 10-terabyte data warehouse, which is designed for CFAR. The RetailLink System extracts the data relevant to Warner-Lambert products (such as Listerine) sales. The data is then stored in the CFAR server. Wal-Mart buyer agents use a spreadsheet (CFAR Workbench) to make a preliminary forecast. A copy of this forecast appears on Warner-Lambert's CFAR server, so Warner-Lambert's planners can add comments and suggested revisions, which is viewed by Wal-Mart planners. After a few iterations, an agreed-upon forecast is made for each product. This is used as a guide for the manufacturing planning at Warner-Lambert and the inventory management at Wal-Mart.

The Warner-Lambert system contains SAP applications to plan the production of Listerine and other products, and the communication between Wal-Mart and Warner-Lambert is done via EDI. The same system is used with other Wal-Mart suppliers.

The CFAR experiments that started in 1996 and concluded in 1998 and are scheduled for implementation in 1999 will provide retailers with:

▶ Accurate (actual) sales and inventory data replacing inaccurate forecasts

▶ Inventory management shift to suppliers

▶ Partners can monitor inventory levels in real time to reduce turns

In addition to Wal-Mart, other major retailers participate in experiments, such as K-Mart and Circuit City. Overall, industry savings are projected to be $150–$250 billion per year.

In addition to CFAR, the data warehouse is used for queries directly from suppliers and buyers (over 12,000 per day in 1998). The system is also used to support internal integrated efforts.

### Questions for Minicase 2

1. Lately, the Web was connected to CFAR. How can the Web be used?

2. What is the role of SAP in the system?

3. How can customers be tied to CFAR? what kind of customers? for what purposes?

4. Why are the major retailers interested in a system such as CFAR?

SOURCE: Darling, C. B., and J. W. Semich, "Extreme Integration," *Datamation,* Nov. 1996, and *InternetWeek,* Feb. 23, 1998, p. 1, 70.

# REFERENCES AND BIBLIOGRAPHY

1. Berry, M., J. A. Linoff, and G. Linoff, *Mastering Data Mining: The Art and Science of CRM,* New York: Wiley, 1999.

2. Blackwell, R., *From Mind to Market: Reinventing the Retail Supply Chain,* New York: HarperCollins, 1997.

3. Blanchard, D., "Agents Infiltrate the Business World," *PC AI,* July/August 1996.

4. Broderick, R., and J. W. Boudreau, "Human Resource Management, Information Technology and the Competitive Edge," *Academy of Management Executives,* Vol. 6, No. 2, 1992.

5. Brown, S. A., *Customer Relationship Management: Linking People, Process, and Technology.* New York: Wiley, 2000.

6. Byan, D., and E. H. Sub, "Human Resource Management Expert Systems Technology," *Expert Systems,* May 1994.

7. Carme, E., et al., "Labor–Management Contract Negotiations in an Electronic Meeting Room: A Case Study," *Group Decisions and Negotiations,* Vol. 2, 1993.

8. Carson, C., "Knowledge-based Product Configuration," *PC AI,* January/February 1996.

9. Farrell, P. B., *Investor's Guide to the Net,* New York: John Wiley & Sons, 1996.

10. Freeman, J., "Turn Your Budgeting Operations into a Profit Center," *Datamation,* 1997.

11. Gilmore, J., and B. J. Pine (eds.), *Markets of One: Creating Customer-Unique Value through Mass Customization,* Boston: Harvard Business School Press, 2000.

12. Hammer, M., and J. Champy, *Reengineering the Corporation,* New York: Harper Business, 1993.

13. James, F., "IT Helps HR Become Strategic," *Datamation,* April 1997.

14. Kalakota, R., and M. Robinson, *e-Business: Roadmap for Success,* Reading, MA: Addison-Wesley, 1999 (Chapter 5).

15. King, J., "Teaching Over the Net," *Computerworld,* June 1997.

16. Kotler, J. P., *Leading Change,* Boston: Harvard Business School Press, 1996.

17. Kotler, P., *Marketing Management,* 9th ed., Englewood Cliffs, NJ: Prentice-Hall, 1996.

18. Martin, J., *Cybercorp: The New Business Revolution,* New York: Amacom, 1996.

19. Martinson, M. G., "Human Resources Management Application of Knowledge-based System," *International Journal of Information Management,* Vol. 17, No. 1, 1997.

20. May, J. H., and L. G. Vargas, "SIMPSON: An Intelligent Assistant for Short-term Manufacturing Scheduling," *European Journal of Operational Research,* January 1996.

21. Meredith, J. R., *The Management of Operations,* 4th ed., New York: Wiley, 1992.

22. Mowren, J. C., and M. Minor, *Consumer Behavior,* Upper Saddle River, N.J.: Prentice Hall, 1998.

23. Narayanan, V., et al., "Simulation: A Tool for Production Planning and Execution," *Information Technology—Journal of SCS,* April 1993.

24. Niehaus, R. J., "Evolution of the Strategy and Structure of Human Resource Planning DSS Applications," *Decision Support Systems,* July 1995.

25. Peppers, D., et al., *The One-to-One Fieldbook,* New York: Currency and Doubleday, 1999.

26. Peppers, D., and M. Rogers, *Enterprise One to One: Tools for Competing in the Interactive Age,* New York: Doubleday, 1999.

27. Petersen, G. S., *Customer Relationship Management Systems: ROI and Results Measurement,* New York: Strategic Sales Performance, 1999.

28. Row, H., "Personal Best," *Webmaster,* September 1996.

29. Saraph, J. V., and T. Guimaraes, "The Role of IS in Manufacturing Automation," *Journal of Information Systems Management,* Winter 1991.

30. Schafer, S., "Super Charged Sell," *Inc. Technology,* No. 2, 1997.

31. Stein, T., "Orders from Chaos" (supply chain systems), *InformationWeek,* June 23, 1997.

32. Trippi, R., and E. Turban, *Investment Management: Decision Support and Expert Systems,* New York: VNR Publishers, 1990.

33. Trippi, R., and E. Turban, *Neural Computing in Investment,* 2nd ed., Ridge Burr, IL: Richard D. Irwin, 1996.

34. Tucker, M. J., "The New Money: Transactions Pour Across the Web," *Datamation,* April 1997.

35. Turban E., et al., *Electronic Commerce: A Managerial Perspective,* Upper Saddle River, NJ: Prentice-Hall, 2000.

36. Tyler, T.C., "Sales and Marketing Software," *Sales and Marketing Management,* December 1992. (A list of about 1,000 commercial software packages is included on p. 61.)

37. Varney, S. E., "Arm Your Salesforce with the Web," *Datamation,* October 1996.

38. Weygandt, J. J., et al. *Accounting Principles,* 5th ed., New York: Wiley, 1999.

39. Wreden, N., "Long Distance Lessons," *Communications Week,* Aug. 18, 1997.

40. Yakhou, M., and B. Rahali, "Integration of Business Functions: Roles of Cross-Functional Information Systems," *APICS,* December 1992.

# CHAPTER 9

# Supporting Management and Decision Making

## Learning Objectives

*After studying this chapter, you will be able to:*

**1** Describe the concepts of management, decision making, and computerized support for decision making.

**2** Justify the role of models in decision making.

**3** Explain how IT supports decision making.

**4** Describe the framework for computerized decision support, and classify problems and support according to the framework.

**5** Describe decision support systems and their benefits, and analyze their role in management support.

**6** Compare regular (personal) decision support systems with organizational decision support systems and analyze the major differences.

**7** Describe executive information systems, and analyze their role in management support.

**8** Explain how computers can enhance idea generation.

**9.1**
**The Managers and Decision Making**

**9.2**
**Decision Support Systems**

**9.3**
**Corporate-Level Decision Support**

**9.4**
**Advanced Decision Support Topics**

# CONNECTIONS

## DATA ANALYSIS AT SHOPKO IS FACILITATED BY DSS

### The Problem

ShopKo is a 130-store Wisconsin-based discount chain which is operating in an extremely competitive environment. The success of such a company depends on the ability to make quick decisions and on superb customer service and vendor (supplier) relations. The information systems that supported the business were highly inflexible. It took a day to get an answer to a simple question and reports were always late and had limited value. Financial and marketing analysts were frustrated. Forecasts were inaccurate and wrong decisions were frequently made. With 130 stores and over 200,000 SKUs it was difficult to know where profits were made and where money was lost.

### The Solution

The company installed a comprehensive DSS software (DSS Agent, from MicroStrategy). This system includes a data warehouse and online analytical processing (OLAP) which supports decision making, report generation, and query capabilities.

THE SYSTEM PROVIDES:

▶ Sales statistics for every SKU, at each store, on a daily basis.
▶ Summarization of sales data, by store, by regions, and so on.
▶ Analysis of the above and similar sales data (e.g., trend analysis, comparison to competitors).
▶ Inventory tracking and analysis.
▶ Sales and expenditures forecasts.
▶ Quick answers to ad-hoc queries.
▶ Customized reports and detailed analysis.
▶ Profitability analysis (by product, by store).
▶ A "drill everywhere" component that automatically allows for exploration of information found along, above, within, or below the current level of details.
▶ Extensive market basket analysis. For example, the company can look at whether customers coming into the stores are buying only items on sale.
▶ Finding the relationship between levels of advertisement and sales per each item.

Using software called DSS Web 4.0, ShopKo permits its vendors to log into its Web page and use standard browsers to see how well their products are selling. This facilitates vendor partnership and assures better customer service (the vendors quickly ship items that are depleted). Some parts of the DSS are integrated with other information systems, especially the pharmaceutical one which is now integrated with medical claim records. The system provides enterprisewide decision support services, including workbenches for sales/marketing, actuarial/claims, medical management, utilization, and government reporting. (See www.shopko.com for more information.)

Of special interest is the DSS application developed for the pharmaceutical business. Costs can be compared over a wide range of variables, including health care providers, treatment protocols, specialties, care plans, patient demographics, and geographical distribution. At a global level, users can "slice and dice" data about a particular medicine or its generic equivalent, the day the drug was prescribed, the prescribing facility, or the physician involved. Complex set-math filtering criteria developed by MicroStrategy lets analysts relate prescriptons to patient diagnoses, so that client firms' medical directors can determine which physicians are prescribing more brand-name than generic drugs for a particular diagnosis.

### The Results

The competitive advantages provided by the DSS solution more than justified ShopKo's investment in the technology. The savings came from the corporate ability to use sophisticated analysis that enabled stores to carry the right merchandise at the right place and time.

**For Further Exploration:** Why do you need a DSS in this case? What is the role of the Web? Distinguish between transaction and analytical processsing.

SOURCE: Condensed from *Stores Magazine*, 1996. Also available at www.strategy.com, 1998.

## 9.1 THE MANAGERS AND DECISION MAKING

The opening case illustrates how the use of a decision support system (DSS) enhanced the *management* of a retailer and helped increase its competitiveness. To better understand, let us review the manager's job and its relationship to decision making.

### THE MANAGER'S JOB

*Management* is a process by which certain goals are achieved through the use of resources (people, money, energy, materials, space, time). These resources are considered to be *inputs*, and the attainment of the goals is viewed as the *output* of the process. The degree of a manager's success is often measured by the ratio between outputs and inputs for which he or she is responsible. This ratio is an indication of the organization's *productivity*.

$$Productivity = \frac{outputs\ (products,\ services\ produced)}{inputs\ (resources\ utilized)}$$

Productivity (sometimes referred to as efficiency) is a major concern for any organization because it deeply influences the well-being of the organization and its members.

To understand how computers support managers, it is necessary first to describe what managers do. Managers do many things, depending on their position in the organization, the type and size of the organization, organizational policies and culture, and the personalities of the managers themselves. Despite this variety, there are several generic frameworks and theories regarding what managers do. Mintzberg (1973) divided the manager's roles into three categories based on his classical studies.

1. *Interpersonal roles:* figurehead, leader, liaison.
2. *Informational roles:* monitor, disseminator, spokesperson.
3. *Decisional roles:* entrepreneur, disturbance handler, resource allocator, negotiator.

Early information systems mainly supported informational roles. In recent years, however, information systems have been developed that support all three roles. In this chapter, we are mainly interested in the support that IT can provide to *decisional* roles. We divide the manager's work, as it relates to decisional roles, into two phases. Phase I is the identification of problems and/or opportunities. Phase II is the decision of what to do about them.

Figure 9.1 provides a flowchart of this process and the flow of information in it. There we see that information comes form both internal and external environments. Internal information is generated from the functional areas. External information comes from sources such as the Internet, online databases, newspapers, industry newsletters, government reports, and personal contacts. Given the large amount of information available, it is necessary to scan the environment and data sources to find the *relevant* information. Collected information is then evaluated for relevancy and importance, and whenever appropriate it is channeled to quantitative and qualitative analysis, which is basically an interpretation

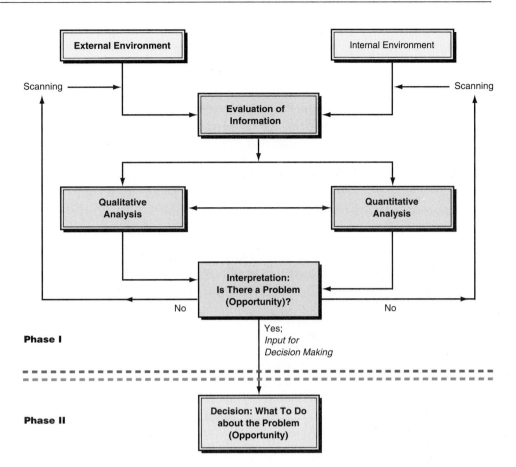

**FIGURE 9.1** Two phases of a manager's decision role and the flow of information in the process.

of the information. Then, a decision by an executive or a group is made on whether a problem or opportunity exists. If it is decided that there is a problem (opportunity), then the problem is transferred as an input to Phase II. In Phase II, alternatives are evaluated and a choice of one alternative is made for solving the problem.

The purpose of various *management support systems (MSS)* is to support the various tasks of the processes in Figure 9.1, such as scanning and analyzing, as well as to support the three managerial roles described earlier. In this chapter, we look mainly at two management support system technologies: decision support systems and executive information systems.

## MANAGERIAL DECISIONS AND COMPUTERIZED SUPPORT

The success of management depends on the skillful execution of the generic managerial functions such as planning, organizing, directing, and controlling. To carry out these functions, managers engage in the continuous process of making decisions.

The ability to make crisp decisions was rated first in importance in a study conducted by the Harbridge House in Boston, MA. About 6,500 managers in more than 100 companies, including many large, blue-chip corporations, were asked how important it was that managers employ certain management practices. They also were asked how well, in their estimation, managers performed these practices. From a statistical distillation of these answers, Harbridge ranked "making clear-cut decisions when needed" as the most important of 10 management practices. Ranked second in managerial importance was "getting to the heart of the problems rather than dealing with less important issues." Most of the remaining eight management practices were related directly or indirectly to decision making. From these evaluations, the researchers also concluded that only 10 percent of the managers thought management performed "very well" on any given practice, mainly due to the difficult decision-making environment. It seems that the trial-and-error method, which might have been a practical approach to decision making in the past, is too expensive or ineffective today in many instances.

Therefore, managers must become more sophisticated, learning how to use the new tools and techniques that are developed to help them make decisions. (See discussion on computerized aids later in this section.) Some techniques use a quantitative analysis approach, and they are supported by computers. Several of these are described in this chapter. Additional computerized techniques that support qualitative and quantitative analysis are described in Chapter 11.

Buyers use DSS and models to make purchasing decisions. Models determine which types of stores are effective outlets for which types of merchandise. This information is used to identify market trends and opportunities to make strategic decisions in the future (better selections of titles, new store title mix, etc.).

— *Kristin Borhofen*

**DECISION SUPPORT.** When making a decision, either organizational or personal, the decision maker goes through a fairly systematic process. Simon (1977) described the process as composed of three major phases: *intelligence, design,* and *choice.* A fourth phase, *implementation,* was added later. Simon claimed that the process is general enough and can be supported by decision aids and modeling. A conceptual presentation of the four-stage modeling process is shown in Figure 9.2 on page 387, which illustrates what tasks are included in each phase. Note that there is a continuous flow of information from intelligence to design to choice (bold lines), but at any phase there may be a return to a previous phase (broken lines).

The decision-making process starts with the intelligence phase, where reality is examined and the problem is identified and defined. In the design phase, a *model* or simplified representation of reality is constructed. This is done by making assumptions that simplify reality and by expressing the relationships among all variables in writing. The model is then validated, and criteria are set for the evaluation of alternative potential solutions that are identified. The choice phase involves selecting a solution, which is tested "on paper." Once this proposed solution seems to be feasible, we are ready for the last phase—implementation. Successful implementation results in resolving the original problem. Failure leads to a return to the previous phases. A DSS attempts to automate several tasks in this process in which modeling is the core.

## MODELING AND MODELS

A model is a *simplified* representation or abstraction of reality. It is usually simplified because reality is too complex to copy exactly, and because much of its complexity is actually irrelevant to a specific problem. With modeling, one performs experiments and analysis on a model of reality rather than on reality itself. The benefits of modeling are:

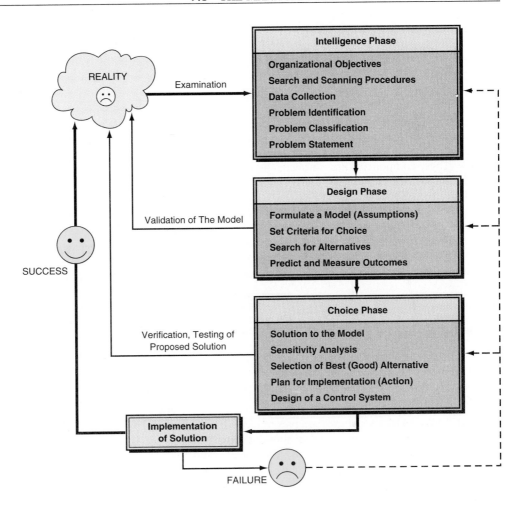

**FIGURE 9.2** The process and phases in decision making/modeling.

1. The cost of modeling is much lower than the cost of similar experimentation conducted with a real system.

2. Models allow for the simulated compression of time. Years of operation can be simulated in seconds of computer time.

3. Manipulating the model (by changing variables) is much easier than manipulating the real system. Experimentation is therefore easier to conduct, and it does not interfere with the daily operation of the organization.

4. The cost of making mistakes during a trial-and-error experiment is much lower when models are used rather than real systems.

5. Today's environment holds considerable uncertainty. Modeling allows a manager to calculate the risks involved in specific actions.

6. Mathematical models allow the analysis of a very large, sometimes infinite number of possible alternatives and solutions. With today's advanced technology and communications, managers frequently have a large number of alternatives from which to choose.

7. Models enhance and reinforce learning and support training.

Representation through models can be done at various degrees of abstraction. Models are thus classified into four groups according to their degree of abstraction: iconic, analog, mathematical, and mental.

# *A Closer Look* BOX 9.1

## ABOUT MODELING AND MODELS

All models are composed of three basic components: decision variables, uncontrollable variables (and/or parameters) and result (outcome) variables (see figure below). These components are connected by mathematical relationships. In a nonquantitative model, the relationships are symbolic or qualitative.

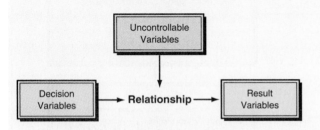

The results (or outcome) of decisions are determined by (1) the decision being made; (2) other factors that are uncontrollable by the decision maker; and (3) the relationships among variables.

**RESULT VARIABLES.** These variables reflect the level of effectiveness of the system; that is, they indicate how well the system performs or attains its goals. The result variables are considered, mathematically, to be *dependent variables*.

**DECISION VARIABLES.** Decision variables describe the alternative courses of action. For example, in an investment problem, how much to invest in bonds is a decision variable. In a scheduling problem, the decision variables are people and jobs. The *values* of these variables are determined by the decision maker. Decision variables are classified mathematically as *independent variables* (or unknown variables). An aim of DSS is to find good enough, or possibly the best, values for these decision variables.

**UNCONTROLLABLE VARIABLES OR PARAMETERS.** In any decision situation there are factors that affect the result variables but *are not under the control* of the decision maker. These factors can either be fixed (and they are called parameters), or they can vary (then they are called variables). Examples are the prime interest rate, a city's building code, tax regulations, and prices of utilities. Most of these factors are uncontrollable because they emanate from the environment surrounding its decision maker. These variables are classified as *independent variables* since they affect the dependent (result) variables.

**INTERMEDIATE VARIABLES.** Intermediate variables are any variables necessary to link the decision variables to the results. Sometimes they reflect intermediate outcomes. For example, in determining machine scheduling, spoilage is an intermediate variable while total profit is the result variable (spoilage affects the total profit).

The components of a quantitative model are tied together by sets of mathematical expressions such as equations or inequalities.

EXAMPLE: A simple financial-type model may look like this: $P = R - C$. $P$ stands for profit, $R$ stands for revenue, and $C$ stands for cost. Another well-known financial-type model is a present-value model, which may look like this:

$$P = \frac{F}{(1+i)^n}$$

where

$P$ = the present value
$F$ = a future single payment in dollars
$i$ = interest rate
$n$ = number of years

Using this model, one can calculate, for example, the present value of a payment of $100,000 to be made five years from today, considering 10 percent interest rate, to be:

$$P = \frac{100,00}{(1.1)^5} = \$62,110$$

Mathematical models, which are the most abstract, contain four types of variables (see Box 9.1). The major types of models are described next.

**ICONIC (SCALE) MODELS.** An iconic model—the least abstract model—is a physical replica of a system, usually based on a different scale from the original. Iconic models may appear to scale in three dimensions, such as models of an airplane, car, bridge, or production line. Photographs are another type of iconic model, but in only two dimensions.

**ANALOG MODELS.** An analog model, in contrast to an iconic model, does not look like the real system but behaves like it. An analog model could be a physical model, but the shape of the model differs from that of the actual system. Some examples include organizational charts that depict structure, authority, and responsibility relationships; maps where different colors represent water or mountains; stock charts; blueprints of a machine or a house; and a thermometer.

**MATHEMATICAL (QUANTITATIVE) MODELS.** The complexity of relationships in many systems cannot conveniently be represented iconically or analogically, or such representations and then the required experimentations may be cumbersome. A more abstract model is possible with the aid of mathematics. Most DSS analysis is executed numerically using mathematical or other quantitative models.

With recent advances in computer graphics, there is an increased tendency to use iconic and analog models to complement mathematical modeling in decision support systems. For example, visual simulation combines the three types of models (see the *IT at Work* example that follows).

---

*IT At Work*     **A DSS FOR PRODUCTION PLANNING IN FINLAND**

*U*SING IT

...in Production &
Operations Management

Dialogos-Team, a consulting company in Espoo, Finland, developed an innovative DSS for production planning (see attached figure).

Running on Windows, the user-friendly DSS creates a master scheduling plan and optimizes customer service, inventory value, and production resources. All the data are gathered into the application, which enables the user to manipulate data with interactive graphics. The software also produces various simulations. The nucleus of the DSS is the planning window, which presents the results of the simulation as they are generated. This product is used in many multinational corporations, such as Nest Chemicals, which uses it in Finland, Sweden, and Belgium.

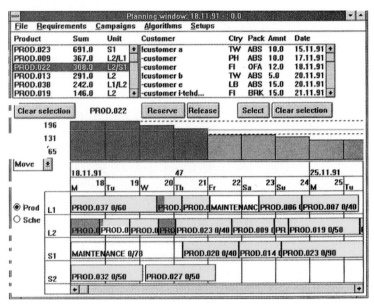

Planning window of the DSS developed by Dialogos-Team.

**For Further Exploration:** How can this DSS facilitate decision making in a multinational corporation? ▲

SOURCE: Condensed from *Finnish Trade Review: Look at Finland,* March 1993, p. 9.

**MENTAL MODELS.** In addition to the explicit models described earlier, people frequently use a behavioral mental model.

A *mental model* of a situation provides a description of how a person thinks about a situation. The model includes beliefs, assumptions, relationships, and flows of work as perceived by an individual. For example, a manager's mental model might say that it is better to promote older workers than younger ones and that such a policy would be preferred by most employees.

Mental models are a conceptual, internal representation used to generate descriptions of a problem structure and make predictions of future related variables. They determine the information we use and the manner in which people interpret (or ignore) information. Mental models are extremely important in environmental scanning where it is necessary to determine which information is important.

Developing a mental model is usually the first step in modeling. Once people perceive a situation, they may then model it more precisely using another type of model. Mental models are subjective and frequently change, so it is difficult to document them. They are important not only for decision making, but also for human-computer interaction (see Staggers and Norcio [1993]).

## COMPUTERIZED DECISION AIDS

We are now ready to answer four basic questions: (1) Why do managers need the support of information technology? (2) How are the information needs of managers determined? (3) Can the manager's job be fully automated? and (4) What IT aids are available to support managers?

### WHY MANAGERS NEED THE SUPPORT OF INFORMATION TECHNOLOGY.

It is impossible to make good decisions without information. Information is needed for each phase and activity in the decision-making process.

Making decisions while processing information manually is growing increasingly difficult due to the following trends:

▶ The *number of alternatives* to be considered is *increasing*, due to innovations in technology, improved communication, the development of global markets, and the use of the Internet and electronic commerce.

▶ Many decisions must be made *under time pressure.* Frequently, it is not possible to manually process the needed information fast enough to be effective.

▶ Due to increased fluctuations and uncertainty in the decision environment, it is frequently necessary to *conduct a sophisticated analysis* to make a good decision. Such analysis usually requires the use of IT.

▶ It is often necessary to rapidly access remote information, consult with experts, or have a group decision-making session.

These trends cause difficulties in decision making, but a DSS can be of enormous help. For example, a DSS can examine numerous alternatives very quickly, can provide a systematic risk analysis, can be integrated with communication systems and databases, and can be used to support group work. How all this is accomplished will be shown later. But first, let's see what information is really needed by managers.

**HOW TO DETERMINE THE INFORMATION NEEDS OF MANAGERS.** An important key to the success of IT is its ability to provide users with the *right information* at the *right time*. Identifying the information needs of managers is not a simple task. Several approaches are available. For example, Wetherbe's approach (1991) consists of a two-phase process. In Phase I, a *structured interview* is conducted to determine managers' perceived information needs. In Phase II, a *prototype* of the information system is quickly constructed. The prototyped system is shown to the managers who then make suggestions for improvements. The system is modified and again shown to the managers. Testing and modification go through several rounds until the detailed requirements are established. The *sources* of information are then identified, and the system can be developed.

The Watson and Frolick approach (1992) is based on the following strategies for *determining* information requirements: *asking* (the interview approach), *deriving* the needs from an existing information system, *synthesizing* from characteristics of the systems, and *discovering* via evolving systems (prototyping).

Several other approaches, some of which are intuitive, can be used to determine the manager's information needs. Representative examples are:

1. Ask managers what questions they would ask upon their return from a three-week vacation.

2. List major objectives in the company's short- and long-term plans, and identify their information requirements.

3. Ask managers (and especially executives) what information they would least like their competition to see.

4. Either through an interview or by observation, determine what information is actually used by managers.

5. Provide more immediate, online access to their current management reports, and then ask managers how you can better tailor the system to their needs. (Managers are much better able to tell you what is wrong with what you have given them than to tell you what they need.)

**CAN THE MANAGER'S JOB BE FULLY AUTOMATED?** The generic decision-making process involves specific tasks (such as forecasting consequences and evaluating alternatives). The process can be fairly lengthy, which is bothersome for a busy manager. Automation of certain tasks can save time, increase consistency, and enable better decisions to be made. Thus, the more tasks we can automate in the process, the better. If the last statement is correct, we may ask a logical question. Is it possible to completely automate the manager's job?

In general, it has been found that the job of middle managers is most likely to be fully automated. Mid-level managers make fairly routine decisions, and these can be automated. Managers at lower levels do not spend much time on decision making. Instead, they supervise, train, and motivate nonmanagers. Even if we completely automate their decisional role, we cannot automate their jobs. The job of top managers is the least routine and therefore the most difficult to automate.

**WHAT INFORMATION TECHNOLOGIES ARE AVAILABLE TO SUPPORT MANAGERS?** Four major information technologies have been successfully used to support managers. Collectively, they are referred to as **management support systems (MSS).** (See Turban and Aronson [1998].) First, DSSs, which have been in use since the mid-seventies, provide support primarily to analytical, quantitative types of decisions. Second, EIS is a technology developed in the mid-eighties, mainly to support the informational roles of executives. Lately, the scope and clientele of EIS have expanded to include analysis and communication, and all levels of managers now have access to EIS. DSS and EIS are discussed in detail in the remainder of this chapter. A third technology, groupware, supports managers working in groups and was discussed in Chapter 5. The fourth technology is intelligent systems, discussed in Chapter 11. These technologies can be used independently, or they can be combined, each providing a different capability. A simplified presentation of such support is shown in Figure 9.3.

Several other technologies can be used to support managers, either by themselves or when integrated with other management support technologies. One example is the **personal information manager (PIM).** A set of tools labeled PIM is intended to help managers be more organized. According to Manheim (1989), a PIM can play an extremely important role in decision support. Manheim showed that PIM tools can support several managerial tasks. For example, most managers are occupied with dozens of routine tasks, each requiring

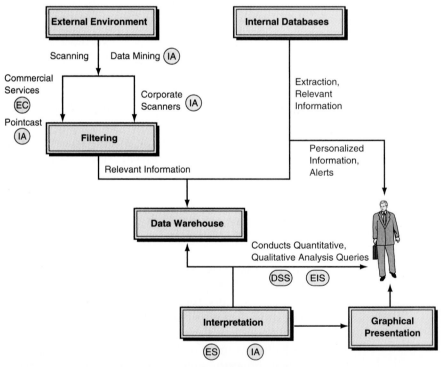

**FIGURE 9.3** Computerized support for decision making. As shown in Figure 9.1, managers need to find, filter, and interpret information to determine potential problems or opportunities and then decide what to do about them. The figure shows the support of MSS tools (circled) as well as the role of the data warehouse, which will be described in Chapter 10. IA = intelligent agents, ES = expert systems, EC = electronic commerce.

several steps for completion. These steps may conflict with each other. The PIM attempts to capture the user's image of the task or problem on which he or she is working. It provides facilities through which the user can analyze this image and operate on it in ways that will increase his or her effectiveness. Representative PIM software includes Organizer (from Lotus Development Corporation). Lotus's Organizer helps in daily planning. It links related tasks, names, and phone numbers. It includes a to-do list, calendar, address books, notepad, and anniversary reminder. It sounds an alarm to remind you to go to a meeting. Using electronic mail, invitations to meetings can be sent. Invitees can accept, decline, or delegate to someone else—with a single mouse click (see www.lotus.com for product description, demo, and loadable software). In 1998 Microsoft provided their customers with a free PIM. To optimize decision aids, we explore the framework in which they provide support.

## A FRAMEWORK FOR COMPUTERIZED DECISION SUPPORT

> I use Excel to tally and organize the sample data that I receive from our field employees about the training and communications products that the corporate training department provides to them. I use this information as a decision support tool when I formulate strategies for training product roll-out. I also use this data to report the needs of the field to upper management.
>
> — *Kristin Borhofen*

A framework for decision support was proposed by Gorry and Scott-Morton (1971), based on the combined work of Simon (1977, originally 1957) and Anthony (1965). The details are as follows.

The first half of the framework is based on Simon's idea that decision-making processes fall along a continuum that ranges from highly structured (sometimes referred to as *programmed*) to highly unstructured (*nonprogrammed*) decisions. *Structured* processes refer to routine and repetitive problems for which standard solutions exist. In structured decisions, all phases—intelligence, design, and choice—are structured. *Unstructured* processes are "fuzzy," complex problems for which there are no cut-and-dried solutions. An *unstructured problem* is one in which *none* of the three phases—intelligence, design, or choice—is structured. In an unstructured problem, human intuition is frequently the basis for decision making. Typical unstructured problems include planning new services to be offered, hiring an executive, or choosing a set of research and development projects for next year.

In a *structured problem,* all phases are structured and the procedures for obtaining the best (or at least a good enough) solution are known. Whether the solution means finding an appropriate inventory level or deciding on an optimal investment strategy, the solution's criteria are clearly defined. They are frequently cost minimization or profit maximization. The manager can use computerized clerical assistance, data processing, or management science models to support structured decisions.

*Semistructured* problems, in which only some of the phases are structured, require a combination of standard solution procedures and individual judgment. Keen and Scott-Morton (1978) give the following examples of semistructured problems: trading bonds, setting marketing budgets for consumer products, and performing capital acquisition analysis. Here, a DSS is most suitable. It can improve the quality of the information on which the decision is based (and consequently the quality of the decision) by providing not only a single solution but also a range of alternatives.

The second half of the framework is based upon Anthony's taxonomy (1965), which defines three broad categories that encompass all managerial activities: (1) *strategic planning*—the long-range goals and policies for resource allocation; (2) *management control*—the acquisition and efficient utilization of resources in the accomplishment of organizational goals; and (3) *operational control*—the efficient and effective execution of specific tasks.

Anthony's and Simon's taxonomies are combined in a nine-cell decision support framework (see Figure 9.4). The right-hand column and the bottom row indicate technologies needed to support the various decisions. Gorry and Scott-Morton suggested, for example, that for the semistructured and unstructured decisions, conventional MIS and management science approaches are insufficient. Therefore, they proposed the use of a DSS.

| Type of Decision | Type of Control | | | Support Needed |
|---|---|---|---|---|
| | **Operational Control** | **Managerial Control** | **Strategic Planning** | **Support Needed** |
| **Structured** | Accounts receivable, order entry   [1] | Budget analysis, short-term forecasting, personnel reports, make-or-buy analysis   [2] | Financial management (investment), warehouse location, distribution systems   [3] | MIS, Management science models, Financial, Statistical |
| **Semistructured** | Production scheduling, inventory control   [4] | Credit evaluation, budget preparation, plant layout, project scheduling, reward systems design   [5] | Building new plant, mergers and acquisitions, new product planning, compensation planning, quality assurance planning   [6] | DSS |
| **Unstructured** | Selecting a cover for a magazine, buying software, approving loans   [7] | Negotiating, recruiting an executive, buying hardware, lobbying   [8] | R & D planning, new technology development, social responsibility planning   [9] | DSS ES Neural Networks |
| **Support Needed** | MIS, Management science | Management science, DSS, EIS, ES | EIS, ES, Neural Networks | |

**FIGURE 9.4** Decision support framework. Technology is used to support the decisions shown in the column at the far right and in the bottom row.

Low-level managers are usually performing the structured and operational control-oriented tasks (cells 1, 2, and 4), whereas tasks in cells 6, 8, and 9 are mainly the responsibility of top executives. Cells 3, 5, and 7 are usually the responsibility of middle managers and/or professional staff. This means that DSS, EIS, expert systems, and neural networks are often applicable for top executives and professionals tackling specialized, complex problems.

**COMPUTER SUPPORT FOR STRUCTURED DECISIONS.** Structured and some semistructured decisions, especially of the operational and managerial control type, have been supported by computers since the 1950s. Decisions of this type are made in all functional areas, especially finance and operations management.

Problems that are encountered fairly often have a high level of structure. It is therefore possible to abstract, analyze, and classify them into standard classes. For example, a "make-or-buy" decision belongs to this category. Other examples are capital budgeting (e.g., replacement of equipment), allocation of resources, distribution of merchandise, and inventory control. For each standard class, a prescribed solution was developed through the use of mathematical formulas. This approach is called *management science/operations research* and is also executed with the aid of computers.

**MANAGEMENT SCIENCE.** The *management science* approach adopts the view that managers can follow a fairly systematic process for solving problems. Therefore, it is possible to use a scientific approach to managerial decision making. This approach, which also centers on modeling, requires the following steps:

1. *Defining* the problem (a decision situation that may deal with a setback or with an opportunity).
2. *Classifying* the problem into a standard category.
3. *Constructing* a standard mathematical model that describes the real-life problem.
4. *Finding* potential solutions to the modeled problem and evaluating them.
5. *Choosing* and recommending a specific solution to the problem.

> Management science most often deals with structured problems. However, in the real world, most problems are unstructured whereby DSS tools are required.
> — *Dave Gehrke*

A list of representative structured management science problems and tools is given in Table 9.1. Software packages are available to solve such problems very quickly.

*Table 9.1* **Representative Structured Management Science Problems and Tools**

| Problem | Tool |
|---|---|
| Allocation of resources | Linear and nonlinear programming |
| Project management | PERT, CPM |
| Inventory control | Inventory management models, simulation |
| Forecasting results | Forecasting models, regression analysis |
| Managing waiting lines | Queuing theory, simulation |
| Transporting and distributing goods | Transportation models |
| Matching items to each other | Assignment models |
| Predicting market share and other dynamically oriented situations | Markov chain analysis, dynamic programming, simulation |

Standard models cannot solve managerial problems that are not structured. These are usually more difficult and important problems of a managerial control and strategic planning nature. Such problems require the use of a DSS.

 ## 9.2 DECISION SUPPORT SYSTEMS

### DSS CONCEPTS

The concepts involved in **decision support systems (DSS)** were first articulated in the early 1970s by Scott-Morton. He defined such systems as "interactive computer-based systems, which help decision makers utilize *data* and *models* to solve unstructured problems" (1971). But the term DSS, like the terms MIS and MSS, means different things to different people. DSS can be viewed as an approach or a philosophy rather than a precise methodology. However, a DSS has certain recognized characteristics that we will present later.

First, let us look at a typical case of a successfully implemented DSS.

---

**IT At Work**     USING A DSS TO DETERMINE RISK

**U**SING IT

...in Finance

**H**ouston Minerals Corporation was interested in a proposed joint venture with a petrochemicals company to develop a chemical plant. Houston's executive vice president responsible for the decision wanted analysis of the risks involved in areas of supplies, demands, and prices. Bob Sampson, manager of planning and administration, and his staff built a DSS in a few days by means of a specialized planning language. The results strongly suggested that the project should be accepted.

Then came the real test. Although the executive vice president accepted the validity and value of the results, he was worried about the potential downside risk of the project, the chance of a catastrophic outcome. Sampson explains that the executive vice president said something like this:

"I realize the amount of work you have already done, and I am 99 percent confident of it. But I would like to see this in a different light. I know we are short of time and we have to get back to our partners with our yes or no decision."

Sampson replied that the executive could have the risk analysis he needed in less than one hour. "Within 20 minutes, there in the executive boardroom, we were reviewing the results of his what-if questions. Those results led to the eventual dismissal of the project, which we otherwise would probably have accepted."

**For Further Exploration:** Why did the DSS results reverse the initial decision? ▲

SOURCE: Information provided by Comshare Corporation.

---

The case demonstrates some of the major characteristics of a DSS. The risk analysis performed first was based on the decision maker's initial definition of the situation, using a management science approach. Then the executive vice president, using his experience, judgment, and intuition, felt that the model should be modified. The initial model, although mathematically correct, was incomplete. With a regular simulation system, a modification of the computer program would have taken a long time, but the DSS provided a very quick analysis. Furthermore, the DSS was flexible and responsive enough to allow managerial intuition and judgment to be incorporated into the analysis.

How can such a thorough risk analysis be performed so quickly? How can the judgment factors be elicited, quantified, and worked into the model? How can the results be presented meaningfully and convincingly to the executive? What are "what-if" questions? We answer these questions in the following sections.

But first, let us review some reasons for the increased use of DSS. Firestone Tire and Rubber Company explained its reasons for implementing DSS as follows:

1. The company was operating in an unstable economy.
2. It faced increasing foreign and domestic competition.
3. Tracking its numerous business operations was increasingly difficult.
4. The company's existing computer system did not properly support the objectives of increasing efficiency, profitability, and entry into profitable markets.

**5.** The IS department could not begin to address the diversity of the company's needs or management's ad hoc inquiries, and business analysis functions were not inherent within the existing systems.

Other reasons for using DSS that were found in surveys are:

▸ Accurate information is needed.

▸ DSS is viewed as an organizational winner.

▸ New information is needed.

▸ Management mandated the DSS.

▸ Timely information is provided.

▸ Cost reduction is achieved.

In Firestone's and other cases, the existing information systems were *not sufficient* to support all the company's critical response activities, described in Chapter 1. A DSS, on the other hand, can do just that. For example, it can provide a competitive advantage to companies as shown in the following example.

---

**IT At Work**  **A DSS FOR IMPROVING PRODUCTIVITY AND PROFITABILITY**

*U*SING IT

...in Production & Operations Management

For American Airlines, maintenance scheduling of 660 airplanes is a nightmare. Being a large airline does not necessarily provide advantages, especially where maintenance is concerned. American Airlines has 10 different fleet types, and each aircraft goes through 30 different maintenance checkups. Some checkups involve overhaul and rebuilding, which is lengthy and expensive (up to $1 million). Every day that an aircraft is not in service costs the airline additional money in lost revenue.

Starting with a five-year plan for major overhauls, planning is becoming a complex and critical activity. A DSS now takes all the variables into consideration. It allows the airline to generate a maintenance plan and perform various what-if analyses. Once a plan has been selected, it is subject to continuous changes, since planners need to react quickly to the rapidly changing maintenance-planning environment. The DSS includes many models, ranging from standard linear programming optimization to complex mathematical programming and simulation.

The DSS helped American Airlines to: (1) improve productivity, (2) reduce (and avoid) maintenance costs by as much as $454 million over the active life of the 227 wide-body aircraft alone, and (3) generate revenues by reducing the time that airplanes are not flying.

A five-year plan, which took weeks to generate manually, takes 1 to 10 minutes with the DSS. Each type of aircraft has its own plan, and each plan includes a resource utilization as well.

**For Further Exploration:** Without the DSS, how easily would American Airlines have been able to grow or compete? ▲

SOURCE: Based on Gray, D. A., "Airworthy-Decision Support for Aircraft Overhaul Maintenance Planning," *OR/MS Today,* December 1992.

---

Another reason for the development of DSS is the end-user computing movement. With the exception of large-scale DSS, end-users build the systems themselves. End users are not programmers, but using DSS development tools they can do this job.

## CHARACTERISTICS AND CAPABILITIES OF DSS

Because there is no consensus of what constitutes a DSS, there is obviously no agreement on the characteristics and capabilities of DSS. The following is presented as an ideal set. Most DSSs have only some of the following attributes.

1. A DSS provides support for decision makers at all management levels, whether individuals or groups, mainly in semistructured and unstructured situations, by bringing together human judgment and computerized information. Such problems cannot be solved (or cannot be solved conveniently) by other computerized systems or by management science.

2. A DSS supports several interdependent and/or sequential decisions.

3. A DSS supports all phases of the decision-making process—intelligence, design, choice, and implementation—as well as a variety of decision-making processes and styles.

4. A DSS is adaptable by the user over time to deal with changing conditions.

5. A DSS is easy to construct and use.

6. A DSS promotes learning, which leads to new demands and refinement of the application, which leads to additional learning, and so forth.

7. A DSS usually utilizes models (standard and/or custom made). Advanced DSSs are equipped with a knowledge management component that allows the efficient and effective solution of very complex problems.

8. A DSS allows the easy execution of sensitivity analysis, which we turn to next.

**SENSITIVITY ANALYSIS: "WHAT-IF" AND GOAL SEEKING. Sensitivity analysis** is the study of the impact that changes in one (or more) parts of a model have on other parts. Usually, we check the impact that changes in input variables have on output variables.

Sensitivity analysis is extremely valuable in DSS because it makes the system flexible and adaptable to changing conditions and to the varying requirements of different decision-making situations. It provides a better understanding of the model and the problem it purports to describe. It may increase the confidence of the users in the model, especially when the model is not so sensitive to changes. A sensitive model means that small changes in conditions dictate a different solution. In a nonsensitive model, changes in conditions do not significantly change the recommended solution. This means that the chances for a solution to succeed are very high. Two popular types of sensitivity analysis are *what-if* and *goal seeking*.

> A DSS such as an electronic spreadsheet is particularly valuable for "what-if" analyses.
> — *Dave Gehrke*

***What-If Analysis.*** A model builder makes predictions and assumptions regarding the input data, many of which are based on the assessment of uncertain futures. When the model is solved, the results depend on these assumptions. **What-if analysis** attempts to check the impact of a change in the assumptions (input data) on the proposed solution. For example, *what* will happen to the total inventory cost *if* the originally assumed cost of carrying inventories is not 10 but 12 percent? Or, *what* will be the market share *if* the initially assumed advertising budget increases by 5 percent?

In a properly designed DSS, managers themselves can easily ask the computer these types of questions as many times as needed for sensitivity analysis.

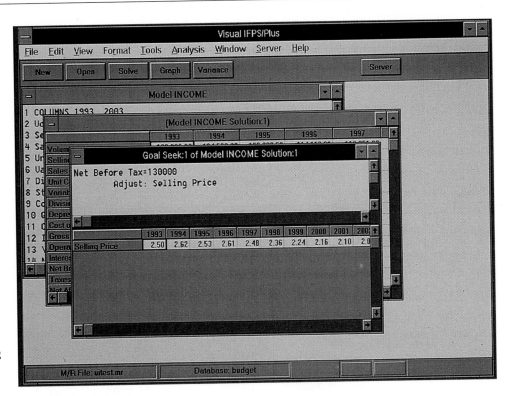

**FIGURE 9.5** Goal-seeking dialogue conducted with IFPS Plus software.

***Goal Seeking.* Goal-seeking analysis** attempts to find the value of the inputs necessary to achieve a desired level of output. It represents a "backward" solution approach. For example, let us say that a DSS solution yielded a profit of $2 million. Management wants to know what sales volume would be necessary to generate a profit of $2.2 million. This is a goal-seeking problem.

A computer printout of a goal-seeking dialogue is shown in Figure 9.5. The user wants to determine the per-unit-selling price necessary to achieve a net gain (before tax) of $130,000 for each of the subsequent years in a multiyear income model. The computer calculates the necessary price (per unit) for each of the years in a planning document. The program also allows the user to find the values of several variables to be adjusted for a desired goal level.

## STRUCTURE AND COMPONENTS

Every DSS consists of at least data management, user interface, and model management components. A few advanced DSSs also contain a knowledge management component. What does each component (subsystem) consist of?

1. *Data management.* Data management includes the *database(s),* and/or the data warehouse which contains relevant data for the situation, managed by a *database management system (DBMS).*
2. *User interface (or human–machine communication) subsystem.* The user can communicate with and command the DSS through this subsystem.

3. *Model management.* This includes software with financial, statistical, management science, or other quantitative models that provide the system's analytical capabilities and an appropriate software management program to manage the models.

4. *Knowledge management.* This subsystem can support any of the other subsystems or act as an independent component, providing knowledge for the solution of the specific problem. This subsystem is available in only a few DSSs.

These components (see Figure 9.6) constitute the software portion of the DSS. They are housed in a computer and can be facilitated by additional software.

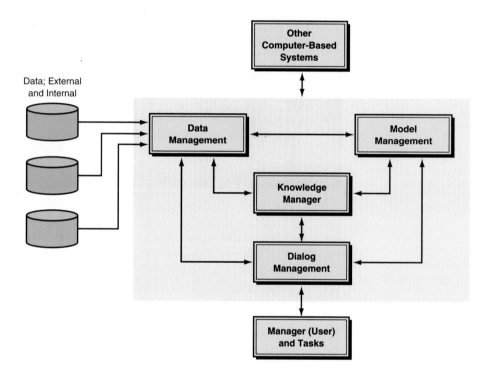

Data; External and Internal

**FIGURE 9.6** Conceptual model of a DSS shows four main software components facilitated by other parts of the system.

The components are put together for DSS either by programming them from scratch, by gluing together existing components, or by using comprehensive tools called DSS generators. End-user constructed DSSs are usually built with integrated tools, such as Excel or Lotus 1-2-3, which include word processors, spreadsheets, graphics, and database management systems.

**DATA MANAGEMENT SUBSYSTEM.** The data management subsystem is similar to any other data management system. The necessary data can flow from several sources and are extracted prior to their entry to a DSS database. In some DSSs, there is no separate DSS database, and data are entered into the DSS as needed. In many DSS applications, data come from a *data warehouse.* A data warehouse (see Chapter 10) includes DSS-relevant data extracted from different sources and organized as a relational database.

**MODEL MANAGEMENT SUBSYSTEM.** The *model base* contains all the models and the models' building blocks used to develop applications to run the system.

The role of the **model base management system (MBMS)** is analogous to that of a DBMS. The major functions (or capabilities) of the MBMS are these:

▶ Creates DSS models easily and quickly, either from scratch, from existing models, or from the building blocks.

▶ Allows users to manipulate DSS models so they can conduct experiments and sensitivity analyses.

▶ Stores and manages a wide variety of different types of models in a logical and integrated manner.

▶ Accesses and integrates the DSS model building blocks.

▶ Catalogs and displays the directory of models.

▶ Tracks models, data, and application usage.

▶ Interrelates models with appropriate linkages through the database.

▶ Manages and maintains the model base with management functions analogous to database management: store, access, run, update, link, catalog, and query.

The model management subsystem of the DSS has several elements: model base; model base management system; modeling language; model directory; and model execution, integration, and command. (For details see Turban and Aronson [1998].)

The model base may contain standard models (such as financial or management science) and customized models as illustrated next.

## IT At Work    DECISION SUPPORT SYSTEM HELPS A SMALL BREWERY TO COMPETE

**U**SING IT

...in Marketing

One of the major problems with a DSS is that it is tailored to a specific application. Guinness Import Co. needed a decision support system for (1) executives, (2) salespeople, and (3) analysts. They did not want separate systems. Using infoAdvisor (from Platinum Technology Inc.), a client/server DSS was constructed. In the past if a manager wanted to look at sales trends it was necessary to ask an analyst to download data from the mainframe and then use a spreadsheet to compute the trend. This took up to a day and was error prone. Now, when Diane Goldman needs such information she queries the DSS herself and gets an answer in a few minutes. Furthermore, she can analyze the data in different ways, quickly. Over 100 salespeople keep track of sales and can do similar analyses, from anywhere, using a remote Internet access.

To expedite the implementation of the system, highly skilled users in each department teach others how to use the DSS. The DSS helped to increase productivity of the employees. ("There's constant pressure to do a lot with a minimum of head count at Guinness.") This enables the company to compete against large companies such as Anheuser-Busch, as well as against microbrewers. The system reduced the salespeople's paperwork load by about one day each month. For 100 salespeople, this means 1,200 extra days a year to sell. And indeed, sales increased by 20 percent in 1997 versus 1996.

Corporate financial and marketing analysts are also using the system to make better decisions.

**For Further Exploration:** What can a DSS do that other computer programs cannot do for this company? ▲

SOURCE: Condensed from *Computerworld*, July 7, 1997. Also, see www.platinum.com.

**THE USER INTERFACE.** The term *user interface* covers all aspects of the communications between a user and the DSS. Some DSS experts feel that user interface is the most important DSS component because much of the power, flexibility, and ease of use of DSS are derived from this component.

The user interface subsystem is managed by software called **user interface management system (UIMS),** which is functionally analogous to the MBMS.

**THE USERS.** The person faced with the problem or decision that the DSS is designed to support is referred to as the *user,* the *manager,* or the *decision maker.* These terms fail to reflect, however, the heterogeneity that exists among users and usage patterns of DSS. There are differences in the positions users hold, ways in which a final decision is reached, users' cognitive preferences and abilities, and ways of arriving at a decision.

The user is considered to be a part of the system. Researchers assert that some of the unique contributions of DSSs are derived from the extensive interaction between the computer and the decision maker.

A DSS has two broad classes of users: managers and staff specialists (such as financial analysts, production planners, and market researchers).

When managers utilize a DSS, they may use it via an intermediary person who performs the analysis and reports the results. There are four types of intermediaries that reflect different types of support for the manager.

1. *Staff assistant.* This person has specialized knowledge about management problems and some experience with decision support technology.
2. *Expert tool user.* This person is skilled in the application of one or more types of specialized problem-solving tools. The expert tool user performs tasks for which the manager does not have the necessary skills or training.
3. *Business (system) analyst.* This person has a general knowledge of the application area, formal business administration education, and considerable skill in DSS construction tools.
4. *Group facilitator.* When group decisions are supported by IT, it is frequently beneficial to use a process facilitator (see Chapter 5).

**KNOWLEDGE MANAGEMENT SUBSYSTEMS.** Many unstructured and semi-structured problems are so complex that they require expertise for their solutions. Such expertise can be provided by an expert system. Therefore, the more advanced DSSs are equipped with a component called *knowledge management.* Such a component can provide the required expertise for solving some aspects of the problem or knowledge that can enhance the operation of the other DSS components.

The knowledge management component is composed of one or more expert (or other intelligent) systems. Like data and model management, knowledge management software provides the necessary execution and integration of the expert system. The capabilities of this component are discussed in Chapter 11.

A decision support system that includes such a component is referred to as an intelligent DSS, a DSS/ES, or a knowledge-based DSS (KBDSS). An example of KBDSS is in the area of estimation and pricing. It is a complex process that requires the use of models as well as judgmental factors. The KBDSS inludes a knowledge management subsystem with 200 rules incorporated with the computational models. For details, see Kingsman and de Souze (1997).

# ▶ 9.3 CORPORATE-LEVEL DECISION SUPPORT

Decision support applications can be segregated into two categories. Those that support individuals, and those that support many users. The first category provides support to functional analysts and to low-level managers. The second category provides support to groups and to upper management. The GDSS technology introduced in Chapter 5 is an example of the latter. Two other corporate support systems, organizational DSS and executive information systems, are described next.

## ORGANIZATIONAL DECISION SUPPORT SYSTEMS

Some decision support systems provide support throughout large and complex organizations (see Carter et al. [1992]). The major benefit of such systems is that many users of DSS become familiar with computers, analytical techniques, and DSS, as illustrated in the *IT at Work* example that follows.

 *IT At Work* **BUILDING AN ODSS FOR KOREA TELECOM**

**I**NTEGRATING IT

...for Finance and Production & Operations Management

**K**orea Telecom (KT) is Korea's largest telecommunications company. It employs 60,000 people in ten district offices and 360 local telephone offices. About half of the employees are in the Operations and Maintenance (O and M) division and work directly

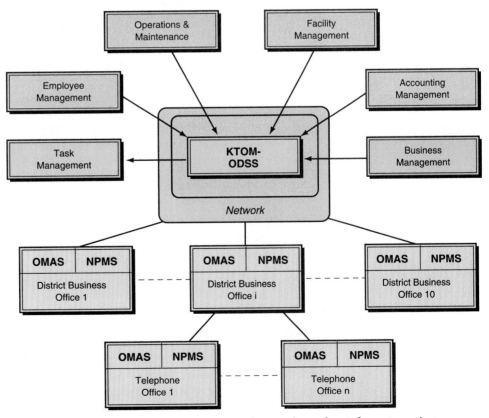

Korea Telecom ODSS supports employees throughout the corporation.

with the customers. For a high level of customer service, the company must invest about 15 percent of its annual budget for improvements and upgrades. The problem is that thousands of alternatives exist to accomplish this. Which alternative is best? The company realized the solution might require the reengineering of its Investment Performance Management activities. In the core of the organizational DSS model is the concept of quality of service. This is composed of four major indicators (operations quality, nonvoice service quality, transmission quality, and connection quality), each involving three to five specific measures. The model also checks the Context Difficulty Index (CDI) that evaluates each local or district office's operating environment.

The CDI evaluation, quality evaluation and O and M performance, determines the O and M budget in a complex model (Korea Telecom Operations and Management Model, KTOM-ODSS). The various organizational units that are involved and the connecting network are shown in the figure on page 403. This DSS is basically a distributed, yet integrated, system.

In addition to the budget allocation, the ODSS is used in decisions such as performance forecasting. The system cuts across functional areas and hierarchical layers (headquarters, districts, and local offices), and deals with many decision makers. The system was upgraded in 1998 with an intelligent component and a data warehouse for OLAP.

**For Further Exploration:** Why do the builders want to reengineer the allocation process first? ▲

SOURCE: Kim et al. (1997) and company's information, 1998.

The **organizational decision support system (ODSS)** was first defined by Hackathorn and Keen (1981), who distinguished between three levels of decision support: individual, group, and organization. They maintained that computer-based systems can be developed to provide decision support for each of these levels. They defined an ODSS as one that focuses on an organizational task or activity involving a sequence of operations and decision makers, such as developing a divisional marketing plan or doing capital budgeting. Each individual's activities must mesh closely with other people's work. The computer support was seen primarily as a vehicle for improving communication and coordination, in addition to problem solving. For a very-large-scale ODSS see El Sherif and El Sawy (1988) and Carter et al. (1992).

George (1991/1992) summarized the following common characteristics of ODSS.

▶ An ODSS is an organizational activity that affects several organizational units or corporate problems.

▶ An ODSS cuts across organizational functions or hierarchical layers.

▶ An ODSS almost necessarily involves computer-based technologies and may also involve communication technologies.

An ODSS often interacts or integrates with an executive information system.

## EXECUTIVE INFORMATION (SUPPORT) SYSTEMS

The majority of personal DSSs support the work of professionals and middle-level managers. Organizational DSSs provide support primarily to planners, analysts, researchers, or to some managers. Rarely do we see a DSS used directly by top- or even middle-level executives. One of the reasons is that DSS does not meet the executives' needs. An **executive information system (EIS)**, also known as an **executive support system (ESS)**, is a technology emerging in response to managers' specific needs, as shown in the following example.

---

**IT At Work**  AN EXECUTIVE INFORMATION
## SYSTEM AT HERTZ CORPORATION

**THE PROBLEM.** Hertz, the largest company in the car rental industry, competes against dozens of companies in hundreds of locations worldwide. Several marketing decisions must be made almost instantaneously (such as whether to follow a competitor's price discount or not). Marketing decisions are decentralized and are based on information about cities, climates, holidays, business cycles, tourist activities, past promotions, competitors' actions, and customers' behavior. The amount of such information is huge, and the only way to process it is to use a computer. The problem faced by Hertz was how to provide accessibility to such information and use it properly.

**I**NTEGRATING IT

...for Marketing and Finance

**THE INITIAL SOLUTION—A DSS.** A mainframe DSS was developed in 1987 to allow fast analysis by executives and managers. But a marketing manager who had a question had to go through a staff assistant, which made the process lengthy and cumbersome. The need for a better system was obvious.

**THE EIS.** In 1988, Hertz decided to add an EIS—a PC-based system used as a companion to the DSS. The combined system gave executives tools to analyze the mountains of stored information and make real-time decisions without the help of assistants. The system is extremely user-friendly and is maintained by the marketing staff. Since its assimilation into the corporate culture conformed to the manner in which Hertz executives were used to working, implementation was no problem.

Executives can now manipulate and refine data to be more meaningful and strategically significant to them and make real-time decisions without the help of assistants. The workload on the mainframe programming resources has been reduced, since the EIS allows executives to draw information from the mainframe, store the needed data on their own PCs, and perform a DSS-type analysis without tying up valuable mainframe time. Hertz managers feel that the EIS creates synergy in decision making. It triggers questions, a greater influx of creative ideas, and more cost-effective marketing decisions. In the late 1990s, the system was integrated with a data warehouse and connected to the corporate intranets and the Internet. Now local managers know exactly all competitors' prices, in real time, and by using supply-demand models, they can assess the impact of price changes on the demand for cars.

**For Further Exploration:** Why was the DSS insufficient by itself, and how did the addition of the EIS make it effective? ▲

SOURCE: Condensed from O'Leary, M., "Putting Hertz Executives in the Driver's Seat," *CIO*, February 1990 and from information provided by Hertz Corporation, 1998.

---

According to Watson et al. (1996), the following factors drive the need for EIS.

EXTERNAL FACTORS

- Increased competition.
- Rapidly changing environment.
- Need to be more proactive.
- Need to access external databases.
- Increasing government regulations.

INTERNAL FACTORS

▶ Need for timely information.

▶ Need for improved communications.

▶ Need for access to operational data.

▶ Need for rapid status updates on different activities.

▶ Need for increased effectiveness.

▶ Need to be able to identify historical trends.

▶ Need for access to corporate databases.

▶ Need for more accurate information.

The terms *executive information system* and *executive support system* mean different things to different people and are sometimes used interchangeably. The following definitions, based on Rockart and DeLong (1988), distinguish between EIS and ESS.

▶ *Executive information system (EIS).* An EIS is a computer-based system that serves the information needs of top executives. It provides rapid access to timely information and direct access to management reports. EIS is very user friendly, is supported by graphics, and provides "exception reporting" and "drill down" capabilities (see below). It is also easily connected with online information services and electronic mail.

▶ *Executive support system (ESS).* An ESS is a comprehensive support system that goes beyond EIS to include analysis support, communications, office automation, and intelligence.

## CAPABILITIES AND CHARACTERISTICS OF EIS

Executive information systems vary in their capabilities and benefits. The following capabilities are common to most EISs.

> This is important. Especially in containerized shipping (international). Top accounts must be able to have their performance reviewed at any time, regardless of where they are located. Managers must be able to sift through layers of data to see how much their accounts are producing.
> — *Nick Fafoutis*

**DRILL DOWN.**   The capability called **drill down** provides details of any given information. For example, an executive may notice a decline in corporate sales in a weekly report. To find the reason, the executive may want to view, without the need of programmers, a detail such as sales in each region. If a problematic region is identified, the executive may want to see further details (sales by product or by salesperson). In certain cases, this drill-down process may continue through several layers of detail. To provide such capability, the EIS may include several thousand menus, submenus, and sub-submenus. Drill down can be also achieved by direct query of databases, and by using a browser. Systems that use intelligent agents to conduct the drill down and bring the results to the user are under development.

**CRITICAL SUCCESS FACTORS AND KEY PERFORMANCE INDICATORS.**   The factors that *must* be considered in attaining the organization's goals are called *critical success factors (CSFs)*. Such factors can be strategic, managerial, or operational, and they are defined mainly from three sources: organizational factors, industry factors, and environmental factors. They can exist at the corporate level as well as at the division, plant, and department level. Sometimes it is even necessary to consider the CSF of individual employees.

Critical success factors, once identified, can be monitored, measured, and compared to standards. One or several key performance indicators, a sample of which is provided in Table 9.2, can measure each CSF. The left side of the table lists CSFs; the right side lists the indicators.

*Table 9.2* **Illustrative Key Performance Indicators for Typical CSFs**

| *CSF* | *Key performance indicators* |
|---|---|
| Profitability | Profitability measures for each department, product, region, etc. Comparisons among departments, and product comparisons with those of competitors. |
| Financial | Financial ratios, balance sheet analysis, cash reserve position, rate of return on investment. |
| Marketing | Market share, advertisement analysis, product pricing, weekly (daily) sales results, customer sales potential. |
| Human Resources | Turnover rates, skills analysis, absenteeism rate. |
| Planning | Corporate partnership ventures, growth/share analysis. |
| Economic Analysis | Market trends, foreign exchange values, industry trends, labor cost trends. |
| Consumer Trend | Consumer confidence level, purchasing habits, demographical data. |

**STATUS ACCESS.** In the *status access mode,* the latest data or reports on the status of key indicators or other factors can be accessed at any time. The *relevance* of information is important here. The *latest data* may require daily or even hourly operational tracking and reporting. In extreme cases, real-time reporting may be required.

**TREND ANALYSIS.** In analyzing data, it is extremely important to identify trends. Are sales increasing over time? Is market share decreasing? Is the competitor's share of the market declining against ours? The executive likes to examine trends, especially when changes in data are detected. **Trend analysis** can be done using forecasting models, which are included in many ESSs, or the executive can activate an adjacent DSS to conduct the trend analysis.

**AD HOC ANALYSIS.** Executive support systems provide for **ad hoc analysis** capabilities instead of merely providing access to the data analysis. Executives can thus use the ESS to do creative analysis on their own. They may even select the programming tools to be used, the outputs, and the desired presentation of information. Several end-user tools provide for ad hoc analysis, which is part of online analytical processing.

Quite a bit of financial management is completed this way (actual profit vs. forecast, actual expenses vs. budget). Exception reporting saves time in directing your attention to items which vary from what you expect them to be.

— *Mike Rewald*

**EXCEPTION REPORTING. Exception reporting** is based on the concept of *management by exception,* in which an executive should give attention to significant deviations from standards. Thus, in exception reporting, an executive's attention will be directed only to cases of very bad (or very good) performance. This approach saves considerable time for both producers and readers of reports.

**EIS TYPES AND ISSUES.** In recent years, the EIS has been enhanced with relational and multidimensional analysis and presentation, friendly data access, user-friendly graphical interface, imaging capabilities, hypertext, intranet access, e-mail, Internet access, and modeling. These are helpful for any executive. We can

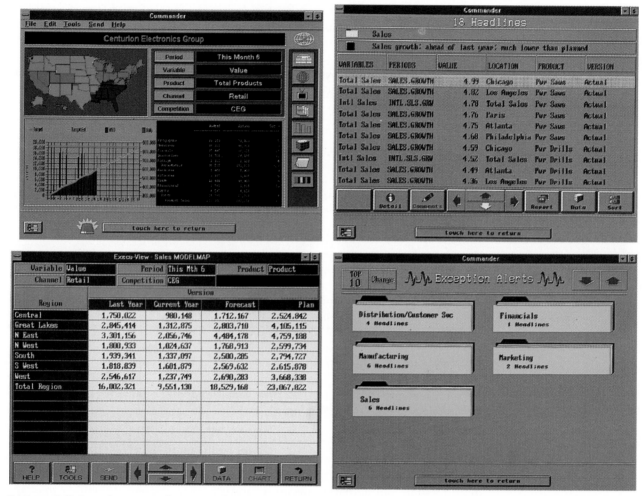

**FIGURE 9.7** Sample screens from Comshare Decision—a modular system for generating an executive information system.

distinguish between two types of EIS: (1) the one designed especially to support top executives, and (2) the EIS that is intended to serve a wider community of users (see Figure 9.7).

The latter type of EIS applications embrace a range of products targeted to support professional decision makers throughout the enterprise. For this reason, some people define the acronym EIS to mean *enterprise* information systems, or *everybody's* information systems. Many recently constructed systems are of this type.

**INTELLIGENT EIS.** In order to save the executive's time in conducting a drill down, finding exceptions, and identifying trends, an intelligent EIS has been developed. Automating these activities not only saves time but also ensures that the executive will not miss any important indications in a large amount of data. Intelligent EIS may include an intelligent agent for alerting management to exceptions. For further details see King and O'Leary (1996) and Liu (1998).

**INTEGRATION WITH DSS.** Executive information systems are useful in identifying problems and opportunities. Such identification can be facilitated by an in-

## *A Closer Look*  BOX 9.2

### AN INTELLIGENT EIS

Using intelligent software agents, Comshare Inc. was able to automate several tasks of an EIS. Specifically, the software can filter through databases or other electronic sources and glean important, relevant information for executives. The information is delivered in a form that is actionable. The software is an expert system that attempts to find irregular things, or exceptions, and then apply special rules to these exceptions. Of special interest is the Exception Monitor, which supplements Comshare's Decision DSS/EIS. It has three components:

1. *Monitor Builder.* This component allows the user to specify the exception-detecting rules, that is, to specify what is an exception or what needs to be detected.

2. *Exception engine.* This software detects variables, data relationships, patterns, and trends according to the specifications of the Monitor Builder.
3. *Desktop alerting.* This component sends messages to users alerting them to the exceptions.

Exception Monitor can save a considerable amount of time in informing executives. It can be designed to follow all the critical success factors and key performance indicators. It provides answers to questions such as why, where, and when exceptions are happening.

SOURCE: Comshare Inc., 1998.

---

telligent component (see Box 9.2). In addition, it is necessary to do something if a problem or an opportunity was discovered. Therefore many software vendors provide EIS/DSS integration tools, as illustrated next.

---

### *IT At Work*  SARA LEE UPGRADES SALES ANALYSIS WITH A DSS/EIS SUITE

*U*SING IT

...in Marketing

As a consumer products manufacturer, Sara Lee Corp. depends on its ability to analyze the sales of the retailers it serves. In 1993, however, the meat division of Sara Lee, which represents about $4 billion of the company's $16 billion in annual sales, was having a tough time performing sales analyses for the brands it supports. The division's DSS was running on an older-generation proprietary IBM mainframe environment that could not be easily upgraded or expanded to accommodate a growing number of users. The solution, which began to be installed in late 1993 and went live in May 1994, was a client/server system that is now known as the IA Decision Support Suite from Information Advantage. The suite is an integrated set of executive information and decision support applications designed to perform multidimensional online analytical processing dynamically against a data warehouse in an open environment. Users can drill down, drill up, skip multiple hierarchy levels, and create personal sets and calculations without having the IS department predefine drill paths or write stored procedures. In doing so, they can identify trends and exceptions, draw comparisons, perform calculations, and get fast answers. Users also benefit from the intuitivity and flexibility of a customizable GUI. The data warehouse is based on a high-speed relational database sorting and indexing engine from Red Brick Systems.

**For Further Exploration:** Point out the EIS/DSS integration. ▲

SOURCE: Condensed from *Chain Store Age*, Vol. 71, No. 9 (Section 3), pp. 22B–22C, Sept. 1995. Also see "How Sara Lee Replaced a Mainframe Decision Support System with Client/Server-based Analysis Tools," *I/S Analyzer Case Studies*, April 1995, Vol. 34, No. 4, pp. 7–11.

## 9.4 ADVANCED DECISION SUPPORT TOPICS

Several topics are involved in implementing DSS (for details see Turban and Aronson [1998]). Four of these are presented in this chapter.

### ONLINE ANALYTICAL PROCESSING

For small problems, data can be entered into an EIS or DSS manually as needed. Data can also be entered into the DSS or EIS model as they are processed or collected (by sensors or from a spreadsheet). For most other situations, the necessary data needs to be transferred electronically from databases or data files. For managers and executives it is very important to simplify the data entry and analysis process. For example, suppose a manager wants to analyze sales data from the last month in order to see the trend. Ideally, the manager should only have to specify the nature of the analysis and the period under consideration; the DSS will do the rest. Similarly, if the executive wants to conduct a drill down, or pose a query, he or she should be able to accomplish it within seconds with a simple request. A process that provides for such analyses is called **online analytical processing (OLAP).** To execute OLAP, the manager needs the appropriate tools for both accessing the databases and performing the analysis and presentation. One approach is the use of data warehouses or data marts, as illustrated in Chapter 10. Without these the manager may need to use a programmer to execute the analysis.

The following illustration demonstrates why OLAP is one of the most beneficial EIS/DSS end-user technologies.

---

*IT At Work* **HOSPITAL TAKES ITS OWN PULSE WITH OLAP SYSTEM**

**U**SING IT

...in Health Care

**I**NTEGRATING IT

...for Production & Operations Management and Finance

In 1993, California's Loma Linda University Medical Center (San Diego) decided to convert its legacy EIS into a client/server-based OLAP system that had the capability to customize future EIS applications, by using its OLAP system as an application development environment. The Loma Linda IS staff realized that the legacy system lacked the speed, convenience, quality, and detail that could be achieved with client/server-based OLAP. The new OLAP system enables EIS users to easily retrieve data in more sophisticated forms. It draws data from many sources, including text files, spreadsheets, databases, and data warehouses and enables managers to quickly drill down into the data to get specific details. The Pilot Decision Support Suite (formerly LightShip) was used by the hospital staff as a developmental environment to create its own customized application.

The OLAP-based EIS provides a wealth of information arranged in different ways. For example, it summarizes hospital financial and operational information by examining the hospital's census (or patient count) at different levels and from different perspectives. A hospital executive can examine the patient load in individual departments, view the overall hospital census in comparison to planned hospital use, look at a rolling 28-day trend, examine the monthly average census for the previous three years, or take an annual view.

EIS information is also used to satisfy hospital regulators that Loma Linda is doing its job. When the hospital was visited by the Joint Commission on Accreditation of Hospital Organizations, the visitors said, "having these types of systems helps show that the hospital really is trying to improve."

**For Further Exploration:** Why is OLAP so important in hospitals? Why can the managers quickly drill down? ▲

SOURCE: Condensed from *InfoWorld,* July 8, 1996, p. 68.

## SIMULATION AND VISUAL INTERACTIVE DECISION MAKING

> Simulation is a valuable tool that can be used in service industries to keep waiting lines to a minimum.
>
> — *Dave Gehrke*

**SIMULATION.** **Simulation** has many meanings. In general, to *simulate* means to assume the appearance of characteristics of reality. In DSS, simulation generally refers to a technique for conducting experiments (such as "what-if") with a digital computer on a model of a management system.

Because DSS deals with semistructured or unstructured situations, it involves complex reality, which may not be easily represented by optimization or other standard models but can often be handled by simulation. Therefore, simulation is one of the most frequently used tools of DSS. (See Fishwick [1995] and Winston [1996].)

*Major Characteristics.* To begin, simulation is not a regular type of model; models in general *represent* reality, while simulation usually *imitates* it. In practical terms, this means that there are fewer simplifications of reality in simulation models than in other models.

Second, simulation is a technique for *conducting experiments.* Therefore, simulation involves the testing of specific values of the decision or uncontrollable variables in the model and observing the impact on the output variables (a kind of sensitivity analysis).

Simulation describes and/or predicts the characteristics of a given system under different circumstances. Once the characteristics' values are computed, the best among several alternatives can be selected. The simulation process often consists of the repetition of an experiment many, many times to obtain an estimate of the overall effect of certain actions. It can be executed manually in some cases, but a computer is usually needed. Simulation can be used for complex decision making, as illustrated in the *IT at Work* example.

## *IT At Work* SIEMENS SOLAR INDUSTRIES SAVES MILLIONS BY SIMULATION

**U**SING IT

...in Production & Operations Management

**S**iemens Solar Industries (SSI) is the world's largest maker of solar electric products. The German company operates in an extremely global competitive market. Before 1994, the company suffered continuous problems in photocell fabrication, including poor material flow, unbalanced resource use, bottlenecks in throughput, and schedule delays. To overcome the problems, the company decided to build a *cleanroom* contamination-control technology. Cleanrooms are standard practice in semiconductor businesses, but they had never been used in the solar industry. The new technology, in which there is perfect control of temperature, pressure, humidity, and air cleanliness, was shown in research to improve quality considerably. In addition, productivity is improved because of fewer defects, better material flow, and reduced cycle times.

Because no one in the solar industry had ever used a cleanroom, the company decided to use a simulation, which provided a virtual laboratory where the engineers could experiment with various configurations of layouts and processes before the physical systems were constructed.

Computer simulation allowed SSI to compare numerous alternatives quickly. The company attempted to find the best design for the cleanroom and evaluate alternative scheduling, delivery rules, and material flows with respect to queue (waiting line) levels, throughput, cycle time, machine utilization, and work-in-progress levels.

The simulation was constructed with a tool called Pro-Model (from ProModel Corp., Orem, UT, http://www.promodel.com). The tool allowed the company to construct simulation models easily and quickly and to conduct what-if analyses. It also included extensive graphics and animation capabilities.

The simulation involved the entire business process, the machines, equipment, workstations, storage and handling devices, operators, and material and information flows necessary to support the process. Using brainstorming, the builders came up with many innovative suggestions that were checked by the simulation.

The solution identified the best configurations for the cleanroom, designed a schedule with minimum interruptions and bottlenecks, and improved material flow, while reducing work-in-progress inventory levels to a minimum.

All in all, the simulation enabled the company to improve the manufacturing process of different solar products significantly. The cleanroom facility has saved SSI over $75 million each year. ▲

**For Further Exploration**: Relate this story to BPR.

SOURCE: Condensed from Vacca, J. R., "Faking It, Then Making It," *Byte*, Nov. 1995.

*Advantages of Simulation.* Simulation is used in DSS because:

1. Simulation can show the effect of compressing time, giving the manager in a matter of minutes some feel as to the long-term effects of various policies.
2. Simulation is descriptive. This allows the manager to ask what-if type questions. Thus, managers who employ a trial-and-error approach to problem solving can do it faster and cheaper, with less risk, using a simulated problem instead of a real one.
3. Simulation can handle an extremely wide variation in problem types such as inventory and staffing, as well as higher managerial level tasks like long-range planning.
4. The manager can experiment with different variables to determine which are important, and with different alternatives to determine which is best.
5. Simulation allows for inclusion of the real-life complexities of problems; only a few simplifications are necessary. For example, simulation may utilize the real-life probability distributions rather than approximate theoretical distributions.

Of the various types of simulation, the most comprehensive is visual interactive simulation.

**VISUAL INTERACTIVE MODELS AND DSS. Visual interactive modeling (VIM)** uses computer graphic displays to represent the impact of different management or operational decisions on goals such as profit or market share. VIM differs from regular simulation in that the user can intervene in the decision-making process and see the results of the intervention. A visual model is much more than a communication device, since it is used as an integral part of decision making and/or problem solving.

A VIM can be used both for supporting decisions and for training. It can represent a static or a dynamic system. Static models display a visual image of the result of one decision alternative at a time. (With computer windows, several results can be compared on one screen.) Dynamic models display systems that evolve over time; the evolution is represented by animation or motion pictures. These are also referred to as real-time simulation, as described next.

One of the most developed areas in VIM is **visual interactive simulation (VIS),** a decision simulation in which the end-user watches the progress of the simulation model in an animated form using graphics terminals. The user may interact with the simulation and try different decision strategies.

Belton and Elder (1994) suggest that VIM is an approach that has, at its core, the ability to allow decision makers to learn about their own subjective values and about their mistakes. Therefore, VIM can be used for training as well as in games, as in the case of Flight Simulator, and as shown in this *IT at Work* example.

---

*IT At Work*    **COMPUTER TRAINING IN COMPLEX LOGGING MACHINES**

**U**SING IT

...in HRM

The forest industry is extremely competitive, and countries with high labor costs must automate tasks such as moving, cutting, delimbing, and piling logs. A new machine, called the "Harvester," replaces 25 lumberjacks.

The Harvester is a highly complex machine that takes six months to learn how to operate. The trainee destroys a sizeable amount of forest, and terrain suitable to practice on is decreasing. In unskilled hands, this expensive machine can also be damaged. Therefore, extensive and expensive training is needed. Sisu Logging of Finland found a solution to the training problem by using a real-time simulation.

In real-time simulation, the chassis, suspension, and wheels of the vehicles have to be modeled together with the forces acting on them, inertia and friction, and the movement equations linked with them have to be solved in real time. This type of simulation is mathematically complex and to date has required equipment investment running into millions or tens of millions of dollars. However, with the help of the simulations program, simulation can be carried out for only one percent of the cost of the traditional method. Inside the simulator are the Harvester's actual controls, which are used to control a virtual model of a Harvester plowing its way through a virtual forest.

The machine sways back and forth on uneven terrain, and the grapple of the Harvester grips the trunk of a tree, fells it, delimbs it, and cuts it into pieces very realistically in real time.

The simulated picture is very sharp and the structures of the bark and annual growth rings are clearly visible where the tree has been cut. In usual simulators, the travelling path is quite limited beforehand, but in this Harvester simulator, you are free to move in a stretch of forest covering two hectares (25,000 square yards).

In addition, different kinds of forest in different parts of the world can be modeled together with the different tree species and climatic conditions. An additional advantage of this simulator is that the operations can be videotaped so that training sessions can be carefully studied afterwards. Moreover, it is possible to practice certain dangerous situations that cannot be done using a real machine. The simulation project was implemented in November 1997.

**For Further Exploration:** Why is the simulated training time shorter? ▲

SOURCE: Condensed from *Finnish Business Report,* April 1997.

---

Animation systems that produce realistic graphics are available from many simulation software vendors (see Swain [1993]). The latest visual simulation technology is tied in with the concept of virtual reality, where an artificial world is created for a number of purposes—from training to entertainment to viewing data in an artificial landscape. (For more on virtual reality, see Chapter 11.)

VIM has been used with DSS in several operations management decisions (see Chau and Bell [1996]). The method consists of priming a virtual interactive model of a plant (or a business process) with its current status. The model is then rapidly run on a computer, allowing management to observe how a plant is likely to operate in the future.

## THE DSS, EIS, AND INTERNET CONNECTION

The Web is a perfect medium for deploying decision support and EIS capabilities on a global basis. Some of those capabilities are discussed next.

**1.** The DSS/EIS builder can access the Web pages and view data of organizations that are related to the DSS project, thus saving time.

**2.** The Web supports interactive DSS-related queries and ad hoc report generation. The users can select a list of variables from a pull down menu when executing a predefined query or report. This gives the builder the ability to customize the DSS/EIS output.

**3.** Web-based application servers download Java applets that execute functions on desktop DSS/EIS programs. This gives users the capabilities of advanced DSS application without requiring client software to be loaded. All users really need is a Web browser. The Web-based processing model is shown in Figure 9.8.

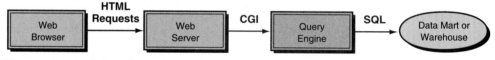

**FIGURE 9.8**  Web-based query.

Most vendors of decision support applications have modified their tools in order for them to work across the Web. An example is Brio Technology Corporation, whose BrioQuery Enterprise, an online analytical processing tool, was converted to Brio's Web Warehouse. Brio's tool enables users to view and manipulate reports created with BrioQuery inside a browser. The user can employ the tool to drill down, pivot, or change the layout and content of the DSS/EIS output. Pilot software www.pilotsw.com and Comshare offer DSS/EIS/Web products. An intranet-based DSS was proposed by Ba et al. (1997). This DSS is also related to intelligent decision support.

Web-based DSS or EIS facilitate the use of these systems and are especially suitable to organizational and enterprisewide EIS. An example is provided next.

---

*IT At Work*   THE UNIVERSITY OF GEORGIA USES A
WEB-BASED DSS FOR THE COURSE APPROVAL PROCESS

**U**SING IT

...in Production &
Operations Management

When the University of Georgia moved from the quarter to the semester system in 1996, the entire curriculum had to be revamped. Every course had to go through the entire course approval process, a lengthy paper trail with approval/modify/reject decisions made at every step. This workflow clearly needed to be automated, since thousands of courses in hundreds of disciplines were involved. The CAPA (Course Approval Process Automation) system was developed to support semester conversion issues; then it became a part of the regular curricula maintenance. Its objectives were to coordinate a process that involved multiple committees, dean's offices, department offices, the Graduate School, and the Vice President of Academic Affairs Office.

CAPA is a Web-based system that runs on the intranet. The Web server provides information to the users, and the SQL database that runs on another system handles queries by the users.

The decision to use a Web server was based on the university's capability to provide Web browsers for clients (to enable PCs on the various local area networks on campus to access databases and software campuswide). The individual colleges and departments incurred no additional hardware or software costs.

The principle benefits of CAPA are that it saves time and is cost effective, especially for the end users; is flexible enough to support various related applications and is extendible to support additional requirements; requires little or no user training; and addresses long-term maintenance/management/upgrade issues.

Appropriate and current information about courses can be accessed from the database to assist the decision makers at the college, departmental, and university levels.

**For Further Exploration:** What made this application so suitable for the Web? ▲

SOURCE: Condensed from an internal report by Anyanwu, K. et al., University of Georgia, Athens, GA, December 1996.

For DSS Web information see http://power.cba.uni.edu/DTP/dssfour.html. Also see www.comshare.com.

## SUPPORTING IDEA GENERATION AND CREATIVITY

One of the major critical response activities we explored in Chapter 1 was the increased use of creativity and innovation. Creativity also plays an important role in decision making. Many DSS builders assume that alternative courses of action are known to the decision makers or are very easy to generate. Although this assumption is probably correct in many structured decisions, there are many semistructured and unstructured situations for which alternative courses of action are not known in advance. Therefore, it is frequently necessary to generate ideas or to be creative.

In the past, it was believed that an individual's creative ability stemmed primarily from personality traits such as inventiveness, independence, individuality, enthusiasm, and flexibility. However, several studies have indicated that individual creativity can be learned and improved, and it is not so much a function of individual traits as was once believed. This understanding has led innovative companies to recognize that the key to fostering creativity may be the development of an idea-nurturing work environment. Idea-generation methods and techniques, to be used by individuals or in groups, are consequently being developed.

Manual methods for supporting idea generation (such as brainstorming in a group) can be very successful in certain settings. However, there are circumstances where such an approach is either not economically feasible or not possible. For example, manual methods will not work or will not be effective in the following situations involving group creativity sessions:

1. There is a poor facilitator (or there is no facilitator).
2. There is no time to conduct a proper idea-generation session.
3. It is too expensive to conduct an idea-generation session.
4. The subject matter is too sensitive for a face-to-face idea-generation session.
5. There are not enough participants, the mix of participants is not optimal, or there is no climate for idea generation.

Thus, manual methods designed to facilitate individual creativity may not work for all individuals or in all types of situations. In such cases, it makes sense to try to electronically induce idea generation (see Elam and Mead [1990] and Marakas and Elam [1997]). Massetti (1996) demonstrated in experiments that computer-enabled people were more creative in problem solving. For creativity and the Web see www.ozemail.com.au/%7Ecareman/creative.

**IDEA-GENERATION SOFTWARE.** *Idea-generation software* is designed to help stimulate a single user or a group with new ideas, options, and choices. The user does all the work, but the software encourages and pushes just like a personal trainer. Although idea-generation software is still relatively new, there are several packages on the market. Representative products are Brainstorm (from Mustang Software), Creative Whackpack (from Creative Think), IdeaFisher (from IdeaFisher Systems), and Think Tank (from Living Videotext).

Various approaches are used by idea-generating software to increase the flow of ideas to the user. One package (IdeaFisher) is unique in that it has an associative lexicon of the English language that cross-references words and phrases (see Box 9.3). These associative links, based on analogies and metaphors, make it easy for the user to be fed words related to a given theme.

Some software packages use questions to prompt the user toward new, un-

---

## A Closer Look    BOX 9.3

### IDEAFISHER SOFTWARE USES ASSOCIATIONS

The first component of IdeaFisher is called the QBank. Questions in QBank are organized to assist the user in more accurately formulating the exact problem that he or she is trying to solve. A series of "modification" questions encourage the user to branch into different lines of thought, and a series of "evaluation" questions help the user to test and compare the quality of "winning" ideas with the original objective. This list of central ideas can then be used to decide what to pursue first in the Idea-Bank and what to save for later.

IdeaBank, the second component, is a database of over 60,000 idea words, concepts, and associations. The result is a cross-reference power of more than 705,000 direct idea associations and an infinite number of secondary (linked) associations. The potential number of associations triggered in the user's mind may easily reach into the millions. The inclusion of polar opposites stimulates an ever-larger group of associations that would never have otherwise occurred to the user.

IdeaBank also lets users add personal associations and phrases to a list of Topical Categories or to create their own Topical Categories, filled with thoughts from personal knowledge along any subject line (i.e., products, customers, or competition).

The third component of the system, the Notepad, allows the two databases to work efficiently together. This frees the user to focus on productive efforts in selecting alternative lines of thought, maximizing the number of quality ideas, and selecting the best ones.

explored patterns of thought. This helps users to break out of cyclical thinking patterns, conquer mental blocks, or deal with bouts of procrastination. Creative Whackpack provides techniques to "whack" the user out of habitual thought patterns.

Idea-generation software for groups works somewhat differently from such software for individuals. Participants in groups create ideas simultaneously. Ideas generated by participants are shown to other participants, stimulating electronic discussion or generation of more ideas. A large number of ideas is usually generated in a short time. These ideas are then organized, debated, and prioritized by the group, all electronically.

The benefits of creativity enhancement afforded by idea-generating software are numerous. A competitive advantage can be realized across all industry spectrums because of the many new ideas and approaches that can be facilitated electronically. Idea-generation software acts as a catalyst to generate alternative solutions that help operations run more efficiently and more competitively. (See the following example.)

---

**IT At Work**   **BRAINSTORMING BUSINESS PROBLEMS USING IDEAFISHER**

**USING IT**
...in Production & Operations Management

**C**EC Instruments (San Dimas, CA) used the IdeaFisher software to cope with shrinking military contracts. In order to survive, the company was looking to the commercial market. Using IdeaFisher, Jim Shenk, manager of contracts, realized that CEC had overlooked an expanding market for its technical instruments in the commercial aviation market.

**Clayton Lee,** an inventor in Houston, TX reduced, with IdeaFisher, the manufacturing costs of a new product from $2,000 to $100 per unit. As a result, the market for the product widened enormously. In addition, IdeaFisher was used to modify existing products so he did not have to think up all the questions that he should be asking himself.

**Infocomp Corporation** (Oceanside, CA) used the IdeaFisher to introduce a cost-reduction program to a daily newspaper (the *Tribune*). The software enabled the company to overcome resistance to the introduction of a new budgeting system. The software also enabled consultants to market and promote new programs to management. ▲

SOURCE: Communication with IdeaFisher Systems, 1998.

---

# ▶ MANAGERIAL ISSUES

1. *Intangible benefits.* MSSs are difficult to justify because they generate mostly intangible benefits, such as the ability to solve problems faster. While the cost of small systems is fairly low and justification is not a critical issue, the cost of a medium-to-large MSS can be very high, and the systems must be justified.

2. *Documenting personal DSS.* Many employees develop their own DSS to increase their productivity and the quality of their work. It is advisable to have an inventory of these DSSs and make certain that appropriate documentation and security measures exist so that if the employee leaves, the productivity tool remains.

3. *Security.* DSS and EIS may contain extremely important information for the livelihood of organizations. Taking appropriate security measures is a must to safeguard data integrity. The problem is that end users who build a DSS frequently ignore appropriate security measures. Management must remember that end users are not professional systems builders. For this reason, there could be problems with data integrity and the quality of the systems developed.

4. *Ready-made commercial DSS.* With the decreased cost of system development, it is possible to find more and more DSS applications sold off the shelf. The benefits of a purchased DSS application (low cost, immediate use) sometimes makes it advisable to change business processes to fit a commercially available DSS rather than to build a custom one. Some vendors are willing to modify their standard software to fit the customer's needs. Commercial DSSs are available for certain industries (hospitals, banking) and for specific tasks (like profitability analysis).

5. *Intelligent DSS.* Introducing intelligent agents into a DSS can greatly increase its functionality. The intelligent component of a system, such as American Express's Credit Card Authorizer, can be less than 3 percent of the entire system (the rest is DSS, databases, and telecommunications). Yet, the contribution of the intelligent component can be incredible.

6. *Organization culture.* The more people recognize the benefits of DSS and the more support is given to it by top management, the more DSS will be used. If the organization's culture is supportive, hundreds of applications can be developed.

7. *Ethical issues.* Corporations with management support systems may need to address some serious ethical issues such as privacy and accountability. For example, a company developed a DSS to help people compute the financial implications of early retirement. However, the DSS developer did not include the tax implications, which resulted in incorrect retirement decisions.

Another important ethical issue is human judgment, which is frequently used in DSS. Human judgment is subjective, and therefore, it may lead to unethical decision making. Companies should provide an ethical code for DSS builders. Finally, the possibility of automating managers' jobs may lead to massive layoffs. Some may ask whether we should do it as well as to what extent.

## KEY TERMS

Ad hoc analysis *407*

Decision support system (DSS) *395*

Drill down *406*

Exception reporting *407*

Executive information system (EIS) *405*

Executive support system (ESS) *405*

Goal-seeking analysis *399*

Management support system (MSS) *392*

Model base management system (MBMS) *401*

Online analytical processing (OLAP) *410*

Organizational decision support system (ODSS) *404*

Personal information manager (PIM) *392*

Sensitivity analysis *398*

Simulation *411*

Trend analysis *407*

User interface management system (UIMS) *402*

Visual interactive modeling(VIM) *412*

Visual interactive simulation (VIS) *413*

What-if analysis *398*

## CHAPTER HIGHLIGHTS  *(L–x means learning objective number x)*

▶ Managerial decision making is synonymous with management. (L–1)

▶ Models allow fast and inexpensive experimentation with systems. Models can be iconic, analog, or mathematical. (L–2)

▶ Decision making is becoming more and more difficult due to the trends discussed in Chapter 1. Information technology enables managers to make better and faster decisions. (L–3)

▶ To a degree, decisions can be structured and are either operational, managerial, or strategic. (L–4)

▶ Decision making involves four major phases: intelligence, design, choice, and implementation. (L–4)

▶ DSS can improve the effectiveness of decision making, decrease the need for training, improve management control, facilitate communication, reduce costs, and allow for more objective decision making. (L–5)

▶ The major components of a DSS are the database and its management, the model base and its management,

and the friendly user interface. An intelligent (knowledge) component can be added. (L–5)

▶ The model base includes standard models and models specifically written for the DSS. (L–5)

▶ Visual interactive modeling decision support is an implementation of GUI that is usually combined with simulation and animation. (L–5)

▶ Organizational DSS deals with decision making across functional areas and hierarchical organizational layers, and it operates in a distributed environment. (L–6)

▶ Discovering the information needs of executives is a very difficult process. Methods such as CSF and BSP are effective, especially if they are followed by prototyping. (L–7)

▶ There is a trend to integrate DSS and EIS to an ESS. Thus, an ESS is basically an EIS with analysis capabilities. (L–7)

▶ Idea generation can be enhanced by software, which uses associations, identification of patterns, and other well-known techniques to facilitate creativity. (L–8)

## QUESTIONS FOR REVIEW

1. Describe the manager's major roles.

2. Define the executive's interpersonal, informational, and decisional roles.

3. Explain the phases of intelligence, design, and choice.

4. What are programmed and unprogrammed problems? Give one example of each in the following three areas: finance, marketing, and personnel administration.

5. Explain what-if analysis, and provide an example.

6. What is goal-seeking analysis? Provide an example.

7. Give two definitions of DSS.

8. Briefly define the major components of a DSS.

9. Describe online analytical processing (OLAP).

10. What is the major purpose of the user interface component in a DSS?

11. List the major classes of DSS users.

12. Describe the relationship of DSS and the Internet/intranet.

13. What is the difference between an EIS and an ESS?

14. What are some of the pressures for the creation of an EIS?

15. What are the major benefits of an EIS?

16. Define drill down, and list its advantages.

17. Explain electronically supported idea generation.

18. Relate DSS and EIS to the Internet.

19. Define visual interactive modeling and simulation.

20. Describe the benefit of simulation in decision support.

## QUESTIONS FOR DISCUSSION

1. What could be the biggest advantages of a mathematical model that supports a major investment decision?

2. Your company is considering opening a branch in China. List several typical activities in each phase of the decision (intelligence, design, choice, and implementation).

3. A hospital desires to know what level of demand for its services will guarantee an 85 percent bed occupancy. What type of sensitivity analysis should the hospital use and why?

4. Some experts believe that the major contribution of a DSS is to the implementation of the decision and not to the intelligence, design, or choice phases. Why?

5. How is the term *model* used in this chapter? What are the strengths and weaknesses of modeling?

6. List some internal data and external data that could be found in a DSS for a company's selection of an investment stock portfolio.

7. List some internal and external data in a DSS that will be constructed for a decision regarding the expansion of a university.

8. If a DSS is employed in finding answers to management questions, what is the EIS used for?

9. Discuss the importance of OLAP in DSS and EIS.

10. American Can Company announced that it was interested in acquiring a company in the health maintenance organization (HMO) field. Two decisions were involved in this act: (1) the decision to acquire an HMO, and (2) the decision of which one to acquire. How can a DSS and an EIS be used in each situation?

11. Why can't a conventional MIS fulfill the information needs of executives?

12. Why is it so difficult to identify the information needs of managers? List a few approaches that can be used to discover the information needs of managers.

13. Describe how critical success factors are measured in your company or in a company with which you are familiar.

14. List the major benefits of integrating EIS and DSS?

15. Discuss the differences between an ODSS and a DSS.

16. Explain how IT can facilitate idea generation. What are its advantages over manual facilitation?

## EXERCISES

1. Susan Lopez was promoted to director of the transportation department in a medium-size university. She controlled the following vehicles: 17 sedans, 9 vans, and 3 trucks. The previous director was fired because there were too many complaints about not getting vehicles when needed. Susan is told not to expect any increase in budget for the next two years, which means there will be no replacement or additional vehicles. Susan's major job was to schedule vehicles for employees, and to schedule maintenance and repair of the vehicles.

Your job is to advise Susan regarding the possibility of using a DSS to improve her manually done job. Susan has a Pentium PC and Microsoft Office, but she is using the computer only for word processing.
   a. Justify use of the proposed DSS. What can this DSS do to improve Susan's job?
   b. Describe the decision variables, result variables, and independent variables of the DSS model.
   c. Which of the Microsoft Office components will you use for the DSS, and for what?

## GROUP ASSIGNMENTS

1. Development of an ESS is proposed for your university. Identify the organization structure of the university and its major existing information systems. Then, identify and interview several potential users of the system. In the interview, you should check the need for such a system and convince the potential users of the benefits of the system.

2. The group should identify current DSS tools and proceed to a computer store to see some of these products. Then make a brief evaluation of at least four products:
   a. An integrated spreadsheet (such as Excel).
   b. An integrated DBMS.
   c. A data access (for EIS) tool such as Visual Basic (check with vendors like Comshare, Inc., Pilot Software, Brio, and Cognos).
   d. Multidimensional presentation, such as Power-Play, CA Compete, or Comshare Decision/Prism.

3. Prepare a report regarding DSS and the Web. As a start go to: http://power.cba.uni.edu/dsstour.html. Also, view Comshare Decision Web (www.comshare.com) and DSS Web (www.strategy.com).

## INTERNET EXERCISES

Note: The URLs included here were current when the book went to press. However, they are subject to change without notice. Please consult the Turban Web site (www.Wiley.com/college/turban2e).

1. Enter the site of Comshare (www.comshare.com) and identify its major DSS and EIS products. Find success stories of customers using these products (try www.comshare.com/customers/. Also, find Comshare's Web-based strategy.

2. Find DSS-related newsgroups. Post a message regarding a DSS issue that is of concern to you. Gather several replies and prepare a report.

3. Several DSS and EIS vendors provide free demos on the Internet. Identify a demo, download it, and report on its major capabilities (try www.strategy.com; www.sas.com, www.comshare.com).

4. Enter the Comshare site and find information about Comshare Decision. Explain the integration of EIS and DSS in this product. E-mail Comshare and identify a successful real-world application using Comshare Decision. Submit a report.

5. Search the Internet for the major DSS and EIS vendors. How many of them market both DSS and EIS tools? (Try www.pilotsw.com)

6. Online analytical processing (OLAP) is becoming an important tool related to DSS and EIS. Browse the Web in search of the latest developments.

7. Enter www.asymetrix.com. Learn about the InfoAssistant decision support tool suite. Download the free software and explain how the software can increase competitive advantage.

8. Find 10 case studies about DSS. Try www.strategy .com, www.infoadvan.com; www.tandem.com, and www.comshare.com. Analyze for DSS characteristics.

---

# ▼ Minicase 1

## Executive Support to Teleglobe Canada

Teleglobe Canada provides the communication link between Canada and all other countries in the world. In the late 1980s, Teleglobe was privatized and became regulated by the Canadian Radio and Telecommunications Commission. At the same time, the company had to report to the parent company in great detail about finance, operations, and marketing activities. Frequently, the parent company asked for information from managers after their assistants had left or even called managers at home. The pressures were mounting.

The corporate president, Jean-Claude Delome, was interested in quick access to data and improved communications even before the privatization. The company had excellent functional MIS, but management wanted a system that can show trends, patterns, and comparisons. So, Delome requested development of a system which would do just that; "a system that will sit on the top of the company databases." Teleglobe had information architecture in place with three layers: strategic planning, management control, and operations control. Each of these layers was composed of numerous systems, but the three layers did not interact easily among themselves. To accommodate the president, the MIS department decided to build an additional layer to address corporate-level issues, such as profits and costs, networks and facilities, rates and tariffs (which are constantly changing), service profitability, and capital investment. They also wanted to provide modeling capabilities and what-if analysis.

The MIS department took the following steps:

1. Looked at the company mission goals and objectives.

2. Prepared a list of critical success factors which distilled the numerous objectives and priorities identified in Step 1.

3. Selected a "champion" for the project—the finance department.

4. Decided to develop an EIS, using Commander EIS (now Comshare Decision).

5. Developed an EIS prototype for the finance department.

6. Improved the prototype and expanded the EIS to all other parts of the company.

7. Developed a total of 30 EIS applications, all using the same information, but with the presentation customized to fit the needs and even the personality of each user.

8. The system's capabilities were basically those described in this chapter. The system became a success. The EIS changed the company and the managers, who became more efficient.

### Questions for Minicase 1

1. Which pressures presented in Chapter 1 can be identified in this case?

2. Which concepts discussed in Chapter 2 can be identified in this case?

3. Why was the EIS needed? Why not use the existing MIS and add a DSS?

4. It was felt that the use of CSFs tied to the corporate mission and objectives was the key to the success of the EIS. Why is this so?

5. It is time now for upgrading the EIS. Based on what you learned in this text and on information you acquired from other sources (vendors, publications), what would you suggest be done now?

SOURCE: This case is based on Comshare Publication #337352, 1995.

# Minicase 2

## A Decision Support System—Or Is It?

John Young, the general manager of a small electric utility company in Colorado, was concerned about the large number of customer complaints. Complaints were received by the customer relations department and distributed to the appropriate departments for consideration. Each complaint was investigated, and a response was provided either orally or in writing.

John completed a course in decision support systems and learned to program with Excel. As a part of the course, he constructed and installed a customers' complaint DSS. Its database includes each complaint, information about it, who is handling it, when it was assigned to an individual department, when it was resolved, and how it was resolved (a copy of the letter to the customer or a copy of the telephone conversation with the customer).

John was very proud of the system. He felt that it increased his control and, because everything is documented, people would handle complaints more effectively. One morning, he had the following conversation with his assistant, Nancy Gray, who also completed a DSS course.

JOHN: What do you think about the success of my DSS?
NANCY: The system works fine, but I am not sure that this is a DSS.
JOHN: You know that I designed it myself. The system is user friendly. I can find the status of any complaint and compute, if necessary, how long it took to solve the complaint.
NANCY: That is all great, but what specific decisions do you support?
JOHN: Well, I can use this information to decide, for example, on rewards for those who handle the complaints most effectively.
NANCY: How?
JOHN: I'm not sure. I may conduct comparisons.

### Questions for Minicase 2

1. Is John's system a DSS? Why or why not?

2. If it is not a DSS, what is necessary to make it a DSS?

## REFERENCES AND BIBLIOGRAPHY

1. Alter, S. L., *Decision Support Systems: Current Practice and Continuing Challenge*, Reading, MA: Addison-Wesley, 1980.

2. Anthony, R. N., *Planning and Control Systems: A Framework for Analysis*, Cambridge, MA: Harvard University Graduate School of Business Administration, 1965.

3. Ba, S. et al., "Enterprise Decision Support Using Intranet Technology," *Decision Support Systems*, Vol. 20, 1997.

4. Belton, V., and M. D. Elder, "DSS: Learning form VIM," *Decision Support Systems*, November 1994.

5. Carter, G. M., et al., *Building Organizational Decision Support Systems*, Cambridge, MA: Academic Press, 1992.

6. Chau, P. Y. K., and P. C. Bell, "A Visual Interactive DSS to Assist the Design of a New Production Unit," *INFOR*, May 1996.

7. Dutta, S. et al., "Designing Management Support Systems," *Communications of the ACM*, June 1997.

8. El Sharif, H., and O. A. El Sawy, "Issue-based DSS for the Egyptian Cabinet," *MIS Quarterly*, December 1988.

9. Elam, J., and A. Mead, "Can Software Influence Creativity?" *Information Systems Research*, January/March 1990.

10. Fishwick, P., *Simulation Model Design and Execution: Building Digital Worlds*, Englewood Cliffs, NJ: Prentice Hall, 1995.

11. George, J. F., "The Conceptualizations and Development of Organizational DSS," *Journal of Management Information Systems*, Vol. 8, No. 3, 1991/1992.

12. Gorry, G. A., and M. S. Scott-Morton, "A Framework for Management Information Systems," *Sloan Management Review*, Vol. 13, No. 1, Fall 1971.

13. Gray, P., and H. J. Watson, *Decision Support in the Data Warehouse Systems*, Upper Saddle River, NJ: Prentice-Hall, 1998.

14. Hackathorn, R. D., and P. G. Keen, "Organizational Strategies for Personal Computing in Decision Support Systems," *MIS Quarterly*, September 1981.

15. Hanson, G., *Automating Business Process Reengineering: Using the Power of Visual Simulation Strategies*, Upper Saddle River, NJ: Prentice Hall, 1996.

16. Holsapple, C. W., and A. B. Whinston, *Decision Support Systems: A Knowledge-Based Approach*, Minneapolis/St. Paul, MN: West Publishing Company, 1996.

17. Keen, P. G. W., and M. S. Scott-Morton, *Decision Support Systems: An Organizational Perspective*, Reading, MA: Addison-Wesley, 1978.

18. Kim, Y. G., et al., "Building an Organizational DSS for Korea Telecom: A Process Redesign Approach," *Decision Support Systems*, April 1997.

19. King, D., and D. O'Leary, "Intelligent Executive Information Systems," *IEEE Expert*, Dec. 1996.

20. Kingsman, B. G., and A. A. de Souza, "A KBDSS for Cost Estimation and Pricing Decisions in Versatile Manufacturing Companies," *Inter. Jour. of Production Economics*, November 1997.

21. Manheim, M. L., "Toward True Executive Support: Managerial and Theoretical Perspective," in *DSS 89 Transactions*, San Diego, CA, 1989.

22. Marakas, G. M., and J. J. Elam, "Creativity Enhancement in Problem Solving: Through Software or Process," *Management Science*, August 1997.

23. Massetti, B., "An Empirical Examination of the Value of Creativity Support Systems in Idea Generation," *MIS Quarterly*, March 1996.

24. Mintzberg, H., *The Nature of the Managerial Work*, New York: Harper & Row, 1973.

25. Mintzberg, H., *Mintzberg on Management*, New York: The Free Press, 1989.

26. Palvia, P., "Information Requirements of a Global EIS: An Exploratory Macro Assessment," *Decision Support Systems*, Vol. 15, 1996.

27. Rai, A., and S. B. Deepinder, "An Empirical Investigation into Factors Relating to the Adoption of EIS," *Decision Sciences*, Fall 1997.

28. Rockart, J. F., and D. DeLong, *Executive Support Systems*, Homewood, IL: Down Jones–Irwin, 1988.

29. Saaty, T. C., *Decisions for Leaders: The Analytic Hierarchy Process*, 2nd ed., Pittsburgh, PA: University of Pittsburgh Press, 1990; Vol. 2, RWS Publishers, 1996.

30. Scott-Morton, M. S., *Management Decision Systems: Computer Based Support for Decision Making*, Cambridge, MA: Harvard University, Division of Research, 1971.

31. Simon, H., *The New Science of Management Decisions*, rev. ed., Englewood Cliffs, NJ: Prentice-Hall, 1977.

32. Sprague, R. H., and H. J. Watson, eds., *Decision Support Systems*, 4th ed., Upper Saddle River, NJ: Prentice-Hall, 1996.

33. Staggers, N., and A. F. Norcio, "Mental Models: Concepts for Human-Computer Interaction Research, *International Journal of Man-Machine Studies*, Vol. 28, 1993.

34. Thalmann, N., and D. Thalmann, *Interactive Computer Animation*, Upper Saddle River, NJ: Prentice Hall, 1997.

35. Turban, E., *Decision Support Systems and Expert Systems*, 3rd ed. New York: Macmillan Publishing, 1993.

36. Turban, E., and J. Aronson, *Decision Support Systems and Intelligent Systems*, 5th ed., Upper Saddle River, NJ: Prentice Hall, 1998.

37. Vandenbosch, B., and S. L. Huff, "Searching and Scanning: How Executives Obtain Information from EIS," *MIS Quarterly*, March 1997.

38. Watson, H. J., and M. Frolick, "Determining Information Requirements for an Executive Information System," *Information Systems Management*, Spring 1992.

39. Watson, H. J., et al., *Building Executive Information Systems*, New York: John Wiley & Sons, 1996.

40. Wetherbe, J. C., "Executive Information Requirements: Getting It Right," *MIS Quarterly*, March 1991.

41. Winston, W. L., *Simulation Modeling Using @ Risk*, Belmont, CA: Wadsworth, 1996.

42. Zopounidis, M., et al., "On the Use of Knowledge-based DSS in Financial Management: A Survey," *Decision Supplement Systems*, July 1997.

# CHAPTER 10

# Data and Knowledge Management

## Learning Objectives

*After studying this chapter, you will be able to:*

❶ Recognize the importance of data, their managerial issues, and their life cycle.

❷ Describe the sources of data, their collection, and quality issues.

❸ Relate data management to multimedia and document management.

❹ Explain the operation of data warehousing and its role in decision support.

❺ Understand the data access and analysis problem and the data mining and online analytical processing solutions.

❻ Describe data presentation methods and explain geographical information systems as a decision support tool.

❼ Discuss the role and provide examples of marketing database.

❽ Explain the concept of knowledge management.

# CONNECTIONS

## PRECISION BUYING, MERCHANDISING, AND MARKETING AT SEARS

### The Problem

SEARS ROEBUCK AND Company, the largest department store chain and the third largest retailer in the United States, was caught by surprise in the 1980s as shoppers defected to specialty stores and discount mass merchandisers, causing the firm to lose market share rapidly. In an attempt to change the situation, Sears used several response strategies, ranging from introducing its own specialty stores (such as Sears Hardware) to reengineering its mail-based stores. Accomplishing this goal required the retooling of its information systems.

Sears had 18 data centers, one in each of 10 geographical regions as well as one each for marketing, finance, and other departments. The first problem was created when the reorganization effort produced only seven geographical regions. Frequent mismatches between accounting and sales figures and information scattered among numerous databases forced users to query multiple systems even when an answer to a simple query was all that was required. Furthermore, users found that data that were already summarized made it difficult to conduct analysis at the desired level of detail. Finally, errors were virtually inevitable when calculations were based on data from several sources.

### The Solution

To solve these problems Sears constructed a single sales information data warehouse. This replaced the 18 old databases which were packed with redundant, conflicting, and sometimes obsolete data. The new data warehouse is a simple depository of relevant decision-making data such as authoritative data for key performance indicators, sales inventories, and profit margins. Sears, known for embracing IT on a dramatic scale, completed the data warehouse and its IT reengineering efforts in under 1 year—a perfect IT turnaround story.

Using an NCR enterprise server, the 1.7 terabyte (1 terabyte equals 1 trillion bytes) data warehouse is part of a project dubbed the Strategic Performance Reporting System (SPRS). SPRS includes comprehensive sales data; information on inventory in stores, in transit, and at distribution centers; and cost per item. This has enabled Sears to track sales by individual items in each of its 1950 stores (including 810 mall-based stores) in the United States and 1600 international stores and catalog outlets. Thus, daily margin by item per store can be easily computed, for example. Furthermore, Sears now fine tunes its buying, merchandising, and marketing strategies with previously unattainable precision.

SPRS is open to all authorized employees, who now can view each day's sales from a multidimensional perspective (by region, district, store, product line, and individual item). Users can specify any starting and ending dates for special sales reports, and all data can be accessed via a highly user-friendly graphical interface. Sears staffers can now monitor the precise impact of advertising, weather, and other factors on sales of specific items. This means that buyers and other specialists can adjust inventory quantities, merchandising, and frequency and placement, along with myriad other variables, almost immediately, so they can respond quickly to environmental changes. SPRS users can also group together widely divergent kinds of products, for example, tracking sales of items marked as "gifts under $25." Advertising staffers can follow so-called "great items," drawn from vastly different departments, that are splashed on the covers of promotional circulars.

### The Results

The ability to monitor sales by item per store enables Sears to create a sharp local market focus. For example, Sears keeps different shades of paint colors in different cities to meet local demands. Therefore, sales and market share have improved.

By the end of 1997, the data warehouse had been used daily by over 3000 buyers, replenishers, marketers, strategic planners, logistics and finance analysts, and store managers. Response time to queries has dropped from days to minutes for typical requests. Overall, the strategic impact of the data warehouse is that it offers everybody a tool for making better decisions, and Sears retailing profits have climbed more than 20 percent annually since SPRS was implemented.

SOURCE: Condensed from "Sears, Roebuck and Co.: Turning Technology into Advantage," *NCR Corp. Publications,* No. sp-6051-0396, 1996. Also see Beitler and Leary (1997).

# ▶ 10.1 DATA MANAGEMENT: A CRITICAL SUCCESS FACTOR

## THE DIFFICULTIES AND THE PROCESS

The opening case illustrates the importance of managing data in the revitalization of a large retailer. Sears consolidated these data in one place, the data warehouse, which, according to *Business Week* (July 31, 1995, p. 61), is the "biggest trend in information management."

**THE DIFFICULTIES.** Data warehousing is only one facet of managing data in organizations, which is a difficult task for the following reasons:

▶ The amount of data increases exponentially; much past data must be kept for a long time, and new data are added rapidly.

▶ Data are scattered throughout organizations and are collected by many individuals using several methods and devices.

▶ Only small portions of an organization's data are relevant for specific decisions.

▶ An ever-increasing amount of external data needs to be considered in making organizational decisions.

▶ Raw data may be stored in different computing systems, databases, formats, and human and computer languages.

▶ Legal requirements relating to data differ among countries and change frequently.

▶ Selecting data management tools can be a major problem because of the huge number of products available.

▶ Data security, quality, and integrity are critical yet are easily jeopardized.

These difficulties, and the critical need for timely and accurate information, have prompted organizations to search for effective and efficient data management solutions. Historically, data management has been geared to supporting transaction processing by organizing the data in a hierarchical format. This format supports efficient high-volume processing; however, it is inefficient for queries and other ad hoc applications. Therefore, relational databases were added to facilitate end-user computing and decision support. With the introduction of client/server environments, databases became distributed throughout organizations, creating problems in finding data quickly and easily. This was the major reason that Sears sought the creation of a data warehouse. As we will see later, the intranet and extranets can also be used to improve data management.

It is now well recognized that data are a *burden*, but their use, in terms of information and knowledge, is *power*. The purpose of appropriate data management is to ease the burden and to enhance the power. The data warehouse is only one building block of effective data management. In this chapter we will look at several others. For example, Sears created a *marketing database* that supported enterprise-level marketing analysis applications. Recently, intranets have been playing a greater role in the support of **information sharing** across the enterprise, and databases accessible through the Internet can be used by almost any organization.

**DATA LIFE CYCLE PROCESS AND KNOWLEDGE DISCOVERY.** To better understand how to manage data and knowledge, it is necessary to trace how and where data flows in organizations. Businesses do not run on data. They run on information and their knowledge of how to put that information to use successfully.

Knowledge fuels results. Everything from innovative product designs to brilliant competitive moves relies on knowledge. Therefore, knowledge has always been an underlying component of business. Knowledge is not readily available, however, especially in today's rapidly changing world. In many cases knowledge is continuously derived from data. However, because of the difficulties cited earlier, such a derivation may not be simple or easy.

The transformation of data into knowledge may be accomplished in several ways. In general, it is a process that starts with data collection from various sources (see Figure 10.1). These data are stored in a database(s). Then the data can be preprocessed and stored in a data warehouse. To discover knowledge, the processed data may go through a transformation that makes them ready for analysis. The analysis is done with data mining tools, which look for patterns, and intelligent systems, which support data interpretation. The result of all these activities is generated knowledge. Both the data, at various times during the process, and the knowledge, derived at the end of the process, may need to be presented to users. Such a presentation can be accomplished by using different presentation tools. The created knowledge may be stored in a *knowledge base*. This process can guide us through the content of the remaining sections of this chapter.

> My company is currently rolling out a state-of-the-art store system. It houses a 2.5 million title database, and that has advanced sales, customer order, title search, and inventory management capabilities. The strategic thrusts behind the implementation of this system are differentiation, cost leadership, innovation, growth, alliance, and time. The targets of this system are our booksellers, suppliers, customers and competitors.
> — *Kristen Borhofen*

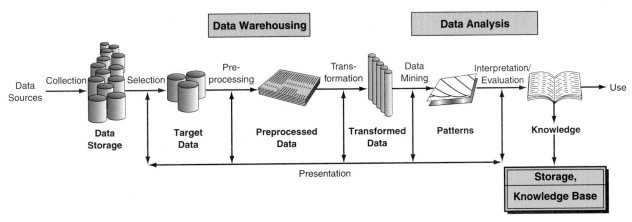

**FIGURE 10.1** Converting data to knowledge. (*Source*: Modified from Fayyad et al. [1996]).

## DATA SOURCES AND COLLECTION

The data life cycle begins with the acquisition of data from data sources. Data can include documents, pictures, maps, sound, and animation and they can be stored and organized in different ways before and after use. Data also include concepts, thoughts, and opinions and can be raw or summarized. Many IS applications use summary or extracted data. Data can also be classified as internal, personal, and external.

**INTERNAL DATA.** An organization's internal data are stored in one or more places. These data are about people, products, services, and processes. For example, data about employees and their pay are usually stored in the corporate database. Data about equipment and machinery may be stored in the maintenance department database. Sales data can be stored in several places—aggregate sales data in the corporate database and details at each regional database, as in the Sears case. Internal data are usually accessible via an organization's computer network.

**PERSONAL DATA.** IS users or other corporate employees may document their own expertise by creating personal data. These include, for example, subjective estimates of sales, opinions about what competitors are likely to do, and certain rules and formulas developed by the users. These data can reside on the user's PC or be placed on some public databases or knowledge bases (some personal data are not documented but are kept in people's memories).

**EXTERNAL DATA.** There are many sources for external data, ranging from commercial databases to sensors and satellites. Data are available on CD-ROMs, on Internet servers, as films, and as music or voices. Pictures, diagrams, atlases, and television are also sources of data. Government reports constitute a major source for external data (see Box 10.1 on page 429). Hundreds of thousands of organizations worldwide place publicly accessible data on their Web servers, flooding us with data. Most external data are irrelevant to a specific application. Yet much external data must be monitored and captured to ensure that important data are not overlooked. Large amounts of external data are available on the Internet.

**THE INTERNET AND COMMERCIAL DATABASE SERVICES.** Some external data flow to an organization on a regular basis through electronic data interchange (EDI) or through other traditional company-to-company channels, but much data are accessible via the Internet.

▶ *The Internet*. Many thousands of databases all over the world are accessible through the Internet. A user can access home pages of vendors, clients, and competitors. He or she can view and download information while conducting research. The Internet, as discussed in Chapter 5, is becoming the major source of external data for many decision situations (see Vassos [1996] for a comprehensive list of Internet data sources).

▶ *Commercial online publishing*. An *online publisher* sells access to specialized databases, newspapers, magazines, bibliographies, and reports. Such a service can provide external data to users in a timely manner and at a reasonable cost. Several thousand services are currently available, most of which are accessible via the Internet. Representative examples of providers are listed in Box 10.1; information related to investors is provided in Chapter 8.

**METHODS FOR COLLECTING RAW DATA.** The diversity of data and the multiplicity of sources make the task of data collection fairly complex, creating quality and integrity problems. Sometimes it is necessary to collect raw data in the field. In other cases it is necessary to elicit data from people. Raw data can be collected manually or by instruments and sensors. Data can also be scanned or

# *A Closer Look* BOX 10.1

## SOURCES OF BUSINESS EXTERNAL DATA—A SAMPLER; MOST AVAILABLE ON THE INTERNET

Thousands of public databases exist, most of which are available on the Internet.

### FEDERAL PUBLICATION

*Survey of Current Business* (Department of Commerce) (continues Business Conditions Digest in short form)—Monthly, general business conditions

*Monthly Labor Review* (Department of Labor)—Monthly employment statistics (a journal with articles)

*Federal Reserve Bulletin* (FEDRB)—Business and economics papers and statistics; government regulations

*Employment and Earnings* (Department of Labor)—Monthly; more detailed than *Monthly Labor Review*

*Commerce Business Daily* (Department of Commerce)—Daily announcements and news provided by the U.S. Department of Commerce

### OTHER

*International Monetary Fund*—Report of balance of payments, including currency rates, for participating countries

*Moody's*—A series of manuals including abstracted information and balance sheets of most large U.S. corporations; intended for investors

*Investext*—Investment reports on 15,000 companies

*Marketing and Advertising Research Service*—Provides information on research

*Thomas Register Online*—Information on over 150,000 U.S. companies and their products

*Standard and Poor's*—Periodically updated report on financial stability of most U.S. corporations

*Advertising Age*—Marketing newspaper, with a great deal of data on marketing

*Annual Editor and Publisher Market Guide*—Annual report of marketing information by standard metropolitan statistical area (SMSA)

*DIALOG* and *Lexis-Nexis*—The major players in the field, providing access to several hundred databases in many disciplines; Business Dateline is included in both

*ABI/Inform*—Available on CD-ROM in many libraries; covers hundreds of business journals for abstracts and full text; now available for a fee on the Internet

### INDEXES (now available for a fee on the Internet)

*Encyclopedia of Business Information Sources*—Gale Research, Inc.; updated annually; bibliographic guide on about 1,000 business subjects, including online databases

*Encyclopedia of Information Systems and Services*—Gale Research, Inc.; updated annually; descriptive guide to databases in electronic form

*The CD-ROM Directory*—TFPL Publishing; updated annually; index of CD-ROM databases

---

transferred electronically. Some examples of manual data collection methods are time studies, surveys, observations, and contributions from experts.

Although a wide variety of hardware and software exists for data storage, communication, and presentation, much less effort has gone into developing software tools for data capture in environments where complex and unstable data exist. Insufficient methods for dealing with such situations may limit the effectiveness of IS development and use.

The collection of data from multiple external sources may be an even more complicated task. One way to improve it, according to Roland (1994), is to use a data flow manager (DFM), which takes information from external sources and puts it where it is needed, when it is needed, in a usable form. A DFM consists of (1) a decision support system, (2) a central data request processor, (3) a data integrity component, (4) links to external data suppliers, and (5) the processes used by the external data suppliers.

Regardless of how they are collected, data need to be validated. A classic expression that sums up the situation is "garbage in, garbage out" (GIGO). Therefore, safeguards on data quality are designed to prevent data problems.

## DATA QUALITY

**Data quality (DQ)** is an extremely important issue since quality determines the data's usefulness as well as the quality of the decisions based on these data. Data are frequently found to be inaccurate, incomplete, or ambiguous, particularly in organizational databases. The economical and social damage from poor-quality data costs billions of dollars (see Redman [1998]). An example of typical data problems, their causes, and possible solutions is provided in Table 10.1. For a discussion of data auditing and controls see Chapter 15.

Strong et al. (1997) conducted extensive research on DQ problems and divided these problems into the following four categories and dimensions (see Wang et al., [1996] and Wang [1998]).

▶ *Intrinsic DQ*: Accuracy, objectivity, believability, and reputation

▶ *Accessibility DQ*: Accessibility and access security

▶ *Contextual DQ*: Relevancy, value added, timeliness, completeness, amount of data

▶ *Representation DQ*: Interpretability, ease of understanding, concise representation, consistent representation

*Table 10.1* **Data Problems**

| Problem | Typical Cause | Possible Solutions (in Some Cases) |
|---|---|---|
| Data are not correct. | Raw data were entered inaccurately. | Develop a systematic way to ensure the accuracy of raw data. Automate (use scanners or sensors). |
| | Data derived by an individual were generated carelessly. | Carefully monitor both the data values and the manner in which the data have been generated. Check for compliance with collection rules. |
| Data are not timely. | The method for generating the data was not rapid enough to meet the need for the data. | Modify the system for generating the data. Move to a client/server system. Automate. |
| Data are not measured or indexed properly. | Raw data were gathered according to a logic or periodicity that was not consistent with the purposes of the analysis. | Develop a system for rescaling or recombining the improperly indexed data. Use intelligent search agents. |
| Needed data simply do not exist. | No one ever stored the data needed now. | Whether or not it is useful now, store data for future use. Use the Internet to search for similar data. Use experts. |
| | Required data never existed. | Make an effort to generate the data or to estimate them (use experts). Use neural computing for pattern recognition. |

SOURCE: Condensed from Alter, Stephen L., *Decision Support Systems*, Reading, MA: Addison-Wesley, 1980, p. 30. New material added in 1998.

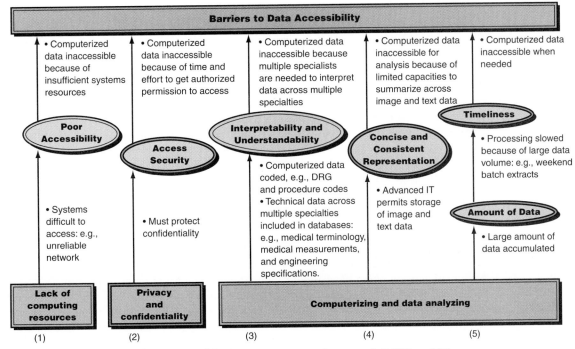

**FIGURE 10.2** Accessibility DQ problem pattern. (*Source*: Strong et al. [1997], p. 106).

Strong et al. (1997) have suggested that once the major variables and relationships in each category are identified, an attempt can be made to find out how to better manage the data. For example, DQ problems in accessibility are shown in Figure. 10.2. Note that some of the problems are technical ones such as capacity, while others relate to potential computer crimes.

One of the major issues of DQ is **data integrity**. Older filing systems may lack integrity. That is, a change made in the file in one place may not be made in the file in another place or department. This results in conflicting data.

Data are collected on a routine basis or for a special application. In either case, it is necessary to organize and store them before they can be used. This may be a difficult task when pictures, complex graphics, or maps are involved. This topic is discussed next.

## MULTIMEDIA AND OBJECT-ORIENTED DATABASES

> Relational database design is important in the real world to maintain data integrity.
> — *Dave Gehrke*

The manner in which data are collected and their intended use dictate the format of their organization and storage. Data are organized and stored in files and databases. The major conventional, logical data organizations are *hierarchical, network,* and *relational.* These are described with other database topics in Technology Guide #3. The object-oriented database is the most widely used of the newest methods of data organization.

An **object-oriented database** is a part of the object-oriented paradigm, which also includes object-oriented programming, operating systems, and modeling. Its technical details are described in Technology Guide #3. It is used for complex applications, such as computer-integrated manufacturing, that require accessibility to pictures, blueprints, and other images, as shown in the case of Daimler-Benz.

## IT At Work   OBJECT-ORIENTED DATABASE AT DAIMLER-BENZ

Daimler-Benz, the German automobile and aerospace multinational corporation known for its Mercedes cars, is a pioneer in the use of object-oriented databases for business applications. The company uses this technology to integrate data stored worldwide, throughout the enterprise, and to expedite decision making. Cooperating with a small software vendor, Daimler-Benz integrated object databases with its existing, or "legacy," information systems. The new technology enables Daimler-Benz to tie its diverse database systems together and to link to customers and suppliers in a network-based, distributed, online information system.

Object-oriented databases have been around since the mid-1980s, but they were used primarily for computer-aided design and graphical information systems. Since the early 1990s, object-oriented databases have become popular for many other business applications as a result of their ability to integrate with existing relational and hierarchical databases and with networks.

This is why Daimler-Benz pioneered the large-scale use of the technology. The company maintains an object database of product-model data based on an automotive industry standard. The databases are used in design, manufacturing, and sales of both automobile and aerospace products. One reason that Daimler-Benz was willing to invest heavily in the emerging technology was that it could meet its business goals of high productivity and quality and at the same time leverage the high investment it had in its legacy information systems.

As of summer 1997, some of the material in these databases is made available to customers on the Internet and to suppliers and other business partners on an extranet.

**For Further Exploration.** Object-oriented databases were used originally for pictures and graphs. Why is Daimler-Benz interested in such capabilities, and why does it want to integrate them with the legacy systems? ▲

SOURCES: Compiled from *Information Week*, November 7, 1994, and corporate information, 1998.

**INTEGRATING IT**

...for Marketing and Production & Operations Management

---

Object-oriented databases are sometimes referred to as **multimedia databases** (see Nwosu et al. [1997]) and are managed by special *multimedia database management systems*. These manage data in a variety of formats in addition to the standard text or numeric fields (see Adjeroh and Nwosu [1997]). The formats include images such as digitized photographs or forms of bit-mapped graphics.

A considerable amount of corporate information resides outside the computer in the form of documents, maps, photos, images, and videotapes. For companies to build applications to take advantage of these rich data types, they must use a multimedia database management system. Database vendors are enhancing their offerings to include the ability to manage and manipulate multimedia data.

There are many applications of a multimedia database, especially in such industries as newspapers and TV, where multimedia plays a critical role, as shown in the case of Southam New Media.

## IT At Work   VIRTUAL NEWSSTAND AT SOUTHAM OF CANADA

Southam New Media, one of the largest newspaper chains in Canada, has created a multimedia database called a virtual newsstand. The Southam Interactive Database allows the entry, filing, and retrieval of data in all formats used by Southam: wire service text, newspaper and magazine text, classified ads, photos, graphics, television, video and

**USING IT**

...in Production & Operations Management

sound, software programs, and Web content. Any unit of data has identifiable attributes that can be stored and retrieved through a single access point. Southam's initial investment was only $500,000—much less than if its newspapers were prepared on different systems. According to Peter Irwin, president of Southam New Media, there is a single access window for retrieval and input, with one export button, with which content can be exported onto the Web or, for example, to a commercial service provider such as America Online. Basically, what the development team did was to write software that allowed extraction from all Southam's newspapers online and tried to make sense of what was in a story. The information was then put into a relational database, which enabled flexibility. The system was set up on Southam's intranet.

Southam owns *Business World*, a Canadian television show. The company plans to put relevant videos from the program into the database using standard video-capturing technology. The videos then can be attached to any story. Future applications include a full electronic distribution of Southam's news.

**For Further Exploration.** Why is the database called interactive, and how is the Web related to this application? ▲

SOURCE: Condensed from Cohen, J.B., "Virtual Newsstand' Debuts Online," *Editor and Publisher*, Vol. 129, No. 24, pp. 86–87, June 15, 1996.

Electronic organization of data is interrelated with the issue of electronic document management.

## DOCUMENT MANAGEMENT

There are several major problems with paper documents. For example, in document maintenance, we can pose the following questions: (1) Does everyone have the current version? (2) How often does it need to be updated? (3) How secured are the documents? and (4) How can the distribution of documents to the appropriate individuals be managed in a timely manner? When documents are provided in electronic form from a single repository (typically a Web server), only the current version is provided. Also, access can be restricted as required. For example, many firms maintain their telephone directories in electronic form on an intranet to eliminate their hardcopy distribution and constant corrections and redistributions. Document management technology grew out of the business community, where, according to the GartnerGroup, some 85 percent of corporate information resides in documents. The need for greater efficiency in handling business documents to gain an edge on the competition has fueled the increased availability of document management systems, also known as electronic document management.

Essentially, **document management systems** (DMS) provide information to decision makers in an electronic format. The Thomas Cook Company, for example, uses a document management system to handle travel refund applications. The system works on the PC desktop and has automated the workflow process, helping the firm double its volume of business while adding only about 33 percent more employees (see Cole [1996]). Another example is the Massachusetts Department of Revenue, which is using imaging systems to increase productivity of tax return processing by about 80 percent (see www.civic.com/pubs, Sept. 1997).

**Document management** is the automated control of electronic documents, page images, spreadsheets, word processing documents, and complex, compound documents through their entire life cycle within an organization, from initial creation to final archiving. Document management allows organizations to exert greater control over production, storage, and distribution of documents, yielding greater efficiency in the reuse of information, the control of a document through a workflow process, and the reduction of product cycle times. The full range of functions that a document management system may perform includes document identification, storage, and retrieval; tracking; version control; workflow management; and presentation.

Document management systems usually include computerized imaging systems that can result in substantial savings, as at USAA.

## *IT At Work*   THE IMAGING SYSTEM AT UNITED SERVICES AUTOMOBILE ASSOCIATION

*INTEGRATING IT*

...for Production & Operations Management, Finance, and Marketing

United Services Automobile Association (USAA) is a large insurance company in San Antonio, Texas, serving about 2 million military officers, former officers, and their dependents. In 1998 the company processed about 130,000 documents every workday.

In the 1980s, the company employed 120 clerks whose only job was to search files (which occupied 39,000 square feet of office space) for information when needed. Searches for one document took anywhere from an hour to 2 weeks, and some documents were never found. However, using an environment called Automated Insurance Environment, USAA has been transformed into a completely paperless company. Since 1993, employees have been able to scan over 50 million pieces of mail per year into a computer database. Agents, using special imaging terminals, then access the database to process information and assist customers. Customers can now obtain *instant* answers to such questions as: "Is the car we bought an hour ago insured against theft?" The system is also used to expedite the treatment of claims. When a customer calls to report a car accident, the telephone call is digitized and stored. Subsequently, all documents (photos, doctors' reports, appraisers' reports, and so on) are scanned into the computer. Once the case is closed, it is stored on a CD-ROM for future reference.

Here is how the data entry works. Every day the company receives almost 25,000 letters as well as thousands of telephone calls; every day the company sends over 60,000 letters and policies. All the documents are indexed on an IBM mainframe and then are scanned to create a digital electronic picture. The imaged documents can then be accessed from anywhere in the company for viewing or processing. Special high-resolution terminals are used for displaying and printing the imaged documents. The company uses *electronic forms* to expedite the preparation of standard documents.

The system improves productivity of employees, reduces the cost of storing documents (most paper documents are destroyed), and improves customer service.

Employee productivity is improved by eliminating the time necessary to search for the appropriate documents. With the new system, all pertinent data can be called to the user's screen within 6 minutes of the request's being issued. With the old system, document collection required an average of 0.5 man-hours. (If any of the documents were not housed in the local facility, the document collection averaged 1.2 hours.) At an average hourly cost of $15 for document handlers, the savings are $7.05 per document, or $70,500,000 for the 10,000,000 documents handled annually.

Most users find the imaging system easier to work with than the old paper-clogged system. The system is also used for scheduling work and monitoring workflow.

**For Further Exploration.** In what other industries can such a system be beneficial? ▲

SOURCE: Based on stories in *Best's Review Magazine*, May 1993; *Datamation*, May 15, 1990; *MIS Quarterly*, December 1991; *IBM Systems Journal*, Vol. 29, No. 3, 1990; and company information, 1998.

The major tools of document management are workflow software, authoring tools, scanners, and databases (object-oriented mixed with relational, known as object-relational database management systems; see Technology Guide #3).

In many organizations, documents are now viewed as multimedia objects with hyperlinks. The Web provides easy access to pages of information. DMSs excel in this area. Web-enabled DMSs also make it easy to put information on an intranet, since many of them provide instantaneous conversion of documents to HTML. BellSouth, for example, saves an estimated $17.5 million each year through its intranet-enabled forms management system. For a discussion of Web-enabled document management systems and a list of products and major vendors, see Haskin (1998).

> Our entire accounting policies and procedures manual is on an intranet Web site. When we make additions or changes everyone gets it—online, and immediately.
> — *Mike Rewald*

McDonnell Douglas distributes aircraft service bulletins to their customers around the world using the Internet. The company used to distribute a staggering volume of bulletins to over 200 airlines, using over 4 million pages of documentation every year. Now it is all on the Web, saving money and time both for the company and for its customers. For details see http://home.netscape.com /comprod/at_work/customer_profile/mcdonnell.html.

Motorola uses DMS not only for document storage and retrieval, but for small group collaboration and companywide knowledge sharing. They develop virtual communities where people can discuss and publish information, all with the Web-enabled DMS.

One of the major vendors of document management is Lotus Development Corporation. Its *document databases* and their replication property provide many advantages for group work and information sharing (see Chapter 5). Document management services are provided by IBM and by Xerox (see *Information Week*, March 6, 1998).

# ▶ 10.2 DATA WAREHOUSING, MINING, AND ANALYSIS

## TRANSACTION VERSUS ANALYTICAL PROCESSING

Data processing in organizations can be viewed either as transactional or analytical. Transaction processing, which has been introduced in Chapter 2 and discussed in Chapter 8, is the routine daily processing of the transactions of the organization such as ordering or billing. The data in such cases are organized mainly in a hierarchical structure (see Technology Guide #3) and are processed by the IS department. The databases and the processing systems involved are known as *operational systems* and the results are mainly summaries and reports.

In today's fast paced and highly competitive marketplace, access to data is critical. The most successful companies are those that can respond quickly and flexibly to market changes and opportunities, and the key to this response is the effective and efficient use of data and information. It is not sufficient, therefore, to conduct transaction processing. A supplementary activity, called *analytical processing*, is done mainly by end users. Placing strategic information in the hands of decision makers aids productivity and empowers users to make better decisions, leading to greater competitive advantage. End users need direct access to corporate data. A good data delivery system therefore should be able to support:

▶ Easy data access by the end users themselves

▶ Quicker decision making

▶ More accurate and effective decision making

▶ Flexible decision making

Such requirements are not met by the traditional database access. Why is this so?

Analytical processing, which includes DSS, EIS, and other end-user activities, is based on data stored in the operational system and possibly on external data. There are basically two options for conducting analytical processing. One is to work directly with the operational systems (the "let's use what we have" approach), using software tools and components known as front-end tools and middleware (see Technology Guide #3). This option can be optimal for companies that do not have a large number of users running queries and conducting analyses against the operating systems. It is also an option for departments (such as engineering) that consist mainly of users who have the technical skills necessary for writing their own programs to generate ad hoc reports and conduct analysis. This option includes extensive use of "fourth-generation" (4GL) tools such as spreadsheets and graphics. Although it is possible to use the 4GLs as query and reporting tools, they may not be effective, flexible, or easy enough to use in many cases.

More recently, there has been a wave of front-end tools that allow end users to ease these problems by directly conducting queries and reporting on data stored in the operational databases. These tools are designed to empower end users with little or no involvement of IS personnel. The problem with this approach, however, is that the tools are only effective with end users that have a medium to high degree of knowledge about the databases—requiring nontechnical personnel, in effect, to think like database administrators. More often than not, IS personnel spend more time supporting the users of these tools than they do generating ad hoc reports and doing analytical processing by themselves. This calls for a better solution.

This improved option of *analytical processing* involves three concepts:

▶ A business representation of data for end users

▶ A client/server environment that gives the users query and reporting capabilities

▶ A server-based repository, the *data warehouse*, that allows centralized security and control over the data

## THE DATA WAREHOUSE AND MARTS

The Sears case illustrates the benefits of a single depository place, called a **data warehouse**. The major benefits are the abilities (1) to reach data quickly, since they are located in one place, and (2) to do it easily, frequently by end users themselves. Let's see what a data warehouse is and what its benefits are.

The purpose of a data warehouse is to establish a *data repository* that makes operational data accessible in a form readily acceptable for analytical processing activities such as decision support, EIS, and other end-user applications. As part of this accessibility, detail-level operational data must be transformed to a relational form, which makes them more amenable to analytical processing. Thus, data warehousing is not a concept by itself but is interrelated with data access, retrieval, analysis, and visualization. (See Gray and Watson [1998].)

The process of building and using a data warehouse is shown in Figure 10.3. Data are stored in operational systems (left side of the figure). Not all data are transferred to the data warehouse, and frequently only a summary of the data is transferred. The data are organized within the warehouse as a relational database so it is easy for end users to access. Also, the data are organized by subject, such as by functional area, vendor, or product. In contrast, operational data are usually organized according to a business process, such as shipping, purchasing, or inventory control. These are basically legacy application systems.

> Until you work for a large company on several computer platforms and versions, you don't realize how important foresight and data warehousing can be.
>
> — *Mike Rewald*

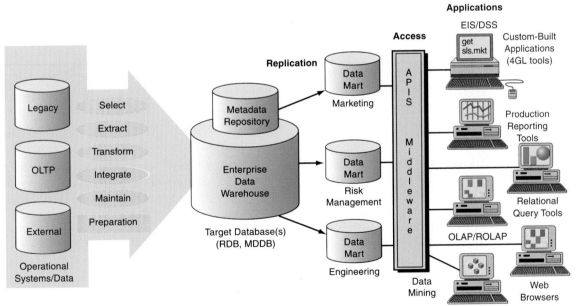

**FIGURE 10.3** Data warehouse framework and views. (*Source*: www.cutter.com and *Data Management Strategies*, Cutter Information Operations, February 1997.)

Data warehouses allow for the storage of **metadata**, which include data summaries that are easier to index and search, especially with Web tools. An optional arrangement is the creation of data marts.

A **data mart** is a replicated subset of the data warehouse and it is dedicated to a functional or regional area. For example, many companies have a marketing data mart, or a data mart for their foreign operations. Some companies have several data marts. Data marts (see Watterson [1996]) can be a substitution for a data warehouse or they can be in addition to it, holding only part of the data warehouse content. In either case, end users can use the warehouse and/or the marts for many applications (shown on the right side of Figure 10.3). These include query, EIS/DSS, reporting, online analytical processing (OLAP), knowledge discovery, and data mining. Some of these applications are described in Chapter 9; others are described later in this chapter. The end users employ a variety of 4GL tools for these applications, including spreadsheets, DBMS, and graphics.

Data marts for industries such as retail, insurance, and telecom, and for special purposes such as financial reporting, can be purchased from leading vendors, so you do not have to build them yourself (see *Datamation*, March 1997, p. 94).

Middleware tools enable access to the data warehouse (see Technology Guide #3).

**CHARACTERISTICS OF DATA WAREHOUSING.** The major characteristics of data warehousing are:

1. *Organization.* Data are organized by detailed subject (e.g., by customer, vendor, product, price level, and region), containing only information relevant for decision support.
2. *Consistency.* Data in different operational databases may be encoded differently. For example, gender data may be encoded 0 and 1 in one place and "m" and "f" in another. In the warehouse they will be coded in a *consistent* manner.
3. *Time variant.* The data are kept for 5 to 10 years so they can be used for trends, forecasting, and comparisons over time.
4. *Nonvolatile.* Once entered into the warehouse, data are not updated.
5. *Relational.* Typically the data warehouse uses a relational structure.
6. *Client/server.* The data warehouse uses the client/server architecture mainly to provide the end user an easy access to its data.

**BENEFITS.** Moving information off the mainframe presents a company with the unique opportunity to restructure its IT strategy. Companies can reinvent the way in which they shape and form their application data, empowering end users to conduct extensive analysis with them in ways that may not have been possible before. Another immediate benefit is providing a consolidated view of corporate data, which is better than providing many smaller (and differently formatted) views. For example, separate production systems may track sales and coupon mailings. Combining data from these different systems may yield insights into the cost efficiency of coupon sales promotions that would not be immediately evident from the output data of either system alone. Integrated within a data warehouse, however, such information can be easily extracted. Another benefit is that data warehousing allows information processing to be off loaded from expensive operational systems onto low-cost servers. Once this is done, the end-user tools can handle a significant number of end-user information requests. Furthermore, some operational system reporting requirements can be moved to decision support systems, thus freeing up production processing.

These benefits can improve business knowledge, provide competitive advantage, enhance customer service and satisfaction, facilitate decision making, and help in streamlining business processes, as happened at the Bank of Ireland.

**IT At Work**    THE BANK OF IRELAND
COMPETES USING A DATA WAREHOUSE

Liberalized banking laws have resulted in stiff competition on a variety of products and services among banks and other financial institutions all over the world. The Bank of Ireland uses a data warehouse to exploit regulatory changes that have opened up myriad opportunities for revenue and profit growth. The warehouse allows managers to access corporate data directly and easily from their PCs, using Microsoft Excel and Access. This access makes for rapid turnout time in getting answers to queries and conducting analyses, such as examination of alternative responses to competitors' activities.

**USING IT**

...in Finance

Easy accessibility to data enables bank employees to analyze large amounts of information quickly, to respond rapidly to changing business conditions, and to determine strategies for gaining competitive advantage. Previously, the IS department was providing answers to queries that are now found by end users, freeing the IS personnel to do system development. (Previously, the bank outsourced most of its systems development.) According to Des Harrold, a sector manager, in a country of only 3.5 million people, companies grow by stealing competitors' customers. In addition to increasing market share at the expense of its main competitor, the bank has saved about $800,000 a year on systems development.

**For Further Exploration.** How were banking deregulations exploited by the bank? How can the bank respond when its competitors also build data warehouses? ▲

SOURCE: Based on "Bank of Ireland Uses Data Warehousing," *Datamation*, March 1997, pp. 18–19.

**COST.** The cost of a data warehouse can be very high, both to build and to maintain. Furthermore, it may difficult and expensive to incorporate data from obsolete legacy systems. Finally, there may be a lack of incentive to share data. Therefore, a careful feasibility study must be undertaken before a commitment is made to data warehousing.

**ARCHITECTURE.** There are several basic architectures for data warehousing. Two common ones are two-tier and three-tier architecture. (See Technology Guide #3.) In three-tier architecture, data from the warehouse are processed twice and deposited in an *additional* multidimensional database, organized for easy multidimensional analysis and presentation, or replicated in data marts.

**PUTTING THE WAREHOUSE ON THE INTRANET.** Delivery of data warehouse content to decision makers throughout the enterprise can be done via an intranet. Users can view, query, and analyze the data and produce reports using Web browsers. This is an extremely economical and effective method of delivering data (see *Information Advantage* [1997] and Eckerson [1997]).

**SUITABILITY.** Data warehousing is most appropriate for organizations in which:

► Large amounts of data need to be accessed by end users.
► The operational data are stored in different systems.
► An information-based approach to management is in use.
► There is a large, diverse customer base (such as in a utility company or a bank).
► The same data are represented differently in different systems.

▶ Data are stored in highly technical formats that are difficult to decipher.

▶ Extensive end-user computing is performed (many end users performing many activities).

Hundreds of successful applications are reported (e.g., see client success stories and case studies at Web sites of vendors such as Brio Technology Inc., Business Objects, Cognos Corp., Information Advantage, Information Builders, NCR Corp., Platinum Technology, Software A&G, Comshare Inc., and Pilot Software). Some of the successful applications are summarized in Table 10.2. For further discussion see McFadden and Watson (1996), Barquin and Edelstein (1997), Gray and Watson (1998), and Inmon (1996). See also www.cait.wustl.edu /cait/papers/rpism/vol1_no1. Also visit the Data Warehouse Institute (www .dw-institute.org).

***Table 10.2*** **Summary of Strategic Uses of Data Warehousing**

| *Industry* | *Functional Areas of Use* | *Strategic Use* |
|---|---|---|
| Airline | Operations and Marketing | Crew assignment, aircraft deployment, mix of fares, analysis of route profitability, frequent flyer program promotions |
| Apparel | Distribution and Marketing | Merchandising, and replenishment |
| Banking | Product Development, Operations, and Marketing | Customer service, trend analysis, product and service promotions. Reduction of IS expenses |
| Credit Card | Product Development and Marketing | Customer service, new information service for a fee, fraud detection |
| Health Care | Operations | Reduction of operational expenses |
| Investment & Insurance | Product Development, Operations, and Marketing | Risk management, market movements analysis, customer tendencies analysis, portfolio management |
| Personal Care Products | Distribution and Marketing | Distribution decision, product promotions, sales decision, pricing policy |
| Public Sector | Operations | Intelligence gathering |
| Retail Chain | Distribution and Marketing | Trend analysis, buying pattern analysis, pricing policy, inventory control, sales promotions, optimal distribution channel |
| Steel | Manufacturing | Pattern analysis (quality control) |
| Telecommunications | Product Development, Operations, and Marketing | New product and service promotions, reduction of IS budget, profitability analysis |

SOURCE: Park (1997), p. 19 (Table 2).

Once the data are in the data warehouse and/or data marts they can be accessed by end users. Users can then conduct several activities with the data, ranging from decision support and executive support analyses, which are discussed in Chapter 9, to knowledge discovery.

## KNOWLEDGE DISCOVERY, ANALYSIS, AND MINING

The process of extracting useful knowledge from volumes of data is known as **knowledge discovery in databases (KDD)**, or just **knowledge discovery**, and it is the subject of extensive research (see Fayyad [1996]). KDD's objective is to identify valid, novel, potentially useful, and ultimately understandable patterns in data. The process starts with identifying which data to consider in the data warehouse and then preprocessing these data (see Figure 10.1) to be ready for analysis.

**THE FOUNDATIONS OF KDD.** KDD techniques are the result of a long process of research and product development. This evolution began when business data were first stored on computers, continued with improvements in data access, and, more recently, generated technologies that allowed users to navigate through their data in real time. KDD is useful because it is supported by three technologies that are now sufficiently mature:

- ▶ Massive data collection
- ▶ Powerful multiprocessor computers
- ▶ Data mining algorithms

Commercial databases are growing at unprecedented rates. According to the Data Warehouse Institute, a 1996 survey of data warehouse projects found that those of 19 percent of the respondents were beyond 50 gigabytes in size, while 59 percent were expected to be there within 6 months. In some industries, such as retail, these numbers can be much larger, reaching terabytes, as at Sears.

**TOOLS AND TECHNIQUES OF KDD.** Knowledge discovery has been done since the 1960s. However, the enabling techniques have been expanded and improved over time. KDD processes have appeared under various names and have shown different characteristics. The evolution of KDD tools over time can be divided into four major stages. These stages are shown in Table 10.3. The table lists the enabling technologies and their characteristics. As time passes the KDD can answer more complex business questions. Data access techniques are discussed in Technology Guide #3 of this book. Online analytical processing and data mining are discussed in this section; multidimensionality is discussed in Section 10.3; and massive databases, as employed in marketing databases, are the subject of Section 10.4.

*Table 10.3*  **Stages in the Evolution of Knowledge Discovery**

| Evolutionary Stage | Business Question | Enabling Technologies | Characteristics |
|---|---|---|---|
| Data Collection (1960s) | What was my total revenue in the last five years? | Computers, tapes, disks | Retrospective, static data delivery |
| Data Access (1980s) | What were unit sales in New England last March? | Relational databases (RDBMS), Structured Query Language (SQL) | Retrospective, dynamic data delivery at record level |
| Data Warehousing & Decision Support (early 1990s) | Drill down to Boston? | Online analytic processing (OLAP), multidimensional databases, data warehouses | Retrospective, dynamic data delivery at multiple levels |
| Intelligent Data Mining (late 1990s) | What's likely to happen to Boston unit sales next month? Why? | Advanced algorithms, multiprocessor computers, massive databases | Prospective, proactive information delivery |

SOURCE: Courtesy of Pilot Software, Inc.

The problem with the data collection and access techniques is that they are not suitable for a large volume of data, nor can they be used effectively by end users. Even though Structured Query Language (SQL) use is becoming more user friendly (due to the use of natural language processors), business questions that can be answered with it are limited. Therefore, better tools are needed.

**ONLINE ANALYTICAL PROCESSSING. Online analytical processing (OLAP)** refers to such end-user activities as DSS modeling using spreadsheets and graphics, which are done online. Unlike online transaction processing (OLTP) applications, OLAP involves many data items (frequently many thousands or even millions) in complex relationships. One objective of OLAP is to analyze these relationships and look for conditions of patterns, trends, and exceptions.

An OLAP database may consist of sales data that have been aggregated by region, product type, and sales channel. A typical OLAP query might access a multigigabyte-multiyear sales database in order to find all product sales in each region for each product type. After reviewing the results, an analyst might further refine the query to find sales volume for each sales channel within region or product classifications. As a last step, the analyst might want to perform year-to-year or quarter-to-quarter comparisons, for each sales channel. This whole process must be carried out online with rapid response time so that the analysis process is undisturbed. OLAP queries can be characterized as online queries that:

▶ Access very large amounts of data—several years of sales data

▶ Analyze the relationships between many types of business elements, such as sales, products, regions, and channels

▶ Involve aggregated data, such as sales volumes, budgeted dollars, and dollars spent

▶ Compare aggregated data over hierarchical time periods—monthly, quarterly, yearly

▶ Present data in different perspectives, such as sales by region versus sales by product or by product within each region

▶ Involve complex calculations between data elements, such as expected profit as calculated as a function of sales revenue for each type of sales channel in a particular region

▶ Are able to respond quickly to user requests so that users can pursue an analytical thought process without being stymied by the system

Here is an example of how OLAP works with a query. An end user makes a request, possibly in a natural language. Some vendors, such as SAS Institute, Inc., provide natural language interfaces (such as SAS English) for this purpose. The query is transformed into an SQL format. This query is delivered via a network to a DBMS that manages the database or the data warehouse. The DBMS finds the answer to the query and delivers it back to the end user. The user can then design a presentation or a report to fit his or her display needs. Today it is possible to access an OLAP database from the Web or a corporate intranet.

Although OLAP is very useful in many cases, it is retrospective in nature and cannot provide the automatic and prospective knowledge discovery that is done by advanced data mining techniques.

**DATA MINING. Data mining** derives its name from the similarities between searching for valuable business information in a large database—and mining a mountain for a vein of valuable ore. Both processes require either sifting through an immense amount of material or intelligently probing it to find exactly where the value resides. Given databases of sufficient size and quality, data mining technology can generate new business opportunities by providing these capabilities:

▶ *Automated prediction of trends and behaviors*. Data mining automates the process of finding predictive information in large databases. Questions that traditionally required extensive hands-on analysis can now be answered directly and quickly from the data. A typical example of a predictive problem is targeted marketing. Data mining can use data on past promotional mailings to identify the targets most likely to favorably respond to future mailings. Other predictive examples include forecasting bankruptcy and other forms of default and identifying segments of a population likely to respond similarly to given events.

▶ *Automated discovery of previously unknown patterns*. Data mining tools identify previously hidden patterns in one step. An example of pattern discovery is the analysis of retail sales data to identify seemingly unrelated products that are often purchased together, such as baby diapers and beer. Other pattern discovery problems include detecting fraudulent credit card transactions and identifying *anomalous data* that may represent data entry keying errors.

When data mining tools are implemented on high-performance parallel processing systems, they can analyze massive databases in minutes. Faster processing means that users can experiment with more *models* to understand complex data. High speed makes it practical for users to analyze huge quantities of data. Larger databases, in turn, yield improved predictions.

Data mining can be conducted by nonprogrammers and it appears under different names, such as knowledge extraction, data dipping, data archeology, data exploration, data pattern processing, data dredging, and information harvesting. The following are the major characteristics and objectives of data mining:

1. Data are often buried deep within very large databases, such as data warehouses, that sometimes contain data stored for several years.
2. In some cases the data are consolidated in a data warehouse and data marts; in others they are kept in Internet and intranet servers.
3. The data mining environment usually has a client/server architecture.
4. Data mining tools help remove the information "ore" buried in corporate files or archived public records.
5. The "miner" is often an end user, empowered by "data drills" and other power query tools to ask ad hoc questions and get answers quickly, with little or no programming skill.
6. "Striking it rich" often involves finding unexpected, valuable results.
7. Data mining tools are easily combined with spreadsheets and other end-user software development tools; therefore, the mined data can be analyzed and processed quickly and easily.
8. Because of the large amounts of data, it is sometimes necessary to use parallel processing for data mining.
9. Data mining yields five types of information: (a) association, (b) sequences, (c) classifications, (d) clusters, and (e) forecasting.
10. Data miners can use several tools and techniques (see the list in Box 10.2).

# A Closer Look BOX 10.2

## DATA MINING TECHNIQUES

The most commonly used techniques for data mining are:

*Case-based reasoning*. The case-based reasoning approach uses historical cases to recognize patterns. For example, customers of Cognitive Systems, Inc., utilize such an approach for help desk applications. One company has a 50,000 query case library. New cases are matched quickly against the 50,000 samples in the library, providing more than 90 percent accurate and automatic answers to queries.

*Neural computing*. Neural computing is a machine learning approach by which historical data can be examined for pattern recognition. These patterns can then be used for making predictions and for decision support (details are given in Chapter 11). Users equipped with neural computing tools can go through huge databases and, for example, identify potential customers of a new product or companies whose profiles suggest that they are heading for bankruptcy.

Many practical applications are in financial services (Trippi and Turban [1996]), in marketing, and in manufacturing.

*Intelligent agents*. One of the most promising approaches to retrieving information from the Internet or from intranet-based databases is the use of intelligent agents. As vast amounts of information become available through the Internet, finding the right information is more difficult. This topic is discussed further in Chapters 5 and 11.

*Association analysis*. This is a relatively new approach that uses a specialized set of algorithms that sorts through large data sets and expresses statistical rules among items. (See Moad [1998] for details.)

*Other tools*. Several other tools can be used. These include decision trees, genetic algorithms, nearest neighbor method, and rule induction. For details, see Inmon (1996).

**A SAMPLER OF DATA MINING APPLICATIONS.** According to a 1997 GartnerGroup report (www.gartnergroup.com), by 2000 at least half of all the Fortune 1000 companies worldwide will be using data mining technology. Data mining can be very helpful as shown by the representative examples that follow. Note that the intent of most of these examples is to identify a business opportunity to create a sustainable competitive advantage.

1. *Retailing and sales*. Predicting sales; determining correct inventory levels and distribution schedules among outlets.
2. *Banking*. Forecasting levels of bad loans and fraudulent credit card use, credit card spending by new customers, and which kinds of customers will best respond to (and qualify for) new loan offers.
3. *Manufacturing and production*. Predicting machinery failures and finding key factors that control optimization of manufacturing capacity.
4. *Brokerage and securities trading*. Predicting when bond prices will change; forecasting the range of stock fluctuations for particular issues and the overall market; determining when to trade stocks.
5. *Insurance*. Forecasting claim amounts and medical coverage costs; classifying the most important elements that affect medical coverage; predicting which customers will buy new policies.
6. *Computer hardware and software*. Predicting disk-drive failures; forecasting how long it will take to create new chips; predicting potential security violations.

7. *Policework*. Tracking crime patterns, locations, and criminal behavior and attributes to assist in solving criminal cases.

8. *Government and defense*. Forecasting the cost of moving military equipment; testing strategies for potential military engagements; predicting resource consumption.

9. *Airlines*. Capturing data on where customers are flying and the ultimate destination of passengers who change carriers in midflight; thus, airlines can identify popular locations that they do not service and check the feasibility of adding routes to capture lost business.

10. *Health care*. Correlating demographics of patients with critical illnesses. Using data mining, doctors can develop better insights on symptoms and their causes and how to provide proper treatments.

11. *Broadcasting*. Predicting what is best to air during prime time and how to maximize returns by interjecting advertisements.

12. *Marketing*. Classifying customer demographics that can be used to predict which customers will respond to a mailing or buy a particular product, as illustrated by Marriott Club International.

---

*IT At Work*    DATA MINING AT MARRIOTT
FOR TARGETED ADVERTISING

Marriott Club International, the nation's largest seller of vacation time-share condos, had a problem. The company had a database with millions of names. Marriott used to send advertisements to all of the customers in the database, at a great expense, but the response was minimal. The company decided to identify the customers in their list who were more likely to respond. By doing so, they have slashed the amount of mail considerably and improved the response rate. Marriott uses neural computing technology in their data mining, the objective of which is to detect patterns by combing through the digitized customer lists.

*USING IT*

...in Marketing

Marriott started with names, mostly hotel guests. Digging into a trove of motor vehicle records, property records, warranty cards, and lists of people who had bought by mail, a computer program enriched the prospect list. It added such facts as the customers' ages, their children's ages, their estimated income, what cars they drove, and whether they played golf. The Marriott system then identifies who is most likely to respond to a mailed flier.

Using these clues, Marriott has been able to cast its net a little more narrowly and catch more fish. Data mining has increased the response rate to Marriott's direct mail time-share pitches to certain hotel guests by 33 percent, for a significant saving.

**For Further Exploration.** How can the detected patterns affect the response rate? Also, like many other companies, Marriott is using information on customers without the customers' knowledge, invading their privacy. What can the company do to act more ethically? ▲

SOURCE: Condensed from Norvack, J., "The Data Miners," *Forbes*, February 12, 1996.

---

## ▶ 10.3 DATA VISUALIZATION TECHNOLOGIES

Once data have been processed they can be presented to users as text, as tables, and via several data visualization technologies.

## DATA VISUALIZATION

Visual technologies make pictures worth a thousand numbers and make IT applications more attractive and understandable to users. **Data visualization** refers to presentation of data by technologies such as digital images, geographical information systems, graphical user interfaces, multidimensional tables and graphs, virtual reality, three-dimensional presentations, and animation. Visualization software packages offer users capabilities for self-guided exploration and visual analysis of large amounts of data. By using visual analysis technologies, people may spot problems that have existed for years undetected by standard analysis methods. Visualization technologies can also be integrated among themselves to create a variety of presentations, as Haworth Corporation has discovered.

---

### *IT At Work*    DATA VISUALIZATION HELPS HAWORTH TO COMPETE

Manufacturing office furniture is an extremely competitive business. Haworth Corporation operates in this environment and has been able to survive and even excel with the help of IT. To compete, Haworth allows its customers to customize what they want to buy. But it may surprise you to learn that an office chair can be assembled in 200 different ways. The customization of all products resulted in 21 million potential product combinations, confusing customers who could not know what the customized furniture looks like until the item was delivered.

The solution was computer visualization software that allowed sales representatives with laptops to show customers exactly what they were ordering. Thus, the huge parts catalogs became more easily understood, and sales representatives were able to configure different options by entering the corporate database, showing what a product would look like, and computing its price. The customers can now make changes until the furniture design meets their needs. The salesperson can do all this from the customer's office by connecting to the corporate intranet via the Internet and using Web tools to allow customers to make the desired changes.

The program allows the company to reduce cycle time. After the last computer-assisted design (CAD) mockup of an order has been approved, the CAD software is used to create a bill of materials that goes to Haworth's factory for manufacturing. This reduces the time spent between sales reps and CAD operators, increasing the time available for sales reps to make more sales calls and increasing customer satisfaction with quicker delivery.

By using this visualization computer program, Haworth has increased its competitive advantage.

**For Further Exploration:** How can the intranet be used to improve the process? ▲

SOURCE: Condensed from *Infoworld*, January 27, 1997, p. 92.

*I*NTEGRATING IT

...for Marketing, Production & Operations Management, and Accounting

---

Data visualization is easier to implement when the necessary data are in a data warehouse. Our discussion here is focused mainly on the data visualization techniques of multidimensionality and geographical information systems. Related topics, such as multimedia and hypermedia, are presented in Technology Guide #2.

### MULTIDIMENSIONALITY

Modern data and information may have several dimensions. For example, management may be interested in examining sales figures in a certain city by product, by time period, by salesperson, and by store (i.e., four dimensions). The more dimensions involved, the more difficult it is to present multidimensional information in one table or in one graph. Therefore, it is important to provide the user with a technology that allows him or her to add, replace, or change dimensions quickly and easily in a table and/or graphical presentation. Such changes are known as "slicing and dicing" of data. The technology of slicing, dicing, and similar manipulations is called multidimensionalty.

Figure 10.4 (page 448) shows three views of the same data, organized in different ways, using multidimensional software, usually available with spreadsheets. In part (a), travel hours of a company's employees by means of transportation and by country are given. The "next year" gives projections automatically generated by an embedded formula. In part (b) the data are reorganized and in part (c) they are reorganized again and manipulated as well. All this is easily done by the end user with one or two clicks of the mouse.

The major advantage of multidimensionality is that data can be organized the way managers like to see them rather than the way that the system analysts do. Furthermore, different presentations of the same data can be arranged and rearranged easily and quickly. Three factors are considered in multidimensionality: dimensions, measures, and time.

▶ *Examples of dimensions*: Products, salespeople, market segments, business units, geographical locations, distribution channels, countries, industries

▶ *Examples of measures*: Money, sales volume, head count, inventory profit, actual versus forecasted results

▶ *Examples of time*: Daily, weekly, monthly, quarterly, yearly

For example, a manager may want to know the sales of product M in a certain geographical area, by a specific salesperson, during a specified month, in terms of units. Although the answer can be provided regardless of the database structure, it can be provided much faster, and by the user himself or herself, if the data are organized in *multidimensional databases*, or in data marts, or if the query tools are designed for multidimensionality. In either case, users can navigate through the many dimensions and levels of data via tables or graphs and then conduct a quick analysis to find significant deviations or important trends. Multidimensional databases are typically more efficient for sharing and processing many dimensions than relational databases. There are several reasons for these advantages:

▶ Data can be presented and navigated with relative ease.

▶ Multidimensional databases are easier to maintain.

▶ Multidimensional databases are significantly faster than relational databases as a result of the additional dimensions and the anticipation of how the data will be accessed by users.

However, multidimensional databases do not replace the data warehouse, so there are additional costs of creating and maintaining them. They actually serve as a data mart (three-tier architecture).

| | | Planes | | Trains | | Automobiles | Travel Hours |
|---|---|---|---|---|---|---|---|
| | | This Year | Next Year | This Year | Next Year | This Year | Next Year |
| Canada | | 740 | 888 | 140 | 168 | 640 | 768 |
| Japan | | 430 | 516 | 290 | 348 | 150 | 180 |
| France | | 320 | 384 | 460 | 552 | 210 | 252 |
| Germany | | 425 | 510 | 430 | 516 | 325 | 390 |
| Country | | | | | | | |

(a)

| | | Hours | |
|---|---|---|---|
| | | This Year | Next Year |
| Planes | Canada | 740 | 888 |
| | Japan | 430 | 516 |
| | France | 320 | 384 |
| | Germany | 425 | 510 |
| Trains | Canada | 140 | 168 |
| | Japan | 290 | 348 |
| | France | 460 | 552 |
| | Germany | 430 | 516 |
| Automobiles | Canada | 640 | 768 |
| | Japan | 150 | 180 |
| | France | 210 | 252 |
| | Germany | 325 | 390 |
| Travel | Country | | |

(b)

**Worksheet1-View1-TUTORIAL**

| | | | Hours | |
|---|---|---|---|---|
| | | | This Year | Next Year |
| Planes | Canada | | 740 | 888 |
| | Japan | | 430 | 516 |
| | | France | 320 | 384 |
| | | Germany | 425 | 510 |
| | Europe | Total | 745 | 894 |
| Trains | Canada | | 140 | 168 |
| | Japan | | 290 | 348 |
| | | France | 460 | 552 |
| | | Germany | 430 | 516 |
| | Europe | Total | 890 | 1068 |
| Automobiles | Canada | | 640 | 768 |
| | Japan | | 150 | 180 |
| | | France | 210 | 252 |
| | | Germany | 325 | 390 |
| | Europe | Total | 535 | 642 |
| Travel | Country | | | |
| | Next Year = (This Year)*1.2 | | | |

- The software adds a *Total* Item
- The software adds formula 2 and calculates *Total*
- Auto-making shades the formulas using two shades of gray

Shows how formula 1 calculates cells (in this case, the cells *Total:Next Year*)

Shows that formula 2 calculates all Total cells.

(c)

**FIGURE 10.4** Multidimensionality views.

Multidimensionality is available with different degrees of sophistication and is especially popular in executive information and support systems. There are several types of software from which multidimensional systems can be constructed, and they often work in conjunction with OLAP tools.

### GEOGRAPHICAL INFORMATION SYSTEMS

A **geographical information system (GIS)** is a computer-based system for capturing, storing, checking, integrating, manipulating, and displaying data using digitized maps. Its most distinguishing characteristic is that every record or digital object has an identified geographical location. By integrating maps with spatially oriented (geographical location) databases (called "geocoding") and other databases, users can generate information for planning, problem solving, and decision making, increasing their productivity and the quality of their decisions, as many banks have done.

*IT At Work* **BANKS USING GEOGRAPHICAL INFORMATION SYSTEMS (GIS) TO SUPPORT MARKETING**

*I*NTEGRATING IT
...for Finance and
Marketing

Banks are using GIS for plotting the following:

▶ Branch and ATM locations
▶ Customer demographics (e.g., residence, age, income level) for each product of the bank
▶ Volume and traffic patterns of business activities
▶ Geographical area served by each branch
▶ Market potential for banking activities
▶ Strengths and weaknesses against the competition
▶ Branch performance

A GIS is used as a geographical spreadsheet that allows managers to model business activities and perform what-if analyses (What if we close a branch or merge branches? What if a competitor opens a branch?). The maps consolidate pages of analysis. Representative pioneering banks are First Florida Banks (Tampa, FL), Marion Bank (Philadelphia, PA), and NJB Financial (Princeton, NJ).

**For Further Exploration.** How can a GIS indicate a bank's strengths and weaknesses against the competition? ▲

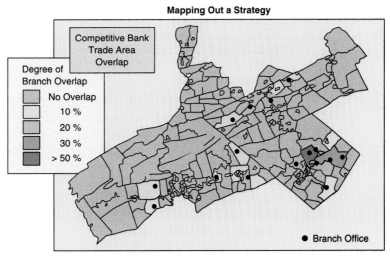

Source: Verdi Ryan Associates

Banks Using Geographical Information Systems (GIS) to Support Marketing.

SOURCE: Condensed from Radding, A., "Going with GIS," *Bank Management*, December 1991.

**GIS SOFTWARE.** GIS software varies in its capabilities from simple computerized mapping systems to enterprisewide tools for decision support data analysis (see Minicase 1). Clearly, a high-quality graphics display and high computation and search speeds are necessary, so most early GIS implementations were developed for mainframes. Since the early 1990s, however, relatively powerful PC implementations have been developed.

**GIS DATA.** GIS data are available from a wide variety of sources. Government sources (via the Internet and CD-ROM) provide some data, while vendors provide diversified commercial data as well (such as CD-ROMs from MapInfo and FirstMap from Wessex Inc.). The field of GIS can be divided into two major categories: functions and applications. According to Mennecke et al. (1995), there are four major functions: spatial imaging, design and planning, database management, and decision modeling. These functions support six areas of applications as shown in Figure 10.5. Of these six, demographics and market analysis, transportation and logistics, and strategic planning and decision making are of special interest.

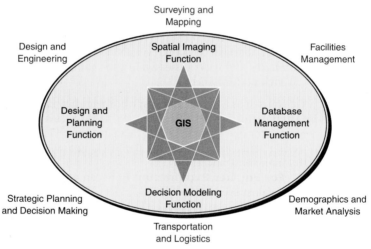

**FIGURE 10.5** GIS functions and applications.
(*Source:* Mennecke, B. E., et al. [1995].)

**GIS AND DECISION MAKING.** Initially, the high cost of GIS prevented its use outside experimental facilities and government agencies. Since the 1990s, however, the cost of GIS software and its required hardware has dropped dramatically. Now relatively inexpensive, fully functional PC-based packages are readily available. GIS provides a large amount of extremely useful information that can be analyzed and utilized in decision making. Its graphical format makes it easy for managers to visualize the data. For example, Janet M. Hamilton, market research administrator for Dow Elanco, a $2 billion maker of agricultural chemicals based in Indianapolis, explains:

> I can put 80-page spreadsheets with thousands of rows into a single map. It would take a couple of weeks to comprehend all of the information from the spreadsheet, but in a map, the story can be told in seconds. (Hamilton [1996], p. 21)

There are countless applications of GIS to improve decision making in the public or private sector. They include the dispatch of emergency vehicles, transit management (see Minicase 1), facility site selection, and wildlife management.

For many companies, the intelligent organization of data within a GIS can provide a framework to support the process of decision making and of designing alternative strategies. Some examples of successful GIS applications are provided by Bidgoli (1995) and Hamilton (1996). Other examples of successful GIS applications are summarized in Box 10.3.

## *A Closer Look* BOX 10.3

### GIS SAMPLE APPLICATIONS

| COMPANY | APPLICATION OF GIS |
|---|---|
| Pepsi Cola Inc., Super Value, Acordia Inc. | Used in site selection for new Taco Bell and Pizza Hut restaurants; combining demographic data and traffic patterns. |
| CIGNA (health insurance) | Uses GIS to answer such questions as "How many CIGNA-affiliated physicians are available within an 8-mile radius of a business?" |
| Western Auto (a subsidiary of Sears) | Integrates data with GIS to create a detailed demographic profile of store's neighborhood to determine the best product mix to offer at the store. |
| Sears, Roebuck & Co. | Uses GIS to support planning of truck routes. |
| Health maintenance organizations | Tracks cancer rate and other diseases to determine expansion strategy and allocation of expensive equipment in their facilities. |
| Wood Personnel Services (employment agencies) | Maps neighborhoods where temporary workers live; for locating marketing and recruiting cities. |
| Wilkening & Co. (consulting services) | Designs optimal sales territories and routes for their clients, reducing travel costs by 15 percent. |
| CellularOne Corp. | Maps its entire cellular network to identify clusters of call disconnects and to dispatch technician accordingly. |
| Sun Microsystems | Manages leased property in dozens of places worldwide. |
| Consolidated Rail Corp. | Monitors the condition of 20,000 miles of railroad track and thousands of parcels of adjoining land. |
| Federal Emergency Management Agency | Assesses the damage of hurricanes, floods, and other natural disasters by relating videotapes of the damage to digitized maps of properties. |
| Toyota (other car manufacturers) | Combines GIS and GPS as a navigation tool. Drivers are directed to destinations in the best possible way. |

**GIS AND THE INTERNET OR INTRANET.** Most major GIS software vendors are providing Web access, such as embedded browsers, or a Web/Internet/intranet server that hooks directly into their software. Thus users can access dynamic maps and data via the Internet or a corporate intranet (see Jacobs [1996]). Big Horn Computer Services, in Buffalo, NY, is using a Web-adapted GIS to develop a custom application for a national television network that wants its affiliate stations to be able to access an intranet containing demographic information about their viewers. Using a Web browser, employees at each station can view thematically shaded maps analyzing their market (see Swenson [1996]).

A number of firms are deploying GIS on the Internet for internal use or for use by their customers. For example, Visa Plus, which operates a network of automated teller machines, has developed a GIS application that lets Internet users call up a locator map for any of the company's 257,000 ATM machines worldwide. As GIS Web server software is deployed by vendors, more applications will be developed. Maps, GIS data, and information about GIS are available over the Web through a number of vendors and public agencies.

**EMERGING GIS APPLICATIONS.** The integration of GIS and global positioning systems (GPS) has the potential to help reengineer the aviation, transportation, and shipping industries. It enables vehicles or aircraft equipped with a GPS receiver to pinpoint their location as they move (Tetzeli [1993]). Emerging applications of GPS include personal automobile mapping systems, railroad car tracking, and earth-moving equipment tracking. The price is dropping with improvements in hardware, increased demand, and the availability of more competing vendors. (A simple GPS costs less than $150 in 1998.) GPS has also become a major source of new GIS data (see Group Assignment 1).

Some researchers have developed intelligent GISs that link a GIS to an expert system (such as applications in irrigation scheduling and forest pest management; see Plant [1993]).

Improvements in the GIS user interface have substantially altered the GIS "look" and "feel." Advanced visualization (three-dimensional graphics) is increasingly integrated with GIS capabilities, especially in animated and interactive maps. GIS can provide information for virtual reality engines and it can display complex information to decision makers. Object-oriented programming and databases are also likely to improve GIS. Multimedia and hypermedia will play a growing role in GIS, especially in help and training systems. Object linking and embedding will allow users to import maps into any document. More GIS will be deployed to provide data and access data over the Web and organizational intranets as "Web-ready" GIS software becomes available. See Clarke (1997) for an overview of GIS, many details, recent developments, and potential advances.

> I travel frequently and often must change itinerary. It's great to know there are Web sites which can provide me a map of, say, Philadelphia, when all I have with me is a Cleveland map.
> — *Mike Rewald*

## ▶ 10.4 MARKETING DATABASES IN ACTION

Data warehouses and data marts serve end users in all functional areas. However, the most dramatic applications of data warehousing and mining are in marketing in what is referred to as **marketing databases** (also referred to as *database marketing*).

In this section we examine how data warehouses, their extensions, and data mining are used and what role they play in new marketing strategies, such as the use of marketing transaction databases in interactive marketing.

### THE MARKETING TRANSACTION DATABASE*

Success in interactive marketing requires a new kind of database, oriented toward targeting the personalizing marketing messages in real time. Such a database provides the most effective means of capturing information on customer preferences and needs and, in turn, enterprises can use this knowledge to create new products and services. Such a database is called a **marketing transaction database (MTD)**. Most current databases are static: they simply gather and store information about customers. They fall under the following categories: op-

*Compiled from Hopkins, W., *GartnerGroup Research Note*, DA-ADP-1171, March 28, 1997, and www.gartner.com/newsltrs/netmarketing.html.

erations databases, data warehouses, and marketing databases. The MTD combines many of the characteristics of these databases and marketing data sources into a new database that allows marketers to engage in real-time personalization and target every interaction with customers.

**MTD'S CAPABILITIES.** The MTD provides dynamic, or interactive, functions not available with traditional types of marketing databases. In marketing terms, a transaction occurs with the exchange of information. With interactive media, each exposure to the customer becomes an opportunity to conduct a marketing "transaction." Exchanging information (whether gathered actively, through registration or use requests, or passively, by monitoring customer behavior) allows marketers to refine their understanding of each customer continuously and to use that information to target him or her specifically with personalized marketing messages.

A comparison of MTDs and other marketing-related databases is given in Table 10.4. Note that MTDs do not eliminate the traditional databases. They complement them by providing additional capabilities.

### *Table 10.4*  **Marketing Databases**

| | *Operational System* | *Data Warehouse* | *Data Marts Marketing Analysis Database* | *Marketing Transaction Database* |
|---|---|---|---|---|
| Purpose | Record transactions | Decision making | Understanding behavior | Targeting and personalization |
| Structure | Rigid—tied to applications and functional rules | Loose—iterative, modifiable | Loose, but marketing specific | Liquid—driven by real-time marketing |
| Update frequency | Real time | Weekly/monthly | Monthly/quarterly | Real time |
| Data level | Transaction detail | Most summarized, some detail | Summarized | Individual detail |
| Data quality | Dubious—most legacy systems have poor quality assurance | Rationalized (cleansed, verified) | Rationalized/house-holded | Focused customer data—verified by individual |
| Data type | Behavioral—based on transactions | Descriptive, behavioral | Descriptive, behavioral, derivative | Combines derivative, behavioral, and descriptive |
| Advantages | Very fast—high transaction volume | Centralized, easy-to-access repository | Organized by marketers for marketing purposes | Allows real-time analysis and decision making |
| Issues | Not oriented or organized the way marketers think | Difficult to implement correctly—typically needs more information for marketing | Generally oriented toward analysis only— little capability for real-time decision making | Emerging—no standards or best practices, not integrated with other systems |
| Event trigger | External | Internal | Internal | External |

SOURCE: The GartnerGroup: www.gartner.com/newsltrs/netmarketing.html, 1997.

**THE ROLE OF THE INTERNET.** Data mining, data warehousing, and MTDs are delivered on the Internet and intranets. The Internet does not simply represent another advertising venue or a different medium for catalog sales; it contains new attributes that smart marketers can exploit to their fullest degree. Indeed, the Internet promises to revolutionize sales and marketing. Dell Computers (see Mini-case 2) offers a good example of how marketing professionals can use the Internet's electronic sales and marketing channels for market research, advertising, information dissemination, product management, and product delivery.

## IMPLEMENTATION EXAMPLES

Fewer and fewer companies can afford traditional marketing approaches, which include big-picture strategies and expensive marketing campaigns. Marketing departments are being scaled down and new approaches such as one-to-one marketing, speed marketing, interactive marketing, and relationship marketing are being employed. The following examples illustrate how companies use data mining and warehousing to support the new marketing approaches.

▶ Alamo Rent-a-Car discovered that German tourists liked bigger cars. So now, when Alamo advertises its rental business in Germany, the ads include information about its larger models.

▶ Burlington Coat Factory tracks families as they grow through the online registry for expectant parents. The company then matches direct-mail material to the different stages of a family's development over time. Burlington also identifies, on a daily basis, top-selling styles and brands. By digging into reams of demographic data, historical buying patterns, and sales trends in existing stores, Burlington determines where to open its next store and what to stock in each store. The company's data warehouse contains 1.5 terabytes of information.

▶ Au Bon Pain Company, Inc., a Boston-based chain of cafes, discovered that the company was not selling as much cream cheese as planned. When it analyzed point-of-sale data, the firm found that customers preferred small, one-serving packaging (like butter). As soon as the package size was changed, sales shot up.

▶ Using U.S. census data along with its own internal data, Spalding Sports profiled thousands of golf courses and pro shops throughout the United States. Promotional materials for each golf course now match the customers' profile (such as upscale golfers versus working-class tourists). They also found that buyers at pro shops were more interested in technical aspects than buyers at retail stores.

▶ Bank of America gets more than 100,000 telephone calls from customers every day. Analyzing their banking activities, the bank determines what may be of interest to the customers. So when a customer calls to check on a balance the bank tries to sell the customer something in which he or she might be interested. The customer database used for this contains about 1 terabyte of data, providing insight into customers' behaviors.

▶ Supermarket chains regularly analyze reams of cash register data to discover what items customers are typically buying at the same time. These shopping patterns are used for issuing coupons, designing floor layouts and products' location (diapers are placed near to beer; can you guess why?), and creating shelf displays.

▶ AT&T and MCI sift through terabytes of customer phone data to fine tune marketing campaigns and determine new discount calling plans.

▶ A pharmaceutical company analyzes the results of its recent sales force activity to improve targeting of physicians who should be first contacted; it also determines which marketing activities will have the greatest impact in the next few months. The data include competitor market activity as well as information about the local health care systems. The results are distributed to the sales force via the Internet, intranets, or a private wide-area network that enables the representatives to review the decision-making recommendations.

▶ A credit card company leverages its vast warehouse of customer transaction data to identify customers most likely to be interested in a new credit product. Using a small test mailing, it identifies the attributes of customers with an affinity for the product. Recent projects have indicated more than a 20-fold decrease in costs for targeted mailing campaigns over conventional approaches.

▶ A diversified transportation company with a large direct sales force applied data mining to identifying the best prospects for its services. Using data mining to analyze its own customer experience, this company can build a unique segmentation identifying the attributes of high-value prospects. Applying this segmentation to a general business database, such as those provided by Dun & Bradstreet, can yield a prioritized list of prospects by region.

▶ A large consumer package goods company applies data mining to improve its sales process to retailers. Data from consumer panels, shipments, and competitor's activity are examined to understand the reasons for brand and store switching. Through this analysis, the manufacturer can select promotional strategies that best reach its target customer segments.

▶ In its data warehouse, the *Chicago Tribune* stores information about customer behavior as customers move through the various newspaper Web sites. Data mining helps to analyze volumes of data ranging from what browsers are used to what hyperlinks are clicked on most frequently (see Figure 10.6).

**FIGURE 10.6** The *Chicago Tribune's* Web page. Every hit is recorded in the data warehouse.

The data warehouses in some companies include 1 terabyte or more of data. They need to use supercomputing to sift quickly through the data. Wal-Mart, the world's largest discount retailer, has a gigantic database.

---

**IT At Work**     DATA MINING POWERS WAL-MART

With more than 20 terabytes of data (in 1998) on two NCR (National Cash Register) systems, Wal-Mart manages one of the world's largest data warehouses. Besides the two NCR Teradata databases, which handle most decision-support applications, Wal-Mart has another 6 terabytes of transaction processing data on IBM and Hitachi mainframes.

Wal-Mart's formula for success—getting the right product on the appropriate shelf at the lowest price—owes much to the company's multimillion dollar investment in data warehousing. "Wal-Mart can be more detailed than most of its competitors on what's going on by product, by store, by day—and act on it," says Richard Winter, a database consultant in Boston. "That's a tremendously powerful thing."

*Using It*

*...in Marketing*

The systems house data on point of sale, inventory, products in transit, market statistics, customer demographics, finance, product returns, and supplier performance. The data are used for three broad areas of decision support: analyzing trends, managing inventory, and understanding customers. What emerges are "personality traits" for each of Wal-Mart's 3000 or so outlets, which Wal-Mart managers can use to determine product mix and inventory levels for each store.

Wal-Mart is rolling out a data mining demand-forecasting application based on neural networking software and a 4000-processor parallel computer. The application "looks at individual items for individual stores to decide the seasonal sales profile of each item," says Rick Dalzell, Wal-Mart's Vice President of Applications Development. The computer keeps a year's worth of data on the sales of 100,000 products and predicts which items will be needed in each store and when.

Wal-Mart is expanding its use of market basket analysis. Data are collected on items that comprise a shopper's total purchase so that the company can analyze relationships and patterns in customer purchases. The data warehouse is available over the Web to store managers and suppliers. In 1997, 3500 users made 20,000 database queries each day.

"What Wal-Mart is doing is letting an army of people use the database to make tactical decisions," says consultant Winter. "The cumulative impact is immense."

**For Further Exploration.** Why is data mining necessary? What kind of competitive advantage can Wal-Mart gain with the system? ▲

SOURCE: Information courtesy of NCR Corp., 1998.

---

## ▶ 10.5 KNOWLEDGE MANAGEMENT

### KNOWLEDGE BASES AND ORGANIZATIONAL LEARNING

Throughout this chapter we have shown how raw data are transformed to information and knowledge. We have demonstrated how knowledge is derived for problem solving and how it is used for forecasting or predicting customer behavior. It only makes sense that the knowledge created for solving problems will be reused whenever the organization faces the same or similar problems (why reinvent the wheel?). This simple idea is the basis for a challenging concept called **knowledge management** or managing knowledge bases. A **knowledge base** is a database that contains knowledge, or the organization's knowhow. The major purpose of an organizational knowledge base is to allow for **knowledge**

**sharing** (see Manville and Foote [1996]). Knowledge sharing among employees, with customers, and with business partners has a huge potential payoff in improved customer service, shorter delivery cycle times, and increased collaboration within the company and with business partners as well. Furthermore, some knowledge can be sold to others or traded for other knowledge.

Sharing knowledge also means facilitating **organizational learning**. Organizational learning is an important discipline that organizations must learn in order to survive (see Senge [1994]). Learning disabilities can be fatal for organizations. Knowledge bases enable companies to learn faster than their competitors, giving them a sustainable competitive advantage. People can learn from the experience of others when this experience is documented in the knowledge base.

## IMPLEMENTING KNOWLEDGE MANAGEMENT SYSTEMS

Building and maintaining organizational knowledge bases is not a simple task and it involves many activities. For example, Andersen Consulting, one of the largest consulting and CPA companies, is pioneering an organizational knowledge base.

*IT At Work* ARTHUR ANDERSEN'S KNOWLEDGE BASE—LEAPFROGGING THE COMPETITORS

For a large consulting company whose very product is knowledge, there is considerable motivation to create a knowledge base to share accumulated knowhow. For this reason, Arthur Andersen and its sister company, Andersen Consulting, began in the early 1990s to create their Global Best Practices (GBP) knowledge base, a central repository of knowledge about world-class business practices.

The GBP contains quantitative and qualitative information about how companies achieve best-in-the-world standards of performance in activities that are common to most companies. Andersen's consultants use this information to provide clients with an ever-growing body of knowledge that can be used for performance improvement. Providing such knowledge to its customers gives a competitive edge to the company. Four years after the GBP was created, it was so successful that it had fundamentally shifted the company's culture and the way it did business. As a matter of fact, the company developed several other knowledge bases, each dedicated to an important topic. Here is how Arthur Andersen gathers knowledge.

**INTEGRATING IT**

...for Production & Operations Management, Marketing, Finance, and Accounting

▶ The Global Best Practices hotline receives more than 250 calls each month, which are sorted into business practice categories.
▶ These data, combined with ongoing research into emerging areas, are used to determine which process areas are to be developed or enhanced for an upcoming release.
▶ Research analysts team with content experts, who serve clients, to develop best practices context and diagnostic tools.
▶ Qualitative and quantitative information and tools are released on a CD-ROM that can be accessed by all Andersen professionals worldwide.
▶ Use in the field with clients generates suggestions that are received by the hotline or captured through formal or informal surveys.

The knowledge base contains information such as:

▶ Best companies' profiles
▶ Relevant Andersen engagement experience
▶ Top 10 case studies and articles

▶ World-class performance measures
▶ Diagnostic tools
▶ Customizable presentations
▶ Process definitions and directory of internal experts
▶ Best control practice
▶ Tax implications

Another corporate knowledge base is the Proposal Toolbox, which contains detailed information on all proposals submitted by Andersen's employees, worldwide, including employees working, resources used, etc. This knowledge base is used to cut the time for preparing new proposals from weeks to days.

The publicly open knowledge base (www.knowledgespace.com) will give you 30 days free trial. The site includes the GBP, current business issues, intelligent search engine using "push" technology, experts' opinions, links, references, and much more. (For details see Kass, E., "Arthur Andersen LLP," *Internet Week*, March 9, 1998).

**For Further Exploration.** Can you think of other topics that might be the subject of a knowledge base in a consulting company? in a university? ▲

SOURCE: Condensed from Burkowitz, W., "In the Know," *CIO*, April 15, 1996, and www.knowledge-space.com (1998).

From the Andersen example, one can see that implementing a knowledge base is not a simple project. The cost of building and maintaining it can be very high and the benefits are difficult to justify. Some implementation issues are: Who will decide on what to include in the knowledge base and how? Who will extract the knowledge from its sources? How will managers and professionals be trained to make effective use of the knowledge? What portion of the knowledge base should be open to outsiders, and how can proprietary and sensitive information be secured? How will the firm integrate the knowledge base with existing databases? And finally, how will managers validate the quality of the knowledge?

Despite these issues, companies are considering not only creating knowledge bases, but also completely reorganizing themselves as **knowledge-based organizations** (see Chapter 19 in Holsapple and Whinston [1996]). Even a new position, titled **chief knowledge officer**, or CKO, has been created (Davenport, [1996]), whose role is to capture and leverage structured knowledge with IT. CKOs have three responsibilities: creating knowledge management infrastructure, building a knowledge culture, and making it all pay off. A related position is the chief learning officer (established in the late 1990s at Coca-Cola and General Electric).

Appointing a CKO may be the first step toward fulfilling Drucker's (1988) prediction that "the typical business will be knowledge based, an organization composed largely of specialists who direct and discipline their own performance through organized feedback from colleagues, customers, and headquarters." Drucker claims that to remain competitive, or maybe even to survive, businesses will have to convert themselves into organizations of knowledge specialists. Based on Drucker's vision, Leonard-Barton (1995) and Holsapple and Whinston (1996) have developed frameworks for the knowledge organizations of tomorrow.

**TOOLS FOR KNOWLEDGE MANAGEMENT.** The GartnerGroup predicts that knowledge management will become a $2 billion market by 2002. Many tools can be used to facilitate knowledge management, as illustrated in Box 10.4.

# *A Closer Look* BOX 10.4

## KNOWLEDGE MANAGEMENT TOOLS

The following were representative knowledge management tools at the end of 1997:

*Knowledge X*. By feeding the software with public documents about employees and investments, this tool attempts to discern relationships that you might otherwise overlook. You can track, for example, the career paths of your competitor's chief executives. (See www.knowledgex.com.)

*Wincite*. This tool tracks market conditions, competitors and trends, and organizes intelligence in a knowledge base. It also distributes knowledge to concerned employees. Information collected comes from both external and internal sources. Included are the corporate analysts' insights and aptitude. (See www.wincite.com.)

*GrapeVine*. It enables employees that use Lotus Notes (Domino) to share their knowledge, such as sales leads, estimates, etc. The tool tries to discover and route existing information stored in Notes databases that it thinks you will be interested in. You may find, for example, that the new project you're embarking on overlaps one already in progress in another corporate unit. (See www.grapevine.com.)

*Sovereign Hill*. This provides a search and index tool, a Web-access layer, and an intelligent database that understands people, places, and things. Once supplied with information about industry news, for example, you can query the tool about your competitors. The answers incorporate hits on your competitor and will try to identify the relationship your competitor has with employees, customers, or suppliers. (See www.sovereignhill.com.)

SOURCE: Compiled from Ginchereau et al. (1997).

**The GrapeVine Solution**

1 To set up the grapeVine system, the Notes administrator builds an Information Resource that corresponds to each document repository in the company, whether it be a Notes database, a server, or the Web. The Information Resource searches the repository for keywords and forwards a copy of each relevant document to the Eureka database.

2 Users can browse the Eureka database for information that serves their needs, or . . .

3 Create a profile of keywords and GrapeVine will forward relevant documents to them through the Notes messaging system.

SOURCE: *InfoWorld*, Nov. 17, 1997, p. 124.

# ▶ MANAGERIAL ISSUES

A number of challenges face companies that are undertaking a data and knowledge management approach.

1. *Cost–benefit issues and justification*. Some of the solutions discussed here are very expensive and are justifiable only in large corporations. Smaller organizations can make the solutions cost effective if they leverage existing databases rather than create new ones. A careful cost–benefit analysis must be undertaken before any commitment to the new technologies is made.

2. *Where to store data physically*. Should data be distributed close to their sources, thereby potentially speeding up data entry and updating but increasing problems of data security, or should data be centralized for easier control, security, and disaster recovery, although they will be more distant from users and create a potential single point-of-failure location?

3. *Legal issues*. Data mining may suggest to a company to send catalogs or promotions to only one group age or one gender. A man sued Victoria's Secret because his female neighbor received a mail order catalog with deeply discounted items and he received only the regular catalog (the discount was actually given for volume purchasing). Discrimination charges can be very expensive.

4. *Disaster recovery*. Can an organization's business processes, which have become dependent on databases, recover and sustain operations after a natural or other type of information system disaster?

5. *Internal or external?* Should a firm invest in internally collecting, storing, maintaining, and purging its own databases of information, or should it pay to subscribe to external databases, where providers are responsible for all data management and data access?

6. *Data security and ethics*. Are the company's competitive data safe from external snooping or sabotage? Are confidential data, such as personnel details, safe from improper or illegal access and alteration? A related question is who owns such personal data? (See Smith [1997].)

7. *Ethics: paying for use of data*. Compilers of public-domain information such as Lexis-Nexis face a problem of people lifting large sections of their work without first paying royalties. The Collection of Information Antipiracy Act (a pending bill) will provide greater protection from online piracy. (See *Interactive Week*, Feb. 16, 1998, for details.)

8. *Data purging*. When is it beneficial to "clean house" and purge information systems of obsolete or non–cost effective data?

9. *The legacy data problem*. One very real problem is what to do with the mass of information already stored in a variety of formats, often known as the *legacy data acquisition* problem. Data in older, perhaps obsolete, databases still need to be available to newer database management systems. Many of the legacy application programs used to access the older data simply cannot be converted into new computing environments without both transparent and procedural access to critical data remaining in the legacy environment. Basically, there are three approaches to solving this problem. One is to create a database front end that can act as a translator from the old system to

> Nothing is ever "safe," especially data. The question is, "How hard can we make it for unauthorized users to access or change it?"
>
> — *Blake Thompson*

the new. The second is to cause applications to be integrated with the new system, so that data can be seamlessly accessed in the original format. The third is to cause the data to migrate into the new system by reformatting it.

10. *Data delivery*. A problem regarding how to move data efficiently around an enterprise also exists. The inability to communicate among different groups in different geographical locations is a serious roadblock to implementing distributed applications properly, especially given the many remote sites and mobility of today's workers.

11. *Privacy*. Collecting data in a warehouse and conducting data mining may result in the invasion of individual privacy. What will companies do to protect individuals? What can individuals do to protect their privacy?

## KEY TERMS

Chief knowledge officer *458*

Data integrity *431*

Data mart *437*

Data mining *442*

Data quality (DQ) *430*

Data visualization *446*

Data warehouse *437*

Document management *433*

Document management system (DMS) *433*

Geographical information system (GIS) *449*

Information sharing *426*

Knowledge base *456*

Knowledge-based organizations *458*

Knowledge discovery *440*

Knowledge discovery in databases (KDD) *440*

Knowledge management *456*

Knowledge sharing *456–57*

Marketing database *452*

Marketing transaction database (MTD) *452*

Metadata *437*

Multimedia database *432*

Object-oriented database *431*

Online analytical processing (OLAP) *442*

Organizational learning *457*

## CHAPTER HIGHLIGHTS  *(L–x means learning objective number x)*

▶ Data are the foundation of any information system and need to be managed throughout their useful lives. (L–1)

▶ Data exist in internal and external sources. Personal data and knowledge are often stored in people's minds. (L–2)

▶ The Internet is a major source of data and knowledge. (L–2)

▶ Many factors that impact the quality of data must be recognized and controlled. (L–2)

▶ The newest types of data organization are object oriented and multimedia. (L–3)

▶ Electronic document management, the automated control of documents, is a key to greater efficiency in handling documents in order to gain an edge on the competition. (L–4)

▶ Warehouses and data marts are necessary to support effective decision making. Relevant data are indexed and organized for easy access by end users. (L–4)

▶ Data mining for knowledge discovery is an attempt to use intelligent systems to scan volumes of data to locate necessary information and knowledge. (L–5)

▶ Online analytical processing is a data discovery method that uses analytical approaches to knowledge discovery. (L–5)

▶ Visualization is important for better understanding of data relationships and compression of information. (L–6)

▶ Multidimensional presentation enables quick and easy multiple viewing of information in accordance with people's needs. (L–6)

▶ A geographical information system captures, stores, manipulates, and displays data using digitized maps. (L–6)

▶ Marketing database provides the technological support for new marketing approaches such as interactive marketing. (L–7)

▶ Marketing transaction databases provide dynamic interactive functions that facilitate customized advertisement and services to customers. (L–7)

▶ Knowledge bases contain shareable knowledge accumulated in organizations. Their management is difficult, but their use can be extremely beneficial. (L–8)

## QUESTIONS FOR REVIEW

1. Define knowledge management.
2. Describe object-oriented database.
3. Define knowledge-based organization.
4. What is a terabyte? (Write the number.)
5. Review the steps of the data life cycle and explain them.
6. List some of the categories of data available on the Internet.
7. Define data quality.
8. Define document management.
9. Describe data warehouse.
10. Describe a data mart.
11. Define online analytical processing (OLAP).
12. Define data mining and describe its major characteristics.
13. Explain the properties of multidimensionality.
14. Describe GIS and its major capabilities.
15. Define marketing transaction database.
16. Define knowledge base and describe its major benefits.
17. Define data visualization.
18. Describe the process of KDD.

## QUESTIONS FOR DISCUSSION

1. Relate knowledge management to organizational learning.
2. Discuss the opportunities that a knowledge base can provide to a pharmaceutical company such as Merck or Johnson & Johnson.
3. Compare data quality to data integrity. How are they related?
4. Discuss some of the advantages of object-oriented databases. How does it relate to multimedia?
5. Discuss the factors that make document management so valuable. What capabilities are particularly valuable?
6. Relate document management to imaging systems.
7. Describe the process of knowledge discovery and discuss the roles of the data warehouse, data mining, and OLAP in this process.
8. Discuss the major drivers and benefits of data warehousing to end users.
9. Discuss how a data warehouse can lessen the stovepipe problem. (See Chapter 4.)
10. A data mart can substitute for a data warehouse or supplement it. Compare and discuss these options.
11. Why is the combination of GIS and GPS becoming so popular? Examine some applications.
12. Discuss the advantages of terabyte marketing databases to a large corporation. Does a small company need a marketing database? Under what circumstances will it make sense to have one?
13. Discuss the difficulties associated with creating and maintaining knowledge bases.
14. Why is the mass marketing approach not effective any more? What is the logic of targeted marketing?
15. Distinguish between operational databases, data warehouse, and marketing data mart.
16. Relate the Sears case at the beginning of this chapter to the phases of the data life cycle.

## EXERCISES

1. Review the list of data management difficulties in Section 10.1. Explain how a combination of data warehousing and data mining can solve or reduce these problems. Be specific.
2. Interview a knowledge worker in a company you work for or to which you have access. Find the data problems they have encountered and the measures they have taken to solve them. Relate the problems to Strong, et al.'s four categories.
3. Prepare a report about knowledge management. Use terms such as "learning organizations," "corporate memory," and "intellectual capital" in your report. Visit www.brint.com/km to discern the ideas driving learning organizations.
4. Ocean Spray Cranberries is a large cooperative of fruit growers and processors. Ocean Spray needed data to determine the effectiveness of its promotions and its advertisements and to make itself able to respond strategically to its competitors' promotions. The company also wanted to identify trends in consumer preferences for new products and to pinpoint marketing factors that might be causing changes in the selling levels of certain brands and markets. Ocean Spray buys marketing data from InfoScan, a company that collects data using bar code scanners in a sample of 2500 stores nationwide. The data for each product include sales volume, market share, distribution, price information, and information about promotions (sales, advertisements).

The amount of data provided to Ocean Spray on a daily basis is overwhelming (about 100 to 1000 times more data items than Ocean Spray used to collect on its own. All the data are deposited in the corporate marketing data mart. In 1998, it was estimated to contain about 2 billion bytes. To analyze this vast amount of data, the company developed DSS. To give end users easy access to the data, the company uses an expert system–based data mining process called CoverStory, which summarizes information in accordance with user preferences. CoverStory interprets data processed by the DSS, identifies trends, discovers cause–effect relationships, presents hundreds of displays, and provides any information required by the decision makers. This system alerts managers to key problems and opportunities.

a. Find information about InfoScan and Ocean Spray by entering Ocean Spray's Web site.

b. Ocean Spray has said that it cannot run the business without the system. Why?

c. What data from the data mart are used by the DSS?

## GROUP ASSIGNMENTS

1. Several applications now combine GIS and GPS:
   a. Survey such applications by conducting literature search and query GIS vendors.
   b. Prepare a list of five applications.
   c. Describe the benefit of such integration.

2. Prepare a report on the topic of "data management and the intranet." Specifically pay attention to the role of the data warehouse, the use of browsers for query, and data mining. Also explore the issue of GIS and the Internet. Finally, describe the role of extranets in support of business partner collaboration. Each student will visit one or two vendors' sites, read the white papers, and examine products (Oracle, Red Bricks, Brio, Siemens Mixdorf IS, Comshare, NCR, SAS, and Information Advantage). Also, visit the Web site of the Data Warehouse Institute (dw-institute.org).

3. Companies invest billions of dollars to support database marketing. The information systems departments' (ISD) activities that have supported accounting and finance in the past are shifting to marketing. According to Tucker (1997), some people think that the ISD should report to marketing. Do you agree or disagree? Debate this issue.

4. In 1996 Lexis-Nexis, the online information service, was accused of permitting access to sensitive information on individuals. Using data mining, it is possible not only to capture information that has been buried in distant courthouses, but also to manipulate and crossindex it. This can benefit law enforcement but invade privacy. The company argued that the firm was targeted unfairly, since it only provided basic residential data for lawyers and law enforcement personnel. Should Lexis-Nexis be prohibited from allowing access to such information or not? Debate the issue.

## INTERNET EXERCISES

Note: The URLs included here were current when the book went to press. However, they are subject to change without notice. Please consult the Turban Web site (www.Wiley.com/college/turban2e).

1. Conduct a survey on document management tools and applications by visiting www.dataware.com, www.documentum.com, and www.aiim.org/aim /publications.

2. Access the Web sites of one or two of the major data management vendors, such as Oracle, Informix, and Sybase, and trace the capabilities of their latest products, including Web connections.

3. Access the Web sites of one or two of the major data warehouse vendors, such as NCR, SAS, or Comshare; find how their products are related to the Web.

4. Access the Web site of the GartnerGroup (www.gartnergroup.com). Examine some of their research notes pertaining to marketing databases, data warehousing, and data management. Prepare a report regarding the state of the art.

5. Explore a Web site for multimedia database applications. Visit such sites as www.leisureplan.com, www.illustra.com, or www.adb.fr. Review some of the demonstrations and prepare a concluding report.

6. Survey some GIS resources such as www.geo.ed .ac.uk/home/hiswww.html and www.prenhall.com /stratgis/sites.html. Identify GIS resources related to your industry and prepare a report on some recent developments or applications. See http://nsdi.usgs .gov/nsdi/pages/what_is_gis.html.

7. Visit the sites of some GIS vendors (such as MAP Info Systems). Join a newsgroup and discuss new applications in marketing, banking, and transportation. Download a demo. What are some of the most important capabilities and new applications?

8. Visit www.brint.com. Review recent information on knowledge management. Write a report.

# Minicase 1

## Geographical Information System at Dallas Area Rapid Transit

Public transportation in Dallas and its neighboring communities is provided by Dallas Area Rapid Transit (DART), which operates buses, vans, and a train system. The service area has grown very fast. By the mid-1980s, the agency was no longer able to respond properly to customer requests, make rapid changes in scheduling, plan properly, or manage security. The solution to these problems was discovered in GIS. A GIS digitizes maps and maplike information, integrates it with other database information, and uses the combined information for planning, problem solving, and decision making. DART maintains a centralized graphical database of every object for which it is responsible.

The GIS presentation makes it possible for DART's managers, consultants, and customers to view and analyze data on digitized maps. Previously, DART created service maps on paper showing bus routes and schedules. The maps were updated and redistributed several times a year, at a high cost. Working with paper maps made it difficult to respond quickly and accurately to the nearly 6000 customer inquiries each day. For example, to answer a question concerning one of the more than 200 bus routes or a specific schedule, it was often necessary to look at several maps and routes. Planning a change was also a time-consuming task. Analysis of the viability of bus route alternatives made it necessary to photocopy maps from map books, overlay tape to show proposed routes, and spend considerable time gathering information on the demographics of the corridors surrounding the proposed routes. The GIS includes attractive and accurate maps that interface with a database containing information about bus schedules, routes, bus stops (in excess of 15,000), traffic surveys, demographics, and addresses on each street in the database. The system allows DART employees to:

▶ Respond rapidly to customer inquiries (reducing response time by at least 33 percent)

▶ Perform the environmental impact studies required by the city

▶ Track where the buses are at any time using a global positioning system

▶ Improve security on buses

▶ Monitor subcontractors quickly and accurately

▶ Analyze the productivity and use of existing routes

For instance, a customer wants to know the closest bus stop and the schedule of a certain bus to take her to a certain destination. The GIS automatically generates the answer when the caller says where she is by giving an address, a name of an intersection, or a landmark. The computer can calculate the travel time to the desired destination as well.

Analyses that previously took days to complete are now executed in less than an hour. Special maps, which previously took up to a week to produce at a cost of $13,000 to $15,000 each, are produced in 5 minutes at the cost of 3 feet of plotter paper.

In the late 1990s, the GIS was combined with a GPS. The GPS tracks the location of the buses and computes the expected arrival time at each bus stop.

### Questions for Minicase 1

1. Describe the role of data in the DART system.

2. What are the advantages of computerized maps?

3. Comment on the following statement: "Using GIS, users can improve not only the inputting of data but also its use."

4. Speculate on the type of information provided by the GPS.

A representative map in DART's database.

SOURCE: Condensed from *GIS World*, July 1993, updated with information provided by DART, 1998.

## Database Marketing Increases Dell's Sales

Dell Computer Corporation has been the world's largest direct-sale vendor of personal computers. One way the company distinguishes itself from other suppliers of PCs is by acting quickly on the masses of data it gathers from customers (the company receives over 50,000 telephone calls or electronic mail messages daily). "Information is a valuable competitive weapon," says Tom Thomas, the chief information officer. "Our whole business system is geared to collect it."

Many of the 50,000 daily messages received by Dell are from potential customers who dial 800 numbers or send e-mail to reach the company's sales representatives; the rest are from current users of Dell machines asking the technical support staff for help. The employees who take these calls work on PCs linked to a computer that contains the company's customer database, which has well over 1 million customer entries. The sales representatives enter information about each call as they receive it, recording names and addresses along with product preferences and/or technical problems. The company stores all this information and much more in a single database shared by employees in various departments, from marketing to product development to customer service.

The data yield significant marketing and sales guidelines. Says Tom Martin, Dell's chief marketer, "We know that if we use a yellow background on a catalog cover, we'll get a 30 percent lower response rate than with gray." The company tailors its mailings even more precisely to each recipient. The rate of response to its mailings to small businesses rose 250 percent once Dell used customer feedback to refine its pitch. At a mailing price of 50¢ to $3 per piece, the benefits of accurate targeting add up quickly.

Experience from the database also guides the sales representatives who receive calls. As they enter information about each caller, sales suggestions automatically pop up on their computer screens. Dell had a 10-fold increase in sales of 3-year warranties after prompting representatives to pitch them to all callers buying systems costing more than a certain dollar amount.

Routine analysis of customer and sales data allows Dell to spot consumer trends such as a shift to larger hard disk drives. At one time, when Dell was shipping most of its systems with drives capable of storing over 120 million characters (120 MB), the customer database alerted management to the fact that new orders for drives with nearly twice the storage capability were rapidly climbing. Dell buyers rushed out, negotiated volume discounts from large disk drive manufacturers, and locked in deliveries before their competitors.

"Know your customer" is a tried and true business rule, and Dell gets the most it can out of it through customer databases.

### Questions for Minicase 2

1. What role do databases play in Dell's marketing strategies?

2. Can you identify any data mining necessary for the information described in the case?

3. Is there any possibility of invasion of privacy of Dell's customers? If so, how can this privacy be protected?

4. The catalog business is supplemented by electronic catalogs; therefore, some suggest that the benefit of "accurate targeting" in electronic catalogs could be lessened or even disappear. Do you agree or not? Discuss.

5. Is the paper catalog eventually going to disappear?

SOURCE: Adapted from *Fortune 1994 Information Technology Guide*, August 1993, and from information provided by the company in 1998.

## REFERENCES AND BIBLIOGRAPHY

1. Adjeroh, D. A., and K. C. Nwosu, "Multimedia Database Management—Requirements and Issues," *IEEE Multimedia*, July/Sept. 1997.

2. Barquin, R., and H. Edelstein, *Building, Using and Managing the Data Warehouse*, Upper Saddle River, NJ: Prentice Hall, 1997.

3. Beitler, S. S., and R. Leary, "Sears' Epic Transformation: Converting from Mainframe Legacy Systems to OLAP," *Journal of Data Warehousing*, April 1997.

4. Bidgoli, H., "Geographic Information Systems: A New Strategic Tool for the 90's and Beyond," *Journal of Systems Management*, May/June, 1995.

5. Clarke, K. C., *Getting Started with Geographical Information Systems,* Upper Saddle River, NJ: Prentice Hall, 1997.

6. Cole, B., "Document Management on a Budget," *Network World,* Vol. 13, No. 8, Sept. 16, 1996.

7. Crosky, W. T. R., et al., *The Handbook of Multimedia Information Management,* Upper Saddle River, NJ: Prentice Hall, 1996.

8. Davenport, T. H., "Think Tank: Knowledge Roles: The CKO and Beyond," *CIO,* April 1, 1996.

9. Davenport, T. H., *Information Ecology,* New York: Oxford University Press, 1997.

10. Drucker, P. F., "The Coming of the New Organization," *Harvard Business Review,* Jan. 1988.

11. Eckerson, W. W., "Web-based Query Tools and Architecture," *Journal of Data Warehousing,* April 1997.

12. Fayyad, U. M., ed., *Advances in Knowledge Discovery and Data Mining,* Boston: MIS Press, 1996.

13. Fayyad, U. M., et al., "The KDD Process for Extracting Useful Knowledge from Volumes of Data," *Communications of the ACM,* Nov. 1996.

14. Fluckiger, F., *Understanding Networked Multimedia: Applications and Technology,* Upper Saddle River, NJ: Prentice Hall ESM, 1996.

15. Forum, "The Data Crisis," *Communications of the ACM,* May 1997.

16. Freeman, E., "Birth of a Terabyte Data Warehouse," *Datamation,* April 1997.

17. Ginchereau, B., et al., "Knowledge Equals Power," *InfoWorld,* Nov. 17, 1997.

18. Gray, P., and H. J. Watson, *Decision Support in the Data Warehouse,* Upper Saddle River, N.J., Prenctice Hall, 1998.

19. Gupta, A., and R. Jain, "Visual Information Retrieval," *Communications of the ACM,* May 1997.

20. Hagel, J., and J. F. Rayport, "The Coming Battle for Customer Information," *Harvard Business Review,* Jan./Feb. 1997.

21. Hamilton, J. M., "A Mapping Feast," *CIO,* Mar. 15, 1996.

22. Haskin, D., "Leverage Your Knowledge Base" (Web-based document management systems), *Internet World,* Feb. 1998.

23. Holsapple, C. W., and A. B. Whinston, *DSS: A Knowledge-Based Approach,* Minneapolis/St. Paul: West Publishing, 1996.

24. *Information Advantage,* "Putting the Data Warehouse on the Intranet," a white paper, www.inforadvan.com/1f.4_int .html, 1997.

25. Inmon, W. H., *Building the Data Warehouse,* New York: Wiley, 1996.

26. Jacobs, A., "Mapping Software Finds the Net," *Computerworld,* Vol. 30, No. 32. 44, Aug. 5, 1996.

27. Kaplan, D., et al., "Assessing Data Quality in Accounting Information Systems," *Communications of the ACM,* Feb. 1998.

28. Kroenke, D. M., *Data Processing: Fundamentals, Design, and Implementation,* 6th ed., Upper Saddle River, NJ: Prentice Hall, 1998.

29. Leonard, Barton D., *Wellsprings of Knowledge,* Boston: Harvard Business Press, 1995.

30. Maybury, M. T., *Intelligent Multimedia Information Retrieval,* Boston: MIT Press, 1997.

31. McFadden, F., and H. J. Watson, "The World of Data Warehousing: Issues and Opportunities," *Data Warehousing,* Vol. 1, No. 1, 1996.

32. Mennecke, B. E., et al., "Using GIS as a Tool for Sensing and Responding to Customers," in Bradley, S. P., and Nolan, R. L. (eds.), *Multimedia and the Boundaryless World,* Boston: Harvard Business School Colloquium, 1995.

33. Moad, J., "Mining a New Vein," *PC Week,* Jan. 5, 1998.

34. Nwosu, K. C., et al., "Multimedia Database Systems: A New Frontier," *IEEE Multimedia,* July/Sept. 1997.

35. Park, Y. T., "Strategic Uses of Data Warehouses," *Journal of Data Warehousing,* April 1997.

36. Redman, T. C., "The Impact of Poor Data Quality on the Typical Enterprises," *Communications of the ACM,* Feb. 1998.

37. Roland, D., "Data Flow Management Can Assist Underwriting," *National Underwriter,* Aug. 29, 1994.

38. Ruthburn, T., "Data Mining in the Financial Markets," *PCAI,* May/June, July/Aug., Sept./Oct. 1997.

39. Senge, P., *The Fifth Discipline: The Art and Practice of the Learning Organization,* New York: Currency/Doubleday, 1994.

40. Smith, H. J., "Who Owns Personal Data?" *Beyond Computing,* Nov./Dec. 1997.

41. Sprague, R. H., "Electronic Document Management: Challenges and Opportunities," *MIS Quarterly,* Mar. 1995.

42. Strong, D. M., et al., "Data Quality in Context," *Communications of the ACM,* May 1997.

43. Swenson, J., "Maps on the Web," *Information Week,* July 8, 1996.

44. Swift, R., "Creating Value Through a Scalable Data Warehouse Framework," *Data Management Review,* Nov. 1996.

45. Tetzeli, R., "Mapping for Dollars," *Fortune,* Oct. 18, 1993.

46. Trippi, R., and E. Turban, eds., *Neural Networks in Finance and Investing,* Chicago: Irwin Professional Publishing, 1996.

47. Tucker, M. J., "Poppin' Fresh Dough" (Database Marketing), *Datamation,* May 1997.

48. Varney, S. F., "Database Marketing Predicts Customer Loyalty," *Datamation,* Sept. 1996.

49. Vassos, T., *Strategic Internet Marketing* Indianapolis: Que, 1996.

50. Vogel, P., "Know Your Business: Build a Knowledge Base," *Datamation,* July 1996.

51. Wang, R. Y., "Total Data Quality Management," *Communications of the ACM,* Feb. 1998.

52. Wang, R. Y., et al., "What Data Quality Means to Data Consumers," *Journal of Management Information Systems,* Vol. 12, No. 4, 1996.

# CHAPTER 11

# Intelligent Support Systems

## Learning Objectives

*After studying this chapter, you will be able to:*

❶ Describe artificial intelligence and compare it to conventional computing.

❷ Identify the characteristics, structure, benefits, and limitations of expert systems.

❸ Describe the major characteristics of natural language processing and voice technologies.

❹ Describe neural computing and its differences from other computer-based technologies.

❺ Define intelligent agents and their role in IT.

❻ Describe virtual reality.

# LIFE IN THE TWENTY-FIRST CENTURY

### Driving to Work

TODAY WHEN YOU drive to work or school, you follow a routine process. You start the car and move it into the street; you try to avoid accidents; you start fighting traffic ("all those people who do not know how to drive"); and finally, you are on the freeway, speeding, trying not to be late. "Sorry," the officer says. "You were speeding." ("Everybody is speeding. Why me?") Finally you arrive at your destination, tired and stressed. For a moment, you close your eyes and say to yourself, "My job is in the marketing department. I am not a paid driver. I wish I could afford a limo." Good news. Your wish may come true in the near future.

You will enter your Autonomous Land Vehicle (ALV). You say, "Go to work, car," and slip into the back seat. The car will then start itself, open the garage door, back out into the street, and carefully drive itself to work. You can relax, watch TV, sip coffee, or just take a nap.

### Supermarket Shopping

There is no food in your place, so you need to do supermarket shopping. You will shop from work or home using the Internet, where you can see pictures of the products, compare prices, click on the items you want to order, and authorize payment by giving your secret password. A delivery is made within a few hours.

### Taking a Vacation

Work and shopping are not much fun. How about taking a trip to Hawaii—a real trip, not a virtual reality one. You can call upon your *intelligent agent* for assistance. Here is how the process works:

**Step 1**. You turn on your PC and enter your desired destination, dates, available budget, special requirements, and desired entertainment.

**Step 2**. Your computer dispatches an intelligent agent that "shops around," entering the Internet and communicating electronically with the databases of airlines, hotels, and other vendors.

**Step 3**. Your agent attempts to match your requirements against what is available, negotiating with the

**Prototypes for Autonomous Land Vehicles are already being tested.** (*Source: Communication of the ACM*, March 1994, p. 5 and *AI Expert*, September 1991.)

vendors' agents. These agents may activate other agents to make special arrangements, cooperate with each other, activate multimedia presentations, or make special inquiries.

**Step 4**. Your agent returns to you within minutes, with one or more suitable alternatives. You have a few questions; you want modifications. No problem. Within a few minutes, it's a done deal. No waiting for busy telephone operators and no human errors. Once you approve the deal, the intelligent agent will make the reservations, arrange for payments, and even report to you about any unforeseen delays in your departure.

How do you communicate with your agent? By voice, of course.

These scenarios are not as far off as they may seem. Prototype ALVs developed at Carnegie Mellon University and in Germany can already drive themselves through city traffic at about 30 mph. (*AI Expert*, September 1991 and April 1994). In California, ALVs can be seen on I-15 near San Diego (see *Los Angeles Times*, Nov. 4, 1996, p. 76 and www.monalite-mis.com/ahs/, 1998). Supermarket shopping on the Internet is a reality now (try www.pea-pod.com) and intelligent agents are moving rapidly to the commercial arena (try www.firefly.com).

SOURCE: Condensed from *Fortune*, June 24, 1994.

## ▶ 11.1 INTELLIGENT SYSTEMS AND ARTIFICIAL INTELLIGENCE

Predictions for the twenty-first century may seem like a dream, but it is only a matter of time before they become reality. Many other scenarios are on the drawing boards of research institutions and technology-oriented corporations worldwide. Common to all these scenarios is the fact that each will include intelligent computer systems. *Intelligent systems* describe the various commercial applications of artificial intelligence (AI). The field of intelligent systems is expanding rapidly. A major management consultant, A.D. Little, estimates that by the year 2000, 15 to 20 percent of all computer applications will include some intelligent systems.

The fundamentals of the major intelligent systems and the support they provide are the subjects of this chapter. We will also discuss a non-AI application, the emerging of a related technology known as virtual reality.

### ARTIFICIAL INTELLIGENCE AND INTELLIGENT BEHAVIOR

*Artificial intelligence (AI)* is a term that encompasses many definitions (see Russell and Norvig [1995] and Ramsay [1996]). Most experts agree that AI is concerned with two basic ideas. First, it involves studying the thought processes of humans; second, it deals with representing those processes via machines (computers, robots, and so on).

One well-publicized definition of AI is "behavior by a machine that, if performed by a human being, would be called *intelligent.*" Winston and Prendergast (1984) list three objectives of artificial intelligence: (1) to make machines smarter (the primary purpose), (2) to understand what intelligence is (the Nobel laureate purpose), and (3) to make machines more useful (the entrepreneurial purpose).

Let us explore the meaning of the term *intelligent behavior.* Several capabilities are considered to be signs of intelligence:

▶ Learning or understanding from experience.

▶ Making sense of ambiguous or contradictory messages.

▶ Responding quickly and successfully to a new situation.

▶ Using reasoning to solve problems and direct actions effectively.

▶ Dealing with complex situations.

▶ Understanding and inferring in ordinary, rational ways.

▶ Applying knowledge to manipulate the environment.

▶ Recognizing the relative importance of different elements in a situation.

Although AI's ultimate goal is to build machines that will mimic human intelligence, the capabilities of current intelligent systems, exemplified in commercial AI products, are far from exhibiting any significant intelligence. Nevertheless, intelligent systems are getting better with the passage of time, and they are currently useful in conducting many tasks that require some human intelligence.

An interesting test to determine whether a computer exhibits intelligent behavior was designed by Alan Turing, a British AI pioneer. According to the **Turing test**, a computer could be considered "smart" only when a human interviewer, conversing with both an unseen human being and an unseen computer, cannot determine which is which.

So far we have concentrated on the notion of intelligence. According to another definition, artificial intelligence is the branch of computer science that deals with ways of representing *knowledge*, using symbols rather than numbers, and heuristics, or rules of thumb, rather than algorithms for processing information. These properties will be explored later.

**KNOWLEDGE AND AI.** AI is frequently associated with the concept of knowledge we defined in Chapter 2. Although a computer cannot have experiences or study and learn as the human mind can, it can use knowledge given to it by human experts. Such knowledge consists of facts, concepts, theories, heuristic methods, procedures, and relationships. Knowledge is also information organized and analyzed to make it *understandable* and *applicable* to problem solving or decision making. The collection of knowledge related to a problem (or an opportunity) to be used in an intelligent system is organized and stored in a **knowledge base**.

## COMPARING ARTIFICIAL AND NATURAL INTELLIGENCE

The potential value of AI can be better understood by contrasting it with natural (human) intelligence. According to Kaplan (1984), AI has several important commercial advantages over natural intelligence.

▶ AI is more *permanent*. Natural intelligence is perishable from a commercial standpoint, because workers may take knowledge with them when they leave their place of employment or they may forget their knowledge. AI, however, is permanent as long as the computer systems and programs remain unchanged.

▶ AI offers *ease of duplication and dissemination*. Transferring a body of knowledge from one person to another usually requires a lengthy process of apprenticeship; some expertise can never be duplicated completely. Knowledge embodied in a computer system can be copied and easily moved to another computer, even across the globe.

▶ AI can be *less expensive* than natural intelligence. There are many circumstances in which buying computer services costs less than having human beings carry out the same tasks.

▶ AI, as a computer technology, is *consistent and thorough*. Natural intelligence is erratic because people are erratic; they may not perform consistently.

▶ AI can be *documented*. Decisions made by a computer can be *easily documented* by tracing the activities of the system. Natural intelligence is difficult to document; for example, a person may reach a conclusion but at some later date be unable to recreate the reasoning process that led to that conclusion or even to recall the assumptions that were a part of the decision.

Natural intelligence has several advantages over AI.

▶ Natural intelligence is *creative*, whereas AI is rather uninspired. The ability to acquire knowledge is inherent in human beings. But with AI, tailored knowledge must be built into a carefully constructed system.

▶ Natural intelligence enables people to benefit from and *directly use sensory experiences*. Many AI systems must first interpret information collected by sensors, thus providing users with indirect sensory experiences.

▶ Natural intelligence enables people to recognize relationships between things, sense qualities, and spot patterns that explain how various items interrelate.

▶ Perhaps most important, human reasoning is always able to make use of a wide *context of experiences* and bring that to bear on individual problems. In contrast, AI systems typically gain their power by having a very narrow focus.

The advantages of natural intelligence result in limitations of applied AI that will be pointed out later on.

**BENEFITS OF AI.** Despite their limitations, AI methods can be extremely valuable. They can make computers easier to use and make knowledge more widely available. The major potential benefits of AI are that it:

▶ Makes the use of some computer applications very friendly.

▶ Significantly increases the speed and consistency of problem solving.

▶ Helps solve problems which cannot be solved by conventional computing.

▶ Helps solve problems with incomplete or unclear data.

▶ Helps in handling the information overload (by summarizing or interpreting information for us).

▶ Significantly increases the productivity of performing many tasks.

▶ Helps in searching through large amounts of data.

Computers can be used to collect information about objects, events, or processes. Of course, computers can process large amounts of information more efficiently than people can. People, however, do some things instinctively that have proven to be very difficult to program into a computer.

## CONVENTIONAL VERSUS AI COMPUTING

Conventional computer programs are based on algorithms. An *algorithm* is a mathematical formula or sequential procedure that leads to a solution. The algorithm is converted into a computer program that tells the computer exactly what operations to carry out. The algorithm then uses data such as numbers, letters, or words to solve problems.

AI software is based on **symbolic processing** of knowledge. In AI, a symbol is a letter, word, or number that represents objects, processes, and their relationships. Objects can be people, things, ideas, concepts, events, or statements of fact. Using symbols, it is possible to create a knowledge base that contains facts, concepts, and the relationships that exist among them. Then various processes can be used to manipulate the symbols in order to generate advice or a recommendation for solving problems.

The major differences between AI computing and conventional computing are shown in Table 11.1.

*Table 11.1* **Conventional versus AI Computing**

| Dimension | Artificial Intelligence | Conventional Programming |
|---|---|---|
| Processing | Include symbolic conceptu- alizations | Primarily algorithmic |
| Nature of input | Can be incomplete | Must be complete |
| Search approach | Frequently uses heuristics | Frequently based on algorithms |
| Explanation | Provided | |
| Focus | Knowledge | Usually not provided |
| Maintenance and update | Relatively easy, changes can be made in self- contained modulars | Data, information Usually difficult |
| Reasoning capability | Yes | No |

**DOES A COMPUTER REALLY THINK?** Knowledge bases and search techniques certainly make computers more useful, but can they really make computers more intelligent? The fact that most AI programs are implemented by search and pattern-matching techniques *leads to the conclusion that computers are not really intelligent.* You give the computer a lot of information and some guidelines about how to use this information. The computer can then come up with a solution. But all it does is test the various alternatives and attempt to find some combination that meets the designated criteria. The computer appears to be "thinking" and often gives a satisfactory solution. But Dreyfus and Dreyfus (1988) feel that the public is being misled about AI, whose usefulness is overblown and whose goals are unrealistic. They claim, and we agree, that the human mind is just too complex to duplicate. *Computers certainly cannot think,* but they can be very useful for increasing our productivity. This is done by several commercial AI technologies.

## THE COMMERCIAL ARTIFICIAL INTELLIGENCE FIELD

The development of machines that exhibit intelligent characteristics draws upon several sciences and technologies, ranging from linguistics to mathematics (see the roots of the tree in Figure 11.1). Artificial intelligence itself is not a commercial field; it is a collection of concepts and ideas that are appropriate for research but cannot be marketed. However, AI provides the scientific foundation for several commercial technologies.

The major intelligent systems are: expert systems, natural language processing, speech understanding, robotics and sensory systems, fuzzy logic, neural computing, computer vision and scene recognition, and intelligent computer-aided instruction. In addition, a combination of two or more of the above is considered a hybrid intelligent system. These are illustrated in Figure 11.1 on page 473 (as the branches of the tree), and some are discussed next.

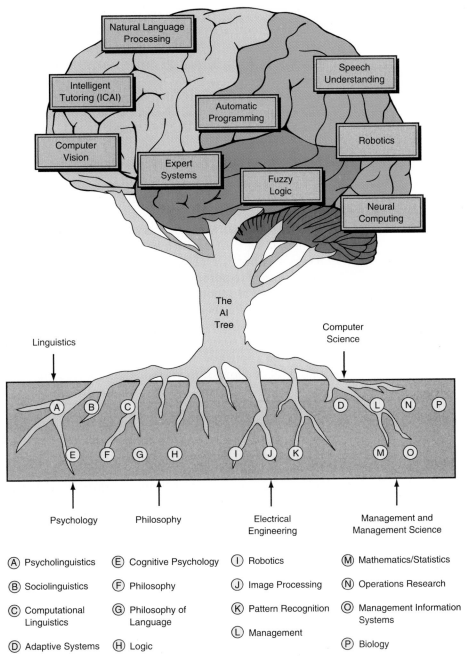

**FIGURE 11.1** The disciplines of AI (the roots) and the major applications. (*Source*: Adapted from Cercone, N., and G. McCalba, "Artificial Intelligence: Underlying Assumptions and Basic Objectives, *Journal of the American Society for Information Science,* September 1984, and from G. S. Tuthill, *Knowledge Engineering,* Blue Ridge Summit, PA: TAB Books, 1990.)

**EXPERT SYSTEMS. Expert systems (ESs)** are computerized advisory programs that attempt to imitate the reasoning processes of experts in solving difficult problems. They are in use more than any other applied AI technology. Expert systems are of great interest to organizations because they can increase productivity and augment workforces in specialty areas where human experts are becoming increasingly difficult to find and retain or are too expensive to use. Expert systems are discussed in Section 11.2 of this chapter.

**NATURAL LANGUAGE TECHNOLOGY. Natural language processing (NLP)** gives computer users the ability to communicate with the computer in human languages. Limited success in this area is typified by systems that can recognize and interpret individual words or short sentences relating to very restricted topics. The field of natural language processing is discussed in detail in Section 11.3.

**SPEECH (VOICE) UNDERSTANDING.** *Speech understanding* is the recognition and understanding by a computer of a *spoken* language. Details are given in Section 11.3.

**ROBOTICS AND SENSORY SYSTEMS.** Sensory systems such as vision systems combined with AI define a broad category of systems generally referred to as *robotics*. A **robot** is an electromechanical device that can be programmed and reprogrammed to automate manual tasks.

Not all of robotics is considered to be part of AI. A robot that performs only the actions it has been preprogrammed to perform is considered to be a "dumb" robot, possessing no more intelligence than, say, an elevator. An "intelligent" robot includes some kind of sensory apparatus, such as a camera, that collects information about the robot's operation and its environment. The intelligent part of the robot allows it to *interpret* the collected information and respond and possibly adapt to changes in its environment, rather than just follow instructions "mindlessly."

Robots combine sensory systems with mechanical motions to produce machines of widely varying abilities. Robotics is used mainly in welding, painting, and simple material handling. Assembly-line operations, particularly those that are highly repetitive or hazardous, are also beginning to be performed by robots. An example of robots' work is provided in the following *IT at Work* illustration.

---

*IT At Work* **HOSPITAL ROBOTS INCREASE QUALITY AND EFFICIENCY**

If you go to a hospital and see a robot dispensing medicine to patients, don't be alarmed. The robot, armed with a gripper, picks up medications from a storage cell and delivers them to bar-coded patient bins. The bins are then brought by hospital technicians to the nursing floors and administered to the patients.

A large hospital dispenses about 12,000 doses of medicines per day. When done manually, the dispensing may involve human errors, sometimes as much as 1 percent a day. An error may kill a patient. The robot (developed by Automated Healthcare) does not make mistakes. Furthermore, the robot keeps track of the dispensed drugs through an inventory control system built into its own software. It also increases efficiency by calculating the shortest paths for medication pickup and delivery.

**For Further Exploration:** What other hospital activities can be performed by robots? Is the robot liable for mistakes? ▲

SOURCE: Condensed from *Computerworld*, January 11, 1993.

Robots are getting more and more capable. In August 1997, the first World Cup Robot Soccer Competition was conducted in Nagoya, Japan. The robots included several AI technologies (see www.robocup.org/Robocup/).

**COMPUTER VISION AND SCENE RECOGNITION. Visual recognition** has been defined as the addition of some form of computer intelligence and decision making to digitized visual information received from a machine sensor. The combined information is then used to perform, or control, such operations as robotics movement, conveyor speeds, and production-line quality control. The basic objective of computer vision is to interpret scenarios. Computer vision is used extensively in performing industrial quality control (such as inspection of products). Would you believe that *every* Tylenol or other brand name pill is checked for defects by computers? Defective pills are removed.

Figure 11.2 illustrates how information collected by a camera (a sensor) is digitized and interpreted by a computer AI program. The computer then instructs a robot to take an action, such as removing a defective product.

**INTELLIGENT COMPUTER-AIDED INSTRUCTION.** *Intelligent computer-aided instruction (ICAI)* refers to the work of machines that can tutor humans. To a certain

> Visual recognition has been the driving force behind the growing use of robotics in industry.
> — *Dave Gehrke*

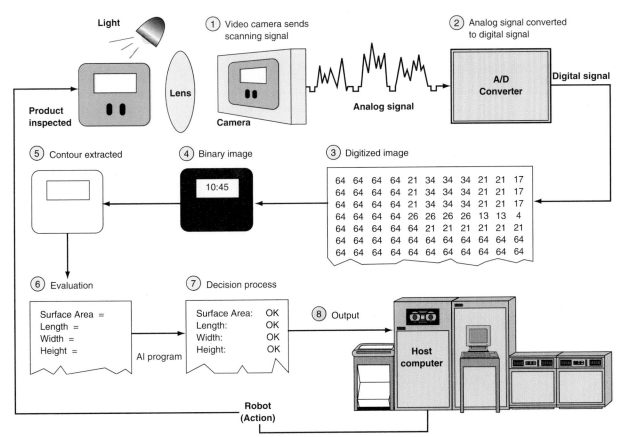

**FIGURE 11.2** Use of computer vision in quality control. (*Source: Introduction to Machine Vision,* Allen-Bradley Publication 2805-2.1, 1985, pp. 1-3.)

extent, such a machine can be viewed as an expert system. However, the major objective of an expert system is to render advice, whereas the purpose of ICAI is to teach.

Computer-assisted instruction (CAI), which has been in use for several decades, brings the power of the computer to the educational process. Now AI methods are being applied to the development of *intelligent* computer-assisted instruction systems in an attempt to create computerized "tutors" that shape their teaching techniques to fit the learning patterns of individual students.

ICAI applications are not limited to schools; as a matter of fact, they have found a sizable niche in the military and corporate sectors. ICAI systems are being used today for various tasks such as problem solving, simulation, discovery, learning, drill and practice, games, and testing. Such systems are also used to support people with physical or learning impairments. An increased number of ICAI programs are now offered on the Internet and intranet, creating virtual schools and universities. This topic is part of the topic of **distance learning** in which teachers and students are in different locations. Another application of ICAI is interpretive testing. Using this approach GMAT and other famously long tests have (or soon will have) shortened their length of time. By being able to better interpret the answers, the test can more accurately pinpoint the strengths and weaknesses of the test takers by asking fewer questions.

**MACHINE LEARNING.** Automated problem solving has been a target for generations, long before computers were invented. After computers were developed, they were used to solve structured problems with quantitative models. Such models, however, cannot solve complex problems where specialized knowledge is needed. Such knowledge can be provided, in some cases, by an expert system (ES). However, the use of an ES is limited by such factors as its rule structure, difficulties in knowledge acquisition, and the inability of the ES to learn from experience. For situations where an ES is inappropriate, we use a different approach called machine learning. **Machine learning** refers to a set of methods that attempt to teach computers to solve problems or to support problem solving by analyzing (learning from) historical cases.

This task, however, is not simple. One problem is that there are many models of learning. Sometimes it is difficult to match the learning model with the type of problem that needs to be solved. Two methods of machine learning, *neural computing* and *fuzzy logic*, are described in Section 11.3. One application is the *learning agents*, described in Section 11.4.

**HANDWRITING RECOGNIZERS.** The dream of any post office in the world is to be able to automate the reading of all handwritten address characters, regardless of their shape. Today's scanners are good at "reading" typed or printed material but they are not very good at handwriting recognition. Handwriting recognition is supported by technologies such as expert systems and neural computing and is available in some pen-based computers. (When you receive an overnight letter or a traffic violation ticket, you will probably sign for it on the screen of a pen-based computer.)

Scanners that can interpret handwritten input are subject to considerable error. To minimize mistakes, handwritten entries should follow very specific rules. Some scanners will flag handwritten entries that they cannot interpret or will automatically display for verification all input that has been scanned.

> I worked at a large restaurant chain that was implementing an online testing module for training and testing its employees. When it detected a wrong answer an illustration would be shown for the right answer.
>
> — *Blake Thompson*

Because handwritten entries are subject to misinterpretation and typed entries can be smudged, misaligned, erased, and so forth, optical scanners have an error rate considerably higher than the error rate for keyed data.

Handwriting interfaces are especially popular with slow typists. Of special interest are products such as a PDA (Technology Guide # 1).

**OTHER APPLICATIONS.** AI can be applied to several other tasks such as automatic computer programming, news summaries, and translation from one language to another. (See special discussion, *IEEE Expert*, April 1996, pp. 12–18.) The ultimate aim of automatic programming is to achieve a computer system that can develop programs by itself, in response to and in accordance with the specifications of a program developer. Some computer programs "read" stories in newspapers or other documents, including those available on the Internet, and make summaries in English or other languages This helps handle the information-overload problem (see the following *IT at Work* example).

## *IT At Work* GENERAL ELECTRIC'S SCISOR ANALYZES FINANCIAL NEWS

**G**eneral Electric's Research and Development Center has developed a natural language system called SCISOR (System for Conceptual Information Summarization, Organization, and Retrieval) that performs text analysis and question answering in a constrained domain. One application of this system deals with analyzing financial news. For example, SCISOR automatically selects and analyzes stories about corporate mergers and acquisitions from an online financial service, Dow Jones. It is able to process news at 10 seconds per story. First, it determines whether the story is about a corporate merger or acquisition. Then, it selects information such as the target, suitor, and price per share. The system allows the user to browse and ask questions such as, "What was offered for Polaroid?" or "How much was Bruck Plastics sold for?" The schematic of this answer retrieval process is shown in the accompanying diagram.

**Scisor System Architecture**

The system's effectiveness was demonstrated in testing, when it proved to be 100 percent accurate in identifying all 31 mergers and acquisitions stories that were included in a universe of 731 financial news releases from the newswire source.

**For Further Exploration:** What is the benefit of analyzing financial news via machine? What other applications might be developed with this type of system? How can such a system be combined with Internet news pushing services such as PointCast? ▲

SOURCE: Condensed from *Management Accounting*, October 1989, supplemented from www.pointcast.com, 1998.

> A vocal typing package can be used to interface with a translator to allow workers to communicate with colleagues who do not speak the same language (for example, an English-speaker can speak into a microphone and have his words displayed in French).
> — *Blake Thompson*

Computer programs are also able to translate words and simple sentences from one language to another. For example, a package called LOGUS is used for translating between English and German.

An interesting application is reported by Wee et al. (1997) where a Web-based personalized news system was developed to track news available in English, Chinese, and Malay, summarize it, and extract desired personalized news in one of these languages. In later sections we describe the major business-related AI applications in more detail.

## ▶ 11.2 EXPERT SYSTEMS

When an organization has a complex decision to make or a problem to solve, it often turns to experts for advice. These experts have specific knowledge and experience in the problem area. They are aware of alternative solutions, chances of success, and costs that the organization may incur if the problem is not solved. Companies engage experts for advice on such matters as equipment purchase, mergers and acquisitions, and advertising strategy. The more unstructured the situation, the more specialized and expensive is the advice. *Expert systems (ES)* are an attempt to mimic human experts. Expert systems are the most widely applied and commercially successful AI technology.

### CONCEPTS OF EXPERT SYSTEMS

In order to explore the concepts involved in ES let us review a well-known application case at General Electric in the following illustration:

 **IT At Work**    GENERAL ELECTRIC'S EXPERT SYSTEM MODELS HUMAN TROUBLESHOOTERS

**THE PROBLEM. General Electric's** (GE) top locomotive field service engineer, David I. Smith, had been with the company for more than 40 years and was expert at troubleshooting diesel electric locomotive engines. Smith was traveling throughout the country to places where locomotives were in need of repair, to determine what was wrong and advise young engineers about what to do. The company was very dependent on Smith. The problem was that he was nearing retirement.

**THE TRADITIONAL SOLUTION.** GE's traditional approach to such a situation was to create apprenticeship teams that paired senior and junior engineers for several months or even years. By the time the older engineers retired, the younger engineers had absorbed

*U*SING IT

...in Production &
Operations Management

enough of their expertise to carry on. It was a good short-term solution, but GE still wanted a more effective and dependable way of disseminating expertise among its engineers and preventing valuable knowledge from retiring with people like David Smith.

**THE ES SOLUTION.** GE decided to build an expert system to solve the problem by modeling the way a human troubleshooter works. The system builders spent several months interviewing Smith and transferring his knowledge to a computer. The computer programming was prototyped over a three-year period, slowly increasing the knowledge and number of decision rules stored in the computer. The new diagnostic technology enables a novice engineer or even a technician to uncover a fault by spending only a few minutes at the computer terminal. The system can also explain to the user the logic of its advice, serving as a teacher. Furthermore, the system can lead users through the required repair procedures, presenting a detailed, computer-aided drawing of parts and subsystems and providing specific how-to instructional demonstrations. It is based on a flexible, humanlike thought process, rather than rigid procedures expressed in flowcharts or decision trees.

The system, which was developed on a minicomputer but operates on PCs, is currently installed at every railroad repair shop served by GE, thus eliminating delays, preserving Smith's expertise, and boosting maintenance productivity.

**For Further Exploration:** If an expert system can replace David Smith, why not replace all experts in the world with expert systems? ▲

Typically, an ES is decision-making software that can reach a level of performance comparable to—or even exceeding that of—a human expert in some specialized and usually narrow problem area. The basic idea behind an ES is simple. *Expertise* is transferred from an expert (or other sources of expertise) to the computer. This knowledge is then stored in the computer. Users can call on the computer for specific advice as needed. The computer can make inferences and arrive at a conclusion. Then, like a human expert, it advises the nonexperts and explains, if necessary, the logic behind the advice. ESs can sometimes perform better than any single expert can.

**EXPERTISE AND KNOWLEDGE.** *Expertise* is the extensive, task-specific knowledge acquired from training, reading, and experience. It enables experts to make better and faster decisions than nonexperts in solving complex problems. Expertise takes a long time (usually several years) to acquire, and it is distributed in organizations in an uneven manner. Figure 11.3 demonstrates a typical distribution of knowledge in an organization.

**FIGURE 11.3** Distribution of expertise: percent successes achieved per decil. A senior expert possesses about 30 times more expertise than a junior expert. (*Source*: Adapted from Augustine, N. R., "Distribution of Expertise," *Defense Systems Management*, Spring 1979.)

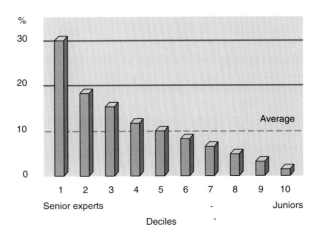

The transfer of expertise from an expert to a computer and then to the user involves four activities: *knowledge acquisition* (from experts or other sources), *knowledge representation* (in the computer), *knowledge inferencing,* and *knowledge transfer* to the user.

Knowledge is acquired from experts or from documented sources. Through the activity of knowledge representation, acquired knowledge is organized as rules or frames (object-oriented) and stored, electronically, in a knowledge base. A unique feature of an expert system is its ability to reason. Given the necessary expertise stored in the knowledge base and accessibility to databases, the computer is programmed so that it can make inferences. The inferencing is performed in a component called the **inference engine** and results in an advice or a recommendation for novices. Thus, the expert's knowledge has been *transferred* to users.

A unique feature of an ES is its ability to explain its recommendation. The explanation and justification is done in a subsystem called the *justifier* or the *explanation subsystem.*

## BENEFITS OF EXPERT SYSTEMS

During the past few years, the technology of expert systems has been successfully applied in thousands of organizations worldwide to problems ranging from AIDS research to the analysis of dust in mines. Other illustrative applications are shown in the following *IT at Work.*

---

### *IT At Work*   INNOVATIVE EXPERT SYSTEMS—A SAMPLER

Of the many innovative expert systems on the market, the following are of particular interest.

*Pitch expert.* This large system was implemented in **Kraft pulp mills** in Canada to analyze and diagnose problems associated with pitch dirt and pitch deposition. The solutions require special expertise, which must be up-to-date. When experts are unavailable, or when the experts are not fully trained, losses of up to $80 million can occur. The system increases productivity in close to 40 Canadian mills representing over 20 companies. Savings there are estimated at $22 million annually.

The system is used also for training employees. Since the problems of pulp mills are similar, the system is used not only by 20 Canadian companies but also by companies in other countries. (SOURCE: Condensed from *AI Magazine,* Fall 1993.)

*Expert configurator.* **Carrier Corporation**, a major air conditioning manufacturer, introduced expert systems into its operations. *Expert* configures a set of part numbers for each particular equipment order based on customer requests. Not only is it necessary to compute the best design combination, but it is also necessary to procure all the parts and subsystems so the orders can be filled on time. Using an ES, Carrier was able to minimize both pricing and configuration errors, reduce cycle time, and increase customer satisfaction as well as profitability. (SOURCE: Based on Heatley, J., et al., "An Evaluation of an Innovative IT—The Case of Carrier *Expert," Journal of Strategic Information Systems,* Vol. 4, No. 3, 1995.)

*Expert auditor.* The **State Street Bank and Trust Company** operates in a highly competitive financial services field. To stay ahead of the competition, it is using expert systems to improve its daily operations. One application electronically audits daily and month-end data against the corresponding general ledger account balance, highlighting any exceptions. The client/server-based application provides online access to the audit exceptions via object request broker technology. Accounting data are examined by audit and proofing processes. The system significantly increased the productivity of the auditors as well as the quality of error detection. (SOURCE: Based on Engler, N., "State Street Bank and Trust Co.," *Computerworld*, August 1996.)

**For Further Exploration:** Is there anything common to these three systems? ▲

---

Why have ESs become so popular? Because of the large number of capabilities and benefits they provide. The major ones are:

**INCREASED OUTPUT AND PRODUCTIVITY.** ESs can work faster than humans. For example, a system called XCON has enabled Digital Equipment Corporation (DEC) to increase fourfold the production preparation of minicomputers customized for clients. The system plans the configuration of components for each customized order of minicomputers and is an example of support to *mass customization* approach.

**INCREASED QUALITY.** ESs can increase quality by providing consistent advice and reducing the error rates. For example, XCON reduced the error rate of configuring computer orders at DEC from 35 percent to 2 percent.

**CAPTURE OF SCARCE EXPERTISE AND ITS DISSEMINATION.** One of the main benefits of ES is its ease of transferring expertise across international boundaries. An example of such a transfer is an eye-care ES for diagnosis and recommended treatment that was developed at Rutgers University. The program has been implemented in Egypt and Algeria, where serious eye diseases are prevalent but eye specialists are rare. The program can be operated by a physician's assistant or nurse.

**OPERATION IN HAZARDOUS ENVIRONMENTS.** Many tasks require humans to operate in hazardous environments. ESs that interpret information collected by sensors enable workers to avoid hot, humid, or toxic environments, such as a nuclear power plant that has malfunctioned.

**ACCESSIBILITY TO KNOWLEDGE AND HELP DESKS.** Expert systems make knowledge (and information) accessible to many people in several locations. People can query systems and receive advice. One area of applicability is in the support of help desks. Over 30 million employees work at help desks in the United States providing information to customers who drop in or call. For example, the IRS provides help to taxpayers, a library provides assistance to students, a receptionist in an office assists visitors. An ES can increase the productivity of help desk employees or even automate it.

**RELIABILITY.** ESs are reliable. They do not become tired or bored, call in sick, or go on strike. They also consistently pay attention to all details and do not overlook relevant information and potential solutions.

**INCREASED CAPABILITIES OF OTHER COMPUTERIZED SYSTEMS.** Integration of an ES with other systems makes the other systems more effective; the integrated systems cover more applications, work faster, and produce higher-quality results.

**ABILITY TO WORK WITH INCOMPLETE OR UNCERTAIN INFORMATION.** In contrast to conventional computer systems, an ES can work with incomplete information, like human experts. The user can respond with a "don't know" or "not sure" answer to one or more of the system's questions during a consultation, and the ES will still be able to produce an answer, although it may not be a certain one.

**PROVISION OF TRAINING.** An ES can facilitate training. Novices who work with an ES become more and more experienced. The explanation facility can serve as a teaching device, and so can notes that may be inserted into the knowledge base.

**ENHANCEMENT OF PROBLEM-SOLVING CAPABILITIES.** ESs enhance problem solving by allowing the integration of top experts' judgments into analysis. Thus, an ES can solve problems where the required scope of knowledge exceeds that of any individual.

**DECREASED DECISION-MAKING TIME.** Using the system's recommendation, a human can make much faster decisions. For example, American Express authorizers make charge authorization decisions in less than 30 seconds versus about three minutes before implementation of the ES.

**REDUCED DOWNTIME.** Many operational ESs are used for diagnosing malfunctions and prescribing repairs. By using ES it is possible to reduce machine downtime significantly. For example, one day of lost time on an oil rig cost as much as $250,000. A system called Drilling Advisor was developed to detect malfunctions in oil rigs. This system saved a considerable amount of money for the company involved by significantly reducing the downtime.

## THE LIMITATIONS

Available ES methodologies are not always straightforward and effective. Here are some problems that have slowed the commercial spread of ES:

▶ Knowledge to be captured is not always readily available.

▶ Expertise is hard to extract from humans.

▶ The approach of each expert to a situation may be different, yet correct.

▶ It is hard, even for a highly skilled expert, to accurately assess situations under time pressure.

▶ Users of expert systems have natural cognitive limits, so they may not use the benefits of the system to the fullest extent.

▶ ES works well only with narrowly defined subject areas such as diagnosing a malfunction in a machine.

▶ Most expert systems have no independent means of checking whether their conclusions are reasonable or correct.

Idioms, slang, and regional terminology are also difficult to program into an ES.

— *Mike Rewald*

▶ The vocabulary, or jargon, that experts use for expressing facts and relations is frequently limited and not understood by others.

▶ Help in building ES is frequently required from knowledge engineers who are rare and expensive—a fact that could make ES construction rather costly.

▶ Lack of trust by end users may be a barrier to ES use.

▶ Knowledge transfer is subject to perceptual and judgmental biases.

▶ Liability for bad advice provided by an ES is difficult to assess.

In addition, expert systems may not be able to arrive at conclusions (especially in early stages of system development). For example, even the fully developed XCON is unable to fulfill about 2 percent of the orders presented to it. Finally, expert systems, like human experts, sometimes produce incorrect recommendations. Some of these limitations may diminish when the forthcoming ES generations mature.

## PROCESSES AND COMPONENTS OF EXPERT SYSTEMS

The following components exist in an expert system: knowledge base, inference engine, blackboard (workplace), user interface, and explanation subsystem (justifier). Future systems will include a knowledge-refining component. The relationships among components are shown in Figure 11.4.

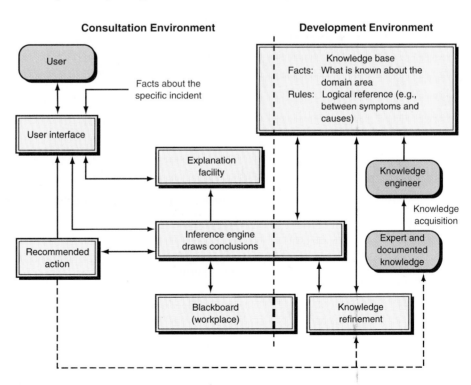

**FIGURE 11.4** Structure and process of an expert system.

**THE PROCESS OF ES.** The process of ES can be divided into two parts: first, the system development (shown as development environment in Figure 11.4), in which the ES is constructed; and second, the consultation environment (left side of Figure 11.4), which describes how advice is rendered to the users.

The development process starts with the knowledge engineer, or the system builder, acquiring knowledge from experts and/or documented sources. This knowledge is programmed in the knowledge base as facts about the subject area (domain) and knowledge in terms of if-then rules.

The consultation environment includes the user, who contacts the system via a user interface to ask for advice. The ES provides advice by activating an inference engine. The engine searches the knowledge base for recommended action based on the facts or symptoms provided by the user and can provide limited explanations. To execute its tasks, the inference engine uses a temporary database called the blackboard. Finally, the knowledge in the database may be refined as experience is accumulated through repetitive consultations. An example of a consultation is provided in the following *IT at Work* illustration.

---

*IT At Work*   HOW TO SELECT AN ADVERTISEMENT MEDIUM—A SAMPLE OF AN ES CONSULTATION

This prototype system will attempt to provide recommendation(s) on the advertising mix so as to maximize the client's product exposure in the market. Presently, the system only makes recommendations on two types of advertising media: television and newspaper.

*U*SING IT
...in Marketing

Sample Printout of Consultation: The system will ask the user several questions, such as the one shown below, to find the requirements and/or symptoms of the problem.

```
EXSYS Pro ══════ You may select ONLY ONE value ══════

        Client prefer
            1   Only TV media
            2   Only Newspaper media
            3   More TV media
            4   More Newspaper media
            5   No preference indicated




                    ⇕ ►► why_
Enter the value number<s> or select with arrow keys and press <ENTER>
WHY  QUIT  <H>-help  Memo <F10>
```

The user may ask the computer *why* (why you need this information). The computer answers by displaying the pertinent rule (#1).

```
EXSYS Pro ══════ RULE NUMBER: 1 ══════

  IF:
       <1> Client prefer ONLY TV media
  THEN:
            All budget on TV - Confidence=8/10

  NOTE:  The client is always right. We should always try to meet the
  client's expectations. If the client prefers only TV as the
  advertising medium for product exposure, we should accomodate it.




IF line # for derivation <K>-known data  <C>-choices
↑or↓ - prev. or next rule <J>-jump  <H>-help <F10>-Memo <ENTER>-Done:
```

The computer continues with questions such as:

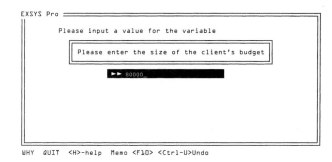

```
EXSYS Pro ════════════════════════════════════════════════

        Please input a value for the variable

      ┌─────────────────────────────────────────────────┐
      │  Please enter the size of the client's budget    │
      └─────────────────────────────────────────────────┘
               ►► 80000_




WHY   QUIT   <H>-help   Memo <F10> <Ctrl-U>Undo
```

Once all questions have been answered by the user, the expert system displays the recommendations:

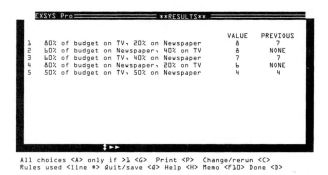

```
EXSYS Pro══════════════════════**RESULTS**═══════════════

                                            VALUE    PREVIOUS
  1    80% of budget on TV, 20% on Newspaper    8        7
  2    60% of budget on Newspaper, 40% on TV    8      NONE
  3    60% of budget on TV, 40% on Newspaper    7        7
  4    80% of budget on Newspaper, 20% on TV    6      NONE
  5    50% of budget on TV, 50% on Newspaper    4        4




            ↕ ►►
All choices <A>  only if >1 <G>   Print <P>   Change/rerun <C>
Rules used <line #> Quit/save <Q> Help <H> Memo <F10> Done <D>
```

Note: Printouts generated with EXSYS PRO (now Resolver) from MultiLogic Corporation. ▲

**THE COMPONENTS OF ES.** A brief description of the major components follows:

▶ The *knowledge base* contains knowledge necessary for understanding, formulating, and solving problems. It includes two basic elements: (1) facts, such as the problem situation and theory of the problem area, and (2) rules that direct the use of knowledge to solve specific problems in a particular domain.

▶ The *blackboard* is an area of working memory set aside for the description of a current problem, as specified by the input data; it is also used for recording intermediate results. It is a kind of database.

▶ The "brain" of the ES is the *inference engine,* essentially a computer program that provides a methodology for reasoning and formulating conclusions.

▶ The user *interface* in ES allows for user-computer dialog, which can be best carried out in a natural language, usually presented as questions and answers and sometimes supplemented by graphics. The dialog triggers the inference engine to match the problem symptoms with the knowledge in the knowledge base and generate advice.

▶ The ability to trace responsibility for conclusions to their source is crucial both in the transfer of expertise and in problem solving. The *explanation subsystem* can trace such responsibility and explain the ES's behavior by interactively answering questions such as the following: *Why* was a certain question asked by the expert system? *How* was a certain conclusion reached? *Why* was a certain alternative rejected? Or *What* is the plan to reach the solution?

▶ Human experts have a *knowledge refining* system; that is, they can analyze their own performance, learn from it, and improve it for future consultations. Similarly, such evaluation is necessary in computerized learning so that the program will be able to improve by analyzing the reasons for its success or failure. Such a component is not available in many commercial expert systems at the moment, but it is being developed in experimental ES.

Expert systems can provide management with inexpensive, innovative solutions to problems requiring expertise. For details see Awad (1996), Beerel (1993), and the next section.

## ILLUSTRATIVE APPLICATIONS

Expert systems are in use today in all types of organizations. They are especially useful in ten generic categories, displayed in Table 11.2. The following examples illustrate the diversity and nature of ES applications.

***Table 11.2*** **Generic Categories of Expert Systems**

| Category | Problem Addressed |
| --- | --- |
| 1. Interpretation | Inferring situation descriptions from observations |
| 2. Prediction | Inferring likely consequences of given situations |
| 3. Diagnosis | Inferring system malfunctions from observations |
| 4. Design | Configuring objects under constraints |
| 5. Planning | Developing plans to achieve goal(s) |
| 6. Monitoring | Comparing observations to plans, flagging exceptions |
| 7. Debugging | Prescribing remedies for malfunctions |
| 8. Repair | Executing a plan to administer a prescribed remedy |
| 9. Instruction | Diagnosing, debugging, and correcting student performance |
| 10. Control | Interpreting, predicting, repairing, and monitoring systems behavior |

### THE U.S. DEPARTMENT OF THE TREASURY FIGHTS CRIMINALS WITH AN EXPERT SYSTEM

***The Problem.*** One of the major tasks of the U.S. Financial Crime Enforcement Network (FinCEN) is to prevent and detect money laundering. One area of investigation is cash transactions over $10,000, which all banks must report. The problem is that there are over 200,000 such transactions every week (over 12,000,000/year). For well-trained analysts to examine all of this requires a large staff, which FinCEN is not budgeted for.

***The Solution.*** The solution was found by the use of a rule-based expert system that contains the expertise of FinCEN's top experts. The expert system is used to detect suspicious transactions and changes in transactions' patterns. These are then checked manually.

*Use and Results.* In the five years since its inception in 1993, the expert system has helped to uncover more than 400 cases of money-laundering activities valued at over $1 billion. (SOURCE: Condensed from *PC AI*, Jan./Feb. 1998.)

### TICKETING AUDITING AT NORTHWEST AIRLINES

*The Problem.* When Northwest Airlines (NWA) acquired Republic Airlines, its volume of operations increased to 70,000 tickets per day. These tickets needed to be audited by comparing a copy of each ticket against fare information including travel agent commissions. Manual comparison was slow and expensive. Therefore, only *samples* of the tickets (about 1 percent) were audited. The sample indicated an error rate of about 10 percent (usually a loss to the airline).

*The Solution.* A ticket-auditing ES was built in which all tickets are scanned electronically and stored in a database. Another database stores all the fares and commission agreements. Then the expert system goes to work. The system first determines the correct fare, using 250 rules. Then the most favorable commission to travel agents is determined. Any discrepancy results in a report to the agent, with a debit or credit and an appropriate explanation. The system also provides information for marketing, contract management, planning, and control.

*The Results.* The system initially processed 70,000 tickets each night on a Sun workstation. Future growth can be handled easily. The reduction in agent errors saves NWA about $10 million annually. (SOURCE: Condensed from Smith and Scott [1991].)

### DUSTPRO—ENVIRONMENTAL CONTROL IN MINES

*The Problem.* The majority of the 2,000 active mines in the United States are medium or small sized. They cannot afford a full-time dust control engineer, whose major job is to reevaluate and reassign facilities, each time operating conditions change. However, if a dust control engineer is not readily available, the mine must be shut down until an expert arrives. Experts are expensive but so is downtime, so any changing conditions can be costly. Operating without appropriate testing and interpretation of results is a violation of federal regulations.

*The Solution.* DustPro is a small rule-based system developed by the U.S. Bureau of Mines. It includes about 200 rules and was developed with a Level 5 shell (from Information Builders) on a microcomputer. The system is now in operation in hundreds of mines.

DustPro advises in three areas: control of methane gas emission, ventilation in continuous operations, and dust control for the mine's machines. Data on air quality is entered manually. The user interface is very friendly. The system is composed of 13 subareas of expertise, and the average consultation time is 10 to 15 minutes.

*System Use.* Through a series of questions, DustPro determines what types of ventilation are used, what the dust standard is, and which type of mine is most affected by the dust. Then, the system can advise the operators what to do if problems are suspected. The system and its variants are used at the U.S. Bureau of Mines Pittsburgh Research Center to diagnose problems telephoned in or e-mailed by mine operators. The staff can now respond more quickly and devote more time to research and development. The system is so successful that more than ten countries have requested permission to use it in their mines. (SOURCE: Condensed from an Information Builders publicity publication.)

## EXPERT SYSTEMS AND THE INTERNET/INTRANET

The relationship between ESs and the Internet and intranets is like a two-way street. The Net supports ESs (and other AI) applications and ESs supports the Net.

**USING ES ON THE NET.** One of the justifications for an ES is the potential to provide knowledge and advice to large numbers of users. By disseminating knowledge to many users, the cost per user becomes small, making ESs very attractive. However, according to Eriksson [1996], attaining this goal has proven to be very difficult. Because advisory systems are used infrequently, they need a large number of users to justify their construction. As a result, a very few ESs were disseminating knowledge to many users. The widespread availability and use of the Internet and intranets provide the opportunity to disseminate expertise and knowledge to mass audiences. Implementing expert systems (and other intelligent systems) as knowledge servers, it becomes economically feasible and profitable to publish expertise on the Net. This implementation approach is described in Eriksson (1996).

ESs can be transferred over the Net not only to human users, but also to other computerized systems, including DSS, robotics, and databases. Another possibility is ES construction over the Net. Here, collaboration between builders, experts, and knowledge engineers can be facilitated by intranet-based groupware. This can reduce the cost of building ES. Knowledge acquisition costs can be reduced, for example, in cases where there are several experts, or where the expert(s) is in a different location from the knowledge engineer. Knowledge maintenance can also facilitate the use of the Net, which is also helpful to users.

Finally, the Web can support the spread of multimedia-based expert systems. Such systems, referred to as *intelimedia systems,* support the integration of extensive multimedia applications and ES. Such systems can be very helpful for remote users, such as in the tourism industry and in remote equipment failure diagnosis (for details, see Fuerst et al. [1995]). The Internet provides an opportunity for the government to disseminate ESs as shown in the *IT at Work* case.

 **WEB-BASED EXPERT SYSTEMS**

USING IT
...in Public Service

*1. The government uses expert systems.* Want to see the latest ES developments at the United States Department of Labor Occupational Safety and Health Administration (OSHA)? Access the OSHA Web site: www.osha.gov. OSHA has an up-and-running Web-based ES developed and deployed in the EXSYS Web Run Time Engine (WREN). Try the Confined Spaces Advisor that provides guidance to help employers protect workers from the hazards of entry into permit-required confined spaces. The system helps determine if a space is covered by OSHA's Permit-Required Confined Spaces Regulation. The software is rich in detail and uses a Web browser as an interface. Run it and see if you need a special government permit to work in your room. The ES is running at http://www.osha.gov

/Wren/csa.html (you can also download a Windows run-time version along with several other safety-advising ESs). More applications are coming soon!

   **2.  *Financial advising system.*** Restricted stocks are those owned by the officers and management within a company, or investors who purchased stocks before the company went public. Many ever-changing rules restrict the sale of such stocks. The laws are complex, and experts on restricted stocks are fairly scarce. MultiLogic Corp. provides a free Web-based expert system that advises you what to do in case you own such stock (www.restrictedstock.com). SOURCE: Condensed from *PC AI*, November/December 1997.

The major potential contributions of intelligent systems to the Internet are summarized in Table 11.3 (for details see O'Leary [1996]).

*Table 11.3*  **Artificial Intelligence Contributions to the Internet**

| Technology | Application |
| --- | --- |
| Intelligent agents | Assist Web browsing |
| Intelligent agents | Assist in finding information |
| Intelligent agents | Assist in matching items |
| Intelligent agents | Filter e-mail |
| Intelligent agents<br>Expert systems | Access databases, summarize information |
| Intelligent agents | Improve Internet security |
| Expert systems | Match queries to users with "canned" answers to frequently asked questions (FAQs) |
| WWW robots (spiders),<br>   Intelligent agents | Conduct information retrieval and discovery, smart search engines ("metasearch") |
| Expert systems | Intelligent browsing of qualitative databases |
| Expert systems | Browse large documents (knowledge decomposition) |
| Intelligent agents | Monitor data and alert for actions (e.g., looking for Web site changes), monitor users and usage. |

   Information about the relationship of expert systems, intelligent agents, and other AI systems and the Internet is readily available on the Internet itself. For example, Hengl (1995) provides a list of over 1,600 AI-related Web sites.

## ▶ 11.3  OTHER INTELLIGENT SYSTEMS: FROM VOICE TO NEURAL COMPUTING

An expert system's major objective is to provide expert advice. However, due to their limitations, expert systems can be used only for special situations. Other intelligent systems can broaden the range of applications. Two approaches can be used: first, other intelligent systems can be integrated with ESs or among themselves, creating hybrid intelligent systems that have many capabilities and enjoy synergy among the various technologies; and second, these technologies can be used alone to solve problems in areas in which they excel. Four such technologies are described next.

## NATURAL LANGUAGE PROCESSING AND VOICE TECHNOLOGY

Natural language processing (NLP) refers to communicating with a computer in English or whatever language you may speak. Today, to tell a computer what to do, you type commands in the keyboard. In responding to a user, the computer outputs message symbols or other short, cryptic notes of information.

Many problems could be minimized or even eliminated if we could communicate with the computer in our own languages. We would simply type in directions, instructions, or information. Better yet, we would converse with the computer using voice. The computer would be smart enough to interpret the input, regardless of its format.

To understand a natural language inquiry, a computer must have the knowledge to analyze and then interpret the input. This may include linguistic knowledge about words, domain knowledge, common sense knowledge, and even knowledge about the users and their goals. Once the computer understands the input, it can take the desired action.

In this section we briefly discuss:

▶ Natural language *understanding*, which investigates methods of allowing a computer to comprehend instructions given in ordinary English, via the keyboard or by voice, so computers are able to understand people.

▶ Natural language *generation*, which strives to allow computers to produce ordinary English language, on the screen or by voice (known as voice synthesis), so people can understand computers more easily.

**APPLICATIONS OF NATURAL LANGUAGE PROCESSING.**  Natural language processing programs have been applied in several areas. The most important are: human–computer interfaces (mainly to databases), abstracting and summarizing text, grammar analysis, translation of a natural language to another natural language, translation of a computer language to another computer language, speech understanding, and composing letters (see Figure 11.5).

By far the most dominant use of NLP is in interfaces, or "front-ends," for

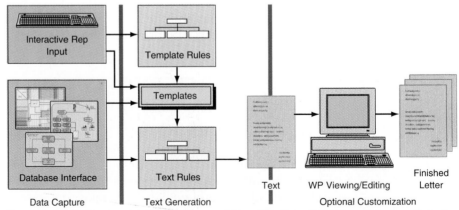

**FIGURE 11.5** Composing letters by machine. The functional breakdown of Ombudsman, a product that was an intelligent correspondence generation (ICG) in composing documents is diagrammed here. (*Source*: Courtesy of Cognitive Systems, New Haven, CT.)

other software packages, especially databases and database management systems. Such *front-end interfaces* are used to simplify and improve communications between application programs and the user. The natural language front-end allows the user to operate the applications programs with everyday language.

**SPEECH (VOICE) RECOGNITION AND UNDERSTANDING. Speech recognition** is a process that allows us to communicate with a computer by speaking to it. The term *speech recognition* is sometimes applied only to the first part of the process—recognizing words that have been spoken without necessarily interpreting their meanings. The other part of the process, wherein the meaning of speech is ascertained, is called **speech understanding.** It may be possible to understand the meaning of a spoken sentence without actually recognizing every word and vice versa. When a speech recognition system is combined with a natural language processing system, the result is an overall system that not only recognizes voice input but also understands it.

**ADVANTAGES OF SPEECH RECOGNITION.** The ultimate goal of speech recognition is to allow a computer to understand the natural speech of any human speaker at least as well as a human listener could understand it. In addition to the fact that this is the most natural method of communication, speech recognition offers several other advantages.

▶ *Ease of access.* Many more people can speak than can type. As long as communication with a computer depends on developing typing skills, many people may not be able to use computers effectively.

▶ *Speed.* Even the most competent typists can speak more quickly than they can type. It is estimated that the average person can speak twice as quickly as a proficient typist can type.

▶ *Manual freedom.* Obviously, communicating with a computer through typing occupies your hands. There are many situations in which computers might be useful to people whose hands are otherwise occupied, such as product assemblers, pilots of military aircraft, and busy executives.

▶ *Remote access.* Many computers are set up to be accessed remotely by telephones. If a remote database includes speech recognition capabilities, you could retrieve information by issuing oral commands into a telephone.

▶ *Accuracy.* In typing information, people are prone to make mistakes, especially in spelling. These are minimized with voice input.

**LIMITATIONS.** The major limitation of speech understanding is its inability to recognize long sentences, or the need to accomplish it very slowly. The better the system the higher the cost. Also, you cannot manipulate wall icons and windows, so speech may need to be combined with the keyboard entry, which slows it down.

**VOICE SYNTHESIS.** The technology by which computers speak is known as **voice synthesis.** The synthesis of voice by computer differs from the simple playback of a prerecorded voice by either analog or digital means. As the term *synthesis* implies, sounds that make up words and phrases are constructed electronically from basic sound components and can be made to form any desired voice pattern.

The current quality of synthesized voice is very good, but the technology remains somewhat expensive. Anticipated lower cost and improved performance of synthetic voice should encourage more widespread commercial applications in the near future. Opportunities for its use will encompass almost all applications that can provide an automated response to a user, such as inquiries by employees pertaining to payroll and benefits. Several banks already offer a voice service to their customers, informing them about their balance, which checks were cashed, and so on. For a list of voice synthesis and voice recognition applications see Table 11.4.

The State of Minnesota's Tax Department is a typical example using an interactive voice system via the telephone. With limited staffing and more than 25

*Table 11.4* **Sample of Voice Technology Applications**

| Company | Applications |
| --- | --- |
| Scandinavian Airlines, other airlines | Answering inquiries about reservations, schedules, lost baggage, etc.[a] |
| Citibank, many other banks | Informing credit card holders about balances and credits, providing bank account balances and other information to customers[a] |
| Delta Dental Plan (CA) | Verifying coverage information[a] |
| Federal Express | Requesting pickups |
| Illinois Bell, other telephone companies | Giving information about services, receiving orders[a] |
| Domino's Pizza | Enabling stores to order supplies, providing price information[a,b] |
| General Electric, Rockwell International, Austin Rover, Westpoint Pepperell, Eastman Kodak | Allowing inspectors to report results of quality assurance tests[b] |
| Cara Donna Provisions | Allowing receivers of shipments to report weights and inventory levels of various meats and cheeses[b] |
| Weidner Insurance, AT&T | Conducting market research and telemarketing[b] |
| U.S. Department of Energy, Idaho National Engineering Laboratory, Honeywell | Notifying people of emergencies detected by sensors[a] |
| New Jersey Department of Education | Notifying parents when students are absent and about cancellation of classes[a] |
| Kaiser-Permanente Health Foundation (HMO) | Calling patients to remind them of appointments, summarizing and reporting results[a] |
| Car manufacturers | Activating radios, heaters, and so on, by voice[b] |
| Taxoma Medical Center | Logging in and out by voice to payroll department[b] |
| St. Elizabeth's Hospital | Prompting doctors in the emergency room to conduct all necessary tests, reporting of results by doctors[a,b] |
| Hospital Corporation of America | Sending and receiving patient data by voice, searching for doctors, preparing schedules and medical records[a,b] |

Output device[a]

Input device[b]

*Source*: Based on Turban (1992).

percent of Minnesota residents without touch-tone dialing service, the Department of Revenue needed to find an innovative solution to meet its increasing tax inquiry phone load and expand its service. In 1993, the department put speech recognition technology into place. As a result, it was able to respond immediately to an additional 100,000 phone inquiries per year from taxpayers that could not have been handled otherwise. (SOURCE: *Communication News,* May 1996.)

American Express Travel Related Services (AETRS) is using a voice recognition system that allows its customers to check and book domestic flights by talking to a computer over the phone. The system asks customers questions such as: Where do you want to travel to? from where? when? and so on. The system can handle 350 city and airport names, and lets callers use more than 10,000 different ways to identify a location.

Compared to telephone served by an operator, reservation transaction cost is reduced by 50 percent. The average transaction time is reduced from 7 to 2 minutes. AETRS offers a similar service on the Web.

## NEURAL COMPUTING

The tools of AI have been mostly restricted to sequential processing and only to certain representations of knowledge and logic. A different approach to intelligent systems is performing computing with architecture that mimics certain processing capabilities of the brain. The results are knowledge representations and processing based on massive parallel processing, fast retrieval of large amounts of information, and the ability to recognize patterns based on experiences. The technology that attempts to achieve these results is called **neural computing** or **artificial neural networks (ANN).**

**BIOLOGICAL AND ARTIFICIAL NEURAL NETWORKS.** Artificial neural networks are biologically inspired. Specifically, they borrow ideas from the manner in which the human brain works. The human brain is composed of special cells called *neurons.* Estimates of the number of neurons in a human brain cover a wide range—up to 150 billion—and there are more than a hundred different kinds of neurons separated into groups called networks. Each network contains several thousand neurons that are highly interconnected. Thus, the brain can be viewed as a collection of neural networks.

An artificial neural network (ANN) is a computer model that emulates a biological neural network. Today's neural computing uses a very limited set of concepts from biological neural systems to implement software simulations of massive parallel processes that involve processing elements interconnected in a network architecture. The artificial neuron receives inputs analogous to the electrochemical impulses biological neurons receive from other neurons. The output of the artificial neuron corresponds to signals sent out from a biological neuron. These artificial signals can be changed, like the signals from the human brain. Neurons in an ANN receive information from other neurons or from external sources, transform the information, and pass it on to other neurons or external outputs.

The manner in which an ANN processes information depends on its structure and on the algorithm used to process the information.

**COMPONENTS AND STRUCTURE OF ANN.** ANNs are composed of artificial neurons; these are the *processing elements.* Each of the neurons receives input(s),

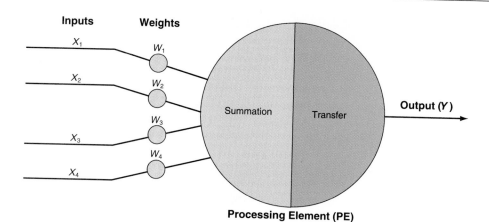

**FIGURE 11.6** Processing information in an artificial neuron.

processes the input(s), and delivers a single or a few outputs. This process is shown in Figure 11.6 (with a single output).

Inputs that describe the attributes of the problem (such as the personal information and income in the case of a request for a loan) are entered into the processing element (PE). First, they are multiplied by "weights," which express the relative strengths of the inputs. These weights are adjusted based on past experience, and continue to be adjusted as new cases are processed. Weights are crucial; it is through repeated adjustments of weights that the network "learns." The output is computed by summing the weighted inputs, and using a special transfer algorithm to do the output calculation. The output can become input for another PE that is situated in another layer of PEs. In Figure 11.7 (see page 495) we show the input layer of PEs, an intermediate layer (called a hidden layer), and an output that may include one (or several) output PEs. Each ANN is composed of three or more layers of PEs. Note the interconnections that exist between any PE and the various PEs at a forward layer.

Like biological networks, neurons can be interconnected in different ways. In processing information, many of the processing elements perform their computations at the same time. This **parallel processing** resembles the way the brain works, and it differs from the serial processing of conventional computing.

**PROCESSING INFORMATION IN THE NETWORK.** Once the structure of a network has been determined and the network constructed, information can be processed. Several concepts related to processing are important.

Each *input* corresponds to the value of a single attribute. For example, if the problem is to decide on the approval or disapproval of a loan, an attribute can be the borrower's income level, age, or ownership of a house. All inputs—including qualitative attributes, voice, signals from monitoring equipment, or pictures—must be preprocessed into binary (0 and 1) equivalencies.

The *output* of the network is the solution to a problem. In the case of the loan application, for example, it may be "yes" or "no." The ANN assigns numeric values, for example, +1 for "yes" and 0 for "no." The purpose of the network is to compute the values of the outputs.

**HARDWARE AND SOFTWARE.** Although neural computing is structured to run on mutiple processors (CPUs), it is considerably less expensive and simpler to

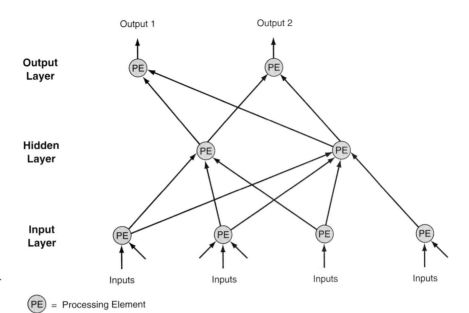

Output 1          Output 2

**Output Layer**

**Hidden Layer**

**Input Layer**

Inputs    Inputs    Inputs    Inputs

PE = Processing Element

**FIGURE 11.7** Neural network with one hidden layer.

run it on a single processor. Current neural network applications use software simulations with a single processor expedited by the use of special acceleration boards. Thus, applications can even run on a PC. In the future, it will eventually become economically feasible to run some ANNs on mutiple processors. Note that supercomputers and some mainframes and midrange computers use parallel processing. But, in neural computing we allow for *massive* interconnections, while in the other types, tasks are divided among the processors and executed independently.

**BENEFITS AND APPLICATIONS OF NEURAL NETWORKS.** The value of neural network technology includes its usefulness for **pattern recognition**, learning, and the interpretation of incomplete and noisy inputs.

Neural networks have the potential to provide some of the human characteristics of problem solving that are difficult to simulate using the logical, analytical techniques of DSS or even expert systems. For example, neural networks can analyze large quantities of data to establish patterns and characteristics in situations where the logic or rules are not known. An example would be loan applications. By reviewing many historical cases of applicants' questionnaires and the decision (yes or no), the ANN can create "patterns" or "profiles" of applications that should be approved, or denied. A new application is matched against the pattern; if it comes close enough, the computer classifies it as a "yes" or "no"; otherwise it goes to a human. Neural networks are especially useful for financial applications such as determining when to buy or sell stock (see Trippi and Turban [1996] for examples).

Neural networks have several other benefits:

▶ *Fault tolerance*. Since there are many processing nodes, damage to a few nodes or links does not bring the system to a halt.

▶ *Generalization*. When a neural network is presented with an incomplete or previously unseen input, it can generalize to produce a reasonable response.

- ▶ *Adaptability*. The network learns in new environments. The new cases are used immediately to retrain the program and keep it updated.
- ▶ *Forecasting capabilities*. Similar to statistics, here, too, prediction is made based on historical data.

Beyond its role as an alternative computing mechanism, neural computing can be combined with other computer-based information systems (CBISs) to produce powerful hybrid systems.

In general, ANNs do not do well at tasks that are not done well by people. For example, speedy arithmetic and transaction processing tasks are not suitable for ANNs and are best accomplished by conventional computers. Specific areas of business that are well suited to the assistance of ANNs include the following:

- ▶ *Tax fraud*—identifying, enhancing, and finding irregularities.
- ▶ *Financial services*—identification of patterns in stock market data and assistance in bond trading strategies, mortgage underwriting, and foreign rate exchange forecast (see Trippi and Turban [1996]).
- ▶ *Loan application evaluation*—judging worthiness of loan applications based on patterns in previous application information (customer credit scoring).
- ▶ *Solvency prediction*—assessing the strengths and weaknesses of corporations and predicting possible failures.
- ▶ *New product analysis*—sales forecasting and targeted marketing.
- ▶ *Airline fare management*—seat demand and crew scheduling.
- ▶ *Evaluation of personnel and job candidates*—matching personnel data to job requirements and performance criteria.
- ▶ *Resource allocation based on historical, experiential data*—finding allocations that will maximize outputs.
- ▶ *Data mining*—finding data in large and complex databases as shown in Chapter 10.
- ▶ *Foreign exchange rate*—including country risk rating.
- ▶ *Identifying takeover targets*—Predicting which companies are most likely to be acquired by other companies.
- ▶ *Stocks, bonds, and commodities selection and trading*—including pricing initial public offerings.
- ▶ *Signature validation*—matching against previous signatures.
- ▶ *Prediction*—employee performance and behavior and personnel requirements.
- ▶ *Credit card fraud detection*—fast detection of fraud by analyzing purchasing patterns (see the following *IT at Work*).

*IT At Work*    VISA CRACKS DOWN ON FRAUD

Only 0.2% of **Visa International's** turnover in 1995 was lost to fraud, but at $655 million it is a loss well worth addressing. Visa is now concentrating its efforts on reversing the number of fraudulent transactions by using neural network technology.

Most people stick to a well-established pattern of card use and only rarely splurge on expensive nonessentials. Neural networks are designed to notice when a card that is

**U**SING IT

...in Finance

usually used to buy gasoline once a week is suddenly used to buy a number of tickets to the latest Andrew Lloyd Webber musical premiere on Broadway.

The Bank of America field tested the cardholder risk identification system (CRIS) and believes that the system has cut fraudulent card use by up to two-thirds. The Toronto Dominion Bank found that losses were reduced while overall customer service improved with the introduction of neural computing. One other bank believes it has saved $5.5 million in six months. In 1994, Visa member banks lost more than $148 million to counterfeiters; by 1995, that figure was down to $124 million—a drop of more than 16 percent. With numbers like that, the $2 million Visa spent to implement CRIS certainly seems worth the investment. In fact, Visa says, CRIS had paid for itself by the end of 1994.

In 1995, CRIS conducted over 16 billion transactions. By 2000, VisaNet (the data warehouse and e-mail operations) and CRIS will handle at least 5,250 transactions per second. By October 1996, CRIS was able to notify banks of fraud within one hour of a transaction. The only downside to CRIS is that occasionally the system prompts a call to a cardholder's spouse when an out-of-the-ordinary item is charged, such as a surprise vacation trip or a diamond ring. After all, no one wants to spoil surprises for loved ones.

**For Further Exploration:** What is the advantage of CRIS over an automatic check against the balance in the account, and against a set of rules such as "call a human authorizer when the purchase price is more than 200 percent of the average previous bill?" ▲

SOURCE: Condensed from: "Visa Stamps Out Fraud," *International Journal of Retail and Distribution Management*, Vol. 23, No. 11, Winter 1995, p. viii; and "Visa Cracks Down On Fraud," *Information Week*, August 26, 1996.

Neural computing is emerging as an effective technology in pattern recognition. This capability is translated to many applications (e.g., see Chen [1996] and Medsker [1995]) and is sometimes integrated with fuzzy logic.

## FUZZY LOGIC

**Fuzzy logic** is a technique developed by Zadeh (1994) that deals with uncertainties by simulating the process of human reasoning, allowing the computer to behave less precisely and logically than conventional computers do.

The rationale behind this approach is that decision making is not always a matter of black and white, true or false; it often involves gray areas where the term *maybe* is more appropriate. In fact, creative decision-making processes are often unstructured, playful, contentious, and rambling.

According to Barron (1993), productivity of decision makers can improve up to 3,000 percent using fuzzy logic. At the present time, there are only a few examples of pure fuzzy logic applications in business (e.g., see Jamshidi et al. [1997]).

Fuzzy logic is used in many cases together with other intelligent systems. As a matter of fact, intelligent systems are frequently integrated with other intelligent systems or other computerized systems (e.g., DSS). The following example illustrates such a hybrid system.

**INTERNATIONAL INVESTMENT MANAGEMENT: STOCK SELECTION.** An international investment company is using a combined fuzzy logic, expert system and an ANN system called FuzzyNet to forecast the expected returns from stocks, cash, bonds, and so on in order to determine the optimal allocation of investment assets. Since many companies invest in global markets, the system determines the creditworthiness of various countries and the estimated performance of key socioeconomic ratios. Then, FuzzyNet selects specific stocks based on company, industry, and economic data. The final stock portfolio must be adjusted according to the forecast of foreign exchange rates, interest rates, and so on—which are handled by a currency exposure analysis. The integrated network architecture of the system is shown in Figure 11.8; it includes the following technologies:

1. *Expert system*. This system provides the necessary knowledge for both country and stock selection.
2. *Neural network*. The neural network conducts a forecasting, based on the data included in the database.
3. *Fuzzy logic*. The fuzzy logic supports assessment of factors for which there are no reliable data. For example, the *credibility* of rules in the rule base is given only as a probability. Therefore, the conclusion of the rule may be expressed either as a probability or as a degree of fuzzy membership.

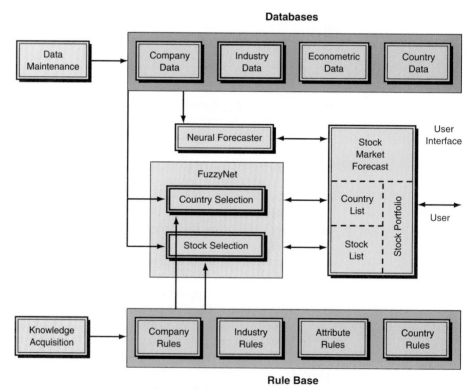

**FIGURE 11.8  FuzzyNet's architecture.** (*Source*: Wong et al., 1992, p. 48. Adapted with permission from *Financial Analysts Journal,* January/February 1992. Copyright 1992, Association for Investment Management and Research, Charlottesville, VA. All rights reserved.)

## ▶ 11.4 INTELLIGENT AGENTS

**Intelligent agents (IA)** represent a new technology with the potential to become one of the most important tools of information technology in the twenty-first century. IA can alleviate the most critical limitation of the Internet—information overflow—and facilitate electronic commerce. Before we look at its capabilities, let us determine what we mean by IA.

There are several names to describe intelligent agents. Notable are: *software agents, wizards, knowbots,* and *softbots*. The names sometime reflect the nature of the agent. Note that the term *agent* is derived from the concept of agency, referring to employing someone to act on your behalf. A computerized agent represents a person and interacts with others to accomplish a predefined task.

There are several definitions of what an intelligent agent is. Each reflects the definer's perspective. Here are some examples:

1. "Intelligent agents are software entities that carry out some set of operations on behalf of a user or another program, with some degree of independence or autonomy and in so doing, employ some knowledge or representation of the user's goals or desires." (SOURCE: The IBM Agent [http://activist.gpl.ibm.com:81/WhitePaper/ptc2.htm].)

2. An agent is anything that can be viewed as perceiving its environment through sensors and acting upon that environment through effectors. (SOURCE: Russell and Norvig [1995], p. 33.)

3. Autonomous agents are computational systems that inhabit some complex dynamic environment, sense and act autonomously in this environment and by doing so realize a set of goals or tasks for which they are designed. (SOURCE: Maes [1994], p. 108.)

## CHARACTERISTICS OF INTELLIGENT AGENTS

While there is no single commonly accepted definition for the term "intelligent agent," there are several traits or abilities that many people think of when they are discussing intelligent agents. These are summarized in Table 11.5 (see page 500). Note that some agents lack some of these characteristics.

## WHAT CAN INTELLIGENT AGENTS DO?

The following are the major tasks that can be performed by IA:

1. *Information access and navigation* are today's major applications of intelligent agents.

2. *Decision support and empowerment.* Knowledge workers need increased support, especially in decision making. IA can facilitate decision making and empower employees, as shown in the next *IT at Work* illustration.

---

 **IT At Work** EMPOWERING EMPLOYEES BY USING SOFTWARE AGENTS AT NIKE AND AT SIGNET BANK

*U*SING IT

...in Human Resources Management

Fringe benefits are frequently likened to a cafeteria—people mix and match what they like within the constraints of what is available and how much they can use. The management of fringe benefits is a very resource-intensive process, especially when thousands of employees are involved. **Nike** and **Signet Bank** both installed special software that empowers employees to access the human resources databases by computer and conduct activities such as selecting and changing benefits or making charitable contributions.

The software agent that supports these activities is called Electronic Workforce (from Edify Corp.). It enables employers to delegate some time-consuming and repetitive tasks, previously conducted by human resources (HR) employees, to any employee supported by a computer. Employees enter and delete data, command the computer, and interpret information. If they make mistakes or request benefits they are not eligible for, the agent automatically alerts them to the problem. Previously, paperwork would have to be routed to an employee for corrections and then back to the HR department. The use of the agents enables companies to increase benefits options, making the employees more satisfied with the same or even fewer human resources employees.

**For Further Exploration:** Can you imagine what the situation was prior to the use of agents? How can an agent know that an employee made a mistake? ▲

SOURCE: Information provided by Edify Corporation, Santa Clara, CA. 1998. For other examples and discussion see Whinston (1997) and Bradshaw (1997).

3. *Repetitive office activity*. There is a pressing need to automate tasks performed by administrative and clerical personnel in functional areas, such as sales or customer support, to reduce labor costs and increase office productivity. Today, labor costs are estimated to be as much as 60 percent of the total cost of information delivery.

4. *Mundane personal activity*. In a fast-paced society, time-strapped individuals need new ways to minimize the time spent on routine personal tasks

**Table 11.5** Characteristics of Intelligent Agents

| Characteristic | Description |
| --- | --- |
| Autonomous | Capable of acting on its own, being goal oriented and collaborative, able to alter its activity if needed (see Maes 1995). |
| Proactive response | The agents response must be corrective (i.e., they must exhibit goal-directed behavior by taking the initiative). |
| Unobstructive | Work without constant attention of its "master," being off-site (remote executions). |
| Module | Transportable across different systems and networks. Many agents are not mobile (e.g., Wizards in spreadsheets). |
| Dedicated and automated | An agent is usually designed to carry on a specific, usually repetitive, normally difficult task. For multifaceted jobs we need a multiagent system. |
| Interactive | Agents are designed to interact with human agents or software programs (see opening case). This is critical for a multiagent system. |
| Conditional processing, practice | Using rule-based or pattern-matching logic (supplied by the user), the agent can make decisions in choosing contexts in which they perceive or send alerts to the user in a timely manner. |
| Friendly and dependable | An effective agent must be believable and exhibit easy interactivity with people. |
| Able to learn | Only a few agents can really do some learning, for example, observing the user and making predictions on his or her future behavior. Agent must be highly autonomous. |

like booking airline tickets so that they can devote more time to professional activities. One specific form of smart agents is the voice-activated interface agent that reduces the burden on the user of having to explicitly command the computer.

5. *Search and retrieval*. It is not possible to directly manipulate a distributed database system in an electronic commerce setting with millions of data objects. Users will have to delegate the task of searching and cost comparison to agents. These agents perform the tedious, time-consuming, and repetitive tasks of searching databases, retrieving and filtering information, and delivering results to the user.

6. *Domain experts*. It is advisable to model costly expertise and make it widely available. "Expert" software agents could be models of real-world agents, such as translators, lawyers, diplomats, union negotiators, stockbrokers, and even clergy.

Here are some management-oriented tasks that an agent can do: advise, alert, broadcast, browse, critique, distribute, enlist, empower, explain, filter, guide, identify, match, monitor, navigate, negotiate, organize, present, query, report, remind, retrieve, schedule, search, secure, solicit, sort, store, suggest, summarize, teach, translate, and watch. An example of a system that conducts several of these follows.

---

 **SALLIE MAE USES INTELLIGENT AGENTS**

**S**allie Mae, the government-sponsored loan services company, is known for its student loan programs. To manage its $30 billion in insured student loans, the company relies on an enterprisewide computer network spanning several states and on large databases. This large information system must operate continuously and must be secured. The networks, servers, and other network resources need to be monitored around the clock, and any irregularities must be reported and fixed quickly. To conduct the above tasks manually would not only cost a fortune; it would also result in major interruptions to the system and poor service to the loan customers.

**U**SING IT

...in Finance

The solution is AgentWorks, which runs with Sun Connect's SunNet Manager, to monitor the system's databases, networks, and applications, working with intelligent agents. The agents are programmed to oversee network management tasks, send alerts, and restore failed procedures.

AgentWorks manages remote resources from a central location. The intelligent agents execute several tasks such as monitoring thresholds at remote locations and taking action when the thresholds are exceeded. The agents are controlled by a command center that can run on its own or be incorporated with other network management systems.

Agents manage over 100 critical business processes. The agents are also used to identify the sources of problems they cannot fix. It is kind of a problem determination drill-down.

Overall, a significant improvement in response time occurred and the number of agents and their tasks are expanding. By using multiple agents, a wide-spectrum solution is provided.

**For Further Exploration:** How can agents assist those who inquire about the status of their loans? ▲

SOURCE: Condensed from Sullivan, K.B., "Sallie Mae Takes on Intelligent Agents," *PC Week*, March 6, 1995.

## APPLICATIONS OF INTELLIGENT AGENTS

We described some intelligent agents applications in Chapters 5, 6, and 10. Here are additional applications.

*User Interface.* For many users, a graphical user interface has been considered difficult to learn and use, especially its nonroutine functions. As capabilities and applications of computers improve, the user interface needs to accommodate the increases in complexity. Intelligent agents can help with both these problems. Intelligent agent technology allows systems to monitor the user's actions, develop models of user abilities, and automatically help out when problems arise.

Of special interest is Microsoft's animated family of agents (e.g., Merlin, Robby, and Genie), which can appear in Web pages, displaying everything from simple idling activities such as yawning to attention-grabbing motions. Thus, even social interaction can be incorporated with the user interface. For details see www.microsoft.com/agent and www.argolink.com/agent. (Source: Barker, D., "Secret Agent Man," *PC AI*, January/February 1998.)

*Operating Systems Agents.* Agents can assist in the use of operating systems. For example, Microsoft Corp. has several agents (called Wizards) in its NT operating system. Some reside on the NT server, while others are on the workstations. These agents assist in the following tasks: add user accounts, group management, manage file and folder access, add printer, add/remove programs, network client administrator, licenses, and install new modems. For details, consult http://www.microsoft.com.

*Spreadsheet Agents.* Spreadsheet agents make the software more friendly. An example of an intelligent agent is the Wizard feature, found in Microsoft's Excel. The Wizard is a built-in package capability that "watches" users and offers suggestions as they attempt to perform tasks by themselves. For example, suppose you are trying to format a group of spreadsheet cells or locations in a particular manner. If you are not skilled at using the spreadsheet package, you might try to format each cell individually. A much faster method is to select the entire group of designated cells and then conduct the format once for all the selected locations.

Suppose a friend of yours was watching you format the cells and noted that you worked on an individual cell basis. Suppose further that your friend was more of an expert on the software package than you were. Presumably, your friend would tell you that you were formatting unproductively. In a similar sense, the Wizard can detect your laborious, repetitive attempts and notify you that there is a better way, or even take the next step and offer to complete the remainder of the formatting task for you.

*Workflow and Task Management Agents.* Administrative management includes both workflow management and areas such as computer/telephone integration, where processes are defined and then automated. In these areas, users need to not only make processes more efficient, but also reduce the cost of human agents. Intelligent agents can be used to ascertain, then automate, user wishes or *business processes.*

Ginkgo is a powerful agent from IBM (Ginkgo is an herbal leaf associated with memory improvement). This agent monitors tasks performed by people (and machines), learns about the tasks and their performance, and makes recommendations based on this knowledge. The agent reminds the user of the most productive ways to complete a task. It can show you how others solved the same problem or executed the same task. The agent has been applied to support the *Physician's Assistant,* a DSS for drug prescription recommendations. The agent is used for many other applications. For details see www.networking.ibm.com/iag /iaghome.html. (SOURCE: Barker, D., "Secret Agent Man," *PC AI*, March/April 1998.)

***Software Development.*** Software development includes many routine tasks that can be carried out or supported by agents. For example, Neural Network Utility (NNU, from IBM) is an intelligent assistant for software developers, which offers the pattern recognition and learning needed for information access. With NNU, the developer can define and graphically connect neural networks, fuzzy rule systems, and data filtering/translation, and then embed them in applications.

***Negotiation in Electronic Commerce.*** A challenging system is one in which agents need to negotiate with each other. Such systems are especially applicable to electronic commerce. Consider the vacation episode in the opening case. There, agents *cooperate* to arrange for a vacation. However, the scenario can be extended to one in which the user's agent will *negotiate* the best price for the car, hotel, airfare, and so on.

## SOFTWARE-SUPPORTED CREATIVITY

The intelligent agents described so far in this chapter can increase productivity and quality—but are they really intelligent? If we check the definition of intelligent behavior, we would probably conclude that today's agents are not intelligent. However, let us look at computer programs that exhibit what we might call *creative behavior.*

Rasmus (July 1995) gives an example of two creativity tools. The first one, called Copycat, is a program that seeks analogies in patterns of alphabetical letters. Identifying patterns is a property of intelligence. Copycat, which consists of several *intelligent agents,* can find analogies to sets or strings of letters, for example, transforming "aabc" to "aabd." This ability can be generalized to other problems that require conceptual understanding and the manipulation of things. The ability of the program to anticipate the meaning of the transformation and to find analogous fits provides evidence that computers can mimic a human being's ability to creat analogies.

The second system, AARON, is a program that can draw. Its output can be considered to be art. Its developer, Harold Cohen, worked for 15 years to create a comprehensive knowledge base to support AARON. Similar programs have been developed to teach computers to write poems, compose music, and create works in other media. The increased size of knowledge bases, processing speed, and storage enable such programs to create artwork of good quality. However, for machines to exhibit more creativity and additional characteristics of intelligence, such as "use reason in solving problems" or "deal with perplexing situations," *multiple agents* are needed that are in a very rudimentary stage of research.

## ▶ 11.5 EMERGING TECHNOLOGY: VIRTUAL REALITY

### WHAT IS VIRTUAL REALITY?

There is no standard definition of **virtual reality (VR).** The most common definitions usually imply that virtual reality is interactive, computer-generated, three-dimensional graphics, delivered to the user through a head-mounted display. Defined technically, virtual reality is an "environment and/or technology that provides artificially generated sensory cues sufficient to engender in the user some willing suspension of disbelief." So in virtual reality, a person "believes" that what he or she is doing is real, even though it is artificially created.

More than one person and even a large group can share and interact in the same environment. VR thus can be a powerful medium for communication, entertainment, and learning. Instead of looking at a flat computer screen, the virtual reality user interacts with a 3-D computer-generated environment. To see and hear the environment, the user wears stereo goggles and a 3-D headset. To interact with the environment, control objects in it, or move around within it, the user wears a computerized behavior-transducing head-coupled display and hand position sensors (gloves). Virtual reality displays achieve the illusion of a surrounding medium by updating the display in real time. The user can grasp and move virtual objects. This capability can be utilized for gaining a competitive advantage, as shown in the following example.

---

*IT At Work*      **VIRTUAL REALITY**
**LEADS TO A WINNER**

Using virtual reality, the city of San Diego was successful in its bid to host the 1996 Republican National Convention. With VR, the city developed a virtual walk-through model of the convention center. Working with an architect, planners developed a seating arrangement that reflected the desires of the Republican National Committee, as well as meeting the requirements of various building and safety codes. The model included both existing and "to be constructed" buildings and even traffic patterns around the center. The model enabled the designer to experiment with various configurations, illustrating how things would appear and identifying potential problems related to the project. Furthermore, it allowed the National Committee to conduct "what-if" scenarios.

The presentation was most impressive, and the Republican National Committee awarded the convention to San Diego, bringing hundreds of millions of dollars to the city's economy. San Diego had a decisive competitive edge—the VR model.

**For Further Exploration:** What could the city presenter do that the competitors could not? ▲

SOURCE: Condensed from Murray, T.J., "Virtual Reality Helps San Diego to Compete," *Public Management,* Vol. 11, No. 1, 1995.

---

### HOW DOES VIRTUAL REALITY WORK?

In a typical virtual reality system, the user views the virtual world either with a head-mounted display or on a screen (with or without 3-D shutter glasses). Delivered over headphones or speakers, 3-D sound provides realistic audio. A tracking system receiver, and one or more transmitters, tell the computer where the user is looking and where the 3-D controller is in space. These connect to the computer through either a serial port or a special interface card. The computer contains the graphics subsystem, spatialized audio subsystem, the databases of the geometry of the objects in the world, the world database (which defines the environment and how objects in it relate to each other), and the sound database (see Figure 11.9).

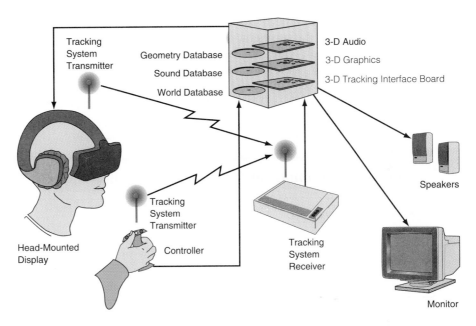

**FIGURE 11.9** The process of virtual reality.

Sophisticated virtual reality systems are interactive and usually simulate real-world phenomena. They often simulate sight, sound, and touch and combine these senses with computer-generated input to users' eyes, ears, and skin. By using a head-mounted display, gloves, and a bodysuit, or large projected images in simulator cabs, users can "enter" and interact with virtual or artificially generated environments. For example, Figure 11.10 shows a skier in the NEC

**FIGURE 11.10** Developing virtual skiing in Japan.

Corporation (Japan) Lab. NEC used the laboratory to develop a ski simulator, which is available in amusement centers. The product is also used for training.

**VIRTUAL REALITY AND THE INTERNET/INTRANET.** A platform-independent standard for VR called **Virtual Reality Markup Language (VRML)** (see Goralski et al. [1997]) makes navigation through online supermarkets, museums, and stores as easy as interacting with textual information. The VRML allows objects to be rendered as an Internet user "walks" through a virtual room. At the moment, users can utilize regular browsers, but VRML browsers will soon be in wide circulation.

Extensive use is expected in marketing (see Burke [1996]). For example, Tower Records offers a virtual music store on the Internet, where customers can "meet" each other in front of the store, go inside, and preview CDs and videos. They select and purchase their choices electronically and interactively from a sales associate. Applications in other areas are shown in Table 11.6.

*Table 11.6* **Examples of Virtual Reality Applications**

| Industry | Application |
|---|---|
| Manufacturing | • Training<br>• Design testing<br>• Virtual prototyping<br>• Engineering analysis<br>• Ergonomic analysis<br>• Virtual simulation of assembly, production, and maintenance |
| Architecture | • Design of building and other structures |
| Military | • Training (pilots, astronauts, drivers)<br>• Battlefield simulations |
| Medicine | • Training surgeons (with simulators)<br>• Planning surgeries<br>• Physical therapy |
| Research/education | • Virtual physics lab<br>• Hurricane studies<br>• Galaxy configurations<br>• Representation of complex mathematics |
| Amusement | • Virtual museums<br>• 3-D race car games (on PC)<br>• Air combat simulation (on PC)<br>• Virtual reality arcades<br>• Virtual reality parks<br>• Ski simulator |

*Source*: Compiled from Adam (1993) and updated.

Virtual supermarkets could spark greater interest in home grocery shopping. In the future, shoppers will enter a virtual supermarket, walk through the virtual aisles, select virtual products, and put them in their virtual cart. This could help in removing some of the resistance to virtual shopping. Virtual malls are designed to give the user the feeling of walking in a shopping mall.

Virtual reality is just beginning to move into many business applications. Three-dimensional worlds on the Internet should prove popular because it is a metaphor to which everyone can relate.

## VIRTUAL REALITY AND DECISION MAKING

Most VR applications to date are used to support decision making indirectly. For example, Boeing developed a virtual aircraft mockup to test designs. Several other VR applications for assisting in manufacturing and for converting military technology to civilian are being utilized at Boeing (see Hedberg [1996]). At Volvo, VR is used to test virtual cars in virtual accidents; Volvo also uses VR in the new model design process. British Airways offers the pleasure of experiencing first-class flying to its Web site visitors.

Another VR application area is data visualization. VR helps financial decision makers make better sense of data by using visual, spatial, and aural immersion virtual systems. For example, some stock brokerages have a VR application in which users surf over a landscape of stock futures, with color, hue, and intensity indicating deviations from current share prices. Sound is used to convey other information, such as current trends or the debt/equity ratio. VR allows side-by-side comparisons with a large assortment of financial data. It is easier to make intuitive connections with 3-D support (see Coy [1996] for details). Morgan Stanley & Co. uses VR to display the results of risk analyses (see *Computerworld*, Feb. 1996, p. 65).

# ▶ MANAGERIAL ISSUES

The implementation of intelligent systems is an extremely important yet difficult task in organizations. Here are some issues to be considered:

1. *Cost-benefit and justification.* While the benefits of some ES are tangible, it is difficult to put a dollar value on the benefits of most intelligent systems. Improved customer service, quality, cycle time, and safety may be more important than tangible benefits.

2. *Heightened expectations.* When there is too much expectation and hope associated with intelligent technologies, management may get discouraged. There is currently a very high failure rate (some people estimate it at 85 percent). More accurate and realistic goals will help increase the chance of success.

3. *Acquiring knowledge.* Intelligent systems are built up on experts' knowledge. How to acquire this knowledge is a major problem, and not just a technical one. For example, how can an expert be motivated to contribute his or her knowledge?

4. *System acceptance.* The acceptance of intelligent systems by the IS department and the integration of such systems with mainstream IT is a critical success factor. There are psychological, social, technical, and political rea-

sons for the IS department to reject the new technologies. Without the cooperation of the IS department, these systems are likely to fail.

5. *System integration.* Intelligent systems can succeed as standalone systems, but they have a broader area of applications when integrated with other CBIS. This is another reason why the IS department must cooperate. Such hybrid systems are complex, but if they are successful, the rewards can be enormous.

6. *System technologies*. Intelligent systems are expected to be found in at least 20 percent of all IT applications in about ten years. It is critical for any prudent management to closely examine the technologies and their business applicability.

7. *Ethical issues.* Finally, there can be ethical issues related to the implementation of expert systems and other intelligent systems. The actions performed by an expert system can be unethical, or even illegal. For example, the expert system may advise you to do something that will hurt someone, or invade the privacy of certain individuals.

## KEY TERMS

Artificial neural network (ANN) *493*

Distance learning *476*

Expert system (ES) *473*

Fuzzy logic *497*

Inference engine *480*

Intelligent agent (IA) *498*

Knowledge base *470*

Machine learning *476*

Natural language processing (NLP) *474*

Neural computing *493*

Parallel processing *494*

Pattern recognition *495*

Robot *474*

Speech recognition *491*

Speech understanding *491*

Symbolic processing *471*

Turing test *470*

Virtual reality (VR) *504*

Virtual Reality Markup Language (VRML) *506*

Visual recognition *475*

Voice synthesis *491*

## CHAPTER HIGHLIGHTS *(L–x means learning objective number x)*

▶ The primary objective of AI is to build computers that will perform tasks that can be characterized as intelligent. (L–1)

▶ The major characteristics of AI are symbolic processing, use of heuristics instead of algorithms, and application of inference techniques. (L–1)

▶ AI has several major advantages: it is permanent; it can be easily duplicated and disseminated; it can be less expensive than human intelligence; it is consistent and thorough; and it can be documented. (L–1)

▶ The major application areas of AI are expert systems, natural language processing, speech understanding, intelligent robotics, computer vision, and intelligent computer-aided instruction. (L–1)

▶ Expert system technology attempts to transfer knowledge from experts and documented sources to the computer, in order to make the knowledge available to nonexperts for the purpose of solving difficult problems. (L–2)

▶ The major components of an ES are a knowledge base, inference engine, blackboard, user interface, and explanation subsystem. (L–2)

▶ The inference engine, or thinking mechanism, is a program of using the knowledge base, a way of reasoning with it to solve problems. (L–2)

▶ The ten generic categories of ES are interpretation, prediction, diagnosis, design, planning, monitoring, debugging, repair, instruction, and control. (L–2)

▶ Expert systems can provide many benefits. The most important are improvement in productivity and/or quality, preservation of scarce expertise, enhancing other systems, coping with incomplete information, and providing training. (L–2)

▶ Natural language processing (NLP) provides an opportunity for a user to communicate with a computer in day-to-day spoken language. (L–3)

▶ Speech recognition enables people to communicate with computers by voice. There are many benefits to this emerging technology. (L–3)

▶ Neural systems are composed of processing elements called artificial neurons. They are interconnected; and they receive, process, and deliver information. A group of connected neurons forms an artificial neural network. (L–4)

▶ Fuzzy logic is a technology that helps analyze situations under uncertainty. The technology can also be combined with an ES and ANN to conduct complex predictions and interpretations. (L–4)

▶ Software agents, some of which are called intelligent, can perform many mundane tasks, saving a considerable amount of time, and improving quality. (L–5)

▶ Virtual reality is a 3-D interactive computing environment that is beginning to support business simulation applications. (L–6)

## QUESTIONS FOR REVIEW

1. What is the Turing test?

2. List the major advantages that artificial intelligence has over natural intelligence.

3. List the major disadvantages of artificial intelligence when compared with natural intelligence.

4. Define a knowledge base.

5. List three major capabilities of an ES.

6. Explain how an ES can distribute (or redistribute) the available knowledge in an organization.

7. Define the major components of an ES.

8. Which component of ES is mostly responsible for the reasoning capability?

9. What is the function of the justifier?

10. Who are the potential users of ES?

11. List the ten generic categories of ES.

12. Describe some of the limitations of ES.

13. Describe a natural language and natural language processing.

14. What are the major advantages of NLP?

15. Distinguish between NLP and natural language generation.

16. List the major advantages of voice recognition.

17. What is an artificial neural network?

18. What are the major benefits and limitations of neural computing?

19. Define fuzzy logic, and describe its major features and benefits.

20. Define software agents. When can an agent be described as intelligent?

21. Define virtual reality.

## QUESTIONS FOR DISCUSSION

1. A major difference between a conventional decision support system and an ES is that the former can explain a "how" question whereas the latter can also explain a "why" question. Discuss.

2. What is the difference between voice recognition and voice understanding?

3. Compare and contrast neural computing and conventional computing.

4. Compare and contrast numeric and symbolic processing techniques.

5. Compare and contrast conventional processing with artificial intelligence processing.

6. Fuzzy logic is frequently combined with expert systems and/or neural computing. Explain the logic of such integration.

7. Describe the advantages of virtual reality over 2-D presentations.

8. Review the various tasks that intelligent agents can perform. Do these tasks have anything in common?

9. How can an intelligent agent alleviate the information overload problem?

10. Deep Blue of IBM defeated the world chess champion, Kasparov, in 1997. If computers cannot think, how is such a defeat possible? Find some recent information about Deep Blue.

11. Why is it that ANN can improve knowledge acquisition in cases where the experts are not available or not cooperating?

## EXERCISES

1. Sofmic is a large software vendor. About twice a year, Sofmic acquires a small specialized software company. Recently, a decision was made to look for a software company in the area of neural computing. Currently,

there are about 15 companies that would gladly cooperate as candidates for such acquisitions.

Bill Gomez, the corporate CEO, asked that a recommendation for a candidate for acquisition be submitted to him within one week. "Make sure to use some computerized support for justification, preferably from the area of AI," he said. As a manager responsible for submitting the recommendation to Gomez, you need to select a computerized tool for conducting the analysis. Respond to the following points:

   **a.** Prepare a list of all the tools that you would consider.

   **b.** Prepare a list of the major advantages and disadvantages of each tool, as it relates to this specific case.

   **c.** Select a computerized tool.

   **d.** Mr. Gomez does not assign grades to your work. You make a poor recommendation and you are out. Therefore, carefully justify your recommendation.

**2.** Table 11.2 provides a list of ten categories of ES. Compile a list of 20 examples, at least two in each category, from the various functional areas in an organization (accounting, finance, production, marketing, personnel, and so on).

**3.** *Debate:* Computers can be programmed to play chess. They are getting better and better and in 1997 they beat the world champion. Do such computers exhibit intelligence? Why or why not?

**4.** *Debate:* Prepare a table showing all the arguments you can think of that justify the position that computers cannot think. Then, prepare arguments that show the opposite.

**5.** *Debate:* Bourbaki (1990) describes Searle's argument against the use of the Turing test. Summarize all the important issues in this debate.

**6.** *Debate:* Lance Eliot made the following comment in *AI Expert* (August 1994, p. 9):

> When you log-on to the network, a slew of agents might start watching. If you download a file about plant life, a seed company agent might submit your name for a company mailing. Besides sending junk mail, such spying agents could pick up your habits and preferences and perhaps make assumptions about your private life. It could note what days you get onto the system, how long you stay on, and what part of the country you live in. Is this an invasion of your privacy? Should legislation prevent such usage of intelligent agents? Perhaps network police (more intelligent agents) could enforce proper network usage.

Prepare arguments to support your perspective on this issue.

**7.** Give five examples, not cited in this book, where voice recognition can be applied, and list the benefit(s) in each case. Be specific.

**8.** Access the U.S. Department of Labor Web site on safety (www.osha.gov). Find the ES www.osha.gov /wren/csa.html. There are Web-based as well as Windows-based applications available to download. Write a report on the capabilities of the ES and its advantages.

**9.** Refer to American Express voice recognition system (AETRS). Compare the voice-based system with the Web-based system offered by the company (advantages and disadvantages).

# GROUP ASSIGNMENTS

**1.** Find recent application(s) of intelligent systems in an organization. Each group member is assigned to a major functional area. Then, from a literature search, material from vendors, or industry contacts, he or she should find two or three recent applications (within the last six months) of intelligent systems in this area. The group will submit the following reports:

   **a.** One-page abstract of the applications found in their functional area.

   **b.** The entire class will conduct an analysis of the similarities and differences among the applications across the functional areas. A possible arrangement is to look at the underlying technology (e.g., compare the use of ANN in marketing against finance or management).

**2.** Each group member composes a list of mundane tasks he or she would like an intelligent software agent to prepare. The group will then meet and compare and draw some conclusions.

**3.** Enter the Web site of MultiLogic Inc. (www.multi-logic.com). Look for the "Resolver" demos. Visit the "restricted stock" page. It shows how the complex subject of restricted stocks can be presented in an easy-to-understand format, using knowledge bases, as well as showing a potential investor how to use an internal broker to trade the restricted stock. Fill in the questionnaire and summarize your experiences in a three-page report.

**4.** It is easy to build a small expert system using a simple ES shell. A Windows version of EXSYS (now Resolver) can be found at www.multilogic.com. It includes demo and tutorial. The system assigned to you is the purchasing of a CD player—a similar demo (for buying a car) is available on the EXSYS demo. Your small demo should include no fewer than 20 rules.

## INTERNET EXERCISES

Note: The URLs included here were current when the book went to press. However, they are subject to change without notice. Please consult the Turban Web site (www.Wiley.com/college/turban2e).

1. Prepare a report on the use of ES in help desks. Collect information from Ginesys Corporation (www.ginesys.com), from (www.multilogic.com), and www.ilog.com.

2. Enter the Web site of Carnegie Mellon University (www.cs.cmu.edu) and identify current activities on the Land Vehicle. Send an e-mail to ascertain when the vehicle will be on the market.

3. There is a considerable amount of interest in intelligent agents at MIT (www.ai.mit.edu). Find the latest activities regarding IA.

4. Enter the site of Tower Records and examine the use of virtual reality in 3-D presentations. Also, visit a VR store (www.vrplace.com) and examine their products. Finally, join a VR newsgroup and try to locate new business applications.

5. Visit ftp://ftp.sas.com/pub/neural/FAZ.html/. Identify links to real-world applications of neural computing in finance, manufacturing, health care, and transportation. Prepare a report on current applications.

6. Enter www.looksmart.com and identify the latest managerial trends and issues related to applied AI technologies.

## ▼ Minicase 1

### Rules of Thumb Schedule Trains in Paris

One of France's busiest train stations is the Gare de l'Est in Paris. Trains are parked at 30 platform tracks and then funneled onto six mainline tracks. Over 1,100 trains come and go every day, including some that cruise at close to 200 miles per hour! That's a train every thirty seconds during busy periods.

Scheduling local and long-distance trains at the 30 platforms is a complex logistical problem. Traffic levels are near the theoretical maximum. Each train must be assigned one of 640 possible routes into and out of the station. Local and long-distance trains share the same platform assignments. One single delayed train can cause a chain reaction that reverberates through the schedule for as long as four hours afterwards. When a track or platform must be taken out of service for repairs, as many as 250 trains each day may have to be diverted. Only specialists at the Gare de l'Est have the skills to reroute these trains without creating delays—skills they have derived from 10 to 15 years of experience working at the station.

The number of possible solutions to such problems is astronomical. As in chess, the moves and countermoves are so numerous that there is no satisfactory algorithmic solution to this problem. To enumerate all possible solutions using a powerful computer may take days to execute. Yet in the real world of railroading, a solution is needed in minutes.

Dispatchers who have solved daily problems manually for scores of years currently handle scheduling.

Until now, the solution for these human experts has been to use rules of thumb—heuristics. These rules are enunciated as constraints that say what may and may not be done in terms of train routes; they also consider the effects of any changes on all the other routes. A basic rule in railroading, for example, is that two trains may not occupy the same track at the same time. The first corollary is that, on a single track, no train can pass another from either direction. These are rules that *must never* be violated. Other rules can be relaxed to solve pressing problems, such as: "Don't assign a train to a platform until the previous debarkees have fully cleared the platform."

The deficiencies of a manual system are the following:

1. When a dispatcher is out sick an extreme amount of pressure is placed on the remaining dispatchers.

2. Due to time constraints, dispatchers can run through only a limited number of possible arrangements for both planning and rerouting, so the best ones may be missed.

3. On holidays, when extra trains are needed, it is necessary to relax some rules. Working under time pressure, dispatchers are not always relaxing the most appropriate rules.

4. Employees fill out paper documents manually, a lengthy process.

**5.** Some dispatchers make mistakes, which may cause significant delays.

**6.** Daily planning and preparation of the semiannual timetable takes too much time.

**7.** The scheduling issue creates a limit on the flow of traffic that is much lower than the physical limit.

**8.** Unnecessary delays may develop when the dispatchers cannot work fast enough to handle emergencies.

Adding more dispatchers is an expensive solution that does not resolve every deficiency. In late 1988, it became clear to management that a computerized support was needed. One proposal suggested the use of an expert system.

Such a system was built in 1989 and has run successfully since. It is interactive and works with a combination of rules and object-oriented programming. When a problem develops, the ES divides it into subproblems. Possible routes are quickly examined. If a potential conflict between trains is indicated, appropriate recommendations for its resolution are provided. The program starts in a batch mode and applies its rule base automatically, listing any situation it cannot solve. Then the dispatcher, in an interactive mode, attempts to solve the

problem with the aid of the computer. The ES increased the productivity of the dispatchers by up to 100 percent, reduced errors, and solved the cited deficiencies.

### Questions for Minicase 1

**1.** A preliminary study concluded that DSS or MIS would not be correct approaches. Why?

**2.** The possibility of using neural computing was examined but quickly discarded. Why?

**3.** Which of the deficiencies listed earlier cannot be removed by an expert system and why?

**4.** Can this system be transferred to train stations in other countries? Why or why not?

**5.** Explain how the improvements are achieved. What is the role of dispatchers now? Do we need dispatchers at all?

**6.** The ES output was designed so the forms and information flow would look exactly the same as that of the manual system. What is the logic of such a design?

SOURCE: Based on information provided by Texas Instruments, the builder of the system.

# Minicase 2

## How the U.N. Automated Its Payroll System

Over 15,000 employees work for the U.N. in more than 100 countries and need to be paid in different currencies. The pay for each employee includes a base pay for the job and entitlements based on location, seniority, and special terms agreed on. The rules and regulations of these entitlements occupied about 1,000 pages in manuals and gave rise to complex, lengthy, and error-prone salary calculations that had resisted automation for decades.

Then the U.N. transferred the rules into an online knowledge base. An expert system was developed to determine which entitlements are relevant for each employee. A formula-based DSS calculates the salaries. Since the system is online, the ES reassesses the entitlements whenever a change to an employee's status gains approval.

The entitlement system maintains data on all U.N. employees and their dependents. It also monitors events such as promotions, relocations, and changes in dependents. The system contains an explanation mech-

anism that clarifies how it determines eligibility, and what the values of the related entitlements are. Explanations are also provided for why some employees are not eligible for certain entitlements.

The U.N. information system was recently converted from a legacy mainframe to a Unix-based client/server architecture. The entitlement application is only one of about 2,000 applications that run on the new $70 million Integrated Management Information System (IMIS). In addition to the entitlement applications, there are financial, accounting, procurement, payroll, and travel applications. The expert system was developed with an object-oriented software. It includes an easy-to-use graphical front end and links to databases as well as other applications. The system includes 20 LANs, and communication between locations is done via secured VANs.

The most difficult part of implementation was building the knowledge base. About 2,000 users at different locations worldwide applied the information requirements in different ways. The maintenance of the rules is now fairly simple since the rules are encapsulated into objects. All that needs to be done is to change the rule and check its consistency with other rules. The object-oriented programs also made it easy to compute backpay, a result of retroactive changes.

Several other ES applications were introduced in the U.N. financial area. For example, an ES analyzes financial data and determines which are debits and credits and which accounts should be consolidated into other accounts. Finally, the system recommends how to close out books at the end of designated financial periods.

The IMIS not only increases the productivity and accuracy of accountants, but it also facilitates planning. Management can make better decisions regarding the deployment of people and other resources. The determination of entitlements is consistent and therefore more equitable. Finally, the expertise of the U.N. experts in New York is now available online, all over the world.

## Questions for Minicase 2

1. Why do employment rules and regulations fit an expert systems approach?

2. Why did the manual process defy automation until the ES approach was used?

3. Why are there links from the ES to databases and IT applications?

4. What are the benefits of consistent handling of equitable entitlements?

5. Today, the IMIS is praised by its users, those who are responsible for the payroll in all locations. Can you ascertain ways to make this system even better?

6. Management said the use of an ES forced them to make objective, rigorous definitions of the regulations. Why?

SOURCE: Condensed from *Datamation*, Nov. 1996, pp. 129–132.

## REFERENCES AND BIBLIOGRAPHY

1. Austin, M., et al., "Security Market Timing Using Neural Network Models," *The New Review of Applied Expert Systems,* 1997.

2. Awad, E. M., *Building Expert Systems,* Minneapolis/St. Paul, MN: West Publishing Company, 1996.

3. Beerel, A., *Expert Systems in Business: Real World Applications,* New York: Ellis Horwood, 1993.

4. Bigus, J. P., *Data Mining with Neural Networks,* New York: McGraw Hill, 1996.

5. Bourbaki, N., "Turing, Searle, and Thought." *AI Expert,* July 1990.

6. Bradshaw, J., ed., *Software Agents,* Boston: MIT Press, 1997.

7. Burke, R. R., "Virtual Shopping," *Harvard Business Review,* March/April 1996.

8. Chen, C. H., *Fuzzy Logic and Neural Network Handbook,* New York, McGraw Hill, 1996.

9. Coy, P., "Finance and Technology," *BusinessWeek,* October 28, 1996.

10. Dreyfus, H., and S. Dreyfus, *Mind Over Machine,* New York: Free Press, 1988.

11. Elofson, G., et al., "An Intelligent Agent Community Approach to Knowledge Sharing," *Decision Support Systems,* Vol. 20, No. 1, 1997.

12. Eriksson, H., "Expert Systems as Knowledge Servers," *IEEE Expert,* June 1996.

13. Etzioni, O., "The WWW: Quagmire or Gold Mine?" *Communications of the ACM,* November 1996.

14. Fuerst, W., et al., "Expert Systems and Multimedia: Examining the Potential for Integration," *Journal of Management Information Systems,* May 1995.

15. Goonatilake, S., ed., *Intelligent Hybrid Systems,* New York: John Wiley & Sons, 1995.

16. Goralski, W. M., et al., *VRML: Exploring Virtual Worlds on the Internet,* Upper Saddle River, NJ: Prentice Hall, 1997.

17. Hengl, T., *Artificial Intelligence on the Internet,* Knowledge Technology Inc., 1995.

18. Hubms, M. N., and M. P. Singh, "Internet-based Agents," Special Issue, *IEEE Internet Computing,* July/Aug. 1997.

19. Hubms, M. N., et al., *Readings in Agents,* Palo Alto: Morgan Kaufman, 1998.

20. Jamshidi, M., et al., eds., *Applications of Fuzzy Logic Towards High Machine Intelligent Quotient Systems,* Upper Saddle Road, NJ: Prentice Hall, 1997.

21. Kaplan, S. J., "The Industrialization of Artificial Intelligence: From By-Line to Bottom-Line," *AI Magazine,* Summer 1984.

22. Liebowitz, J., et al., *The Explosion of Intelligent Systems by the Year 2000,* New York: Bowker & Reed Elsevier, Inc., 1996.

23. Liu, N. K., and K. K. Lee, "An Intelligent Business Advisor System for Stock Investment," *Expert Systems,* Aug. 1997.

24. Maes, P., "Agents that Reduce Work and Information Overload," *Communications of the ACM,* July 1994.

25. Medsker, L. R., *Hybrid Intelligent Systems,* Norwell: Kluwer Academic Publishing, 1995.

26. O'Hare, G. M. P., and N. R. Jennings, *Foundations of Distributed AI,* New York: John Wiley & Sons, 1996.

27. O'Leary, D., "AI and Navigation on the Internet and Intranet," *IEEE Expert,* April 1996.

28. Poh, H. L., "A Neural Approach for Decision Support," *International Journal of Applied Expert Systems,* Vol. 2, No. 3, 1994.

29. Ramsay, A. M., ed., *Artificial Intelligence: Methodology, Systems, and Applications,* Amsterdam: IOS Press, 2nd ed., 1996.

30. Rasmus, D. W., "Creativity and Tools," *PC AI,* Part 1: May/June 1995; Part 2: July/August 1995; Part 3: September/October 1995.

31. Russell, J., and P. Norvig, *Artificial Intelligence: A Modern Approach,* Upper Saddle River, NJ: Prentice Hall, 1995.

32. Saver, J., and R. Bruns, "Knowledge-based Scheduling System in Industry and Medicine," *IEEE Expert,* Jan./Feb. 1997.

33. Smith, R., and C. Scott, *Innovative Applications of Artificial Intelligence #3,* Menlo Park, CA: AAAI Press/MIT Press, 1991.

34. Trippi, R., and E. Turban, eds., *Neural Computing Applications in Investment and Financial Services,* Burr Ridge, IL: R. D. Irwin, 2nd ed., 1996.

35. Turban, E., *Expert Systems and Applied AI,* New York: Macmillan, 1992.

36. Turban, E., and J. Aronson, *Decision Support Systems and Intelligent Systems,* Upper Saddle River, NJ: Prentice Hall, 1998.

37. "Virtual Reality," a special issue of the *Communications of the ACM,* May 1996.

38. Wallace, W. A., and Grabowski, M., eds., *Advances in Expert Systems for Management,* Greenwich: Jai Press, 1996.

39. Wee, L. K., et al., "DeNews—A Personalized News System," *Expert Systems with Applications,* November 1997.

40. Whinston, A., "Intelligent Agents as a Basis for Decision Support Systems," *Decision Support Systems,* Vol. 20, No. 1, 1997.

41. Winston, P. H., and K. A. Prendergast, eds., *The AI Business,* Cambridge, MA: MIT Press, 1984.

42. Wong, F. S., et al., "Fuzzy Neural Systems for Stock Selection," *Financial Analysts Journal,* January/February, 1992.

43. Zadeh, L., "Fuzzy Logic, Neural Networks, and Self Computing," *Communication of the ACM,* March 1994.

Note: An integrated case study for Part III, *Nabisco Net Brings Sweet Success,* is available on the Turban Web site (www.wiley.com/college/turban2e).

# PART IV
## MANAGING IT

### PART I
#### IT In the Organization

1. Organizations, Environments, and Information Technology
2. Information Technologies: Concepts and Management
3. Strategic Information Systems
4. Supply Chain, Enterprise Resources Planning, and Business Process Reengineering

### PART II
#### Networks and IT

5. Network Computing: Discovery, Communication, and Collaboration
6. Electronic Commerce
7. Impacts of IT on Organizations, Individuals, and Society

### PART III
#### Using IT

8. Transaction Processing, Innovative Functional Systems, and Integration
9. Supporting Management and Decision Making
10. Data and Knowledge Management
11. Intelligent Support Systems

### PART IV
#### Managing IT

12. Planning for Information Technology and Systems
13. Information Technology Economics
14. Systems Development
15. Managing Information Resources, Control, and Security

| Hardware | Software | Databases | Telecommunications and Internet |

In the previous parts we demonstrated how information systems are used to enhance productivity, profitability, quality, customer service, creativity, decision making and so on. We assume that such systems are available. However, information systems are basically enablers which must be planned for, justified, constructed, operated, and maintained. Although many of these activities are executed by the IS department, the end users must be involved in most activities. Furthermore, end users may conduct many of these activities in their own functional areas. For example, end users need to justify the purchasing of PCs and maintain their security.

This part opens with Chapter 12, which provides a comprehensive overview of the planning process for IT infrastructure. It also reviews the related topic of the various IT architectures and their planning.

Chapter 13 deals with several issues which are related to the economics of IT. First, the IT productivity paradox is examined to see why it is difficult to capture the relationship between IT expenditure on a macro level and productivity improvement. From an individual organization's point of view we examine issues such as justification and cost-benefit analysis (several methods), outsourcing versus in-house delivery of IT, and financing of IT infrastructure (e.g., with a chargeback approach).

Developing information systems applications can be done by using several approaches. Chapter 14 provides an overview of the major approaches, starting with the traditional System Development Life Cycle and ending with modern approaches such as object-oriented and prototyping. Some major issues related to systems development are discussed. They range from buy versus make options to major supporting tools. Special attention is given to developing Internet and intranet applications.

Closing the book is Chapter 15, which deals with multiple issues related to the management of IT resources. First, the role of the IS department in the organization and its relationship with end users are described. It is followed by a description of the organization of the IS department. The chapter also reviews all the major issues involved in information security. The chapter ends with an example of a current important issue: the handling of the Year 2000 problem. Also, a conclusion to the book is provided.

Part IV ends with an integrated case about Capital One, a major credit card issuer. This case, which is available on the book's Web site, deals with many issues ranging from outsourcing to the management of the IS department.

## CHAPTER 12

# Planning for Information Technology and Systems

### Learning Objectives

*After studying this chapter, you will be able to:*

1. Discuss the major issues addressed by information systems planning.

2. Demonstrate the importance of aligning information systems plans with business plans.

3. Explain the four-stage model of information systems planning.

4. Describe several different methodologies for conducting strategic information systems planning.

5. Identify the different types of information technology architectures and outline the processes necessary to establish an information architecture.

6. Apply specific questions to establish what kind of information systems planning is needed in an organization.

517

## HOW TRUSERV PLANNED ITS INFORMATION TECHNOLOGY

### The Problem

TRUSERV CORP. (www.trusrv.com) was created in 1997 by a merger of Cotter & Co. and Servistar Corp. TruServ is a $5 billion retail giant. A major problem was to merge the information systems of the two companies, a task which is planned for completion in 1999. To do so, Paul Lemerise, the CIO of TruServ, will rely on a *strategic IT plan* rather than putting together blueprints.

### The Solution

Lemerise turned first to Ernst & Young, a major CPA/IT consultant with which he had worked before on external auditing. He created a planning team that included the consultants and executives from the two merging companies. Lemerise did not include IT executives because he wanted strong input from the business side. He felt that he and the consultants know enough about IT.

The team decided to include both a short-term tactical plan and a long-term strategic plan. The short-term plan was aimed at supporting the immediate needs of TruServ. It ensured that projects such as the Year 2000 compliance would be on track. It also established a help desk. The long-term plan examined such issues as the use of the Internet and introducing intranets and electronic commerce.

The team examined the merger plans and the business plan of the new corporation. Interviews were conducted with 30 top executives regarding business goals and technology wish lists. Of special importance were long meetings with the CEO. Lemerise said that during the interview the CEO got very excited and started to think not just about IT but about the business.

Once the interviews were completed, Lemerise met with all the executives together in an attempt to get a consensus about the priorities of IT projects and the entire strategic plan. The formal IT strategic plan was completed in July 1997. It includes all major initiatives for three years, such as the move to one common retail system, and delineating how the company will use the Internet and intranet. The topics ranged from the use of radio-frequency (RF) technologies in the warehouses to electronic commerce.

### The Results

The plan will remain fluid; it will be reevaluated and updated with new business goals every six months. The company decided not to plan for more than three years ("Anything beyond planning for three years often doesn't happen.").

The plan includes an ROI part with such intangible items as improving communication with customers.

SOURCE: Condensed from Blodgett (1998).

## ▶ 12.1 IT PLANNING—A CRITICAL ISSUE FOR ORGANIZATIONS

The Case of TruServ demonstrates to us the need for a formal IT strategic plan, especially for large corporations. It also demonstrates to us that there are different types of plans (e.g., tactical and strategic), and that end users must be involved in planning as well as the CEO.

The topic of IT planning is very important for end users for the following reasons:

1. End users do IT planning for their own units.
2. End users must participate in the corporate IT planning. Therefore they must understand the process.

**3.** Corporate IT planning determines how the IT infrastructrure will look. The future of every unit in the organizations will be impacted by the infrastructure.

## BUSINESS IMPORTANCE AND CONTENT

A survey of 301 IT executives, conducted in Oct. 1997 by CIO Communication Inc., revealed that IT strategy is the number-one concern for CIOs. Strategic planning used to rank at the top of the list in the late 1980s and early 1990s, then it retreated to the middle of the list. Now it is back in style with an increased emphasis on aligning IT and business planning.

Why this renewed interest in formal strategic planning? According to Blodgett (1998), as the demands of an increasingly competitive workplace call for closer integration of IT goals and the business mission, strategic plans for the whole enterprise become more important. "I remember a time when IS strategic plans came forward from an IS perspective. 'This is what IS thinks,' " says John Braucksieker, corporate director of IS for the International Wire Group Inc. in St. Louis. "We in IS were on this side and the business people were on the other side, afraid to show us to customers, and there was not much dialogue between the two groups.

"Now, a good IS plan has to keep in mind the internal customers as well as the external customers and vendors, and IS has to work closely with the business side to make sure IS is helping the company stay competitive," he continues. "The two sides have to work together or a plan will fail" (pp. 1, 2).

CIOs in the early 1990s were busy cutting costs and outsourcing, leaving no time for strategic planning. But now, due to the business pressures described in Chapter 1, strategic planning is a must.

What's in a plan? Simply put, a strategic information systems plan identifies a set of computer-based applications that will help the company reach its business goals. To create a plan that is truly strategic, the CIO and the CEO must work together. Strategic planning is a complex process based on relationships and communications. IT planning has similarities and differences as compared to any business planning. For example, planning and forecasting are not the same thing. *Forecasting*, which is a part of planning, predicts the future; *planning* is preparing for that future. Given the many changes that are occurring in today's business environment, forecasting is particularly difficult. But just because the future is very uncertain and forecasting it is a daunting task does not mean that IT planning can be deferred or neglected. Certain assumptions about the environment—and about technology—must be made, even if some of them may later prove to be wrong.

This chapter focuses on the critical issues of IT planning—on developing an overall plan for all of an organization's IT applications and infrastructure. (Planning for developing individual applications is discussed in Chapter 14.)

This chapter first describes the evolution of, and special problems of, information technology systems planning (abbreviated **IT planning**). Then it presents a four-stage model of information systems planning: strategic planning, requirements analysis, resource allocation, and project planning. Next it discusses methodologies for operationalizing the model, with primary emphasis on the stages of strategic planning and requirements analysis. In addition, it describes a number of specific planning approaches. In particular, it discusses issues relative to building an information technology architecture. Finally, there is a discussion of some general guidelines for IT planning, planning of interorganizational systems, and ethical considerations.

## THE EVOLUTION OF IT PLANNING

Initial efforts to establish planning and control systems for IT started in the late 1950s and early 1960s. During these early years, information technology resources went into developing new applications and revising existing systems. These two areas became focal points for the first planning and control systems. Organizations adopted methodologies for developing systems, and installed project management systems to assist with planning new applications. These included the use of well-defined project phases, specified deliverables, formal user reviews, and sign-off procedures. Efficient operation of completed systems also became important, with an emphasis on high availability and reliability. The information systems department (ISD) implemented automated operations planning and scheduling systems.

These initial mechanisms addressed *operational* planning. As organizations became more sophisticated in their use of information systems, emphasis shifted to *managerial* planning, or resource allocation control. A manifestation of this shift was the organization of the ISD into a corporate computing utility. A form of **chargeback** or **chargeout** (i.e., users pay for the computing and information services they use, by charging the corporate IT expenditures to the users; see Chapter 13) was implemented in an attempt to shift accountability for IT expenditures to users. Some questioned the effectiveness of chargeback as a cost-control tool but, at least in theory, chargeback fostered greater user attention to benefits versus costs and resulted in more effective planning and utilization.

Collectively, these measures increased the amount of planning, and processes for identifying demand for information services were also developed. Typically, annual planning cycles were established to identify potentially beneficial IT services, to perform cost-benefit analyses, and to subject the list of potential projects to resource allocation analysis. Often the entire process was conducted by an IT *steering committee* (see Chapter 15) composed of key managers representing major functional units within the organization. The steering committee was created to oversee the ISD, to ensure that adequate planning and control processes were present, and to focus IT activities on long-range organizational objectives and goals. The steering committee reviewed the list of potential projects, approved the ones considered to be beneficial, and assigned relative priorities. The approved projects were then mapped onto a development schedule, usually encompassing a one- to three-year time frame. This schedule became the basis for determining IT support requirements such as long-range hardware, software, personnel, facilities, and financial requirements.

Some organizations extend this planning process by developing additional plans for longer time horizons. They have a long-range IT plan, sometimes referred to as the "strategic" IT plan. (See Ward and Griffiths [1996].) This plan typically does not refer to specific projects; instead it sets the overall direction in terms of infrastructure and resource requirements for IT activities for five to ten years in the future. The next level is a medium-term, "master plan" that identifies the **applications portfolio,** a list of major approved IS projects that are consistent with the long-range plan. Since some of these projects will take more than a year to complete, and others will not start in the current year, this plan extends over several years. The third level is a "tactical" plan with budgets and schedules for current-year projects and activities. In reality, because of the rapid pace of change in technology and the environment, short-term plans may include items not anticipated in the other plans. All these projects would be from the *master plan.*

The planning process just described is currently practiced by many organizations. Specifics of the IT planning process, of course, vary among organizations. For example, not all organizations have a high-level IT steering committee. Project priorities may be determined by the IT director, by his or her superior, by company politics, or even on a first-come, first-served basis. Organizations with decentralized ISD often employ integrative mechanisms, such as formal review and consolidation meetings, to determine their overall IT plan. In cases of strong divisional autonomy, no centralized planning may be attempted; rather, a process similar to that just described may be utilized by each divisional IS group. Planning must be continously monitored and adjusted if needed. Some organizations adjust their IT long plan every 6 months, due to the rapid technological changes. Short and medium plans must also be reviewed periodically.

## ISSUES IN IT PLANNING

Improving the planning process for information systems has long been one of the top concerns of ISD management. The Society for Information Management (SIM) (www.simnet.org) found this to be the number-one issue in surveys of senior IS executives. Although the issue declined to number three in the 1990 survey and number 10 in the 1994 survey, IT planning still represents a challenging issue for IS executives (Brancheau et al., 1996). As indicated earlier, planning was at the top of the list in a different survey in 1997.

Basic information systems planning addresses the following four general issues:

1. Aligning the IT plan with the organizational business plan (e.g., see Reich and Benbasat [1996]).
2. Designing an IT architecture for the organization in such a way that users, applications, and databases can be integrated and networked together.
3. Efficiently allocating information systems development and operational resources among competing applications.
4. Planning information systems projects so that they are completed on time and within budget and include the specified functionalities.

**ALIGNMENT OF THE IT PLAN WITH THE ORGANIZATIONAL PLAN.** The first task of IT planning is to identify information systems applications that fit the priorities established by the organization. Surprisingly, organizational strategies and plans are often not available in written form, or they may be formulated in terms that are not useful for information systems planning. Therefore, it is often difficult to ascertain the strategies and goals to which the information systems plan should be aligned. Nevertheless, without this alignment, the information systems plan cannot get and keep long-term organizational support. If selecting and scheduling information systems projects are based solely on proposals sub-

Good communication is the most crucial element here. If the IT department, accounting department, and upper management can't communicate in simple English (rather than "tech-ese" or "accountant-ese"), no plan will be successful.

— *Mike Rewald*

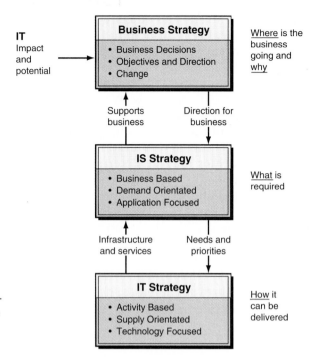

**FIGURE 12.1** The relationship between business, IS, and IT strategies. (*Source*: Ward and Griffiths [1996], p. 31.)

mitted by users, the projects will reflect existing computer-use biases in the organization, managers' aggressiveness in submitting proposals, and organizational power struggles, rather than the overall needs and priorities of the organization. Figure 12.1 graphically illustrates the alignment of IS strategy, business strategy, and IT strategy and deployment.

**DESIGN OF AN INFORMATION TECHNOLOGY ARCHITECTURE.** The term **information technology architecture,** or **information architecture,** refers to the overall (high-level) structure of all information systems in an organization. This structure consists of applications for various managerial levels (operational control, management planning and control, and strategic planning) and applications oriented to various functional-operational activities such as marketing, R&D, production, and distribution. The information architecture also includes infrastructure (e.g., the databases, supporting software, and networks needed to connect applications together). An information architecture for an organization should guide long-range development as well as allow for responsiveness to diverse, short-range information systems demands. The configuration of these architectures is discussed in Section 12.4.

**ALLOCATION OF RESOURCES.** Rational, optimal allocation of information systems resources among competing organizational units is difficult. This is especially true if the portfolio of potential applications does not mesh with an overall organizational plan, and if the functional or organizational unit requirements have not been integrated into a planning framework that establishes completeness and priority. Sometimes organizational dynamics, such as relative power and aggressiveness, are used in place of rational allocation. This can result in a precarious political situation for ISD management.

**COMPLETION OF PROJECTS ON TIME AND WITHIN BUDGET.** Few IS projects (applications) are completed on time or within budget. A common saying in the IT field is that projects often "take twice as long and cost four times as much" as originally planned. Consequently, organizational performance and ISD management's credibility suffer. Project plans are seldom accurate, as time and resource requirements are generally underestimated.

Often, under the pressure to finish a project on time and/or within budget, certain promised features are omitted. This reduction in functionality and/or quality frequently leads to user dissatisfaction with the resultant systems. Missing or inadequate features must be added later in what is usually called "system maintenance." Better project planning could avoid or reduce the impact of such mishaps. Chapter 14 discusses project planning methods and tools that can help control the schedule and budget of IT applications.

**PROBLEMS WITH IT PLANNING** IT planning can be an expensive and time-consuming process. A study of five large-scale planning projects (Goodhue et al. [1992]) found that these projects involved 10 or more employees, on a half-time or full-time basis, for periods lasting from 10 weeks to a year. The estimated costs of these projects ranged from $450,000 to $1.9 million. A survey of 80 firms with formal IT planning projects (Lederer and Sethi [1988]) found that 53 percent were dissatisfied with their experiences in actually carrying out the plans they developed.

These research findings suggest that, although IT planning is desirable, organizations should be careful not to devote an excessive amount of resources to these efforts. They should also beware of the pitfall of allowing IT planning to become an end in itself. To achieve the potential benefits of IT planning, organizations need to focus greater effort on actually implementing the plans they develop. This plan should be realistic and of high quality.

## A FOUR-STAGE MODEL OF IT PLANNING

Several models were developed to facilitate IT planning (e.g., see Ward and Griffiths [1996]). Of special interest is Wetherbe's (1993) **four-stage model of planning**, which is based on observation of planning efforts, promotional literature, and analysis of various methodologies used in the planning process. The model (depicted in Figure 12.2 and summarized in Table 12.1) consists of four major activities: strategic planning, requirements analysis, resource allocation, and project planning. These activities correspond to the four general issues of IT planning listed in the previous section.

**FIGURE 12.2** Basic four-stage model of IS planning.

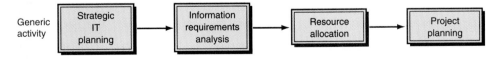

Most organizations engage in each of the four stages, but their involvement tends to be sporadic and influenced by problems as they occur, instead of reflecting a systematic, stage-by-stage process. If they use a formal planning methodology, it is important that the selection reflects what is most appropriate for each stage of IT planning, rather than the persuasive arguments of consultants.

**Table 12.1**  **IT Planning Stages**

| Major IT Planning Activity | Description |
| --- | --- |
| Strategic IT planning | Establishing the relationship between the overall organizational plan and the IT plan. |
| Information requirements analysis | Identifying broad, organizational information requirements to establish a strategic information architecture that can be used to direct specific application development projects. |
| Resource allocation | Allocating both IT application development resources and operational resources. |
| Project planning | Developing a plan that expresses schedules and resource requirements for specific information systems projects. |

The four-stage model can be expanded to include major activities and outputs of the four stages, as shown in Figure 12.3. With additional detail, the model moves from a high level of abstraction to a more concrete formulation of IT planning activities. The expanded methodologies useful for conducting each planning stage are discussed in the following pages.

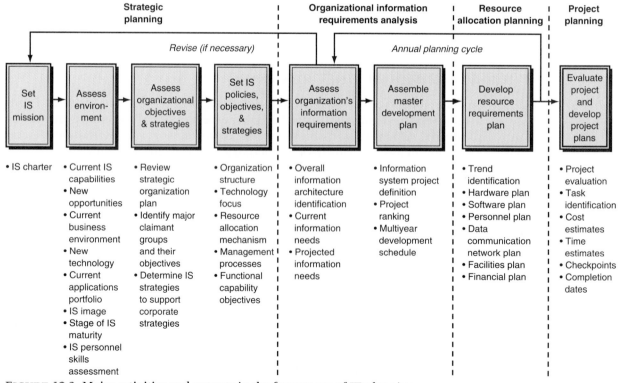

**FIGURE 12.3** Major activities and outputs in the four stages of IT planning.

The four-stage planning model is the foundation for the development of an applications portfolio of new information systems. There is also a relationship between the four-stage planning model and the various versions of the system development life cycle (SDLC) described in Chapter 14. The four-stage planning model identifies projects and general resource requirements necessary to achieve organizational objectives.

## ▶ 12.2 STRATEGIC INFORMATION PLANNING

In my experience with IT systems implementation, this step is often overlooked or lacks detail.
— *Dave Gehrke*

The first stage of the IT planning model is **strategic information planning (SIP).** It includes several somewhat different types of activities. On the one hand, it refers to identifying a set of new applications—a portfolio—through which an organization will conduct its business. These applications make it possible for the organization to implement its business strategies in a competitive environment. This type of activity is evidenced in the opening case of this chapter.

On the other hand, SIP can also refer to a process of searching for *strategic information systems (SIS)* applications that enable an organization to develop a competitive advantage rather than just maintaining its position, as discussed in Chapter 3 and in Lederer and Sethi (1988).

Another type of activity is planning for a specific project (a topic which will be discussed in Chapter 14) or a set of issue-related projects, such as the Year 2000 case discussed in the following *IT at Work* story.

---

### *IT At Work*   PLANNING FOR THE YEAR 2000 PROBLEM IN CALIFORNIA

USING IT

...in Public Service

The Year 2000 situation (Chapter 15) can be especially serious in governmental systems. John Flynn, the CIO of the state of California, initiated a major attack on the problem as of Feb. 19, 1998, when a special conference was called. Flynn said: "Beneficiaries may not receive welfare checks, prisoners may become prematurely eligible for parole, every elevator in the state could stop functioning, the 911 system might fail . . . ." Actually, the state and local governments have been working on the problem for years. The situation intensifies since many government computers are interconnected. Welfare data, for example, are passed from the county to the state to federal agencies. The Feb. 19 meeting attempted to establish standards so that repairs are compatible across different systems. In the conference people welcomed the initiative. Los Angeles County officials said: "We know that the state is doing repair work, but they haven't told the counties what format they want to see data in." As a result some repairs already made by the counties might have to be redone to make them compatible with the state standards. Of the 70,000 computer programs used in Los Angeles, roughly 30,000 are affected by the Year 2000 problem. The 500 conference participants believe that with appropriate planning the problem will be solved in time, and at worst, there will be some inconveniences and delays in a few government services.

**For Further Exploration:** Explore the similarities and differences between governments and large corporations. Which of them can be more complex and why? ▲

SOURCE: *Los Angeles Times,* Feb. 16 and Feb. 20, 1998.

In either case, SIP must be aligned with overall organizational planning (see Ward and Griffiths [1996]). To accomplish this alignment, the organization must do the following:

▶ Set the IT mission.

▶ Assess the environment.

▶ Assess existing systems availabilities and capabilities.

▶ Assess organizational objectives and strategies.

▶ Set IT objectives, strategies, and policies.

▶ Assess the potential impacts of IT.

The output from this process should include the following: a new or revised IT charter and assessment of the state of the ISD; an accurate evaluation of the strategic aspirations and directions of the organization; and a statement of the objectives, strategies, and policies for the IT effort.

To carry out the above tasks there exist several methodologies; the major ones are: Business Systems Planning (BSP), Nolan's Stages of IT Growth model, ends/means (E/M) analysis, and critical success factors (CSFs). We look at each of these methodologies next.

## BUSINESS SYSTEMS PLANNING (BSP)

One of the earliest IT planning methodologies was **Business Systems Planning (BSP).** It was developed by IBM and has influenced other planning efforts such as Andersen Consulting's *Method/1* and James Martin and Clive Finkelstein's *Information Engineering.* BSP is a top-down approach that starts with business strategies. It deals with two main building blocks—**business processes** and **data classes**—which become the basis of an information architecture. From this architecture the planners can define organizational databases and identify applications that support business strategies, as illustrated in Figure 12.4.

Business processes are groups of logically related decisions and activities required to manage the resources of the business. The recognition that *processes*

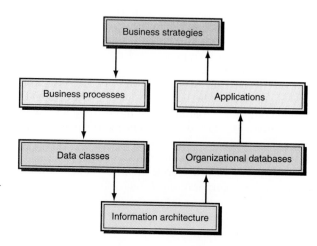

**FIGURE 12.4 Business Systems Planning (BSP) approach.** (*Source*: Derived from *Business Systems Planning—Information Systems Planning Guide,* Application Manual GE20-0527-3, 3rd ed., IBM Corporation, July 1981.)

(such as filling a customer order) are a more fundamental aspect of business than departments or other organizational arrangements is at the heart of much of the current business process reengineering activity discussed in Chapter 4.

Figure 12.5 shows the steps in a Business Systems Planning study. Note that the study is conducted by a study team, which may include representatives from

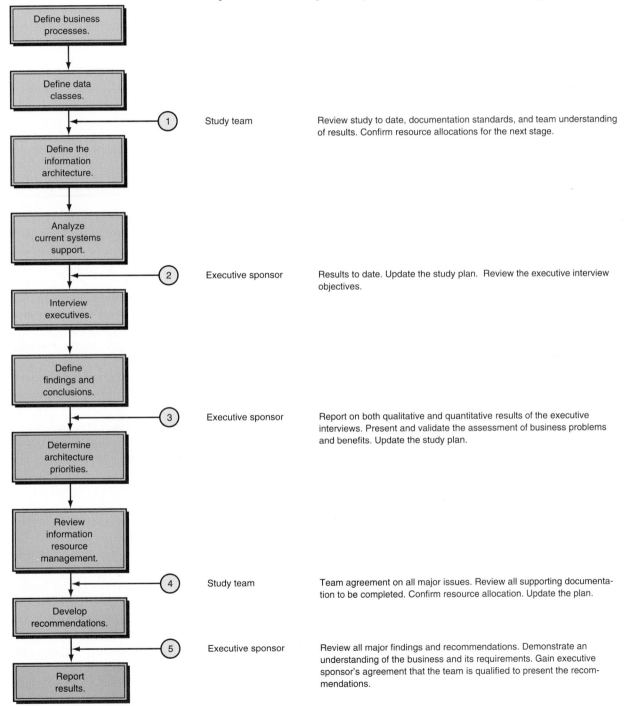

Define business processes.

Define data classes.

① Study team — Review study to date, documentation standards, and team understanding of results. Confirm resource allocations for the next stage.

Define the information architecture.

Analyze current systems support.

② Executive sponsor — Results to date. Update the study plan. Review the executive interview objectives.

Interview executives.

Define findings and conclusions.

③ Executive sponsor — Report on both qualitative and quantitative results of the executive interviews. Present and validate the assessment of business problems and benefits. Update the study plan.

Determine architecture priorities.

Review information resource management.

④ Study team — Team agreement on all major issues. Review all supporting documentation to be completed. Confirm resource allocation. Update the plan.

Develop recommendations.

⑤ Executive sponsor — Review all major findings and recommendations. Demonstrate an understanding of the business and its requirements. Gain executive sponsor's agreement that the team is qualified to present the recommendations.

Report results.

**FIGURE 12.5** Steps in BSP study, including five control points.

the IT group and representatives from end-user groups. The study team works under the sponsorship of a senior organizational executive. The process includes five control points, as identified in the figure. At each of these control points, the outputs of the process are subjected to a formal review prior to going on to the next steps.

BSP relies heavily on the use of matrices in the analysis of processes and data with the ultimate goal of developing the information architecture. For details see *Business Systems Planning* (1981).

## STAGES OF IT GROWTH

Richard Nolan developed a different approach to IT planning. His research (Nolan [1979]) indicates that organizations go through six **Stages of IT Growth** (called IS growth at that time). In each stage (see Box 12.1 on p. 529), four processes are active, to varying degrees. They are the application portfolio, users' role and awareness, IT resources, and management planning and control techniques.

The *application portfolio* is the mix of computer applications that the ISD has installed or is in the process of developing on behalf of the company. The *user's role and awareness* is the extent to which the user community is actively involved in identifying and promoting IT applications in its areas of responsibility. *IT resources* are the hardware, software, staff, and management available to provide information services to the company. Finally, *management planning and control* are the various tools and techniques, such as long-term or strategic planning and chargeback schemes, used to manage information resources.

The $y$ axis in the figure in Box 12.1 refers to IT expenditure. Note that the IT expenses *growth rate* is low during data administration, medium during initiation and maturity, and high during expansion (contagion) and integration. In addition to serving as a guide for expenditure, the model helps in determining the seriousness of problems.

Nolan's model became the basis of a strategic information systems planning methodology (known as the Nolan-Norton Methodology), and this model has been quite influential among IS practitioners. Academic researchers subsequently conducted studies to evaluate its validity, but they did not find a lot of support for specific aspects of the model (Benbasat et al. [1984]).

Even if it does not have strong empirical support, Nolan's model does represent a useful perspective for conceptualizing how new information technologies develop and how they should be planned and managed. For example, the development of the World Wide Web on the Internet in the 1990s seems to correspond in many organizations to the early stages of Nolan's model. The initiation stage extended through 1994. During this period, few organizations outside the academic and research worlds had any demand for Web sites. The expansion stage started around 1995 with a large increase in organizational activities on the Internet. In 1996 and 1997, some organizations expressed concern about the tremendous costs in relation to uncertain benefits, indicating an interest in moving on to the control stage. Development and use of organizational intranets and extranets in 1997/1998 corresponds to the integration stage.

King and Teo (1997) have taken Nolan's concept and applied it to the evolution of IT planning within organizations. Their research indicates that IT planning moves over time through the following four stages of growth:

1. *Separate planning*—weak relationship between IT and business planning.
2. *One-way linked planning*—IT plans are based on business plans.
3. *Two-way linked planning*—business and IT plans are coordinated.
4. *Integrated planning*—IT planning is an integral part of business planning.

## *A Closer Look* BOX 12.1

### NOLAN'S SIX STAGES OF IS GROWTH

The six stages (see figure below) are:

1. *Initiation:* Initial introduction of computers to the organization. Batch processing to automate clerical operations to achieve cost reduction, operational systems focus, lack of management interest, and Centralized ISD.
2. *Expansion (contagion):* Centralized rapid growth as users demand more applications based on high expectations of benefits, move to online systems as ISD tries to satisfy all user demands. Little control if any. IT expenses increase rapidly.
3. *Control:* In response to management concern about cost vs. benefits, systems projects are expected to show a return, plans are produced and methodologies/standards enforced. Often produces a backlog of applications and dissatisfied users. Planning and controls are introduced.
4. *Integration:* Considerable expenditure on integrating (via telecommunications and databases) existing

systems. User accountability for systems established, and ISD provides a service to users, not just solutions to problems. At this time there is a transition in computer use and an approach from data processing to information and knowledge processing (transition between the two curves).

5. *Data administration:* Information requirements rather than processing drive the applications portfolio and information is shared within the organization. Database capability is exploited as users understand the value of the information and are willing to share it.
6. *Maturity:* The planning and development of IT in the organization is closely coordinated with business development. Corporatewide systems are in place. The ISD and the users share accountability regarding the allocation of computing resources. IT has truly become a strategic partner.

SOURCE: Compiled from Nolan (1979).

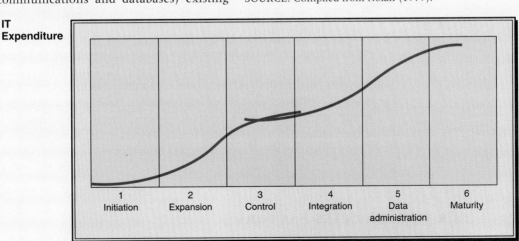

Nolan's six stages of IS growth.

### ENDS/MEANS ANALYSIS

**Ends/means (E/M) analysis,** the third SIP model we introduce, is a planning technique that IT planners can use to determine information requirements at the organizational, departmental, or individual manager level (Wetherbe and Davis [1982]). Based on general systems theory, this technique focuses first on the *ends,* or outputs (goods, services, and information), generated by an organizational process. Next, the technique is used to define the *means* (inputs and processes) used to accomplish these ends. The ends or outputs from one process—whether it is an organizational, departmental, or individual process—are the inputs to some other process. For example, the inventory process supplies parts to the production process, the accounting process generates budget information for other organizational processes, and the marketing process offers products to customer processes.

Ends/means analysis is concerned with both the effectiveness and the efficiency of generating outputs from processes. In this approach, *effectiveness* refers to how well outputs from a process match up with the input requirements of other processes. *Efficiency* refers to the amount of resources required to transform inputs into outputs.

For example, in developing information requirements using E/M analysis, an inventory manager might produce the following:

1. *Ends specification.* The output, or end result, of the inventory management function is an inventory kept as low as possible but at an acceptable level of availability.
2. *Means specification.* The inputs and processes to accomplish the ends are items such as: forecasts of future needs, amounts on hand and on order, items that are obsolete or in unusable condition, stock safety policy, demand variations, cost of ordering and holding inventory, and cost of items.
3. *Efficiency measures* needed for inventory management are the following: number and cost of orders placed, cost of holding inventory, and loss from disposal of obsolete or unusable inventory.
4. *Effectiveness measures* needed for inventory management are the following: number of items out-of-stock, and seriousness of stock-outs (in terms of lost business).

Information requirements determined by this approach are usually more extensive than those generated using other techniques. The problem with most information planning tools is that they usually result in information systems that provide only efficiency-oriented information. However, managers agree that it is more important to be effective than to be efficient. Ends/means analysis identifies effectiveness considerations in information requirements. Such considerations typically transcend departmental boundaries, so ends/means analysis is especially useful for database and other shared IT resources planning efforts.

### CRITICAL SUCCESS FACTORS

The final technique—the **critical success factors (CSF)** approach—was developed by Rockart (1982) to help identify the information needs of managers. The fundamental assumption is that in every organization there are three to six key functions. If these functions are done well, the organization will do well. Therefore organizations should continuously measure performance in these areas, taking corrective action where necessary.

Critical success factors vary by broad industry categories—manufacturing, service, or government—and by specific industries within these categories. For organizations in the same industry, CSFs will vary depending on whether the firms are market leaders or weaker competitors, where they are located, and what competitive strategies they follow. Environmental issues, such as the degree of regulation or amount of technology used, influence CSFs. In addition, CSFs change over time based on temporary conditions, such as high interest rates, or long-term trends.

IT planners identify CSFs by interviewing managers in an initial session, and then refine these CSFs in one or two additional sessions. The first step is to determine the organizational objectives for which the manager is responsible, and then the factors that are critical to attaining these objectives. To illustrate these concepts, Rockart points out that the objectives in the automobile industry are growth in earnings per share and high return on investment. The CSFs for attaining these objectives are: (1) attractive styling of the product line; (2) an efficient dealer organization; and (3) effective cost control in manufacturing.

The critical success factors approach encourages managers to identify what is most important to their performance and then develop good indicators of performance in these areas. Because there is more than one interview, it is less likely that key items will be overlooked. On the other hand, the emphasis on critical factors avoids the problem of collecting too much data, or including some data just because they are easy to collect. Table 12.2 provides a sample of questions in the CSF approach.

---

### *Table 12.2* Critical Success Factors Questions

1. What objectives are central to your organization?
2. What are the critical factors that are essential to meeting these objectives?
3. What decisions or actions are key to these critical factors?
4. What variables underlie these decisions, and how are they measured?
5. What information systems can supply these measures?

---

Once the CSFs are identified we can examine the *information needs* to achieve them by using the approach discussed in the next section.

## ▶ 12.3 INFORMATION REQUIREMENTS ANALYSIS

The goal of the second stage of the model, the *information requirements analysis*, is to ensure that the various information systems, databases, and networks can be integrated to support decision making and operations.

In the first step of **requirements analysis,** IT planners assess what information is needed to support current and projected decision making and operations in the organization. This is different from the detailed information requirements analysis associated with developing individual application systems (i.e., identifying required outputs and the inputs necessary to generate them, which we describe in Chapter 14). Rather, information requirements analysis is at a more comprehensive level of analysis, which encompasses infrastructures such as the data needed in a large number of applications (e.g., in data warehouse) of the whole organization.

## CONDUCTING A REQUIREMENTS ANALYSIS

There are several alternative approaches for conducting the requirements analysis. One of them is presented as a five-step model in Figure 12.6. The steps of the process are:

**STEP 1: DEFINE UNDERLYING ORGANIZATIONAL SUBSYSTEMS.** The first step of requirements analysis is to identify the underlying organizational processes, such as order fulfillment or product analysis.

**STEP 2: DEVELOP SUBSYSTEM MATRIX.** Once the underlying organizational processes are identified, the next phase of the requirements analysis exercise is to relate specific managers to organizational processes. This relationship can be represented by a matrix. The matrix is developed by reviewing the major decision responsibilities of each middle-to-top manager and relating them to specific processes. (For details see Premkumar and King [1994].)

**STEP 3: DEFINE AND EVALUATE INFORMATION REQUIREMENTS FOR ORGANIZATIONAL SUBSYSTEMS.** In this phase of the requirements analysis, managers with major decision-making responsibility for each process are interviewed in groups by the information analysts in order to obtain the information requirements of each organizational process.

**STEP 4: DEFINE MAJOR INFORMATION CATEGORIES AND MAP INTERVIEWS INTO THEM.** The process of defining information categories is similar to how data items for individual information systems are factored into entities and attributes.

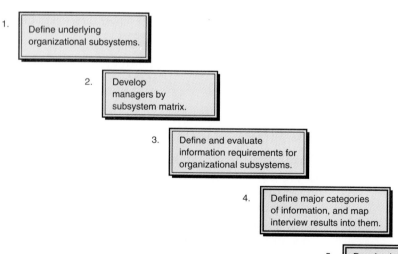

**FIGURE 12.6** Planning model for information requirements analysis.

**STEP 5: DEVELOP INFORMATION/SUBSYSTEM MATRIX.** Mapping information categories against organizational subsystems creates an information-categories-by-organizational-process matrix. Information categories can be accounts receivable, customers' demographics, or products' warranties. In each cell of the matrix an importance value is inserted.

## USING THE REQUIREMENTS ANALYSIS FOR PLANNING

The results of the requirements analysis exercise are threefold. It identifies high-payoff information categories, it provides an architecture for information projects, and it guides in resource allocation.

**IDENTIFYING HIGH PAYOFFS.** The organization can identify categories with high scores of the importance values to consider them first for feasibility studies. Planners use a special matrix, an information-categories-by-organizational-process matrix, to identify high payoff, but this matrix does not tell us whether it is technically, economically, or operationally feasible to develop systems for each information category. The matrix merely indicates the relative importance of information. Feasibility studies and other project-related tasks must still be performed, as described in Chapter 14. This step requires substantial creativity (e.g., see Ruohonen and Higgins [1998]).

**PROVIDING AN ARCHITECTURE.** Clearly defining the intersection of information and processes helps an organization avoid separate, redundant information systems for different organizational processes. When an organization decides to improve information for one process, other processes that need such information can be taken into consideration. By completing the conceptual work first, an organization can identify information systems projects that offer the most benefit and lead to cohesive, integrated systems. The resulting systems are far better than the fragmented, piecemeal systems that are continually being reworked or abandoned because they do not mesh with the organization's general requirements. To develop such integrated systems requires planning deliberately from the top down, rather than randomly from the bottom up, and this is done in the architecture phase.

**GUIDANCE IN RESOURCE ALLOCATION.** Once high-payoff areas of IT have been identified it is reasonable to allocate resources to them with high priority. Such an allocation is described next.

## RESOURCE ALLOCATION

**Resource allocation,** the third stage of the model for information planning, consists of developing the hardware, software, data communications, facilities, personnel, and financial plans needed to execute the master development plan as defined in the requirements analysis. This stage provides the framework for technology and labor procurement, and identifies the financial resources needed to provide appropriate service levels to users. The financial aspect will be discussed briefly here (with a more in-depth discussion in the next chapter).

Resource allocation is a contentious process in most organizations because opportunities and requests for spending far exceed the available funds. This can lead to intense, highly political competition between organizational units, which makes it difficult to objectively identify the most desirable investments.

Funding requests from the ISD fall into two categories. Some projects and infrastructure are necessary for the organization to stay in business. For example, it may be imperative to purchase or upgrade hardware if the network, or disk drives, or the processor on the main computer are approaching capacity limits. Obtaining approval for this type of spending is largely a matter of communicating the gravity of the problems to decision makers.

On the other hand, the IT planning process identifies an information architecture that usually requires additional funding for less critical items: new projects, maintenance or upgrades of existing systems, and infrastructure to support these systems and future needs. Approval for projects in this category may become more difficult to obtain because the ISD is already receiving so much funding for mandatory projects.

After setting aside funds for the first category, the organization can use the remainder of the IT budget for projects related mainly to the improved information architecture. The organization can prioritize spending among items in the architecture developed by using information requirements analysis. In addition to formally allocating resources through budgeting decisions, an organization can use chargeback mechanisms to fund corporate-level projects. In addition, management may encourage individual units to make their own decisions about IT expenses. Chapter 13 discusses chargeback, cost-benefit analysis, and other, more sophisticated analyses that can also be used to assess investment in individual IT projects and infrastructure investments.

## PROJECT PLANNING

The fourth and final stage of our model for information systems planning, **project planning,** provides an overall framework within which specific applications can be planned, scheduled, and controlled. Since this stage is associated with systems development, it will be covered in Chapter 14.

The relationship between the four stages of the IT model, the execution methods, and the output of each stage are shown in Figure 12.7 (p. 535). The figure summarizes the discussion in the previous sections and ties it in with the remainder of this chapter and to Chapters 13 and 14. A major output of the planning process is the IT architecture, which is discussed next.

## ▶ 12.4 PLANNING INFORMATION TECHNOLOGY ARCHITECTURES

*Information technology architecture* is the field of study and practice devoted to understanding and deploying information systems components in the form of an *organizational infrastructure*. In the simplest view, an IT architecture consists of a description of the combination of hardware, software, data, personnel, and telecommunications elements within an organization, along with procedures to employ them.

An information architecture is a high-level, logical plan of the information requirements and the structures or integration of information resources needed

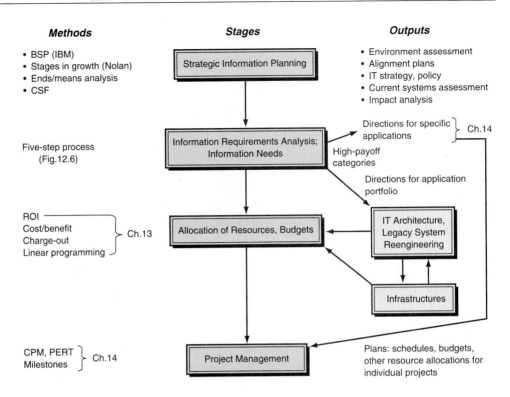

**FIGURE 12.7** IT planning: stages, methods, and outputs.

to meet those requirements. An *information technology architecture* specifies the technological and organizational infrastructure that physically implements an information architecture.

Three types of technology architectures are described in some detail: centralized, noncentralized, and client/server. The descriptions of the three categories are followed by a discussion of issues to be considered in choosing among them. The issue of **legacy systems**—holdovers from earlier architectures still in use after an organization migrates to a new architecture—is also discussed.

## CENTRALIZED ARCHITECTURE

The issue of *centralized* versus noncentralized (decentralized or distributed) computing is perhaps the foremost IT architectural issue with the most far-reaching impacts on other issues. **Centralized computing** has been the mainstay of corporate computing since the mid-1960s. As organizations migrate from centralized computing with mainframes to noncentralized architectures (usually with smaller computers) they still have to deal with their centralized systems, which have become *legacy* systems—hardware, software, and databases—on which they remain dependent.

Centralized computer systems are centered around a large computer, known as the "host," that provides computational power and internal storage. Several devices that lack self-contained computer processors, such as "dumb" terminals and printers, are connected to the mainframe. These devices are merely machines through which information is entered, distributed, stored, or communicated. There are five basic types of these devices: *terminals* for direct, temporary interaction with people (usually via a typewriter-like keyboard and an electronic monitor or screen); *output devices* such as printers and plotters for generating permanent outputs; *input devices* such as bar-code scanners for reading data; *communications devices* for exchanging data with other computer systems; and *storage devices* for electronically storing data. (See Technology Guide #1 for a review of computer hardware.) In each case, the host computer, usually a mainframe, is responsible for computer processing and it is centrally connected to each device. All information processing is orchestrated by the host, and much of it is carried out by the devices. This arrangement (Figure 12.8) is simple, direct, and easily controlled.

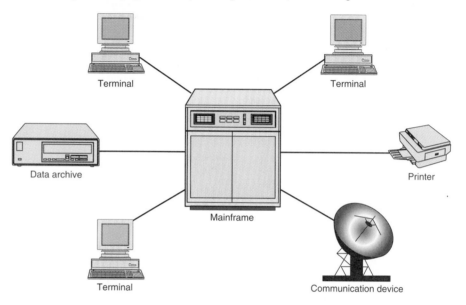

**FIGURE 12.8 An example of a centralized architecture.** (*Source*: Figures 12.8 through 12.10 are reprinted by permission from James C. Wetherbe and Nicholas Vitalare, *Systems Analysis and Design: Best Practices,* St. Paul, MN: West Publishing, copyright 1994 West Publishing Co. All rights reserved.)

*Mainframe computers* are relatively large computers built to handle large corporate-size databases, thousands of user terminals with fast response times, and millions of transactions. Mainframes have been responsible for the far-reaching growth in business computing and for bringing about the Information Age. But mainframe computing—as a technology and as a concept—is changing.

Although mainframes have represented the dominant centralized form of computing for over 30 years, minicomputers, workstations, and powerful PCs are challenging that dominance. Centralized computing, as an architecture, can include *all* sizes of computer processors, including a conglomeration of computers acting in parallel. Mainframes, by themselves, no longer "rule the roost," but they are still an important part of an IT architecture, along with smaller computers ranging down to palmtops. Whereas architectural decisions were relatively simple with one computer—the mainframe—they are now much more varied and complex with a wide range of computers available.

There is a large market for migrating legacy code to a client/server architecture.
— *Blake Thompson*

Mainframes have traditionally been expensive to purchase, operate, and maintain. Indeed, the cost of mainframes is the primary reason industry analysts predict their demise. But the acquisition and operational costs of mainframes continue to decline, because of technological improvements (such as cheaper, more powerful processors and peripheral equipment) and production cost reductions. Operational costs are also declining through modern managerial techniques such as "lights out" automated operations, which reduce the need for personnel to operate and maintain the mainframe system. Built-in monitoring tools allow for control of the mainframe and problem detection without the need of any human presence.

There are still many business applications for which mainframes reign. For high-volume, rapid-pace, transaction-intensive applications—such as airline reservation systems or stock trading systems—the mainframe still plays a vital role. Continuous availability and rapid response, as well as the benefits of reliability and security, are all available from the typical mainframe package, making it worthy of ongoing attention. Whether mainframe sales will continue at the same level, however, is still a controversial topic.

## NONCENTRALIZED COMPUTING

Noncentralized computing architectures are *decentralized* or *distributed*. **Decentralized computing** breaks centralized computing into *functionally equivalent* parts, with each part essentially a smaller, centralized subsystem. Almost all telephone utilities operate this way. Local switching stations contain local, centralized computers for the telephones in their immediate areas—each switching center is functionally identical. **Distributed computing,** on the other hand, breaks centralized computing into many computers that may not be (and usually are not) functionally equivalent. For a bank with many regional centers, for example, one location may process loan applications, another foreign currency transactions, and another business and individual deposit accounts. All branches can access all data, but certain computing functions are distributed across different regional centers.

As smaller, midrange computers (commonly called *minicomputers*) appeared, and as businesses increasingly required systems capable of sharing information and resources, computing evolved toward **peer-to-peer architectures** (see Figure 12.9). In this architecture, which is basically *distributed computing*, one computing resource shares processing with other computing resources. As peers, they also share devices and data with each other, although one "peer" may be more important than another for certain tasks or for controlling devices such as print-

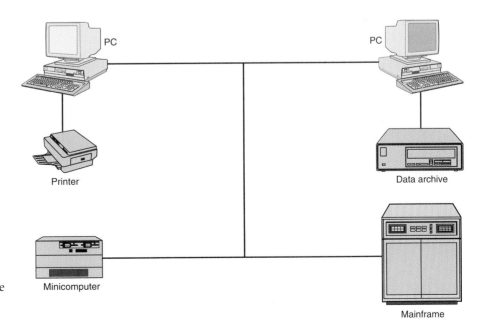

FIGURE 12.9 An example of peer-to-peer architecture.

ers. Such peer-to-peer relationships became even more common as PCs began to proliferate in offices, and as they were linked together for communications.

There is nothing inherently good or bad about a decision to centralize versus a decision to distribute an IT architecture. Instead, there are benefits and limitations to each approach. Most organizations would normally be categorized somewhere along a continuum between the extremes of completely centralized and completely distributed architectures.

Many older organizations that started out centralized have either evolved toward distributed computing in some way or developed new information systems based on distributed computing. As is true with any decision based on relative advantages and disadvantages, some organizations that completely abandoned centralized computing are now finding that their move was ill-timed. Likewise, some firms that fully embraced distributed computing wonder how anyone could operate otherwise. One of the most interesting varieties of distributed computing is client/server architecture.

## CLIENT/SERVER ARCHITECTURE

The increasing linkage of computers led to a new type of relationship, called **client/server** (see Figure 12.10). In one sense, it is a blending of host-based and peer-to-peer architectures. In the client/server model, servers provide for the data and processing needs of clients as in a centralized relationship, but the clients themselves are *fully capable computer processors* that have peer-to-peer relationships among themselves as well. A client can bring locally controlled computing directly to a user's desktop—while still sharing computing, devices, and data resources with other users.

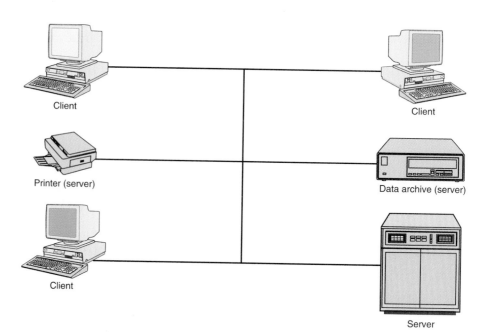

**FIGURE 12.10** An example of client/server architecture.

**DEFINITIONS.** Since client/server computing is a recent phenomenon, definitions from different sources may vary. A **client** is generally agreed to be any sys-

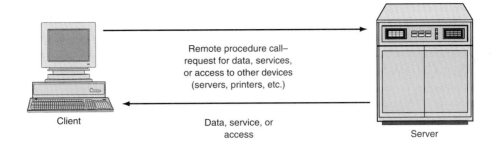

**FIGURE 12.11**
Client/server relationship.

tem or process that can *request and make use of* data, services, or access to other systems provided by a server. This arrangement is illustrated in Figure 12.11. An example of a client might be a desktop PC used by a financial analyst to request data from a corporate mainframe. Or it might be a laptop used by a salesperson to get pricing and availability information from corporate systems, calculate and print an invoice, and order goods directly—all from a client's office.

A **server** is generally considered to be any system or process that *provides* data, services, or access to other systems for clients, most often for multiple clients simultaneously (as a shared resource). In order to serve multiple clients, most servers—mainframes, minicomputers, workstations, and sometimes high-end PCs—are considerably more powerful than individual clients. An example of a server might be a powerful PC that controls network traffic in an office setting or a minicomputer that provides access to a corporate database.

There is a working relationship among clients and servers, in which requests for service from clients go to servers that attempt to fulfill those requests. Clients and servers process information independently but in conjunction with one another. Thus, we normally refer to this integral relationship by denoting it as "client/server" (as opposed to "client or server" or "client and server"). This may appear to be only a subtle difference, but it is an important one architecturally. Independence in a practical sense gives client/server systems the ability to be reconfigured rapidly—clients and servers can be easily added or subtracted, giving IT managers previously unheard-of architectural flexibility. As a result of this flexibility and high degree of functionality at a user's desk, client/server usage has grown rapidly. Some data on its growth are given in Box 12.2 (page 540).

**SPECIALIZATION.** Because servers may have to handle the needs of many clients in diverse operational conditions, they tend to be specialized in the types of services provided. For example, a *file server* may be used to manage data files, a *network server* may control network connections, and an *image server* may provide digitized office documents. Typical servers are dedicated to specific activities such as file management, database management, network management, groupware management, processing/transaction management, Internet, and so forth.

> A wide variety of jobs require a knowledge of client/service architecture.
> — *Blake Thompson*

Computing clients are not supposed to be bothered by server details, such as the location of the server, internal processes of the server, or how and where data are stored. It should not make any difference whether the client is getting data from a server on the other side of the building, or on the other side of the country. This hiding of server details is referred to as "service transparency," and it is an important architectural feature. Service transparency gives IT managers the ability to change servers and server processing without affecting clients, and vice versa.

# *A Closer Look*   BOX 12.2

## THE GROWTH OF CLIENT/SERVER APPLICATIONS

In the early 1990s, client/server systems were primarily used for non-mission-critical applications due to experiences with (or fears of) poor system stability and lack of robustness. However, the type of usage appears to be changing. Studies by International Data Corporation (IDC) and IDC Research Services in 1994 showed a significant increase in the number and size of installed business client/server systems—especially for critical online transaction processing.

IDC's study of 200 IS departments in different organizations found that 36 percent had large-scale client/server applications—ones with more than 50 users and dealing with applications critical to the organization. IDC found that 62 percent of 100 IS organizations surveyed were developing or planning to develop mission-critical applications in client/server environments. Finally, another IDC survey found that 31 percent of 280 organizations were using or developing mission-critical, online transaction processing client/server applications.

The studies also showed other interesting facts. The first IDC survey found that financial applications were the most prevalent client/server application, with operations, manufacturing, sales and marketing, human resources, and executive support following. This suggests that financial applications were the most prevalent to begin with, but it also points out that organizations had enough confidence in client/server systems to use them for critical financial applications.

Another interesting finding concerned changes or improvements that organizations wanted most to see in their client/server systems. First on the list was ease of use, followed by compatibility, lower cost, improved support, speed or performance, and finally documentation.

Results of a 1998 study indicated that client/server was voted as the second most important IT technology for 1998 (43% of the voters).

SOURCE: Adapted from "Client/Server Applications Grow Up," *ComputerWorld*, August 1994. © 1994 by *ComputerWorld*, Inc. For IDC studies see www.idcresearch.com.

**CLIENT/SERVER RESPONSIBILITIES.** Decisions must be made regarding the amount of work to be performed on a client versus the amount of work to be performed on a server. In any given setup, more work performed on one side is referred to as "fat" on that side. For example, if a client were a desktop PC for a financial analyst who calculated various financial reports on the PC and simply used the server to upload and download data, the client would be considered a "fat client" since most of the work is done by a client processor. The issue of where to distribute the processing load is technically important, and it can also have significant practical implications for users in terms of response time and resource availability.

A distributed application can be split in various ways across a client/server setup. Data can reside on the server and be used by a client, or they can reside on the client and be only partially shared (or not shared at all) with the server. Application processing can take place on the client, or it can take place on one or more servers—or both. Displaying computational or analytical results usually takes place on the client, the device directly interfacing with a human user, but even this can be partially split with the server by having the server determine what is displayed or by controlling the display shown on the client.

If this sounds complex, it *is*. As with most things, the advantage of flexibility brings the baggage of complexity. While client/server architectures give IT managers unprecedented flexibility to tune their systems and adjust to changing business needs, that flexibility also carries the burden of dealing with highly complex systems—planning, documenting, implementing, and maintaining them. Client/server systems put a premium on good IT management principles, people, and execution.

When the client/server architecture first appeared, many IT analysts believed that it would lower costs because the typical servers were much less expensive (in relation to processing power) than mainframe computers. However, because of the complexities of linking many different types of hardware and software, as well as the relative immaturity of the technology, it appears that client/server applications may actually be substantially more expensive to operate than mainframe applications. The International Technology Group estimated in 1996 that computing on a client/server system cost an average of $6,982 per user per year, versus $2,127 on a mainframe system (Depompa [1996]). However, other experts provided substantially different results.

In summary, client/server architectures offer the potential to use computing resources more effectively through division of labor among specialized processing units. A client desktop PC can use its strengths for calculations and visually displaying results, but it can also access the specialized functionality of a file server for the required data. This configuration also facilitates sharing hardware such as printers and plotters, and sharing data throughout the organization via an intranet. The client/server model fits well in an environment of disparate computing needs that are distributed throughout an organization, in an environment that is unstable or changes frequently, and in an environment characterized by risk and uncertainty. In today's business environments, we can fully expect that client/server architectures will continue to increase in popularity and sophistication.

> The vast majority of my company is on a client/server model: Some 60–70 separate servers service most of the offices across the country. Smaller LANs link via T1 lines to a larger WAN. I use our main server as an information resource, but manipulate much of the data I need after I have extracted it via my client PC.
>
> —*Kristin Borhofen*

## IT INFRASTRUCTURE CONSIDERATIONS

Different organizations have different infrastructure requirements. Broadbent et al. (1996) looked at how the characteristics and environments of organizations influenced their IT infrastructure. They identified five "core" infrastructure services provided in all of the firms, plus 18 others provided by some of the firms. They found the following infrastructure relationships in a sample of 26 large firms:

▶ *Industry*—manufacturing firms use less infrastructure services than retail or financial firms.

▶ *Market volatility*—firms that need to change products quickly use more infrastructure services.

▶ *Business unit synergy*—firms that emphasize synergies (e.g., cross-selling) use more infrastructure services.

▶ *Strategy and planning*—firms that integrate IT and organizational planning, and track or monitor the achievement of strategic goals, use more infrastructure services.

Broadbent et al. also studied the "reach and range" of IT services in these firms. *Reach* indicates how far the firm can connect. Reach is a continuum with the following end points: some firms can only connect within a single business unit while others can connect with "anybody, anywhere." *Range* refers to another continuum: the level of functionality of services provided at different locations. At the low end is the ability to send messages, while the highest level is performing complex transactions on multiple applications.

Based on analysis of their data, Broadbent et al. developed the model shown in Figure 12.12. This model indicates that two general factors influence infrastructure levels. The first factor is *information intensity,* the extent to which products or processes incorporate information. The second factor is *strategic focus,* the level of emphasis on strategy and planning. Firms with higher levels of these two factors use more infrastructure services, and have greater reach and range in their use of these services.

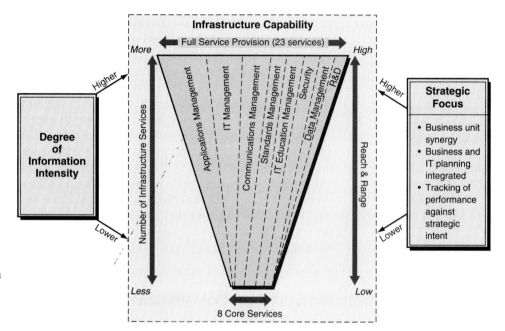

**FIGURE 12.12** Model of relationship between firm context and IT infrastructure. (*Source*: Broadbent, M., et al. [1996], p. 186.)

## CHOOSING AMONG ARCHITECTURE OPTIONS

Notice that the definition of IT architecture emphasizes the need to deal appropriately with the information needs of the business. A poorly organized IT architecture can disrupt a business by hindering or misdirecting information flows. Each organization—even within the same industry—has its own particular needs and preferences for information, and it therefore requires an IT architecture specifically designed and deployed for its use.

Unfortunately, many organizations have allowed their IT architecture to evolve over time without a systematic and explicit plan of what the architecture should be. In many organizations today, there is a wide mixture of IT components that do not fit well together and do not fit well with the needs of the business. Moreover, patching and fixing may continue to occur even though the business is highly dependent on the architecture to keep things running. Businesses usually do not have the luxury of stopping in midstream and "starting clean" with the development of a brand-new IT architecture.

Historically, developing an IT architecture was a somewhat mundane task. It merely involved identifying a desirable configuration, with a mainframe as a centralized computing device and terminals for access to this centralized mainframe. Decisions on hardware, software, databases, and telecommunications were all made periodically, based upon the notion that the centralized system was the key to running the business and dealing with its information needs.

However, with client/server systems, intranets, and extranets, IT architecture decisions are now much more complex and far reaching.

Another important facet of IT architecture deals with distributing, using, and managing information. Indeed, technology should not be selected and adopted by an organization merely to have technology in place, but rather to accomplish desired business goals (such as ensuring that information flows effectively and efficiently between functional areas of the business or out to customers and suppliers). Otherwise, an organization can end up with costly equipment that provides little return to the business on the technology investments.

Specialists who concern themselves with designing and deploying IT architecture are sometimes called **information engineers.** Information engineering is a top-down approach to information planning and implementation that also examines, describes, or reengineers (as necessary), and guides the direction of an existing IT architecture on an ongoing basis.

IT architecture is as much a *managerial issue* as it is a technological issue. Failure to deal with the managerial issues will lead even the best information technology architecture into a hopeless morass of components that do not fit the needs of the business. The IT architecture should be viewed from an enterprisewide computing perspective, and it should include the managerial issues and perspectives. Box 12.3 provides some suggestions for meeting enterprisewide information processing needs.

## *A Closer Look*  BOX 12.3

### SOME ENTERPRISE ARCHITECTURE PRINCIPLES

IT structures are becoming more dynamic in order to provide flexibility and yet maintain a stable focus on meeting future needs. To help ensure an IT architecture can achieve these often-conflicting goals, Richardson et al. (1990) argue that IT architectures must be *principle-based*, a premise that is even more compelling as we enter the twenty-first century. The following are examples of suggested enterprise IT principles in four areas.

*Organization principles.* All IT professionals in each business unit should report either directly or indirectly to the person responsible for the IT function in that business unit. Technology areas need to collaborate in order to provide the best service possible in application development and support—and to eliminate artificial internal competition. The IT function in a business unit must be organized to make IT a strategic tool, and IT professionals need to acquire the necessary skills to use and exploit IT as a strategic asset for the business.

*Applications principles.* Information systems planning must be an integral part of the strategic business planning process. Information systems should be developed using formal planning and software engineering methodologies. Successful projects require proactive user and sponsor involvement to ensure proper functionality and ultimate business success. Information systems development should provide for portability across various

hardware and software systems. Information systems need to be periodically reviewed in regard to their ability to meet current business needs and the possibility of technological obsolescence. Information systems should be managed as an enterprise asset.

*Data principles.* Data is to be viewed as a corporate asset and managed as such. Enterprise data plans need to be developed and maintained independent of the applications and the storage technologies. The user of an application should be responsible for the content and consistency of the data that the application provides or uses. A "steward" should be responsible for the security of the data associated with each specific application.

*Infrastructure principles.* An infrastructure architecture, generated through data modeling techniques, can facilitate information systems development and data sharing. A high level of connectivity and compatibility among all hardware, software, and communications components is necessary (and possibly could be attained through an intranet).

It is interesting to note that new IT solutions such as the data warehouse, client/server architecture, and extranets are very much in line with these four principles.

SOURCE: Richardson, G. L., et al., "A Principles-Based Architecture," *MIS Quarterly,* December 1990.

In today's computing environment, IT architectures are becoming increasingly complex, yet they still must be responsive to changing business needs. These requirements call for tough decisions about a number of architectural issues. The choices between *centralized computing, noncentralized computing,* and *end-user and enterprise computing* architectures are discussed below.

**CENTRALIZED COMPUTING.** As discussed earlier, this architecture has been the foundation of corporate computing for over 30 years. With increasing use of client/server systems, however, the role of the mainframe computer has shifted toward a more collaborative relationship with other computing resources within an organization. Although some proponents of PCs claim that the mainframe is dead, many experts agree that the mainframe is likely to exist for many years, particularly as a repository for data that can be centrally maintained for enterprisewide use. In a client/server model, the mainframe could be a large-scale file server, processing server, or database server. In other words, the mainframe—like other types of computers—can be assigned to specific kinds of information-processing tasks that are appropriate for the type of IT being used and the business needs being fulfilled. Mainframes, like other computers, are beneficial when used appropriately.

Providing access to and analyzing very large quantities of data are uses for which mainframes are still very appropriate. This is especially important in banking, insurance, airlines, and large retailing. The notion of treating data or information as an item of inventory has led to a movement toward *data warehousing.* Drawing upon the principles of inventory management, we can apply warehousing techniques to the timely and proper collection, cleansing, maintenance, and distribution of data and information. However data—and information—are only valuable if they are accessible. The Internet and intranets can be extremely useful in distributing information stored on mainframe (and smaller) computers. Building and managing intranets can be a daunting task, but it is becoming an essential task for many organizations.

**IN FAVOR OF CENTRALIZED COMPUTING.** Centralized computing can exploit the economies-of-scale that arise whenever there are a large number of IS applications and users in an organization. It may be more cost-effective to have one large-scale computing resource that is used by many than it is to have many small-scale computing resources used by many. The cost of a centralized facility can be divided among many users, usually reducing duplication of effort and more efficiently managing an operation (this applies to housing the computer, providing support services, etc.).

Centralized approaches can also offer easier control from an enterprise perspective. If important corporate data are stored on a centralized computing platform, a company is able to impose strict physical access controls to protect the data. When data are spread throughout an organization, securing and preserving data becomes much more difficult.

**IN FAVOR OF DISTRIBUTED COMPUTING.** A distributed approach argues that choices for computing are best handled at the point of the computing need; individual needs are best met with individualized computing. The rise in popularity of PCs, with their decreasing costs and increasing performance, has led many organizations to embrace decentralized computing, giving users direct control over their own computing. Application data can be entered, verified, and maintained closer to its source.

Distributed computing can also offer a high degree of flexibility and system redundancy. When an organization expands, it may be much easier and less expensive to add another local, distributed processor than to replace a centralized mainframe with an even larger mainframe. Moreover, a malfunctioning distributed computer ordinarily does not prevent other distributed computers from working, especially if data are partially or fully duplicated around the system, such as in the case of Lotus Notes/Domino or some intranets.

On the other hand, a centralized approach has a single point of failure—the central computer. When it goes down, no one computes. Consider an organization that sells by catalog: if its order processing system goes down for a day in the holiday season, it could lose hundreds of thousands of dollars in sales. Also, if the centralized computer is some distance away from a user, it may be noticeably slower to respond than a localized computer.

**BLENDING CENTRALIZED AND DISTRIBUTED COMPUTING.** As noted earlier, computing does not have to be entirely centralized or entirely decentralized—it can be a blending of the two models. In some circumstances, the mainframe (centralized resource) is viewed as a kind of peripheral device for other (distributed) computing resources. The mainframe can be a large file server that offers the economies-of-scale and data control that are desirable in most organizations, and yet still allows processing and handling of local needs via distributed computing resources. *What* to distribute *where* (and what not to distribute) then become key issues.

## END-USER COMPUTING ARCHITECTURE ISSUES

As computing has spread throughout organizations—especially in the form of personal computers—users themselves increasingly have taken on some duties and responsibilities of IT specialists. This phenomenon, commonly called *end-user computing,* is a field of study and practice that focuses on users and their ability to cope directly with IT.

> A smaller cluster of our developers work in peer-to-peer networking environments. These developers work in clusters for rapid sharing of code and easy access to each others' work without going through a server. Our financial center uses a mainframe to poll stores for sales and to track sales and book information. A number of dedicated dumb terminals are used to access this information.
> — *Kristin Borhofen*

IT executives, managers, and technical specialists should never forget that information systems are created for *people* to use. This section focuses on the relevant architectural and managerial issues for *end users*. In this book, **end-user computing** is defined as the use and/or development of information systems by the principal users of the systems' outputs or by their staffs. (See Chapter 14.)

**INFORMATION ARCHITECTURES AND END-USER COMPUTING.** Like an automobile, a personal computer gives its user great flexibility, power, and freedom. But just as the user of an automobile needs access to an infrastructure of highways, the user of a personal computer needs access to an infrastructure of databases and communication networks, including the Internet and possibly intranets. Creating such an architecture for end-users invariably involves addressing PC linkage issues.

There are five basic configurations of PCs for end users.

1. Centralized computing with the PC functioning as a "dumb terminal."
2. A single-user PC not connected to any other device.

3. A single-user PC connected to other PCs or systems using ad hoc telecommunications (such as dial-up telephone connections).
4. Workgroup PCs connected to each other in a small peer-to-peer network.
5. Distributed computing with many PCs fully connected by LANs or an intranet.

The key issue is to provide an architecture consistent with a division of responsibilities agreed upon by the ISD and user groups. If corporate control of data is paramount (perhaps for security reasons), then an architecture leaning toward centralized computing is appropriate. On the other hand, if data access and sharing are preeminent (perhaps among sales and production staffs), then a distributed architecture is probably better.

There are clear benefits and risks, but end-user computing with interconnected desktop PCs is inevitable. It is important that organizations maximize corporate business benefits and, at the same time, minimize risks and undue constraints on user initiative, business knowledge, and unity.

## REENGINEERING LEGACY SYSTEMS

Older systems that have become keystones for business operations are described as legacy systems. These systems may continue in use even after an organization switches to an architecture that is different from, and possibly incompatible with, the architectures on which they are based. They may still be capable of meeting business needs (and might not require any immediate changes), or they may be in need of reengineering to meet current business needs, requiring significant changes. Each legacy system has to be examined on its own merits, and a judgment made regarding the current and future value of the system to the organization. This type of decision—to keep, improve, or replace—can present management with agonizing alternatives. On one hand, keeping a legacy system active offers stability and return on previous investments ("if it ain't broke, don't fix it"). On the other hand, increasing processing demands and high operational costs make replacement attractive if not imperative. Newer systems, however, may be more risky and less robust.

**Reverse engineering** is the process of examining legacy systems to determine their present status, and to identify whatever changes are necessary to allow the system to meet current and future business needs. The results of this process can then guide the redesign and redevelopment of the system. Some reverse engineering tools automatically generate up-to-date documentation for legacy systems. Other tools in this category help programmers convert code in older programs into a more efficient form.

Legacy systems are not just mainframe systems. A legacy system might consist of PC programs that need to be reengineered and "ported" to a mainframe, which is sometimes called *upsizing* the system. Or a legacy system might be a mainframe application that needs to be reengineered and "rehosted" onto PCs, an example of *downsizing* a system. In each instance, a business is trying to effectively "rightsize" a legacy system to meet evolving business requirements.

Finally, but perhaps most importantly, organizations should reengineer legacy systems in concert with business process reengineering. (Refer to the "retooling" in Chapter 4.) Changes to the computerized or automated side of a business should synchronize with changes in other business processes. While reengineering legacy systems might be justified solely on a cost or efficiency basis, significant business gains can also be made when it is a coordinated part of reengineering the entire business to improve efficiency and effectiveness.

# ▶ 12.5 OTHER ISSUES IN IT PLANNING

IT planning is a complex process (e.g., see Ward and Griffiths [1996]). Of the many special topics in this category, we elected to present the following:

## GUIDELINES FOR IT PLANNING

At the beginning of this chapter we identified major issues in information systems planning, which are directly addressed by the four-stage planning model. Within the framework of the model, a set of appropriate methodologies is applied to each stage.

The model provides practical guidance for IS planning. It can help recognize the nature of planning problems in a specific project as well as identify the appropriate stage of planning to emphasize. Too often, this is not done. For example, some organizations view their IS function as making minimal contributions to strategic organizational objectives. In seeking to resolve this problem, they install a chargeback system (an issue in resource allocation) to make IT pay its own way. Other organizations have conducted a requirements analysis planning exercise to resolve the same problem. Although these activities may result in improved IT services, the IT planning model suggests they are probably not the appropriate methodologies for the given situation. If the ISD is not contributing to the attainment of organizational objectives, the four-stage IT planning model indicates that *a strategic planning effort* should precede requirements analysis and resource allocation planning.

To determine how much IT planning is needed, an organization should assess the extent to which each stage of IT planning has been accomplished. It can implement this assessment through a series of questions related to major activities and outputs in each of the stages of the four-stage planning model in Figure 12.2. After determining the IT planning needs at each stage, it can select appropriate methodologies.

**STRATEGIC PLANNING.** Each of the four stages of the IS planning model raises specific questions. In assessing the strategic planning stage, organizations need to answer questions such as:

▶ Is an IT mission clearly expressed in an IT charter?

▶ Is there a comprehensive assessment of the environment? Are the IT capabilities adequately assessed? Have new opportunities been identified? Is the current business environment understood? Is the current applications portfolio defined and documented? Is the ISD image healthy?

▶ Is there a clear definition of organizational objectives and strategies? Has the strategic organizational plan been reviewed? Have strategic applications been identified to improve strategic advantage?

▶ Are IT policies, objectives, and strategies defined? Is the ISD structure appropriate for the overall organization? Is the IS technology focus appropriate to the technology focus of the organization? Are the objectives for allocating IT resources appropriate? Are the IS management processes appropriate? Are the functional capability objectives appropriate?

If answers to these questions (some of which will be discussed in Chapter 15) indicate a weakness, strategic planning is required.

**REQUIREMENTS ANALYSIS.** To conduct an assessment of the requirements analysis stage, an organization should answer the following questions:

▶ Is there an adequate assessment of the organizational information requirements? Is the overall information architecture identified? Is there a good understanding of current information needs of the organization? Is there a good understanding of projected information needs of the organization? Are the major databases and their relationships defined?

▶ Is there a master IT development plan? Are IT projects well defined? Are projects ranked by priority? Is there a multiyear development schedule?

If an organization does not have acceptable answers to these questions, a requirements analysis planning exercise is in order.

**RESOURCE ALLOCATION.** To assess the resource allocation stage, an organization should answer the following questions:

▶ Does the organization have a resource requirements plan? Are trends identified? Is there a hardware plan? Is there a software plan? Is there a data management plan? Is there a data communications plan? Is there a personnel plan? Is there a facilities plan? Is there a financial plan?

▶ Does the organization have an adequate procedure for resource allocation?

If an organization does not have acceptable answers to these questions concerning the resource allocation stage, resource allocation planning is needed.

**PROJECT PLANNING.** This issue is covered in more detail in Chapter 14. However, to have a complete review of the IT planning process, an organization should answer the following questions in regard to project planning:

▶ Is there a procedure for evaluating projects in terms of difficulty or risk?

▶ Are project tasks usually identified adequately?

▶ Are project cost estimates generally accurate?

▶ Are project time estimates generally accurate?

▶ Are checkpoints defined to monitor progress of projects?

▶ Are projects generally completed on schedule?

If an organization does not get satisfactory answers to the project planning questions, it should review the project planning techniques that are discussed in Chapter 14.

**SELECTING METHODOLOGIES.** Revisiting the basic four-stage model, we see that it provides considerable insight into IT planning issues and reduces confusion about competing planning methodologies. For example, an organization that follows the planning model may find that it should postpone using a resource allocation methodology until it has resolved issues related to requirements analysis or strategic planning. Keep in mind, however, that the planning model does not indicate which methodology should be used for any particular planning stage. Some organizations find that using several methodologies provides additional useful perspectives that are unavailable when only one is used.

## INTERORGANIZATIONAL AND INTERNATIONAL SYSTEMS

Information technology planning may get more complicated when several organizations are involved, as well as when we deal with multinational corporations.

**PLANNING FOR INTERORGANIZATIONAL SYSTEMS.**  Internal information systems of business partners must talk with each other effectively and efficiently. In Chapters 5 and 6 we introduce IT technologies such as EDI, e-mail, and extranets, which facilitate communication and collaboration between companies. IT planning that involves several organizations may be complex (see the opening case). The problem is that some information systems may involve hundreds or even thousands of business partners. IT planners should use focus groups of customers, suppliers, and other business partners, especially during the strategic information planning as well as during the information requirements analysis. Planning for project management of IOSs can be fairly complex. IT planners may create virtual planning teams that will work together on projects such as extranets or EDI. Such cooperation is especially important in strategic planning that involves infrastructure. Questions such as who is going to pay for what, can become critical factors in cost/benefit analysis and justification of information systems applications.

> My company has eight divisions running four distinctly different types of accounting software. It takes weeks to consolidate financials, which if they were on the same system, would take minutes. That's poor planning.
> — *Mike Rewald*

Using an extended supply chain approach and adopting enterprise software can be examples of joint planning. If company A will use SAP and company B will use Baan software, there could be additional expenses for joint projects.

**MULTINATIONAL CORPORATIONS.**  Multinational corporations face a complex legal, political, and social environment which complicates corporate IT planning. Therefore, many companies prefer to decentralize their IT planning and operations, empowering their IT managers. However, such a policy may be self-defeating since communication, coordination, and collaboration may require large expenses. Mobil Oil Corp. was forced to centralize its IT operations because of the high expenditures, as shown in the *IT at Work* example that follows.

---

*IT At Work*   **IT PLANNING AND CENTRALIZATION AT MOBIL OIL**

*U*SING IT
...in Production &
Operations Management

With sales approaching $100 billion a year and operating in over 125 countries, **Mobil Oil** is a true multinational corporation. The company originally preferred to decentralize its information resources. Spending $1 billion a year on IT, the company realized that in the decentralized environment, local managers were making IT decisions independent of the decisions made in other business units. Communication among business units was poor, resources were wasted, and end-users complained. It became clear that it was necessary to reengineer the corporate IT.

The process started with the establishment of a planning team that worked with IT consultants. Analysis of the existing system revealed many duplications and redundancies. The team recommended a new, centralized architecture based on one operating system and a standard set of applications. The planning team estimated a 40 percent reduction in the IS staff and a huge saving of software purchasing cost, due to the large quantity purchased (volume discounts). To move to the centralized system, Mobil consolidated 6 mainframe data centers into two. All pending IT projects were discontinued, and an evaluation of all IS staff was done to determine their competence levels. The IS staff was reduced from 4,400 to 2,400 in 1997. To assure success, Mobil appointed its first-ever CIO, Ellen McCoy. She introduced a strict system for examining requests for nonstandard hardware and software. Furthermore, nonstandard items must be paid for only from end-user accounts.

By educating both functional managers and IS managers about IS and business issues, McCoy facilitated a better understanding and cooperation in the managerial ranks.

**For Further Exploration:** Why was it possible to reduce the IS staff? What are the benefits of the centralized architecture? ▲

SOURCE: Condensed from Gross, D., "Getting the Lead Out," *CIO*, April 15, 1997.

▶ MANAGERIAL ISSUES

1. *Importance.* Getting IT ready for the future—that is, planning—is one of the most challenging and difficult tasks facing all of management, including IS management. Each of the four steps of the IT strategic planning process—setting the mission, assessing the environment, including the organization's goals and objectives, and, finally, setting the IS objectives, strategies, and policies—presents its own unique problems. Yet, without planning, or with poor planning, the organization may be doomed.

2. *Organizing for planning: Many issues.* What *should* be the role of the ISD? How should it be organized? staffed? funded? How should human resources issues, such as training, benefits, and career paths for IS personnel, be handled? What about the environment? the competition? the economy? governmental regulations? emerging technologies? What is the strategic direction of the host organization? What are its key objectives? Are they agreed upon and clearly stated? Finally, with these strategies and objectives and the larger environment, what strategies and objectives should IS pursue? What policies should it establish? What type of information architecture should the organization have: centralized or not centralized? How should investments in IT be justified? The answer to each of these questions must be tailored to the particular circumstances of the ISD and the larger organization of which it is a part.

3. *Fitting the IT architecture to the organization.* Management of an organization may become concerned that their IT architecture is not suited to the needs of the organization. In such a case, there has likely been a failure on the part of the IT technicians to determine properly the requirements of the organization. Perhaps there has also been a failure on the part of management to understand the type and manner of IT architecture that they have allowed to develop or that they need.

4. *IT architecture planning.* IT specialists versed in the technology of IT must meet with business users and jointly determine the present and future needs for the IT architecture. In some cases, IT should lead (e.g., when

business users do not understand the technical implications of a new technology); in other cases, users should lead (e.g., when technology is to be applied to a new business opportunity). Plans should be written and published as part of the organizational strategic plan and as part of the IT strategic plan. Plans should also deal with training, career implications, and other secondary infrastructure issues.

5. *IT policy.* IT architectures should be based on corporate guidelines or principles laid out in policies. These policies should include the roles and responsibilities of IT personnel and users, security issues, cost-benefit analyses for evaluating IT, and IT architectural goals. Policies should be communicated to all personnel who are managing or directly affected by IT.

6. *Ethical and legal issues.* Conducting interviews for finding managers' needs and requirements must be done with full cooperation. Measures must be taken to protect privacy.

   In designing systems one should consider the people in the system. Reengineering IT means that some employees, for example, those who have worked many years as COBOL programmers and systems analysts, will have to completely reengineer themselves. Some may feel too old to do so. Also, a client/server environment requires sharing. Some employees may have developed systems on their free time. These systems may be their private intellectual property. Appropriate planning must take these and other issues into consideration.

7. *IT strategy.* In planning IT it is necessary to examine three basic strategies.

   a. Be a *leader* in technology. Companies such as FedEx, Dell, and Wal-Mart are known for their leading strategy. The advantages of being a leader are the ability to attract customers, to provide unique services and products, and to be a cost leader. However, there is a high development cost of new technologies and high probability of failures.

   b. Be a *follower.* This is a risky strategy of being left behind. However, you do not risk failures, and you implement new technologies at a fraction of the cost.

   c. Be an *experimenter,* on a small scale. This way you minimize your research and development investment and the cost of failure. Yet, if new technologies prove to be successful you can move fairly fast for full implementation.

# KEY TERMS

## CHAPTER HIGHLIGHTS *(L–x means learning objective number x)*

▶ Information technology and systems planning can help organizations meet the challenges of a rapidly changing business and competitive environment. (L–1)

▶ The major information systems planning issues are strategic alignment, architecture, resource allocation, and time and budget considerations. (L–1)

▶ Aligning IT plans with business plans makes it possible to prioritize IS projects on the basis of contribution to organizational goals and strategies. (L–2)

▶ The four-stage IT planning model includes strategic planning, requirements analysis, resource allocation, and project planning. (L–3)

▶ Strategic information systems planning involves methodologies such as Business Systems Planning (BSP), Stages of IT Growth, ends/means (E/M) analysis, and critical success factors (CSFs). (L–4)

▶ Information technology architectures can be centralized, distributed, or client/server. (L–5)

▶ Organizations can use enterprise architecture principles to develop an information technology architecture. (L–5)

▶ Specific questions can help identify stages of the four-stage model that require additional planning activities. (L–6)

## QUESTIONS FOR REVIEW

1. Briefly discuss the evolution of IT planning.

2. What are some of the problems associated with IT planning?

3. Define and discuss the four-stage model of IT planning.

4. Identify the methods used for strategic planning, and review their characteristics.

5. Define and discuss the steps necessary to build an information architecture.

6. What is information technology architecture, and why is it important?

7. What are the three fundamental IT architectures, and what are their primary differences?

8. What are the advantages and disadvantages of centralized computing architectures?

9. What are some types of noncentralized computing architectures? What are their advantages and disadvantages compared to centralized computing architectures?

10. What is a legacy system? Why do companies have legacy systems?

11. Describe the client/server model and how it works.

## QUESTIONS FOR DISCUSSION

1. Discuss how strategic planning, as described in this chapter, could help an electric utility plan its future.

2. How might an organization with a good strategic idea be limited in its ability to implement that idea if it has an inferior or inappropriate information architecture? Provide an example.

3. What type of problems might an organization encounter if it focuses only on resource allocation planning and project planning?

4. What are the advantages of a "top-down" approach to information planning? Are there any disadvantages?

5. Why is it so important to align the IT plan with organizational strategies? What could happen if the plan is not aligned with these strategies?

6. Discuss possible pitfalls to avoid in a large strategic information planning project. What are the potential impacts on the information systems department if it does not avoid these pitfalls?

7. Some organizations feel that IT planning is a waste of time, because the competitive environment and technologies are changing so rapidly. They argue that their plans will be obsolete before they are completed. Discuss.

8. What factors should a firm consider when evaluating a move from a mainframe computing system to a client/server system? What factors should not be considered?

9. Should there be a correlation between a firm's human organization architecture and its IT architecture (e.g., centralized IT for a centralized organization)?

10. Review the opening case. What approach was used to develop an information systems plan?

## EXERCISES

1. Using the ends/means analysis method of strategic planning, identify new strategic initiatives that a university might make using information technology.

2. Visit with managers of an ISD in some medium-size or large organization, and find out which of the four stages of the information systems planning model they have used.

3. In a computer publication, find an article that describes the IT architecture at a large multinational corporation. Evaluate the reasons behind the architecture. Do they seem to be valid?

4. Find a local organization that uses a mainframe, and interview IT managers to determine the rationale. Are there plans to stop using a mainframe? If so, why? If not, why not?

5. Find a local organization that has a client/server system. Interview IT managers to determine the major problems in managing it.

6. What kind of planning is done in your university or place of work to assure that the Internet demand in the future will be met?

7. It was the third time in 14 months that John Henderson had to go to Methodist Hospital. He had broken a wrist playing basketball 14 months ago, only to break an ankle 6 months later playing volleyball. Now this past week, he experienced chest pains that turned out to be a pulled muscle in his chest as a result of weightlifting at the gym.

   John found it incredible that each time he went to the hospital he was a complete stranger. Each time he had to provide a medical history, insurance information, employment information, and demographic information. It took up to an hour to get all of this data recorded and for him to be admitted. Finally, in a moment of extreme frustration during his third attempt to get admitted, he said "Don't you people have any corporate memory? Don't you have any way to determine or keep track of the fact that I have been here before?"

   Wendy Brown, a physician overhearing the comments, brought up the issue at a staff meeting the following week. The hospital was interested in what it might do to avoid such frustration to patients and reduce the cost of having to capture information over and over again every time a patient was admitted. As a result, the staff met with the information systems group to determine what could be done to improve the admission process.

   a. Use strategic planning methods to determine what Methodist Hospital should do to improve its competitive position.

   b. Based on the ideas that you came up with in (a), decide how these ideas might be assessed and selected. What types of project planning might be appropriate for proceeding with them?

## GROUP ASSIGNMENTS

1. Divide into groups of six people or less. Each group will be entrepreneurs attempting to start some kind of nationwide company. Each group should describe the IT architecture it would build, as well as the expected benefits from, and potential problems with, the IT architecture they have chosen.

2. Have teams from the class visit IT project development efforts at local companies. The team members should interview members of the project team to ascertain the following information:

   a. How does the project contribute to the goals and objectives of the company?

   b. Is there an information architecture in place? If so, how does this project fit into that architecture?

   c. How was the project justified?

   d. What planning approach, if any, was used?

   e. How is the project being managed?

3. Assign groups to the following industries: banking, airlines, healthcare, insurance, and large retailing. Each group will investigate the use of the mainframe in one industry and prepare a report on the future of the mainframe.

## INTERNET EXERCISES

Note: The URLs included here were current when the book went to press. However, they are subject to change without notice. Please consult the Turban Web site (www.Wiley.com/college/turban2e).

1. Go to the Web page at www.city.grande-prairie.ab.ca/webs_sbp.htm#Information_Technology_Plans. Then follow the links to pages covering Strategic Planning for Information Technology and Telecommunications. Use the links in this section to go to other places, and try to find references to aligning IT (including telecommunications) plans with organizational strategy. Prepare a summary report on your findings.

2. Review the IT architecture at www.ai.org/dpoc/html/II.html. Can you think of anything that should be included in this architecture but isn't?

3. Go to the Web page at www.dwinc.com/strat.htm and read the content. Compare and contrast the approach on this page to other approaches to strategic information systems planning.

4. Enter www.cio.com. Review the latest IT planning surveys and reviews reported. Start with the Oct. 1997 survey done by CIO Communications Inc.

# Minicase 1

## Oregon Geographic Information System Plan

Geographic information systems (GISs) are becoming increasingly important to governmental agencies in conducting their business and serving the public. The state government in Oregon recognized the increasing importance of GIS as a tool, and the potential benefits of coordination among agencies to avoid duplicated efforts and incompatible data. It therefore created a Geographic Information Council, consisting of 22 people from agencies at the federal, state, and local level, to develop a strategic plan to promote the effective use of GIS in Oregon. The planning process commenced in 1995 and produced a comprehensive plan dated March 1996. The plan identified and prioritized goals and strategies, including leadership responsibilities and time frames for each major item. The council circulated the draft plan to GIS personnel in different organizations, to obtain a peer review before finalizing the document.

The plan starts with a "Vision for GIS," a scenario for potential types and levels of usage by the year 2000. This vision incorporates potential advances in technology such as multimedia, organizational structures including a statewide centralized GIS data administration function, a high-bandwidth telecommunications infrastructure, and adequate funding for GIS activities.

▶ **Benchmarks for Success** The plan identified criteria for evaluating its own validity:

- ▶ GIS integrated into governmental processes ("as common as word processing").

- ▶ Geographic data gathered and managed cooperatively and made available to the public.

- ▶ Statewide standards for spatial data.

- ▶ Centralized catalog of statewide GIS data.

- ▶ GIS as an integral part of curriculum for K–12 and higher education throughout the state.

▶ **Goals and Strategies.** The plan established specific goals, strategies for achieving them, agencies with lead responsibilities, and target dates. The goals include data such as: (1) currency and completeness; (2) security; (3) ease of use and accessibility; (4) incorporation of metadata indicating applicability; (5) coordination of collection and maintenance; (6) standardization.

For technology, the goals include: (1) network access for agencies and public; (2) compatible data exchange formats; (3) real-time update capability; (4) master contracts for hardware/software/training; (5) integration with global positioning system (GPS) technology; (6) centralized data repository.

For people and organizations, the goals include: (1) stable funding and resources; (2) recruitment and retention of GIS employees; (3) definition of a model GIS organizational structure; (4) develop an educational program; (5) effective marketing of Oregon GIS program.

▶ **Follow-up.** The planning group recognized that this plan would lose its value if not maintained, or if there were no follow-up on its recommendations. Therefore the plan includes the following ongoing strategies: (1) monthly meetings of the planning group; (2) workgroups to address specific recommendations; (3) development of GIS plans at other state agencies; (4) distribution of supplements and updates four times a year; (5) measurement against benchmarks and revision of the plan for the next two-year period.

### Questions for Minicase 1

1. Which stage(s) and activities of the four-stage planning model is/are included in the Oregon GIS planning effort?

2. Based on material presented in this chapter and your own personal evaluation, identify things that the planners did well in this project.

3. Can you see any problems or weaknesses with this planning effort?

4. Discuss possible differences in IT planning for governmental agencies, as discussed in this minicase, versus in business organizations.

5. Identify businesses and other private organizations that might want to use GIS data created and maintained by public agencies in Oregon. Discuss how (or whether) public agencies should charge private organizations for such data.

SOURCE: Condensed from Oregon Geographic Information System Plan at www.sscgis.state.or.us/coord/ogisplan.html, 1997, 1998.

# Minicase 2

## Computer Problems at Oxford Health Plans

Oxford Health Plans was a successful HMO and a stock market favorite. But in late October 1997 the company stock plunged almost 75 percent in a few days. A major reason was a long list of troubles with its computer information system: how it was designed, how it was installed, and how Oxford executives managed it.

Oxford is one of the largest HMOs in the United States. The company started to plan its computerized system in 1993 when it had only 217,000 members. However, the system was completed in October 1996, when there were 1.5 million members. Thus, the system was outdated by the time it was completed. For example, processing a new-member signup took 15 minutes instead of the planned 6 seconds. Oxford continued to sign up new members but the office infrastructure was unable to process the applications.

What happened? Oxford locked into an inflexible design in 1993, which made it difficult to quickly adjust to subsequent technological improvements as the project moved forward. Moreover, Oxford tried to convert the bulk of its membership-billing database to a new system in one sweeping conversion. This proved to be too difficult. They should have used some kind of prototyping, according to experts (e.g., put all the small customers on the new system and see how it goes). On top of this, Oxford's old software was riddled with seemingly innocuous errors in member records. This created an enormous problem in the new system.

The new software is very unforgiving. "If you don't get it right, you don't get it in," said Seth Lefferto, Oxford's IT manager. So, when the program detected a single mistake, for example, in a 1000-member account, it kicked out the entire group—delaying billing for all members by weeks, or even months. Attempts to fix the problem with the database vendor took months. Oxford had no backup system. As a result there were many delays and customers received flawed invoices.

By the time Oxford started to catch up on long-overdue accounts, contacting customers for the first time in months, many refused to pay and others said they had quit the HMO long ago. By Fall 1997, Oxford had to write off $111 million in uncollectible bills and admitted it had overestimated its membership by 30,000.

Oxford's failure to process claims on time angered many star physicians and renowned teaching hospitals whose participation was a key selling point of Oxford. Oxford was unable to pay many physicians and hospitals. So they started losing important health services providers. By February 1998, Oxford's stock dipped to around $15 (from $89 a few months earlier). Some providers took legal action. An additional blow came to Oxford when it was discovered that the company lost track of its actual medical costs—critical information for reacting to unforeseen problems, setting reserves, and projecting future liabilities. Oxford's executives were not getting the data they needed to make accurate estimates of costs incurred but not reported.

The large-scale conversion to the 1996 system was too much for the corporate ISD, which grew too fast but did not change its operations. There was little IT planning, no intermediate goals, no coordination of multiple IT projects, etc.

By the time that this case was written (Feb. 1998), Oxford was still in big trouble, desperately looking for dozens of IS employees and managers to rescue its information systems.

### Questions for Minicase 2

1. Why was it difficult to plan the new system?

2. How could prototyping have been beneficial in this case?

3. Assume you were the IT director at Oxford in 1993. Your responsibility was to prepare the conversion. You knew that you were going to grow, but you had no clue that the growth was going to be so explosive. Use some of the principles of planning you learned and prepare a high-level IT plan for the conversion.

# REFERENCES AND BIBLIOGRAPHY

1. Benbasat, I., et al., "A Critique of the Stage Hypothesis: Theory and Empirical Evidence," *Communications of the ACM*, Vol. 27, No. 5, May 1984.

2. Blodgett, M., "Game Plans" (strategic plans), *CIO Magazine*, Jan. 1998.

3. Brancheau, J. C., et al., "Key Issues in Information Systems Management: 1994–1995 SIM Delphi Results," *MIS Quarterly*, Vol. 20, No. 2, June 1996.

4. Broadbent, M., et al., "Firm Context and Patterns of IT Infrastructure Capability," *Proceedings of the 17th International Conference on Information Systems*, Cleveland, December 16–18, 1996.

5. *Business Systems Planning—Information Systems Planning Guide*, Application Manual GE20-0527-3, 3rd ed., IBM Corporation, July 1981.

6. Callon, J. D., *Competitive Advantage Through Information Technology*, New York: McGraw-Hill Companies, 1996.

7. Depompa, B., "Rising from the Ashes," *Information Week*, May 27, 1996.

8. Goodhue, D. L., et al., "Strategic Data Planning: Lessons from the Field," *MIS Quarterly*, Vol. 16, No. 1, March 1992.

9. Gray, P., et al., eds., *Management of Information Systems*, 2nd ed., Fort Worth, TX: Dryden Press, 1994.

10. Ives, B., and G. P. Learmonth, "The Information System as a Competitive Weapon," *Communications of the ACM*, Vol. 27, No. 12, December 1984.

11. King, W. R., and T. S. H. Teo, "Integration Between Business Planning and Information Systems Planning: Validating a Stage Hypothesis," *Decision Sciences*, Spring 1997.

12. Lederer, A. L. and V. J. Sethi, "The Implementation of Strategic Information Systems Planning Methodologies," *MIS Quarterly*, Vol. 12, No. 3, September 1988.

13. McLean, E. R., and J. V. Soden, *Strategic Planning for MIS*, Wiley-Interscience, 1977.

14. McNurlin, B. C., and R. H. Sprague, Jr., *Information Systems Management in Practice*, 4th ed., Upper Saddle River, NJ: Prentice-Hall, 1998.

15. Nolan, R. L., "Managing the Computer Resource: A Stage Hypothesis," *Communications of the ACM*, Vol. 16, No. 3, March 1973.

16. Nolan, R. L., "Managing the Crises in Data Processing," *Harvard Business Review*, March/April 1979.

17. Premkumar, G., and W. R. King, "Organizational Characteristics and Information Systems Planning: An Empirical Study," *Information Systems Research 5*, No. 2, June 1994.

18. Raghunathan, B., and T. S. Raghunathan, "Adaptation of a Planning System Success Model to Information Systems Planning," *Information Systems Research 5*, No. 3, September 1994.

19. Reich, B. H., and I. Benbasat, "Measuring the Linkage Between Business and Information Technology Objectives," *MIS Quarterly*, March 1996.

20. Rockart, J. F., "Chief Executives Define Their Own Data Needs," *Harvard Business Review*, March/April 1979.

21. Ruohonen, M., and L. F. Higgins, "Application of Creativity Principles to IS Planning," *Proceedings HICSS*, Hawaii, Jan. 1998.

22. Ward, J., and P. Griffiths, *Strategic Planning for Information Systems*, 2nd ed., Chichester: John Wiley & Sons, 1996.

23. Wetherbe, J. C., "Executive Information Requirements: Getting It Right," *MIS Quarterly*, Vol. 15, No. 1, March 1991.

24. Wetherbe, J. C., "Four-Stage Model of MIS Planning Concepts, Techniques, and Implementation," in Banker, R., R. Kaufman, and M. Mahmood, eds., *Strategic Information Technology Management: Perspectives on Organizational Growth and Competitive Advantage*, Harrisburg, PA: Idea Group Publishing, 1993.

25. Wetherbe, J. C., and G. B. Davis, "Strategic MIS Planning Through Ends/Means Analysis," University of Minnesota, *Management Information Systems Research Center Working Paper Series*, 1982.

# CHAPTER 13

# Information Technology Economics

## Learning Objectives

*After studying this chapter, you will be able to:*

① Identify the major aspects of the economics of information technology.

② Explain the "productivity paradox."

③ Demonstrate how to define and measure tangible information technology benefits.

④ Show how to evaluate intangible information technology benefits.

⑤ Identify the advantages and disadvantages of approaches to charging end users for IT services.

⑥ Identify the advantages and disadvantages of outsourcing.

⑦ Describe causes of systems development failures.

⑧ Discuss the concept of "increasing returns" as it relates to the Internet and to software production.

557

## PILKINGTON PLC: TOTAL OUTSOURCING AT HEADQUARTERS

Pilkington PLC is a major international supplier of glass products, with headquarters at St. Helens in Great Britain. In the early 1990s it downsized its headquarters staff in an effort to reduce costs in a period of declining profitability. Management needed to decide how to handle Head Office IT services in the context of this downsizing. Pilkington considered retaining the IT function (IS department) until after the downsizing, or spinning it off as a subsidiary that would sell services to outside organizations as well as to internal business units. However, it decided that most aspects of its IT were essentially commodities, and that a reasonable option would be outsourcing them to a vendor.

The next decision was whether to outsource IT on a piecemeal basis to multiple vendors, or to obtain all services from one vendor. Pilkington decided to use a single source, to minimize management involvement with the outsourcing. This approach would allow management to focus on strategic issues related to its core competencies. Using a single vendor would also facilitate a transition from a mainframe system to client/server systems.

Pilkington narrowed the choices to four vendors and, after extensive analysis, signed a contract with EDS-Scicon in January 1992. EDS offered support for IS technologies from multiple vendors and had strong technical capabilities, and its worldwide coverage paralleled Pilkington's multinational operations. Another consideration was the favorable working conditions and career opportunities for employees who would transfer to the vendor.

**Network Technology**

Pilkington's key concerns in the arrangement were to minimize risk and to maintain in-house capabilities related to the strategic management of IT. Pilkington negotiated a two-year contract with a renewal option. This flexible arrangement reduced the risk of outsourcing problems that other Pilkington units had experienced. Only six key IS professionals remained on Pilkington's payroll. Two managed the vendor contract, while the others were responsible for strategic policy and technology issues.

In January 1994, EDS successfully replaced the Head Office mainframe with a local area network. Important financial reports are now available faster than before. The outsourcing contract saved $1.85 million over two years. Pilkington renewed the contract for two more years, and has provided references to other companies considering contracts with EDS.

Pilkington is satisfied with the current arrangement but faces additional questions for the future. Should it continue to use EDS? Should it bring the IT function back into the corporation now that the transition from the mainframe to a LAN is complete? Or should it outsource functions at its operating units that are still in-house?

SOURCE: Condensed from Willcocks, L., and G. Fitzgerald (1996). A full version of this case is available on www.wiley.com/turban/cases.

## ▶ 13.1 ECONOMIC AND FINANCIAL TRENDS

The Pilkington case illustrates an interesting economic issue: the relative benefits of using internal IT services versus obtaining them via outsourcing. There are several other economic issues related to IT, and the unique aspects of IT make its economics different in many respects from the economics of other aspects of business. This chapter explores these issues and the factors that shape them.

## TECHNOLOGICAL AND FINANCIAL TRENDS

Information technology capabilities are advancing at a rapid rate, and this trend should continue for at least another ten years. Expanding power and declining costs enable new and more extensive applications of information technology, which makes it possible for organizations to improve their efficiency and effectiveness. However, the increasingly diverse uses of this new potential make it more and more difficult to get a true picture of the benefits relative to the associated costs.

On the hardware side, capabilities are growing at an exponential rate. **Moore's Law,** named for one of the founders of Intel Corp., is illustrated in Figure 13.1. Moore suggested in a 1965 article that the number of transistors, and thus the power, of an integrated circuit (computer chip) would double every year while the cost remained the same. Moore later revised this estimate to a slightly less rapid pace: doubling every 18 months (Moore [1995]). In Figure 13.1 power is measured in MIPS, or millions of (computer) instructions per second. He has also applied the law to the Web, electronic commerce, and supply chain management (see Moore [1997]).

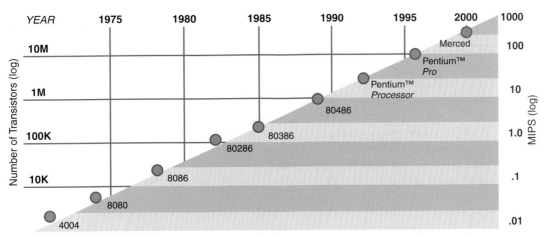

**FIGURE 13.1** Moore's Law as it relates to Intel microprocessors. (*Source*: Intel Corporation, http://www.intel.com/product/tech-briefs/man_bnch.htm.)

At the current rate of growth in computing power, organizations will have the opportunity to buy, for the same price, twice the processing power in 1½ years, four times the power in three years, eight times the power in 4½ years, and so forth. Another way of saying this is that the **price-to-performance ratio** will continue to decline exponentially. Limitations associated with current technologies could end this trend for silicon-based chips in 10 or 20 years (or possibly earlier; see Pountain [1998]), but new technologies will probably allow this phenomenal growth to continue.

What does this mean in economic terms? First, most organizations will perform existing functions at decreasing costs over time and thus become more efficient. Second, creative organizations will find new uses for information technology—based on the improving price-to-performance ratio—and thus become more effective. They will use the technology for new or enhanced products or services, or operational activities, that are technically feasible only with higher levels of computing power. They will also enable the application of technology to activities that are technically feasible at current power levels but will not be economically feasible until costs are reduced. Information technology will become an even more significant factor in the production and distribution of almost every product and service and will be physically embedded in many products, including commonplace low-technology items (for example, automobile tires).

These new and enhanced products and services will provide competitive advantage to organizations that have the creativity to exploit the increasing power of information technology. They will also provide major benefits to consumers, who will benefit from the greater functionality and lower costs. Moreover, applications of advanced information technologies are becoming increasingly diverse, with greater emphasis on intangible benefits. Increasing flexibility and ability to make better decisions are examples of *intangible benefits*—factors that are important but difficult to express in monetary values. These trends make it difficult to identify and evaluate the true financial impact of IT projects.

In the early days of data processing, economic analyses did not need to be as sophisticated as they are required to be today. Computer systems typically replaced portions of existing, well-defined manual processes on a one-to-one basis. Consider an automated payroll system implemented in the 1950s. This application replaced the activities of looking up withholding factors in tables, calculating deductions and net pay, typing checks, and filing results for use in the next cycle. It was easy to define the benefits: $x$ hours of labor by accounting clerks, at a specified pay rate, were replaced by a smaller number of hours of labor by data entry personnel at a lower rate of pay. Computers processed a limited number of applications one at a time in batch mode, so it was not difficult to generate reasonable estimates of the direct and indirect costs. The benefits were usually tangible savings that were typically substantially larger than the costs, so it really did not matter if the cost allocations were somewhat inaccurate or omitted a few items.

Forty years later, the situation is very different. Most of the simple replacements of computer capabilities for manual processes, with well-defined cost savings, have already been accomplished, at least in industrialized countries. To achieve further cost reductions it is usually necessary to reorganize (reengineer) processes to optimize the efforts of technology and personnel working together, rather than to simply replace manual with automated activities. Such business process reengineering typically produces intangible side-effects—for example, faster response or improved quality—whose value is more difficult to quantify than cost savings.

The alternative to reducing costs is increasing revenues by creating better products through IT. Organizations are also using IT to make their marketing and customer service more effective. In contrast to simple cost displacement, but similar to reengineering, many of the benefits of enhanced products and services are intangible and difficult to objectively quantify.

The remainder of this chapter focuses on evaluating the costs, benefits, and other economic aspects of information technology. First we address the so-called **productivity paradox,** the lack of evidence for a payoff from massive IT investments in the 1970s and 1980s. Following that discussion is a section on the measurement and evaluation of information technology benefits. We follow this with a discussion of several general perspectives on identifying desirable information technology investments. Subsequent sections cover accounting and charging for IT costs, outsourcing as a means of improving the economics of information technology, and the economic impacts of IS project failures. The chapter concludes with a discussion of the "increasing returns" often found in software production and electronic commerce.

## THE PRODUCTIVITY PARADOX

Over the last 50 years, organizations have invested trillions of dollars in information technology. Total worldwide annual spending on IT in 1996 was estimated at over a *trillion* dollars, about half in the United States (Strassmann [1997]). These expenditures have unquestionably transformed organizations: the technologies have become an integral aspect of almost every business process. The business and technology presses publish many "success stories" about major benefits from information technology projects at individual organizations. It seems self-evident that these investments must have increased productivity, not just in individual organizations, but throughout the economy.

On the other hand it is very hard to demonstrate, at the level of a national economy, that the IT investments really have increased outputs or wages. Most of the investment went into the service sector of the economy which, during the 1970s and 1980s, was showing much lower productivity gains than manufacturing. Nobel prize winner in economics Robert Solow quipped: "We see computers everywhere except in the productivity statistics." The discrepancy between measures of investment in information technology and measures of output at the national level is described as the "productivity paradox."

**PRODUCTIVITY.** To understand this paradox, we first need to understand the concept of productivity. Economists define *productivity* as outputs divided by inputs. Outputs are calculated by multiplying units produced, for example, number of automobiles, by their average value. The resulting figure needs to be adjusted for price inflation and also for any changes in quality (such as increased safety or better gas mileage). If inputs are measured simply as hours of work, the resulting ratio of outputs to inputs is **labor productivity.** If other inputs—investments and materials—are included, the ratio is known as **multifactor productivity.** Box 13.1 (p. 562) shows an example of a productivity calculation.

## EXPLAINING THE PRODUCTIVITY PARADOX

Economists have studied the productivity issue extensively in recent years and developed a variety of possible explanations of the apparent paradox. These explanations are grouped into the following three categories, which we discuss in more detail next.

## *A Closer Look* BOX 13.1

### CALCULATING LABOR PRODUCTIVITY AT THE DRISCOLL COMPANY

The Driscoll Company uses 10 employees who manually process 1,000 customer service inquiries per day. Unit sales are increasing at 5 percent per year, and the number of inquiries is increasing at about the same rate. Turnover among these customer service representatives is 20 percent: on the average two of these employees leave the company every year.

The company purchased an automated call answering and customer service system, which should make it possible to increase output per employee by 50 percent. However, the Driscoll Company values its employees. Rather than having a layoff to achieve the 50 percent productivity gain right away, it will wait until there is a need to hire new employees to replace those who leave.

The following calculations compare productivity with the previous system and new systems.

**PRODUCTIVITY WITH THE MANUAL SYSTEM:**

1000 inquiries / 10 employees = 100 inquiries handled per employee per day

**PRODUCTIVITY WITH THE AUTOMATED SYSTEM (ONE YEAR LATER):**

1050 inquiries / 8 employees = 131 inquiries handled per employee per day

Productivity increase = 31%

Productivity will increase further as additional employees leave.

---

> ▶ Problems with data or analyses hide productivity gains from IT.
> ▶ Gains from IT are offset by losses in other areas.
> ▶ IT productivity gains are offset by IT costs or losses.

**DATA AND ANALYSIS PROBLEMS HIDE PRODUCTIVITY GAINS.** Productivity numbers are only as good as the data used in their calculations. For manufacturing, it is fairly easy to measure outputs and inputs. General Motors, Ford, and Chrysler produce motor vehicles, relatively well-defined products whose quality changes gradually over time. It is not difficult to identify, with reasonable accuracy, the inputs used to produce these vehicles. However, the trend in the United States and other developed countries is away from manufacturing and toward services.

> My company has these same problems. How do you quantify an investment in IT which provides quicker, easier to read, and more accurate billing invoices? It's tough to justify via simple cost-benefit analysis because the benefits aren't always tangible.
> — *Mike Rewald*

In service industries, such as finance or health care delivery, it is more difficult to define what the products are, how they change in quality, and how to allocate to them the corresponding costs. For example, banks now use IT to handle a large proportion of deposit and withdrawal transactions through automated teller machines (ATMs). The ability to withdraw cash from ATMs 24 hours per day, 7 days per week is a substantial quality increase in comparison to the traditional 9 A.M. to 4 P.M. hours for live tellers. But what is the value of this quality increase in comparison with the associated costs? If the incremental value exceeds the incremental costs, then it represents a productivity gain; otherwise the productivity impact is negative.

Another important consideration is the amount of time it takes to achieve the full benefits of new technologies. Economists point out that it took many decades to start achieving the productivity impacts of the industrial revolution. We all know that it takes time to learn to use new software: productivity actually decreases during the initial learning period and then increases over a period of a year or longer. Economic analyses that fail to consider the *time lags* between IT investments and IT benefits may underestimate the productivity impacts.

Hitt and Brynjolfsson (1996) point out that answers to questions about the value of IT investments depend on how the issue is defined. They emphasize that productivity is not the same thing as profitability. Their research indicates that IT increases productivity and value to consumers but does not increase organizational profitability.

**IT PRODUCTIVITY GAINS ARE OFFSET BY LOSSES IN OTHER AREAS.** It is possible that IT produces gains in certain areas of the economy, but these gains are offset by losses in other areas. One company's IT usage could increase its share of market at the expense of other companies. Total output in the industry, and thus productivity, remains constant even though the competitive situation is different.

Offsetting losses can also occur within organizations. Consider the situation where an organization installs a new computer system that makes it impossible to increase output per employee. If the organization reduces its production staff but increases employment in unproductive overhead functions, the productivity gains from information technology will be dispersed.

**IT PRODUCTIVITY GAINS ARE OFFSET BY IT COSTS OR LOSSES.** The third possibility is that IT in itself really does not increase productivity. This idea seems contrary to common sense: why would organizations invest tremendous amounts of money in something if it really does not improve performance? On the other hand, there are considerations that support this possibility. Figure 13.2 shows an analysis from Strassmann (1997) which suggests little or no relationship between IT spending and corporate profitability.

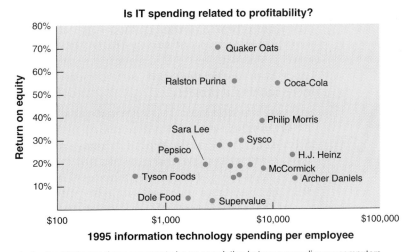

**FIGURE 13.2** Comparing relative IT spending and profitability at a sample of corporations. (*Source*: www.strassmann.com/pubs/datamation0297/.)

In the food industry, there appears to be no correlation between spending on computers and profitability.

*The dots without names stand for companies whose names did not fit into the graphic.

As mentioned earlier, productivity is the ratio of outputs divided by inputs. To determine whether IT increases productivity, it is not enough to simply measure changes in outputs for a new system. If outputs increase 40 percent but inputs increase 50 percent, the result is a decline in productivity rather than a gain. Or consider a situation where a new system is developed and implemented but then, because of some major problems, is replaced by another system. Even though the second system has acceptable performance, an analysis that includes the costs of the unsuccessful system could indicate that IT did not increase productivity, at least in the short run.

Productivity evaluations must include changes in inputs, especially labor, over the total life cycle, including projects that are not implemented. These inputs need to include not just the direct labor required to develop and operate the systems, but also indirect labor and other costs required to maintain the system. Examples of factors that, under this broader perspective, reduce productivity include:

> *Support costs.* The GartnerGroup estimates the total cost of a networked PC at $13,000 per year (Munk [1996]). Technical support accounts for 27 percent of this cost, and administration for another 9 percent. The additional employees required for these support activities could offset a significant portion of the productivity benefits from the hardware and software.

> *Wasted time.* Personal computers make it possible to work more productively on some tasks but also result in nonproductive activities. A survey of 6000 workers indicated the average PC user loses 5 hours per week waiting—for programs to run, reports to print, tech support to answer the phone, and so on—or "futzing" with the hardware or software (Munk [1996]). The GartnerGroup estimates that businesses lose 26 million hours of employee time per year to these nonproductive activities, and that they account for 43 percent of the total cost of a personal computer on a network. The cartoon in Figure 13.3 highlights the issue of wasted time.

> *Software development problems.* Some information systems projects fail; they are not completed. Others are abandoned, completed but never used. Others are **runaway projects,** systems that are eventually completed but require much more time and money than originally planned. This is not an uncommon problem: a recent survey (King [1997]) found that 73 percent of software projects at 360 U.S. corporations were canceled, over budget, or late. Labor hours associated with these projects can offset productivity gains from more successful projects.

> *Software maintenance.* This expense, which includes fixing bugs and modifying or enhancing system functionality, now accounts for up to 80 percent of IS budgets. Many of the modifications—for example, updates to payroll systems to reflect tax law changes—do not increase outputs. They are necessary just to keep the system at the same level of performance, so productivity declines because labor increases while output volumes do not.

One of the most frustrating portions of my job is "down time." I work with a desktop publishing program called PageMaker, and it is a resource hog. Some of my publications are quite lengthy, and the PC can't support these sizable documents. When this happens, everything freezes (sometimes I lose work)—I shut the PC down, reboot, etc. The day slips away.

— *Kristin Borhofen*

**FIGURE 13.3** Dilbert analyzes the productivity paradox. (*Source*: Dilbert reprinted by permission of United Feature Syndicate, Inc.)

The "Year 2K Problem" (see Chapter 15) is a notable example of software maintenance that does not add to productivity. The cost to update software throughout the world just to handle dates in the twenty-first century is estimated to be as high as $600 billion, which does not include legal liabilities for system failures. To deal with this problem, Merrill Lynch in 1997 had an 80-person team working 24 hours per day in shifts seven days a week, even though "our return on investment is zero" (Vistica et al. [1997]).

The complexity of this problem is shown in Figure 13.4. According to Kappelman et al. (1998), the Society for Information Management (www.sim.net) calculated this cost as over 30 percent of an organization's annual IS operating budget.

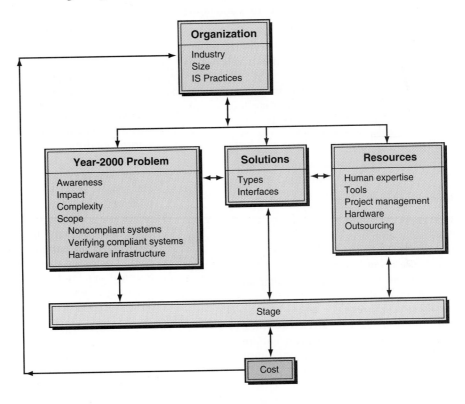

**FIGURE 13.4** Kappelman-Fent Year-2000 enterprise cost model. It includes four main categories of cost influence: the nature of the problem, the organization, the proposed solution, and the resources. (*Source*: Kappelman [1998], p. 31.)

▶ *Incompatible systems and workarounds.* Although individual systems produce productivity gains, the increased labor required to get them to work together (or at all) could offset these benefits.

One major phenomenon that can waste time and reduce productivity is known as *junk computing* (see Box 13.2 on p. 566).

To a large extent these productivity-offsetting factors reflect problems with the administration of information technology, rather than with the technologies themselves. In many cases they are controllable through better planning or more effective management techniques. For organizations, the critical issue is not whether and how IT increases productivity in the economy as a whole, but how it improves their own productivity. The next three sections cover ways organizations can evaluate IT benefits and costs and target their IT development and acquisition toward systems that will best contribute to the achievement of organizational goals.

## *A Closer Look* BOX 13.2

### CONTROLLING JUNK COMPUTING

Guthrie and Gray (1996) coined the expression "junk computing" to describe "the use of information systems in a way that does not directly advance organizational goals." They created this expression as an analogy to the concept of junk mail. The subjects of their research identified 19 different types of junk computing activities, and mentioned seven items most frequently. Games and doing personal work were at the top of the list, followed by:

▶ *Junk reporting*—creating unnecessary reports.
▶ *Excessive computerization*—automation that is not an improvement over manual systems.
▶ *Excessive detail*—for example, inputting minor activities into a scheduling system rather than focusing on milestones and higher priority projects.
▶ *Excessive attention to presentation,* such as elaborate formatting for simple memos.
▶ *E-mail*—for example, sending copies to large distribution lists or responding to unimportant messages.

The causes of junk computing include:

▶ *Excessiveness.* Although the computerized activity is valid in itself, employees may devote more time to it than is necessary to achieve the desired result.
▶ *Physical environment*—for example, incompatible hardware or systems that require manual effort to transfer or integrate data.
▶ *Cultural or social pressures.* Other employees or the organization may encourage excesses, for example, large reports or very elaborate presentations.
▶ *Individual behavioral styles.* Some employees are very oriented toward computers and try to do as much work as they can with them.
▶ *Miscommunication and mismanagement.* Managers may ask for or indirectly signal employees that they want elaborate work, or try to implement technical

solutions instead of dealing with the people or procedures that are causing problems.

Guthrie and Gray note that junk computing is not always counterproductive. Experimentation—for example, using advanced features of a word processing program to format a memo—may develop skills that the employee can subsequently use in a formal report that requires a more elaborate layout. Or playing a quick game of solitaire may provide a relaxing break to an employee, after which she or he can go back to work with renewed vigor.

The following recommendations can help managers control junk computing:

▶ *Increase awareness.* Recognize junk computing as an organizational productivity problem.
▶ *Control environmental factors.* Set policies against inappropriate use, mandate standard formats for documents and presentations to prevent excessive effort, and remove game software from computers.
▶ *Control behavior* through training that covers appropriate and inappropriate computer uses, and through chargeback of computing costs (see Section 13.4).
▶ *Controlling mismanagement.* Encourage appropriate computer usage through effective managerial communications, and by creating an environment that encourages employees to manage their own computer use consistent with organizational needs.

Note: With the advancement of the Web, the problem of junk computing has been accelerating because employees use corporate time for private viewing. Controlling this problem can be a major issue (see Chapter 15).

SOURCE: Condensed from Guthrie, R., and P. Gray, "Junk Computing: Is It Bad for an Organization?" *Information Systems Management,* Winter 1996, pp. 23–28.

## ▶ 13.2 EVALUATING IT: BENEFITS, COSTS, AND PERFORMANCE

Organizations face the ongoing problem of trying to most efficiently allocate their limited resources to maintain or improve performance. Information technology is very much a part of this problem, since IT is becoming a significant component of almost everything organizations do (including using spreadsheets to analyze resource allocation decisions). Evaluating the costs and benefits of IT is therefore an important aspect of the allocation process.

The rapid rate of change contributes to the difficulty of making decisions about information technology. Newer technologies offer capabilities that are very different from what is currently available, and they make existing technologies obsolete. Costs of processing power per unit of computing are declining rapidly, which can have a great impact on the timing and nature of IT investment decisions.

A major problem in evaluating IT is that many of its benefits are intangible: they are real and important, but it is not easy to accurately estimate their value. The fact that organizations use IT for different purposes further complicates the evaluation process. For example, IT assists decision making, automates processes, and provides an infrastructure that supports other uses. Methods of evaluating IT reflect the different types of uses, as we discuss below.

## THE VALUE OF INFORMATION IN DECISION MAKING

People in organizations use information to help them make decisions that are better than they would have been if they did not have the information. Senior executives make decisions that influence the profitability of an organization for years to come, while operational employees make decisions that affect production on a day-to-day basis. In either case, the value of information is the difference between the net benefits—benefits adjusted for costs—of decisions made using the information and decisions without the information. The value of the net benefits with information obviously needs to reflect the additional costs of obtaining the information.

$$\text{Value of information} = \left\{ \begin{array}{l} \text{Net benefits} \\ \text{with} \\ \text{information} \end{array} \right. - \left\{ \begin{array}{l} \text{Net benefits} \\ \text{without information} \end{array} \right.$$

One of the best-known models of the value of information for decision making is the value of perfect information and its extension to imperfect information, as shown in Box 13.3 on page 568.

One way to estimate the value of information for more complex decisions is to experiment, comparing decisions with and without information, either in real-world situations or in laboratory experiments that simulate some of the decision processes. Unfortunately, there are problems with both approaches. Organizations might experiment with small problems where the consequences of failure are limited, but for major decisions they usually cannot afford to test alternatives that are less likely to be successful. Laboratory experiments are much less risky, but it is not easy to translate the results into an accurate reflection of the value of information in real-world situations.

The remaining alternative is to have the decision maker subjectively estimate the value of the information. This person is most familiar with the problem and has the most to lose from a bad decision. If this person identifies a specific value for the information and it is obtainable for that cost or less, the organization probably should make the investment to acquire the information or develop a system to produce it. However, to make sure the estimates are not inflated in order to get an approval, the organization needs to make the decision maker accountable for the cost of the information. Before we deal with such accountability we will examine the methodologies of evaluating automation of business processes with IT.

## *A Closer Look* BOX 13.3

### VALUE OF PERFECT INFORMATION

When decisions are made under the condition of risk, information about future consequences becomes very valuable. In such cases one is not sure about the results of each alternative course of action. Generally speaking, the more information you have, the better you can assess these results. At the extreme, information can tell you *exactly* what the results will be. In such a case we talk about **perfect information.** If the information will improve your knowledge, but will not tell you the results for sure, we are dealing with **imperfect information.** In quantitative decision analysis one can compute the expected value of perfect information (EVPI) as the average of a series of repetitive decisions:

$$EVPI = \left\{ \begin{array}{l} \text{Expected yield with} \\ \text{perfect information} \end{array} \right\} - \left\{ \begin{array}{l} \text{Expected yield without} \\ \text{perfect information} \end{array} \right\}$$

For the case of imperfect information one can use Bayes' theorem. For examples of both computations see any management science or decision analysis text (e.g., Turban and Meredith [1994]).

The EVPI is then compared with its cost. If EVPI is larger than its cost, then acquisition of additional information should be considered.

The issue of acquisition of information for decision making may be very complex. The following questions need to be considered:

1. What information is needed and is it available?
2. Is there time to acquire the information?
3. What is the quality of the additional information? Information can have very different levels of quality. This issue will be explored later in this chapter.
4. What is the value of the information?
5. What is the cost of obtaining the information?
6. Should the information be acquired?

## EVALUATING AUTOMATION BY COST-BENEFIT ANALYSES

Automation of business processes is an area where it is necessary to define and measure IT benefits and costs. In automation, mechanical equipment under the control of information technology replaces or enhances human labor. For example, automation was implemented in the organization's business offices when word processing replaced typing and spreadsheet programs replaced accounting pads and 10-key calculators. In the factory, robots weld and paint automobiles on assembly lines. In the warehouse, incoming items are recorded by bar-code scanners.

> You can talk a lot about how great computers and computer systems are, but if you don't provide a breakdown of how it will benefit the company financially, you'll never get it approved.
>
> — *Blake Thompson*

The decision of whether to automate is a capital investment decision, which can be analyzed by **cost-benefit analyses** that compare the total value of the benefits with the associated costs. Organizations often use net present value (NPV) calculations for cost-benefit analyses. In an NPV analysis, analysts convert future values to their present value equivalent by discounting them at the organization's cost of funds. Figure 13.5 illustrates the concept of future value and

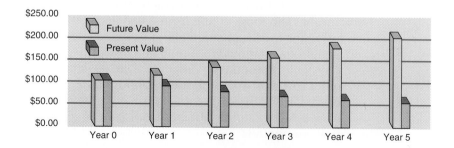

**FIGURE 13.5** Future value and present value of $100 at 15%.

present value. The chart indicates that, in an organization earning a 15 percent return, $100 would grow to about $200 five years in the future. Similarly $100 five years in the future would be worth about $50 at present.

The NPV analysis works well in situations where the costs and benefits are well defined or "tangible," so that it is not difficult to convert them into monetary values. For example, if human welders are replaced by robots that produce work of comparable quality, the benefits are the labor cost savings over the usable life of the robots. Costs include the capital investment to purchase and install the robots, plus the operating and maintenance costs. Box 13.4 shows a simplified NPV analysis for this example.

---

## *A Closer Look*  BOX 13.4

### CALCULATING NET PRESENT VALUE

|  | Year 0 | Year 1 | Year 2 | Year 3 | Year 4 | Year 5 | Total |
|---|---|---|---|---|---|---|---|
| Cash Flow | $(50,000) | $20,000 | $20,000 | $20,000 | $20,000 | $20,000 | $50,000 |
| Discount Factor | 1.00 | 1.15 | 1.32 | 1.52 | 1.75 | 2.01 | |
| Discounted Cash Flow | $(50,000) | $17,391 | $15,123 | $13,150 | $11,435 | $9,944 | $17,043 |

In this example, a small business invests $50,000 in robotic equipment. This amount is shown as a negative value in Year 0. Projected cash flows of $20,000 per year in Year 1 through Year 5 result from labor savings, reduced material costs, and tax benefits. The business plans to replace the robots with more modern ones after 5 years and does not expect them to have any scrap value.

The equipment generates a total of $100,000 in savings over five years, or $50,000 more than the original investment. However, a dollar saved in the future is worth less than a dollar invested in the present. If the business estimates its return on investment as 15 percent, then $1.00 should be worth $1.15 in one year, $1.32 after two years with compound interest, and so on. Cash flows are divided by these "discount factors" to estimate what they are worth at present. The total cash flow after this discounting is a positive value, $17,043, which indicates the project is economically justified. This figure is then compared to those derived in other proposed projects, and money is allocated first to those projects with the highest NPV.

---

It would make life easier for financial analysts if all automation decisions were this simple. In many cases, however, the information technology aspect of the new equipment generates benefits such as increased quality, faster product development, greater design flexibility, better customer service, or improved working conditions for employees. These are very desirable benefits but it is difficult to place an accurate monetary value on them. The analyst could ignore intangible benefits, but this implies that their value is zero and may lead the organization to reject investments that could substantially increase its revenues and profitability. Therefore, financial analyses need to consider not just tangible benefits but also intangible benefits, in such a way that the decision reflects their potential impact.

**HANDLING INTANGIBLE BENEFITS.** The most straightforward solution to this problem is to make *rough estimates* of monetary values for all intangible benefits, and then conduct the financial analysis. The simplicity of this approach is attractive, but in many cases the assumptions used in these estimates are debatable. If the technology is acquired because decision makers assigned too high a value to intangible benefits, the organization could find that it has wasted some valuable resources. On the other hand, if the valuation of intangible benefits were too low, the organization might reject the investment and then find that it is losing market share to competitors who did implement the technology.

Downing (1989) discusses these issues and suggests eight ways to evaluate intangible benefits. Here are a few of them:

▶ *Use "concrete indicators."* Instead of subjectively estimating the value, find some measurable effects resulting from the benefit. For example, automating a monotonous process could improve working conditions. Estimate how much this could reduce employee turnover, and then use the savings in hiring and training costs as the value of this intangible benefit.

▶ *Solve for an unknown.* Calculate the net present value without including any value for intangible benefits. If the net present value is negative, calculate the shortfall—the required value of the intangible benefits needed to make NPV positive. If the intangible benefits are worth at least this value, the project can be approved. With this approach, it is not necessary to accurately estimate the ultimate value of intangible benefits. Instead it is sufficient just to evaluate whether the shortfall is a reasonable estimate of the low end of the range of possible values of intangible benefits.

▶ *Prevent competitive disadvantage.* The typical investment analysis assumes that the financial situation will not change if the investment is not made. In reality, however, competitors may adopt a new technology, which could reduce income for the organization that does not make an investment in that technology. Thus, it is necessary to include an estimate of not just the gain from the investment, but also the losses from failing to adopt the new technology.

## EVALUATING IT INFRASTRUCTURE THROUGH BENCHMARKS

Information systems projects are usually not standalone applications. In most cases they depend for support on enabling technologies already installed in the organization. These *infrastructure technologies* include mainframe computers, operating systems, networks, database management systems, utility programs, development tools, and more. Since many of their benefits are intangible and are spread over many different present and future applications, it is hard to estimate their value or evaluate the desirability of enhancements or upgrades. In other words, it is much more difficult to evaluate infrastructure investment decisions than investments in specific information systems application projects.

One approach to evaluating infrastructure is to focus on objective measures of performance known as *benchmarks*. These measures are often available from trade associations within an industry or from consulting firms. The benchmark approach implicitly assumes that investments in infrastructure are justified if they are managed efficiently. A comparison of measures of performance or expenditures with averages for the industry, or with values for the more efficient performers in the industry, indicates how well the organization is using its infrastructure. If performance is below standard, corrective action is indicated.

Benchmarks come in two very different forms. **Metric benchmarks** provide numeric measures of performance, for example:

▶ IT expenses as percent of total revenues.

▶ Percent of "downtime" (when the computer is not available).

▶ CPU usage (as percent of total capacity).

▶ Percent of IS projects completed on time and within budget.

These types of measures are very useful to managers, even though sometimes they lead to the wrong conclusions. For example, a ratio of IT expenses to revenues that is lower than the industry average could indicate that a firm is operating more efficiently than its competitors. Or it might indicate that the company is investing less in IT than it should and will become less competitive as a result.

> It's important to have benchmarks to know if you're doing good. You may be doing fine for yourself but how do you stack up to others?
> — *Blake Thompson*

Metric benchmarks can help diagnose problems, but they do not necessarily show how to solve them. Therefore, many organizations also use **best practice benchmarks.** Here the emphasis is on how information system activities are actually performed rather than numeric measures of performance. For example, an organization might feel that its local area networks are very important to its performance. It could obtain information about best practices in this area, such as the way other organizations—or its own more efficient units—operate and manage their LANs. The organization would then implement these best practices for all its LANs, to bring performance up to the level of the leaders. An example of the benefits of benchmarking at several large corporations is provided in the next *IT at Work*.

## IT At Work    USING BENCHMARKING
## AT LARGE CORPORATIONS

**U**SING IT

...in Production &
Operations Management

The **Estee Lauder** cosmetics company used best practices benchmarking to identify ways to speed up internal systems projects and reduce development cycle times. Visiting other companies to develop benchmark information also generated ideas on how to develop a new inventory management system. The project was successful, and now benchmarking is "a way of life for Estee Lauder Information Services."

**Honeywell Europe** wanted to identify the most appropriate role for its IT unit within the organization. Benchmarking indicated that in "best in class" organizations, the IT units act as consultants working in partnership with the business units. Benchmarking also confirmed the validity of Honeywell's previous commitment to total quality management in IT activities.

**Pfizer** used benchmarking to help identify promising new technologies. It assigned 25 of its technical experts to transformation study teams that visited leading companies. Pfizer included companies that had problems in its study, because the pressures to achieve a turnaround could result in creative new approaches. The results of their data collection and analysis indicated that Pfizer needed to provide additional training to IT employees. Although their skills with large computers were good, employees needed additional skills for an environment in which the focus was shifting to desktop computing.

Benchmarking provided answers to **Amoco Corporation** on how to handle various aspects of technology planning and management. Instead of having a large group that studies technology, the IT group now works together with users to select appropriate technologies. It stopped producing annual technology forecasts after finding that other companies generally did not do this. Benchmarking also provided information on appropriate IT roles after the company decentralized many of its IT personnel into the business units. Amoco discovered that it was inappropriate for the central IT unit to try to act as a watchdog and enforce a large number of standards in a decentralized environment.

**American Express** initiated a benchmarking study because the IT unit needed to be able to respond faster to business needs, and because IT costs were increasing faster than business revenues. The benchmarking findings led to specific recommendations to the executive committee about increasing the alignment of IT with business functions, and increased the credibility of these recommendations.

**For Further Exploration:** How can an organization determine whether it needs to conduct a benchmarking study, or how much it should spend on this type of study? ▲

SOURCE: Condensed from Greene, C. B., *Benchmarking the Information Technology Function,* New York: The Conference Board, 1993.

## EVALUATING IT PERFORMANCE: SERVICE LEVEL AGREEMENTS

One of the biggest problems with an information systems department (ISD) is that it is difficult to identify exactly what it does for the organization. The concepts of "computing power" and "communications services" are rather vague and do not relate very well to specific activities on the floor of the factory or in the marketing department. The **service level agreement (SLA)** approach bridges this communication gap by establishing measures of performance based on the functional requirements of the users of IS services.

The first step in the SLA approach is to meet with a client to determine what IT service he or she needs. Working together, the client and IS representative then determine the most relevant and objective methods of measuring and calculating how well the service is meeting the client's needs. They also determine how, and how often, to report the performance measurements, and what happens if service levels fail to meet the standards. The final result is a written document specifying all the responsibilities of the IS group under the agreement (Belitsos [1989]).

The major advantage of the SLA approach is that it gives users a much better understanding of, and much more control over, the IS services they require in order to operate. Clients can also use these agreements to compare the costs and performance of the internal IS group to that of outside vendors. Such comparisons encourage the ISD to hold down its costs, while the detailed performance specifications provide some protection from outside bids that omit important aspects of the services being compared.

A common use of service level agreements is to establish performance levels for internal computer support hotlines or help desks. Typical SLAs require the IS unit to resolve a large percentage of the problems, say 95 percent, during the first call. The SLAs also require a solution for most of the remaining problems within four hours, and for all the rest within five working days. For further discussion of SLAs, see Chapter 15.

## OTHER METHODS AND COMMERCIAL SERVICES

Several other methods can be used to assess the value of information. Table 13.1 (p. 573) lists some of the traditional methods with their advantages and disadvantages (including the NPV discussed earlier). Traditional methods may not be useful in cases of some of the newest technologies (e.g., see Violino [1997]). Consider the case of acquiring expert systems, as shown below:

| COSTS | BENEFITS |
|---|---|
| *One Time* | *Quantifiable* |
| Software Expert System Purchase | Improved Decision Speed |
| Software Development | Improved Decision Quality |
| Other Software Purchase | Automation of Tasks |
| Hardware Platform Lease or Purchase | Ability to Perform New Tasks |
| Communication Equipment | Standardization of Decisions |
| Office Space and Furnishings | Shorter Employee Training Time |
| Training and Documentation | |
| | |
| *Ongoing (Recurrent)* | *Intangible* |
| Operating Personnel | Synergy With Other Projects |
| Communication Lines | Expanded Long-Term Opportunities |
| Hardware Maintenance | Strategic Positioning |
| Software Upgrades | Job Enrichment |
| Office Space and Utilities | Recording of Knowledge |

For this reason there are special methodologies for dealing with investment in IT and its special technologies. For example, Smith and Dagli (1992) surveyed all the methodologies that can be used for assessing expert systems. (See also Lucas et al. [1996].) Also, there are many computerized models that help with investment decisions. (One such model is shown later in Box 13.7, p. 578.)

Some of the methods cited by Violino (1997) (see also Section 13.3) and found at http://techweb.cmp.com/iw/ are:

***Table 13.1*** **Traditional Methods of Evaluating Investments**

| *Method* | *Advantages* | *Disadvantages* |
|---|---|---|
| Internal Rate of Return (IRR) | Brings all projects to common footing. Conceptually familiar. | Assumes reinvestment at same rate. Can have multiple roots. No assumed discount rate. |
| Net Present Value or Net Worth (NPV or NW) | Very common. Maximizes value for unconstrained project selection. | Difficult to compare projects of unequal lives or sizes. |
| Equivalent Annuity (EA) | Brings all project NPVs to common footing. Convenient annual figure. | Assumes projects repeat to least common multiple of lives, or imputes salvage value. |
| Payback Period | May be discounted or nondiscounted. Measure of exposure. | Ignores flows after payback is reached. Assumes standard project cash flow profile. |
| Benefit-to-Cost Ratio | Conceptually familiar. Brings all projects to common footing. | May be difficult to classify outlays between expense and investment. |

SOURCE: Compiled from Seitz, N. E., *Capital Budgeting and Long-Term Financing Decisions*, Hinsdale IL: Dryden Press, 1989.

▶ Compare technological speeds and feeds, using price/performance and other measures.

▶ Measure shareholder value.

▶ Use risk analysis.

▶ Use "modern portfolio theory" (used in stock market investment).

▶ Economic value added (similar to value analysis, Section 13.3).

**TOTAL COST OF OWNERSHIP.** An interesting approach for evaluating the value of IT is the **Total Cost of Ownership (TCO).** TCO is a formula for calculating the cost of owning and operating a PC. The cost includes hardware, technical support, maintenance, software upgrades, help desk and peer support. By identifying such cost, organizations get more accurate cost-benefit analyses and also reduce the TCO if it is too high (see Hildebrand [1998]). Many commercial companies help in evaluating IT investments (see Box 13.5).

---

## *A Closer Look*  BOX 13.5

### COMMERCIAL IT EVALUATIONS

Dozens of consultants and cost justification software products are available on the market. Here are some examples:

*Total Cost of Ownership* (TCO) is offered by Interpose (www.interpose.com) and Microsoft. The software attempts to aid in comprehending the direct and indirect costs of "owning or using an IT component throughout its life cycle." The direct costs include "hardware, software, IS management labor, development, communication fees and other IS cost center budgeted expenses."

The indirect costs focus on elements not normally budgeted and usually overlooked by many organizations. Items include "end user, self and peer support, casual learning, and productivity losses due to downtime."

*Product Data Management* (www.pdmic.com) offers a cost management tool kit. It is an Excel-based program that will assist in "determining current status and associated costs" and "calculating specific cost savings areas for implementing product data management technology."

---

One of the major IT industry research firms is International Data Corporation (www.idcresearch.com). They conduct industrywide studies on rate of return on investment (ROI).

## ▶ 13.3 EVALUATING IT: PERSPECTIVES ON INTANGIBLE BENEFITS

### ASSESSING INTANGIBLE BENEFITS

Some information technology investment decisions are easy. Occasionally the benefits, especially cost savings, are quite measurable and carry little or no risk of failure. In other cases the project is necessary for the organization to stay in business: for example, the Internal Revenue Service is requiring businesses to switch to electronic systems for filing their tax returns. These types of investments do not require firms to do a lot of analysis.

Unfortunately, considerations related to most potential IT investments are not usually so well defined. One possible way of dealing with this issue is to limit

IT investments to situations, such as regulatory compliance, where there is a compelling justification. However, the pressures of the competitive environment make this approach impractical for most organizations. They face a continuing need to improve their performance, and IT can produce many benefits that could improve performance. IT can speed up business processes, provide more accurate information for decision making and management control, improve communications, and make it easier for employees to work together.

These kinds of benefits are often difficult to measure by themselves, and their impact on organizational performance is even less measurable. Many people would agree that e-mail improves communications, but it is not at all clear how to measure the value of this improvement. A network administrator can provide statistics on the number of e-mail messages but cannot prove that communication within the organization is, say, 10 percent better because employees now receive an average of four e-mail messages per day. Managers are very conscious of the bottom line, but no manager can prove that e-mail is responsible for so many cents per share of the organization's total profits. So, what is the solution? Even though the relationship between intangible IT benefits and performance is not clear, some investments should be better than others. How can organizations increase the probability that their IT investments will improve their performance? Several available methodologies are of special interest. They are: value analysis, information economics, management by maxim, and option valuation. Briefly:

▶ Value analysis allows users to evaluate intangible benefits on a low-cost, trial basis before deciding whether to commit to a larger investment.

▶ Information economics focuses on the application of IT in areas where its intangible benefits contribute to performance on key aspects of organizational strategies and activities.

▶ Management by maxim provides a means of rationalizing IT infrastructure investments.

▶ Option valuation takes into account potential future benefits that current IT investments could produce.

The remaining parts of this section describe how each of these methodologies work.

## VALUE ANALYSIS

Peter Keen (1981) developed the **value analysis** method to assist organizations considering investments in decision support systems (DSSs). The major problem with justifying DSS is that most of the benefits are intangible; they are not readily convertible into monetary values. Some—such as better decisions, better understanding of business situations, and improved communication—are difficult to measure even in nonmonetary terms. These problems in evaluating DSS are similar to the problems in evaluating intangible benefits for other types of systems. Therefore, value analysis should be applicable to other types of IT investments in which a large proportion of the value derives from intangible benefits.

The value analysis approach includes eight steps, grouped into two phases. The first phase works with a low-cost prototype, which, depending on the initial results, is followed by a full-scale system in the second phase. In the first phase the decision maker identifies the desired capabilities and the (generally intangi-

> Often the valuation of an IT project involves intangible benefits, which must be quantified to gain project acceptance.
> — *Dave Gehrke*

ble) potential benefits. The developers estimate the cost of providing the capabilities and, if the decision maker feels the benefits are worth this cost, a small-scale prototype of the DSS is constructed.

The results of the first phase provide information that helps with the decision about the second phase. The user has a better understanding of the value of the benefits, and of the additional features the full-scale system needs to include, after using the prototype. The developers can make a better estimate of the cost of the final product. The question at this point is: What benefits are necessary to justify this cost? If the decision-maker feels that the system can provide these benefits, development proceeds on the full-scale system. Figure 13.6 illustrates the steps in the value analysis approach.

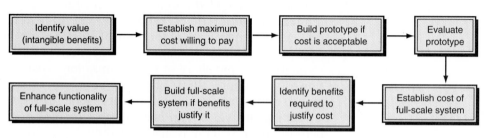

**FIGURE 13.6** Steps in the value analysis approach.

The value analysis approach was designed for DSS, but it is not limited to this type of system. It is applicable to any information technology that can be tested on a low-cost basis before deciding whether to make a full investment. The current trend of buying rather than developing software, along with the increasingly common practice of offering softwear on a free-trial basis for 30 to 90 days, provide ample opportunities for the use of this approach. Organizations may also have opportunities to "pilot" the use of new systems in specific operating units, and then to implement them on a full-scale basis if the initial results are favorable.

## INFORMATION ECONOMICS

The **information economics** approach is similar to the concept of critical success factors (discussed in Chapter 12) in that it focuses on key organizational objectives. Information economics incorporates the familiar technique of scoring methodologies, which are used in many evaluation situations.

To use a **scoring methodology,** the analyst first identifies all the key performance issues and assigns a weight to each one. Each product in the evaluation receives a score on each factor, usually between zero and 100 points, or zero and ten. These scores are multiplied by the weighting factors and then totaled. The item with the highest score is judged the best product. Box 13.6 (p. 577) shows an example of using a scoring methodology to evaluate geographical information systems from several vendors.

The information economics approach uses organizational objectives to determine which factors to include, and what weights to assign, in the scoring methodology. The approach is flexible enough to include other factors in the analysis, such as impacts on customers and suppliers (the value chain). Executives in an organization determine the relevant objectives and weights at a given point in time, subject to revision if there are changes in the environment. These factors and weights are then used to evaluate IT alternatives; the highest scores go to the items that have the greatest potential to improve organizational performance.

## *A Closer Look*   BOX 13.6

### SCORING GEOGRAPHIC INFORMATION SYSTEMS

| Criterion | Weight | Systems/Scores Atlas GIS | MapInfo | Maptitude |
|---|---|---|---|---|
| Map creation and modification | 150 | 93.75 | 112.50 | 93.75 |
| Data query and display | 150 | 93.75 | 93.75 | 93.75 |
| Spatial queries | 100 | 62.50 | 62.50 | 62.50 |
| Geocoding | 100 | 75.00 | 62.50 | 50.00 |
| Reporting | 75 | 56.25 | 56.25 | 56.25 |
| Expandability | 75 | 56.25 | 56.25 | 37.50 |
| Import and export | 75 | 37.50 | 37.50 | 46.87 |
| Speed | 50 | 37.50 | 37.50 | 25.00 |
| Documentation | 25 | 15.62 | 15.62 | 15.62 |
| Support | 100 | 62.50 | 75.00 | 62.50 |
| Pricing | 100 | 75.00 | 50.00 | 100.00 |
| Overall score (total divided by 100) | | 6.5 | 6.5 | 6.4 |

Individual scores are derived by multiplying the weight of each criterion by its rating, where:

Excellent = 1.0—outstanding in all areas
Very good = 0.75—meets all essential criteria and offers significant advantages
Good = 0.625—meets essential criteria and includes some special features
Satisfactory = 0.5—meets essential criteria
Poor = 0.25—falls short in essential areas
Unacceptable or N/A = 0.0—fails to meet minimum standards or lacks this feature

For example, the Atlas GIS was rated Good at map creation. Therefore the weight of 150 points was multiplied by 0.625 to arrive at the score of 93.75 on this item.

SOURCE: Compiled from *InfoWorld*, July 31, 1995.

Note that this approach can incorporate both tangible and intangible benefits. If there is a strong connection between a benefit of IT investment—such as quicker decision making—and an organizational objective—such as faster product development—the benefit will influence the final score even if it does not have a monetary value. Thus the information economics model helps solve the problem of assessing intangible benefits by linking the evaluation of these benefits to the factors that are most important to organizational performance.

This approach is very flexible and it can be carried out by software packages such as Expert Choice (www.expertchoice.com). The analysis can vary the weights over time; for example, tangible benefits might receive heavier weights at times when earnings are weak. The approach can also take risk into account, by using negative weights for factors that reduce the probability of obtaining the benefits. Box 13.7 (p. 578) shows an analysis of a decision of whether to develop a system in-house or buy it from Oracle Corporation. The analysis uses Oracle's CB-90 model, which is based on the information economics concept.

## *A Closer Look*   BOX 13.7

### ANALYZING A BUILD VS. BUY DECISION USING ORACLE'S CB-90 MODEL

*Tangible ROI with Enhanced Analysis*
*($thousands)*

|  | Build Only (A) | | | | Buy and Build (B) | | | |
|  | 1993 | 1994 | 1995 | 1996 | 1993 | 1994 | 1995 | 1996 |
|---|---|---|---|---|---|---|---|---|
| *Standard Tangible Savings:* (Reduced Head Count) | 0 | 0 | $75 | $200 | 0 | 0 | $175 | $275 |
| *Overlooked Tangible Savings:* | 0 | 0 | $375 | $575 | 0 | 275 | $600 | $625 |
| *Total Tangible Savings:* | 0 | 0 | $450 | $775 | 0 | 275 | $775 | $900 |
| Cost of New System: | $150 | $100 | $50 | $50 | $250 | $175 | $100 | $100 |
| Net Annual Savings: | ($150) | ($100) | $400 | $725 | ($250) | $100 | $875 | $800 |
| Cumulative Savings: | ($150) | ($250) | $150 | $875 | ($250) | ($150) | $525 | $1,325 |

| | Build Only (A) | Buy and Build (B) |
|---|---|---|
| Gross Four-Year Savings From Each Choice: | $1,225 | $1,950 |
| Four-Year Cost of Each Choice: | $350 | $825 |
| *Net Four-Year Saving from Each Choice:* | $875 | $1,325 |
| *Net Present Value (NPV) from Each Choice (at 6.5%):* | $709 | $1,100 |
| Inernal Rate of Return (IRR): | 150 | 124 |

*Choice Based on NPV Analysis: Buy/Build (B)*
*Choice Based on IRR Analysis: Build Only (A)*

SOURCE: Condensed from *Datamation*, Jan. 7, 1994, p. 46.

## MANAGEMENT BY MAXIM FOR IT INFRASTRUCTURE

Organizations that are composed of multiple business units, including large, multidivisional ones, need frequently to make decisions about the appropriate level and types of infrastructure that will be shared among and support their individual operating units. These decisions are important because infrastructure can amount to over 50 percent of the total IT budget, and because it can increase effectiveness through synergies across the organization. However, because of substantial differences among organizations—in their culture, structure, and environment—what is appropriate for one will not necessarily be suitable for others. The fact that many of the benefits of infrastructure are intangible further complicates this issue.

Broadbent and Weill (1997) suggest a method called **management by maxim** to deal with this problem. This method brings together corporate executives, business unit managers, and IT executives in planning sessions to determine appropriate infrastructure investments through the following steps:

▶ *Consider strategic context.* Identify long-term goals, potential synergies where sharing of services or data across units could improve performance, and degree of emphasis on autonomy or cooperation across business units.

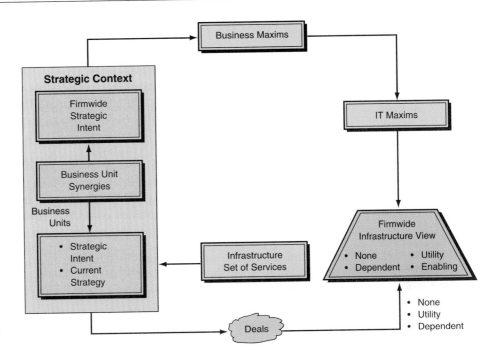

**FIGURE 13.7** Management by maxim: linking strategy and infrastructure. (*Source*: Broadbent and Weill [1997], p. 79.)

▶ *Articulate business maxims.* Develop short, well-defined statements of organizational strategies or goals in key areas such as costs, quality, flexibility, growth, human resources, and management philosophy.

▶ *Identify IT maxims.* Develop statements of the IT strategies or goals required to support the business maxims. For example, a business maxim might be "price products/services at lowest cost." A corresponding IT maxim could be "use IT to reduce costs by eliminating duplicated effort."

▶ *Clarify the firm's view of its IT infrastructure.* Reach consensus on which category of infrastructure the business and IT maxims require. The four possibilities are:

1. None—each business unit maintains its own infrastructure.

2. Utility—sharing across units is done primarily to reduce costs.

3. Dependent—primarily supports the requirements of current strategies of business units, including increasing revenues.

4. Enabling—goes beyond current strategies of business units to support long-term goals.

▶ *Specify infrastructure services.* Identify infrastructure services required to achieve the business and IT maxims, in the context of whichever of the above infrastructure categories is appropriate for the firm.

These steps are diagrammed in Figure 13.7, which also shows a line at the bottom through an item labeled "Deals." This represents an alternative approach in the absence of appropriate maxims, where the IT manager negotiates with individual business units to obtain adequate funding for shared infrastructure. This approach can work where there is no shared infrastructure, or where the infrastructure category is a utility. However, Broadbent and Weill have not found any cases of firms that developed an enabling infrastructure via deals.

### OPTION VALUATION OF IT INVESTMENTS

A promising new approach for evaluating IT investments is to recognize that they can increase an organization's options in the future. Current IT investments, especially for infrastructure, make it possible to respond quickly to unexpected and unforeseeable challenges and opportunities in later years. If the organization waits until the benefits have been established, it may be very difficult to catch up with competitors that have already invested in the infrastructure and have become familiar with the technology.

The concept of **option valuation** is well known in the securities markets. In addition to stocks, investors can purchase options on stocks. These options give their owners the right to buy or sell the stock at a given price within a specified time period. For example, an investor could buy stock now in a major computer manufacturer at $80 per share, or he or she could pay around $8 now for the right to buy a share of that same stock at $80 any time in the next three months.

The key aspect of an option is that it offers an opportunity for a large profit in the future. If the stock in our example goes to $96—a 20 percent increase in value—the option to buy at $80 is now worth $16, which is a 100 percent gain over its original price. Therefore investors are willing to pay $8 for the option to pay $80 to buy a stock that is currently selling for $80, even though the actual value of the option at this point is zero.

Applying this concept to IT, the costs of a proposed investment could exceed the tangible benefits. However, if the project creates opportunities for additional projects in the future, the investment also has an options value that should be added to its other benefits.

The mathematics of option valuation are well established but unfortunately too complex for many managers. (See Dixit and Pindyck [1995] for details.) On the other hand, it is relatively easy to estimate **expected value (EV)** of possible future benefits by multiplying the size of the benefit by the probability of its occurrence. For example, an organization might consider investing in a corporate intranet. If there is a 50 percent probability that this would lead to better analyses, which would result in new business worth $10 million in additional profits, the value of this specific benefit would be 50 percent times $10 million or $5 million. The calculations could also include an estimate of value for unspecified, totally unforeseeable benefits, based on the fact that they have occurred in the past (i.e., computerized airline reservation systems unexpectedly made it possible to establish "frequent flyer" and other yield management marketing programs).

The expected value approach does not, however, provide any estimate of the option value of an IT investment that makes it possible for the organization to either enter into or decide against other projects in the future. Box 13.8 (p. 381) shows an example of option valuation calculations.

## ▶ 13.4 ACCOUNTING FOR COSTS: CHARGEBACK AND OUTSOURCING

In addition to identifying and evaluating the benefits of IT, organizations also need to account for its costs. Ideally the accounting systems will effectively deal with two issues. First, they should provide an accurate measure of total IT costs for management control purposes. Second, they should charge users for shared (usually infrastructure) IT investments and services in a manner that contributes

## *A Closer Look* BOX 13.8

### VALUING AN IT INFRASTRUCTURE INVESTMENT THAT GIVES FUTURE OPTIONS

Suppose an organization faces a decision about a $10 million current investment in IT infrastructure. If this infrastructure were available, the organization would be able to develop new services with substantial market potential. At this point in time, the costs of producing the new services (including amortization of subsequent investments) are fairly clear, but the revenues are uncertain. If the organization waits until the revenue potential becomes more visible in two years, it will probably be too late to make the initial investment. The time required to establish and become proficient with the new infrastructure will make it difficult or impossible to compete with other organizations that make such investments before the potential becomes clear.

The table below shows the calculations. To simplify the analysis, all future revenues and costs over the life span of the new services are converted to present values. At the time of the analysis, there are three possible scenarios for revenues, which result in profits (NPV) of $39 million, or $6 million, or a loss of $27 million. Each of these three outcomes is equally likely. Multiplying each outcome by its probability of one-third, and adding these weighted values together, results in an expected value (EV) of $6 million. Since the infrastructure investment of $10 million is greater than this expected value, the organization would probably reject the investment.

On the other hand, the organization could invest in the IT infrastructure now but wait two years to decide whether to produce the new services. The organization will know then which scenario is most accurate. Under scenario A or B, it will produce the new services because revenues will exceed costs, but it will avoid the new market under scenario C, because costs will exceed revenues. Providing the ability to avoid future losses justifies the $10 million infrastructure investment by raising its expected value to $15 million. The $9 million difference in expected values—$15 million rather than $6 million—is the *option value* of the investment.

| Scenario (Probability) | Present Value | | Net Present Value of Profit | First Weighted NPV | Second Weighted NPV |
|---|---|---|---|---|---|
| | Revenues | Costs | | | |
| A (1/3) | $82 MM | $43 MM | $39 MM | $13 MM | $13 MM |
| B (1/3) | 46 MM | 40 MM | 6 MM | 2 MM | 2 MM |
| C (1/3) | 10 MM | 37 MM | (27 MM) | (9 MM) | 0 MM |
| | | | Total EV: | $6 MM | $15 MM |

to the achievement of organization goals. These are two very challenging goals for any accounting system, and the complexities and rapid pace of change make them even more difficult to achieve in the context of IT.

In the early days of computing it was much easier to identify costs. Computers and other hardware were very expensive and were managed by centralized organizational units with their own personnel. Most application software was developed internally rather than purchased. IT was only used for a few well-defined applications, such as payroll, inventory management, and accounts payable/receivable.

In contrast, nowadays computers are cheap and software is increasingly purchased rather than made. The overwhelming majority of the total processing power is located on the collective desktops of the organization rather than in centralized computer centers, and it is managed by individual organizational units rather than a centralized IS department. A large proportion of the costs are in "hidden," indirect costs that are often overlooked.

These trends make it very difficult just to identify, let alone effectively control, the total costs of IT. As a practical matter, many organizations track costs associated with centralized IS and leave management and cost accounting for desktop IT to the user organizations. However, the trend toward attaching personal computers to networks, and the availability of network management software, make it easier to track and manage costs related to desktop IT. Some organizations indicate "six-digit" savings by using network management software to identify which computers use what software, and then reducing the site licenses to correspond to the actual usage.

## CHARGEBACK

Although it is hard to accurately measure total IT costs, organizations can still use accounting systems to influence organization IT usage in desirable directions. Large organizations typically require individual operating and support units to develop annual budgets and justify variances. Services from the central IS department represent a significant budget item for most of these units, so the way they are charged for these services will influence how much they use them.

In some organizations, the ISD functions as an *unallocated cost center*. All expenses go into an overhead account. The problem with this approach is that IT is a "free good" that has no explicit cost, so there are no incentives to control usage or avoid waste.

> We tried chargeback for 6 months. After 3, we found that computers had viruses, backups weren't completed, and service wasn't maintained because department managers didn't want to pay for it. It was a terrible idea for us.
>
> — *Mike Rewald*

One alternative is to distribute all costs of IT to users as accurately as possible, based on actual costs and usage levels. This approach is one form of **chargeback** (also known as chargeout, or cost recovery). Although accurate allocation sounds desirable in principle, it can create problems in practice. The most accurate measures of use may reflect technological factors that are totally incomprehensible to the user. If fixed costs are allocated on the basis of total usage throughout the organization, which varies from month to month, charges will fluctuate for an individual unit even though its own usage does not change. These considerations can reduce the credibility of the chargeback system.

A third approach is to have a **behavior-oriented chargeback** system. The primary objective of this type of system is influencing users' behavior. Although more difficult to develop, it recognizes the importance of IT—and its effective management—to the success of the organization. A behavior-oriented system not only avoids the unallocated-cost-center's problem of overuse of "free" resources; it can also reduce the use of scarce resources where demand exceeds supply even with fully allocated costs. In addition to increasing the organization's efficiency through better cost control, a behavior-oriented system can encourage more effective use of IT. Fully allocated costs often discourage the testing of new technologies—ones that could offer substantial benefits in the future—because the high initial costs are spread over a limited number of early users. On the other hand, behavior-oriented chargeouts can encourage experimentation and organizational learning of targeted technologies by offering them on a subsidized basis. Table 13.2 (p. 583) provides examples of considerations relevant to behavior-oriented chargeback systems.

There are three steps in implementing a behavior-oriented chargeback system:

► *Determine objectives.* This should involve IS staff, executives familiar with organizational plans, accounting personnel, and possibly consultants with related expertise. Within the context of organizational goals and plans, current

---

***Table 13.2*** **General Objectives of a Behavior-Oriented Chargeback System**

---

*Efficiency—Doing Things Right*
- Reduce wasted resources.
- Reduce use of scarce resources.
- Encourage use in off-peak hours (load leveling).
- Discourage "false economies" and suboptimizing behavior (actions that appear to help the individual unit but are bad for the organization as a whole).

*Effectiveness—Doing the Right Things*
- Encourage IT usage consistent with organizational strategies and goals.
- Encourage experimentation, technology assimilation, and organizational learning.
- Encourage more productive use of surplus resources.
- Encourage data sharing across organizational units.
- Encourage reuse of software instead of new development.
- Improve communications between users and IS department.

---

and projected IT capabilities, and industry and technological trends, this group determines the general goals and specific behaviors that the chargeback system needs to encourage or discourage.

▶ ***Determine appropriate measures.*** The success of a chargeback system depends on having measures that users can understand and control, and that they perceive as fair rather than arbitrary. It is better to use physical outputs, for example, number of invoices processed, rather than abstract computer jargon such as "CPU seconds." Calculations should be simple, verifiable, and consistent from month to month. However, caution is necessary with measures that correspond to services offered by vendors, because they initially may provide lower quality or price services at less than cost to attract business.

▶ ***Implement and maintain the system.*** The final step is to put the new chargeback system into operation. Like other information systems, it will probably have initial bugs and users will identify desirable features to add to the system. In addition, the system will need updates on a regular basis to reflect changes in technologies, organizational operations, strategies, and plans.

There are various methods of chargeback. The reason is that it is very difficult to approximate costs, especially in companies where multiple independent operating units are sharing a centralized system. For a review of methods see McAdam (1996). The difficulties in chargeback may be one of the drivers of IT outsourcing.

## OUTSOURCING AS AN ECONOMIC STRATEGY

If organizations can effectively define and measure information technology costs and benefits, as we discussed in the preceding sections, they are in a better position to effectively manage their IT. On the other hand, they still may not be able to manage it as well as firms that specialize in managing IT. For such organizations, outsourcing may be the most effective strategy for obtaining the economic benefits of IT and controlling its costs.

Information technology is now a vital part of almost every organization and plays an important supporting role in most functions. However, IT is not the primary business of many organizations. Their *core competencies*—the things they do best and that represent their competitive strengths—are in manufacturing, or retailing, or services, or some other function. IT is complex, expensive, and constantly changing. It is difficult to manage IT, even for organizations with above-average management skills. Because of these considerations, some organizations have decided to use outside vendors rather than internal IS units as their primary source of IT services. Obtaining services from vendors, rather than from within the organization, is known as **outsourcing.**

The idea of outsourcing itself is not new. Organizations have always faced the choice of buying goods and services externally or producing them internally. The decision usually considers two factors: (1) which source is less expensive? and (2) how much control is necessary? Most organizations buy their power from electric utilities because this is cheaper than operating their own generating equipment. However, a few (hospitals, for example) have their own emergency power generating systems. These internal systems give them more control over their operations; they do not have to shut down if a disaster causes a power failure.

Outsourcing IT functions, such as payroll services, has been around since the early days of data processing. Contract programmers and computer timesharing services are longstanding examples. What is new is that, since the late 1980s, as illustrated in the opening case, *many* organizations are outsourcing the majority of their IT functions rather than just incidental parts. The trend became very visible in 1989 when Eastman Kodak announced it was transferring its data centers to IBM under a 10-year, $500 million contract. This example, at a prominent multibillion-dollar company, gave a clear signal that outsourcing was a legitimate approach to managing IT.

However, outsourcing remains a very debatable issue as demonstrated below.

### IT At Work — XEROX VERSUS CAPITAL ONE: CONTRADICTORY APPROACHES

When Patricia Wallington, **Xerox**'s CIO, was told to curtail costs to help Xerox get ready for the twenty first century, her solution was to outsource much of the company's IS operations—including telecommunications, mainframe management, and PC support. "The legacy environment is so important, but it is very hard to get focused on the move to the future, so we figured separating the two environments would help us move forward," Wallington says. "And we focused on doing a global contract so we could benefit from the consistency."

For its outsourcing needs, Xerox chose EDS in a 10-year, $3.2 billon deal that started in 1995. About 2,000 Xerox employees were moved to EDS, leaving Xerox's internal IS organization with a staff of just 700 people. Of Xerox's annual $800 million IS budget, about $300 million now goes to EDS every year. By 1997 it was clear that the EDS deal has required more attention than Xerox anticipated. "We spend more time co-managing than we expected," says Wallington. The company has 12 people internally devoted to contract management from a financial perspective alone. Wallington declines to be specific, but she admits that the contract has cost more than Xerox had hoped. Still, according to her, the deal appears to be providing the necessary savings to pay for Xerox's business process reengineering efforts. (SOURCE: Compiled from Knowles, A., "Copy This!" *Datamation*, June 1997.)

In 1990, Signet Bank had outsourced all of the company's information systems to EDS to raise much-needed capital. In 1994 management of **Capital One**, a spinoff from Signet Bank (see case on our Web site), wanted them back. Bringing back the systems—all of the company's main functions, including general ledger, purchasing, payroll, and personnel—was a first step in unifying IT and laying the groundwork for future architectures.

It cost the company $49 million to break the contract. After reviewing each system's contract, the CIO opted to leave the deposit system used for Capital One's secured credit-card accounts—those that require an initial deposit by the consumer—at EDS. That decicion, he says, was unpopular. "No one wanted to do [business with] EDS. The business people didn't want to deal with them, and there were problems on the technological side. But no one could give me a solid business case for why bringing this piece of business in house was more profitable than leaving it where it was." The deposit system remained with EDS. SOURCE: Compiled from Asbrand, D., "A Profitable Synchronicity," *Datamation*, Sept. 1997.

**For Further Exploration:** How come we have such a contradiction? ▲

In a typical situation, the outsourcing firm hires the IS employees of the customer and buys the computer hardware. The cash from this sale is an important incentive for outsourcing by firms with financial problems. The outsourcer provides IT services under a five- to ten-year contract that specifies a baseline level of services, with additional charges for higher volumes or services not identified in the baseline.

Many smaller firms provide limited-scale outsourcing of individual services, but only the largest outsourcing firms can take over large proportions of the IT functions of major organizations. In the mid-1990s, IBM, EDS, and Computer Sciences Corp. were winning approximately two-thirds of the largest outsourcing contracts. Figure 13.8 shows outsourcing revenues for all IT suppliers on a worldwide basis. It indicates a market of almost $130 billion in 1996, which is projected to more than double by 2000.

> With outsourcing, management is able to get the technologically most advanced staff at a moment's notice. It's like leasing employees.
>
> — *Blake Thompson*

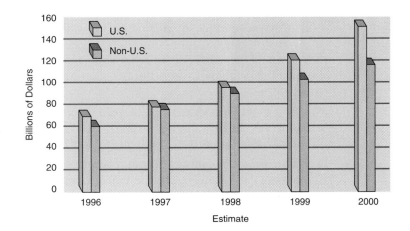

**FIGURE 13.8** World IT outsourcing market forecast (estimated vendor revenues). (*Source*: The Yankee Group, 1996. http://www.ibm.com/Other-Voices/YankeeGroup /March2597215921.html.)

**OUTSOURCING ADVANTAGES AND DISADVANTAGES.** Outsourcing advocates describe IT as a commodity, a generic item like electricity or janitorial services. They note the benefits summarized in Table 13.3. In particular, the advo-

*Table 13.3* **Potential Outsourcing Benefits**

*Financial*
- Avoid heavy capital investment, thereby releasing funds for other uses.
- Improve cash flow and cost accountability.
- Realize cost benefits from economies-of-scale, and from sharing computer housing, hardware, software, and personnel.
- Release expensive office space.

*Technical*
- Be freer to choose software due to a wider range of hardware.
- Achieve technological improvements more easily.
- Have greater access to technical skills.

*Management*
- Concentrate on developing and running core business activity.
- Delegate IT development (design, production, and acquisition) and operational responsibility to supplier.
- Eliminate need to recruit and retain competent IT staff.

*Human Resources*
- Draw on specialist skills, available from a pool of expertise, when needed.
- Enrich career development and opportunities for staff.

*Quality*
- Clearly define service levels.
- Improve performance accountability.
- Earn quality accreditation.

*Flexibility*
- Respond quickly to business demands.
- Handle IT peaks and valleys more effectively.

cates claim that outside vendors can provide IT services at 10 to 40 percent lower cost, with higher quality, for the following reasons:

▶ **Hardware economies of scale.** With multiple customers, outsourcers can use more cost-efficient larger computers or get discounts on volume purchases of hardware. They also can operate their computers with less excess capacity because peak loads from different customers will not all occur at the same time.

▶ **Staffing economies of scale.** A larger customer base also makes it possible for outsourcers to hire highly skilled, specialized technical personnel whose salaries would be hard to justify in smaller IS groups.

▶ **Specialization.** Providing computer services is one of the core competencies of the oursourcing firm, rather than an incidental part of its business.

▶ **Tax benefits.** Organizations can deduct outsourcing fees from current income, in contrast to depreciating computer hardware purchases over three to five years.

To evaluate claims about the benefits, Lacity and Hirschheim (1993) conducted interviews with 14 companies that outsourced or considered outsourcing. They found that outsourcing was not necessarily less expensive, and that it could create problems. They point out the following issues:

▶ *Limited economies of scale.* Although outsourcers can negotiate larger discounts on hardware, the advantage is not large, especially over the five-year life of a mainframe.

▶ *Staffing.* For the most part, customers are served by their former employees rather than more highly skilled vendor staff. In some cases, the outsourcer shifts the better former employees to other accounts.

▶ *Lack of business expertise.* In addition to losing former employees to other accounts, the remaining staff members tend to become more technically oriented and have less knowledge of the business issues in the customer's industry.

▶ *Contract problems.* Some customers did not adequately specify service levels and had to pay "excess fees" for services not in the contract, or for volumes greater than the averages written into the contract.

▶ *Internal cost reduction opportunities.* Organizations can achieve many of the cost savings of outsourcing by improving their own IT management, for example, through:

Economies of scale from consolidating multiple data centers into one location

More efficient resource usage as a result of implementing chargeout systems

Increased control over user abuses of IT services through prioritization and formal procedures

The implementation of Internet-based technologies and especially electronic commerce encourages the use of outsourcing, as can be seen in the following *IT at Work* example.

---

### *IT At Work*  CANADIAN IMPERIAL BANK OF COMMERCE (CIBC) OUTSOURCES INTERNET TECHNOLOGIES

In the spring of 1996 the competitors of this bank were ahead in implementing Internet banking and CIBC started to lose market share. A decision was made to move quickly.

Being a bank and not an IT expert, this was a challenge. So the bank decided to outsource the job to IBM's Global Services. Together, CIBC and IBM were able to implement home banking in six months. By 1998 the bank regained market share, having 200,000 online clients (see www.pcbanking.cibc.com).

IBM admitted that CIBC's dilemma is becoming a familiar story in just about every industry. Time constraints brought on by competitive challenges, security issues, and a shortage of skilled system developers in the Internet/intranet field contribute to a boom in the outsourcing business. Implementing EC applications forces companies to outsource mission-critical applications. This was never done before on such a grand scale. This will result, according to the GartnerGroup, in the tripling of IT outsourcing in three years. Forrester Research found that 90 percent of the companies they polled use or plan to use Internet-related outsourcing.

**For Further Exploration:** What will happen to the outsourcers once the Internet/EC infrastructure is in place? ▲

SOURCE: Condensed from Duvall (1998).

---

A special consideration is the implementation of extranets. Implementing an extranet is very difficult due to security issues and the need to have the system be rapidly expandable (some companies report 1000% growth for EC activities in a year; e.g., see www.hotmail.com). General Electric Information Services (www.geis.com), an extranet outsourcer, charges $100,000–$150,000 to set up an extranet, and a $5,000+/month service fee. However, users of these services admit an ROI of 100 to 1,000 percent. For details see (Duvall [1998]).

**OUTSOURCING RECOMMENDATIONS.** Some organizations may decide to outsource because they just do not have the skills to manage the IT function, or because they need to sell off IT assets to generate funds. For these situations, Lacity and Hirschheim (1993) offer 14 suggestions shown in Table 13.4. Other sources (e.g., Marcolin and McLellan [1998]) offer additional recommendations such as:

---

*Table 13.4* **Suggestions for Successful Outsourcing**

---

1. Discard the vendor's standard contract and develop a version more appropriate for the specific situation.
2. Do not sign incomplete contracts.
3. Hire technical and legal experts in outsourcing to assist with negotiations.
4. Measure all IT activities during the baseline period that determines the terms of the contract.
5. Develop specific and complete service level agreements and measures.
6. Develop service level reports that make it possible to monitor vendor performance.
7. Specify escalation procedures for failures to meet service levels.
8. Include cash penalties for nonperformance.
9. Specify service level growth rates that reflect the impact of decreasing IT costs on demand.
10. Include provisions for business changes, such as mergers or divestitures, that could significantly increase or decrease service requirements.
11. Specifically identify the vendor's account manager for the organization.
12. Include a termination clause and be sure that it provides for a transition period.
13. Take special care with clauses that require additional charges for functions that are different ("change of character") from the baseline.
14. Be considerate of the interests of the organization's IS employees who will shift to the outsourcer or move on to some other employment.

---

SOURCE: Condensed from Lacity, M. C., and R. Hirschheim, "The Information Systems Outsourcing Bandwagon," *Sloan Management Review,* Fall 1993, pp. 73–86.

▶ *Write short-period contracts.* Outsourcing contracts are often written for 5- to 10-year terms. Because IT and the competitive environment change so rapidly, it is very possible that some of the terms will not be in the customer's best interests after five years. If a long-term contract is used, it needs to include adequate mechanisms for negotiating revisions where necessary.

▶ *Subcontracting.* Vendors may subcontract some of the services to other vendors. The contract should give the customer some control over the circumstances, including choice of vendors, and any subcontract arrangements.

▶ *Selective outsourcing.* This is a strategy used by many corporations who prefer not to outsource the majority of their IT, like Kodak, but rather outsource certain areas (such as connectivity or network security).

A comprehensive discussion of outsourcing, vendors, conditions, and recommendations is provided by Field (1997).

At this point, the phenomenon of large-scale IT outsourcing is approximately ten years old. The number of organizations that have used it for at least several years is still small, but it is growing. Business and IT-oriented periodicals have published numerous stories about their experiences. The general consensus of this anecdotal information is that the cost savings are not large—perhaps around 10 percent—and that not all organizations experience them. This still leaves the question of whether outsourcing IT can improve organizational performance by making it possible to focus more intensely on core competencies. Further research is necessary to answer this question.

An interesting example is the case of DuPont, the giant chemical concern. *Chemical Week,* March 12, 1997, reports that DuPont transferred its IT data center with 4,000 IT employees to Andersen Consulting and Computer Services Corp. This deal enables DuPont and its outsourcers to form a partnership that markets IT services to others.

Finally, a new approach is that of *strategic outsourcing* (Garner [1998]), where you can generate new business, retain skilled employees, and best manage emerging technologies.

## ▶ 13.5 OTHER ECONOMIC ASPECTS OF INFORMATION TECHNOLOGY

### NEGATIVE IMPACTS OF FAILURES AND "RUNAWAYS"

Information technology is difficult to manage. One symptom of this problem is the trend to let somebody else manage IT through outsourcing. Another symptom is the high proportion of IS development projects that either fail completely or fail to meet some of the original targets for features, development time, or cost. The following definitions indicate the range of possibilities for the various types of failures:

▶ *Outright failure.* The system is never completed, and little or nothing is salvaged from the project.

▶ *Abandoned.* The system is completed, including some or all of the originally specified features, but either it is never used or usage stops after a short period.

▶ *Scaled down.* The system is completed and used, but lacks much of the functionality of the original specifications.

▶ *Runaway.* The project requires much more money and time than planned, regardless of whether it is ever completed or used.

> My company is halfway through a revenue control runaway project which will never work even if it's completed. Sometimes it's best to cut your losses and start from scratch.
> — *Mike Rewald*

Many failures occur in smaller systems that handle internal processes within an organization, and they usually remain corporate secrets. The total investment is not large, the failure does not have a major economic impact, and the effects are generally not visible to outsiders. On the other hand, some IS failures result in losses in excess of ten million dollars and may severely damage the organization, as well as generating a lot of negative publicity. Failures in large public organizations such as the IRS or Social Security are well advertised. The CONFIRM reservation system and the Taurus stock exchange projects, which both resulted in losses of over one hundred million dollars, are described in the following *IT at Work.*

*IT At Work*    NINE-DIGIT FAILURES

**THE CONFIRM HOSPITALITY INDUSTRY RESERVATION SYSTEM PROJECT. AMR Corp.** announced plans in 1988 for CONFIRM, a $50 million dollar car rental and hotel reservations system. AMR is the parent of American Airlines, which developed the highly successful SABRE airline reservation system. The project also included Marriott Corp. and Hilton Hotels, as well as Budget Rent-a-Car.

Within six months the project was in trouble. The IS group at AMR (AMRIS) hired an IBM consulting group in April 1989 to do an outside review. The consultants reported that "the CONFIRM project is in dire need of . . . immediate corrective action. . . . Not doing so will assuredly result in a failure." The other partners say that they did not receive copies of this report, but AMR claims they were aware of the findings.

The project continued for three more years. In April 1992, AMRIS announced that completion could be 18 months past the already delayed target date. In September 1992, AMRIS sued its partners for breach of contract, claiming they had caused the delays by requesting thousands of changes after completion of the original specifications. The partners responded by suing for damages in excess of $500 million, with Budget claiming that AMRIS had lied to them to obtain continued funding for the project.

AMR wrote off $165 million in 1992, over three times the original budget for the project. The partners received out-of-court settlements estimated at $160 million. AMR incurred substantial legal fees, as well as damage to its reputation as a provider of IS services (Zellner [1994]).

**LONDON STOCK EXCHANGE TAURUS SYSTEM.** The original budget for the **Taurus** automated securities trading system was £6 million. The London Stock Exchange finally canceled the project in 1993 after 11 years of development and £75 million in spending. However, this was just a small part of the total losses. In response to the requirements of the stock exchange, brokerage firms had modified their own systems to be "Taurus-compliant" and, in aggregate, they incurred costs of over £400 million.

**For Further Exploration:** Why do organizations keep investing money in projects in spite of clear evidence that they are failing? What are the issues in a decision to terminate a failing project? ▲

---

Spectacular, highly visible failures are evidence of problems in IS development. However, publicity on a few very large IT projects does not demonstrate how widespread these problems are throughout the field. The Standish Group International reports that a large majority of projects experienced some form of failure. Their 1995 survey of 365 large organizations indicates that 31 percent of projects are not completed. Some 53 percent are completed, but with an average cost overrun of 189 percent; in other words, they cost almost three times the budget. Many of these completed projects did not contain all the functionalities of the original specifications. Only 16 percent were completed on time and on budget.

These high failure levels are in marked contrast to experience with design and development in other areas of the economy. Architects and engineers design houses, buildings, and bridges, and then contractors construct them. Engineers design automobiles that are subsequently mass-produced in factories. Failures are rare, and they usually result from unusual situations such as natural disasters or gross negligence.

The number of system development problems is large enough to represent a market opportunity for consulting firms. For example, KPMG Peat Marwick has a unit that will help with the management of runaway projects (Rothfeder [1988]). A KPMG Peat Marwick survey in Britain provides another indicator of the magnitude of problems in this area. When using contractors to develop information systems, organizations had threatened legal action on 20 percent of the projects and actually went into court on 4 percent. This level of legal involvement is much greater than in other types of business dealings.

What are the causes of the high failure rates? One problem is that computer systems are highly abstract and complex. Architects create drawings that eventually become houses or buildings, which are solid and visible and easily understandable by nontechnical people.

In contrast there are two end results of programming: (1) code that requires a lot of effort even for other programmers to understand; and (2) systems that are comprehensible to users only in terms of a limited number of printouts and screen displays, rather than all the other things that need to occur within the hardware, software, and network to produce these outputs. Their inherent complexity means that systems development projects need more effective management than other organization activities.

Because of the complexity and associated risks, some managers refuse to develop systems beyond a certain size. The "one, one, ten rule" says not to develop a system if it will take longer than one year, has a budget over one million dollars, and will require more than ten people. Following this strategy, an organization will need to buy rather than develop large systems, or do without them.

Purchasing can be the safest strategy for very large and complex systems, especially those that involve multiple units within an organization. For example, the SAP AG software firm offers a family of integrated, "enterprise-level," large-scale information systems (see Chapter 8). These systems are available in versions tailored for specific industries, including aerospace, banking, utilities, retail, and so forth. Many organizations feel that buying from a good vendor reduces their risk of failure, even if they have to change their business processes to be compatible with the new system. The economics of software production suggest that, for relatively standardized systems, purchasing can result in both cost savings and increased functionality (see Box 13.9).

---

## *A Closer Look* BOX 13.9

### THE ECONOMICS OF BUY VERSUS MAKE

A large bank needs a system to handle a variety of customer checking and savings accounts. It has two options:

▶ Spend $5 million to internally develop its own system, which, *if the project is successful,* will match up exactly with the way it does business, or

▶ Spend $3 million to purchase a system from an outside vendor. The purchased system will require an additional $500,000 for customization, and for changes within the organization to accommodate it. The new system includes desirable features that might not be available if the bank develops its own system, but it does not include certain other features that the bank views as important but not critical. The vendor spent $20 million developing the software, because it expects to sell the system to at least 10 banks. Several other banks are already using the system and recommend it, so there is very little risk of failure.

**For Further Exploration:** Should the bank buy the system or develop its own? What other information would be helpful in making this decision?

## THE NEW ECONOMICS OF IT

In the preceding sections, our focus has been on the economics of the use of IT in organizations to assist in performing other activities. In this section, we turn to the economics of IT as a product in itself rather than playing a supporting role.

In 1916, David Sarnoff attempted to persuade his manager that the American Marconi company should produce inexpensive radio receivers to sell to the consumer market. Others in the company (which subsequently became RCA) opposed the idea because it depended on the development of a radio broadcasting industry. They did not expect this to happen, because they could not see how broadcasters could generate revenues by providing a service without any charges to the listeners.

The commercial development of radio, and the even greater success of television, proved that Sarnoff was right. If it is possible to provide a popular service to a large audience at a low cost per person, there will be ways of generating revenues. The only question is: how?

The World Wide Web on the Internet resembles commercial broadcasting in its early days. Fixed costs—initial investments and production costs—can be high in themselves, but they are low in terms of average cost per potential customer. The incremental or variable costs of delivering content to individual customers, or processing transactions, are very low.

The market is large—at least one-third of the population of the United States, plus foreign markets, now have access to the Internet—and it is growing rapidly. Many people who do not have computers at home can access the Internet through computers at work, schools, or libraries. The arrival in 1995 of Web TV adapters for television sets made it possible for homes without computers to get on the Internet for as little as $400. These trends could lead to a situation of "universal connectivity," in which almost every citizen in the industrialized countries has access to the Internet.

The Web is also different from broadcasting in ways that increase its economic potential. At present, typical Web users have above-average incomes and education. Users can view most Web content at any time, rather than just at the scheduled times of broadcast programs. The Web can reach smaller, very specialized "niche" markets better than the mass media.

Chapter 6 provides detailed information on specific applications of electronic commerce. These applications demonstrate how favorable economic factors are leading to a wide variety of approaches to generating income using the Web or other aspects of the Internet. We now turn to the economic concepts of increasing returns, which applies both to the Internet and to software production.

## INCREASING RETURNS

Stanford economist Brian Arthur (1996) is the leading proponent of the economic theory of increasing returns, which applies to the Web and other forms of information technology. He starts with the familiar concept that the economy is divided into different sectors, one that produces physical products, and another that focuses on information. Producers of physical products—foodstuffs, petroleum, automobiles—are subject to diminishing returns. Although they may have initial increasing economies of scale, they eventually reach a point where costs go up and additional production becomes less profitable.

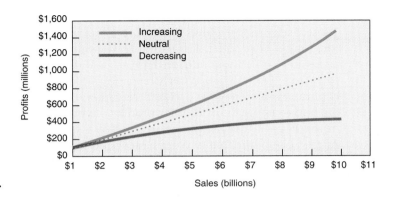

FIGURE 13.9 Increasing versus decreasing returns.

Arthur notes that in the information economy the situation is very different. For example, initial costs to develop new software are very high, but the cost of producing additional copies is very low. The result is **increasing returns,** where profitability rises more rapidly than production increases. A firm with a high market share can use these higher profits to improve the product, or enhance the marketing, to strengthen its leading position. Figure 13.9 illustrates the difference between increasing and decreasing returns. Box 13.10 provides an example of increasing returns in the software business.

In addition to higher profitability, two other factors favor firms with higher market share. The first is **network effects.** Leading products in an industry at-

---

## *A Closer Look*   BOX 13.10

### HIGH VERSUS LOW SHARE OF A SOFTWARE MARKET

Two companies produce comparable software that sells for $325 a copy. Each invested $250 million to develop its version, and they have costs of $50 per copy for packaging, marketing, and so on. The only difference is that one company has 90 percent, and the other 10 percent, of a market of 10 million copies. Financial results are summarized below:

| Financial Results at Software Price of $325 | | |
|---|---|---|
| | Leading Firm | Competitor |
| Units Sales | 9,000,000 | 1,000,000 |
| Gross Revenue | $2,925,000,000 | $325,000,000 |
| – Production Costs | (450,000,000) | (50,000,000) |
| – Development Costs | (250,000,000) | (250,000,000) |
| = Profit Before Taxes | $2,225,000,000 | $25,000,000 |
| Return on Investment | 890% | 10% |

The data above show that, although the sales of the leading firm were nine times higher, its profits and return on investment were 89 times higher (890% vs.

10%). The following table shows what would happen if the leading company reduced the price to $250 per copy, forcing its competitor to also lower its price, with unit sales rising to 12.3 million as a result of the lower price:

| Financial Results at Software Price of $250 | | |
|---|---|---|
| | Leading Firm | Competitor |
| Unit Sales | 11,100,000 | 1,200,000 |
| Gross Revenue | $2,775,000,000 | $300,000,000 |
| – Production Costs | (555,000,000) | (60,000,000) |
| – Development Costs | (250,000,000) | (250,000,000) |
| = Profit Before Taxes | $1,970,000,000 | ($10,000,000) |
| Return on Investment | 788% | (4)% |

In this situation, sales of the leading firm are still around nine times higher. However, its profits and return on investment have declined only slightly, while its competitor is now losing money.

SOURCE: Compiled from Gurley, as quoted in Aley (1996).

tract a base of users, and this leads to development of complementary products. These users and products constitute a "network" that enhances the position of the dominant product. For example, the open architecture of the IBM PC made it possible to develop add-on hardware and to create clones that run the same software. The market for PCs became much larger than the market for Apple computers, which have a closed architecture. Software companies shifted production to PC versions of their products, which further enhanced the dominance of the PC. All this happened in spite of a substantial amount of evidence that Apple's computers really were better products.

The second factor is the **lock-in effect.** Most new software is hard to learn, so users typically will not switch to a different product unless it is much more powerful or they are forced into making the change. The end result of these factors is that when a firm establishes a clear lead over its competitors, it tends to become stronger and stronger in its market.

The potential for increasing returns requires management strategies that are very different from those in other industries. Arthur (1996) suggests the following:

▶ *Build up a large customer base through low prices.* Netscape allows individual consumers (as opposed to organizations) to download its Web browser at no charge. This accelerated development of the Web and established Netscape's leading position. It also increased the market for browsers and related software that Netscape sells to organizations as well as to individual consumers through retail outlets.

▶ *Encourage development of complementary products.* Novell provided support and assistance for developers to create applications or modify existing applications to run on its network operating system. The availability of this application software strengthened Novell's market position, which in turn increased the size of the market for the developers of these applications.

▶ *Use "linking and leveraging."* In addition to encouraging outside suppliers, firms can acquire or internally develop products that complement existing products. They can also capitalize on a large customer base for existing products. Microsoft's Windows operating system provides capabilities that make its word processing and spreadsheet software more competitive. The market for the Windows operating system is also enhanced because it is required in order to run these strong products. In addition, Microsoft generates a large proportion of its revenues by selling upgrades to customers who own previous versions of its products.

## Market Transformation Through New Technologies

In some cases, IT has the potential to completely transform the economics of an industry. For example, until recently the encyclopedia business consisted of low-volume sales, primarily to schools and libraries. The physically very bulky product resulted in relatively high manufacturing and shipping costs, which made the price even higher. The high price, and the space required to store the books, reduced potential sales to the home market.

Two things happened to change this situation. First, CD-ROM technology was adapted from storing music to storing other digital data including text and images. Second, since the mid-1990s this technology has been a standard component of a majority of computers sold for the home market. Encyclopedia producers began selling their products on CD-ROMS, in some cases at reduced prices that reflected the lower production costs. These CD-ROM versions include new features made possible by the technology, most notably sound and hyperlink cross references to related material in other sections. Lower prices and additional features have the potential to substantially increase the size of the total market. The hypothetical example in Box 13.11 shows how the economics of this business could change.

---

## *A Closer Look*  BOX 13.11

### THE ENCYCLOPEDIA ATLANTICA

The table below shows a financial analysis for an aggressive scenario in which the Encyclopedia Atlantica immediately shifts all its production from the traditional hardbound book format to a CD-ROM version. Note that manufacturing and shipping costs drop from $150 to $10 per unit. The cost of the contents increases by $2 million, reflecting the addition of sound, greater use of graphics, and the effort required to set up hyperlinks between different sections. The price per unit is reduced by 50 percent, from $700 to $350, while unit sales more than double and marketing expenses increase in proportion to unit sales. Despite the lower price and higher costs for content and marketing, the profit margin on the CD-ROM version is projected at 19.6 percent versus 16.7 percent on the hardbound version.

In practice, some customers in Atlantica's traditional markets will continue buying the hardbound version for many years to come. Additional scenarios are necessary to show a more gradual transition to a market dominated by CD-ROM versions.

The scenarios also need to include additional revenues from customers after the initial sale. Customers can receive annual updates for $25 per year, as well as

| | Hardbound | CD-ROM |
|---|---|---|
| Unit Sales | 30,000 | 70,000 |
| Price Per Unit | $700 | $350 |
| Gross Revenue | $21,000,000 | $24,500,000 |
| − Cost of Content | −10,000,000 | −12,000,000 |
| − Manufacturing & Shipping Costs | −4,500,000 | −700,000 |
| − Marketing Costs | −3,000,000 | −7,000,000 |
| = Profit Before Taxes | $3,500,000 | $4,800,000 |
| Profit Margin | 16.7% | 19.6% |

the opportunity to buy new editions at a 50 percent discount every five years.

Some interesting questions may be raised regarding this situation: Should Atlantica cut the price of the CD-ROM version to reflect economies of production and shipping, and to dramatically increase the size of the total market? Or should it set the price at the same level as the hardbound version, and try to market the CD-ROM version as a low-volume, high-margin, premium product? What will happen if Atlantica starts to publish on the Web? Should they?

---

## ▶ MANAGERIAL ISSUES

Information technology has certain characteristics that differentiate it, and its economics, from other aspects of the organizational world. Therefore IT requires management practices that are more effective than, and in some cases different from, those that are adequate for non-IT activities. Managers need to be aware of and responsive to the following issues:

1. *Constant growth and change.* The power of the microprocessor chip doubles every two years while the cost remains constant. This ever-increasing power creates both major opportunities and large threats as its impacts ripple across almost every aspect of the organization and its environment.

Managers need to continuously monitor developments in this area to identify new technologies relevant to their organizations, and to keep themselves up-to-date on their potential impacts.

2. *Shift from tangible to intangible benefits.* Few opportunities remain for automation projects that simply replace manual labor with IT on a one-for-one basis. The economic justification of IT applications will increasingly depend on intangible benefits, such as increased quality or better customer service. In contrast to calculating cost savings, it is much more difficult to accurately estimate the value of intangible benefits prior to the actual implementation. Managers need to understand and use tools that bring intangible benefits into the decision-making processes for IT investments.

3. *Not a sure thing.* Although IT offers opportunities for significant improvements in organizational performance, these benefits are not automatic. Managers need to very actively plan and control implementations to increase the return on their IT investments.

4. *Chargeback.* Users have little incentive to control IT costs if they do not have to pay for them at all. On the other hand, an accounting system may allocate costs fairly accurately to users but discourage exploration of promising new technologies. The solution is to have a chargeback system that has the primary objective of encouraging user behaviors that correspond to organizational objectives.

5. *Risk.* Investments in IT are inherently more risky than investments in other areas. Managers need to evaluate the level of risk before committing to IT projects. The general level of management involvement as well as specific management techniques and tools need to be appropriate for the risk of individual projects.

6. *Outsourcing.* The complexities of managing IT, and the inherent risks, may require more management skills than some organizations possess. If this is the case, the organization may want to outsource some or all of its IT functions. However, if it does outsource, the organization needs to make sure that the terms of the outsourcing contract are in its best interests both immediately and throughout the duration of the agreement.

7. *Increasing returns.* Industries whose primary focus is IT, or that include large amounts of IT in their products, often operate under a paradigm of increasing returns. In contrast, industries that primarily produce physical outputs are subject to diminishing returns. Managers need to understand which paradigm applies to the products for which they are responsible and apply management strategies that are most appropriate.

## KEY TERMS

Behavior-oriented chargeback *582*

Best practice benchmarks *571*

Chargeback *582*

Cost-benefit analysis *568*

Expected value (EV) *580*

Imperfect information *568*

Increasing returns *593*

Information economics *576*

Labor productivity *561*

Lock-in effect *594*

Management by maxim *578*

Metric benchmarks *571*

Moore's Law *559*

Multifactor productivity *561*

Network effects *593*

Option valuation *580*

Outsourcing *584*

Perfect information *568*

Price-to-performance ratio *559*

Productivity paradox *561*

Runaway project *564*

Scoring methodology *576*

Service level agreement (SLA) *572*

Total Cost of Ownership (TCO) *574*

Value analysis *575*

## CHAPTER HIGHLIGHTS *(L–x means learning objective number x)*

▶ The power of computer hardware should continue increasing at an exponential rate for at least 10 years, doubling every 18 months, while costs remain at the same levels as before. (L–1)

▶ Although organizations have spent tremendous amounts of money on IT, it is difficult to prove that this spending has increased national productivity. (L–1) (L–2)

▶ Approaches to measuring IT benefits include: the value of information, cost-benefits analyses of automation projects, and benchmarking IT infrastructure performance. (L–3)

▶ Decision-makers can evaluate intangible benefits of IT by using the value analysis, information economics, and option valuation methods. (L–4)

▶ Behavior-oriented chargeback systems, if properly designed, encourage efficient and effective usage of IT resources. (L–1) (L–5)

▶ Outsourcing may reduce IT costs and can make it possible for organizations to concentrate their management efforts on issues related to their core competencies. (L–1) (L–6)

▶ Computer systems are highly abstract and inherently very complex, which magnifies the impacts of weaknesses in the management of the development process. (L–7)

▶ Industries in the information sector of the economy experience increasing returns, which provide a major advantage to firms that have large shares of markets. (L–1) (L–8)

## QUESTIONS FOR REVIEW

1. What are the impacts of exponentially increasing computer hardware power and declining price-to-performance ratios on business production activities and new product development?

2. What is the productivity paradox and why is it important?

3. Why is it generally more difficult to evaluate the benefits of IT projects now than it was 20 years ago?

4. Write and explain the formula for calculating the value of information.

5. Identify examples of intangible benefits of IT.

6. Describe both metric and best practice benchmarks and give examples.

7. What are the results when an organization does not charge users for IT services?

8. Identify circumstances that could lead a firm to outsource its IT functions rather than continue with an internal IS unit.

9. Describe the different types of failure than can occur in IS development projects.

10. Identify some industries that operate with diminishing returns, and some that have increasing returns.

## QUESTIONS FOR DISCUSSION

1. What are the general implications for managers, organizations, and consumers of constantly increasing computer capabilities and declining costs?

2. Discuss what is necessary to achieve productivity gains from IT investments.

3. Why is it more difficult to measure productivity in service industries?

4. Identify arguments for including estimated values for intangible benefits in net present value (NPV) analyses of IT investments, and contrast them with the arguments for excluding such estimates.

5. What is IT infrastructure and why is it important to an organization?

6. Explain how a behavior-oriented chargeback system can be superior to an accounting system that charges users fairly accurate estimates of the costs of services they use.

7. Discuss the pros and cons of outsourcing IT, including alternatives to outsourcing.

8. How can an organization evaluate the quality of its customer service to make sure that the productivity gains of IT are not offset by poorer service?

9. Compare and contrast chargeback systems and outsourcing as alternative approaches for reducing costs and more effectively managing the IS function.

10. Identify and discuss reasons why IS projects are more vulnerable to failure than other types of projects.

11. Discuss how giving products away can be a profitable strategy in industries with increasing returns.

12. Is an NPV analysis appropriate for projects where there is a high risk of failure? If so, does the NPV model need to be modified? How?

## EXERCISES

1. Conduct research on how long exponential growth in computer hardware capabilities (Moore's Law) will continue.

2. Create a scoring methodology that reflects your personal requirements and use it to evaluate two competing software products in the same category (for example, two word processing programs or two spreadsheet programs).

3. If you have access to a large organization, conduct research on the methods it uses to charge users for IT services and how the users feel about these charges.

4. Identify several large corporations that have out-sourced major portions of their IT and compare their stock market performance to the S&P 500 stock index over the same period.

5. Do scoring systems (Box 13.6) always provide valid results? Consider a system where each individual component (hardware, software, operating system, database, and users) receives a high score. However, the database functions poorly because it was designed to work with a later version of the operating system. What adjustments to the scoring system are necessary to generate valid scores in a situation where interaction—how well the components work together—is critically important?

## GROUP ASSIGNMENTS

1. Group members should use the Web and periodical indexes, such as ABI/Inform, to find information about IT failures with total losses of at least $50 million. Each group will produce a five-page report on at least three major failures. The report should identify the factors that led to each individual failure, emphasizing factors that were common to more than one project. The report should also identify management actions that could have prevented or reduced the impacts of these failures.

2. Considerable discussions and disagreements exist among IS professionals regarding outsourcing. Divide the group into two parts: One will defend the strategy of large-scale outsourcing. One will oppose it. Start by collecting recent material at www.datamation.com and www.cio.com.

## INTERNET EXERCISES

Note: The URLs included here were current when the book went to press. However, they are subject to change without notice. Please consult the Turban Web site (www.Wiley.com/college/turban2e).

1. Read the speech at www.kurzweiledu.com/handicaps1 .htm. Based on this material, prepare a summary report on the relationship of Moore's Law to new technologies that can assist persons with disabilities.

2. Look at the work of Brynjolfsson and Hitt regarding the "productivity paradox" (two abstracts at web.mit .edu/cisr/www/oldabs.html, and a paper at ccs.mit .edu/CCSWP162/CCSWP162.html). Then look at Paul Strassmann's article at www.strassmann.com /pubs/datamation0297/. Compare the different findings in these two sources and prepare a summary report.

3. Read the *Information Week* article at www.techweb .com/se/directlink.cgi?IWK19970630S0038. Compare and contrast the approaches to evaluating intangible benefits in the article to those suggested in this textbook.

4. Enter the Web sites of the GartnerGroup (www .gartnergroup.com), The Yankee Group (www .yankeegroup.com), and *CIO* (www.cio.com). Search for recent material about outsourcing, and prepare a report on your findings.

5. Enter the Web site of IDC (www.idc.com) and find how they evaluate ROI on intranets, supply chain, and other IT projects.

6. Enter www.interpose.com. Find information about the total cost of ownership model. Write a report on the state of the art.

# Minicase 1

## Intranets: Invest First, Analyze Later?

The traditional approach to information systems projects is to analyze potential costs and benefits before deciding whether to develop the system. However, for moderate investments in promising new technologies that could offer major benefits, organizations may decide to do the financial analyses after the project is over. A number of companies took this latter approach in regard to intranet projects initiated prior to 1997.

### Judd's

Located in Strasburg, Virginia, Judd's is a conservative, family-owned printing company that prints *Time* magazine, among others. Richard Warren, VP for IS, pointed out that Judd's "usually waits for technology to prove itself . . . but with the Internet the benefits seemed so great that our decision proved to be a no-brainer." Judd's first implemented Internet technology for communications to meet needs expressed by customers. After this it started building intranet applications to facilitate internal business activities. One indication of the significance of these applications to the company is the bandwidth that supports them. Judd's started with 56 Kbps connections, upgraded to 1.5 Mbps in 1996, and was considering another upgrade to 45 Mbps in 1997.

### Eli Lilly & Company

A very large pharmaceutical company with headquarters in Indianapolis, Eli Lilly has a proactive attitude toward new technologies. It began exploring the potential of the Internet in 1993. Managers soon realized that, by using intranets, they could reduce many of the problems associated with developing applications on a wide variety of hardware platforms and network configurations. Because the benefits are so obvious, the regular financial justification process is waived for intranet application development projects. The IS group that helps user departments develop and maintain intranet applications increased its staff from three to ten employees in 15 months.

### Needham Interactive

Needham, a Dallas advertising agency, has offices in various parts of the country. Needham discovered that, in developing presentations for bids on new accounts, employees found it helpful to use materials from other employees' presentations on similar projects. Unfortunately, it was very difficult to locate and then transfer relevant material in different locations and different formats. After doing research on alternatives, the company identified intranet technology as the best potential solution.

Needham hired EDS to help develop the system. It started with one office in 1996 as a pilot site and plans to extend it to all its employees over a one- to two-year time frame. Although the investment is "substantial," Needham did not do a detailed financial analysis before starting the project. David King, a managing partner explains: "The system will start paying for itself the first

time an employee wins a new account because he had easy access to a co-worker's information."

### Cadence Design Systems

Cadence is a consulting firm located in San Jose, California. It wanted to increase the productivity of its sales personnel by improving internal communications and sales training. It considered Lotus Notes but decided against it because of the costs. With the help of a consultant, it developed an intranet system. Because the company reengineered its sales training process to work with the new system, the project took somewhat longer than usual.

International Data Corp., an IT research firm, helped Cadence do an after-the-fact financial analysis. Initially the analysis calculated benefits based on employees meeting their full sales quotas. However, IDC later found that a more appropriate indicator was having new sales representatives meet half their quota. Startup costs were $280,000, average annual expenses were estimated at less than $400,000, and annual savings are projected at over $2.5 million. Barry Demak, director of sales, remarked: "We knew the economic justification . . . would be strong, but we were surprised the actual numbers were as high as they were."

### Questions for Minicase 1

1. Where and under what circumstances is the "invest first, analyze later" approach appropriate? Where and when is it inappropriate? Give specific examples of technologies and other circumstances.

2. How long do you think the "invest first, analyze later" approach will be appropriate for intranet projects? When (and why) will the emphasis shift to traditional project justification approaches? (Or has the shift already occurred?)

3. What are the risks of going into projects that have not received a thorough financial analysis? How can organizations reduce these risks?

4. Based on the numbers provided for Cadence Design System's intranet project, use a spreadsheet to calculate the net present value of the project. Assume a five-year life for the system.

5. Do you see any relationship between the "invest first, analyze later" approach to financial analysis and the use of behavior-oriented chargeback systems?

6. Relate the Needham case to Knowledge Base (Chapter 10).

SOURCE: Korzenioski, P., "Intranet Bets Pay Off," *InfoWorld*, January 13, 1997.

# Minicase 2

## Money Mastery

Controlling costs is important for every organization. Formal procedures and organizational policies help control costs, but they can sometimes be an obstacle to necessary investments. Astute chief information officers (CIOs) practice what Forrester Research (www .forrester.com) calls "money mastery." These CIOs know how to work within the constraints of their organizations to make sure that their IT expenditures are productive and contribute to organizational goals. Successful financial tactics in various organizations include the following:

▶ **Agway, Inc.** outsources all of its systems development activities. By doing so, it converted from the fixed costs of an in-house development group to variable costs. This makes it possible to substantially increase development when necessary to meet business needs, without worrying about the burden of high ongoing costs if the economy turns down.

▶ **Texas Instruments** reorganized its IS operation into separate units ("Centers of Excellence"). Instead of dealing with a single, monolithic IS group, the business units deal with smaller, more focused IS units that provide specific types of services. It is easier to compare the costs and services from these units to what is available from outside vendors.

▶ **Shell Oil** spun off its IS unit into a separate company that markets its IS capabilities to internal business units, in competition with outside vendors. It also sells its services outside the corporation.

▶ **American Red Cross** obtained an external Web site and internal intranet, even though it did not have funds to pay for the systems. It convinced a vendor to do the development in exchange for future usage fees from the organization's 1,600 chapters and 200 units affiliated with the armed forces.

▶ **Fruit of the Loom** created a Web site template to give to its distributors. Because of the promotional aspects of the project, the CIO sought funding for the $2 million project as an advertising expense.

▶ **L. L. Bean** has its business units, rather than its IS group, take responsibility for presenting IT project funding requests to senior management. The IS group helps these units with the cost aspects, as

well as identifying potential additional benefits elsewhere in the organization.

▶ **Thiokol Corp.** has its IS unit conduct offsite meetings with business units to jointly prioritize IT spending. These meetings are designed to help users understand IS costs, and to emphasize their responsibility to help control these costs.

▶ **Amdahl Corp.** recognizes that it needs to spend "whatever it takes" in critical areas such as customer service. Amdahl spent $6 million on a system that reduced response time to customers to less than two hours, in comparison to 21 hours with the previous system.

### Questions for Minicase 2

1. What risks does Agway, Inc. incur by totally outsourcing development? Can you think of some organizations, or some types of development, that should not be outsourced?

2. What are the pros and cons of setting up a company's IS unit as a separate, profit-making company?

3. Should business units in an organization be free to purchase IS services from outside vendors, rather than obtaining them from the organization's IS unit? Why or why not?

4. What are the pros and cons of having a vendor finance a project in exchange for future revenues, as the Red Cross did?

5. From an organizational perspective, is it very likely that the IS unit will be able to obtain significant funding from non-IS sources such as the advertising budget at Fruit of the Loom? Under what circumstances might this approach be successful?

6. What are the potential problems in financing infrastructure in organizations such as L. L. Bean, where business units have primary responsibility for obtaining IS funding approvals? What are some possible ways of dealing with these problems?

SOURCE: Maney, R., and J. H. Meringer, "Money Mastery: Digging for Dollars Is a Key Skill for High Performance CIOs," *CIO*, Dec 1, 1996.

# REFERENCES AND BIBLIOGRAPHY

1. Aley, J., "Give It Away and Get Rich," *Fortune,* June 10, 1996.

2. Arthur, W. B., "Increasing Returns and the New World of Business," *Harvard Business Review,* July–August 1996.

3. Aubert, B. A., et al., "Assessing the Risk of IT Oursourcing," *Proceedings HICSS 31,* Hawaii, January 1998.

4. Barua, A., and W. Richmond, "Economics of Information Systems," Special Issue, *Decision Support Systems,* February 1997.

5. Belitsos, B., "A Measure of I/S Success," *Computer Decisions,* January 1989.

6. Broadbent, M., and P., Weill, "Management by Maxim: How Business and IT Managers Can Create IT Infrastrucures," *Sloan Management Review,* Spring 1997.

7. Brynjolfsson, E., "The Productivity Paradox of Information Technology," *Communications of the ACM,* December 1993.

8. Brynjolfsson, E., and L. M. Hitt, "Beyond the Productivity Paradox," *Communication of the ACM,* August 1998.

9. Campbell, I., "The Intranet: Slashing the Cost of Business," *International Data Corporation,* 1997.

10. Connally, P., "Blood Test: The ROI of Testing Tools," *Datamation,* May 1997.

11. Dewan, S., and Kramer, K. L., "International Dimentions of the Productivity Paradox," *Communication of the ACM,* August 1998.

12. Dixit, A. K., and Pindyck, R. S., "The Options Approach to Capital Investment," *Harvard Business Review,* May–June 1995.

13. Downing, T., "Eight New Ways to Evaluate Automation," *Mechanical Engineering,* July 1989.

14. Duvall, M., "Companies Size Up Outsourcing," *Interactive Week,* January 12, 1998.

15. Earl, M. J., "The Risks of Outsourcing IT," *Sloan Management Review* Spring 1996.

16. Farbey, B., et al., "Appraisal and Evaluation of Information Systems," special issue of the *European Journal of Informtion Systems* (forthcoming).

17. Field, T., "An Outsourcing Buyer Guide: Caveat Emptor," *CIO Magazine,* April 1, 1997.

18. Garner, R., "Strategic Outsourcing: It's Your Move," *Datamation,* February 1998.

19. Green, C. B., *Benchmarking the Information Technology Function,* New York: The Conference Board, 1993.

20. Gutert, F. "How to Manage Your Outsourcer," *Datamation,* March 1, 1996.

21. Hildebrand, C., "The PC Price Tag," *CIO Magazine,* October 15, 1997.

22. Hitt, L. M., and E., Brynjolfsson, "Productivity, Business Profitability, and Consumer Surplus: Three Different Measures of Information Technology Value," *MIS Quarterly,* June 1996, pp. 121–142.

23. Kappelman, L. A., et al., "Calculating the Cost of the Year-2000 Compliance," *Communications of the ACM,* February 1998.

24. Keen, P. G. W., "Value Analysis: Justifying DSS," *Management Information Systems Quarterly,* March 1981.

25. King, J., "IS Reins In Runaway Projects," *Computerworld,* February 24, 1997.

26. Lacity, M. C., and R., Hirschheim, "The Information Systems Outsourcing Bandwagon," *Sloan Management Review,* Fall 1993.

27. Lacity, M. C., et al., "The Value of Selective IT Outsourcing," *Sloan Management Review,* Spring 1996 (also in *Harvard Business Review,* May–June 1995).

28. Lucas, H. C., et al., "A Reengineering Framework for Evaluating a Financial Imaging System," *Communications of the ACM,* May 1996.

29. Marcolin, B. L., and K. L. McLellan, "Effective IT Outsourcing Arrangements," *Proceedings HICSS 31,* Hawaii, January 1998.

30. McAdam, J. P., "Slicing the Pie: Information Technology Cost Recovery Models," *CPA Journal,* February 1996.

31. Moore, G. E., "Cramming More Components on Integrated Circuits," *Electronics,* April 19, 1965.

32. Moore, G. E., *Inside the Tornado,* New York: HarperCollins, 1995.

33. Moore, G. E., "Moore's Law," *CIO,* January 1, 1997.

34. Munk, N., "Technology for Technology's Sake," *Forbes,* October 21, 1996.

35. Pountain, D., "Amending Moore's Law," *Byte,* March 1998.

36. Rothfeder, J., "It's Late, Costly, Incompetent—But Try Firing a Computer System," *Business Week,* November 7, 1988.

37. Smith, A. E., and C. H. Dagli, "Analysis of Worth," in Turban E., and J. Liebowitz, *Managing Expert Systems,* Harrisburg, PA: Idea Group 1992.

38. Strassmann, P. A., *The Squandered Computer,* New Canaan, CT: Information Economics Press, 1997.

39. Turban, E., and J. Meredith, *Fundamentals of Management Science,* 6th ed., Burr Ridge, IL: Irwin, 1994.

40. Violino, B., "Return on Investment Profiles: The Intangible Benefits of Technology Are Emerging as the Most Important of All," *Information Week,* June 30, 1997.

41. Vistica, G. L., et al., "The Day the World Shuts Down," *Newsweek,* June 2, 1997.

42. Willcocks, L., and G. Fitzgerald, "Pilkington PLC: A Major Multinational Outsources Head Office IT Function," in Turban, E., et al., *Information Technology for Management,* 1st ed., New York: John Wiley & Sons, 1996.

43. Zellner, W., "Portrait of a Project as a Total Disaster," *Business Week,* January 19, 1994.

# CHAPTER 14

# Systems Development

## Learning Objectives

*After studying this chapter, you will be able to:*

❶ Explain the concept of a systems development life cycle (SDLC).

❷ Compare and contrast prototyping and traditional SDLC approaches to systems development.

❸ Discuss the benefits and shortcomings of rapid application development (RAD).

❹ Identify advantages and disadvantages of object-oriented (OO) development.

❺ Evaluate alternatives to in-house systems development.

❻ Compare and contrast Internet and intranet application development with other forms of systems development.

❼ Identify advantages and disadvantages of CASE tools.

❽ Describe alternative approaches to software process quality improvement.

# CONNECTIONS

## CORNING DEVELOPS FLEXIBLE TOOLS TO PROVIDE SUPERB SERVICE TO CUSTOMERS

CORNING INC.'S TELECOMMUNICATION Product Division is the world's largest manufacturer of fiber optic waveguides. The demand for the products increases rapidly, so production must be expanded quickly (75% in 3 years). Due to technological development the demand characteristics are constantly changing; Corning must be very responsive.

Information technology supports the work of product developers, who must be very flexible in their work. They also must become productive quickly, which is difficult to do with all of the changes.

To build flexible information systems and do it quickly the company created a development team. The team decided that a distributed client/server environment for the applications will provide flexibility, and that object-oriented (OO) technology will yield the best IT tools.

The team decided to use an *integrated* tool set (from Forte Systems). The developers found that the training time for using the OO tools was only a few weeks. The team also purchased design and analysis tools to expedite the development. The OO tools led to improved programmers' productivity, since modules developed for one application can be used by several. The first application enables collection and formatting of data needed to ship with fiber optic cable orders. Such a system has the flexibility to provide customers with data they want within 24 hours. The second application was a factory floor application that makes production responsive to constantly changing demand requirements.

The development team created a library of reusable objects and distributed OO services. These can be shared by future applications.

The first application was developed by a team of six in nine months, the second by a team of two in three months. The larger the history of objects, the faster is the application development. In building the applications the team used some off-the-shelf software. Also, integration with databases was needed. This was done with Visual C++ (from Microsoft).

This application won the 1997 Innovation award from *Application Development Trends* magazine.

SOURCE: Condensed from Desmond, J., "Distributed Applications Built with OO Tools Get Corning's Waveguides to Customers," *Application Development Trends,* April 1997.

## ▶ 14.1 THE CONCEPT OF A SYSTEMS DEVELOPMENT LIFE CYCLE

The Corning case demonstrates the use of object-oriented tools (Technology Guide #2) for rapid development of flexible applications. The case also indicates that the development team used several purchased packages, and that by using object-oriented tools, future systems are expected to be developed even faster.

The topic of this chapter is **systems development,** which refers to all the activities used to create information systems in an organization and the processes of their accomplishment.

Since specific organizational environments and general technologies change over time, organizations need new systems, or major revisions to existing systems, to continue to meet their objectives. Therefore, systems development is an ongoing process in all organizations that use it.

At the same time, information systems are expensive, and systems development is prone to failure. Therefore it is very desirable to acquire new systems through some kind of process that will (1) reduce the risk of failure; and (2) result in systems that really do increase the effectiveness of the organization. This chapter discusses systematic approaches that can help meet both these objectives.

In the early years of data processing, many software developers did not use any kind of formal approach. They would simply ask users a few questions about what the system was supposed to do and then start programming. Sometimes this approach resulted in desirable outcomes, and sometimes it failed. The failures were frequent enough to indicate that more formal approaches were necessary.

In this chapter we discuss various approaches to development that can increase the probability of favorable outcomes. We initially discuss the concept of a systems development life cycle, which provides a comprehensive framework for design and development activities. After laying this foundation, we discuss various system development alternatives. The first is the prototyping approach, in which the developers create limited versions of a system before coding the full-scale version. This section also includes a discussion of rapid application development tools and methods. Next is a section on object-oriented development, which capitalizes on the strengths of the object-oriented programming model. Subsequent sections cover end-user development, acquiring systems from outside sources, deciding between development approaches, developing Internet/intranet applications, and using quality management and project planning techniques to improve outcomes of the development process.

## WHAT IS A SYSTEMS DEVELOPMENT LIFE CYCLE?

To understand the concept of a systems development life cycle (SDLC) consider this analogy. A business firm moves from one city to another. Someone has to acquire property in the new city. Someone has to arrange for telephone and utility services at the new location. People need to pack, ship, unpack, and install furniture and equipment at the new location. The actual list of tasks will have many additional items.

The moving project therefore requires a very detailed plan. It should identify every significant task and assign each one to individuals or groups within or outside the organization. Every task needs a start date and a completion date, and some tasks cannot start until after the completion of others. Therefore the plan needs to coordinate the start and completion dates of the individual tasks within the limitation of the target completion date for the whole project.

Looking at the plans for several such moving projects, we would find many of the same tasks. With a little more effort, we could group the tasks into logically related categories and then arrange the categories in a sequence corresponding to the different phases of a moving project over time. These general categories would apply to most moving projects, even though the individual tasks could vary from project to project.

Substitute the words "information systems development" for the word "moving" in the above paragraphs and you have the concept of a **systems development life cycle (SDLC).** An SDLC represents a set of general categories that show the major steps, over time, of an information systems development project. Within these general categories are individual tasks. Some of these tasks are present in most projects, while others would apply only to certain types of projects. For example, smaller projects may not require as many tasks as larger ones.

Note that there is no universal, standardized version of the SDLC. Consulting firms, as well as IS groups within organizations, develop individualized versions appropriate to their own operations. They may give their versions unique names; for example, Andersen Consulting calls its version Method/1. The Microsoft certification programs include training in its Solution Development Discipline (SDD) methodology. Most of the description of this chapter's version of an SDLC is relevant to other SDLCs.

Another consideration is that the phrase "systems development life cycle" has *two distinct meanings*. An SDLC can be a general conceptual framework for all the activities involved in systems development or acquisition. An SDLC can also be a very structured and formalized design and development process, in contrast to less structured approaches such as prototyping and rapid application development, which are discussed in later sections. The following discussion is from the perspective of the SDLC as a general conceptual framework. For a formal SDLC development methodology, see Kendall and Kendall (1998).

## AN EIGHT-STAGE SDLC

Figure 14.1 provides a graphic model of an SDLC that has eight stages. That is, we grouped all the major tasks into eight groups. Others group theirs into six, seven, eight, or even nine. Even if others use eight groups, the content of each stage may differ somewhat. Note also that the stages overlap: a subsequent stage may start before the previous stage ends. This is in contrast to the traditional **waterfall method,** in which the work flows completely through the tasks in one

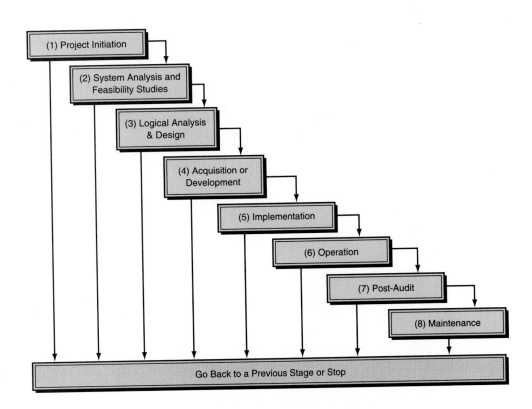

**FIGURE 14.1** An eight-stage SDLC.

stage before dropping down to the next stage. Also note that the process can go backward more than one stage, if necessary. These overlapping stages provide flexibility for adapting quickly to the volatile demands of the current business environment.

An organization can use this framework to develop its own comprehensive checklist of tasks and subtasks. Project managers can then use the checklist to identify activities required for specific projects. The following discussion outlines the individual stages and their major tasks.

**STAGE 1: PROJECT INITIATION.** Somebody needs to start the project. Usually it is a manager outside the IS organization who has a problem or sees an opportunity related to the area where he or she works. A formal planning process also may identify new systems that can help the organization meet its objectives. Sometimes the IS group initiates projects that will improve its own operations or deal with common problems among the user areas.

**STAGE 2: SYSTEMS ANALYSIS AND FEASIBILITY STUDIES**

*Systems Analysis.* Once a project is initiated, the **systems analysis** phase begins. Systems analysis refers to the investigation of the existing situation. It may be the status of a problem that the information system is expected to solve. It is a process that may take weeks, or months, involving many activities (see Kendall and Kendall [1998] for details). Some of the major activities include isolating the symptoms of a problem and determining its cause. Other activities are the identification of the business processes and their interrelations and the flow of information related to these processes. Systems analysis aims at providing a thorough understanding of the existing organization, its operation, and the situation relevant to the system one wants to build. Systems analysis deals also with the people and procedures involved, the existing information system technology, and the environment surrounding the problem area.

Systems analysis methods include observations, review of documents, interviews, and performance measurement. Several methods exist for the execution of systems analysis and some of them are supported by software. Systems analysis also includes the concept of the proposed system and its anticipated contribution to the solution of the problem.

> Including end-users in the feasibility study not only could save a logistics disaster down the road, but also gets the users to feel like part of the team, making eventual implementation much easier.
>
> — *Mike Rewald*

*Feasibility Studies.* To determine the probability of success of the proposed solution **feasibility studies** are conducted. Such studies, which may be conducted several times throughout the systems development life cycle, are designed to determine whether the solution is achievable, given the organization's resources and constraints and the impact of the surrounding environment. The major areas of investigation are:

▶ *Technology.* Are the performance requirements achievable utilizing current information technologies? If not, are they attainable through capabilities that will be available by the time the project finishes? Will newer technologies supersede those in the proposed project before the organization recovers its investment?

▶ *Economics.* Are the expected benefits greater than the costs? Can the organization afford the costs, in terms of spending and personnel requirements? Are the risks, including the possibility of cost and schedule overruns, acceptable for an investment of this size?

> ▶ *Organizational factors.* Is the proposed system reasonably compatible with the organizational culture, internal political considerations, and work rules? Are the skill levels to use the new system consistent with the employees who will operate it?

> ▶ *Legal, ethical, and other constraints.* Is the new or automated process ethical to employers or customers? Does it meet all regulatory requirements? Are any of the constraints in danger of being violated?

If the initial analysis indicates that the project could be feasible, the organization should conduct a more comprehensive analysis, using financial analysts and technology specialists as appropriate for the size and complexity of the project. This study needs to verify the findings of the initial analysis and develop more detailed information about costs and benefits for net present value or other formal financial analyses. If the detailed study verifies the feasibility (and the sponsors are still interested), the project can go on to the next stage.

**STAGE 3: LOGICAL ANALYSIS AND DESIGN.** At this point, one or more systems analysts determine two major aspects of the system: (1) what it needs to do; and (2) how it will accomplish these functions. The emphasis at this stage is on **logical design.** The analyst identifies *information requirements* and specifies processes and generic IS functions such as input, output, and storage, rather than writing programs or identifying hardware. Determining information requirements, as discussed in Chapter 9, may be a very difficult task. Then, the logical analysis and design that lays out the components of the system and their relationships can start. The analysts often use modeling tools such as data flow diagrams (DFDs, see Figure 14.2) and entity-relationship diagrams (ERDs, see Figure 14.3 on page 608) to represent logical processes and data relationships.

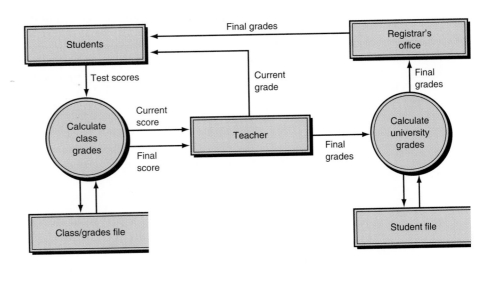

**FIGURE 14.2** Data flow diagram student grades example.

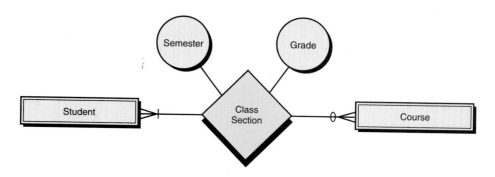

FIGURE 14.3 Entity-relationship diagram of students, courses, and grades.

The development team needs to involve the users in the process but not put a large burden on them. Users are a major source of information about the functional requirements of the system. Involving them can also increase their feelings of ownership of the system, which can lead to a more successful implementation. The following *IT at Work* illustration provides an example of user involvement.

## IT At Work    CITY OF PHOENIX GETS USERS INVOLVED IN AN HR SYSTEM PROJECT

USING IT

...in Public Service

USING IT

...in Human Resources Management

The City of Phoenix did not just acknowledge the importance of user involvement; it made involvement a key aspect of the development and implementation of a client/server human resources (HR) system.

Carl Myers, the assistant information technology director, recruited two key, high-level users to work on the project. Mike Ingersoll was the city's deputy personnel direction. However, for two years Ingersoll and the deputy controller worked full-time on the HR system project as "transition managers." Other employees handled their previous duties during this period.

Myers feels that this strategy reduced the risks of the project, saying: "The biggest challenge of client/server is dealing with cultural change among users. You have to sell it to the business unit, and transition managers who are members of the IS project have a lot of credibility with end users." With senior managers from the end-user areas, Myers estimates that it took 50 percent less time to accomplish the reengineering aspects of the project.

**For Further Exploration:** Does user involvement guarantee the success of a systems project? In what types of projects is user involvement most important? least important? ▲

SOURCE: Condensed from "In City Hall," *Computerworld*, November 25, 1996, p. 72.

Logical design is followed by a **physical design,** which translates the abstract logical model into the specific technical design (the "blueprints") for the new system.

The trend toward purchasing software, instead of developing it, is changing both the general emphasis and the specific tasks in the logical analysis and design phase. Analysts still need to identify user requirements. However, they now spend more time comparing requirements to features of available software, and less time on designing systems. They only need to prepare detailed specifications when the functionality that users need is not available in software in the marketplace. They also have to identify configuration requirements for commercial packages that offer a wide range of customization options.

**STAGE 4: ACQUISITION OR DEVELOPMENT.** The logical design of the new system guides the actual development or acquisition, just as blueprints guide the construction of a new building. IS personnel use the specifications to purchase the hardware and software required for the system and then to configure it as needed. Programmers write code for parts of the system where commercial sources are not appropriate. Technical writers develop documentation and training materials. IS personnel *test* the system, and users should also do some testing prior to the actual implementation. The testing identifies bugs and also compares system performance to the specifications in the design.

**STAGE 5: IMPLEMENTATION.** Implementation is obviously an important stage; the system can fail here even if it has all the specified functionality. The project team should plan the implementation very carefully, to avoid problems that could lead to resistance. The users need training in the mechanics of the system, to reduce frustration and to minimize productivity losses in the transition period. In addition to developing technical skills, the training should also attempt to motivate users, for example, by stressing the benefits the system brings to the organization.

Even in the best circumstances, the implementation process will reveal bugs and other unexpected problems. The implementation team needs to resolve these as soon as possible, to retain its credibility with the users and maintain the progress of the conversion.

In most cases, implementing a new system requires a *conversion* from a previous system. Approaches to conversion include:

▶ *Parallel conversion.* The old and new systems operate concurrently for a test period, and then the old system is discontinued. **Parallel conversion** is the safest approach, but also the most expensive.

▶ *Direct cutover.* The old system is turned off, and the new system is turned on. This **direct cutover** is the fastest and least expensive approach, but also the most risky.

▶ *Pilot conversion.* The new system is implemented in a subset of locations—for example, some of the branches in a large banking chain—and extended to remaining locations over time. The **pilot conversion** approach is like a direct cutover for the pilot locations but, for the organization as a whole, it is similar to a parallel conversion. Both risks and costs are relatively low.

▶ *Phased (or modular) conversion.* Large systems often are built from distinct "modules." For example, an order-fulfillment system could have an inventory module, an order processing module, and an accounts receivable module. If the modules were originally designed to be relatively independent, it may be possible to replace the modules one at a time. **Phased conversion** is probably safer than a direct conversion but takes longer and may require more testing, because it is necessary to test other parts of the system every time a new module is implemented.

**STAGE 6: OPERATION.** After a successful conversion, the system will operate for an indefinite period of time, until the system is no longer adequate or necessary, or cost effective.

**STAGE 7: POST-AUDIT EVALUATION.** An organization should evaluate all its larger systems projects after their completion. If the implementation was successful, an audit should occur after the system's operations have stabilized. If the project failed, the audit should be done as soon as possible after the failure.

Many organizations do not conduct formal evaluations of their systems projects. They see no need for the extra effort if the project was successful and would rather avoid the issue if it failed. Nevertheless these evaluations are important. The feedback from comparisons of actual performance to specifications can help analysts learn to make better estimates on future projects. Identifying the causes of failures can help IS groups avoid the same problems on subsequent systems. **Post-audits** introduce an additional element of discipline into the development process.

**STAGE 8: MAINTENANCE.** Every system needs two kinds of maintenance. Bugs are more frequent in the beginning, but problems can appear even years later. In addition to fixing bugs, programmers need to *update* systems to accommodate changes in the environment. Examples include adjusting for tax law changes and dealing with the "Year 2000" problem. These corrections and updates usually do not add any additional functionality; they are just necessary to keep the system operating at the same level.

An additional form of maintenance adds new features to existing systems. This work is somewhat similar to the development of new systems; however, because the new features must be installed without disturbing the operation of the existing system, it is more difficult and less flexible.

Regardless of type, maintenance is expensive, accounting for up to 80 percent of organizational IS budgets. Therefore it is important that the design and development stages produce systems that include, in the initial versions, all the essential functionality. The developer should also use appropriate software engineering methodologies and produce good documentation for the system, to make the inevitable maintenance easier.

## TRADITIONAL VERSUS MODERN SDLCS

There are two major problems with systems development life cycle methodologies. First, many systems projects fail, even though the project management incorporates a formal SDLC approach. Second, the environment is very different from what it was thirty years ago. Organizations need to respond much more rapidly to their markets and competitors. Information technology is much more powerful and includes features such as graphical user interfaces, intranets, and client/server architectures that are very different from earlier forms of programming.

Do these problems mean that project managers should abandon the SDLC concept? Not really. All the stages in Figure 14.1 are either absolutely necessary or highly desirable for larger projects. The benefits described above are still important. The increasing complexity of systems development means that some form of structure is even more necessary now than thirty years ago. However, the general organization of the SDLC needs to change to adjust to the realities of the current environment. IS groups considering the implementation of a formal SDLC methodology and associated tools for managing projects should look for the following characteristics:

▶ *Minimal overhead.* One of the problems with older SDLCs and other project management techniques is that they require a great deal of record keeping and data entry. These tasks divert resources away from actual development activities. A modern SDLC needs to provide tools that capture most of this information automatically, and facilitate data entry for the rest.

▶ *Flexibility and responsiveness.* The traditional SDLC does not handle changes in specifications very well. However, the ability to handle change is more important now than ever before. The fast pace of the current world means that, for projects to be successful, systems developers need the flexibility to respond rapidly to environmental opportunities and threats even in the midst of the project.

▶ *Concurrent tasks.* The traditional life cycle is essentially sequential: some stages focus on the early part of the project, while others occur toward the end. To meet the demands of the current environment, a new SDLC needs to allow developers to perform some tasks in different stages concurrently, or even to do tasks from "later" stages before tasks in "earlier" stages. For example, the developers may code, test, implement, and evaluate (post-audit) critical parts of the system before doing the logical analysis and design of other parts.

▶ *Focused analysis.* Another problem with the conventional approach is that it tends to emphasize analysis as an end in itself. Analysis is very important, but it needs to be focused on areas where it adds the most value to the project.

Yourdon proposes the modern "structured" project life cycle in Figure 14.4 He does not address the record-keeping issue, but his approach is highly concurrent. With an emphasis on developing an initial top-down framework for the system and then filling the details in later, this approach should also be very flexible.

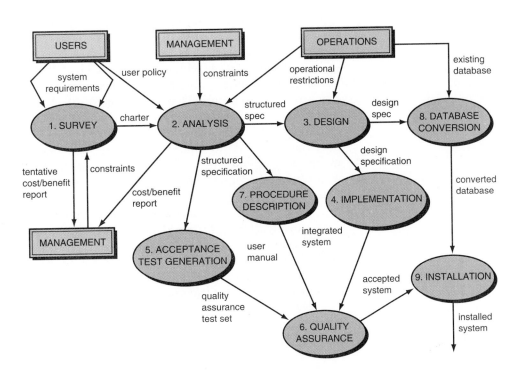

**FIGURE 14.4** A modern structured project life cycle. (*Source:* Yourdon, E. [1989], p. 89.)

## ▶ 14.2 METHODS FOR COMPLEX OR QUICKLY NEEDED SYSTEMS

The traditional systems development life cycle approach works best on projects in which users have a clear idea about what they want. The typical automation project is a good example because, in this type of project, computer systems replace manual labor with only minimal changes in processes. Unfortunately, simple automation projects are becoming less common. Nowadays projects tend to require either major changes in existing processes, through reengineering, or development of processes that are new to the organization. Furthermore, the need to build interorganizational and international systems using Web technologies such as extranets, and the need to build or modify systems quickly (see Minicases 1 and 2), created a major shift in the nature of information systems. This shift in emphasis, along with the high failure rate in traditional systems development, indicates a need for alternatives to conventional SDLC methodologies. Prototyping, rapid application development, and object-oriented development are three possible alternatives.

### PROTOTYPING

Prototyping is a very good way to spark interest in a system or project. Management makes important decisions on tangible results.

*— Blake Thompson*

The **prototyping** approach to systems development is, in many ways, the very opposite of an old-style SDLC. Instead of spending a lot of time producing very detailed specifications, the developers find out only generally what the users want. The developers do not develop the complete system all at once. Instead they *quickly* create a prototype, which either contains portions of the system of most interest to the users, or is a small-scale working model of the entire system. After reviewing the prototype with the users, the developers refine and extend it. This process continues through several iterations until either the users approve the design or it becomes apparent that the proposed system cannot meet their needs. If the system is viable, the developers create a full-scale version that includes additional features.

In this approach, which is also known as *evolutionary development*, the emphasis is on producing something quickly for the users to review. To speed up the process, programmers may use a fourth-generation language (4GL) and other tools such as screen generators or spreadsheet software for parts of the prototype. After the users approve the prototype, the programmers can finish development making whatever changes are necessary for acceptable performance and for meeting organizational standards for that type of system. This could involve programming it in a third-generation language, using the prototype as a model.

Prototyping can be a complete developmental methodology in itself. However, newer versions of the SDLC often incorporate it as an alternative, or supplement, to the analysis and design stage. Figure 14.5 (page 613) shows a flowchart of the prototyping process, using a relational database for the initial versions of the system. Note that in this version, the prototyping process creates the specifications, and the project then goes back into a conventional SDLC.

Neither the users nor the systems personnel know how many times the prototyping process will go through the loop of reviews and revisions. In a sense, prototyping is like a speeded-up version of the maintenance stage of a regular

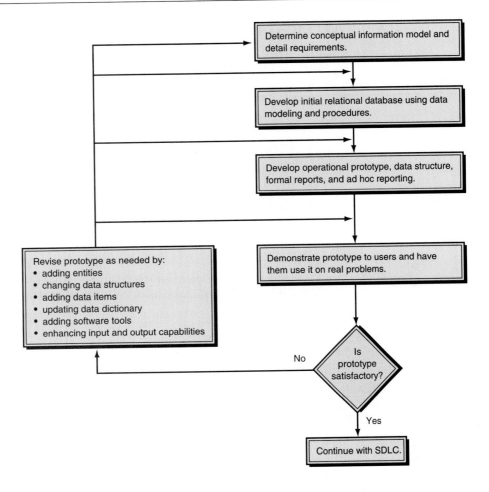

FIGURE 14.5 Model of prototyping process.

SDLC, in which users ask the IS group to add functionality to existing systems. However, it is much less expensive to make these changes over a short period on a model of the system, rather than spread over time on the operational version.

Prototyping is particularly useful for situations, such as decision support (DSS) or executive information systems (EIS), in which user interaction is especially important. It is also good for IS projects that substantially change business processes. For users of these types of systems, prototyping allows opportunities to work with the model, and identify necessary changes and enhancements, before making a major commitment to development. Users should also consider prototyping if it is necessary to start using the system as soon as possible, even before it is complete.

Prototyping does have some disadvantages. It largely replaces the formal analysis and design stage of a conventional SDLC. As a result, the systems analysts may not need to produce much formal documentation for the programmers during the project. If managers do not follow up on this, the documentation may be inadequate years later when the system needs maintenance. Another problem is that users, after working with the final prototype, may not understand why additional work and associated charges are necessary to bring the system up to organizational standards.

## RAPID APPLICATION DEVELOPMENT

**Rapid application development (RAD)** methodologies and tools make it possible to develop systems faster, especially systems where the user interface is an important component. Another area is the rewriting of legacy applications. An example of how quickly experienced developers can create applications with RAD tools is provided in the following *IT at Work* illustration.

---

*IT At Work*    PHÔNE-POULENCE USES RAPID APPLICATION DEVELOPMENT FOR QUICKLY DEVELOPING APPLICATIONS

Phône-Poulence S.A. of Paris, France is the world's seventh largest pharmaceutical and chemical company, operating in 160 countries. Its North American division had a problem; its IT department was unable to build critical IT applications for the users in a timely manner. Because there are 12 different businesses in the United States, and because the market for most of the products is extremely competitive, the new applications were needed quickly.

**U**SING IT
...in Marketing

To solve the problem the company reengineered its Information Technology department, including a new autonomous RAD team. The RAD team was chartered to look across both functional boundaries and manufacturing facilities for new mission-critical applications. The RAD unit selected RAD tools, including Delphi (from Borland International).

One of the first RAD projects was to develop a sales force automation application to be used by field representatives equipped with laptop computers. Sales data are extracted daily to a file where they are analyzed by this application, according to guidelines provided by the field representatives. Results are automatically e-mailed to the representatives. The system also helps in pricing and approvals.

Several components of this application will be reused in other applications (for example, the automatic e-mail dissemination component), cutting both development time and cost.

**For Further Exploration:** Why is the RAD unit needed? ▲

SOURCE: Condensed from *Borland Online* (www.borland.com/delphi/cases/phonepou.html). Feb. 1998.

---

What are the components or tools and capabilities of a RAD system? Typical packages include:

▶ *GUI development environment*—the ability to create many aspects of an application by "drag-and-drop" operations. For example, the user can create a report by clicking on file names, and then clicking and dragging fields from these files to the appropriate locations in the report.

▶ *Reusable components*—a library of common, standard "objects" such as buttons and dialog boxes. The developer drags-and-drops these items into the application.

▶ *Code generator.* After the developer drags-and-drops them into the design, the package automatically writes computer programs to implement the reports, input screens, buttons and dialog boxes, and so forth.

▶ *Programming language*—such as BASIC (in Visual Basic), Object Pascal (in Delphi), or C++. This component includes an *integrated development environment*

*(IDE)* for creating, testing, and debugging code. It may be possible to use drag-and-drop operations to create up to 80 percent of the code for a system.

The RAD process is similar to the prototyping process. Both are highly iterative and emphasize speed of development. Prototyping often uses specialized languages, such as 4GLs and screen generators, while RAD packages include different tools with similar capabilities. With RAD tools, developers enhance and extend the initial version through multiple iterations until it is suitable for operational use. The tools work together as part of an integrated package. They produce functional components of a final system, rather than mockups or limited-scale versions. Typical RAD products are suitable for development on a wide variety of platforms, especially the increasingly popular client/server ones.

RAD projects are substantially different from conventional systems projects. This suggests that managers should not use a traditional SDLC to handle them. Linthicum (1995) proposes the parallel development model shown in Figure 14.6. Systems personnel work with the users in an iterative prototyping mode to develop the interface. At the same time programmers write code for calculations and other operational functions.

In addition to the benefits of speed and portability, RAD is used to create applications which are easier to maintain and to modify. However, RAD packages also have some disadvantages. Like prototyping, the iterative development process can continue indefinitely if there is no unambiguous criterion for ending it. RAD packages may have capabilities to document the system, but having these features does not guarantee that developers will produce appropriate documentation.

Linthicum (1995) indicates that RAD packages are most appropriate in situations that focus primarily on data. Typical applications include accessing databases for sales reporting and decision support. On the input side, RAD applications are good for activities such as order processing and inventory control. However, RAD is not the best approach for applications that require extensive

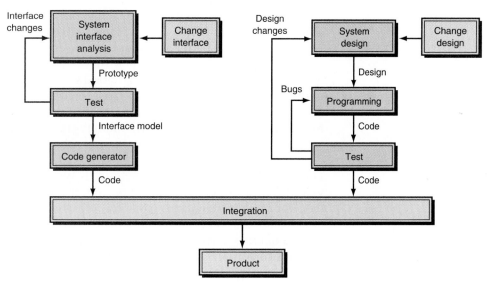

**FIGURE 14.6 A rapid application development SDLC.** (*Source:* Linthicum, D. S. [1995], p. 70. See www.byte.com/art/9508/img/503083b2.htm.)

calculations, such as engineering or financial analysis. RAD is also inappropriate for real-time applications where processing speed is very important. For more information, vendors, and Web sites see Ruber (1998).

## OBJECT-ORIENTED DEVELOPMENT

SDLC development projects often run beyond schedule and over budget and result in systems that are too rigid, have too many defects, and do not meet user requirements closely enough. These problems illustrate the *software crisis* facing organizations today. An alternative approach is object-oriented development.

**Object-oriented development** (Technology Guide #2) is based on a fundamentally different view of computer systems than that found in traditional SDLC approaches. Traditional approaches provide specific step-by-step instructions in the form of computer programs, in which programmers must specify every procedural detail. They usually result in a system that performs the original task but may not be suited for handling other tasks, even when the other tasks involve the same real-world entities. For example, a billing system will handle billing but probably will not be adaptable to handle mailings for the marketing department or generate leads for the sales force, even though the billing, marketing, and sales functions all use similar data such as customer names, addresses, and current and past purchases.

An object-oriented (OO) system begins not with the task to be performed, but with the aspects of the real world that must be modeled to perform that task. Therefore, if a firm has a good model of its customers and its interactions with them, this model can be used equally well for billings, mailings, and sales leads.

**BENEFITS OF THE OBJECT-ORIENTED APPROACH.** The OO approach to software development can lead to many benefits. First, it reduces the complexity of systems development and leads to systems that are easier and quicker to build and maintain, because each object is relatively small, self-contained, and manageable. Second, the OO approach improves programmers' productivity and quality. Once an object has been defined, implemented, and tested, it can be reused in other systems. Third, systems developed with the OO approach are more flexible. These systems can be modified and enhanced easily, by changing some types of objects or by adding new types. Fourth, the OO approach allows the systems analyst to think at the level of the real-world system (as users do) and not at the level of the programming language. The basic operations of an enterprise change much more slowly than the information needs of specific groups or individuals. Therefore, software based on generic models (the OO approach) will have a much longer life span than programs written to solve specific, immediate problems.

Fifth, the object-oriented approach is ideal for developing Web applications. For example, to speed development of its Web site, so it could be the first to provide ticketing on the Internet, Southwest Airlines used OO development. The data and code were encapsulated into reusable components, each of which could be developed and enhanced independently. This increased development speed and flexibility, as well as reducing system maintenance. The airline found that answers to complex queries are processed by the OO database 10 to 100 times faster. (See Harrison [1997] for details.) An example of using an intranet to facilitate objects' reuse is provided in the next *IT at Work.*

**IT At Work**   MCI USES AN INTRANET
TO SHARE OBJECTS

Although software reuse is a good idea in theory, it may not be easy to achieve in practice. MCI Communications Corp. failed in several previous attempts to get its developers to share components and reuse them in new applications. However, it is having more success with a software repository it established on the corporate intranet. This repository is easier to access and use than the previous versions that were based on Lotus Notes.

The new system supports over 6,000 developers, managers, and support staff. Although the teams are scattered across the United States, they may be working on similar projects and thus could benefit from software sharing. The system also facilitates communication among these dispersed employees and promotes employee morale. Mike Kremer, manager of MCI's Object Technology Group, says: "We save a lot of time and money just by putting people in touch with one another . . . people feel better knowing that they are not the only ones on this development journey."

The system has monitoring capabilities, which provide information on which development teams are using individual objects. This information will make it easier to evaluate the new system and promote a new corporate policy of increasing software reuse.

Speed is another advantage of implementing this on an intranet. Kremer decided to use this approach in July 1996. His staff of six people started building the repository in September and had it in operation by mid-October. The repository started with 20 components, and had grown to around 150 by mid-1997.

Kremer's advice is to not take an authoritarian approach in a project like this. "Don't say, `Here it is. Use it.' " Instead he recommends getting users involved in the project, so they will have more interest in using the system.

**For Further Exploration:** Why is it hard to get developers to reuse software? ▲

SOURCE: Condensed from "MCI Puts Object Repository Online," *Computerworld Intranets,* May 26, 1997, p. 10.

> It's really hard to optimize program code when you're writing for platform independence. It's the same old speed vs. flexibility tradeoff.
>
> — *Blake Thompson*

On the other hand, there are some disadvantages to the OO approach. OO systems, especially those written in Java, generally run more slowly than those developed in other programming languages. Many programmers have little skill and experience with OO languages, so retraining may be necessary in organizations that want to start using OO programming in their systems development projects.

**OBJECT-ORIENTED ANALYSIS AND DESIGN.** The development process for an object-oriented system is in many respects similar to that for a conventional system. This process would include the same steps as the generic eight-stage SDLC presented in Section 14.1. The developers could use a formal SDLC methodology to manage this process, or use the prototyping or RAD approaches. The major difference is that, in the logical analysis and design stage, the analysts can use specialized modeling diagrams that are more appropriate for representing object-oriented concepts.

Figure 14.7 provides an example from an article on object-oriented analysis (Rescigno and Batt [1997]). It shows two objects: Major Field of Study and Student. The systems analyst diagrams each object as a box with three parts. The top part contains the object name, the middle part lists the attributes or data associated with the object, and the bottom part lists the methods that implement the

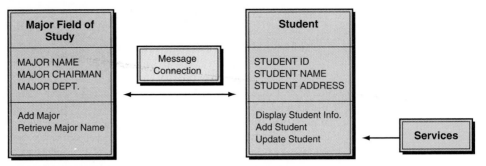

**FIGURE 14.7** **Object-oriented analysis diagram.** (*Source:* Rescigno, G., and W. Batt [1997], p. 46.)

behaviors of the objects. Arrows between objects show messages. In Figure 14.7 a Student object can send a message to a Major Field of Study object to retrieve Major Name. The arrow is two-headed, showing that messages could also go in the other direction. A Major Field of Study object could send a message to Student objects to Display Student Info, for example, to create a list of students in that major.

## 14.3 SYSTEMS DEVELOPED OUTSIDE THE IS DEPARTMENT

The methodologies presented earlier are usually used by the IS department. Their execution requires highly skilled employees, and the methodologies are fairly complex. The result is a backlog in application development, and a high failure rate. Therefore, many organizations are using approaches that shift the construction task from the ISD to others. Of the various ways of doing it, three are most common: let users build their own systems; let end users and/or the ISD use packages; or outsource the entire systems development process. These options are described next.

### END-USER DEVELOPMENT

In the early days of computing, an organization housed its computer in a climate-controlled room, with locked doors and restricted access. The only people who interacted with the computer (most organizations had only one computer) were specialists: programmers, computer operators, and data entry personnel. Over the years, computers became cheaper, smaller, and more widely dispersed throughout the organization. Now almost everybody who works at a desk has a computer.

Along with this transfer of hardware, many computer-related activities shifted out into the work area. Users now handle most of their own data entry. They create many of their own reports and print them locally, instead of waiting for them to arrive in the interoffice mail after a computer operator has run them at a remote data center. They provide unofficial training and support to other workers in their area. And users also design and develop an increasing proportion of their own applications, sometimes even relatively large and complex systems.

This trend toward such **end-user computing** is not surprising. Given the increasing demand for more and better information to support decision making and operations, it is clear that not enough computer programmers can be trained to handle the entire workload. This situation is similar to the one faced by telephone companies years ago. Had switchboards not been automated, everyone in the workforce today would have to be a telephone operator to handle the telephone dialing workload. Automating switchboards, however, did make all of us telephone operators to some degree: the phone company shifted more and more of the manual workload to telephone users. Today, we get assistance from a telephone operator only when we can't make a call on our own.

The evolution of phone dialing is analogous to what is happening with computer programming. In the early days of computers, users were totally dependent on computer technicians, but the increasing availability of user-friendly languages and system interfaces is allowing users to do more and more of their own development. The computer technician's role, like the telephone operator's, may evolve into helping users to help themselves. Computer technicians and information systems professionals will still be necessary to manage and control the increasing complexity of hardware, software, and databases needed to support this new environment. But because users will not have to depend on a technician to provide everything they need, overall productivity may significantly increase. Professional programmers will still write and update complex software, while users will do more ad hoc programming.

## TRENDS FAVORING END-USER DEVELOPMENT

The following summary lists existing factors that lead to higher levels of end-user development. Note that many of these factors represent continuing trends, and therefore this form of development could become even more important in the future.

▶ *Increasingly powerful desktop hardware.* This makes it possible to run powerful software that allows users, even with limited technical skills, to develop applications and systems.

▶ *Declining hardware costs.* In the early years, computers cost over a million dollars. Now for a few thousand dollars, users can acquire PCs that are much more powerful than those old mainframes. Declining costs make it possible for almost everybody to have a computer, increasing the market potential for powerful software tools to support end-user developers.

▶ *Increasingly diverse software capabilities.* Early mainframes primarily handled accounting, finance, and inventory applications. Early personal computers did word processing, spreadsheets, and databases. Although these categories still account for the majority of usage, the proportion and range of other applications is very large and growing. Many of the new packages are programmable: with macros and other features, users can automate activities for themselves or others in their work unit. Other packages, including the RAD tools discussed in the previous section, make it easier for users to develop even relatively large systems.

▶ *Increasingly computer-literate population.* Computers are becoming common at work, in homes, and at schools. Perhaps half the population in the United

At my location, every employee is "empowered" to do their own end-user computing.
— *Dave Gehrke*

States under 65 now has some basic computer skills. With experience and study, some of these people move into the category of "power users," persons who are highly skilled with various kinds of software and able to develop applications.

▶ **Backlog of IS projects.** In most organizations, the internal IS unit has a large backlog of new systems development projects. In the absence of a priority, users may have to wait several years for work on their project to even start. This makes alternate sources, including end-user development, relatively attractive.

▶ **Development speed.** Even if the users have a priority, a formal systems development project by the central IS unit may take longer than having an end-user develop the system.

▶ **Business orientation.** One reason why end-users may develop systems faster is that they understand their own business processes better than the technology-oriented staff in the IS unit.

▶ **Small applications.** Many office tasks can benefit from automation, even though they are far too small to be suitable for a formal systems project. For example, it is easier to enter a one-page table with 20 entries into a spreadsheet than it is to compute the total with a calculator and then type the table with a typewriter. It is far easier to update the same report when the data changes the following month. End-user development is the only option for many small applications.

▶ **Control.** Managers often perceive the IS unit as unresponsive and therefore prefer to have the developers under their own direct control.

▶ **Apparent cost savings.** If the systems developer is already on the payroll of the user organization, the marginal costs may negligible and far lower than a quotation from the central IS unit. Not recognizing the possibility of hidden costs, such as higher maintenance in the future, managers may bias their decisions in the direction of end-user development.

**TYPES OF END-USER COMPUTING.** Rockart and Flannery (1983) identify the six end-user computing categories shown in Table 14.1. Note that the last four of these categories participate in some form of development. With experience, end users can migrate into the development categories, or advance from doing limited to more extensive development.

---

**Table 14.1** Categories of End-User Computing

| Category | Activities |
|---|---|
| 1. Nonprogramming end users | Enter data, use application |
| 2. Command-level users | Access data, print reports |
| 3. End-user programmers | Develop applications for personal use |
| 4. Functional support personnel | Develop applications for others to use |
| 5. End-user computing support personnel* | Training, hotline, develop applications |
| 6. Programmers* | Work on a contract basis |

*Note: Support personnel and programmers are typically not employees of user work groups.

In the 1980s many large organizations set up **information centers** to help their employees learn how to use the emerging technology of personal computing. These information centers had their own office space and a variety of personal computer hardware and software, as well as employees in Category 5 in Table 14.1. Although some organizations have closed their information centers, they typically continue to provide end users with help desk and training functions from other locations or through outsourcing.

## PROBLEMS WITH END-USER DEVELOPMENT, AND SUGGESTED SOLUTIONS

Although the underlying trends and the advantages are favorable to end-user development, managers need to be aware of potential problems. End users who develop applications may claim that they need more expensive hardware and additional software. Although they tend to exaggerate their requirements, some additional spending will usually be necessary.

In addition to explicit costs, end-user developers can also incur hidden costs. Although the end user is already on the unit's payroll, developing systems takes time away from other responsibilities. The employee may also create support costs elsewhere in the organization, even if the unit does not receive charges for them. Different units may duplicate efforts by producing separate systems that do essentially the same thing. Development of localized systems and databases may conflict with organizational goals for increased data sharing among operating units.

Another problem is that managers outside the IS area generally have limited technical skills, which makes it difficult for them to evaluate end-user development activities. Although their managers may not realize it, some end-user developers are much less competent than others. In some cases a lack of competency may result in failed projects: systems that do not work at all. In other cases, applications that appear to function adequately may actually produce inaccurate outputs that lead to bad decisions.

End users often fail to produce adequate documentation for their systems, which can create maintenance problems later, especially if the developer leaves the organization. Security is also a potential problem area: end users may not understand, or be able to implement, organizational standards for data security. As a result, they may fail to appropriately safeguard confidential data or properly back up data and programs. In some cases the maintenance or security problems revert back to the central IS unit.

> Although the bridging application was a "gift" and adopted in a few departments, we still had troubles. As time progressed, some of us had updated versions and some earlier. There wasn't any documentaion, and there was a little confusion. We were better-off with the application and confusion, rather than without it, but a hidden lesson-documentation and a concurrent upgrade schedule is essential.
> — *Kristin Borhofen*

**RESEARCH ON END-USER COMPUTING PROBLEMS.** Researchers have generated a substantial amount of data on the problems that can occur with spreadsheets, which represent the most common basis for end-user applications. In regard to spreadsheets, Panko and Halverson (1996) report that "every study that has looked for errors has found them . . . in disturbingly high numbers." One of their experiments required MBA students, each of whom had hundreds of hours of previous experience developing and debugging spreadsheets, to individually develop a pro-forma income statement with 21 formula cells. Over half (56%) of these very experienced developers had at least one error in their spreadsheets. The following *IT at Work* demonstrates a spreadsheet error notable for its sheer magnitude.

*IT At Work*   A $2.4 BILLION SPREADSHEET ERROR AT MAGELLAN FUND

If a mutual fund has a net profit on holdings sold during the year (a realized capital gain), U.S. tax laws require it to distribute the gain to shareholders, who must then report it as income. In estimating this information for the year 1994, an accountant at Magellan Fund entered a $1.2 billion loss in a spreadsheet without a minus sign in front of the number. The spreadsheet therefore added $1.2 billion rather than subtracting it from the total, so the result was off by $2.4 billion. To help its shareholders with tax planning, Magellan informed them in November that they would receive a capital gains distribution of around $4.32 per share. Because of tax laws and individual circumstances, it would have been advantageous for certain shareholders to sell shares prior to a distribution of this size. For other investors, it could have been advantageous to delay purchasing Magellan until after the distribution.

A subsequent review detected the error. In terms of realized capital gains, the fund had a net loss, so shareholders received no capital gains distribution for 1994. However, Magellan's net asset value per share, based on the market prices of its holdings, declined 4.4 percent between the initial announcement and the correction. So the error worked in favor of anyone who decided—on the basis of the erroneous forecast—either to sell Magellan or to defer a purchase.

**For Further Exploration:** Was this primarily a technology problem, or primarily a management problem? Can better spreadsheet technologies, or other information technologies, help avoid this type of error? Would such an error be possible in a system developed with the SDLC? ▲

SOURCE: Condensed from Savitz, E. J., "Magellan Loses Its Compass," *Barron's*, December 12, 1994.

Edberg and Bowman (1996) evaluated end-user computing from the perspective of development using database rather than spreadsheet software. They used undergraduate computer information systems (CIS) majors as surrogates for information systems professionals, and MBA students to represent end-user computing personnel. Comparing performance on the same development assignments, they found that the CIS majors were much more productive, in terms of the functionality and quality of their applications, than the MBA end-user developers. Their findings suggest that organizations may do better by shifting some of

*Table 14.2* **Performance Developing the Same Database Systems**

| Team Averages | CIS Majors (IS Professionals) | MBAs (End-User Developers) |
|---|---|---|
| Hours worked on project | 154 | 162 |
| Lines of code (LOC) | 991 | 359 |
| Function points | 130 | 54 |
| Defects | 2.8 | 6.0 |
| Quality points (55 possible) | 40 | 22 |
| % Defects/LOC | 0.3% | 1.7% |

SOURCE: Edberg and Bowman (1996), p. 177.

**Table 14.3** Guidelines for Avoiding Spreadsheet Errors

1. Randomly audit a sample of 25 to 50 spreadsheet applications, especially mission-critical ones, and make corrections where necessary. If this initial review indicates substantial problems, extend the audit to other important spreadsheets.

2. Use the built-in cell protection features of the spreadsheet package to prevent changes in the formulas. (Some other types of packages also have security mechanisms, which developers should use wherever available.)

3. Establish organizational spreadsheet policies regarding good coding style, identifying who is responsible for the validity of the outputs, and determining who will do the maintenance if the original author leaves the organization.

4. Check new spreadsheets manually using existing data with known results (e.g., previous financial statements).

5. Spreadsheet developers need to spend time creating detailed designs of their spreadsheets before plunging into the development.

their end-user development activities back to IS professionals. They recommend that organizations provide end users with training in development methods and procedures, especially in regard to quality assurance. Table 14.2 summarizes the results of their study.

**IMPROVING END USERS' SYSTEMS DEVELOPMENT.** To prevent or control spreadsheet errors, Panko (quoted in Ross [1996]) recommends the five-step program outlined in Table 14.3. To avoid problems with other systems, managers could consider applying or adapting these recommendations to end-user development with databases and other types of software also.

**DIVIDING COMPUTING RESPONSIBILITIES.** A management strategy to encourage the beneficial aspects of end-user computing and to minimize its risks is to divide computing responsibilities among groups—including IS groups. One approach is first to brainstorm a list of required computing activities, making the list as long as possible before eventually cutting it down to the most important activities. Each activity is then assigned either to an IS group or to end users. Some types of activities that should be examined for divisional responsibilities are listed in Table 14.4.

Dividing responsibilities can be done in several ways, one of which is shown in the *IT at Work* on the next page.

**Table 14.4** Computing Activities for Divided Responsibility Decisions

- Standards for hardware and software acquisition.
- Purchase authority for hardware and software.
- Economic cost-justification standards and procedures.
- Responsibility for developing and maintaining types of applications.
- Data security, integrity, and privacy.
- Electronic access to local and corporate data.
- Authority and responsibility for entering and modifying data.

## IT At Work — END-USER SUCCESS AT 3M

3M is a large manufacturer of office supplies, plastics, and chemicals. Recognized by Tom Peters and Robert Waterman in their book on outstanding management, *In Search of Excellence,* 3M Corp. has a corporate culture that encourages entrepreneurship. This is possible because the more than 60 divisions operate like small, independent companies. 3M also wants to maintain corporatewide financial and human resources management and corporatewide career path planning in order to benefit from economies-of-scale. What 3M does *not* want is a central bureaucracy to inhibit the competitiveness of its divisions.

**U**SING IT

...in Production & Operations Management

3M resolved this situation by having a centralized computing system and staff for financial and human resources systems, and a decentralized computing system and staff for logistical and operational systems. However, all decentralized technology is as compatible as possible, in order to aid technology transfer and allow staff to be reassigned without being retrained.

For the logistical and operational systems, the corporate IS staff plays a key role in planning and coordination. These staffers facilitate technology transfer of applications between divisions.

At 3M, there is one task of IS that is close to sacred and will likely never be decentralized: planning. Without centralized planning, it is too easy to miss opportunities for shared efforts and resources.

**For Further Exploration:** Relate 3M's IT architecture to its organizational structure and mode of operation. How does IT contribute to 3M's being recognized as a well-managed company? ▲

SOURCE: Authors' experience.

## APPLICATION SOFTWARE PACKAGES AND OUTSOURCING

As more and more organizations began to use computers, relying on internal IS units to develop applications and operate the hardware, they found that, at times, the IS units needed additional staff or specialized skills for some projects. To meet these needs, they could hire experienced programmers who were willing to "moonlight" (work a second job) or who preferred to work on a project-by-project basis. These were the first contract programmers, and they represented the start of the outsourcing trend.

Externally developed software and outsourcing have become much more important since these early beginnings. The market for mainframe (and mini-computer) software expanded with the sales growth of these larger machines. Table 14.5 on page 625 shows estimated software sales for leading companies in this industry. IBM, which is usually considered a computer hardware manufacturer, is also the leading software producer in the world. Several other computer hardware companies are also among the top ten software producers. Microsoft Corp. was the number-two software producer in the world in 1996. International Data Corp. projected total worldwide software sales for 1997 at $121.4 billion, a 13 percent increase over 1996 (Gross [1997]).

**ENTERPRISE SOFTWARE.** A recent trend in the software business is **enterprise software** (see Chapter 8). One of the major attractions of enterprise packages is that they incorporate many of the "best practices" in the various functional areas. Organizations thus have the opportunity to upgrade their processes

*Table 14.5* **Leading Software Producers**

| Company | Estimated 1996 Software Revenues (billions) |
|---|---|
| IBM | $12.9 |
| Microsoft Corp. | 9.4 |
| Hitachi | 5.5 |
| Fujitsu | 4.8 |
| Computer Associates | 3.2 |
| NEC | 2.3 |
| Oracle | 2.3 |
| SAP | 1.7 |
| Novell | 1.2 |
| Digital Equipment | 1.2 |

SOURCE: Rucker, M. J., "A Juggling Act Between Old and New," *Datamation,* July 1996.

at the same time they install the new software. Another advantage is that they handle dates beyond 1999 correctly, so organizations can migrate to these systems to avoid the problems of identifying and upgrading in-house software to deal with the Year 2000 problem.

Major suppliers in this category include SAP/AG, Oracle, Baan, and People-Soft. Since these companies sell their products to a large number of customers, they can hire more specialized personnel and spend more on development than an individual organization would spend to develop its own systems.

**OUTSOURCING DEVELOPMENT.** The chart in Figure 13.8 in Chapter 13 shows that worldwide outsourcing revenues, projected at $154 billion in 1997, are somewhat higher than the projections of $121 billion in software sales cited above. However, development is a relatively small part of these outsourcing revenues, so purchasing software is still much more important than outsourcing development. Outsourcing is especially popular in the development of Web sites, as can be seen at *Readers Digest,* illustrated in the next *IT at Work.*

**IT At Work** *READER'S DIGEST* **OUTSOURCES ITS WEB SITE DEVELOPMENT**

*U* **SING IT**

...in Marketing

*Reader's Digest* (www.readerdigest.com) is a popular magazine read by over 100 million people around the world in 19 languages. The company revenues ($2.8 billion in 1997) are derived not only from the monthly magazine, but from direct-market (mail) sales of books, videos, music, and audio books. Such sales seemed to be ideal for the Web. However, *Reader's Digest* resisted the frenzied rush to get on the Web that many companies followed in 1995 and 1996. Instead, they conducted comprehensive market research in 1996. This study indicated that the company should not publish content supported by advertising revenues, but rather use the Web for direct marketing.

Further research indicated that rather than hiring staff to build and maintain the

Web site, the company should outsource it. This allows the company to concentrate on its core competencies.

Several vendors were used: Connect Inc. was selected as the primary technology provider, including handling all online transactions using the vendor's OneServe product. Nicholson N.Y. was hired as a site designer and engineer, and Modern Media was entrusted with placing advertisements, promotions, and drawing people to the site.

A major problem is to make sure that technology will keep pace with the site's growing popularity. Of special importance is the Web server. Therefore the company conducted a post-audit evaluations. The site was launched in October 1996 and relaunched in November 1996 (for Thanksgiving) and December 1996 (for Christmas). It is expected to be profitable in three to five years. Revenue comes not only from direct sales and advertising, but also from generating a list of visitors that is used for targeted advertisement by mail. Keith Fox, director of media, believes that the development of this kind of Web site and its maintenance will actually never stop, and use of vendors is the only way to go.

**For Further Exploration:** Why do you need to work with several vendors? If this is a continuous job, why not hire your own employees? ▲

SOURCE: Condensed from *Infoworld,* Jan. 5, 1998, p. 74.

## ▶ 14.4 COMPARING ALTERNATIVES FOR ACQUIRING NEW SYSTEMS

Managers have a wide variety of ways to acquire new systems. In-house IS professionals can handle development, using either a traditional structured programming methodology or an object-oriented methodology. Professionals can develop systems using prototyping or rapid application development. End users can also develop systems. Or managers can obtain systems from outsiders, either by outsourcing development or by purchasing generic packages. In this section we discuss considerations relevant to choosing among these different options.

### DESIRABLE OUTCOMES AND IMPLEMENTATION ISSUES

Before we discuss specific approaches to acquiring systems, let us consider in more detail what constitutes desirable outcomes of the acquisition process. The most prominent considerations are:

▶ *On-time.* Completion and implementation of the system on or before the scheduled target date.

▶ *On-budget.* The system cost is equal to or less than the budget.

▶ *Full functionality.* The system has all the features in the original specifications.

> Involving the end users in the development phase of new systems can significantly reduce user acceptance problems. Including them gives them a feeling of empowerment, and really can't hurt the development phase.
>
> — *Mike Rewald*

These outcomes are very desirable, especially since fewer than half of all systems projects achieve all three. However, it is possible to succeed on each of these criteria but still have a system that does not increase the effectiveness of the organization. Therefore, the following outcomes are also important:

▶ *User acceptance.* Some systems perform poorly or even fail solely because of resistance from the users. One reason for resistance is a poor user interface that makes a system difficult to learn or use. Perceptions that the system shifts power from one part of the organization to another, or increases management control over employees, can also lead to resistance.

▶ ***Favorable costs-to-benefits ratio.*** A system may have all the specified functionality but still not help the organization because actual benefits and/or operating costs differ substantially from the initial estimates. This unfavorable outcome is becoming more common as organizations exhaust the possibilities for automation projects that replace manual labor with computer functionality. Decision makers must increasingly use intangible benefits, which are much harder to predict, to justify new systems.

▶ ***Low maintenance.*** Up to 80 percent of the operational ISD budget now goes for maintenance of existing systems. This implies that a more expensive system, which is easier to maintain or has greater functionality, could be more beneficial to an organization than one that is difficult to update or needs subsequent enhancements in its functionality.

▶ ***Scalability.*** Processing volumes can increase as usage levels expand and as organizations grow. It may therefore be necessary to migrate a system to another hardware platform with greater capabilities. If the original system is based on software that is portable to different platforms, for example, a common database management system, the migration should be cheaper and less difficult.

▶ ***Integration with other systems.*** A system may achieve all its own design objectives but not coordinate well with other systems in an organization. For example, some of its data may overlap files in other locations. The end result would be less organizational cost savings than available through more integrated systems.

▶ ***Minimal negative cross impacts.*** A new system may be successful by itself but create major problems for an organization in other areas. For example, a new system could put unacceptably large demands on limited computing resources and result in unacceptable delays on other systems during peak demand.

▶ ***Reusability.*** Ideally, some of the more general code developed for the new system would be reusable. If so, it could save money in future systems development projects. An example of code reuse is given in the following *IT at Work.*

---

**IT At Work**    THE STATE OF WISCONSIN REDUCES DEVELOPMENT COSTS THROUGH CODE REUSE

**USING IT**

...in Public Service

Wisconsin's Department of Health and Family Services had problems with its information systems. These included 20 applications, most running on mainframes, that performed 22 different functions. Data was stored in separate files for individual applications, in inconsistent formats, so it was difficult to share data between applications. Mark Clement, the development services manager, indicates that "the largest problem was the inability to ask a single question to multiple systems and get a consistent answer."

To solve these problems, the department created a team including Clement, two analysts, four system developers, and some end users. This team's initial responsibility is to analyze business processes to identify which should be retained, or eliminated, or transferred to other departments or agencies. The ultimate goal was to reduce the 20 previous applications to eight integrated client/server systems.

The project is to be done in three phases, starting with the Bureau of Licensing and Regulation. This phase was budgeted at $1.2 million and started in February 1996, with a target completion of September 1997.

One of the key aspects of the project is object reuse. Clement notes that some activities, such as sending a license request through the system or extracting data, are common to many departments. The initial phase will develop objects to perform these activities for one department. The developers plan to incorporate these objects into systems for other departments in the second and third phases of the project.

Clement estimates that this approach will cut development efforts in half for later projects. For example, the Children's Licensing Office (for day care centers) expected to spend $950,000 to upgrade its systems. However, by waiting to reuse objects developed for another office, this unit cut its costs by almost 35 percent.

**For Further Exploration:** Can you think of possible disadvantages to this strategy of reusing objects? ▲

SOURCE: Condensed from "Revamp Streamlines State IS," *Computerworld*, August 11, 1997, pp. 55–56.

---

> This is a valuable list that is often overlooked when buying commercial software packages.
> — *Dave Gehrke*

**SELECTING COMMERCIAL SOFTWARE PACKAGES.** The criteria listed above can be used to select specific software packages, either for development and/or applications. Other criteria that can be used are:

▶ Cost and financial terms

▶ Upgrade policy and cost

▶ Vendor's reputation and availability for help

▶ Vendor's success stories (visit their Web site, contact clients)

▶ System flexibility

▶ Ease of Internet interface

▶ Availability and quality of documentation

▶ Necessary hardware and networking resources

▶ Required training (check if provided by vendor)

▶ Security

▶ Learning (speed of) for developers and users

▶ Graphical presentation

▶ Data handling

▶ Environment and hardware

Several independent organizations and magazines conduct software package comparisons from time to time.

For smaller packages you can use "trialware" from the Internet before purchase is made. Most vendors will give you the software for a limited testing time. Also, they will come and demonstrate the software (let them use *your* data).

## MANAGEMENT CONSIDERATIONS

Since organizations and their systems requirements vary along many dimensions, it is not possible to neatly match all types of systems projects with the acquisition approaches identified in this chapter. Therefore, in many cases it might be advisable to use a combination of approaches.

Below we provide general considerations related to the different approaches. These considerations should be reviewed in the context of the desirable outcomes discussed earlier. If coupled with good judgment, these considerations may help managers make better decisions regarding new systems' acquisition.

**TRADITIONAL SDLC METHODOLOGY.** The SDLC approach often works well for large projects with well-defined requirements, where there is *not* a lot of pressure to finish the project quickly. Use of this approach requires appropriate and effective management, possibly including a user as the leader if the project is not highly technical.

**PROTOTYPING.** Prototyping is especially useful in situations where the requirements (and therefore the costs) are poorly defined and/or when speed is needed. However, it requires effective management to make sure that the iterations of prototyping do not continue indefinitely. It is important to have tools such as 4GLs and screen generators when using this approach. If the project is large, it is probably better to establish the information requirements through prototyping and then use a more formal SDLC to complete the system.

**RAPID APPLICATION DEVELOPMENT (RAD).** This is an obvious candidate when new systems are needed very quickly. RAD tools can work well for developing client/server systems or front-ends for mainframe systems. RAD may be less appropriate than conventional programming languages for larger projects, or for developing systems with a lot of calculations or real-time processing.

**OBJECT-ORIENTED DEVELOPMENT.** OO development is becoming increasingly popular, but usage is limited by a shortage of personnel with OO skills. Java is an OO language that is especially suitable for developing network applications. However, OO languages in general, and Java in particular, tend to run slowly. Reusability of code is a potential advantage of OO development, but reuse will not occur without appropriate cataloging, search engines, and experienced and motivated employees.

**END-USER DEVELOPMENT.** Although most appropriate for small projects, end-user development is also a possibility for larger projects whose priorities are not high enough to lead to a timely response from the central IS unit. Managers should beware of end-user development in situations where problems with the system can lead to significant risks for the organization such as system failures, inaccurate results, disclosure of confidential data, inefficiency, incompatibility with other systems, and inability to maintain the system if the developer leaves.

**PURCHASING OR OUTSOURCING.** For large and complex systems with a significant risk of failure, organizations should *always* consider using an outside source. The exception to this rule is that in-house development may be necessary if the system is highly strategic or incorporates critical proprietary information. If scalability is important to the organization, it may be advisable to buy rather than make, even for smaller systems. However, managers need to be aware of relatively high additional implementation costs when purchasing enterprise software packages.

# ▶ 14.5 SOME IMPORTANT SYSTEMS DEVELOPMENT ISSUES

Building information systems, either by the ISD or by end users, involves many issues not discussed in the preceding sections. Some of the issues which may be of interest to managers and end users are discussed here.

## BUILDING INTERNET AND INTRANET APPLICATIONS

Web browsers and Internet communication operate on very simple, least-common-denominator technologies. Therefore it is very easy to adapt them to any operating system, and to any personal computer hardware. This feasibility avoids most of the incompatibility problems and integration difficulties that have plagued the computer industry since its early days. It doesn't matter whether the user has a PC or an Apple computer, or whether the operating system is Windows, OS/2 or Unix.

The Web browser represents a highly intuitive and nearly universal interface that is easy to learn to use. The hyperlinks feature of Web pages represents an extremely powerful capability for organizing information into a usable and accessible form. Because of its simplicity and universal acceptance, the Web browser represents an ideal interface for many applications. It requires less skill to develop Web pages in hypertext markup language (HTML), or using Web page development tools, than it takes to write code in programming languages such as C or COBOL. This simplicity means that applications can be developed rapidly. Implementations are easy because most users already know how to work with a browser. Although there are some major potential security problems, the simplicity of the browser and the HTML language reduce the risks of failure in development.

These considerations suggest that developing Internet (and intranet) applications should be fast and inexpensive and should result in high returns on investment (ROI). The experience in many organizations has verified these theoretical benefits. For example, General Electric Corp. developed a Web site with 1500 pages in two months, for $100,000. In some cases, as illustrated in Minicase 1 in Chapter 13, the benefits are so obvious that organizations do not even bother to do cost/benefit analyses.

**AN INTERNET AND INTRANET DEVELOPMENT STRATEGY.** Because the technology is so new yet so simple, most organizations have not been using the SDLC approach for Internet/intranet development. Much of the activity has been on a low-budget, experimental basis to gain experience with the technologies. However, most organizations have now gained some experience, so it is probably appropriate for them to start implementing more formal planning and development policies.

The first planning issue is to identify the objectives for organizational Web sites. These should align with and support organizational strategies. The objectives will vary depending on whether the sites are on: (1) the Internet, which represents the organization to the general public; (2) an extranet, for use with business partners; or (3) an intranet, to serve the needs of organizational employees.

This initial planning also needs to adequately cover infrastructure requirements as well as security and legal issues. Organizational servers and communications links need to have capabilities consistent with the importance of the site to the organization's activities and business strategies. If the site is critical, it needs to have enough capacity to avoid breakdowns or delays during peak periods. The organization also needs to have specialized personnel, including Webmasters to operate and maintain Web sites, and may want to establish a steering IT committee to develop and monitor compliance with policies regarding organizational sites.

Security provisions need to be appropriate to the intended use of each site, with adequate **firewalls** (see Chapter 15) to protect data and programs, and with mechanisms to protect the security of customer transactions. The legal department needs to address potential liability issues related to the sites and set policies to prevent improper use of intellectual property.

After the planning issues have been resolved, the organization can identify and prioritize potential projects. Management may choose to fund the more promising applications, leaving the others to be developed later, or by end users. The steering committee should monitor end-user projects to make sure that they comply with organizational standards in relation to communications with external customers, and with internal security requirements.

## JAVA, A PROMISING TOOL

Internet and intranet Web pages are coded primarily in HTML, a simple language that is most useful for displaying static content to viewers. HTML has very limited capabilities for interacting with viewers, or for providing information that is continually being updated. It is not suitable for collecting information, such as names and addresses, or for providing animation or changing information such as stock quotes. To do these types of things it is necessary to add programs written in some form of programming language to the HTML for a Web site.

**Java** is relatively new, but it has already established itself as the most important programming language for putting extra features into Web pages. It has many similarities to the C language, but omits some of the more complex and error-prone features of C. Java was specifically designed to work over networks: Java programs can be sent from a Web server over the Internet and then run on the computer that is viewing the Web page. It has numerous security features to prevent these downloaded programs from damaging files or creating other problems on the receiving computer.

Java is an object-oriented language, so the concepts of object-oriented development are relevant to its use. However, the Java Web page programs, called **applets,** need to be relatively small to avoid delays in transmitting them over the Internet. Java programs run more slowly than other languages, such as C, which is another reason to keep them small. Therefore it is not necessary that Java developers use the very formal development methodologies appropriate for large system projects. Prototyping is probably the most suitable approach for developing Java applets, because it provides for a high level of interaction between the developers and users in regard to the critical issues of the appearance and ease-of-use of the Web page.

## CASE TOOLS

For a long time, computer programmers resembled the cobbler in the old story. He was so busy mending his customers' shoes that he didn't have time to repair the holes in his own children's shoes. Similarly, programmers were so busy developing systems to increase the productivity of other functions, such as accounting and marketing, that they didn't have time to develop tools to enhance their own productivity. However, this situation has changed with the emergence of **computer-aided software engineering (CASE)** tools, which are marketed as individual items or in a set (tool kit) that automates various aspects of the development process. For example, a systems analyst could use a CASE tool to create data flow diagrams on a computer, rather than drawing them manually (see Technology Guide #2).

**MANAGERIAL ISSUES REGARDING CASE.** CASE can be used in two different ways. Individual system personnel or IS groups may use a variety of specific CASE tools to automate certain SDLC activities on a piecemeal basis. Or the IS group may acquire an integrated (I-CASE) package, whose components are tightly integrated and which often embodies a specific systems development methodology. (See Technology Guide #2). These two approaches are quite different in terms of their implications for the organization.

Using tools independently can provide some significant productivity benefits. Since they are acquired on an individual basis, the organization has many options and can select the ones that offer the best performance for the cost and are best suited to the organization's needs. The tools can be used independently as needed so users have the option of learning, at their own pace, the tools that are most helpful to them.

On the other hand, with integrated packages the components are specifically designed to work well together and therefore offer the potential for higher productivity gains. However, the learning pace for these packages is much slower than for individual tools. This means that after adoption productivity will initially decline, which may be unacceptable for an organization with a large backlog of high-priority IS projects. Some components of an I-CASE package may not be as good as corresponding tools that can be purchased separately.

The relatively high turnover rate among systems personnel also creates problems for use of I-CASE systems. New employees will need to take the time to learn the integrated package. Existing employees may resist using the package, because they feel it will reduce their opportunities to move to other organizations that use either: (1) traditional development methods, or (2) some other I-CASE package that is incompatible with the one at the present organization.

In addition to the costs of training and productivity losses, organizations need to purchase the actual I-CASE systems. In the past, this often required purchasing workstations in addition to software. With the availability of much more powerful PCs and servers in client/server systems, many organizations may not find it necessary to buy any additional hardware (except possibly a plotter for printing large diagrams). On the other hand, buying an I-CASE system will cost more than buying a few of the most helpful individual tools.

**Table 14.6** Levels of the Capability Maturity Model

| Level | Characteristics |
|---|---|
| **1:** Initial | Processes are ad hoc, undefined, possibly chaotic. Success depends on individual efforts and heroics. |
| **2:** Repeatable | Basic project management tracks cost, schedule, and functionality. On similar applications, organization is able to repeat earlier successes. |
| **3:** Defined | Project management and software engineering activities are documented, standardized, and integrated into development through an organization-specific process (i.e., an SDLC). |
| **4:** Managed | Both software process activities and quality are measured in detail and are quantitatively understood and controlled. |
| **5:** Optimizing | Processes are improved continuously based on feedback from quantitative measures, and from pilot projects with new ideas and technologies. |

SOURCE: Compiled from Herbsleb, J., et al. (June 1997), p. 32.

## SOFTWARE QUALITY IMPROVEMENT AND IS-9000

The success of quality management in manufacturing suggested that it might also be helpful in dealing with the problems of information systems development. To implement this concept for systems development, the Software Engineering Institute at Carnegie Mellon University developed the Capability Maturity Model (CMM). The original purpose of the CMM was to provide guidelines for the U.S. Department of Defense in selecting contractors for software development. The CMM identifies five levels of maturity in the software development process, as summarized in Table 14.6.

As an organization moves to higher maturity levels of the CMM, both the productivity and the quality of its software development efforts should improve. Results of a case study, summarized in Table 14.7, verified substantial gains in both areas through software process improvement (SPI) programs based on the capability maturity model.

Organizations need to understand, however, that software process improvement efforts require significant spending and organizational effort. The case study mentioned above found costs ranging from $490 to $2,004 (median $1,375) per software engineer. Well over half the respondents found that SPI efforts cost more and took longer than expected.

**Table 14.7** Improvements from Capability Maturity Model Implementations

| Category | Range | Median | # of Cases |
|---|---|---|---|
| Productivity gain | 9–67% | 35% | 4 |
| Faster time to market | 15–23% | NA | 2 |
| Reduction in defects | 10–94% | 39% | 5 |

SOURCE: Compiled form Herbsleb, J., et al. (June 1997), pp. 30–40.

**ISO 9000-3.** Another approach to software quality is to implement the ISO 9000-3 software development standards. These international standards are very extensive: they identify a large number of actions that must be performed to obtain certification. However, the specifications do offer a substantial amount of leeway in many areas. For example, Section 5.1 in ISO 9000-3 requires an organized life cycle (SDLC) for software development, but allows the organization to use any SDLC that includes the following (Kehoe and Jarvis [1996]):

▶ *Contract review*—covering scope, responsibilities, risks, and ownership of resulting software.

▶ *Purchaser's requirements specification*—including performance requirements that are quantitatively measurable.

▶ *Development planning*—including schedule, inputs and outputs for each phase, and appropriate project status verification and progress control mechanisms.

▶ *Quality planning*—including specific plans for verifying the quality of the software being developed.

▶ *Design and implementation*—using design methodologies, with reviews of outputs of design process and adherence to organizational standards.

▶ *Testing and validation*—including test environment, test cases, types of testing, schedules, and completion criteria.

▶ *Acceptance*—testing by purchaser.

▶ *Replication, delivery, and installation*—mechanisms for transferring software to user.

▶ *Maintenance*—provisions for enhancing and updating the software.

The ISO standards identify the responsibilities of the software developer, and also the responsibilities of the purchaser or client, in developing quality software. The purchaser needs to clearly identify the requirements and have an established process for requesting any necessary changes in these requirements.

Under ISO 9000-3, the supplier needs to have documented processes for developing software. The supplier's senior management is responsible for developing the *quality policy* document, a short statement that requires employees to use generally accepted quality practices in all areas of the organization. This quality policy is implemented through a *quality system,* which documents the development and quality control processes that implement the quality policy. The quality system requires preparation of *quality plans* for types of products and processes. To ensure compliance with the plans, there needs to be an internal auditing process. ISO 9000-3 requires appropriate funding for quality activities, and appointment of personnel and assignment of responsibilities necessary to implement the program.

## PROJECT PLANNING

Chapter 12 provided a four-stage model for information systems planning for IT infrastructure projects. The final stage of this process, **project planning,** is also used in system development of individual applications. Project planning provides an overall framework with which the systems development life cycle can be planned, scheduled, and controlled. Some of the tools of project management

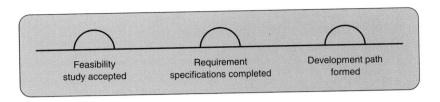

**FIGURE 14.8** Milestones.

are milestones; critical path method (CPM) and its variant known as program evaluation and review technique (PERT); and Gantt charts.

**MILESTONES.** Milestone planning techniques allow projects to evolve as they are developed. Rather than try to predict all project requirements and problems in advance, management allows the project to progress at its own pace. **Milestones,** or checkpoints, are established to allow periodic review of progress so that management can determine whether a project merits further commitment of resources, requires adjustments, or should be discontinued.

Milestones can be based on time, budget, or deliverables. For example, a project's progress might be evaluated weekly, monthly, or quarterly. It might be evaluated after a certain amount of resources are used, such as $50,000. However, milestones are most effective when they identify that specific events have occurred, such as the completion of a feasibility study. Figure 14.8 illustrates the simplicity of a milestone chart.

The following *IT at Work* illustrates how Microsoft Corporation uses milestones in its software development projects.

**IT At Work**   USING MILESTONES AT MICROSOFT

Microsoft Corporation produces software packages that are extremely large and complex. Windows 95, for example, has over 11 million lines of code; its development team included over 200 programmers and testers.

For such large software projects, many companies use a very structured waterfall-type SDLC. The developers initially develop complete specifications and then "freeze" them so that they can focus on completing the remainder of the project.

Microsoft, however, finds that this approach is not flexible enough to meet the needs of the rapidly changing PC software market. Therefore its strategy is to use prototyping, namely to produce a workable product relatively early in the development process. Subsequent development adds more features to the limited functionality of this initial version. Microsoft's projects have three major milestones. At the first, the product has one-third of its features (the most important ones), plus the interface and any other shared components. At the second milestone, the developers add the next-most-important one-third of the features, and the last milestone marks the completion of the remaining features. Individual programmers and small teams (three to eight developers) are responsible for developing individual features.

One key aspect of this approach is "synchronization and stabilization." The project "buildmaster" compiles a working version of the whole package, including any new or revised components from individual teams, at the end of every day. If it is not possible to compile this latest version, the team whose code caused the failure must correct the problem immediately. In this way, all teams are able to work with a copy of the latest version every morning. In addition, every day Microsoft has a working version that it can test with users, distribute to beta testers, or finalize for production at that level of functionality.

**For Further Exploration:** Would this development approach work for other companies in different industries? Is it possible to maintain as high a level of quality with this

**USING IT**

...in Production &
Operations Management

approach as with more structured approaches? What are the characteristics of the employees an organization would need in order to be successful with this approach? ▲

SOURCE: Based on Cusamono, M. A., and R. W. Selby, "How Microsoft Builds Software," *Communications of the ACM*, June 1997, pp. 53–61.

**CRITICAL PATH METHOD (CPM), PERT, AND GANTT CHARTS.** These generic project management tools are suitable for system development projects. Many off-the-shelf software packages are available for planning, organizing, and controlling projects.

**PROJECT PROPERTIES AND PRIORITIES.** Setting budget and time frames prior to defining the system design constraints is perhaps the greatest mistake made in project planning. For example, management may decide to install a new order entry system in nine months, for which it is willing to spend $1 million. This leaves one important issue undefined: What will the new system do? By default, management has constrained the functionality of the new system.

The proper sequence for managing a project is first to get a good functional definition of what the system is designed to do, and then to have people with experience and expertise in information systems and in project management develop a budget and schedule. If management cannot accept the schedule or budget, then the capabilities of the new system can be scaled down to meet the schedule and/or budget constraints.

In developing a budget, schedule, and specifications for a system, managers need to consider and understand several properties of projects and their management. The following five properties most significantly influence the overall nature of an IT project.

1. *Predefined structure.* The more predefined structure a project is, the more easily it can be planned and controlled.
2. *Stability of technology.* The greater the experience with a given technology to be used for a new system, the more predictable the systems development process is.
3. *Size.* The larger the project, the more difficult it is to estimate the resources (time and costs) required to complete it.
4. *User proficiency.* The more knowledgeable and experienced users and managers are in their functional areas and in developing systems, the more proficient they will be relative to information technology and the easier it will be to develop systems for them.
5. *Developer proficiency.* The more knowledge and experience the systems analyst assigned to a project has, the easier the project will go, and vice versa.

Projects can possess variations of each of the preceding properties. For example, a project can have predefined structure but use unstable technology, or it can be a massive undertaking and have low user and developer proficiencies (e.g., most initial online airline reservations systems could be described in this fashion).

Using appropriate project management concepts and tools could be critical to the success or failure of complex systems as illustrated in the *IT at Work* that follows.

## IT At Work   IBM SUCCEEDED IN THE 1998
## OLYMPICS WITH PROPER PROJECT MANAGEMENT

Building an Olympic IT and Web site is not an easy task, even for IBM. Based on its experiences in Atlanta, IBM used rapid development tools, project management, and heavy testing in developing the Nagano Winter Olympics in February 1998.

Developing such an information system is much more complex than many people think. To begin with the deadlines must be met; the games are not delayed if the supporting IT is not in place. The users are from over 80 countries with diverse cultures and expectations. The 7,000 users speak many different languages and the system must handle all the data of the games, including athlete accreditation, press feeds, results, accommodations arrangements, food, logistics, and more.

The hardware includes two S/390 mainframes, more than 100 R/S 6000 servers, and over 4000 PCs. It took IBM 14 months, hundreds of employees, and millions of dollars to develop the system. It was a major challenge for IBM, since its system for the 1996 Olympics had many problems, including spitting out inaccurate information. So quality became a major objective. IBM learned that many shortcomings of the Atlanta systems were the fault of project management. Some of the systems were tested too late, including the Info '96 intranet, so IBM was unable to run data for some events.

To improve project management IBM prepared a project plan as follows: use proven technology, test the full system early, and foster tight communications with the diverse system users, ranging from Olympic committees to athletes. Finding the information requirements of these users was difficult. For every sport a test was designed to find gaps between what users wanted and what the system delivered. Gaps were found with report generation, format of reports, names, and so on. The project management software planned all tests such that corrective actions could be made prior to the opening. Time was needed because different users (e.g., Olympic committees, sport federations, and the press) had different requirements that needed to be negotiated into an agreed-upon format.

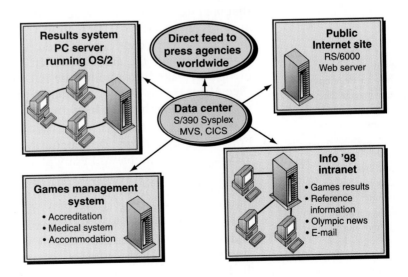

To coordinate the entire project IBM created an end-to-end plan, using CPM-based software management package. Actually, there were 10 major projects, and they were interrelated. The software simulated the ripple-through effect when one piece falls behind. The software was also used to make adjustments in both simulated and real time. IBM also reviewed all potential changes in the 10 projects and their impacts. Extensive testing was a key success factor. The testing found many requirements that were not included in the initial design.

On February 7, 1998, the Nagano games started. Over 100 million hits were recorded on the Web site. Everything worked as planned; IBM, the largest computer company in the world, did not fail this time. Most companies will never develop such enormous and complex systems.

What about cost/benefits? In the short run, IBM invested so much money that its earnings per share for the first quarter of 1998 declined by over $100 million. The benefits are difficult to measure, but IBM's reputation is the major one, so IBM is already preparing for the Sydney Games in 2000.

**For Further Exploration:** Find some information about IBM and the Sydney Olympic Games. Why is IBM willing to lose money on this system? ▲

SOURCE: Condensed from Guth, R., and L. Radosevich, "IBM Crosses the Olympic Finish Line," *InfoWorld*, February 9, 1998.

# ▶ MANAGERIAL ISSUES

1. *Importance.* Some general and functional managers believe that system development is a technical topic that should be of interest only to technical people. This is certainly not the case. Appropriate construction of systems is necessary for their success. Functional managers must participate in the development process and should understand all the phases. They must also participate in the make-or-buy decisions and software selection decisions. Inappropriate development methodologies can result in the system's failure.

2. *Building interorganizational and international information systems.* Building systems that connect two or more organizations, or one organization that operates in different countries, can be very complicated. (See Tractinsky and Jarvenpaa [1995]). As seen in Chapter 12, you need to carefully plan for such systems, considering different requirements and cultures. In addition to planning, the analysis, design, and other phases of system development must take into account the information needs of the various parties. (See Minicase 2.) One of the major problems with international systems is that what is ethical or legal in one country may be unethical or illegal in another.

3. *Ethical and legal issues.* Developing systems across organizations and countries could have problems in any phase of system development. For example, in developing the Nagano Olympics system in 1998, IBM found at the last minute that pro-North-Korea groups in Japan took offense at a reference to the Korean War written on the Web site. Although the material was taken from the *World Book Encyclopedia,* it offended some people. IBM had to delete the reference and provide an apology. IBM commented: "Next time we're going to do a ton of research first versus just do it and find out the hard way."

    A special difficulty exists with Internet-related projects, where legislation is still evolving.

4. *User involvement.* The direct and indirect users of a system are likely to be the most knowledgeable individuals concerning requirements and which alternatives will be the most effective. Users are also the most affected by a new information system. Information systems analysts and designers, on

My company acts responsibly as they are developing our new system. They realize that programmers aren't retailers and retailers aren't programmers. There is a high level of involvement from executives, field personnel, and office personnel from all divisions and departments. As the system is put to the test, the users give feedback to the systems developers. The process is cyclical in nature and comes full circle when users see the changes or are made aware that certain modifications cannot be made.

— *Kristin Borhofen*

the other hand, are likely to be the most knowledgeable individuals concerning technical and data managerial issues as well as the most experienced in arriving at viable systems solutions. The right mixture of user involvement and information systems expertise is crucial.

5. *Traditional approaches vs. prototyping.* The traditional development approach stresses detailed, lockstep development with established decision points; prototyping stresses flexible development based on actual use of partially functional systems. Experience has shown that the traditional approach can be better for low-risk, environmentally stable, and technology-simple situations; prototyping is often better under the opposite conditions.

6. *Tool use by developers.* Development tools and techniques can ensure that developers consider all necessary factors and standardize development, documentation, and testing. Forcing their use, on the other hand, may unnecessarily constrain innovation, development efficiency, and personnel productivity.

7. *Quality assurance vs. schedules.* Quality counts in the short term and the long term, but it can lengthen development and increase developmental costs. Trying to meet tight development schedules can induce poor quality—with even worse schedule, cost, and morale problems.

8. *Behavior problems.* Information systems are primarily for people to use. People may react to new systems in unexpected ways, however, making even the best technically designed systems useless. Changes brought about by information systems need to be managed effectively. Of special interest is the issue of motivating programmers to increase their productivity by learning new tools and reusing preprogrammed modules.

9. *Perpetual development.* Information systems are designed to meet organizational needs. When they don't accurately meet these needs, or these needs change, information systems need to be redeveloped. Developing a system can be a major expense, but perpetually developing a system to maintain its usefulness is usually a much larger expense.

## KEY TERMS

Applets (Java) *631*

Computer-aided software engineering (CASE) *632*

Direct cutover *609*

End-user computing *619*

Enterprise software *624*

Feasibility study *606*

Firewalls *631*

Information center *621*

Java *631*

Logical design *607*

Milestones *635*

Object-oriented development *616*

Parallel conversion *609*

Phased conversion *609*

Pilot conversion *609*

Post-audit *610*

Project planning *634*

Prototyping *612*

Physical design *608*

Rapid application development (RAD) *614*

Systems analysis *606*

Systems development *603*

Systems development life cycle (SDLC) *604*

Waterfall method *605*

## CHAPTER HIGHLIGHTS *(L–x means learning objective number x)*

▶ A systems development life cycle (SDLC) identifies the major steps, or stages, in the development or acquisition of an information system. Organizations may use a proprietary SDLC methodology to help manage systems projects. (L–1)

▶ The prototyping approach is an iterative process that creates simple versions of a system to help users identify their requirements. Traditional SDLCs try to complete much of their analysis and design activities before starting development and are more appropriate where requirements are easier to identify. (L–1) (L–2)

▶ Rapid application development (RAD) packages can speed development. However, systems developed via RAD may not run as efficiently, or be as scaleable, as systems developed with more conventional methodologies. (L–3)

▶ Object-oriented development makes it easier to develop very complex systems rapidly and with relatively few errors. It is also easier to reuse code from object-oriented systems. However, object-oriented systems may not run as fast as those developed in other languages, and many programmers lack OO skills. (L–4)

▶ Outsourcing custom development or purchasing generic systems are alternatives to in-house development. (L–5)

▶ Internet and intranet applications are easy to develop and implement. However, organizations need to establish consistent policies and practices to make sure that Web page development activities support organizational goals. (L–6)

▶ CASE tools can substantially increase programmer productivity. However, the more integrated packages are difficult to learn, which initially reduces productivity and can lead to resistance to implementation within IS groups. (L–7)

▶ Software quality can be improved by implementing the capability maturity model (CMM) or ISO 9000-3 standards. (L–8)

## QUESTIONS FOR REVIEW

1. Describe the major stages of the SDLC.

2. Explain why it is important to understand the concept of SDLC.

3. List four different approaches to converting from one system to another. Which is most risky? least risky?

4. Describe post-audit activities. Why is it important to do an audit after a system has been completed and put into operation?

5. Describe the tools that are commonly included in rapid application development (RAD) packages. What capabilities can they provide?

6. Describe object-oriented development and its increasing importance.

7. Identify trends that encourage more systems development by end users.

8. What are the risks inherent in end-user development? How can they be minimized?

9. List the advantages and disadvantages of purchasing generic software versus using in-house staff or outsourcers to develop customized applications.

10. Describe Java and its role in Internet development.

11. Identify and explain the five levels of the capability maturity model (CMM).

12. List the issues in controlling the quality of systems development. What is the role of IS-9000?

## QUESTIONS FOR DISCUSSION

1. Why is it advisable in some systems development projects to use prototyping to find information needs? Why can't the analyst just ask the users what they want and use the SDLC?

2. What types of incentives could an IS group provide to its programmers to encourage reuse of objects and other software they develop?

3. What type of development approaches would be most appropriate for developing small systems? very large systems? Why? What other factors need to be considered?

4. End-user systems developers usually work for managers whose IT knowledge is limited. Discuss the types of problems to which this situation could lead, and suggest possible ways of dealing with these problems.

5. Although the CASE concept—automated tools to increase programmer productivity—seems valid, many IS organizations do not use integrated (I-CASE) packages. Discuss the barriers to the increasing use of I-CASE.

6. Some programmers feel that implementing the capability maturity model (CMM) will make the development process too rigid and bureaucratic, thus stifling their creativity. Discuss the pros and cons of this issue.

7. Building Internets and intranets can be a fast and fairly easy process. Based on Chapters 5, 6, and 14, can you explain why? What are the long-term implications of this for IS professionals? end-user systems developers? outsourcing firms?

## EXERCISES

1. Contact a major information systems consulting firm and ask for literature on its systems development life cycle methodology (or search for it on the Internet). Compare and contrast the proprietary methodology to the eight-stage SDLC described in this chapter.

2. Identify and interview some end users who develop systems at their organizations. Ask them whether their organization has any standards for documenting and testing systems developed by end users. If it has such policies, are they enforced? If not, what do the end-users do to ensure the accuracy and maintainability of the systems they develop?

3. Contact an administrator at your university or work place and find out what purchased systems, especially larger ones, are in use. Do these systems meet the organization's needs, or are some important features missing that should be included in these packages?

4. Contact IS managers at some large organizations, and find out whether their IS developers use any CASE tools. If the IS units use an integrated (I-CASE) tool, what things do they like and dislike about it? If the units do not use I-CASE tools, what are the reasons for not using them?

## GROUP ASSIGNMENTS

1. Divide the class into two teams. Have both teams collect information on SAP's integrated enterprise management software, and on Oracle's comparable software packages. After the teams analyze the data, stage a debate with one team arguing that the SAP products are the most desirable and with the other team supporting Oracle (or other vendor).

2. Study the IBM systems at the 1996 and 1998 Olympics. Find information about the two systems. Why did the 1996 system fail, and why was the 1998 successful? Assign one group each to 1996 and 1998 and one to the comparisons.

## INTERNET EXERCISES

Note: The URLs included here were current when the book went to press. However, they are subject to change without notice. Please consult the Turban Web site (www.Wiley.com/college/turban2e).

1. Explore the General Electric site at www.ge.com, and then compare it to the Kodak site at www.kodak.com. Try to identify the organizational objectives for these two different types of sites. In the context of these objectives, discuss the advantages and disadvantages of having either: (1) a relatively simple site with limited graphics, or (2) a site that contains extensive graphics.

2. Go to the site at www.geocities.com/~rfinney/case .htm. Follow the links on the page to look at the features of several CASE tool packages. Prepare a report on the capabilities of one or two packages with multiple features.

3. Look at the Netron Renovator site (www.netron.com /products/renovatr.htm). Prepare a report on Netron's approach to, and tools for, renovating and maintaining legacy systems.

# ▼Minicase 1

## Do or Die

A direct cutover from an existing system to a new one is risky. If the system is critical to the operations of the organization, the risks are magnified to an even higher level. Yet Quantum Corp., a Milpitas, California disk drive manufacturer, did just that—and lived to tell about it. The vendors and consultants on the project claim that this was one of the largest-ever direct cutovers of a distributed business system.

Quantum realized that it had to take action. The limitations of its existing systems were making it difficult for the company to compete in the disk drive market. Sales representatives needed to determine how much of a specific item—in inventory or in production—had not yet been committed to other customers. However, because databases did not share information, it was very difficult for them to get this information.

Quantum was especially interested in a piece of information known as available-to-promise (ATP). This indicates how many units of a given item could be delivered, by what date, to specific locations throughout the world. Calculating these values requires coordination and real-time processing of sales, inventory, and shipping data. If Quantum implemented its new system by phasing in the modules one at a time, the conversion would take much longer. Furthermore, the system would not be able to provide this key information until the end of the transition.

Quantum felt that the business risks of this kind of delay were greater than the technical risks of a direct cutover. The company was also concerned about possible resistance in some departments if the full implementation took a long time. The departments had enough autonomy to implement other systems if they lost confidence in the new system and, if they did, Quantum would lose the benefits of having an integrated system.

Although the actual cutover took eight days, the planning and preparation required over three years. The initial analysis was in October 1992, and Quantum sent out requests for proposals in April 1993. In March 1994, the company chose Oracle, Hewlett-Packard, and Price Waterhouse as its business partners on the project.

Quantum created a project team of 100 people, composed of key employees from each business unit and the IS department, and moved them into a separate building. The purchase of the disk drive business of Digital Equipment Corp. in October 1994, which brought in another set of legacy applications and assorted hardware platforms, set the project back by about four months.

In February 1995, Quantum started a public relations campaign with a three-day conference for the users. The following month, "project evangelists" made presentations at all organizational locations.

In August 1995, the team conducted a systems validation test. It failed. The team worked intensely to solve the problems and then tested the system again for four weeks starting in December 1995. This time, it was successful.

In March 1996, Quantum provided a very extensive and absolutely mandatory user training program. In April, it conducted final briefings, tested the system at all locations throughout the world, and set up a "mission control" center.

At 5 P.M. on April 26, Quantum shut down the old system. Hank Delavati, the CIO, said: "Business as we know it stopped . . . we could not place an order, we could not receive material, we could not ship products. We could not even post cash." Data records from the old system were loaded into the new system. At 4 P.M. on May 5, the new system started up successfully.

Mark Jackson, an executive vice president at Quantum, noted afterward that the relatively large project budget was not the company's primary concern. He said: "We could have figured out how to save 10 percent of the project's cost . . . but that would have raised the risk to an unacceptable level. To succeed, you have to spend the money and take care of the details."

### Questions for Minicase 1

1. Estimate Quantum Corporation's chances of survival if this project failed. Provide some reasons to support your estimate.

2. What did Quantum do to minimize the risks of this direct cutover?

3. Evaluate the claim that, because of business and organizational issues, this direct cutover was less risky than a phased conversion.

4. Under what, if any, circumstances would you recommend this kind of direct cutover for critical operational systems?

5. Discuss the impact of this project on the internal power relationships between the IS department and the other departments in the organization.

6. It appears that Quantum spent a substantial amount of money on this project and was willing to increase spending when it seemed necessary for the success of the project. Discuss the risks of a "whatever it takes" approach.

SOURCE: Condensed from Radosevich, L., "Quantum's Leap," *CIO*, February 15, 1997.

# Minicase 2

## Autodesk Implements SAP R/3

Autodesk is a medium-sized company that produces CAD/CAM (computer-aided design/computer-aided manufacturing) software. Its headquarters are in San Rafael, California, but it has software developers in five locations in the United States and Switzerland, and 20 overseas subsidiaries in Europe and Asia. Because of its rapid growth and a transition to global operations and marketing, it found that its processes and applications systems were no longer adequate to support the business requirements of the organization.

To meet the increasing challenges, Autodesk initiated a project, called "System 2000," to reengineer its business processes and information systems. Key objectives of the project included:

▶ *Global capabilities.* Software should support multiple languages and currencies, as well as country-specific tax calculations and accounting procedures.

▶ *Data available in real-time*—on customers, orders, product availability, pricing, costs, profitability, and so on.

▶ *Speed up processes.* Customer orders should be handled within ten minutes, and products should be shipped within 24 hours.

▶ *Inventory management*—close to 100 percent accuracy.

▶ *Software should run on a client/server architecture.*

Autodesk established a team, with representatives from all major functional areas, to evaluate how to meet these goals. The team selected the R/3 system from SAP as the driving software.

A large-scale project, which replaces many existing systems, could be very risky. Therefore, Autodesk decided to implement the parts of the system that offered the most potentially favorable results in a short period. The initial implementation included the following modules: financial accounting, controlling, materials management, and sales/distribution.

To further reduce the risks, the project team created a model of the company, which it called "Mini-Autodesk," to be a pilot for the implementation. Within this model company, the team reengineered and then tested 25 core processes, with 240 subprocesses. After this it installed R/3 in Mini-Autodesk, as a precursor to subsequent installations throughout the company. The team accomplished the actual, companywide implementation in only six months.

Bill Kredel, Autodesk's CIO, indicates that the inventory costs savings alone covered the cost of the R/3 system in less than six months. Implementing the new systems simplified the company's operations: for example, it reduced the number of order codes for different versions of the company's products from 20,000 to 1,600. The new system also reduced internal conflicts about defining materials codes, product lines, and customer accounts, by forcing different business units to conform to the standards in the R/3 system.

The next step in the implementation is to expand into electronic commerce. Autodesk plans to integrate the R/3 with an Internet system, to improve communications with customers, suppliers, dealers, and employees.

### Questions for Minicase 2

1. Discuss the advantages, disadvantages, and risks of a "quick hit" strategy, as used by Autodesk, versus a more prolonged transition to a new system.

2. Discuss the advantages and disadvantages of a purchased system that forces different organizational units to change their business processes and policies to conform to the new system. Identify situations where this standardization would be desirable, and other situations where it would be undesirable.

3. Can you think of circumstances where a company might want to install an enterprise management system, such as SAP's R/3, even though it appears that this would be significantly *more* expensive than developing a comparable system in-house? Discuss.

SOURCE: Condensed from Buck-Emden, R., and J. Galimow, *SAP R/3 System: A Client/Server Technology,* Harlow, England, 1996, and from *CIO,* June 15, 1996. Also, www.sap.com, 1998.

# REFERENCES AND BIBLIOGRAPHY

1. Baskerville, R. L., and J. Stage, "Controlling Prototype Development through Risk Analysis," *MIS Quarterly,* December 1996.

2. Bordoloi, B., et al., "A Framework to Limit Systems Developers' Legal Liabilities," *Journal of MIS,* Spring 1996.

3. Edberg, D. T., and B. J. Bowman, "User-Developed Applications: An Empirical Study of Application Quality and Developer Productivity," *Journal of Management Information Systems,* Summer 1996.

4. Edmondson, G., et al., "Silicon Valley on the Rhine," *Business Week,* November 3, 1997.

5. Gross, N., "Software," *Business Week,* January 13, 1997.

6. Harrison, D., "Southwest Air Gives Netizens Ticket to Ride," *Interactive Week,* Nov. 17, 1997.

7. Henderson, J. C., and J. G. Cooprider, "Dimensions of I/S Planning and Design Aids: A Functional Model of CASE Technology," *Information Systems Research,* September 1990.

8. Herbsleb, J., et al., "Software Quality and the Capability Maturity Model," *Communications of the ACM,* June 1997.

9. Kehoe, R., and A. Jarvis, *ISO 9000-3: A Tool for Software Product and Process Improvement,* New York: Spring-Verlag, 1996.

10. Keil, M., "Pulling the Plug: Software Project Management and the Problem of Project Escalation," *MIS Quarterly,* Dec. 1995.

11. Kendall, K. E., and J. E. Kendall, *Systems Analysis and Design,* 4th ed., Englewood Cliffs, NJ: Prentice Hall, 1998.

12. Linthicum, D. S., "The End of Programming," *Byte,* August 1995.

13. Marcos, M. L., and R. I. Benjamin, "Change Agentry—The Next IS Frontier," *MIS Quarterly,* Dec. 1996.

14. Marlow, E., *Web Visions,* New York: Van Nostrand Reinhold, 1997.

15. Newman, M., and R. Sabherwal, "Determinants of Commitment to Information Systems Development: A Longitudinal Investigation," *MIS Quarterly,* March 1996.

16. Newman, M., and R. Sabherwal, "Determinants of Longitudinal Investigation," *MIS Quarterly,* March 1996.

17. Panko, R. R., and R. H. Halverson, "Are Two Heads Better than One (at Reducing Spreadsheet Errors)?" *Proceedings of the Second AIS Americas Conference on Information Systems,* August 16–18, 1996.

18. Rescigno, G., and W. Batt, "Understanding Object Oriented Analysis by the Structured Analyst," *Journal of Computer Information Systems,* Spring 1997.

19. Rockart, J. F., and L. S. Flannery, "The Management of End-User Computing," *Communications of the ACM,* October 1983.

20. Ross, J. A., "Spreadsheet Risk," *Harvard Business Review,* September–October 1996.

21. Ruber, P., "Today's Power Tools," *Beyond Computing,* March 1998.

22. Subramanian, G. H., and G. E. Zarnich, "An Examination of Some Software Development Efforts and Productivity Determinants in I-CASE Tool Projects," *Journal of MIS,* Spring 1996.

23. Tractinsky, M., and S. L. Jarvenpaa, "Information Systems Design Decisions in a Global v Domestic Context, *MIS Quarterly,* December 1995.

24. Wang, S., "Toward Formalized Object-Oriented Management Information Systems Analysis," *Journal of MIS,* Spring 1996.

25. Wood-Harper, A. T., et al., "How We Profess: The Ethical Systems Analyst," *Communications of the ACM,* March 1996.

26. Yourdon, E., *Modern Structured Analysis,* Englewood Cliffs, NJ: Prentice-Hall, 1989.

**CHAPTER 15**

# Managing Information Resources, Control, and Security

## Learning Objectives

*After studying this chapter, you will be able to:*

1. Recognize the difficulties in managing information resources.

2. Understand the role of the IS department and its relationships with end users.

3. Discuss the role of the chief information officer.

4. Compare the alternative structures of the IS department.

5. Recognize information systems' vulnerability and the possible damage from malfunctions.

6. Distinguish between security measures and disaster planning and recovery.

7. Describe the Year 2000 issue, its magnitude, and possible solutions.

# CONNECTIONS

## THE BOMBING OF THE WORLD TRADE CENTER

ON FRIDAY, FEBRUARY 26, 1993, a bomb ripped apart the subbasement of the 110-story World Trade Center in New York City. The bombing, which killed six people and injured over 1,000, forced an evacuation of the huge office complex. Apart from the human tragedy, hundreds of resident financial firms were thrown into a state of chaos because they could not return to their offices for several weeks. Most of these companies faced the enormous and unprecedented task of restoring their networked distributed computer systems in order to resume business.

The problem was further complicated because those companies that used distributed systems relied on LANs. In contrast with users in mainframe environments, who typically have standard procedures and a plan for recovery from disasters, the users of LANs are generally unprepared. In a distributed environment it is not enough to find a recovery site with backup systems, an approach typically used in mainframe environments. Instead, it is necessary to find office space where workers can reestablish their networks to resume continuous transactions. This means it is necessary to equip a temporary space with computers (primarily PCs), communication lines, and LANs. In addition, the employees need full office support, ranging from telephone lines and faxes to duplicating machines. To prepare ahead of time for a disaster to a distributed system may require very costly arrangements.

Another issue that complicated the situation for several of the firms in the center was the unclear assignment of security responsibility between the central IS department and various end-user departments such as finance or marketing.

Fortunately for those companies that had planned ahead, the transition was fairly smooth, even though they were operating in a distributed environment. For example, Dean Witter Financial Services Group enacted a contingency plan, using an office equipped with PCs that was set aside earlier for emergency use. By the following Monday, the company was running business as usual.

Dean Witter Reynolds' temporary setup after the World Trade Center bombing

Other corporations were less fortunate. Some restored their networks but could not secure telephone lines. Others had problems with their networks and, in some cases, even their contingency plans were not effective. For example, several companies with arrangements for a temporary site as a backup to their mainframe operations either had problems accessing the tapes from the vaults in the World Trade Center building or found the tapes contaminated by smoke particles.

Disaster recovery experts say that most of the companies were simply unprepared, but the situation was especially severe for LAN-based companies. Ken Brill, president of a data-center infrastructure consulting company in Santa Fe, NM, summarized the situation: "I can protect a 20,000-square-foot data center, but how do I safeguard a million square feet of office space?"

SOURCE: Based on McPartlin, J. P., and J. C. Panettieri, "Towers Without Power," *Information Week*, March 8, 1993.

# ▶ 15.1 THE INFORMATION SYSTEMS DEPARTMENT

## INFORMATION RESOURCES

Throughout this book, we have seen that information systems are used to increase productivity and help achieve quality. Most large, many medium, and even some small corporations around the world are strongly dependent on IT. Their information systems have considerable strategic importance. However, the World Trade Center case showed us that information systems can become a dangerous and expensive problem when they break down.

The opening case demonstrates that:

▶ Information resources that include computers, networks, programs, and data are vulnerable to unforeseen attacks.

▶ Protection of networked systems can be a complex issue.

▶ The responsibility for protecting and managing information resources is divided among the IS department and end users; the division may not be clear.

▶ Only a few companies used disaster planning and recovery at the World Trade Center.

The actions of people or of nature can cause an information system to function in a way different from what was planned. It is important, therefore, to know how to ensure the continued operation of an IS and to know what to do if the system breaks down.

These and similar issues are of concern to the management of information resources, the subject of the concluding chapter of this book.

*Information resources management (IRM)* encompasses all activities related to the planning, organizing, acquiring, maintaining, and controlling of IT resources. IT resources are very diversified and they include, according to Ross et al. (1996), technology assets, personnel assets, and IT relationship assets. IRM activities are conducted both at the information systems department (ISD) level and in the end-user departments, units, and teams. Here we look at the following IRM issues: (1) the distributions of IRM between the ISD and the end users, (2) how the ISD and the end users work together, (3) the role of the chief information officer, (4) the management of the ISD, (5) the information security and control issue, and (6) the Year 2000 problem.

## THE IS DEPARTMENT IN THE ORGANIZATION

The management of information resources is divided among the ISD and end users as discussed in Chapter 2. The division of activities between the two parties depends on many factors, beginning with the amount and nature of duties involved in IRM, and ending with outsourcing policies. Decisions about the roles of each party are made during the IS planning and are not discussed here (for some insights see Wysocki and DeMichiell [1996]).

A major decision that must be made by senior management is where the ISD is to report. Partly for historical reasons, a common place to find the ISD is in the accounting or finance organization. In such situations, the ISD normally reports to the controller or the vice president of finance. The ISD might also report to one of the following: (1) a vice president of administration, (2) the senior executive of an operating division, (3) an executive vice president, or (4) the CEO. In the latter case, the **chief information officer (CIO)**\* usually carries the title of vice president. The actual title may be vice president of IS, vice president of administrative services, or vice president of information resources. The four possibilities are marked and shown in Figure 15.1.

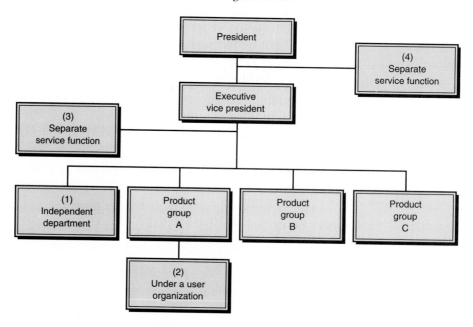

**FIGURE 15.1**  Four alternative locations for the ISD.

The *title* of CIO and the position to whom this person reports reflect, in many cases, the degree of support being shown by top management to the ISD. The *reporting relationship* of the ISD is important in that it reflects the focus of the department. If ISD reports to the accounting or finance area, there is often a tendency to emphasize accounting or finance applications at the expense of those in the marketing, production, and logistical areas. To be most effective, the ISD needs to take as broad a view as possible.

The *name* of the ISD is also important. Originally the Data Processing (DP) department, the name was changed to the Management Information Systems department and then to the Information Systems Department (ISD). Today we find, in addition to ISD, names such as Information Services Department, Information Technology Department, Corporate Technology Center, and so on. In very large organizations the ISD is a division, or even an independent corporation (such as at the Bank of America and Boeing). The name depends on the IT role, its size, and so forth. When the information function is given the title of information resources management or information technology, the organization often has the charter to do much more than just provide information system services. In these instances, the department usually involves itself in strategic corporate planning, in BPR, in electronic commerce, and sometimes in selling IS services to other organizations.

---

\*To show the importance of the IS area, some organizations call the director of IS a CIO, chief information officer, similar to chief financial officer (CFO) and chief operating officer (COO). Typically, only senior vice presidents receive such titles. CIOs exist mainly in organizations that are heavily dependent on IT, such as banks, insurance companies, and airlines.

The increased role and importance of IT and its management by both a centralized unit and end users requires careful understanding of the manner in which ISD is organized as well as the relationship between the ISD and end users. These topics are discussed next.

## THE IS DEPARTMENT AND END USERS

It is extremely important to have a good relationship between the ISD and end users; unfortunately, these relationships are not always optimal. The development of end-user computing and outsourcing was motivated—in part—by the poor service that end users felt they received from the ISD. Conflicts occur for several reasons, ranging from the fact that priorities of the ISD may differ from those of the end users to a simple lack of communication. Also, there are some fundamental differences between the personalities, cognitive styles, educational backgrounds, and gender proportion of the end users versus the ISD staff (more males in the ISD) that could contribute to conflicts. An example of such conflict is illustrated in the following *IT at Work* scenario.

*IT At Work* **MINNESOTA'S DEPARTMENT OF TRANSPORTATION VIOLATES PROCEDURES**

*U*SING IT

...in Public Service

The Department of Transportation in Minnesota had come across a hybrid PC system that would allow road surveys to be accomplished with less time and effort, and greater accuracy. The system would require two people to conduct a survey instead of the usual three, and because of the precision of the computer-based system, the survey could be done in half the time.

The department ran into a problem because the ISD for the State of Minnesota had instituted standards for all PCs that could be purchased by any state agency. Specifically, a particular brand of IBM PC was the only PC purchase allowed, without going through a special procedure. The red tape, as well as the unwillingness of the ISD to allow any deviation from the standard, caused a great deal of frustration.

As a last resort, the Department of Transportation procured the hybrid PC and camouflaged the transaction as engineering equipment for conducting surveys. From that point on, its staff decided they would do what they needed to do to get their jobs done, and the less the ISD knew about what they were doing, the better. When asked why they behaved this way, the administrator of the Department of Transportation simply said, "We have to do it this way because the ISD will either try to stop or hold up for a long period of time any decision we want to make, because they just are not familiar enough with the issues that we are facing in our department."

**For Further Exploration:** What are the organizational risks when the Transportation Department takes this attitude? How can the conflict be resolved? ▲

SOURCE: Author's experience.

Generally, the IS organization can take one of the following four approaches toward end-user computing:

1. *Let them sink or swim.* Don't do anything—let the end user beware.
2. *Use the stick.* Establish policies and procedures to control end-user computing so that corporate risks are minimized.

3. *Use the carrot.* Create incentives to encourage certain end-user practices that reduce organizational risks.
4. *Offer support.* Develop services to aid end users in their computing activities.

Each of these responses presents the IS executive with different opportunities for facilitation and coordination.

## FOSTERING THE ISD/END-USER RELATIONSHIP

This paragraph sums up why my BA is in Finance and my MBA in IS. Any individual who can bridge the interpersonal gap between IS and accounting is worth his weight in gold.
— *Mike Rewald*

The ISD is a service organization that manages the IT infrastructure needed to carry on end-user applications, so a partnership between the ISD and the end user is a must, as indicated by Wysocki and DeMichiell (1996). This is not an easy task since the ISD is basically a technical organization that may not understand the business and the users. The users, on the other hand, may not understand information technologies. In order to foster the relationship between the two, organizations can employ several strategies. For example, the ISD of the Housing Development Board in Singapore uses the following strategies (per Tung and Turban [1996]):

▶ Introducing a special end-user support unit that coordinates quality assurance, data administration and office systems.
▶ Introducing an end-user training and development unit that is responsible for training and certification in IS software packages.
▶ Giving high priority and visibility to end-user computing.
▶ Training ISD employees to understand the business.
▶ Implementing a special conflict resolution team that quickly handles ISD/end-user conflicts.
▶ Recognizing the CIO as a member of the top executive organizational team.
▶ Empowering ISD employees to make decisions on the spot in order to minimize interferences and delays to end users.
▶ Developing a malfunction recovery plan for each end-user unit to minimize interferences with work when a system fails.

The ISD and end users also employ three common strategies used in many other organizations: the steering committee, service level agreements, and the information center.

## THE STEERING COMMITTEE

The corporate **steering committee** is a group of managers representing various organizational units that is set up to establish IT priorities and to ensure that the ISD is meeting the needs of the enterprise. The committee's major tasks are:

1. *Direction setting.* In linking the corporate strategy with the IT strategy, planning is the key activity.
2. *Rationing.* The committee approves the allocation of resources for and within the information systems organization.
3. *Structuring.* The committee deals with how the ISD is positioned in the organization. The issue of centralization–decentralization of IT resources is resolved by the committee.

4. *Staffing.* Key IT personnel decisions involve a consultation-and-approval process made by the committee. Notable is the selection of the CIO.

5. *Communication.* It is important that information regarding IT activities flows freely.

6. *Evaluating.* The committee should establish performance measures for the ISD and see that they are met. This includes the initiation of service level agreements.

## SERVICE LEVEL AGREEMENTS

**Service level agreements (SLAs)** are formal agreements regarding the division of computing responsibility among end users and the ISD. Such divisions are based on a small set of critical computing decisions that are made by *end-user management.* The way managers make these decisions commits them to accept certain responsibilities and to turn over others to the ISD. Since end-user management makes the decisions, they are free to choose the amount and kind of support they feel they need. This freedom to choose provides a check on the ISD. If the ISD is to meet its objectives of coordinating and facilitating end-user computing, it must develop and deliver support services to meet these needs. An effective approach to managing end-user computing must achieve both facilitation and coordination. Service level agreements do this by (1) defining computing responsibilities, (2) providing a framework for designing support services, and (3) allowing end users to retain as much control as possible over their own computing.

An approach based on SLA offers several other advantages. First, it reduces "finger pointing" by clearly specifying responsibilities. When a microcomputer malfunctions, everyone knows who is responsible for fixing it. Second, it provides a structure for the design and delivery of end-user services by the ISD. Third, incentives are created for end users to improve their computing practices, thereby reducing computing risks to the firm. By clearly stating what has to be done to qualify for better IS service, end-user management is in a better position to make trade-offs in its computing decisions. Finally, SLA provides a means for the ISD to coordinate end-user computing. The same staff people who provide support services also monitor and report on end-user activities. Some end-user computing will remain outside these coordination efforts, but those activities are recognized to be the responsibility of end-user managers.

Establishing SLA requires four steps:

1. Defining levels.
2. Dividing computing responsibility at each level.
3. Designing the details of the service levels.
4. Implementing service levels.

The process of establishing and implementing SLA may be applied to each of the *major* computing resources: hardware, software, people, data, networks, and procedures.

Due to the introduction of new tools for simplifying the task of monitoring enterprise networks, more attention has recently been given to service level agreements, according to *Communications Week,* May 1997. This is especially important when SLAs are made between outsourcing vendors and end users. Because most networks involve multivendor and multiproduct configuration, measuring network performance by its components accurately is critical.

### THE INFORMATION CENTER

An interesting change in organizational structure related to computer technology is the introduction of the **information center (IC)**.* The concept was conceived by IBM, Canada, as a response to the increased number of end-user requests for new computer applications. This demand created a huge backlog in the IS department, and users had to wait several years to get their systems built. Today, the ICs concentrate on end-user support with PCs, client/server applications, and the Internet/intranet.

The IC is set up to help users get certain systems built quickly and provide tools that can be employed by users to build their own systems. The concept of the IC, furthermore, suggests that the few people working as a team or as individuals in the center should be especially oriented toward the user in their outlook. This attitude should be shown in the training provided by the staff at the center and in the way the staff helps users with any problems they might have. There can be one or several ICs in an organization that report to the ISD and/or the end-user departments (see Fuller and Swanson [1992]).

The IC can also be used as a place to house a few "commandos," or "guerrilla warriors" who can be available to build important user systems very quickly. The staff of the IC can construct systems, like standalone decision support systems, much more quickly than such systems can be built with traditional software and systems development methods. Because of the impact of such systems and the rapidity with which they can be made available, the ISD often gets a very good reputation in the user community.

**PURPOSES AND ACTIVITIES.** The three main functions of an IC are (1) to provide assistance to end users in dealing with computing problems, (2) to provide general technical assistance, and (3) to provide general support services. Typical activities associated with these functions are shown in Box 15.1 (see page 653).

The importance of ICs may diminish in the future as users become more computer literate, end-user software development tools become more friendly, hardware becomes more reliable, and intelligent diagnostic and training tools provide some of the services provided by ICs. Finally, management views ICs as cost centers whose benefits are intangible and difficult to justify.

The steering committee, SLAs, and ICs help to foster the ISD/end-user relationship that also depends, to a large extent, on the manner in which the ISD is structured and managed.

## ▶ 15.2 MANAGING THE IS DEPARTMENT

Managing the ISD is similar to managing any other organizational unit. The unique aspect of the ISD is that it operates as a service department in a rapidly changing environment, thus making projections and planning difficult. The equipment purchased and maintained by the ISD is scattered over the entire enterprise, adding to the complexity of ISD management. Here we will discuss only two issues. The first issue describes the CIO and his or her relationship with other managers and executives. The second issue deals with the internal structure of the ISD and how it interacts with end users.

---

*Other names for similar organizational units are *information resources center* and *users' service center*.

## *A Closer Look* BOX 15.1

### ACTIVITIES OF INFORMATION CENTERS

END-USER COMPUTING:

- Training and education.
- Assisting in application development.
- Assisting in the selection of intranet applications.
- Providing debugging assistance.
- Identifying networking requirements.
- Consulting with the user to determine whether a particular application is appropriate for end-user development.
- Providing a formal means for users' communication with management and with the traditional data processing staff.
- Cooperating with database administrators to improve access to shared data resources.
- Generating a catalog or library of existing applications for future use.
- Assisting in Internet/intranet applications.

TECHNICAL ASSISTANCE:

- Directing security and control issues.
- Providing guidance in the selection of hardware and software.

- Helping in the selection and evaluation of application packages and other development tools.
- Assisting in software installation and updates.
- Assisting in using query and report languages and/or packages.
- Assisting in the installation and use of hardware.
- Assisting in the installation and use of communication devices.
- Establishing database (or file) backups, recovery, and archive guidelines.

GENERAL SUPPORT SERVICES:

- Providing clearing house functions for receiving and disseminating information on relevant personal computing issues.
- Establishing a "hotline" for interrupt-driven user requests for information on software, hardware, or application systems.
- Chairing user group meetings on a regular and ad hoc basis.

SOURCE: Compiled from Jacobson and Cardullo (1983).

### THE CHIEF INFORMATION OFFICER

The changing role of the ISD highlights the fact that the CIO is becoming an important member of the organization's top management team.

**THE ROLE OF THE CIO.** A survey conducted in 1992 found that the prime role of the CIO is to align IT with the business strategy (see Table 15.1 see page 654). Now, CIO roles are also supplemented by activities related to the Internet and electronic commerce.

Two recent roles of the CIO are decision making about enterprise software and outsourcing.

- Enterprise software (such as SAP, Baan, and PeopleSoft [see Chapter 8]) will have a strong impact on the ISD as well as on the entire organization (like in BPR and in productivity improvement). The evaluation, selection, and implementation of SAP-like packages are a new role for the CIO.

- Outsourcing, which was discussed in Chapters 12 and 13, is also an important topic related to the job of the CIO. Note that both outsourcing and SAP reduce the IS staff and thus may diminish the importance of the ISD.

Information technology has become a strategic resource for many organizations. Coordinating this resource requires strong IT leadership and ISD/end-user cooperation within the organization. Therefore, the CIO-CEO relationships are crucial for effective, successful utilization of IT, especially in organizations that greatly depend on IT, where the CIO joins the top management "chiefs" group.

### *Table 15.1* The Roles of the CIO

CIOs were asked to name their top priority in helping to improve their organizations' efficency and performance. The results are:

| | |
|---|---|
| Align technology with the business strategy | 24% |
| Implement state-of-the-art solutions | 12% |
| Provide and improve information access | 12% |
| Enhance customer service | 9% |
| Create links within the organization | 7% |
| Train and empower employees | 7% |
| Create links with external customers | 6% |
| Enhance current systems | 4% |
| Support business reengineering | 4% |
| Act as change agent/catalyst | 4% |
| Educate business units about IT | 3% |
| Evaluate emerging technologies | 3% |
| Implement standard systems and architecture | 3% |
| Others | 2% |

SOURCE: Kiely (1992), p. 30. Reprinted through the courtesy of *CIO*. © 1992 CIO Communications Inc.

The chief information officer is a member of the corporate *executive committee*, which has responsibility for strategic business planning and response, the most important committee in any organization. Its members include the chief executive officer and the senior vice presidents. The executive committee provides the top-level oversight for the organization's information resources. It guides the IS steering committee, usually chaired by the CIO. Related to the CIO is the emergence of the chief knowledge officer (see Chapter 10). A CIO may report to the CKO, or the same person may assume both roles, especially in smaller companies.

According to Sitonis and Goldberg (1997) and McNurlin and Sprague (1998), the major challenges facing CIOs are:

▶ Understanding the complexity inherent in doing business in a competitive, global environment.

▶ Managing the accelerating pace of technological change.

▶ Understanding that IT may reshape organizations which could become technology driven.

▶ Realizing that often IT is the primary enabler of business solutions.

▶ Knowing the business sector in which your company is involved.

▶ Understanding your company's organizational structure and operating procedures.

▶ Using business, not technology, terms when communicating with corporate management.

▶ Gaining acceptance as a member of the business management team.

▶ Establishing the credibility of the IS department.

▶ Increasing the technological maturity of the company.

► Creating a vision of the future of IT and selling it.

► Implementing IT architecture that will support the vision.

To handle such challenges the CIO must acquire new skills, such as:

► Understanding the business.

► Maintaining technology competency.

► Understanding networking on a global basis.

► Facilitating change.

► Managing safety and security.

► Providing education to other executives.

► Understanding and setting industry standards.

► Balancing priorities.

The diversity of skills is evidenced in the high salaries of CIOs (up to $1,000,000/year in large corporations) and the high turnover of CIOs (see McGee [1996] and Sitonis and Goldberg [1997]). As technology becomes central to business, the CIO becomes a key mover in the ranks of upper management. For example, in a large financial institution executive committee meeting, modest requests for additional budgets by the senior vice presidents for finance and for marketing were turned down after hours of debates. But, at the same meeting the CIO's request for a tenfold addition was approved in only a few minutes.

It is interesting to note that CEOs are acquiring IT skills. According to *InfoWorld* (June 16, 1997), a company's best investment is a CEO that knows technology. If both the CIO and the CEO have the necessary skills for the Information Age, their company has the potential to flourish.

Two factors stand out in those organizations that tend to be successful computer users: the high degree of support shown for the ISD by the organization's senior management, and the consequent image the ISD has in the organization. Some of the actions CEOs can take are obvious, and others are subtler. Among the more obvious are (1) putting the IS VP's office next to the CEO's, (2) supporting an executive training series in IT and attending the sessions in an uninterrupted manner, and (3) elevating the head of ISD to the level of vice president reporting directly to the CEO. Less obvious is that a CEO can use the organizational reward system to show support for IT. Budget commitment to the ISD, plus the undertaking of a major IS project affecting the entire organization, are other signs of support for IT.

## THE ORGANIZATIONAL STRUCTURE OF THE IS DEPARTMENT

**MANAGERIAL EFFICIENCY VERSUS USER SERVICE.** IS departments can be organized in many different ways. A major factor that determines the structure of the ISD is the balancing of two conflicting goals: achieving efficiency of the ISD resources while providing a high level of service to the end users.

The traditional ISD was composed of three major components: system analysis, programming, and operations. However, as shown in Minicase 2, Chapter 2 (Mead Corporation), today's **internal IS structure** includes several other components such as networks, technology planning, decision support, and the

Internet and intranets. The first issue is how to organize the systems analysts and programmers who constitute a major portion of the ISD.

From an efficiency standpoint, an IS manager would probably prefer to structure the system development part as an independent unit of the ISD. The beauty of this organization is that it is very flexible. If new systems development requirements come along, it is easy to assign persons from the analysis and programming pool to do the job. The difficulty, especially from a user perspective, is that the analysts and programmers assigned to certain projects may have no experience with the problem or familiarity with the user's area. In addition, they are often an unknown quantity, since they may not have worked with this user before.

To ease these problems some organizations add a special subunit called *user liaison*. The people in this subunit, who should be experienced senior analysts, are responsible for working with the user organizations *to determine* their information needs and with the analysts and programmers *to meet* these needs. One problem with this structure is that there is often confusion about the responsibilities and authority of the user liaison and those of the users or systems analysts.

Another structure that tries to balance managerial need and user requirements is a matrix organization, as shown in Figure 15.2. In a matrix organization, there is a pool of programmers and a pool of analysts. These people report to a supervisor with a title such as manager of programming. In addition there is a unit composed of project leaders who report to a supervisor with a title such as manager of project development. This organizational form is very efficient, but it has the disadvantage that each analyst and programmer has two bosses because each reports to a project leader for project-related matters and to the manager of their function for overall matters (broken lines). The functional manager evaluates performance with input from project leaders with whom an individual has worked. This system has high potential for difficulties when conflicts arise. For this reason there is a trend toward an end-user-oriented structure and a virtual IS organization.

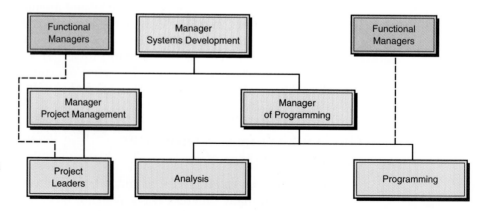

**FIGURE 15.2** Information systems organization in matrix form.

### END-USER-ORIENTED STRUCTURE AND THE VIRTUAL IS ORGANIZATION.

An end-user-oriented structure could be prominent in future ISD. This is a team-based organization in which analysts, programmers, and other IS professionals with diverse skills are grouped into teams, each to service a particular user

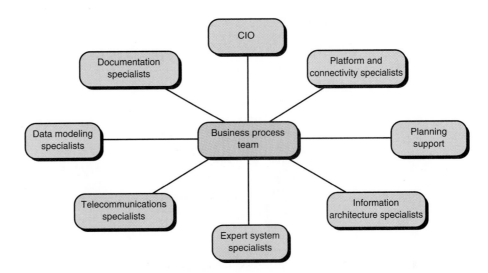

**FIGURE 15.3** Model of business process team drawing from specified sources for virtual team members.

group. A team may not have all the skills it needs so it may bring in a "virtual" team member for specialized skills as needed (see Figure 15.3). Such a structure is referred to as a *virtual IS organization.*

The **virtual IS organization** can be arranged in several configurations, one of which is shown in Box 15.2 (see page 658). A team-based structure is also shown in the Mead Corporation Minicase in Chapter 2.

The team-based structure can be difficult to manage when slack resources may exist in one team while another is overloaded. The shortcoming is balanced by the fact that over time, the systems development personnel become very familiar with the business function they are serving. Furthermore, by working together on many projects, team members form many strong interpersonal relationships, which usually work well to ease communication and system implementation problems.

An alternative team-based structure is known as *centers of excellence,* in which IS members are organized into teams according to their technical expertise. Transforming IS organizations into centers of excellence is not simple and may fail if appropriate measures are not taken. Clark et al. (1996) provides valuable insights based on the experience of Bell Atlantic Corporation.

**CENTRALIZATION VERSUS DECENTRALIZATION.** Computing equipment and IS activities are distributed among end users throughout the organization. The ISD is basically a centralized unit, but some of its activities such as systems development and maintenance can be decentralized. In a decentralized structure, some ISD employees are assigned to user departments so they are closer to local problems and get to know the business better. Decentralization of IS personnel is frequently combined with the decentralization of supporting resources.

The major advantages of centralization are ease of planning and control. Consolidation of financial and operating data for evaluation and reporting purposes, management of personnel and personnel changes, and the location of more and specialized people in one place allow flexibility and increase productivity. In contrast, in a decentralized structure it is easier to control cost, since the IS employees are more empowered because they know better the end-user problems and response time is shorter.

# A Closer Look BOX 15.2

## THE VIRTUAL IS ORGANIZATION

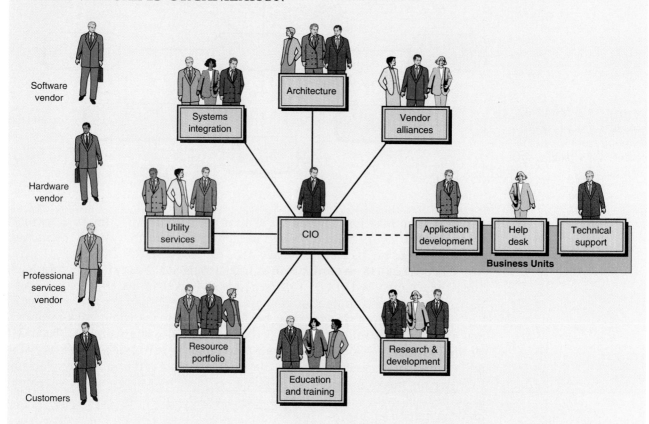

Virtual IS organizations are emerging in several different forms, but generally the central IS staff works with departmental IS (end-user computing), business managers, outside vendors, and even corporate customers. This changes the nature and culture of the traditional IS hierarchical structure to more open, interactive struture (see the figure above).

Some characteristics of the new structure are the following:

▶ **IS personnel**, particularly those involved in application development, are incorporated into the business units, sometimes even reporting directly to the business managers.

▶ **The boundary of the virtual IS organization** doesn't end at the company's walls; vendors and customers may be part of the team as well.

▶ **The rest of the virtual IS organization** is coming to rely on what is left of central IS functions to develop an overall technical architecture that meets the needs of the entire corporation.

▶ **Central IS plays a prominent role as technology scouts**, surveying the stream of new products and technologies for those most suitable for the company.

SOURCE: Condensed from Moad (1994). Figure reprinted with permission of *Datamation*, February 1, 1994. © 1994 by Cahners Publishing Company.

**Centralized IS** resources tend to be best suited to the following situations:

1. Information systems designed for top-level management (executive information systems).
2. Organizationwide, homogeneous functions such as payroll, personnel, and common accounting functions.
3. When rapid response time of development is not required.
4. Organizational functions that are too small to justify appropriate computing equipment and/or staff.
5. Situations where integration of information technically requires centralized processing (e.g., airline reservations).

Decentralized IS resources tend to be best suited to the following situations:

1. Situations where rapid and flexible response time for development and/or production is required.
2. Situations where the systems are unique and heterogeneous to a decentralized operation (a conglomerate may own several companies that are in different businesses).
3. Information systems for which there is no compelling reason to centralize (a standalone inventory system).

Finally, in a decentralized environment it is more difficult to provide high levels of computing security, a topic we discuss next.

# 15.3 IS VULNERABILITY AND COMPUTER CRIMES

Information resources are scattered throughout the organization. Furthermore, employees travel with and take home corporate computers and data. Information is transmitted to and from the organization and among the organization's components. IS physical resources, data, software, procedures, and any other information resources may therefore be vulnerable in many places at any time.

Before we describe the specific problems with information security and proposed solutions here is some of the terminology of the field:

▶ *Backup*—an extra copy of the data and/or programs kept in a secured location(s).
▶ *Decryption*—transformation of scrambled code into readable data after transmission.
▶ *Encryption*—transformation of data into scrambled code prior to its transmission.
▶ *Exposure*—the harm, loss, or damage that can result if something has gone wrong in an information system.
▶ *Fault tolerance*—the ability of an information system to continue to operate (usually for a limited time and/or at a reduced level) when a failure occurs.
▶ *Information system controls*—the procedures, devices, or software that attempt to ensure that the system performs as planned.
▶ *Integrity (of data)*—a guarantee of the accuracy, completeness, and reliability of data. System integrity is provided by the integrity of its components and their integration.

▶ *Threats (or hazards)*—the various dangers to which a system may be exposed.

▶ *Risk*—the likelihood that a threat will materialize.

▶ *Vulnerability*—given that a threat exists, the susceptibility of the system to harm caused by the threat.

## INFORMATION SYSTEMS BREAKDOWNS

In the opening case, we illustrated the danger faced by businesses that are dependent on computers when a disaster strikes. Information systems, however, can be damaged for many other reasons. The following incidents illustrate representative cases of breakdowns in information systems.

**INCIDENT 1.** A Tarrant County, TX jury found Donald Gene Burleson guilty of harmful access to a computer, a third-degree felony with a maximum penalty of 10 years in prison and a $5,000 fine. Jurors were told that Burleson planted a virus in the computer system that was used to store records at USPA & IRA Company, a Fort Worth–based insurance and brokerage firm. The virus was programmed like a time bomb and was activated two days after Burleson was fired from his job. The virus eliminated 168,000 payroll records, which resulted in a one-month delay in issuing employee payroll checks. (SOURCE: Condensed from *Stars and Stripes,* September 22, 1988.)

**INCIDENT 2.** On Sunday, May 8, 1988, a fire disabled a major Illinois Bell switching center in Hinsdale, IL. The outage affected the voice and data telecommunications of more than one-half million residents and hundreds of businesses during a period ranging from two days to three weeks. The major effects on businesses were the following:

▶ Dozens of banks were hindered in cashing checks and transferring funds.

▶ At least 150 travel agencies were hindered in their ability to make reservations and print tickets.

▶ About 300 automated teller machines were shut down.

▶ Most of the cellular phone and paging systems in the area were disrupted.

▶ Hundreds of companies were hindered in their communications, both inside and outside the immediate area.

The business cost was conservatively estimated to be $300 million.

**INCIDENT 3.** For almost two weeks in the spring of 1993, a seemingly legitimate automated teller machine (ATM) operating in a shopping mall near Hartford, Connecticut, gave customers apologetic notes that said "sorry, no transactions are possible." Meanwhile, the machine recorded the card numbers and the personal identification numbers that hundreds of customers entered in their vain attempts to make the machine dispense cash. On May 8, 1993, while the dysfunctional machine was still running in the shopping mall, thieves started tapping into the 24-hour automated teller network in New York City. Using counterfeit bank cards encoded with the numbers stolen from the Hartford customers, the thieves removed about $100,000 from the accounts of innocent customers.

The criminals were successful in making an ATM machine do what it was supposedly not designed to do: breach its own security by recording bank card numbers together with personal security codes.

**INCIDENT 4.** According to the *Wall Street Journal*, the Bank of Tokyo–Mitsubishi branch in New York and the National Westminster Bank in the UK reported losses of tens of millions of dollars in 1996 due to errors in their options and derivatives trading models. In both cases the losses went undetected for a long time. In the first case the trading model was found to be inaccurate, in the second case the model was fed inaccurate data.

**INCIDENT 5.** In 1996 the *Los Angeles Times* reported: "Computer makes $850-million error in Social Security." The glitch shortchanged about 700,000 Americans in retirement benefits and had been undetected for almost 23 years until it was discovered during an audit in 1994. While the newspaper blamed the computer, the fault was actually that of the programmers who were unable to properly automate the complex computations of the benefits. It took more than three years to fix the problem.

**INCIDENT 6.** Netscape security is aimed at scrambling sensitive financial data such as credit card numbers and sales transactions so they would be safe from break-ins, by using a powerful 128-bit program. However, using 120 powerful workstations and two supercomputers, in 1996 a French student breached the encryption program in eight days, demonstrating that no program is 100 percent secure.

**INCIDENT 7.** In April 1998 an Israeli teenager was arrested on suspicion of hacking his way into the Pentagon and 700 other sensitive computer systems worldwide. The story was published on the cover page of the *L.A. Times* (April 27, 1998). The hacker became a folk hero in Israel and has already received several lucrative employment contracts.

**INCIDENT 8.** In 1994 a Russian hacker (who did not know English!) broke into a Citibank electronic fund transfer system and stole more than $10 million by wiring it to accounts around the world. Since then, Citibank, a giant bank that moves half a trillion dollars a day, increased its security measures, requiring customers to use electronic devices that create new passwords very frequently.

These incidents illustrate the vulnerability of information systems and diversity of causes of computer security problems and the substantial damage to organizations.

## SYSTEMS VULNERABILITY — HOUSE ALARM

Information systems are made up of many components that may be in several locations. Thus, each information system is vulnerable to many potential *hazards*. Figure 15.4 presents a summary of the major threats to the security of an information system. Figure 15.4, along with the incidents just described, illustrates that information systems can be very vulnerable (see page 662).

The **vulnerability** of information systems is increasing as we move to a world of networked computing. Theoretically, there are hundreds of points in a

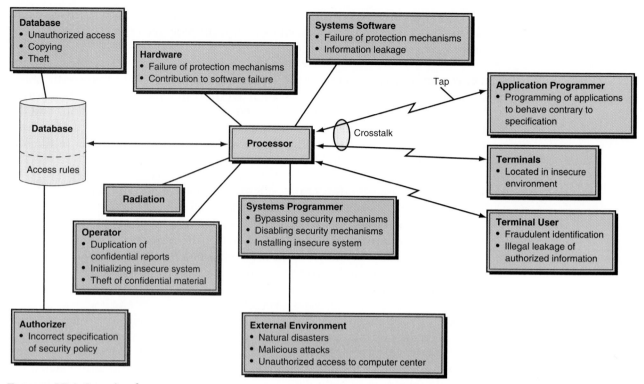

**FIGURE 15.4 Security threats.** (*Source*: Gallegos and Wright [1988], p. 12. © [1988], Warren, Gorham & Lamont. Used with permission.)

corporate information system that can be subject to some threat. These threats can be classified as *unintentional* or *intentional.*

**UNINTENTIONAL THREATS.** These can be divided into three major categories: human errors, environmental hazards, and computer system failures (Box 15.3).

## *A Closer Look* BOX 15.3

### A COMPUTER MALFUNCTION CRIPPLES SINGAPORE

On October 12, 1994, at 11:31 A.M. two-thirds of Singapore's telecommunication system was knocked out of business. Telephones, fax machines, wireless telephones, pagers, and credit cards were useless. The disruption lasted about five hours. Hundreds of thousands of people were affected.

What happened? Singapore was expanding its telecommunication system. In order to cope with increased demand, new computer software was installed. But the new software was unable to do its job. A software bug corrupted one of two common channel signaling systems that link the country's 28 telephone exchanges. Within minutes the problem spread to 26 exchanges. Unfortunately, there were no software backups. A complete disaster was prevented only because the older system was still running side-by-side with the new one. The deputy president of Singapore Telecom, Mr. Lee, said that this sort of thing should not happen. "Unfortunately," he added, "with computer software, a certain amount of risk has to be taken, and it is the job of Singapore Telecom to make sure that this risk is kept at a minimum."

Several computer problems result from *human error.* Errors can occur in the design of the hardware and/or information system. They can also occur in the programming, testing, data collection, data entry, authorization, and instructions. Human errors contribute to the vast majority of control- and security-related problems in many organizations.

*Environmental hazards* include earthquakes, hurricanes, severe snow, sand, storms, floods, tornadoes, power failures or strong fluctuations, fires (the most common hazard), defective air-conditioning, explosions, radioactive fallout, and water cooling system failures. In addition to damage from combustion, computer resources can incur damage from other elements that accompany fire, such as smoke, heat, and water. Such hazards may disrupt normal computer operations and result in long waiting periods and exorbitant costs while computer programs and data files are recreated. *Computer systems failures* can be the result of poor manufacturing or defective materials. Unintentional malfunctions can happen for other reasons ranging from lack of experience to incompatibility of software as was demonstrated in Box 15.3.

**INTENTIONAL THREATS.**   Computer systems may be damaged as a result of intentional actions. Here are some examples:

▶ Theft of data.

▶ Inappropriate use of data (e.g., manipulating inputs).

▶ Theft of mainframe computer time.

▶ Theft of equipment and/or programs.

▶ Deliberate manipulation in handling, entering, processing, transferring, or programming data.

▶ Labor strikes, riots, or sabotage.

▶ Malicious damage to computer resources.

▶ Destruction from viruses and similar attacks.

▶ Miscellaneous computer abuses and crimes.

## COMPUTER CRIMES

According to the Computer Security Institute, 64% of all corporations experienced computer crimes in 1997 (*Los Angeles Times,* March 5, 1998, p. D2). The number, magnitude, and diversity of computer crimes and abuse are increasing rapidly. Lately, increased fraud related to the Internet and electronic commerce is in evidence.

**TYPES OF COMPUTER CRIMES AND CRIMINALS.**   In many ways, computer crimes resemble conventional crimes. They can occur in four ways. First, the computer can be the *target* of the crime. For example, a computer may be stolen or destroyed, or a virus may destroy data. Second, the computer can be the *medium* of the attack by creating an environment in which a crime or fraud can occur. For example, false data are entered into a computer system to mislead individuals examining the financial condition of a company. Third, the computer can be the *tool* by which the crime is perpetrated. For example, a computer is used to plan a crime, but the crime does not involve a computer. Fourth, the computer can be used to *intimidate* or *deceive.* For instance, a stockbroker stole

$50 million by convincing his clients that he had a computer program with which he could increase their return on investment by 60 percent per month.

Crimes can be performed by *outsiders* who penetrate a computer system (frequently via communication lines) or by *insiders* who are authorized to use the computer system but are misusing their authorization. **Hacker** is the term often used to describe outside people who penetrate a computer system. A **cracker** is a *malicious hacker* who may represent a serious problem for a corporation. Computer criminals, whether insiders or outsiders, have a distinct profile and are driven by several motives (see Box 15.4). Ironically, many employees fit this profile, but only a few of them are criminals. Therefore, it is difficult to predict who will be a computer criminal. Criminals use various and frequently innovative attack methods.

---

## *A Closer Look*    BOX 15.4

### THE COMPUTER CRIMINAL—PROFILE AND MOTIVATION

**THE PROFILE**

**Sex:** White males between the age of 19-30 with no criminal record. (Women tend to be accomplices.)

**Occupation:** Application programmer, system user, clerical personnel, student, or manager.

**IQ:** High IQ, bright, personable, and creative.

**Appearance:** Outwardly self-confident, eager, and energetic.

**Approach to work:** Adventurous, willing to accept technical challenge, and highly motivated.

**THE MOTIVATION**

**Economic:** Urgent need for money (e.g., due to extravagant lifestyle, gambling, family sickness, or drug abuse).

**Ideological:** Deceiving the establishment is viewed as fair game because "the establishment deceives everyone else."

**Egocentric:** Beating the system is fun, challenging, and adventurous. Egocentricity seems to be the most distinguishing motive of computer criminals.

**Psychological:** Getting even with the employer who is perceived by the employee as cold, indifferent, and impersonal.

**Other:** The employee views himself as a "borrower" of software, for example, not a thief.

SOURCE: Based on Bologna (1987).

---

**METHODS OF ATTACK.** Two basic approaches are used in deliberate attacks on computer systems: data tampering and programming techniques.

**Data tampering** ("data diddling") is the most common approach and is often used by insiders. It refers to entering false, fabricated, or fraudulent data into the computer or changing or deleting existing data. For example, to pay for his wife's drug purchases, a savings and loan programmer transferred $5,000 into his personal account and tried to cover up the transfer with phony debit and credit transactions.

Computer criminals also use *programming techniques* to modify a computer program, either directly or indirectly. For this crime, programming skills and knowledge of the targeted systems are essential. **Programming fraud** schemes appear under many names as shown in Table 15.2. Due to their frequency, viruses merit special mention here.

We use antivirus software (McAfee) extensively at my work place. I've seen what viruses can do to a hard drive.

— *Dave Gehrke*

**VIRUSES.** The most publicized attack method, the **virus** receives its name from the program's ability to attach itself to other computer programs, causing them to become viruses themselves. A virus can spread throughout a computer system very quickly. Due to the availability of public-domain software, widely used

*Table 15.2* **Programming Fraud Schemes**

| Programming Technique | Definition |
|---|---|
| Virus | Secret instructions inserted into programs (or data) that are innocently run during ordinary tasks. The secret instructions may destroy or alter data, as well as spread within or between computer systems. |
| Worm | A program which replicates itself and penetrates a valid computer system. It may spread within a network, penetrating all connected computers. |
| Trojan horse | An illegal program, contained within another program, that "sleeps" until some specific event occurs, then triggers the illegal program to be activated and cause damage. |
| Salami slicing | A program designed to siphon off small amounts of money from a number of larger transactions, so the quantity taken is not readily apparent. |
| Super zapping | A method of using a utility "zap" program that can bypass controls to modify programs or data. |
| Trap door | A technique that allows for breaking into a program code, making it possible to insert additional instructions. |

telecommunications networks, and the Internet, viruses can also be spread to many organizations as shown in the previous incidents. Viruses are known to spread all over the world. Some of the most notorious viruses are "international," such as Michelangelo, Pakistani Brain, and Jerusalem.

When a virus is attached to a legitimate software program, the program becomes infected without the owner of the program being aware of the infection (see Figure 15.5). Therefore, when the software is used, the virus spreads, causing damage to that program and possibly to others. Thus, the legitimate software is acting as a *Trojan horse*.

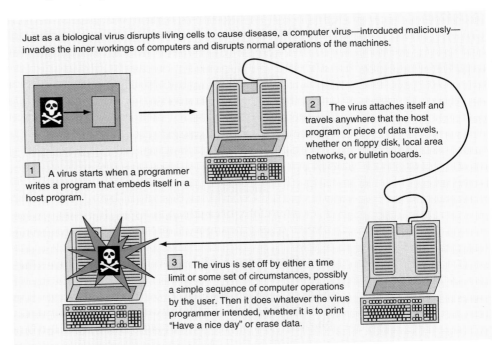

**FIGURE 15.5** How a computer virus can spread. (*Source*: Courtesy of Thumbscan.)

**REPRESENTATIVE FEDERAL LAWS DEALING WITH COMPUTER CRIME.** According to the FBI, an average robbery involves $3,000; an average white-collar crime involves $23,000; but an average computer crime involves about $600,000. The following are some federal statutes dealing with computer crime.

▶ Counterfeit Access Device and Computer Fraud Act (passed in October 1984).

▶ Computer Fraud and Abuse Act (1986).

▶ Computer Abuse Amendment Act of 1994 (prohibits transmission of viruses).

▶ Computer Security Act of 1987.

▶ Electronic Communications Privacy Act of 1986.

▶ Electronic Funds Transfer Act of 1980.

## ▶ 15.4 PROTECTING INFORMATION SYSTEMS

### SECURITY AND THE ROLE OF CONTROLS

Knowing about major potential threats to information systems is important, but understanding ways to defend against these threats is equally critical. Defending information systems is not a simple or inexpensive task for the following reasons:

▶ Hundreds of potential threats exist.

▶ Computing resources may be situated in many locations.

▶ Many individuals control information assets.

▶ Computer networks can be outside the organization and difficult to protect.

▶ Rapid technological changes make some controls obsolete as soon as they are installed.

▶ Many computer crimes are undetected for a long period of time, so it is difficult to "learn from experience."

▶ People tend to violate security procedures because the procedures are inconvenient.

▶ Many computer criminals who are caught go unpunished, so there is no deterrent effect.

▶ The amount of computer knowledge necessary to commit computer crimes is usually minimal. As a matter of fact one can learn hacking, for free, on the Internet.

▶ The cost of preventing hazards can be very high. Therefore, most organizations simply cannot afford to protect against all possible hazards.

▶ It is difficult to conduct a cost-benefit justification for controls before an attack occurs since it is difficult to assess the value of a hypothetical attack.

Therefore, organizing an appropriate defense system is one of the major activities of any prudent IS or functional manager who controls information resources.

Protection of IT is accomplished by inserting controls—defense mechanisms—intended to *prevent* accidental hazards, *deter* intentional acts, *detect* problems as early as possible, *enhance damage recovery*, and *correct problems*. Controls can be integrated into hardware and software during the system development phase (a most efficient approach). They can also be implemented once the system is in operation or during its maintenance. The important point is that defense should stress *prevention*; it does no good after the crime. Since there are many threats, there are also many defense mechanisms. In this section, we describe some representative controls.

Controls are designed to protect all the components of an information system, specifically data, software, hardware, and networks.

**DEFENSE STRATEGIES: HOW DO WE PROTECT?**  The selection of a specific strategy depends on the objective of the defense and on the perceived cost-benefit. The following are the major *defense strategies:*

1. *Controls for prevention and deterrence.* Properly designed controls may prevent errors from occurring, deter criminals from attacking the system, and better yet, deny access to unauthorized people. Prevention and deterrence are especially important where the potential damage is very high.
2. *Detection.* It may not be economically feasible to prevent all hazards, and deterring measures may not work. Therefore, unprotected systems are vulnerable to attack. Like a fire, the earlier it is detected, the easier it is to combat and the less is the damage. Detection can be performed in many cases by using special diagnostic software.
3. *Limitation.* This means to minimize losses once a malfunction has occurred. Users typically want their systems back in operation as quickly as possible. This can be accomplished by including a *fault-tolerant system* that permits operation in a degraded mode until full recovery is made. If a fault-tolerant system does not exist, a quick (and possibly expensive) recovery must take place.
4. *Recovery.* A recovery plan explains how to fix a damaged information system as quickly as possible. Replacing rather than repairing components is one route to fast recovery.
5. *Correction.* Correcting damaged systems can prevent the problem from occurring again.

The defense strategy may involve the use of several controls as described next.

## GENERAL AND APPLICATION CONTROLS

A typical secured system is shown in Figure 15.6. Insiders who want to access the computer follow the footsteps until they reach a computer. The outsiders access via the telephone or networks. Note the physical shield that the user must pass through (follow the footsteps). Solid lines with arrows show the nonphysical (logical, administrative) controls. There are several other types of controls; some are intended to protect against human errors, while others are designed to protect against natural forces.

**Information systems controls** can be divided into two major groups: general (system) controls and application controls. **General controls** are established to protect the system regardless of the specific application. For example, protecting hardware and controlling access to the data center are independent of the specific application. **Application controls** are safeguards that are intended to protect specific applications.

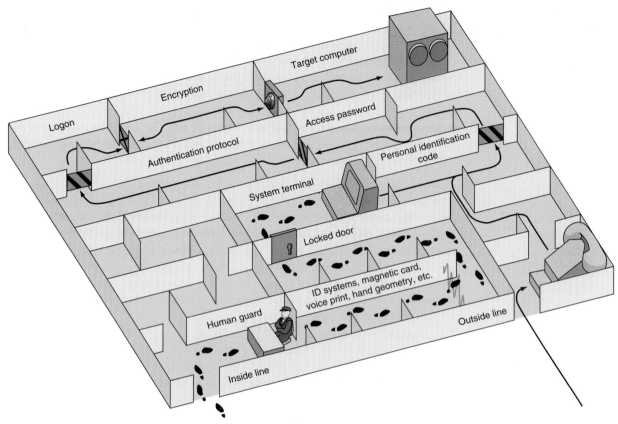

**FIGURE 15.6 The defense.** (*Source*: Joe Lertola.© 1983 *Discover* magazine.)

**GENERAL CONTROLS.** The major categories of general controls are physical controls, access controls, data security controls, communications (networks) controls, and administrative controls.

***Physical Controls.*** Physical security refers to the protection of computer facilities and resources. This includes protecting physical property such as computers, data centers, software, manuals, and networks. Physical security is the first line of defense and usually the easiest to construct. It provides protection against most natural hazards as well as against some human hazards. Appropriate physical security may include several controls such as the following:

1. Appropriate design of the data center. For example, the site should be non-combustible and waterproof.
2. Shielding against electromagnetic fields.
3. Good fire prevention, detection, and extinguishing systems, including sprinkler system, water pumps, and adequate drainage facilities. A better solution is fire-enveloping Halon gas systems.
4. Emergency power shutoff and backup batteries, which must be maintained in operational condition.
5. Properly designed, maintained, and operated air-conditioning systems.
6. Motion detector alarms that detect physical intrusion.

***Access Control.*** Access control is the restriction of unauthorized user access to a portion of a computer system or to the entire system. To gain access, a user must first be *authorized*. Then, when the user attempts to gain access, he or she must be *authenticated*. Access to a computer system basically consists of three steps: (1) physical access to a terminal, (2) access to the system, and (3) access to specific commands, transactions, privileges, programs, and data within the system. Access control software is commercially available for large mainframes, minicomputers, personal computers, local area networks, and dial-in communications networks. Access control to the network is executed through firewalls and will be discussed later in this section.

Access procedures match every valid user with a unique user identifier (UID). They also provide an authentication method to verify that users requesting access to the computer system are really who they claim to be. User identification can be accomplished when the following identifies each user:

▶ Something only the user *knows,* such as a password.

▶ Something only the user *has,* for example, a smart card or a token.

▶ Something only the user *is,* such as a signature, voice, fingerprint, or retinal (eye) scan. It is implemented via biometric controls.

A **biometric control** is defined as an "automated method of verifying the identity of a person, based on physiological or behavioral characteristics." The most common biometrics are the following.

▶ ***Photo.*** The computer takes a picture of your face and matches it with a pre-stored picture. In 1997, this method was successful in correctly identifying users except in cases of identical twins. (e.g., see www.mrpayroll.com).

▶ ***Fingerprints.*** Each time a user wants access, matching a fingerprint against a template containing the authorized person's fingerprint (see Figure 15.7) identifies him or her.

▶ ***Hand geometry.*** Similar to fingerprints except the verifier uses a television-like camera to take a picture of the user's hand. Certain characteristics of the

**FIGURE 15.7** Fingerprint identification control system.

hand (e.g., finger length and thickness) are electronically compared against the information stored in the computer.

▶ **Blood vessel pattern in the retina of a person's eye.** A match is attempted between the pattern of the blood vessels in the back-of-the-eye retina that is being scanned and a prestored picture of the retina.

▶ **Voice.** A match is attempted between the user's voice and the voice pattern stored on templates.

▶ **Signature.** Signatures are matched against the prestored authentic signature. This method can supplement a photo-card ID system.

▶ **Keystroke dynamics.** A match of the person's keyboard pressure and speed against prestored information.

▶ **Others.** Several other methods exist such as *facial thermography* and *iris scan*.

**Data Security Controls.**  Data security is concerned with protecting data from accidental or intentional disclosure to unauthorized persons, or from unauthorized modification or destruction. Data security functions are implemented through operating systems, security access control programs, database/data communications products, recommended backup/recovery procedures, application programs, and external control procedures. Data security must address the following issues: *confidentiality of data, access control, critical nature of data*, and *integrity of data*.

Two basic principles should be reflected in data security.

1. **Minimal privilege.** Only the information a user needs to carry out an assigned task should be made available to him or her.

2. **Minimal exposure.** Once a user gains access to sensitive information, he or she has the responsibility of protecting it by making sure only people whose duties require it obtain knowledge of this information while it is processed, stored, or in transit.

**Data integrity** is the condition that exists as long as accidental or intentional destruction, alteration, or loss of data *does not* occur. It is the preservation of data for its intended use.

**Communications (Network) Controls.**  Network protection is becoming extremely important as the use of the Internet, intranets, and electronic commerce increases. We will discuss this topic in more detail later in this section.

**Administrative Controls.**  While the previously discussed controls were technical in nature, administrative controls deal with issuing guidelines and monitoring compliance with the guidelines. Representative examples of such controls include the following:

▶ Appropriately selecting, training, and supervising employees, especially in accounting and information systems.

▶ Fostering company loyalty.

▶ Immediately revoking access privileges of dismissed, resigned, or transferred employees.

▶ Requiring periodic modification of access controls (such as passwords).

▶ Developing programming and documentation standards (to make auditing easier and to use the standards as guides for employees).

▶ Insisting on security bonds or malfeasance insurance for key employees.

▶ Instituting separation of duties, namely dividing sensitive computer duties among as many employees as economically feasible in order to decrease the chance of intentional or unintentional damage.

▶ Holding periodic random audits of the system.

*Other General Controls.* Several other types of controls are considered general. Representative examples include the following:

▶ *Programming controls.* Errors in programming may result in costly problems. Causes include the use of incorrect algorithm or programming instructions, carelessness, inadequate testing and configuration management, or lax security. Controls include training, establishing standards for testing and configuration management, and enforcing documentation standards.

▶ *Misunderstandings or misinterpretations.* Manuals are often a source of problems because they are difficult to interpret or may be out of date. Accurate writing, standardization updating, and testing are examples of appropriate documentation control. Intelligent agents can be used to prevent such problems.

▶ *System development controls.* System development controls ensure that a system is developed according to established policies and procedures. Conformity with budget, timing, security measures, and quality and documentation requirements must be maintained.

**APPLICATION CONTROLS.** General controls are intended to protect the computing facilities and provide security for hardware, software, data, and networks. However, general controls do not protect the *content* of each specific application. Therefore, controls are frequently built into the applications (that is, they are part of the software) and are usually written as validation rules. They can be classified into three major categories: *input controls, processing controls,* and *output controls.*

*Input Controls.* Input controls are designed to prevent data alteration or loss. Data are checked for accuracy, completeness, and consistency. Input controls are very important; they prevent the GIGO (garbage-in, garbage-out) situation. Examples of input controls are the following:

▶ *Completeness.* Items should be of a specific length (e.g., nine digits for a Social Security number). Addresses should include a street, city, state, and zip code.

▶ *Format.* Formats should be a standard form. For example, sequences must be preserved (zip code comes after an address).

▶ *Range.* Only data within a specified range are acceptable. For example, zip code ranges between 10,000 to 99,999, the age of a person cannot be larger than say, 120, and hourly wages cannot exceed $50.

▶ *Consistency.* Data collected from two or more sources need to be matched. For example, in medical history data, males cannot be pregnant.

***Processing Controls.*** Processing controls ensure that data are complete, valid, and accurate when being processed and that programs have been properly executed. These programs allow only authorized users to access certain programs or facilities and monitor the computer's use by individuals.

***Output Controls.*** Output controls ensure that the results of computer processing are accurate, valid, complete, and consistent. By studying the nature of common output errors and the causes of such errors, management can evaluate possible controls to deal with problems. Also, control ensures that outputs are sent only to authorized personnel.

## NETWORK PROTECTION AND FIREWALLS

Due to the increased importance of the Internet and intranets, and the fact that security is considered a major limitation to the wide use of the Internet and electronic commerce, we discuss network protection here in detail. Security issues regarding the Internet are also discussed in Chapters 5 and 6.

**SECURITY MEASURES.** Many measures can be employed to protect the Internet and electronic commerce (Stallings [1995] and Carrol [1996]). The most common are: access control that includes authentication and passwords, encryption, cable testers, and firewalls.

*Access Control.* An access control system guards against unauthorized dial-in attempts. Many companies use an access protection strategy that requires authorized users to dial in with a preassigned personal identification number (PIN). This strategy may be enhanced by a unique and frequently changing password. A communications access control system authenticates the user's PIN and password. Some security systems proceed one step further and accept calls only from designated telephone numbers. Access controls also include biometrics.

*Encryption.* **Encryption** encodes regular digitized text into unreadable scrambled text or numbers to be decoded upon receipt. Encryption accomplishes three purposes: (1) identification (helps identify legitimate senders and receivers), (2) control (prevents changing a transaction or message), and (3) privacy (impedes eavesdropping). A widely accepted encryption algorithm is the Data Encryption Standard (DES), produced by the U.S. National Bureau of Standards. Many software products are available for encryption. *Traffic padding* can further enhance encryption. Here a computer generates random data that are intermingled with real data, making it virtually impossible for an intruder to identify the true data.

Encryption is used extensively in electronic commerce for protecting payments and privacy. Public key/private key systems were described in Chapter 6. For further discussion see www.sra.com.

To ensure secure transactions of the Internet, VeriSign and VISA developed encrypted digital certification systems for credit cards that allow customers to make purchases on the Internet without giving their credit card number. Cardholders create a digital version of their credit card, VeriSign confirms validity of the buyer's credit card, and then it issues a certificate to that effect—even the merchants do not see the credit card number. The SET (see Chapter 6) has now been adopted as the standard for credit card transactions on the Internet.

***Cable Testers.***  A popular defense of LANs is troubleshooting. For example, a *cable tester* can find almost any fault that can occur with LAN cabling. Another protection can be provided by *protocol analyzers,* which allow the user to inspect the contents of information packets as they travel through the network. Recent analyzers use *expert systems,* which interpret the volume of data collected by the analyzers. Some companies offer integrated LAN troubleshooting (a tester and an intelligent analyzer).

**FIREWALLS.**  A *firewall* is a system, or group of systems, that enforces an access control policy between two networks. It is commonly used as a barrier between the secure corporate intranet, or other internal networks, and the Internet, which is assumed to be unsecured (see Chapter 5).

> We use a firewall in our Lockheed Martin intranet to keep "outsiders" out.
> — *Dave Gehrke*

Firewalls are used to implement control access policies. The firewall follows strict guidelines that either permit or block traffic; therefore, a successful firewall is designed with clear and specific rules about what can pass through. Several firewalls may exist in one information system (see Oppliger [1997]).

***Why Firewalls?***  Hacking is a growing phenomenon; even the Pentagon's system, considered a very secure system, experiences more than 250,000 hacker infiltrations per year, many of which are undetected (*Los Angeles Times,* Apr. 24, 1998). It is believed that hacking costs U.S. industry several billion dollars each year. Hacking is such a popular activity that over 80,000 Web sites are dedicated to it and anyone can download, at no cost, tools that are needed to break into computerized systems (see Internet Exercise 11). Firewalls provide the most cost-effective solution the problem of hacking.

Firewalls are also used as a place to store public information. While visitors may be blocked from entering the company networks, they can obtain information about products and services, download files and bug-fixes, and so forth.

An example of how Fidelity Investments uses firewalls to protect privacy and security is shown in the *IT at Work* scenario that follows.

---

*IT At Work*    **FIREWALLS AT FIDELITY INVESTMENT**

**U**SING IT ⟶

...in Finance

Fidelity Investments, the largest U.S. mutual fund company and a stock broker, allows its customers and prospective customers to personalize their access to information available on Fidelity's Web site, including their own account access and transactional information. This service, called Web Express, was pioneered by Fidelity and includes information about balances and stock positions, historical transactions, online registration for new accounts, secure log-ins, real-time quotes on equities, mutual funds, options, and indices, and trading capabilities. A major concern is the protection of security and privacy, a difficult task since even simple transactions require complex operations, including dynamically generated HTML.

The highly secure system is shown in the figure on the next page. The customer enters the Web site, and her or his information is encrypted, using SSL encryption, and passes through the firewall to the Netscape commerce server. The server, acting as a client, sends a transaction remote procedure call (RPC) to a second firewall in a replica-

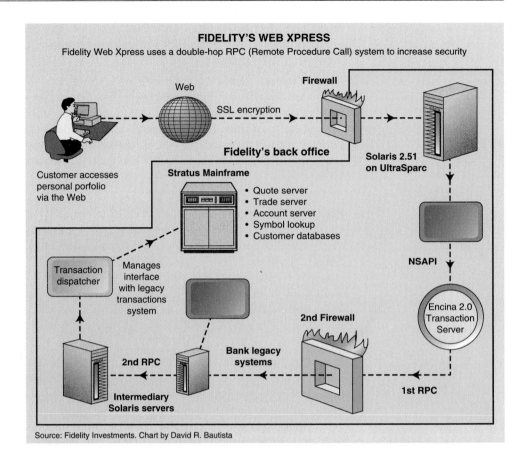

**FIDELITY'S WEB XPRESS**

Fidelity Web Xpress uses a double-hop RPC (Remote Procedure Call) system to increase security

Source: Fidelity Investments. Chart by David R. Bautista

tion server. This server generates a second RPC that goes to a transaction dispatcher that connects it to the mainframe servers and databases. ▲

SOURCE: Information provided by Fidelity Investments, 1998.

*What Firewalls Cannot Do.* Because so many viruses exist (18,000 in 1998, growing by 30% a year according to the National Computer Security Association), firewalls cannot protect against them very well.

Viruses can pass through firewalls, so the question is, What can you do to protect yourself? Some solutions to virus penetrations are provided in Table 15.3 (see page 674). Antivirus software is available (e.g., see www.symantec.com). However, it does not protect against all viruses (see *Internet World*, Jan. 1998, pp. 37–40, and *Interactive Week*, Jan. 19, 1998, p. 34).

*Cost.* Firewalls may cost over $100,000 while less effective systems cost only $20,000. But compared to the possible damage that hackers can cause, the cost is not prohibitive for medium or large organizations.

**Table 15.3** Protecting Against Viruses

| Possible Entrance of Viruses | Countermeasure |
| --- | --- |
| Viruses pass through firewalls undetected (from the Internet) | User must screen all downloaded programs and documents before use |
| Virus resident on networked server; all users at risk | Run virus scan daily; comprehensive backup to restore data; audit trail |
| Infected floppy; local server system at risk; files shared or put on server can spread virus | Virus checker to screen floppies locally |
| Mobile or remote users exchange or update large amounts of data; risk of infection is greater | Scan files before upload or after download; make frequent backups |

SOURCE: Compiled from Nance (1996), p. 171.

## AUDITING INFORMATION SYSTEMS

Controls are established to ensure that information systems work properly. Controls can be installed in the original system; the ISD, end users, or others (e.g., vendors) can add them once a system is in operation. Installing controls is necessary but not sufficient. It is also necessary to answer questions such as the following: Are controls installed as intended? Are they effective? Did any breach of security occur? If so, what actions are required to prevent reoccurrence? These questions need to be answered by independent and unbiased observers. Such observers perform the information system *auditing* task.

An **audit** is an important part of any control system. In an organizational setting, it is usually referred to as a regular *examination* and *check* of financial and accounting records and procedures. Specially trained professionals who may be internal employees or external consultants execute auditing. In the information system environment, auditing can be viewed as an additional layer of controls or safeguards.

**TYPES OF AUDITORS AND AUDITS.** There are two types of auditors (and audits): internal and external. An *internal auditor* is usually a corporate employee who is not a member of the ISD.

An *external auditor* is a corporate outsider. This type of auditor reviews the findings of the internal audit and the inputs, processing, and outputs of information systems. The external audit of information systems is frequently a part of the overall external auditing performed by a certified public accounting (CPA) firm.

IT auditing (which used to be called electronic data processing auditing) can be very broad, so only its essentials are presented here. Auditing looks at all potential hazards and controls in information systems. It focuses attention on topics such as new systems development, operations and maintenance, data integrity, software application, security and privacy, disaster planning and recovery, purchasing, budgets and expenditures, chargebacks, vendor management, documentation, insurance and bonding, training, cost control, and productivity. Several guidelines are available to assist auditors in their jobs. SAS No. 55 is a comprehensive guide provided by the American Institute of Certified Public Accountants. Also, guidelines are available from the Institute of Internal Auditors, Orlando, Florida.

Auditors attempt to answer questions such as these:

▶ Are there sufficient controls in the system?

▶ Which areas are not covered by controls?

▶ Which controls are not necessary?

▶ Are the controls implemented properly?

▶ Are the controls effective; that is, do they check the output of the system?

▶ Is there a clear separation of duties?

▶ Are there procedures to ensure compliance with the controls?

▶ Are there procedures to ensure reporting and corrective actions in case of violations of controls?

Two types of audits are used to answer these questions. The *operational audit* determines whether the ISD is working properly. The *compliance audit* determines whether controls have been implemented properly and are adequate.

**HOW IS AUDITING EXECUTED?** IT auditing procedures can be classified into three categories: auditing *around* the computer, auditing *through* the computer, and auditing *with* the computer.

*Auditing around the computer* means verifying processing by checking for known outputs using specific inputs. Therefore, it is assumed that there is no need to check the processing if the correct output is obtained. The best application of this approach is in systems that produce a limited range of outputs. It is fast and inexpensive, but it may give false results. For example, two errors may compensate for each other, resulting in correct output.

In *auditing through the computer,* inputs, outputs, and processing are checked. This approach is more complex and is usually supported by special tools. Some methods used by auditors are reviewing program logic, test data, and controlling processing and reprocessing.

*Auditing with the computer* means using a combination of client data, auditor software, and client and auditor hardware. It allows the auditor to perform tasks such as simulating payroll program logic using live data.

Auditors use several tools to increase their effectiveness and efficiency. Typical tools are checklists, formulas, and charts. These can be executed manually or computerized. Several computer programs are available to support the auditor's job. These include programs for testing, summarizing, sampling, and matching. Generalized Audit Software (GAS) is a set of programs designed to support auditing. Expert systems and neural computing also can be used to facilitate IT auditing.

**SOURCES OF INFORMATION FOR AUDITOR'S REPORTS.** Auditors gather information from sources such as samples of inputs and outputs, interviews with end users and information systems employees, application programs tested using the auditor's data, and reviews of previous audit reports. Audit results are presented in special reports submitted to the audit committee. These reports call attention to weaknesses and deficiencies and suggest possible remedies. They also highlight positive aspects of the system.

Often it is necessary to trace a transaction through each processing step (when, where, by whom, and so on). The procedure (or document) that describes such tracing is called an **audit trail**. In manual systems it is fairly easy to conduct an audit trail. However, in computerized systems, this may not be so easy. One task of auditing is to provide procedures for audit trails and to execute them when needed.

Auditors and security consultants may try to break into a computer system, in what is called a *simulated attack,* in order to find weak points in the system (see Box 15.5 and Steefora and Cheek [1994]). In some cases, companies hire famous hackers to do the job.

---

## *A Closer Look*  BOX 15.5

### "HACKERS" AUTHORIZED TO BREAK INTO THE STATE OF ILLINOIS INFORMATION SYSTEM

Auditors for the State of Illinois issued a public statement on July 1, 1993, in which they notified the State that they were successful in their mission of breaking into the Central Computer Facility which serves 109 state agencies. The auditors pulled off their mission with "disturbing ease." An authorized hacker, operating from a remote location, was able to break into the system, and read, modify, and delete data such as payroll and prison records. Real hackers could have altered the security structure and negated system integrity. The security system, which was thought to be satisfactory, was enhanced immediately and all known security flaws were fixed.

---

### IMPLEMENTING CONTROLS

Implementing controls in an organization can be a very complicated task, particularly in large, decentralized companies where administrative controls may be difficult to enforce. For example, Lee (1990) suggests that IT auditing be expanded to include end-user computing. Of the many issues involved in implementing controls, two are described here: planning and organizing, and disaster recovery planning.

**PLANNING AND ORGANIZING.** A comprehensive control and security management program must begin with the establishment of a formal, documented, organizationwide *security policy,* endorsed by the highest levels of management in the organization. Such a program was developed by Fine (1983). Fine's *total computer security* can be envisioned as a horizontal beam supported by nine pillars. Three of the pillars are technical issues: *physical security, control,* and *system security.* These three support the integrity and confidentiality of an organization's information systems.

The other six pillars are managerial and they are:

▶ A defined and documented computer security policy.

▶ Standards and procedures.

▶ An assignment of responsibility for computer security.

▶ A personnel security program.

▶ A complete asset-threat inventory.

▶ Introduction of user awareness.

Each of the program's pillars must be carefully planned and properly managed. This may not be a simple task, since the pillars are fairly broad. For example, the responsibility pillar includes 15 topics, each of which can be further broken down into several subtopics.

Developing a security policy begins with a detailed analysis of current equipment, functions performed, data contained, ease of access, security devices, and potential losses. Following this analysis, a policy can be drafted that will focus on employees as well as other assets (hardware, software, and data). Any security policy developed should deal with threats proactively, not just reactively. For each identified threat, the policy should describe not only the necessary protection, but also the actions to be taken if the threats materialize. Stringent policies, surprise audits, and strenuous *security awareness* programs are excellent ways of protecting the company's information systems.

Security administration is the responsibility of both the IS department and the line managers. Line managers are responsible for protecting all resources in their possession and for ensuring that their subordinates are aware of and abide by established security policies and procedures.

## Disaster Recovery Planning

As described, disasters may occur in many places without warning. According to Strassman (1997), the best defense is to be prepared. Therefore, an important element in any security system is the **disaster recovery** plan. Destruction of all (or most) of the computing facilities can cause significant damage as shown in the opening case. Therefore, it is difficult for many organizations to obtain insurance for their computers and information system without showing a satisfactory disaster prevention and recovery plan.

Disaster recovery is the chain of events linking planning to protection to recovery. The following are some key thoughts by Knoll (1986):

▶ The purpose of a recovery plan is to keep the business running after a disaster occurs. Both the IS department and line management should be involved in preparation of the plan. Each function in the business should have a valid recovery capability plan.

▶ Recovery planning is part of *asset protection*. Every organization should assign responsibility to management to identify and protect assets within their spheres of functional control.

▶ Planning should focus first on recovery from a total loss of all capabilities.

▶ Proof of capability usually involves some kind of what-if analysis that shows that the recovery plan is current.

▶ The plan should be kept in a safe place; copies should be given to all key managers; and the plan should be audited periodically.

▶ All critical applications must be identified and their recovery procedures addressed in the plan.

▶ The plan should be written so that it will be effective in case of disaster, not just in order to satisfy the auditors.

Disaster recovery planning can be very complex, and it may take several months to complete (see Butler [1992]). Using special software, the planning job can be expedited (see Box 15.6).

---

## A Closer Look  BOX 15.6

### PC-BASED SOFTWARE PROVIDES A USEFUL DISASTER RECOVERY

Hurricane Hugo hit Charleston, South Carolina, on Friday, September 20, 1989. Electrical power was knocked out for nine days. However, Heritage Trust Credit Federal (a credit union) resumed normal operation by the following Tuesday.

The credit union had developed a disaster recovery plan supported by battery-operated, PC-based software (Recovery Pac, from Computer Security Consultants, Ridgefield, CT). Both internal and external auditors were involved in the plan. When a disaster occurred, the software was to be activated. The software tracks the crisis and suggests the best method of handling it. The software is flexible enough to guide users through problems that have not been anticipated in the tests or the original plan. Other representative software products include the Total Recovery Planning System and PANAMAX.

---

**Disaster avoidance** is an approach oriented toward *prevention*. The idea is to minimize the chance of avoidable disasters (such as fire or other human-caused threats). For example, many companies use a device called uninterrupted power supply (UPS), which provides power in case of a power outage.

**BACKUP ARRANGEMENTS.** In the event of a major disaster, it is often necessary to move a centralized computing facility to another **backup** location. External *hot-site* vendors provide access to a fully configured backup data center. To appreciate the usefulness of such an arrangement, consider the following example:

On the evening of October 17, 1989, a major earthquake hit San Francisco, California, and Charles Schwab and Company was ready. Within a few minutes, the company's disaster plan was activated. Programmers, engineers, and backup computer tapes of October 17th transactions were flown on a chartered jet to Carlstadt, New Jersey. There, Comdisco Disaster Recovery Service provided a hot-site. The next morning, the company resumed normal operation. Montgomery Securities, on the other hand, had no backup recovery plan. On October 18, the day after the quake, the traders had to use telephones rather than computers to execute trades. Montgomery lost revenues of $250,000 to $500,000 in one day.

A less costly alternative arrangement is external *cold-site* vendors that provide empty office space with special flooring, ventilation, and wiring. In an emergency, the stricken company moves its own (or leased) computers to the site.

Physical computer security is an integral part of a total security system. Cray Research, a leading manufacturer of supercomputers (now a subsidiary of Silicone Graphics, Inc.), has incorporated a corporate security plan, under which the corporate computers are monitored automatically and controlled centrally. *Graphic displays* show both normal status and disturbances. All the devices controlled are represented as icons on floor-plan graphics. These icons can change colors (e.g., green means normal, red signifies a problem). The icons can flash as well. Corrective action messages are displayed whenever appropriate. The alarm system includes over 1,000 alarms. Operators can be alerted, even at remote locations, in less than one second.

Of special interest is the disaster planning for Web-based systems, as shown in the following *IT at Work* example.

---

### *IT At Work*    DISASTER PLANNING AND THE INTERNET AT REUTERS LTD.

...in Finance

Reuters is a multinational information delivery corporation with great interest in the Web. One of its subsidiaries, Realty Online (www.moneynet.com) builds and operates online stock trading services for well-known brokerage houses, such as Paine Webber, Inc. If Reuters' information system were to fail outright, it would take more than 15 brokerage houses with it. The costs, not to mention the legal ramifications, can be tremendous. There is very little experience in how to plan for Web-based disasters. Both traditional vendors, such as Comdisco Inc. and Internet-based specialists, such as Exodus Communications, are trying to grab a share of this developing market. Reuters implemented an Internet disaster recovery plan with SunGard Corp. In addition the company operates three redundant Web sites in different locations from coast to coast. In case all of them were to fail, a hot site, which is constantly updated with information from the main Reuters server, would be used to assure continuous operation.

**For Further Exploration:** How safe is this triple level of security? Are Web-based systems like this more vulnerable to disasters? Why? ▲

SOURCE: Condensed from *Interactive Week,* March 9, 1998, p. 7.

---

### RISK MANAGEMENT AND COST-BENEFIT ANALYSIS

It is not economical to prepare protection against every possible threat. Therefore, an IT security program must provide a process for assessing threats and deciding which ones to prepare for and which ones to ignore, reduce, or eliminate. Installation of control measures is based on a balance between the cost of controls and the need to reduce or eliminate threats. Such analysis is basically a **risk management** approach, which helps identify threats and select cost-effective security measures.

Major activities in the risk management process can be applied to existing systems as well as to systems under development. These are summarized in Figure 15.8.

**RISK MANAGEMENT ANALYSIS.** Risk management analysis can be enhanced by the use of DSS software packages. A simplified computation is shown here:

$$\text{Expected Loss} = P1 \times P2 \times L$$

where:

$P1$ = probability of attack
$P2$ = probability of attack being successful
$L$ = loss occurring if attack is successful

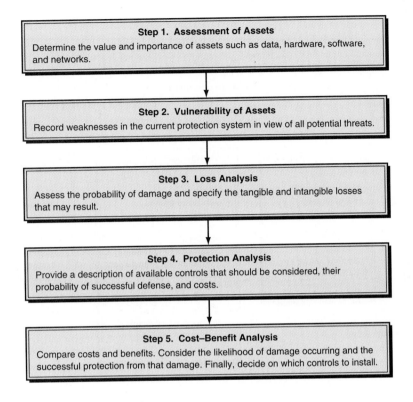

**FIGURE 15.8** The risk management process.

> **Step 1. Assessment of Assets**
> Determine the value and importance of assets such as data, hardware, software, and networks.
>
> **Step 2. Vulnerability of Assets**
> Record weaknesses in the current protection system in view of all potential threats.
>
> **Step 3. Loss Analysis**
> Assess the probability of damage and specify the tangible and intangible losses that may result.
>
> **Step 4. Protection Analysis**
> Provide a description of available controls that should be considered, their probability of successful defense, and costs.
>
> **Step 5. Cost–Benefit Analysis**
> Compare costs and benefits. Consider the likelihood of damage occurring and the successful protection from that damage. Finally, decide on which controls to install.

*Example:*

$$P1 = .02$$
$$P2 = .10$$
$$L = 1,000,000$$

Then, expected loss = $2000.

The expected loss can then be compared against the cost of preventing it. The value of software programs lies not only in their ability to execute complex computations, but also in their ability to provide a structured, systematic framework for ranking both threats and controls.

***How Much to Secure?*** The National Computer Security Center (NCSC) of the Department of Defense published a book containing guidelines for security levels. The government uses these guidelines in its requests for bids on jobs where vendors must meet specified levels. The seven levels are shown in Figure 15.9 (see page 682). The level of security increases from left to right. Vendors are required to maintain a certain security level depending on the security needs of the job.

## CONTROL AND SECURITY IN THE TWENTY-FIRST CENTURY

As we reach the next millenium, computer control and security are receiving increased attention. For example, according to a 1997 Dataquest survey, almost 70 percent of all U.S. corporations have battled computer viruses. Therefore, the lat-

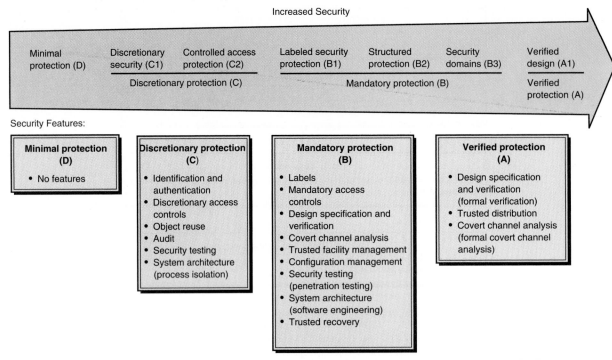

**FIGURE 15.9** The NCSC provides an excellent guideline for determining an appropriate level of security.
(*Source*: Chokhani (1992), p. 68. © 1992, Association for Computing Machinery Inc.)

est technologies need to be employed to protect against viruses. Several important trends including the following are evidenced:

**INCREASING THE RELIABILITY OF SYSTEMS.** The objective here is to use **fault tolerance** to keep the information systems working, even if some parts fail. Compaq Computer and other PC manufacturers provide a feature that stores data on more than one disk drive at the same time. So, if one disk fails or is attacked, the data are still available. Several brands of PCs include a built-in battery that is automatically activated in case of power failure.

**INTELLIGENT SYSTEMS FOR EARLY DETECTION.** Detecting intrusion in its beginning is extremely important, especially for classified information and financial data. Expert systems and neural networks are used for this purpose. For example, a new approach, called *intrusion-detecting systems,* is especially suitable for local area networks and client/server architectures. This approach compares users' activities on a workstation network against historical profiles and analyzes the significance of any discrepancies. The purpose is to detect security violations. The approach is pursued by several government agencies (e.g., Department of Energy and the U.S. Navy) and large corporations (e.g., Citicorp, Rockwell International, and Tracor). It detects other things as well, for example, compliance with security procedures. People tend to ignore security measures (20,000–40,000 violations were reported each month in a large aerospace company in California). The system detects such violations so improvements can be made.

**INTELLIGENT SYSTEMS IN AUDITING.** Intelligent systems are used to enhance the task of IS auditing. For example, expert systems evaluate controls and analyze basic computer systems while neural networks can be used to detect fraud.

**ARTIFICIAL INTELLIGENCE IN BIOMETRICS.** Expert systems, neural computing, voice recognition, and fuzzy logic can be used to enhance the capabilities of several biometric systems.

**EXPERT SYSTEMS FOR DIAGNOSIS, PROGNOSIS, AND DISASTER PLANNING.** Expert systems can be used to diagnose troubles in computer systems and to suggest solutions. The user provides the expert systems with answers to questions about symptoms. The expert system uses its knowledge base to diagnose the source(s) of the trouble. Once a proper diagnosis is made, the computer provides a restoration suggestion. Panas Group sells intranet-based business recovery planning expert systems that are part of a bigger program called Self-Assessment. The program is used to evaluate a corporation's environment for security, procedures, and other risk factors.

**SMART CARDS.** Smart card technology can be used to protect PCs on LANs. An example is Excel MAR 10 (from MacroArt Technology, Singapore), which offers six safety levels. These include identification of authorized user, execution of predetermined programs, authentication, encryption of programs and files, encryption of communication, and generation of historical files. This product can also be integrated with fingerprint facility. The user's smart card is authenticated by the system using signatures calculated with a secret key and the encryption algorithm. Smart cards containing embedded microchips can generate unique passwords (used only once) that confirm a person's identity.

 **15.5 A FUTURE ISSUE**

*The CIO and the ISD focus on many problems as technologies change, new innovations appear, and experience is accumulated. We pointed out many issues throughout the book, ranging from the outsourcing debate to the electronic commerce payment system selection. To conclude the book, we present an interesting issue that may cost organizations dearly if not handled properly. This is the Year 2000 programming issue.*

### THE YEAR 2000 PROBLEM

> Y2K is certainly a buzz-word right now in my company, as programmers scramble to update legacy payroll systems. It's this hype and fear that got management to spend more money in IS and IT.
>
> — *Mike Rewald*

In early 1997, a government computer system sent a notice to a contractor notifying him that he was delinquent on his contract for the Defense Department for the year 97. When the amazed contractor called for an explanation, he was told that the computer thought the contract's completion date was 1900 instead of 2000. This incident is an indication of the problem the world may face due to a computer-programming mistake that created what is known as "the Year 2000 (Y2K) problem."

**THE PROBLEM.** When the clock clicks over to January 1, 2000, many computer systems may crash unless their operating codes are rewritten to recognize

"00" as 2000 and not 1900. When most systems were designed, CPU cycles and storage were at a premium. Programmers saved memory by using a two-digit instead of a four-digit entry for the year, such as "66" for 1966. Twenty to 40 years ago, programmers realized this approach would not work in the next century. However, even when memory and storage became cheaper, there was little interest in dealing with the issue because the typical IS shop was very busy handling program maintenance needed immediately rather than many years in the future. IS personnel were also reluctant to address this issue because of the risk of introducing "bugs" into programs that were functioning adequately and were important to the operations of the organizations. Finally, many optimistically believed that organizations would replace most of the programs that had this problem long before 2000.

> As my company rolls out our new computer system to our stores, we must pay attention to and address those stores whose antiquated systems are not Y2K compliant.
>
> — *Kristin Borhofen*

It turns out that many of these programs were updated again and again—they became "immortal software"—rather than being replaced. Unfortunately, in most cases, the maintenance did not address the date problem. The fact that programming is not standardized—programmers code the same application in different ways—adds to the complexity of the situation. Corrective software is available to analyze programs and help to identify problems in the Y2K area, but it cannot detect all the codes that need maintenance. However, many organizations are unable to take full advantage of whatever capabilities such software does offer, because they do not even have a complete inventory of all the programs they use.

But when 2000 arrives, computers programmed only to recognize a two-digit entry for the year may interpret "00" as 1900, spelling disaster for our computer-dependent society. This computer glitch could eliminate electronic money transfers, mix up retiree database systems, affect our military missions, and even wipe out academic, financial, medical, and personnel records. Chaos could erupt in any system programmed with a year, like airline schedules, driver's license expirations, banking records, and federal benefit check distribution.

**THE SOLUTION.** Several solutions exist to deal with the problem. The following is an example of how one company approaches the problem.

### *IT At Work*    BLUE CROSS/BLUE SHIELD SAVES MILLIONS IN YEAR 2000 PROJECT

*U*SING IT

...in Health Care

Blue Cross/Blue Shield of South Carolina has more than 17 million lines of legacy code. To avoid problems such as "receivable due in the year 2000 might be automatically written off as 100 years past due," management began in 1994 to study the potential impact of the problem and assess possible solutions. The company established a task force whose first job was to determine the size of the problem. They found it to be huge: over 10,000 data sets contained dates in 110 applications. Initially, the proposed solutions were estimated to cost from $30 million to $50 million. However, an innovative approach by the task force resulted in a solution that will only cost $10 to $11 million.

The solution includes three steps: (1) rewrite the legacy system using expanded databases and client/server technology; (2) expand the date field to include a four-digit year/century and modify the code accordingly, and (3) use a special technology that assumes a century of "19" or "20" depending on a comparison with a year between 1900 and 2000.

Furthermore, using a special system development methodology, the company hopes to complete the project by the end of 1998 so a budget system and other applications that project dates a year in advance can be implemented in time. To accomplish the program, the ISD assigned a special Y2K coordinator and special teams. A pilot project was executed first to ensure the reliability of the solution. Then, the teams prioritized the 110 applications so that the most difficult ones were tackled first. A savings of this magnitude helps Blue Cross/Blue Shield provide quality care at a reasonable cost to over 1,000,000 subscribers.

**For Further Exploration:** Why were the most difficult applications tackled first? Evaluate some methods and tools that are used to rectify the problem. ▲

SOURCE: Condensed from Warner, R. W., "Blue Cross/Blue Shield Saves Big Bucks in the Year 2000 Project," *Datamation*, January 1997.

The Y2K problem is very difficult because the CIO may not be able to provide a solution on his own. Take EDI as an example. An enterprise cannot control what its business partners will do to resolve the problem or when they will resolve it. According to the GartnerGroup, there are no standards-based guidelines to follow; therefore, most enterprises using EDI will be affected by the problem. To solve the problem, the GartnerGroup suggests the following strategy:

1. Identify all the EDI systems that are deployed throughout the company including all vendors, platforms, and versions in production.
2. Determine all transactions being exchanged via EDI, the trading partners involved with each transaction, and the target applications within the company.
3. Locate all EDI maps that are in use, identifying versions of standards being supported for each of the transactions and trading partners.
4. Gather all trading partner elements that may be in place with business partners.
5. Create a trading partner Year 2000 information kit. Develop a proposal on how to handle the date problem with each of the transaction sets involved, and send a copy of the proposal to each of the trading partners.

> Year 2000 problems have to be quantified (cost) and then the impact has to be estimated if nothing is done. Then, compare and decide.
>
> *— Dave Gehrke*

Obviously, such an approach takes time and money. And indeed, according to *Datamation*, U.S. companies will spend $71 billion to make their applications Y2K compliant. In addition, because of the costs associated with database repairs, hardware upgrades, and so forth, the total bill could reach $276 billion. The ISD is responsible for handling the problem (for sources of help see Jones [1997], and de Jager [1997]). In 1998, the cost estimates reached $600 billion. One area that may result in large expense is the potential lawsuits. Because of the interdependency among organizations (e.g., suppliers, service providers), there is a need for a comprehensive preparation (see Hock [1998]). For example, carefully drafted contracts with customers will help head off lawsuits and will reduce the liability if one does develop.

A similar problem, the *Euro Bug* (*Business Week*, March 30, 1998, p. 18) exists in Europe, where the currencies of at least nine countries will be replaced in 2002 by one currency. The cost to fix the problem may exceed $175 billion.

Soon, Y2K will be history and new and challenging problems will face the ISD. No one knows what they will be, but as the relative importance of IT increases, so does our dependence on computerized systems. Managing information resources is becoming more difficult and important with time; that is why every manager, in any organization, must learn about IT and its management.

# CONCLUSION TO THE BOOK

Throughout this book we have emphasized the important role of IT in the modern organization. We have illustrated how IT is helping foster *connections* among the various units and employees inside organizations as well as between organizations and their business partners. In this chapter we highlighted the connections between the ISD and the rest of the organization. McLeod (1995) developed an integrative IRM feedback model that summarizes this connection. According to this five-part model, shown in Figure 15.10, IRM provides an organization with a competitive advantage within its business environment (#1).

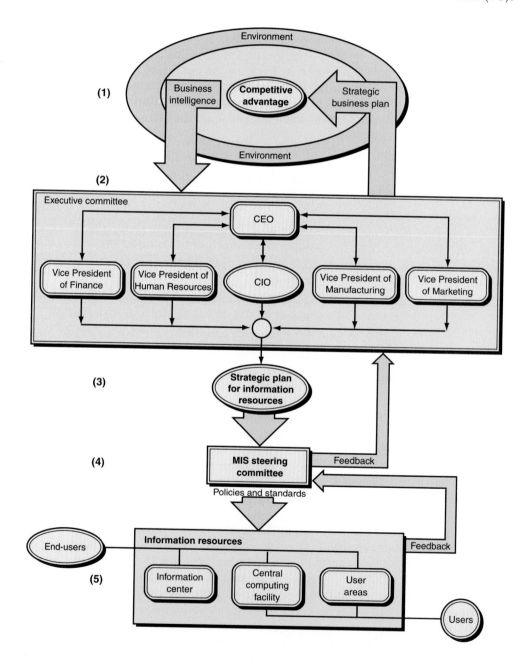

**FIGURE 15.10** The IRM model. (*Source*: McLeod [1995], p. 10 Figure 6.)

Using business intelligence, the executive committee (#2) can prepare the strategic plan necessary to achieve competitive advantage.

The executive committee, chaired by the CEO, involves the CIO as a member in addition to representatives from the functional areas. The committee drafts the strategic plan for IRM (#3). This plan is presented to the MIS steering committee (#4) that provides feedback to the executive committee. After one or more iterations, the steering committee develops the necessary policies and procedures for IRM by both the ISD and the end users (#5). The feedback from the resource users, which may include an information center, helps to refine the plan at all levels, and consequently improves the competitive advantage of the organization.

The interactions of IS with the organization that are shown in McLeod's model and discussed earlier in this chapter were subject to intensive IT research. Topics such as the proximity of the CEO/CIO relationship, the impact of different ISD structures, and the distribution of IRM activities between the ISD and end users were found to significantly impact innovation, quality, and sustainable competitiveness (for empirical evidence in several Southeast Asian countries see Jain [1997]). In order to best respond to the business pressures described in Chapter 1, Rockart et al. (1996) proposed the following eight imperatives for the ISD, which they call the "new IT organization."

▶ *Achieve two-way strategic alignment.* As discussed in Chapter 12 and McLeod's model, it is necessary to align IT strategy with the organization's business stragegy. This must be a two-way effort in which IT executives contribute.

▶ *Develop effective relations with line management.* IT personnel at all levels must develop strong, ongoing *partnerships* with end-user managers so both business and technology capabilities are integrated into effective solutions for organizational problems, as shown in this chapter.

▶ *Develop and implement new system.* Innovative applications must be developed *quickly* and *effectively* by the ISD, the users, and the outsourcers. System delivery includes effective system development, procurement, and integration. Firms are recognizing that they do not have the time, money, expertise, or inclination to develop large integrated systems necessary for in-house BPR, and increasingly rely on outsourcers and commercially integrated packages. This approach is discussed in Chapters 3, 4, 8, 13, and 14.

▶ *Build and manage infrastructures.* The ISD is responsible for creating and managing an effective infrastructure. As discussed in Chapters 12 and 13, an architecture must first be developed to guide infrastructure implementation. Managers must understand the value of the infrastructure (Chapter 12). Because of the increased role of the network, a major component of the infrastructure is networked. As a result, organizations create a new role—a **chief network officer (CNO)**, who reports to the CIO.

▶ *Reskill the IT organization.* The new role of the ISD discussed in Chapter 2 and the present chapter requires new skills. Retraining is one solution, some of which is available on the Web (for example, see www.zdnet.com). Finding employees with new technological skills becomes a difficult task that can be alleviated with the help of the Web, as described in Chapter 6.

▶ *Manage vendor relationships.* Since outsourcing is an increasingly sensible option, especially for those activities that the ISD does not have the necessary skills to complete, it is important to properly manage the outsourced work and the vendors (see Earl [1996]). Vendor relationships must not just be transactional and contractual, but also strategic and joint.

▶ *Build high performance.* Like any other unit in the organization, the ISD must strive to meet increasingly demanding performance goals. IT budgets are rising rapidly, and as shown in Chapters 13 and 14, justification is not a trivial thing. The ISD should use all modern management methods to improve its own operations. Systems must be developed quickly and in the most efficient manner, yet, quality must be superb. Motorola, for example, has introduced Six-Sigma performance goals (about 99 percent accuracy) in their IT quality program.

▶ *Redesign and manage the "federal" IT organization.* As stated earlier, the responsibility of managing IRM is divided between the ISD and end users. The exact locus of all or part of IT decision-making power is critical, and getting the right distribution of managerial responsibilities is thus an important imperative for IT management. This situation is analogous to power sharing between the U.S. federal and state governments, and has been debated for decades under the name of the "centralization–decentralization" issue (see Group Assignment 4).

Information technology, as shown throughout this book, is playing a critical role in the livelihood of many organizations, small or large, private or public, throughout the world. Furthermore, the trend is for even more IT involvement. Therefore, according to Rockart et al. (1996), the ISD will be even more critical to its firm's operations. Effective ISDs will help their firms apply IT to redesign processes and access needed information on a tight budget. Following the eight imperatives suggested here is mandatory for an organization's survival in a fast-changing, competitive world.

Participants in *Beyond Computing*'s 1997 Executive Forum (Kleinschrod [1997]) discovered that they have a lot in common. Most notably, they found that information technology is helping to *reshape* their organizations in *dramatic* ways.

This book is about IT use and its management throughout the organization and it provides a comprehensive view of the most important issues in IT management. It is our hope that the knowledge presented here will prepare the reader to be an effective manager as we enter the next millenium.

# ▶ MANAGERIAL ISSUES

The following are the major issues related to this chapter.

1. *To whom should the IS department report?* This issue is related to the degree of IS decentralization and to the role of the CIO. Reporting to a functional area may introduce biases in providing IT priorities to that functional area, which may not be justifiable.

2. *Who needs a CIO?* This is a critical question that is related to the role of the CIO as a senior executive in the organization. Giving a title without author-

ity can damage the ISD and its operation. Asking the IS director to assume a CIO's responsibility, but not giving the authority and title, can be just as damaging. Any organization that is heavily dependent on IT should have a CIO.

3. *How to organize the IS department.* There are many possibilities. However, the department's organization should depend on its role, its size, and the degree of importance of IT to the organization. Also, the corporate strategy of outsourcing IS services needs to be considered. Lately there is a trend to use both permanent and temporary teams as the core of the ISD. The transformation to a team-based ISD is not simple and the entire concept requires careful examination (see Garmer [1997]).

4. *End users are friends, not enemies, of the IS department.* The relationship between end users and the ISD can be very delicate. In the past, many ISDs were known to be insensitive to end-user needs. This created a strong desire for end-user independence, which can be both expensive and ineffective. Successful companies develop a climate of cooperation and friendship between the two parties.

5. *Ethical issues.* The reporting relationship of the ISD can result in some unethical behavior. If the ISD reports, for example, to the finance department, the finance department may misuse information about individuals or other departments.

6. *Responsibilities for security should be assigned in all areas.* It is important to make sure that people know who is responsible and accountable for what. The vast majority of information resources is in the hands of end users. Therefore, functional managers must understand and practice IT security management.

7. *Security awareness programs are important for any organization that is heavily dependent on IT.* Such programs should be corporatewide and supported by senior executives. In addition, monitoring security measures and assuring compliance with administrative controls are essential to the success of any security plan. For many people, following administrative controls means additional work, which they prefer not to do.

8. *Auditing information systems should be institutionalized into the organizational culture.* You do it not because your insurance company may ask for it, but because it can save you considerable amounts of money. On the other hand, overauditing is not cost effective.

9. *Multinational corporations.* Organizing the ISD in a multinational corporation is a complex issue. Some organizations prefer a complete decentralization, having an ISD in each country, or even several ISDs in one country. Others keep a minimum of centralized staff. Some companies, like Mobil Oil, prefer a highly centralized structure. Legal issues, government constraints, and the size of the IS staff are some factors that determine the degree of decentralization.

## KEY TERMS

Application controls *667*

Audit *675*

Audit trail *677*

Backup *679*

Biometric control *669*

Centralized IS *659*

Chief information officer (CIO) *648*

Chief network officer (CNO) *687*

Cracker *664*

Data integrity *670*

Data tampering *664*

Disaster avoidance *679*

Disaster recovery *678*

Encryption *672*

## CHAPTER HIGHLIGHTS  *(L–x means learning objective number x)*

▶ Information resources scattered throughout the organization are vulnerable to attacks, and therefore are difficult to manage. (L–1)

▶ The responsibility for IRM is divided between the ISD and end users. (L–1)

▶ Steering committees, information centers, and service level agreements can reduce conflicts between the ISD and end users. (L–2)

▶ ISD reporting locations can vary, but a preferred location is to senior management. (L–2)

▶ The chief information officer is a new position demonstrating the importance and changing role of IT in organizations. (L–3)

▶ ISD can be centralized or decentralized, depending on the nature of the organization. (L–4)

▶ There are alternative ISD structures; however, a team approach, focusing on business processes, is becoming more common. (L–4)

▶ Data, software, hardware, and networks can be threatened by many internal and external hazards. (L–5)

▶ The damage to an information system can be caused either accidentally or intentionally. (L–5)

▶ There are many potential computer crimes; some resemble conventional crimes (embezzlement, vandalism, fraud, theft, trespassing, and joyriding). (L–5)

▶ Computer criminals are driven by economic, ideological, egocentric, or psychological factors. Most of the criminals are insiders, but outsiders (such as hackers, crackers, and spies) can cause major damage as well. (L–5)

▶ A virus is a computer program hidden within a regular program that instructs the regular program to change or destroy data and/or programs. (L–5)

▶ Information systems are protected with controls such as security procedures, physical guards, or detecting software. These are used for *prevention, deterrence, detection, recovery,* and *correction* of information systems. (L–6)

▶ General controls include physical security, access controls, data security controls, communication (networks) controls, and administrative controls. (L–6)

▶ Biometric controls are used to identify users by checking physical characteristics of the user (e.g., fingerprints, and retina of the eye). (L–6)

▶ Encrypting information is a useful method for protecting transmitted data. (L–6)

▶ Application controls are usually built into the software. They protect the data during input, processing, or output. (L–6)

▶ A detailed internal and external IT audit may involve hundreds of issues and can be supported by both software and checklists. (L–6)

▶ Disaster recovery planning is an integral part of effective control and security management. (L–6)

▶ It is extremely difficult and expensive to protect against all possible threats. Therefore, it is necessary to use cost-benefit analysis to decide how many and which controls to adopt. (L–6)

▶ Many older computer programs do not differentiate the year 2000 from 1900 (or 2100), possibly creating chaos. Fixing the problem may cost billions of dollars. (L–7)

## QUESTIONS FOR REVIEW

1. What are possible reporting locations for ISD?

2. Why has ISD historically reported to finance or accounting departments?

3. What are the considerations for centralizing or decentralizing ISD?

4. What are the internal structures for ISD presented in the chapter?

5. What is a virtual ISD structure?

6. What is a steering committee?

7. Define SLAs and the roles they play.

8. What are the services to end users provided by an information center?

9. Define controls, threats, vulnerability, and backup.

10. What is the purpose of a control system?

11. What is a computer crime?

12. List the four major categories of computer crimes.

13. What is the difference between hackers and crackers?

14. Describe the profile of a computer criminal.

15. Describe the major motivations of computer criminals.

16. Explain a virus.

17. Describe prevention, deterrence, detection, recovery, and correction.

18. List five factors that make it difficult to protect an information system.

19. Distinguish between general controls and application controls.

20. What is the difference between authorized and authenticated users?

21. Explain encryption.

22. Distinguish between internal and external auditing.

23. Distinguish between auditing around, through, and within the computer.

24. What is a security policy?

25. Define and describe a disaster recovery plan.

26. What do "hot" and "cold" sites for recovery mean?

27. List and briefly describe the steps involved in risk analysis of controls.

28. Define firewalls.

29. Explain the Y2K problem.

## QUESTIONS FOR DISCUSSION

1. What is a desirable location for ISD to report to and why?

2. Why is a team approach focusing on business processes preferable for the ISD structure? Compare with a team organized by technical expertise.

3. In an organization with a business unit and charge-back system, is it more likely to find a centralized or a decentralized structure? Why?

4. Why should information control and security be a prime concern to management?

5. Compare the computer security situation with that of insuring a house.

6. Explain what firewalls protect and what they do not protect.

7. Why is it so important to have firewalls?

8. Describe how IS auditing works and how it is related to traditional accounting and financial auditing.

9. Review Fine's (1983) total security framework. Explain the need for all eight pillars.

10. Some insurance companies will not insure a business unless the firm has a computer disaster recovery plan. Explain why.

11. Explain why risk management should involve the following elements: threats, exposure associated with each threat, risk of each threat occurring, cost of controls, and assessment of their effectiveness.

12. It was suggested recently to use viruses and similar programs in wars. What is the logic of such a proposal? How can it be implemented?

13. What are some of the advantages and disadvantages of the virtual IS organization?

14. A senior IBM manager was appointed as a CIO of a large bank. After a short time, he resigned because the CEO felt that he did not understand the business. His next job was CIO at a large airline where he became very successful. Discuss.

15. How important is it for a CIO to have an extensive knowledge of the business?

16. Why is it necessary to use SLA with vendors? What are some of the potential problems in such situations?

17. Why may the Year 2000 problem cause chaos in our society?

## EXERCISES

1. Examine Table 15.1 on page 654. Read some new material on the CIO and add new roles. Which of the roles in the table seem to have gained importance and which seem to have lost importance?

2. The daily probability of a major earthquake in Los Angeles is .0007. The chance of your computer center being damaged during a quake is 5 percent. If the center is damaged, the average estimated damage will be $1.6 million.
   a. Calculate the expected loss (in dollars).
   b. An insurance agent is willing to insure your facility for an annual fee of $15,000. Analyze the offer, and discuss it.

3. Robert T. Morris, a computer wizard and graduate student at Cornell University, introduced a damaging program to thousands of computers on the ARPANET network. He was fined $10,000, sentenced to three years of probation, and ordered to perform 400 hours of community service and to pay the cost of his probation supervision. This verdict caused a debate that lingered for three years. It finally reached the U.S. Supreme Court which refused to hear the case (see *ComputerWorld,* January 29, 1990; May 7, 1990; May 14, 1990; and October 14, 1991). In your view, is the punishment too high, too low, or just right? Why?

4. Expert systems can be used to analyze the profile of computer users. This may enable better intrusion detection. Should an employer notify employees that their usage of computers is being monitored by an expert system (see *Datamation,* February 1, 1990)?

5. Ms. M. Hsieh worked as a customer support representative for the Wollongong Group, a small software company (Palo Alto, CA). She was fired in late 1987. In early 1988, Wollongong discovered that someone was logging onto its computers at night via a modem and had altered and copied files. During investigation, the police traced the calls to Ms. Hsieh's home and found copies there of proprietary information valued at several million dollars. It is interesting to note that Ms. Hsieh's access code was canceled the day she was terminated. However, the company suspects that Ms. Hsieh obtained the access code of another employee. (SOURCE: Based on *BusinessWeek,* August 1, 1988, p. 67.)
   a. How was the crime committed? Why were the controls ineffective? (State any relevant assumptions.)
   b. What can Wollongong do in order to prevent similar incidents in the future?

6. In Spring 1998 a malfunction in the AT&T network prevented millions of customers from accessing the Internet. Many banking functions and other electronic commerce were interrupted. It took 24 hours to restore the service, but more than a week to find the cause of the problem and fix it (*L.A. Times,* Apr. 27, 1998).

   a. Find some information about this incident.
   b. Why was the service restored in a day, while the cause was found only in a week?
   c. What can AT&T do to prevent such problems in the future?

7. Refer to the opening case of this chapter. You were hired as a consultant to one of the financial services companies that were evacuated from the World Trade Center. The company asked your advice on the following:
   a. Should they continue their work with networks or use a centralized mainframe, which is easier to protect?
   b. Will the companies that return to the World Trade Center need to prepare for potential disasters?
   c. How can they calculate the amount of money that they should invest in disaster planning and recovery management?

8. Research the status of the Federal Encrypted Communication Privacy Act written by Dr. Denning (www.cose.georgetown.edu/~denning). Describe the encryption debate and the position of both sides.

9. Find information about a virus called MDMA. Describe the potential damage of the virus and the possible protection against it.

10. Twenty-five-thousand messages arrive at an organization each year. Currently there are no firewalls. On the average there are 1.2 successful hackings each year. Each successful hacking costs $130,000. A firewall is proposed at a cost of $66,000. The estimated life is three years. The chance that an intruder will break through the firewall is 0.0002. In such a case, the damage will be $100,000 (30 percent) or $200,000 (50 percent), or no damage. There is annual maintenance cost of $20,000 for the firewall.
    a. Should management buy the firewall?
    b. An improved firewall that is 99.9988 percent effective costs $84,000, with a life of three years, and annual maintenance cost of $16,000 is available. Should this one be purchased?

## GROUP ASSIGNMENTS

1. The class is divided into groups. Each group will visit an IS department and present the following in class: an organizational chart of the department; a discussion on the department's CIO (director) and her or his reporting status; information on a steering committee (composition, duties); information of SLA; and a report on the extent of IT decentralization in the company.

2. Each group is to be divided into two parts. The first part will interview students and business people and record the experiences they have had with computer problems. The second group will visit a computer store (read the literature or use the Internet) to find out what software is available to fight computer security problems. Then, the group will prepare a presentation in which they describe the problems and identify which of the problems could have been prevented with the use of commercially available software.

3. Create groups to research the status of the Year 2000 problem. Working students may report on the status in their organizations. Other students in the group

may consult sources on the Web such as: www.data-mation.com, www.simnet.org, www.gartner.com, www.itaa.org, and www.stsc.hill.af.mil.

4. Research the issue of centralization versus decentralization of IT in organizations. Begin with Rockart et al. (1996), imperative 8. In addition to a literature search, visit organizations and interview both the CIO and end users.

## INTERNET EXERCISES

Note: The URLs included here were current when the book went to press. However, they are subject to change without notice. Please consult the Turban Web site (www.Wiley.com/college/turban2e).

1. Explore some job-searching Web sites (such as www.jobcenter.com; www.careermosaic.com) and identify openings for CIOs. Examine the job requirements and the salary range. Report.

2. Access www.datamation.com and www.cio.com and find some information regarding CIOs, their roles, salaries, and so forth.

3. Access the site of Comdisco Corporation. Locate and describe the latest disaster recovery services.

4. Access the site of IBM (www.ibm.com) and find out the latest products and services regarding security and virus protection.

5. Access the Web sites of the major antivirus vendors (www.symantec.com, www.mcafee.com, and www.drsalmas.com). Find out what the vendors' research centers are doing.

6. Many newsgroups are related to computer security (alt.comp.virus; comp.virus; maous.comp.virus). Access any of these sites to find information on the most recently discovered viruses.

7. Many security software packages are available on the Internet (such as in www.shareware.com). Download a program such as McAfee's Virusscan. Unzip the program and use it to scan your hard drive. Prepare a short report.

8. Access the Electric Library program (elibrary@infonautics.com) or Yahoo. Find recent articles on disaster planning. Prepare a short report on recent developments in disaster recovery planning.

9. The use of smart cards for electronic storage of user identification, user authentication, changing passwords, and so forth is on the rise. Surf the Internet and report on recent developments. (Try the Web site of Security Dynamics Technologies, Inc.)

10. Surf the Internet to collect information about the following viruses: Concept, Airwolf, Hare, Good Times, and Jerusalem.

11. Access the Web site www.2600.com and read the *2600 Magazine*. Also try Hack and Crack Web sites at home.earthlink.net/~mumbv/index.html.   Explore tools such as Electronic Mail Bomb, SATAN, Password Sniffers, Sandmail, and wu-ftp. Prepare a report that shows how easy it is to hack successfully.

12. Enter www.ncsa.com and find information about "why hackers do the things they do." Write a report.

## ▼ Minicase 1

### The CIO/CEO Connection at Xerox Paid Off

Xerox Corp., the "king" of copying, has been fighting for its life, facing challenges from new technologies, and strong competitors that are constantly transforming the markets where Xerox does business. Electronic documents, which count for only 10 percent of the business in 1990, are expected to capture 70 percent of the market by 2000 (www.idcresearch.com).

Xerox had to reengineer itself. In 1993 Xerox made history when it outsourced its IT operations, in the largest ever and first global deal of a $3.2 billion, 13-year contract. Despite the outsourcing, Xerox kept its CIO, Pat Wallington, at a very high corporate position. As a matter of fact she is a member of the top management team. She engineered the outsourcing, and so far she has kept her job for six years. The average job tenure in her profession lasts less than three years. The CEO places lots of importance on the CIO's job, even though the IS area is small. The CEO said that Xerox gave Pat long-term projects with long-term payoff. Her job is to get Xerox ready for the twenty-first century.

Wallington developed a strategic plan called IM 2000 (IM for Information Management). The plan includes three key strategies: outsourcing, replacing propriety infrastructure with a standard one, and creating an investment fund to support the reengineering of IT. Xerox reengineered four key areas: customer service, sale cycle (time-to market), integrated supply chain, and superb employee relations.

The key to Wallington's success is considered to be her ability to create a roadmap for others to follow. She had a vision and she knows how to implement it through special teams, like the one that put together the outsourcing deal.

People say that Pat's success is also due to her ability in painting an accurate and compelling vision. It may cause some controversy—nothing this important is easy—but she is able to sustain the vision and sustain executive management support for it.

As IT continues to play an increasingly important role in enabling companies to become more competitive, CIOs and other IT executives must think beyond glass-house borders. But perhaps most important is the ability to find the right people both in the IS organization and among the end users to implement visions.

Wallington works with an IS steering committee (called IM Council) which includes IS experts from each business unit. One of the major tasks of the committee is to review the IT project requests of the units, which are submitted annually. The IM Council meets once a month to discuss IT strategy and implementation.

In addition, Wallington created the office of the CIO, consisting of herself and her two assistants, the director of IT operations, and the director of IT finance. This committee meets almost daily to run the IM organization.

### Questions for Minicase 1

1. Why is a CIO needed if the IS function is basically outsourced?

2. The CIO's job is basically a man's job with a tenure of only three years. Find some research on why this is so, and why Pat is lasting on the job much longer in a major corporation.

3. It is said that the CIO/CEO relations are critical, and that Pat had the backing of the CEO to make bold decisions. Comment.

4. Pat was extensively using the "IS by committee" approach. What are the major benefits of it?

5. Comment on the relationships between Pat's strategy and Xerox's need for BPR.

6. People repeatedly said that Pat's vision was the key to her success. What do they mean by that?

SOURCE: Condensed from Knowles, A., "CIO/CEO Spotlight on Xerox—Copy This," *Datamation*, June 1997.

# Minicase 2

## Flyhigh Corporation

Flyhigh is a large aerospace corporation (fictitious name, real incident) that regularly performs projects for the military and other government organizations. A virus attack that caused significant damage resulted in an investigation. The investigation revealed the following:

▶ While there are clear instructions not to use common names (such as Smith, Lee, or Brown) as passwords, these names are in use.

▶ While there are clear instructions to change passwords once a month, many people neglect to do so. In fact, some employees have not changed their password for more than a year.

▶ Violations are especially prevalent among top managers and top scientists. The higher the individuals are in the organizational hierarchy, the more likely it is that they will ignore the instructions.

▶ In the past, notices were mailed to violators, but most of the notices were ignored.

▶ The responsibility for security issues is decentralized.

The database administrator is responsible for security in the IS department and for the LAN. Various individuals were assigned responsibility in users' departments, mainly for microcomputers. However, some departments do not have anyone formally assigned for computer security, while others do not have any formal procedures regarding security management.

### Questions for Minicase 2

1. What do you suggest should be done about the violators?

2. Would you change the responsibility scheme (structure)? How?

3. The actual loss to the corporation from the virus attack is estimated at $1,600,000. Should somebody be punished? Justify your answer, if punishment is recommended. What should it be, and who should be punished?

# REFERENCES AND BIBLIOGRAPHY

1. Applegate, L. M., and J. J. Elam, "New Information Systems Leaders: A Changing Role in a Changing World," *MIS Quarterly,* December 1992.

2. Behar, R., "Who's Reading Your E-mail?", *Fortune,* February 3, 1997.

3. Butler, J., "How to Stay in Business When Disaster Strikes," *Software,* August 1992.

4. Carrol, J. M., *Computer Security,* 3rd ed., Stoneham, MA: Butterworth-Heinemann, 1996.

5. Chao, P. Y. K., "Reexamining a Model for Evaluating Information Center Success Using a Structural Equation Modeling Approach," *Decision Sciences,* Spring 1997.

6. Chapman, C., "Before Disaster Strikes," *Internal Auditor,* December 1996.

7. Chapman, D. B., and E. D. Zwicky, *Building Internet Firewalls,* Sebastopal, CA: O'Reilly and Associates, 1995.

8. Chavez, G., "How Expert Systems Can Help Controllers," *Global Finance,* July 1996.

9. Clark, C. E., et al., "Building a Change-Ready IS Organization at Bell Atlantic," *SIM* 1996 International Paper Award Winner, www.simnet.org, 1996.

10. Coderre, D. G., "Computer Assisted Auditing Tools and Techniques," *Internal Auditor,* February 1993.

11. de Jager, P., "Year 2000—A Matter of Honor," *Datamation,* March 1997.

12. Earl, M. J., ed., *Information Management: The Organizational Dimension,* Oxford: Oxford University Press, 1996.

13. Earl, M. J., and D. F. Feeny, "Is Your CIO Adding Value?" *Sloan Management Review,* Spring 1995.

14. Feeny, D. F., et al., "Understanding the CEO/CIO Relationship," *MIS Quarterly,* December 1992.

15. Fine, L. H., *Computer Security—A Guide for Management,* London: Heinemann, 1983.

16. Ford, J. C., "Expert Systems in Auditing," in Umbaugh, R. E., ed., *Handbook of MIS Management,* Boston: Auerbach Publishers, 2nd ed. 1991.

17. Fuller, M. K., and E. B. Swanson, "Information Centers as Organizational Innovation," *Journal of Management Information Systems,* Vol. 9, No. 1, Summer 1992.

18. Gallegos, F., and D. M. Wright, "Evaluating Data Security," Jour. of Information Systems Management, Spring 1988.

19. Garmer, K., "Still an Excellent Adventure?" *ComputerWorld,* March 31, 1997.

20. Gupta, Y. P., "The Chief Executive Officer and the Chief Information Officer: The Strategic Partnership," *Journal of Information Technology,* Vol. 6, 1991.

21. Hock, S. L., "The Year 2000 Legal Crisis," *Beyond Computing,* January/February 1998.

22. Jain, R., "Key Constructs in Successful IS Implementation: South-East Asian Experience, *Omega,* Vol. 25, No. 3, 1997.

23. Jenne, S. E., "Audits of End-user Computing," *Internal Auditor,* December 1996.

24. Jones, C., "Year 2000: What's the Real Cost?" *Datamation,* March 1997.

25. Kiely, T., "The Shape of Excellence," *CIO,* August 1992.

26. Kleinschrod, W. A., "Technology Transformations," *Beyond Computing,* July/August 1997.

27. Knoll, A. P., *Disaster Recovery: An Organization View,* Chicago, IL: IBM Information Systems Management Institute, 1986.

28. Lee, D. R., "Changing Responsibilities for Audit and Security Information Resources," *Information Executive,* Spring 1990.

29. Loch, K. D., et al., "Threats to Information Systems: Today's Reality, Yesterday's Understanding," *MIS Quarterly,* June 1992.

30. McGee, M. K., "Over the Rainbow" (CIOs' salaries), *InformationWeek,* July 8, 1996.

31. McLeod, R., Jr., "Systems Theory and Information Resources Management: Integrating Key Concepts," *Information Resources Management Journal,* Spring 1995.

32. McNurlin, B. C., and R. H. Sprague, Jr., *Information Systems Management in Practice,* 4th ed., Upper Saddle River, NJ: Prentice Hall, 1998.

33. Mirani, R., and W. R. King, "Impacts of End-User and Information Center Characteristics on End-User Computing Support," *Journal of Management Information Systems,* Vol. 11, No. 1, 1994.

34. Moad, J., "Welcome to the Virtual IS Organization," *Datamation,* February 1, 1994.

35. Moynihan, T., "What Chief Executives and Senior Managers Want from Their IT Department," *MIS Quarterly,* March 1992.

36. Nance, B., "Keep Networks Safe from Viruses," *Byte,* November 1996.

37. Oppliger, R., "Firewalls and Beyond," *Communications of the ACM,* May 1997.

38. Ovans, A., "Improve IS-Department Relations!" *Datamation,* October 1996.

39. Rockart, J. F., et al., "Eight Imperatives for the New IS Organization," *Sloan Management Review,* Fall 1996.

40. Ross, J. W., et al., "Develop Long-term Competitiveness Through IT Assets," *Sloan Management Review,* Fall 1996.

41. "Security, Special Report," *ComputerWorld,* February 10, 1997.

42. Shah, H. U., et al., "Bridging the Cultural Gap Between Users and Developers," *Journal of Systems Management,* July 1994.

43. Sitonis, J. G., and B. Goldberg, "Changing Role of the CIO," *InformationWeek,* March 24, 1997.

44. Stallings, W., *Network and Internetwork Security: Principles and Practices,* Upper Saddle River, NJ: Prentice Hall, 1995.

45. Steefora, A., and M. Cheek, "Hacking Goes Legit," *Industry Week,* February 7, 1994.

46. Steinberg, R. M., and R. N. Johnson, "Implementing SAS No. 55 in a Computer Environment," *Journal of Accountancy,* August 1991.

47. Stephens, C. S., et al., "Executive or Functional Manager? The Nature of the CIO's Job," *MIS Quarterly,* December 1992.

48. Strassman, P., "What Is the Best Defense? Being Prepared," *ComputerWorld,* March 31, 1997.

49. Tung, L. L., and E. Turban, "Housing Development Board: Reengineering the IT Function," in Neo, B. S., *Exploiting Information Technology for Business Competitiveness,* Singapore: Addison-Wesley, 1996.

50. Wilder, C., and J. Angus, "Pace of Change: Here's How CIOs at Some of the Most Successful Companies Keep Up," *InformationWeek,* July 21, 1997.

51. Wysocki, R. K., and R. L. De Michiell, *Managing Information Across the Enterprise,* New York: John Wiley & Sons, 1996.

Note: An integrated case study for Part IV, *Capital One,* is available on the Turban Web site (www.wiley.com/college/turban2e).

# TECHNOLOGY GUIDE 1:

# Hardware

## T1.1
### What Is a Computer System?

## T1.2
### The Evolution of Computer Hardware

## T1.3
### Types of Computers

## T1.4
### The Microprocessor and Primary Storage

## T1.5
### Input/Output Devices

## ▶ T1.1 WHAT IS A COMPUTER SYSTEM?

Computer hardware is composed of the following components: central processing unit (CPU), input devices, output devices, primary storage, secondary storage, and communication devices. (These devices are described in Technology Guide #4). Each of the hardware components plays an important role in computing. The **input devices** accept data and instructions and convert them to a form that the computer can understand. The output devices present data in a form people can understand. The **CPU** manipulates the data and controls the tasks done by the other components. The **primary storage** (internal storage) temporarily stores data and programs instructions during processing. It also stores intermediate results of the processing. The **secondary storage** (external) stores data and programs for future use. Finally, the **communication devices** provide for the flow of data from external computer networks (e.g., Internet, intranet) to the CPU, and from the CPU to computer networks. A schematic view of a computer system is shown in Figure T-1.1.

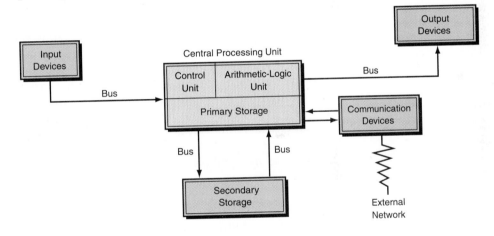

**FIGURE T-1.1** The components of computer hardware. A "bus" is a connecting channel.

### REPRESENTING DATA, PICTURES, TIME, AND SIZE IN A COMPUTER

**ASCII.** Today's computers are based on integrated circuits (chips), each of which include millions of subminiature transistors which are interconnected on a small (less than !s-inch square) chip area. Each transistor can be in either an "on" or "off" position.

The "on-off" states of the transistors are used to establish a binary 1 or 0 for storing one **binary digit,** or **bit.** A sufficient number of bits to represent specific characters—letters, numbers, and special symbols is known as a **byte,** usually 8 bits. Because a bit only has two states, 0 or 1, the bits comprising a byte can represent any of $2^8$, or 256, unique characters. Which character is represented depends upon the bit combination or coding scheme used. The two most commonly used coding schemes are **ASCII (American National Standard Code for Information Interchange),** pronounced "ask-ee," and **EBCDIC (Extended Binary Coded Decimal Interchange Code),** pronounced "eb-sa-dick." EBCDIC was developed by IBM and is used primarily on large, mainframe computers. ASCII has emerged as the standard coding scheme for microcomputers. These coding schemes, and the characters they present, are shown in Figure

| Character | EBCDIC Code | ASCII Code | Character | EBCDIC Code | ASCII Code |
|-----------|-------------|------------|-----------|-------------|------------|
| A | 11000001 | 10100001 | S | 11100010 | 10110011 |
| B | 11000010 | 10100010 | T | 11100011 | 10110100 |
| C | 11000011 | 10100011 | U | 11100100 | 10110101 |
| D | 11000100 | 10100100 | V | 11100101 | 10110110 |
| E | 11000101 | 10100101 | W | 11100110 | 10110111 |
| F | 11000110 | 10100110 | X | 11100111 | 10111000 |
| G | 11000111 | 10100111 | Y | 11101000 | 10111001 |
| H | 11001000 | 10101000 | Z | 11101001 | 10111010 |
| I | 11001001 | 10101001 | 0 | 11110000 | 01010000 |
| J | 11010001 | 10101010 | 1 | 11110001 | 01010001 |
| K | 11010010 | 10101011 | 2 | 11110010 | 01010010 |
| L | 11010011 | 10101100 | 3 | 11110011 | 01010011 |
| M | 11010100 | 10101101 | 4 | 11110100 | 01010100 |
| N | 11010101 | 10101110 | 5 | 11110101 | 01010101 |
| O | 11010110 | 10101111 | 6 | 11110110 | 01010110 |
| P | 11010111 | 10110000 | 7 | 11110111 | 01010111 |
| Q | 11011000 | 10110001 | 8 | 11111000 | 01011000 |
| R | 11011001 | 10110010 | 9 | 11111001 | 01011001 |

**FIGURE T-1.2** Internal computing coding schemes.

T-1.2. In addition to characters, it is possible to represent commonly agreed-upon symbols in a binary code. For example, the letter k is 10101011 in ASCII.

The 256 characters and symbols that are represented by ASCII and EBCDIC codes are sufficient for English and Western European languages but are not large enough for Asian and other languages that use different alphabets. **Unicode** is a 16-bit code that has the capacity of representing more than 65,000 characters and symbols. The system employs the codes used by ASCII and also includes other alphabets (such as Cyrillic and Hebrew), special characters (including religious symbols), and some of the "word writing" symbols used in various Asian countries.

**REPRESENTING PICTURES.** Pictures are represented by a grid overlay of the picture. The computer measures the color (or light level) of each cell of the grid. The unit measurement of this is called a **pixel**. Figure T-1.3 shows a pixel representation of the letter A and its conversion to an input code.

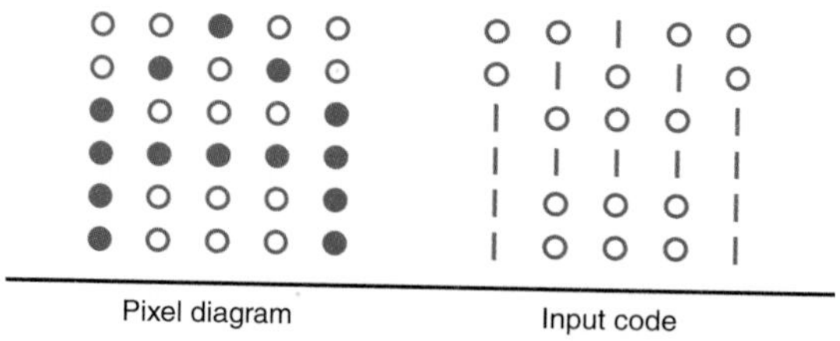

**FIGURE T-1.3** Pixel representation of the letter "A."

Pixel diagram          Input code

**REPRESENTING TIME AND SIZE OF BYTES.** Time is represented in fractions of a second. The following are common measures of time:

▶ **Millisecond** = 1/1000 seconds
▶ **Microsecond** = 1/1,000,000
▶ **Nanosecond** = 1,1000,000,000
▶ **Picosecond** = 1/1,000,000,000,000

Size is measured by the number of bytes. Common measures of size are:

▶ **Kilobyte** = 1,000 bytes (actually 1024)
▶ **Megabyte** = 1,000 kilobytes = 106 bytes
▶ **Gigabyte** = $10^9$ bytes

▶ **Terabyte** $= 10^{12}$ bytes
▶ **Petabyte** $= 10^{15}$ bytes
▶ **Exabyte** $= 10^{18}$ bytes

# T1.2 THE EVOLUTION OF COMPUTER HARDWARE

Computer hardware has evolved through four stages, or generations, of technology. Each generation has provided increased processing power and storage capacity, while simultaneously exhibiting decreases in costs (see Table T-1.1). The generations are distinguished by different technologies that perform the processing functions.

**Table T-1.1** Hardware Generations

| | Generations | | | | | |
|---|---|---|---|---|---|---|
| *Feature* | *1st* | *2nd* | *3rd* | *4th (early)* | *4th (1988)* | *4th (2000)* |
| Circuitry | Vacuum tubes | Transistors | Integrated circuits | LSI and VLSI | ULSI | GSI |
| Primary storage | 2 KB | 64 KB | 4 MB | 16 MB | 64 MB | 128 MB |
| Cycle times | 100 millisecs | 10 microsecs | 500 nanosecs | 800 picosecs | 2,000 picosecs | 4,000 picosecs |
| Average cost | $2.5 million | $250 thousand | $25 thousand | $2.5 thousand | $2.0 thousand | $1.5 thousand |

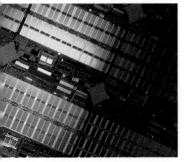

A chip showing circuit lines.

The *first generation* of computers, 1946–1956, used vacuum tubes to store process information. Vacuum tubes consumed large amounts of power, generated much heat, and were short-lived. Therefore, first-generation computers had limited memory and processing capability.

The *second generation* of computers, 1957–1963, used **transistors** for storage and processing information. Transistors consumed less power than vacuum tubes, produced less heat, and were cheaper, more stable, and more reliable. Second-generation computers, with increased processing and storage capabilities, began to be more widely used for scientific and business purposes.

*Third-generation* computers, 1964–1979, used **integrated circuits** for storing and processing information. Integrated circuits are made by printing numerous small transistors on silicon chips. These devices are called *semiconductors*. Third-generation computers employed software that could be used by nontechnical people, thus enlarging the computer's role in business.

Early to middle *fourth-generation* computers, 1980–1995, used **very large-scale integrated (VLSI)** circuits to store and process information. The VLSI technique allows the installation of hundreds of thousands of circuits (transistors and other components) on a small chip. With **ultra large-scale integration (ULSI),** 10 million transistors could be placed on a chip. These computers are inexpensive and widely used in business and everyday life.

Late *fourth-generation computers*, 1996–present, use **grand-scale integrated (GSI)** circuits to store and process information. With GSI, 1,000 million transistors can be placed on a chip.

## FIFTH-GENERATION COMPUTERS

The first four generations of computer hardware are based on the Von Neumann architecture, which processed information sequentially, one instruction at a time. The fifth generation of computers uses **massive parallel processing** to process multiple instructions simultaneously. Massively parallel computers use flexibly connected networks linking thousands of inexpensive, commonly used chips to address large computing problems, attaining supercomputer speeds. With enough chips networked together, massively parallel machines can perform more than a trillion floating point operations per second—a teraflop. A *floating point operation (flop)* is a basic computer arithmetic operation, such as addition or subtraction, on numbers that include a decimal point.

## FUTURE GENERATIONS

Two major innovations are in experimental stages:

**DNA COMPUTERS.** DNA is an acronym for deoxyribonucleic acid. Scientists are experimenting now with DNA computing, which takes advantage of the fact that information can be written onto individual DNA molecules. The information uses the alphabet of four bases that all living organisms use to record genetic information. A DNA computation is done by coding a problem into the alphabet and then creating conditions under which DNA molecules are formed that encode all possible solutions of a problem. The process produces billions of molecules encoding wrong answers, and a few encoding the right one. Modern molecular genetics has chemical procedures that can reliably isolate the few DNA molecules encoding the correct answer from all the others.

DNA computers process in parallel and are potentially twice as fast as today's fastest supercomputers. In addition, modern storage media store information at a density of one bit per 1,012 nanometers (one billionth of a meter), while DNA computers have storage densities of one bit per cubic nanometer, a trillion times less space.

**OPTICAL COMPUTERS.** Scientists are working on a machine that uses beams of light instead of electrons. Called *optoelectronic,* these computers are expected to process information several hundred times faster than current computers.

## ▶ T1.3 TYPES OF COMPUTERS

Computers are distinguished on the basis of their processing capabilities. Computers with the most processing power are also the largest and most expensive.

### SUPERCOMPUTERS

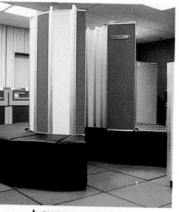

Supercomputers are the computers with the most processing power. The primary application of supercomputers has been in scientific and military work, but their use is growing rapidly in business as their prices decrease. Supercomputers are especially valuable for large simulation models of real-world phenomena, where complex mathematical representations and calculations are required, or for image creation and processing. Supercomputers are used to model the weather for better weather prediction, to test weapons nondestructively, to design aircraft (e.g., the Boeing 777) for more efficient and less costly production, and to make sequences in motion pictures (e.g., *Jurassic Park*). Supercomputers generally operate at 4 to 10 times faster than the next most powerful computer class, the mainframe. By the year 2000, supercomputers were able to compute one trillion operations per second. This represented a 1,000-fold speed increase over 1990's most powerful computers. In 2000, the prices of supercomputers range from $100,000 to $20 million or more.

A supercomputer.

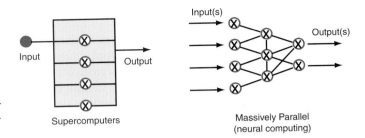

**FIGURE T-1.4** Supercomputers vs. neural computing (⊗ is a CPU).

Supercomputers use the technology of **parallel processing.** However, in contrast to neural computing, which uses massively parallel processing, supercomputers use noninterconnected CPUs. The difference is shown in Figure T-1.4. Parallel processing is also used today in smaller computers where 2 to 64 processors are common.

## MASSIVELY-PARALLEL COMPUTERS

The development of massively-parallel computers has led some people to confuse these computers with supercomputers. The massively-parallel computers are a relatively new type of computer that uses a large number of processors. The processors divide up and independently work on small chunks of a large problem. Modern problems in science and engineering, such as structural engineering, fluid mechanics, and other large scale physical simulations, rely on high-performance computing to make progress. These problems are so enormous as to swamp the computational power of conventional computers, so massively-parallel computers must be used. In 2000, the prices of massively-parallel computers range from $100,000 to $4 million or more.

## MAINFRAMES

Mainframes are not as powerful and generally not as expensive as supercomputers. Large corporations, where data processing is centralized and large databases are maintained, most often use mainframe computers. Applications that run on a mainframe can be large and complex, allowing for data and information to be shared throughout the organization. In 2000, a mainframe system had anywhere from 50 megabytes to several gigabytes of *primary storage*. Online secondary storage may use high-capacity magnetic and optical storage media with capacities in the gigabyte to terabyte range. Additionally, offline storage often uses high-capacity magnetic tape systems. Several hundreds or even thousands of online computers can be linked to a mainframe. In 2000, mainframes are priced as high as $5 million.

A mainframe computer.

## MINICOMPUTERS

Minicomputers, also called midrange computers, are smaller and less expensive than mainframe computers. Minicomputers are usually designed to accomplish specific tasks such as process control, scientific research, and engineering applications. In 2000, a minicomputer system had anywhere from 10 megabytes to over 1 gigabyte of primary storage, and the prices ranged from $10,000 to $250,000.

Larger companies gain greater corporate flexibility by distributing data processing with minicomputers in organizational units instead of centralizing computing at one location. These minicomputers are connected to each other and often to a mainframe through telecommunication links. The minicomputer is also able to meet the needs of smaller organizations that would rather not utilize scarce corporate resources by purchasing larger computer systems.

## WORKSTATIONS

Vendors originally developed workstations to provide the high levels of performance demanded by these users. Workstations are often based on RISC (reduced instruction set computing) architecture and provide both very high-speed calculations and high-resolution graphic displays. These computers have found widespread acceptance within the scientific community and, more recently, within the business community.

A workstation has more powerful mathematical and graphical processing capability. In 2000, a workstation system had anywhere from 8 megabytes to 300 megabytes of primary storage and ranged in price from $5,000 to $50,000. However, the distinction between workstations and personal computers is rapidly blurring. The latest PCs have the computing power of recent workstations. Low-end workstations are now indistinguishable from high-end PCs.

## MICROCOMPUTERS (PCs)

Microcomputers, also called micros or personal computers (PCs), are the smallest and least expensive category of general-purpose computers. In general, modern microcomputers have between 8 and 64 megabytes of primary storage, one 3.5-inch floppy drive, a CD-ROM drive, and one gigabyte or more of secondary storage. They may be subdivided into four classifications based on their size: desktops, laptops, notebooks, and palmtops.

The **desktop personal computer** is the typical, familiar microcomputer system. It is usually modular in design, with separate but connected monitor, keyboard, and CPU. **Laptop computers** are small, easily transportable, lightweight microcomputers that fit easily into a briefcase. **Notebooks** are smaller

(a)

(b)

(c)

A desktop computer (*a*), an IBM thinkpad laptop (*b*), and a laptop Notebook computer (*c*).

laptops (also called mini-laptops), but sometimes are used interchangeably with laptops. Laptops and notebooks are designed for maximum convenience and transportability, allowing users to have access to processing power and data without being bound to an office environment.

**Palmtop computers** are hand-held microcomputers small enough to carry in one hand. Although still capable of general-purpose computing, palmtops are usually configured for specific applications and limited in the number of ways they can accept user input and provide output.

**A Palmtop PDA.** (*Source: Palm VII, from 3Com Corp.*)

**PERSONAL DIGITAL ASSISTANT.** A **personal digital assistant (PDA)** is a palmtop computer that combines a fast processor with a multitasking operating system using a pen for handwriting recognition rather than keyboard input. PDAs differ from other personal computers in that they are usually specialized for individual users. The PDA may be thought of as a computing appliance, rather than a general-purpose computing device. In 2000, PDAs often weigh under a pound and are priced from $300 to $1,000. Some PDAs enable users to communicate via fax, electronic mail, and paging, or to access online services. PDAs are very popular for special applications, such as the New York Stock Exchange.

PDA from 3Com Corp. emerges as a solid wireless communications tool. The Palm VII features a built-in modem that allows users to wirelessly connect to the Internet, plus send and receive e-mail. To view Web content, the Palm VII uses technology the company calls "Web clipping." Web clipping is an efficient way for people on the move to access Web information without a PC.

**SMART CARDS.** An even smaller form of computer is the **smart card,** which has resulted from the continuing shrinkage of integrated circuits. Similar in size and thickness to ordinary plastic credit cards, smart cards contain a small CPU, memory, and an input/output device that allow these "computers" to be used in everyday activities such as person identification and banking.

Uses for smart cards are appearing rapidly. People are using them as checkbooks; a bank ATM (automatic teller machine) can "deposit money" into the card's memory for "withdrawal" at retail stores (see Chapter 6). Smart cards are being used to transport data between computers, replacing floppy disks. Adding a small transmitter to a smart card can allow businesses to locate any employee and automatically route phone calls to the nearest telephone.

Smart cards.

## NETWORK COMPUTERS AND TERMINALS

The computers described so far are considered "smart" computers. However, mainframe and midrange computers use "dumb" terminals, which are basically input/output devices. However, as time passed, these terminals, which are called *X terminals,* were also used for limited processing. Two extensions of these terminals are discussed here.

**NETWORK COMPUTERS.** A **network computer (NC),** also called a "thin" computer, is a desktop terminal that does not store software programs or data permanently. Similar to a "dumb" terminal, the NC is simpler and cheaper than a PC and easy to maintain. Users can download software or data they need from a server on a mainframe over an intranet or the Internet. There is no need for hard disks, floppy disks, CD-ROMs and their drives. The central computer can save any material for the user. The NC's cost in 2000 is $300 to $600. At the same time, simple PCs are selling for $600 to $800. Since the price advantage is not so large, the future of NCs is not clear. However, there is a saving in the maintenance cost that can be substantial. The NCs provide security as well. However, users are limited in what they can do with the terminals.

**WINDOWS-BASED TERMINALS (WBTs).** WBTs are a subset of the NC. Although they offer less functionality than PCs, WBTs reduce maintenance and support costs and maintain compatibility with Windows operating systems. WBT users access Windows applications on central servers as if those applications were running locally. As with the NC, the savings are not only in the cost of the terminals, but mainly from the reduced support and maintenance cost.

The WBT is used by some organizations as an alternative to NCs. However, because the NCs use Java and HTML languages, they are more flexible and efficient and less expensive to operate than a WBT.

## ▶ T1.4 THE MICROPROCESSOR AND PRIMARY STORAGE

### THE CENTRAL PROCESSING UNIT

The central processing unit (CPU) is also referred to as a microprocessor because of its small size. The CPU is the center of all computer-processing activities, where all processing is controlled, data are manipulated, arithmetic computations are performed, and logical comparisons are made. The CPU consists of the control unit, the arithmetic-logic unit (ALU), and the primary storage (or main memory).

The arithmetic-logic unit performs required arithmetic and comparisons, or logic, operations. The ALU adds, subtracts, multiplies, divides, compares, and determines whether a number is positive, negative, or zero. All computer applications are achieved through these six operations. The ALU operations are performed sequentially, based on instructions from the control unit. For these operations to be performed, the data must first be moved from the storage to the

A CPU.

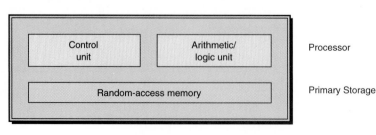

Control unit | Arithmetic/logic unit — Processor

Random-access memory — Primary Storage

arithmetic registers in the ALU. **Registers** are specialized, high-speed memory areas for storing temporary results of ALU operations as well as for storing certain control information.

## PRIMARY STORAGE

**Primary storage,** or **main memory,** stores data and program statements for the CPU. It has four basic purposes.

1. To store data that have been input until they are transferred to the ALU for processing.
2. To store data that have been input until they are transferred to the ALU for processing.
3. To hold data after processing until they are transferred to an output device.
4. To hold program statements or instructions received from input devices and from secondary storage.

Primary storage in today's microcomputers utilizes **integrated circuits,** which are interconnected layers of etched semiconductor materials forming electrical transistor memory units with "on-off" positions that direct the electrical current passing through them. The "on-off" states of the transistors are used to establish a binary 1 or 0 for storing one binary digit, or bit.

## BUSES

Instructions and data move between computer subsystems and the processor via communications channels called buses. A **bus** is a channel (or shared data path) through which data is passed in electronic form. Three types of buses link the CPU, primary storage, and the other devices in the computer system. The **data bus** moves data to and from primary storage. The **address bus** transmits signals for locating a given address in primary storage. The **control bus** transmits signals specifying whether to "read" or "write" data to or from a given primary storage address, input device, or output device. The capacity of a bus, called **bus width,** is defined by the number of bits they carry at one time. (The most common PC in 2000 was 64 bits.) Bus speeds are also important, currently averaging about 66 megahertz (MHz).

## CONTROL UNIT

The **control unit** reads instructions and directs the other components of the computer system to perform the functions required by the program. It interprets and carries out instructions contained in computer programs, selecting program statements from the primary storage, moving them to the instruction registers in the control unit, and then carrying them out. It controls input and output devices and data-transfer processes from and to memory. The control unit does not actually change or create data; it merely directs the data flow within the CPU. The control unit can process only one instruction at a time, but it can execute instructions so quickly (millions per second) that it can appear to do many different things simultaneously.

The series of operations required to process a single machine instruction is called a **machine cycle.** Each machine cycle consists of the *instruction cycle,* which sets up circuitry to perform a required operation, and the *execution cycle,* during which the operation is actually carried out.

## ARITHMETIC-LOGIC UNIT

There are two categories of memory: the register, which is part of the CPU and is very fast, and the **internal memory chips,** which reside outside the CPU and are slower. A register is circuitry in the CPU that allows for the fast storage and retrieval of data and instructions during the processing. The control unit, the CPU, and the primary storage all have registers. Small amounts of data reside in the register for very short periods, prior to their use.

The **internal memory** is used to store data just before they are processed by the CPU. Immediately after the processing it comprises two types of storage space: RAM and ROM.

**RANDOM-ACCESS MEMORY. Random-access memory (RAM)** is the place in which the CPU stores the instructions and data it is processing. The larger the memory area, the larger the programs that can be stored and executed.

With the newer computer operating system software, more than one program may be operating at a time, each occupying a portion of RAM. Most personal computers as of 2000 need 32 to 64 megabytes of RAM to process "multimedia" applications which combine sound, graphics, animation, and video, thus requiring more memory.

The advantage of RAM is that it is very fast in storing and retrieving any type of data, whether textual, graphical, sound, or animation-based. Its disadvantages are that it is relatively expensive and volatile. This volatility means that all data and programs stored in RAM are lost when the power is turned off. To lessen this potential loss of data, many of the newer application programs perform periodic automatic "saves" of the data.

Many software programs are larger than the internal, primary storage (RAM) available to store them. To get around this limitation, some programs are divided into smaller blocks, with each block loaded into RAM only when necessary. However, depending on the program, continuously loading and unloading **blocks** can slow down performance considerably, especially since secondary storage is so much slower than RAM. As a compromise, some architectures use high-speed **cache memory** as a temporary storage for the most frequently used blocks. Then the RAM is used to store the next most frequently used blocks, and secondary storage (described later) for the least used blocks.

Since cache memory operates at a much higher speed than conventional memory (i.e., RAM), this technique greatly increases the speed of processing because it reduces the number of times the program has to fetch instructions and data from RAM and secondary storage.

**Dynamic random access memories (DRAMs)** are the most widely used RAM chips. These are known to be volatile since they need to be recharged and refreshed hundreds of times per second in order to retain the information stored in them.

**Synchronous DRAM (SDRAM)** is a relatively new and different kind of RAM. SDRAM is rapidly becoming the new memory standard for modern PCs. The reason is that its synchronized design permits support for the much higher bus speeds that have started to enter the market.

**READ-ONLY MEMORY. Read-only memory (ROM)** is that portion of primary storage that cannot be changed or erased. ROM is nonvolatile; that is, the program instructions are continually retained within the ROM, whether power is supplied to the computer or not. ROM is necessary to users who need to be able to restore a program or data after the computer has been turned off or, as a safeguard, to prevent a program or data from being changed. For example, the instructions needed to start, or "boot," a computer must not be lost when it is turned off.

**Programmable read-only memory (PROM)** is a memory chip on which a program can be stored. But once the PROM has been used, you cannot wipe it clean and use it to store something else. Like ROMs, PROMs are non-volatile.

**Erasable programmable read-only memory (EPROM)** is a special type of PROM that can be erased by exposing it to ultraviolet light.

**OTHER MEASURES.** Several other types of memories are on the market. Noteable are the fast static RAM (SRAM) chips and the Flash Memory.

## MICROPROCESSOR SPEED

The speed of a chip depends on four things: the clock speed, the word length, the data bus width, and the design of the chip. The *clock,* located within the control unit, is the component that provides the timing for all processor operations. The beat frequency of the clock (measured in megahertz [MHz] or millions of cycles per second) determines how many times per second the processor performs operations. In 2000, PCs with Pentium III, P6, PowerPC, or Alpha chips were running at 450–600 MHz. All things being equal, a processor that uses a 600 MHz clock operates at twice the speed of one that uses a 300 MHz clock. A more accurate processor speed within a computer is millions of instructions per second (MIPS).

*Word length* is the number of bits that can be processed at one time by a chip. Chips are commonly labeled as 8-bit, 16-bit, 32-bit, and 64-bit devices. A 32-bit chip, for example, can process 32 bits of data in a single cycle. The larger the word length, the faster the chip speed.

The *width of the buses* determines how much data can be moved at one time. The wider the data bus (e.g., 64 bits), the faster the chip. Matching the CPU to its buses can affect performance significantly. In some personal computers, the CPU is capable of handling 32 bits at a time, but the buses are only 16 bits wide. In this case, the CPU must send and receive each 32-bit word in two 16-bit chunks, one at a time. This process makes data transmission times twice as long.

## PARALLEL PROCESSING

A computer system with two or more processors is referred to as a *parallel processing system.* Today, some PCs have 2–4 processors while workstations have 20 or more. Processing data in parallel speeds up processing. Larger computers may have a hundred processors. For example, IBM is building a supercomputer for the U.S. Energy Department with 8,192 processors working in tandem and able to execute 10 trillion calculations per second (about 150,000 times faster than the 1999 PC).

Systems with large numbers of processors are called *massively parallel processor* (MPP) systems. They are related to neural computing and complex scientific applications.

*Table T-1.2* **Evolution of Microprocessors**

| Chip | Introduction Date | Clock Speed | Bus Width | Number of Transistors | Addressable Memory |
|---|---|---|---|---|---|
| 4004 | 11/71 | 108 KHz | 4 bits | 2,300 | 640 bytes |
| 8008 | 4/72 | 108 KHz | 8 bits | 3,500 | 16 Kbytes |
| 8080 | 4/74 | 2 MHz | 8 bits | 6,000 | 64 Kbytes |
| 8086 | 6/78 | 5–10 MHz | 16 bits | 29,000 | 1 Mbyte |
| 80286 | 2/82 | 8–12 MHz | 16 bits | 134,000 | 16 Mbytes |
| 80386 DX | 10/85 | 16–33 MHz | 16 bits | 275,000 | 1 Gbytes |
| 80386 SX | 6/88 | 16–20 MHz | 16 bits | 275,000 | 1 Gbytes |
| 80486 DX | 4/89 | 25–50 MHz | 32 bits | 1.2 M | 4 Gbytes |
| 80486 SX | 4/91 | 16–33 MHz | 32 bits | 1.185 M | 4 Gbytes |
| Pentium | 3/93 | 60–166 MHz | 32 bits | 3.1 M | 4 Gbytes |
| Pentium Pro | 3/95 | 150–200 MHz | 32 bits | 5.5 M | 4 Gbytes |
| Pentium II | 1996 | 233–300 MHz | 32 bits | 5.5 M | 4 Gbytes |
| P6 | 1997 | up to 400 MHz | 32 bits | 7.5 M | 4 Gbytes |
| Merced (IA64) | 1998/99 | 500–600 MHz | 64 bits | 9 M | 4–8 Gbytes |
| Pentium III | 1999 | 450–600 MHz | 64 bits | 9.5 M | 10–12 Gbytes |
| Itanium (Merced) | 2000 | 800–1,000 MHz | 64 bits | 20 M | 16 Gbytes |

## MICROPROCESSOR EVOLUTION

Table T-1.2 shows the evolution of the microprocessor from the introduction of the 4004 in 1971 to 2000's Pentium III and P6 microprocessors. Over the twenty-eight years, microprocessors have become dramatically faster, more complex, and denser, with increasing numbers of transistors embedded in the silicon wafer. As the transistors are packed closer together and the physical limits of silicon are approached, scientists are developing new technologies that increase the processing power of chips.

Chips are now being manufactured from gallium arsenide (GaAs), a semiconductor material inherently much faster than silicon because electrons can move through GaAs five times faster than they can move through silicon. GaAs chips are more difficult to produce than silicon chips, resulting in higher prices. However, chip producers are perfecting manufacturing techniques that will result in a decrease in the cost of GaAs chips.

Intel has incorporated MMX (multimedia extension) technology in its Pentium microprocessors. MMX technology improves video compression/decompression, image manipulation, encryption, and input/output processing, all of which are used in modern office software suites and advanced business media, communications, and Internet capabilities.

A prototype plasma-wave chip has been developed that transmits signals as waves, not as packets of electrons as current chips do. Developers use an analogy with sound. Sound travels through the air, not as batches of air molecules that leave one person's mouth and enter another's ear. If sound worked in that fashion, there would be a long delay while the sound-carrying molecules negotiated their way through the other air molecules. The new chips have the potential of operating speeds in the gigahertz range, or billions of cycles per second.

## MICROPROCESSOR ARCHITECTURE

The arrangement of the components and their interactions is called computer *architecture*. Computer architecture includes the instruction set and the number of the processors, the structure of the internal buses, the use of caches, and the types and arrangements of input/output (I/O) device interfaces.

Every processor comes with a unique set of operational codes or commands that represent the computer's instruction set. An *instruction set* is the set of machine instructions that a processor recognizes and can execute. Today, the two instruction set strategies, **complex instruction set computer (CISC)** and **reduced instruction set computer (RISC),** dominate the processor instruction sets of computer architectures. These two strategies differ by the number of operations available and how and when instructions are moved into memory. A CISC processor contains more than 200 unique coded commands, one for virtually every type of operation. The CISC design goal is for its instruction set to look like a sophisticated programming language. Inexpensive hardware can then be used to replace expensive software, thereby reducing the cost of developing software. The penalty for this ease of programming is that CISC processor–based computers have increased architectural complexity and decreased overall system performance. In spite of these drawbacks, most computers still use CISC processors.

The other, most recent approach is RISC processors, which eliminate many of the little-used codes found in the complex instruction set. Underlying RISC design is the claim that a very small subset of instructions amounts for a very large percentage of all instructions executed. The instruction set, therefore, should be designed around a few simple "hardwired" instructions that can be executed very quickly. The rest of the needed instructions can be created in software.

## ▶ T1.5 INPUT/OUTPUT DEVICES

The input/output (I/O) devices of a computer are not part of the CPU, but are channels for communicating between the external environment and the CPU. Data and instructions are entered into the computer through **input devices**, and processing results are provided through **output devices.** Widely used I/O devices are the cathode-ray tube (CRT) or visual display unit (VDU), magnetic storage media, printers, keyboards, "mice," and image-scanning devices.

I/O devices are controlled directly by the CPU or indirectly through special processors dedicated to input and output processing. Generally speaking, I/O devices are subclassified into secondary storage devices (primarily disk and tape drives) and peripheral devices (any input/output device that is attached to the computer).

## SECONDARY STORAGE

Secondary storage is separate from primary storage and the CPU, but directly connected to it. An example would be the 3.5-inch disk you place in your PC's A drive. It stores the data in a format that is compatible with data stored in primary storage, but secondary storage provides the computer with vastly increased space for storing and processing large quantities of software and data. Primary storage is volatile, contained in memory chips, and very fast in storing and retrieving data. On the other hand, secondary storage is nonvolatile, uses many different forms of media that are less expensive than primary storage, and is relatively slower than primary storage. Secondary storage media include magnetic tape, magnetic disk, magnetic diskette, optical storage, and digital videodisk.

**Magnetic tape** is kept on a large reel or in a small cartridge or cassette. Today, cartridges and cassettes are replacing reels because they are easier to use and access. The principal advantages of magnetic tape are that it is inexpensive, relatively stable, and long lasting, and that it can store very large volumes of data. A magnetic tape is excellent for backup or archival storage of data and can be reused. The main disadvantage of magnetic tape is that it must be searched from the beginning to find the desired data. The magnetic tape itself is fragile and must be handled with care. Magnetic tape is also labor intensive to mount and dismount in a mainframe computer.

**Magnetic disks** (called hard disks) alleviate some of the problems associated with magnetic tape by assigning specific address locations for data, so that users can go directly to the address without having to go through intervening locations looking for the right data to retrieve. This process is called *direct access*. Most computers today rely on hard disks for retrieving and storing large amounts of instructions and data in a nonvolatile and rapid manner. The hard drives of 2000 microcomputers provide six to thirteen gigabytes of data storage.

A **hard disk** is like a phonograph containing a stack of metal-coated platters (usually permanently mounted) that rotate rapidly. Magnetic read/write heads, attached to arms, hover over the platters. To locate an address for storing or retrieving data, the head moves inward or outward to the correct position then waits for the correct location to spin underneath.

The speed of access to data on hard disk drives is a function of the rotational speed of the disk and the speed of the read/write heads. The read/write heads must position themselves, and the disk pack must rotate until the proper information is located. Advanced disk drives have access speeds of 5 to 10 milliseconds.

Magnetic disks provide storage for large amounts of data and instructions that can be rapidly accessed. Another advantage of disks over reel is that a robot can change them. This can drastically reduce the expenses of a data center. Storage Technology is the major vendor of such robots. The disks' disadvantages are that they are more expensive than magnetic tape and they are susceptible to "disk crashes."

A magnetic tape cartridge (right) and its drive (left).

In contrast to large, fixed disk drives, one current approach is to combine a large number of small disk drives each with 9 to 23 gigabyte capacity, developed originally for microcomputers. These devices are called **redundant arrays of inexpensive disks (RAID).** Because data are stored redundantly across many drives, the overall impact on system performance is lessened when one drive malfunctions. Also, multiple drives provide multiple data paths, improving performance. Finally, because of manufacturing efficiencies of small drives, the cost of RAID devices is significantly lower than the cost of large disk drives of the same capacity.

Hard disks are not practical for transporting data of instructions from one personal computer to another. To accomplish this task effectively, developers created the **magnetic diskette,** also called the "floppy disk." The floppy disk is a 3.5-inch, removable, flexible magnetic platter encased in a plastic housing. Unlike the hard disk drive, the read/write head of the floppy disk drive actually touches the surface of the disk. As a result, the speed of the floppy drive is much slower, with an accompanying reduction in data transfer rate. However, the diskettes themselves are very inexpensive, thin enough to be mailed, and able to store relatively large amounts of data. A standard high-density disk contains 1.44 megabytes. **Zip disks** are larger than conventional floppy disks, and about twice as thick. Disks formatted for zip drives contain 250 megabytes.

**Optical storage devices** have extremely high storage density. Typically, much more information can be stored on a standard 5.25-inch optical disk than on a comparably sized floppy (about 400 times more). Since a highly focused laser beam is used to read/write information encoded on an optical disk, the information can be highly condensed. In addition, the amount of physical disk space needed to record an optical bit is much smaller than that usually required by magnetic media.

Another advantage of optical storage is that the medium itself is less susceptible to contamination or deterioration. First, the recording surfaces (on both sides of the disk) are protected by two plastic plates, which keep dust and dirt from contaminating the surface. Second, only a laser beam of light comes in contact with the recording surface, not a flying head; the head of an optical disk drive comes no closer than 1 mm from the disk surface. Optical drives are also less fragile, and the disks themselves may easily be loaded and removed. Three common types of optical drive technologies are CD-ROM, WORM, and rewritable optical.

**Compact disk read-only memory (CD-ROM) disks** have high capacity and low cost. CD-ROM technology is very effective and efficient for mass producing many copies of large amounts of information that does not need to be changed, for example, encyclopedias, directories, and online databases.

A CD-ROM inside a drive.

CD-ROMs are generally too expensive for mastering and producing unique, one-of-a-kind applications. For these situations, **write once, read many (WORM)** technology is more practical. The storage capacity and access for WORMs is virtually the same as for CD-ROMs. Companies use CD-ROM/WORM for the following applications: publishing their corporate manuals, disseminating training information, and sending samples of products or their description to customers. Once you write on a WORM it becomes a regular CD-ROM. You cannot change anything on the disk.

When information needs to be changed or updated, and companies do not want to incur the expense of mastering and producing a new CD-ROM, **rewritable optical disks** are needed (also called floptical, magneto-optic). The surface of the disk is coated with a magnetic material that can change magnetic polarity only when heated. To record data, a high-powered laser beam heats microscopic areas in the magnetic medium that allows it to accept magnetic patterns. Data can be read by shining a lower-powered laser beam at the magnetic layer and reading the reflected light.

**DIGITAL VIDEO DISK (DVD). DVD** is a new storage disk that offers higher quality and denser storage capabilities. In 2000, the disk's maximum storage capacity was 17 Gbytes, which is sufficient for storing about five movies. It includes superb audio (six-track vs. the two-track stereo). Like CDs, DVD comes as DVD-ROM (read-only) and DVD-RAM.

## INPUT DEVICES

Users can command the computer and communicate with it by using one or more input devices. Each input device accepts a specific form of data; for example, keyboards transmit typed characters while handwriting recognizers "read" handwritten characters. Users want communication with computers to be simple, fast, and error free. Therefore, a variety of input devices fits the needs of different individuals and applications (see Table T-1.3). Some of these devices are shown in Figure T-1.5 together with their usage.

**Table T-1.3** **Representative Input Devices**

| Categories | Examples |
|---|---|
| **Keying devices** | • Punched card reader<br>• Keyboard<br>• Point-of-sale terminal |
| **Pointing devices**<br>*(devices that point to objects on the computer screen)* | • Mouse (including rollerballs and trackballs)<br>• Touch screen<br>• Touchpad (or trackpad)<br>• Light pen<br>• Joy stick |
| **Optical character recognition**<br>*(devices that scan characters)* | • Bar code scanner<br>• Optical character reader<br>• Wand reader<br>• Cordless reader<br>• Optical mark reader |
| **Handwriting recognizers** | • Pen |
| **Voice recognizers** *(data are entered by voice)* | • Microphone |
| **Other devices** | • Magnetic ink character readers<br>• Digital cameras<br>• Automatic teller machines (ATM)<br>• Smart cards<br>• Digitizers (for maps, graphs, etc.) |

**KEYBOARD.** The most common input device is the keyboard. The keyboard is designed like a typewriter but with many additional special keys. Most computer users utilize keyboards regularly. Unfortunately, a number of computer users have developed repetitive stress injury, which they allege comes from excessive use of poorly designed keyboards (see Chapter 7). As a result, new keyboards have been

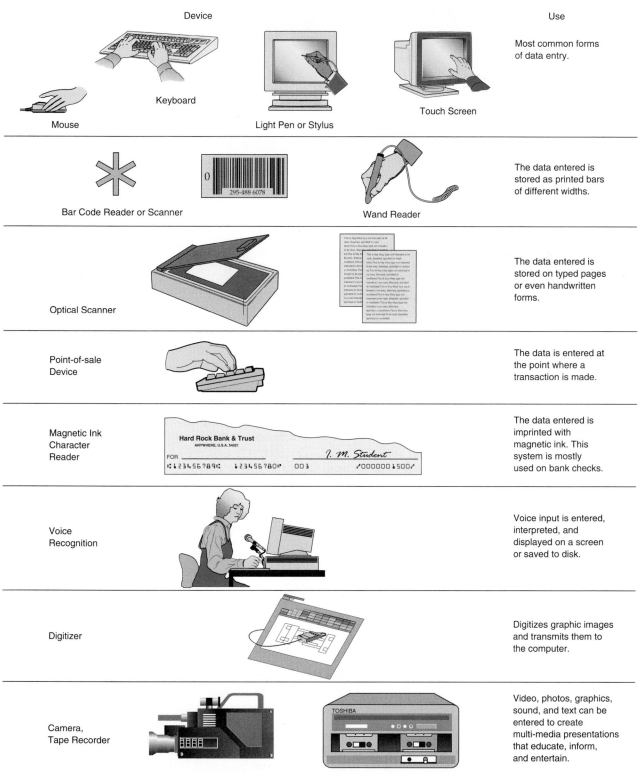

| Device | | | Use |
|---|---|---|---|
| Mouse / Keyboard | Light Pen or Stylus | Touch Screen | Most common forms of data entry. |
| Bar Code Reader or Scanner | | Wand Reader | The data entered is stored as printed bars of different widths. |
| Optical Scanner | | | The data entered is stored on typed pages or even handwritten forms. |
| Point-of-sale Device | | | The data is entered at the point where a transaction is made. |
| Magnetic Ink Character Reader | | | The data entered is imprinted with magnetic ink. This system is mostly used on bank checks. |
| Voice Recognition | | | Voice input is entered, interpreted, and displayed on a screen or saved to disk. |
| Digitizer | | | Digitizes graphic images and transmits them to the computer. |
| Camera, Tape Recorder | | | Video, photos, graphics, sound, and text can be entered to create multi-media presentations that educate, inform, and entertain. |

**FIGURE T-1.5** Typical input devices. Each input device reads a different form of data for processing by the CPU. (*Source*: *Computing in the Information Age*, Stern and Stern, 1993, p. 172. Copyright© 1993 John Wiley and Sons, Inc. Reprinted by permission of John Wiley and Sons, Inc.)

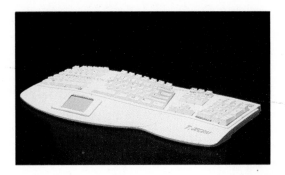

A split keyboard.

developed that are ergonomically designed. For example, some keyboards are now "split" in half, loosely approximating the natural angle of the arms and wrists.

Of the many attempts to improve the keyboard, one of the most interesting is the DataHand keyboard, which consists of two unattached pads. Rather than a conventional array of keys, this device has touch-sensitive receptacles (or finger wells) for the fingers and thumbs. Each finger well allows five different commands, which are actuated by touching one of the sides or the bottom of the finger wells. Complex commands can be programmed so that a single flick of the finger can be used to enter frequently used sequences of commands or chunks of data.

**MOUSE.** The mouse is a hand-held device used to point a cursor at a desired place on the screen, such as an icon, a cell in a table, an item in a menu, or any other object. Once the arrow is placed on an object, the user clicks a button on the mouse, instructing the computer to take some action. The use of the mouse reduces the need to type in information or use the slower arrow keys.

Special types of mice are *rollerballs* and *trackballs,* used in many portable computers. A new technology, called glide-and-tap, allows fingertip cursor control in laptop computers.

**TOUCH SCREEN.** An alternative to the mouse or other screen-related devices is a touch screen. The user activates an object on the screen by touching it with his or her finger.

**TOUCHPAD.** A touchpad or trackpad is a small, flat, rectangular pointing device that is sensitive to pressure and motion.

**LIGHT PEN.** A light pen is a special device with a light-sensing mechanism, which is used to touch the screen. Pointing with a light pen is more accurate than touch screens because you can point at very small objects.

**JOYSTICK.** Joysticks are used primarily at workstations that can display dynamic graphics. They are also used in playing video games. The joystick moves and positions the cursor at the desired object on the screen.

**AUTOMATED TELLER MACHINES.** Automated teller machines (ATMs) are interactive input/output devices that enable people to obtain cash, make deposits, transfer funds, and update their bank accounts instantly from many locations. ATMs can handle a variety of banking transactions, including the transfer of funds to specified accounts. One drawback of ATMs is their vulnerability to computer crimes and to attacks made on customers as they use outdoor ATMs.

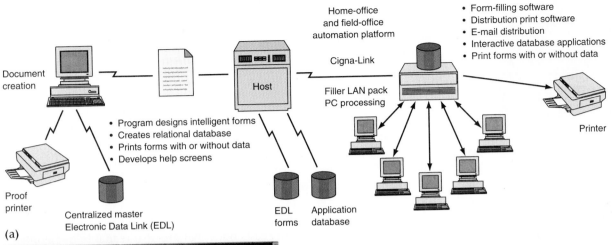

(a)

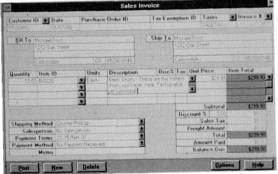

(b)

FIGURE T-1.6 Form interaction. The upper part shows the process of using electronic forms, and a completed form is shown on the left. (a) Intelligent electronic form processing (paperless). (*Source*: Reprinted with permission from the November 1993 issue of *BYTE* magazine, by McGraw-Hill, Inc., New York, NY. All rights reserved.)
(b) A standard "service invoice" form. The form appears online to the user who fills in the appropriate information. The program executes automatic routing computations (such as sales tax).

**ELECTRONIC FORMS.** In **form interaction,** the user enters data or commands into predesignated spaces (fields) in a form (see Figure T-1.6). The headings of the form serve as a prompt for the input. The computer may produce some output after input is made, and the user may be requested to continue the form interaction process. **Electronic forms** can alleviate many of the resource-intensive steps of processing forms. Traditional typesetting and printing steps become unnecessary. Finally, processing centers do not need to rekey data from paper-based forms, since the data remains in electronic format throughout the process.

**WHITEBOARD.** A **whiteboard** is an area on a display screen that multiple users can write or draw on. Whiteboards are a principal component of teleconferencing applications because they enable visual as well as audio communication.

## SOURCE DATA AUTOMATION

Source data automation captures data in computer-readable form at the moment the data are created. Point-of-sale systems, optical bar-codes scanners, other optical character recognition devices, handwriting recognizers, voice recognizers, digitizers, and cameras are examples of source data automation. Source data automation devices eliminate errors arising from humans keyboarding data and allows for data to be captured directly and immediately, with built-in error correction. The major devices are:

**POINT OF SALE TERMINALS.** Many retail organizations utilize point of sale (POS) terminals. The POS terminal has a specialized keyboard. For example, the

A POS terminal.

POS terminals at McDonald's include all the items on the menu, often labeled with the picture of the item. POS terminals in a retail store are equipped with a scanner that reads the bar-coded sales tag. POS devices increase the speed of data entry and reduce the chance of errors. POS terminals may include many features such as scanner, printer, voice syntheses, which pronounces the price by voice, and accounting software.

**BAR CODE SCANNER.** Bar code scanners scan the black-and-white bars written in the Universal Product Code (UPC). This code specifies the name of the product and its manufacturer (product ID). Then a computer finds in the database the price equivalent to the product's ID. Bar codes are especially valuable in high-volume processing where keyboard energy is too slow and/or inaccurate. Applications include supermarket checkout, airline baggage stickers, Federal Express, and other transport companies' packages. The wand reader is a special hand-held bar code reader that can read codes that are also readable by people.

**OPTICAL CHARACTER READER (OR OPTICAL SCANNER).** With an optical character reader (OCR), source documents such as reports, typed manuscripts, and books can be entered directly into a computer without the need for keying. An OCR converts text and images on paper into digital form and stores the data on disk or other storage media. OCRs are available in different sizes and for different types of applications. The publishing industry is the leading user of optical scanning equipment. Publishers scan printed documents and convert them to electronic databases that can be referenced as needed. Similarly, they may scan manuscripts instead of retyping them in preparation for the process that converts them into books and magazines. Considerable time and money are saved, and the risk of introduction of typographical errors is reduced.

**HANDWRITING RECOGNIZERS.** Today's scanners are good at "reading" typed or published material, but they are not very good at handwriting recognition. Handwriting recognition is supported by technologies such as expert systems and neural computing and is available in some pen-based computers.

Scanners that can interpret handwritten input are subject to considerable error. To minimize mistakes, handwritten entries should follow very specific rules. Some scanners will flag handwritten entries that they cannot interpret or will automatically display for verification all input that has been scanned. Because handwritten entries are subject to misinterpretation and typed entries can be smudged, misaligned, and/or erased, optical scanners have an error rate much higher than the error rate for keyed data.

Pen-based input devices transform the letters and numbers written by users on the tablet into digital form, where they can be stored or processed and analyzed. At present, pen-based devices cannot recognize free-hand writing very well, so users must print letters and numbers in block form.

**VOICE RECOGNIZERS.** The most natural way to communicate with computers is by voice, using a natural language. The process of doing this is called *natural language processing*. Voice recognition devices convert spoken words into digital form. Voice recognition devices are extremely important because they work fast, free the user's hands, and result in few entry errors. They also allow people with visual or other disabilities to communicate with computers. When voice technology is used in combination with telephones, people can call their computers from almost any location. While voice technologies have certain limitations such as size of the vocabulary, they are rapidly being improved. In 2000, the price of some voice recognizers is as low as $60, and they have a vocabulary of 30,000 to 80,000 words (e.g., Via Voice from IBM and Naturally Speaking from Dragon Systems).

Recognizing words is fairly easy, but understanding the content of sentences and paragraphs is much more difficult. To understand a natural language inquiry, a computer must have sufficient knowledge to analyze the input in order to interpret it. This knowledge includes linguistic knowledge about words, domain knowledge, common sense knowledge, and even knowledge about users and their goals.

**MAGNETIC INK CHARACTER READERS.** Magnetic ink character readers (MICR) read information printed on checks in magnetic ink. This information identifies the bank and the account number. On a canceled check, the amount is also readable after it is added in magnetic ink.

**DIGITIZERS.** Digitizers are devices that convert drawings made with a pen on a sensitized surface to machine-readable input. As drawings are made, the images are transferred to the computer. This technology is based on changes in electrical charges that correspond to the drawings. Designers, engineers, and artists use digitizers.

**DIGITAL CAMERAS.** Regular video cameras can be used to capture pictures that are digitized and stored in computers. Special cameras are used to transfer pictures and images to storage on a CD-ROM. A digital camera can take photos and load them directly from the camera, digitally, to a main storage or secondary storage device.

Digital cameras use a charge-coupled device (CCD) instead of a film. Once you take pictures you can review, delete, edit, and save images. You can capture sound or text annotations and send the results to a printer. You can zoom or shrink images and interface with other devices. Images can be transmitted from the camera to a PC, printer, or other cameras, even via telephone lines. Digital cameras work with or without computers.

In addition to instant prints you can do many other things with your digital camera (cost $200–$1,000). For example, you can stop scribbling notes and can instead digitally capture the teacher's (presenter's) notes, slides, and other visual exhibits.

A digital camera.

## OUTPUT DEVICES

The output generated by a computer can be transmitted to the user via several devices and media. The presentation of information is extremely important in encouraging users to embrace computers. The major output devices are shown in Figure T-1.7 and are discussed next.

**MONITORS.** The data entered into a computer can be visible on the computer monitor, which is basically a video screen that displays both input and output. Monitors come in different sizes, ranging from inches to several feet, and in different colors. The major benefit is the interactive nature of the device.

Monitors employ the cathode ray tube (CRT) technology, in which an electronic "gun" shoots a beam of electrons to illuminate the pixels on the screen.

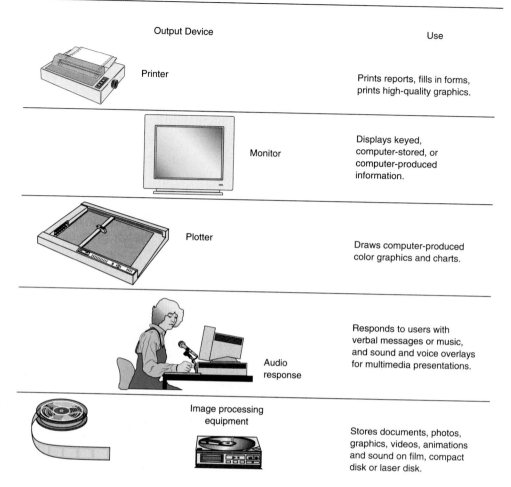

FIGURE T-1.7 Representative output devices and their use. (*Source: Computing in the Information Age*, Stern and Stern 1993, p. 199. Copyright© 1993 John Wiley and Sons, Inc. Reprinted by permission of John Wiley and Sons, Inc.)

An LCD Monitor

They are 21-inch or smaller. The more pixels on the screen, the higher the resolution. Portable computers use a float screen consisting of a liquid crystal display (LCD). Gas Plasma monitors offer larger screen sizes (more than 42 inches) and higher display quality than LCD monitors but are much more expensive.

In 2000, the monitor's depth was still large. We see more and more thin and flat monitors on the market, but the cost is still very high ($1,000 to $5,000).

**IMPACT PRINTERS.** Like typewrites, impact printers use some form of striking action to press a carbon or fabric ribbon against paper to create a character. The most common impact printers are the dot matrix, daisy wheel, and line. Line printers print one line at a time; therefore, they are faster than one-character type printers.

Impact printers are slow and noisy, cannot do high-resolution graphics, and are often subject to mechanical breakdowns. They have largely been replaced by nonimpact printers.

**NONIMPACT PRINTERS.** Nonimpact printers overcome the deficiencies of impact printers. Laser printers are of higher speed, containing high-quality devices that use laser beams to write information on photosensitive drums, whole pages at a time; then the paper passes over the drum and picks up the image with toner. Because they produce print-quality text and graphics, laser printers are used in desktop publishing and in reproduction of artwork. Thermal printers create whole characters on specially treated paper that responds to patterns of heat produced by the printer. Ink-jet printers shoot tiny dots of ink onto paper. Sometimes called bubble jet, they are relatively inexpensive and are especially suited for low-volume graphical applications when different colors of ink are required.

**PLOTTERS.** Plotters are printing devices using computer-driven pens for creating high-quality black-and-white or color graphic images—charts, graphs, and drawings. They are used in complex, low-volume situations such as engineering and architectural drawing and come in different types and sizes.

Laser printers.

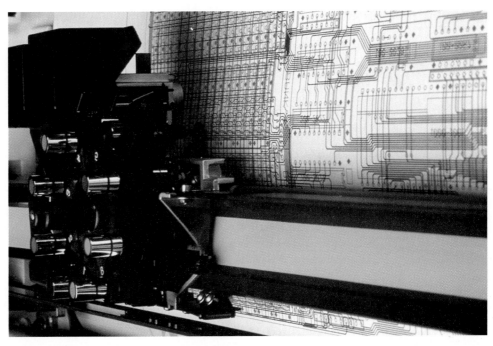

A large plotter and its output (on the right).

**VOICE OUTPUT.** Some devices provide output via voice—synthesized voice. This term refers to the technology by which computers "speak." The synthesis of voice by computer differs from a simple playback of a prerecorded voice by either analog or digital means. As the term "synthesis" implies, the sounds that make up words and phrases are constructed electronically from basic sound components and can be made to form any desired voice pattern. The quality of synthesized voice is currently very good, and relatively inexpensive.

## MULTIMEDIA

**Multimedia** refers to a group of human-machine communication media, some of which can be combined in one application. In information technology, an interactive multimedia approach involves the use of computers to improve human-machine communication by using a combination of media. The con-

**Table T-1.4** Communications Media

**Computer**
- CRT and terminals
- CD-ROM
- Computer interactive videodisc
- Digital video interactive
- Compact disc interactive
- Computer simulation
- Teletext/videotext
- Intelligent tutoring system
- Hypertext
- Image digitizing
- Scanners
- Screen projection
- Object-oriented programming

**Motion image**
- Videodisc (cassette)
- Motion pictures
- Broadcast television
- Teleconference/videoconference
- Animation
- Virtual reality

**Projected still visuals**
- Slide
- Overhead

**Graphic materials**
- Pictures
- Printed job aids
- Visual display

**Audio**
- Tape/cassette/record
- Teleconference/audioconference
- Sound digitizing
- Microphone
- Compact disc
- Music

**Text**
- Printouts

SOURCE: Based on Chao, P., et al., "Using Expert Systems Approaches to Solve Media Selection Problems: Matrix Format," *Proceedings of the Association of Computer Interface System*, November 1990, IEEE.

struction of a multimedia application is called *authoring*. Multimedia also merges the capabilities of computers with television sets, VCRs, CD players, and other entertainment devices. Communications media are listed in Table T-1.4. The multimedia software is described in Technology Guide #2.

# REFERENCES AND BIBLIOGRAPHY

1. Athens, G., "Supercomputer Tops 1 Teraflop," *ComputerWorld*, January 2, 1997, p. 124.

2. Barry, B. Brey, "The Intel Microprocessors : 8086/8088, 80186/80188, 80286, 80386, 80486, Pentium, Pentium Pro, Pentium II Processors," Prentice Hall, August 1999.

3. Hansen, B., "The Dictionary of Computing & Digital Media : Terms & Acronyms," Abf Content, May 1999.

4. Halfhill, R., "Cheaper Computing," *Byte,* April 1997.

5. Jacobs, A., and S. Gaudin, "Can the NC Deliver?" *ComputerWorld*, November 4, 1996, p. 45.

6. Katz, M., ed., "Technology Forecast: 1997" (also 1998, 1999, 2000), Menlo Park, CA: Price Waterhouse World Technology Center, 1997 (1998), (1999), (2000).

7. Lohr, S., "The Network Computer as the PC's Evil Twin," *New York Times,* November 4, 1996.

8. Loudermilk, S., "A Fresh Look at RAID," Lantimes Online, http://www.wcmh.com:80/Lantimes/archive/506a07a.html, June 5, 1995.

9. Markcott, J., "Innovative to Double Chip Power May Cut Life Span of Computers," *New York Times,* September 17, 1997.

10. Mossberg, W., "MMX Has Much to Offer, But Less than Hype Suggests," *Wall Street Journal,* February 13, 1997, p. 124.

11. Mueller, S., *Upgrading and Repairing PCs*, (11th Ed.), Que Corp, September, 1999.

12. "120 MB Floppies," Datamation, Vol. 42, No. 8, April 15, 1996, p. 7.

13. Ouellette, T., "Big Iron Rebounds," *ComputerWorld,* November 11, 1996, p. 45.

14. Peleg, A., et al., "Intel MMX for Multimedia PCs," *Communications of the ACM* 40, No. 1, January 1997.

15. Radding, A., "RISC Servers Still Have the Advantage," *ComputerWorld,* November 11, 1996, p. 97.

16. Ramstad, E., "Texas Instruments Makes Chip Offering Huge Boost in Power," *Wall Street Journal,* January 31, 1997, p. B3.

17. Selker, T., "New Paradigms for Using Computers," *Communications of the ACM* 39, No. 8, August 1996.

18. Tredennick, N., "Microprocessor-based Computers," *Computer,* October 1996.

19. Vaughan-Nichols, S., "To NC or Not to NC?" *Networker* 1, No. 1, March/April 1997.

20. White, T., "Rx for 400 Billion Characters," *Beyond Computing,* special advertising section, April 1996.

21. Wohl, A.D., "Defining DVD," *Beyond Computing,* November/December 1997.

# TECHNOLOGY GUIDE 2:

# Software

## ▶ T2.1 TYPES OF SOFTWARE

Computer hardware cannot perform a single act without instructions. These instructions are known as **software** or computer programs. Software is at the heart of all computer applications. Computer hardware is, by design, general purpose. Software, on the other hand, enables the user to tailor a computer to provide specific business value. There are two major types of software: application software and systems software.

**Application software** is a set of computer instructions, written in a programming language. The instructions direct computer hardware to perform specific data or information processing activities that provide functionality to the user. This functionality may be broad, such as general word processing, or narrow, such as an organization's payroll program. An **application program** applies a computer to a need, such as increasing productivity of accountants or improved decisions regarding an inventory level. **Application programming** is either the creation or the modification and improvement of application software.

**Systems software** acts primarily as an intermediary between computer hardware and application programs and knowledgeable users may also directly manipulate it. Systems software provides important self-regulatory functions for computer systems, such as loading itself when the computer is first turned on, as in Windows 98; managing hardware resources such as secondary storage for all applications; and providing commonly used sets of instructions for all applications to use. **Systems programming** is either the creation or modification of systems software.

Application programs primarily manipulate data or text to produce or provide information. Systems programs primarily manipulate computer hardware resources. The systems software available on a computer provides the capabilities and limitations within which the application software can operate (See Figure T-2.1).

Unlike computer hardware, which can be designed and manufactured on automated assembly lines, software must be programmed by hand. Computer hardware power grows roughly by a factor of two every 18 months, but computer software power barely doubles in eight years. This lag presents a great challenge to software developers and to information systems users in general.

Both application software and systems software are written in coding schemes called **programming languages** which are also presented in this guide.

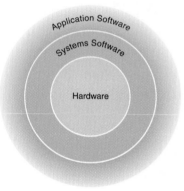

**FIGURE T-2.1** Systems software serves as intermediary between hardware and functional applications.

## ▶ T2.2 APPLICATION SOFTWARE

### TYPES OF APPLICATION SOFTWARE

Because there are so many different uses for computers, there are a correspondingly large number of different application programs, some of which are special-purpose or "packages" tailored for a specific purpose (e.g., inventory control or payroll). A package is a commonly used term for a computer program (or group of programs) that has been developed by a vendor and is available for purchase in a prepackaged form. If a package is not available for a certain situation, it is necessary to build the application using programming languages or software development tools. There are also general-purpose application programs that are not linked to any specific business task, but instead support general types of information processing. The most widely used general-purpose application packages are spreadsheet, data management, word processing, desktop publishing, graphics, multimedia, and communications.

Some of these general-purpose tools are actually *development tools*. That is, you use them for building applications. For example, you can use Excel to build decision support applications such as resource allocation, scheduling, or inventory control. You can use these and similar packages for doing statistical analysis, for conducting financial analysis, and for supporting marketing research.

Many decision support and business applications are built with programming languages rather than with general-purpose application programs. This is especially true for complex, unstructured problems. Information systems applications can also be built with a mix of general-purpose programs and/or with a large number of development tools ranging from editors to random number generators. Of special interest are the software suites, such as Microsoft Office. These are integrated sets of tools that can expedite application development. Also of special interest are CASE tools and integrated enterprise software, which are described later in the guide.

## GENERAL-PURPOSE APPLICATION PROGRAMS

**SPREADSHEETS. Spreadsheet software** transforms a computer screen into a ledger sheet, or grid, of coded rows and columns. Users can enter numeric or textual data into each grid location, called a cell. In addition, a formula or macro can also be entered into a cell to obtain a calculated answer displayed in that cell's location. The term *macro* is used to refer to a single instruction or formula that combines a number of other simpler instructions. A user-defined macro can enhance and extend the basic instructions and commands that are furnished with the spreadsheet. Spreadsheet packages include a large number of already programmed statistical, financial, and other business formulas. They are known as *functions*.

With spreadsheet software, you create worksheets that contain numeric data arranged in rows and columns.

Computer spreadsheet packages are used primarily for decision support such as in financial information processing (e.g., such as income statements or cash flow analysis). However, they also are relevant for many other types of data that can be organized into rows and columns. Spreadsheets are usually integrated with other software, such as graphics and data management, to form *software suites.*

**DATA MANAGEMENT.**   Data management software supports the storage, retrieval, and manipulation of data. There are two basic types of data management software: simple **filing programs** patterned after traditional, manual data filing techniques, and **database management systems (DBMSs)** that take advantage of a computer's extremely fast and accurate ability to store and retrieve data in primary and secondary storage (see Technology Guide #3).

A file is a simple collection of related records organized alphabetically, chronologically, hierarchically in levels, or in some other manner. File-based management software is typically simple to use and often very fast, but it is difficult and time-consuming to modify because of the structured manner in which the files are created. Database management software was developed to rectify such problems with file-based management software. A **database** is a collection of files serving as the data resource for computer-based information systems. In a database, all data are integrated with established relationships. An example of database software is provided in Figure T-2.2.

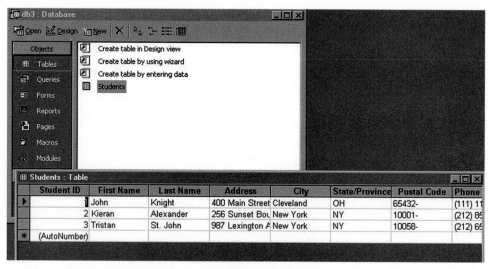

**FIGURE T-2.2** Database software.

**WORD PROCESSING.   Word processing** software allows the user to manipulate text rather than just numbers. Modern word processors contain many productive writing features. A typical word processing software package consists of an integrated set of programs, including an editor program, a formatting program, a print program, a dictionary, a thesaurus, a grammar checker, a mailing list program, and integrated graphics, charting, and drawing programs. WYSIWYG (**W**hat **Y**ou **S**ee **I**s **W**hat **Y**ou **G**et) word processors have the added advantage of displaying the text material on the screen exactly—or almost exactly—as it will look on the final printed page (based on the type of printer connected to the computer).

**DESKTOP PUBLISHING.**   In the past, newsletters, announcements, advertising copy, and other specialized documents had to be laid out by hand and then typeset. **Desktop publishing** software allows microcomputers to perform these tasks directly. Photographs, diagrams, and other images can be combined with text, including several different fonts, to produce a finished, camera-ready document. When printed on a high-resolution laser printer, the product is difficult to distinguish from that which was produced by a professional typesetter.

**GRAPHICS.** Graphics software allows the user to create, store, and display or print charts, graphs, maps, and drawings. Graphics software enables users to absorb more information more quickly, to spot relationships and trends in data more easily, and to make points more emphatically. There are three basic categories of graphics software packages: presentation graphics, analysis graphics, and engineering graphics.

*Presentation Graphics.* This software allows users to create pseudo-three-dimensional images, superimpose multiple images, highlight certain aspects of a drawing, and create freehand drawings. These packages typically contain drawing tools, presentation templates, various font styles, spell-checking routines, charting aids, and tools to aid in assembling multiple images into a complete presentation. Many packages have extensive built-in tutorials and libraries of clip-art—pictures that can be electronically "clipped out" and "pasted" into the finished image.

*Analysis Graphics.* These applications additionally provide the ability to convert previously analyzed data—such as statistical data—into graphic formats like bar charts, line charts, pie charts, and scatter diagrams. The charts may also include elements of different textures, labels, and headings. Some packages will prepare three-dimensional displays.

*Engineering Graphics.* Various engineering software programs are available to shorten development time of applications and to increase productivity of draftspersons and engineers. Most notable are computer-aided design and computer-aided manufacturing (for details see Chapter 8).

**MULTIMEDIA.** There are two general types of multimedia software: presentation and interactive. Presentation software presents a sequential procession of information similar to a movie or television show. The order of events is fixed, although the presentation can be stopped and started. Speakers and trade show booths often use multimedia for marketing purposes. Interactive software allows a user to alter the sequence or flow of information, similar to looking at an encyclopedia or a photo album. Educational, interactive multimedia products are popular at museums or at information kiosks and show great potential for public and private education both within and outside the classroom.

**COMMUNICATIONS SOFTWARE.** Computers are often interconnected in order to share or relate information. To exchange information, computers utilize communications software. This software allows computers located close together or far apart to exchange data over dedicated or public cables, telephone lines, satellite relay systems, or microwave circuits (see Technology Guide #4).

When communications software exists in both the sending and receiving computers, they are able to establish and relinquish electronic links, code and decode data transmissions, verify transmission errors (and correct them automatically), compress data streams for more efficient transmission, and manage the transmission of documents. Communications software establishes the switched routings needed to ensure successful "end-to-end" transmissions, establishes electronic contact ("handshaking") between computers, and assures that data

Two popular software suites are Lotus Smart-Suite and Microsoft Office 2000.

will be sent in the proper format and at the proper speed. It detects transmission speeds and codes, and routes information to the appropriate hardware. Communication software checks for and handles transmission interruptions or conflicting transmission priorities. Other communication software include terminal emulators, remote control software, and fax programs.

**SOFTWARE SUITES.** Software suites are collections of application software packages in a bundle. Software suites can include word processors, spreadsheets, database management systems, graphics programs, communications tools, and others. Microsoft Office, Corel Perfect Office, and Lotus SmartSuite are widely used software suites for personal computers. Each of these suites includes a spreadsheet program, word processor, database program, and graphics package with the ability to move documents, data, and diagrams among them. In addition to end-user type suites, such as described above, there are software kits for system developers, such as CASE tools, which are described later.

**WORKGROUP SOFTWARE.** Workgroup software, or **groupware**, helps groups and teams work together by sharing information and by controlling workflow within the group. The use of this type of software has grown because of a need for groups to work together more effectively, coupled with technological progress in networking and group support products.

Many groupware products are designed to support specific group-related tasks such as project management, scheduling (called calendaring), workflow, and retrieving data from shared databases. For example, Lotus Notes is designed as a system for sharing text and images, and contains a data structure that is a combination of a table-oriented database and an outline. Using Lotus Notes, groups of users working together on projects are able to see each other's screens, share data, and exchange ideas and notes in an interactive mode. Such capabilities increase the productivity of work groups.

Other groupware products focus primarily on the flow of work in office settings. These products provide tools for structuring the process by which information for a particular task is managed, transferred, and routed. Other groupware systems are basically e-mail systems extended by classifying messages and using those classifications to control the way messages are handled. Of special interest is *group decision support systems (GDSS)*, which are presented in Chapter 5.

**ENTERPRISEWIDE INTEGRATED SOFTWARE.** Enterprise software consists of programs that manage a company's vital operations, from order taking to manufacturing to accounting. Integrated enterprise software supports supply chain management as well as human resources management and financial management. The major vendors of enterprise software are SAP, Oracle, J. D. Edwards, Peoplesoft, and Baan, with SAP being the largest (for details see Chapter 8).

**OTHER APPLICATION SOFTWARE.** There exist hundreds of other application software products. Of special interest to business managers are:

- Idea generation (creativity) software
- DSS and EIS generators
- Expert systems development tools
- Project management software
- Financial management
- Marketing management
- Productivity improvement
- Accounting and auditing
- Human resources management
- Manufacturing and operations management
- Training software

Examples of information systems in the above areas are provided throughout the book.

## ▶ T2.3   SYSTEMS SOFTWARE

Systems software is the class of programs that controls and supports the computer hardware and its information processing activities. Systems software also facilitates the programming, testing, and debugging of computer programs. It is more general than applications software and is usually independent of any specific type of application. Systems software programs support application software by directing the basic functions of the computer. For example, when the computer is turned on, the initialization program (a systems program) prepares and readies all devices for processing. Systems software can be grouped into three major functional categories:

- **System control programs** are programs that control the use of hardware, software, and data resources of a computer system during its execution of a user's information processing job. An **operating system** is the prime example of a system control program.

- **System support programs** support the operations, management, and users of a computer system by providing a variety of services. System utility programs, performance monitors, and security monitors are examples of system support programs.

- **System development programs** help users develop information processing programs and procedures and prepare user applications. Major development programs are language compilers, interpreters, and translators.

## SYSTEM CONTROL PROGRAMS

The most important system control programs are:

**OPERATING SYSTEMS.** The main component of systems software is a set of programs collectively known as the operating system. The operating system, such as Windows 98, supervises the overall operation of the computer, including monitoring the computer's status, handling executable program interruptions, and scheduling of operations, which include the controlling of input and output processes.

Mainframes and minicomputers contain only one CPU, but they perform several tasks simultaneously (such as preparation and transfer of results). In such cases, the operating system controls which particular tasks have access to the various resources of the computer. At the same time, the operating system controls the overall flow of information within the computer.

On a microcomputer, the operating system controls the computer's communication with its display, printer, and storage devices. It also receives and directs inputs from the keyboard and other data input sources. The operating system is designed to maximize the amount of useful work the hardware of the computer system accomplishes.

Programs running on the computer use various resources controlled by the operating system. These resources include CPU time, primary storage or memory, and input/output devices. The operating system attempts to allocate the use of these resources in the most efficient manner possible.

The operating system also provides an interface between the user and the hardware. By masking many of the hardware features, both the professional and end-user programmers are presented with a system that is easier to use.

*Portability*, a desirable characteristic of operating systems, means that the same operating system software can be run on different computers. An example of a portable operating system is the Unix system. Versions of Unix can run on hardware produced by a number of different vendors. However, there is no one standard version of Unix that will run on all machines.

***Operating System Functions.*** The operating system performs three major functions in the operation of a computer system: job management, resource management, and data management.

*Job management* is the preparing, scheduling, and monitoring of jobs for continuous processing by the computer system. A job control language (JCL) is a special computer language found in the mainframe-computing environment that allows a programmer to communicate with the operating system.

*Resource management* is controlling the use of computer system resources employed by the other systems software and application software programs being executed on the computer. These resources include primary storage, secondary storage, CPU processing time, and input/output devices.

*Data management* is the controlling of the input/output of data as well as their location, storage, and retrieval. Data management programs control the allocation of secondary storage devices, the physical format and cataloging of data storage, and the movement of data between primary storage and secondary storage devices.

A variety of operating systems are in use today. The operating system used on most personal computers is Microsoft's Windows and NT. Many minicomputers use the Unix operating system. Mainframes use primarily the operating systems called virtual memory system (VMS) or multiple virtual system (MVS). Although operating systems are designed to help the user in utilizing the resources of the computer, instructions or commands necessary to accomplish this process are often user-unfriendly. These commands are not intuitive and a large amount of time must be spent to master them. Intelligent agents (Chapters 5 and 11) provide some help in this area.

**GRAPHICAL USER INTERFACE OPERATING SYSTEMS.** The graphical user interface (GUI) is a system in which users have direct control of visible objects (such as icons) and actions that replace complex command syntax. The next generation of GUI technology will incorporate features such as virtual reality, sound and speech, pen and gesture recognition, animation, multimedia, artificial intelligence, and highly portable computers with cellular/wireless communication capabilities.

The most well-known GUIs are Windows from Microsoft Corporation and the built-in interfaces in Apple's computers. Windows 95 is a 32-bit operating system that provides a streamlined GUI that arranges icons to provide instant access to common tasks. It can support software written for DOS and Windows but it can also run programs that take up more than 640 K of memory. Windows 95 and 98 feature multitasking, multithreading (the ability to manage multiple independent tasks simultaneously), and networking capabilities, including the ability to integrate fax, e-mail, and scheduling programs.

Windows NT can provide extensive computing power for new applications with large memory and file requirements. It can support multiprocessing with multiple CPUs. Unlike OS/2, Windows NT is not linked exclusively to computer

This graphical user interface incorporates icons that function like Web links, and news and weather Web pages pushed onto the desktop. (*Source:* C/netNews.com.)

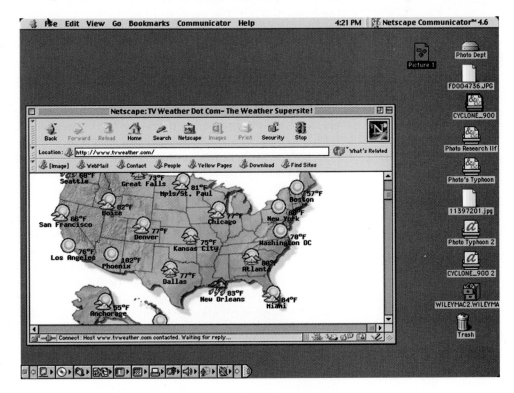

hardware based on Intel microprocessors. It can run on microcomputers and workstations using microprocessors from Mips Computer Systems, Inc. or DEC's Alpha chip. Windows 2000 is an upgrade to the Windows 98 and Windows NT operating systems.

OS/2 is a 32-bit operating system that is used with Intel microprocessors. OS/2 supports multitasking, accommodates larger applications, allows applications to be run simultaneously, and supports networked multimedia and pen computing applications. The latest version of OS/2 is called OS/2 Warp 4.

Mac OS 9, for use on Apple Macintosh microcomputers, features multitasking and powerful graphics capabilities. An extension of Mac OS 9, called Quick-Time4, allows users to integrate video clips, stereo sound, and animated sequences with conventional text and graphics software.

Linux is a free Unix-type operating system. Linux includes true multitasking, virtual memory, shared libraries, demand loading, proper memory management, TCP/IP networking, and other features consistent with Unix-type systems. Due to the very nature of Linux's functionality and availability, it has become quite popular worldwide.

**PROCESSING TASKS.** Operating systems manage processing activities with some task management features that allocate computer resources to optimize each system's assets. The most notable features are:

*Multiprogramming and Multiprocessing.* **Multiprogramming** involves two or more application modules or programs placed into main memory at the same time. The first module is executed on the CPU, until an interrupt occurs, such as a request for input. The input request is initiated and handled while the execution of a second application module is started. The execution of the second module continues until another interruption occurs, when execution of a third module begins. When the processing of the interrupt has been completed, control is returned to the program that was interrupted, and the cycle repeats. Because switching among programs occurs very rapidly, all programs appear to be executing at the same time.

In a **multiprocessing** system, more than one processor is involved. The processors may share input/output devices, although each processor may also control some devices exclusively. In some cases, all processors may share primary memory. As a result, more than one CPU operation can be carried on at exactly the same time; that is, each processor may execute an application module or portion of an application module simultaneously. Multiprogramming is implemented entirely by software, where multiprocessing is primarily a hardware implementation, aided by sophisticated software.

*Time-Sharing.* **Time-sharing** is an extension of multiprogramming. In this mode, a number of users operate online with the same CPU, but each uses a different input/output terminal. An application module of one user is placed into a partition (i.e., a reserved section of primary storage). Execution is carried on for a given period of time, a time slice, or until an input/output request (an interrupt) is made. As in multiprogramming, modules of other users have also been placed into primary storage in other partitions. Execution passes on to another application module at the end of a time slice and rotates among all users.

**VIRTUAL MEMORY.** Virtual memory allows the user to write a program as if primary memory were larger than it actually is. Users are provided with "virtually" all the primary storage they need. With virtual memory, all the pages of an application module need not be loaded into primary memory at the same time. As the program executes, control passes from one page to another. If the succeeding page is already in primary memory, execution continues. If the succeeding page is not in primary memory, a delay occurs until that page is loaded. In effect, primary memory is extended into a secondary storage device.

***Virtual Machine Operating System.*** A virtual machine is a computer system that appears to the user as a real computer but, in fact, has been created by the operating system. A virtual machine operating system makes a single real machine appear as multiple machines to its users, each with its own unique operating system. Each user may choose a different operating system for his or her virtual machine. As a result, multiple operating systems may exist in the real machine at the same time.

The most popular virtual machine operating system is IBM's VM/ESA. A control program supervises the real machine and keeps track of each virtual machine's operation. The conversational monitoring system (CMS) provides the user with a highly interactive environment coupled with easier access to translators, editors, and debugging tools. Of the newest tools, *Java's Virtual Machine* is of special interest.

## SYSTEMS SUPPORT PROGRAMS

**SYSTEM UTILITY PROGRAMS.** System utilities are programs that have been written to accomplish common tasks such as sorting records, merging sets of data, checking the integrity of magnetic disks, creating directories and subdirectories, restoring accidentally erased files, locating files within the directory structure, managing memory usage, and redirecting output. TestDrive, for example, allows you to download software; you try it, and TestDrive helps you either with a payment or with removal of the software.

**SYSTEM PERFORMANCE MONITORS.** System performance monitors monitor computer system performance and produce reports containing detailed statistics concerning the use of system resources, such as processor time, memory space, input/output devices, and system and application programs.

**SYSTEM SECURITY MONITORS.** System security monitors are programs that monitor the use of a computer system to protect it and its resources from unauthorized use, fraud, or destruction. Such programs provide the computer security needed to allow only authorized users access to the system. Security monitors also control use of the hardware, software, and data resources of a computer system. Finally, these programs monitor use of the computer and collect statistics on attempts at improper use.

## SYSTEM DEVELOPMENT PROGRAMS

Translating user computer programs written in source code into object or machine code requires the use of compilers or interpreters, which are examples of system development programs. Another example is computer-aided software engineering (CASE) programs.

# ▶ T2.4 PROGRAMMING LANGUAGES

Programming languages are the basic building blocks for all systems and application software. Programming languages allow people to tell computers what to do and are the means by which systems are developed. Programming languages are basically a set of symbols and rules used to write program code. Each language uses a different set of rules and the *syntax* that dictates how the symbols are arranged so they have meaning.

The characteristics of the languages depend on their purpose. For example, if the programs are intended to run batch processing, they will differ from those intended to run real-time processing. Languages for Internet programs differ from those intended to run mainframe applications. Languages also differ according to when they were developed; today's languages are more sophisticated than those written in the 1950s and the 1960s.

## THE EVOLUTION OF PROGRAMMING LANGUAGES

The different stages of programming languages over time are called "generations." The term *generation* may be misleading. In hardware generation, older generations are becoming obsolete and are not used. All software generations are still in use. They are shown in Figure T-2.3 and are discussed next.

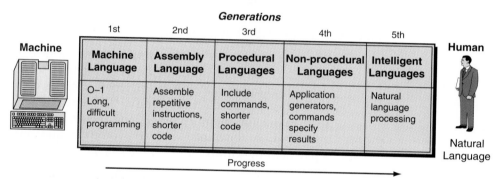

**FIGURE T-2.3** The evolution of programming languages. With each generation progress is made toward humanlike natural language.

**Generations**

| | Machine | 1st Machine Language | 2nd Assembly Language | 3rd Procedural Languages | 4th Non-procedural Languages | 5th Intelligent Languages | Human Natural Language |
|---|---|---|---|---|---|---|---|
| | | 0–1 Long, difficult programming | Assemble repetitive instructions, shorter code | Include commands, shorter code | Application generators, commands specify results | Natural language processing | |

Progress →

**MACHINE LANGUAGE.** Machine language is the lowest-level computer language, consisting of the internal representation of instructions and data. This machine code—the actual instructions understood and directly executable by the CPU—is composed of binary digits. A program using this lowest level of coding is called a *machine language program* and represents the first generation of programming languages. A computer's CPU is capable of executing only machine language programs which are machine dependent. That is, the machine language for one type of central processor may not run on other types.

Machine language is extremely difficult to understand and use by programmers. As a result, increasingly more user-oriented languages have been developed. These languages make it much easier for people to program, but they are impossible for the computer to execute without first translating the program into machine language. The set of instructions written in a user-oriented language is called a *source program*. The set of instructions produced after translation into machine language is called the *object program*.

**ASSEMBLY LANGUAGE.** An assembly language is a more user-oriented language that represents instructions and data locations by using mnemonics, or memory aids, which people can more easily use. Assembly languages are considered the second generation of computer languages. Compared to machine language, assembly language eases the job of the programmer considerably. However, one statement in an assembly language is still translated into one statement in machine language. Because machine language is hardware dependent and assembly language programs are translated mostly on a one-to-one statement basis, assembly languages are also hardware dependent.

A systems software program called an assembler accomplishes translating an assembly language program into machine language. An assembler accepts a source program as input and produces an object program as output. The object program is then process data (see Figure T-2.4).

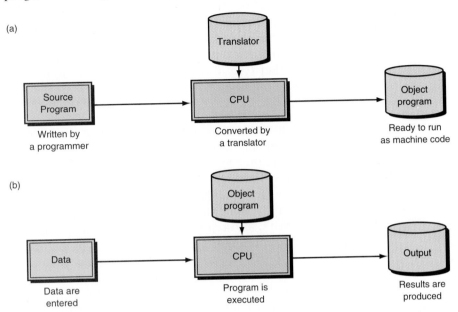

FIGURE T-2.4 The language translation process.

## HIGH-LEVEL LANGUAGES

High-level languages are the next step in the evolution of user-oriented programming languages. High-level languages are much closer to natural language and therefore easier to write, read, and alter. Moreover, one statement in a high-level language is translated into a number of machine language instructions, thereby making programming more productive.

**PROCEDURAL LANGUAGES: THIRD GENERATION.** Procedural languages require the programmer to specify—step by step—exactly how the computer will accomplish a task. A procedural language is oriented toward how a result is to be produced. Because computers understand only machine language (i.e., 0's and 1's), higher-level languages must be translated into machine language prior to execution. This translation is accomplished by systems software called language translators. A language translator converts the high-level program, called *source code*, into machine language code, called *object code*. There are two types of language translators—compilers and interpreters.

*Compilers.* The translation of a high-level language program to object code is accomplished by a software program called a compiler, and the translation process is called compilation.

*Interpreters.* An interpreter is a compiler that translates and executes one source program statement at a time. Therefore, interpreters tend to be simpler than compilers. This simplicity allows for more extensive debugging and diagnostic aids to be available on interpreters.

*Examples of Procedural Languages.* FORTRAN (**For**mula **Tran**slator) is an algebraic, formula-type procedural language. FORTRAN was developed to meet scientific processing requirements.

COBOL (**Co**mmon **B**usiness **O**riented **L**anguage) was developed as a programming language for the business community. The original intent was to make COBOL instructions approximate the way they would be expressed in English. In this way, the programs would be "self-documenting." There are more COBOL programs currently in use than any other computer language.

The C programming language has experienced the greatest growth of any language in the 1990s. C is considered more transportable than other languages, meaning that a C program written for one type of computer can generally be run on another type of computer with little or no modification. Also, the C language is easily modified. Other procedural languages are Pascal, BASIC, APL, RPG, PL/1, ADA, LISP, and PROLOG.

**NONPROCEDURAL LANGUAGES: FOURTH GENERATION.** Another type of high-level language, called nonprocedural or fourth-generation language (4GL), allows the user to specify the *desired results* without having to specify the detailed procedures needed for achieving the results. A nonprocedural language is oriented toward what is required. An advantage of nonprocedural languages is that they may be manipulated by nontechnical users to carry out specific functional tasks. 4GLs, also referred to as *command languages,* greatly simplify and accelerate the programming process as well as reduce the number of coding errors.

The term *fourth-generation language* is used to differentiate these languages from machine languages (first generation), assembly languages (second generation), and procedural languages (third generation). For example, *application (or program) generators* are considered to be 4GLs, as are *query* (e.g., MPG's RAMIS), *report generator* (e.g., IBM's RPG), and *data manipulation languages* (e.g., ADABASE's Natural) provided by most *database management systems* (DBMSs). DBMSs allow users and programmers to interrogate and access computer databases using statements that resemble natural language. Many graphics languages (Powerpoint, Harvard Graphics, Corel Draw, and Lotus Freelance Graphics) are considered 4GLs. Other 4GLs are FOCUS, PowerHouse, Unifare, Centura, Cactus, and Developer/2000.

**FIFTH-GENERATION LANGUAGES. Natural language programming languages (NLP)** are the next evolutionary step and are sometimes known as fifth-generation languages. Translation programs to translate natural languages into a structured, machine-readable form are extremely complex and require a large amount of computer resources. Examples are INTELLECT and ELF. These are usually front-end to 4GLs (such as FOCUS) improving the user interface with the 4GLs. Several procedural artificial intelligence languages (such as LISP) are labeled by some as 5GLs. Initial efforts in artificial intelligence in Japan were called the Fifth Generation Project. A comparison of the five generations is shown in Table T-2.1

**SIXTH-GENERATION LANGUAGES.** Although some people call advanced machine learning languages (see neural computing, Chapter 11) sixth-generation languages, there are no current commercial languages that are closer to human or natural languages than NLP. Some research institutions are working on the concept of such languages which could be commercialized in the future.

## NEW PROGRAMMING LANGUAGES

Several new languages have been developed in the last 10 to 15 years. These languages were designed to fit new technologies such as multimedia, hypermedia, document management, and the Internet. The major languages are described next.

*Table T-2.1* **Language Generation Table**

| Language Generation | Features | | | | |
|---|---|---|---|---|---|
| | Portable (Machine independent)? | Concise (One-to-many)? | Use of Mnemonics & Labels? | Procedural? | Structured? |
| 1st—Machine | no | no | no | yes | yes |
| 2nd—Assembler | no | no | yes | yes | yes |
| 3rd—Procedural | yes | yes | yes | yes | yes |
| 4th—Nonprocedural | yes | yes | yes | no | yes |
| 5th—Natural language | yes | yes | yes | no | no |

**OBJECT-ORIENTED PROGRAMMING LANGUAGES.** Object-oriented programming (OOP) models a system as a set of cooperating objects. Like structured programming, object-oriented programming tries to manage the behavioral complexity of a system, but it goes beyond structured programming, also trying to manage the information complexity of a system. The object-oriented approach involves programming, operating systems environment, object-oriented databases, and a new way of approaching business applications.

The object-oriented (OO) approach views a computer system as a collection of interacting objects. These objects have certain features, or attributes, and they can exhibit certain behaviors. Further, similar objects in a computer system can be grouped and classified as a specific class of things. The objects in a computer system can interact with each other, and people and objects can interact as well. People interact with objects by sending them messages telling them what to do. Objects also interact by sending each other messages.

*Concepts of the Object-Oriented Approach.* The basic concepts of OO are objects, classes, message passing, encapsulation, inheritance, and polymorphism. Since these concepts sound very complex and technical at first, it may be helpful to relate them to aspects of graphical user interfaces in popular operating systems, such as Windows and Mac OS 9 for Apple's computers. These interfaces were developed through object-oriented programming, and incorporate object-oriented features.

Object-oriented systems view software as a collection of interacting objects. An **object** models "things" in the real world. These things may be physical entities such as cars, students, or events. They may be abstractions such as bank accounts, or aspects of an interface such as a button or a box to enter text.

When we refer to an object, we can have two possible meanings: a class or an instance. A **class** is a template or general framework that defines the methods and attributes to be included in a particular type of object. An object is a specific **instance** of a class, able to perform services and hold data. For example, "student" may be a class in a student registration system. A particular student, John Kim, can be an instance of that class, and thus an object.

Objects have data associated with them. The data elements are referred to as **attributes**, or as variables because their values can change. For example, the John Kim object could hold the data that he is a senior, majoring in management information systems, and registering for the fall quarter.

Objects exhibit **behaviors,** which are things that they do. The programmer implements these behaviors by writing sections of code that perform the **meth-**

**ods** of each object. Methods are the procedures or behaviors performed by an object that will change the attribute values of that object. Methods are sometimes referred to as the operations that manipulate the object. Common behaviors include changing the data in an object and communicating information on data values. By clicking on a "check box" in a Windows system, a user initiates the behavior that changes the attribute to "checked" and shows an X or check mark in the box.

Objects interact with each other using **messages**. These messages represent requests to exhibit the desired behaviors. The object that initiates a message is the sender and the object that receives a message is the receiver. When we interact with objects, we send messages to them and they may also send messages to us. Clicking on a button, selecting an item from a menu, and dragging and dropping an icon are ways of sending messages to objects. These messages may activate methods in the recipient objects and in turn new messages may be generated.

Message passing is the only means to get information from an object, because an object's attributes are not directly accessible. The inaccessibility of data in an object is called **encapsulation** or information hiding. By hiding its variables, an object protects other objects from the complications of depending on its internal structure. The other objects do not have to know each variable's name, the type of information it contains, or the physical storage format of the information. They only need to know how to ask the object for information.

With **inheritance,** a class of objects can be defined as a special case of a more general class, automatically including the method and variable definitions of the general class. Special classes of a class are **subclasses**, and the more general class is a superclass. For example, the student class is a subclass of human being, which is the superclass. The student class may be further divided into in-state students, out-of-state students, or scholarship students, which would be subclasses of the student class. This type of organization results in class hierarchies. The subclass can *override* or *add to* the definitions of the superclass attributes and methods. In other words, subclasses *inherit* all the characteristics of higher-level classes.

Inheritance is particularly valuable because analysts can search through predefined class hierarchies, called **class libraries**, to find classes that are similar to the classes they need in a new system. This process saves large amounts of time. For example, if the end user needs to deal with students as a class of objects, the analyst may be able to find a general class that is similar to the student class as viewed by the end user. Therefore, the analyst can reuse information from an existing class instead of starting from the beginning to define a student class. The relationship between classes and subclasses are shown in Figure T-2.5.

**Polymorphism** is the ability to send the same message to several different receivers (objects) and have the message trigger the desired action. For example, suppose that there are three classes of objects in a tuition-and-fee system: in-state students, out-of-state students, and scholarship students. We must calculate tuition and fees for all three types of student (classes) while noting that the tuition and fees will differ for the three classes. Polymorphism allows us to send the same "calculate tuition and fees" message to these three different classes and have the correct tuition and fees calculated for each one.

***Programming With OO.*** Building programs and applications using object-oriented programming languages is similar to constructing a building using prefabricated parts. The object containing the data and procedures is a programming building block. The same objects can be used repeatedly, a process called **reusability**. By

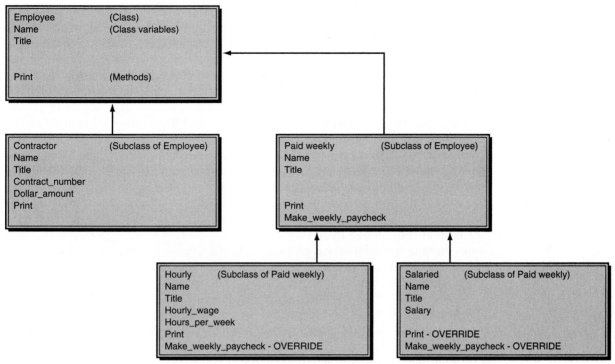

**FIGURE T-2.5** **Object classes, subclasses, inheritance, and overriding.** (*Source*: © Courtesy of Apple Corporation. Used with permission.)

reusing program code, programmers can write programs much more efficiently and with fewer errors. Object-oriented programming languages offer advantages such as reusable code, lower costs, reduced errors and testing, and faster implementation times. Popular object-oriented programming languages include Smalltalk, C++, and Java.

***Smalltalk.*** Smalltalk is a pure object-oriented language developed at Xerox Palo Alto Research Center. The syntax is fairly easy to learn, being much less complicated than C and C++.

***C++.*** C++ is a direct extension of the C language, with 80 to 90 percent of C++ remaining pure C.

**VISUAL PROGRAMMING LANGUAGES.** Programming languages that are used within a graphical environment are often referred to as visual programming languages. Visual programming allows developers to create applications by manipulating graphical images directly, instead of specifying the visual features in code. These languages use a mouse, icons, symbols on the screen, or pull-down menus to make programming easier and more intuitive. Visual Basic, DELPHI, CA Visual, Power Objects, and Visual C++ are examples of visual programming languages.

## INTERNET-ORIENTED LANGUAGES

**HYPERTEXT MARKUP LANGUAGE.** The standard language the Web uses for creating and recognizing hypermedia documents is the **Hypertext Markup Language (HTML)**. HTML is loosely related to the Standard Generalized

Markup Language (SGML), which is a method of representing document formatting languages. Languages such as HTML that follow the SGML format allow document writers to separate information from document presentation. That is, documents containing the same information can be presented in a number of different ways. Users have the option of controlling visual elements such as fonts, font size, and paragraph spacing without changing the original information.

HTML is very easy to use. Web documents are typically written in HTML and are usually named with the suffix ".html." HTML documents are standard 7- or 8-bit ASCII files with formatting codes that contain information about layout (text styles, document titles, paragraphs, lists) and hyperlinks. The HTML standard supports basic hypertext document creation and layout, as well as interactive forms, and defined "hot spots" in images.

**Hypertext** is an approach to data management in which data are stored in a network of nodes connected by links (called **hyperlinks**). Users access data through an interactive browsing system. The combination of nodes, links, and supporting indexes for any particular topic is a hypertext document. A hypertext document may contain text, images, and other types of information such as data files, audio, video, and executable computer programs.

The World Wide Web uses **Uniform Resource Locators (URLs)** to represent hypermedia links and links to network services within HTML documents. The first part of the URL (before the two slashes) specifies the method of access. The second part is typically the address of the computer where the data or service is located. A URL is always a single unbroken line with no spaces.

**Dynamic HTML** is the next step beyond HTML. Dynamic HTML provides advances that include the following:

▶ It provides a richer, more dynamic experience for the user on Web pages, making the pages more like dynamic applications and less like static content. It lets the user interact with the content of those pages without having to download additional content from the server. This means that Web pages using Dynamic HTML provide more exciting and useful information.

▶ Dynamic HTML gives developers precise control over formatting, fonts, and layout, and provides an enhanced object model for making pages interactive.

▶ It serves as the foundation for **crossware**, a new class of platform-independent, on-demand applications built entirely using Dynamic HTML, Java, and JavaScript. Netscape Netcaster, a component of Netscape Communicator, is Netscape's first crossware application.

***XML.*** XML (eXtensible Markup Language) is optimized for document delivery across the Net. It is built on the foundation of SGML. It is easy to write and it supports Web authoring and indexing (see *Interactive Week*, February 16, 1998, p. 12; www.interactive.week.com). XML is especially suitable for electronic commerce applications.

***Java.*** Java is an object-oriented programming language developed by Sun Microsystems. The language gives programmers the ability to develop applications that work across the Internet. Java is used to develop small applications, called applets, which can be included in an HTML page on the Internet. When the user uses a Java-compatible browser to view a page that contains a Java applet, the applet's code is transferred to the user's system and executed by the browser.

*JavaBeans.* This is the platform-neutral, component architecture for Java. It is used for developing or assembling network-aware solutions for heterogeneous hardware and operating system environments, within the enterprise or across the Internet. JavaBeans extends Java's "Write Once, Run Anywhere" capability to reusable component development. JavaBeans runs on any operating system and within any application environment.

*ActiveX.* ActiveX is a set of technologies from Microsoft that combines different programming languages into a single, integrated Web site. ActiveX is not a programming language as such, but rather a set of rules for how applications should share information.

**VIRTUAL REALITY MODELING LANGUAGE.** The **Virtual Reality Modeling Language (VRML)** is a file format for describing three-dimensional interactive worlds and objects. It can be used with the Web to create three-dimensional representations of complex scenes such as illustrations, product definitions, and virtual reality presentations. VRML can represent static and animated objects and it can have hyperlinks to other media such as sound, video, and image. For further discussion see Chapter 5.

**WEB BROWSERS.** The major software tool for accessing and working with the Web is the **browser**. It includes a point-and-click GUI that is controlled via a mouse or some keyboard keys. Browsers can display various media and they are used also to activate the hyperlinks. Netscape Navigator and Communicator and Microsoft's Explorer are the major competing browsers.

# ▶ T2.5 SOFTWARE DEVELOPMENT AND CASE TOOLS

Most programming today is done by taking a large process and breaking it down into smaller, more easily comprehended modules. This method is commonly described as top-down programming, stepwise refinement, or structured programming.

Structured programming models a system similar to a layered set of functional modules. These modules are built up in a pyramid-like fashion, each layer a higher-level view of the system. Even with this approach, however, many systems have developed severe complexity. Thousands of modules with cross-links among them are often called "spaghetti code." The ability to break a programming job into smaller parts enables the deployment of special productivity tools, the best known of which is CASE.

## CASE

Computer-aided software engineering (CASE) is a tool for programmers, systems analysts, business analysts, and systems developers to help automate software development and at the same time improve software quality.

CASE is a combination of software tools and structured software development methods. The tools automate the software development process, while the methodologies help identify those processes to be automated with the tools. CASE tools often use graphics or diagrams to help describe and document sys-

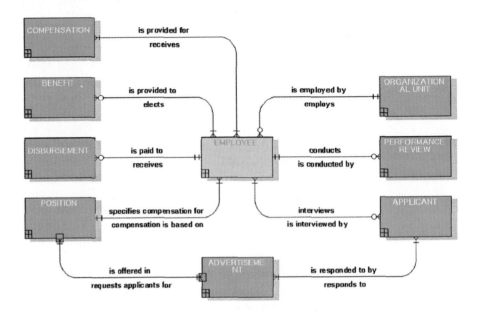

**FIGURE T-2.6** A CASE display.

tems and to clarify the interfaces or interconnections among the components (see Figure T-2.6). They are generally integrated, allowing data to be passed from tool to tool.

**CATEGORIES OF CASE TOOLS.** CASE tools support individual aspects or stages of the systems development process, groups or related aspects, or the whole process. Upper CASE (U-CASE) tools focus primarily on the *design* aspects of systems development, for example, tools that create data flow or entity-relationship diagrams. Lower CASE (L-CASE) tools help with *programming* and related activities, such as testing, in the later stages of the life cycle. Integrated CASE (I-CASE) tools incorporate both U-CASE and L-CASE functionality and provide support for many tasks throughout the SDLC.

CASE tools may be broken down into two subcategories: tool kits and work benches. A tool kit is a collection of software tools that automates one type of software task or one phase of the software development process. A CASE work-bench is a collection of software tools that are interrelated based on common assumptions about the development methodology being employed. A workbench also uses the data repository containing all technical and management information needed to build the software system. Ideally, workbenches provide support throughout the entire software development process and help produce a documented and executable system.

CASE tools have several advantages:

▶ CASE improves productivity by helping the analyst understand the problem and how to solve it in an organized manner.

▶ CASE facilitates joint application and design (JAD) sessions, resulting in better interaction among users and information systems professionals.

▶ CASE makes it easier to create prototypes, so that users can see what they are going to get at an early stage in the development process.

▶ CASE makes it easier to make system design changes as circumstances change.

Tasks that are repeated may be automated with CASE tools, for example, drawing dataflow diagrams (a graphical technique for representing the system under development) or drawing system charts. Effectiveness results from forcing the developer to do the task in an organized, consistent manner as dictated by the CASE tool.

Because most CASE tools are graphical in nature and have the ability to produce working prototypes quickly, nontechnically trained users can participate more actively in the development process. They can see what the completed system will look like before it is actually constructed, resulting in fewer misunderstandings and design mistakes.

Using CASE can help make revising an application easier. When revisions are needed, one need only change specifications in the data repository rather than the source code itself. This also enables prototype systems to be developed more quickly and easily. Some CASE tools help generate source code directly, and the benefits can be significant.

CASE tools also have disadvantages. A lack of management support for CASE within organizations can be a problem. CASE is very expensive to install, train developers on, and use properly. Many firms do not know how to measure quality or productivity in software development and therefore find it difficult to justify the expense of implementing CASE. In addition, the receptivity of professional programmers can greatly influence the effectiveness of CASE. Many programmers who have mastered one approach to development are hesitant to shift to a new method.

Also, the insistence on one structured method in a CASE program is good for standardization but can be stifling for creativity and flexibility. If an analyst is in an organization that does not use a structured methodology to accompany CASE, then the effectiveness of CASE will be greatly reduced. Creating software often entails imaginative solutions to procedural problems; being constrained to one methodology and the tools included in the CASE package can be constricting. Finally, CASE tools cannot overcome poor, incomplete, or inconsistent specifications. Popular CASE tools are Oracle's Designer/2000, Seer Technologies' Seer*HPS, and Texas Instruments' Composer. For a comprehensive list of CASE tools see Table T-2.2, page 742.

# ▶ T2.6 SOFTWARE ISSUES AND TRENDS

The importance of software in computer systems has led to the emergence of several issues and trends. These issues include software licensing, software upgrades, shareware and freeware, and software selection.

## SOFTWARE LICENSING

Vendors spend time and money in software development, so they must protect their software from being copied and distributed by individuals and other software companies. Vendors can copyright software, but this protection is limited.

*Table T-2.2* **The Major Tools of CASE**

| Category | Comments |
|---|---|
| Analysis and design tools | • Create data flow, entity-relationship, etc. diagrams<br>• Generic, or specific to proprietary systems design methodologies |
| Code or application generators | • Some convert specifications directly into code<br>• Often have drag-and-drop capabilities for developing applications and interfaces |
| Prototyping tools | • Screen and menu generators<br>• Report generators/4GLs |
| Programming language support | • Templates for common code sequences in specific languages<br>• Subroutine libraries for common functions |
| Testing tools | • Produce data for testing programs<br>• Monitor program execution<br>• Check systems analysis diagrams for completeness and consistency |
| Problem-tracking tools | • Identify responsibility for fixing bugs and track progress in solving them |
| Change management/version control tools | • Repository of different versions of code, with "check out" and "check in" capabilities<br>• Allow access only to authorized personnel<br>• Maintain information on changes between versions of programs |
| Project management tools | • Critical path method (PERT charts)<br>• Gantt charts<br>• Time and expense tracking |
| Estimation tools | • Estimate personnel requirements and costs for systems development projects |
| Documentation generators | • Create flowcharts, other documentation for systems with poor or no documentation |
| Reverse engineering tools | • Help restructure code in legacy systems |
| Business process reengineering tools | • Analyze and improve existing processes<br>• Design new processes |

Another approach is for firms to use existing patent laws, but this approach has not been fully accepted by the courts.

The Software & Information Industry Association (formerly the Software Publishers Association) enforces software copyright laws in corporations through a set of guidelines. These guidelines state that when information systems (IS) managers cannot find proof of purchase for software, they should get rid of the software or purchase new licenses. IS managers need to take inventory of their software assets to ensure that they have the appropriate number of software licenses.

As the number of desktop computers continues to increase and businesses continue to decentralize, it becomes more and more difficult for IS managers to manage their software assets. As a result, many firms specialize in tracking software licenses for a fee.

## SOFTWARE UPGRADES

Software firms revise their programs constantly and sell new versions. The revised software may offer valuable enhancements, but, on the other hand, may offer little in terms of additional capabilities. Also, the revised software may contain bugs. Deciding whether or when to purchase the newest software can be a major problem for companies.

## SHAREWARE AND FREEWARE

Shareware (software where the user is expected to pay the author a modest amount for the privilege of using it) and freeware (software that is free) are available to users and help to keep their software costs down. Shareware and freeware are often not as powerful (do not have the full complement of features) as the professional versions, but some users get what they need at a good price. These are available now on the Internet in large quantities.

## SOFTWARE SELECTION

There are dozens or even hundreds of packages to choose from for almost any topic. Software selection becomes a major issue in systems development and is discussed in Chapter 14.

## REFERENCES AND BIBLIOGRAPHY

1. Baum, D., "Putting the Web in its Place," *InfoWorld,* July 22, 1996.

2. Booker, E., "Better Java," *Internet Week,* Feb. 16, 1998.

3. Cortese, A., et al., "The Software Revolutions," *Business Week,* December 4, 1995.

4. Courter, G., and Marquis, A., "Mastering Microsoft Office 2000 : Premium Edition," *Sybex,* July 1999.

5. Cox, B., *Object-Oriented Programming: An Evolutionary Approach,* Reading, MA: Addison Wesley, 1987.

6. Dorfman, M., and R. H. Thayer, *Software Engineering,* Los Alamits, CA: IEEE Computer Society Press, 1996.

7. "Employers Sabotage Office Computer Games," *Wall Street Journal,* February 6, 1995, pp. B1, B5.

8. Fayad, M., and M. P. Cline, "Aspects of Software Adaptability," *Communications of the ACM,* No. 10, October 1996.

9. Feibus, A., "A Garden of Visual Delights," *Information Week,* July 1, 1996.

10. Hutheesing, N., "Speaking with One Voice: Using the C++ Programming Language," *Forbes,* September 23, 1996.

11. Katz, H., ed., *Technology Forecast: 1998* (also 1999, 2000). Menlo Park, CA: Price Waterhouse World Technology Center, 1998, 1999, 2000.

12. Korson, T., and V. Vaishnave, "Managing Emerging Software Technologies: A Technology Transfer Framework," *Communications of the ACM* 35, No. 9, September 1992.

13. Pancake, M., "The Promise and the Cost of Object Technology: A Five-Year Forecast," *Communications of the ACM* 38, No. 10, October 1995.

14. Semich, B., and D. Fisco, "Java Internet: Toy or Enterprise Tool?" *Datamation,* March 1, 1996.

15. Wallace, N., "ActiveX Template Library Development With Visual C++ 6.0," *Wordware Publishing,* May 1999.

16. "What's New for COBOL?" *Information Week,* February 21, 1994.

17. Welsh, M., M. Dalheimer, K., Kaufman, K. and Welsh, K. "Running Linux," O'Reilly & Associates, August, 1999.

# TECHNOLOGY GUIDE 3:

# Data and Databases

## ▶ T3.1 FILE MANAGEMENT

### INTRODUCTION

A computer system organizes data in a hierarchy that begins with bits, and proceeds to bytes, fields, records, files, and databases (see Figure T-3.1). A **bit** represents the smallest unit of data a computer can process (i.e., a 0 or a 1). A group of eight bits, called a **byte**, represents a single character, which can be a letter, a number, or a symbol. A logical grouping of characters into a word, a group of words, or a complete number is called a **field**. For example, a student's name would appear in the name field. A logical group of related fields, such as the student's name, the course taken, the date, and the grade, comprise a **record**. A logical group of related records is called a **file**. For example, the student records in a single course would constitute a data file for that course. A logical group of related files would constitute a **database**. All students' course files could be grouped with files on students' personal histories and financial backgrounds to create a students' database.

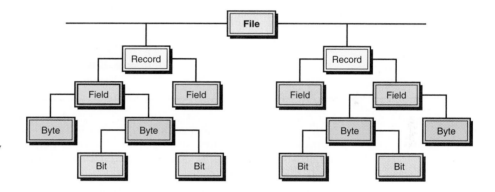

**FIGURE T-3.1** Hierarchy of data for a computer-based file.

Another way of thinking about database components is that a record describes an **entity**. An entity is a person, place, thing, or event on which we maintain information. Each characteristic or quality describing a particular entity is called an **attribute** (corresponds to a field).

Every record in a file should contain at least one field that uniquely identifies that record so that the record can be retrieved, updated, and sorted. An identified field is called the **key field**. For example, a student record would probably use the Social Security number as its key field.

### ACCESSING RECORDS FROM COMPUTER FILES

Records can be arranged in several ways on a storage medium, and the arrangement determines the manner in which individual records can be accessed. In **sequential file organization** data records must be retrieved in the same physical sequence in which they are stored. In **direct** or **random file organization**, users can access records in any sequence, without regard to actual physical order on the storage medium. Magnetic tape utilizes sequential file organization, where magnetic disks use direct file organization.

## PROBLEMS ARISING FROM THE FILE ENVIRONMENT

Organizations typically began automating one application at a time. These systems grew independently, without overall planning. Each application required its own data, which were organized into a data file. This approach led to many problems. Figure T-3.2 uses a university file environment as an example.

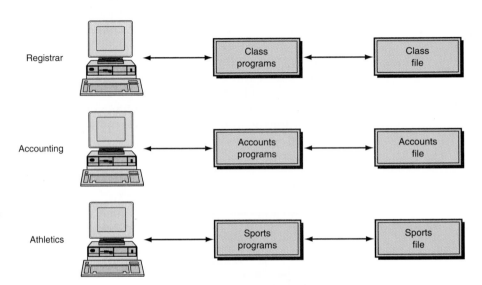

**FIGURE T-3.2** Computer-based files of this type cause problems such as redundancy, inconsistency, and data isolation.

The applications (e.g., registrar, accounting, or athletics) would share some common core functions, such as input, report generation, querying, and data browsing. However, these common functions would typically be designed, coded, documented, and tested, at great expense, for each application. Moreover, users must be trained to use each application. File environments often waste valuable resources creating and maintaining similar applications, as well as in training users how to use them.

Other problems arise with file management systems. The first problem is **data redundancy**. As applications and their data files were created by different programmers over a period of time, the same piece of information could be duplicated in several files. In the university example, each data file will contain records about students, many of whom will be represented in other data files. Therefore, student files in the aggregate will contain some amount of duplicate data. This wastes physical computer storage media, the students' time and effort, and the clerks' time needed to enter and maintain the data.

Data redundancy leads to the potential for **data inconsistency**. Data inconsistency means that the actual values across various copies of the data no longer agree. For example, if a student changes his or her address, the new address must be changed across all applications in the university that require the address.

File organization also leads to difficulty in accessing data from different applications, a problem called **data isolation**. With applications uniquely designed and implemented, data files are likely to be organized differently, stored in different formats (e.g., height in inches versus height in centimeters), and often physically inaccessible to other applications. In the university example, an administrator who wanted to know which students taking advanced courses were also starting players on the football team, would most likely not be able to get the answer from the computer-based file system. He or she would probably have to manually compare printed output data from two data files. This process would take a great deal of time and effort and would ignore the greatest strengths of computers—fast and accurate processing.

**Security** is difficult to enforce in the file environment, because new applications may be added to the system on an ad hoc basis.

The file environment may also cause **data integrity** problems. Data values must often meet integrity constraints. For example, the students' Social Security data field should contain no alphabetic characters, and the students' grade-point-average field should not be negative. It is difficult to place data integrity constraints across multiple data files.

Finally, applications should not have to be developed with regard to how the data are stored. That is, applications and data in computer systems should be independent **(application/data independence)**. In the file environment, the applications and their associated data files are dependent on each other.

Storing data in data files that are tightly linked to their applications eventually led to organizations having hundreds of applications and data files, with no one knowing what the applications do or what data they require. There is no central listing of data files, data elements, or definitions of the data. The numerous problems arising from the file environment approach led to the development of **databases**.

# ▶ T3.2   DATABASES AND DATABASE MANAGEMENT SYSTEMS

## DATABASES

A database is an organized logical grouping of related files. In a database, data are integrated and related so that one set of software programs provides access to all the data, alleviating many of the problems associated with data file environments. Therefore, data redundancy, data isolation, and data inconsistency are minimized, and data can be shared among all users of the data. In addition, security and data integrity are increased, and applications and data are independent of one another.

## DATABASE MANAGEMENT SYSTEMS

The program (or group of programs) that provides access to a database is known as a **database management system (DBMS)**. The DBMS permits an organization to centralize data, manage them efficiently, and provide access to the stored data by application programs. (For a list of capabilities and advantages of the DBMS, see Table T-3.1 on page 748.) The DBMS acts as an interface between application programs and physical data files (see Figure T-3.3 on page 748) and provides users with tools to add, delete, maintain, display, print, search, select, sort, and update data. These tools range from easy-to-use natural language interfaces to complex programming languages used for developing sophisticated database applications.

DBMSs are installed in a broad range of information systems. Some are loaded on a single user's personal computer and used in an ad hoc manner to support individual decision making. Others are located on several interconnected

**Table T-3.1** Advantages and Capabilities of DBMS

- Access and availability of information can be increased.
- Data access, utilization, security, and manipulation can be simplified.
- Data inconsistency and redundancy is reduced.
- Program development and maintenance cost can be dramatically reduced.
- Captures/extracts data for inclusion in databases.
- Quickly updates (adds, deletes, edits, changes) data records and files.
- Interrelates data from different sources.
- Quickly retrieves data from a database for queries and reports.
- Provides comprehensive data security (protection from unauthorized access, recovery capabilities, etc.).
- Handles personal and unofficial data so that users can experiment with alternative solutions based on their own judgment.
- Performs complex retrieval and data manipulation tasks based on queries.
- Tracks usage of data.
- Flexibility of information systems can be improved by allowing rapid and inexpensive ad hoc queries of very large pools of information.
- Application-data dependence can be reduced by separating the logical view of data from its physical structure and location.

mainframe computers and are used to support large-scale transaction processing systems, such as order entry and inventory control systems. Still others are interconnected throughout an organization's local area networks, giving individual departments access to corporate data. Because a DBMS need not be confined to storing just words and numbers, firms use them to store graphics, sounds, and video as well.

There are many specialized databases, depending on the type or format of data stored. For example, a **geographical information database** (see Chapter 10) may contain locational data for overlaying on maps or images. Using this

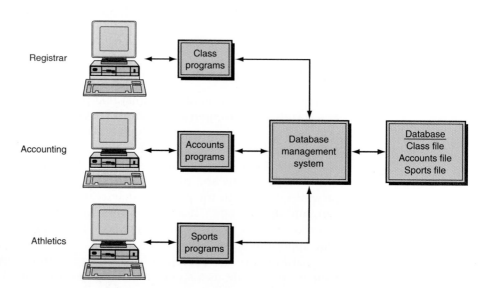

FIGURE T-3.3 Database management system provides access to all data in the database.

type of data, users are able to spatially view customer and vendor locations instead of simply reading the actual addresses. A **knowledge database** (knowledge base, see Chapters 10 and 11) can store decision rules used to evaluate situations and help users make decisions like an expert. A **multimedia database** (see Chapter 10) can store data on many media—sounds, video, images, graphic animation, and text.

Database management systems are designed to be relatively invisible to the user. To interact with them, however, one needs to understand the procedures for interacting, even though much of their work is done behind the scenes and is therefore invisible or "transparent" to the end user. Most of this interaction occurs by using DBMS languages.

A DBMS contains three major components: a data definition language, a data manipulation language, and a data dictionary. The **data definition language (DDL)** is the language used by programmers to specify the content and structure of the database. The DDL is essentially the link between the logical and physical views of the database. ("Logical" refers to the way the user views data and "physical" refers to the way the data are physically stored and processed.)

A DBMS user defines views or schemes using the DDL. The **schema** is the logical description of the entire database and the listing of all the data items and the relationships among them. A **subschema** is the specific set of data from the database that is required by each application.

The DDL is used to define the physical characteristics of each record, the fields within a record, and each field's logical name, data type, and character length. The DDL is also used to specify relationships among the records. Other primary functions of the DDL are the following:

▶ Provide a means for associating related data

▶ Indicate the unique identifiers (or keys) of the records

▶ Set up data security access and change restrictions

The **data manipulation language (DML)** is used with a third- or fourth-generation language to manipulate the data in the database. This language contains commands that permit end users and programming specialists to extract data from the database to satisfy information requests and develop applications. The DML provides users with the ability to retrieve, sort, display, and delete the contents of a database. The DML generally includes a variety of manipulation verbs (e.g., CREATE, MODIFY, DELETE) and operands for each verb.

Requesting information from a database is the most commonly performed operation. Because users cannot generally request information in a natural language form, query languages form an important component of a DBMS. **Structured Query Language (SQL)** is the most popular relational database language, combining both DML and DDL features. SQL offers the ability to perform complicated searches with relatively simple statements. Keywords such as SELECT [to specify desired attribute(s)], FROM [to specify the table(s) to be used], and WHERE (to specify conditions to apply in the query) are typically used for the purpose of data manipulation. For example, a state legislator wants to send congratulatory letters to all students from her district graduating with honors from a state university. The university information systems staff would query the student relational database with an SQL statement such as SELECT (Student Name), FROM (Student Relation), WHERE (Congressional District=7 and Grade Point Average>=3.4).

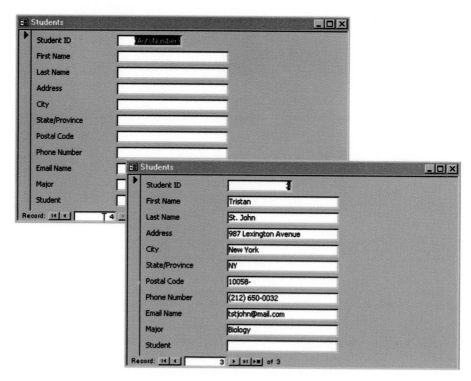

The QBE capabilities of Microsoft Access.

When using a PC, the SQL is not normally used and instead an approach called **query-by-example (QBE)** is employed. The user selects a table and chooses the fields to be included in the answer. Then the user enters an example of the data he wants. The QBE provides an answer based on the example.

The third element of a DBMS is a **data dictionary**, which is a file that stores definitions of data elements and data characteristics such as usage, physical representation, ownership (who in the organization is responsible for maintaining the data), authorization, and security. A **data element** represents a field. Besides listing the standard data name, the dictionary lists the names that reference this element in specific systems and identifies the individuals, business functions, applications, and reports that use this data element.

## ▶ T3.3 LOGICAL DATA ORGANIZATION

Just as there are many ways to structure business organizations, there are many ways to structure the data those organizations need. A manager's ability to use a database is highly dependent on how the database is structured logically and physically. The DBMS separates the logical and physical views of the data, meaning that the programmer and end user do not have to know where and how the data are actually stored. In logically structuring a database, businesses need to consider the characteristics of the data and how the data will be accessed.

There are three basic models for logically structuring databases: hierarchical, network, and relational. Three additional models are emerging: multidimensional, object-oriented, and hypermedia. Using these models, database designers can build logical or conceptual views of data that can then be physically implemented into virtually any database with any DBMS. Hierarchical, network, and object-oriented DBMSs usually tie related data together through linked lists. Relational and multidimensional DBMSs relate data through information contained in the data. In this section we will present the three basic models. (Others are described in Chapter 10.)

## THE HIERARCHICAL DATABASE MODEL

The **hierarchical model** relates data by rigidly structuring data into an inverted "tree" in which records contain two elements:

1. A single root or master field, often called a key, which identifies the type location, or ordering of the records.

2. A variable number of subordinate fields that defines the rest of the data within a record.

As a rule, while all fields have only one "parent," each parent may have many "children." An example of a hierarchical database is shown in Figure T-3.4.

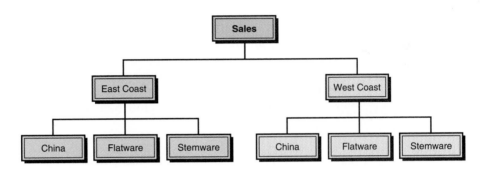

**FIGURE T-3.4**
Hierarchical database model.

The hierarchical structure was developed because hierarchical relationships are commonly found in many traditional business organizations and processes.

The strongest advantage of the hierarchical approach is the speed and efficiency with which it can be searched for data. This speed is possible because so much of the database is eliminated in the search with each "turn" going down the tree. As shown in Figure T-3.4, half the records in the database (East Coast Sales) are eliminated once the search turns toward West Coast Sales, and two-thirds of the West Coast Sales are eliminated once the search turns toward stemware.

Finally, the explicit child/parent relationships in a hierarchical model mean that the integrity of the database is strongly maintained. Every child in a hierarchical database must belong to a parent, and if a parent is eliminated from the database, all its children automatically become children of the parent's parent.

But the hierarchical approach does have some deficiencies. In the hierarchical model, each relationship must be explicitly defined when the database is created. Each record in a hierarchical database can contain only one key field, and only one relationship is allowed between any two fields. This can create a problem because real-world data do not always conform to such a strict hierarchy. For example, in a matrix organization, an employee might report to more than one manager, a situation that would be awkward for a hierarchical structure to handle. Moreover, all data searches must originate at the top or "root" of the tree and work downward from parent to child.

Another significant disadvantage of the hierarchical model is the fact that it is difficult to relate "cousins" in the tree. In the example shown in Figure T-3.4, there is no direct relationship between china sales on the East Coast and china sales on the West Coast. A comparison of companywide china sales would entail two separate searches and then another step combining the search results.

## THE NETWORK DATABASE MODEL

The **network model** creates relationships among data through a linked-list structure in which subordinated records (called members, not children) can be linked to more than one parent (called an owner). Similar to the hierarchical model, the network model uses explicit links, called pointers, to link subordinates and parents. That relationship is called a *set.* Physically, pointers are storage addresses that contain the location of a related record. With the network approach, a member record can be linked to an owner record and, at the same time, can itself be an owner record linked to other sets of members (see Figure T-3.5. In this way, many-to-many relationships are possible with a network database model—a significant advantage of the network model over the hierarchical model.

Compare Figure T-3.5 to Figure T-3.4. In Figure T-3.5, sales information about china, flatware, and stemware is in one subordinate or member location. Information about each has two parents or owners, East Coast and West Coast. The problem of getting a complete picture of nationwide china sales that exists with the hierarchical model does not occur with the network model. Moreover, searches for data do not have to start at a root—there may not even be a single root to a network—which gives much greater flexibility for data searches.

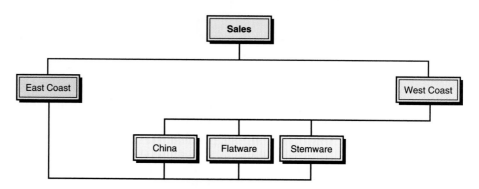

**FIGURE T-3.5** Network database model.

The network model essentially places no restrictions on the number of relationships or sets in which a field can be involved. The model, then, is more consistent with real-world business relationships where, for example, vendors have many customers and customers have many vendors. However, network databases are very complex. For every set, a pair of pointers must be maintained. As the number of sets or relationships increases, the overhead becomes substantial. The network model is by far the most complicated type of database to design and implement.

## THE RELATIONAL DATABASE MODEL

While most business organizations have been organized in a hierarchical fashion, most business data have traditionally been organized into tables of columns and rows, especially accounting and financial data. Tables allow quick comparisons by row or column, and items are easy to retrieve by finding the point of intersection of a particular row and column. The **relational model** is based on this simple concept of tables in order to capitalize on characteristics of rows and columns of data, which is consistent with real-world business situations. In a relational database, these tables are called **relations**, and the model is based on the mathematical theory of sets and relations. In this model, each row of data is equivalent to a *record*, and each column of data is equivalent to a *field.* In the relational model terminology, a row is called a **tuple**, and a column is called an **attribute**. A relational database is not always, however, one big table (usually called a *flat file*) consisting of all attributes and all tuples. That design would likely entail far too much data redundancy. Instead, a database is usually designed as a collection of several related tables.

One of the greatest advantages of the relational model is its conceptual simplicity and the ability to link records in a way that is not predefined (that is, they are not explicit as in the hierarchical and network models). This ability provides great flexibility, particularly for end users. The relational or tabular model of data can be used in a variety of applications. Most people can easily visualize the relational model as a table, but the model does use some unfamiliar terminology.

Consider the relational database example on East Coast managers shown in Figure T-3.6. The table contains data about the entity called East Coast managers. Attributes or characteristics about the entity are name, title, age, and division. The tuples, or occurrences of the entity, are the two records on A. Smith and W. Jones. The links among the data, and among tables, are implicit, as they are not necessarily physically linked in a storage device but implicitly linked by the design of the tables into rows and columns.

East Coast Mgrs.

| NAME | TITLE | AGE | DIVISION |
|------|-------|-----|----------|
| Smith, A. | Dir., Accntg | 43 | China |
| Jones, W. | Dir., TQM | 32 | Stemware |

**FIGURE T-3.6** Relational database model—a table.

This property of implicit links provides perhaps the strongest benefit of the relational model—flexibility in relating data. Unlike the hierarchical and network models, where the only links are those rigidly built into the design, all the data within a table and between tables can be linked, related, and compared. This ability gives the relational model much more data independence than the hierarchical and network models. That is, the logical design of data into tables can be more independent of the physical implementation. This independence allows much more flexibility in implementing and modifying the logical design. Of course, as with all tables, an end user needs to know only two things: the identifier(s) of the tuple(s) to be searched and the desired attribute(s).

The relational model has some disadvantages: Because large-scale databases may be composed of many interrelated tables, the overall design may be complex and therefore have slower search and access times (as compared to the hierarchical and network models). The slower search and access time may result in processing inefficiencies, which lead to an initial lack of acceptance of the relational model. These processing inefficiencies, however, are continually being reduced through improved database design and programming. Second, data integrity is not inherently a part of this model as with hierarchical and network models. Therefore, it must be enforced with good design principles.

**OBJECT-RELATIONAL DATABASE SYSTEMS.** Object-relational database products are replacing purely relational databases. Object-relational database management systems (ORDBMSs) have some of the capabilities of object-oriented database systems as well as additional unique capabilities. (For details, see Katz [1998].)

## COMPARING THE THREE BASIC DATABASE MODELS

The main advantage of the hierarchical and network database models is processing efficiency. The hierarchical and network structures are relatively easy for users to understand because they reflect the pattern of real-world business relationships. In addition, the hierarchical structure allows for data integrity to be easily maintained.

Hierarchical and network structures have several disadvantages. All the access paths, directories, and indices must be specified in advance. Once specified, they are not easily changed without a major programming effort. Therefore, these designs have low flexibility. Hierarchical and network structures are programming-intensive, time-consuming, difficult to install, and difficult to remedy if design errors occur. The two structures do not support ad hoc, English-language-like inquiries for information.

The advantages of relational DBMSs include high flexibility in regard to ad hoc queries, power to combine information from different sources, simplicity of design and maintenance, and the ability to add new data and records without disturbing existing applications. The disadvantage of relational DBMSs is their relatively low processing efficiency. These systems are somewhat slower because they typically require many accesses to the data stored on disk to carry out the select, join, and project commands. Relational systems do not have the large number of pointers carried by hierarchical systems.

Large relational databases may be designed to have some data redundancy in order to make retrieval of data more efficient. The same data element may be stored in multiple tables. Special arrangements are necessary to ensure that all copies of the same data element are updated together. A visual comparison of the three modes is shown in Figure T-3.7. The lines with arrows in the relational models show the duplication of information.

## ▶ T3.4 CREATING DATABASES

To create a database, designers must develop a conceptual design and a physical design. The **conceptual design** of a database is an abstract model of the database from the user or business perspective. The **physical design** shows how the database is actually arranged on direct access storage devices.

The conceptual database design describes how the data elements in the database are to be grouped. The design process identifies relationships among data elements and the most efficient way of grouping data elements together to meet information requirements. The process also identifies redundant data elements and the groupings of data elements required for specific applications. Groups of data are organized, refined, and streamlined until an overall logical view of the relationships among all of the data elements in the database appears. To produce optimal database design, entity-relationship modeling and normalization are employed. These are described next.

## ENTITY-RELATIONSHIP MODELING

Database designers often document the conceptual data model with an **entity-relationship (ER) diagram**. ER diagrams consist of entities, attributes, and relationships. In ER diagrams, the boxes represent entities, ovals represent attrib-

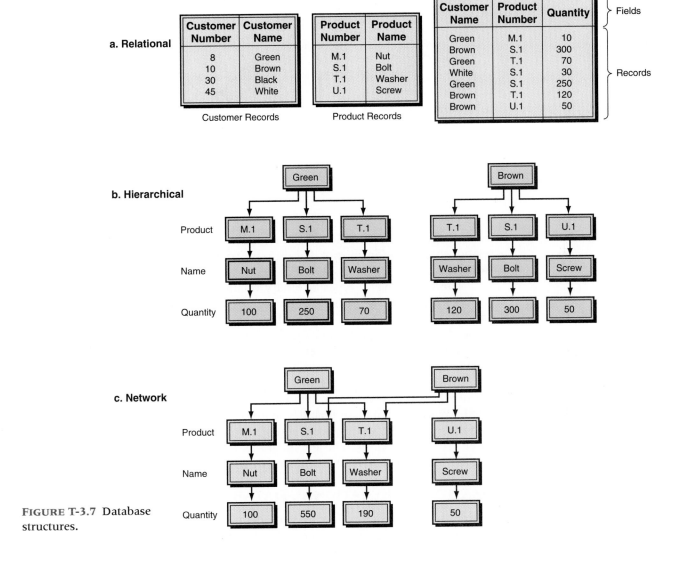

a. Relational

| Customer Number | Customer Name |
|---|---|
| 8 | Green |
| 10 | Brown |
| 30 | Black |
| 45 | White |

Customer Records

| Product Number | Product Name |
|---|---|
| M.1 | Nut |
| S.1 | Bolt |
| T.1 | Washer |
| U.1 | Screw |

Product Records

| Customer Name | Product Number | Quantity |
|---|---|---|
| Green | M.1 | 10 |
| Brown | S.1 | 300 |
| Green | T.1 | 70 |
| White | S.1 | 30 |
| Green | S.1 | 250 |
| Brown | T.1 | 120 |
| Brown | U.1 | 50 |

Fields

Records

b. Hierarchical

c. Network

**FIGURE T-3.7** Database structures.

utes, and the diamonds represent relationships. The attributes for each entity are listed next to the entity (see Figure T-3.8, page 756).

An **entity** is something that can be identified in the users' work environment. In the university example, STUDENT and PROFESSOR are examples of entity. An **instance** of an entity is the representation of a particular entity, so John Smith is an instance of the STUDENT entity and Sara Douglas is an instance of the PROFESSOR entity.

Entities have **attributes**, or properties, that describe the entity's characteristics. In our example, attributes for STUDENT would be Name, IDNumber, and Major. Examples of attributes for PROFESSOR would include Name, Department, and ClassTaught.

Entity instances have **identifiers**, which are attributes that identify entity instances. For example, STUDENT instances can be identified with IDNumber. These identifiers are underlined on ER diagrams.

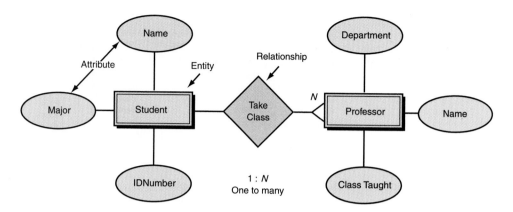

FIGURE T-3.8 Entity-
relationship diagrams.

Entities are associated with one another in **relationships**, which can include many entities. The number of entities in a relationship is the degree of the
relationship. Relationships of degree 2 are common and are called **binary relationships**.

There are several types of binary relationships. For example, one student
can take several classes as shown by the 1:N symbol in Figure T-3.8. We can expand the diagram to N:N relationships, meaning one student can take many
classes from several professors, and each professor can teach several classes and
have many students in each. Several other relationships can be shown on the diagram.

The ER diagrams are supported by tables. The diagrams help to ensure that
the relationships among the data elements in the database are logically structured. When the database includes many files it is difficult to navigate and find
data there. The ER acts like conceptual blueprints of the database. It represents
all entity relationships. The ER diagrams are often consulted to determine a
problem with a query or the complement changes.

## NORMALIZATION OF RELATIONAL DATABASES

In order to use a relational database model effectively, complex groupings of data
must be streamlined to eliminate redundant data elements and awkward many-
to-many relationships. The process of creating small, stable data structures from
complex groups of data is called **normalization**.

Normalization is a method for analyzing and reducing a relational database
to its most parsimonious or streamlined form for minimum redundancy, maximum data integrity, and best processing performance. Specifically, normalization
has several goals:

▶ Eliminate redundancy caused by fields repeated within a file, fields that do
not directly describe the entity, and fields that can be derived from other
fields.

▶ Avoid update anomalies (i.e., errors from inserting, deleting, and modifying
records).

▶ Represent accurately the item being modeled.

▶ Simplify maintenance and information retrieval.

Several levels of normalization exist, which build upon each other addressing increasingly specialized and complex normalization problems.

**THE NORMALIZATION PROCESS.** The concepts of functional dependency and keys are fundamental to normalization. A **functional dependency** is a relationship between or among attributes, where, given the value of one attribute, we can obtain (or look up) the value of another attribute. For example, in Figure T-3.9 if we know the value of IDnumber, we can find the student's major. Therefore, we say that a student's major is functionally dependent on the student's identification number, and that the student's identification number is a **determinant** of the student's major.

| IDNumber | Major | Lab | Fee |
|---|---|---|---|
| 3244 | Management | Inorganic Chemistry | 25 |
| 1697 | Economics | Physics | 25 |
| 9611 | Accounting | Organic Chemistry | 125 |
| 1234 | Marketing | Physics | 25 |

**FIGURE T-3.9** LAB Relation (Single Key)— First Normal Form.

## T3.5 EMERGING DATABASE MODELS

Many of today's applications require database capabilities that can store, retrieve, and process diverse media and not just text and numbers. Full motion video, voice, photos, and drawings can be handled effectively or efficiently by either hierarchical, network, or relational databases and the DBMS. For multimedia and other complex data we use special data models.

The most common database models are:

▶ *Multimedia database.* This is an additional database that enables end users to quickly retrieve and present complex data that involve many dimensions (see Chapter 10).

▶ *Deductive databases.* Hierarchical, network, and relational DBMSs have been used for decades to facilitate data access by users. Users, of course, must understand what they are looking for, the database they are looking at, and at least something about the information sought (like a key and some field or attribute about a record). This approach, however, may not be adequate for some knowledge-based applications that require deductive reasoning for searches. As a result, there is interest in what is called deductive database systems.

▶ *Object-oriented databases.* In order to work in an object-oriented environment, it is necessary to use OO programming and OO databases. This topic is presented in this section. Also see the description in Chapter 10.

▶ *Multimedia and hypermedia databases.* These are analogous to contemporary databases for textual and numeric data; however, they have been tailored to meet the special requirements of dealing with different types of media materials (see Chapter 10).

## THE OBJECT-ORIENTED DATABASE MODEL

Although there is no common definition for *object-oriented database,* there is agreement as to some of its features. Terminology in the object-oriented model, similar to object-oriented programming languages, consists of objects, attributes, classes, methods, and messages (see Technology Guide #2).

Object-oriented databases store both data and procedures acting on the data, as objects. These objects can be automatically retrieved and processed. Therefore the OO database can be particularly helpful in multimedia environments, such as in manufacturing sites using CAD/CAM. Data from design blueprints, photographic images of parts, operational acoustic signatures, and test or quality control data can all be combined into one object, itself consisting of structures and operations. For companies with widely distributed offices, an object-oriented database can provide users with a transparent view of data throughout the entire system.

Object-oriented databases can be particularly useful in supporting temporal and spatial dimensions. All things change; sometimes keeping track of temporal and spatial changes, rather than just the latest version, is important. Related but slightly different versions of an object can easily be maintained in an object-oriented database. Object-oriented databases allow firms to structure their data and use it in ways that would be impossible, or at least very difficult, with other database models. An OO database is slow and therefore cannot be used efficiently for transaction processing-type data. Therefore, as indicted earlier, it is sometimes combined with a relational database.

## HYPERMEDIA DATABASE MODEL

The **hypermedia database model** stores chunks of information in the form of nodes connected by links established by the user. The nodes can contain text, graphics, sound, full-motion video, or executable computer programs. Searching for information does not have to follow a predetermined organizational scheme. Instead, users can branch to related information in any kind of relationship. The relationship between nodes is less structured than in a traditional DBMS. In most systems, each node can be displayed on a screen. The screen also displays the links between the node depicted and other nodes in the database. Like OO databases, this database model is slow.

## ▶ T3.6 DATA WAREHOUSES

A **data warehouse** is an additional database that is designed to support DSS, EIS, online analytical processing (OLAP), and other end-user activities, such as report generation, queries, and graphical presentation. It can provide an "executive view" of data and a unified corporate picture to the end-users by combining the data from many operational systems and incompatible databases without affecting the performance of the running operational systems. It can also provide the decision support system environment in which end users can analyze timely information, and it increases the ability of end users to exploit such information effectively by using data mining tools or OLAP. The topic is discussed at length in Chapter 10.

A **data mart** is smaller, less expensive, and more focused than a large-scale data warehouse. Data marts can be a substitution for a data warehouse, or they can be used in addition to it. In either case, end users can use the warehouse and/or the marts for many applications, such as query, DSS/EIS, reporting, OLAP, knowledge discovery and data mining. It can increase the productivity of the end users. Also see the description in Chapter 10.

# ▶ T3.7 PHYSICAL DATABASE ORGANIZATION

Once a database is logically structured based on its characteristics, relationships, and access methodology, it must be physically implemented with specific software and hardware so users can access data in real-world applications. Data organized into databases are usually stored and accessed through DBMSs, which are themselves organized under various processing arrangements or topologies. Each database management system uses one or more of the various digital storage and access methods, which can significantly affect the amount of required storage space and the speed of data retrieval.

## DATABASE TOPOLOGY

A database is a collection of related files that need to be in one physical location. Where those related files are located can greatly affect user accessibility, query response times, data entry, security, and cost. In general, database files can be centralized or distributed.

A **centralized database** has all the related files in one physical location. Centralized database files on large mainframe computers were the main database topology for decades, primarily because of the enormous capital and operating cost of other alternatives. Not only do centralized databases save the expenses associated with multiple computers, but they also provide database administrators with the ability to work on a database as a whole at one location. Files can generally be made more consistent with each other when they are physically kept in one location because file changes can be made in a supervised and orderly fashion. Files are not accessible except via the centralized host computer, where they can be protected more easily from unauthorized access or modification. Also, recovery from disasters can be more easily accomplished at a central location.

Like all centralized systems, however, centralized databases are vulnerable to a single point of failure. When the centralized database computer fails to function properly, all users suffer. Additionally, access speed is often a problem when users are widely dispersed and must do all of their data manipulations from great distances, thereby incurring transmission delays.

A **distributed database** has complete copies of a database, or portions of a database, in more than one location, which is usually close to the user. A **replicated database** has complete copies of the entire database in several locations, primarily to alleviate the single point-of-failure problems of a centralized database as well as to increase user access responsiveness. There is significant overhead, however, in maintaining consistency among replicated databases, as records are added, modified, and deleted. A **partitioned database** is subdivided, so that each location has a portion of the entire database (usually the portion meeting users' local needs). This type of database provides the response speed of localized files without the need to replicate all changes in multiple locations.

## PHYSICAL VERSUS LOGICAL DATA VIEW

As mentioned earlier, the key benefits from a database, as opposed to multiple unrelated files, come from the ability of many different users to efficiently and effectively share data and process resources. But as there can be many different users, there are many different database needs. How can a single, unified database meet the differing requirements of so many users? For example, how can a single database be structured so that sales personnel can see customer, inventory, and production maintenance data while maintaining restricted access to private personnel data?

A DBMS minimizes these problems by providing two "views" of the database data: a physical view and a logical view. The **physical view** deals with the actual, physical arrangement and location of data in the direct access storage devices (DASD). Database specialists use this view to make efficient use of storage and processing resources. Users, however, may wish to see data differently from how it is stored, and they do not want to know all the technical details of physical storage. After all, a business user is primarily interested in using the information, not in how it is stored.

The **logical view**, or user's view, of a database program represents data in a format that is meaningful to a user and to the software programs that process that data. One strength of a DBMS is that while there is only one physical view of the data, there can be an endless number of different logical views—one specifically tailored to every individual user, if necessary. This process allows users to see database information in a more business-related way rather than from a technical, processing viewpoint. Clearly, users must adapt to the technical requirements of database information systems to some degree, but DBMS logical views allow the system to adapt to the business needs of the users.

## ▶ T3.8 DATABASE MANAGEMENT

Database management, outside of purely technical hardware and software considerations, consists primarily of two functions: *database design and implementation,* and *database administration.*

In designing and implementing databases, specialists should carefully consider the individual needs of all existing and potential users in order to design and implement a database, which optimizes both processing efficiency and user effectiveness. The process usually starts by analyzing what information each user (or group of users) needs and then producing logical views for each. These logical views are analyzed as a whole for similarities that can lead to simplification, and then related so that a single, cohesive logical database can be formed from all the parts. This logical database is implemented with a particular DBMS in a specific hardware system.

**Database administrators** are responsible for ensuring that the database fulfills the user's business needs, in terms of functionality as well for the data itself. User needs, like business in general, do not remain constant. As the business environment changes, and organizational goals and structures react, the database that the firm depends on must also change to remain effective. The computer hardware on which the DBMS software is installed must change to meet changing environments or to take advantage of new technology. This brings accompanying constraints and/or new opportunities for the DBMS's processing performance.

Further, database administrators need to ensure the reliability of databases under their care by managing daily operations, including planning for emergency contingencies by providing backup data and systems to ensure minimal loss of data in the event of a disaster. Security is always a data administration concern when there are multiple accesses to databases that contain all the corporate data. Administrators must balance the business advantages of widespread access with the threat of corporate espionage, sabotage by disgruntled employees, and database damage due to negligence. Database administrators play a significant role in training users about what data is available and how to access it. Finally, administrators are responsible for ensuring that the data contained in the database are accurate, reliable, verifiable, complete, timely, and relevant—a daunting task at best. Otherwise-brilliant business decisions, based on wrong information, can be disastrous in a highly competitive market.

## REFERENCES AND BIBLIOGRAPHY

1. Connolly, T. M., et al., *Database Systems,* 2nd ed., Reading, MA: Addison-Wesley, 1998.

2. Date, C. J., *An Introduction to Database Systems,* 7th ed., Reading, MA: Addison-Wesley, 1999.

3. Elmasri, R., and S. Navathe, *Fundamentals of Database Systems,* Reading, MA: Addison-Wesley, 1999.

4. Goodhue, D., et al., "The Impact of Data Integration on the Costs and Benefits of Information Systems," *MIS Quarterly* 16, No. 3, September 1993.

5. Gray, P., and H. J. Watson, *Decision Support in the Data Warehouse,* Upper Saddle River, NJ: Prentice Hall, 1998.

6. Gupta, A., and J. Ranesh, "Visual Information Retrieval," *Communications of the ACM* 40, No. 5, May 1997.

7. Halper, M., "Welcome to 21st Century Data," *Forbes,* Vol. 157, No. 7, April 8, 1996.

8. Katz, M., ed., *Technology Forecast: 1998,* (also 1999, 2000), Menlo Park, CA: Price Waterhouse World Technology Centre, 1998, 1999, 2000.

9. King, J., "Sorting Information Overload," *ComputerWorld,* December 2, 1996.

10. Kroenke, D., *Database Processing: Fundamentals, Design, and Implementation,* 6th ed., Upper Saddle River, NJ: Prentice Hall, 1997.

11. Ramakrishnan, R., and Gehrke, J. *Database Management Systems,* New York: McGraw Hill, 1999.

12. Silberschatz, A., et al. *Database Systems Concepts,* New York: McGraw Hill, 1997.

13. Sperley, E., *The Enterprise Data Warehouse: Planning, Building, and Implementation,* Upper Saddle River, NJ: Prentice Hall, 1999.

14. Stonebreaker, M., and D. Moore, *Object-Relational DBMS: The Next Great Wave,* San Francisco: Morgan Kaufmann, 1996.

15. Ulman J. D., and J. Widam, *A First Course in Database Systems,* Upper Saddle River, NJ: Prentice Hall, 1997.

16. Zaniolo C., et al., *Advanced Database Systems,* San Francisco: Morgan Kaufmann, 1997.

# TECHNOLOGY GUIDE 4:

# Telecommunications and the Internet

### T4.1
Telecommunication Concepts

### T4.2
Communications Media (Channels)

### T4.3
Network Architecture: Protocols, Standards, Interfaces, and Topologies

### T4.4
Network Processing: Open Systems and Enterprise Networking

### T4.5
The Internet

## ▶ T4.1  TELECOMMUNICATION CONCEPTS

The term **telecommunication** generally refers to all types of long-distance communication through the use of common carriers, including telephone, television, and radio. **Data communications** is the electronic collection, exchange, and processing of data or information, including text, pictures, voice, and other information that is digitally coded and intelligible to a variety of electronic machines. Today's computing environment is dispersed both geographically and organizationally, placing data communications in a strategic organizational role. Data communications is a subset of telecommunication and is accomplished through the use of telecommunication technologies.

In modern organizations, there is an integration of communications technologies. Businesses are finding electronic communications essential for minimizing time and distance limitations. Telecommunication plays a special role when customers, suppliers, vendors, and regulators are part of a multinational organization in a world that is continuously awake and doing business somewhere 24 hours/day, 7 days/week. Figure T-4.1 represents a model of an integrated computer and telecommunication system common in today's business environment.

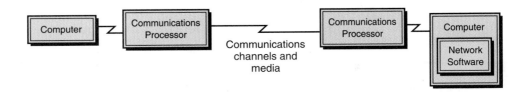

**FIGURE T-4.1**  An integrated computer and telecommunication system.

### TELECOMMUNICATION SYSTEM

A **telecommunication system** is a collection of compatible hardware and software arranged to communicate information from one location to another. These systems can transmit text, graphics, voice, documents, or full motion video information.

A typical telecommunication system is shown in Figure T-4.2. Such systems have two sides: the transmitter of information and the receiver of information.

The major components are:

1. *Hardware.* In addition to a host computer, there is a need for a front-end processor, such as a PC or a mainframe terminal. Other communication processors include controllers, multiplexors, modems, and so on.

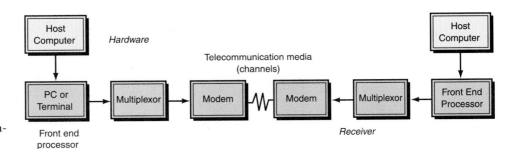

**FIGURE T-4.2**  A telecommunication system.

2. *Communications media*—the physical media through which **electronic signals** are transferred; including wireless media.

3. *Communications networks*—the linkages among computers and communications devices.

4. *The communications processes device*—This device shows how data communication occurs.

5. *Communications software*—software that controls the process.

6. *Data communications providers.* These agencies are either regulated utilities or private firms.

7. *Communication protocols*—the rules for transferring information.

8. *Communications applications.* These applications include EDI, teleconferencing, electronic mail, facsimile, electronic funds transfer, among others.

To transmit and receive information, a telecommunication system must perform the following separate functions that are transparent to the user:

▶ Transmit information.

▶ Establish the interface between the sender and the receiver.

▶ Route messages along the most efficient paths.

▶ Process the information to ensure that the right message gets to the right receiver.

▶ Edit the data to check for errors and rearrange the format if necessary.

▶ Convert messages from another speed into the speed of a communications line or from one format to another.

▶ Control the flow of information by routing messages, polling receivers, and maintaining the network.

▶ Secure the information at all times.

## ELECTRONIC SIGNALS

Telecommunications media can carry two basic types of signals, **analog** and **digital** (see Figure T-4.3). **Analog signals** are continuous waves that "carry" information by altering the characteristics of the waves. Analog signals have two parameters, **amplitude** and **frequency**. For example, voice and all sound is analog, traveling to human ears in the form of waves—the higher the waves (or amplitude), the louder the sound; the more closely packed the waves, the higher the frequency or pitch. Radio, telephones, and recording equipment historically transmitted and received analog signals, but they are beginning to change to digital signals.

**Digital signals** are discrete on-off pulses that convey information in terms of 1s and 0s, just like the central processing unit in computers. Digital signals have several advantages over analog signals. First, digital signals tend to be less affected

**FIGURE T-4.3** Analog vs. digital signals.

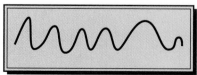

Analog data transmission
(wave signals)

Digital data transmission
(pulse signals)

by interference or "noise." Noise (e.g., "static") can seriously alter the information-carrying characteristics of analog signals, while it is generally easier, in spite of noise, to distinguish between an "on" and an "off." Because of this, digital signals can be repeatedly strengthened for long distances without ever accumulating noise. Second, because computer-based systems process digitally, digital communications among computers require no conversion from digital to analog to digital.

## COMMUNICATIONS PROCESSORS

**MODEM.** The public telephone system (called POTS for "plain old telephone service") was designed as an analog network to carry voice signals or sounds in an analog wave format. In order for this type of circuit to carry digital information, that information must be converted into an analog wave pattern. The conversion from digital to analog is called **modulation**, and the reverse is **demodulation**. The device that performs these two processes is called a **modem**, a contraction of the terms *modulate/demodulate* (see Figure T-4.4). Modems are always used in pairs. The unit at the sending end converts digital information from a computer into analog signals for transmission over analog lines; at the receiving end, another modem converts the analog signal back into digital signals for the receiving computer. Like most communications equipment, a modem's transmission speed is measured in bits per second (bps). In 2000, typical modem speeds range from 14,400 to 56,600 bps.

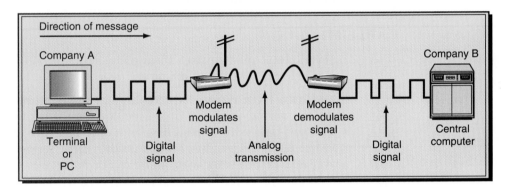

**FIGURE T-4.4** A modem converts digital to analog signals and vice versa. (*Source*: Stern and Stern, 1996, p. 334.)

The amount of data actually transferred from one system to another in a fixed length of time is only partially dependent on the transmission speed. Actual throughput speed, or the effective throughput speed (usually measured in characters per second), varies with factors such as the use of data compression or electrical noise interference.

**MULTIPLEXOR.** A **multiplexor** is an electronic device that allows a single communications channel to carry data transmissions simultaneously from many sources. The objective of a multiplexor is to lower communication costs by allowing efficient use of circuits through sharing. Multiplexing makes more efficient use of an existing communications channel by merging the transmissions of several terminals at one end of the channel, while a similar unit separates the individual transmissions at the receiving end. This process is accomplished through frequency division multiplexing (FDM), time division multiplexing (TDM), or statistical division multiplexing (SDM).

**FRONT-END PROCESSOR.** With most computers, the CPU has to communicate with several devices or terminals at the same time. Routine communication tasks can absorb a large proportion of the CPU's processing time, leading to degraded performance on more important jobs. In order not to waste valuable CPU time, many computer systems have a small secondary computer dedicated solely to communication. Known as a **front-end processor**, this specialized computer manages all routing communications with peripheral devices.

The functions of a front-end processor include coding and decoding data, error detection, recovery, recording, interpreting, and processing the control information that is transmitted. It can also poll remote terminals to determine if they have messages to send or are ready to receive a message. In addition, a front-end processor has the responsibility of controlling access to the network, assigning priorities to messages, logging all data communications activity, computing statistics on network activity, and routing and rerouting messages among alternative communication links and channels.

## ▶ T4.2 COMMUNICATIONS MEDIA (CHANNELS)

For data to be communicated from one location to another, some form of pathway or medium must be used. These pathways are called **communications media (channels)**, and include twisted pair wire, coaxial cable, fiber optic cable, microwave transmission, and satellite transmission. The essentials of these communications media are as follows:

### CABLE MEDIA

Several cable media exist and in many systems a mix of media (e.g., fiber-coax) can be found. The major media are:

**TWISTED-PAIR WIRE.** Twisted-pair wire is the most prevalent form of communications wiring, because it is used for almost all business telephone wiring. **Twisted-pair wire** consists of strands of copper wire twisted in pairs. As shown in Figure T-4.5, it is usually enclosed inside a cable. It is relatively inexpensive, widely available, easy to work with, and it can be made relatively unobtrusive by running it inside walls, floors, and ceilings. However, twisted-pair wire has some important disadvantages. It emits electromagnetic interference, is relatively slow for transmitting data, is subject to interference from other electrical sources, and it can be easily "tapped" for gaining unauthorized access to data by unintended receivers.

**FIGURE T-4.5** Twisted pair telephone cable, coaxial cable, and fiber-optic cable.

**COAXIAL CABLE.** **Coaxial cable** consists of *insulated* copper wire, and is much less susceptible to electrical interference and can carry much more data than twisted-pair wire. For these reasons, it is commonly used to carry high-speed data traffic as well as television signals (i.e., in cable television). However, coaxial cable is 10 to 20 times more expensive, more difficult to work with, and relatively inflexible. Because of its inflexibility, it can increase the cost of installation or recabling when equipment must be moved. The advantages and disadvantages of twisted-pair cables are compared in Table T-4.1 with that of other media.

**FIBER OPTICS.** Fiber-optic technology, combined with the invention of the semiconductor laser, provides the means to transmit information through clear glass fibers in the form of light waves, instead of electric current. **Fiber-optic cables** consist of thousands of very thin filaments of glass fibers. These fibers can

*Table T-4.1* **Advantages and Disadvantages of Communications Media**

| Medium | Advantages | Disadvantages |
|---|---|---|
| **Twisted pair** | • Inexpensive<br>• Widely available<br>• Easy to work with<br>• Unobtrusive | • Emits electromagnetic interference<br>• Slow (low bandwidth)<br>• Subject to interference<br>• Easily tapped (low security) |
| **Coaxial cable** | • Higher bandwidth than twisted pair<br>• Less susceptible to electromagnetic interference | • Relatively expensive and inflexible<br>• Somewhat difficult to work with<br>• Easily tapped (low to medium security) |
| **Fiber optic cable** | • Very high bandwidth<br>• Smaller and lighter than coaxial cable<br>• Difficult to tap | • Difficult to work with (difficult to splice)<br>• Expensive<br>• Relatively inflexible |
| **Microwave** | • Very high bandwidth<br>• Relatively inexpensive | • Must have unobstructed line-of-sight<br>• Subject to interference from rain |
| **Satellite** | • Very high bandwidth<br>• Large coverage on earth | • Must use encryption for security<br>• Expensive<br>• Must have unobstructed line-of-sight<br>• Signals experience propagation delay<br>• Must use encryption for security |

conduct light pulses generated by lasers at transmission frequencies that approach the speed of light.

Besides significant size and weight reductions over traditional cable media, fiber-optic cables provide increased speed, greater data-carrying capacity, and greater security from interferences and tapping. A single hairlike glass fiber can carry up to 30,000 simultaneous telephone calls, compared to about 5500 calls on a standard copper coaxial cable. Until recently, the costs of fiber and difficulties in installing fiber-optic cable slowed its growth. Fiber optics are used as the high-speed backbone of most networks (including the Internet) and are just starting to connect isolated devices to the backbone.

**PHOTONICS.** The technology of generating and harnessing light and other forms of radiant energy whose quantum unit is the photon is called **photonics**. This science includes light emission, transmission, deflection, amplification, and detection by optical components and instruments, lasers and other light sources, fiber optics, electro-optical instrumentation, related hardware and electronics, and sophisticated systems. The range of applications of photonics extends from energy generation to detection to communications and information processing. Photons allow gobs of data to move at gigabit speeds across more than 1000 wavelengths per fiber strand.

## WIRELESS MEDIA

Cables present several problems, notably the expense of installation and change, as well as a fairly limited capacity, with the exception of fiber-optic cables. The alternative is **wireless communication**. Common uses of wireless data transmission include pagers, cellular telephones, microwave transmissions, communications satellites, mobile data networks, personal communications services, and personal digital assistants.

**MICROWAVE. Microwave** systems are widely used for high-volume, long-distance, point-to-point communication. These systems were first used extensively to transmit very high frequency radio signals in a line-of-sight path between relay stations spaced approximately 30 miles apart (due to the earth's curvature). To minimize line-of-sight problems, microwave antennas were usually placed on top of buildings, towers, and mountain peaks. Long-distance telephone carriers adopted microwave systems because they generally provide about 10 times the data-carrying capacity of a wire without the significant efforts necessary to string or bury wire. Compared to 30 miles of wire, microwave communications can be set up much more quickly (within a day) and at much lower cost.

The fact that microwave requires line-of-sight transmission severely limits its usefulness as a practical large-scale solution to data communication needs, especially over very long distances. Additionally, microwave transmissions are susceptible to environmental interference during severe weather such as heavy rain or snowstorms. Although still fairly widely used, long distance microwave data communications systems have been replaced largely by satellite communications systems.

**SATELLITE.** A major advance in communications in recent years is the use of communications satellites for digital transmissions. Although the radio frequencies used by satellite data communication transponders are also line-of-sight, the enormous "footprint" of a satellite's coverage area from high altitudes overcomes the limitations of microwave data relay stations. For example, a network of just three evenly spaced communications satellites in stationary "geosynchronous" orbit 22,300 miles above the equator is sufficient to provide global coverage.

Currently, there are three types of orbits in which satellites are placed: geostationary earth orbit, medium earth orbit, and low earth orbit.

**Geostationary earth orbit (GEO)** satellites orbit 22,300 miles directly above the equator and maintain a fixed position above the earth's surface. These satellites are excellent for sending television programs to cable operators and broadcasting directly to homes. However, transmissions from GEO satellites take a quarter of a second to send and return (called *propagation delay*), making two-way telephone conversations difficult. Also, GEO satellites are large and expensive, and the equatorial orbit cannot hold many more GEO satellites than the 150 that now orbit there.

**Medium earth orbit (MEO)** satellites are located about 6,000 miles above the earth's surface, in orbits inclined to the equator. While fewer satellites are needed to cover the earth than in LEO orbits, telephones need more power to reach MEO satellites than to reach LEO satellites.

**Low earth orbit (LEO)** satellites are located 400 to 1000 miles above the earth's surface. These satellites are much closer to the earth, reducing or eliminating apparent signal delay. They can pick up signals from weak transmitters, meaning that handheld telephones need less power and can use smaller batteries. They consume less power and cost less to launch than GEO and MEO satellites. However, moving data across constellations of many satellites will be complex and the technology remains untested.

Satellites have a number of unique characteristics. Some are advantages while others are restrictions that render satellite use either impractical or impossible for other applications.

### Advantages of Satellites

▶ Cost of transmission is the same regardless of the distance between the sending and receiving stations within the footprint of a satellite.

▶ Cost remains the same regardless of the number of stations receiving that transmission (simultaneous reception).

▶ They have the ability to carry very large amounts of data.

▶ They can easily cross or span political borders, often with minimal government regulation.

▶ Transmission errors in a digital satellite signal occur almost completely at random. Thus, statistical methods for error detection and correction can be applied efficiently and reliably.

▶ Users can be highly mobile while sending and receiving signals.

### Disadvantages of Satellites

▶ Any one-way transmission over a satellite link has an inherent propagation delay of approximately one-quarter of a second. This delay makes the use of satellite links inefficient for some data communications needs (voice communication and "stepping-on" each other's speech).

▶ Due to launch weight limitations, they carry or generate very little electrical power. Low power of signal coupled with distance can result in extremely weak signals at the receiving earth station.

▶ Signals are inherently not secure because they are available to all receivers within the footprint—intended or not.

▶ Some frequencies used are susceptible to interference from bad weather or ground-based microwave signals.

Several large corporations are busy building satellite systems as shown in Table T-4.2.

**GLOBAL POSITIONING SYSTEMS.** A **global positioning system (GPS)** is a wireless system that uses satellites to enable users to determine their position anywhere on the earth. GPS equipment has been used extensively for navigation by

---

**Table T-4.2**  **Satellites Under Construction or Recently Completed**

| Type | Company(ies) | Miles Above Earth | Number | Cost | Year Completed |
|------|--------------|-------------------|--------|------|----------------|
| GEO  | Hughes Electronics | 22,300 | 8 | $3 billion | 2000 |
| MEO  | ICO Global | 6,434 | 10 | $3.7 billion | 2000 |
| MEO  | TRW and Teleglobe (Odyssey) | 6,434 | 12 | $3.2 billion | 2001 |
| LEO  | Loral Space, Qualcomm | 763 | 48 | $2.5 billion | 1999 |
| LEO  | McCaw Cellular Comm | 420 | 840 | $9 billion | 2002 |

commercial airlines and ships and for locating tracks. GPS is supported by 24 U.S. government satellites that are shared worldwide. Each satellite orbits the earth once in 12 hours, on a precise path at an altitude of 10,900 miles. At any point in time, the exact position of each satellite is known, because the satellite broadcasts its position and a time signal from its on-board atomic clock, accurate to one-billionth of a second. Receivers also have accurate clocks that are synchronized with those of the satellites. Knowing the speed of signals (186,272 miles per second), it is possible to find the location of any receiving station (latitude and longitude) within an accuracy of 50 feet by triangulation, using the distance of three satellites for the computation. GPS software computes the latitude and longitude and converts it to an electronic map. GPS has many applications; several are discussed in this book. An interesting application is now available from several car manufacturers (e.g., Toyota) as a navigation system for finding your way to gas stations, and so on. GPS are also available on cell phones, so you can know where the caller is located. This feature is now available to hikers in the form of handheld devices costing as little as $90.

**RADIO.** **Radio** electromagnetic data communications do not have to depend on microwave or satellite links, especially for short ranges such as within an office setting. Radio is being used increasingly to connect computers and peripheral equipment or computers and local area networks. The greatest advantage radio has for data communications is that no metallic wires are needed. Radio waves tend to propagate easily through normal office walls. The devices are fairly inexpensive and easy to install.

However, radio media can create reciprocal electrical interference problems—with other office electrical equipment, and from that equipment to the radio communication devices. Also, radio transmissions are susceptible to snooping by anyone similarly equipped and on the same frequency.

**INFRARED.** **Infrared light** is red light, not commonly visible to human eyes, that can be modulated or pulsed for conveying information. The most common application of infrared light is with television or videocassette recorder remote control units. With computers, infrared transmitters and receivers (or "transceivers") are being used for short-distance connection between computers and peripheral equipment, or between computers and local area networks. Many mobile phones have a built-in infrared (IrDA) port, which supports data transfer speed up to 14.4 kbps.

Advantages of infrared light include no need for metallic wires, equipment is highly mobile, no electrical interference problems, no Federal Communications Commission (FCC) permission required to operate an infrared transmitter, no certification needed before selling an infrared device, and fairly inexpensive devices exist with very high data rates. Disadvantages of infrared media include susceptibility to fog, smog, smoke, dust, rain, and air temperature fluctuations.

**CELLULAR RADIO TECHNOLOGY.** Telephone users for data communications are increasingly employing **cellular radio technology**. The basic concept is relatively simple. The FCC has defined geographic cellular service areas; each area is subdivided into hexagonal cells that fit together like a honeycomb to form the backbone of that area's cellular radio system. Located at the center of each cell is a radio transceiver and a computerized cell-site controller that handles all cell-site control functions. All the cell sites are connected to a mobile telephone switching office that provides the connections from the cellular system to a wired telephone network and transfers calls from one cell to another as a user travels out of the cell serving one area and into another.

The cellular telephone infrastructure has primarily been used for voice transmission, but recent development of a transmission standard called Cellular Digital Packet Data (CDPD) has made it possible for the infrastructure to support two-way digital transmission.

In 1999, the Internet started to meet the cellular network. **Wireless Application Protocol (WAP)** provides a universal open standard that enables users to access Web-based interactive information services and applications from the screens of mobile phones.

It is the trend that mobile phones cannot really compete without Internet access. A WAP-enabled mobile phone with a WAP-enabled microbrowser, can let users access any WAP-supporting Web sites. WAP is designed to work with most wireless networks such as TDMA, CDSMA, GSM, etc. It can also be built on any operating system. The communication language being used between the Internet and the mobile phone is **Wireless Markup Language (WML)**. WAP's WML uses the XML standard that is widely used in Web sites. The WAP technology will greatly encourage the prosperity of electronic commerce. It is expected that in 2002, more than half of the e-commerce transactions will be conducted with mobile phones.

Another new technology for wireless connectivity is **Bluetooth**. It allows wireless communication between mobile phones, laptops, and other portable devices. In the first half of 2000 Bluetooth technology is being built in to many mobile PCs, mobile telephones, and PDAs.

**MOBILE COMPUTING. Mobile computing** refers to the use of portable computer devices in multiple locations. It occurs on radio-based networks that transmit data to and from mobile computers. Computers can be connected to the network through wired ports or through wireless connections. Mobile computing, especially if wireless, provides for many applications (see Table T-4.3, page 772).

Another type of mobile data network is based upon a series of radio towers constructed specifically to transmit text and data. Ram Mobile Data (jointly owned by Ram Broadcasting and BellSouth) and Ardis (jointly owned by IBM and Motorola) are two publicly available networks that use these media for national two-way data transmission.

**PERSONAL COMMUNICATION SERVICE.** Personal communication service (PCS) uses lower-power, higher frequency radio waves than does cellular technology. The lower power means that PCS cells are smaller and must be more numerous and closer together. The higher frequency means that PCS devices are effective in many places where cellular telephones are not, such as in tunnels and inside office buildings. PCS telephones need less power, are smaller, and are less expensive than cellular telephones. They also operate at higher, less-crowded frequencies than cellular telephones, meaning that they will have the bandwidth necessary to provide video and multimedia communication.

**PERSONAL DIGITAL ASSISTANTS.** Personal digital assistants (PDAs) are small, pen-based, handheld computers capable of entirely digital communications transmission (see discussion in Technology Guide #1). They have built-in wireless telecommunications capabilities. Applications include Internet access, e-mail, fax, electronic scheduler, calendar, and notepad software.

## CHARACTERISTICS OF COMMUNICATIONS MEDIA

Communications media have several characteristics that determine their efficiency and capabilities. These characteristics include the speed, direction, mode, and accuracy of transmission.

### *Table T-4.3* Mobile and Wireless Applications

Mobile computing enables existing and entirely new kinds of applications, for example:

- *Mobile personal communications capabilities*, such as the new personal digital assistants (PDAs) for networked communications and applications (a networked extension of the portable palmtop style of computing).
- *Online transaction processing*, for example, where a salesperson in a retail environment can enter an order for goods and also charge a customer's credit card to complete the transaction.
- *Remote database queries*, for example, where a salesperson can use a mobile network connection to check an item's availability or the status of an order, directly from the customer's site.
- *Dispatching*, which means any kind of dispatching application such as air traffic control, rental car pickup and return, delivery vehicles, trains, taxis, cars, and trucks.
- *Front-line IT applications*, where instead of the same data being entered multiple times as it goes through the value chain, it is entered only once, typically at the beginning of the cycle or where first created.

Wireless communications enables both mobile computing applications and low-cost cable replacement applications, for example:

- *Temporary offices* can be set up quickly and inexpensively by using wireless network connections (often just running the wires to a standard office can cost hundreds of dollars).
- *Wireless connections* to permanent office locations are often practical in difficult wiring environments (e.g., in historic buildings where installed wired connections could cause damage, or in buildings where there is asbestos insulation, and wire installation could produce a health risk).
- *Campus area network backbones*, where installing a wireless connection can replace leased lines that are used to connect LANs, thus eliminating the costs of monthly line leases.
- *Preconfigured LAN installations*, where the software and the network is preconfigured, preloaded, and pretested as a sort of LAN-in-a-box so that anyone can install the network instead of having to use an expensive network installation specialist.

There are mobile and wireless application opportunities in many industries, such as:

- *Retail*—the most successful application to date, particularly in department stores where there are frequent changes of layout; retail sales personnel could conduct inventory enquiries or even sales transactions on the retail floor with wireless access from their PCs.
- *Wholesale/distribution.* Many distributors currently use wireless networking for inventory picking in warehouses with PCs mounted directly on forklifts and for delivery and order status updates, with PCs inside distribution tractor trailers.
- *Field service/sales.* Dispatching, online diagnostic support from customer sites, and parts ordering/inventory queries are typical applications in all types of service and sales functions.
- *Factories/manufacturing*—process control, hostile environments, clean rooms; applications could include mobile shop-floor quality control or wireless applications that give added flexibility for temporary setups.
- *Healthcare/hospitals.* Healthcare personnel need to access and send data to patient records or consult comparative diagnosis databases wherever the patient or the healthcare worker may be located (different hospital rooms, departments, outpatient sites, and so forth).
- *Education.* Interesting pilot applications involve equipping students with PCs in the lecture halls, linked by a wireless network, for interactive quizzes, additional data and graphics lecture support, and online handout materials.
- *Banking/finance.* Mobile transactional capabilities can assist in purchasing, selling, inquiry, brokerage, and other dealings.

SOURCE: Advertisement from the Digital Equipment Corporation.

**TRANSMISSION SPEED. Bandwidth** refers to the range of frequencies available in any communications channel. Bandwidth is a very important concept in communications because the transmission capacity (stated in bits per second, *bps*) is largely dependent on its bandwidth. In general, the greater the bandwidth the greater the channel capacity. For many data communications applications, a small bandwidth (2400 to 14,400 bps) is usually adequate. The speed of a transmission is measured in **bits per second (bps)** (i.e., the number of bits that can be transmitted in one second). On the other hand, graphical information requires a much greater bandwidth than textual data (in the range of millions of bits per second, or *Mbps*). Note the difference between the **signal frequency** that is measured in Hertz that designates the number of times per second that a signal is changing, and a bps.

Channel capacity is subdivided into three bandwidths: *narrowband, voiceband, and broadband* channels. Slow, low-capacity transmissions, such as those transmitted over telegraph lines, make use of **narrowband** channels while telephone lines utilize **voiceband** channels. The channel bandwidth with the highest capacity is **broadband**, used by microwave, cable, and fiber-optic lines.

The amount of data that can be transmitted through a communications channel is called the **baud rate** and is measured in bits per second. A baud represents a signal change from positive to negative or vice versa. The baud rate is not always the same as the bit rate. At higher transmission speeds, a single signal change can transmit more than one bit at a time, so the bit rate can be greater than the baud rate.

One signal change, or cycle, is necessary to transmit one or more bits per second. Therefore, the speed of a channel is a function of its frequency: the number of cycles per second that can be transmitted through a channel measured in Hertz.

Communications channels have a wide range of speeds based on the technology used and the enhancements. Transfer rates for various types of transmission media are as follows:

| | |
|---|---|
| Twisted pair | up to 128 Mbps (million bits per second) |
| Coaxial cable | up to 200 Mbps |
| Fiber-optic cable | 100 Mbps to 2 Gbps (billions bits per second) |
| Broadcast radio | up to 2 Mbps |
| Microwave | 45 Mbps |
| Satellite | 50 Mbps |
| Cellular radio | 9600 bpts to 14.4 Kbps (thousand bits per second) |
| Infrared | 1 to 4 Mbps |

**OPTICAL NETWORKING.** One effective innovation that increases the capacity of fiber optics is *dense wave division multiplexing* (DWDM). It facilitates the process of managing signals as wavelengths or colors of light, not electrical streams of bits. Eventually, an all-optic network, where signals coming into the network are immediately converted to colors of light and managed at an optical layer, will become economically feasible. The increased capacity will be very significant.

## TRANSMISSION DIRECTION

Data transmission occurs in one of three directions: simplex, half-duplex, or full-duplex.

A **simplex data transmission** uses one circuit in one direction only—similar to a doorbell, a public announcement system, or broadcast television and radio. Simplex transmission is simple and relatively inexpensive but very constraining, since communication is one way only.

**Half-duplex transmission** also uses only one circuit, but it is used in both directions—one direction at a time. Examples include an intercom or a citizen's band radio where users can receive or transmit, but cannot do both simultaneously. Two-way data transfer makes half duplex much more useful than simplex, but coordination of half-duplex communications could be difficult.

**Full-duplex transmission** uses two circuits for communications—one for each direction simultaneously (for example, a common telephone). Full-duplex is easier to use than half-duplex, but the cost of two circuits can be significant, especially over long distances. Most data devices can operate in both half- and full-duplex directions.

## TRANSMISSION MODE

Data transmissions may be either asynchronous or synchronous. In an **asynchronous transmission**, only one character is transmitted or received at a time. During transmission, the character is preceded by a start bit and followed by a stop bit that lets the receiving device know where a character begins and ends. There is typically idle time between transmission of characters, so synchronization is maintained on a character-by-character basis. Asynchronous transmission is inherently inefficient due to the additional overhead required for start and stop bits, and the idle time between transmissions. It is generally used only for relatively low-speed data transmission (up to 56K bps).

In a **synchronous transmission**, a group of characters is sent over a communications link in a continuous bit stream while data transfer is controlled by a timing signal initiated by the sending device. The sender and receiver must be in perfect synchronization to avoid the loss or gain of bits; therefore, data blocks are preceded by unique characters called sync bits that are encoded into the information being transmitted. The receiving device recognizes and synchronizes itself with a stream of these characters. Synchronous transmission is generally used for transmitting large volumes of data at high speeds.

## TRANSMISSION ACCURACY

An electrical communications line can be subject to interference from storms, signals from other lines, and other phenomena that introduce errors into a transmission. Telephone line cables may be mishandled by repair personnel, accidentally cut by construction workers, or subjected to power surges while data are being transmitted. These events might cause one bit or several bits to be "dropped" during transmission, thus corrupting the integrity of the information. Because the loss of even one bit could alter a character or control code, data transmission requires accuracy controls. These controls consist of bits called *parity bits* that are like check sums added to characters and/or blocks of characters at the sending end of the line. Parity bits are checked and verified at the receiving end of the line to determine whether bits were lost during transmission.

**T4.3 NETWORK ARCHITECTURE: PROTOCOLS, STANDARDS, INTERFACES, AND TOPOLOGIES**

Network architectures facilitate the operation, maintenance, and growth of the network by isolating the user and the application from the physical details of the network. Network architectures include protocols, standards, interfaces, and topologies.

### PROTOCOLS

Devices that are nodes in a network must access and share the network to transmit and receive data. These components work together by adhering to a common set of rules that enable them to communicate with each other. This set of rules and procedures governing transmission across a network is a **protocol**. The principal functions of protocols in a network are line access and collision avoidance. Line access concerns how the sending device gains access to the network to send a message. Collision avoidance refers to managing message transmission so that two messages do not collide with each other on the network. Other functions of protocols are to identify each device in the communication path, to secure the attention of the other device, to verify correct receipt of the transmitted message, to verify that a message requires retransmission because it cannot be correctly interpreted, and to perform recovery when errors occur.

The simplest protocol is *polling*, where a master device (computer or communications processor) polls, or contacts, each node. Polling can be effective because the speed of mainframe and communications processors allows them to poll and control transmissions by many nodes sharing the same channel, particularly if the typical communications are short.

In the **token passing approach**, a small data packet, called a token, is sent around the network. If a device wants to transmit a message, it must wait for the token to pass, examine it to see if it is in use and pass it on, or use the token to help route its message to its destination on the network. After transmission is completed, the token is returned to the network by the receiving terminal if it is not needed. IBM token ring networks use this access method.

The **Transmission Control Protocol/Internet Protocol (TCP/IP)** is a file transfer protocol that can send large files of information across sometimes-unreliable networks with assurance that the data will arrive in uncorrupted form. TCP/IP allows efficient and reasonably error-free transmission between different systems and is the standard protocol of the Internet and intranets.

### COMMUNICATION STANDARDS

Networks typically have hardware and software from a number of different vendors which must communicate with each other by "speaking the same language" and following the same protocols. Unfortunately, commercially available data communication devices speak a variety of languages and follow a number of different protocols, causing substantial problems with data communications networks.

Attempts at standardizing data communications have been somewhat successful, but standardization in the United States has lagged behind other countries where the communication industry is more closely regulated. Various organizations, including the Electronic Industries Association (EIA), the Consultative Committee for International Telegraph and Telephone (CCITT), and the International Standards Organization (ISO), have developed electronic interfacing standards that are widely used within the industry. The major types of standards are *networking standards, transmission standards, and software standards.*

**NETWORKING STANDARDS.** Typically, the protocols required to achieve communication on behalf of an application are actually multiple protocols existing at different levels or layers. Each layer defines a set of functions that are provided as services to upper layers, and each layer relies on services provided by lower layers. At each layer, one or more protocols define precisely how software programs on different systems interact to accomplish the functions for that layer. This layering notion has been formalized in several architectures. The most widely known is the Reference Model of Open Systems Interconnection (OSI). There is a peer-to-peer communication between software at each layer and a reliance on underlying layers for services to accomplish communication.

The OSI model has seven layers, each having its own well-defined function.

*Layer 1: Physical layer.* Concerned with transmitting raw bits over a communications channel; provides a physical connection for the transmission of data among network entities and creates the means by which to activate and deactivate a physical connection.

*Layer 2: Data link layer.* Provides a reliable means of transmitting data across a physical link; breaks up the input data into data frames sequentially and processes the acknowledgment frames sent back by the receiver.

*Layer 3: Network layer.* Routes information from one network computer to another; computers may be physically located within the same network or within another network that is interconnected in some fashion; accepts messages from source host and sees to it they are directed toward the destination.

*Layer 4: Transport layer.* Provides a network-independent transport service to the session layer; accepts data from session layer, splits it up into smaller units as required, passes these to the network layer, and ensures all pieces arrive correctly at the other end.

*Layer 5: Session layer.* User's interface into network; where user must negotiate to establish connection with process on another machine; once connection is established the session layer can manage the dialogue in an orderly manner.

*Layer 6: Presentation layer.* Here messages are translated from and to the format used in the network to and from a format used at the application layer.

*Layer 7: Application layer.* Includes activities related to users, such as supporting file transfer, handling messages, and providing security.

*The SNA Standard.* The Systems Network Architecture (SNA) is a standard developed by IBM that is widely used in private networks. Similar to OSI, SNA uses a layered approach; however, the layers are somewhat different.

**TRANSMISSION STANDARDS.** A number of network bandwidth boosters address the need for much greater bandwidth on networks for advanced computing applications. These boosters include FDDI (fiber distributed data interface), ATM (asynchronous transfer mode), switching hubs, and ISDN (integrated services digital network).

Like token-ring networks, the **fiber distributed data interface (FDDI)** passes data around a ring, but with a bandwidth of 100 Mpbs—far faster than a standard 10–13 Mbps token-ring or bus network. Although the FDDI standard can use any transmission medium, it is based on the high-speed, high-capacity capabilities of fiber optics. FDDI can significantly boost network performance, but this technology is about 10 times more expensive to implement than most LAN networks.

**Asynchronous transfer mode (ATM)** networks are based on switched technologies, allowing for almost unlimited bandwidth on demand. They are packet-switched networks, dividing data into uniform cells, each with 53 groups of eight bytes, eliminating the need for protocol conversion. ATM allows channel mixing and matching of varying bandwidths and data types (e.g., video, data, and voice) and much higher speeds because the data are more easily "squeezed" in among other very small packets. ATM currently requires fiber-optic cable.

**Switched hub technologies** are often used to boost local area networks. A switched hub can turn many small LANs into one big LAN. A network need not be rewired nor adapter cards replaced when changes are made; all that is needed is the addition of a switching hub. Switched hub technology can also add an ATM-like packet switching capability to existing LANs, essentially doubling bandwidth.

**Integrated services digital network (ISDN)** is a high-speed data transmission technology that allows users to simultaneously transfer voice, video, image, and data at high speed. ISDN uses existing telephone lines and provides two levels of service: basic rate ISDN and primary rate ISDN. Basic rate ISDN serves a single device with three channels. Two channels are B (bearer) channels with a capacity to transmit 64 Kbps of digital data. The third or D channel is a 16-Kbps channel for signaling and control information. Primary rate ISDN provides 1.5 Mbps of bandwidth. The bandwidth contains 23 B channels and one D channel. A second generation of ISDN is broadband ISDN (BISDN), which provides transmission channels capable of supporting transmission rates greater than the primary ISDN rate. BISDN supports transmission from 2 Mbps up to much higher, but as yet unspecified, rates.

**SOFTWARE STANDARDS.** Three types of software standards are necessary for an **open system**. An open system refers to the ability of different devices, from different vendors, to conveniently "talk" to each other.

*Operating Systems.* No standard exists, resulting in many differing versions of operating systems, such as DOS, Unix, Windows NT, OS/2, OSF (Open Software Foundation), and Linux.

*Graphical User Interface Standard.* X Windows is the standard for GUI. It runs on all types of computers and is used with Unix and the DEC VAX/VMS operating systems. It permits one display of several applications on one screen and allows one application to use several windows.

*Software Application Standards.* The U.S. government is attempting to establish a standard for all its systems. It will cover operating systems, DBMS, user interfaces, programming languages, electronic data interchange, and so on.

## INTERFACES

An *interface* is a physical connection between two communications devices. One important concept of interfacing concerns the types of data transfer—parallel or serial. **Parallel data transfer**, most often used for local communication, employs a communications interface with a series of dedicated wires, each serving one purpose. In parallel communication, both data and control signals are transmitted simultaneously.

A **serial data transfer**, most often used for long-distance communications, is bit by bit rather than many bits in parallel. Most data communications devices transmit in serial fashion. While much slower than parallel data transfer, serial transfer is simpler and requires much less on the part of the receiving system.

## NETWORK TOPOLOGY

The **topology** of a network is the physical layout and connectivity of a network. Specific protocols, or rules of communications, are often used on specific topologies, but the two concepts are different. Topology refers to the ways the channels connect the nodes, where protocol refers to the rules by which data communications takes place over these channels. Neither concept should be confused with the *physical cabling* of the network. There are three basic network topologies: bus, ring, and star (see Figure T-4.6):

**BUS.** In a bus topology, nodes are arranged along a single length of twisted-pair wire, coaxial cable, or fiber-optic cable that can be extended at the ends. Using a bus topology, it is easy and inexpensive to add a node to the network and losing a node in the network will not cause the network to fail. The main disadvantages to the bus topology are that a defective bus causes the *entire network* to fail and providing a bus with inadequate bandwidth will degrade the performance of the network.

**RING.** In a ring topology, nodes are arranged along the transmission path so that a signal passes through one station at a time before returning to its originating node. The nodes, then, form a closed circle. It is relatively easy and inexpensive

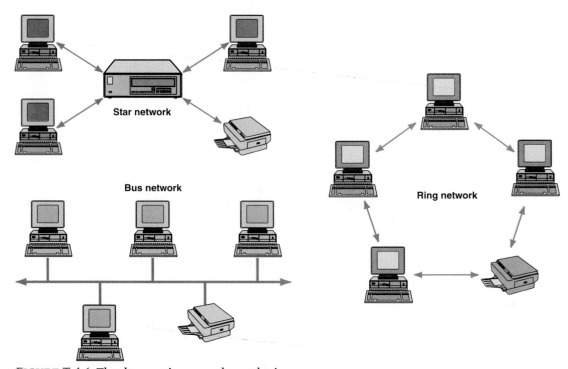

**FIGURE T-4.6** The three main network topologies.

to add a node to the network, and losing a node does not necessarily mean that the network will fail.

**STAR.** A star network has a central node that connects to each of the other nodes by a single, point-to-point link. Any communication between one node and another in a star topology must pass through the central node. It is easy to add a node in a star network and losing a peripheral node will not cause the entire network to fail. However, the central computer must be powerful enough to handle communications in a star network. Too many devices in the star can overload the central computer and cause degradation in performance across the network. The star topology is typically used in low-cost, slow-speed data networks.

Each topology has strengths and weaknesses. When an organization is choosing a topology, it should consider such performance issues as delay, throughput, reliability, and the network's ability to continue through, or recover after, the failure of one or more of its nodes. A company should also consider such physical constraints as the maximum transmission speed of the circuit, the distances between nodes, the circuit's susceptibility to errors, and the overall system costs.

## NETWORK SIZE

Because people need to communicate over long as well as short distances, the geographic size of data communications networks is important. There are two general network sizes: local area networks and wide area networks. A "metropolitan" area network falls between the two in size.

**LOCAL AREA NETWORKS.** A **local area network (LAN)** connects two or more communicating devices within a short distance, (e.g., 2,000 feet) so that every user device on the network has the potential to communicate with any other device. LANs are usually intraorganizational, privately owned, internally administered, and not subject to regulation by the FCC. LANs do not cross public right-of-ways and do not require communications hardware and software that are necessary to link computer systems to existing communications networks. A LAN allows a large number of its intelligent devices to share corporate resources (such as storage devices, printers, programs, and data files) and integrates a wide range of functions into a single system. Many LANs are physically connected as a star, meaning that every device is connected to a hub.

In an office, a LAN can give users fast and efficient access to a common collection of information while also allowing the office to pool resources, such as printers and facsimile machines. A well-constructed LAN can also eliminate the need to circulate paper documents by distributing electronic memos and other materials to each worker's terminal.

The network gateway connects the LAN to public networks or other corporate networks so that the LAN can exchange information with networks external to it. A **gateway** is a communications processor that can connect dissimilar networks by translating from one set of protocols to another. A **bridge** connects two networks of the same type. A **router** routes messages through several connected LANs or to a WAN.

A LAN consists of cabling or wireless technology linking individual devices, network interface cards (special adapters serving as interfaces to the cable), and software to control LAN activities. The LAN network **interface card** specifies the data transmission rate, the size of message units, the addressing information attached to each message, and the network topology.

*Private Branch Exchange.*   A **private branch exchange (PBX)** is strongly related to the LAN. The PBX is a special-purpose computer that controls telephone switching at a company site. PBXs can carry both voice and data and perform a wide variety of functions to make communications more convenient and effective, such as call waiting, call forwarding, and voice mail. PBXs also offer functions directed at decreasing costs, such as reducing the number of outside lines, providing internal extensions, and determining least-cost routings. Automatic assignment of calls to lines reduces the required number of outside lines. Providing internal extension numbers permits people to make calls within the same site using only extension numbers and without making a chargeable outside call.

**WIDE AREA NETWORKS.** **Wide area networks (WANs)** are long-haul, broadband (analog), generally public access networks covering wide geographic areas that cross right-of-ways and are provided by common carriers. WANs include *regional networks* such as telephone companies or *international networks* such as global communications service providers. They usually have very large capacity circuits with many communications processors to use these circuits efficiently.

WANs may combine switched and dedicated lines, microwave, and satellite communications. Switched lines are telephone lines that a person can access from his or her computer to transmit data to another computer, the transmission being routed or switched through paths to its destination. Dedicated (or leased) lines, or nonswitched lines, are continuously available for transmission and a lessee typically pays a flat rate for total access to the line. The lines can be leased or purchased from common carriers or private communications media vendors. Dedicated lines are often higher speed than switched lines and are used for high-volume transactions.

A leased line may handle digital data only, or it may be capable of handling both voice and digital data just as a standard telephone line does. When leased lines have been designed specifically for data transmission, they produce less static and fewer transmission errors than regular telephone lines and they are more secure from wiretapping and other security risks. Most importantly, the central processor is always accessible through the leased line, and the line usually transmits data at speeds faster than a standard telephone line.

Some WANs are commercial, regulated networks, while others are privately owned, usually by large businesses that can afford the costs. Some WANs, however, are "public" in terms of their management, resources, and access.

*Value-Added Networks.*   A **value-added network (VAN)** is a type of WAN. VANs are private, multipath, data-only, third-party-managed networks that can provide economies in the cost of service and network management because they are used by multiple organizations. VANs can add message storage, tracking, and relay services; teleconferencing services; and more closely tailor communications capabilities to specific business needs.

VANs offer several valuable services; customers do not have to invest in network hardware and software or perform their own error checking, editing, routing, and protocol conversion. Subscribers realize savings in line charges and transmission costs because many users share the costs of using the network.

Value-added networks also provide economies through **packet switching**. Packet switching breaks up a message into small, fixed bundles of data called packets. The VAN continuously uses various communications channels to send the packets. Each packet travels independently through the network. Packets of data originating at one source can be routed through different paths in the network, and then may be reassembled into the original message when they reach their destination.

*Frame Relay.* **Frame relay** is a faster and less expensive version of packet switching. Frame relay is a shared network service that packages data into "frames" that are similar to packets. Frame relay, however, does not perform error correction, because modern digital lines are less error prone than older lines and networks are more effective at error checking. Frame relay can communicate at transmission speeds of at least 50 megabits per second (in 1999).

Frame relay is essentially used for transmitting data. It is not recommended for any transmissions that are sensitive to varying delay, such as voice or digital video traffic, and it cannot easily control network congestion.

*Virtual Private Networks.* **Virtual private network (VPN)** refers to a set of hardware and software that provides a gateway between a corporate LAN and the Internet. VPN is a means for allowing access to a private network's e-mail, shared files, or intranet via an Internet connection. A VPN server handles the security, such as authentication, permitting access from the Internet to an intranet. The data, from business partners, or corporate commuters, travels over the Internet—but it is encrypted. To provide this level of security without VPN it is necessary to make a long distance call to connect to a Remote Access Service (RAS) dialup. With VPN, this cost is eliminated. In addition, VPN is less expensive than RAS and can provide more services. There are several types of VPNs on the market, and they are priced differently. VPNs are especially suited for extranets, since they allow the use of the Internet between business partners instead of using a more expensive VAN. VPNs are especially important for international trade where long-distance calls, or VANs, are very expensive.

## ▶ T4.4  NETWORK PROCESSING: OPEN SYSTEMS AND ENTERPRISE NETWORKING

When two devices on a network are directly connected, there is a **point-to-point connection**. When the two devices have the same relative standing, as with two microcomputers, there is a **peer-to-peer connection**. If, however, there is a point-of-sale terminal dialing into a credit card checking mainframe via modem, there is a point-to-point, but not peer-to-peer connection. In this latter example, there is a client/server, point-to-point network.

### CLIENT/SERVER ARCHITECTURE

The basic structure of **client/server architecture** is a client device(s) and a server device(s) that are distinguishable, but interact with each other (i.e., independent processing machines in separate locations that can perform operations separately, but can operate more efficiently when operating together). This architecture divides processing between "clients" and "servers." Both are on the network, but each processor is assigned functions it is best suited to perform.

In a client/server approach, the components of an application are distributed over the enterprise rather than being centrally controlled. There are three application components that can be distributed: the presentation component, the applications (or processing) logic, and the data management component. The *presentation component* is the application interface or how the application appears to the user. The *applications logic* is created by the business rules of the application. The *data management component* consists of the storage and management of the data needed by the application. The exact division of processing tasks depends on the requirements of each application including its processing needs, the number of users, and the available resources.

There are five models of client/server implementation, depending on the partitioning of the three components between the server and the client (See Figure T-4.7). With **distributed presentation**, all three components are on the server, but the presentation logic is distributed between the client and the server. With **remote presentation**, applications logic and database management are on the server, and the presentation logic is located on the client. With **distributed function**, data management is on the server and presentation logic is on the client, with application logic distributed between the two. **Remote data management** means that database management is on the server, with the other two components on the client. **Distributed data management** has all three components on the client, with database management distributed between the client and the server.

These models lead to the ideas of "fat" clients and "thin" clients. **Fat clients** have large storage and processing power, and the three components of an application can be processed. **Thin clients** may have no local storage and limited processing power, meaning that thin clients can handle presentation only (such as in a network computer).

The client is the user point-of-entry for the required function, and the user generally interacts directly with only the client portion of the application, typically through a graphical user interface. Clients call on the server for services rendered by the application software. When a client needs information based on files in the server, the client sends a message (or remote procedure call) requesting the information from the server.

The server has the data files and the application software. The server stores and processes shared data and performs "back-end" functions not visible to users, such as managing peripheral devices and controlling access to shared databases. When a client makes a remote procedure call, the server processes file data and provides the information, not the entire file(s), to the client.

The advantages of client/server architecture include: no overloading of the network with entire files being transferred back and forth; file integrity much

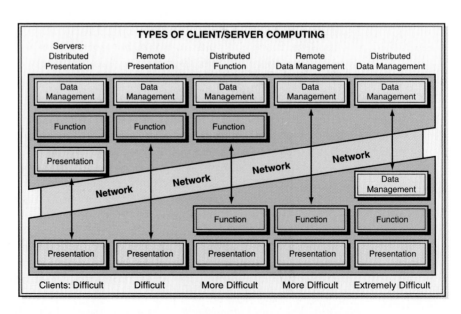

**FIGURE T-4.7**
Client/server configuration. (*Source: Datamation,* February 21, 1994, p. 30.)

easier to maintain, because only the server actually updates the files; and the file security easier to maintain with server in full control of file data.

The limitations of the client/server architecture include: difficulty in writing software that divides processing among clients and servers; specific servers can be slowed when too many clients need service; and microcomputers with independent processing power are more difficult to coordinate and administer on a network. For further discussion, see Chapter 12.

## PEER-TO-PEER ARCHITECTURE

A **peer-to-peer network architecture** allows two or more computers to pool their resources together. Individual resources like disk drives, CD-ROM drives, and even printers are transformed into shared, collective resources that are accessible from every computer. Unlike client/server networks, where network information is stored on a centralized file server and made available to many clients, the information stored across peer-to-peer networks is uniquely decentralized. Because peer-to-peer computers have their own disk drives that are accessible by all computers, each computer acts as both a client and a server. Each computer has transparent access (as assigned for security or integrity purposes) to all files on all other computers.

Popular peer-to-peer network operating systems include Microsoft's Windows 95 and 98, Windows NT, Artisoft's LANtastic, and Netware Lite. Most of these operating systems allow each computer to determine which resources will be available for use by other users. When one user's disk has been configured so that it is "sharable," it will usually appear as a new drive to the other users.

There are several advantages of peer-to-peer architecture:

▶ There is no need for a network administrator.

▶ The network is fast and inexpensive to set up and maintain.

▶ Each computer can make backup copies of its files to other computers for security.

▶ It is the easiest network to build.

## OPEN SYSTEMS AND ENTERPRISE NETWORKING

Open systems can provide flexibility in implementing IT solutions, optimization of computing effectiveness, and the ability to provide new levels of integrated functionality to meet user demands. Open systems require connectivity across the various components of the system.

**Connectivity** is the ability of the various computer resources to communicate with each other through network devices without human intervention. Connectivity allows for application portability, interoperability, and scalability. **Portability** is the ability to move applications, data, and even people from one system to another with minimal adjustments. **Interoperability** refers to the ability of systems to work together by sharing applications, data, and computer resources. **Scalability** refers to the ability to run applications unchanged on any open system where the hardware can range from a laptop PC to a super computer.

Open systems and connectivity have enabled networks to completely span organizations. Most firms have multiple LANs and may have multiple WANs, which are interconnected to form an enterprisewide network (see Figure T-4.8). Note that the enterprisewide network shown in Figure T-4.8 has a backbone network composed of fiber-optic cable using the FDDI protocol. The LANs are called **embedded LANs** because they connect to the backbone WAN. These LANs are usually composed of twisted-pair wire.

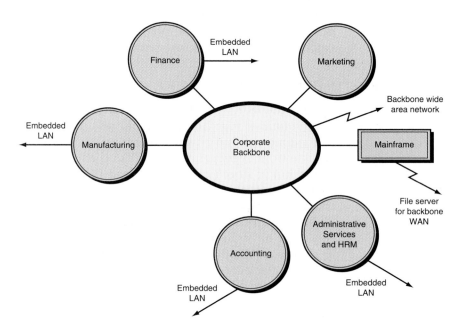

**FIGURE T-4.8** Enterprisewide computing.

## ▶ T4.5  THE INTERNET

### WHAT IS THE INTERNET?*

The **Internet** is a network that connects hundreds of thousands of internal organizational computer networks worldwide. Examples of internal organizational computer networks are a university computer system, the computer system of a corporation such as IBM or McDonald's, a hospital computer system, or a system used by a small business across the street from you. Participating computer systems (called **nodes**) include PCs, local area networks, database(s), and mainframes. A node may include several networks of an organization, possibly connected by a wide area network. The Internet connects to hundreds of thousands of computer networks in more than 200 countries so that people can access data in other organizations, and can communicate and collaborate around the globe, quickly and inexpensively. Thus, the Internet has become a necessity in the conduct of modern business.

### BRIEF HISTORY

The Internet grew out of an experimental project of the Advanced Research Project Agency (ARPA) of the U.S. Department of Defense, which was initiated in 1969 as ARPAnet to test the feasibility of a wide area computer network over which researchers, educators, military personnel, and government agencies could share data, exchange messages, and transfer files.

*For an up-to-date overview see www.whatis.com. and "Internet 101" at www.northernwebs.com/bc.

From four nodes at its initiation, the Internet has grown to millions of nodes today. The major growth occurred after commercial organizations were allowed to join ARPAnet, renamed the Internet in 1993. Each node may connect many individual users, sometimes tens of thousands of them. It is estimated that, in 2000, there were over 300 million Internet users.

The computers and organizational nodes on the Internet can be of different types and makes. The networks are connected to each other not by hardware but by data lines (of different speeds). The main network that links the nodes is referred to as the **backbone**, a fiber-optic network currently operated mainly by the telecommunications company, MCI.

It is interesting to note that no central agency manages the Internet. The cost of its operation is shared among hundreds of thousands of nodes, and therefore the cost for any one organization is small. Organizations must pay a small fee if they wish to register their name, and they need to have their own hardware and software for the operation of their internal networks. The organizations are obliged to move any data or information that enters their organizational network, regardless of its source, to its internal destination, at no charge to the senders. The senders, of course, pay the telephone bill for using the backbone or regular telephone lines.

**NEXT GENERATION INTERNET SERVICES.** Very High-Speed Backbone Network Service (vBNS) is a high-speed network designed to support the academic Internet2 and the government-sponsored Next-Generation Internet (NGI) initiatives. The vBNS was first implemented as an OC-3 (155-Mbps) backbone but has been upgraded to OC-12 (622Mbps). The goal is to increase the vBNS backbone to OC-48 (2.4Gbps).

**INTERNET2.** Internet2 is a collaborative effort by large U.S. research universities, working with industry and government, to develop advanced Internet technologies and applications to support the research and education goals of higher education. Announced in October 1996 with 34 universities, Internet2 had 122 member universities by mid-1998. In October 1997 the University Corporation for Advanced Internet Development (UCAID) was formed to administer the Internet2 project. Internet 2 will use part of vBNS as a backbone for providing high-speed connectivity to many of its member universities.

**NEXT-GENERATION INTERNET.** The NGI initiatives is a multiagency U.S. federal government research and development program that is developing advanced networking technologies and revolutionary applications that require advanced networking. The broad goals of the NGI initiative are to research and develop advanced end-to-end networking technologies, focusing primarily on reliability, robustness, security, QoS guarantees for multicasting and video, and bandwidth allocation. To this end, NGI is building two test beds, one at speeds at least 100 times faster than today's Internet, and the other 1000 times faster.

## BASIC CHARACTERISTICS AND CAPABILITIES

**ACCESSING THE INTERNET.** There are several ways to access the Internet. From your place of work or your university, you can access an Internet-connected file server on your organization's LAN. A campus or company backbone connects all the various LANs and servers in the organization to the Internet. You can also log into the Internet from your home or on the road; wireless connections are also possible. Using a modem you can connect to your campus or company network from any place that offers a dial tone. Connection to the Internet is also available through commercial providers such as America Online (AOL), for which you pay a fee. Many telephone providers, such as AT&T and MCI, also sell Internet access, as do computer companies such as Microsoft.

**THE TV AS A CHANNEL TO THE INTERNET.** For people who do not own a computer, television can also provide access to the Internet. Using a television set, a special connection device, and a telephone connection, viewers can surf the World Wide Web in their living rooms. The concept was pioneered by Web TV Networks, which manufacturers an add-on device for the television, but several other companies are also developing similar devices. At the present time (2000) the quality of the Web image on a television screen is poor compared to what you see on a computer screen. It may take a few years before this situation improves.

An alternative is a combined PC and TV. This is a PC with a TV feature. It takes advantage of the convergence of telecommunications, television, and computer to deliver video and other multimedia content over the Internet at low cost. Technologies are now available to enable PCs to decode TV signals, and to receive full-motion video over the Internet. TV sets also have the ability to access the Internet through a $100 set-top box.

**OTHER ACCESSES.** There have been several attempts to make access to the Net cheaper, faster, and/or easier. Special Internet terminals called "Internet Lite" or *network computers (NC)* (see Technology Guide #1) are used by some companies. Also, **Internet kiosks** are terminals placed in public places like libraries and coffee houses and even in 7-Eleven stores for use by those who do not have computers of their own. (For examples see Payphone Cyberbooth at www.atcominfo.com.) Accessing the Internet from cell phones and pagers is growing very rapidly.

## THE TCP/IP PROTOCOL

Procedures and rules for transferring data across the Internet are called telecommunication protocols. The original participants of the Internet, mostly universities, used the TCP/IP (described earlier), which is now the dominant protocol of the Internet. The information that passes through the Internet is divided into small portions, called **packets**, whose creation and transmission are governed by TCP/IP to provide for more consistent delivery and control. One member of the TCP/IP family of protocols is **Telnet,** a service that allows users to connect to computers other than their own and interactively search for files, text, software, and so forth. This enables researchers who commute to conduct their research without interruption. You can also use Telnet to connect to your organization's computer system when you are traveling, so you can check your e-mail, send messages, or conduct other activities.

## INTERNET RESOURCES

Some information sources on the Internet are free. For example, using Telnet, you can access libraries and conduct research. Alternatively, the information may be owned by a commercial online service. An **online service** sells access to large (usually nationwide) databases. Such services can be used to add external data to a corporate information system in a timely manner and at a reasonable cost. Several thousand services are currently available. Representative services are Dow Jones Information Service, Mead Data Central, and Compustat (see Chapter 10).

Several magazines deal exclusively or mainly with the Internet (such as *Internet Business Advantage* (www.zdjournals.com/iba) *Internet World* (www.iw.com), *NetGuide* (www.netguide.au.com), *IEEE Internet, and Wired*). There are also many online magazines such as *TechWeb* (www.techweb.com). Finally, there are several associations and societies through which members participate in activities related to the Internet, such as the *Internet Society* (www.isoc.org) and the *Electronic Frontier Foundation* (www.eff.org).

## WIDE AREA INFORMATION SERVERS (WAIS)

WAIS is an Internet directory designed to help end users find and retrieve information over the networks by providing efficient search methods. Users can ask for general topics, searching for key words and phrases.

## BROWSING AND THE WORLD WIDE WEB

When you visit a library or a bookstore, you may browse through the books and magazines, reading a page in one and looking at a picture in another. Similarly, you can browse through the vast resources of the Internet. Initially, the amount of information on the Net was relatively small, so by going through catalogs and indices, it was possible to browse and find things quickly. But when the amount of information became very large, it was necessary to make the browsing more efficient. In 1991, a new way to organize information was introduced—the World Wide Web (WWW).

The **World Wide Web** (or the Web) is a vast collection of interconnected pages of information that are stored on computers around the world that are connected to the Internet. The Web allows quick access to information that is stored as text, pictures, video, and so on. The Web is based upon a set of standards for storing, retrieving, and manipulating information, using a special tool called a Web **browser**. In 2000, the most widely used browers are Netscape Navigator and Microsoft Explorer. These use GUI interfaces and require multimedia hardware and software. Similar capabilities, but without graphics, are provided by Lynx, a text-based browser developed by the University of Kansas.

Documents accessible on the Web contain **links** to other documents. Such links or **hyperlinks** are used to link documents, either internal or external. A **Web site** is a computer network, such as the one in your university, that has a connection to the Internet.

The links are basically an implementation of *hypertext*. When you click on a link, the browser will automatically display the associated document, called a **Web page**, on the topic you are exploring, regardless of where it is located on the Web. The home page is the starting point for your search. From a single Web page located on a computer attached to the Internet you can browse the Web by clicking on any interesting links you see.

The Web is based on client/server architecture. The browser that runs on your PC is the client. When you search for information and services, Internet (or Web) servers process your request.

## CREATING WEB DOCUMENTS

To write a Web document for the Internet or an intranet, the **HyperText Markup Language (HTML)**, Dynamic HTML (DHTML), eXtensible Markup Language (XML), and Virtual Reality Modeling Language (VRML) (see Technology Guide #2) can be used.

Creating Web documents is becoming easier with the introduction of new tools. One of the most useful is **Java**, which we described in Technology Guide #2. Applications programmed in Java essentially become plug-and-play objects that operate on any operating system.

Java "applets" are small applications designed to expand the capabilities of the Web browser. They can be programmed rapidly and are reusable and portable. Using the applets, it is easy to develop special applications in finance, manufacturing, marketing, and education. Some of these include features such as animation. Java applications are easily distributed on the networks.

## SEARCH ENGINES

Browsing is a fascinating activity; you can click on the links and discover a wealth of information new to you. But a random search may be inefficient when you are looking for specific information. The solution then is to use a search engine.

A **search engine** is a tool that makes your browser more effective. It enables you to locate information by using *key words* in the same way that you would search online library resources (for example, ABI Inform). The search engine matches the key words with abstracts and presents the results to you. The abstracts contain links to the source documents so you can view them in full.

Some of the major Internet-based search engines include Yahoo, Lycos, hotBot, WebCrawler, Infoseek, Altavista, and Excite. Each engine uses a slightly different approach, syntax, and presentation mode, and yet they all have similar capabilities. Search engines can be reached directly by entering their address in the location box of most browsers. Yahoo's address, for example, is http://www.yahoo.com. When you enter the Yahoo site, you are presented with many resources that can be reached by the hyperlinks found here. For example, by requesting "Option Trading," you can receive information about this topic. With sites such as Yahoo, Infoseek, and Excite constantly beefing themselves up into the online equivalent of mega-malls, the online resources are astounding, and expanding daily. Some new search engines do nothing but search. Google is one such search engine. It uses sophisticated next-generation technology to produce the most relevant search results fast with every query.

To get better even results, **metasearch engines** (such as *Spider, Savvy Search, Metacrawler, All-in-One,* and *Web Compass*) integrate the findings of the various search engines to answer queries posted by the users.

## INTERNET ADDRESSES

A **uniform resource locator (URL)** indicates the location (or address) of a Web site you want to visit. The address consists of several parts. For example, Yahoo's address (http://www.yahoo.com) tells us that we use a **hypertext transfer protocol (http)**, which is a procedure for retrieving hypermedia and hypertext documents. "WWW" indicates that you are making a request of a Web server. "Yahoo" is the name of the company, and ".com" refers to a commercial organization (as opposed to an educational one—".edu"). The URLs are classified into generic domains. In addition to .com and .edu, we have .net, .gov, .firm, .store, .info, .art, .web, .rec, and .nom. Addresses can be even more detailed, including the specific name of a document at a site.

## GOPHER

Not every file or document on the Internet is accessible on the Web. A predecessor to the Web, **Gopher**, is a "burrowing tool" that provides access to a wide range of *textual information* available on the Internet. It is a delivery system for retrieving documents from the Internet, based on a set of menus, submenus, and sub-submenus (down to many levels). Although the Web is rapidly eclipsing it, there are still thousands of Gopher servers worldwide providing access to hundreds of thousands of documents. Gopher can be reached directly via your browser by typing www.gopher.com.

## DOWNLOADING SOFTWARE AND FILES

Tens of thousands of software packages can be downloaded. Many of them are free either as public domain (*cheapware*), or copyrighted, but given away (*freeware*). Others are called *shareware*, meaning you can use them on a trial basis, and are expected to purchase them if you like them (see www.shareware.com). Internet users can also retrieve documents including graphics, voice, and other media for use on their PCs. Working with the Web or Gopher, it is usually fairly easy to do so. Many of the documents are transferable from the Internet using a member of the TCP/IP family called **File Transfer Protocol (FTP)**. Using special FTP software, you can easily download files stored in an *FTP site,* a server that archives such files.

## ELECTRONIC MAIL

**Electronic mail (e-mail)** allows multiple-access communication delivered exclusively on a computer network. With e-mail, a person can send letters to anyone connected to the system. When a message is sent, it arrives at an individual's "mailbox." The receiver, when connected to the network, is notified that he or she has mail. The receiver can then read the mail, send a reply, edit the mail, save it, or forward it to another person.

E-mail is becoming an important communication tool in many organizations. The primary advantages of e-mail are that it can:

- ► Send and receive messages very quickly.
- ► Conduct paperless communication.
- ► Connect to the network from any location that has a telephone line (using a portable computer and a modem). It is also possible to connect to the networks with wireless technologies.
- ► Send messages to many users simultaneously.
- ► Trace any correspondence (who sent what to whom, when, and so on).
- ► Communicate with millions of people, worldwide.
- ► Work easily with others on the same task.
- ► Rapidly access information stored in databases at many locations.
- ► Send anything you can create or view on a PC including pictures, voice, video, audio, film clips, text, maps, and animation.
- ► Contain a good word processing text editor and a spelling checker.
- ► Allow you to color documents in dozens of combinations.
- ► Retrieve messages from your in-box, bulletin boards, and other electronic devices.
- ► Search for a document by a key word.
- ► Use "return receipt," which notifies you when the recipient actually retrieves a message.
- ► Print, prioritize, forward, and store messages.
- ► Send a group reply; that is, reply to everyone who received the current message.
- ► Create different folders and archives to keep track of your electronic mail.
- ► Create public bulletin boards where everyone in the organization can post and view messages.
- ► Share text messages and application files across popular computer platforms.
- ► Deliver and receive faxes.
- ► Send copies of messages.
- ► Schedule meetings.

However, there are limitations on e-mail, such as the following:

▶ It does not provide for face-to-face communication.

▶ Some e-mail systems are not very user friendly.

▶ Confidentiality and privacy cannot always be assured.

Several vendors produce e-mail software. Some well-known software packages are cc: Mail, QuickMail, Microsoft Outlook, BeyondMail, Netscape Messenger, Eudora Pro, and Em@iler. Windows-based e-mail and mail-enabled applications that are enterprisewide are increasing the attractiveness, friendliness, and capabilities of e-mail. E-mail is also becoming connected to voice mail and sometimes the two are integrated. Netscape and Microsoft browsers include e-mail capabilities and so do online services such as AOL.

Many Web-based e-mail providers offer e-mail accounts for free (such as Hotmail, Coolmail, and Yahoo! Mail). People can send and receive messages from any computer connected to the Internet.

## CHAT PROGRAMS

Chat programs allow you to send messages to people who are connected to the same channel of communication *at the same time*. It is like a global conference call system. Anyone can join in the online conversation. Messages are displayed on your screen as they arrive, even if you are in the middle of typing a message. You can even use voice chat, which, like voice e-mail, is free of charge, even if it is long distance. Two major types of chat programs exist: (a) a Web-based program, called Webchat, which allows you to send messages to Net users using a Web browser and visiting a Webchat site (the Budweiser Web site, for example, has a popular chat program), and (b) on e-mail-based (text only) program called **Internet Relay Chat (IRC)**. A business can use IRC to interact with customers, provide online experts' answers to questions, and so on.

*ICQ ("I Seek You")* is a popular chat program that informs users who's online at any time and enables users to contact them at will. With ICQ, people can chat, send messages, files, and URLs, and play games.

## NEWSGROUPS

Using a chat program requires you to communicate in real time. It may also be a waste of time, if the chatterers are not focused on a topic of interest to you. The solution is to join (subscribe to) a **newsgroup** (also known as Usenet, or just News). Newsgroups are organized in a directory and are divided into categories and subcategories. Once you join such a group (and there are many thousands of them, each of which is dedicated to a specific topic), you can read all the messages sent by other members. You can respond by posting a message for all members, or e-mail to just one individual. In contrast to a chat room, where all communication is done in real time, here communication is done via messages in a different time/different place mode.

Not all newsgroups may be available at your site; they are so numerous that they create a great deal of Internet traffic, so your management may block some. You may try access services such as America Online to reach more newsgroups. AOL and similar services have their own newsgroups. Newsgroups are popular for discussion and posting business opportunities such as creating partnerships or selling items.

Many newsgroups have a FAQ specific to the subject of the newsgroup. FAQ is an acronym for *Frequently Asked Questions*. FAQs are compilations of information that are usually the result of certain questions constantly being asked in a newsgroup. Before asking a question in a newsgroup, check out the appropriate FAQs. If you cannot find the answer to your question there, then you can post your question to the newsgroup.

Participation in chat or newsgroup forums can be anonymous (you can use a nickname). Make sure your messages will not cause embarrassment or offend anyone. This may be difficult to do since you are not acquainted with all possible readers.

## MAILING LISTS AND ELECTRONIC BULLETIN BOARDS

Similar to newsgroups are e-mail-based *discussion* or *mailing lists*. To add your e-mail name and address to a mailing list, you **subscribe** to it; to remove your name, you **unsubscribe** from the mailing list. Some mailing lists are called LIST-SERVs, named after a popular mailing list of software products. It is important to note the difference between the name of the list you are subscribed to (and to which you will send your messages), and the name of the listserver that maintains the list. The name of the list is usually subject@somesite.edu (for example isworld@listserve.heanet.ie).

**Electronic bulletin boards (EBBs)** are mailing lists on which users can leave messages for other people and receive massive amounts of information (including free software). They are similar to the Web newsgroups, but initially they resided on the noncommercial Internet and on private information providers' networks. To access an EBB, you need to be a member and sometimes pay a nominal fee. Special interest groups, like users of specific software, display messages on these boards and exchange experiences about the software. Universities and schools use the EBB to advertise classes and special programs.

## PORTALS

A **portal** is a Web site designed to offer a variety of Internet services from a single convenient location. Most portals offer the following services: search engine; news, sports, and weather; reference such as yellow pages and maps; shopping malls; e-mail; and chat rooms. Popular portals include Altavista, Excite, Infoseek, Lycos, Microsoft Internet Start, Netscape Netcenter, Snap, and Yahoo!

## REFERENCES AND BIBLIOGRAPHY

1. Baca, H., et al., *Local Area Networks with Novell,* Belmont, CA: Wadsworth, 1995.

2. Comer, D. E., Droms, R. E., *Computer Networks and Internets,* Upper Saddle River, NJ: Prentice-Hall, 1996.

3. Dodd, A. Z., *The Essential Guide to Telecommunications,* Upper Saddle River, NJ: Prentice-Hall, 1999.

4. Fitzgerald, J., *Business Data Communications: Basic Concepts, Security, and Design,* 5th ed., New York: John Wiley & Sons, 1996.

5. Gauntt, J., Jurin, B., and Katz, M., "E-Business Technology Forecast," PricewaterhouseCoopers Global, May 1999.

6. Keen, P. G. W., and J. M. Cummings, *Networks in Action: Business Choices and Telecommunications Decisions,* Belmont, CA: Wadsworth Publishing Company, 1994.

7. Kim, B. G., and P. Wang, "ATM Network: Goals and Challenges," *Communications of the ACM* 38, No. 2, February 1995.

8. Lyon, J., "Blast onto the Net by Satellite," *PC Computing,* March 1997, p. 71.

9. Minoli, D., and Schmidt, A. "Internet Architectures," New York: John Wiley & Sons, 1999.

10. Mueller, M., "Universal Service and the Telecommunications Act: Myth Made Law," *Communications of the ACM* 40, No. 3, March 1997.

11. Quelch, J. A., and L. R. Klein, "The Internet and International Marketing," *Sloan Management Review,* Spring 1996.

12. Rose, F., "New Modems Are Fast, Cheap," *Wall Street Journal,* February 11, 1997.

13. Simpson, D., "Cut Costs with Client/Server Computing? Here's How!" *Datamation,* October 1, 1995.

14. Singleton, J. P., and M. M. Schwartz, "Data Access Within the Information Warehouse Framework," *IBM Systems Journal,* Vol. 33, No. 2, 1994.

15. Stewart, T. A., "Managing in a Wired Company," *Fortune,* July 11, 1994.

16. Sullivan, D., *The New Computer User,* 2nd ed., Orlando, FL: Harcourt Brace, 1997.

17. Vetter, R. J., "ATM Concepts, Architectures, and Protocols," *Communications of the ACM* 38, No 2, February 1995.

18. Wilson, C., "Optical Networking," White Paper, *Interactive Week,* February 21, 1998.

# GLOSSARY*

**Ad hoc** reports are issued in reply to a special request, in contrast with periodical reports.

**Application controls** are designed to protect specific applications.

**Application portfolio** is the collection of corporate IT applications, sometimes including those under development.

An **application program** is a set of computer instructions written in a programming language, the purpose of which is to provide functionality to a user.

**Artificial intelligence (AI)** is a subfield of computer science concerned with symbolic reasoning and problem solving.

**Artificial neural network (ANN)** is a computer technology attempting to build computers that will operate like a human brain. ANN programs can work with ambiguous information.

An **audit** is a regular examination or check of systems, their inputs, outputs, and processing.

An **audit trail** lists all changes made to a file for checking or control purposes.

A **backup** is a copy of software or data.

**Batch processing** processes inputs at fixed intervals as a file and operates on it all at once; interactive (or online) processing operates on a transaction as soon as it occurs.

**Backbone** is the long-distance, high-capacity and -speed network that links the major Internet computer nodes.

A **behavior-oriented chargeout system** sets IS service costs in a way that encourages usage consistent with organizational objectives, even though the charges may not correspond to actual costs.

**Best practice benchmarks** identify activities and methods that the most effective organizations use to operate and manage various IS functions.

**Biometric** controls are security controls that involve physical or behavioral unique characteristics of people, such as fingerprints or voice.

**Business pressures** are forces, such as global competition, in the organization's environment that create pressures on the organization's operations.

A **business process** is a collection of activities that take one or more kinds of inputs and create an output.

**Business process reengineering (BPR)** is a methodology for introducing a fundamental change in specific business processes, usually supported by an information system.

**Business systems planning (BSP)** concentrates on identifying problems and related decisions, based on business processes and data classes. (An IBM methodology.)

A **byte** is a number of bits (usually eight) used to represent one alphanumeric character.

**CD-ROM** (**c**ompact **d**isc-**r**ead **o**nly **m**emory) is a secondary digital storage medium that uses laser-made pits in plastic to represent bits.

A **central processing unit (CPU)** is the "brain" of a computer—controlling all computational, input, output, and storage activities.

**Centralized computing** puts all processing and control authority within one computer to which all other computing devices respond.

**Centralized IS** refers to the corporate information system department which controls the shared IT, such as corporate infrastructure, from a central location.

**Channel systems** is a network of the materials and product distribution system within an organization, and between the organization and its suppliers and customers.

**Chargeback** systems treat the MIS function as a service bureau or utility charging organizational subunits for MIS services with the objective of recovering MIS expenditures.

**Chargeout** (see chargeback).

A **Chief Information Officer (CIO)** is the director of the IS department in a large organization, analogous to a CEO, COO, or CFO.

**Chief Knowledge Officer (CKO)** is the title given to the director assigned to capture and leverage structured knowledge with IT in a knowledge-based system.

**Chief Network Officer (CNO)** is a title given to the director of telecommunications to reflect the importance of the role.

**Client/server architecture** is a type of distributed architecture where end-user PCs (clients) request services or data from designated processors or peripherals (servers).

A **code of ethics** is a group of ethical behavior rules developed by organizations or by professional societies.

**Collaboration** is defined as the mutual efforts by two or more individuals who perform activities in order to accomplish certain tasks.

**Competitive advantage** is an advantage over a competitor such as lower cost or quicker deliveries.

The **competitive forces model** is a business framework of Porter, depicting the five forces in a market (e.g., bargaining power of customers).

**Competitive intelligence** refers to the activities conducted by companies, frequently with the aid of IT and the Internet, to spy on their competitors.

*Key terms for the Technology Guides are not included here but can be found on the Website (www.wiley.com/college/turban).

A **computer** is an electronic device capable of storing and manipulating data and instructions.

**Computer-aided design (CAD)** software allows designers to design and "build" production prototypes in software, "test" them as a computer object under given parameters, compile parts and quantity lists, outline production and assembly procedures, and then transmit the final design directly to milling and rolling machines.

**Computer-aided engineering (CAE)** enables engineers to execute complex engineering analysis on a computer.

**Computer-aided manufacturing (CAM)** software uses a digital design such as that from a CAD system to directly control production machinery.

**Computer-aided software engineering (CASE)** is an integrated set of systems development tools.

**Computer architecture** is the arrangement of computer components and their relationships.

**Computer-based information systems (CBIS)** are information systems that include a computer for their operation.

**Computer graphics** present data in two or virtual three-dimensional form such as bar charts, histograms, pie charts, or grids on a display screen or plotter to highlight data variations.

**Computer-integrated manufacturing (CIM)** integrates several computerized systems, such as CAD, CAM, MRP, and JIT into a whole, in a factory.

**Continuous improvement** refers to programs done by corporations on a regular basis to improve productivity, quality, and operations.

**Cookie** is a text string stored on the user's hard drive file to record the history of the user of this computer in particular Web sites.

**Cooperative processing** teams two or more geographically dispersed computers to execute a specific task.

A **cost–benefit analysis** helps in decisions on spending or investments by determining if the benefits (possibly including intangible ones) exceed the costs. With **increasing returns**, which often occur in the software industry, a given percentage increase in sales or share of market leads to a larger increase in profitability.

**Cost leadership** is the ability of a company to produce quality products at the lowest cost in its industry group.

A **cracker** is a malicious hacker.

**Critical Path Method (CPM)** is a method for planning and adjusting projects. It is usually computerized.

**Critical response activities** are the major activities used by organizations to counter the *business pressures.*

**Critical success factors (CSF)** are those few things that must go right in order to ensure the organization's survival and success.

**Cross-functional activities** are those that are performed in several functional areas along the same business processes.

**Cyberbanking** is managed over the Internet or private networks, enabling people to bank from home or on the road.

**Cybermall** is an electronic shopping center on the Internet (may include thousands of stores).

**Cycle time reduction** refers to the reduction of the time required to execute a task or produce a product. It is usually done by using information technologies.

**Data** are raw facts that can be processed into accurate and relevant information.

**Data Class** One of the two main building blocks that became the basis of an information architecture. *See also* business processes

**Data communications** is the process of exchanging data or information electronically.

**Data conferencing** refers to data sent along with voice and/or video.

**Data encryption** is encoding data so that they cannot be understood unless they are decoded; used to protect data from unauthorized users.

**Data integrity** is the accuracy and accessibility of data.

**Data mart** is a subset of the data warehouse, usually originated to a specific purpose or major data subject.

**Data mining** is the process of searching for unknown information or relationships in large databases using tools such as neural computing or case-based reasoning.

**Data quality (DQ)** is a measure of the accuracy, objectivity, accessibility, relevance, timeliness, completeness, and other characteristics that describe useful data.

**Data tampering** is deliberately entering false data, or changing and deleting true data.

**Data visualization** refers to visual presentation of data and information by graphics, animation, or any other multimedia.

**Data warehouse** is a repository of historical data, subject oriented and organized, integrated from various sources that can easily be accessed and manipulated for decision support.

A **database** is a collection of files serving as a data resource for computer-based information systems.

A **database management system (DBMS)** is a software program (or group of programs) that manages and provides access to a database.

**Decentralized computing** breaks centralized computing into functionally equal parts with each part essentially a smaller, centralized subsystem.

A **decision room** is an arrangement for a group DSS in which terminals are available to the participants.

A **decision support system (DSS)** is a computer-based information system that combines models and data in an attempt to solve semistructured problems with extensive user involvement.

A **decision system** provides the framework for determining what information is required.

A **decryption** is the restoration (uncoding) of scrambled data into the original format using some key.

The **Delphi method** is a qualitative forecasting methodology using anonymous questionnaires done in several iterations to find consensus.

**Differentiation (of product or service)** is a strategy of gaining competitive advantage by providing a product (or service) of the same cost and quality as a competitor, but with some additional attribute(s), that makes it different from the competition.

A **digital signature** is added to electronic messages usually encrypted in the sender public key.

A **disaster avoidance plan** is a comprehensive plan to avoid a controllable catastrophe in the corporate information systems.

A **disaster recovery plan** is a plan to operate an IS area after a disaster (such as an earthquake) and to restore the functioning of the systems.

**Distance learning** An ICAI learning approach in which teachers and students are in different locations.

**Distributed computing** breaks centralized computing into many semiautonomous computers that may not be (and usually aren't) functionally equal.

**Distributed processing** (see distributed computing).

**Document management** refers to the automated management and control of digitized documents throughout their life cycle.

**Domain name** refers to the major category in an Internet name (URL).

**Drilldown** is the ability to investigate information in increasing detail; e.g., find not only total sales, but also sales by region, by product, or by salesperson.

An **edutainment** is the delivery of education online in combination with some entertainment. It combines learning and fun.

**Electronic banking** (see cyberbanking).

**Electronic bartering** is the exchange of commodities and/or services between business partners.

**Electronic benefits transfer (EBT)** refers to transfer of direct payments made by the government to recipients' bank accounts or smart cards.

**Electronic bulletin boards** are public-access electronic mail message centers where authorized people can leave messages for everyone to read (e.g., interest groups in Internet).

**Electronic cash (e-cash)** is a computerized stored value that can be used as cash. It is stored on a smart card or on a computer's hard drive.

**Electronic catalogs** refer to vendors' catalogs available online.

**Electronic certificates** are provided by a trusted third party, verifying that specific public encryption keys belong to specific individuals.

**Electronic checks (e-checks)** enable payments made with electronic rather than paper checks.

**Electronic commerce** is the exchange of products, services, information, or money with the support of computers and networks. It is business done online.

**Electronic communities** refers to groups of people with similar interests who use the Internet to communicate or collaborate.

**Electronic credit cards** allows online payments with the characteristics of regular credit cards (e.g., pay within 30 days).

**Electronic data interchange (EDI)** is a computer-to-computer direct communication of standard business transactions between or among business partners.

**Electronic funds transfer (EFT)** is the transmission of funds, debits and credits, and charges and payments electronically between banks and their customers.

**Electronic mail (e-mail)** is computer-based messages that can be electronically manipulated, stored, combined with other information, and exchanged with other computers.

An **electronic mall** is an online shopping center with many (sometimes thousands) stores in one Web site.

**Electronic markets** are the networks of interactions and relationships where products, services, information, and payments are exchanged.

**Electronic purse** (or wallet) refers to the device that enables the storage and distribution of e-cash.

**Electronic retailing** refers to online selling products or services to individuals, similar to regular retailing.

**Electronic surveillance** refers to the tracking of people's activities, online or offline. It is often done with the aid of computers (e.g., monitoring e-mail).

An **encryption** is scrambling of data so that they cannot be recognized by unauthorized readers.

**End-user computing** is the use or development of information systems by the principal users of the systems' outputs or by their staffs.

**Ends/Means Analysis (E/M Analysis)** determines information requirements based on desired ends (effectiveness) and available means (efficiency) to achieve the ends.

**Enterprise-computing** (or **enterprisewide systems**) are information systems that are used throughout the enterprise.

**Enterprise resources planning (ERP)** is an integrated process of planning and managing of all resources and their use in the entire enterprise. It includes contacts with business partners.

**Enterprise software** is an integrated software that supports enterprise computing. Most notable is SAP R/3.

An **enterprisewide system** is one that encompasses the entire enterprise. It is implemented on a companywide network.

**Entities** are people, places, or things about which we want to collect, store, and maintain information.

**Ergonomics** is the science of adapting machines and work environments to people.

**Ethics** is a branch of philosophy that deals with what is considered to be "right" and "wrong."

**Exception reporting** calls attention only to results that deviate from a standard by a certain percentage or exceed a threshold.

**Executive information systems (EIS)** are specifically designed to support executive work.

An **executive support system (ESS)** is an executive information system that includes some analytical and communication capabilities.

**Expected value** is a weighted average. It is achieved by multiplying values by their relative importance or frequencies and totaling the results.

An **expert support system** is an expert system that supports problem solving and decision making.

An **expert system (ES)** is a computer system that applies reasoning methodologies or knowledge in a specific domain to render advice or recommendations—much like a human expert.

An **extranet** is a secured network that allows business partners to access portions of each other's intranets.

**Fault-tolerance** is the ability to continue operating satisfactorily in the presence of faults.

A **feasibility study** seeks an overview of a problem and a rough assessment of whether feasible solutions exist prior to committing resources. Also done in systems development.

A **file** is a group of data with some form of commonality.

**Firewalls** protect organizations' internal networks from hacking and other unauthorized access.

**Flaming** is anonymous insulting or angry messaging on the Internet. They are frequently in response to spamming or to mistakes of inexperienced Internet users.

**Flattened organizations** have fewer levels of management and a larger span of control.

**Four-stage model of planning** is a generic information systems planning model based on four major, generic activities: strategic planning, information requirements analysis, resource allocation, and project planning.

**Freeware** is a software available on the Internet for unloading, without the need to pay or get permission to use.

**Fuzzy logic** is a way of reasoning that can cope with uncertain or partial information; a characteristic of human thinking and some expert systems.

**General controls** are physical, access, communication, administrative, and data security controls aimed at protecting a system in general rather than specific applications.

**Geographical information systems** use spatial data such as digitized maps, and can combine this data with other text, graphics, icons, and symbols.

**Global business drivers** are entities that benefit from global economies of scale and add value to a global business strategy.

**Goal-seeking (analysis)** is asking what values certain variables must have in order to attain desired goals.

A **graphical user interface (GUI)** is an interactive, user-friendly interface in which icons and similar graphical devices enable a user to control a computer.

A **group DSS (GDSS)** is an interactive, computer-based system that facilitates finding solutions to semistructured problems by using a set of decision makers working together as a group.

**Group support systems (GSS)** support the working process of groups (e.g., communication and decision making).

**Groupware** is a generic term for several computerized technologies and tools that aim to support people working in groups.

**Hackers** are people who illegally or unethically access a computer system.

A **hard disk** is a hard, metal platter coated with a material that can be magnetized in spots to represent bits, primarily for secondary storage.

**Hardware** is the physical equipment, media, and attached devices used in a computer system.

**Help desk** refers to an organizational unit that provides information or assistance to people.

**Heuristic design** or prototyping is an approach to systems development that exploits advanced technologies for using trial-and-error problem solving.

**Hidden unemployment** refers to cases in which people are considered fully employed but actually working only part of the time.

The **hierarchical model** relates data by structuring data into an inverted "tree" in which records refer to a senior field and any number of subordinate fields (i.e., one "parent" and several "children").

A **hierarchical organization** is a traditional multilevel structure, like a military command, with each level supervising the level below it.

**Hyperlink** is the process of automatically moving from a certain Web page to another by clicking on a highlighted word or icon.

**Hypertext Markup Language (HTML)** is a programming language that uses hypertext to establish dynamic links (see hyperlink) to other documents stored in the same or other computers on the Internet or intranets.

**Icons** are pictures of features or functions that can be graphically "selected" for execution.

**Imperfect information** Information that improves your knowledge, but does not tell you the results for sure.

**Increasing returns** is a concept in economics that points to increased benefits with the volume of operation (the larger, the better).

An **inference engine** is the part of an expert system that performs a reasoning function.

**Information** is data that are processed or operated on by a computer.

An **information architecture** is a conceptualization of the manner by which information requirements are met by the system.

**Information centers** train and support business users with end-user tools, testing, technical support information, and standard certification.

**Information content** is an approach to identify strategic information systems by the importance of the information to the organization.

**Information economics** is an approach to cost–benefits analysis that incorporates organizational objectives in a scoring methodology to assess more accurately the value of intangible benefits.

**Information engineers** are specialists for IT architecture design.

An **information infrastructure** is the physical arrangement of hardware, software, databases, networks, and so forth.

**Information intensity** is the amount of information that measures the actual, or planned, usage of information

**Information privacy** refers to privacy issues related to the use of information systems, such as invasion of privacy in databases.

**Information requirements** are those items of information needed by information systems users for decision making.

**Information sharing** refers to users permitting each other to view information in their possession.

The **information superhighway** is a national information infrastructure to interconnect computer users.

An **information system** is a physical process that supports an organizational system by providing information to achieve organizational goals.

**Information systems controls** are used to counter computer hazards (such as crime and human errors).

**Information technology (IT)** is the technology component of an information system (a narrow definition), or the collection of the entire systems in an organization (broad definition used in this book).

**Information technology architecture** is the field of study and practice devoted to understanding and planning information systems components in the form of an organizational infrastructure.

An **input device** is a computer system component that accepts data from the user (e.g., a keyboard or mouse).

**Inputs** are the resources introduced into a system for transformation into outputs.

An **input/output (I/O) device** transfers data into or out of a computer.

**Integrated CASE tools** support prototyping and reusable systems components, including component repositories and automatic computer code generation.

**Integrated circuits** are interconnected layers of etched semiconductor materials forming electronic transistor circuit units with "on–off" positions that direct the electrical current passing through them.

**Intellectual property** refers to the right of individuals and companies to receive royalties for copyrighted original work such as writing books, composing music, or developing software.

**Intelligence support systems** are intelligent systems designed to support knowledge workers.

**Intelligent agents** are expert or knowledge-based systems embedded in computer-based information systems (or their components).

**Intelligent systems** include a knowledge component, such as an expert system or neural network.

**Interactive marketing (intermarketing)** is an interactive customized relationship between vendors and buyers for advertisement and sales transactions.

**Intermarketing** is a new interactive style of marketing, allowing personal contact with customers and providing marketing organizations with greater ability to understand the customer, market, and competition.

The **internal IS structure** is the organizational structure of an IS department.

**Internet** is a self-regulated network of computer networks connecting millions of computers all over the world.

**Internet kiosks** enable people that do not have computers to access the Internet from public locations.

**Interorganizational information systems (IOS)** refers to information systems between two or more organizations that support efficient, routine flow of transaction processing data.

The **intranet** is a corporate network that functions with Internet technologies, such as browsers and search engines, using Internet protocols.

**IT outsourcing** is using outside vendors to create, maintain, or reengineer IT architectures and systems.

**IT planning** is the organized planning for IT infrastructure and applications portfolios done at various levels of the organization.

**Job content** refers to the elements of a job as reflected in its description.

**Job stress** refers to the stress experienced by individuals from performing their job.

**Just-in-time (JIT)** is a concept in which material and parts arrive at a work place when needed, minimizing inventory, waste, and interruptions.

**Knowledge** is the understanding, awareness, or familiarity acquired through education or experience.

A **knowledge base** is a collection of facts, rules, and procedures organized in one place.

**Knowledge-based organizations** are organized as networks that capture, store, and utilize knowledge as a major activity, with the help of IT.

**Knowledge discovery** (see knowledge discovery in databases).

**Knowledge discovery in databases (KDD)** refers to the process of extracting knowledge from volumes of data in databases (e.g., in data warehouses).

**Knowledge workers** are people who use knowledge as a significant part of their work responsibility.

**Labor productivity** is the ratio of the value of outputs to the quantity of labor required to produce these outputs.

**Laser printers** are nonimpact printers that produce high-quality printed output.

**Legacy systems** are older systems that have become central to business operations and may be still capable of meeting these business needs; they may not require any immediate changes, or they may be in need of reengineering to meet new business needs.

A **local area network (LAN)** is a system for interconnecting two or more closely located communicating devices supporting full connectivity so that every user device on the network has the potential to communicate with any other device.

A **lock-in effect** occurs when it is difficult to switch to a competing product because of the difficulty in learning to use a different product, or other factors that discourage change.

**Logical design** refers to the design of information systems from the user's point of view.

**Long-range planning** is a corporate or IT plan usually for five years or longer.

**Lotus Notes** is an integrated groupware software package that also provides application developers an environment for quickly creating cross-platform client/server applications.

**Machine learning** is a method by which a computer can learn from past experiences (e.g., from historical data).

**Mainframe computers** are relatively large computers built to handle very large databases, thousands of user terminals with fast response times, and millions of transactions.

**Management by maxim** guides investment in IT infrastructure by identifying infrastructure requirements that correspond to organizational strategies and objectives.

**Management information systems (MIS)** are designed to provide past, present, and future routine information appropriate for planning, organizing, and controlling the operations of a functional area in an organization.

**Management support systems (MSS)** are three major IT technologies designed to support managers: decision support systems, executive support systems, and groupware technologies.

**Manufacturing resource planning (MRP II)** is a planning process that integrates production, inventory, purchasing, financing, and labor in an enterprise.

**Marketing databases** are large databases that contain marketing related data and are used for determining advertisement and marketing strategies.

**Marketing transaction database (MTD)** is an interactive marketing database oriented toward targeting messages and marketing in real time.

**Mass customization** refers to the production of a very large quantity of customized products, such as computers (e.g., by Dell Computers).

**Material requirements planning (MRP)** is a planning process (usually computerized) that integrates production, purchasing, and inventory management of interrelated products.

**Metadata** are data about data, such as indices or summaries.

**Metamalls** refer to online supermalls that serve several online malls by providing them with unified services, such as search engines.

**Metric benchmarks** provide numeric measures of IS performance relative to other numerical factors such as organizational revenues, CPU capacity, etc.

**Microcomputers** are the smallest and least expensive category of general-purpose computers; also known as **micros** and **personal computers**.

**Micropayments** refers to small payments (few dollars or cents) for products or services purchased on the Internet.

**Milestones**, or checkpoints, are established to allow periodic review of progress so that management can determine if a project merits further commitment of resources, if it requires adjustments, or if it should be discontinued.

A **minicomputer** is a relatively smaller, cheaper, and more compact computer that performs the same functions as a larger, mainframe computer, but to a more limited extent.

A **model base management system (MBMS)** is a software program to establish, update, and use a model base.

A **modem** is a device that **mo**dulates and **dem**odulates signals.

**Moore's Law** indicates that the power of a microprocessor will double every 18 months while the cost stays at the same level.

**Multifactor productivity** is the ratio of the value of outputs to the value of the inputs—including labor, investments, materials, etc.—used to produce these outputs.

**Multimedia** is the combination of at least two media for input or output of data; these media can be audio (sound), voice, animation, video, text, graphics, and/or images.

In a **multimedia database** data and procedures are stored as objects containing various multimedia (e.g., video clips).

A **natural language processor (NLP)** is an knowledge-based user interface that allows the user to carry on a conversation with a computer-based system in much the same way as he or she would converse with another human.

**Netiquette** is the rules of conduct over the Internet, especially in newsgroups, chat rooms, and bulletin boards.

**Netizen** is a member who surfs the Internet.

A **network** is a telecommunications system that permits the sharing of resources such as computing power, software, input/output devices, and data.

**Network computer (NC)** is a network-based terminal, similar to a "dummy" terminal in a mainframe, that allows communication and use of information on the network, but it does not have a CPU.

**Network effects** are the support that leading products in an industry receive from their large user base and the complementary products marketed to these users.

**Networked computing** is a corporate information infrastructure that provides the necessary networks for distributed computing. Users can easily contact each other or databases and communicate with external entities.

**The networked enterprise** comprises one seamless network, extending the corporate contacts to all the entities a company does business with.

**Neural computing** The technology that attempts to achieve knowledge representations and processing based on massive parallel processing, fast retrieval of large amounts of information, and the ability to recognize patterns based on experiences.

**Nominal group technique (NTG)** is a group dynamic procedure to improve the process of people working in a group.

**Object-oriented database** refers to a database that is organized and managed using an object-oriented approach for data presentation and management.

**Object-oriented development** is based on interchangeable software components (objects) that model the behavior of persons, places, things, or concepts in the real world.

**Object-oriented programming (OOP)** models a system as a set of cooperating objects.

**Office automation systems (OAS)** are used to increase the productivity of office workers and the quality of office work.

**Online analytical processing (OLAP)** is the processing of data as soon as transactions occur.

**Online data entry** inputs data directly to and is immediately used by a computer.

**Online transaction processing (OLTP)** is a transaction processing system, created on a client/server architecture, that saves money by allowing suppliers to enter the TPS and look at the firm's inventory level or production schedule.

**Operating system** software supervises the overall operation of a computer, including such tasks as monitoring the computer's status, handling executable program interruptions, and scheduling of operations.

An **optical character reader (OCR)** is an input device that scans textual data.

**Optical scanners** scan text and graphics forms for input to a computer system.

**Option valuation** is the process of assigning a value to future benefits that could result from a current investment.

**Organization transformation** is a radical change in an organization involving structure, culture, and the manner in which business is conducted.

An **organizational decision support system (ODSS)** is a network DSS that serves people at several locations.

**Organizational learning** is the process of organizations coping with major changes such as BPR. Such learning can be facilitated by knowledge bases.

An **output device** is the part of a computer system that produces processed data or information.

**Outputs** are the completed products or services of a system.

**Outsourcing** is acquiring IS services from an external organization rather than through internal employees.

**Parallel conversion** is a process of converting to a new information system by using the old and new systems concurrently until the new system is demonstrably stable and reliable.

**Parallel processing** is executing several processing instructions at the same time (in parallel) rather than one at a time (serial or sequential processing).

**Pattern recognition** is the ability of a computer to classify an item to a predetermined category by matching the item's characteristics with that of a stored category.

**Peer-to-peer** network relationships stress processing on an equal basis among all processors, sharing devices and data on a mutual basis.

**Perfect information** refers to an information that enables a user to predict results with a complete certainty (such as the yield from a certificate of deposit).

**Periodic reports** are routine reports executed at predetermined times (in contrast with ad hoc reports).

**Personal information manager (PIM)** is a software package for a manager's personal use combining the features of project management software and desktop organizers.

**Phased conversion** is switching from an old system to a new system in several phases.

**Physical design** is the process of translating the logical design of a system into the technical design.

**Pilot conversion** is switching from an old system to a complete, new system in parts of an organization, one part at a time.

**Post-audit** refers to the auditing conducted on information systems after their implementation and use.

The **price-to-performance ratio** indicates the relative cost, usually on a per-MIPS (millions of instructions per second) basis, of the processing power of a computer.

**Primary storage**, or main memory, stores data and code for the CPU.

**Privacy policies** are organizational policies designed to protect individuals' privacy.

**Private key** refers to a security encryption/decryption code that is known *only* to its user/owner.

**Process innovation** is stepping back from a process to inquire into its overall business objectives, and then effect creative and radical change to realize order-of-magnitude improvements in a way that accomplishes objectives.

The **productivity paradox** is the seeming contradiction between extremely large investments in IT in the economy, in contrast to indications of low productivity growth in the sectors that have received the largest IT investments.

**Program evaluation and review technique (PERT)** is a planning and control tool representing the network of tasks in diagram form required to complete a project, establishing sequential dependencies and relationships among the tasks.

**Project planning** is the fourth stage of the model for information systems planning, providing an overall framework with which the system development life cycle can be planned, scheduled, and controlled.

A computer **processor** is a device that processes inputs into outputs.

**Prototyping** is an approach to systems development that exploits advanced technologies for using trial-and-error problem solving.

A **public key** is the code of a certain individual that is distributed to authorized people so they can encrypt or decrypt messages with it.

**Push technology** delivers only information users want per their preference profile.

**Quality of life** is the measure of how well we achieve a desirable standard of living.

The three **R's of reengineering** are redesign, retool, and re-orchestrate.

**Random-access memory (RAM)** is digital storage or memory that can be directly written to and read.

**Rapid application development (RAD)** is a methodology that enables the rapid construction of information systems applications by using special tools.

**Read-only memory (ROM)** is digital storage or memory that can be read directly.

**Reengineering** is the introduction of fundamental and radical changes to a process; the complete restructuring of an existing system. (Same as BPR.)

**Requirement analysis** refers to the stage in a system development life cycle where the goals (outputs) of a system are evaluated against the needs of the users.

**Resource allocation** is the third stage of the model for information systems planning, consisting of developing the hardware, software, data communications, facilities, personnel, and financial plans needed to execute the master development plan defined in an OIRA.

**Response management** is the strategy of responding to competitors or market developments rather than being a leader.

**Return on investment (ROI)** is the percentage return computed by ROI = net return ÷ required investment.

**Reverse engineering** is the process of converting the code, files, and databases of legacy systems into components that can be used to create new (usually client/server) applications.

**Risk management** is the process of determining the potential risk associated with a project or a problem and considering this risk in cost–benefit analysis.

**Robot** An electromechanical device that can be programmed to automate manual tasks.

**Robotics** is the science of using a machine (a robot) to perform complex manual functions without human intervention.

**Role ambiguity** refers to the possibility of the creation of unclear or fuzzy job descriptions when organizational changes occur. This may confuse the employees.

A **runaway project** is a systems development project that requires much more spending and time to complete than budgeted and scheduled.

**Sales automation software** is the software used to automate the work of salespeople.

**Sales-force automation** refers to the hardware and software used by salespeople, usually in the field, to automate some of their tasks (e.g., using wireless computers to generate proposals at clients' sites).

**SAP R/3** is the leading EPR software (from SAP AG Corp.). It is a highly integrated package containing more than 70 modules.

A **scoring methodology** evaluates alternatives by assigning weights and scores to various aspects and then calculating the weighted totals for comparison.

**Screen sharing** enables two or more participants to see the same screen and make changes on it that can be seen by all.

**Secondary storage** stores data in a format that is compatible with the data stored in primary storage, but provides space for storing and processing large quantities of software and data for long periods.

**Self-directed teams** make their own decisions and have authority (and responsibility) to execute specific tasks.

**Sensitivity analysis** studies the effect of a change in one or more input variables on a proposed solution.

**Server** Any system or process that *provides* data, services, or access to other systems for clients.

**Service level agreements (SLA)** are made between the IS department and end users to specify what, when, and how IS services are expected to be rendered.

**Shareware** refers to a downloadable software that the user can try without fee, but is expected to pay for if he or she wants to use it.

**Simulation** is a process of imitation of reality. It is usually done for computerized experiments with proposed solutions.

**Smart cards** are storage media the size of a credit card that contain a microprocessor capable of storing and processing information.

**Social responsibility** refers to social issues that are of concern to a corporation—for example, improve the air pollution or health level in the community.

**Software** is instructional coding that manipulates the hardware in a computer system.

**Software agents** are autonomous software programs that execute mundane tasks for the benefit of their users. Also known as intelligent agents.

**Spamming** refers to indiscriminate distribution of messages (e.g., junk mail) without consideration for their appropriateness.

**Span of control** is a measure of the number of employees who report to one supervisor or manager.

**Speech recognition** A process that allows us to communicate with a computer by speaking to it.

**Speech understanding** is the ability of computers to understand the meaning of sentences, in contrast with *recognizing* individual words.

Information system **stages of growth** are six commonly accepted stages that all organizations seem to experience in implementing and managing an information system from conception to maturation (Nolan's model).

A **steering committee** is composed of key managers representing major functional units within the organization to oversee the IS function, to ensure that adequate planning and control processes were present, and to direct IS activities in support of long-range organizational objectives and goals.

**Strategic alliances** are business alliances among companies that provide strategic benefits to the partners.

**Strategic information systems (SIS)** are information systems that provide, or help to provide, strategic advantage.

**Strategic planning**, the first stage of the planning model, aligns IS strategic planning with overall organizational planning by assessing organizational objectives and strategies, setting the IS mission, assessing the environment, and setting IS policies, objectives, and strategies.

**Strategic systems** are those that *significantly* impact the operation of an organization, its sucess or even survival.

**Supercomputers** have the most processing power of computers generally available.

A **supply chain** describes all the activities related to the acceptance of an order from a customer and fulfilling it. In its extended format, it also includes connections with suppliers, customers, and other business partners.

**Support activities** do not add value directly to a firm's product or service under consideration but support the primary activities that do add value.

**Symbolic processing** uses symbols, rather than numbers, combined with rules of thumb (or heuristics) to process information and solve problems.

**Synchronous (real-time) communication** means that messages sent at a certain time are received immediately, almost simultaneously.

A **system** is a set of elements that acts as a single, goal-oriented entity.

**System development** refers to the structuring of hardware and software to achieve the effective and efficient processing of information.

**System development life cycle (SDLC)** is a model for developing a system based on a traditional problem-solving process with sequential steps and options for revisiting steps when problems appear.

**System software** is a set of instructions that act as the intermediary between the computer hardware and application programs.

**Telecommuting** generally refers to all types of electronic high-speed long-distance voice and data communication usually through the use of common carriers.

**Teleconferencing** refers to the ability to confer with a group of people by telephone or computer systems.

**3 R's of Reengineering** The key activities of reengineering organized into three phases: redesign, retool and reorchestrate.

**Total cost of ownership** is a formula for calculating the cost of owning and operating a PC.

**Total quality management (TQM)** is an organization-wide effort to improve quality and make it the responsibility of all employees.

A **transaction processing system (TPS)** processes an organization's basic business transactions such as purchasing, billing, and payroll.

**Trend analysis** is the analysis of performance over time, attempting to show future direction using forecasting methods.

**Turing tests**, named after the English mathematician, Alan Turing, are designed to measure if a computer is intelligent or not.

**User interfaces** facilitate communications between a user (a person) and an information system and may be tailored uniquely for an individual.

**Validation** ensures that a system meets documented and approved system requirements established during the design stage.

**Value added networks** are networks that add communications services to existing, common carriers.

**Value analysis** facilitates decision making in situations where intangible benefits are important, by evaluating benefits and costs through an initial prototype prior to development of a complete system.

**Value chain model** (by Porter) shows the primary activities that sequentially add value to the profit margin. Also shown are the support activities.

**Value systems** in Michael Porter's value chain model include producers, suppliers, distributors, and buyers (all with their own value chains).

**Video mail** refers to the ability to transmit photos, pictures, and documents among conversing people, including conferencing.

**Video teleconferencing** is a teleconferencing with the added capability of the participants seeing each other as well as documents or other objects.

**Virtual corporations** may operate from various locations, usually through telecommunications, without a permanent headquarters.

**Virtual IS organization** is a team-based IS organization that includes vendors and other business partners.

**Virtual reality** is a pseudo–3D interactive technology which provides a user with a feeling that he or she is physically present in a computer-generated world.

**Virtual Reality Markup Language (VRML)** A platform-independent standard for virtual reality (VR).

A **virus** is software that can damage or destroy data or software in a computer.

**Visual interactive modeling (VIM)** is a method of modeling situations for problem solving where users can interact with the system and the results of their action are displayed.

**Visual interactive simulation (VIS)** is a VIM where simulation is used as the problem-solving tool.

**Visual recognition** refers to the computer's ability to interpret scenes. Also known as computer vision.

**Voice mail** is digitized spoken messages that are stored and transferred electronically to receivers.

**Voice recognition** is the ability of a computer to understand the meaning of spoken words.

**Voice synthesis** transforms computer output to voice or audio output.

**Vulnerability** (in security) refers to a system exposure to potential hazards, either intentional or accidental.

**Wand readers** are handheld optical readers for scanning data.

**Waterfall method** refers to the process of system development where work flows down from one stage to the next only after it is completed.

**"What-if" analysis** seeks to determine the effect of changing some of the input data on solutions.

**Wide area networks (WANs)** are networks that generally span distances greater than one city and include regional networks such as telephone companies or international networks such as global communications services providers.

**Work group** Two or more individuals who act together to perform a task.

**Workflow systems** use group support software for scheduling, routing, and monitoring specific tasks throughout an organization.

**WYSIWYG** (**w**hat **y**ou **s**ee **is w**hat **y**ou **g**et) means that material displayed on a computer screen will look exactly—or almost exactly—as it will look on a printed page.

## Chapter 1

Figure 1-7: Courtesy International Business Machines Corporation. Page 30: Courtesy Port of Singapore Authority.

## Chapter 2

Figure 2-2: Courtesy American Airlines. Page 51: Courtesy Heimann Systems Co. Figure 2-4: Courtesy Lotus Development Corp. Page 63: Courtesy BYTE magazine, June 1993. Reproduced with permission.

## Chapter 5

Figure 5-1a: ©Gabe Palacio/Leo de Wys, Inc. Figure 5-1b: ©James King-Holmes/Science Photo Library/Photo Researchers. Figures 5-1c and 5-1f: Courtesy International Business Machines Corporation. Figure 5-1d: Courtesy Apple Computers. Figure 5-1e: Courtesy Sony Pictures Entertainment Company. Figure 5-1g: ©Blair Seitz/Photo Researchers. Figure 5-4: Courtesy Hewlett Packard. Figure 5-5: Group room photo of Ventana Corporation's Falls Church, Virginia, offices. GroupSystems is a registered trademark of Ventana Corporation. Figure 5-6: Courtesy Changepoint Corp.

## Chapter 6

Page 221: Screenshot supplied by GlobalMall.com, a division of Global Marketing Group, Grayslake, IL. Page 231: Courtesy Wells Fargo and Company. Page 232: Courtesy Security First Network Bank. Page 236: The screen shot is the property of Ameritrade Holding Corporation and is being displayed with the permission of Ameritrade Holding Corporation, all rights in the copyrightable content and trademarks are owned and reserved by Ameritrade Holding Corporation. Page 239: Courtesy Egghead.com. Page 266: Courtesy VISA International. Page 267: Courtesy Motorola, Inc.

## Chapter 7

Page 300 (top, right and left and bottom right): Courtesy WorkSmart. Page 300 (bottom, left): Courtesy ErgoView Technologies. Page 303: Courtesy U.C.-Davis. Page 305: ©James Keyser. Page 320: Courtesy Granite Communications.

## Chapter 8

Page 353: Courtesy Tandy Corporation.

## Chapter 9

Page 389: Courtesy Dialogos-Team Oy. Figure 9-5: Courtesy Comshare, Inc. Figures 9-7a-d: Courtesy Comshare, Inc.

## Chapter 10

Figure 10-6: ©Chicago Tribune Company. All rights reserved. Used with permission. Page 434: Courtesy USAA. Page 464: Courtesy Dallas Area Rapid Transit.

## Chapter 11

OPENING CASE: Courtesy The Robotics Institute/Carnegie Mellon University. Figure 11-10: Courtesy NEC Corporation.

## Chapter 13

Figure 13-3: DILBERT, reprinted by permission of United Feature Syndicate, Inc.

## Chapter 15

OPENING CASE: Courtesy Dean Witter Reynolds, Inc. Figure 15-7: Courtesy Startek Engineering, Inc.

## Tech Guide 1

Page 699, 701, 703 (top left and top center) and 704: Courtesy International Business Machines Corporation. Page 700: Courtesy SGI/Cray Research. Page 703 (top right): Acer America. Page 703 (center margin): Courtesy Palm, Inc. Page 703 (bottom): ©GEM Plus. Page 710 (left): Courtesy Conner Peripherals. Page 710 (right): Courtesy Sony Electronics, Inc. Page 711 and 714: Courtesy International Business Machines Corporation. Page 715: Courtesy Great Plains Software, Inc. Page 716: Courtesy Avnet, Inc. Computer Marketing Group. Page 717: Courtesy Sony Electronics, Inc. Page 718: Jody Dole/The Image Bank. Page 719 (top): Courtesy Fujitsu Computer Products of America, Inc. Page 719(bottom): ©Dick Luria/Photo Researchers.

## Tech Guide 2

Page 723, 724, and 726: Courtesy Microsoft Corporation. Page 729: Courtesy tvweather.com.

## Tech Guide 3

Page 750: Courtesy Microsoft Corporation.

## Tech Guide 4

Page 766: Phil Degginger/Tony Stone Images.

# NAME INDEX

# GLOBAL INDEX